The Encyclopedia
of
War Journalism
1807 – 2015

The Encyclopedia
of
War Journalism
1807 – 2015

Third Edition

MITCHEL P. ROTH

Grey House
Publishing

PUBLISHER: Leslie Mackenzie
EDITORIAL DIRECTOR: Laura Mars
MANAGING EDITOR: Diana Delgado
PRODUCTION MANAGER: Kristen Thatcher
MARKETING DIRECTOR: Jessica Moody

AUTHOR: Mitchel P. Roth
COMPOSITION & DESIGN: Lumina Datamatics®

Grey House Publishing, Inc.
4919 Route 22
Amenia, NY 12501
518.789.8700 FAX 845.373.6390
www.greyhouse.com
e-mail: books@greyhouse.com

Publisher's Cataloging-In-Publication Data
(Prepared by The Donohue Group, Inc.)

Roth, Mitchel P., 1953-
    The encyclopedia of war journalism, 1807-2015 / Mitchel P. Roth. -- Third edition.

     pages : illustrations ; cm

    First edition published with title: Historical dictionary of war journalism.
    Includes bibliographical references and index.
    ISBN: 978-1-61925-745-0 (hardcover)

    1. War--Press coverage--Encyclopedias. 2. War correspondents--Biography--Encyclopedias. I. Title.

PN4784.W37 R68 2015
070.4/333/03

This book is dedicated to journalists around the world
who have given their lives in the pursuit of reporting the truth.

Table of Contents

Preface ix

Introduction and Study Guide xi

Encyclopedia of War Journalism A – Z 1

Primary Documents and Photographs 413

Timeline 571

Appendices 587

    A   Mexican-American War Correspondents and the Battles They Covered 587

    B   Crimean War Correspondents 588

    C   American Indian War Correspondents 589

    D   American Civil War Correspondents 590

    E   Franco-Prussian War Correspondents 596

    F   Russo-Turkish War Correspondents 597

    G   Correspondents Covering the Sudan and Egyptian Campaigns, 1882-1899 598

    H   Greco-Turkish War Correspondents 599

    I   Spanish-American War Correspondents 600

    J   Boer War Correspondents 603

    K   Russo-Japanese War Correspondents, 1904-1905 605

    L   World War I Correspondents 606

    M   Spanish Civil War Correspondents, 1936-1939 608

    N   World War II Accredited U.S. War Correspondents 610

    O   BBC War Correspondents with the Allied Expeditionary Force,
               June 6, 1944–May 5, 1945 631

    P   Korean War Correspondents 632

    Q   Vietnam War Correspondents 634

    R   Pulitzer Prizes Awarded for War Reporting, 1917-2010 636

    S   War Artists 637

    T   War Photographers/Cameramen 638

    U   Films that Portray War Correspondents 640

    V   Iraq War Correspondents, 2003-2015 643

    W   Afghanistan War Correspondents, 2001-2015 644

    X   Journalists Killed in Somalia, 1992-2014 645

    Y   Syrian Civil War Correspondents 646

    Z   Libyan Civil War Correspondents 647

    AA   Robert Capa Gold Medal Winners 648

    BB   Bayeux Calvados Awards for War Correspondents, 1994-2014 649

Bibliography 654

Index 659

About the Author 675

Preface

The first war correspondent, like the first war photographer, remains a somewhat shadowy and elusive figure. There is still a lack of consensus as to who exactly should be the first individual to be accorded the moniker "war correspondent," especially since Isaiah Thomas' eyewitness account of the Battle of Concord appeared in the *Worcester Massachusetts Spy* in 1775 and in 1837 Charles Lewis Gruneison covered the Carlist War in Spain as a special correspondent for the *London Morning Post*. In any case, by most accounts it was the Mexican-American War of 1846–1848 that introduced the first identifiable war correspondents. What elevated the reporters of the Mexican-American War to the status of first modern war journalists was their access to the telegraph and the penny presses, as well as the advent of photography, all of which combined to lend an air of immediacy to this developing enterprise and satisfy a readership thirsting for timely war news. The first war journalist was undoubtedly male, and probably worked out of the strategically located city of New Orleans. Since newspaper bylines were rarely used until the twentieth century, journalism was a relatively impersonal endeavor, with journalists reporting in virtual anonymity, except for the occasional use of initials or pseudonyms.

Anyone writing a reference book or a larger history of war journalism history faces the daunting task of identifying hundreds if not thousands of anonymous and pseudonymous journalists who reported from the field without bylines well into the nineteenth century. Several guidelines have been followed in selecting the various entries for this book. While conducting research over the past several years, I have found references to literally thousands of correspondents who covered wars over the past 200 years. It has been estimated that perhaps 5,000 individuals covered some part of the Vietnam War, over 1,600 the Korean War and over 204 for the Iraq War. It is beyond the scope of any one book to include every one of these, particularly since it would require listing the names of journalists from most countries in the developed world as well, a task that would require translating references from myriad languages. War journalists were selected who covered significant conflicts and events and left behind more than a fleeting trace of their presence at the frontlines. Except in a few cases, to be considered a war reporter, photographer, or artist, an individual must either represent or be somehow affiliated with a newspaper, a magazine, radio, television or digital news source. Restricting entries with this criterion excludes army officers, many freelancers and other eyewitnesses. Other entries include significant events, persons, or terms relevant to the history of war journalism. Each entry concludes with references for further information on the subject and cross-references within the text are cited by an asterisk. I have used several reference books, which are cited by their better-known acronyms. *DAB* refers to the *Dictionary of American Biography*, *DNB* is the *Dictionary of National Biography*, and *DLB* refers to the *Dictionary of Literary Biography*.

This third edition of *The Encyclopedia of War Journalism, 1807-2015* is designed to fill many of the existing gaps in the history of war journalism, as well as to update and enhance the first edition (*Historical Dictionary of War Journalism*, 1997). Much has changed since the last edition, including new wars, new technologies and the ubiquity of the World Wide Web/Internet as a news source. There are several new features in this new edition that will assist anyone wanting to learn more about war journalism, including a Timeline, and a fully annotated Primary Documents and Photographs section covering the subject up to 2015.

The twenty-first century has been the deadliest era for the world's journalists, whether covering wars, drug cartels, or political instability. According to the Committee to Protect Journalists (CPJ), between 2003 and 2009 at least 139 journalists were killed covering the Iraq war alone. During this period Algeria in 1995 was the deadliest year for journalists, when 24 were killed there. The CPJ only lists a journalist killed on duty if the individual died "as a result of a hostile action" which can include "reprisal for his or her work, or crossfire while carrying out a dangerous assignment." This criteria then leaves out journalists killed in typical car accidents and plane crashes or by health conditions. So, in effect, a journalist can be considered killed in action only as the result of hostile "human action" such as shooting down a plane, or aggressive action resulting in a car crash. While most accounts focus on Western journalists the brunt of danger is carried by the indigenous correspondents or non-embedded unilateral journalists. Many of those killed were abducted and murdered away from the battlefront. What's more, during urban combat a whole nation can be considered a battlefront.

In this third edition of the book, I have updated and revised previous entries, and added more than 200 new ones. Many of the new entries reflect the changing battlegrounds of the 21st century. With the withdrawal of most foreign forces from Afghanistan and Iraq over the past several years, new battle lines have been drawn as geopolitics and the Arab Spring have stimulated new bloodshed, while conflicts in Africa have continued to expand and take more lives. Syria and Libya have been among the most dangerous war zones in history, and many of the new entries chronicle individuals who have given their lives in the pursuit of war reporting. In previous editions of this work, the focus has been on coverage by Western war journalists. However, with the introduction of new forms of communication technologies, from satellites to YouTube and iPhones, indigenous war reporting has filled an important news void in regions off-limits to outside journalists. Conflict zones in the Ukraine and Syria have become virtual no-go zones for Western journalists. This new edition highlights the contributions being made by these brave journalists, many of them citizen journalists, unsupported by any monolithic new organization.

This past year has been a particularly deadly one for war journalists. According to the International Federation of Journalists, Pakistan and Syria were the most dangerous places to be a journalist, not just those reporting wars, but those simply looking to report the truth. Afghanistan, Palestine, Iraq and Ukraine have become almost equally perilous, with these six countries accounting for more than 50% of all confirmed killings of reporters in 2014. The world has been particularly riveted and appalled by the media coverage of the beheadings of Western reporters in Syria by the Islamic State.

As I have mentioned in previous books, no author writes a book alone. This book has benefited from the help and guidance of managing editor Diana Delgado, who has never shied away from gently reminding me of deadlines. Thanks are also due to my editor, Laura Mars, who guided this book to completion. Kudos are also due to my research assistant and current teaching fellow Elizaweh Weisz for her assistance in tracking down recent obituary information. However, no one deserves more thanks than my wife Ines Papandrea and son E. J. Roth, who have never wavered from their support of my seemingly endless writing projects.

Introduction and Study Guide

The Encyclopedia of War Journalism 1807 – 2015 is the third edition. It has been significantly revised, and includes a substantial amount of new material.

Content

This new edition of *The Encyclopedia of War Journalism* includes over **1,100 A-Z entries,** 200 more than the previous edition. These new entries include women journalists, modern conflicts, significant new media and organizations, how war correspondents are paid, how technology like iPhones affect the job, and new insight on the danger of this work. This A-Z section includes correspondents, illustrators, photographers, periodicals, publishers, wars, war zones, news organizations, and relevant awards. Each entry includes additional sources to facilitate individual research, and cross-references throughout.

Following the entries is **Primary Documents and Photographs.** This 100-plus page section is comprised of carefully selected and annotated writings and photographs, chronological by war. Strengthened by its own Table of Contents and Introduction, here you will find 56 documents and photographs. These were chosen to represent not only a variety of approaches to war coverage, but how improved communication has affected the work of correspondents and photographers. They include article and book excerpts, government safety guidelines, and a war journal blog. Photographs range from the Crimean War in the 1850s, to a 2014 photo of Iraq War journalist James Foley.

Next is a **Timeline** with historical context crucial in understanding how covering a war has changed. It has been updated to include significant technical advances, history-making firsts, censorship, news scoops, award winners and more.

Appendices include individual correspondents and photographers for specific wars, Pulitzer Prize winning war correspondents, correspondents who appeared in war films and correspondents killed in a several different wars.

The 29 Appendices are followed by a **Selected Bibliography,** updated with recently published works, and **Index.**

The Encyclopedia of War Journalism offers unique, historical in-depth coverage of individuals and their accomplishments, along with experienced insight at how war coverage is linked to public opinion. It will prove invaluable to students of war, history, journalism, political science, and public opinion.

Abend, Hallett Edward
(1882-1955)

Born in Portland, Oregon, and educated at Stanford University, Abend was the Far Eastern correspondent for the *New York Times* from 1926 to 1940 and was bureau chief in Shanghai when the Japanese attacked in 1937. He was one of the earliest casualties among Western correspondents in China, and one of the first of World War II*, when he was injured during an aerial bombardment of the city. Abend developed his own intelligence service using sources in both the Chinese and Japanese armies prior to American entry into the war. Any information he received was passed directly to either the State Department or the armed forces. In September 1940, he delivered one of his greatest news scoops four days before the official announcement which revealed that Japan was about to conclude a military alliance with Germany and Italy.

He joined the Washington bureau of the *Times* in April 1941, but left in August to cover New Zealand, Australia, and the Dutch East Indies for *Reader's Digest*. When the war in Asia came to a close in 1945, Abend was among the journalists reporting the story of the Air Transport Command and how it accomplished its task flying weapons and soldiers over the Himalayas between India and China when the Burma Road was closed. Among his many books on Asia are *Ramparts of the Pacific* (1942), *Pacific Charter* (1943), *Japan Unmasked* (1941), and *My Life in China* (1943).

REFERENCES: Robert W. Desmond. *Tides of War*. 1984; Eric Downton. *Wars Without End*. 1987.

Abkey, Sheikh Nur Mohamed
(c. 1958–2011)

This Somalian journalist was murdered while working for Radio Mogadishu-Voice of Somali Republic in that country's capital city. Abkey was already a prominent reporter and news anchor, having worked for at least two decades for a variety of news sources, including radio station HornAfrik, East Africa Radio, and the Somali News Agency. He trained journalists at Radio Mogadishu in collaboration with the Somali Information Industry. Under almost constant threat, Abkey refused most entreaties to live at the radio station for his own protection. On May 4, 2011 the journalist was abducted early in the day and then shot near his home. Subsequently, someone called in to the radio station from Al–Shabaab terrorist group, claiming to be responsible for the killing. Witnesses reported seeing his lifeless body dumped on the streets of Mogadishu.

REFERENCE: https://cpj.org/killed/2010/sheikh-nur-mohamed-abkey.php.

Abrams, Alexander St. Clair
(1845-1931)

The Louisiana native had served in the Confederate army and as a reporter for the *Vicksburg Whig* during the siege of Vicksburg before turning full-time to journalism with the *Atlanta Intelligencer* after the campaign. His account of the siege of Vicksburg was carried in both the *Whig* and the *Mobile Advertiser and Register*. Fellow war correspondent John H. Linebaugh* ranked Abrams' report as the most complete account of the siege. Later that year his dispatches were collected and published as *The Siege of Vicksburg*. In 1864 he covered the Atlanta campaign and produced the best account of the Battle of Oostanaula for the *Intelligencer*. Abrams' dispatches appeared above his sobriquet "St. Clair" until he left wartime journalism in July 1864. A champion of the foot soldier, he wrote several articles detailing the mistreatment of soldiers by officers.

REFERENCE: J. Cutler Andrews. *The South Reports the Civil War*. 1970.

Abyssinian War

See ETHIOPIAN WAR.

Active Service

Stephen Crane's* 1899 novel revolves around fictional *New York Eclipse* war correspondent Rufus Coleman and the 1897 Greco-Turkish War.* The novel is based in part on some of Crane's observations as a war correspondent during the conflict. In this romantic potboiler Coleman follows his fiancee to Greece after her classics-professor father drags her away in an attempt to keep her from marrying too far down the evolutionary ladder. However, after the intrepid correspondent on "active service" rescues the professor, his students, and family from the vile Turks, Coleman wins the consent of the professor to marry his daughter.

REFERENCES: Stephen Crane. *Active Service*. 1899; Howard Good. *The Image of War Correspondents in Anglo-American Fiction*. 1985.

Adams, Edward "Eddie" T. (1933–2004)

Born on February 20, 1933, in Kensington, Pennsylvania, Adams joined the *Philadelphia Bulletin* as a photographer in 1959. In 1962 he moved to the Associated Press* and later to *Time* magazine in 1972. From 1976 to 1980 he worked as a special correspondent for the Associated Press.

In 1969, he was on his third tour of Vietnam for the AP* when he took probably one of the most famous photos of the Vietnam War.* During the Tet offensive he recorded Brigadier General Nguyen Ngoc Loan, commander of the Vietnam National Police, executing a prisoner with a pistol shot to the head at point-blank range. Adams won a Pulitzer Prize* and a place in photographic history. Following the war the police commander moved to America and opened a restaurant in Virginia. Since 1980 Adams has worked as a freelance photojournalist.

REFERENCE: Clarence R. Wyatt. *Paper Soldiers: The American Press and the Vietnam War*. 1993; Pittsburgh Post Gazette, Sept. 20, 2004.

Adan, Barkhad Awale (1950–2010)

Adan was a Somali journalist and director of Radio Hurma in Mogadishu. He had been working there for four years when he rushed to cover the aftermath of a suicide bombing at the Hotel Muna that killed 33 people. Adan was apparently helping a technician fix his radio station's roof transmitter when he was fatally shot in the abdomen by a stray bullet. He was caught in the crossfire of a battle between Al-Shabaab fighters and AMISOM (African Union Mission in Somalia) soldiers during what became known as the Battle of Mogadishu.

REFERENCES: Committee to Protect Journalists, "Burhat Awale," Aug. 24, 2010; Reporters without Borders, "Journalist Killed in Mogadishu fighting," Aug. 26, 2010.

Addario, Lynsey (b. 1973)

Born in Norwalk, Connecticut and educated at the University of Wisconsin-Madison, she began her professional career in photojournalism in 1996 with Argentina's *Buenos Aires Herald*. She would later transition to freelancing for the Associated Press. She started covering conflict zones in 2000, when she traveled to Afghanistan to chronicle the Taliban. Since then Addario has covered conflicts in Iraq, Darfur, the Congo, Israel, Libya, and Haiti. Her work has appeared in the *New York Times, Newsweek,* and *National Geographic*. In March 2011 she went missing along with the *New York Times* reporters Anthony Shadid,* Stephen Farrell, and Tyler Hicks.* were also captured. They were all captured and released within a week by Libyan soldiers, but not before Addario reported being "groped" by them. In November, 2011 she was strip searched and forced through an x-ray scanner three times by Israeli soldiers, although she reported telling them she was pregnant. The *Times* sent a letter of complaint on her behalf to the Israeli government after receiving these allegations. Addario claimed that she had never been subjected to "such blatant cruelty." The Israeli Defense ministry later issued an apology to both the reporter and her newspaper. Addario was the recipient of numerous awards including a MacArthur Fellowship ($500,000) in 2009. That same year she shared a Pulitzer Prize with other *New York Times* reporters for International Reporting. In 2015 her much ballyhooed memoir, *It's What I Do,* was published, describing her experiences in combat zones.

REFERENCE: http://www.lynseyaddario.com.

Adie, Kate (b. 1945)

Educated at Newcastle University, where she specialized in Scandinavian studies, Adie worked in southern Lapland before entering broadcast journalism with a local Durham radio station. She came to prominence in 1980 covering the Iranian embassy siege in London. She delivered a dramatic on-the-scene account of the Strategic Air Services (SAS) rescue of the hostages. According to one source she was the first woman on British television to broadcast live from such a potentially dangerous situation. In 1986 she covered the U.S. bombing of Tripoli, Libya, for the BBC. Adie received the International News Story of 1986 Award for her coverage.

Over the next three years she continued to report from the world's hot spots, including Armenia, Afghanistan, Africa, and Libya once more. In 1989 she covered the student revolt in China's Tiananmen Square and witnessed the massacre of Chinese students. For her courage under fire the BBC created a special position for her as chief news correspondent. Adie reported the attempted coup in Trinidad in 1990, the Palestine refugee problem, and the 1991 Gulf War.* She noted that her most dangerous assignment was the Yugoslavian conflict. She is the author of several books including *Corsets and Camouflage: Women and War* (2003).

REFERENCE: Anne Sebba. *Battling for News*. 1994.

Adler, Martin (1958–2006)

Born in Stockholm, Sweden he turned to journalism after studying anthropology in London. He covered wars in more than twenty war zones including El Salvador, Rwanda, the Republic of Congo, Angola, Sierra Leone, Liberia, Chechnya, Bosnia, Afghanistan, Somalia, Iraq, Sri Lanka, and Sudan. He emphasized the poverty, corruption, and human rights abuses that often took place in the war zones he covered. Adler worked for several media outlets including the Swedish daily *Aftonbladet*. He was shot to death on June 23, 2006 by an unknown killer while covering a rally for peace in Mogadishu. Apparently some of the demonstrators had just set an Ethiopian flag on fire when a hooded man shot Adler in the left side of the chest, killing him instantly. According to Somali journalists working with

Indicates a separate entry.

Reporters Without Borders,* the killing was probably motivated by anti-Western sentiments. Adler won various awards, including the Amnesty International Media Award (2001), the Silver Prize for Investigative Journalism (2001), and the Rory Peck Award for Hard News (2004). In 2007 the Rory Peck Trust established the Martin Adler Prize to honor Adler's career as "journalist, filmmaker and storyteller." Winners of the award include freelance camera men and women, journalists, fixers, drivers, and translators for their role in reporting important news stories.

REFERENCES: "Swedish Man Shot Dead in Somalia," http://news.bbc.co.uk/2/hi/africa/5108958sm, BBC, June 24, 2006; "Director-General Condemns the Murder of Journalist and Photographer Martin Adler in Mogadishu," http://portal.unesco.org/ci/en/ev.php; Reporters without Borders, "Swedish Freelance Photographer Gunned Down on Mogadishu Street," June 23, 2006.

Ahmad, Sardar (c. 1974–2014)

Ahmed entered the journalism field in 2001, working as a translator for Japanese reporters following the fall of the Taliban in Afghanistan. Beginning in 2003 he covered the daily briefings given by the U.S. coalition representatives at Bagram airbase for *Agence France-Press* (AFP). He became a familiar presence in the Afghan media and was well-respected for his "rigorous reporting" of the Afghanistan insurgency. By the time of his death in 2014 he had risen to senior correspondent for AFP. In the run up to the Afghanistan national elections, the Taliban was making a violent resurgence. Ahmad was dining with his family at Kabul's Serena Hotel on the night of March 20 when Taliban gunmen smuggled weapons into the restaurant complex and attacked the diners, killing nine, including Ahmad, his wife, daughter, and youngest son. In a subsequent statement the Taliban insisted that Ahmad was not targeted and even apologized for the murders of the children.

REFERENCE: http://www.theguardian.com/world/2014/mar/21/sardar-ahmad-afghan-journalist-killed-taliban.

Ahmed, Abdulkadir (1987–2014)

A freelance journalist covering the Somalian conflict for Somali Channel TV, Star FM, and Radio Baidoa, Ahmed was among the fifteen killed in a suicide car bomb attack on a restaurant in Baidoa on December 5, 2014. Cameraman Mohamed Isaq* was also killed in the attack.

REFERENCE: https://cpj.org/killed/2014/Abdulkadir-ahmed.php.

al-Deeri, Mahran (c. 1983–2014)

Born in Sheikh Miskeen, the Syrian journalist studied at Damascus University. Al-Deeri worked for the Syrian government news agency SANA, only leaving with the outbreak of the Syrian conflict to work as an independent journalist. In October 2013 he began freelancing for Al Jazeera.* While covering the civil war he reported the rebel capture of a government position on the outskirts of his hometown. On December 10, 2014 he was killed while covering the battles between rebel and government forces outside of Sheikh Miskeen. He was killed after his car crashed into a rebel vehicle. For security reasons he had been driving without lights to avoid government forces. Three other journalists were killed covering the violence during the three days of fighting there.

REFERENCE: http://cpj.org/killed/2014/mahran-al-deeri.php.

Aldrich, Thomas Bailey (1836-1907)

Better known today as a poet, editor, and writer of children's books, Bailey was born in Portsmouth, New Hampshire. Rejected in his attempts to secure a military appointment at the outbreak of the American Civil War,* he joined the *New York Tribune* as a war correspondent in late 1861. He accompanied General Louis Blenker's German division, part of the Army of the

Potomac in Virginia. He left his assignment early the following year. He went on to a long, distinguished literary career.

REFERENCE: Ferris Greenslet. *The Life of Thomas Bailey Aldrich.* 1908.

Alexander, Peter Wellington (c. 1820-1866)

Described as the "Prince of Correspondents" by one Southern newspaper, the Georgian-born Alexander practiced both law and journalism before becoming one of the most important reporters for the South during the American Civil War.* His accounts appeared in the *Savannah Republican,* the *Atlanta Confederacy,* the *Columbus Sun,* the *London Times,* and many others. He covered the 1861 Manassas campaign, during which he criticized the performance of Brigadier General Richard Ewell. He also covered the Battle of Shiloh, and the Maryland and Virginia campaigns in 1862. His report on the Battle of Fredericksburg was based on second-hand accounts due to problems of military censorship. He later reported the Battles of Chancellorsville, Antietam, Gettysburg, Chickamauga, Chattanooga, the Wilderness, Spotsylvania, and Petersburg, as well as the fall of Atlanta. His accounts of the poor conditions confronting the common soldier enhanced his popularity among the ranks. After the war he returned to his law practice in Georgia.

REFERENCES: J. Cutler Andrews. *The South Reports the Civil War.* 1970; Stewart Sifakis. *Who Was Who in the Civil War.* 1988.

al-Jabar, Ali Hassan (1955–2011)

Born in Doha, Qatar, al-Jabar studied cinematography at the Academy of Fine Arts in Cairo, Egypt. He began his career with Qatar TV in Dohar as head of the filming department between 1979 and 2001. He left Doha to join a local Al Jazeera* affiliate several years later. In 2011 he

became the first foreign journalist killed during the Libyan civil war.* He was mortally wounded in Suluq as he was returning to Benghazi to file a news report. He died from a gunshot wound in a local hospital.

REFERENCES: Matt Wells, "Al-Jazeera Cameraman Chased and Shot Dead by Gaddafi Regime Supporters," London Guardian, Mar. 14, 2011; "Ali Hassan al-Jabar," www.cpj.org/killed/2011/ali-hassan-al-jaber.php.

Al Jazeera

In November 1996, Al Jazeera (which refers to the Arabian Peninsula) was established as an Arabic news and current affairs satellite TV channel. Based in Doha, Qatar, it has now branched into most other forms of media, featuring specialty TV channels in a number of languages. In its early days it was applauded for its willingness to broadcast dissenting views, leading in some cases to controversies in the Arab countries of the Persian Gulf region. Al Jazeera rose to international prominence after the outbreak of war in Afghanistan* after the 9/11 attacks in America. It was the only channel to cover the war live, thanks to its Kabul offices, established before war broke out. On April 1, 2003, Al Jazeera's Baghdad bureau was bombed by a U.S. plane, killing a reporter. While the Americans claimed it was an error, others insisted that the Qatar government had given the United States a precise map of the bureau to protect it from just such an event. In 2006 Al Jazeera launched the English language channel, Al Jazeera International, and in 2013 it purchased Current TV in the United States, offering an American news channel eight months later. As Al Jazeera has branched out into other countries, it has been embroiled in controversies and subject to criticism. The Algerian government has often targeted it for its criticism of the Algerian military. Contretemps have ensued in Bahrain, Egypt, Iraq, Syria, the Palestinian National Authority, and in Israel, where the news network was accused of biased reporting of the Gaza conflict. The United States has described

Indicates a separate entry.

its reportage of the war in Iraq as anti-American and inciting violence by featuring graphic war footage and materials on national security. Al Jazeera's coverage of the invasion of Iraq in 2003 was chronicled in the 2004 award-winning documentary, *Control Room*. No matter its detractors, Al Jazeera has earned numerous accolades from the international journalism community, leading U.S. Secretary of State Hillary Rodham Clinton in March 2011, to state that the channel provides more news coverage than the opinion-laden American mass media. Other Al Jazeera channels include Al Jazeera English (2006), Al Jazeera Mubasher Al-'Amma (2005), Al Jazeera Balkans (2011), Al Jazeera Turk (2014), and Al Jazeera Documentary (2007).

REFERENCES: http://www.allied-media.com/aljazeera/jazeera_history.html; Hugh Miles. *Al Jazeera; The Inside Story of the Arab News Channel That Is Challenging the West*. 2006.

Allen, Jay (1900-c. 1974)

Allen began his career in journalism with the *Chicago Tribune* in 1924 and over the next decade followed stories throughout Europe. It was during this time he became familiar with a number of personalities that would play important roles on both sides of the looming Spanish Civil War*. He covered the war for two years and became the first foreign correspondent to interview general and future Spanish president Francisco Franco in July 1936. The following month he was reportedly the only American journalist to witness the mass executions in Badajoz. This resulted in the Nationalists placing a bounty on his life. He returned to the United States in 1936. Allen was fired by the *Chicago Daily Tribune* because its owner disagreed with his pro-Republican position. He went to France to cover the opening rounds of World War II before American entry, working as a correspondent for the North American Newspaper Alliance. He won prominence for having had the first exclusive interview with

Marshal Petain after he became dictator of France. He was also noticed after he was taken prisoner by the Germans while trying to cross between occupied and unoccupied France without a permit. He was released not long after, and went on to cover the campaign in North Africa, before returning to the States in 1942. He continued his career in journalism until he died.

REFERENCES: Paul Preston. *Foreign Correspondents in the Spanish Civil War.*; Curt Riess, ed. *They Were There.* 1944.

Allen, Laurence Edmund (1908-1975)

Born in Mt. Savage, Maryland, he gained early experience on papers in Ohio, West Virginia, and Washington, D.C. He worked for the Associated Press* beginning in the 1930s, when he was stationed in Prague. With the outbreak of World War II* Allen worked out of the Rome bureau. In 1942 he was awarded the Pulitzer Prize for his coverage of the British fleet in the Mediterranean. He was aboard the *Illustrious* in January 1941 when it weathered a seven-hour attack by German planes before being put out of action at Malta. Later that year he was on a British cruiser when it was torpedoed while protecting Crete from a German sea attack. Allen spent almost an hour in the water before being rescued and would spend several months recovering from a bout with pneumonia.

He returned to the Mediterranean in mid-1942 and took part in a British commando raid on Tobruk. He was aboard the destroyer *Sikh* when it was sunk in Tobruk harbor. Allen was captured by Italian forces and began a twenty-month internment. While being transferred to German custody he escaped but was eventually recaptured after being severely wounded. He was released in an exchange of wounded prisoners in May 1944. The next year he was the recipient of the Bronze Star, for defending freedom of the press as a prisoner of war.

Following the war he served as foreign correspondent in Poland, Moscow, Tel Aviv, and the Caribbean. Allen served as war correspondent in Southeast Asia during the 1950s French war in Indochina and was awarded the Croix de Guerre from the French High Command for his frontline reporting in 1952.

REFERENCE: Robert W. Desmond. *Tides of War.* 1984.

Allis, Sebastian Albert Dutton (1821–1878)

Born in New Haven, Connecticut, he worked as a newspaper clerk for the *New Orleans Daily Picayune* during the 1840s and served as a sergeant in the U.S. Army with the Louisiana Brigade during the Mexican-American War.* He was appointed postmaster in Vera Cruz, Mexico in 1847. Allis fought at Monterrey but still kept in touch with former colleagues from his newspaper days, with one historian describing Allis as "a special favorite of the New Orleans press." His skill in handling mail at Vera Cruz led General Winfield Scott to grant him an early discharge from his unit, feeling his talents could be better used in the transfer of mail. He was not disappointed, as Allis developed a system that avoided the usual post-office barriers, placing mail directly into the hands of ship captains and thus speeding the delivery of mail and news.

REFERENCES: Tom Reilly. *War with Mexico!: American Reporters Cover the Battlefront*, edited by Manley Witten. 2010; "Descendants of William Allis of Dagenham, Essex, England 1613-x," rootsweb.ancestry.com.

Alpert, Max (1899-1980)

A pioneer in the field of Soviet photojournalism, Alpert published his first photographs in 1924. As a war photographer* and correspondent for TASS during World War II* he covered the battles of the Fourth Ukrainian Front in Czechoslovakia and the siege of Stalingrad. In addition he reported and photographed Maxim Gorky's return from Italy, the rescue of General Nobile's expedition, and construction of the first Five-Year Plans. Following the war he worked for the Soviet Information Bureau, *Novosti,* and *Pravda.*

REFERENCE: Daniela Mrazkova and Vladimir Remes, eds. *The Russian War: 1941-1945.* 1975.

Alpi, Illaria (1961–1994)

Born in Rome, Alpi graduated from the Department of Oriental Studies of the Sapienza University of Rome and became conversant in Arabic, French, and English. Her language skills led to her becoming the first Italian journalist to be stationed from Cairo for *Pase Sera* and *L'Unita.* While covering the Somalian conflict for public station Radiotelevisione Italiana (RAI 3) she was murdered along with the Slovenian cameraman Miran Hrovatin in Mogadishu on March 20, 1994. Initially a parliamentary inquiry blamed their deaths on bandits during a botched kidnapping attempt. More recently, evidence suggests they were killed from ambush by a seven-man hit team, while traveling by jeep back to Mogadishu after apparently witnessing the delivery of toxic waste to Bosaso by Italian gangsters. In 2009 a former member of the 'Ndrangheta organized crime group reported that the journalists had been murdered because they were about to expose the illegal shipping of toxic waste to Bosaso, Somalia. This theory has some credibility, since at the time of her death she was investigating illegal weapons and toxic waste trafficking, which she claimed involved the Italian Army and other high-level officials. Her life was dramatized in the 2002 Italian film, *Ilaria Alpi-Il piu crudele dei giorni.* Her life was also chronicled in the 2009 book, *Passion Reporter*, by Daniel Biacchesi. During her career she was the recipient of numerous journalism awards.

REFERENCES: Reporters without Borders, "Swedish Freelance Photographer Gunned Down on Mogadishu Street," June 23, 2006; Phillip Willan, "Establishment Hit by Fresh Accusations in Toxic Waste Scandal," Herald, Sept. 20, 2009.

* Indicates a separate entry.

Alqasim, Mohammed (d. 2014)

Alqasim was studying English literature at Damascus University as the Syrian civil war* broke out. He withdrew from university fearing arrest by Syrian security forces for his participation in the uprising against President Bashar al-Assad. He returned home to the city of Idleb, where he worked as a citizen journalist prior to transitioning to professional news affiliated positions. His work appeared in a variety of Arab news outlets, including the Dubai-based Al-Aan TV and Al Jazeera* before becoming a correspondent for Syrian Radio Rozana Radio in northern Syria. He was killed on September 10, 2014, while trying to interview a rebel commander near Idleb. It was reported that as he interviewed the commander, members of a competing rebel faction opened fire on them, killing both.

REFERENCES: https://cpj.org/killed/2014/mhammed-al-qasim.php; Project SalamaTech, "Prominent Syrian Citizen Journalist Mohammed Alqasim Killed in Idleb," Sept. 15, 2014.

al-Sayed, Basil (1987–2011)

Al-Sayed was living in Homs, when he began documenting the Syrian civil war* as a so-called citizen journalist. As a resident of Homs he was in position to cover news events off limits to the international media. Formerly a carpenter, he was working at an aluminum factory when he began posting videos on YouTube, recorded with his red Samsung video camera. He was apparently shot in the head by the security forces at the end of November while in the act of filming. At his death the conflict was not even a year old. He became the second Syrian journalist to be killed covering the civil war (after Ferzat Jarban*).

REFERENCE: http://www.npr.org/blogs/thetwoway/2011/12/29/144448779/basil-al-sayed-who-chronicled-the-syrian-uprisingis-dead.

al-Washli, Khaled (d. 2015)

He worked as a correspondent for the insurgent Houthi-controlled Al Masirah TV in Yemen. He was the station's first journalist to be killed while covering the growing violence in Yemen between the rebels and government forces. At the time of his death the Houthi movement was closing in on the capital city of Sana'a and Dhamar, taking over several towns. Al-Washli was killed on January 4, 2015 as he watched militia members defuse a bomb. The explosion also killed a number of others including five members of a local Houthi security force.

REFERENCE: https://cpj.org/killed/2015/khaled-al-washli.php.

Amanpour, Christiane (b. 1958)

Amanpour was born in London to an Iranian father and English mother. She grew up in Iran and went to private school in England and then college in the United States. After studying journalism at the University of Rhode Island she landed her first job in television and then in 1983 she joined CNN. She has covered the first Persian Gulf War, the conflicts in the Balkans, the U.S. intervention in Somalia, the Arab-Israeli conflict, and the war against the Taliban in Afghanistan. She began covering the invasion of Iraq in 2003.

REFERENCES: Michelle Ferarri and James Tobin. *Reporting America at War*. 2003.

American Civil War

The Civil War was the most thoroughly documented war of its era. While the Northern press gave it the most attention, there were contingents of correspondents representing the Confederate states as well as members of the European press, more significantly from Great Britain.

The British press generally favored the Confederacy. On various occasions British journalists reportedly accepted bribes to write and publish Southern propaganda. While the *London Daily News* gave the most evenhanded account of the war, the first British paper to send a correspondent was the *Times,* when William Howard Russell* arrived in New York in March 1861 prior to the actual outbreak of hostilities. Russell, the preeminent war reporter of his time, did not endear himself to the American military when he criticized the Union Army in a dispatch to the *Times* after the debacle at Bull Run in July. After copies of his reports were circulated in Washington, D.C., he was derided as "Bull Run Russell." In March 1862 his permission to accompany the Union armies was revoked and he returned to England.

Other British correspondents of note spent stints in America covering the war, including Antonio Gallenga* and Charles MacKay* for the *Times,* Edwin Godkin* for the *London Daily News,* and Frank Vizetelly* of the *Daily News.* Additional coverage was supplied by George Augustus Sala* and Edward James Dicey* of the *Daily Telegraph,* and Samuel P. Day* of the *Morning Herald.*

The Reuters* News Agency is credited with providing the most consistent coverage for the British press. Both the *Times* and Reuters chartered dispatch boats to insure that war news reached a public clamoring for information in a timely fashion. These boats intercepted incoming ships which had arranged to relay special dispatches by tossing them overboard in watertight cylinders attached to floating devices. At night these canisters were made visible with flares. They would then be picked up in nets and brought to shore to be telegraphed to London. By means of private telegraph lines secretly extended to the most western reaches of the Irish coast, Reuters received telegraph transmissions eight hours before its competition.

Despite the presence of pools of European correspondents, most of the news of the war reported in Europe was based on Union press coverage. Close to three hundred special correspondents represented the Northern press at some point during the war. The Union press representation became so unwieldy that the War Department required that all war reports be accompanied by a byline. The tradition of reportorial anonymity was broken with the Civil War. Dispatches appeared above either a correspondent's initials, pen name, or birth names.

Of the more than three hundred reporters covering Union armies during the Civil War, the average age was in the early twenties, with at least six still in their teens. Several had prior experience reporting foreign wars. Many were well educated, with degrees from Harvard, Yale, Columbia, and Amherst. Several were killed by enemy gunfire and at least six perished from camp diseases.

The best coverage in the North was provided by the *New York Herald.* Publisher James Gordon Bennett* was well prepared for this conflict, having dispatched correspondents to Southern cities before the war broke out. Close to forty reporters would eventually accompany the Union Army for the *Herald.* As publisher of the best-represented newspaper at the front, Bennett paid his writers the highest wages and could afford the best correspondents, ever cognizant that he could easily recoup his investment with enough news scoops. Leading *Herald* reporters included Charles Henry Farrell, Bradley Osbon,* Henry Villard,* George Hosmer, George Alfred Townsend,* William Young, and William F. G. Shanks.*

The *New York Tribune* claimed up to twenty reporters in the field, with Albert Deane Richardson,* Junius Henri Browne,* George W. Smalley,* Henry E. Wing,* Homer Byington,* Samuel Wilkeson,* and James Wilkeson the most recognizable names. The *New York Times* offered excellent coverage, having up to three dozen reporters with the Union Army. Among the more notable representatives were William Conant Church,* Henry J. Raymond,* Franc B. Wilkie,* Major Benjamin Truman,* William Swinton,* and Lorenzo Crounse.* Other important war correspondents for the North included Sylvanus Cadwallader* for the *Chicago Times,* Charles Carleton Coffin* of the *Boston Journal,* Murat Halstead* and James R. McCullagh for

Indicates a separate entry.

the *Cincinnati Commercial,* and Uriah Painter* for the *Philadelphia Inquirer.*

More than one hundred Southern reporters covered the war at various times. They ranged from the paid "specials" to volunteers, officers, and enlisted men who regularly sent letters and telegrams from the different theaters of operation. Among the best-known Southern correspondents were Peter Alexander* of the *Mobile Advertiser* and the *Richmond Dispatch,* Felix Gregory de Fontaine* of the *Courier,* Dr. William Shepardson* and James Sener of the *Richmond Dispatch,* and John H. Linebaugh* for the *Memphis Appeal.* The *Mobile Register* was well represented, with an aggressive staff that included Henry Watterson, Albert Street,* Israel Gibbons,* and Samuel Reid Shepardson. In addition, the Confederate Press Association* provided war reports for newspapers that could not afford their own special correspondents.

Compared to their Union counterparts, Southern reporters were allowed to operate with an unusual degree of freedom, although Southern authorities made various ineffective attempts at censorship. During President Jefferson Davis' inauguration ceremony he promised freedom of the press, and never closed down a newspaper during the conflict, unlike his Union counterpart. Initially, reporters were allowed to view camp conditions as long as no dispatches were filed detailing troop strengths, movements, or other logistical information. However, in January 1862 the Army of the Potomac banned all correspondents, and any security breach by the press would be a viewed as a criminal act. Following this new policy, reporters had to filter telegraphic dispatches through military censors.

The federal government prosecuted newspapers that published information that could be construed as helpful to the enemy. Several papers were closed temporarily for printing false rumors harmful to the Union war effort, and the *Chicago Times* was ordered to cease publication simply for attacking the Lincoln administration.

War correspondents came under vitriolic attacks on both sides of the Mason-Dixon Line. Confederate general Braxton Bragg had several reporters arrested for jeopardizing security and often instituted censorship of telegraph dispatches. Other Southern generals who expressed outward hostility to the press included Earl Van Dorn, Joseph E. Johnston, P.G.T. Beauregard, John Bell Hood, Thomas "Stonewall" Jackson, and Robert E. Lee.

Union reporters fared little better. General William Tecumseh Sherman loathed correspondents and barred them from his encampments. He was hostile to all "specials" and once suggested hanging *New York Herald* correspondent Thomas W. Knox.* On one occasion General George G. Meade took umbrage with reporter Edward Crapsey, and had him placed backward on a horse with the sign "Libeler of the Press" tied around his neck, and had him escorted out of camp to the tune of the "Rogue's March." Crapsey's colleagues rallied to his defense by eliminating Meade's name from any future dispatches, and in the process probably thwarted his political career. General Henry W. Halleck expelled several dozen journalists from the western theater in 1862 and General Burnside would have shot William Swinton* of the *New York Times* had not General Ulysses Grant intervened.

By 1864, Secretary of War Edwin Stanton was so concerned over public morale as the war dragged on and casualties continued to mount that he began reporting the war himself. He altered casualty figures and issued his own reports.

REFERENCES: J. Cutler Andrews. *The North Reports the Civil War.* 1955; J. Cutler Andrews. *The South Reports the Civil War.* 1970; Ian F. W. Beckett. *The War Correspondents: The American Civil War.* 1993; Hodding Carter. *Their Words Were Bullets: The Southern Press in War, Reconstruction and Peace.* 1969; Emmet Crozier. *Yankee Reporters, 1861-65.* 1956; Robert Neil Mathis. "Freedom of the Press in the Confederacy: A Reality," *Historian.* 1975; Louis M. Starr. *The Bohemian Brigade.* 1954; Bernard A. Weisberger. *Reporters for the Union.* 1953.

American Indian Wars

War reporting during the western Indian Wars between 1860 and 1890 offered correspondents many more challenges than the American Civil War.* As opposed to the Civil War, where reporters had access to towns, railroads, and telegraph lines, Indian War correspondents were rarely afforded such luxuries. Journalists were required not only to share the hardships of the various campaigns but also to participate in the fighting when required. Press coverage of various Indian campaigns began following the Civil War.

In 1867 and 1868 several correspondents accompanied the campaigns of Generals Philip Sheridan and Winfield Scott Hancock in Kansas and Oklahoma. Correspondents with Sheridan included Henry Stanley* of the *St. Louis Democrat*, artist Theodore R. Davis* of *Harper's Weekly*, and Randolph Debenneville Keim* for the *New York Herald*. They filed their stories by military mail couriers and regular mail. The most newsworthy story to come out of Sheridan's campaign was the Battle of the Washita River between General George Armstrong Custer's Seventh Cavalry and the Cheyennes in 1868.

In 1872-1873 the Modoc War broke out in southern Oregon and California when 160 Modoc Indians went on the warpath, terrorizing and killing local settlers. Among the contingent of correspondents covering this campaign were Robert D. Bogart* and H. Wallace Atwell* of the *San Francisco Chronicle*, Alex McKay* of the *Yreka Union*, and Edward Fox* of the *New York Herald*. This was the first Indian War covered by a foreign correspondent, with William Simpson* of the *Illustrated London News* serving a short stint in the field.

The most significant era and most active phase of warfare for Indian War correspondents was from 1875 to 1881. The biggest battle of the wars was the Battle of the Rosebud in southern Montana in June 1876. Five correspondents reported this epic battle, including John

F. Finerty* of the *Chicago Times*, Reuben Briggs Davenport* of the *New York Herald*, Robert Strahorn* of the Denver-based *Rocky Mountain News*, Thomas C. MacMillan* representing the *Chicago Inter-Ocean*, and Joe Wasson* of the *Alta California, Philadelphia Press*, and the *New York Tribune*. Most of these correspondents plus Jerome B. Stillson* of the *New York Herald* were present with Generals George C. Crook and Alfred Terry at the Battle of the Little Big Horn. Only the ill-fated Mark Kellogg* of the *Bismarck Tribune* accompanied General Custer's command to his death, the lone correspondent to perish in the Indian Wars.

Following the Battle of the Little Big Horn other correspondents were drawn to the battlefield. Among the most notable were Charles Sanford Diehl* of the *Chicago Times*, Barbour Lathrop* of the *San Francisco Evening Bulletin*, James J. O'Kelly* of the *New York Tribune*, and representing the *Chicago Tribune*, James William Howard.* Diehl, Stillson, Lathrop, O'Kelly, Howard, and Finerty reported the Nez Perce War from 1877 to 1879.

In 1890 a new field of operations seemed to be developing in South Dakota, drawing a new group of correspondents. Of the almost two dozen journalists, less than a handful would witness any action. Among the best-known were Charles W. Allen of the *New York Herald*, William F. Kelley of the *Lincoln State Journal*, Charles (Will) Cressey of the *Omaha Bee*, Teresa Dean* of the *Chicago Herald*, and Frederic Remington* for *Harper's Weekly*. The Sioux Indian disturbances, as they came to be known, had certain trappings of a war story, but could hardly be called a war. From 1890 to 1891 the Sioux were attempting to hold on to their lands and retain their cultural identity as the reservation system became more pervasive and restrictive. The massacre of over two hundred men, women, and children at Wounded Knee on the Pine Ridge Reservation signaled an end to the Indian Wars. Most sources indicate that only three correspondents witnessed this tragedy,

* Indicates a separate entry.

including Charles W. Allen, Charles H. Cressey, and William F. Kelley.

REFERENCES: Robert W. Desmond. *The Information Process.* 1978; Oliver Knight. *Following the Indian Wars.* 1960; George R. Kolbenschlag. A *Whirlwind Passes: Newspaper Correspondents and the Sioux Indian Disturbances of 1890-91.* 1990; Roger L. Nichols. "Printer's Ink and Red Skins: Western Newspapermen and the Indians," *Kansas Quarterly.* 1971; Elmo Scott Watson. "The Indian Wars and the Press, 1866-67," *Journalism Quarterly.* December 1940; Elmo Scott Watson. "A Checklist of Indian War Correspondents, 1866-1891," *Journalism Quarterly.* December 1940; Elmo Watson. "The Last Indian War, 1890-91-A Study of Newspaper Jingoism," *Journalism Quarterly.* September 1943.

Amery, Leopold Charles Maurice Stennett (1873-1955)

Born in India, he obtained his first newspaper job with the *Manchester Guardian,* which gave him a free hand covering events in the Near East. Soon after, the Oxford-educated journalist and future politician became assistant to the foreign editor of the *Times* in 1899, where he organized its correspondents for the Boer War.* A schoolmate of Winston Churchill's* at Harrow, he became the chief war correspondent for the *Times.*

Amery was authorized to accompany Boer forces until being expelled by Boer general Petrus Joubert. He was not unsympathetic to the Boers, having taken time to learn the Afrikaner language. He shared a tent with Churchill prior to his capture by the Boers; however, as luck would have it, Amery elected to stay in the tent as his ex-schoolmate went out to board the armored train that was later waylaid by Boer forces. Following the war he edited the seven-volume *Times History of the War in South Africa.* In 1902 he was called to the bar before embarking on a long political career. A Conservative M.P., he represented South Birmingham from 1911 to 1945.

During World War I* he organized some of the first recruiting campaigns and worked as an intelligence officer in the Balkans. Amery was

on the *Caledonian* when it was torpedoed in the Mediterranean. He escaped the submarine attack by hiding in the masts of a small boat that was later rescued by a hospital ship. Of his two sons, his eldest, John, was executed for treason during World War II.*

REFERENCES: Dennis Griffiths, ed. *The Encyclopedia of the British Press.* 1992; *DNB,* 1951-1960; Phillip Knightley. *The First Casualty.* 1975.

Anannin, Mikhail (b. 1912)

Born in Minsk, he joined the staff of *Pravda* in 1931. With the outbreak of World War II* he covered the front as a photographer-correspondent and fought with partisan forces. He suffered permanent injuries from several wounds he received in the fighting. After his injuries his wife Alexandra assisted him, as they worked as a correspondent team for *Soviet Union* magazine. Together they recorded the discovery of the mass grave at Katyn and the Polish campaign.

REFERENCE: Daniela Mrazkova and Vladimir Remes, eds. *The Russian War: 1941-1945.* 1975.

Anderson, Finley (?)

He covered the American Civil War* for the *New York Herald.* Anderson cultivated an especially close relationship with General Winfield Scott. During the siege of Vicksburg Admiral Porter attempted to run gunboats through Confederate batteries. In February 1863, Anderson was among the three reporters aboard the gunboat-ram *Queen of the West* when it came under heavy fire. Despite taking at least a dozen hits, it made it through one battery and continued downstream, where it was put out of commission by another Confederate battery when it ran aground. The indecisive Anderson was captured while waiting for the captain to return to destroy the ship and spent a year in a Confederate prison in Texas, while his compatriots Joseph Burbridge McCullagh* of the *Cincinnati Commercial* and Albert Bodman* of the *Chicago Tribune* managed to escape with the rest of the crew.

Anderson would return to the battlefront in 1864, where on May 9, three months after his release from prison, he was wounded in the arm at the Battle of Spotsylvania Court House following the Wilderness campaign. Faced with increasing censorship, in order to have his account of the Battle of Petersburg published, he acceded to Stanton's demand that he reduce the number of Union casualties in his report by two thousand, or one third of the actual figure.

Following the Civil War Anderson was made the *Herald's* London correspondent and reported the Austro-Prussian War* of 1866. He cabled the full speech of the king of Prussia announcing the end of the war to the *Herald* at a cost of $6,500 gold. This was reportedly the first newspaper story carried by the Atlantic cable.

REFERENCES: J. Cutler Andrews. *The North Reports the Civil War*. 1955; Louis M. Starr. *Bohemian Brigade*. 1954.

Anderson, John R. L. (1911-1981)

Anderson was dismissed from the British Indian Army prior to World War II* after he contracted a case of amoebic dysentery. Soon after he found employment as a reporter for the *Manchester Guardian*. Within a month the energetic ex-soldier was promoted to military correspondent,* beginning a twenty-five-year relationship with the paper. During the last year of the war in Europe he was the paper's chief correspondent in Germany.

REFERENCE: David Ayerst. *The Manchester Guardian: Biography of a Newspaper*. 1971.

Anderson, Jon Lee (b. 1957)

Anderson is a widely traveled correspondent and biographer. He has worked for *The New Yorker* as war correspondent and international investigative reporter. Anderson entered journalism as a reporter for Peru's *Lima Times* in 1979 and during the following years covered conflicts in

Central America. He has covered war zones in Afghanistan, Iraq, Uganda, Israel, El Salvador, Ireland, Lebanon, and Iran. His articles have also appeared in the *New York Times, Harper's, Life,* and *Nation*. Anderson is probably best known for his best-selling biography, *Che Guevara: A Revolutionary Life* (1997). While conducting research for the book he unraveled the mystery of what happened to Che Guevara's remains, which were exhumed in 1997 and reburied in Cuba. He demonstrated his narrative verve once again in the widely praised, *The Fall of Baghdad* (2004).

REFERENCE: http://www.newyorker.com/contributors/jon-lee-anderson.

Anderson, Scott (1959)

Anderson, the brother of war journalist Jon Lee Anderson,* grew up in East Asia. He began his writing career in 1994 with an article on Northern Ireland published in *Harper's Magazine*. While he has covered wars sporadically he is probably best known as a novelist and nonfiction author. By most accounts the 2007 film, *The Hunting Party,* was based on his reportage in Bosnia. In 2013 he was shortlisted for the National Book Critics Circle Award for biography for *Lawrence in Arabia: War, Deceit, Imperial Folly and the Making of the Modern Middle East*. Anderson has also collaborated with his brother on several books, including *War Zones* and *Inside the League*.

REFERENCES: http://www.thehalfking.com/info/scott.htm; Anne Goodwin Sides, "Under a Guise of Fiction, Realities of War," New York Times, May 22, 2006.

Anglo-Saxon Press

During the Mexican-American War* numerous correspondents and printers founded newspapers in Mexico's occupied cities rather than simply sending the news back to their home offices in the States. These fledgling enterprises became known collectively as the "Anglo-Saxon" press. Beginning with the *Corpus Christi Gazette,* they

Indicates a separate entry.

would eventually number twenty-five in fourteen cities. Most were ephemeral in nature, although some lasted until the end of the conflict. The first English-language newspaper to be published in Mexico City was the *American Star,* founded during the occupation of the Mexican capital by two enterprising journalists from New Orleans, John H. Peoples* and John R. Barnard. Having already established the *Vera Cruz Eagle* and other papers, they set to work in Mexico City publishing proclamations, military orders from American officers, and sundry news items. The real significance of these newspapers to the American public was that they offered more reliable news than releases coming through official and military channels.

REFERENCES: Robert W. Johanssen. *To the Halls of the Montezumas: The Mexican War in the American Imagination.* 1985; Lota M. Spell, "The Anglo-Saxon Press in Mexico, 1846-1848," *American Historical Review.* October 1932.

Angly, Edward (1898-1950)

Angly was born in Palestine, Texas, and attended the University of Texas before beginning a ten-year affiliation with the Associated Press as foreign correspondent in 1920. He joined the *New York Herald Tribune* as chief correspondent and chief of the London bureau in 1930. In 1940 he covered the French front, the British Expeditionary Force in retreat from Flanders, and then the Russian war before moving to the *Chicago Sun* in 1941 as its Far East correspondent. He was one of the first three war correspondents to reach Pearl Harbor from the United States following the surprise attack, and beginning in March 1942, was the first correspondent to report the arrival of U.S. troops in Australia. Later that year he covered action in New Guinea and the Southwest Pacific theater.

Angly later reported developments in the Soviet Union and the Baltic states and was one of only two journalists to cover the Teheran Conference in 1943. He then covered the war on the western front against Germany and headed

the Paris bureau for the *Sun* in 1944. Following the war he turned to freelance writing.

REFERENCE: Robert W. Desmond. *Tides of War.* 1984.

Aquino, Jr., Benigno Simeon "Ninoy" (1932–1983)

Best known as a Filipino politician and for his opposition to the Ferdinand Marcos government, he was brazenly assassinated as he stepped off a plane at Manila International Airport, as he made his way home from self-imposed exile. Less well-known was his stint in journalism for the *Manila Times.* At the age of 17 he became the youngest war correspondent to chronicle the Korean War* for the newspaper. His courage was rewarded the following year when he was awarded the Philippine Legion of Honor award from the country's president.

REFERENCE: "Benigno Aquino," *Encyclopedia of World Biography,* http://www.notablebiographies.com/An-Ba/ Aquino-Benigno.html.

Archibald, James Francis Jewell (1871-1934)

Archibald was born in New York and educated at Ohio Wesleyan University. He served in the Sino-Japanese War, was with General Nelson Miles in the Sioux and Apache campaigns and was with the Fifth Army Corps through the Spanish-American War.* Representing the *San Francisco Post* during the Spanish-American War, he was the first American wounded, albeit superficially, in the first encounter with Spanish troops.

Archibald was among the seven war correspondents permitted to accompany General Shafter aboard the flagship *Seguranca* during the initial American invasion. During the El Caney operation he was an aide-de-camp on the general's staff with the First Division. He was responsible for leading soldiers into El Caney in the search for hidden Spanish soldiers. In the process they were to destroy or confiscate weapons and arrest ambulatory civilians. *Leslie's* published a series of articles by Archibald and illustrated by Howard Chandler Christy* detailing this action. He also witnessed the surrender of Spanish troops after the fall of Santiago.

Following the war he continued to report from the battlefront. He covered the Chippewa campaign on Leach Lake, was with the army of occupation in Cuba, and in 1899 was with British forces in the Sudan on the staff of General Ludlow. During the Boer War* he covered the Boer army and later reported on Castro's army during the Barcelona campaign in Venezuela. He was with the Philippine constabulary in its campaign against the Ladrones and covered the Russian army during the Russo-Japanese War* for *Collier's Weekly.*

In 1910 Archibald was with the French army in Morocco and then with the Turkish army during the revolution in Albania. The following year saw him in Lisbon during the Portuguese revolution, and two years later he was with Chinese troops during the revolution in China. He accompanied Austrian and German armies at the outset of World War I,* but was arrested and then released by British authorities for violating war censorship.He wrote *Blue Shirt and Khaki* and *Tales from the Trenches.*

REFERENCES: Charles H. Brown. *The Correspondents' War.* 1967; *Who's Who in* America. 1910-1911.

Armit, R. H. (?)

During the Franco-Prussian War* the *Manchester Guardian* hired naval officer Armit to cover German forces throughout the hostilities. When not with military expeditions he was in the company of a British volunteer ambulance. His routine exemplified the freedom afforded correspondents prior to the twentieth century. Often he traveled alone across the battlefields at night with only a compass and the light of a cigar to guide him. His dispatches took up to two weeks to reach his paper and were characterized by

detailed but precise descriptions of each battle of the war.

REFERENCE: David Ayerst. *The Manchester Guardian: Biography of a Newspaper.* 1971.

Arnett, Peter (b. 1934)

Born in Riverton, New Zealand, on November 13, 1934, Arnett entered the American consciousness, vilified as "Baghdad Pete" by Senator Alan Simpson during Operation Desert Storm, for broadcasting for CNN from the Iraqi capital of Baghdad. In reality Arnett has been one of the most dependable war correspondents for the last thirty-five years.

He worked for various Australian newspapers and the *Bangkok World* while still in his twenties before becoming a stringer* for the Associated Press (AP) in Laos. Arnett continued to work for the AP in the Far East throughout the early 1960s. He began his coverage of South Vietnam in June 1962 and was one of the few correspondents to cover the conflict through the fall of Saigon thirteen years later. The often controversial Arnett probably saw more action than any other reporter during the Vietnam debacle. In 1966 he won the Pulitzer Prize for his coverage.

After Vietnam he made the shift from print reporter to what he described as "a video version of the Associated Press" working for the fledgling CNN in 1980. The first war he covered outside Southeast Asia was Cyprus in 1974 after the Turkish army invaded. In the early 1980s he reported the carnage in El Salvador and Nicaragua, as well as the Israeli invasion of Lebanon in 1982. That same year Arnett made his first trip into Afghanistan to cover the resistance of the mujahedin to the Soviet invasion.

He covered the aftermath of the Panama invasion in 1989 and the subsequent capture of strongman Manuel Noriega, which he described as "the first war as media event." Perhaps his greatest scoop took place during the Gulf War,*

* Indicates a separate entry.

when a U.S. military raid destroyed a shelter, killing more than three hundred civilians. The United States claimed it was a legitimate military target despite Arnett's firsthand account, which found no evidence of an Iraqi military presence. Arnett became a controversial figure during the Gulf War, denounced in Congress as the "Joseph Goebbels of Saddam Hussein's Hitler-like regime," and labeled a turncoat, a "video Benedict Arnold," and a traitor by a conservative spokesman. CNN, to its credit, resisted attempts to have him fired. Besides the Pulitzer*, Arnett has won numerous other awards such as the George Polk Memorial Award, an Emmy, and three ACE awards from the National Cable Television Association. In his autobiography, *Live from the Battlefield* (1994), Arnett counters charges that his reporting was manipulated by Saddam Hussein. In March 2003 he covered the U. S. invasion of Iraq for NBC and *National Geographic*. He retired as field reporter in 2007.

REFERENCES: Peter Arnett. *Live from the Battlefield.* 1994; Phillip Knightley. *The First Casualty.* 1975.

Arnot, Charles P. (1917-1998)

Arnot worked as a frontline correspondent in various capacities over a forty-eight-year career. He covered World War II,* the 1967 Arab-Israeli War, the Indo-Chinese War of 1962, Vietnam,* and other conflicts. He was affiliated with the Associated Press for more than a quarter century. Following his retirement he wrote several books, including *Don't Kill the Messenger* (1994), which recounts his life as a war correspondent and the deaths of numerous foreign correspondents since 1935.

REFERENCES: Charles P. Arnot. *Don't Kill the Messenger: The Tragic Story of Welles Hangen and Other Journalistic Combat Victims.* 1994; Robert W. Desmond. *Tides of War.* 1984.

Artist-Correspondents

The birth of the artist-correspondent coincided with the rise of pictorial journalism. By 1842 print technology made it possible for woodblocks of pictures to be printed next to type for long runs. Illustrated papers like the *Illustrated London News* were instantly popular with an increasingly literate public clamoring for information. The popularity of British illustrated papers was in part connected with the colonial wars of the Victorian era.

There have always been war artists, but artist-correspondents variously known as war artists or "specials" working for the pictorial press served a different purpose. They had to serve a dual function as artist and journalist. Artist-correspondents were expected to supplement their sketches with a written report. Engravers employed by the paper would then take the sketch and redraw it on a block, often embellishing the original product.

Besides the professionally trained artists and the "specials" of the illustrated journals, there were artists hired by publishers to produce paintings of frontline action that could be reproduced as lithographic prints. This method was particularly fashionable in the 1850s and 1860s. While there was no inherent news value in these images, they were produced by eyewitnesses and were considered colorful war souvenirs. Sets of lithographic prints were sold in sets complemented by detailed captions. Currier and Ives in America, and Day and Son in Great Britain, were the preeminent lithographic printers of this era. One of the most outstanding practitioners of this method was William Simpson,* who covered the Crimean War* for a London print seller. The Crimean War produced several outstanding war artists, such as Joseph A. Crowe,* Edward A. Goodall,* Robert T. Landells,* and the aforementioned Simpson.

Until the founding of the *Graphic* in 1869, the *Illustrated London News* was unchallenged by major competition in Great Britain. But soon after the publication of the *Illustrated London News,* imitators cropped up in America and throughout Europe, creating new markets for the growing pool of artist-correspondents.

The two best-known American pictorials were *Frank Leslie's Illustrated Newspaper,* founded in 1855, and *Harper's Weekly,* founded by Fletcher Harper* two years later. Both publications made remarkable contributions to the visual record of the American Civil War.* Among the most outstanding artist-correspondents of the Civil War were Edwin Forbes* and Henri Lovie,* who were two of more than eighty artists representing *Leslie's,* while *Harper's* could boast the talents of Alfred and William Waud,* Thomas Nast,* Winslow Homer,* and Theodore R. Davis.*

Most Civil War artists covered only one theater of operations. Alfred Waud, for example, spent the whole war in Virginia, and Alex Simplot* covered the western river war. There were of course exceptions, such as Lovie, who covered both the East and the West; William Waud, who reported from the West and the Deep South; and the peripatetic Theodore R. Davis, who covered more ground than any of his colleagues.

Civil War artists carried a minimum of accoutrements. Although Alf Waud wore a holstered pistol, most did not carry weapons, unlike their British counterparts, who often took part in the colonial wars. Battle sketches were usually done in pencil, while crayon and charcoal was the medium of choice for camp scenes. Other essential equipment included powerful field glasses, drawing supplies, a horse, rations, and a rolled blanket. The most skilled artists developed a kind of shorthand with sweeping lines filling in for the horizon or distant trees, a wavering circle in place of shells exploding in the air, and short lines representing troop formations. Notes were then written in the margins for the engravers, in order to avoid consuming time with minute details. In this way veteran war artists could produce sketches in minutes. Once the special artists completed their work, the sketches were rushed by mail or courier to the offices of the illustrated weeklies in New York. It generally took from three to four weeks for sketches to reach the newspaper page from the sketch pad.

The main obstacles faced by Civil War artists were lack of time and limited visibility. While the shorthand method was best for saving time, they worked on horseback as often as possible in order to cover the entire field of operations. They would avoid getting too close to the front lines, which were usually obscured by battle smoke, instead opting for vantage points such as elevated ridges, rooftops, and even balloons.

Artist-correspondents relied on engravers to reproduce their field sketches. Good engravers could improve the quality of poor sketches, while careless engravers ruined many fine examples of battle art. The best lithographers could be found at *Leslie's.* Frank Leslie,* himself a skilled engraver, supervised the preparation of each illustration. Prior to the 1860s war illustrators were often uncredited. At the outset of the Civil War, artists who produced the sketches for engraving were seldom acknowledged, quite often because they neglected to sign their sketches.

The siege of Paris in 1870-1871 during the Franco-Prussian War* was a watershed for war correspondents and artists. The *Graphic* editorialized that the war artist had come of age during the Franco-Prussian War. The golden years for war illustrators ended in the late nineteenth century. Some of the most recognized war artists plied their trade at this time, including the preeminent war illustrator of the era, Melton Prior,* the legendary Frederic Villiers,* W. T. Maud,* Charlie Fripp,* Frederic Remington,* Howard Chandler Christy,* and Charles Sheldon.* By the 1880s photographic methods began to replace the block drawings of the engravers and never again would the artist-correspondent have such fame and influence.

During World War I the U.S. Army hired eight artists to document the American Expeditionary Forces (AEF) in 1918. These included William J. Aylward,* Walter J. Duncan,* Harvey T. Dunn,* George M. Harding,* Wallace Morgan,* Ernest C. Peixotto,* J. Andre Smith,* and Harry E. Townsend.* At one time or another their work appeared in such venues as *Stars and*

* Indicates a separate entry.

Stripes*, Harper's, Scribner's, Collier's, Saturday Evening Post, Century, and other popular major magazines. All would go on to successful careers as artists in a variety of capacities. Although artists "developed their own agendas and individual styles of operation," Wallace Morgan, for example, was never without a sketchbook, typically about five by six inches, where he made notes in pencil, "little more than shorthand scribbles," that would be used as memory aids and the basis of the finished drawings he completed in the studio.

REFERENCES: Pat Hodgson. *The War Illustrators.* 1977; The Library of Congress. *An Album of American Battle Art.* 1947; Frederic E. Ray. *"Our Special Artist," Alfred R. Waud's Civil War.* 1994; Philip Van Doren Stem. *They Were There: The Civil War in Action As Seen by Its Combat Correspondents.* 1959; W. Fletcher Thompson, Jr. *The Image of War: The Pictorial Reporting of the American Civil War.* 1959; Alfred Emile Cornebise. *Art from the Trenches.* 1991.

Ashmead-Bartlett, Ellis
(1881-1931)

He witnessed his first war as special correspondent during the 1897 Greco-Turkish War.* Unfortunately, while in the company of Turkish forces he was captured by Greek troops. Following the war he enlisted in the Second Bedfordshire Regiment at the outset of the Boer War.* In 1904 he represented the *Daily Telegraph* during the Russo-Japanese War,* reporting the conflict from the Japanese side. In 1907 he covered the French campaign in Morocco and two years later was with the Spanish army in Morocco during the war against the inhabitants of the Riff Mountains.

Ashmead-Bartlett was again at the front for the *Telegraph* in 1911, when he accompanied the Italian army on its advance toward Tripoli, and the next year was stationed at Turkish headquarters in the First Balkan War. The following year he reported the conflict from the Serbian side. With the outbreak of World War I* he hurried from London to the Continent, the first London correspondent to do so. He was present during the German bombardment of Rheims, but soon after was arrested by French forces for ignoring censorship restrictions. Because of the obstacles presented by the censors of the War Office, many reporters gave up covering the war in the winter of 1914-1915. Ashmead-Ellis joined the Red Cross in order to follow the action, while acting as ambulance attendant and hospital orderly.

In 1915, he was chosen by the National Press Association to cover the Dardanelles expedition for the London press. The campaign was a disaster, but due to harsh censorship restrictions he was barred from reporting the debacle. Any attempt to publish realistic accounts or casualty figures was intercepted by War Office censors. After he circumvented the censor, William Maxwell, and attempted to smuggle reports of the bungled Gallipoli campaign to Prime Minister Asquith, he was expelled and deprived of his accreditation. Ashmead-Bartlett returned to London and testified in front of the Dardanelles Committee, providing information which ultimately led to the dismissal of the commanding officer at Gallipoli, Sir Ian Hamilton. Except for a short stint at the French front in 1916, his career as a war correspondent was cut short when his name appeared on the War Office blacklist. Following the war he published his account of the Gallipoli campaign in *Despatches from the Dardanelles* (1918) and *Some of My Experiences in the Great War* (1918).

REFERENCES: Emmet Crozier. *American Reporters on the Western Front 1914-1918.* 1959; Phillip Knightley. *The First Casualty.* 1975.

Asmi, Rami

See YOUSEF EL-DOUS.

Aspell, Thomas Francis "Tom"
(1950–2013)

Aspell was born in New Zealand. He covered most major conflicts and world hotspots over a career that spanned more than forty years. He began his career as foreign correspondent as a cameraman with Visnews in 1970. He covered the Vietnam War* and was among the few journalists who remained in Southeast Asia to chronicle the fall of Saigon to communist forces in April 1975. Between 1975 and 1978 he was a freelance cameraman in the Middle East and in 1978 joined CBS as cameraman covering Beirut and the Lebanon Civil War. He worked there as a producer for ABC News from 1981 to 1985, when he was hired by NBC News as a producer, based in Cyprus. He would go on to cover major events and war zones, including the 1990 Iraq invasion of Kuwait and in 1992 the Bosnian conflict. During his 28 years with NBC he covered the wars in Afghanistan and Iraq, Chechnya, and the Arab Spring upheavals. He died on February 11, 2013, following a two-year bout with lung cancer.

REFERENCE: Christopher Harper, "No More Wars for a Real Pro; Rest in Peace," Tom Aspell," Washington Times, Feb. 20, 2013.

Associated Press (AP)

The AP was created in 1846 after five New York newspapers jointly shared and funded a pony express route that enabled riders passing through Alabama to get the news from the Mexican American War* faster to New York than the U.S. Post office could. The five papers involved in this cooperative news gathering and news wholesaling venture included *The New York Sun*, *The Journal of Congress*, *The Courier and Enquirer*, *The New York Herald* and *The Express*. In 1875 the AP secured its first leased telegraph wire, a 226-mile line connecting New York, Philadelphia, Baltimore and Washington allowing the news service to move news quicker by eliminating competition for other wire services. The following year Mark Kellogg* perished with Custer at the Battle of the Little Big Horn, becoming the first AP reporter to die in the line of duty. By 1914 it adopted teletype machines which allowed words to be transmitted by wire from a keyboard to far-flung printers. Before the end of the decade AP was delivering news to

overseas news organizations and in 1921 it ended its tradition of writer anonymity. In 1935 AP introduced AP Wirephoto, the world's first wire service for photographs. This allowed newspapers to use pictures the day they were taken instead of relying on the mail. In 1941 AP entered the age of broadcasting with its new radio wire. This method involved radio stations receiving teletype reports which were then read on air. In 1945 AP reporter Joe Morton* became the only known journalist to be executed by the Axis forces during World War II.* Just 25 years later AP would enter the "age of electronic news transmission" when it used a computer in Atlanta to news and broadcast services in seven southern states. By 1972 computers were beginning to take the place of typewriters for writing, editing and filing stories. By 2007 AP had won 49 Pulitzer Prizes,* more than any other news organization, including 19 for writing and 30 for pictures. By 2015 the AP had lost 35 journalists who died on assignment. AP President Gary Pruitt issued a detailed statement at the gathering of the Foreign Correspondents Club in Hong Kong on March 30, 2015 offering suggestions for better protection of journalists who cover increasingly dangerous war zones across trhe globe. He suggested that there should be new international legal mechanisms for protecting reporters, including one that would make the killing or abduction of a journalist a war crime.

REFERENCES: Walter R. Mears. "A Brief History of AP." In *Breaking News*, Princeton Architectural Press, 2007, pp. 403-413; Oliver Gramling. *AP: The Story of News.* 1940; http://www.ap.org/Content/Press-Release/2015/Dying-in-pursuit-of-the-news.

Atkins, John Black (1871-1954)

Educated at Cambridge, he joined the *Manchester Guardian* as its first special correspondent in 1897, when he covered the thirty-day Greco-Turkish War.* The next year he reported the Spanish-American War* from Cuba. Following this short-lived conflict, Atkins was sent to cover the Boer War* from 1899 to 1900. During the war, correspondents were instructed to send only very short news telegrams, these to be followed up by more detailed accounts by mail several weeks later. He was promoted to London editor in 1901. In 1907 he left this position to assume the assistant editor position with the *Spectator*. Besides his war dispatches Atkins also wrote *The Relief of Mafeking* and the two-volume *The Life of Sir William Howard Russell, the First Special Correspondent* (1911).

REFERENCE: David Ayerst. *The Manchester Guardian: Biography of a Newspaper.* 1971.

Atkinson, George (1822-1859)

Atkinson served as artist with the Bengal Engineers in India between 1840 and 1859. He published several collections of lithographs based on his experiences in the British army during the Indian Mutiny (1857-1859), including *Pictures from the North* (1848), *The Campaign in India* (1859), and *Curry and Rice* (1860). The *Illustrated London News* published lithographs of several of his Indian sketches.

REFERENCE: Pat Hodgson. *The War Illustrators.* 1979.

Atwell, H. Wallace (c. 1832-1888)

Writing under the pen name "Bill Dadd the Scribe" for the *Sacramento Record,* he covered the Modoc War (1872-1873). Born in Windsor, Vermont, he moved to California and had a peripatetic twenty-two-year newspaper career before covering the Modoc War. Atwell would eventually replace Robert D. Bogart* as the correspondent for the *San Francisco Chronicle* when Bogart was arrested and court-martialed for an old embezzlement charge. While covering the Three Days' Fight at the Lava Beds, Atwell and the other two correspondents, Edward Fox* and Alex McKay,* figured out a way to pool their reports, presaging an arrangement which would become more refined during World War II.*

During this battle Atwell narrowly missed getting killed in an ambush.

Ultimately, Atwell would serve as war correspondent during the Modoc War for not only the *Sacramento Record* and the *Chronicle,* but the *New York Herald* and the *Chicago Inter-Ocean* as well. He was the only reporter to cover the entire conflict from February to October. Following the end of the uprising and the capture of the Modoc leader Captain Jack, Atwell unsuccessfully sought justice for the prisoners. The Modoc War was the first American Indian War* to be so extensively covered, with correspondents competing to get their news into print. On his way home at the conclusion of the conflict Atwell had the misfortune to be riding a stagecoach that was waylaid by highwaymen near Yreka. When queried as to his valuables Atwell responded "two bits," whereupon they let him keep it. Upon his return to California he remained in journalism, doing stints with the *Visalia Delta* and the *Sunset Route.*

REFERENCES: Oliver Knight. *Following the Indian Wars.* 1960; Keith A. Murray. *The Modocs and Their War.* 1959.

Ault, Phillip H. (c. 1914-2001)

After graduating from DePauw University he took a bike trip 2,200 miles across Europe in 1937, as Germany prepared for war, building fortifications along the border between Germany and France (the Siegfried Line). In 1941 he returned to Europe to cover the Battle of the Atlantic for the United Press* from Iceland. He went on to cover the North African campaign in 1942, where he remembered wading ashore with advance troops near Oran "carrying my portable typewriter above my head. That was the war correspondent's only weapon." He covered the Tunisian campaign, including the tank and infantry battles at Kasserine Pass, Maknassa, and El Guettar. He reported the London Blitz and was one of three correspondents who wrote the

United Press's main story about the Normandy invasion from the safety of General Eisenhower's press office in England. While at the UP* office in London he mentored a young Walter Cronkite*.

REFERENCES: "Philip H. Ault," Indiana Journalism Hall of Fame, 1998; "Legendary Journalist Phil Ault '35 Remembered," July 31, 2001.

Aultman, Otis A. (1874-1943)

Born in Holden, Missouri, he was a pioneer in motion picture work. He was employed with the International News Service and then Pathe News during the Mexican Revolution. Between 1916 and 1917 he was under contract with Pancho Villa. He covered the major events of the Mexican Revolution as a commercial photographer and news cameraman, including Villa's raid on Columbus, New Mexico. He died in El Paso, Texas.

REFERENCES: Turner Browne and Elaine Partnow. *Photographic Artists and Innovators*. 1983; Raymond Fieldong. *The American Newsreel 1911-1967*. 1972.

Austin, Alexander Berry (1903-1943)

With the outbreak of World War II* Austin joined the RAF and became a member of the press section of the Fighter Command until the Battle of Britain, which he covered as an air correspondent and accredited war correspondent for *The Daily Herald*. Austin received high praise when he accompanied and trained with the commandos who made the ill-fated raid on Dieppe in 1942. He was the only representative of the British press to witness this action.

Austin covered the First Army throughout the Tunisian campaign before joining the Fifth Army for the landing at Salerno. He was killed on the road to Camarelle in Italy. Besides his war dispatches he wrote three books on his battle exploits, including *Fighter Command*, about the Battle of Britain; *The Birth of an Army*, about the Tunisian campaign; and his account of the Dieppe raid, *We Landed at Dawn*.

REFERENCES: Robert W. Desmond. *Tides of War*. 1978; Dennis Griffiths, ed. *The Encyclopedia of the British Press*. 1992.

Austro-Italian War

The Austro-Italian war, also known as the Austro-Piedmont War, lasted from April to July 1859. It began when Austrian military forces invaded Piedmont on the Italian peninsula. French intervention led to the formation of the kingdom of Italy in 1861 and ultimately to the unification of Italy in 1870. Besides the invasion and the July armistice the main actions of the war took place at the Battles of Magenta and Solferino.

Few correspondents were on hand to cover the war. The Piedmont military commander had threatened to hang any that he caught in his camp. The only French press representative on hand was the artist-correspondent Charles Emile Yriarte of the *Monde Illustre*. The best reportage was produced by British correspondents led by Joseph A. Crowe* and Ferdinand Eber of the *Times*, both reporting the war from the Piedmont side. Other correspondents reporting from the Piedmont side included Henry Wreford and Antonio Gallenga,* also for the *Times*. Coverage from the Italian side was provided by the stringer* Mrs. Jessie White Mario for the *Daily News*, Frank Vizetelly* of the *London Illustrated Times*, and with the *New York Times* Henry J. Raymond* and Dr. W. E. Johnstone, whose reports appeared under the name "Malakoff."

REFERENCE: Robert W. Desmond. *The Information Process*. 1978.

Austro-Prussian War

The seven-week Austro-Prussian War began on June 16, 1866. The war was triggered by the Prussian seizure of the duchy of Holstein. The Germanic states of Hanover, Bavaria, and Saxony sided with Austria against Prussia, which was supported by Italy. Since the military controlled the press in the countries involved in the war, the best coverage was provided by the British press,

Indicates a separate entry.

which was represented by five London papers. William Howard Russell* and C. B. Brackenbury* were there for the *Times* and George Alfred Henty* for the *Standard*. Other prominent war correspondents included Frank Vizetelly* and Hilary Skinner* of the *Daily News* and Edward Dicey* of the *Daily Telegraph*. American correspondents included Finley Anderson* of the *New York Herald,* and George W. Smalley* and Henry Villard* for the *New York Tribune.*

REFERENCE: Robert W. Desmond. *The Information Process.* 1978.

Axe, David (b. 1978)

Currently a military correspondent based in Washington, D.C., Axe has also worked as a contributing editor at *Warships International Fleet Review*. He is best known for his publications and blogs on military conflicts and barracks life. He has covered warfare and related activities from the United Kingdom, Iraq, Lebanon, Japan, East Timor, Afghanistan, Somalia, Chad, Nicaragua, Kenya, Gabon, Congo, and elsewhere. A man of many hats, he has shot video footage for Voice of America and has published articles in a range of publications including *Diplomat* and *Wired*. He coauthored with Tim Hamilton, *Army of God: Joseph Kony's War in Central Africa* (2013). Axe also maintains a "War is Boring" website (http://medium.com/war-is-boring). His graphic novel war memoir, *WAR FIX* (2006), was his best-selling book.

REFERENCES: http://www.warisboring.com/authors/25/david-axe; http://www.worldpoliticsreview.com/authors/25/david-axe.

Axelsson, George (1899-1966)

Born in Sweden, he moved to the United States in his teens and began his newspaper career in California. He returned to Europe in 1926 to work for the Paris edition of the *Chicago Tribune*. During the Spanish Civil War* he accompanied General Francisco Franco's forces as correspondent for the *New York Times*. Following

the outbreak of World War II* and the fall of France in 1940 he witnessed the French surrender ceremony in the Compiegne Forest and Hitler's famous jig of triumph, captured for posterity by photographers. Prior to American entry into the war he worked at the *Times* Berlin bureau, before moving to the Stockholm bureau.

REFERENCE: Robert W. Desmond. *Tides of War.* 1984.

Ayers, Chris (b. 1975)

Ayres was born in Newcastle upon Tyne, England and rose to prominence as a best-selling author and journalist. During the 2003 invasion of Iraq he was embedded with U.S. forces, chronicling the war in his book *War Reporting for Cowards*, detailing how he made the transition from business correspondent to war correspondent for the *Times* of London. The book is currently being developed as a motion picture. In 2004 he was nominated as "Foreign Correspondent of the Year" at the British Press Awards.

REFERENCE: http://www.chrisayres.net.

Aylward, William James (1875-1957)

Born in Milwaukee, Aylward studied art in both the United States and Europe before beginning his career as an illustrator and writer. His work appeared in *Scribner's Magazine* and *Harper's*. His subject matter early on was typically related to nautical life and he illustrated various works such as Jack London's* *Sea Wolf* (1904) and *Twenty Thousand Leagues Under the Sea* (1925) by Jules Verne. He was selected as an official Army artist and was commissioned in March 1918. He was headquartered in Chaumont, France. Following the Armistace he covered the occupation forces as they converged on Germany before returning to France. He was one of only eight official combat artists of the American Expeditionary Forces during World War I.

REFERENCE: Alfred Emile Cornebise. *Art from the Trenches.* 1991.

B

Bagby, George W. (1828-1883)

Prior to the American Civil War* Bagby was a Lynchburg physician. He hesitantly entered the field of journalism with several articles for the *Lynchburg Virginian* and as Washington correspondent for the *Richmond Whig* and the *Charleston Mercury*. He served as editor of the *Southern Literary Messenger* in Richmond for most of the war. Bagby had joined the Confederate Army at one point but was found unfit for the field. He returned to journalism as occasional correspondent for almost twenty Southern publications. Among his sobriquets during the war were "Hermes" for the *Charleston Mercury*, "Gamma" for the *Mobile Register,* and "Pan" for the *Columbus Sun* of Georgia. In the words of at least one Southern editor, he was "literally the best newspaper writer in the Confederate States."

Bagby was one of the first journalists to call attention to Stonewall Jackson. In 1862 he reported from the perimeter of the Battle of Seven Pines, and in 1864 from Petersburg, the closest he would come to witnessing live combat. After the war he continued in the newspaper business in New York but was forced to retire when his eyesight deteriorated. He returned to Virginia and went on a highly successful lecture circuit. Toward the end of his career he worked as state librarian and wrote several short works.

REFERENCES: J. Cutler Andrews. *The South Reports the Civil War.* 1970; Joseph Leonard King. *Dr. William Bagby, a Study of Virginian Literature, 1850-1880.* 1927; Stewart Sifakis. *Who Was Who in the Civil War.* 1988.

Baillie, Hugh (1890-1966)

Born into a newspaper family in Brooklyn, New York, Baillie got his start in the business with the *Los Angeles Record* as a police reporter. In 1912 he began a lifelong affiliation with the United Press*. By the outbreak of World War II* he had risen to president of the United Press; however, this did not deter him from traveling to the combat zones, reporting the air offensive over Germany and from the Sicilian campaign in 1943 and the following year from France. His dispatches were collected and published in his book *Two Battlefronts* in 1943. In 1945 Baillie was injured in a jeep accident near the city of Aachen. After visiting First Army units near the German city, Baillie was thrown through the windshield of the jeep and was saved only by his steel helmet. He later reported the occupation of Japan. Baillie chronicled some of his wartime exploits in *High Tension* (1959). In addition to his coverage of World War II, Baillie interviewed both Hitler and Mussolini, and reported from the Spanish Civil War* and the Korean War.*

REFERENCE: Robert W. Desmond. *Tides of War.* 1984.

---

* Indicates a separate entry.

Bajbouj, Atallah (d. 2014)

Bajbouj was a founding member and field reporter for the Syrian opposition-associated Nabaa Media Foundation.* He posted videos of the Syrian conflict* in the vicinity of Daraa on YouTube and Facebook under his pen name "Abou Daniel el Hourani." While covering the Daraa fighting he suffered a severe head injury from shrapnel during a mortar attack and died a week later in a Jordanian hospital on October 15, 2014.

REFERENCE: "Atallah Bajbouj," http://cpj.org/killed/2014/atallah-bajbouj.php.

Baker, George (1915-1975)

Born in Lowell, Massachusetts, at the outbreak of World War II* Baker was a cartoonist for Disney Studios. After enlisting in the army in 1941 he found an outlet for his talent on the staff of *Yank** magazine. His most enduring contribution to the war was his creation of the cartoon character "Sad Sack," which became a weekly strip in the magazine. Baker traveled the world as unofficial ambassador for *Yank*, promoting the magazine wherever it was distributed. Following the war "Sad Sack" went into world syndication and was reproduced in newspapers, books, and even a Paramount movie starring Jerry Lewis in the title role. However, as the war era faded from memory, the comic strip lost its appeal.

REFERENCE: Art Weithas. *Close to Glory*. 1991.

Baldwin, Hanson W. (1903-1991)

Born in Maryland and educated at the U.S. Naval Academy, he began his newspaper career as a police reporter for the *Baltimore Sun*. He joined the *New York Times* in 1929 and eight years later became its military and naval correspondent. In 1943 he received the Pulitzer Prize for a series of articles on his tour of the Solomon Islands and South Pacific war area. Although he was not an official war correspondent he visited many battle areas in his capacity as military correspondent.* In 1943 he visited the North African battlefront and the next year was with the invasion fleet during the Normandy invasion, joining Allied forces in the advance to Paris in July.

REFERENCE: Robert W. Desmond. *Tides of War*. 1984.

Baldwin, Herbert (?)

He was assigned by the Central News Agency to report the 1912 Balkan War. He started out following Turkish forces. His account was published as A *War Photographer in Thrace-An Account of Personal Experience During the Turco-Balkan War, 1912* in 1913. He apparently chafed under the restrictions imposed on press photographers by the Ottoman armies, which forbade photographing Turkish women and prevented any real action pictures. In one instance he was afforded the opportunity to take battle images during the Turkish retreat following Lula-Burgas but his camera malfunctioned. Baldwin noted that the best way to secure good combat photos was to be on the losing side because the retreat process presented more opportunities for action shots than an offensive attack, which most often left the photographer stranded behind the front lines.

REFERENCE: Jorge Lewinski. *The Camera at War*. 1978.

Balibo

During the 1975 war in Timor five correspondents employed by Australian television networks arrived in Timor to cover the fighting between the Indonesian government forces and nationalist Fretilin guerrillas from Portuguese Timor in eastern part of the island. Only two had previous war reporting experience. They were in the village of Balibo on October 16th when Indonesian soldiers entered the village. As the journalists pointed their cameras in their direction the Indonesians fired at them. One went down immediately. They pointed to their "safe house" with an Australian flag painted on the side and shouted that they were

"Australians." Nonetheless all five were killed by the soldiers. By most accounts the Indonesians were under orders to kill all journalists in the area to keep them from reporting the brutal war. Historian Philip Knightly put it best, noting "The Indonesians came across the correspondents but did not understand what they were doing in a battle zone and killed them anyway because the concept of a correspondent as an observer whose neutrality is to be respected is a western one, and to have believed that this concept offered any protection in a remote guerrilla was a fatal mistake." Several months later another Australian journalist came to investigate what happened and was captured by Indonesian soldiers and shot in a firing squad.

REFERENCE: Phillip Knightley. *The First Casualty*. 2004 edition.

Baltermans, Dmitri (1912-1990)

He was born in Moscow and studied mathematics at the University of Moscow. A self-taught photographer, Baltermans took up the profession of photography while still teaching mathematics in Moscow in 1936. During World War II* he was a photo-reporter for the Red Army and *Izvestia* and *Na Razgrom Varaga (To Destroy the Enemy)* newspapers. He covered most of the important battlefronts during the war, including the defense of Moscow and Sebastopol, the Battle of Stalingrad, the occupation of Poland, the liberation of the southern Soviet Union, and the climactic battles for Berlin. Following the war he spent three decades as chief press photographer for *Ogonjok* magazine.

REFERENCES: *Contemporary Photographers*. 1982; Jorge Lewinski. *The Camera at War*. 1978; Daniela Mrazkova and Vladimir Remes, eds. *The Russian War: 1941-1945*. 1975.

Bang Bang Club

This refers to four photojournalists who risked their lives to cover the death squads of South Africa

during the early 1990s. The exploits of Ken Oosterbroek, Kevin Carter, Greg Marinovich and Joao Silva are chronicled in the 2001 book *The Bang Bang Club* by Marinovich and Silva. Oosterbroek was killed by a stray bullet while taking pictures. Carter would commit suicide in Sudan, probably traumatized by his experiences there covering the deadly famine; he earned a Pulitzer Prize for his photo of a child starving to death under the watchful eye of a vulture.

REFERENCES: Greg Marinovich and Joao Silva. *The Bang Bang Club*. 2001; Paul L. Moorcroft and Philip M. Taylor. *Shoooting the Messenger*. 2008.

Bangert, Christoph (b. 1978)

Bangert is a German photographer who has covered conflict zones in Palestine, Japan, Darfur, Afghanistan, Indonesia, Pakistan, Lebanon, Nigeria, Zimbabwe, and Iraq, where he spent nine months on assignment for the *New York Times* in 2005 to 2006. The publication of his book, *War Porn* in 2014 made him a figure of some controversy in the war journalism community. The book features a number of horrific images from Iraq and other conflict and disaster zones, with most featuring graphic death and violence.

REFERENCE: http://www.christophbangert.com/cv.php.

Barber, Noel (1909-1988)

Author and foreign correspondent Noel Barber reported for the *Yorkshire Post* and the *Manchester Daily Express*. He left journalism during World War II* to serve in the RAF. Following the war he worked eight years for the *Continental Daily Mail* before joining the *Daily Mail* in 1953. He was wounded twice while covering combat stories. In 1954 he was wounded in Morocco while covering the North African War, and in 1956 he was again injured while reporting the Hungarian uprising. He went on to a prolific career writing both fiction and nonfiction works.

REFERENCE: Noel Barber. *The Natives Were Friendly.* 1985.

Barber, Wilfred C. (d. 1935)

Will Barber was a sportswriter for the Associated Press and a member of the Paris staff of the *New York Herald* before going to Addis Ababa to report the Ethiopian War.* Shortly after he arrived in Ethiopia he was stricken with malaria and died, the only correspondent to perish in the campaign. In 1936 he was awarded posthumously a Pulitzer Prize for "distinguished service."

REFERENCES: Robert W. Desmond. *Tides of War.* 1984; John Hohenberg. *The Pulitzer Prizes.* 1974.

Baring, Maurice (1874-1945)

Baring was born in Mayfair, London. He left Cambridge early to enter the diplomatic service in 1898. After serving at various European postings he joined the *Morning Post* as a war correspondent in 1904 to cover the Russo-Japanese War,* which he reported from the Russian side. He was present at the Battle of Liaoyang. His exploits during the war are chronicled in *With the Russians in Manchuria.* His detailed scholarly dispatches from Manchuria led his editor to call him back to London, where he was promoted to drama critic. However, in 1905 he was again reporting under hostile conditions, from Russia, where he remained until 1909.

In 1912 Baring was hired as the Balkan correspondent by the *Times,* and he was stationed in the Balkans until the outbreak of World War I.* He chronicled his early exploits as a war correspondent in *The Puppet Show of Memory* (1922). During World War I he joined the Intelligence Corps, rising to the rank of major. After demobilization from the military in 1918 he continued his career in journalism and wrote numerous volumes of poetry, and articles on Russia.

REFERENCES: *DNB;* Dennis Griffiths, ed. *The Encyclopedia of the British Press.* 1992; Phillip Knightley. *The First Casualty.* 1975.

Barnard, George N. (1819-1902)

Barnard was a skilled photographer at the outbreak of the American Civil War,* when he became an army photographer under Captain Poe, chief engineer of the Military Division of the Mississippi. Due to the nature of the photographic process, photographers were forced to remain content recording the aftermath of battles rather than the action as it occurred. The complexities of the collodion wet-plate process remained a barrier to actual battle coverage until the twentieth century. In his capacity as the Union's official photographer, Barnard was typically called on to take plates of bridges, railways, and military structures. However, he was responsible for some of the most enduring and earliest images of the conflict. Barnard accompanied William Tecumseh Sherman on his "March to the Sea," and his series of photographs are considered classics. Following the war he remained active in photojournalism.

REFERENCE: Pat Hodgson. *Early War Photographs.* 1974.

Barnes, Ralph W. (1899-1940)

He was born in Salem, Oregon, and garnered his first newspaper assignment with the *Brooklyn Daily Eagle* in 1924. Later that year he joined the staff of the *New York Herald Tribune.* He served in the Paris and Rome bureaus before becoming Moscow correspondent in 1931. He went on to report from Berlin (1935-1939) and then London (1939). He also covered the Italian campaign in Egypt, the British desert campaign, and British combat over the Mediterranean, Barnes was killed when the British bomber in which he was flying was shot down over Yugoslavia in November 1940, while he was covering the Italo-Greek campaign. The plane was reportedly heavily armed with bombs and received a direct mid-air hit. He was the first American correspondent killed in World War II,* a year before the United States entered the conflict.

REFERENCES: Richard Kluger. *The Paper.* 1986; Doral Chenoweth, *54 War Correspondents K.I.A. WWII,* 2003.

Bartholomew, Frank Harmon (1898-1985)

The Oregon-born Bartholomew began his fifty-year affiliation with the United Press in 1921. Prior to entering the field of journalism he attended the University of Oregon and joined the Student Army Training Corps during World War I.* Already a veteran of several local newspapers, in 1921 he was made Portland bureau manager for the United Press.

Following the Japanese attack on Pearl Harbor in 1941, Bartholomew headed war news coverage for the San Francisco division of the UP before assuming the role of war correspondent accredited to the Pacific theater of operations. In 1943 he covered the New Guinea campaign and then the Aleutian campaign from 1943 to 1944. In 1945 he was with the Tenth Army in Luzon, Philippines, and then with the Thirty-eighth Division. While covering the Okinawa campaign he became the first correspondent to enter Naha, the capital of the island. His last story of World War II* covered the Japanese surrender aboard the USS *Missouri* in Tokyo Bay in 1945.

Bartholomew reported the Bikini atomic bomb tests in 1946 and the Korean War* four years later. In 1954 he covered the last year of the French war in Indochina. One of his greatest scoops occurred when he reported the story of the U.S. Strategic Air Command's "fail safe" strategy for national defense during the Cold War. He retired from journalism in 1972.

REFERENCES: Robert W. Desmond. *Tides of War.* 1984; *New York Times,* March 28, 1985.

Barzini, Luigi (1874-1947)

The Italian journalist and caricaturist worked for the Fanfulla from 1898 to 1900, before joining Italy's largest newspaper, *Corriere della Sera,* for the next quarter century. His name became so linked to the paper that newsboys touted issues by announcing, "Article by Barzini." He also sporadically contributed to the *London Daily Telegraph.* He took his first photographs in China while reporting the Boxer Rebellion* in 1900. He was by most accounts equally adept with both pen and the camera.

In 1904 Barzini traveled to the Far East to cover the Russo-Japanese War.* Most reporters tired quickly of Japanese censorship restrictions and departed, leaving Barzini and two other correspondents to cover the war. As the only correspondent to witness the pivotal Battle of Mukden, he amassed several hundred photos, and hundreds of pages of notes and diagrams. His chronicle of the battle is reportedly still studied in Japanese military schools. According to one authority he was the only correspondent to comprehend the significance of the first war in which Asian forces defeated a Western nation. Following the Russo-Japanese War, Barzini covered two Balkan conflicts, the Mexican Revolution, and then World War I.* His son, the writer Luigi Barzini, Jr., stated that Barzini took his last war photograph during the Italo-Turkish War of 1911, recording the Italian cavalry in action at Tripoli.

Although Barzini covered eight wars as a reporter and became one of the most famous European journalists of his time, he was the rare breed in a time of wars in that he did not glorify the slaughter. He eschewed military decorations from foreign governments, ever cognizant these could be construed as some type of payment for services rendered. He directed several papers, wrote books and articles, and in 1934 was elected to the Italian senate.

Indicates a separate entry.

REFERENCES: Phillip Knightley. *The First Casualty*. 1975; Nicolas Monti. *Africa Then*. 1987.

Bass, John Foster (1866-1931)

The largest contingent of war correspondents covering the 1897 Greco-Turkish War* for any one paper was from the *New York Journal*, led by John Foster Bass from Chicago. He had prior experience on the front lines as the only American press representative covering the Egyptian-Sudan campaign in 1894 for the *Chicago Record*. Bass later covered the Spanish-American War* for the *New York Evening Post* and then the subsequent Philippines campaign for the *Journal*.

He left the Philippines in 1901 for a posting in St. Petersburg for the *Chicago Daily News*. During the Russo-Japanese War* he headed the *Daily News* war coverage and witnessed the final engagements of the war, including the surrender at Port Arthur. Following the war he returned to St. Petersburg, remaining until 1915. During World War I* he reported the German capture of Warsaw and was wounded while covering the Russian front in 1916. After recovering from his wounds he covered campaigns in France, Italy, and the Balkans. He also took part in various government missions and covered the 1919 Peace Conference.

REFERENCES: Robert W. Desmond. *The Information Process*. 1978; Robert W. Desmond. *Windows on the World*. 1980.

"Battle Fog" Policy

Prussian military theorist Carl von Clausewitz described the chaos of swiftly moving events as "the fog of war." One recent attempt to control press access to the battlefield has been referred to as "battle fog" policy. This involves blocking foreign correspondents from covering combat zones during the first crucial days of the conflict. This policy was employed by the Israelis during the invasion of Lebanon. The policy has been heavily criticized for heightening the suspicion among the foreign press concerning Israel's true goals in the region. Journalists resorted to deception in an attempt to find unauthorized routes to the war zone. Most sources have concluded that the "battle fog" policy was counterproductive during the 1982 campaign.

REFERENCE: Derrik Mercer, Geoff Mungham, Kevin Williams. *The Fog of War: The Media on the Battlefield*. 1987.

Bayeux-Calvados War Correspondents Awards

Each year correspondents and photographers are awarded with this honor for risking their lives and reporting conflicts around the world. Four cash awards of $10,000 USD are given in categories relating to television, radio, print and photography. Four other awards worth $5,000 each are given to young reporters under the age of 28 for similar criteria. According to the awards committee, an entry "should report on a conflict and its consequence for the civilian population, or an event concerning the defense of the press, freedom and democracy." A monument to more than 1,800 journalists who died while reporting stands in the City of Bayeux, in partnership with Reporters Without Borders.

REFERENCE: http://www.prixbayeux.org/index.php?id=46&L=1.

BBC Effect

See CNN EFFECT.

Bean, Charles Edwin Woodrow (1879-1968)

Born in Bathurst, New South Wales, Australia, Bean attended Oxford on scholarship, graduating with honors in 1902. He was called to the bar the following year. For several years he practiced law in Australia while writing articles sporadically for several Sydney newspapers. In 1908 he left law for journalism when he joined the staff of the *Sydney Morning Herald*. When World War I* broke out he began writing a "War Notes" column for the *Herald*. In 1915 Bean became the official press correspondent with the Australian Imperial Force (AIP), beginning with the disastrous 1915 Gallipoli campaign. As a member of the expeditionary force, Bean would remain a citizen, but wear an officer's uniform without badges or identifying emblems. The army equipped him with a horse and rations, and he was made an honorary captain of the mess.

Bean was one of three correspondents to witness the Gallipoli landings on April 25, 1915. According to Bean's biographer, the movie director Peter Weir used Bean's account for some of the battle recreations in Weir's movie *Gallipoli*. Rather than watch the battles from the safety of the warships, Bean shared the danger and rigors of the frontline soldiers. He began keeping a diary with the notion of writing the official history of Australian participation in World War I. Over the next four and a half years Bean filled 120 handwritten diaries. Following Gallipoli, Bean reported the western front in France and began compiling a photographic record of the campaign. In 1942 he completed the last of his six volumes in the series *The Official History of Australia in the War of 1914-1918*.

REFERENCES: Kevin Fewster, ed. *Gallipoli Correspondent: The Frontline Diary of C.E.W. Bean*. 1983; Denis Winter, ed., Making the Legend: The War Writings of C.E.W. Bean, 1992.

Beato, Felice A. (c. 1825-c. 1909)

Born in Venice, Italy, he became a naturalized British citizen during the heyday of the British Empire. He has been described as the first photographer to convincingly record the true face of war. The photographic technology of his time precluded reproducing actual combat scenes. Although identified with his graphic war photographs, Beato was primarily interested in landscape photography. From 1852 to 1865 he was a partner of James Robertson's.* They arrived in the Crimea at about the time Roger Fenton* departed. Their photographic business was known as Robertson, Beato and Company and was active in the Middle and Far East. Their most lasting images document the Crimean War* and the Indian Mutiny.

Beato was also active outside the partnership, taking pictures on his own at the siege of Lucknow and the Opium War. With an interest in architectural photography, Beato was commissioned by the War Office to photograph the destruction of the buildings at Lucknow. In 1860, following the assault on the Taku forts during the Second China War, Beato took pictures of the interior of the forts littered with corpses, some of the most memorable and graphic images of nineteenth-century warfare. According to one witness he asked the soldiers burning the dead not to move them until he had finished his work. According to a recent book by Duncan Anderson, Beato's 1858 photos in the aftermath of the battle for Lucknow "was the first time the dead had been shown after a battle."

He was one of the first European photographers to work in Japan, where in 1864 he took perhaps his earliest action photographs, capturing the French landing force debarking at Akama Fort. He photographed the Korean War of 1871 and the Wolseley Nile expedition of 1884-1885. Beginning in the late 1880s he worked as a trader and photographer in Burma.

REFERENCES: Christopher Hibbert. *The Dragon Awakes*. 1970; Pat Hodgson. *Early War Photographs*. 1974; Lawrence James. *Crimea, 1854-56*. 1981; Duncan Anderson. *War: A Photo History*. 2006.

Beattie, Jr., Edward W. (b. 1909)

A graduate of Phillips Exeter Academy and Yale University, Beattie was on holiday in Germany in 1931 when he joined the staff of the United Press in Berlin. He covered most of the major events of the developing world war, including the

* Indicates a separate entry.

Ethiopian War,* the "China Incident," Dunkirk, and the fall of France in 1940, at which time he was accredited to the British Expeditionary Forces (BEF) in France. He returned to London in 1940, where he reported the Battle of Britain. He reported the D-Day landings for the U.S. media from London in 1944 and returned to France in September, where he was captured along with two other correspondents and held by the Germans as a prisoner of war. Beattie was held at the Moorsburg prison camp for transfer to a camp at Luckenwalde. He was released when Red Army forces liberated it in April 1945.

REFERENCES: Richard Collier. *Fighting Words: The War Correspondents of World War H*. 1989; Robert W. Desmond. *Tides of War*. 1984.

Beatty, Elizabeth Mary "Bessie" (1886–1947)

Bessie Beatty was born in Los Angeles, California, beginning her career in journalism with the *Los Angeles Herald* while still in college. Following a decade as a columnist with the *San Francisco Bulletin* in 1917, she accompanied journalists Rheta Childe Dorr,* Albert Rhys Williams, Louise Bryant, and John Reed* to Russia during the period of the Russian Revolution and the First World War. She would cover Russia during the First World War for *Good Housekeeping* and in 1917 began a series entitled, "Around the World in Wartime," for the *San Francisco Bulletin*, visiting Japan, China, and Russia over an eight-month period. She spent a week in the trenches with the Women's Battalion of Death and witnessed the Bolshevik uprisings. In 1918 she chronicled her adventures in the book *The Red Heart of Russia*. During her tour in Russia she interviewed Leon Trotsky and interviewed members of the Russian Army. She was among the first civilians to enter the Winter Palace after the fall of the provisional government to the Bolsheviks. Beatty spent most of her foreign correspondent career as a freelancer.

REFERENCES: "Bessie Beatty, 61, Commentator, Dies," New York Times, Apr. 7, 1947; John Simkin, "Bessie Beatty," http://spartacus-educational.com/RUSbeatty.htm, Sept. 1997, updated Aug. 2014.

Beech, Keyes (1913-1990)

Prior to covering the Korean War* for the *Chicago Daily News*, Beech had been a Marine combat correspondent at the Battle of Iwo Jima. He was in his third year covering the Asian scene when Communist forces broke South Korean lines and advanced on Seoul. Beech narrowly escaped to Japan, where he filed his account of the Communist breakthrough. He returned to Korea in July 1950, representing the *London Evening Standard* as well as the *Daily News*. Reporting the Communist victory at Taejon, Beech described it as "the Americans' worst defeat." The ex-Marine sergeant remained throughout the conflict a critic of American war preparedness. In 1951 he was awarded the Pulitzer Prize for his informed dispatches from the Korean war front.

Following the Korean War, Beech reported the American buildup of the Vietnam War* to its conclusion in 1975. Beech, like other members of the war correspondent contingent from World War II* and Korea, chided the reporting of the younger journalists in Vietnam as "lopsided" in their criticism of the Saigon regime and the U.S. war effort. Beech worked for the *Chicago Daily News* until its demise in 1978. He worked briefly for the *Los Angeles Times* in Asia before retiring in 1983.

REFERENCES: Michael Emery. *On the Front Lines*. 1995; William Prochnau. *Once upon a Distant War*. 1995; John Toland. *In Mortal Combat: Korea, 1950-1953*. 1991.

Belden, Jack (1910-1989)

Belden was born in Brooklyn, New York, and educated at Colgate University. Following graduation he traveled to China, where he spent a decade before turning to reporting first with United Press International News Service and then *Time* magazine. He worked as an independent war correspondent in China between 1937 and 1942. During World War 11* he accompanied General Joseph Stilwell's forces on the Burma Road, which he chronicled in his book *Retreat with Stilwell.*

In 1943 he covered the British Eighth Army in North Africa and then Italy, where he was wounded. During the 1943 Sicilian campaign he took part in the amphibious landings at Gela and later at Salerno. In 1945 he covered the German breakthrough in the Ardennes.

Belden wrote *Still Time to Die* (1975) and *China Shakes the World* (1949), which was one of the few books published after the war about Communist guerrillas in the civil war era (1946-1949). Following the rise of Mao in China and the concomitant rise of McCarthyism in America few books saw the light of day that portrayed the Communists in a favorable manner. Belden felt that his book *China Shakes the World,* a classic in war reporting from the Communist side of the conflict, was poorly reviewed due to McCarthyism, and turned away from writing books. He spent the last twenty years of his life in Paris, where he supported himself driving a taxi. He made one last visit to China in the early 1970s, where journalists with the Nixon entourage reported him in such dire straits that he did not even possess a winter coat. He was apparently ill and was researching a book on Lin Piao.

REFERENCES: Robert Desmond. *Tides of War.* 1984; Peter Rand. *China Hands.* 1995.

Bell, Martin (b. 1938)

Bell was born in East Anglia and joined the BBC as a reporter in 1962. He moved to London in 1965 and for over almost thirty years covered conflicts and events in almost eighty countries. Among the almost dozen war zones he covered were the Arab and Israeli Wars of 1967 and 1973, Vietnam, Nigeria, Angola, Zimbabwe, El Salvador, the first Gulf War, Croatia, Bosnia, and the North Ireland troubles. In 1992 he was awarded the OBE and was also seriously wounded by shrapnel from a grenade fired by Serbian forces. His books include *In Harm's Way: Reflections of a War Zone Thug* (1995), relating his experiences in Bosnia, and *Through the Gates of Fire: A Journey into World Disorder* (2003). Since the 1990s he has been more involved in politics than reporting and served as a Member of Parliament from 1997-2001.

REFERENCE: www.redhammer.ifo/clients/martin-bell;

Benjamin, Anna Northend (1874-1902)

Born in Salem, Massachusetts, Benjamin set new standards for female reporters in an era when men dominated the medium. She represented *Leslie's* during the Spanish-American War,* covering American preparations for the conflict in Tampa and Key West. Although the army attempted to block her access to the hostilities in Cuba, she was one of only two women correspondents to reach the front lines at Santiago, where the combined might of the army and navy defeated Spanish forces.

Benjamin was one of the first reporters to break the mold of the woman correspondent. Prior to the Cuban conflict, female reporters were expected to report from the "women's angle," emphasizing stories concerning their own gender, chance meetings, health problems, and care of the wounded in the hospitals. Her dispatches were devoid of the usual sentimental renderings of the military camp life. She investigated the bad food, unsanitary conditions, and unsuitable uniforms issued to soldiers. Her reports deglamorized the conflict, depicting Theodore Roosevelt's Rough Riders as "Teddy's Terrors," as they stole pigs and chickens and generally terrorized the civilians of Tampa. Following the war she became a popular figure on the lecture circuit, delivering her accounts of adventure as a war correspondent.

Following the Spanish-American War she reported the Philippine insurrection for the *New York Tribune* and *San Francisco Chronicle*. Her reports were mostly filed behind her male counterparts' but were deeper and more detailed. Eschewing the telegraph, she usually would mail in her reports. She was in Manila when it came under attack by rebel fire. Benjamin was in Peking for the *Tribune,* where she narrowly escaped the Boxer Rebellion.* August of 1900 found Benjamin reporting the construction of the Trans-Siberian Railroad; she compared the primitive conditions she encountered to the nineteenth-century American West. Besides writing for the *Tribune,* Benjamin published articles in the *Atlantic Monthly* and *Outlook.* She died in France from a brain tumor at the age of twenty-seven.

REFERENCES: Charles B. Brown. "A Woman's Odyssey: The War Correspondence of Anna Benjamin," *Journalism Quarterly.* Fall 1969, pp. 522-530; Charles H. Brown. *The Correspondents' War.* 1967.

Bennett, James Gordon
(1795-1872)

Born in Scotland, Bennett emigrated to the United States in 1819. After working as a proofreader and book salesman in Boston, Bennett discovered his bailiwick when he became Washington correspondent for the *New York Enquirer* in 1827. Within eight years he had saved enough to establish his own penny daily, the *New York Herald.* He is credited with many innovations related to war journalism. During the Mexican-American War* he inaugurated an overland express service to facilitate delivering war news to New York City. In order to accelerate the delivery of news from Europe, he began using fast dispatch boats to intercept New York-bound ships fifty to a hundred miles away from landfall. In the course of the American Civil War* Bennett employed sixty-three different correspondents to report war news. He was the first editor to employ European correspondents, the first to use illustrations for news stories, and the first

to hawk papers through newsboys. His son was James Gordon Bennett, Jr.,* the so-called father of yellow journalism.*

REFERENCE: John Hohenberg. *Foreign Correspondence: The Great Reporters and Their Times.* 1964.

Bennett, Jr., James Gordon
(1841-1918)

The son of James Gordon Bennett,* the younger Bennett, born on May 10, 1841, founded the *New York Herald* and was the so-called father of yellow journalism.* Educated in Europe, he returned to the United States and served in the Union Navy during the American Civil War.* Following the war, after a training stint in each department, he assumed the post of editor in 1866. On his father's retirement the following year, he assumed the directorship of the *Herald,* presiding over it for more than fifty years. His interest in news of the exotic variety led to his sponsorship of various foreign expeditions, most notably Henry Stanley's* search for David Livingstone in Africa. While on assignment Stanley covered the British invasion of Abyssinia. With the rise of competing papers in the 1880s the *Herald* suffered a loss of prestige and circulation. Bennett died of heart disease in France.

REFERENCE: Richard O'Connor. *The Scandalous Mr. Bennett.* 1962.

Bennett, Lowell (d. 1975)

Well suited to the life of a foreign correspondent, by the time Bennett was twenty-one he had already experienced a lifetime of adventures. He had worked his way across the American continent and voyaged to Australia in 1939, where he joined the Royal Australian Air Force. He had to resign when it was revealed he was an American citizen. Next, he went to England and joined an international brigade organized by Kermit Roosevelt to fight for Finland in the Russo-Finnish

War. However, by the time the young sergeant reached the front the fighting had ceased.

Prior to the capitulation of France he joined the French Foreign Legion, but again resigned when he learned that Americans, as neutrals, were prohibited from serving in combat units. He next joined the American Volunteer Ambulance Corps and was captured by the Germans shortly before the French surrendered. He was imprisoned in a concentration camp for five months. Following his release he made his way to England, where he joined the Free French Army. In 1940 he served in an ambulance corps during the London blitz and parachuted with the French resistance until once again U.S. citizenship hastened his departure.

In July 1941 Bennett joined the International News Service as correspondent in London. In 1943 he reported the entire Tunisian campaign and was one of three correspondents who flew with paratroopers who captured an airfield near the Algerian-Tunisian border. While accompanying a U.S. Air Force bombing run over Berlin in December 1943, his aircraft was disabled by a German interceptor plane and he was forced to bail out at a four-mile altitude. He was taken prisoner again but eventually escaped when he was being transferred between vehicles. However, it was not long before he was recaptured and held in Stalag Luft No. 1 in Pomerania. In the spring of 1945 he was freed by the advancing Allied armies. Bennett returned to the United States following the end of the war in Europe.

REFERENCE: Robert W. Desmond. *Tides of War.* 1984.

Benson, Eugene (1839-1908)

Benson made the switch from struggling art student to war artist at the outbreak of the American Civil War.* His renderings of the attack on Fort Sumter were published in *Frank Leslie's Illustrated Newspaper.* He continued to work for the paper until leaving journalism to continue his art studies in Europe.

REFERENCE: Stewart Sifakis. *Who Was Who in the Civil War.* 1988.

Bentley, Henry (?)

Bentley covered Union forces in the American Civil War* for the *Philadelphia Inquirer.* He witnessed the Battle of Shiloh, where he was captured. He escaped and returned to Philadelphia with his eyewitness account of the battle from behind Confederate lines. He accompanied Burnside's Roanoke Island expedition (1862), and his account was the first published of the Battle of Roanoke Island.

REFERENCE: J. Cutler Andrews. *The North Reports the Civil War.* 1955.

Bernstein, Walter (b. 1919)

Born in Brooklyn, New York, he graduated from Dartmouth College, where he edited the college newspaper and contributed articles to the *New Yorker.* With the outbreak of World War II* he joined the army, transferring to *Yank** magazine from the Eighth Infantry in 1942. Bernstein reported from army training camps and later covered the Italian campaign. In 1944 he interviewed the Yugoslavian leader Tito. Following the war, Bernstein became a successful screenwriter and director of such films as *Fail Safe, The Molly Maguires, Yanks,* and many others. He chronicled his experiences as a blacklisted writer during the 1950s in the movie *The Front.*

REFERENCE: Art Weithas. *Close to Glory.* 1991.

Berry, Ian (b. 1934)

Born in Preston, Lancashire, England, he entered the ranks of photojournalism as press photographer for the *Daily Mail* and later for *Drum* magazine, both based in Johannesburg, South Africa. He covered his first conflict in 1960 when he photographed the massacre of protestors in Sharpeville for *Drum;* however, because of political censorship these pictures were never published. Between 1960 and 1964 Berry made at least six trips to the Congo to cover the conflict there. He covered skirmishes between the Katangan insurgents and mercenaries at Leopoldville, Elizabethville, and the most spectacular fight of the war when Belgian paratroopers stormed the rebel stronghold at Stanleyville. He left war photojournalism after his years in Africa, shifting to more tranquil settings for his subject material as a freelancer and photographer for Magnum Photos.

REFERENCES: *Contemporary Photographers.* 1982; Jorge Lewinski. *The Camera at War.* 1978.

Bewley, Cyril (1904-1944)

Born in Rotherham, England, he covered World War II* for the *Sheffield Telegraph and Star.* Reporting preparations on the British Isles for a German invasion in 1939, he was one of the first reporters from a provincial paper to be accorded accreditation with the Northern Command. He covered the campaign in Africa (1943) before being transferred to Italy to follow the Fifth and Eighth Armies. In May 1944, Bewley was on his way to cover the capture of Cassino with correspondent Roderick MacDonald when one of them stepped on a land mine, killing both men.

REFERENCES: Robert W. Desmond. *Tides of War.* 1984; Dennis Griffiths, ed. *The Encyclopedia of the British Press.* 1992.

Bickham, William Denison (1827-1894)

He reported the Union side of the American Civil War* for the *Cincinnati Commercial.* Almost immediately upon his arrival in the camp of the newly renamed Army of the Cumberland he became the favorite of fellow Ohioan Major General William S. Rosecrans. Partisan politics came into play when the staunchly Republican Rosecrans designated Bickham his volunteer aide-de-camp with the rank of captain and the reporter wrote complimentary articles about the general. Bickham, sometimes referred to as "Rosecrans' Boswell," came under criticism from rank-and-file soldiers in the field for what seemed inflated accounts of Rosecrans' successes.

Bickham covered the Battle of Rich Mountain (July 1861) and the Seven Days' Battles. He witnessed the Battle of Murfreesboro (1862) and in 1863 published his account of it in *Rosecrans Campaign.* In 1863 he ended his short career as a war reporter to begin his new paper, the *Dayton Journal.*

REFERENCES: J. Cutler Andrews. *The North Reports the Civil War.* 1955; Stewart Sifakis. *Who Was Who in the Civil War.* 1988.

Bicycles

Bicycles were sometimes used by correspondents on campaign during the Victorian era. Frederic Villiers* was one of the most notable boosters of this vehicle and used one in the Sudan. A prototype of a bike for correspondents was developed. One report described this as being sturdy and noted that "upon the handlebar is to be attached a typewriter," which the rider could use to record impressions of the battlefront in his path. There are no reports of anyone having put such a contraption to use. During the 1912 Balkan War photographer-correspondent Herbert Baldwin* of the Central News Agency suggested that the bicycle was a better mode of transportation than the horse.

REFERENCE: Pat Hodgson. *The War Illustrators.* 1977.

Biddle, George (1885-1973)

During World War II,* at the age of fiftyeight, he was recruited as an artist-correspondent by *Life* magazine from the army's short-lived art unit. He was born into a socially well-connected Philadelphia family and knew President Roosevelt by his first name from their days together at

Harvard. During the Depression Biddle collaborated with Roosevelt on the establishment of the Federal Art Project under the Works Progress Administration. He covered the North African and Italian campaigns from 1943 to 1944. His sketches and paintings strove to capture the horrors of war rather than upbeat and life-affirming imagery.

REFERENCE: Frederick Voss. *Reporting the War.* 1994.

Bigart, Homer (1907-1991)

Though he was handicapped by a slow writing style and a bad stutter, his career as a newspaper reporter spanned forty years. For half of this period (1943-1963) he acted predominantly as a war correspondent, first for the *Herald Tribune* (1927-1955), where he won two Pulitzer Prizes, and then the *New York Times* (1955-1972).

Born in Hawley, Pennsylvania, he enrolled in the New York University School of Journalism before dropping out in 1929 to work at the *Herald Tribune* full-time. Promoted to war correspondent in 1942, he covered the London blitz, the bombing of Germany, and campaigns in North Africa, Italy, and southern France. As a charter member of the Writing 69th,* Bigart was named by fellow member Robert Perkins Post* "least likely to return" from a bombing run. But Post was the only reporter to die on its first and only mission. Following V-E Day Bigart covered the final months of the Pacific theater in the Philippines, Guam, and Japan, for which he won his first Pulitzer. He was one of the earliest Americans to enter Hiroshima after the nuclear bomb was dropped.

With the end of the war Bigart spent the remainder of the 1940s reporting from Prague and Warsaw (1946), Palestine (1946-1947), and in 1948 Greece, Yugoslavia, and Hungary. In 1951 he won his second Pulitzer while covering the Korean War,* leading *Newsweek* to laud him as "the best war correspondent of an embattled generation." In the years to come his controversial

reportage would see him summarily evicted from a host of countries, including Hungary, Egypt, Syria, Lebanon, Jordan, Saudi Arabia, Oman, and Vietnam.

Recognizing that the *Herald Tribune* was on the decline and only a few years from expiration, he jumped ship to the *New York Times,* but not without regrets. Known for his memorable prose style, he covered World War II,* the Greek Civil War, the Korean War,* and finally the Vietnam War* as a member of the Saigon press corps.

REFERENCES: Richard Kluger. *The Paper: The Life and Death of the New York Herald Tribune.* 1986; Betsy Wade, ed. *Forward Positions: The War Correspondence of Homer Bigart.* 1992.

Bigelow, Poultney (1856-1954)

The son of diplomat John Bigelow, Poultney Bigelow was educated in Europe and was a classmate of Kaiser Wilhelm of Germany. He was hired by the *New York Herald* and the *London Times* to cover the Spanish-American War,* but lost his credentials to travel with the army to Cuba when he criticized the quality of American officers and the efficiency of the army organization in an article in the May *28, 1898 Harper's Weekly.* Richard Harding Davis* joined the chorus of outrage directed at the Englishman, although in private he shared Bigelow's opinions concerning the preparedness of the army.

REFERENCE: Charles H. Brown. *The Correspondents' War.* 1967.

Billman, Howbert (?)

Billman reported the Spanish-American War* for the *Chicago Record.* Unlike many of his colleagues he witnessed much of the conflict first-hand. He was present at the five-hour battle for Cusco Hill, which gave American forces the control of Guantanamo Bay. Billman also covered the El Caney operation, one of the most difficult engagements of the war, and the Spanish surrender following the capitulation of Santiago.

REFERENCE: Charles H. Brown. *The Correspondents' War.* 1967.

Birch, Michael (1944–1968)

Educated in Tasmania, this Australian journalist demonstrated an affinity for journalism at a very young age, not surprising since he was the scion of a family that included a number of other journalists going back several generations. By 1965 he was reporting from Canberra for *The West Australian.* Following his dream of becoming a foreign correspondent in 1967 he was selected over 100 other applicants to cover the Vietnam War,* rising to senior Australian Associated Press correspondent. Birch often placed himself in harm's way, leading to his death while covering the 1968 Tet Offensive. On May 5 he was covering the events with three other journalists in a Saigon suburb when they were ambushed and killed by Vietcong soldiers. The other victims were *Time* magazine's John Cantwell, Reuters' Bruce Pigott, and Ronald Laramy.

REFERENCES: "Michael Birch," http://www.answers. com/topic/michael-birch-journalist; "Michael Birch (Journalist)," http://netlibrary.net/articles/michael_birch_ (journalist).

Blair, Eric Arthur (1903-1950)

Better known as the author George Orwell, Blair was born at Motihari, Bengal. Following his education he departed from tradition by turning away from the university to join the Imperial Police in Burma for a five-year stint. Following this experience he traveled around Europe on a shoestring budget, as chronicled in his book *Down and Out in Paris and London* (1933).

His work was already leaning toward an anticapitalist philosophy when he volunteered for the Republican army in the Spanish Civil War.* Orwell went to Spain as a freelance reporter but ended up fighting in Barcelona. Early on he noted that totalitarianism was present on both sides of the battlefield, but the *New Statesman* refused to print his reports. He enlisted in the Twenty-ninth POUM, also known as the Rovira Division. Six months later he was severely wounded when shot through the neck by a sniper's bullet. Orwell was told he would never get his voice back, but several months later his voice suddenly returned. Returning to writing in the following months, he produced work characterized by anti-Stalinist rhetoric. His book *Homage to Catalonia* recounts his six months at war and was seen as a tough sell by his publisher because of its then unpopular political stance. When he died in 1950, less than a thousand copies had been sold. Orwell is best remembered for his apocalyptic vision of the future in *Nineteen Eighty Four* (1949). He also wrote *The Road to Wigan Pier* (1937), *The Lion and the Unicorn* (1941), and *Animal Farm* (1945).

REFERENCES: *DNB,* 1941-1950; Phillip Knightley. *The First Casualty.* 1975; Peter Wyden. *The Passionate War.* 1983.

Bloom, David (1963-2003)

Born in Edina, Minnesota, Bloom came to prominence as an investigative journalist and the White House anchor for NBC news beginning in 1989. He covered conflicts in Bosnia, Somalia, Israel, Kuwait and Pakistan. To cover the Iraq War in 2003 he created what became known as the "Bloom Mobile." This $500,000 retrofitted Army tank recovery vehicle had its own live television and satellite transmission equipment, which would allow him to file reports as he accompanied the 3rd Infantry Division moving toward Baghdad. He suddenly died from deep vein thrombosis and a pulmonary embolism brought on by many hours in a cramped posture within the vehicle.

REFERENCES: "David Bloom, 39, of New York." MSNBC obituary; Donald Matheson and Stuart Allan. *Digital War Reporting.* 2009.

Blundey, David (1945-1989)

Born in London, England, he began his newspaper career with the *Burnley Star* in 1967, and then later the *Evening Post,* before embarking on a sixteen-year stint with the *Sunday Times* in 1970. He served as the paper's Middle East correspondent from 1981 to 1986, when he reported the carnage in Beirut, the massacres in the Palestinian refugee camps, and the American retaliatory raids on Libya. He joined the recently created *Sunday Correspondent* in 1989 as its Washington correspondent and on his next assignment went to Central America. On November 17, 1989, Blundey was mortally wounded while covering warfare in San Salvador.

REFERENCE: Dennis Griffiths, ed. *The Encyclopedia of the British Press.* 1992.

Bodman, Albert (?)

Bodman covered the 1863 Vicksburg campaign for the *Chicago Tribune* and was aboard the Union gunboat-ram *Queen of the West* when it was scuttled after an encounter with a Confederate battery. Of the three correspondents on board the vessel only Finley Anderson* was captured. Bodman was one of the first on the Union side to enter Vicksburg following its capitulation on July 3. He also covered the Chattanooga campaign.

REFERENCE: J. Cutler Andrews. *The North Reports the Civil War.* 1955.

Boer War

The Boer War, variously referred to as the Second Boer War or South African War, was the most widely reported British war up to the twentieth century, with as many as three hundred correspondents spending time in the field. The two Boer republics of South Africa declared war on Great Britain on October 11, 1899, inaugurating the longest and bloodiest conflict fought by British forces between 1815 and World War I.

The war began when Boers laid siege to the cities of Mafeking,* Kimberly, and Ladysmith.*

The best-represented British press organizations were the *Times* and Reuters.* Well prepared, with correspondents already in South Africa, Reuters would supply close to one hundred stringers* and staff during the two-and-a-half-year conflict, with two fatalities. Among the best-known correspondents for the news agency were H. A. Gwynne,* J. de Villiers Roos,* William Hay Mackay, and Roderick Jones.* Reuters had a reputation for fairness that contributed to its accessibility to both sides of the war.

Correspondents for the *Times* included Lionel James,* Angus Hamilton, Percival Landon,* and Bron Herbert. While few journalists from outside Great Britain reported the war, other British papers sent reporters soon after the outbreak of hostilities. The *Daily Mail* organized a special war service pool which included George Warrington Steevens,* Charles E. Hands,* Frederick Slater Collett, Edgar Wallace,* and Americans Richard Harding Davis* and Julian Ralph.* Bennet Burleigh* and Percy S. Bullen represented the *Daily Telegraph,* and the *Morning Post* sent Winston Churchill* and Edward Frederick Knight,* who would lose his right arm to a dumdum bullet during the Modder River campaign.

Other British war veterans of the press included Melton Prior* for the *Illustrated London News,* Frederic Villiers* and Harry H. S. Pearse* for the *Daily News,* Henry W. Nevinson* and George Lynch* for the *Daily Chronicle,* John Black Atkins* for the *Manchester Guardian,* and William T. Maud* of the *Graphic.* In addition to the British press corps, noted authors Rudyard Kipling* and Arthur Conan Doyle* spent stints covering the brutal war. In addition to the print journalists numerous photographers were on hand to report the conflict. The London illustrated papers reportedly existed almost solely on Boer War photographs. One of the distinguishing features of this war was the prevalence of

* Indicates a separate entry.

photographers led by the teams from the *Daily Mail* and the *Black and White*. The *Black and White* sent fifteen artists, correspondents, and cameramen, resulting in increased circulation of more than a half million, while the *Mail* published illustrated supplements to the paper bound up and sold as *With the Flag in Pretoria*. Also present were the first cameramen to record moving pictures of a war for the British public. Early newsreels* from the Biograph Company depict General Redvers Buller's troops leaving Southhampton for war, as well as British Red Cross crews coming under fire on the South African veldt, although this was discovered to have been fabricated on a studio back lot safe in Great Britain.

Fifteen correspondents were killed during the war and are commemorated by a plaque in the crypt of St. Paul's Cathedral in London. An additional thirty-seven were wounded and several taken prisoner. The only non-British correspondent to perish in the conflict was Colonel De Villebois-Mareuil of the Paris-based *Liberte*.

REFERENCES: Byron Farwell. *The Great Anglo-Boer War.* 1976; Thomas Pakenham. *The Boer War.* 1979; Raymond Sibbald. *The War Correspondents: The Boer War.* 1993; Frederic William Unger.* *With Bobs and Kruger: Experiences and Observations of an American War Correspondent in the Field with Both Armies.* 1901.

Boer War Siege Newspapers

During the siege of Ladysmith,* Natal, in December 1899 several newspapers were published by journalists attempting to relieve the monotony of the siege. These included the *Ladysmith Bombshell* and *Ladysmith Lyre*. The *Mafeking Mail* was supervised by Baden-Powell during the siege of Mafeking,* Cape Province, from November 1, 1899 to June 15, 1900. As the siege wore on newsprint ran out, and the remaining issues were printed on ledger paper.

REFERENCE: Byron Farwell. *The Great Anglo-Boer War.* 1976.

Boettcher, Mike (b. 1954)

Boettcher was born in Ponca City, Oklahoma and educated at the University of Oklahoma. He began covering conflicts around the world in the 1980s and became a familiar presence during the early years of CNN*. He covered the El Salvador civil war, South African apartheid, and the fall of the Berlin Wall. As CNN's national security correspondent he covered riots in Miami, the Cuban refugee boatlift, the Grenada invasion, the Israeli invasion of Lebanon, the Falklands War, and the kidnapping of General Dozier in Rome. More recently he covered the Iraq and Afghanistan wars while embedded with American troops. He was among the first current war reporters to publicly discuss his bout with a serious posttraumatic stress disorder (PTSD).* He left war journalism to teach as a visiting professor at his alma mater. His many accolades include a Peabody Award, four Emmys, and a National Headliner award. He was credited as the first reporter to present a live satellite report on CNN.

REFERENCES: "Veteran Journalist Mike Boettcher Featured Speaker at OU Ceremony," The Oklahoman, Dec. 17, 2009; "Oklahoma Journalism Hall of Fame Inductions, Oklahoma Press Association, Apr. 9, 2010; Kevin Canfield, "Oklahoma Journalist and Ponca City Native Mike Boettcher Keeps Reporting from Dangerous Areas," Tulsa World, Apr. 2, 2012.

Bogart, Robert D. (b. 1842?)

He reported the Modoc War for the *San Francisco Chronicle* after a stint in the U.S. Navy and working on the staff of the *New York Sun*. Of the four correspondents who reported the conflict, he reportedly produced the least accurate work, usually basing his accounts on second-hand information.

The New Jersey-born Bogart had been in California for less than a year when the Modoc War broke out. He had edited a newspaper in Hoboken, New Jersey, and had been a paymaster in the navy before his western exploits.

On March 5, 1873, he was replaced in the field by his paper for making irresponsible charges in an attempt to stir up controversy over the peace negotiations. Soon after, he was arrested by the navy and court-martialed for allegedly embezzling while he was employed as paymaster in 1869. Sentenced to two years' imprisonment, he escaped from a navy ship. It is unknown what transpired afterward. His only paper trail consists of several articles he wrote in 1878 for the *San Francisco Daily Stock* and the *Boston Commercial Bulletin*.

REFERENCE: Oliver Knight. *Following the Indian Wars.* 1960.

Bohemian Brigade

The term "Bohemian Brigade" was invoked half seriously by members of the Northern press to describe themselves during the American Civil War.* Many of them reveled in a "nomadic, careless, half-literary" lifestyle. In the late 1850s and early 1860s the Bohemian movement was transported to America from Paris. So-called Bohemians met in coffeehouses to discuss art and politics and drink wine. Many of the era's newspaper reporters and artists of the illustrated weeklies were drawn to spots such as Pfaff's Cafe in New York where they could rub shoulders with prominent literary figures like Walt Whitman and William Dean Howells. By the time of the Civil War the term was used in reference to the Northern war reporters, particularly from New York City. Correspondent Junius Browne* defined a Bohemian as a person "of aesthetic and luxurious tastes, born out of place, and in opposition to his circumstances."

REFERENCES: Joseph J. Mathews. *Reporting the Wars.* 1957; Louis M. Starr. *Bohemian Brigade.* 1954.

Bohrod, Aaron (1907-1992)

He was invited to join the army's art unit in 1943. At that time he was artist in residence at Southern Illinois University. Bohrod was trained at the Art Institute of Chicago and the Art Students League in New York City. Assigned to the Pacific theater, he accompanied the first wave of American forces during the amphibious assault at Rendova. While in the field he made rough sketches and took photographs which ultimately would be used to produce a series of paintings chronicling the Rendova campaign.

Soon after, Congress disbanded the army art unit, but in late 1943 he was a war artist for *Life* magazine. Bohrod was transferred to the European war in May 1944. He landed at Normandy's Omaha Beach shortly after the initial beachhead was gained. Too late to sketch any fighting, he captured massive movement of arms and equipment onto the French shores. He followed American forces into Germany and sketched the last days of the war. His portrait, with a backdrop of rubble and debris, appeared on the cover of *Life* on April 30, 1945.

REFERENCE: Frederick S. Voss. *Reporting the War.* 1994.

Bonsal, Stephen (1865-1951)

Born in Baltimore, Maryland, he was a student in Germany before entering journalism in 1885, when he accompanied the Bulgarian army during the Bulgarian-Serbian War. Following the war he returned to the United States to continue his journalism career. He returned to Europe in 1887 as a representative of the *World* and then the *New York Herald.* In 1890 he established his reputation with several articles repudiating accusations of Turkish atrocities in Macedonia. The next year he reported social upheaval in Africa, which is chronicled in his book *Morocco As It Is.* He served in the Foreign Service from 1893 to 1897 in a variety of Asian postings and also reported the Sino-Japanese War of 1894-1895.

In 1897, prior to American involvement in Cuba, Bonsal took a fact-finding tour of the island, where he found hundreds of thousands of Cubans forced from their homes by Weyler's "depopulation by proclamation program" and on the brink of mass starvation. The looming tragedy was chronicled the following year in his book *The Real Condition of Cuba Today*.

With the outbreak of hostilities, Bonsal headed for the action as a member of *McClure's Magazine*. He witnessed the Battle of El Caney and the appalling treatment of the wounded at Siboney. In August 1898 Bonsal transferred to the Philippines to cover the outbreak of the insurrection and subsequent political developments for the *New York Herald*.

In 1900 Bonsal remained in the Far East, where he covered the Boxer Rebellion* and four years later the Russo-Japanese War* from the Japanese side. Prior to World War I* he reported the Balkan Wars and was in Mexico City when President Diaz was forced out of office. Later he served as interpreter for President Woodrow Wilson during the 1919 Versailles Peace Conference. Among his books are *The Real Condition of Cuba* (1897), *The Fight for Santiago* (1899), *Heyday in a Vanished World* (1937), and *Unfinished Business, Paris-Versailles*, 1919 which garnered him a Pulitzer Prize for history in 1945.

REFERENCES: Charles H. Brown. *The Correspondent's War.* 1967; Gerald W. Johnson, Frank R. Kent, H. L. Mencken, and Hamilton Owens. *The Sunpapers of Baltimore, 1837-1937.* 1937.

Borthwick, Jessica Elvira (1888–1946)

Borthwick was the daughter of General George Colville Borthwick, commander-in-chief of the Turkish army during the 1913 war between the Ottoman Empire and the Balkan states of Greece, Bulgaria, Serbia, and Montenegro. Her story parallels the development of early film history. On her own volition and due to her father's military and journalistic connections, she was able to cover aspects of the Balkan war using motion picture and still photography. Her father's Bulgarian connections allowed her to make a year-long Balkan expedition "armed with a still camera, Newman cinematograph camera and a revolver." According to one of her biographers, she made a habit of relieving dead soldiers on her peregrinations of their weapons. She embedded herself with the Bulgarian army and was stricken with cholera. Covering the Serbian war in Macedonia, some of her equipment was damaged by an errant shell, but fortunately her film survived. Following her Balkan adventures she returned to Britain and went on tour with her films and photos. While her lecture tour proved rather lackluster, she reportedly exhibited her films of the war at London's Scala Theatre, under the title, "The Aftermath of the Balkan War." During World War I* she returned to the battlefront as an ambulance worker on the Western Front, where she was wounded and made an honorary officer in the Belgian army. Borthwick helped refugees escape Ostend on her steam yacht, the *Grace Darling*. She lived the remainder of her life among Bohemian artists in South Kensington where she worked as a sculptor under the name "Nell Foy" and developed a taste for pipe smoking. Her Balkan war films have vanished.

REFERENCES: Luke McKernan, "Jessica Borthwick Homepage," Women and Silent British Cinema, http://womenandsilentbritishcinema.wordpress.com/the-women/Jessica-borthwick; Kevin Brownlow. *The War the West and the Wilderness.* 1979.

Boss, Gerard William (1917–2007)

Born in Kingston, Ontario, Boss was a virtual Renaissance man, conversant in English, French, German, Dutch, and Russian; he was equally accomplished in the world of music as musician and composer and founded the Ottawa Concert Orchestra while working as a part-time journalist for the local newspaper. Boss rose to prominence in war journalism while covering World War II* and the Korean War.* Better known as Bill Boss, or simply by the initials "bb," he became known for his ginger-colored beard and for eating "censors for breakfast." In 1943 he went to Italy with the Canadian Corps as a Public Relations officer, a position that often required him to transport other journalists to the battlefront. The following year he was hired as a war correspondent to cover the Allied penetration into Italy and Northwest Europe. In 1945 he covered the liberation of the Netherlands. He stayed on with the Canadian Press as a foreign correspondent and went on to cover the outbreak of the Korean War* in 1950. He reported from Busan, South Korea while accompanying Princess Patricia's Canadian Light Infantry. He found himself at loggerheads with censorship authorities, leading him to cover the war separately from the armed forces. He covered the major battles of the war in which Canadian forces were involved, including the Battle of Kapyong, the Battle of Chuam-ni, and the Battle of Maehwa-San. Boss often found himself at odds with other reporters, who attempted to have him banned from the battlefront because he refused to censor his reporting. This became a public matter after he reported on various war crimes allegedly committed by Canadian troops. In one case he filed a report charging several Canadian soldiers of beating and raping two Korean women; however, it was never printed after it was intercepted by American occupation officials in Tokyo and sent to Canadian Army headquarters. Following the war he put his Russian language skills to work, opening the first Canadian news bureau for Canadian Press in Moscow.

REFERENCE: Stephen Thorne, "Tribute to Former Canadian Press War Correspondent," Canadian Press, Oct. 17, 2007.

Boulat, Alexandra (1962-2007)

The daughter of noted *Life* photographer Pierre Boulat, Alexandra developed an early affinity for photojournalism. She left art school to cover the war in the Balkans for Sipa press in 1989. From there she went on to chronicle the spreading violence in Croatia, Kosovo and Bosnia in the 1990s. She would go on to cover even worse conflagrations in Rwanda and Afghanistan, and then Iraq, Isreal

and Lebenon. Her last assignment took her to the Gaza Strip where in the summer of 2007 she covered the fighting between Fatah and Hamas militants. Her work was cut short when she suffered a stroke in the West Bank. She would never recover and died in Paris that October.

REFERENCE: Jan McGirk. "Alexandra Boulat, Photojournalist who recorded the injustices wrought on ordinary people by war". *The Guardian*. October 13, 2007.

Bourchier, James David (1850-1920)

Born in Limerick County, Ireland, he was educated at Trinity College, Dublin, and King's College, Cambridge. After ten years as a teacher at Eton and afflicted with increasing deafness he joined the staff of the *Times* in 1892. He had been in Sofia, Bulgaria, since 1888 seeking medical treatment for his hearing loss before being assigned to head up the Sofia bureau for the *Times,* a post he would hold until World War I.* With a reputation as an authority on Balkan affairs he was often called on to serve as an intermediary between Cretan freedom fighters and Greek authorities.

In 1903 he was present when Bulgarian peasants in Macedonia attempted to overthrow the Ottoman rulers. Bourchier, sympathetic to the patriots, publicized Turkish atrocities. In 1915, he was unprepared for news that Bulgaria had chosen to align itself with Austria-Hungary and Germany. Since he was supposedly an expert on the region, his reports lost much of their credibility after this unforeseen turn of events. His paper lost faith in his reporting and Bourchier moved to neighboring Rumania, where he remained until 1917. When the country was overrun by the Central Powers, Bourchier relocated first to Odessa, and then to Petrograd. While in Russia he covered the October Revolution and was granted rare interviews with Lenin and Trotsky. He returned to England in 1918 and spent the remainder of his life as an unofficial spokesman for Bulgaria and other Balkan states.

Indicates a separate entry.

His affinity for the region led to his 1920 appointment as Bulgaria's consul general in London. Before assuming this position he made a final visit to Bulgaria. He died in Sofia shortly after his arrival and was buried with high honors.

REFERENCES: Robert W. Desmond. *Windows on the World*. 1980; DNB. 1912-1921.

Bourke-White, Margaret (1906-1971)

One of the greatest photojournalists of the twentieth century, Bourke-White joined the staff of *Life* at its inception in 1935. She gained early prominence for photo stories on daily life in quintessentially American small towns. Her first wartime assignment promised to be her first scoop, or so it seemed, when she found herself the only photojournalist in Russia on June 22, 1941 as Nazi troops invaded the Soviet Union. Unfortunately, Russian authorities had issued an edict forbidding any photos of the invasion under penalty of death. Instead, Bourke-White opted for the safety of her suite as the world plunged further into chaos.

However, only days after the invasion she was in position atop the American embassy to record raids by the Luftwaffe. Among her memorable pictures in 1941 was a spread of Joseph Stalin, Bourke-White being the first American photographer to be granted such access. Her tenure in Russia resulted in many classic war photos.

Margaret often had to overcome discrimination by the military brass in order to gain permission to accompany the troops into battle. She covered the North African campaign and was on board a ship torpedoed by a U-boat; this yielded her another photo scoop, on the hazards of the war at sea. On January 22, 1943, she became the first woman to fly on an American combat mission. Among the most lasting images of World War II* are her photographs of the liberation of the German concentration camps.

While covering the Korean War* she noticed the first symptoms of Parkinson's disease, which effectively ended her career as a war correspondent. In addition to her other work she went on to write six books.

REFERENCES: Julia Edwards. *Women of the World*. 1988; Frederick Voss. *Reporting the War*. 1994.

Bowen, Jeremy (b. 1960)

Born in Cardiff, Wales, Bowen joined the BBC in 1984 and has covered numerous war zones since 1989 when he reported the El Salvadoran civil war. He has purportedly reported from over 70 countries, mostly in the Middle East and the Balkans. He covered the Bosnia-Herzegovina civil war and the 1999 Kosovo war. Bowen described the death of a friend and colleague under fire in Lebanon in 2000 as "the pivotal moment of his life." It took place as the Israel Defense Forces (IDF) were withdrawing from southern Lebanon and Bowen's car came under fire from IDF tank fire, killing his "fixer" and driver, Abed Takkoush. After this, Bowen suffered from posttraumatic stress disorder* and left the frontlines to work in the television studio as a presenter for two years. Chafing at the confines of the studio in 2003 he covered the invasion of Iraq from Baghdad and eventually returned to the field as a foreign correspondent. In 2005 after the BBC created the position of Middle East editor, he was selected as the first one. He covered the Israeli-Palestinian conflict and once more found himself under fire. In 2011 he was credited as the first British journalist to interview Muammar Gaddafi since the outbreak of the Libyan Civil War* earlier in the year. In 2013 Bowen was covering protests in Egypt when he escaped serious injury despite being shot in the head with shotgun pellets. He is one of the few journalists still reporting the war in Syria from inside the country. He nabbed an exclusive BBC interview with President Bashar al-Assad in February 2015. He is the author of several books including *War Stories* (2006).

REFERENCE: "Jeremy Bowen: Man in the Middle," Independent, Dec. 11, 2006.

Bowlby, Thomas William (1818–1860)

Born in Gibraltar, Bowlby was educated in the law and became a solicitor in the 1840s. In 1848 he worked as a special correspondent in Berlin, Germany for the *London Times*. In between the 1840s and his death in 1860 he was involved in a variety of business ventures, especially those connected with the fledgling railroad industry. In 1860 he agreed to go to China as a special correspondent for the *Times* once more. His reports from there were informative and popular with readers. He was in Tien-tsin on August 23, 1860 when he was captured along with Admiral Hope and several others as they made their way to Tang-chow to arrange some of the preliminaries for getting the peace process underway. They were waylaid and captured by the Tartar general, San-ko-lin-sin, and imprisoned. The captives were apparently tortured over several days and Bowlby died from his injuries less than a month later.

REFERENCE: http://en.wikisource.org/wiki/Bowlby,_Thomas_William_%28DNB00%29.

Boxer Rebellion

Following the Japanese victory over China in the Sino-Japanese War of 1894-1895, secret societies began forming in China in response to a mounting antiforeigner sentiment. Some of these societies banded together into a league whose name, translated into English, meant "Fists of Righteous Harmony," or "Boxers," and whose main goal was to drive out foreigners. After several riots and violent attacks on foreign residents the Chinese government was called on to suppress the Boxers. When it failed to respond adequately, a coalition of eight governments sent forces into China between June and August 1900.

As eighteen thousand British, French, U.S., Japanese, Russian, and German troops assisted various besieged foreign legations, war correspondents began flocking to China. Among them were numerous correspondents who had been following the Philippine insurrection, including Frederick Palmer,* Stephen Bonsal,* Oscar King Davis,* Robert M. Collins,* David Morris, and Martin Egan,* in addition to Ralph D. Paine* and Charles E. Kloeber. Other correspondents, including Dr. Robert Coltman,* Thomas F. Millard,* and Wilmott Harsant Lewis,* had prior China experience. Joseph Medill Patterson,* George Lynch,* Dr. Emile Joseph Dillon,* and Dr. George Morrison* also contributed outstanding firsthand accounts of the conflict.

Foreign correspondents were in abundance as well during this multinational operation. Gaston Chadbourne and Louis Marie Julien Viaud,* better known as the novelist Pierre Loti, represented French papers, and Luigi Barzini* was in China for the Milan-based *Corriere della Sera*.

Those reporting the Boxer campaign faced more than their share of logistical hardships. Transportation and communication activities were impeded by the tremendous distances and cost of sending dispatches from China to Europe by way of Siberia. Rates varied between $1.62 and $1.72 per word for dispatches bound for London or New York.

REFERENCES: Robert W. Desmond. *The Information Process.* 1978; Peter Fleming. *The Siege at Peking.* 1959; Henry Keown-Boyd. *Boxer Rebellion.* 1995; Richard O'Connor. *The Spirit Soldiers.* 1973.

Boyle, Frederick (1841-1914)

Boyle covered the 1868 Abyssinian War and the 1873 Ashanti campaign for the *Daily Telegraph*. He witnessed the victorious British entry into the fortress at Essaman. Four years later he reported the Russo-Turkish War* for the *Standard*, but was expelled for violating military security in one of his dispatches, as he chronicled in his 1877 book, *Narrative of an Expelled Correspondent*. He also wrote *Through Fanteeland to Commmassie: A Diary of the Ashantee Campaigns in Africa* (1874).

REFERENCE: Robert Wilkinson-Latham. *From Our Special Correspondent.* 1979.

---

* Indicates a separate entry.

Brabazon, James Martin (b. 1972)

He is a British journalist and documentary film-maker. Educated at Cambridge he began his photojournalism career in London and Paris and then relocated to Nairobi, Kenya to work for the Kenyan agency Camerapix as a television news producer. Over his career he has specialized in conflict and politics and worked in over 50 countries, including Eritrea, Kashmir, Kosovo, Israel, Zimbabwe, and Northern Ireland. He rose to prominence covering conflict zones in Africa. By most accounts he was the only journalist to film the Liberians United for Reconciliation and Democracy (LURD) rebel group fighting to topple President Charles Taylor during what has been dubbed the Second Liberian Civil War in 2002. During his travels with LURD, he reported the group's alleged atrocities against government soldiers and civilians. In 2003 he hooked up with the photojournalist Tim Hetherington* on a trip to Liberia. While covering the Liberian conflict he met the noted South African mercenary, Nick du Toit. Brabazon hired him as a bodyguard and then chronicled their friendship and du Toit's escapades in the failed Equatorial Guinea coup attempt in the book *My Friend the Mercenary* (2011). He produced the HBO documentary, *Which Way Is the Frontline From Here? The Life and Time of Tim Hetherington*. Brabazon's Liberian experiences were documented in his documentaries *Liberia: A Journey Without Maps* (2002) and *Liberia: An Uncivil War* (2004).

REFERENCE: Robert Young Pelton, *The World's Most Dangerous Places*, 5th ed. 2003.

Brackenbury, Charles Booth (1831-1900)

London born, he graduated from the Royal Military Academy at Woolwich in 1847 and was commissioned as a lieutenant in the royal artillery. After service in the Crimean War* he was promoted to captain and became an instructor at his alma mater. In 1866 he was hired as a war correspondent by the *Times*. While accompanying the Austrian army during the Austro-Prussian War* he witnessed the Battle of Koniggratz. He also reported the Franco-Prussian War* and was with Prince Frederick Charles during the Le Mans campaign. He covered the Russo-Turkish War* in 1877, crossing into the Balkans with General Gourko's forces.

Following his years as a war reporter he resumed his military career, eventually rising to colonel in the army and, in 1899, to director of the artillery college at Woolwich. He died of a heart attack in June 1900. He published a variety of works on warfare and tactics.

REFERENCE: *DNB*, 245-246.

Brady, Mathew B. (1823-1896)

The son of Irish immigrants, Brady was born in Warren County, New York. He was named after Matthew in the Bible and added the B. to his name to lengthen it, but it stood for nothing, like the "S" in Harry S. Truman. Brady came to photography after a short stint as a itinerant portrait painter. In 1841, his art teacher introduced him to Samuel Morse, inventor of the telegraph and an early practitioner of daguerreotype* photography. In 1844 Brady opened his first studio, Brady's Daguerrian Miniature Gallery, and embarked on his photographic career. An innovator, entrepreneur, and tireless self-promoter, he created daguerreotype portraits of the most celebrated Americans of the mid-nineteenth century. Brady gained fame and medals as these images were widely exhibited.

In 1854 he shifted from daguerreotypes to the wet-plate process. Alexander Gardner* joined Brady two years later as the manager of his Washington studio; then Brady began to specialize in life-size portraits when Gardner introduced him to enlarging techniques. Photographs from the Brady studio were widely used for engravings by illustrated publications such as *Harper's Weekly* and *Frank Leslie's Illustrated Newspaper*. In 1860 he took the first of eventually thirty-five photographs of Lincoln. Lincoln, in part, attributed his election to that first picture, noting that "Brady and the Cooper Union speech made me President."

With the outbreak of the American Civil War* Brady turned from social portraiture to war photography* when he obtained official permission to follow the campaigns. Brady's motivations for recording the war were both commercial and historical. Maintaining his staff of from ten to twenty photographers would ultimately lead to his financial ruin. During the war he supported four field units which covered thirty-five bases of operation in three states. He was able to outfit his traveling darkrooms with large-format cameras and a profusion of equipment and supplies on an open expense account. In addition he maintained the practice of purchasing the work of other battlefield photographers. Since he was a man of business rather than action, there persists much controversy as to whether Brady himself spent much time at the front lines. His collection of war photographs, however, offers the most complete documentation of any nineteenth century war. In the early months of the conflict all photographs taken by his employees carried the attribution "from a photograph of Brady." Only a portion of the photographs attributed to Brady were actually his work, since he spent time in Washington overseeing his extensive network. Following the war his associate Gardner finally received credit for his contributions. But, it is clear that Brady was on hand for the initial Union debacle at Bull Run, Chancellorsville, and the aftermath of Gettysburg and Antietam. With eyesight failing he took great risks to cover the Battles of Fredericksburg and Petersburg. Following Gardner's exit in 1862 and the financial burdens of his wartime project, Brady slowly inched toward financial ruin. When his Washington studio went out of business he attempted to sell his photographic collection to Congress for $100,000. By this time the value of

his prints had plummeted as the public interest in the war declined. Faced with public and congressional indifference and his failing eyesight, he put his work into storage, but when he was unable to pay his storage bill the priceless images were sold at auction to clear his debt. The War Department purchased the collection for $2,840, the price of the debt, and Brady remained uncompensated.

Brady's great achievement was completing a comprehensive visual record of the war. Ultimately he was forced into bankruptcy in both New York and Washington between 1868 and 1873. However, in 1874 he received $25,000 from the War Department, as his collection began to deteriorate in storage. In the 1880s he suffered from a cornucopia of maladies including rheumatism, blindness, and injuries from a carriage accident. His health crisis was augmented by depression and alcoholism. He died in the paupers' ward of a New York hospital from kidney disease and assorted ailments on January 15, 1896. While much of his priceless work is catalogued in the National Archives and the Library of Congress, many prints are still missing.

REFERENCES: James D. Horan. *Mathew Brady: Historian with a Camera.* 1955; Jorge Lewinski. *The Camera at War.* 1978; Roy Meredith. *Mathew Brady's Portrait of an Era.* 1982.

Breckinridge, Marvin Mary (1905–2002)

Born in New York City and educated at Vassar College, Breckinridge met Edward R. Murrow* when she founded the National Student Federation of America while still a student. She adopted her middle name Marvin as her first name to distinguish herself from her cousin Mary who founded the Frontier Nursing Service. She also probably thought it would open more doors in this era having a masculine given name. In the 1930s Breckinridge traveled extensively and had her photographs published in most of the popular news magazines of her time, including

National Geographic, Look, Life, and others. Murrow hired her in 1939 at the outbreak of the Second World War, making here the first female news broadcaster for the CBS Radio Network. She covered stories in various European hotspots and was recognized as the first woman member of the legendary CBS reporting staff known by the sobriquet "Murrow's Boys." During the early years of the war she reported from Ireland, Norway, England, Amsterdam, France and Germany. Her career as a war reporter ended almost as soon as it began when she married in 1940, forcing her to give up broadcasting and photojournalism. However, the decision was forced on her by law. Since she was married to the first secretary of the. U.S. embassy in Berlin, the State Department was obliged to censor anything written by a diplomat's spouse. In 2010 her wartime photojournalism and radio broadcasts were included along with those of seven other female journalists and photographers in the exhibit, "Women Come to the Front: Journalists, Photographers and Broadcasters during World War II."

REFERENCES: "Marvin Breckinridge," *Vassar Encyclopedia,* https://vcencyclopeida.vassar.edu/alumni/marving-breckinridge.html; Wolfgang Saxon, "Mary Patterson, Philanthropist and Wartime Broadcaster, 97," New York Times, Dec. 22, 2002.

Brelis, Dean (1924–2006)

Born Constantinos Christos Brelis in Newport, Rhode Island, Brelis joined the army in 1942 and was assigned to work in military intelligence for the Office of Strategic Services (OSS). After the war he attended Harvard before beginning his journalism career in 1949 with the *Boston Globe.* Between 1949 and 1954 he worked for Time-Life. During the 1960s he reported for NBC, filing dispatches from the Middle East, North Africa, Cyprus, and Vietnam before settling down to anchor the nightly news in 1967 on Los Angeles KNBC-TV Channel 4. In 1974 he left the staid confines of the television studio to cover conflicts,

politics, and disasters for *Time* magazine as a foreign correspondent. He retired in 1986. He covered the impact of the Vietnam War with photojournalist Jill Kremetz in *The Face of South Vietnam* (1968) and with William R. Peers, his experiences in Burma during World War II in *Behind the Burma Road: The Story of America's Most Successful Guerrilla Force* (1963). He also wrote several novels in the 1950s and 1960s loosely based on his wartime experiences.

REFERENCE: "Dean Brelis, 82; Foreign Correspondent also Wrote Nonfiction, Novels," Los Angeles Times, Nov. 22, 2006.

Brigham, Charles D. (1819-1894)

Born and raised in upper New York State, Brigham had been the editor of the *Troy Whig* prior to the American Civil War.* He was the Charleston correspondent for the *New York Tribune* during parts of 1860 and 1861 reporting the opening salvos of the Civil War. Northern reporters were subject to tar and feathering or worse if caught by local vigilance committees. In February 1861 he was arrested by the Charleston police and given an ultimatum to leave town. Following his departure, the *Tribune* replaced him with pairs of correspondents, which the paper rotated periodically. Southern newspaper coverage was considered so dangerous for Northern reporters that the *Tribune* usually held one man in reserve in case his colleague was arrested. Brigham was assigned to edit the dispatches to make their letters appear the work of one individual. Most Southern newspapers and Northern competitors refused to believe the newspaper had correspondents in Charleston and accused the *Tribune* of publishing synthetic correspondence fabricated at the home desk. Following his prewar experiences in the South he covered the western theater of operations. In 1862 Brigham reported one of the major stories of the war in a twenty-two-page telegram to the *Tribune* recounting the battle of the ironclads *Monitor* and *Merrimac* at Hampton Roads. Brigham later reported the 1863 Chattanooga campaign and was rebuked by General Hooker for his criticism of his actions during the operation; Hooker went as far as requesting Secretary Edwin Stanton to expel Brigham from the field. In 1864 Brigham left the *Tribune* to join the *Pittsburgh Commercial* as managing editor.

REFERENCES: J. Cutler Andrews. *The North Reports the Civil War.* 1955; Louis M. Starr. *Bohemian Brigade.* 1954.

Brines, Russell (1911-1982)

Brines was an AP journalist who covered World War II* in the Philippines and Japan; the Korean War;* and the Indo-Pakistani conflict in 1965 Brines joined the Associated Press in 1935 in Honolulu. Among his first assignments was the search for Amelia Earhart when she disappeared in 1937. He covered World War II from Manila, where he was captured in 1941 and repatriated two years later. He covered the war in the Pacific until the fall of Japan and became the chief of the AP Tokyo Bureau. He wrote the *Indo Pakistani Conlict* (1968) and *MacArthur's Japan* (1948).

REFERENCE: Russell Brines Scholarship in International or Political Reporting, University of Florida Foundation website.

Brodie, Howard (1915-2010)

Born in Oakland, California, and educated at various art schools, Brodie was a staff artist for the *San Francisco Chronicle* before becoming the best-known artist for *Yank** magazine. In addition to working for *Yank*, Brodie served as staff artist for *Life, Collier's,* the Associated Press, and CBS News. As sketch artist for *Yank* magazine during World War II* Brodie was teamed with writer Mack Morriss.* Together they covered the war in New Georgia and Guadalcanal in the Pacific theater, and in the European theater of operations they covered the Huertgen Forest Battle and the Ardennes breakthrough during the Battle of the Bulge. Brodie was awarded the Bronze Star for his coverage of the war. As

sketch artist he went on to cover the Korean* and Vietnam Wars.* His war drawings were collected in *Howard Brodie's War Drawings* in 1963. The dean of CBS courtroom artists, Brodie sketched some of the most notorious trials of the twentieth century, including those of Jack Ruby, James Earl Ray, Sirhan Sirhan, My Lai murderer William Calley, Charles Manson, and the Chicago Seven; he also sketched the Watergate hearings.

REFERENCE: Art Weithas. *Close to Glory.* 1991.

Broun, Heywood (1888-1939)

The seemingly perpetually disheveled Broun, at six foot four and 250 pounds, was regarded as one of the most respected journalists of his era. He was originally a drama critic, but his claustrophobia forced him to give up the theater for the outdoors. Born in Brooklyn, New York, he was educated in private schools and then Harvard. He left college after his second year to work for the *New York Morning Telegraph,* covering sporting events. In 1911 he left the penurious *Telegraph* over a rejected pay raise and joined the *Tribune* for even less money.

With the outbreak of war in Europe, in 1917 Broun accompanied General Pershing's Allied Expeditionary Forces to France. On October 19, Frederick Palmer* chided him for being absent without leave, having left the monotony of the front lines for Paris along with other correspondents. Broun breached military censorship on several occasions and often expressed contempt for the news reporting restrictions set by the military. His credentials were revoked over his critical pieces on the army and Pershing, of whom he wrote that American soldiers would never call the imperious general "Papa." But his short stint in Europe as a war correspondent resulted in two books the following year, *The A.E.F.: With General Pershing and the American Forces* and *Our Army at the Front.* He went on to work for a succession of newspapers and wrote eleven more books, but never covered another war.

* Indicates a separate entry.

REFERENCES: Emmet Crozier. *American Reporters on the Western Front, 1914-18*. 1959. Richard O'Connor. *Heywood Broun: A Biography*. 1975.

Brown, Cecil (1907-1987)

Brown was born in New Brighton, Pennsylvania, and educated at Western Reserve University and Ohio State University. After a short life at sea and stints with various newspapers he became a freelance writer in Europe. On the strength of his freelance articles he was hired by the International News Service to cover Paris and Rome in 1931.

In 1940 CBS hired Brown to report German and Italian developments that could draw the United States into the rapidly developing conflict. The following year he was expelled from Italy by Fascist officials. Brown next reported the war from Belgrade, Yugoslavia, where he reported the advance of Nazi forces, barely escaping himself. He went on to report the war from Turkey, Syria, and Cairo, and transmitted news of the German invasion of Crete for CBS. He was awarded the Distinguished Service Award for his coverage of the escape of Greece's King George from German forces. He continued to report from North Africa before being transferred to Singapore at the end of 1941. Brown was aboard the British battleship *Repulse* when it was torpedoed during a Japanese bomber attack on December 10, 1941. He was among the two thousand survivors plucked from the water several hours later. Brown received a National Headliners' Club award for his CBS broadcast of the sinking.

Shortly after, Brown was banned from broadcasting news stories from Singapore by British authorities for painting a bleak picture of the worsening situation in Singapore and Malaya. Continuing his broadcasts from the Far East, he was next stationed in Australia where he reported that the British were unready for a Japanese invasion.

After the war he continued his association with CBS, before jumping to ABC in 1957 and then NBC the following year. He left journalism and broadcasting in 1967 to assume a teaching post in communications and international affairs at California State Polytechnic University. He wrote *Suez to Singapore* (1942).

REFERENCE: Robert W. Desmond. *Tides of War*. 1984.

Brown, Stephen R. (b. 1947)

He was initially assigned to cover the landing of the U.S. Marines in Beirut in 1982. Originally scheduled to cover the Lebanese conflict for a few days, he stayed for two months. According to Brown he will not partake of war coverage again.

REFERENCE: Frances Fralin. *The Indelible Image*. 1985.

Browne, Junius Henri (1833-1902)

He was born in Seneca Falls, New York, and educated at St. Xavier College in Cincinnati. He entered the newspaper trade at the age of eighteen. After working for several Cincinnati papers he joined the *New York Tribune* as a war correspondent when the American Civil War* broke out. He covered the campaigns in the Southwest and along the Mississippi River, including the Battle of Vicksburg in 1863. He was among a group of journalists captured by Confederate forces when their ship was sunk by batteries on the cliffs protecting Vicksburg. Browne and his *Tribune* colleague Albert D. Richardson* were not immediately released with some of the others, due to their connections with the *Tribune*, which was associated with the abolition movement. For over a year he was incarcerated in various Confederate prisons, including the notorious Libby Prison. Browne, Richardson, and several other prisoners finally escaped from Salisbury Prison, after which they endured a four-hundred-mile trek through enemy country before reaching the Union lines at Knoxville. His book *Four Years in Secessia* (1865) was an account of his experiences following the Battle of

Vicksburg. He covered Fremont's Missouri campaign and the Battle of Fort Donelson, where he actually took up arms himself.

Following the Civil War Browne worked for various newspapers and contributed articles to several popular magazines. He wrote *The Great Metropolis* (1869) and *Sights and Sensations in Europe* (1871), as well as a series of books on the French Revolution.

REFERENCES: J. Cutler Andrews. *The North Reports the Civil War.* 1955; Stewart Sifakis. *Who Was Who in the Civil War.* 1988.

Browne, Malcolm W. (1931-2012)

Born in New York City and educated at Swarthmore College, Browne worked as a chemist following college until he was drafted during the Korean War.* In Korea he drove a tank before landing a position on the staff of *Stars and Stripes.**

He reported his next war in Vietnam,* beginning a five-year stint in 1961 as bureau chief for the Associated Press. Browne's greatest scoop of the war came when he photographed the self-immolation of a monk in Saigon. His 1964 Pulitzer Prize-winning photograph was only the first of hundreds that would chronicle the Buddhists' revolt against President Ngo Dinh Diem in South Vietnam. Browne's pictures reportedly led President Kennedy to withdraw his support of the Diem regime, and on November 1, 1963, Diem was overthrown and assassinated. In 1965, disillusioned by the war, Browne resigned from the AP but stayed in Saigon with ABC television and then the *New York Times.* Browne spent a total of ten years in Indochina, only exiting when Saigon fell in 1975. According to Browne, he was the oldest journalist to cover the Gulf War.* He is currently a senior writer for the *New York Times.*

REFERENCES: Malcolm W. Browne. *Muddy Boots and Red Socks: A War Reporter's Life.* 1993; William Prochnau. *Once upon a Distant War.* 1995.

Bryan, Ann (1932–2009)

Born Grace Ann Bryan in Ballinger, Texas and educated at Texas Tech University, she left a local Texas paper for New York City where she worked as a freelance reporter for a year, before making a go at being a stewardess, ending up in Germany in 1959. Bryan found work with the Overseas Family and spent five years there as many of the soldiers she covered were shipping out to Vietnam. She following suit and in 1965, the newly minted Ann Bryan was covering Saigon for the Asian edition of *Overseas Weekly* (some regarded it more as the "Oversexed Weekly"). She is widely regarded as one of the first female war correspondents of the Vietnam War.* She often found herself at loggerheads with the military brass, even while working for the "scrappy German-based tabloid that saw itself as an irreverent alternative to the semiofficial *Stars and Stripes.** Aimed at a mostly GI audience, the Asian edition of the *Overseas Weekly* featured 12 pages of color comics and "a weekly buffet of bosomy beauties." However, under her direction the paper would cover a number of issues often left out of standard news reports on army life in Vietnam. Controversial pieces featured the misdeeds of military officers, war profiteering, and officers involved in black-market activities, as well as drug abuse among soldiers and racism in the Army. Bryan's paper proved a muckraking embarrassment to the military, so much so that the Defense Department banned it from newsstands and post exchanges in Vietnam and the rest of Asia. In response, Bryan's paper filed a lawsuit in 1966 accusing the Secretary of Defense Robert McNamara of violating the 1st amendment by barring the distribution of the paper in the Pacific region. Not one to stand idly by while the suit languished in court, Bryan connived to have the paper published in Hong Kong and then flown into Saigon to be sold on the city's streets and outside military barracks by local newsboys. The *Overseas Weekly* lost in the first round of the suit but won on appeal in

Indicates a separate entry.

1967. Bryan fought for the right to publish her paper, and then became embroiled in the fight to gain access to the war front from the Pentagon. Ultimately she played a role in the Pentagon lifting the ban on female war correspondents. She moved back to the states for several years, still working on a freelance basis. She returned in 1973 and when Saigon fell in 1975, helped her former colleagues escape the city.

REFERENCES: http://www.latimes.com/local/obituaries/la-me-ann-bryan-mariano9-2009mar09-story.htm; Harold G. Moore and Joe Galloway. *We Were Soldiers Once ... and Young.* 1992.

Bryson, George Eugene (d. 1912)

An old Cuban hand at the time of the Spanish-American War,* Bryson initially covered Cuban affairs for the *New York Herald* and the *New York World* before moving to the *New York Journal* in early 1897. Bryson made a name for himself prior to the outbreak of the war with a series of sensational stories which inflamed American public opinion against Spain. His story of the machete executions of hospital patients, and the arrest and subsequent imprisonment of several nuns by the Spanish, made front page news in the *Journal* in early 1897. Not long after, Bryson reported the imprisonment by Spanish officials of a beautiful young woman who became better known in the press as the "Cuban Girl Martyr." Known simply as Evangelina, she was apparently related to the former president of the Cuban Republic. His story created another *cause celebre,* and when he attempted to secure her release Bryson was expelled from the country. Evangelina eventually bought her way out of prison.

The following year he smuggled his account of the sinking of the *Maine* out of Cuba. Based on slim evidence, his early report that the *Maine* was destroyed by a torpedo provided impetus for the increasing anti-Spanish fervor gripping America. The *Journal,* ever vigilant for a news scoop, ran Bryson's dispatch under the headline "WAR! SURE!" accompanied by Bryson's intelligence: "*Maine* DESTROYED BY SPANISH ... THIS PROVED ABSOLUTELY BY DISCOVERY OF THE TORPEDO HOLE." Bryson's scoop led to one of the most hysterical newspaper campaigns in American history. It is ironic that the reporter who contributed so much to the outbreak of the war left once the actual bloodletting began. Following the war Bryson went into business in Havana, where he owned and operated an independent news bureau.

REFERENCES: Charles H. Brown. *The Correspondents' War.* 1967; Joyce Milton. *The Yellow Kids.* 1989.

Buckley, Christopher (d. 1950)

Buckley was a veteran war correspondent for the *Daily Telegraph* when he was killed reporting the Korean War.* During World War II* he covered the North African desert war, including the pivotal battle of El Alamain on October 25, 1942. The following year he reported the Sicilian operation before moving across the Strait of Messina to cover the Italian campaign. In 1944 he landed with the first wave during the invasion of Normandy before accompanying the British Second Army pushing into Belgium and Holland later that year. He was covering the Burma theater when the war ended. Buckley died in August 1950 when the jeep he shared with the *Times'* Ian Morrison* struck a land mine, killing both correspondents.

REFERENCES: Richard Collier. *Fighting Words.* 1989; Robert W. Desmond. *Tides of War.* 1984.

Bugbee, Charles "Charley" (d. 1849)

During the Mexican-American War* Bugbee worked as an express rider, successfully eluding wartime guerrillas, only to be shot and killed in a stagecoach robbery near Jalapa, Mexico, while still working as an agent for the *New York Sun.* During the early 1840s Bugbee developed a reputation in Boston for "enterprise and speed in boarding English steamers and selling the news they carried before American papers could issue extra editions." According to the *Boston Daily* of that era, "Young Bugbee was one of the best specimens of a live Yankee we ever knew…We wager our best beaver that Bugbee will come back from the war worth $10,000 in cash, and twice that amount in 'glory.'" During the Mexican-American War* he rode as a special courier for the *New Orleans Picayune's* George Wilkins Kendall*. "Kendall's letters by 'Bugbee Express' became a byword among the journalists in Mexico," with the *Picayune* observing that he was "shot at again and again while riding express for Mr. Kendall." Kendall and Bugbee could often be observed riding together advancing with American troops toward the frontlines of the next battle. Kendall would then spend time interviewing army personnel after the battles gathering detailed lists of wounded and killed. These would appear after the initial battle reports in the *Picayune*. As soon as Kendall compiled his accounts he gave them to Bugbee and he set off immediately for the port city of Vera Cruz. He became an expert at evading pursuing guerrilla bands on the six-hour, 50-mile ride. Once he reached Vera Cruz he boarded a steamer and ten days later as the ship slowly made its way up the Mississippi, Bugbee debarked, grabbed a horse, and rode 30 miles into New Orleans. Kendall's letters were then set in type and an extra edition was out that same day, making the *Picayune* the nation's main source for news on the conflict, that is until the telegraph began to transmit the news north quicker, but only in short summaries. But if readers wanted the complete story it would come on the pony express deliveries that followed a week later. The paper's careful planning and enterprise insured that it often beat its competitors with details of momentous events.

REFERENCES: Tom Reilly. War *with Mexico!: America's Reporters Cover the Battlefront*, Manley Witten, ed. 2010.

Bugbee Express

See CHARLES "CHARLEY" BUGBEE.

Bulgarian Atrocities

Beginning in May 1876, word leaked out of Bulgaria that demonstrators against Turkish rule had fallen victim to harsh retaliation. Rumors emanated from Constantinople that thousands of Christians had been massacred and many villages destroyed. The British government, which had been allied with Turkey since the Crimean War,* attempted to suppress the rumors, worried that Russia, as defender of the Christian faith, might intrude. When correspondent Januarius MacGahan* offered to investigate these rumors for his paper the *New York Herald* he was rebuffed. But the *London Daily News* accepted his offer and he set off for Bulgaria. In a series of articles in the summer of 1876, MacGahan substantiated the rumors of Turkish atrocities. These dispatches were collected and published as a booklet. The accuracy of his reports were confirmed by an investigation the following year, when it was found that over twelve thousand men, women, and children had been murdered. Russia responded to the confirmation by declaring war on Turkey in April 1877, inaugurating the Russo-Turkish War* of 1877-1878. MacGahan, who died of typhus soon after war broke out, is viewed as a national hero by Bulgarians; his actions were commemorated at an annual mass for years after his death.

REFERENCES: Robert W. Desmond. *The Information Process.* 1978; Phillip Knightley. *The First Casualty.* 1975.

Bull, Rene (1872-1942)

Born in Ireland, Bull was one of the first war correspondents employed by the newly established *Black and White* in 1890. He served as writer, artist, and photographer for the new journal, which attempted to use photographs rather than sketches whenever possible. Stationed as special artist in Constantinople, he reported the Armenian massacres before leaving for India to cover the plague in Bombay.

In 1897 he reported the Greco-Turkish War* along with Bennet Burleigh* of the *Daily Telegraph*. He was captured by the Greeks after attempting to recover some personal items he left behind when the Turks took Volo. Firmly established as a member of the war correspondent establishment, he next ventured to India and the North West Frontier, where Pathan tribesmen were wreaking havoc. He was with the British advance into the Maidan Valley and the Tirah Valley Expedition. Bull and Melton Prior* of the *Illustrated London News* were with a Sikh column when they were attacked by Aridis warriors. In one episode the correspondents were cut off with several Sikhs from the main party when they were ambushed. Pressed into battle, where the correspondents reportedly acquitted themselves quite well.

In 1896 Bull reported Kitchener's expedition to reconquer the Sudan. In 1898 he witnessed the Battle of Omdurman and afterward toured the battlefield littered with thousands of dead Mahdist warriors. The following year found Bull reporting the Boer War.* He along with Bennet Burleigh narrowly escaped the siege of Ladysmith* at the outset of the conflict. Bull accompanied the Ladysmith relief column under General Buller in December 1899. On December 15, 1899, he reported the British advance on Colenso, where Buller's army marched into a deadly trap and was decimated.

On February 24, 1900, the *Black and White* published Bull's account of the Battle of Spion Kop - the last battle of 1899 and a terrible defeat for the British, who lost over 1,700 men taking a hill that they withdrew from the following day. Following the defeats of Colenso and Spion Kop, Ladysmith was not relieved until March. In 1901 he was severely wounded and returned to England for recuperation. Bull's career as a war artist and reporter ended with the Boer War, after which he turned to book illustrating. He served in the Royal Navy Volunteer Reserve and the RAF during World War I.*

REFERENCES: Pat Hodgson. *The War Illustrators*. 1977; Robert Wilkinson-Latham. *From Our Special Correspondent*. 1979.

Bunker, William Mitchell (b. 1850)

Born in Nantucket, Massachusetts, he reported the Modoc War of 1872-1873. A third-generation newspaperman, he was one of the top reporters for the *San Francisco Evening Bulletin* when the conflict broke out in the Lava Beds. Most of the stories at the end of the campaign, including the capture of Captain Jack, the Modoc leader, came from Bunker's pen. Following the war he continued his journalism career in San Francisco. Having risen to city and news editor of his oiginal newspaper, he acquired a paper of his own two years after the war when he purchased the *Daily Evening Report*.

REFERENCE: Oliver Knight. *Following the Indian Wars*. 1960.

Burchett, Wilfred (1911-1983)

Born in Melbourne, Australia, in 1911, he became one of the most controversial journalists of the Cold War era. Burchett acquired his radical bent in his youth when he was exploited along with other unskilled workers in the cane fields of Queensland during the 1930s Depression. Consistently accused of being a KGB agent and a Communist sympathizer, for seventeen years he and his family were denied passports by the Australian government for reporting the Communist side.

Burchett acquired his first posting as a war correspondent with the Australian-based *Digest*, and then the *Sunday Telegraph*. Shortly after arriving in China, he joined the staff of the *Daily Express* for which he covered the Pacific theater of World War II* from 1941 to 1943. In January 1942 he was sent to cover the Japanese invasion of Burma. He reported the invasions of the Marianas, Guam, and Peleliu. Burchett was the first Western reporter to reach Hiroshima after the dropping of the atom bomb in August 1945. His story debunked the American claims that there could be no atomic sickness because the bomb had been detonated at a height that avoided any "residual radiation."

He covered the Chinese Revolution in the 1950s as well as the Korean War.* As a champion of radical causes Burchett became embroiled in the Korean and Vietnam Wars,* and he counted Premier Chou En-Lai and Ho Chi Minh among his intimate acquaintances.

At the age of seventy he survived ambush by Khmer Rouge in Cambodia. He completed the last of thirty-five books, *Shadows of Hiroshima,* shortly before his death in 1983.

REFERENCES: Wilfred Burchett. *At the Barricades.* 1981; Ben Kiernan, ed. *Burchett Reporting the Other Side of the World.* 1986.

Burke, John (1843-1900)

Burke was a professional British photographer in the Punjab of India. He was hired by the Indian government as a civilian to take pictures during the Second Afghan War in 1878-1880. Burke was one of a number of professional photographers in India who earned their living taking portraits of British soldiers. Most sources note that India was better served photographically because there were so many experienced photographers on the scene. Many, like Burke, were hired to accompany various punitive expeditions. Terms of payment usually included a fee, honorary rank, and free transportation and food for the photographer and his servants. Burke accompanied the First Division of the Peshawar Valley Field Force in 1879 and spent the winter in Kabul. He captured the signing of the peace treaty, which was soon after broken by the murder of Major Sir Louis Cavagnari, head of the peace mission. Sketches of Burke by a war artist appeared in the *Graphic.* With the murder of Cavagnari in

September 1879, Burke's photograph of the peace mission provided him with a real scoop when an engraving made from his picture appeared in the *Graphic.*

REFERENCE: Pat Hodgson. *Early War Photographs.* 1974.

Burleigh, Bennet (c. 1840-1914)

Born in Glasgow, Scotland, as a young man he fought for the Confederate Army during the American Civil War* and twice escaped death sentences by firing squads. After the war he entered journalism as an editor for the *Houston Telegraph,* but left for England shortly after. He turned to war reporting in 1882, covering the Arabi Revolt for the Central News Agency before transferring to the *Daily Telegraph* later that year. As the newspaper's preeminent special war correspondent he covered numerous campaigns between 1882 and 1911.

Burleigh was the premier special during the 1882 Sudan expedition for the *Daily Telegraph.* He covered the Sudan campaign of 1884-1885, reporting and witnessing the Battles of El Teb and Tamai in March 1884. After Gatling guns jammed, rifles malfunctioned, and bayonets and swords bent like "hoop-iron" at the Battle of Abu Klea, Burleigh wrote a critical dispatch on the poor quality and inefficiency of British weapons.

During the Battle of Abu Kru several noted war correspondents were killed by friendly fire, and Burleigh narrowly escaped death when he was hit in the throat by a ricocheting bullet. However, it did not penetrate, only raising an egg-size lump under his ear. Virtually all of the war correspondents covering this action were wounded by the haphazard shooting and subsequent ricocheting of bullets.

Burleigh's major scoop of the campaign came when he courageously rode through hostile territory to Dongola, where he telegraphed his paper and the world the stunning news of General Gordon's martyrdom at Khartoum.

Indicates a separate entry.

He covered the Greco-Turkish War* from the Turkish side and reported from the 1895 Ashanti campaign. During the Sudan campaign of the late 1890s against the Mahdist forces, he reported and took part in the Battle of Atbara, and in 1898 the Battle of Omdurman. The *Times* also printed his account of the battle when it lost both of its correspondents to battle wounds at Omdurman. His book on Atbara, *Sirdir and Khalifa,* was published in July 1898, barely three months after the battle. The following year he was in South Africa covering the Boer War* for the *Daily Telegraph.* He escaped from Ladysmith* shortly before the siege began. Apparently, due to excessive censorship his main coups during the war were interviewing Boer General Joubert and carrying news of peace past the military censors. In 1903 he reported the minor punitive expedition to Somaliland and the following year covered the Russo-Japanese War.* In his seventies he witnessed his last war while reporting the 1912 Balkan conflict. Burleigh has often been compared to William Howard Russell* for the quality of his work and the value of his criticism in leading to the improved efficiency of the British military system. He died in June 1914, shortly before the outbreak of World War I.*

REFERENCES: F. Lauriston Bullard. *Famous War Correspondents.* 1914; Robert Wilkinson-Latham. *From Our Special Correspondent.* 1979.

Burns, George (1902-1964)

Born in Albany, New York, he wrote for the *Albany Times Union* before enlisting in the army and joining the staff of *Yank** magazine during World War II.* Burns served in the Pacific theater of operations, where he covered the landings in the Marianas, Leyte, Iwo Jima, and Okinawa. He executed one of *Yank's* greatest scoops when he witnessed and reported in both print and photographs the attempted suicide of Japanese prime minister Tojo in Tokyo at the conclusion of the war.

He narrowly missed another classic scoop at the flag raising on Iwo Jima. He photographed the event with Joe Rosenthal* of the Associated Press. However, Rosenthal's negatives went directly through to the AP, while Burns' was held up by the Signal Corps labs. Following the war Burns continued his career as a photojournalist with *Life, Look,* and the *Saturday Evening Post.* He won numerous awards, including Photographer of the Year in 1964.

REFERENCE: Art Weithas. *Close to Glory.* 1991.

Burns, John Fisher (b. 1944)

Born in Nottingham, England, he studied Russian at Harvard and Chinese at Cambridge University in the 1980s. He also speaks French and German. He began his journalism career as a local reporter for the Canadian *Globe and Mail* in the early 1970s and became one of the first Western journalists to visit China during the Cultural Revolution. In 1975 he began his 39-year career with the *New York Times,* reporting from South Africa, the first of ten foreign bureaus he would work for. In 1978 he was a co-winner of the George Polk Award for foreign reporting on Africa. Burns was the recipient of two Pulitzer Prizes. In 1993 he won for International Reporting and his coverage of the devastation in Sarajevo and the ethnic cleansing during the war in Bosnia-Herzegovina. In 1997 he won another one, "For his courageous and insightful coverage of the harrowing regime imposed ion Afghanistan by the Taliban." Burns covered the lead up to the Iraq War from Baghdad and has continued to cover it over the succeeding years. In an interview with Charlie Rose in 2010, Christopher Hitchens who had spent time with Burns covering the war in Sarajevo, lauded Burns as "the greatest war correspondent of our time." Burns came to prominence for his portrait of a cellist playing on Sarajevo's main thoroughfare as artillery shells burst nearby.

REFERENCE: "Reporter Ends Acclaimed Run," New York Times, Mar. 26, 2015.

Burroughs, Edgar Rice (1875-1950)

Best known for his pulp fiction and the creation of popular cultural icon Tarzan in 1912, Burroughs was born in Chicago. He attended several private schools including the Michigan Military Academy. His affinity for the military life led to stints with the 7th Cavalry in Arizona (1896-97) and the Illinois Reserve Militia (1918-1919). Burroughs was among the more than 300 international correspondents sent by British newspapers to cover the Boer War*.

REFERENCES: John Taliaferro. *The Life of Edgar Rice Burroughs: Creator of Tarzan.* 2002; Duncan Anderson. *War: A Photo History.* 2006.

Burrows, Larry (1926-1971)

Born in London, he began his career in photojournalism as a laboratory technician in London's *Life* office in the early 1940s. In 1944, during the Normandy invasion, Burrows had been traditionally blamed for destroying most of Robert Capa's* D-Day photos by applying too much heat to the negatives while working as a laboratory technician. In 1998, author John G. Morris claimed in his book *Get the Picture: A Personal Account of Photojournalism*, that blame actually belonged to a different technician named Dennis Banks.

Burrows covered the Vietnam War* for nine years as well as conflicts in Africa and the Middle East. He was killed along with three other photographers on February 10, 1971, when the Vietnamese helicopter shuttling them over Laos was shot down by antiaircraft fire. The last pictures he took were of the accidental bombing of South Vietnamese soldiers by U.S. naval planes. He received the Overseas Press Club's Robert Capa Award twice and in 1966 was named Magazine Photographer of the Year. His book *Larry Burrows-Compassionate Photographer* was posthumously published in 1972.

REFERENCE: Frances Fralin, ed. *The Indelible Image.* 1985. New York: Random House.

Burton, James (b. 1871)

Born in London, he came to the United States in 1894. Burton worked as an illustrator for the *New York Herald, Harper's, Leslie's,* and other New York and London papers. He covered the Spanish-American War* as a photographer for *Harper's Weekly.* He recorded the Battles of San Juan Hill* and El Caney, and the advance on Santiago. Burton noted the impossibility of taking action shots when he came under fire on the front lines while accompanying the Seventh Infantry Regiment at San Juan Hill. He commented that shooting actual battle scenes was out of the question because of the distance at which the fighting was conducted and the long grass and thickly wooded topography. Following the Battle of El Caney, Burton took one of the few pictures of American dead to be published during the conflict. It appeared in *Harper's* on July 30, 1898, under the caption "Killed on the Field of Battle."

REFERENCES: Susan D. Moeller. *Shooting War.* 1989; *Who's Who in America.* 1910-1911.

Buschemi, John (d. 1944)

Prior to World War II* he was a news photographer for the *Gary Post Tribune.* Following his induction into the army in 1941 he joined the staff of *Yank* the next year. Between 1942 and 1944 he covered the fighting in New Georgia, Guadalcanal, Munda, Tarawa, and Kwajalein. He was killed at the battle on Eniwetok Island.

REFERENCE: Art Weithas. *Close to Glory.* 1991.

Bush, Asahel "Ace" (1910-1944)

Hired by the AP in 1939, he was just the latest in his family to work in the newspaper business dating back to a great-grandfather who established Oregon's first newspaper. In 1943 he left San Francisco to cover the Pacific theater of World War Two. He was reporting from the American-occupied city of Tacloban on the Philippine Island of Leyte on October 24, 1944 when he was killed by a Japanese bomb, becoming the first American correspondent to die in the Philipppines in the war. Before his death he had covered most of General Douglas MacArthur's operations.

REFERENCE: AP Wall of Honor, www.ap.org/wallof-honor/1940_1949.html.

Byington, Aaron Homer
(1826-1910)

A newspaper reporter since the age of fourteen, Byington was the editor and owner of the Norwalk, Connecticut, *Gazette* at the start of the American Civil War* and a part-time correspondent for the *New York Tribune*. He scored one of the biggest news scoops of the war when he organized a crew to repair telegraph lines in Hanover, Pennsylvania, following the Union victory at Gettysburg. For his services Byington was given a monopoly on the wire for two days. Once this agreement concluded he returned to the battlefield only sixteen miles away, where he interviewed witnesses to the first two days of the pivotal battle. His dispatch was the first complete account of the first two days of Gettysburg to hit the newsstands on July 4, 1863. The *Tribune* sold sixty-five thousand copies of this extra before noon. By August 1863, Byington had been made chief of the *Tribune* war correspondents with the Army of the Potomac. He later reported the Mine Run campaign and the Battles of the Wilderness.

REFERENCES: J. Cutler Andrews. *The North Reports the Civil War.* 1955; Louis M. Starr. *Bohemian Brigade.* 1954.

C

Cadwallader, Sylvanus (b. 1826)

Born in Ohio in 1826, he served as city editor of the *Milwaukee Daily News*. During the American Civil War* he was persuaded by the *Chicago Times* to replace its star reporter, who was languishing in a military prison for ignoring journalistic protocol. The owners of the *Times* begged the thirty-six-year-old Cadwallader to obtain a personal interview with Grant and to report on the movements of the western army. Described as distant and unsociable, he somehow gained a reputation for successfully obtaining news that had eluded his fellow war correspondents. However, this success was not the result of some uncanny resourcefulness. It was later revealed Cadwallader had helped Grant escape rebuke for a drinking binge on board the *Diligent* during the Vicksburg campaign, and that the reporter's reward was a pass that allowed him unprecedented access to Grant's forces. Cadwallader was the only newspaperman on board the steamer *Magnolia*, which was Grant's headquarters during the siege of Vicksburg. On the battlefield his tent was usually located next to Grant's, and he was permitted to use the general's official mail pouch to send off his dispatches.

Much of the credit for Cadwallader's success as a war reporter was due to his ability to respect the confidentiality of much that he was privy to. He followed Grant through his western campaign in Tennessee and Mississippi, including the Battles of Vicksburg and Chattanooga, and was at the general's side in 1865 during the peace signing at Appomattox, Virginia. He was captured by Confederate forces twice, and both times escaped by means of chicanery. The *Herald* promoted him to the supervisory position of correspondent-in-chief in charge of more than a dozen reporters after his second escape. Shadowing Grant from 1862 through 1865, he had an unrivaled position to observe the Union command.

After the war he became head of the *Herald's* Washington news bureau. In 1896, at the age of seventy, he finished a manuscript chronicling his wartime career. It was not published at the time, languishing in a library before being edited and published in 1955. Recent scholarship suggests that Cadwallader might not have witnessed firsthand much of what he reported, instead gleaning information from camp gossip.

REFERENCES: J. Cutler Andrews. *The North Reports the Civil War.* 1955; Sylvanus Cadwallader. *Three Years with Grant,* edited by Benjamin P. Thomas. 1955; Stewart Sifakis. *Who Was Who in the Civil War.* 1988.

Cagnoni, Romano (b. 1935)

Born in Pietrasanta, Italy, he was self-taught in photography. Cagnoni is predominately a freelance photographer whose pictures have appeared in the *Observer, Paris-Match, Life, Stern, L'Espresso, Newsweek,* and many other magazines. He was the only photographer to cover the entire war in Biafra and in 1965 was the first independent photographer admitted into North Vietnam after the fall of Dien Bien Phu eleven years earlier. He appeared in Afghanistan shortly after the Soviet invasion and secretly photographed the conflict through his partly unbuttoned coat.

Cagnoni is recognized as one of the first photojournalists to become deeply attached to the people he covered, often living among them during conflicts. During the Biafran conflict he would often blacken his face; otherwise Nigerians would have taken him for one of the hated white mercenaries. He was present as the Biafran resistance in Nigeria crumbled and General Ojukwu made his final escape. His scoop was featured in *Life* magazine.

While in North Vietnam, Cagnoni was denied access to combat missions but witnessed several American bombing raids. He also covered the war in Cambodia in 1974. His work has been collected in *Presenting Romano Cagnoni.*

REFERENCES: *Contemporary Photographers.* 1982; Jorge Lewinski. *The Camera at War.* 1978.

Caldwell, Erskine (1903-1987)

Born in Moreland, Georgia, Caldwell is best remembered as a writer of realistic novels such as *Tobacco Road* and short stories portraying poor southerners. He collaborated with his wife and *Life* photographer Margaret Bourke-White* on a series of articles on wartime Moscow. In 1941 he represented *PM*, the New York daily, in Russia. His account of his wartime exploits in Russia is chronicled in *All Out on the Road to Smolensk.* In late 1941 he visited Chungking, China, in the aftermath of the recent Japanese invasion.

REFERENCE: Robert W. Desmond. *Tides of War.* 1984.

Callahan, Charles (d. 1856)

Born in New York City, Callahan joined the *New Orleans Picayune* as a printer, later moving on to city reporter and war correspondent during the Mexican-American War.* From October 1847 to January 1848 he was the newspaper's main correspondent in Mexico City, filling in for George Wilkins Kendall* who had returned to New Orleans. He transferred to the *North American*, helping William Tobey* run the paper until it folded that March. He returned to the *Picayune* as a backup correspondent. He earned a reputation for his eloquence and personality and was evidently well-respected within the war journalism community. However, he lacked Kendall's connections and experience, and his letters were considered less analytical then Kendall's. Callahan would be among the first reporters to leave the war zone. After the war, he traveled to San Francisco and then was attracted to filibustering in Latin America. He was killed on September 14, 1856 at San Jacinto, Nicaragua, while fighting with William Walker's ill-fated filibuster expedition. Callahan ended up with the expedition by most accounts, to cover the invasion for the *Picayune*, but decided instead to join the filibuster army, leading to his death in the failed attempt to capture Nicaragua.

REFERENCE: Tom Reilly. *War with Mexico!: America's Reporters Cover the Battlefront*, Manley Witten, ed. 2010.

Cameron, James (1911-1985)

Born in London, he entered journalism with several newspapers in Manchester and Dundee. He was rejected for wartime service in the 1940s and spent ten years with the *Sunday Post*. A committed pacifist, he became a lifelong opponent of nuclear weapons.

Representing the *Picture Post*, he arrived with the rest of the British press corps at the beginning of the Korean War,* in time to report the Pusan breakout. Cameron was accompanied by veteran photographer Bert Hardy,* who had covered World War II* and had been Mountbatten's personal photographer in the Far East. From the start, the pacifist Cameron felt the war was futile and was skeptical of America's true war goals.

Cameron demonstrated he was capable of covering a large-scale military operation when he reported the successful landing of United

Nations forces at Inchon on September 15, 1950. He witnessed the bombardment and took part in the landing operation. Cameron started a furor when he described atrocities perpetrated by South Korean soldiers on political opponents of the Syngman Rhee regime. After a slew of similar stories by other British correspondents, Douglas MacArthur, the commanding general, imposed full military censorship on the press. Cameron departed shortly after the restrictions went into effect.

In 1952 Cameron left the *Picture Post* for the *News Chronicle,* with which he remained until 1960, shortly before its demise. In the 1960s he visited Hanoi as both a print and television journalist and reported the Vietnam* conflict from the North Vietnamese perspective. His experiences with Communist forces is chronicled in the book *Witness* (1966) by Romano Cagnoni* and Malcolm Aird.

REFERENCE: Trevor Royle. *War Report.* 1987.

Cameron, John Alexander
(d. 1885)

Born in Inverness, Scotland, he left his position as a bank clerk for India, where he quickly rose through the ranks of the *Bombay Gazette* to acting editor by 1878. In 1879 he reported the Afghan War for the *Standard* while accompanying the relief column to Kandahar under General Phayrer. He reached a telegraph with news of General Roberts' victory, a day and a half before his competitors. His dispatch from the battlefield of Maiwand (1880) elevated him to the top ranks of war reporters of his day.

With the outbreak of the First Boer War in December 1880, he traveled from Bombay to Natal, again beating his competitors to the news. In January 1881 he witnessed the Battles of Laing's Nek and Ingogo before being captured after the debacle at Majuba Hill in February. His account of the defeat of British forces at Majuba Hill (1881), later published by the *Illustrated London News* with illustrations by Melton

Prior,* is considered a classic. In June 1882, following the denouement of the Boer insurrection, Cameron reported the combined bombardment of Alexandria by French and British forces in retaliation for the massacre of Christians in the vicinity. He witnessed the British bombardment of the city on board the flagship *Invincible.* He covered the subsequent Egyptian campaign and later reported from Madagascar.

Cameron next accompanied French forces to Indochina and was in Tonkin when the French were beaten back by the Black Flags. Thereafter English correspondents were barred from covering the conflict, and on his way back to Britain he stopped at Suez to cover the advance of Osman Digma on Suakin. Cameron barely escaped alive from the defeat of Baker Pasha's forces by the Arabs.

He returned to North Africa in 1884 with the British expeditionary force and covered the battles of Trinkiat, El Teb, and Tamanieb. After a brief return to England he joined the 1884 Nile expedition and was with General Gordon at the siege of Khartoum. On January 19, 1885, Cameron was killed at the Battle of Abu Kru, where he was reporting Wolseley's unsuccessful attempt to move south to rescue Pasha Gordon. A tablet in the crypt at St. Paul's Cathedral commemorates the deaths of Cameron and six other correspondents who sacrificed their lives covering the 1883-1885 Sudan campaigns.

REFERENCES: *DNB;* Robert Wilkinson-Latham. *From Our Special Correspondent.* 1979.

Campbell, Archibald Doon
(1920-2003)

Born in Annan, Dumfriesshire, he worked for several newspapers in Scotland between 1938 and 1941 before joining Reuters* in 1941 as the youngest war correspondent accredited to Allied headquarters in Algiers. While covering the Royal Marine Commandos at Sword Beach during the D-Day landing he was reportedly the first correspondent to come ashore. In 1945 he crossed the Rhine inside a glider with the Seventeenth American Airborne Division. He was awarded the American Glider Wings and the Combat Star for his wartime reporting. He continued with Reuters until 1973. In 1984 he received the Order of the British Empire.

REFERENCE: Robert W. Desmond. *Tides of War*. 1984; The Guardian, June 2, 2003.

Campbell, Gerald Fitzgerald (1872-1933)

Following short stints with *Punch* and the *World* he joined the *Times* in 1908. He was one of the first reporters to witness the action at the western front with the French. Returning to France in 1915 after a fact-finding mission in Switzerland, he was arrested for espionage. However, his paper, with the help of the British legation in Berne, interceded and he was released. The following two years he covered French headquarters before returning to the western front. He wrote *Verdun to the Vosges* (1916).

REFERENCE: Robert W. Desmond. *Windows on the World*. 1980.

Cannon, James Monroe III (1918–2011)

Born in Sylacauga, Alabama, during World War II he served in the Office of Strategic Services (OSS). In 1949 he was hired by the *Baltimore Sun* and sent to cover the Korean War* in 1950. Over the next 18 months he covered a number of important battles including the American retreat from the Yalu River. He was wounded and left the battlefront for good. He left the *Sun* in 1954 and worked for *Time* and then *Newsweek*. From the late 1960s on he served as either assistant or aide for Governor Nelson A. Rockefeller, Senator Howard H. Baker, and President Ronald Reagan.

REFERENCE: http://www.koreanwar-educator.org/topics/p_war_correspondents.htm.

Cantlie, John (b. 1971)

Cantlie is a British war photographer and correspondent who had the unenviable distinction of having been kidnapped twice by Islamist extremists in Syria. The first time was in July 2012, when he was captured with Dutch photographer Jeroen Oerlemans as they crossed illegally into Syria from Turkey. A week after their kidnapping, they were rescued by members of the Free Syrian Army. Both journalists were shot and wounded during the escape, with Cantlie suffering a gunshot to his left arm, damaging his ulnar nerve, resulting in the loss of feeling and use of the hand. This excursion had been Cantlie's second to Syria, and in March 2012 he was credited as the first Western photographer to witness government troops attacking a city in an attempt to take back territory from the rebels. In November 2013 he was kidnapped for the second time along with James Foley.* They had been working together on a film about Cantlie's first brush with abduction. Cantlie disappeared for more than a year before he resurfaced in an Islamic State (ISIS) video on September 18, 2014. Between that day and February 9, 2015, ISIS released seven videos as part of its *Lend Me Your Ears* series. This British hostage held by the Islamic State* was "forced" to act as a combat reporter in a propaganda video from the Syrian city of Kobani, chronicling how the town was about to fall to ISIL in the face of repeated American air attacks. On February 9, 2015, the ISIS released a new 11-minute video, featuring Cantlie, its last known Western hostage. As in past videos, it features the war correspondent narrating a news-broadcast-quality report from the Aleppo vicinity.

The more recent videos portray Cantlie as a Western journalist rather hostage. The propaganda value initially depicted ISIS in a more favorable light than did the Western media.

His video persona has undergone a metamorphosis over this time, from simple captive to actual war correspondent. In his first video, posted September 18, 2014, Cantlie was featured wearing the orange jumpsuit worn by other Western hostages prior to their executions. In a subsequent video he was dressed in black, which one scholar said marked him as a captive and subordinate. The evolution of his wardrobe next found him on January 3, 2015 dressed in casual Western clothes, and even showed him walking through streets and riding a motorcycle as he made his reports. The aforementioned expert on ISIS suggests that this is part of a message; that ISIS is projecting the erstwhile war correspondent as an ordinary individual making an objective assessment of what is going on, rather than a hostage forced to make these observations under penalty of death. By most accounts no matter what is said in the videos, this propaganda and reportage reflects wishful thinking on the part of ISIS rather than a reality in which the group is suffering heavy casualties and territorial losses. As of March 2015, Cantlie was the last known Western hostage still alive.

REFERENCE: Mitchell Prothero, "Hostage's Talent May Be Raising Hi Value," Houston Chronicle, Feb. 10, 2015, A11.

Capa, Cornell (1918-2008)

Born in Budapest, Hungary, as Komel Friedmann on April 10, 1918, he graduated from Madach Imre Gymnasium in 1936. A photojournalist like his more famous brother Robert, he served as staff photographer for *Life* from 1946 to 1954. He covered the Israeli Six Day War in 1967, the Argentine Revolution, and the Somoza assassination.

REFERENCES: Richard Whelan. *Robert Capa: A Biography*. 1985; NY Times, May 24, 2008.

Capa, Robert (1913-1954)

Born Andrei Friedmann in Budapest, Hungary, he studied journalism in Berlin. In 1932 he began his career as a freelancer for *Life, Time,* and other magazines. In 1935 he changed his name to Robert Capa, under the impression he would make more money if he was thought to be an American photographer. He was also associated with Magnum Photos, which he cofounded in 1947.

Capa covered the Spanish Civil War* with his lover and photography partner Gerda Taro*; she was crushed to death under a Loyalist tank in the confusion of retreat. In 1938, he was watching raw soldiers attacking a well-guarded machine gun nest when he caught in a series of photographs his most famous image, a soldier frozen in his moment of death. This shot of the "Falling Soldier," also known as the "Death of a Loyalist Soldier,"* identified the name "Capa" with war photojournalism for posterity. In years to come he would justify his success by noting that "if your pictures aren't good, you aren't close enough."

Following the Spanish Civil War, he reported the Japanese invasion of China in 1938. Capa was initially prevented from covering World War II* due to his classification as an enemy alien because of his Hungarian citizenship. In 1942 he was informed that in the interest of national security he had to turn in his photographic equipment and not stray more than ten miles from New York City. However, in March 1943 he received the elusive accreditation and travel permits that would allow him to cover another war.

He covered the European theater of the war for *Life* from 1943 to 1945. His greatest scoop of the war was covering the D-Day invasion in 1944. One of only four news photographers allowed to accompany the invasion forces, Capa was among the first soldiers to land on the Normandy beach as he took pictures of men desperately trying to stay alive. His six hours of photos were sent to the processing lab aboard the USS *Chase*. However, a week later he learned his shots, which were the best of the invasion, were ruined by an overzealous darkroom assistant who in his excitement used too much heat on the negatives. Only 11 of 106 pictures survived this calamity. Later in the war he jumped with parachutists into Germany, covered the Anzio invasion, and was almost killed by friendly fire

Indicates a separate entry.

in Belgium when American soldiers mistook him for a German soldier. A week after the German surrender, *Life* featured on its cover another famous Capa photo, an American corporal offering a mock Nazi salute in front of the huge swastika on Nuremberg's sports stadium.

Following the war Capa and other unemployed war photographers formed the Magnum Picture Agency. He served as its first president and anchor until his death in 1954. He covered the birth of Israel from 1948 to 1950. In 1954 *Life* asked him to cover the French war in Indochina. On May 25, bored with waiting at a Viet Minh roadblock, Capa headed up the road in search of action when he triggered a land mine. He was found with a hole in his chest and one foot blown off.

REFERENCES: Robert E. Hood. *12 at War.* 1967; Frederick S. Voss. *Reporting the War.* 1994; Richard Whelan. *Robert Capa: A Biography.* 1985.

Caputo, Philip (b. 1943)

Caputo served in the marines from 1960 to 1967, including sixteen months in Vietnam. He chronicled his experiences in Vietnam in the highly acclaimed 1977 book *A Rumor of War.* In 1972 Caputo joined the staff of the *Chicago Tribune* and shared the Pulitzer Prize for investigative reporting. Following a stint as Rome correspondent he was assigned to cover the Middle East, where he was captured by Palestinian guerrillas. He was a recipient of the Overseas Club's George K. Polk* Award for his account of his captivity. He returned to Vietnam in 1975 and covered the final stages of the Vietnam conflict. Later that year he was shot in both legs while reporting the Lebanese civil war in Beirut. After recuperating he was reassigned to Moscow. His 1983 novel *DelCorso's Gallery* tells the story of combat photographer Nick DelCorso. The fictional DelCorso rushes from war to war attempting to exorcise the demons that still haunt him from pictures he took in the Vietnam War during a village burning by American paratroopers ten years earlier.

REFERENCES: Philip Caputo. A *Rumor of War.* 1977; Philip Caputo. *DelCorso's Gallery.* 1983; Howard Good. *The Image of War Correspondents in Anglo-American Fiction.* 1985.

Carpensian, Mile (1975–2010)

Born in Timisoara, Romania, he began his journalism career as a local correspondent for Antena 1. Over the next decade he worked for Antena 1 and Antena 3, rising to prominence as one of Romania's first international correspondents. He covered wars in Iraq and Kosovo, the revolution in Belgrade, and natural disasters in Indonesia and elsewhere. In 2009 he left Antena 1 to ply his trade as a freelancer. Despite his often risky coverage of war and floods, he died after a boil brought on septic shock, succumbing to the infection in his hometown hospital. Carpenisan was the only Romanian reporter covering Kosovo from the first to last day of the 1999 conflict. In 2003 he was embedded with the U.S. Army covering the invasion of Baghdad.

REFERENCE: http://en.wikipedia.org/wiki/Mile_C%C4%83rpeni%C8%99an.

Carpenter, Iris (1904-1997)

Born in England, after a short stint as a film critic for the *London Daily Express* Carpenter opted for staying home to raise a family before returning to the *Daily Express* and then the *London Daily Herald* to cover the London blitz and bombings in 1940. It was a common conceit in the early war years that women were acceptable for covering the home front but should not be allowed to accompany the armed forces to the Continent. When Carpenter applied for accreditation with the British Expeditionary Force in 1942 she was rebuffed. Not easily dissuaded, she circumvented the process by becoming an American reporter for the *Boston Globe,* and accompanied the American First Army instead. Carpenter noted that the American War Department was much more tolerant than the British

War Office when it came to allowing women to report the war. While General Montgomery flatly vowed that "we will not tolerate them," American officials were of the notion that there were certain aspects of the war better covered by women.

After the Normandy invasion Carpenter followed the army through Caen, across the River Orne around Falaise. However, the Supreme Headquarters Allied European Forces (SHAEF) prevented women from witnessing the jubilation of the liberation of Paris. When she finally made it to Paris Carpenter accompanied French liberation troops as they hunted down the remaining Germans left in the city. She suffered a shattered eardrum from the bombing at St. Lo, which became infected and led to a case of mastoiditis. Rather than leaving the front lines she moved with the hospital, staying close to the action, compiling stories about how Americans cared for their wounded.

Carpenter went on to cover the Battle of Arnhem and followed American troops through Antwerp and Aachen and ultimately to the Rhine. She was accredited to the First Army, with whom she witnessed the Battle of Huertgen Forest. From there she retreated from the developing Battle of the Bulge, but accompanied troops toward the Rhine and the Remagen bridge. She reported the breakup of Nazi Germany and the liberation of the concentration camps as well as the meeting of the Allied and Russian armies. After the war Carpenter continued to write and worked for the Voice of America. In 1946 she published *No Woman's World,* about her exploits as a woman war correspondent.

REFERENCE: Lilya Wagner. *Women War Correspondents of World War II.* 1989.

Carrier Pigeons

Training pigeons to carry messages goes as far back as the fourth century B.C. Egypt. Other accounts report that they were used by the ancient Romans and in the Middle East by the twelfth century at the latest. As late as the present century Japan used pigeons to return film from a news event to the home office. By the late 1830s the *Times* of London was using carrier pigeons to send news from the European continent across the English Channel. Beginning in 1840, the *Boston Daily Mail* introduced what became known as the "pigeon express." Thirty years later, carrier pigeons were used to get news out of besieged Paris, during the Franco-Prussian War.*

REFERENCE: Robert W. Desmond. *The Information Process.* 1978.

Cartier-Bresson, Henri
(1909-2004)

Born near the French village of Chanteloup, he first studied painting before turning to photography in 1931. Cartier-Bresson rose to the top of his profession with a minimum of equipment, most often resorting to his Leicas. In 1937 he and Jean Renor made a documentary film about the Loyalists during the Spanish Civil War* entitled *Return to Life.* Cartier-Bresson was a corporal in the French army in 1940 when the Germans invaded France. He was captured and spent almost three years in a prison camp. He escaped in 1943 on his third attempt and joined the French resistance. Soon after he joined a resistance group and helped other prisoners and escapees.

Following World War II* he cofounded the international distribution agency Magnum along with Robert Capa* and David Seymour.* He covered the 1947 war in Kashmir from both sides. The following year he arrived in China shortly before Mao Tse-tung's forces took control of Peking. After spending five weeks covering the Communist forces he was in Nanking when Chiang Kai-shek and his followers departed. In September 1948 he left China for India and the police action against the Hyderabad state.

His photographs have been widely reprinted and published in collections such as *The Decisive Moment* (1952), *People of Moscow* (1955), *China in Transition* (1956), and *the World of*

Henri Cartier-Bresson (1968). He was the first photographer to have his works exhibited at the Louvre.

REFERENCE: Robert E. Hood. *12 at War.* 1967.

Casey, Robert Joseph (1890-1962)

Born in Beresford, South Dakota, Casey earned a reputation for his adventurous exploits. He served as correspondent for the *Chicago Daily News* from 1920 to 1947. Prior to joining the paper he had served as a captain in World War I* and had reported for the *Des Moines Register and Leader.* He covered World War II* action in the company of British, American, and French forces in campaigns from the Middle East to the Mediterranean, and in the South Pacific. He covered the British army in Egypt and Libya in 1941, and the following year was with the U.S. fleet in the South Pacific during the Battles of Wake Island, Coral Sea, Midway, and the Marshall Islands. Casey was with the British navy in the Adriatic, the Mediterranean, and the Middle East before reporting the invasion of Normandy in 1944. He accompanied the U.S. First Army through France, Belgium, Luxembourg, and then Germany. He wrote over two dozen books based on his exploits including *I Can't Forget,* the story of the German invasion of Holland and France, and *Torpedo Junction,* which chronicles his experiences as a foreign correspondent on a U.S. warship in the South Pacific.

REFERENCE: Jack Stenbuck, ed. *Typewriter Battalion.* 1995.

Cassidy, Henry C. (b. 1910)

Cassidy became European correspondent for the Associated Press in 1936 and began his career as a war correspondent two years later when he covered the Battle of the Ebro from the Spanish Republican side of the Spanish Civil War.* With the outbreak of World War II,* he was accredited to the French armies in 1939, before covering

the British army and air force in France. He remained in Paris until German forces entered the city following the defeat of France in 1940. Soon after, he went to Berlin and then to Moscow as chief of the AP bureau. His experiences in Russia are recounted in *Moscow Dateline.*

REFERENCE: Robert W. Desmond. *Crisis and Conflict: World News Reporting Between Two Wars, 1920-1940.* 1982.

Cave, Peter (b. 1952)

One of Australia's most prominent journalists, Cave has covered major hotspots around the world for more than three decades. He started his forign postings in Japan in the 1980s and is a five-time winner of Australian journalism's most prestigious award, the Walkley Award, for his coverage of the Tiananmen Square massacre, the fall of the Berlin Wall, and an Iraq hostage investigation. He has chronicled the end of Apartheid in South Africa, the Palestinain intifadas in the Occupied Territoies, the break-up of Yugolslavia and the wars that followed in Slovenia, Croatia, Bosnia, Kosovo and later Lebanon. Other major conflicts he has reported on have been the two Gulf Wars, the troubles in Northern Ireland, the Coconut War in the New Hebrides, and the first Bali terrorist bombing. In 2011 he covered the Egyptian revolution and the Libyan civil war. More recently he covered the Syrian civil war and has dedicated much of his attention to helping fellow journalists with trauma training and peer support.

REFERENCE: www.abc.net.au/profiles/content/s1888147. htm.

Chandler, Edmund (1874-1926)

Born in Norfolk, England, and educated at Cambridge, he was hired as special correspondent for the *Daily Mail* to cover the British expedition to Tibet in 1904. At the Battle of Hot Springs Chandler was wounded in twelve places when attacked by four Tibetans.

With the outbreak of World War I* he was assigned by the *Times* and the *Daily Mail* to cover the western front. He covered the Mesopotamia campaign between 1915 and 1918, the same year he became the *Times* correspondent in the Middle East. He wrote several books, including A *Vagabond in Asia* (1899), *The Unveiling of Lhasa* (1905), and *Youth and the East* (1924). He died on January 4, 1926.

REFERENCE: Robert Wilkinson-Latham. *From Our Special Correspondent*. 1979.

Chapelle, Georgette "Dickey" (1918-1965)

It is somewhat ironic that Dickey Chapelle, the daughter of pacifist parents, grew up to become the first American woman war correspondent killed in action and the first woman photographer accredited to the war in the Pacific. Chapelle left the Massachusetts Institute of Technology early to pursue a career in aviation. After her nearsightedness contributed to her crash landing a plane she was forced to abandon her first ambition. She stayed in the aviation field as a publicist for several airlines and took a course in photography, eventually marrying her instructor, TWA publicity photographer Tony Chapelle, in 1940. After her husband enlisted in the navy following Pearl Harbor, she applied for photography jobs with various news services. In 1944 Chapelle was assigned to a hospital ship bound for Iwo Jima.

Photographer-correspondent Chapelle was a latecomer to World War II* reportage when she took one of the most famous photos of the war. On board the hospital ship *Samaritan,* which was steaming toward the Battle of Iwo Jima, she snapped a photo of a seriously wounded marine being lifted on board the ship. The picture, "The Dying Marine," would be used in countless blood drives for the remainder of the war. She was thereafter assigned by the navy to photograph casualties for possible use in future blood drives for the mounting numbers of wounded in the Pacific campaign. She survived the Battles of Iwo Jima and Okinawa, as well as some of the most deadly kamikaze attacks of the war.

In 1956 Chapelle covered the revolt in Hungary for *Life* magazine and was jailed in Budapest for three months by the Soviets for helping the freedom fighters. This experience would lead to a lifelong disdain for Communism, reflected in much of her coverage of the Cuban Revolution and the Vietnam War.* In 1958 she was sent to document the Algeria war for independence. Her investigation revealed that the French were using NATO weapons in their campaign to protect their African possessions. Her photos became poignant reminders of the brutality and inhumanity of colonialism. Later that year Chapelle covered the landing of the marines in Lebanon and Castro's revolt against the Batista regime in Cuba. During the Cuban campaign she witnessed four engagements in Oriente Province and was injured when her jeep overturned during a mortar attack. The next year she was on hand at Quemoy Island, off the coast of China, when it was bombarded by Communist forces.

Beginning in 1961 Chapelle witnessed the Vietnam conflict as a freelancer, which required the endorsement of two news agencies, in this case the *National Observer* and the *Wall Street Journal*. Already an accomplished pilot, Chapelle gained the respect of troops by parachuting with them in full combat gear. She would eventually repeat this exercise over thirty times during five different tours of duty. In 1962 Chapelle took the first photographs of combat-ready American advisors in Vietnam, which were featured in her picture-story "Helicopter War in South Viet Nam" in *National Geographic* magazine. She received the 1962 George Polk* Award "for the best reporting, any medium, requiring exceptional courage and enterprise abroad." In 1965 Chapelle accompanied U.S. Marines when they landed in the Dominican Republic. On November 4, 1965, she was with a marine patrol during Operation Black Ferret in Vietnam when someone triggered a booby trap made of a grenade wired to an 81 mm mortar round. Hit in the throat by shrapnel, Chapelle died almost instantly.

REFERENCES: Dickey Chapelle. *What's a Woman Doing Here?* 1961; Julia Edwards. *Women of the World: The Great Foreign Correspondents.* 1988; Roberta Ostroff. *Fire in the Wind: The Life of Dickey Chapelle.* 1992.

Chapman, Frank C. (?)

Chapman is credited with one of the greatest news scoops of the American Civil War.* However, the *New York Herald* correspondent was accused of lacking scruples for the way he delivered it. Following the Battle of Shiloh, Chapman was granted access to the army telegraph facility on the pretense that he was on General Ulysses S. Grant's staff. Chapman's controversial account soon came under fire for its inaccuracies as well as its exaggeration of Grant's role in the battle.

After General Halleck expelled all reporters from the western army Chapman transferred to the East, where he was rewarded for his Shiloh scoop with the position of chief correspondent with General John Pope's army. The intrepid reporter resorted to subterfuge once more after the first day of the Battle of Gettysburg. Reaching Baltimore ahead of his competition, Chapman telegraphed his account using the services of the only two telegraphers on duty to speed up his transmissions. As they quickly relayed his account a correspondent from the *Tribune* breathlessly arrived to send his dispatch. In order to stall the telegraphers Chapman handed them a copy of the Bible and told them to add it to his transmission until he returned. Since protocol insured that telegraph messages should be sent in order of arrival, Chapman was able to control the wires throughout the day as his competitors waited powerlessly in line.

Throughout the war, the *Herald* spared no expense in the pursuit of war news. On one occasion, following the insignificant Battle of Mine Run, Chapman offered five hundred dollars to a sutler's clerk to smuggle newspaper reports through enemy territory to Washington.

REFERENCES: J. Cutler Andrews. *The North Reports the Civil War.* 1955; Louis M. Starr. *Bohemian Brigade.* 1954.

Chauvel, Patrick (b. 1949)

This French-born war photographer has covered more than twenty conflicts, including the Arab-Israel Six Days War and the Vietnam War.* In 1995 he received the World Press Photo commendation for Spot News Stories for his coverage of the Battle of Grozny during the First Chechen War. While covering the U.S. invasion of Panama in 1989 he narrowly survived after being shot twice in the abdomen by an American soldier. He has produced several documentaries as well as the autobiographical book *Rapporteur de guerre* (*War Reporter*) in 2003.

REFERENCE: http://www.historynet.com/interview-with-war-photographer-patrick-chauvel.htm.

Chenery, Thomas (1826-1884)

Born in Barbados, he was educated at Eton and Cambridge. While serving in Constantinople as officer of the East India Company's army, in 1854 he joined the *Times* as its Constantinople correspondent during the Crimean War.* Prior to the war Chenery had been a barrister in London. His descriptive reports of the primitive conditions at the hospital of Scutari and the inadequate medical care afforded the wounded aroused public indignation back in England. His dispatches, along with W. H. Russell's,* are credited with bringing Florence Nightingale's nurses to the Crimea.

The eclectic and eccentric Chenery was an ex-professor of Arabic and a linguist fluent in French, German, Greek, and Turkish. In the 1860s and 1870s he produced several works of Arabic scholarship as well as the publication *Suggestions for a Railroad Route to India.* In 1878 he became editor of the *Times.*

REFERENCES: *DNB*; Robert Wilkinson-Latham. *From Our Special Correspondent*. 1979; Oliver Woods and James Bishop. *The Story of THE TIMES*. 1983.

Chester, Thomas Morris
(1834-1892)

He was born in Harrisburg, Pennsylvania, the son of a former slave. At the age of eighteen he sailed to Liberia, where he opened a school and founded a newspaper. He returned to the United States in early 1863, shortly after the government authorized the creation of a black volunteer regiment. Chester was appointed captain of the regiment and shortly after was hired by former war correspondent John Russell Young* of the *Philadelphia Press* to report the American Civil War.*

His coverage of the war lasted from August 1864 to June 1865. Chester's dispatches describe camp life, the reaction and responses of Confederates and civilians to black troops, various military engagements, and the initial stages of Reconstruction. He participated in and reported action during the expedition against Fort Fisher, North Carolina, and the battles leading up to the fall of Petersburg and Richmond. He was one of the first reporters to enter Richmond, and was with the black troops of the Twenty-fifth Army Corps, which were symbolically the first to enter the Confederate capital.

Following the war Chester became the European agent for a freedman's aid society and traveled widely through the continent. He earned a law degree in Great Britain and was the first black American to join the English bar. He came back to the States in 1871, settling in New Orleans, where he remained active in politics and practiced law.

REFERENCES: R.J.M. Blackett, ed. *Thomas Morris Chester: Black Civil War Correspondent*. 1989.

Chetwyd-Talbot, John (1910-1991)

Born in Sidmouth, Devon, and educated at Eton, he entered journalism with Reuters* in 1929. At the outbreak of World War II* he reported from the Ministry of Information before transferring to the battlefront in June 1941, when he covered Admiral Vian's assault on Spitzbergen. He reported Russian naval operations before switching to the Mediterranean theater, where he accompanied the Malta convoys.

He narrowly missed death at sea on several occasions. Fate intervened for the first time when he left the battleship *Hood* shortly before it was sunk by the *Bismarck*. Then he just missed a posting on the Far Eastern voyage of the *Prince of Wales*, which Japanese bombers sunk several months later along with the *Repulse* off the coast of Malaya.

Using the sobriquet of John Talbot he covered the Operation Torch invasion of North Africa in 1942, following which he became the first reporter to cover Marshal Tito's guerrillas in Yugoslavia. Early on he was captured by German forces and prepared for execution, but was saved at the last moment by the intervention of an American news photographer. He spent the next several months as a prisoner of war. Following the war he continued to work for Reuters in Europe and Africa before retirement in 1975.

REFERENCES: Robert W. Desmond. *Tides of War*. 1984; Dennis Griffiths, ed. *The Encyclopedia of the British Press*. 1992.

China Hands

"China Hands" refers to a small corps of eccentric Western writers and journalists who lived and reported from China between 1900 and the formation of the People's Republic of China in 1949.

REFERENCE: Peter Rand. *China Hands*. 1995.

Christy, Howard Chandler
(1873-1952)

Born in Morgan City, Ohio, he began working for the illustrated periodicals in the early 1890s. He achieved prominence as a war artist for

Leslie's Weekly during the Spanish-American War.* He witnessed the landing of American troops in Cuba on June 22, 1898. Following the first land battle of the war at Las Guasimas on June 24 Christy sketched the wounded returning to camp. His articles and sketches appeared in both *Leslie's* and *Harper's* during the war, and he was one of the illustrators for Wright's history of the war. Following the war he became well known as a poster and portrait artist.

REFERENCE: Pat Hodgson. *The War Illustrators.* 1977.

Church, William Conant "Pierrepont" (1836-1917)

Church was born in Rochester, New York. He entered journalism as co-owner of the *New York Chronicle,* a religious daily newspaper, with his father, a Baptist clergyman. Prior to the American Civil War,* Church was publisher of the *New York Sun.* At the outbreak of war he headed the *New York Times* war correspondence staff and was a member of the Bohemian Brigade.* He was considered one of the most outstanding of the 150 accredited war correspondents during the war. Under the pseudonym "Pierrepont," he reported the 1861 Port Royal operation and was wounded in the leg by a bullet during the Battle of Fair Oaks. His wound did not keep him from producing an account of the battle that filled the entire front page of the *Times* on June 3, 1862. Church took a six-month respite from the Civil War to serve as a roving reporter in Europe in 1862 and later served as a captain in the Union Army for nine months. In 1863 he cofounded the *Army and Navy Journal* with his brother, fellow *Times* war correspondent Francis P. Church. Church became perhaps the greatest military expert within the ranks of American journalism, and he presided over the military journal until his death in 1917. He also cofounded *Galaxy* magazine, which would eventually merge with the *Atlantic Monthly.*

REFERENCES: J. Cutler Andrews. *The North Reports the Civil War.* 1955; George H. Phillips. "The *Army and Navy Journal* Before Two Wars," *Journalism Quarterly.* Fall 1961. Louis M. Starr. *Bohemian Brigade.* 1954.

Churchill, Sir Winston Leonard Spencer (1874-1965)

One of the greatest statesmen of the twentieth century, he was one of its preeminent men of letters as well. Born at Blenheim Palace on November 30, 1874, he was educated at Sandhurst. In 1895 he was commissioned in the Fourth Queen's Own Hussars. In October of that same year he journeyed to Cuba in order to observe the insurrection against the Spanish. Reporting for the *Daily Graphic,* he witnessed action for the first time on his twenty-first birthday. His coverage appeared in the paper in a five-part series entitled "The Insurrection in Cuba." For his service he was awarded the Spanish Order of the Red Cross.

Following his excursion to Cuba he took a respite in London before setting out with his regiment for India. While on leave in the summer of 1897 he contracted with two papers to cover the conflict with the Pathans on the North West Frontier. Writing for the *Daily Telegraph,* Churchill was criticized for overstepping the scope of typical war reporting by commenting on political issues in order to further his own career. The result of his reportage was *The Story of the Malakand Field Force* (1898). Thanks to his American-born mother's connections he was next assigned to the Twenty-first Lancers as they advanced on Khartoum in September 1898, where he took part in the last British cavalry charge during the Battle of Omdurman. The following year Churchill completed *The River War,* his highly praised account of the Sudan expedition.

In October 1899 he arranged to cover the Boer War* for the *Morning Post.* After his arrival in Durban, South Africa, he was caught in a Boer ambuscade while aboard an armored freight train and taken prisoner. Shortly after, he escaped from Pretoria. With a bounty on his head, after a perilous journey he made it back to Durban, where he joined the South Africa Light Horse. It is worth noting here that his dual service as correspondent-officer during the previous 1898 Nile campaign led to a prohibition against such an arrangement. However, Churchill was able to circumvent this rule to perform the same role during the Boer War, one of only several soldiers to do so. During the Sudan campaign he disguised his reports as private letters addressed to a fictitious "my dear" who in reality was the editor Oliver Borthwick of the *Morning Post*. In June 1900 he returned to England to write several books based on his South African exploits. His books *London to Ladysmith, via Pretoria* (1900) and *Ian Hamilton's March* (1900) were based on his reports for the *Morning Post*. His career as a war correspondent was short and amazingly successful, with four profitable books to his credit by the time he was twenty-six. However, his career as writer and statesman was just beginning. He died on January 24, 1965.

REFERENCES: Keith Alldritt. *Churchill, the Writer*. 1992; Winston Churchill. *The Boer War*. 1990; *DNB, 1961-1970*; Robert Wilkinson-Latham. *From Our Special Correspondent*. 1979.

Civil War

See AMERICAN CIVIL WAR.

Clapper, Raymond Lewis (1892-1944)

Clapper was born in La Cygne, Kansas, and educated at the University of Kansas. He began writing for the *Kansas City Star* while still in college. He joined the staff of United Press International in 1917, serving in the nation's capital for the next sixteen years. Disgusted by the nepotism, graft, and political patronage of the city, he wrote *Racketeering in Washington* (1933). The next year he joined the *Washington Post* and became a popular syndicated columnist with his daily column "Between You and Me."

During World War II* he became a traveling war correspondent, reporting the invasion of Sicily and the bombing of Rome, before transferring to the Pacific theater in late 1943 to cover action from New Britain, New Guinea, and Guadalcanal. He was reporting the invasion of the Marshall Islands in 1944 when the plane that was carrying him over the devastated airfield at Eniwetok hit another American bomber, killing all on board. Following his death colleagues established the Raymond Clapper Memorial Association, which annually rewards a Washington correspondent. Its first recipient was war correspondent Ernie Pyle.* Clapper's collected work was published as *Watching the World* in 1944.

REFERENCES: Robert W. Desmond. *Tides of War*. 1984; *DAB 3*.

Clark, Gregory (1892–1977)

The Canadian journalist, soldier, and outdoorsman was educated at the University of Toronto and began his newspaper career with the *Toronto Star*, working for the paper from 1911 to 1947. During World War I* he served with the 4th Canadian Mounted Rifles and won the Military Cross as an infantry lieutenant (or major) at the Battle of Vimy Ridge. After the war he returned to Toronto, going on to cover the major news events of his lifetime. Rejected as too old for active service in World War II,* he went overseas as the next best thing—a war correspondent—going on to report from the United Kingdom, Sicily, Italy, and France. He was recognized for his service by being named an Officer of the Order of the British Empire (OBE) and was awarded the Service Medal of Canada.

REFERENCE: http://www.thecanadianencyclopedia.ca/en/article/greg-clark/.

Clark, Willis Gaylord (1827-1898)

Born in New York, he served as both coeditor and frontline reporter for the Confederate newspaper the *Mobile Register.* Clark studied law in Illinois before moving to Mobile to practice. He first entered journalism as editor for the Democratic *Southern Magazine* before moving over to the *Mobile Daily Advertiser,* which merged with the *Register* at the outbreak of the war. He left war reporting for a career in manufacturing and railroading.

REFERENCE: Stewart Sifakis. *Who Was Who in the Civil War.* 1988.

Clarke, Sir Basil (1879-1947)

Born in Cheshire, England, he was educated at Oxford before entering the banking profession. In 1904 he joined the *Manchester Guardian* as a special correspondent. He assumed the same position in 1910 with the *Daily Mail.* When World War I* broke out he covered the German invasion of Belgium in 1914. In 1915 he reported the Balkan campaign and the following year witnessed warfare in Holland and Scandinavia as well as the naval blockade of Germany. Joining Reuters* that same year, he was with the British army at the Battle of the Somme. Following the war he left journalism for the Special Intelligence Branch of the Ministry of Reconstruction, with which he remained for the next twelve years. He continued his career with the Ministry of Health and was knighted in 1923.

REFERENCE: Dennis Griffiths, ed. *The Encyclopedia of the British Press.* 1992.

Clarke, Thomas (1884-1957)

Clarke was born in Bolton, England, and entered journalism while still in his teens. In 1903 he was hired by the *South China Morning Post* in Hong Kong. Soon after, he was covering events in French Indochina for the *Daily Mail* and the *Chicago Tribune.* He reported the Russo-Japanese War* and returned to England shortly after the conflict.

In 1911 Clarke joined the staff of the *Daily Mail* on a full-time basis. He went on to hold a variety of posts with several other papers as well as serve in World War I.* During World War II* he worked as a news broadcaster for the BBC Latin American service. He wrote several books, including two about the power of the press, *Northcliffe in History* (1950) and *My Northcliffe Diary* (1931).

REFERENCE: *DNB.* 1951-1960.

Clifford, Alexander Graeme (1909-1952)

Prior to becoming Berlin correspondent for Reuters* in 1939 he had covered the Spanish Civil War* for the news agency. With the outbreak of World War II* Clifford went to the British headquarters in France as an "eyewitness"* for the entire British press establishment. By 1940 he was with the *Daily Mail* reporting the conflict in Greece and Yugoslavia before accompanying the British Expeditionary Force to North Africa during the Egyptian-Libyan desert campaign the following year. During the winter of 1943-1944 Clifford was on the Italian front, where he was cited for the second time for "gallant and distinguished services." In 1944 he returned to France after five years to cover the post-D-Day campaign. Following the liberation of Paris Clifford accompanied the British Second Army on its push into Belgium, Holland, and finally Germany.

REFERENCES: Richard Collier. *Fighting Words.* 1989; Robert W. Desmond. *Tides of War.* 1984.

CNN Effect

In 1990s with the rise of cable news it became de rigueur to refer to the instant transmission of news as either the "BBC Effect" or the "CNN Effect." Either phrase alludes to the notion that, when instant news is broadcasted and received, it often leads to "instant decision-making," or "instant diplomacy" by the world powers.

REFERENCES: Greg McLaughlin. *The War Correspondent.* 2002; Paul L. Moorcraft and Philip M. Taylor. *Shooting the Messenger.* 2008.

Cobb, Irvin Shrewsbury
(1876-1944)

Cobb was born in Paducah, Kentucky, and got his start in journalism working for his hometown newspaper. Primarily remembered as a humorist, Cobb worked for a variety of papers, often doubling as a political reporter and humor columnist. While employed by the *Saturday Evening Post* he was twice sent to Europe to cover World War I.* He reported the battles at Chateau-Thierry, Louvain, and Mons, and the occupation of Brussels. He was bedridden in a London hotel when German zeppelins bombed the city in 1918. During the war he viewed combat from an observation balloon above the Aisne River and was nearly shot as a spy by a Prussian officer. Following each of his European stints he went on the lecture circuit once back home.

In 1922 he left the *Post* for Hearst's *Cosmopolitan* magazine. Cobb continued to write books and articles, met seven presidents, and wrote for vaudeville and silent films.

REFERENCES: Emmet Crozier. *American Reporters on the Western Front 1914-18.* 1959; Fred Gus Neuman. *Irvin S. Cobb: His Life and Achievements.* 1934.

Cockburn, Claud (1904-1981)

Born in Peking, Cockburn was one of the most eccentric and controversial reporters to cover the Spanish Civil War.* He was educated at Oxford and was a cousin of the writer Evelyn Waugh.* Following graduation he entered journalism with the *Times* and by 1929 was a fulltime journalist and foreign correspondent. However, within four years he had drifted toward radical politics and resigned. He established the *Week,* which published stories not typically handled by the establishment press. The London-based paper reported the developing conflict in Spain well ahead of its competition.

By the summer of 1936 Cockburn was in Spain himself, joining the ranks of the Fifth Regiment. He would be one of many journalists who took up arms during the Spanish Civil War. After several weeks in the field he was persuaded to return to journalism, where his talent for propaganda could be better put to use. Upon his return to London he turned his efforts to overturning England's policy of nonintervention in the conflict. The publication of his polemic, *Reporter in Spain,* and his pro-Communist sympathies led the British government to deny him a visa due to his participation in the Republican militia. Despite efforts to bar his return, several weeks later Cockburn was sending dispatches to the *Week* and the *Daily Worker* from Spain.

One of his best pieces on the war involved an event which never occurred. From August 1936, the border between Spain and France had been closed to arms traffic, which the Republic forces drastically needed. Cockburn convinced the French prime minister, Leon Blum, to reopen the border in March 1938 by concocting a story of a major Nationalist setback in Morocco. He was heavily criticized for distorting the truth and using the press to achieve his political goals.

In 1941 Cockburn's paper the *Week* was banned along with the *Daily Worker* because of their antiwar stance. Except for a brief stint in the field at the onset of the war Cockburn functioned more as propagandist than war correspondent. His request for accreditation as a war correspondent was denied on account of his Communist leanings and his potential for impairing morale within the armed forces. Following the war he lived in Ireland and kept his hand in journalism as a regular contributor to the *Irish Times,* the *New Statesman,* and other periodicals.

REFERENCES: Phillip Knightley. *The First Casualty.* 1975; Trevor Royle. *War Report.* 1987; Peter Wyden. *The Passionate War.* 1983.

Coffin, Charles Carleton
(1823-1896)

Born in Boscawen, New Hampshire, Coffin was, according to some sources, the only reporter to cover all four years of the American

Civil War.* He worked for several Boston newspapers, including the *Boston Journal,* which released him soon before the outbreak of the Civil War. Coffin covered the Battle of Bull Run at his own expense, figuring at worst he could sell his story to another paper. The *Journal* was so impressed by his reporting of the battle that he was rehired as a "special" to cover the war. During the conflict his letters appeared regularly in the Boston papers under the pen name "Carleton."

Along the front linies Coffin became a familiar fixture with his notebooks and topographical maps on hand to ensure accuracy. His reputation for precision was enhanced by the fact that he was one of the few reporters to include diagrams with his dispatches. His simultaneous coverage of both the western and eastern battle fronts was also a rarity. Among his feature scoops were Grant's victory at Fort Donelson, Tennessee, and the Union recapture of Charleston. He reported on the Battles of Antietam, Gettysburg, and the Wilderness, as well as Lincoln's Gettysburg Address and the capture of Richmond. In the process he gained national prominence as one of the foremost reporters of the war. After the war he embarked on a lecture tour around the world recounting his wartime exploits. He wrote thirteen books ranging from travel and children's stories to novels. Among his works recounting his career as a war reporter were *My Days and Nights on the Battlefield* (1864), *Following the Flag* (1865), *Four Years of Fighting* (1866), and *Marching to Victory* (1888). Coffin entered the political arena in 1884, serving a term in the Massachusetts state assembly before entering the state senate in 1890. He died of apoplexy in Boston on March 2, 1896, hard at work on a speech concerning his life as a war correspondent.

REFERENCES: J. Cutler Andrews. *The North Reports the Civil War.* 1955; Patricia Faust, ed. *Historical Times Illustrated Encyclopedia of the* Civil War. 1986; William Elliot Griffis. *Charles Carleton Coffin.* 1898; Louis M. Starr. *Bohemian Brigade.* 1954.

Colburn, Robert T. (?)

Colburn covered the western theater of the American Civil War* for the *New York World.* He was one of the first reporters to arrive at Cairo, Illinois, in early 1862, as the Western Army of Tennessee prepared to move up the Tennessee River to strike at the heart of the Confederacy. He was captured along with correspondents Junius Browne* and Albert Deane Richardson* while attempting to run the batteries at Vicksburg and reach Grant's command. Colburn was released within a month, while his colleagues endured almost two years in seven different Confederate prisons. Confederate authorities explained that the disparity in the sentences was due to the other reporters' affiliation with the *New York Tribune,* which they blamed for inaugurating the war.

REFERENCES: J. Cutler Andrews. *The North Reports the Civil War.* 1955; Louis M. Starr. *Bohemian Brigade.* 1954.

Cole, Carolyn (b. 1961)

Cole studied photojournalism at the University of Texas and began her career with the *El Paso Herald-Post* in 1986. After two years she was hired by the *San Francisco Examiner* and continued to work for a variety of papers as her reputation grew. In 1994 she covered the upheaval in Haiti for the *Los Angeles Times* and the following year was working in Russia. Her photos of the Los Angeles bank robbery shoot-out in 1997 helped her paper earn a Pulitzer Prize for its coverage of the mayhem. In 1999 Cole reported on the crisis in Kosovo and in 2001 spent several months in Afghanistan. Cole was frequently recognized for her fine work. In 2002 she was recognized as the National Press Photographers Association Newspaper Photographer of the Year. In 2002 she covered the conflict in Liberia and was in Monrovia reporting on the siege of the nation's capital as rebels demanded the resignation of President Charles Taylor. She won the 2004 Pulitzer Prize for her coverage of the civil war in

Liberia. In 2004 she became the first photojournalist to win all three of America's top photojournalism awards in the same year.

REFERENCE: http://carolyncoleart.com.

Coleman, Kit

See WATKINS, KATHLEEN "KIT" BLAKE.

Collingwood, Charles Cummings (1917-1985)

Born in Three Rivers, Michigan, the future Rhodes scholar was hired by Edward R. Murrow as a network correspondent for CBS radio during World War II.* Following graduation from Cornell University he attended Oxford on a scholarship, intending to pursue a law career. In 1940 he went to work for the United Press.

Joining the likes of William L. Shirer,* Howard K. Smith,* and Eric Sevareid,* all recruited by Murrow to make up the CBS broadcast team during the war, Collingwood was first assigned to North Africa, where he would be awarded the rank of captain as war correspondent with the British army. In 1943 he won the Peabody Award for best foreign reporting and was sent stateside. He went on to a successful career in television newscasting, winning another Peabody Award in 1963. In the 1960s he began covering American involvement in Vietnam* and in 1968 was one of the first American news reporters permitted broadcast access to North Vietnam. He received Emmy awards for his coverage of the Vietnam War in 1968 and 1969.

REFERENCES: Dennis Griffiths, ed. *The Encyclopedia of the British Press.* 1992; *New York Times.* October 4, 1985.

Collins, Robert Moore (1868-1937)

As Reuters* correspondent he covered the Boxer Rebellion,* the Philippine insurrection, and the Russo-Japanese War* as the chief Reuters correspondent in China. He returned to England soon after the Portsmouth Treaty was signed and worked for the Associated Press until 1925.

REFERENCE: Dennis Griffiths, ed. *The Encyclopedia of the British Press.* 1992.

Coltman, Robert (1862-1931)

Coltman was born in Washington, D.C., and graduated from Jefferson Medical College in Philadelphia. He was practicing medicine in Peking as well as reporting for the *Chicago Record* from 1895. When the Boxer Rebellion* broke out in 1900, Coltman chronicled the siege from inside the city. He was able to smuggle the news scoop of the Boxer siege through the Boxer pickets with the assistance of a local beggar, and was thereby responsible for alerting the outside world to the siege of Peking. He wrote *The Chinese: Medical, Political and Social* (1891) and *Yellow Crime, or Beleaguered in Peking* (1901).

REFERENCE: M. L. Stein. *Under Fire: The Story of American War Correspondents.* 1968.

Colvin, Marie Catherine (1956–2012)

Born in Astoria, New York, Colvin was educated at Yale University, making the transition from studying either anthropology or marine biology to English literature after working for the university newspaper. She began international reporting with Universal Press International,* first from Washington and New York and then France as Paris bureau chief. During her time in France she worked as a stringer for the *Sunday Times* and in 1986 became its Middle East correspondent, replacing David Blundy,* who had left for another job. She worked her way up to *Sunday Times* foreign correspondent in 1995 and became more prominent while covering international conflicts. The British Press awarded the American of Irish ancestry with the foreign reporter of the year award in 2001 and 2010.

*Indicates a separate entry.

Colvin became the first reporter to interview Libyan strongman Muammar Gaddafi, after the American bombing of Tripoli in 1986, during Operation El Dorado Canyon. She would cover conflicts in Chechnya, Kosovo, Sierra Leone, Zimbabwe, Timor, and Sri Lanka. She was hailed for helping save the lives of hundreds of women and children besieged by Indonesian forces during the carnage in East Timor in 1999. In 2000, she was recognized with the International Women's Media Foundation award for Courage in Journalism for her reporting activities in Kosovo and Chechnya.

In 2001, Colvin was covering the civil war in Sri Lanka when she lost her left eye to a shrapnel burst from a rocket-propelled grenade fired by the Sri Lanka Army. Her black eye-patch "became something of a trademark" for her. After sustaining the injury the 44-year old journalist was able to walk some 30 miles through the jungle and meet her deadline with a 3,000-word article on the conflict. In the aftermath of these events Colvin was forced to seek treatment for posttraumatic stress disorder.*

During the 2011 Arab Spring Colvin scored the first interview with Gaddafi in Libya since the war broke out. Granted permission to bring along two other journalists she chose Christiane Amanpour* and Jeremy Bowen.* Colvin's last assignment was in Syria to cover the civil war in 2012. Despite Syrian government prohibitions against foreign coverage of the war she was able to make it to the beleaguered city of Homs, describing the shelling of the city by government forces "the worst conflict" she had ever witnessed. Colvin was killed along with French photojournalist Remi Ochlik,* dying from injuries received in an IED (improvised explosive device) stuffed with nails. According to the *Sunday Times* she had died after Ochlik attempted to get their shoes in order to flee the bombardment of a building they were using for shelter. Fellow journalists have suggested that the building had been specifically targeted by the Syrian Army, after intercepting satellite telephone signals.

REFERENCES: Roy Greensdale, "Marie Colvin Obituary," Guardian, Feb. 22, 2012; Charles Walford and Nabila Ramdani, "Veteran American War Reporter Marie Colvin Killed When Syrian Army Shells Media Center Just Hours after Her Last TV Broadcast," Daily Mail, Feb. 22, 2012.

Committee to Protect Journalists (CPJ)

In 1981 this independent and nonprofit organization was launched to defend the rights of journalists and protect them from reprisals while covering conflicts. The CPJ was created by a coterie of American journalists concerned about the harsh treatment often meted out to their counterparts in other countries. It investigates and chronicles attacks on the press and classifies cases in categories that include, Abducted, Attacked (wounded or assaulted), Censored, Expelled, Harassed (denied access or detained for less than 48 hours), Imprisoned, Killed, Legal Action, Missing, and Threatened. According to the CPJ, in order for a journalist to be considered in the line of duty the mishap must be the result of a hostile action. The CPJ does not include in its database journalists killed in accidents such as car and plane crashes; nor does it include journalists who died from health-related issues.

REFERENCES: Herbert N. Foerstel. *Killing the Messenger*. 2006; http://cpj.org/reports/2008/07/journalists-killed-in-iraq.php.

Confederate Press Association

During the American Civil War* many Southern newspapers could not afford special war correspondents and relied on the members of the Confederate Press Association, also known as the Press Association of the Confederate States. Established on March 1, 1863, the new organization encompassed all Confederate dailies east of the Mississippi River. Once Dr. Robert W. Gibbes, the editor of the *Columbia South Carolinian*, was elected president and headquarters was established in Atlanta, correspondents were recruited and telegraph facilities were arranged with both the military and Southern telegraph companies. Each newspaper that subscribed to the association paid twelve dollars a week for a news report that could not exceed 3,500 words. In order to control access to the service the association copyrighted its reports.

Correspondents were instructed to eliminate opinion from their dispatches and to stress factual reporting. They achieved a creditable record for objective reporting, eschewing rumor and unsubstantiated information. Leading journalists for the association included Bartholomew Riordan, John Hatcher, Jonathan Albertson, A. J. Wagner, and W. O. Woodson.

REFERENCES: J. Cutler Andrews. *The South Reports the Civil War.* 1970; Hodding Carter. *Their Words Were Bullets: The Southern Press in War, Reconstruction and Peace.* 1969.

Conniff, Frank (1914-1971)

Born in Danbury, Connecticut, and educated at the University of Virginia, Conniff joined the Hearst newspaper chain following graduation. Beginning in 1944 he covered most theaters of conflict during World War II,* including Africa, Italy, and Germany. He was with Allied forces after the capture of Rome and was part of the International News Service French invasion team. After World War II he reported the Korean War.* Following his interview of Soviet premier Khrushchev in 1955 he received the Pulitzer Prize along with fellow correspondents Howard Kingsbury Smith and W. R. Hearst, Jr. He retired from journalism in 1967.

REFERENCE: Jack Stenbuck, ed. *Typewriter Battalion.* 1995.

Cook, George S. (1819-1902)

Born in Connecticut and failing at business, he moved to New Orleans where success also evaded him. He began experimenting with the newly invented dagguereotype in 1842 and ended up

living in Charleston, South Carolina. In April 1861 he managed to get permission to enter Fort Sumter and photograph its leader Major Robert Andserson, who had refused to surrender the garrison at the opening of the Civil War.* Within a few weeks his photographic cards were selling in New York City at fifty cents a piece. One recent account suggests that Cook had previously worked for Mathew Brady.* In any case he was one of the few photographers to represent the Confederacy during the war. In 1863 he photographed U.S. monitors bombarding Fort Moultrie from the ruins of Ft. Sumter. The destruction of most of his photos in a fire in 1864 is a huge loss for students of the Civil War and war photography.

REFERENCE: Duncan Anderson. *War: A Photo History.* 2006.

Cooke, George Wingrove (1814–1865)

Born in Bristol, England, Cooke was educated at Jesus College, Oxford and the University of London, where he studied law, joining the bar in 1835. He published several books on British politics and history as well as a biography of the first Earl of Shaftesbury. Cooke visited the Crimea in 1855, chronicling the Crimean War* in his 1856 book *Inside Sebastopol.* In 1857 he covered the Second Opium War in China as a special correspondent for *The Times.* His dispatches from the battlefront and the British expedition were collected and republished in book form in 1858.

REFERENCE: W.P. Courtney; Jonathan Harris, revision, "Cooke, George," *Oxford Dictionary of National Biography.* 2004.

Cooke, John Esten (1830-1886)

Cooke was the leading war correspondent for the *Southern Illustrated News* during the American Civil War.* He served as staff officer on different occasions for Generals J.E.B. Stuart and

Thomas J. "Stonewall" Jackson. In addition to the *Illustrated News* he filed dispatches with other Richmond papers. His coverage of the Battle of Fredericksburg while with Stuart is one of the best accounts of the engagement and appeared in the *Richmond Whig* under his pen name "J.E.C."

REFERENCE: J. Cutler Andrews. *The South Reports the Civil War.* 1970.

Cooper, Anderson Hays (b. 1967)

A scion of the Vanderbilt family, Cooper was born in New York City and educated at Yale University. After a short interlude interning with the Central Intelligence Agency (CIA) he gravitated toward the journalism profession, although he had no training. Initially Cooper attempted to find work with ABC, but could not find entreé despite his lofty connections. Instead he began working as a fact checker for Channel One, a news agency, and on his own forged a press pass that allowed him to cover events in then-closed Burma. In the early 1990s he moved to Vietnam for a year and was able to convince Channel One to loan him a Hi-8 video camera, with which he started making low-tech documentaries on Vietnam. These were featured on the station, which specialized in youth-oriented news broadcasts for American junior high and high schools. As Cooper began to travel to brutal conflict areas he claimed to have become inured to violence, especially after witnessing the aftermath of the Rwanda genocide. In 1995 he was hired as correspondent by ABC News. In 2001 he joined CNN.* He has covered a number of conflict zones including Bosnia, Haiti, Israel, Somalia, and Rwanda, but is probably best known for his ubiquitous presence on broadcast television. In recent years he has covered conflicts in Egypt and Syria and the Cedar Revolution in Beirut. In 2006, his book *Dispatches from the Edge*, chronicling his foreign and domestic reporting during the previous year became a New York Times best-seller.

REFERENCES: "Anderson Cooper Profile," http://www.cnn.com/profiles/anderson-copper-profile; Po Bronson, "Anderson Cooper's Private War," Men's Journal, Mar. 2007.

Cooper, James Lees (1907-1980)

Born in Darwen, Lancashire, he joined the *Darwen News* before leaving for the *Daily Express*. In 1941 he became its war correspondent, covering the Malta Convoys, the Eighth Army campaign in North Africa, and action in Sicily, Italy, and Madagascar. Following the war he returned to Fleet Street before becoming the first staff reporter for the paper in Canada. He left the *Daily Express* in 1958 to return to London and join the *Globe and Mail*. The next year he returned to Toronto, where he was promoted to *Globe and Mail*'s editor and publisher. He retired in 1974.

REFERENCE: Dennis Griffiths, ed. *The Encyclopedia of the British Press.* 1992.

Cooper, Robert Wright "Bob" (1904-1992)

Born in Toronto, he joined the *Times* in 1924 and became its sports reporter. In 1939 he became a war correspondent covering French forces. After the debacle at Dunkirk, Cooper fled back to England before reporting from India, Orde Wingate's Burmese campaign, the Normandy invasion on D-Day, the liberation of Paris and Belgium, and finally the surrender of German forces. He received accolades for his coverage of the Nuremberg trials, following which he became the chief *Times* correspondent in Germany.

REFERENCES: Robert W. Desmond. *Tides of War.* 1984; Dennis Griffiths, ed. *The Encyclopedia of the British Press.* 1992.

Courtenay, William Ashmead (1831–1908)

Courtenay was born in Charleston, South Carolina and worked in his brother's book business before joining the White Light Infantry in 1851. He continued to work for his brother while performing militia duties and in 1860 became a business manager for one of the South's leading secessionist newspapers, the *Charleston Mercury*. Less than a week after Abraham Lincoln was elected president, his militia unit was dispatched by the governor of South Carolina to take the U.S. Arsenal in his hometown. He was involved in the first actions of the war after South Carolina seceded. In 1861 he began covering the conflict for the *Mercury*, under the alias, "Kiawah." In a time before actual bylines, journalists covering the war selected pseudonyms for their own protection and to facilitate the gathering of information. His reportage captured the minutiae and misery of camp life. Courtenay was with the South Carolina Palmetto Guard during the First Battle of Bull Run in Manassas, Virginia in October 1861. Consistently appalled by the lack of Army efficiency when it came to feeding and clothing soldiers, he published a number of pieces in his newspaper with recommendations for providing better food and running supplies through the Union blockade. His continuous criticism of conditions angered members of the Palmetto Guard who felt his comments reflected poorly on their chivalry, especially when he noted that the soldiers were "getting disgusted" sitting around doing nothing. Comments by members of the Palmetto Guard were published, which he felt challenged his honor, leading him into two duels. The first took place on November 21, 1861 and ended with both duelists missing their targets. They walked away after this apparently satisfied. In March of the following year another duel was narrowly averted over similar comments published in the *Mercury*. However, after hectic correspondence between the two men the duel never took place. Courtenay proved a consistent critic of army conditions and was never at a loss with suggestions to improve them.

After his true identity was revealed following the duel, Kiawah was transferred to an outpost far from the field of battle for the rest of the war. His war reportage now finished, his articles for the *Mercury* consisted of bits of information about casualties and other information gleaned from others, his career as war correspondent effectively over, but not before he challenged an officer to a duel for insulting him. As General William T. Sherman's forces moved toward Atlanta in 1864 he had his last opportunity to report on a battle at the Battle of Honey Hill, which took place near his base in Hardeeville, South Carolina. According to Courtenay's biographer, his description of the battle is considered the definitive account of the affair, in which outnumbered Confederates turned back Federal troops, losing only eight men to the Union's loss of 746 soldiers. He later returned to Charleston where he started a successful shipping business and sired ten children. As the nineteenth century closed the quick-to-take offense former reporter had accrued a fortune and had become one of the richest men in the South. In his last decades, now a philanthropist, he devoted his money and time trying to preserve South Carolina's historic legacy and the state's contribution to the Civil War.

REFERENCE: Patricia G. McNeely, "William Ashmead Courtenay: A Knight on the 'Field of Honor,'" *Knights of the Quill*, 2010, 27-44.

Cowan, Ruth (1902-1993)

Born in Salt Lake City, she graduated from the University of Texas before joining the staff of the *San Antonio Evening News* in 1928. Her first assignment as a war correspondent was in Algiers in 1942. She was reassigned to London, where she would stay until the Normandy invasion. Her coverage of the evacuation and treatment of the wounded contributed to her permanent assignment to follow the U.S. armies for the duration of the war. During her two and a half years as a war correspondent, Cowan interviewed Generals Eisenhower, Bradley, and Patton, and covered major battles such as the Battle of the Bulge. Shortly before V-E Day she returned to the United States and a posting with the

Washington Bureau of the Associated Press. In 1956 she married Bradley D. Nash, the undersecretary of commerce, and retired from the AP.

REFERENCE: Lilya Wagner. *Women War Correspondents of World War Two*. 1989.

Cowles, Virginia (1910-1983)

Born in Brattleboro, Vermont, Cowles entered journalism in the early 1930s with the *Boston Breeze*. She covered the Spanish Civil War* for the *Daily Telegraph,* the *Sunday Times,* and the Hearst newspapers. With the outbreak of World War II* she reported the Russo-Finnish War and the fall of France for the *Sunday Times,* before returning to England. In 1941 she published *Looking for Trouble,* and from 1942 to 1943 she was special assistant to the American ambassador to London.

Cowles reported the North African campaign for the *Chicago Sun* and the London *Sunday Times.* She eventually covered the conflict from Germany, Russia, and Czechoslovakia. Following the war she remained in London, marrying future British cabinet official and member of Parliament Aidan Crawley in 1945. Cowles died in an automobile accident near Biarritz while revisiting sites from her Spanish Civil War days. She published numerous biographies and works of nonfiction including *Winston Churchill: The Era and the Man* (1953), *The Phantom Major: The Story of David Stirling and His Desert Command* (1958), and *The Russian Dagger: Cold War in the Days of the Czars* (1969).

REFERENCES: Robert W. Desmond. *Tides of War.* 1984; Library of America. *Reporting World War H.* 1995; Anne Sebba. *Battling for News: The Rise of the Woman Reporter.* 1994.

Cox, Sir Geoffrey Sandford (1910-2008)

Born in New Zealand he entered journalism in 1935 with the *News Chronicle,* going on to chronicle the Spanish Civil War* from Madrid before covering the early events of World War Two in Vienna and Paris for the *Daily Express.* He later covered the war from Finland, but was prescient enough to suggest that the Red Army would eventually defeat the German Army. He served in the war with the New Zealand army, seeing action in North Africa and Crete. He was the author of a number of books including *Defence of Madrid* (1937), *The Red Army Moves* (1941), *The Road to Trieste* (1947), and *A Tale of Two Battles* (1987).

REFERENCE: Obituary, Dominion Post, April 10, 2008.

Coyne, Catherine (1907-1992)

Born in Portland, Maine, Coyne graduated from Boston University and then joined the *Boston Herald.* She was one of the few female correspondents to cover World War II in Europe. She reported the London Blitz and interviewed wounded soldiers returning to military hospitals in England after the Normandy invasion. In April 1945 she witnessed the the Russians crossing the Elbe into Germany. Coyne covered the Nuremberg War Trials and filed reports from Germany, France and England during the conflict.

REFERENCES: Stenbuck, ed. *Typewriter Battalion.*; Lilya Wagner. *Women War Correspondents of World War II.* 1989.

Crane, Stephen (1871-1900)

Born in Newark, New Jersey, he broke into journalism with his brother's local newspaper, covering the New Jersey coastal resorts. He moved to New York City, publishing occasional articles in local newspapers and working on his novel *Maggie: A Girl of the Streets,* which he self-published under the pseudonym Johnston Smith in 1893. He wrote for several periodicals while completing *The Red Badge of Courage.* Sent to Cuba to cover the insurrection in 1896, he was on a ship that went down off the coast of Florida just after the new year. His thirty-hour fight for life on a small raft was the grist for his *Scribner's* story "The Open Boat."

In 1897 Crane covered the Greco-Turkish War* for the *New York Journal* and the following year the Spanish-American War* for the *New York World*. He witnessed the landing of the marines at Guantanamo as well as most of the battles of the short war. His health began to decline, resulting in his evacuation. After a dispute over finances he left the *World* for the *Journal,* and returned to cover the action on Puerto Rico. His novel *Active Service** (1899) tells the story of war correspondents in action. Richard Harding Davis,* the preeminent war correspondent of his era, called Crane the best correspondent of the war. Crane died from tuberculosis at the age of twenty-eight.

REFERENCES: James B. Colvert. *Stephen Crane.* 1984; *DAB 2.*

Crawford, Kenneth Gale (1902-1983)

Crawford was born in Sparta, Wisconsin, and educated at Beloit College. He joined the United Press in 1924 and five years later became its Washington correspondent. In 1943 he was hired by *Newsweek* as a war correspondent. He covered action in North Africa, the Middle East, France, and Italy. He was reportedly the first American reporter to hit the beaches at Normandy during the D-Day invasion. His wartime reporting led to various awards, including the European Theater Ribbon, the Navy Commendation, and the French Liberation Medal.

In 1945 he returned to Washington as editor of the local *Newsweek* bureau. After a long career at the magazine he retired from journalism in 1970. He died of lung cancer on January 13, 1983. He wrote *The Pressure Boys* (1939) and *Report on North Africa* (1943).

REFERENCES: Robert W. Desmond. *Tides of War.* 1984; *New York Times.* January 14, 1983.

Crawfurd-Price, Walter (1881-1967)

Born in London and educated at the University of Wales, Crawfurd-Price covered the Turkish counterrevolution for the *Daily Mail* in 1909. In 1911 he joined the *Times* as special correspondent for Greece and Macedonia. He covered the Turkish army during the First Balkan War (1912) and was with the Greek army the following year. During World War I* he accompanied the Serbian army. He covered the signing of the 1919 Peace Treaty for the *Sunday Times* and stayed with the paper until 1925. Among his numerous travel books is *A Tangier Visit* (1935).

REFERENCE: Dennis Giffiths, ed. *The Encyclopedia of the British Press.* 1992.

Creelman, James (1859-1915)

Born in Montreal, Canada, Creelman moved to New York at the age of twelve. Six years later, he found work as a cub reporter for the *New York Herald.* Presaging his future fame, he received plaudits for his coverage of the Hatfield-McCoy feud while under gunfire as well as for interviewing Sitting Bull and surviving a crash in a gas airship. In 1889 he became editor of the London branch of the *Herald.* In 1893, after several stints with other papers, he was hired by Joseph Pulitzer's *New York World* to cover events in Asia, including the Sino-Japanese War. Creelman followed the Japanese armies and covered the Battles of Pyongyang and Port Arthur and the naval engagement of Yalu. He received the first of several combat-related wounds while accompanying the army in Manchuria, when the explosion of an artillery shell threw him off his horse, causing several injuries. In December 1894 he was involved in perhaps his most controversial story when his account of a massacre of Chinese civilians at Port Arthur hit the newsstands.

In 1896 Creelman covered the insurrection in Cuba, again publicizing atrocities, before being expelled by Spanish authorities for his investigative proclivities. He was responsible for giving Captain-General Weyler, the Spanish commander in Cuba, his moniker "The Butcher."

Successfully lured away from the *World* by Hearst's *New York Journal,* he was assigned to Europe, where he covered the Greco-Turkish War.* He would claim to be the first correspondent to cross the frontier to the Turkish lines. In June 1898 he was sent to Cuba to cover the Spanish-American War.* He ended up leading the charge against fortifications at El Caney when it turned out he was the only American who knew the back way up the hill. He was wounded while explaining surrender terms to a Spanish officer. Later that same year Creelman was wounded twice more while covering the American conflict with the insurgents in the Philippines.

Creelman returned to the *New York World* in 1900, and then spent short stints with several other papers over the next decade. In 1915 he was sent to cover what would be his last battle in Europe; he died of Bright's disease in Berlin shortly after his arrival. He published several books, with *On the Great Highway: The Wanderings and Adventures of a Special Correspondent* (1901) being the most notable.

REFERENCES: Willis J. Abbott. *Watching the World Go By.* 1933; *DAB* 2. 533; Jeffrey M. Dowart. "James Creelman, the *New York World* and the Port Arthur Massacre," *Journalism Quarterly.* 1973, pp. 697-701.

Crimean War

The Crimean War broke out in October 1853 when Turkey declared war on Russia. This conflict was an outgrowth of an ongoing territorial dispute between Russia and Turkey which resulted in Russian forces occupying the Danubian Principalities to coerce Turkey into accepting certain concessions. Great Britain joined France in a declaration of war on Russia in March 1854. In September a combined Anglo-French force landed in the Crimea and advanced against the Russians at Sebastopol. Subsequent battles occurred at the Alma River, Balaklava, and Inkerman. The war ended in December 1856 when the Austrians threatened to join the alliance. Both Turkey and Russia made concessions, but more significantly, Turkey was drawn closer into the sphere of Western nations.

Compared to the Mexican War,* which was covered more by solitary correspondents, the Crimean War attracted groups of correspondents on foreign assignment, in numbers not seen before. The majority of reporters were members of the London press, with the *Times* the best represented. In addition artistcorrespondents* covered their first war, and pioneer war photographers* such as Roger Fenton,* James Robertson,* and Karl Baptist von Szathmari* provided considerably more photographic coverage than in any previous wars.

The Crimean War introduced the legendary William Howard Russell* to the annals of wartime journalism. Over the next two decades he became the preeminent war correspondent of the nineteenth century. Russell is best remembered for contributing the phrase "the thin red line" in his description of the British infantry at Balaklava. His report of "the charge of the Light Brigade" reportedly inspired Alfred Lord Tennyson's poem of the same title.

This war also introduced a prejudicial attitude among the high command toward war correspondents. The commander of the Crimean expedition, Lord Raglan, and General Sir Arthur Wellesley, later better known as Lord Wellington, expressed objections to their presence and would have nothing to do with them. General Sir William Simpson perhaps more eloquently christened war reporters as "the curse of modern armies."

With war reportage still in its infancy, the rules of this craft were still being written. Correspondents were expected to be self-supporting, providing their own shelter, food, transportation, and communication channels. Other correspondents besides Russell represented the *Times,* including Dr. Humphrey Sandwith, John Barkley,

Thomas Chenery,* Ferdinand Eber, Frederick Hardman,* Andrew Archibald Paton, and T. M. O'Bird. Several of their group perished, some of the first casualties of this profession. Henry Stowe died of enteric fever and Charles Naysmith was killed in battle.

Other reporters reporting the war included Edwin L. Godkin* of the *Daily News,* George Alfred Henty* of the *Morning Post,* and Nicholas A. Wood for the *Morning Chronicle.* There were many others as well. Some spent only short stints in the Crimea and others stayed for over a year. Among the more notable artist-correspondents were William Simpson* of the *Illustrated London News* and Joseph A. Crowe* of the *Daily News.* The more strictly controlled Russian press provided little coverage, relying on official reports instead. An important innovation stimulated by the war effort was the extension from Vienna to the Black Sea coast of Bulgaria of telegraph services, which the British extended to Sebastopol and Balaklava.

REFERENCES: Nicholas Bentley, ed. *Russell's Despatches from the Crimea, 1854-1856.* 1967; Lawrence James. *Crimea, 1854-1856: The War with Russia from Contemporary Photographs.* 1981; Andrew Lambert and Stephen Badsey. *The War Correspondents: The Crimean War.* 1994.

Crockett, Edward Harry (1911-1943)

Born in Lowell, Massachusetts, he entered journalism with the AP in Boston in 1937. Crockett started covering World War II* in 1942 reporting on the conflict from Northern Africa. He covered General Field Marshal Erwin Rommel's last offensive at Bir Hacheim. Crockett was killed on February 5, 1943 when the ship he was traveling on was torpedoed in the Mediterranean Sea. In a Maine shipyard the following year, Crockett's wife christened a new Liberty ship, named after her husband.

REFERENCES: AP Wall of Honor, www.ap.org/wallofhonor/1940_1949.html.

Croft, Steve (b. 1945)

Born in Kokomo, Indiana he graduated from Syracuse University in 1967. During the Vietnam War Kroft served with the U.S. Army as a correspondent and photographer for Pacific *Stars and Stripes*.* Before joining CBS 60 Minutes in 1989 he had worked as a foreign correspondent covering international terrorism in the Middle East and Europe. He covered the war in Beirut, the sectarian violence in North Ireland, the civil war in El Salvador and the invasion of Grenada*. He is the only 60 Minutes correspondent to win two Peabody Awards in the same year. He has been the recipient of many other awards including 10 Emmys.

REFERENCE: www.cbsnews.com/ stories/1998/07/09/60minutes/bios/main13544.shtml.

Cromie, Robert (1909–1999)

Born in Detroit, Michigan and educated at Oberlin College, his first journalism job was with the *Pontiac Daily Press* in 1935. Two years later he moved over to the *Chicago Tribune.* In 1942 he went overseas to cover World War II* as a war correspondent. He was with the U.S. Marine landing at Guadalcanal on August 7. During the battle he was often seen helping wounded soldiers out of harm's way. In January 1943 he landed in New Caledonia and spent two weeks in the hospital with malaria. Later that year he was aboard a B-24 Liberator with the moniker "Satan's Sister" on a bombing raid over Raibaul, New Guinea. After his 17-month tour in the Pacific he returned to Chicago and was then off to London to cover the European theater of the war in 1944. He covered the Normandy invasion and accompanied General George S. Patton's Third Army as it moved toward Paris and the subsequent liberation of the city. In 1944 he was on a B-26 during a bombing raid when it was hit by anti-aircraft fire and forced to crash-land in England. Without missing a beat Cromie transferred to another bomber bound for a bombing raid over Germany. Cromie covered the Battle of the Bulge in France and Belgium and only returned to Chicago in May 1945. In July he returned to the Pacific campaign to chronicle the end of the Japanese war. He was in Tokyo by August 1945 and reported on the war-crimes trial of General Tomoyuki Yamashita from the Philippines. His war reporting career ended;with the conclusion of the war he went on to earn prominence as a sportswriter and nonfiction author.

REFERENCES: Diane Struzzi, "Robert Cromie, 90, Long-time Tribune Reporter," Chicago Tribune, May 24, 1999; Katherine Warner,"Robert Cromie," American World War II Correspondents, Jeffrey B. Cook, ed., 2012, 52-59.

Cronkite, Jr., Walter Leland (1916-2009)

Born in St. Joseph, Missouri, Cronkite became the elder statesman of American newscasting. He gravitated toward a career in journalism while still in high school. In the 1930s he left the University of Texas before graduating and went to work for the *Houston Post*. After several other jobs in newscasting and public relations he was hired by the United Press in 1940. With the outbreak of the war in Europe Cronkite rose to prominence as one of the first American journalists accredited to cover the conflict. Posted to London in 1942, he participated in many bombing raids and witnessed the North African campaign, the invasion of Normandy, and the Battle of the Bulge. He continued to report from Europe after the war, including the Nuremberg trials.

He returned to the States in 1948 and continued to make a name in radio and television broadcasting. In 1962 he became the CBS anchorman. He made several visits to Southeast Asia and Vietnam in the 1960s, but his career as a war correspondent ended with World War II.*

REFERENCES: Les Brown. *The New York Times Encyclopedia of Television*. 1977; Gary Gates. *Air Time: The Inside Story of CBS News*. 1978.

Crosby, Charles E. (d. 1897)

Born in Great Britain, Crosby had been a soldier and a civil engineer in Latin America when the conflict in Cuba began to develop in the late 1890s. He covered the Cuban insurrection prior to the Spanish-American War* for the *Chicago Record*. Landing at Havana in January 1897, Crosby headed for the insurgent stronghold of General Maximo Gomez. After sending back several dispatches under his pen name "Don Carlos," he was killed in March during an engagement between the rebels and Spanish forces. Although his pseudonym was an attempt to evade Spanish authorities, some of his work had fallen into enemy hands. The Spanish had apparently posted a description of Crosby and were actively searching for him when he was killed.

REFERENCE: Charles H. Brown. *The Correspondents' War*. 1967.

Cross, Henry (1855-1898)

Born in Bedfordshire and educated at Oxford, Cross covered the Sudan campaign for the *Manchester Guardian*. Cross had agreed to pay his own expenses like many of his colleagues, and had arranged to be paid for each article or "letter" he sent back to the paper. He witnessed the defeat of the Mahdist forces at the Battle of Omdurman on September 2, 1898. Shortly after the battle he was stricken with enteric fever and died. However, his account of the pivotal battle was published three days after his death. In good faith the newspaper paid Cross' estate twenty-five percent more than the agreed upon rate for the story.

REFERENCES: David Ayerst. *The Manchester Guardian: Biography of a Newspaper*. 1971; E. N. Bennett. *The Downfall of the Dervishes*. 1899.

Crost, Lyn (1915-1997)

Crost began her newspaper career writing for the *Providence Star-Tribune* while still a student at Brown University. After graduation she moved to Hawaii and in 1944 was hired by the *Honolulu Star-Bulletin* to report on the American-born Japanese soldiers, known as the Nisei, who were fighting in Europe. She covered their actions in Italy, Germany, and France, concentrating on the human side of the war rather on combat stories. Crost wrote the first story about the Nisei hero and future senator, Lieutenant Daniel Inouye, who won the Distinguished Service Cross during the Po Valley campaign. She was one of the first American correspondents to arrive at Buchenwald. After the war she worked as the Washington correspondent for the *Star-Bulletin* and as a special assistant in the White House during Eisenhower's first term.

REFERENCE: Lilya Wagner. *Women War Correspondents of World War Two*. 1989.

Crounse, Lorenzo L. (1834-1909)

Born in Sharon, New York, Crounse demonstrated an affinity for the newspaper profession by the age of twelve, when he traveled thirty miles in a wagon in response to an advertisement for a printer's apprentice. Initially rebuffed because of his youth, two years later he landed a job on the *Milwaukee Free Democrat*. Less than eight years later he had risen to editor and co-owner of the paper. With the outbreak of the American Civil War* Crounse took to the field for various western newspapers before joining the staff of the *New York World* and then the *New York Times*.

Crounse and William Swinton* would become the preeminent correspondents for the *New York Times* covering the Army of the Potomac. During the war he had two horses shot from under him and in 1862 lost the use of his arm when struck by a shell fragment. On another occasion he was captured by Mosby's raiders, who confiscated his notebooks and turned the news over to Richmond newspapers. For much of the conflict Crounse was accompanied by his

brother Silas, who served as his dispatch courier. In 1863 he traded the front lines for the night editor position with the *Times*.

Crounse lost his first horse while reporting the Peninsular campaign for the *New York World* following the Battle of Gaines Mill. In addition to the *World* he represented the *Cincinnati Commercial* and the *Chicago Tribune* during the expedition against Roanoke Island in 1862.

He delivered one of his greatest scoops with his account of the Battle of Chancellorsville for the *New York Times*. In June 1863 Crounse reported the cavalry battle at Beverly's Ford and Brandy Station. By the time of the Gettysburg campaign Crounse was chief correspondent for the *Times* with the Army of the Potomac. He narrowly escaped capture on his way to Gettysburg when he stumbled upon Confederate troops. Crounse claimed that his reconnaissance report to Major General John Reynolds of Confederate troop movements toward Gettysburg precipitated the battle. During the battle he had another horse shot from under him and witnessed the annihilation of General Pickett's division during its attack on Cemetery Ridge.

Crounse later covered the Battle of Wauhatchie, the capture of Lookout Mountain, the fall of Richmond, and the surrender of General Robert E. Lee. Following the war he became a top Washington correspondent for the *Times*.

REFERENCES: J. Cutler Andrews. *The North Reports the Civil War*. 1955; Louis M. Starr. *Bohemian Brigade*. 1954.

Crowe, Sir Joseph Archer (1825-1896)

Best known for his histories of painting, Crowe was born in London. Son of a newspaper correspondent, he went to work for the *Morning News* and then the *Daily News*. One of the first of the "special artists," Crowe, a watercolorist, was the artist for the *Illustrated London News* in the Crimean War* and a correspondent for the *Daily News* (1846-1852) and the *Times* during the Indian Mutiny. Crowe arrived at Balaklava in September 1854, where he witnessed the Russian attack on the heights of Balaklava and later reported that he had had a good view of the charge of the Light Brigade. He was with the Ninety-fifth Regiment at the Battle of Inkerman in November 1854. Following the battle Crowe was stricken with a serious case of frostbite and was forced to return to England. While home he lectured on the war and was well enough to return to the Crimea in June 1855. In September he witnessed the fall of Sebastopol.

Following the Crimean War he became the superintendent of an art college in India. In the late 1850s he pursued the craft of art history and acted as correspondent during the Indian Mutiny. He left India in 1859 due to poor health before reporting the Austro-Italian War* that same year for the *Times,* during which he reported the Battle of Solferino. He entered the Foreign Office in 1860 when he was appointed consul general for Saxony, in which capacity he represented French interests at Leipzig during the Franco-Prussian War* of 1870. In 1872 he was appointed consul general for Westphalia and the Rhenish provinces and in 1880 was made commercial attache to the embassies at Vienna and Berlin. After leaving journalism Crowe embarked on a career as a diplomat and art critic. He died shortly after retiring as commercial attache in Paris.

REFERENCES: *DNB*; Pat Hodgson. *The War Illustrators.* 1977.

Crozier, Emmet (1893-1982)

Crozier was a correspondent and founding member of the American Newspaper Guild. He began his newspaper career with the *Kansas City Star* in 1912; next he worked for the *New York Herald Evening World* and then the *New York Tribune,* for which he served as a war correspondent during World War II* covering the Pacific theater of operations. He was the author of several books on war journalism history,

Yankee Reporters: 1861-65 (1956) and *American Reporters on the Western Front: 1916-18* (1959).

REFERENCE: M. L. Stein. *Under Fire.* 1968.

Cunningham, Alfred (1870-1918)

Born in London, Cunningham became one of the preeminent and best-traveled war correspondents of his day. He first became a special correspondent in 1894 when he covered the Sino-Japanese War* for the Central News Agency. Two years later he was in the Philippines with Spanish forces while covering the Spanish-American War* for the *New York Journal.* In 1900 he reported the Boxer Rebellion* and the relief expedition into Peking for the *Daily Mail* and the *New York Sun.* Five years later he represented the same two papers during the Russo-Japanese War* and was awarded the Imperial Japanese Order of the Rising Sun. He wrote many books, including *The French in Tonkin and South China, The Chinese Soldier and Other Sketches,* and *Today in Egypt.*

REFERENCES: Dennis Griffiths, ed. *The Encyclopedia of the British Press.* 1992; Robert Wilkinson-Latham. *From Our Special Correspondent.* 1979.

Cunningham, Ed (1913-1984)

He was the first *Yank** correspondent sent overseas at the start of World War II.* On his way overseas his plane was forced off course in a storm, crashing in the Brazilian jungle, where he was rescued ten days later. During the war he served in the China-Burma-India theater under General Joseph Stilwell. He landed several exclusive interviews with the general by charting his privy schedule so he could join him in privacy. Once they were sitting together the general confided his concerns about combat-related problems. Cunningham also covered the fighting in the Middle East, North Africa, and the last advance of the German army during the Ardennes breakthrough.

REFERENCE: Art Weithas. *Close to Glory.* 1991

Curtis, Peter Theo (b. 1968)

Born Peter Theophilus Padnos in Atlanta, Georgia, Curtis is fluent in French, German, and Russian. He received his PhD in comparative literature from the University of Massachusetts at Amherst. After first teaching poetry to prisoners in a Vermont jail, Curtis relocated to Yemen and chronicled his times there under the pen name Theo Padnos. He began studying Islam in Yemen and then enrolled in an Islamic religious school in Damascus, Syria. He published *Undercover Muslim: A Journey into Yemen*, about Islamic extremism. He changed his name to Peter Theo Curtis after its publication to distance himself from the controversial book so he could travel under the radar in the Middle East. In 2012 he made the transition to freelance journalist and moved to Antakya, Turkey, near the border with Syria. In October of that year he was kidnapped and held in a Syrian prison. Ransom requests from the Al-Nusrah Front and then Abu Mariya al-Qahtani were in the millions of dollars. He was eventually released by the latter in August 2014 after almost two years in captivity. Apparently no ransom was paid and representatives from Qatar were able to mediate his release "on a humanitarian basis." He would later reveal that he managed to escape twice from the Al Nusrah Front, but was returned to them each time by the Free Syrian Army. His release took place just one week after the beheading of James Foley.*

REFERENCE: Dean Schaber, "Released Hostage Peter Theo Curtis Back in US," ABC News.

Cutuli, Maria Grazia (1962–2001)

Born in Catania, Italy and educated at the University of Catania, she began her journalism career with *La Sicilia*. Cutuli moved to Milan in 1990 and over the next eleven years covered a variety of subjects, writing magazine articles and freelance pieces to burnish her credentials as a foreign correspondent from such hotspots as Israel, Sudan, and Rwanda. In 1997 she began working for *Corriere della Sera*. She was covering the fall of the Taliban in Afghanistan and the American invasion in the aftermath of the September 11, 2001 terrorist attacks, when she was murdered along with three other journalists, including the Australian cameraman Harry Burton, Afghan-born photographer Azizullah Haidari,* and the Spanish reporter Julio Fuentes. Cutuli was the first female and first Italian journalist killed in the conflict. On November 19, 2001 the journalists were shot in the back after being pulled from their vehicle while traveling in a convoy of eight vehicles between Jalalabad and Kabul. By most accounts the convoy was stopped at a bridge by self-identified Taliban members. When they started shooting and throwing rocks, the last four vehicles were able to turn back and return safely to Jalalabad. Cutuli, in one of the first two cars, was raped before she was killed with four gunshots and had an earlobe sliced off with a sharp instrument, apparently to steal a piece of jewelry. Earlier in the day Cutuli had just filed her last story reporting the discovery of a chemical factory. In honor of her career she was posthumously promoted to "Special Correspondent" by her newspaper. Her attacker was identified as Reza Khan. During his interrogation he admitted that the Taliban had ordered the murders. He was sentenced to death in 2004 and three years later was executed by a firing squad along with 14 other murderers, some also implicated in the murder of the journalists just 90 kilometers from Kabul. Thousands attended her funeral in Sicily and a national journalism award was created in her name.

REFERENCES: "Italy Mourns Murdered Journalist," CNN.com, Nov. 24, 2001; Reporters without Borders, "Two More Death Sentences in 2001 Murders of Four Journalists," Oct. 31, 2005; https://cpj.org/killed/2001/maria-grazia-cutuli.php.

Daguerreotype

Commercially popular between 1841 and 1860, this photographic technique was developed by the French physicist and artist Louis Jacques Mande Daguerre in 1839. The process does not require a negative image, so each daguerreotype is a one-of-a-kind positive image that cannot be reproduced. In the daguerreotype process an illuminated image is exposed to a polished surface coated with an iodine vapor, and later separately treated with mercury and a sodium solution. This technique was phenomenally popular in mid-nineteenth-century America, where more daguerreotypes were produced than anywhere else in the world.

The first examples of war photography were daguerreotypes taken during the 1846-1848 Mexican War,* but technical limitations made it impossible to photograph actual combat scenes. Only twelve images from this conflict were known to exist until 1981, when an additional thirty-eight daguerreotype portraits were discovered in a Connecticut barn. By the time of the American Civil War* wet-plate photography had replaced the daguerreotype, although it remained an occasional alternative.

REFERENCES: Pat Hodgson. *Early War Photographs.* 1974; Martha A. Sandweiss, Rick Stewart, and Ben W. Huseman. *Eyewitness to War.* 1989.

Damon, Arwa (b. 1977)

Born in Boston, Massachusetts and educated at Skidmore College, she decided to become a journalist after the 9/11 attacks, and relocated to Iraq to cover the subsequent invasion and war. Prior to joining CNN* in 2006 she covered the Middle East as a freelance producer for CNN, PBS, FOX News, and other new outlets. Having grown up speaking Arabic, French, Turkish, and English, the multilingual journalist was in high demand over the past decade, covering numerous military and civil events during the invasion and subsequent occupation of Iraq. She covered the U.S. Army during the Battle of Najaf against the Mehdi Army as well as the operation to retake Samarra in 2004. Damon also covered the offensive in Fallujah and Operation Steel Curtain near the Syrian border. Beginning in late 2010 she covered the Arab Spring events in Libya and Egypt and was one of the first reporters to arrive at Benghazi after the attack in 2012 that left Ambassador J. Christopher and several others dead. She was credited with retrieving the ambassador's personal diary. She was awarded the Courage in Journalism Award in 2014, given by the International Women's Media Foundation.

REFERENCES: http://www.cnn.com/CNN/anchors_reporters/damon.arwa.html; "Arwa Damon: 2014 Courage in Journalism Award," http://www.iwmf.org/arwa_damon.

Daniel, John Moncure
(1825-1865)

Born in Stafford County, Virginia, Daniel briefly studied law and worked as a superintendent
in a library before entering the newspaper business in the 1840s. After a short stint as editor
of the *Southern Planter* he moved over to the
Richmond Examiner in the same capacity in
1847 and soon became the sole proprietor of
the paper. He left journalism for several years
when President Pierce appointed him to a diplomatic post in Sardinia. He returned to the
States and the editorial desk at the *Examiner*
in late 1860.

During the American Civil War* Daniel sporadically left his desk to report the progress of
the Confederate armies on the battlefields. He
traveled with General A. P. Hill's army as his
aide and was present at the Battle of Gaines'
Mill in June 1862. He soon returned to his paper
and was wounded in a duel with the Confederate treasurer in 1864. He became ill the following year and died shortly before his plant was
torched after the capture of Richmond.

REFERENCE: J. Cutler Andrews. *The South Reports the
Civil War.* 1970.

Daniell, Tania Long (1913-1998)

Born in Berlin to a British journalist father and
Russian mother, the family moved to Scandinavia and later the United States following the
outbreak of the First World War. After the war
they moved back to Germany and Tania completed her education in Pairis and London. Following the break-up of her marriage in 1936 she
found work writing for what was then the *Newark Ledger*. As the Second World War beckoned
on the horizon, circumstances found her back in
Berlin, where she caught on as an assistant for
the *New York Herald Tribune* chief. She helped
evacuate her family members out of harm's way

and ended up in England where she covered the
London Blitz and the bombing of Coventry and
other cities. In 1941 she was awarded the Newspaper's Women's Club Award for coverage of the
London war-front and its impact on its civilians.
Long married *New York Times* correspondent
Raymond Daniell in 1941. She reported mostly
from London before making it to France several
weeks after the 1944 Normandy invasion. She
was in Paris to cover the aftermath of its liberation by the Allies and contributed articles from
other liberated towns in France. Along with her
husband she covered the Nuremburg Trials as
well as the tribulations of war refugees for the
Times. Since she spoke all four languages used
in the trials (English, French, German, and Russian) she was much in demand. She committed
suicide after a number of lengthy illnesses.

REFERENCES: Lilya Wagner. *Women War Correspond-
ents of World War II.* 1989; M.L. Stein. *Under Fire.* 1968;
Jim Yardley. "Tania Long, 85, a Reporter For the Times in
World War II; New York Times, September 6, 1998.

Da Ponte, Durant (1825-1894)

Da Ponte moved to New Orleans from Illinois
when he was twelve years old. The grandson of
the composer of the libretto for the opera *Don
Giovanni* began working for the *New Orleans
Crescent* as a reporter in his early teens. In 1861
he covered the Virginia campaign beginning with
the Battle of Manassas for the *New Orleans
Delta*. Following the battle he returned to New
Orleans before joining General Johnston's army
as a reporter and captain on the staff of Major
General Earl Van Dorn. By 1862 Da Ponte had
risen to editor of the *Delta* and left the field of
battle temporarily. When federal troops took
New Orleans later that year he moved to Richmond, Virginia.

REFERENCES: J. Cutler Andrews. *The South Reports the
Civil War.* 1970; John Howard Brown, The Cyclopedia of
American Biography, 1899.

---

* Indicates a separate entry.

Darnton, Byron (1897-1942)

Born in Adrian, Michigan, he was inspired to enter journalism by the career of his uncle, a drama critic for Pulitzer's *Evening World*. After high school he enlisted in the National Guard to fight in World War I. He arrived in France in 1918, taking part in the battles of Oise, the Aisne, the Meuse-Argonne and the attack on the Kriemhilde-Stellung; and was on hand when troops entered German territory in 1918. Following the war he went to the University of Michigan where he edited the campus paper but left college before graduation to tour the former battlefields of France and Germany. When he came back to America he won his first newspaper job. He worked for several papers, including the noted Henry L. Mencken at the *Baltimore Sun* (who tried to talk him into leaving journalism for fiction writing). In 1940 Darnton found himself on roving assignment for the *New York Times*, which he had joined five years earlier. He was an early reporter to cover the Pacific theater of World War II. He was in the process of embedding with American troops headed to the Philippines when, on October 18, 1942, an accident killed him in New Guinea.

REFERENCE: Doral Chenoweth, 54 War Correspondents Killed in Action in World War Two, Chapter 3. 2003.

Das Schwarze Korps (*The Black Corps*)

This Nazi magazine was published between 1935 and 1945. *The Black Corps* was published under the direction of the High Command of the SS and was considered "the official weekly newspaper and propaganda agency" of the SS. Every member of the SS was expected to read it. Its hands-on director was Gunter d'Alquen. In 1939 he was selected to take over the newly created War Correspondents Company (SS-Kriegsberichter Kompanie). Leadership of the newspaper was then taken over by Kurt Eggers* until his death in battle in 1943. By most accounts it was the only uncensored paper in Nazi Germany.

REFERENCE: www.jewishvirtuallibrary.org/source/Holocaust/DasSchwarzeKorps.html.

Davenport, Reuben Briggs (c. 1852-1932)

Born in New York City, Davenport graduated from the College of the City of New York in 1871 before joining the *New York Herald* the following year. He covered the American Indian Wars* from 1875 to 1881. After covering the Jenny-Newton expedition into the Black Hills in 1875 he rode alone through hostile country to report negotiations with the Sioux over the purchase of the Black Hills. He was reportedly unpopular with military commanders because of his penchant for criticism.

In 1876 Davenport joined the Crook expedition into the Black Hills for the *New York Herald*. At the Battle of the Rosebud he took part in the fighting and later covered the Battle of Slim Buttes, in which he corrected the total number of soldiers killed in the battle. He was with General George Crook during the advance to the Little Big Horn. A constant critic of General Crook, he labeled Crook incompetent. One of Davenport's articles even cast doubt on the general's supposed spartan lifestyle, suggesting that each night he was brought an excess of supplies by a mule packer. However, one of Crook's staunchest supporters challenged this. Charles King, in his *Campaigning with Crook* (1880), labeled Davenport a coward; Davenport threatened a libel suit, forcing King to retract his charge.

Following the Crook expeditions Davenport remained with the *Herald* until 1882. He went on to a career with several other top-flight papers including the *Morning News* and the *New York Times*. Davenport later established the *New Haven Morning News* in Connecticut and covered the Spanish-American War* for the Associated Press. He worked as a foreign correspondent for the *New York Times* and as chief editorial writer for the *Herald's* Paris edition from 1920 until his death in 1932.

REFERENCES: Robert W. Desmond. *The Information Process.* 1978; Oliver Knight. *Following the Indian Wars.* 1960.

Davies, Charles Maurice (1828-1910)

Born in Wales, he attended Durham University and University College. He left his position as headmaster of the West London Collegiate School for a journalism career in 1868. He covered his only war when he reported the Franco-Prussian War* from the French side for the *Daily Telegraph.* In one incident he was arrested as a spy while searching for fellow correspondent George Augustus Sala.*

REFERENCE: *DNB,* 1901-1911.

Davis, Elmer (1890-1958)

Formerly a CBS radio news commentator, he was appointed by President Roosevelt in June 1942 to head the Office of War Information (OWI). This appointmenet placed Davis firmly in the journalistic coverage of World War II. While not technically a war reporter, as the chief of the Office of War Information in September 1943, he complained to President Roosevelt that censorship was doing the American people a disservice by shielding them from the less heroic aspects of war. He campaigned to lift the embargo on pictures of dead American soldiers. Davis struck a chord with someone since thereafter *Life* magazine published a photo (by George Strock) of three dead American soldiers on a Pacific beach.

REFERENCES: Frederick S. Voss. *Reporting the War.* 1994.

Davis, Neil (1934-1985)

Born in Australia, Davis was a well-known cameraman and photojournalist fom the 1960s until his untimely death in 1985. He worked first for the Australian Broadcasting Commission (ABC) and the Visnews. During the Vietnam War he covered both U.S. and Vietcong forces in the field and filmed the war in Cambodia and Laos. Davis covered his first conflict in 1965, filming the clash between Indonesia and Malaysia from Borneo. He covered the 1968 fighting in Saigon and Hue during the Tet Offensive. He was seriously wounded several times while covering wars in Indochina. He left Visnews for freelance work in 1973 and was in Vietnam for the end of the war. Among his most memorable achievements was the filming of the North Vietnamese troops and the tank that broke through the gates to the Presidential Palace in Saigon. Following Vietnam he covered hot spots in Angola, Sudan, Uganda, and Beirut. He was killed by shrapnel from a round of ammunition fired from a Thai rebel tank in 1985 during his filming of the Thai Army coup. Tim Bowden chronicled Neil Davis's life in *One Crowded Hour* (1987).

REFERENCE: Tim Bowden. *One Crowded Hour: Neil Davis, Combat Cameraman.* 1987.

Davis, Oscar King (1866-1932)

Born in Baldwinsville, New York, Davis reported his first foreign assignment when he covered the Spanish-American War* in the Philippines for the *New York Sun, Harper's Weekly,* and the Laffan News Bureau. In 1900 he joined the exodus of correspondents from the Philippines to China to report the Boxer Rebellion* and four years later was in Tokyo following the developments of the Russo-Japanese War.* Following his stint as a war correspondent in the Far East, Davis settled down to a long career spent mainly in Washington, D.C.

REFERENCE: Robert W. Desmond. *The Information Process.* 1978.

Davis, Richard Harding (1864-1916)

The preeminent journalist and war correspondent of his time was born in Philadelphia. An

Indicates a separate entry.

indifferent student, Davis attended Lehigh and Johns Hopkins Universities before embarking on a journalism career with the *Philadelphia Record* and the *Philadelphia Press* beginning in 1886.

In 1892 he headed out west to write a series of articles for *Harper's Weekly*. During his trip he got his first taste of war reporting when he accompanied the U.S. Cavalry in its pursuit of Mexican revolutionaries near Laredo. This assignment apparently led to his fascination with the military.

As one of the best-known reporters in New York while still in his twenties, Davis was sent by Hearst to cover the Cuban rebellion in 1896 with Frederic Remington* for the *New York Journal*. However, he resigned when Hearst altered one of his dispatches. After his resignation he left for England, where he was hired by the *Times*. Following his coverage of Queen Victoria's Diamond Jubilee he was sent to report the Greco-Turkish War* in April 1897. While covering his first engagement at the Battle of Velestino, his rivalry with Stephen Crane* turned into genuine animosity, with Davis criticizing Crane for reporting the battle by using secondhand information.

In 1898 Davis returned to Cuba to cover the Spanish-American War.* He accompanied General Schafter and his troops aboard the *Seguranca*. However, Schafter would not allow anyone but soldiers to disembark with the first landing party. Consequent to this incident Davis would never write a positive comment about the general. Davis linked up with the Rough Riders and followed them through several actions, taking part in the fighting at Las Guasimas and San Juan Hill.* A critic of American strategy during the war, he witnessed the fall of Santiago and the occupation of Puerto Rico.

He next covered the Boer War* from 1899 to 1900 for the *New York Herald*. Although he was sympathetic to the Boers, he joined the British so that he could watch a more modem and newsworthy army in action. Davis found British

censorship and protocol vexing, to say the least. He accompanied the British troops into Ladysmith* after the lifting of the 118-day siege. He next decided to view the war from the Boer side. Davis compared them to the minutemen during the American Revolution. Recently married, he brought his wife with him, nearly getting trapped between the two armies. His coverage from the Boer side resulted in a public backlash in England, leading to a decline in his popularity. Davis ultimately found the Boer War unjust and wasteful.

In 1904 he reported the Russo-Japanese War,* and then the Matos Revolution in Venezuela, the border conflict between Mexico and America, and the American occupation of Veracruz. His last war coverage was during World War I,* for the *Daily Chronicle*. Among his most vivid accounts are descriptions of the German advance into Brussels and the burning of Louvain. Davis was with a group of correspondents following the German army in 1914 and was arrested three times. The Germans suspected him of spying and being a British officer because of a passport photo in which he was wearing a West African Field Force uniform that he had found comfortable eight years earlier. While it did not look like a military uniform then, by the time war had broken out, English soldiers had adopted the look in a variety of divisions. He recounts these exploits and his brush with a firing squad in *With the Allies* (1914). He left the front for good in 1916 and was at work on what would be his last book, *With the French in France and Salonika* (1916), when he died of a heart attack in Mount Kisco, New York. Davis was a prolific writer with seven novels, twelve volumes of short stories, and several plays to his credit. His most memorable works based on his war reportage are *Cuba in War Time* (1897), *A Year in a Correspondent's Notebook* (1898), *The Cuban-Porto Rico Campaign* (1899), *With Both Armies in South Africa* (1900), *Notes of a War Correspondent* (1910), *The Notes of a War*

Correspondent (1912), and *With the French in France and Salonika* (1916).

REFERENCE: Arthur Lubow. *The Reporter Who Would Be King.* 1992.

Davis, Theodore Russell (1840-1894)

Born in Boston and educated at Rittenhouse Academy in Washington, he joined *Harper's Weekly* in March 1861 as a traveling artist, reporting on the South before the war. Although he had many close calls covering the American Civil War,* he described this trip as the most harrowing of his journeys. Along with Al Waud,* he was one of the magazine's most important artists during the Civil War. One of the most widely traveled and prolific artists of the war, he recorded the capture of Port Royal, the battle between the *Monitor* and the *Merrimac,* the Battle of Shiloh, the capture of Corinth, the Battle of Antietam, the surrender of Vicksburg, the Battle of Chattanooga, and Sherman's march to the sea. He was the only artist with Sherman during the Atlanta campaign in 1864.

Subscribing to the notion that artists must see the actual carnage of battle, Davis often dangerously compromised his health by exposing himself to the dangers of the front lines. He was wounded twice in battle, and one report described him threatening at the point of a gun doctors who attempted to amputate his leg. His technique in recording frontline action was to make sketch notes and later complete the details.

Following the war he was on assignment to the western states, where his stagecoach was attacked at Smokey Hill Spring by hostile Indians. Davis was the first reporter to accompany an Indian campaign. Along with Henry Stanley,* he was attached to the command of General Winfield S. Hancock and Lieutenant Colonel George A. Custer in the 1867 expedition to Nebraska and Kansas. Davis secured firsthand knowledge of western warfare. He witnessed several Indian skirmishes with the Sioux and was present when the remains of Lieutenant L. S. Kidder and ten of his men were found in Kansas.

He returned to New York after his 3,000-mile western trip and turned to freelancing in 1884. Few of his original sketches still exist. His published illustrations, however, which were redrawn or traced on woodblocks before the engraving process, are still in existence. He died from Bright's disease.

REFERENCES: Pat Hodgson. *The War Illustrators.* 1977; Edgar M. Howell. "A Special Artist in the Indian Wars," *Montana, the Magazine of Western History.* Spring 1965; Robert Taft. *Artists and Illustrators of the Old West, 1850-1900.* 1953.

Dawson, Albert Knox (1885–1967)

Born in Vincennes, Indiana, Dawson developed an early affinity for photography and not surprisingly became a professional cameraman. He established his own photographic business, Brown & Dawson, in 1912. He covered the European front of World War I* beginning in 1914 with the American Correspondent Film Company. He continued to cover the war into 1916 and his newsclips were regularly distributed through the company of Underwood & Underwood. His work while attached to the German, Austrian, and Belgian armies appears in a host of documentary motion pictures chronicling the conflict. His four-reel film, *The Battle of Przemysl,* was among his best work, and most controversial, since it was accused of portraying German and Austrian forces in such a favorable light. Between 1917 and 1918 he was among the most prominent American photographers covering the war.

REFERENCE: Kevin Brownlow. *The War, The West and the Wilderness.* 1979.

Day, Samuel Phillips (?)

Samuel P. Day was one of a score of British correspondents who covered parts of the American Civil War.* He covered the opening salvos of the war while with the Confederate Army. After being granted a pass by General Beaureguard he reported the First Battle of Bull Run. He was affiliated with the London publications the *Spectator* and *Macmillan's Magazine*.

REFERENCE: Joseph Mathews. *Reporting the Wars.* 1957.

Dean, Teresa Howard (d. 1935)

Born in New York, she moved to Wisconsin in 1855, while still a young girl. She was educated at Lawrence College, where she gravitated from painting toward journalism. On the strength of several essays she was hired by the *Chicago Herald*. Dean covered church activities. and then the Ghost Dance troubles among the Dakota Sioux on the Pine Ridge Reservation in 1891, following Wounded Knee. There were numerous other reporters on the scene by the time Dean arrived, and plans had been made to have a group picture taken. However, the consensus was that Dean should be excluded because of the emasculating effect a fashionably dressed woman would have on the death-defying image the reporters had been conveying in their newspaper reports. The closest she came to experiencing action was when she accompanied fifty soldiers and assorted Sioux scouts and Indian policemen investigating the killing of a Sioux woman and her three children. She was present when one of the Sioux policemen identified the slain woman as his sister.

Dean later reported for the *Chicago Inter-Ocean* and then *Town Topics*. She went on to cover the Pennsylvania coal strikes in 1896, the Spanish-American War* from Cuba, the Philippine insurrection, the 1900 Boxer Rebellion,* the Army of Cuba pacification in 1906, and the Mexican Revolution of 1913-1914. One source describes Dean as the first woman war correspondent.

REFERENCES: Douglas C. Jones. "Teresa Dean: Lady Correspondent Among the Sioux Indians," *Journalism Quarterly.* Winter 1972; George R. Kolbenschlag. A *Whirlwind Passes.* 1990.

"Death of a Loyalist Soldier"

First published on Spetember 23, 1936 in the French magazine, *Vu*, this iconic photo is officially known as "Loyalist Militiaman at the Monument of Death, Cerro Muriano, September 5, 1936," but more often is referred to as "The Falling Soldier." It is one of the most famous war photographs of all time. But from at least the mid-1970s, its authenticity has been challenged. According to many photojournalists who were veterans of the conflict, the forging of pictures was a relatively common occurrence.

Robert Capa* had arrived in Spain in early 1936 devoted to the Loyalist cause. His photograph of a Loyalist Soldier in his moment of death made Capa and international celebrity. However, in the 1970s, veteran correspondent O.D. Gallegher* became the first to question the authenticity of the image as well as to candidly state that the picture was a planned fake. Gallegher claimed he had shared a room in Spain with Capa, when he recounted how Franco's troops often dressed in uniforms for simulated combat replete with smoke bombs and defensive strategems. Capa explained that he had taken some photographs of attacking troops being repulsed; Gallagher later noted that these were reprinted in newspapers and identified authentic, although the locality and identification of the military units were unknown. Gallegher was convinced that it was during these re-creations that Capa took his immortalized picture. Gallegher further claimed that Capa had explained to him how to get "lifelike action shots" by keeping the camera slightly out of focus and slowly moving the camera when taking the shot. Gallegher insists that no shot better exemplifies this technique than the "Death of the Loyalist Soldier." However, author John Hersey* refuted this claim, noting that Capa had told him a different story. According to his account, Capa was covering heavy fighting in Andalusia and had sought refuge in a trench with Republican soldiers. These soldiers were untrained and so zealous in their support of the Republican cause they charged Nationalist machine-guns placements on several occasions only to be mowed down. The way Capa told it was that as they attacked once more, he raised his camera over the top of the trench without looking and snapped the button at the sound of the first machine-gun fire. Two months after sending his film to Paris to be developed, he found out he was famous, since the picture had been reprinted throughout the world. Many fellow war correspondents, including Martha Gellhorn,* believed this was Capa's way of joking. Both Gellhorn and Herbert Matthews* were convinced of the picture's authenticity.

There are still many questions surrounding the photograph, although it has been generally accepted as authentic. However, the identification of the soldier as Federico Borrell in the mid-1990s, and who died in the location claimed by Capa, seened to support the picture's legitimacy. Capa had originally reported that the photograph was taken on September 5, 1936. An amateur historian decided to plumb the military archives in Madrid and Salamanca and found that only one man died that day at Cerro Muriano, a mill worker by the name of Federico Borrell. With the help of another intrepid investigator, the amateur historians located his widow who confirmed the picture was of her husband and in the process has rehabilitated Capa's Spanish Civil War reputation.

In 2009, attention was once again directed at this iconic image after an investigation of the image by Jose Manuel Susperregui, a professor of communications at the Universidad del Pais Vasco. Susperregui has made a convincing argument that the photo was actually taken 35 miles away from the site north of Cordoba, where Capa claims he took it. The investigator came to his conclusion by examining the background of the series of images taken in the same sequence as the "Falling Soldier." After consulting librarians and historians in the Cordoba region, the only town experts that recognized the back-

groung were from the town of Espejo, 35 miles away. Further investigations by the Spanish press seemed to confirm that is was a "perfect match." Nonetheless, in 2010, there is still no consensus as to the authenticity of the photograph.

REFERENCES: Philip Knightley. *The First Casualty*. 1975; Jorge Lewinski. *The Camera at War*. 1978; Larry Rohter. "New Doubts Raised Over Famous War Photo." *New York Times*. August 18, 2009.

De Blowitz, Henri Stefan Opper (1825-1903)

Prior to joining the *Times*, de Blowitz had emigrated from Bohemia to France, where he taught German and foreign literature for many years. He was in Marseille in 1870, when he was reportedly hired to travel to the besieged city of Paris, then in the grip of the revolutionary Commune. Arriving in Paris in January 1871, he met Laurence Oliphant,* chief correspondent for the *Times*. He invited the intrepid de Blowitz to become his assistant. De Blowitz reported the preliminary peace negotiations in Versailles while Oliphant reported from Paris. In February 1875, he was promoted to Paris correspondent, a position he would hold until 1902. His greatest news scoop was his coverage of the Berlin Congress of 1878.

REFERENCES: Robert W. Desmond. *The Information Process*. 1978; Oliver Woods and James Bishop. *The Story of THE TIMES*. 1983.

Deedes, William Frances (1913-2007)

Best known by his initials, W.F. Deedes reveled in the fact that he was probably the inspiration for William Boot, the main character in Evelyn Waugh's* classic novel on war correspondents *Scoop*.* Deedes even went as far as writing a book on the subject, *At War With Waugh: The Real Story of Scoop* (2003). They did in fact spend three months together reporting Mussolini's invasion of Abyssinia in 1935. The non-fictional

*Indicates a separate entry.

Deedes began his journalism career as a reporter for the *Morning Post* in 1931. He joined the *Daily Telegraph* after it took over the *Post*. He fought in World War II with the King's Royal Rifles and is considered the only officer to serve in the unit for the entire war. He also helmed the *Daily Telegraph* as editor between 1974-1986, to be replaced by Max Hastings.* By most accounts he is the only person in England "to have been a member of the cabinet and editor of a major daily newspaper, leading to his moniker the "Grand Old Man of Fleet Street.". While there were similar parallels between the fictional Boot and Deedes, ultimately Deedes admitted he despised war, calling it "a disgrace to the human race" whereas Waugh relished it, at least in Abyssinia and on more than one occasion chided other journalists for their cowardice. During his last years Deedes once more turned to reporting, albeit from a different perspective, traveling war zones and countries plagued by famine, disease and natural disasters, such as Afghanistan, Angola, Darfur, Bagladesh, Zimbabwe, Bosnia and Iraq. He worked with the late Diana, Princess of Wales in a joint campaign against landmines well into his seventies. His 76 years as an active journalist is considered an unofficial record.

REFERENCES: BBC NEWS. "Journalist Lord Deedes dies at 94." Augsut 17, 2007; "Did Bill Deedes inspire Evelyn Waugh's Boot?" www.telegraph.co.uk. March 9, 2008; W.F. Deedes. *At War With Waugh.* 2003.

Deepe, Beverly (b. 1936)

Following graduation from the University of Nebraska and the Columbia School of Journalism, Deepe traveled around the world, before settling in Saigon in 1961. She remained in Saigon until 1969 covering the Vietnam* conflict as a stringer* for the *London Daily Express,* the *Christian Science Monitor,* and *Newsweek.* In 1963 she reported the overthrow of President Diem and the Buddhist protests. Her reports to *Newsweek* describing the killing of dozens of Buddhists by the Diem government turned American public opinion against the government. However, a United Nations investigation three months later concluded that there was no evidence of any monks being killed.

By 1964 Deepe was also reporting for the *New York Herald Tribune* prior to its demise the next year. Consistently challenged for inaccuracies in her dispatches, she became increasingly unpopular with American authorities. By the following year she was the only American reporter regularly excluded from official briefings. Deepe reported the Tet offensive from Saigon in a three-part series for the *Christian Science Monitor.* She left Vietnam in 1969 and after a brief stint in 1970 at the Pentagon left journalism to start a family.

REFERENCE: Virginia Elwood-Akers. *Women War Correspondents in the Vietnam War, 1961-1975.* 1988.

De Fontaine, Felix Gregory (1834-1896)

He was born in Boston, the son of a French nobleman who had accompanied Charles X into exile in Edinburgh. He entered the newspaper world as a Washington congressional reporter before moving to Charleston, South Carolina, on the eve of the American Civil War.* In 1860 he founded the *Daily South Carolinian,* in which he published many articles regarding the worsening sectional crisis. In 1861 the *New York Herald* began publishing accounts of Southern conditions. His friendship with the Confederate Beauregard allowed him to witness the attack on Fort Sumter, his first major news scoop. His account was the first to appear in the Northern press.

He accompanied a South Carolina regiment throughout the Civil War as a correspondent and was accorded the rank of major. In 1861 De Fontaine reported the Manassas campaign and the following year the Battle of Shiloh, the Corinth campaign, the Seven Days' Battles, and the Virginia campaign. His dispatches on the Battle of Antietam are considered his outstanding achievement of the war and the best account of it in the Southern press.

In 1863 he covered the Union assaults on Charleston and Battery Wagner, the Chattanooga campaign, the Battle of Lookout Mountain, and the Knoxville campaign. Absent from the field for most of 1864, he was active again in 1865 reporting the Atlanta campaign and the Federal occupation of Columbia.

His reportage appeared under the pen name "Personne" in the *Charleston Courier* until the end of 1863, when he became co-owner and editor of the *Columbia Daily South Carolinian*. When Sherman entered Columbia he destroyed De Fontaine's press. After the Civil War De Fontaine moved to New York, where he continued his writing career with the *Telegram* and the *Herald*. A Southern sympathizer to the end, at his death he was writing a book on the missing records of the Confederate cabinet from documents he had gathered in 1865.

REFERENCES: J. Cutler Andrews. *The South Reports the Civil War*. 1970; *DAB*; Stewart Sifakis. *Who Was Who in the Civil War*, 1988.

Delahaye, Luc (b. 1962)

Delahaye is a photojournalist who has worked independently or has been commissioned by Western news magazines such as *Newsweek*. He worked for Magnum Photos from 1994 to 2004 and has been a contract photographer for *Newsweek* beginning in 1994. In the 1980s and 90s he covered wars in Lebanon, Afghanistan, Rwanda, Chechnya, and Bosnia. Among his many awards are Robert Capa Gold Medals for covering Sarajevo in 1993 and Afghanistan in 2002.

REFERENCE: http://getty.museum.news/press/delahaye.

Della Casa, Nick (1960-1991)

Della Casa was a freelancer for the Frontline News Television Agency* when he was killed along with his wife Rosanna della Casa (1960-

1991) and brother-in-law Charles Maxwell (1952-1991) while attempting to cross the mountains into Kurdistan from Turkey. They were there to chronicle Kurdish resistance against the Saddam Hussein regime for a BBC documentary as the first Gulf War moved to conclusion. By most accounts they were murdered by their Turkish guide in an argument over his fee. He was sentenced to 26 years in prison. While the bodies of both men were found, Rosanna's was not found for three years. Nick had covered conflicts and hotspots in Tibet, and Afghanistan and had survived an 18-month captivity by Mozambique RENAMO rebels.

REFERENCES: Julie Flint. "Who Killed Rosanna?" www.independent.co.uk, January 23, 1994; David Loyn. Frontline. 2005.

Della Casa, Rosanna

See DELLA CASA, NICK.

Della Gattina, Ferdinando Petruccelli (1815–1890)

Della Gattina is regarded as one of the greatest journalists of the nineteenth century and a pioneer in his craft. However, he is best known for his war reporting. He started his career in Naples, Italy with the *Omnibus* in 1838. A political activist for liberal causes he often found himself embroiled in controversy or threatened with arrest under the Bourbon Dynasty. He had to flee Italy for France after being sentenced to death and having his property confiscated. In 1851 he fought alongside French republicans against the coup d'état orchestrated by Napoleon III (Louis-Napoleon Bonaparte). His correspondence was published in numerous French, Belgian, and British newspapers. In 1859 he covered the Second Italian War of Independence and the following year Giuseppe Garibaldi's "Expedition of the Thousand," chronicling it from Calabria to Naples. He was present at the birth of the Kingdom of Italy and sat on the Italian parliament for several years. During the Third Italian War of Independence in 1866 he covered the conflict for the *Journal des Debats*. He also covered the Franco-Prussian War,* and reported on the ill-fated Paris Commune and its bloody aftermath. He was expelled from France for his support of the vanquished communards.

REFERENCE: http://en.wikipedia.org/wiki/Ferdinando_Petruccelli_della_Gattina#cite_ref-4.

De Luce, Daniel (1911-2002)

De Luce was born in Yuma, Arizona, and educated at the University of California. He began his newspaper career with the *Los Angeles Examiner* and in 1939 went to London for the Associated Press. Later that year, while stationed in Eastern Europe, he reported German preparations in Czechoslovakia for the invasion of Poland. He went on to witness the Italian conquest of Albania and the fall of Greece. De Luce was the only correspondent in Iran covering British-Soviet operations there in October 1941. The intrepid foreign correspondent's penchant for globe-trotting for news led fellow AP reporters to say of him while he was in the field that "De Luce is on da loose."

In 1942 he was sent to Burma, where he reported the fighting before fleeing to India just ahead of Japanese forces. The next year found him covering Allied operations from North Africa to Sicily and the subsequent Italian campaign. His greatest scoop came in 1943 when he became the first war correspondent to enter the war zone controlled by Marshal Tito's partisan forces along the coast of Yugoslavia, although he stayed for only several days. His series of five articles on the Yugoslav partisans led to a Pulitzer Prize in 1944. In 1944 he was among the first correspondents to enter Rome, and his dispatch datelined from the city was the first by an American correspondent since December 1941.

REFERENCE: Frederick S. Voss. *Reporting the War.* 1994.

De Monfried, Henri (1879-1974)

Born in La Franqui, France, he left his uneventful life as a businessman to travel to the Red Sea coast in 1911. Six years later he was selling weapons and diving for pearls near Djibouti. After being expelled from Ethiopia for his political views he returned in 1936 as a photographic war correspondent during the Ethiopian War.* In 1940 he was arrested by the British army and exiled to Kenya, where he stayed until returning to France in 1948. He continued to travel and photograph Africa, and disappeared at sea for several weeks near Mauritius while in his late seventies.

REFERENCE: Turner Browne and Elaine Partnow. *Photographic Artists and Innovators.* 1983.

DeMorse, Charles (c. 1816–1887)

Born in Leicester, Massachusetts, he became an attorney and sought adventure in Texas, heading there with a group of like-minded volunteers in 1835 intent on fighting in the Texas war for independence. After his discharge following the war, in 1837 he returned to law, married, and served as a reporter for a small newspaper before starting his own newspaper in Clarksville, 135 miles northeast of Dallas. DeMorse was 46 years old in 1862, when the veteran Texas newspaper editor received permission to raise a cavalry regiment to fight in the Civil War. He went on to create the 29th Texas Cavalry and served as its colonel. He fought in at least three battles and several smaller affairs in the Trans-Mississippi West Theater of the war. In between skirmishing he found time to provide war correspondence in his hometown *Clarksville Standard* newspaper. His reports on these battles were especially important since few journalists reported from this region of the war. According to his biographer, he distinguished himself from his fellow correspondents by sending back dispatches under three different names: his full real name, and the monikers "Private" or "A Soldier of the Twenty-Ninth."

The well-educated correspondent was especially wide-ranging in his interests and his reports were often full of arcane scientific material and goings on in Indian Territory. By most accounts he was a dependable reporter in terms of objectivity. DeMorse and his men faced their first actual battle at Elk Creek on July 17, 1863, a battle fought during the Battle of Honey Springs near Fort Gibson. It turned out to be an embarrassing defeat for the Confederates, made worse for DeMorse when he suffered a serious arm wound. It was during this battle that DeMorse accorded the Confederate's Indian allies a high level of respect. In early 1864 he was once more reporting from the battlefront during the Red River campaign in Arkansas, and that April could take solace in his first victory against federal forces. Left out of his battle reportage was the massacre of the Union's 1st Kansas Colored by his Choctaw and Chickasaw troops. Following the carnage at Poison Spring his unit was ordered back to Indian Territory where they would take part in their last battle, at Cabin Creek in September 1864. This battle also featured a repeat of the previous one, with a number of black Union soldiers from the 1st Kansas Colored massacred while gathering hay. General Robert E. Lee's surrender on May 26, ended his career in war journalism, as he returned home and once more took over as editor of the *Standard*. He became an outspoken critic of radical Republican control of the South and an unapologetic supporter of white supremacy, a view he would hold the rest of his life. In 1873 he was elected to head the Texas Press and Editorial Association. He went on to play an important role in creating the Texas Constitution of 1876.

REFERENCE: Mary M. Cronin, "Charles DeMorse: Reporting from the Indian Territories," *Knights of the Quill*, 2010.

Denny, Harold Norman (1899-1945)

Born in Des Moines, Iowa, and educated at Drake University, he worked on newspapers in Des Moines, St. Paul, and Minneapolis between 1913 and 1922, when he joined the *New York Times*. He reported the Moroccan War in 1922, the 1927-1928 Nicaraguan crisis, and the Cuban crisis of 1930-1931. In 1934 he began a five-year stint in Moscow. This assignment was interrupted when he covered the beginning of the Ethiopian War* in 1935 and then again two years later when he reported further developments in the conflict. He covered the Moscow treason trials of 1936-1938, the 1938 German invasion of Czechoslovakia, and the Russo-Finnish War the following year.

With the outbreak of the war in Europe he was accredited with the British Expeditionary Force in France and later covered the Libyan campaign. In 1941 he was captured by Rommel's forces in North Africa. Denny was a neutral correspondent when he was initially held in Italy, but his status was changed to enemy correspondent when Pearl Harbor was attacked, and he was moved to a Berlin prison. His subsequent account of his imprisonment was published as *Behind Both Lines*. Following a prisoner exchange in June 1942 he returned to the States and became the *Times* correspondent in Spain. In 1944 he covered the invasion of France, and he was slightly wounded covering the fighting in the Ardennes during the Battle of the Bulge.

REFERENCES: Robert W. Desmond. *Crisis and Conflict*. 1982; Robert W. Desmond. *Tides of War*. 1984' Ben Fox, "Pultizer Prize Winner DeLuce Dies," Associated Press, January 30, 2002.

Depardon, Raymond (b. 1942)

The French photographer served as a war reporter in Algeria while in the French army during the 1960s. Following Algerian independence he covered wars in Chile, Chad, Lebanon, and Afghanistan. He has produced numerous documentaries and is a member of Magnum, originally founded by Robert Capa.*

REFERENCE: Frances Fralin, ed. *The Indelible Image*. 1985.

* *Indicates a separate entry.*

"Derelict, The"

Richard Harding Davis' 1902 short story is based on his impressions of the horde of correspondents who were drawn to the Spanish-American War.* It was suggested when the story was first published that the title character was based on Stephen Crane.*

REFERENCE: Howard Good. *The Image of the War Correspondent in Anglo-American Fiction*. 1985.

De St. Jorre, John (b. 1936)

Born in London, he graduated from Oxford and entered the diplomatic service. He served as an officer in Malaya during the 1950s insurgency. He was stationed at the British embassy in the Congo during the turbulent postindependence years of 1960-1961. He later was posted to other African assignments. He turned to journalism in 1963, resigning from the foreign service to write for the *Observer* and other papers. He covered the conflict surrounding Rhodesian independence in 1963-1965 and from 1966 to 1967 he reported conflicts in Zambia, Congo, Uganda, Aden, and Nigeria. De St. Jorre reported from both sides during the Nigerian civil war and was with the first correspondents allowed access to the war zones following the capitulation of Biafra. He became Paris correspondent for the *Observer* beginning in 1969.

REFERENCE: John de St. Jorre. *The Brothers' War*, 1971.

Deuell, Peggy Hull

See HULL, PEGGY.

Diament, Rafail (b. 1907)

Diament began publishing his photographs in the 1920s. In 1937 he moved to Moscow and became a professional photojournalist. During World War II* he served as a correspondent with the Russian navy in the North Sea.

REFERENCE: Daniela Mrazkova and Vladimir Remes, eds. *The Russian War: 1941-1945*. 1975.

Dicey, Edward James Stephen (1832-1911)

Born near Lutterworth, Leicestershire, England, he attended King's and Trinity Colleges before receiving his degree from Cambridge in 1854. Following college he traveled and dabbled in business and foreign politics. In 1861 he published *Rome in 1860* and *Cavour-A Memoir*. That same year he began his affiliation with the *Daily Telegraph*. In 1862 he reported the American Civil War* for *Macmillan's Magazine* and the *Spectator*, and in 1863 his Civil War experiences resulted in the poorly received *Six Months in the Federal States*.

His acumen on foreign issues led to a full-time position on the staff of the *Telegraph* by 1862. Dicey covered the Schleswig-Holstein War in 1864 and the Austro-Prussian War* of 1866. His accounts of these wars are collected in *The Schleswig-Holstein War* (1864) and *The Battlefields of 1866* (1866). In the late 1860s his travels in Egypt, Russia, and Turkey resulted in several travel books, and in 1869 he accepted the post of editor for the *Daily News*, which he held for three months. Shortly after, Dicey filled a similar post with the *Observer*, which he held for almost two decades.

REFERENCES: *DNB*, 1901-1911; Joseph J. Mathews. *Reporting the Wars*. 1957.

Dickenson, Edith Charlotte Musgrave (1851-1903)

During the Boer War* Dickenson reported from South Africa under the byline ECM Dickenson. She rose to prominence for her reports on the grave conditions faced by women and children interned in the Bethulie concentration camp. The book *The Brunt of the War and Where It Fell*, written by Emily Hobhouse, makes substantial use of Dickenson's observations. As a result Hobhouse was barred from returning to South Africa due to her political views. According to Dickenson's grandson she faced little difficulty from the authorities "likely due to influential relatives throughout the British military."

REFERENCE: Steve Lipscombe. "Special Correspondent Edith Dickenson." Ww.bwm.org.au/site/Edith_Dickenson.asp.

Diehl, Charles Sanford (1854-1946)

Born in Flintstone, Maryland, and raised in Illinois, he was hired to replace special correspondent Mark Kellogg,* who was the only reporter to die with Custer at the Battle of Little Big Horn. Diehl made his reputation covering the American Indian Wars* on the Plains in the 1870s and early 1880s. He had been with the *Chicago Times* for three years when he was assigned to cover General Alfred Terry's command following the Custer debacle. According to Diehl, Terry showed him a copy of the directive issued Custer prior to his last expedition. Terry added that Custer would have been court-martialed had he survived. Diehl interviewed Terry, attempting to get the "real" story of the Custer defeat.

In 1877, on his second assignment to Indian country he was given the opportunity to interview Sitting Bull when he accompanied Terry's peace mission to Canada, where the Sioux chief had taken sanctuary. When Sitting Bull agreed to turn himself over to the American government in 1880, Diehl was sent to cover the surrender at Fort Buford. In the thick of winter Diehl traveled 175 miles by army sleigh and bobsled through blizzard conditions to reach his destination. When the Sioux balked at coming into the fort, Diehl joined the skirmish line that attacked the Indian camp, which they found empty. An artillery barrage brought the Indians out of their hiding places in the woods and after a brief action many of the Sioux surrendered; however, Sitting Bull was not among them. After the

Poplar River fight Diehl returned to his paper, albeit without his story of the legendary chief's surrender.

After his career with the *Chicago Times,* Diehl became the assistant general manager for the Associated Press. He was in charge of the Associated Press' coverage of the Spanish-American War.* Following his tenure with the AP he purchased the *San Antonio Light*, with which he was still affiliated at his death. Diehl chronicled his exploits as a correspondent in *The Staff Correspondent* in 1931.

REFERENCES: Charles H. Brown. *The Correspondents' War.* 1967; Oliver Knight. *Following the Indian Wars.* 1960.

di Giovanni, Janine (b. 1961)

Di Giovanni's first foray into conflict-zone reporting dates back to the late 1980s, when she covered the First Palestinian Intifada. Since then she has covered most major violent conflicts around the world. In 1993 she was featured in the documentary on women war reporters, *No Man's Land*, which covered her work in Sarajevo. She has focused much of her attention on the Balkan conflict and its postconflict resolution. She was one of the few reporters to witness the fall of Grozny, Chechnya. During the Kosovo war she accompanied the Kosovo Liberation Army (KLA) through occupied Kosovo. She narrowly missed being killed when the unit she was traveling with was attacked in what turned out to be a bloody bombing raid. Her 1999 *Vanity Fair* article on this event and her other experiences during the Balkan Wars, "Madness Visible," won a National Magazine award, and was later expanded into a book. In 2013 di Giovanni was recognized as one of the 100 most influential people in the world of armed violence by the organization Action on Armed Violence (AOAV).

REFERENCE: http://www.janinedigiovanni.com/biography/.

* Indicates a separate entry.

Dillon, Emile Joseph (1854-1932)

Born in Dublin, Ireland, and educated at several European universities, Dillon could reportedly speak twenty-six different languages and write newspaper leaders in five. One of the greatest philologists of his day, Dillon was reputed to possess a "cloak and dagger complex." He taught comparative philology at the University of Kharkov in Russia, where he entered journalism first with *Le Musson* and then the *Odessa Messenger*. In 1887 he began a twenty-seven-year affiliation with the *Daily Telegraph*. In 1894, he circumvented the Sultan's edict prohibiting journalists from Armenia, when he covered the conflict disguised as a Russian officer, Kurdish chief, and Turkish woman. He again donned disguise in 1897 as a rebellious monk when he covered the Greco-Turkish War.*

During the Spanish-American War* he covered the Spanish side of the conflict, and in 1900 he was in China during the Boxer Rebellion.* While employed by the *Daily Telegraph*, Dillon was stationed in St. Petersburg from 1886 until the beginning of World War I.* He accompanied Russian troops to Peking via the Trans-Siberian Railroad and later covered the second Dreyfus trial, the Portsmouth Peace Conference at the end of the Russo-Japanese War,* and the Paris Peace Conference (1919). He retired from the newspaper in 1919 and lived in Mexico and Spain until his death. He wrote numerous books, including *Leaves from My Life* (1932).

REFERENCES: Robert W. Desmond. *Windows on the World*. 1980; *DNB*, 1912-1921; Dennis Griffiths, ed. *The Encyclopedia of the British Press*. 1992.

Dimbleby, Richard (1913-1965)

Born into a newspaper family, he began his career in journalism with the family-owned *Richmond and Twickenham Times*, in Surrey, England. By the age of twenty-one he was news editor for *Advertiser's Weekly*. In 1936 he joined the BBC, where he came to prominence with his radio commentaries on the Spanish Civil War.*

Dimbleby was an innovator for the BBC, introducing the first mobile recording van, essential for on-the-spot interviews and providing a sense of participation that most newspaper reporting lacked. At the outset of World War II* Dimbleby was with the British Expeditionary Force headquarters in France. In 1941 he was one of the earliest arrivals at the Greek front before covering action in Iraq, Syria, Lebanon, and Iran later that year. In 1942 he reported the resumption of the desert campaign in North Africa.

In 1943 he was one of seven observers flying in RAF Liberator bombers in a night attack on Berlin. More significantly, this was the first major action outside Britain in which correspondents were allowed to participate. The following year he covered the D-Day landings for the BBC. During the crossing of the Rhine into Germany, he was injured when his glider crash-landed. He witnessed the liberation of the Belsen concentration camp and the taking of Berlin. Following the war he became a well-known television personality while continuing to publish in newspapers and magazines.

REFERENCES: Richard Collier. *Fighting Words*. 1989; Robert W. Desmond. *Tides of War*. 1984.

Dinwiddie, William (1867-1934)

Born in Charlottesville, Virginia, Dinwiddie was a war photographer* and journalist for *Harper's Weekly* during the Spanish-American War.* He covered both the Cuban and the Puerto Rican campaigns in 1898. Following the war he became the magazine's chief correspondent on Cuban affairs. One of his most memorable photographs was of American troops at Daiquiri in June 1898. He also took one of the few action photographs of the war when he captured Captain Capron's artillery firing on the Spanish during the Battle of El Caney.

He later covered the Philippine insurrection for the *New York Herald,* where he became an islands administrator during the first year of American occupation. Soon after he left for South Africa to report the Boer War* and then later the Russo-Japanese War* in 1904 for the *Herald.* He wrote *War Sketches, in Truth, Puerto Rico and Its Possibilities* (1899), *The War in the Philippines,* and *The War in South Africa.*

REFERENCES: Robert W. Desmond. *The Information Process.* 1978; Susan D. Moeller. *Shooting War: Photography and the American Experience of Combat.* 1989.

Disher, Leo S. (1912-1969)

Educated at Duke University, Disher was a war correspondent for the United Press beginning in 1939. In November 1942 he was badly wounded by Vichy troops while accompanying the British navy near Oran, Algeria. He became the first civilian to be awarded a Purple Heart during the war. Disher coauthored *Springboard to Berlin,* based on the Battle of Oran. He returned to the war in 1943, accredited to the British Home Fleet. Disher covered the North Africa landings and the Normandy invasion.

Following the war he headed the United Press bureaus in Czechoslovakia, Bulgaria, and Romania. In 1948 he left Eastern Europe and joined the United Information Service.

REFERENCE: Robert W. Desmond. *Tides of War.* 1984.

Dixie, Lady Florence Caroline (1857-1905)

Better known as a travel writer, she was born Florence Douglas in London and educated primarily at home. In 1875 she married Sir Alexander Churchill Dixie and in 1878-1879 traveled through Patagonia, describing her experiences in *Across Patagonia* (1880). Dixie represented the *Morning Post* in South Africa during the 1879 Zulu War. Competitors ridiculed the *Post* when it sent out probably the first woman war

correspondent. Dixie shared with her two brothers a predilection for eccentricity. One of her brothers was killed while climbing the Matterhorn and another had the dubious distinction of being the ninth marquis of Queensberry, who established the rules for the sport of pugilism.

By the time she arrived in South Africa the hostilities had ceased and the peace conference was under way. Dixie supported the release of Zulu chief Cetewayo and the restoration of Zululand following the British intrusion. Ultimately her efforts were rewarded when the king was freed and returned home to Zululand. She chronicled her exploits and views on the Zulu conflict in A *Defence of Zululand and Its King* (1882) and *In the Land of Misfortune* (1882). She later became involved in the women's movement in Great Britain and became an advocate for the prevention of animal cruelty with her books *Horrors of Sport* (1891) and *The Mercilessness of Sport* (1901).

REFERENCES: *DNB,* 1901-1911; Robert Wilkinson-Latham. *From Our Special Correspondent.* 1979.

Dobson, George (1850-1938)

Fluent in Russian, he was the *Times* correspondent in Russia for over a quarter century. He covered the Czar's army during the Russo-Turkish War* and witnessed the siege of Plevna. His book *Russia's Railway Advance into Central Asia* was based on his adventures as the first Englishman to travel Russia's newly built military railway to Samarkand.

Upon leaving the *Times* he joined Reuters* and wrote for various English papers. He resumed his relationship with the *Times* to cover the Russian Revolution. He was working in the British embassy when Soviet troops attacked it, killing a captain and imprisoning Dobson and several associates for five weeks. Following a stint with the War Office Intelligence Section Dobson continued to play an important role in evacuating British civilians and Russian colleagues from the beleaguered country. He wrote *Russian Under the Red Terror and Harmsworth's History of the Great War* (1919).

REFERENCE: Robert W. Desmond. *Windows on the World: World News Reporting, 1900-1920.* 1980.

Donohoe, Martin (1869-1927)

Born in Galway, Ireland, in the early 1890s he emigrated to Australia, where he entered journalism in 1892 with the *Sydney Courier Australian.* After stints with several other papers, he joined the *London Daily Chronicle,* and reported the Boer War* in South Africa beginning in 1899. He covered the advance of Methuen's forces from the Orange River to Magersfontein and witnessed Hector "Fighting Mac" MacDonald's engagement at Koodoesberg Drift, after which he reported Lord Roberts' forces near Enslin. Captured after the battle of Paardeberg, he was released following the fall of Pretoria.

In 1905 Donohoe covered the Russo-Japanese War* while with the Japanese forces. He accompanied the Japanese First Army during the Battles of Yalu, Motien Pass, Towan, Liaoyang, and the Shaho. Throughout the war he was continuously hampered by restrictions and press censorship. Following the war he shifted his attention to conflict in the Balkans. He reported the Turkish revolution (1909) and the capture of Constantinople by the Young Turks, and was the first reporter to be granted an interview by the newly installed Sultan.

In the years leading up to World War I* he covered the Portuguese revolution (1910), the Italo-Turkish War, and the Balkan War (1912-1913). During World War I Donohoe was in demand by the British intelligence corps due to his experience in foreign affairs and proficiency in linguistics. He served in the Balkans, Russia, and the Middle East.

REFERENCE: Robert W. Desmond. *Windows on the World.* 1980.

Dorr, Rheta Childe (1873-1948)

Don was born in Omaha, Nebraska, and attended the University of Nebraska for two years. She entered journalism with the *New York Evening Post* in 1902, editing the women's pages. During her four years in this position Don gathered notes for what would become her first book, *What Eight Million Women Want* (1910). She became active in the suffragette movement and edited the *Suffragist.* In the years leading up to World War I* she remained active as a freelance journalist, writing for *Collier's, Cosmopolitan,* and other magazines.

Dorr had already covered several European assignments prior to the war. In 1906 she reported the coronation of King Haakon of Norway, before traveling at her own expense to St. Petersburg, Russia, where she covered the Duma as it attempted to defuse the developing revolutionary conflict. An activist for women's rights, she visited Great Britain in 1912 and 1913, reporting the suffrage movement there.

In her forties, she began her second career as war correspondent and foreign correspondent, and returned, in 1917, to Russia following the February revolution. She covered women soldiers at the Russian front, noting in one dispatch that half had been killed or wounded. She reported World War I for the *New York Evening Mail* and a syndicate representing over twenty newspapers. Following the war she was a foreign correspondent in Prague and wrote A *Woman of Fifty* in 1924.

REFERENCE: Julia Edwards. *Women of the World: The Great Foreign Correspondents.* 1989.

Dos Passos, John Roderigo (1896-1970)

Best known as author and playwright, he was born in Chicago, the illegitimate son of a corporate lawyer. As a child he was known as John Madison, adopting his father's surname upon entering Harvard University in 1912. With a pre-dilection for socialist politics and a wish to serve in World War I* in some volunteer capacity, upon graduation in 1916 he followed his father's wishes instead and studied architecture in neutral Spain.

After his father's death the following year he returned to New York City and socialized with well-known radicals Emma Goldman and Max Eastman. Soon after he joined an ambulance corps and returned to France, where he later witnessed his first war during the Battle of Verdun. By November 1917 he was with a Red Cross unit in Italy, but the following spring was discharged for writing letters critical of American intervention. He then joined the Army Medical Corps and served in Europe until the 1918 armistice.

Although he was never affiliated with a newspaper he went to Spain during the Spanish Civil War* to observe the activities of Loyalist forces, for whose cause he had great sympathy. Some of his best work on the war was published in *Esquire* magazine. Among his most prominent books are *Three Soldiers, Manhattan Transfer, Nineteen Nineteen,* and *Adventures of a Young Man.*

REFERENCE: Virginia Spencer Can. *Dos Passos: A Life.* 1984.

Dowling, James Graham (d. 1955)

Born in Philadelphia and educated at the University of Notre Dame, Dowling worked for the *Chicago Times* and the *Newark Star-Ledger* before joining the *Chicago Sun* in 1941. During World War II* he reported from the Pacific war fronts, including the Battle of Guadalcanal, where he landed with the second wave of the amphibious assault. In 1943 he was with U.S. naval forces involved in the Solomon Islands campaign, and the following year he injured both ankles while parachuting with the Eleventh Airborne Division on the island of Luzon in the Philippines and was awarded paratrooper wings. He saw his

last action in Burma in the waning months of the war. Following World War II he joined *Time* magazine as Singapore bureau chief. Dowling died tragically in a plane crash with twenty-four others on June 16, 1955 in Paraguay.

REFERENCES: Robert W. Desmond. *Tides of War.* 1984; Jack Stenbuck, ed. *Typewriter Battalion.* 1995.

Downing, John (b. 1940)

Born in Wales, he became a skilled photographic printer before joining the *Daily Express* as a free-lance photographer in 1962. During his twenty-eight-year career with the paper he has covered major conflicts in Vietnam,* Beirut, the Falkland Islands* and the Persian Gulf. He accompanied guerrilla forces in Sudan, Nicaragua, and Afghanistan. His imprisonment by Idi Amin in Uganda led to a widely published photo from inside the prison. He was also present when the IRA bombed the Grand Hotel in Brighton. He has received many awards for his photojournalism, including the Member of British Empire in 1992.

REFERENCE: Dennis Griffiths, ed. *The Encyclopedia of the British Press.* 1992.

Downs, Jr., William Randall "Bill" (1914–1978)

Bill Downs was born in Kansas City, Kansas and educated at the University of Kansas. He began his career in journalism in 1937 with the United Press. After three years he was posted to London as foreign correspondent from 1940-1942. It was here that he fell into the orbit of fellow journalists Edward R. Murrow* and Charles Collingwood.* Downs' timing was fortuitous since Murrow was looking for a replacement for Larry LeSeuer* as Moscow correspondent for CBS, where he covered the war from 1942 to 1944. Downs chafed under the heavy censorship of his Russian minders, and along with other correspondents, was reliant on Soviet authorities to allow them to cover the battlefront. He reported on the aftermath of

* *Indicates a separate entry.*

the Battle of Stalingrad and the Russian summer counteroffensive on the Central Front. After the liberation of Kiev by Soviet forces he was among the reporters taken to the scene of the Babi Yar mass executions. Downs would later cover the British landing at Normandy and on June 14, 1944 made the first live broadcast from the invasion zone to the United States. For the rest of the war, Downs accompanied the 21st Army Group on its advance toward Paris and the subsequent Battle of the Falaise pocket. While covering the Battle of Arnhem in the Netherlands he established a lifelong friendship with fellow UP reporter Walter Cronkite.* In the waning days of the European theater of conflict Downs was among the reporters drawing lots to see who would parachute into Berlin to cover the battle raging there and deliver the first broadcast to the United States. He parachuted (for the first time) but was forced to pool his broadcast with the rest of the networks. It became a moot point when the Soviets captured Berlin beforehand. Downs was honored with the National Headliner's Club Award for his eyewitness coverage of Germany's unconditional surrender. He would cover the last days of the Pacific theater of operations, reporting the Soviet invasion of Manchuria and the signing of the Japanese surrender. Downs covered subsequent Cold War events and was selected to cover the 1948 Berlin blockade due to his war zone experience. He covered various aspects of the Korean War* between 1950 and 1953, but most of his latter coverage was accomplished by radio and television. He continued in broadcast journalism but never achieved the prominence of some of the other "Murrow Boys," in part due to his gruff voice and his charisma-challenged demeanor.

REFERENCE: http://billdownscbs.blogspot.com/p/about_28.html.

Downton, Eric (1917-1999)

Downton covered his first war as a young journalist for the *Daily Worker* during the Spanish Civil War.* By the late 1930s Downton was night editor of the English-language *Singapore Free Press*. In 1939 he arrived in Shanghai, China, and the following year became chief editor for Reuters'* Far Eastern organization. After a three-year term in the Royal Canadian Navy he rejoined Reuters, covering the war in Europe beginning in 1944. As war correspondent with the Third Army Downton reported the execution of prisoners, the Battle of the Bulge, and bombing raids over Germany; he also learned to parachute.

Following the war he covered the Greek Civil War and the first Arab-Israeli War in 1948 before taking over the New Delhi bureau for the *Daily Telegraph*. In the 1950s he reported the Korean War,* witnessed the French Foreign Legion in action during the war in Indochina, and during the 1953-1955 Mau Mau uprising in Kenya claimed to wear a firearm for the first and last time. Downton would return to Africa in 1960 to report the troubles in the Congo for the *Daily Telegraph*. Throughout the postwar era he reported coups in Nigeria, Ghana, Sudan, Somalia, the Congo, Zaire, and Rwanda. Downton went on to report the revolt in Yemen, the Greek-Turkish conflict on Cyprus, the Vietnam War,* and the civil war in Lebanon.

REFERENCE: Eric Downton. *Wars Without End*. 1987.

Doyle, Sir Arthur Conan (1859-1930)

The creator of Sherlock Holmes was born in Edinburgh, Scotland. The son and grandson of artists and men of letters, Doyle was educated at Stonyhurst and Edinburgh University. He practiced medicine at Southsea from 1882 to 1890. His first novel, A *Study in Scarlet* (1887), introduced the world to one of its most enduring fictional characters, Sherlock Holmes.

During the Boer War* he acted as senior physician in a field hospital and wrote an early account of the war entitled *The Great Boer War* (1900). He accompanied Lord Roberts on his advance against Johannesburg and Pretoria, and his account appeared under "Days with the Army" in the *Strand*. Doyle was knighted following the war and became an important voice for army reform. Besides his Holmes novels he wrote several Napoleonic War stories, and several works on World War I.* The latter included A *History of the British Campaign in France and Flanders* (six vols., 1916-1920) and A *Visit to Three Fronts* (1916), a series of sketches based on his visits to France and Italy, where he narrowly missed being killed by an Austrian shell while at the front lines. He died on July 7, 1930.

REFERENCES: John Dickson Carr. *The Life of Sir Arthur Conan Doyle*. 1949; *DNB*, 1922-1930.

Dozier, Kimberly (b. 1966)

Dozier was born in Honolulu, Hawaii and educated at Wellesley College and the University of Virginia, where she earned a master's degree in foreign affairs (Middle East). Her first jobs in journalism from 1988 to 1991 revolved around Congressional policy and industry regulation in the nation's capital. She began her foreign correspondent career doing freelance work in Cairo from 1992-1995 for CBS Radio News and Voice of America, and the *Washington Post* and other print media. She served as a reporter for CBS News television between 1996 and 2002, covering the war in Iraq and Afghanistan, the refugee crisis in the Balkans, the North Ireland Peace process, and the Kohbar barracks bombing in Dharan. On May 29, 2006 she was covering the war in Iraq from Baghdad alongside Iraqi security forces when they were targeted by a car bomb. It killed her cameraman, soundman, a U.S. army captain and his interpreter and seriously wounded Dozier. It took her months to recuperate and nearly two dozen surgeries to repair her shattered femurs, apply skin grafts to badly burned legs and remove shrapnel from her head. In 2007 she was honored by the Overseas Press Club and the following year she became the first woman

to receive the Congressional Medal of Honor Foundation's Reagan "Tex" McCrary's Award for Excellence in Journalism. She chronicled her brush with death in *Breathing the Fire: Fighting to and Get Back to the Fight*, (2011).

REFERENCES: http://election.cbsnews.com/stories/2003/09/19/broadcasts/main574141.shtml; www.kimberlydozier.com.

Dring, Simon (b. 1945)

Born in Fakenham, England, he dropped out of school at the age of seventeen to see the world. In 1963, while still in his teens, he entered journalism as a feature writer for the *Bangkok World* newspaper in Thailand. The following year he was doing freelance work for the *London Daily Mail* and the *New York Times* covering Laos. In the mid-1960s he covered the Vietnam War* for Reuters.* From his beginning as the youngest correspondent for Reuters, over the next thirty years his reportage was featured in Reuters, the *Daily Telegraph*, the BBC, and numerous other news outlets as he covered more than twenty conflicts in Europe, the Middle East, Asia, Africa, and Latin America. In 1971 Dring was the only foreign correspondent covering the carnage of the Bangladeshi war for independence from Pakistan. For his coverage of the massacres that left perhaps one million dead in 1971, he was awarded honorary citizenship by Bangladesh. In 2002 he was expelled from the country after the government closed the only independent television station in Dhaka. By most accounts the closing of the station and the expulsion of Dring was the result of the radical Islamist government hardline campaign to control the media. Dring has been the recipient of many awards, including UK Reporter of the Year for his coverage of the Dhaka massacres at the onset of the Bangladesh civil war. He continues to work in the field of journalism in a variety of capacities other than covering the battlefront.

REFERENCE: Alastair Lawson-Tancred, "'Hero' Journalist Expelled from Bangladesh," Daily Telegraph, Oct. 2, 2002.

* *Indicates a separate entry.*

Dubois, Jules (1910-1966)

Dubois was a prominent Latin American correspondent who covered dozens of taut situations over a career lasting more than 30 years, in the process earning the enmity of Argentina strongman Juan Peron who labeled Dubois, "The Number One Gangster of Yankee Journalism." He entered journalism as a reporter for the *New York Tribune*. He then relocated to Panama and wrote for several papers. In 1931 he covered the last Sandino War for *Universal News Service*. During World War II he served as an intelligence officer during the conflict in Panama, North Africa, and the European theater of the war. In the course of his career he published four books and was decorated by a number of Latin American countries. After the war he joined the *Chicago Tribune* until his death by heart attack at a conference in Bogota. He received his greatest prominence for conducting the first interview with Fidel Castro after the Cuban Revolution, a world scoop in January 1959.

REFERENCES: Jules Dubois. Freedom is My Beat! 1959; Chicago Herald Tribune obituary, August 17, 1966.

Dufka, Corinne (b. 1958)

Prior to her career as a photojournalist, Dufka spent ten years in San Francisco working as a psychiatric social worker. She left for El Salvador to continue her social work for several years and in the process made the transition to human rights investigator, cataloguing the abuses of Salvadoran death squads. At the same time she was teaching herself the intricacies of photography and beginning her journalism career as a freelancer for Reuters and other news sources. In 1989 she was hired full-time by Reuters and following the end of the El Salvadoran conflict in 1992 transitioned to covering Europe and then Africa. She rose to prominence for her photographic renderings of the horrors endured by civilians during wars and campaigns of ethnic cleansing. In 1993 she was badly injured by a land mine in Bosnia. She covered war zones in 25 African countries for Reuters. She left Reuters after eleven years in 1999 and moved to Africa to open a field office for Human Rights Watch. In 1997 she was the recipient of the Courage in Journalism Award from the International Women's Media Foundation.

REFERENCE: Award Winners, http://www.iwmf.org/category/award-winners/)CorinneDufka.

Duncan, David Douglas (b. 1916)

Born in Kansas City, Missouri, sometime during his college years at the University of Miami and the University of Arizona he took up photography as a hobby. He began freelancing for newspapers in 1938. Two years later he was assigned to accompany the Chile-Peru expedition of the American Museum of Natural History as its photographer.

In 1943 he joined the U.S. Marine Corps and was soon photographing military operations for the South Pacific Air Transport Command, covering guerrilla fighting in the Fiji Islands, marine combat aviation on Okinawa, the Battle of Bougainville. and the official Japanese surrender aboard the USS *Missouri* in 1945.

Following the war he joined *Life* magazine. Duncan covered the Korean War* in 1950. He was present at the Battle of Pusan Perimeter and the retreat of the marines from Chosin Reservoir in North Korea after Chinese Communist forces crossed the Yalu River, which he chronicles in *This Is War!* Before leaving *Life* in 1956 he reported from South Africa, French Guinea, Morocco, and Egypt.

In 1967 he began covering the Vietnam War* for *Life* and ABC news and then became a special correspondent for *Collier's*. In 1968 his collected photographs of the war were published as *I Protest*. He received the Overseas Press Club Award twice and was awarded the U.S. Camera Gold Medal for his book *This Is War!* Royalties from this book are contributed to a fund for the families of marines killed in action. Duncan also was the recipient of a Legion of Merit, a Purple Heart, two Distinguished Flying Crosses, and other medals testifying to his bravery under fire. In 1970 he published *War Without Heroes*.

REFERENCES: Davis Douglas Duncan. *Yankee Nomad: A Pictorial Odyssey*. 1966; Robert E. Hood. *12 at War*. 1967.

Dunn, Harvey Thomas (1884-1961)

Dunn was perhaps the best known of the eight official artists of the American Expeditionary Forces (AEF) during the First World War. He was born on a homestead in what was then the Dakota Territory. He studied with the noted artist-teacher Howard Pyle from 1904 to 1906 before opening his own studio and beginning his career as an illustrator and teacher. He was commissioned as a war artist in March 1918. At the conclusion of the war, he visited French battlefields in preparation for a long run documenting the war for the AEF, but he was discharged in 1919. While he made a number of sketches, he finished just thirty while in the service of the AEF, many fewer than by his fellow AEF artists. During the conflict Dunn was attached to Company A, 1st Battalion, 167th Infantry and by most accounts covered military operations in the vicinity of St. Mihiel and Chateau-Thierry. During World War II Dunn declined to return to the war zone but instead threw his lot in with the United Service Organization (USO), for whom he traveled to military hospitals and training camps, where he drew portraits of wounded soldiers.

REFERENCE: Alfred Emile Cornebise. *Art from the Trenches*. 1991.

Dunn, William J. (1906–1992)

Born in Rosedale, Indiana, he dropped out of college to pursue a journalism career, first with the *South Bend News-Times* in 1923. Three years

later he joined United Press International (UPI). In 1938 he joined CBS News in New York City. In 1941 with war with Japan on the horizon, Dunn was sent to report on Far East developments from the Philippines. His early assignments had him arranging radio communications in various Asian countries and hiring stringers.* He was in Burma when Pearl Harbor was attacked, effortlessly making the transition from foreign correspondent to war correspondent. In February he was with Dutch forces and was reportedly the first reporter to cover the Battle of the Java Sea and the invasion of Java by Japanese forces on March 1, 1941. In order to avoid capture he escaped aboard a Dutch freighter along with several other journalists, ending up in Australia. Running into General Douglas MacArthur, who he had met prior to the war in the Philippines, he was asked to accompany him, promising to take him back to Manila, a promise that would take almost three years to fulfill. In November 1942 Dunn covered New Guinea for several weeks before returning to the United States for a five-week leave. He would cover marine assaults on Cape Gloucester on New Britain in January 1944. The following month he accompanied the crew of a B-25 on a bombing run over the Admiralty Islands. Dunn was one of a handful of reporters selected by MacArthur to accompany his forces as they headed for the Philippines. He covered the Battle of Leyte Gulf and waded ashore along with MacArthur after debarking from a landing craft. Dunn played a role in burnishing the reputation of MacArthur, often countering inaccurate articles about the celebrated general with pieces presenting him in a more favorable light. Dunn covered the rest of the Philippines campaign, and was present at the liberation of Manila. He accompanied Australian forces as they captured Tarakan Island, an important oil source for the Japanese military. He was in the States on leave, only his second of the war, when the conflict ended after the atomic bombings of Hiroshima and Nagasaki. He made it back to Asia in time to witness MacArthur accepting the Japanese surrender aboard the USS

Indicates a separate entry.

Missouri on September 2, 1945. Dunn remained in Asia for CBS until 1947.

In 1950 he was hired by NBC to cover the Korean War* for six months. Following the end of the war in 1953 he left journalism for advertising and then the writer's life. Returning to the Philippines in 1977 for the dedication of the Leyte Landing Memorial, he was surprised to find out that one of the seven bronze figures in a reflecting pool memorial was his likeness carrying his typewriter as he accompanied MacArthur on the famous landing at Leyte. According to his biographer William P. McEvoy, Dunn was the "only broadcast journalist to cover American involvement in World War II in the Pacific theater" from 1941 until the surrender in 1945.

REFERENCES: Raymond Hernandez, "William J. Dunn, CBS Radio Correspondent, 86," New York Times, Sept. 21, 1992; William P. McEvoy, "William J. Dunn," *American World War II Correspondents*, Jeffrey B. Cook, ed., 2012, 81-86.

Dunning, John P. (c. 1863-1907)

Dunning was a foreign correspondent for the Western Associated Press beginning in the late nineteenth century. In 1889 he was sent to the Samoan Islands to report a disagreement between the United States, Germany, and Great Britain over who controlled the islands. While on this assignment he witnessed one of the most catastrophic hurricanes to ever strike the South Seas. In 1891 Dunning was the only American correspondent reporting the civil war raging in Chile. Beginning in 1898 he reported the Spanish-American War* in Cuba and then the Philippines. He was one of six correspondents to witness the battle of Las Guasimas on the advance to Santiago, Cuba. He was also credited with telegraphing the scoop of the Battle of Santiago.

REFERENCES: Charles H. Brown. *The Correspondents' War*. 1967; Robert W. Desmond. *The Information Process*. 1978.

DuPont, Ghislaine (1956–2013)

She grew up in Africa and later studied journalism in Paris. DuPont entered the field of journalism with *Quest-France* and *Temoigagne Chretien* and in 1986 Radio France Internationale (RFI). Africa remained the focus of her reporting until her death in 2013, reporting on conflicts in the Democratic Republic of Congo, Ethiopia, Rwanda, Sudan, Algeria, and the Ivory Coast. Dupont was in Mali to chronicle the first round of the presidential election, when she was killed along with the technician Claude Verlon* on November 2, 2013, after being abducted in northeastern Mali. They had been interviewing the separatist leader Ambeiry Ag Rhissa, from the National Movement for the Liberation of Azawad (MNLA), a Tuareg separatist group, for Radio France Internationale. The reporters were forced into a truck as they left the leader's house. Originally it was reported their bodies were found with their throats cuts eight miles from the town of Kidal in the Sahara. However, subsequent investigation of the deaths by the Committee to Protect Journalists* described their bodies as being found riddled with bullets. French military sources reported pursuing the abductors shortly after the two journalists were taken, chasing them with military vehicles and helicopters. The abductors realized they would not be able to make their escape with their captives in tow, so they killed them and dumped the bodies. Al-Qaeda in the Islamic Maghreb later claimed responsibility for the deaths.

REFERENCE: Adam Nossiter, "Two French Journalists are Kidnapped and Killed by Gunmen in Mali," New York Times, Nov. 3, 2013.

Duranty, Walter (1884-1957)

Born in Liverpool, England, he was an only child and lost his parents in a train accident when he was ten. After graduating with honors from Cambridge, he traveled widely through the United States and Europe, intermittently writing articles for Frank Munsey's *Argosy* magazine.

He gained his first full-time position in journalism when he joined the staff of the *New York Times* in Paris in 1913. He served as war correspondent for the paper at French army headquarters and on the western front during World War I.* He cowrote with fellow *Times* correspondent Wythe Williams* one of the best accounts of the Battle of Verdun in 1916. After covering the Paris Peace Conference in 1919 he traveled to the Soviet Union, where he reported political unrest and famine in the Baltic states following the Russian Revolution. In Finland he received his first glimpse of the repercussions of the revolution, noting in a dispatch the bitter fighting and executions.

Duranty served as Moscow correspondent for the *Times* from 1922 to 1934. In 1932 he was awarded the Pulitzer Prize for his economic reporting in Russia. During this era he became recognized as an expert on Soviet affairs and was one of the most controversial analysts of the Stalinist period. He interviewed Stalin twice and reported Lenin's death in 1924, the same year he lost his left foot in a train wreck in France. After resigning from the Moscow post in 1934 he was a roving reporter, spending parts of each year in the Soviet Union. He later covered the Spanish Civil War* in 1936 and the early years of World War II.* He wrote *I Write As I Please* in 1935.

REFERENCE: Michael Emery. *On the Front Lines: Following America's Foreign Correspondents Across the Twentieth Century.* 1995.

Durborough, Wilbur H.
(1882–1946)

Born in New Castle, Delaware, he had worked for several newspapers in Chicago and Philadelphia before joining the Newspaper Enterprise Association as a press photographer. This agency provided features news stories to members of the syndicate—both photos and text. Durborough photographed Pancho Villa in Mexico in 1914 during the events surrounding the Mexican Punitive Expedition. He garnered his greatest coup when he arranged

permission from German authorities to record the aftermath of the German campaign on the eastern front. He would spend seven months with the German Army in 1915-1916 filming the First World War.

REFERENCES: Cooper C. Graham, "The Kaiser and the Cameraman: W.H. Durborough and the Eastern Front, 1915," *Film History: An International Journal*, Vol. 22, 2010, 22-40; James W. Castellan and Ron van Dopperan, eds. *American Cinematographers in the Great War*, 1914-1918. 2015.

Durivage, John "Jack" E.
(1813–1869)

Durivage was a former Boston and New York journalist. He happened to be working as an actor and writer in New Orleans when the Mexican-American War broke out. He was hired by George Wilkins Kendall's* *Picayune* to cover the progress and actions of General Zachary Taylor's forces. He missed the Battle of Buena Vista and during the rest of 1847 reported on camp life and scouting expeditions. When he couldn't find battle news to report he expressed the growing concerns about the criminal misbehavior of the volunteer soldiers. His 68 letters and reports published in the *Picayune* appear under his pen name, "J.E.D." Durivage covered the high rate of sickness among the soldiers. In August 1847 he was appointed a civilian aide on General John E. Wool's staff, awarding him the pay and privileges of a major, without the actual military rank. Wool apparently intended to use Durivage to burnish his claim of having selected Buena Vista's battlefield in a "modest public relations campaign." With most of the fighting over by October 1847, he decided to return to New Orleans after spending eight months covering the American occupation in northern Mexico. After leaving the *Picayune* for good, he spent several years as part owner of the *Alta California* in San Francisco. In 1851 he sold his interest in the paper and returned to Boston

REFERENCES: Tom Reilly. *War with Mexico!: America's Reporters Cover the Battlefront*, Manley Witten, ed. 2010; Francis Samuel Drake. *Dictionary of American Biography*. 1879.

---

* Indicates a separate entry.

Edwards, Henry Sutherland (1828-1906)

Born in Hendon, England, he was educated in France. After a brief interlude as a staff writer for *Punch* he wrote several light farces for the London stage. Fluent in French, he covered the 1852 coup d'etat in Paris and four years later represented the *Illustrated Times* in Russia at the coronation of Czar Alexander II.

Edwards reported the Polish insurrection for the *Times* in 1862 and 1863 before being expelled by Russian authorities for his favorable coverage of the Polish rebels. From these experiences he wrote *Polish Captivity, an Account of the Present Position of the Poles in Austria, Prussia and Russia,* (two vols., 1863) and *The Private History of a Polish Insurrection* (two vols., 1865). In 1871 he reported the Franco-Prussian War* while attached to the Prussian army for the *Times*. His observations were collectively published as *The Germans in France, Notes on the Method and Conduct of the Invasion*. Besides his work as a war correspondent, Edwards became the first editor of the *Graphic* in 1869, and wrote books on foreign affairs and musical history, as well as several novels.

REFERENCE: *DNB*, 1901-1911.

Egan, Martin (1872-1938)

Egan covered the Philippine insurrection during the Spanish-American War* for the *San Francisco Chronicle* in 1899. The following year he represented the Associated Press in China during the Boxer Rebellion.* By the outbreak of the Russo-Japanese War* Egan was chief of the AP bureau in Tokyo. He reported from the Japanese side during the conflict. Egan left the AP in 1907 to become editor of the *Manila Times*. He continued in this role for seven years, then moved to New York as public relations advisor to J. P. Morgan and Company, a position he held until his death in 1938.

REFERENCES: Robert W. Desmond. *Windows on the World*. 1980; David Shavit. *The United States in Asia*. 1990.

Eggers, Kurt (1905-1943)

Eggers was born in Berlin. He worked for several radio stations between 1933 and 1936. He was the author of a number of plays, poems and songs. He finished his studies in theology in 1929, became a priest and left the clergy two years later. He turned to freelance writing and began publishing a nationalistic newspaper. He joined the Nazi SS in 1935 and held various positions before taking the field with the Waffen-SS in 1939. He was the editor of the SS magazine *Das Schwarze Korps* beginning in 1939. He was killed in battle in Russia when his tank took a direct hit. In Eggers' memory the various War Correspondents units of the SS wore his name on their uniforms.

* Indicates a separate entry.

REFERENCE: www.feldgrau.com/ss-st-ke.html; www.axishistory.com/index.php?id=2008.

Ehrenburg, Ilya (1891–1967)

The well-known Russian writer served as correspondent with the Red Army during World War II.* He reported the Russo-German war for *Red Star* magazine and Moscow-based *Izvestia* and chronicled the Battle of Stalingrad. His propagandizing dispatches with their vehemently anti-German slant were widely reprinted in the West prior to American entry into World War II. His accounts of the German death camps in August 1944 were some of the earliest descriptions of the German final solution. These accounts were reprinted in many American newspapers.

REFERENCES: Robert W. Desmond. *Tides of War.* 1984; Phillip Knightley. *The First Casualty.* 1975.

Eldon, Daniel "Dan" (1970–1993)

Born in London and raised in Kenya, in his short life Eldon visited 46 different countries. In 1992 he landed a job with Reuters* and began following the famine then raging in neighboring Somalia. He covered the story for Reuters and witnessed the landing of U.S. Marines in Mogadishu. Over the next several months his photographs appeared in newspapers and magazines around the world. As the violence continued to spiral out of control in 1993, against his better judgment he stayed behind to chronicle it. Along with reporters Hansi Krauss,* Anthony Macharia, and Hos Maina, Eldon was on the scene when the United Nations tried to arrest the warlord Aidid. In the process 74 women and children were killed and more than 100 wounded. The innocent survivors asked the journalists to leave their hotel to come document the errant raid. From the supposed safety of a protected convoy, the four journalists were stoned and beaten to death by a mob as they were photographing the bombed-out area.

REFERENCE: "Young Photographer Exposed Somalia's Horrors," CNN, Dec. 7, 1997.

el-Dous, Yousef (d. 2014)

El-Dous began covering the Syrian civil war* in Daraa as a media activist prior to joining *Orient News* as a correspondent. El-Dous was traveling with two crew members from the Syrian opposition TV station when their car was hit with a missile on December 8, 2014. They were on their way to cover a firefight in the village of Sheikh Miskeen. Correspondent Rami Asmi and cameraman Salem Khalil were with el-Dous when their car was hit a guided missile fired by government forces. Although the car was not marked as a media vehicle, it would have been easy to recognize with the six-foot satellite dish it was carrying.

REFERENCE: https://cpj.org/killed/2014/yousef-el-dous.php.

Eliott, Richard Smith (1817–1890)

Born in Pennsylvania, during the Mexican-American War,* Elliott served as the *St. Louis Reveille's* main war correspondent. At the time of the war he was a lieutenant in the Missouri Volunteers. Self-educated, he was inspired by the life of Benjamin Franklin to become a printer. Elliott's father owned a local newspaper that allowed his son to realize his ambition, and at the age of 18 his father left him the newspaper as its editor and owner. However, the young printer soon ran into financial troubles and he left town for a spell, all the while working at other newspapers. Seeking more exciting prospects as an Indian agent, Elliott went west around 1843. During the 1840s he established a reporting arrangement with the *St. Louis Reveille*, sending back dispatches under the nom de plume of "John Brown." With the outbreak of war in 1846 he was elected a first lieutenant with the Laclede Rangers, a volunteer mounted rifle company organized by his friend Thomas Hudson, who served as its captain. However, Elliott seemed to just barely miss most of the action. He accompanied Colonel Kearny's Army of the West as it took Santa Fe without any shooting and served as part of the occupying

* *Indicates a separate entry.*

force, as the action took place elsewhere. Due to the exigencies of fate he just barely missed the Battle of Chihuahua, action in Taos, and elsewhere before taking part in a campaign along the Santa Fe Trail. His one year tour of duty ended in mid-1857 and he returned home. His coverage of the war consisted of almost 70 letters written for his St. Louis paper, appearing on its pages between June 1846 and July 1847. He was probably the most prolific correspondent on the war for the *Reveille* and could be counted on for dependable news from the "seat of war."

REFERENCE: Mark L. Gardner and Marc Simmons, eds. *The Mexican War Correspondence of Richard Smith Elliott.* 1997.

Embedded Journalists

The news industry has changed drastically over the past twenty years. Nowhere is this more obvious than when covering Americans at war. In order to witness the war in Iraq or Afghanistan journalists must have Pentagon approval. In the 2nd Gulf War the US military introduced a new word into journalistic usage—"embedding." In reality, there is nothing new about the principle—as far back as the Crimean War,* William Howard Russell* was "embedded" with the British Army when he witnessed the Charge of the Light Brigade.

Embedding requires a compromise between freedom and access. At one extreme was the First World War, when reporters gave up all freedom of movement in return for officer status, comfortable billets in chateaux set back from the front line, and safe escorted day trips up to see the troops. At the other extreme was the Vietnam War—where reporters could go almost anywhere they wanted using US helicopters to move around. Embedded reporters in Iraq would be attached to individual units, dependent on them for food and transport, if they hoped to catch even a glimpse of the war. The more practical reason for accepting embedded status, however, is the "guaranteed" protection of the armed

services. Signing up as an embed effectively puts you officially among the troops. According to a 2003 Pentagon memo, "embedded media will live, work, and travel as part of the units with which they are embedded to facilitate maximum, in depth coverage of U.S. forces in combat and related operations." If, on the other hand, individuals acted as "unilateral*" or "unembedded" reporters, they faced covering the war without military protection. One unilateral gamely responded to the risks by noting "if I wanted your protection [the military's], I wouldn't be in this business. I'm not looking for protection from the military. I'm trying to cover them." Critics of embedding charge there is a tendency for embedded reporters to report the war from the soldier's point of view; by identifying with their protectors, they risk the danger of losing objectivity.

REFERENCES: Herbert N. Foerstel. *Killing the Messenger.* 2006; Public Affairs Guidance on Embedding Media. 2003.

Emeny, Stuart (1904-1944)

He reported the Italian invasion of Ethiopia for the *Daily Chronicle* in 1935. His battle reportage while accompanying Haile Selassie's forces was widely distributed. Following the war he returned to England before covering conflict in Palestine, where he barely survived an ambush.

During World War II* he reported the Bengal famine in 1942, as well as a disastrous tidal wave. He rode on U.S. air bomber missions before being assigned to cover General Orde Wingate's Chindit guerrillas behind enemy lines in Burma. He was killed on March 24, 1944, along with colleague Stanley Wills* when Wingate's aircraft crashed, killing all aboard.

REFERENCE: Robert W. Desmond. *Tides of War.* 1984.

Emerson, Gloria (1929-2004)

Emerson left her position as reporter for the women's section of the *New York Journal*

American in 1956 and bought a one-way ticket to Saigon to visit a boyfriend in the marines. Returning to the States the following year, she joined the *New York Times*. By 1960 she was with the Paris bureau. Over the next ten years she covered stories in the Middle East, Africa, Eastern Europe, and London. She also reported the Nigerian civil war in 1968 and the conflict in Northern Ireland the following year.

Arriving in Saigon for the *New York Times* in 1970, she became an outspoken critic of the war, concentrating on the effect of the war on the Vietnamese people. In 1971 she was the recipient of the George Polk* Memorial Award for excellence in foreign reporting from Vietnam.* Her freelance work has appeared in *New Yorker, Harper's, Saturday Review,* and many other magazines. Her book *Winners and Losers: Battles, Retreats, Gains, Losses and Ruins from the Vietnam War* (1976) is a scathing portrait of American military intervention in Southeast Asia.

REFERENCE: Virginia Elwood-Akers. *Women War Correspondents in the Vietnam War, 1961-1975.* 1988.

Engel, Richard (b. 1973)

Raised on New York's Upper East Side and educated at Stanford, Engel has lived in the Middle East for more than a decade and is fluent in Arabic, Italian, and Spanish. The ubiquitous NBC foreign correspondent has covered the Iraq war since its inception in 2003. He was given the Edward R. Murrow Award in 2006 for his report *Baghdad E.R.*, and in 2008, the Medill Medal for Courage in Journalism for his documentary *War Zone Diary*. He joined NBC in 2003 and in 2008 was named its chief foreign correspondent. Engel has chronicled his years covering Iraq in the books *A Fist in the Hornet's Nest* (2004) and *War Journal: My Five Years in Iraq* (2008). Besides Iraq, Engel has covered other regional conflicts including the 2006 war between Israel and Hezbollah. In 2011 he reportred on the Egyptian

revolution and the Libyan Civil War*. In that same year he was recognized for his reporting with the Daniel Pearl Award, the David Bloom Award and the Overseas Press Club Award. In December 2010, Engle and four crew members were abducted in Syria, but freed five days later. There has been some dispute over who captured the journalists, nonetheless they were released unharmed. He chronicled this episode for *Vanity Fair* in 2013, in "The Hostage."

REFERENCES: Barret Sheridan. "An Iraq Diary." www.stanfordalumni.org/news/magazine/2008/sepoct/pc/engel.html; http://www.nbcnews.com/id/5424809/ns/nightly_news-about_us.

Esper, George (1932-2012)

Born and raised in Uniontown, Pennsylvania, Esper worked for the AP for 42 years, covering the Vietnam War* for ten, then the First Gulf War* in 1991, and several U.S. peace missions in Somalia and Bosnia. As AP bureau chief Esper stayed calmly at his post in Saigon as North Vietnamese troops entered the city. He famously served the first enemy soldiers he saw Coca-Cola and stale pound cake and then wrote the bulletin announcing the fall of South Vietnam. Esper was forced to leave five weeks later, long after most reporters had been expelled. He returned in 1993 to open up AP's first postwar bureau in Hanoi. According to the AP's most recent history, during his decade as a reporter in Vietnam, Esper "produced more than twice as many words as any other journalist in Vietnam." He retired in 2000, and now teaches journalism at his alma mater, West Virginia University.

REFERENCE: *Breaking News.* 2007.

Ethiopian War

The Ethiopian War of October 1935-May 1936 between Ethiopia and Fascist Italy is also known as the Italo-Ethiopian War or the Abyssinian War. In December 1934 Italian troops clashed

---

Indicates a separate entry.

with Ethiopian forces on the Italian Somaliland frontier. Fascist Italy, intent on creating its own African empire, signed an agreement with France in January 1935 which recognized Italian claims in Africa and was thought a form of reassurance for France against Nazi aggression. In October 1935 Italian troops crossed into Ethiopia from Italian Eritrea and the Somaliland. The war was protested by the League of Nations, Great Britain, and other countries. However, France, Germany, and Japan raised no objections. After the war ended in an Italian victory in May 1936, Italy withdrew from the League of Nations and formally annexed Ethiopia.

War correspondents descended on Rome following the outbreak of hostilities in Ethiopia. Among the 120 Anglo-American correspondents who reported the conflict were O. D. Gallegher,* Evelyn Waugh,* newsreel* cameraman Laurence Stallings, photographer Alfred Eisenstaedt, and George Steer* of the *Times*. Sympathy was over-whelmingly in favor of the embattled African country and its emperor Haile Selassie. Italian dictator Mussolini launched a juggernaut of 250,000 troops against the ancient kingdom defended by barefoot troops armed with swords and daggers.

Almost two hundred Italian reporters and writers were accredited to cover the war. Following the war, many produced books of poetry or history, or plays chronicling the war. Italian authorities would eventually invite forty foreign correspondents and various film units to record the war. The only two American or British correspondents with the Italian forces at the outset were Webb Miller* of the UP and Floyd Gibbons* representing the *Chicago Tribune*. Other correspondents reporting the onslaught of the Italian army included Will Barber* of the *Chicago Tribune*, Robinson Maclean for the *Toronto Telegram*, John T. Whitaker* of the *New York Herald Tribune*, and William W. Chaplin of Universal Service. Jim Mills of the AP was among the correspondents covering the Ethiopian side of the conflict.

Sometime after December 6, 1935, Haile Selassie ordered all journalists to return to his capital of Addis Adaba, where they would remain until the end of the war. On one hand, Selassie was afraid tribesmen were unable to tell the difference between Italians and friendly Europeans, and he could not guarantee their safety outside the city. On the other hand, he suspected some of the reporters of being spies. By the beginning of the new year, only three correspondents from America, and one from Great Britain, were still with Italian forces, including Reynolds Packard* of the UP, Eddie Neil of the AP, Christopher Holme* of Reuters,* and Herbert Matthews* of the *New York Times*. Correspondents found it virtually impossible to get anywhere near the main front in the north, and many out of sheer boredom left the country before the conclusion of the war.

Each correspondent had to go through the accreditation process with the Abyssinian Foreign Office, which required each newspaper's guarantee that a certain sum of money would be made available to the Foreign Office in the event a reporter was "required to leave the country by reason of a misdemeanor." Communication lines out of the country were primitive if they existed at all. Cables often arrived at various newspapers so unintelligible that they needed a team of cryptographers to decipher them. This was in part due to the fact the Ethiopian cable operators did not understand the cacophony of languages they were faced with transmitting, although they still managed to send dispatches totaling 30,000 words per day.

REFERENCES: Angelo Del Boca. *The Ethiopian War, 1935-1941.* 1969; Robert W. Desmond. *Crisis and Conflict.* 1982; James Dugan and Laurence Lafore. *Days of Emperor and Clown.* 1973; John Hohenberg. *Foreign Correspondence.* 1964; Phillip Knightley. *The First Casualty.* 1975.

"Eye-Witness"

Beginning with World War I* the British military imposed censorship restrictions on the wartime press. Lord Kitchener and the War Office were unusually suspicious of reporters and refused to allow any newspapermen near the western front. Their solution was to appoint an official "eye-witness" to relay the army's official daily reports to the journalists. Each report was scrutinized by Kitchener and other generals before being released to the public under the byline "Eye-witness."

The Allied general staffs adapted the World War I "eyewitness" system for World War II as well. However, instead of employing an army officer to fill the role of "eyewitness," journalist Alexander Clifford* was appointed to this role.

REFERENCE: Phillip Knightley. *The First Casualty*. 1975.

F

Faas, Horst (1933-2012)

Born in Berlin, he began his career in photojournalism in 1951 with Keystone, a British newsphoto agency in Munich. Five years later he joined the Associated Press. From 1956 to 1960 he covered West German politics. In 1961 he covered the conflict in the Congo, where he was beaten by Katangan rebels and forced to eat his United Nations pass. He next covered the Algerian independence movement before establishing his name as a war correspondent in Vietnam* beginning in 1962. His pictures from the bloody battle of Dong Xoai in 1965 appeared in *Life* magazine. In 1965 he became the first cameraman to win the Pulitzer Prize and the Robert Capa* Award in the same year.

REFERENCE: Robert E. Hood. *12 at War.* 1967.

Falklands War

The 1982 Falkland War between Great Britain and Argentina was triggered by Argentinean attempts to reclaim the British possessions of South Georgia and the Falkland Islands through the use of armed force. From the start the British military attempted to exclude war correspondents from the campaign. A compromise was worked out with the Ministry of Defence, with the task force agreeing to allow six correspondents to accompany the expedition. This was eventually increased to twelve, including a camera team and representatives from the British Broadcasting Corporation (BBC) and the Independent Television News (ITN). A consortium of Fleet Street newspaper editors and proprietors exerted further pressure to add more press representation. The military authorities relented and allowed fifteen correspondents and photographers to travel with the task force. They would be joined by thirteen more members of the press who would follow in the converted civilian liner *Canberra.*

British authorities controlled not only how many correspondents would cover the war but which organizations would be represented. No foreign correspondents were included, and the only international news agency represented was London-based Reuters.* The accreditation system for determining the selection process was severely flawed. There was no agreement concerning censorship guidelines, and some journalists formally agreed to the Officials Secrets Act, while others did not. Many of the journalists were inadequately briefed, clothed, and equipped for the military action.

The most recognized correspondent to come out of this abbreviated war was Max Hastings* of the *London Standard.* His fame was ensured when he made the front pages as "the First Man into Stanley." The Falklands War presented reporters with problems akin to those endured by their Victorian-era counterparts. Separated by eight thousand miles from England, they found communications difficult. Reporters relied on the navy communications systems to relay

Indicates a separate entry.

dispatches back to London. Since no provisions had been made for live television coverage, and the Ministry of Defence was lukewarm to facilitating any live transmissions, film had to be returned to London by plane or ship. At the heart of the controversy over live coverage was the lingering American experience of the Vietnam War* and how it had impacted morale at home. Military censors demanded that pictures of body bags be deleted from film footage.

The Ministry of Defence initiated a set of rules for newspaper editors called "D" notices. Each day briefings were conducted by Ian McDonald, a member of the ministry's public relations department. His job was not unlike the "Five O'Clock Follies"* briefings of the Vietnam War. His task was to provide the official spin on the day's activities.

War correspondents were assigned to various units and were dependent on their relationship with the commanding officer. Besides Hastings, Brian Harahan and Michael Nicholson provided excellent coverage considering the media environment, reporting engagements at Goose Green and at San Carlos. Other journalists regularly broadcasting from the conflict included Robert Fox of the BBC, Kim Sabido for the Independent Radio News, and John Shirley and John Witherow of the *Sunday Times*. The Falklands War demonstrated that 130 years after the Crimean War,* war still sold news.

REFERENCES: Derrik Mercer, Geoff Mungham, and Kevin Williams. *The Fog of War: The Media on the Battlefield.* 1987; Trevor Royle. *War Report: The War Correspondent's View of Battle from the Crimea to the Falklands.* 1987; *Sunday Times* of London Insight Team. *War in the Falklands.* 1982.

Fall, Bernard (1926-1967)

He was born in Vienna, Austria, and grew up in France. His parents were killed by the Nazis, and he fought with the French resistance and then the French army during the liberation of France. Following the war he worked as an investigator

for the Nuremberg War Crimes Tribunal and then began his college education at the University of Paris in 1948. He went on to receive his M.A. and Ph.D. from Syracuse before taking an academic position in international relations at Howard University in 1956.

After completion of his doctoral research on the Viet Minh insurgency in 1953, Fall became a recognized authority on the former French colony. His exploits with French troops in the field during the First Indochina War are chronicled in his *Street Without Joy* (1961). He continued to visit Southeast Asia throughout the early 1960s and subsequently wrote numerous articles and essays which were collected in *Viet-Nam Witness* (1966). His book *Hell in a Very Small Place,* published that same year, is a classic study of the French debacle at the Battle of Dien Bien Phu.

As the foremost authority of his generation on Vietnam, Fall warned that the capacity of the Vietnamese people to endure great hardships would thwart American efforts to defeat Vietnamese nationalism. Fall demonstrated great affection for Vietnam and its people and was an implacable critic of both colonialism and the Communist Viet Minh. Fall was diagnosed with an incurable disease shortly before he was killed by a Viet Minh land mine while accompanying a marine unit in the field.

REFERENCES: *DAB 8*; Bernard Fall. *Last Reflections on a War.* 1967; *New York Times.* February 22, 1967.

Fallaci, Oriana (1930–2006)

The renowned Italian foreign correspondent arrived in South Vietnam in 1967, and reported her first battle of the war at Dak To that November. No stranger to war, Fallaci grew up in Fascist Italy, where her father fought with the partisans. Oriana participated as a child in the war against the Axis by assisting downed fliers and escaped prisoners of war along underground escape routes.

Fallaci spent only several months in Vietnam* on her first stint in 1967. She returned the following year intending to report the Tet Offensive, but did not arrive on the battlefront until the after the final Battle of Hue. In May 1968 she was under fire once again during a mortar attack at Dak To. That October, Fallaci covered the student protests in Mexico City against the Olympic Games. She was with the students when Mexican soldiers fired into them. Fallaci was seriously wounded, lying alone for hours before being taken to a hospital.

She returned to Vietnam for the last time in 1972 to interview President Nguyen Van Thieu. Following the war in Vietnam, Fallaci remained an active and controversial journalist, interviewing and antagonizing world figures from the Ayatollah Khomeini to Libya's Muammar Khadafy. In 1981 she was the subject of a *Playboy* interview. Fallaci wrote the critically acclaimed novel *A Man* in 1980 and several works chronicling her career in journalism, including *Interview with History* (1976) and *Nothing, and So Be It* (1972).

REFERENCE: Virginia Elwood-Akers. *Women War Correspondents in the Vietnam War, 1961-1975.* 1988.

Faust, Frederick (1892-1944)

Better known for his fiction under the pen name Max Brand, Faust was the author of the scripts for the highly successful *Dr. Kildare* series of motion pictures. He was killed by German mortar fire while covering the 1944 Italian campaign for *Harper's* magazine.

REFERENCE: Robert W. Desmond. *Tides of War.* 1984.

Feinstein, Anthony (c. 1959)

Feinstein is a professor of psychiatry at the University of Toronto and the Director of the Neuropsychiatry Programme at Sunnybrook and Women's College Science Centre. He has studied the psychological effects of covering war zones for twenty years and has produced a number of important books and peer-reviewed studies on the topic including, *Dangerous Lives: War and the Men and Women Who Report It* (2003), *In Conflict* (1998), *Journalists Under Fire: The Psychological Hazards of Covering War* (2006), and *Battle Scarred: Hidden Costs of the Border War* (2011). Feinstein produced the documentary *Under Fire*, based on his research on journalists in war zones, and in 2012 it received a Peabody Award and was shortlisted for an Academy Award.

REFERENCES: http://conflict-study.com/biography. html; http://sunnybrook.ca/research/team/member. asp?t=10&m=56&page=172.

Fenton, Roger (1819-1869)

Fenton had been a leader in British photography prior to the Crimean War.* Educated at University College, London, following graduation he studied painting before turning to law in 1844. But it was during his study of painting that photography first piqued his interest, and in 1847 he helped found a photographic club. Six years later he was a founding member of the Photographic Society, later to become better known as the Royal Photographic Society.

With the intense interest in the Crimean War at home in England, Fenton was hired and financed by Thomas Agnew, a Manchester publisher, to take photographs which Agnew would sell for a profit. Although Fenton has often been referred to as the first war photographer, he was preceded by others who covered the 1846-1848 Mexican War* and the 1848-1849 Second Sikh War in the Punjab.

By 1854 Fenton had an impressive portfolio as a landscape and portrait photographer. He could count the royal family as among his clients, and thanks to their support and patronage he was able to document the Crimean War. In addition, letters of introduction to British commanders from Lord Raglan on down made his stay in the Crimea comfortable and relatively free from restrictions. It was hoped Fenton would photograph scenes that would counter negative accounts concerning the hardships faced by British forces in the Crimea. Although his over three hundred images of the conflict are devoid of graphic war scenes, his work has been described as the first extensive photodocumentation of a war. Wood engravings made from several of his images were published in the *Illustrated London News*.

Fenton was sick for much of his stay in the Crimea, which only lasted from March through June 1855. He took 360 photographs during these three months. Upon his return to England, the quality of his war images greatly impressed Napoleon III of France, who thus sent several French photographers to capture the rest of the conflict.

A full account of Fenton's Crimean venture can be found in the January 1856 *Journal of the Photographic Society*. He reportedly used the wet collodion process, which was first made public in 1851. The wet-plate process utilized a glass plate which had to be wet through the entire process. This process entailed first submerging the glass plate in a sensitizing solution, which was then exposed in the camera, then taken out and developed. The process necessitated the constant availability of a portable darkroom. Fenton's photographic van replete with photographic equipment was a frequent target of enemy artillery. Although his images of military encampments, forts, and harbors are priceless documents for this era, they are little more than posed sets, which when compared to Mathew Brady's* war images compromise the true horror of war. This was in part due to the technology of the day, which required exposures of three to twenty seconds. Any movement within this time span would result in blurring, making it necessary to pose each shot. Since part of his mission was to reassure the British public, Fenton knew that portraits of the dead would be unacceptable.

In October 1855 an exhibition of most of his photographs was held in London. The exhibition toured throughout England, eliciting much excitement and public interest. Several large folios of Fenton's prints were published, but interest in the conflict was declining. Following the

end of the fighting and the fall of Sebastopol in September 1855, and the subsequent peace negotiations, Fenton auctioned off his remaining stock of war photos.

In 1859 he recorded the horrors of war for the last time when he accompanied troops to the Piedmont in several battles with Austrian forces during the Austro-Italian War.* It was said the carnage distressed him to such an extent that he never covered the front lines again. In 1862, at the zenith of his fame he retired from photography to practice law.

REFERENCES: Helmut and Alison Gernsheim. *Roger Fenton: Photographer of the Crimean War.* 1973; Pat Hodgson. *Early War Photographs.* 1974; Lawrence James. *Crimea, 1854-56.* 1981; Jorge Lewinski. *The Camera at War.* 1978.

Filkins, Dexter (b. 1961)

Raised in Florida, and educated at Oxford University and the Univeresity of Florida. Filkins is a prizewinning correspondent for the *New York Times*. He came to prominence covering the second Iraq War. Previous to this he covered conflict in Afghanistan. He has also worked for the *Los Angeles Times* and *Miami Herald*. From 2003-2006 he covered Iraq for the Baghdad Bureau of the *New York Times*. He won the George Polk Award for his coverage of the assault on Fallujah in November 2004. During the attack he was embedded* with a company of Marines that took 25% casualties in eight days. His best known work is *The Forever War* (2008), which chronicles his Iraq experiences. He has twice been a finalist for the Pulitzer Prize for his war reporting in Afghanistan and Iraq.

REFERENCES: http://dexterfilkins.net/authot.html; Dexter Filkins. *The Forever War.* 2008.

Fincastle, Viscount Alexander Edward Murray (1871-1962)

Born in London, he joined the army in 1891 following his graduation from Eton. He served as

* Indicates a separate entry.

an assistant to the viceroy of India from 1895 to 1897 and during the Frontier War he fought in the Battle of Landaki while serving as a special for the *Times*. He received the Victoria Cross for his attempt to save the life of Lieutenant Greaves, a reporter for the *Times of India*. Fellow correspondent Winston Churchill* attempted to quickly publish his collected dispatches of the campaign but was beaten to the publisher by Fincastle. Fincastle rose to captain and served in the Boer War* and World War I.* Better known as Lord Dunmore beginning in 1907, he won the Distinguished Service Order during the Somme campaign. He is the only journalist to have been awarded the Victoria Cross.

REFERENCE: Dennis Griffiths, ed. *The Encyclopedia of the British Press*. 1992.

Finerty, John F. (1846-1908)

He is best known for his coverage of the American Indian Wars* from 1876 to 1881 for the *Chicago Times*. Born in County Galway, Ireland, he was the son of a newspaper editor. In 1864, he fled Ireland and a possible jail sentence after a brief flirtation with the Irish freedom movement. Upon his arrival in America he enlisted in the Union Army to serve in the American Civil War.*

Following the war, the classically educated Finerty moved to Chicago, where he found employment with the *Chicago Republican* in 1868. In 1871 he switched his allegiance to the *Chicago Tribune*, where he would remain until 1875. when he moved to the *Chicago Times*. His first assignment was to cover General George Crook's 1876 expedition against the Sioux and the Northern Cheyennes. Finerty was not content to play the passive reporter and often took part in the fighting. He participated in the skirmish on the Tongue River, the Battle of the Rosebud, and the Sibley Scout, all resulting in citations for bravery.

In 1879 he covered Nelson Miles' expedition against the Sioux along the Canadian border.

That same year he covered the suppression of the Ute uprising. In 1881 he went into the field during the Apache uprising. However, in the last two campaigns he saw no action. Tall and lanky, he was sometimes referred to as "Long John." After his career as an Indian War correspondent he served as a Washington correspondent and was active in various Irish societies.

REFERENCES: John Finerty. *War-Path and Bivouac*. 1961; Oliver Knight. *Following the Indian Wars*. 1960.

Fiorillo, Luigi (active 1860-1909)

The Italian photographer specialized in portraits from the Middle East before covering the Egyptian army rebellion led by Arabi Pasha in 1881. He witnessed the naval bombardment of Alexandria on July 11, 1882. His images of this incident are collected in *Album Souvenir d'Alexandrie: Ruines*. In 1887 he documented the Italian campaign in Abyssinia as a guest of an artillery officer.

REFERENCE: Nicolas Monti. *Africa Then*. 1987.

First Casualty, The

The 1975 book *The First Casualty, from the Crimea to Vietnam: The War Correspondent as Hero, Propagandist, and Myth Maker*, by Phillip Knightley, takes a controversial and updated look at the history of war reporting. The title refers to California senator Hiram Johnson's warning about American intervention during World War I,* that "the first casualty when war comes is truth."

REFERENCE: Phillip Knightley. *The First Casualty*. 1975.

Fisher, Philip D. (?)

Originally from Ohio, Fisher went west as a civil engineer for the Union Pacific Railroad following his service in the Union Army during the American Civil War.* He was in Kansas during the 1867 Indian troubles and shortly before the arrival of *Harper's* sketch artist Theodore R. Davis.* Several of Fisher's sketches of the American Indian War* were published by *Harper's* that year. Among them was a drawing of the Hancock expedition at Fort Harker.

REFERENCE: Peggy and Harold Samuels. *Samuels' Encyclopedia of Artists of the American West*. 1985.

Fisk, Robert (b. 1946)

Born in Maidstone, Kent, the British journalist has covered a host of conflicts for *The Independent* over thirty years. While he is most asscociated with the Middle East, during the 1970s he covered the North Ireland troubles, the Portuguese Revolution (1974), the Lebanese Civil War, and the Iranian Revolution in 1979. He then covered the Soviet-Afghanistan war, the Iran-Iraq War, the Algerian civil war, the Gulf War, and the 2003 inavsion of Iraq. Most notably he interviewed Osama bin Laden on three occasions in the mid-1990s. Fisk is one of the few war reporters with a Ph.D., which he received in Political Science from Trinity College, Dublin in 1985. He has spent a number of years in Lebanon, lived in Beirut through its civil war. and was among the few journalists to visit the sites of the Sabra and Shatilla massacre. Fisk has been the recipient of a number of awards and has been named British Press Awards' International Journalist of the year seven times. He is the author of six books, including *Pity the Nation: Lebanon at War (1990)* and *In Time of War: Ireland, Ulster and the Price of Neutrality (1983)*.

REFERENCES: http://en.wikipedia.org/wiki/Robert_Fisk; Ethan Bronner. "A Foreign Correspondent Who Does More Than Report." *New York Times*, November 19, 2005.

Fiske, Stephen Ryder (1840-1916)

Born in New Brunswick, New Jersey, Fiske demonstrated an early interest in the newspaper business. By the time he was fourteen he had published several articles and edited a small newspaper. After being expelled from Rutgers University for writing a novel satirizing one of his professors he was hired by the *New York Herald*. During the American Civil War* he served briefly as a war correspondent and then as the paper's drama critic. He left for Europe in 1866 and was with Giuseppe Garibaldi in Rome during the revolution. Fiske returned to the States in 1879 and founded the *New York Dramatic Mirror*. He remained active in the theater as a critic and playwright up to his death.

REFERENCE: Robert B. Downs and Jane B. Downs. *Journalists of the United States*. 1991.

Fitzgerald, Frances (b. 1940)

The well-connected Fitzgerald was the daughter of a former deputy director of the CIA. She went to Vietnam* as a freelance journalist in 1966. Intending to stay only a month she remained for a year. She returned to Vietnam five years later to cover the 1971 elections. When her highly acclaimed book *Fire in the Lake* was released in 1972 she was praised for her deep insights into Vietnamese culture; that book went on to become a bestseller and Pulitzer Prize* winner. The next year she was honored with the George Polk* Memorial Award for her Vietnam coverage. In 1973 Fitzgerald covered the Vietnam cease-fire. Over the next year she reported form Cuba, Syria, and Lebanon, and in late 1974 was in Hanoi for a nineteen-day fact-finding trip.

REFERENCE: Virginia Elwood-Akers. *Women War Correspondents in the Vietnam War, 1961-1975*. 1988.

"Five O'Clock Follies"

"Five O'Clock Follies" was the derisive term used by reporters to describe daily briefings given by the Joint United States Public Affairs Office (JUSPAO) in Saigon each day at five o'clock during the Vietnam War.* The briefings were controlled by the Military Assistance Command-Vietnam (MACV), which compiled data related to

Indicates a separate entry.

current military operations. It came under criticism for its penchant to inflate enemy casualty counts and underestimate enemy successes. It did just the opposite with American gains and losses.

REFERENCES: Daniel C. Hallin. *The "Uncensored War": The Media and Vietnam.* 1986; Clarence R. Wyatt. *Paper Soldiers: The American Press and the Vietnam War.* 1993.

Fleeson, Doris (1901-1970)

Fleeson was born in Sterling, Kansas, and entered journalism with the *Pittsburg Star* in Kansas. In 1934 she joined the *New York Daily News* and in 1943 became war correspondent for the *Woman's Home Companion,* covering the Sicilian campaign and the D-Day landing at Omaha Beach. Following the war she became the first woman political columnist to be syndicated.

REFERENCE: Robert B. Downs and Jane B. Downs. *Journalists of the United States.* 1991.

Fleischer, Jack (1903-1966)

Born in Luxembourg and educated at the University of Missouri, Fleischer joined the International News Service in 1929. Five years later he headed up its Berlin bureau. He covered German military affairs until the fall of France in 1940. Prior to American entry into World War II* he was allowed to cover German forces up to the Soviet frontier. However, beginning in October 1941 the Nazi government introduced censorship restrictions that barred foreign journalists from covering the developing war with the Soviet Union. In December 1941 he was among the American journalists arrested in Berlin. He eventually joined the U.S. Army, after the bombing of Pearl Harbor, but did not see any combat. Following the war he returned to journalism with the INS and the Hearst Headline Service as a columnist, reporter, and United Nations correspondent.

REFERENCES: Robert W. Desmond. *Tides of War.* 1984; Jack Stenbuck, ed. *Typewriter Battalion.* 1995.

Fletcher, Martin (b. 1947)

Born in London and educated at the University of Bradford he began his journalism career as a television news programming writer for VisNews in 1970. He joined NBC News as a cameraman in 1977 an in 1982 became NBC's network correspondent in Tel Aviv. A war reporter for almost thirty years, Fletcher covered his first war during the 1973 Yom Kippur War in Israel. He has chronicled his long career in the book *Breaking News* (2008). Fletcher has covered conflicts in Afghanistan and Kosovo, and was in China during the aftermath of the Tiananmen Square massacre. Fletcher scored one of his greatest coups when he interviewed Somalian warlord General Aidid, as American and NATO soldiers searched for him following the *Blackhawk Down* episode that resulted in the deaths of 18 soldiers. On another occasion he was the first correspondent to enter Cambodia with the Khmer Rouge guerrillas. Most recently he has served as the NBC News Bureau Chief in Tel Aviv and has focused most of his reporting on the Israeli-Palestinian conflict and other Middle East hotspots from Tel Aviv. In 2010 he left his Tel Aviv Post after 32 years to concentrate on his writing career, but still reports as a freelance Special Correspondent.

REFERENCES: martinfletcher.net. www.artsopolis.com/event/detail/57161;

Fly, Camillus Sidney (1849-1901)

Better known as "C.S." or "Buck," Fly was one of the best known photographers of the late-nineteenth century American West. His studio was located in Tombstone, Arizona beginning in 1879. The famous "Gunfight at the OK Corral" in 1881 took place close to his studio and Sheriff John Behan hid in it. Fly reportedly left the studio and disarmed a mortally wounded Billy Clanton. He didn't take pictures of the aftermath of the shootout. By some accounts he was warned not to by the Earps. In 1886 he accompanied General George C. Crook to photograph the peace negotiations with the Apache chief Geronimo. His photographs of the notorious Apache and his warriors are some of the most famous from the waning days of the Indian wars.

REFERENCE: Duncan Anderson. *War: A Photo History*. 2006.

Flynn, Sean (1941-1970)

The son of movie legend Errol Flynn was freelancing and on assignment for *Time* magazine in Cambodia when he was captured by Vietnamese Communists and reportedly executed. Flynn and Dana Stone* of CBS news were riding motorcycles along Route 1 near Chi Pou, close to the South Vietnamese border, when they were seized. Flynn and Stone were two of eleven journalists, photographers, and members of television camera teams seized at a Vietnamese roadblock during the first week of April 1970. They were just several of the 37 journalists who were killed or disappeared during the 1970-1975 Cambodian campaign that pitted the U.S.-backed Lon Nol administration against the North-Vietnamese-backed Khmer Rouge. Contrary to accounts that he was simply an adventure seeker with a death wish, Flynn was an accomplished professional photographer and cameraman; he had published work in *Time*, and had news footage broadcast on the CBS television network. In March 2010 searchers claimed to have found Flynn's remains, although at this writing the results of forensic tests had not yet been released. Freelance "bone hunters" and others have been looking for missing Americans for years, and not always with the best intentions. There have been some cases in which fraudsters have swindled grieving families with false hopes and remains. Flynn's mother, a former French movie star named Lili Damita, reportedly spent millions of her own money to find Sean. But ultimately in 1984 she had her son declared dead. Several documentaries and books

have been written about this case. The author of the dual biography of Sean and Errol Flynn, Jeffrey Meyers, claimed he found records insinuating that he died from poor medical care for malaria, and that it was possible he was buried alive. However, most other reports support the claims of execution. According to his biographer, at least three novels have been inspired by aspects of the life (and death) of Sean Flynn, including Jean Larteguy's *Presumed Dead* (1974); J.D. Hardin's *Highway of Death* (1989); and Gordon Chaplin's *Joyride* (1982).

REFERENCES: Charles C. Amot. *Don't Kill the Messenger*. 1994; Perry Deane Young. *Two of the Missing*. 1975; Helen Kennedy. "Remains of Errol Flynn's son, photographer Sean Flynn, may have been found in Cambodia mass grave." *NY Daily News*, March 29, 2010; Jeffrey Meyers. *Inherited Risk*. 2002.

Foa, Sylvana (b. 1945)

Born in Buffalo, New York and educated at Barnard College, Foa began her journalism career in 1970 covering the Saigon beat as a stringer* for *Newsweek*. Following the 1971 death of the news magazine's Indo-China foreign correspondent Francois Sully* in Cambodia, Foa took over Sully's Phnom Penh position. Over the following years Foa proved to be a thorn in the side of the American military establishment and in April 1973 she was kicked out of Cambodia, following a directive from the U.S. Embassy, after she started reporting on the American violation of the Cooper-Church Amendment, which had been passed in response to the American invasion of Cambodia. The amendment prohibited American advisors from helping the Cambodian army, as well as banned air operations in support of the Cambodian forces.

Following her stint in Cambodia, Foa reported as a stringer for *Newsweek* and United Press International (UPI). She landed a position with UPI in Hong Kong and in October 1973 landed an interview with Prince Sihanouk from Beijing. She became one of the first American

*Indicates a separate entry.

reporters to be permitted to visit China, as it was still convulsed by the Cultural Revolution. Over the next decade Foa would report from various postings around the world from Rome and Vienna to Bangkok and New Delhi. In 1982 she became UPI's Asia Pacific News Editor. Much of the rest of her journalism career was editorial or management in nature. In 1986 she became the first woman news director of an American television network, when she became Vice President for News and News Director of the Spanish language network Univision. In the 1990s she became the first woman to serve as Spokesman for the Secretary General of the United Nations. Foa was nominated for the Pulitzer Prize for her coverage of the assassination of Indian Prime Minister Indira Gandhi and for her reporting on the tenth anniversary of the end of the Vietnam War.

REFERENCE: http://www.un.org/press/en/1995/19951117.sga614.html.

"Fog of War, The"

See "BATTLE FOG" POLICY.

Foley, James Wright "Jim" (1973–2014)

Born in Evanston, Illinois, Foley was educated at Marquette University (1996), the University of Massachusetts, Amherst (2003), and Northwestern University's Medill School of Journalism (2008). He began reporting from the warfront in 2010 as an embedded journalist* with U.S. troops in Iraq. The following year he was hired by *Stars and Stripes** to cover Afghanistan. However, three months later he resigned from the position after being apprehended by military police with a small amount of marijuana for personal use. He found work with the Boston-based *GlobalPost* covering the Libyan revolt against Muammar Gaddafi by embedding himself with rebel fighters. In April 2011 he was detained with several other journalists by loyalist forces. During the attack in which he was captured, journalist

Anton Hammerl* was killed. Some 44 days later Foley was released from captivity along with Spanish photographer Manu Brabo and freelance reporter Clare Morgana Gillis. Foley returned to the United States but was back in Libya in time to witness the capture of Gaddafi along with *GlobalPost* correspondent Tracey Shelton.

Foley came to international prominence after he was kidnapped along with his interpreter and British journalist John Cantlie* by a gang after leaving an Internet café on their way from Syria to the Turkish border. In subsequent negotiations his captors, supporters of the Syrian regime, demanded the equivalent of $132 million from Foley's family, his employer *GlobalPost,* and the U.S. government. Efforts to bring Foley home were ongoing and his location was discovered several times, until it appeared he was being held in a Damascus prison, along with the journalist Austin Tice,* Foley was able to get a final message to his family in June 2014, describing the conditions in which he was being held. The following month a Special Forces rescue operation was launched, but the hostages had been moved. Foley suffered regular torture and beatings, as well as mock executions. On August 19, 2014, Foley appeared in a video uploaded on YouTube by ISIS,* entitled "A Message to America." After a preface denouncing the American role in the Middle East, the camera cut to the now iconic image of the orange-suited Foley kneeling next to a black-clad ISIS fighter. Foley was forced to read a final message condemning American airstrikes, and was then beheaded. The execution took up less than ten seconds of the four-and-a-half minute tape, and unlike similar execution videos did not show the entire execution, but did show his corpse after his murder. It was revealed at this time that ISIS was holding hostage journalist Steven Sotloff,* who they threatened to kill in a similar fashion if America did not end its air campaign. The day after the video was shown American intelligence officials verified the murder was authentic; however, there was still some debate as to exactly when and where it took.

Subsequent investigation suggests that Foley was executed in hills south of Raqqa, Syria.

REFERENCES: Jonathan Mahler, "James Foley," New York Times Magazine, Dec. 28, 2014, 22-23; Rukmini Callimachi, "Militant Group Says It Killed American Journalist in Syria," New York Times, Aug. 20, 2014.

Forbes, Archibald (1838-1900)

Born in Morayshire and educated at Aberdeen and Edinburgh, after a course taught by the preeminent war correspondent of his day, William Howard Russell,* Forbes enlisted in the Royal Dragoons in 1857. He published his first war pieces with the *Morning Star* and *Cornhill Magazine* while still in the military.

He left the army and published a weekly journal called the *London Scotsman* from 1867 to 1871. In 1870 his career as a war correspondent was given a boost when he was assigned by the *Morning Advertiser* and then the *Daily News* to cover the siege of Metz during the Franco-Prussian War.* At the Battle of Metz he suffered a minor leg wound which became gangrenous, nearly necessitating amputation. Forbes recovered and went on to cover the siege of Paris and was the first correspondent to enter the city after its fall in January 1871.

Formerly, most correspondents had made only occasional use of the war telegram. However, as competition among the newspapers for coverage intensified, one of Forbes' contributions to his craft was his making full use of the telegraph to effectively relay his eyewitness accounts.

Forbes made his reputation as one of the foremost war correspondents of his era while engaged by the *Daily News*. Entering Paris with the victorious Prussian army he was nearly drowned by French citizens who suspected him of being a German spy. After covering the Franco-Prussian War and the subsequent carnage of the Paris Commune (1871), he witnessed the Carlist fighting in Spain and the Russo-Turkish War,* and accompanied the Khyber Pass force to Jalalabad (1878-1879). During the Russo-Turkish War

Forbes accompanied the Russian army and witnessed the key Battles of Plevna and Schipka Pass. When the Czar was informed of the Russian victory at Schipka Pass through Forbes' dispatch he was so elated that he awarded the war correspondent the highest Russian award for valor.

In 1880 Forbes reported the Zulu War and rode 110 miles following the Battle of Ulundi to Landman's Drift in less than a day. Two days later he appeared 170 miles away with news of the British victory and was able to wire his dispatch to England before official sources. His death-defying journey of 300 miles in fifty hours, better known as the "Ride of Death" was a journalistic coup, widely hailed but little rewarded. While some members of parliament thought a Victoria Cross was in order, he did not receive so much as a campaign medal. Coincidentally, it was also his last war.

Although he was just into his forties, Forbes' health began to decline after all the years of hardships on the battlefield, and he retired to England, where he lectured and continued to write over the last two decades of his life. Besides his voluminous war reportage Forbes published numerous books related to distinguished soldiers and his military exploits, including *My Reminiscences: 1870-71* (1871), *War Correspondence of the Daily News* (1878), *Glimpses Through Cannon Smoke* (1880), *The Afghan Wars of 1839 and 1879* (1892), *The Soldiers I Have Known, Memories and Studies of War and Peace* (1895), and the Men of Action series.

REFERENCES: Robert W. Desmond. *The Information Process.* 1978; *DNB*; Robert Wilkinson-Latham. *From Our Special Correspondent.* 1979.

Forbes, Edwin (1839-1895)

Forbes, an American Civil War* illustrator, devoted much of his career to rendering his sketches into paintings and an elaborate book of illustrations, which was published as *Life Studies of the Great Army.*

*Indicates a separate entry.

In 1861, he was hired by *Frank Leslie's Illustrated Newspaper* to follow the Army of the Potomac under General George McClellan. He performed the dual functions of artist and reporter while covering the Union troops from 1862 to 1864. In 1862 he sketched most of Stonewall Jackson's campaigns in the Shenandoah as well as the Second Battle of Bull Run. He went on to witness the Battles of Gettysburg (1863), the Wilderness (1864), Cold Harbor and the Spotsylvania Courthouse, and many others. After the war Forbes recollected that the Battle of Antietam was the most "picturesque" battle that he had covered. Like most other sketch artists employed by the press, he made quick drawings on the battlefield, and completed them later in the studio. Some of his techniques in covering the field of battle contradict the popular image of the war correspondent. At one battle he sat on his stoic mount, Kitty, on an elevated ridge almost half a mile from the action, sketching the battle through his binoculars. He wrote and illustrated his memoirs of the war in the two-volume *Thirty Years After, An Artist's Story of the Great War* (1891). An artist to the end, he became paralyzed on his right side shortly before his death. Assisted by his wife, he taught himself successfully to draw with his left hand up until his death in 1895.

REFERENCES: Pat Hodgson. *The War Illustrators.* 1977; W. Fletcher Thompson, Jr. *The Image of War.* 1960; Philip Van Doren. *They Were There.* 1959.

Forsyth, Fredrick (b. 1938)

He worked for Reuters* from 1961 to 1965. The future best-selling novelist of *The Day of the Jackal* and *Dogs of War* was criticized by his superiors for injecting "imagination and language" into his journalism. He wrote *The Biafra Story* after spending many months in Biafra, but according to Nigerian civil war historian John de St. Jorre,* Forsyth's book is disappointing not only for its partisanship but for its failure to give an accurate portrait of life in Biafra.

REFERENCES: John de St. Joffe. *The Brothers' War.* 1972; Donald Read. *The Power of News.* 1992.

Forsyth, John (1812–1877)

Forsyth was an editor for the *Mobile Advertiser and Register* in Alabama and was considered politically significant during his lifetime. He also owned the *Columbus (Ga.) Times.* He only served as a Civil War correspondent for three weeks, but his role as newspaper editor and staunch advocate for slavery and the Confederacy often put him in the center of the national debate over sectional discord. Forsyth joined the Georgia bar in 1834 before moving to Mobile the following year. In the late 1830s he became increasingly involved in journalism and politics. In the following decade he purchased the *Columbus Times* and was selected as a local postmaster by President James K. Polk. While involved with the *Times* he served in the Mexican-American War* for five months as a lieutenant and adjutant in the 1st Georgia Regiment. It was at this time that he first covered warfare for a newspaper, sending accounts of his military life in the war back to his newspaper.

Forsyth's Civil War correspondence was published during the last months of 1862 as he served alongside General Braxton Bragg during the campaign in Kentucky. Bragg had a notoriously tense relationship with the press and was considered the "Sherman of the Confederacy" due to his arrest of so many war correspondents and civilians for perceived treasonous transgressions. Bragg needed to repair his censorious image and hoped this could be achieved by hiring his close friend Forsyth to join him on the Kentucky campaign. In September Forsyth reported the prelude to the Battle of Perryville for the *Mobile Advertiser and Register.* However, he was captured before the battle and quickly paroled. This experience turned him into a more vehement foe of the North and he made plans to create a newspaper office to accompany Bragg's army through Kentucky. His only actual battle reportage during the war came in October as he sent back reports from Harrodsburg, Kentucky. Forsyth would defend the actions of Bragg's forces against all critics who suggested that the Kentucky campaign had been a failure. His biased coverage of the campaign led the Kentucky Provisional Governor Richard Hawes to describe Forsyth's accounts of the campaign as "replete with erroneous statements" and cast the blame squarely on the shoulders of Forsyth's friend Bragg.

Forsyth hewed closer to the role of editor for the rest of the war making every effort to keep up public morale as the tide of war washed over the South. In 1865 he fled Mobile as the Union army approached. Ever the journalist he also brought with him the printing equipment and staff that made up his stock in trade, hoping to set up a paper in Confederate territory.

REFERENCE: Erika J. Pribanic-Smith, "John Forsyth: Love and Hate in the Strife-Torn South," *Knights of the Quill*, 2010, 203-215.

Fortescue, Granville Roland (1875-1952)

Fortescue was born in New York City. He dropped out of the University of Pennsylvania to serve in the Spanish-American War,* where he caught the attention of Colonel Theodore Roosevelt, who later selected him as a White House military aide. During the short war he served as a private, corporal, and in the 1st U.S. Volunteer Cavalry, better known as the "Rough Riders." In 1907 he accompanied an expedition exploring the Orinoco River in South America.

Fortescue served as a military observer during the Russo-Japanese War,* where he began a long friendship with correspondent Ellis Ashmead-Bartlett.* In 1909 Fortescue covered the Spanish Army in the Riff War in Morocco, his first assignment as a war correspondent, at the behest of Ashmead-Bartlett for the *London*

Standard. Fortescue happened to be on vacation with his family on the North Sea coast when Germany invaded Belgium in 1914. Ashmead-Bartlett arranged to have him cover the story for the *Daily Telegraph,* resulting in a first-rate eyewitness account from the fighting near Liege for the paper, and future assignments with the *New York Tribune.* He later covered the French, English, Russian, and Turkish armies on fronts in Russia and France. Fortesecue was commissioned as a major in 1917 and was wounded in France. In 1928 he retired from the Army. During his military career he was awarded the Certificate of Merit and Distinguished Cross, the Spanish War Medal, the Philippine Insurrection Medal, the Order of the Purple Heart, the Order of the Rising Sun (from Japan), and the Japanese War Medal. His best known books included *At the Front With Three Armies* (1914), *Russia, the Balkans and the Dardanelles* (1915), and *Frontline and Deadline* (1937). He is buried in Arlington National Cemetery.

REFERENCES: Emmet Crozier. *American Reporters on the Western Front, 1914-18.* 1959; Robert W. Desmond. *Windows on the World.* 1980; Edward J. Renehan, Jr., "A Secret Roosevelt," 2003, http:www.arlingtoncemetery.net/fotesc.htm.

Fox, Edward (d. 1895)

Fox covered the Modoc War of 1872-1873 for the *New York Herald.* An Englishman who had served in the British army, he was often compared to Henry Stanley* for his courage under fire. Fox had been the yachting editor back in New York when the war broke out, and he journeyed overland to San Francisco and by stage to the mining town of Yreka on the outskirts of the conflict. He covered the first meeting of the peace commission and got his first scoop when he rode alone into hostile country to successfully interview the Modoc leader Captain Jack. The *Herald* headlined one of his stories about the Modoc chief with the fanciful "Rob Roy

Mac-Modoc." Fox's interview has been described as perhaps the most outstanding individual feat of the war.

He later covered the Three Days' Fight after peace negotiations failed and some officers were ambushed. He narrowly escaped being killed in an ambush. He left for New York shortly before the end of the war. Following his battle exploits he was nicknamed "Modoc" Fox by New York newspapermen. Fox returned to California to cover the execution of Captain Jack in October 1873.

In 1874 he exposed management corruption at the Red Cloud Agency and testified before a congressional committee the following year. He continued with the *Herald*, then worked on Wall Street before moving back to England. He fought in several duels and was instrumental in establishing the Anglo-colonial paper the *British Australian*. In 1894 he moved to Australia to enter the mining business and died in a yachting accident near Perth.

REFERENCE: Oliver Knight. *Following the Indian Wars.* 1960.

Fox, John Jr. (1862–1919)

Fox was best known for his fiction, having written *New York Times* best-sellers in 1903, 1904, 1908, and 1909. His best-known works were *The Little Shepherd of Kingdom Come* (1903) and *The Trail of the Lonesome Pine* (1908). Born in Stony Point, Kentucky, Fox graduated from Harvard and began his reporting career in New York City. He worked for several newspapers before covering his first war in 1898, serving as war correspondent for *Harper's Weekly* in Cuba during the 1898 Spanish American War.* During the short conflict he served with Theodore Roosevelt's "Rough Riders." In 1904 he covered the Russo-Japanese War* for *Scribner's Magazine*, ending his war reporting career.

REFERENCE: http://en.wikipedia.org/wiki/John_Fox,_Jr.

Franco-Prussian War

The Franco-Prussian War began on July 19, 1870, and ended with a Prussian victory on May 10, 1871. The ten-month war witnessed one of the great battles in history at Sedan and several long sieges. The siege of Paris from September 19 to January 28 saw revolution break out in Paris as well as the creation of a temporary government. The outbreak of the Franco-Prussian War in 1870 signaled a new era in European war reporting. Two records for press coverage emerged from the conflict. Not only was it the most expensive war to date to cover up, but it also marked the first use of wireless for transmitting news from the scene of battle. Overall this was the most thoroughly covered European conflict up to that time. While the Crimean War* and subsequent campaigns were reported by mostly British correspondents, the press of at least six countries covered the Franco-Prussian War.

Initially the French government prohibited foreign war correspondents from the field, while the Prussians were more accommodating to the press. The best coverage of the war was provided by the French daily *Le Gaulois,* with twenty-six correspondents. Eventually neutral journalists could be found with both armies. *Daily Telegraph* correspondents included John Merry Lesage,* George Augustus Sala,* and Frank Lawley.* Reporting for the *Times* were Frederick Hardman,* Laurence Oliphant,* and William Howard Russell* with Prussian forces reporting his last war. Reporting for the *Daily News* were Archibald Forbes,* Hilary Skinner,* Henry Labouchere,* and four members of the Vizetelly* family. Only a handful of American correspondents appear in the annals of war literature on the conflict, with Januarius MacGahan,* beginning a short but eventful career as a war reporter, being the most recognizable.

The Franco-Prussian War marked a new era in war reporting. With the departure of William Howard Russell from the battlefield, his place was taken by a new breed of war reporter that would depend on the telegraph and cable facilities to speed news reports to the public regardless of the cost. Accurate, succinct, but precise accounts replaced the florid, subjective descriptions which had been the norm prior to the American Civil War.* During the four-month siege of Paris, carrier pigeons* and balloons were used to facilitate the transmission of news through Prussian forces. However, no outcome of the war was more significant than the emergence of the German Empire, the unification of Italy, and the establishment of the French Republic.

REFERENCES: Robert Desmond. *The Information Process.* 1978; Michael Howard. *The Franco-Prussian War.* 1961.

Francois, Didier (b. 1961)

Didier is a reporter for the French radio station Europe One. He has covered numerous conflict zones prior to being kidnapped in Syria and held by ISIS. He was held for more than ten months along with Nicholas Henin, Pierre Torres, and Edouard Elias. They were found blindfolded and handcuffed but alive near the Turkish border on April 19, 2014. He covered the wars in Bosnia for the French daily *Liberation.* During a firefight in Sarajevo, he was credited with rescuing and saving the life of the badly injured British photographer Tom Stoddart. After Bosnia, Francois covered danger zones in Kosovo, Chechnya, Afghanistan, and Africa.

REFERENCE: Janine Di Giovanni, "In Syria, Reporters are Targets for Kidnapping," Newsweek, May 9, 2014.

Fraser, David (1869-1953)

The Scottish-born correspondent left a banking career in 1900 for military service in Lumsden's Horse during the Boer War.* Following the war he was initially rebuffed in his attempts to land a position as foreign correspondent for the *Times,*

but another interview resulted in a posting as an assistant to the Far East correspondent. During the Russo-Japanese War* he followed the Japanese land forces while his supervisor covered the naval campaign. Fraser's account of General Kuroki's victory at the Battle of the Yalu River was widely printed. After the Battle of Shako he ceased to cover the land war and returned to London to join the staff of the *Times.* Over the next few years he reported from the Indian subcontinent, Turkey, and China. He retired as Far East correspondent in 1940.

REFERENCE: Robert W. Desmond. *Windows on the World.* 1980.

Freaner, James L. (d. 1852)

Freaner was one of the outstanding war correspondents of the Mexican-American War* and George Wilkins Kendall's* strongest competitor during the conflict. Representing the *New Orleans Delta,* he wrote articles appearing under his nickname "Mustang," a sobriquet bestowed on the reporter following the Battle of Monterrey, where Freaner killed a Mexican lancer officer and took his steed. During the Battle of Monterrey and other actions in the Valley of Mexico campaign he served with McCulloch's Texas Rangers. He was with the American army as it made its way from Veracruz to Mexico City.

Prior to entering the newspaper profession, Freaner wandered through Texas and Louisiana before accompanying a New Orleans regiment to the Rio Grande, at the outset of the war. He later joined a Texas Ranger company led by Captain Jack "Coffee" Hays. Freaner copied Kendall's method of sending stories by special courier as news competition became intense toward the close of the war.

Freaner was involved in the controversial publication of the "Leonidas letter," a hoax which overstated the importance and accomplishments of General Pillow during the Mexican War. On separate occasions Freaner personally transported important official documents. In November 1847 he carried dispatches to Washington on behalf of General Winfield Scott, and in February 1848 he conveyed the Peace Treaty of Guadalupe Hidalgo from peace emissary Nicholas Trist to President Polk. Following the war, Freaner was hired to cover the story of the California gold rush. He was killed along with three companions in California by Indians as they were surveying a wagon road under state contract.

REFERENCES: F. Lauriston Bullard. *Famous War Correspondents.* 1914; Fayette Copeland. *Kendall of the Picayune.* 1943; Tom Reilly, *War with Mexico!,* 2010.

Fredenthal, David (1914-1958)

The Detroit artist-correspondent was one of the members of the army art unit who joined *Life* after the dissolution of the unit in 1943. Assigned to the Pacific in late 1943, he covered military operations under General Douglas MacArthur, including three island invasions. His most memorable work came during the American assault on Arawe in New Britain. In September 1944 he was transferred to Europe to cover partisan activities against the Germans in Yugoslavia. He witnessed the liberation of Belgrade by partisan and Russian forces.

REFERENCE: Frederick Voss. *Reporting the War.* 1994.

Friend, The

Before the Boer War* an English-language newspaper called *The Friend of the Sovereignty and Bloemfontein Gazette* was published in Bloemfontein. The chief press censor of the British army asked a group of correspondents to transform it into the first army newspaper, called *The Friend* starting on March 16, 1900. During its one-month run, it published articles by most of the Boer War correspondents, including Bennet Burleigh,* Lionel James,* and even Rudyard Kipling.*

REFERENCE: Byron Farwell. *The Great Anglo-Boer War.* 1976.

Fripp, Charles Edwin (1854-1906)

Born in Hampstead, London, the son of a successful landscape painter, Fripp received his art training at the Royal Academy in Munich. He covered his first conflicts as a special artist for the *Graphic* during the Kaffir War (1878) and the Zulu War of 1879. His eccentric manner made him the subject of endless anecdotes among his colleagues. On one occasion during the Zulu War, Fripp, an avid swimmer, insisted on swimming despite intermittent sniper fire. He refused an officer's order to leave the water and had to be removed by force. In another incident the reportedly mild-mannered artist had to be restrained from slugging General Buller, "who annoyed him."

In 1881 he covered conflict in South Africa and in 1885 he reported the Sudan campaign. During the Sino-Japanese War* he was with the Chinese forces. Beginning in 1890 his sketches appeared in the new *Daily Graphic* as well as the *Graphic.* He covered the Sino-Japanese War from 1894 to 1895, and then the Second Matabele War in 1896-1897. In the late 1890s he traveled throughout the American West before accompanying American forces in the Philippine campaign during the Spanish-American War* in 1899. The year 1900 found Fripp covering the Boer War.* Some of his sketches were drawn from notes provided by soldiers in the field. Following the war he relocated to Canada, where he recorded the Klondike story.

REFERENCES: Pat Hodgson. *The War Illustrators.* 1977; Robert Wilkinson-Latham. *From Our Special Correspondent.* 1979.

Frontline Television News Ltd.

The brainchild of Peter Jouvenal*, Rory Peck*, Vaughan Smith* and Nicholas Della Cassa*, it was created as a "cooperative of freelance cameramen" in 1989. Over the next fifteen years they covered the most dangerous conflicts in the world, losing at least eight affiliated journalists and cameramen. Some of the members had military backgrounds and local knowledge about the cultures of the regions they would be working in. By most accounts Frontline was also in the forefront of the media revolution going on in the 1990s and the 2000s, introducing innovations such as small Hi8 Cameras and then using live satellite newsfeeds. The news cooperative was disbanded in 2003 but lives on in the the Frontline Club* and various trusts honoring members who died while filming the news.

REFERENCE: David Loyn. *Frontline*. 2005.

Frontline Club

This London club was set up in 2003 following the deaths of two of the of the four founders of Frontline Television News*. It has since become a popular stopping place for war correspondents and has provided a forum for the discussion of journalism related issues, films and general safety concerns while in the field. It was set up by Vaughan Smith* with the intention of honoring his former comarades. It has about 850 members who pay an annual fee of $475USD. The vast majority are members of the news media (70%) and freelancers are given discounted memberships. The club itself is reserved for members, while there is a restaurant open to the public.

REFERENCES: Eric Pfanner. "IN London, a Haven and a Forum for War Reporters," New York Times, August 28, 2006; http://frontlineclub.com/club/about.php.

Fuller, Sarah Margaret
(1810-1850)

Fuller was born in Cambridge, Massachusetts, and is considered by some authorities to be the first woman war correspondent. Better known for her feminist and transcendentalist writings, her book *Woman in the Nineteenth Century* (1845) was an important influence on the 1848 Seneca Falls convention on woman's rights.

In 1844 she joined the staff of Horace Greeley's *New York Tribune* as literary critic. Two years later she was made a foreign correspondent and sent to Europe, where she reported on social conditions in Great Britain, interviewed notable political and artistic figures, and became embroiled in the Roman revolution. From Italy she reported the French bombardment and capture of Rome. While in Rome she married Angelo Ossoli and had a son. She served as both nurse and reporter on the battlefield, which saw her husband fighting on the Italian side. Following the capitulation of Rome, Fuller and family fled the country by sea. They perished when their ship was lost off the coast of Fire Island in July 1850, shortly before her fortieth birthday.

REFERENCES: John Hohenberg. *Foreign Correspondence*. 1964; Ishbel Ross. *Ladies of the Press*. 1936.

Furlong, Charles Wellington
(1874–1967)

Born in Cambridge Massachusetts, after graduating from college he taught at Cornell for about decade before leaving for a life of adventure. He is credited with discovering the wreck of the U.S. frigate *Philadelphia* in Tripoli harbor in 1904 and three years later became the first American and the second white man to explore the interior of Tierra del Fuego. In Patagonia he lived among Ona and Yahgan tribes and in 1909 wrote his first book, *Gateway to the Sahara*, based on his explorations in North Africa. He then returned to South America where he traveled extensively and in 1915 sailed a schooner from the United States back to North Africa, where he took a position as a correspondent to cover World War I.* He eventually joined the army and became an aide to President Woodrow Wilson during the Paris Peace Conference. Following World War I he lived the life of a cowboy and later published *Let 'Er Buck* (1921). He left war journalism after his first war but kept busy as a colonel in the army reserve, treasure hunting in Bolivia, and recovering relics from Henry Stanley's expedition in Africa.

REFERENCES: Charles Wellington Furlong. *Let 'Er Buck.* 1921; W.K. Stratton. *Chasing the Rodeo.* 2005.

Furnas, Joseph Chamberlain "J.C." (1905–2001)

J.C. Furnas was born in Indianapolis, Indiana and educated at Harvard University, where he wrote for the *Crimson*. He worked a variety of jobs before turning to freelance writing after the 1929 stock market crash. He turned to war reporting after the Japanese attack on Pearl Harbor. Too old for the draft and with poor eyesight and hearing, his only option for contributing to the war effort was reporting the war. In January 1942 he obtained a job with *Reader's Digest* and set sail from Halifax, Nova Scotia on antisubmarine patrol aboard a Royal Canadian Navy corvette. With not even a brush with a submarine and the ship developing engine problems, Furnas headed back to Ottawa by train. His next assignment was with the *Saturday Evening Post* in spring 1945, which agreed to cover his expenses for traveling to the South Pacific. He was among a group of war reporters in Manila who were permitted to accompany General Douglas MacArthur to witness the landing at Borneo in the Netherlands East Indies (current-day Indonesia). It turned out to be the last amphibious action of the war. Prior to the end of the war he flew on several bombing missions with the Thirteenth Air Force over the island of Morotai. After the war Furnas went on to a prolific, if undistinguished, career writing popular history.

REFERENCES: Katherine Warner, "J.C. Furnas," *American World War II Correspondents*, Jeffrey B. Cook, ed. 2012, 87-96; "J.C. Furnas, Wry Historian of American Life, Dies at 95," New York Times, June 12, 2001, A31.

Fyfe, Henry Hamilton (1869-1951)

Born in London, he followed his father onto the staff of the *Times*. In 1902 he transferred to the *Morning Advertiser* before moving to the *Daily Mirror* the following year. In 1907 he began an eleven-year affiliation with the *Daily Mail*. He covered the developing revolution in Russia in 1911, and two years later was in Mexico covering Carranza's revolution, on special assignment for the *Times*. Fyfe returned briefly in 1916, the only foreign news correspondent during this period of the conflict. Shortly afterward the Irish troubles in Ulster became a major story and Fyfe was called back to Europe.

With the outbreak of World War I* in 1914, he was soon reporting from France and Belgium. His reputation soared after his telegram to the *Daily Mail* reporting the retreat from Mons was reprinted in the *Times*. His coverage portrayed the true horrors of war and dissuaded anyone of the notion that the war would be of short duration. Fyfe came under fire from government censors. He was threatened with arrest if he reported from the Western Front, after Lord Kitchener, the War Minister, banned journalists from this theater of the war. Fyfe thought he could evade the authorities by joining the French Red Cross, allowing himself a few more months of reporting from France. However, he soon left to cover the Eastern Front, where few restrictions on reporting existed. He spent the last year of the war reporting once more from the Western Front. In 1915-1916 he reported the war in Russia and the killing of the court mystic, Rasputin. The following year he was sent on diplomatic missions to the United States. Besides his journalistic activities, Fyfe wrote numerous works of fiction and nonfiction, plays, and biographies.

REFERENCES: Robert W. Desmond. *Windows on the World.* 1980; *DNB,* 1951-1960.

G

Gallagher, James Wesley "Wes" (1911-1997)

Born in Santa Cruz, California, Gallagher was educated at various California schools and the University of San Francisco before joining the *Register Pajaronian* in Watsonville as a sportswriter in late 1929. He gradually moved into other areas of news reporting, and received a master's degree in journalism from Louisiana State University in 1935. He just missed witnessing the assassination of Governor Huey Long, but was on the scene soon enough to make one of the earliest accurate reports of the incident.

After being hired by the Associated Press in 1938, he was assigned to its Buffalo bureau, and later was transferred to New York, where he was promoted to foreign correspondent. He was on his way to cover the Russo-Finnish War, but the conflict ended before he got there. He was in Copenhagen when the German army invaded in April 1940, and he covered the final stages of the Norwegian campaign.

He was in Yugoslavia when Italy invaded Greece, and he covered the Albanian front until he was hospitalized with jaundice. By 1942 he was back in action covering the invasion of North Africa as head of the AP news crew. The following year he suffered back and face injuries when his jeep overturned. In 1944 Gallagher was placed in charge of the AP field crew covering the Normandy invasion and later directing postwar European coverage. From his

wartime experiences came *Free Men Are Fighting* (1944).

Following the war he continued his career with the AP, rising to general manager in 1962. The AP continued to develop under his tenure and in 1976 he was made director of the Gannett Company. He also wrote *Back Door to Berlin: The Full Story of the American Coup in North Africa* (1943).

REFERENCES: *DLB*, 254-255; Library of America. *Reporting World War H*. 1995.

Gallagher, O'Dowd "O. D." (b. 1913)

South African-born O.D. Gallagher represented the *London Daily Express* during the Ethiopian War.* According to one source, the inexperienced reporter was selected merely for being an African native. He left Ethiopia prior to the end of the war when he was assigned to interview Emperor Haile Selassie, who was in exile in Jerusalem. The resulting interview was carried in the *Express* under the headline "Gallagher Sees Emperor," and was a minor sensation.

Gallagher covered the Spanish Civil War,* first with the Nationalists and then with the Republicans. He was one of the few journalists to report virtually the entire war, although he was twice expelled from the country by Falangist insurgents. According to Phillip Knightley,

Gallagher claimed that Robert Capa* insinuated to him that his famous photograph "Death of a Loyalist Soldier"* had been faked. When Madrid fell in March 1939 Gallagher was the only fulltime war correspondent on hand to observe the entry into the city of the victorious Nationalist troops. While hiding in the Ritz Hotel the intrepid journalist was able to smuggle several short dispatches to the telegraph office before he was captured by Nationalist authorities and narrowly escaped being shot.

In 1939 he covered the war in France, before transferring to the Pacific theater. He was aboard the ill-fated battle cruiser *Repulse* only days after Pearl Harbor when he witnessed the worst British naval disaster of the war. On December 10, 1941, Japanese torpedo bombers sank the *Repulse* and the battleship *Prince of Wales* in the Gulf of Siam, with a heavy loss of life. Gallagher and his notes survived a plunge into the oily sea and, after he was rescued with the only other two correspondents to witness the engagement, was taken back to Singapore, where he filed his scoop, much to the chagrin of the slow-footed censors. He later reported the 1942 Burma campaign for the *Daily Express*.

REFERENCES: Robert W. Desmond. *Crisis and Conflict.* 1982; Robert W. Desmond. *Tides of War.* 1984; Phillip Knightley. *The First Casualty.* 1975.

Gallenga, Antonio (1810-1895)

Born in Italy, he became a naturalized British citizen in 1846. Gallenga was a professor of foreign languages in Nova Scotia and of Italian literature at University College before returning to Italy in 1859. Even though he was a British subject he was allowed to hold a seat in the Piedmontese parliament. It was during this time that he began his affiliation with the *London Daily News* and the *Times*.

In 1863 he was assigned to report the American Civil War.* He reported from the western theater of the war, and among his first stories was an account of the internecine bloodshed on the Kansas-Missouri border. He chronicled the advance of the Union Army of the Cumberland under Rosecrans and the Battle of Chickamauga. Gallenga returned to England in December 1863, claiming ill health. However, most sources indicate he had tired of restrictions imposed by Federal authorities which prohibited any member of the *Times* from accompanying armies in the field.

REFERENCE: Ian F. W. Beckett. *The War Correspondents: The American Civil War.* 1993.

Galloway, Joseph L. (b. 1941)

Raised in Refugio, Texas, Galloway spent more than twenty years as a foreign and war correspondent and bureau chief for United Press International. He followed that with another twenty years with *U.S. News and World Report* before moving to media company Knight Ridder in 2002. He has been posted in Japan, Vietnam, India, Indonesia, Singapore and Moscow. He spent four tours covering the Vietnam War and took part in the "first major battle" of the war at Ia Drang. During the battle he was decorated for rescuing wounded soldiers under heavy fire and became the only civilian awarded the Bronze Star by the U.S. Army during the war. His participation in the battle was chronicled in the bestselling book which he co-authored with Harold G. Moore, *We Were Soldiers Once ... and Young: Ia Drang—The Battle that Changed the War in Vietnam* (1992). In *We Were Soldiers*, the 2002 movie version of the film, starring Mel Gibson, Galloway was portrayed by actor Barry Pepper. Galloway also covered the 1971 India-Pakistan War and Desert Storm in 1990-1991. He covered the war with the 24th Infantry Division (Mech) on assignment for *U.S. News*. General H. Norman Schwarzkopf called Galloway "the finest combat correspondent of our generation—a soldier's reporter and a soldier's friend." He co-authored the book *Triumph Without Victory: The Untold*

History of the Persian Gulf War (1992) and also co-authored *We Are Soldiers Still: A Journey Back to the Battlefields of Vietnam* (2008).

REFERENCES: www.huffingtonpost.com/joe-galloway; www.google.com/profiles/gallowayjoseph380.

Garanin, Anatoly (1912-1990)

Born and educated in Moscow, Garanin was self-taught in photography. Prior to World War II* he worked as a photojournalist for several publications. He was not limited to covering the front lines, having carved a career in both scenic and theater photography. During the conflict he was a reporter for *Frontovaya Illustracia*. His photograph, "Death of a Soldier," taken on the Crimean front in 1942 for TASS, is considered a classic. Following the war he worked as special correspondent for *Soviet Union* magazine and for the Moscow Theater.

REFERENCES: *Contemporary Photographers.* 1982; Daniela Mrazkova and Vladimir Remes, eds. *The Russian War: 1941-1945.* 1975.

Garcia-Navarro, Lourdes (?)

Also known by the moniker "Lulu," Garcia-Navarro has covered numerous conflict zones. Much of her career has been spent with National Public Radio (NPR). Educated at Georgetown University and City University London, she broke into freelance reporting with BBC World Service and Voice of America. In 1999 she was hired by Associated Press Television News as a producer and reporter. In 1999 she covered Kosovo, Afghanistan in 2001, Israel in 2002, and Iraq between 2002 and 2004. She was one of the few journalists to cover the invasion of Iraq as a unilateral reporter. In 2008 she was posted to Baghdad to oversee NPR's coverage of the Iraq war. In 2011 she was on the scene as one of the first reporters to chronicle the growing uprising in eastern Libya. She reported the conflict for several months from rebel-held sites in Benghazi,

Tripoli and the western mountains as the conflict against the Gadhafi regime intensified. In 2011 she was recognized with the George Foster Peabody Award, a Lowell Thomas Award from the Overseas Press Club, and several other prestigious broadcasting and reporting awards.

REFERENCE: http://www.npr.org/people/4462099/lourdes-garcia-navarro.

Gardner, Alexander (1821-1882)

Born in Paisley, Scotland, Gardner worked as a jeweler's apprentice from 1835 to 1843. At the same time he pursued interests in chemistry and optics. Prior to moving to America in 1856 and working as Mathew Brady's* assistant, Gardner worked as a reporter for the *Glasgow Sentinel*. Gardner, self-taught in wet-plate photography, introduced Brady to the techniques of enlargement. In 1858 he operated Brady's Washington studio, but within five years he resigned to strike out on his own. As one of Brady's most important photographers, he felt he had not been given enough credit or payment for his work.

Gardner opened his own portrait establishment, where he advertised a set of "Photographic Incidents of the War." Soon after, he was named official photographer for the Army of the Potomac, although he continued to photograph the progress of the war by deploying teams much in the tradition of Brady. In 1866 Gardner published *Sketch Book of the War*, which was comprised of one hundred original photographs by various photographers. In 1867 he became the official photographer for the Union Pacific Railroad and went west to photograph the frontier. While Gardner is most often identified with the American Civil War,* he also documented some remarkable events such as execution of the Lincoln conspirators, Lincoln's funeral procession, the trial and execution of Andersonville commandant Wirz, and the life of the Great Plains Indians.

* Indicates a separate entry.

REFERENCES: Alexander Gardner. *Gardner's Photographic Sketch Book of the Civil War.* 1959; D. Mark Katz. *Witness to an Era: The Life and Photographs of Alexander Gardner.* 1991.

Garrels, Anne (b. 1951)

Educated at Harvard University's Radcliffe College (1972), she entered the journalism profession with ABC serving a variety of positions for almost ten years. In 1982 she was expelled from Moscow where she was serving as a bureau chief. Between 1984 and 1985 she served as the Central America bureau chief. After serving as an NBC News correspondent at the U.S. State Department she joined NPR in 1988 and went on to cover such hotspots as Chechnya, Bosnia, Kosovo, Afghanistan, Pakistan, Israel, and the West Bank. In 2003 she was one of the 16 Western journalists who stayed in Baghdad to witness the early events of the Iraq War.* She would chronicle her experiences during the invasion in her memoir, *Naked in Baghdad: The Iraq War as Seen by NPR's Correspondent* (2003). In November 2004 she was embedded with the U.S. Marines during the Battle of Fallujah. She would return to cover the war on several occasions. In 2003 she was awarded a Courage in Journalism Award from the International Women's Media Foundation and the following year the George Polk Award* for Radio Reporting for her Iraq War coverage.

REFERENCES: "NPR's Anne Garrels Wins Prestigious Polk Award," www.npr.org/about/press/040219.garrels. html; Anne Garrels. *Naked in Baghdad: The Iraq War as Seen by NPR's Correspondent.* 2003.

Gellhorn, Martha (1908-1983)

Born in St. Louis, she dropped out of Bryn Mawr College a year before graduation to pursue her goal of becoming a foreign correspondent. Her first steps in journalism were taken with the *New Republic* and the *Albany Times Union.* In the early 1930s she traveled in Europe and wrote her first novel, *What Mad Pursuit,* published in 1934. In 1936 she met Ernest Hemingway,* who would eventually become her husband. In 1937 Gellhorn joined Hemingway in Spain, where she was persuaded by *Collier's* to become its special correspondent. She returned to the States to drum up support for the Loyalist side in the Spanish Civil War.* In late 1937 she was back in Spain writing from the battlefront. During the conflict she worked in field hospitals and visited the Loyalist fronts.

In 1939 she covered the Russian invasion of Finland and then the developing Asian theater of the war, reporting from Singapore, the Dutch East Indies, and the Burma Road. By the time Pearl Harbor was bombed she was already a seasoned war reporter and the wife of Hemingway. She became aware that some had attributed her literary success to her relationship with the best-known writer in the world and took steps to keep her name from being forever linked with his.

Sent to London in 1943 by *Collier's,* she became its official war correspondent. After she requested that Hemingway join her in London, he took out his displeasure at having been left behind in the States by offering his services to *Collier's.* The U.S. press corps protocol allowed for only one frontline correspondent per magazine and Gellhorn lost her position to her husband. She left Hemingway after this and covered the war on her own, having lost her accreditation. However, while Hemingway was with the official war correspondents preparing for the Normandy invasion, Gellhorn secretly boarded a hospital ship that preceded the landing craft with the correspondents, infuriating Hemingway in the process. Scooping Hemingway on this story should have been her best revenge, but her story was accorded secondary status by *Collier's* whereas Hemingway's eyewitness account was the front-page story.

Gellhorn went on to cover the British Eighth Army and the Battle of the Bulge. She collaborated with Virginia Cowles* on the play *Love Goes to War* (1946), a comedy about war correspondents. She also reported the Indonesian rebellion against the Dutch and the Nuremberg war crime trials. After the war she returned to novel and travel writing before reporting the Vietnam War* in 1966 as correspondent for the *Guardian*, the 1967 Six Day War, and the 1980s wars in Central America. Her best-known work is probably *The Face of War*, a collection of her war reportage (1986). In summer 2010 it was announced Nicole Kidman will portray Gellhorn in a forthcoming movie.

REFERENCES: Bernice Kert. *The Hemingway Women*. 1983; Lilya Wagner. *Women War Correspondents of World War H*. 1989.

Gerretsen, Chas (b. 1943)

Born in Groningen, Netherlands, Gerretsen ended up in the United States in 1963, where he purchased his first movie camera and was on the road to becoming an award-winning war photojournalist. In 1968 he traveled through Laos and Cambodia and ended up in South Vietnam. It was here that he really began his career as a freelance photojournalist and cinematographer. Several months after arriving he joined UPITN (United Press International News) as a staff cameraman, but chafed under the restrictions inherent in working for a traditional news outlet and went back to his freelance work, working at times for ABC TV, and selling some of his pictures to Time/Life, *Newsweek*, and UPI. In 1969 the Vietnam War had calmed down and many freelancers went elsewhere. However, things heated up in 1970 during the American invasion of Cambodia and soon Gerretsen was back in the region. He joined the French photo agency Gamma in 1972 and the following year won the Robert Capa Gold Medal Award* with David Burnett and Raymond Depardon.*

REFERENCE: http://www.nederlandsfotomuseum.nl/nl/component/content/article/51-collecties/fotograaf/153-beschrijving-chas-gerretsen.

Geyer, Georgie Anne (b. 1935)

The Chicago-born Geyer entered the journalism profession in 1960 with the *Chicago Daily News*. A graduate of Northwestern University, prior to joining the *News*, Geyer studied overseas on a Fulbright scholarship, and reported for the *Southwest Economist*. In 1965 she covered her first foreign assignment when she was dispatched to the Dominican Republic to cover the revolution there. Over the next several years she developed a reputation as a specialist in Latin American affairs.

By most accounts Geyer began covering the Vietnam War* in 1967 after falling in love with correspondent Keyes Beech,* who was stationed in Saigon for the *Chicago Daily News*. Their relationship ended abruptly but led Geyer to one of her greatest scoops when she obtained an interview with Prince Sihanouk of Cambodia after all other journalists had been expelled from the country. Apparently Geyer hid the fact that she was actually a journalist, although the Cambodian leader later sent her a cable noting how pleased he was with the objectivity of her final report. She left Vietnam in early 1969, but not before writing a series of articles noting the disillusionment among American servicemen. Following the war she continued as a foreign correspondent, specializing in Latin America, and became a columnist for the Universal Press Syndicate.

REFERENCE: Virginia Elwood-Akers. *Women War Correspondents in the Vietnam War, 1961-1975*. 1988.

Gibbes, Robert W. Jr. (1809–1866)

Gibbes became a journalist in 1840 and early on developed an appreciation for collaboration within the newspaper business. He enlisted in the Confederate Army at the outbreak of hostilities and was later appointed South Carolina's surgeon general. Although Gibbes never actually reported from the battlefield during the American Civil War,* he came to prominence as an advocate for war correspondents and as the president of the Press Association of the Confederate States of America, which was created in 1863 by the Confederacy's newspaper editors in Augusta, Georgia. He probably came closest to the battlefront witnessing the war-torn devastation of Columbia, South Carolina in February 1865, days after the city was destroyed by Sherman's army. Chroniclers of his life credit his actions with making it easier for journalists to report on the war. He helped found the South's first wire service and made every effort to exempt journalists from being drafted into the army and helped gain them better access to army officers and battlefronts.

REFERENCE: Debra Reddin van Tutll and Patricia G. McNeely, "Robert W. Gibbes: The 'Mind' of the Confederacy," *Knights of the Quill*, 2010, 95-103.

Gibbons, Floyd (1887-1939)

Born in Washington, D.C., Gibbons was educated at Georgetown University before being expelled for pranksterism. After trying his hand at police reporting with the *Minneapolis Daily News*, and then the *Milwaukee Free Press*, he joined the *Minneapolis Tribune*. In 1912 he landed a job with the *Chicago Tribune*. Two years later he was sent by the paper to cover the American mobilization along the Mexican border during the Mexican Revolution. Among his much-publicized exploits was his warm relationship with Pancho Villa, who outfitted a special railroad car for the intrepid reporter despite his threat to hang the first American reporter to fall into his hands. He also reported the Battle of Ciudad Juarez from El Paso. In 1916 Gibbons accompanied General John J. Pershing's expedition to punish Villa for his raid on New Mexico.

In 1917 he was assigned to cover World War I* in Europe for the *Tribune*. Gibbons almost made a fatal mistake when he ignored instructions to cross the Atlantic on the *Frederick VIII*, which carried a German ambassador, and instead opted for the SS *Laconia*, which was torpedoed by U-boats two hundred miles off the coast of Ireland. His account of the sinking was widely printed and was probably his greatest scoop.

While covering the war in France, Gibbons parted ways from the carefully controlled press column and, on his own initiative, left for training with the Sixth Field Artillery for six weeks, resulting in several news scoops. Gibbons was almost killed while accompanying a marine assault in the Belleau Wood. He was attempting to aid a gravely wounded major who was trapped by machine-gun fire when he was hit in the arm, shoulder, and head. One bullet ricocheted off a rock and tore out his left eye. He returned to the States and the lecture circuit wearing what would become his trademark eye patch.

He returned to Europe following the war unsatisfied by his new management position. In 1919 he covered the Sinn Fein rebellion and the next year was the only reporter at the front during the Polish-Russian conflict. In 1921 he scored one of his greatest scoops as the first reporter to cover the Russian famine. In 1925 he covered the French and Spanish war with the people of the Riff Mountains in Morocco.

He ended his fifteen-year relationship with the *Tribune* in 1926 and wrote the biography of the German war ace Baron von Richthofen, which was serialized for twenty-six weeks in *Liberty* magazine. His attempts at fiction writing were, however, unsuccessful. He moved into radio broadcasting with NBC in 1929 and was an immediate success with his rapid-fire delivery. His radio contract contained a provision that if a war broke out he could break his contract and head to the front. In 1931 he covered the Sino-Japanese conflict for Hearst's International News Service. In the meantime he still broadcast reports for NBC. His interview in Mukden with the commander of Japanese forces was the first radio broadcast from the headquarters of an army in the field and the first to bridge the Pacific Ocean from the Asian continent. Gibbons went on to cover Italy's 1935 invasion of Ethiopia* and the Spanish Civil War* in 1936, which he described as the most brutal and inhumane of the nine wars he covered. He became one of the most recognized personalities of his day. He died of a heart attack on September 24, 1939. Gibbons wrote several books, including *How the Laconia Sank*, and *The Militia Mobilization on the Mexican Border: Two Masterpieces of Reporting* (1917).

REFERENCES: *DAB 22*, Supp. 2, 230-231; Edward Gibbons. *Floyd Gibbons, Your Headline Hunter*. 1953; Douglas Gilbert. *Floyd Gibbons, Knight of the Air*. 1930.

Gibbons, Israel (?)

The Northern-born Gibbons reported the American Civil War* from the Southern side. Prior to the war he worked as a compositor and local reporter for the *New Orleans Crescent*. He described Confederate camp life in his trademark folksy style at the outset of the conflict. He was one of the few Confederate war correspondents to cover the opening of the 1862 campaign in the West, reporting the fall of Nashville and the siege and bombardment of Island Number 10. After a furlough in Mobile he rejoined General Braxton Bragg's army in September 1863. Following the federal takeover of New Orleans in 1862, Gibbons reported for the *Mobile Register*.

REFERENCE: J. Cutler Andrews. *The South Reports the Civil War*. 1970.

Gibbs, Sir Philip Armand Hamilton (1877-1962)

Born in Kensington, England, Gibbs never attended public school due to lack of money and was homeschooled by his father. He joined the publishing house of Cassell at the age of 22. There he wrote *Founders of the Empire* (1899). After a short spell as literary editor he joined the *Daily Mail* and then Pearson's *Daily Express* before moving to the *Daily Chronicle*. He continued

to move from one paper to another before rejoining the *Daily Chronicle* in 1908, when he reported the siege at Sydney Street and helped expose as a hoax Dr. Cook's claim to have reached the North Pole first. In 1912 he covered the Balkan War for the *Daily Graphic*. By most accounts, this was where he developed his skills as a war correspondent, which would be put to the test in 1914.

In Paris at the outbreak of World War I,* Gibbs was appointed correspondent to the British Expeditionary Force. He was one of only five reporters allowed to wear the green brassard which distinguished the expedition correspondents. His dispatches were widely printed and syndicated in the United States. Gibbs became one of the preeminent British war correspondents of World War I, winning in the process the accolade of "Fleet Street's Finest War Correspondent." He was knighted in 1920 and made a chevalier of the Legion of Honor. Among his books on the war are *The Soul of War* (1915), *The Battle of the Somme* (1917), *From Bapaume to Passchendaele* (1918), *Realities of War* (1920), and *Now It Can Be Told* (1920).

Following the war he turned to freelance journalism and writing fiction, producing almost fifty books. During World War II* he reported from France for the *Daily Sketch*. He narrowly averted blindness in the 1940s when improvements in eye surgery were made available. Gibbs wrote several volumes chronicling his years on Fleet Street. He died on March 10, 1962.

REFERENCES: Robert W. Desmond. *Windows on the World*. 1980; *DNB*, 1961-1970; Martin J. Farrar. *News from the Front*. 1998.

Gibney, Frank Bray (1924-2006)

Born in Scranton, Pennsylvania and raised in New York City, he left college at Yale to fight in World War II, serving as an intelligence officer. After the war he was posted to Japan. He began working for *Time* magazine in 1947, covering Europe and Asia. He was the Time-Life bureau

Indicates a separate entry.

chief in Japan when the Korean War* started. During the war he shuttled back and forth between Korea and his Tokyo office. He reported the paucity of resources available to war reporters in the conflict noting "Never since and including the Civil War have correspondents had so few of the facilities vital to their trade." Press policy was improvised during the conflict and there was only one military phone line connecting Korean press headquarters to Tokyo, which was only available between 12 midnight and 4 am. He narrowly escaped death when the South Korean army prematurely detonated a bridge he was on during the evacuation of Seoul. After the war Gibney became a noted authority on Asian affairs and on postwar Japan. He wrote almost a dozen books, including several seminal books on Japan. His 1992 book *The Pacfic Century* was turned into a 10-part PBS series.

REFERENCES: Michelle Ferrari. *Reporting America at War*. 2003; Adam Bernstein. "Frank Gibney, 81; Authored Seminal Books on Japan." *Washington Post*, April 13, 2006; Margalit Fox. "Frank Gibney, Writer and Authority on Asia, Dies." *NYT*, April 14, 2006.

Gilbertson, Ashley (b. 1978)

Born in Melbourne, Australia, he developed an early affinity for photography. His early professional work focused on social issues in Australia and war zones in Southeast Asia and the South Pacific. Between 1999 and 2002 he focused on various international refugee crises throughout the world. In 2003 he covered the American-led invasion of Iraq and one of his photos was featured in that years' *Time Magazine's* "Pictures of the Year." Gilbertson covered the Battle of Fallujah in 2004 and was honored with the Robert Capa Award for his photographic work and bravery. He covered the Iraq War* for the *New York Times* until 2008. His work during the war was collected in *Whiskey Tango Foxtrot: A Photographer's Chronicle of the Iraq War* (2007). He continues to cover conflict, but in a way unlike any other photojournalist. In 2014 his book

Bedrooms of the Fallen was published featuring black-and-white photos depicting the bedrooms left behind by 40 American, Canadian, and European servicemen and -women (there are 40 soldiers in a platoon).

REFERENCE: http://www.ashleygilbertson.com/about. html.

Giles, Geoffrey Douglas (1857-1923)

An accomplished painter of the sporting life with exhibitions at prestigious galleries, Giles represented the *Graphic* during the Boer War,* accompanying the Kimberley Relief Column. He had prior military experience, having retired as an officer in the Indian army in 1884.

REFERENCE: Pat Hodgson. *The War Illustrators*. 1977.

Gishu, Nakayama (1900–1969)

Born Takama Yoshide in what is now the city of Shirakawa, his early career was spent teaching middle school. In the 1930s he began pursuing a literary career under the pen name Gishu Nakayama. His only foray into war reporting was as war correspondent during World War II.* His short story, *Teniyan no matsujitsu*, published in 1948, was inspired by his war experiences and tells the story of two intellectuals who died in the Mariana Islands campaign towards the end of the conflict. He became a well-known writer of historical fiction and short stories.

REFERENCE: http://en.wikipedia.org/wiki/ Gish%C5%AB_Nakayama.

Glover, Ridgeway (1831-1866)

Born in New Jersey, he developed an early interest in photography and by his thirties was a freelance photographer covering Fort Phil Kearny in Wyoming at the outbreak of the 1866 American Indian War.* Before leaving Philadelphia he made arrangements to send back news reports and photographs to the Philadelphia *Photographer* and *Frank Leslie's Illustrated Newspaper*. He also received sponsorship from The Smithsonian. In a journal he kept, Ridgeway described the difficulties of developing pictures on the frontier, citing limits imposed by the lack of good, clean, water sources. Although Glover was aware of hostile Indian activity around the fort, he persisted in venturing out alone, armed only with his photographic equipment and a butcher knife. He was killed by Arapahos on September 17, 1866, during one of his solitary excursions. Glover was apparently attempting to photograph Red Cloud's Sioux warriors near the fort. *Leslie's* published letters from the post chaplain and an officer detailing the demise of Glover on October 27 in an article entitled "The Fate of a Frank Leslie Special." He was reportedly the first photographer killed while attempting to take news photos in America. His photos never made it back home and are considered lost. These included rare photos he took at the 1866 treaty conference at Ft. Laramie.

REFERENCES: Michael L. Carlebach. *The Origins of Photojournalism in America.* 1992; Oliver Knight. *Following the Indian Wars.* 1960; Judy, "Frontier Photographer— Ridgeway Glover," http://writing.com/main/view_item/item_id/982344-Frontier-Photographer-Ridgeway-Glover.

Godkin, Edwin Lawrence (1831-1902)

Godkin was born in Moyne County, Wicklow, and educated at Queen's College, Belfast. He left his law studies for journalism and a writing career shortly after his graduation in 1851. His early interest in military affairs is exemplified by the publication of his first book, *The History of Hungary and the Magyars from the Earliest Period to the Close of the Late War* (1853). In 1853 he was hired as special correspondent by the *London Daily News* to cover the outbreak of the Crimean War* in Turkey and was one of the first correspondents on the scene. With the outbreak of the conflict he accompanied Omar

Pasha's army and remained in the Crimea until the cessation of hostilities in September 1855. His experiences during the conflict led to a lifelong disdain for warfare. He noted in his autobiography that the most significant outcome of the Crimean War was the creation of the profession of war journalism.

Shortly after moving to the United States in 1856 he toured the South, conducting a study of the slavery system, and in 1860 he became a member of the New York State bar. He was touring Europe in 1861 when the American Civil War* broke out. Unlike many of his countrymen he was a fervent supporter of the Union. Upon his return to the States in 1862 he covered the conflict for the *London Daily News* and also for American papers such as the *New York Times* and the *North American Review,* although not from the front lines.

In 1865 he established the *Nation,* a weekly magazine of opinion, which he edited and wrote for until selling it to the *Evening Post* in 1881. A confirmed advocate of peace, later in life he opposed the Spanish-American War,* the Boer War,* and America's annexation of Hawaii and the Philippines.

REFERENCES: Robert W. Desmond. *The Information Process.* 1978; Edwin Godkin. *Reflections and Comments.* 1895; Rollo Ogden. *Life and Letters of E. L. Godkin.* 1907.

Goldenberg, Suzanne (b. 1962)

This Canadian-born journalist began covering foreign events in 1988 for *The Guardian*. She has worked as that paper's South Asia and Middle East Correspondent, covering the Palestinian Intifada in 2000-2002 and the U.S. invasion of Iraq from Baghdad in 2003. She has covered a number of conflict zones, including the war in Chechnya, Georgia, and Nagorno Karabakh, and the Taliban takeover of Afghanistan. In 2009 she made the transition to U.S. environment correspondent for *The Guardian*. During her years as a war reporter she won a Bayeux-Calvados Award* for her Iraq reporting, and was recognized as Reporter of

Indicates a separate entry.

the Year by *What the Papers Say* for her reportage on the Israeli-Palestinian conflict.

REFERENCE: http://www.suzannegoldenberg.com/pages/author.html.

Goltz, Thomas (b. 1954)

Born in Japan and educated at New York University, this American journalist has been recognized for his reporting of the conflicts in the Caucasus region in the 1990s. For over a decade he has covered events in Turkey and the Caucasus region of the former Soviet Union. He covered the war between Azerbaijan and Armenia over Karabakh, the war of secession in Abkhazia from Georgia, and the Chechen conflicts. His fluency in German, Turkish, Arabic, Azeri, and Russian has helped him navigate the complex mélange of cultures in this region. He chronicled the years between the Karabakh War and the rise of Heydar Aliyev in Azerbaijan in the years following its separation from the Soviet Union in the book *Azerbaijan Diary*. His book *Chechnya Diary* details the story behind the 1995 Samashki Massacre.

REFERENCE: http://www.thomasgoltz.com/.

Goodall, Edward Angelo (1819-1908)

Goodall was a landscape artist with exhibitions at the Royal Academy and the Old Watercolour Society to his credit when he turned to war journalism in 1855. He served as war artist for his only campaign when he represented the *Illustrated London News* during the Crimean War.* However, the pioneer war photographer* Roger Fenton* criticized his sketches for "their total want of likeness to the reality." Following the war he returned to landscape painting.

REFERENCES: Helmut and Alison Gemsheim. *Roger Fenton, Photographer of the Crimean War.* 1973; Pat Hodgson. *The War Illustrators.* 1977.

Goode, Sir William Athelstane Meredith (1875-1944)

Born in Newfoundland to missionary parents, after attending Foyle College in Londonderry, Ireland, Goode went to sea, and in 1892 enlisted in the U.S. cavalry. He entered journalism in 1898, when he represented the Associated Press of America during the Spanish-American War.* He accompanied Admiral Sampson on board his flagship for most of the war. His exploits at sea are recorded in *Sampson Through the War* (1899). Following Lieutenant Hobson's courageous sinking of the *Merrimac* at the entrance to Havana harbor under an intense shelling, Goode scooped the competition by getting Hobson's only interview immediately after the action.

Goode was assigned to London as special correspondent from 1898 until 1904, when he joined the *Standard*. In 1911 he became joint news editor of the *Daily Mail*. During World War I* he organized various relief committees and was a member of the British delegation at the Peace Conference. In the postwar years he was best known for his reports on economic conditions and relief missions to Central Europe. He was knighted in 1918.

REFERENCES: Charles H. Brown. *The Correspondents' War.* 1967; *DNB*, 1941-1950; Oliver Gramling. AP: *The Story of News.* 1969.

Goralski, Robert Stanley (1928–1988)

Born in Chicago, Goralski served in the Navy during World War II.* He served as an NBC news correspondent between 1961 and 1975, during which time he covered the Vietnam War* for two years and the Arab Israeli War of 1967. He would also provide witness testimony during the My Lai massacre trials.

REFERENCE: "Robert Goralski, News Correspondent, 60," New York Times, Mar. 21, 1988.

Gorbatov, Boris (1908-1954)

Born in Ukraine, he published his first book in 1928. During the 1930s he covered the Urals and Siberia for PRAVDA. The Soviet novelist reported the Red Army's capture of Berlin and the subsequent bloody streetfighting. In his dispatch "In Berlin's Neighborhoods" he noted the surrender of Germans using baby diapers as surrender flags.

REFERENCE: http://www.sovietlit.com/war/inberlin. html.

Gore, Al (b.1948)

An outspoken critic of the Vietnam War in the 1960s and 70s, the future Senator, Vice President, Presidential candidate, and foe of global warming decided to enlist in the Army in 1969. Some have suggested he did so to salvage the political career of his father, Senator Al Gore, Sr. by neutralizing his father's political opponents' claims, during a tight Senatorial election in Tennessee, that Al Gore, Sr. was too tolerant of social protest. By some accounts the Nixon administration held up young Al's orders to go to Vietnam, fearful that he might be harmed and thus help his father's reelection. The senior Gore ultimately lost the 1970 Senate election, and in January 1971 his son was sent to Vietnam (one of about a dozen Harvard graduates out of the 1,115 in his 1969 graduating class). He was assigned to the 20th Engineer Brigade in Bien Hoa where he functioned as a reporter for *The Castle Courier*. He was awarded an honorable discharge five months later.

REFERENCES: David Maraniss and Ellen Nakashima. *The Prince of Tennessee*. 2000; Bill Turque. *Inventing Al Gore*. 2000.

Gore, William W. "Billy" (c. 1871-1935)

Born in Norfolk, England, he went to sea as a young man and then lived in Canada. In the 1890s he returned to England and became one of the first photographers with the London News Agency. He covered his first war from Tripoli during the Italian invasion, before moving to the *Daily Sketch,* and covering the 1912 Balkan War. While with the Bulgarian army he finagled permission to fly in one of the earliest air reconnaissance missions over a battlefield and in the process took the first aerial war photographs.

With the outbreak of World War I* in 1914 he took the first photographs of the war while with the *Daily Sketch* in Belgium. In 1920 he covered the conflict in Ireland for the *News Chronicle* and narrowly escaped being executed in a firing squad. For the next fifteen years he continued to work for the same paper, landing one of his greatest coups when he took aerial photos of the Dartmoor mutiny.

REFERENCE: Dennis Griffiths, ed. *The Encyclopedia of the British Press*. 1992.

Gorrell, Henry T. (1911-1958)

Born to American parents in Florence, Italy, Gorrell entered the newspaper business with the United Press in Kansas City in 1930. Three years later he was assigned to the Buenos Aires bureau. With the outbreak of the Ethiopian War,* Gorrell was dispatched to Rome as assistant United Press manager. He went on to cover the Spanish Civil War* and World War II* as war correspondent for the United Press.

In 1936 he was captured first by Republican soldiers and two weeks later was arrested by Spanish rebel forces. At the outset of World War II he was attached to the British fleet. In early 1941 he was with British and Greek troops under attack by German forces in Athens before moving on to Egypt, where he was accredited to the British Middle East Command.

In 1943 he received the Air Medal for saving the life of an injured bomber crewman while under heavy German fire during the raid on Navarino Bay on the Greek coast. He was also recognized

* Indicates a separate entry.

by the Headliners' Club for his coverage of the war in Greece. Following his excursion with the British Eighth Army in Libya, Gorrell moved on to Algiers, where he flew with a U.S. bomber group on raids over Italian naval forces in Naples. He went on to report the landing at Salerno during the Italian campaign and the 1943 Cairo Conference.

In 1944 Gorrell covered the D-Day landings and the capture of the port of Cherbourg. He covered the French campaign into 1945, before accompanying Allied forces into Germany for the final phase of the war in Europe. He was the first correspondent to cross into Germany, as a passenger in the lead vehicle as it entered Roetgen on September 11, 1945. After retiring from the UP later that year he joined *Veteran's Report* as its editor and publisher.

REFERENCES: Robert W. Desmond. *Tides of War.* 1984; Jack Stenbuck, ed. *Typewriter Battalion.* 1995; Henry T. Gorrell. *Soldier of the Press.* 2009.

Goto, Kenji (1967–2015)

Born in Sendai, Japan and educated at Hosei University, Goto was an active journalist between 1991 and his death in 2015. He founded Independent Press, a news website that covered conflict, refugee situations, and poverty. During his frequent foreign reporting stints he preferred to focus on the impact war has on the lives of ordinary people, concentrating much of his work in Africa and the Middle East. On several occasions he was warned by Japanese officials not to return to Syria. Over their protestations Goto made the fatal decision to go back. On October 24, 2014 he crossed into Syria from Turkey in hopes of helping rescue another Japanese hostage, Haruna Yukawa, captured by the Islamic State (ISIL)* in August. Goto was captured just a day later by ISIL members. On January 20, 2015 ISIL released a video demanding $200 million from the Japanese government for the release of the two hostages. Four days later another video appeared with Goto holding a photograph of his beheaded colleague. He was apparently forced to read a

message blaming his government for the execution and claiming that his life would be spared in exchange for unsuccessful suicide bomber, Sajida al-Rishawi, being held in Amman, Jordan. This is when negotiations became really complicated. On January 27 the Islamic State released another video threatening to kill Goto and captured Jordanian pilot Muath Kaseasbeh if al-Rishawi was not released. Jordanian officials agreed to release the failed suicide bomber but only if Goto and the Jordanian pilot were exchanged. The deal never came to pass and despite concerted efforts by human rights and journalism organizations, a video was released on January 31, 2015 showing Goto being decapitated. It later came out that Goto had been moved near the Turkish border in preparation for the possible prisoner exchange but when it appeared this wouldn't take place he was taken back to the vicinity of Raqqa and executed.

REFERENCES: "Kenji Goto," https://cpj.org/killed/2015/kenji-goto.php; Justin McCurry, "Isis Video Purports to Show Beheading of Japanese Hostage Kenji Goto," Guardian, Jan. 31, 2015.

Gotto, Basil (1866-1954)

Basil Gotto was a professional sculptor who turned to war journalism to cover the Boer War.* He sculpted the Army and Navy Club war memorial and the Newfoundland battle memorial. Following the war he served as a staff officer during World War I.*

REFERENCE: Robert Wilkinson-Latham. *From Our Special Correspondent.* 1979.

Govin, Charles (1873-1896)

Govin was a young correspondent for the Key West *Equator-Democrat* when he was assigned to cover the Cuban insurrection in 1896. Three days after landing he was killed ignominiously by a Cuban officer. He was apparently captured while in the company of insurgent forces. When the Cuban army officer found out he was an American, Govin was tied to a tree and hacked to death with machetes. Because he was a member of a prominent Key West family, his death caused a minor sensation in the United States.

REFERENCE: Charles H. Brown. *The Correspondents' War.* 1967.

Gowran, Clay (1914-1972)

Following graduation from Northwestern University he worked for the *Evansville Review* before joining the *Chicago Tribune* as a reporter, beginning a thirty-four-year relationship with the paper. He began covering World War II* in 1942. The first major operation he covered was the Allied counteroffensive against Japanese forces in the South Pacific during an amphibious landing at New Georgia Island in the Solomons. In 1943 he received the Edward Scott Beck Award for excellence for his account of a Japanese surprise attack that was repulsed by marines after they had slogged through water up to their necks in a counterattack during the Solomon Islands campaign. In 1944 he accompanied the Allied advance into Greece. Gowran was among the nine correspondents who flew on Superfortress bombing runs, the first American B-29 bombing attacks over Japan in June 1944.

Following the war he was engaged as foreign correspondent in the Middle East. He went on to cover conflicts and revolutions in Italy, Yugoslavia, Greece, Lebanon, and Palestine. During the campaign to create the state of Israel, Gowran joined the Jewish underground in Jerusalem to write a first-person account of the Stern gang, one of the militant Zionist groups trying to establish the Jewish homeland.

REFERENCES: Jack Stenbuck, ed. *Typewriter Battalion.* 1995; Lloyd Wendt. *Chicago Tribune: The Rise of a Great American Newspaper.* 1979.

Graham, George Edward (b. 1866)

Born in Albany, New York, Graham covered the Spanish-American War* for the Associated Press. He was with Admiral Schley aboard the flagship *Brooklyn* when the Spanish fleet attempted to escape from Santiago Harbor. He witnessed the subsequent naval battle which secured Santiago and virtually ended the war. He was the only noncombatant to witness the destruction of Cervera's fleet. He chronicled his wartime exploits in the 1902 book *Schley and Santiago.*

REFERENCES: Charles H. Brown. *The Correspondents' War.* 1967; Oliver Gramling. *AP: The Story of News.* 1940.

Grebnev, Viktor (b. 1907)

Grebnev began his career in photojournalism in the 1930s. With the outbreak of World War II* he began reporting for the army newspaper *Krasnaya Zvezda* or *Red Star.* He later transferred to the *Frontovik* or *Frontline Fighter* to get closer to the battlefield. He accompanied several other photographers raising the Soviet Banner of Victory over the Reichstag after the fall of Berlin. Following the war he worked as a journalist in Soviet occupied Germany and then turned to sportswriting upon his return to the Soviet Union.

REFERENCE: Daniela Mrazkova and Vladimir Remes, eds. *The Russian War: 1941-1945.* 1975.

Greco-Turkish War

In 1897 revolutionaries on Crete attempted to overthrow Turkish rule. The Greek government supported the movement by declaring war on Turkey. The conflict lasted five weeks and ended with a Turkish victory on May 21, 1897. The war drew a large contingent of war correspondents. While the majority came from Great Britain, the best-represented newspaper was the *New York Journal.*

American correspondents included *Journal* correspondents John Foster Bass,* Richard Harding Davis,* Stephen Crane,* James Creelman,* and Julian Ralph.* Other Americans on the scene of note were Sylvester Scovel* for the

Indicates a separate entry.

New York World, Frederick Palmer* for the *New York Press,* and Percival Phillips* for the *Pittsburgh Press.*

Among the formidable British war correspondents were Dr. Emile Joseph Dillon* and Bennet Burleigh* of the *Daily Telegraph,* Melton Prior* of the *Illustrated London News,* Francis Scudamore* of the *Daily News,* Frederic Villiers* for the *Standard,* and W. T. Maud* of the *Graphic.* Representing the *Times* were James David Bourchier,* Clive Bingham, and Edward Frederick Knight.* Other war reporters included George Warrington Steevens* of the *Daily Mail,* Henry W. Nevinson* for the *Daily Chronicle,* and John B. Atkins* of the *Manchester Guardian,* and for Reuters* W. Kinnaird Rose, H. A. Gwynne,* and Fergus Ferguson. Journalists accompanied armies on both sides of the conflict.

There is no evidence that any Greek or Turkish reporters were in the field. The only major continental power to have provided identifiable correspondents was France, with German, Russian, Austrian, and Italian representatives noticeably absent.

REFERENCES: Robert W. Desmond. *The Information Process.* 1978; Robert Wilkinson-Latham. *From Our Special Correspondent.* 1979.

Grenada Invasion

On October 25, 1983, the United States launched a massive invasion of the Communist-governed island nation of Grenada. Noticeably absent were any members of the press. This was the first American military campaign from which the Defense Department successfully excluded all journalists. With no independent reportage the media were forced to improvise. The *Washington Post* attempted to monitor developments through ham operator transmissions which gave conflicting accounts of the military operation. Networks resorted to three-dimensional maps, models, and file footage. Two days after

the invasion, reporters were permitted to visit Grenada. On the first day fifteen journalists and photographers were flown in for several hours, accompanied by a military escort. On the next day twenty-four were given permits and fifty more the following day. These military-directed pooling arrangements came under intense criticism. The fact that two days following the invasion there were 369 journalists waiting for accreditation in Barbados to report a war against approximately six hundred Cuban soldiers, comments on how unwieldy the presence of the news media can become on the battlefield.

REFERENCES: Derrik Mercer, Geoff Mungham, and Kevin Williams. *The Fog of War: The Media on the Battlefield.* 1987; Donald Atwell Zoll. "The Press and the Military: Some Thoughts After Grenada," *Parameters, Journal of the U.S. War College.* 1984.

Greenway, H. D. S. "David" (b. 1935)

Greenway began covering from conflict zones in 1967 when he was posted to Southeast Asia at the height of the Vietnam War* by *Time* magazine. During the war he was awarded a Bronze Star for helping rescue a wounded Marine and left Saigon by helicopter as the American embassy fell into enemy hands. He was with Sean Flynn* hours before he disappeared in Cambodia and escorted author John le Carre around Southeast Asia as he researched his book, *The Honorable Schoolboy.* In 1972, tired of the heavy-handed editing of his editors, Greenway joined the *Washington Post* and then the *Boston Globe* six years later. During his journalism career, he covered the Khmer Rouge siege of Phnom Penh alongside Sidney Schanberg* and Dith Pran, the civil war between east and west Pakistan, the civil war and bombing in Lebanon, the Balkans conflicts, both Gulf wars, and from both Iraq and Afghanistan as they drifted into turmoil. Greenway opened the *Post's* first bureau in Israel and covered the collapse of the Soviet Union. Prior to his retirement in 2000, Greenway had visited 96 countries. He chronicled his career in the book, *Foreign Correspondent: A Memoir* (2014).

REFERENCES: H.D.S. Greenway. *Foreign Correspondent: A Memoir*. 2014; Jonathan Yardley, "A Long-time Foreign Reporter Reflects on His Career," Washington Post, Aug. 8, 2014.

Gregg, Josiah (1806–1850)

Born in Overton, Tennessee, he began studying law, but health issues led him to move to Santa Fe in 1831 in hopes of recuperation. Gregg would go on to become a naturalist, explorer, and the author of *Commerce of the Prairies* (1844), a noted book on the geography, botany, and geology of the American Southwest and Northern Mexico. He reportedly brought the first printing press to New Mexico in 1834. He sold it and it was used to print the territory's first newspaper. Gregg learned Spanish and studied medicine for several semesters at the University of Louisville School of Medicine. He was heading back to Santa Fe when the Mexican American War* began, and left the convoy of wagons he was accompanying to join up with General John E. Wool's Arkansas Volunteers as an unofficial news correspondent and interpreter. Gregg by then was an accomplished and prominent authority on the Southwest and Wool figured he could act as a scout and advisor. But this arrangement did not work out, due to their acrimonious relationship. During the war he covered the Battle of Buena Vista, with his reports appearing in the *Louisville Journal* as well as the *Caddo Gazette* and the *St. Louis Daily Reveille*. His coverage consisted of personal letters sent to the newspaper editor, who had the option to decide whether to publish them or not. In the case of Buena Vista, where Gregg remained for five weeks after the battle continuing to gather information on events, the paper considered him "our interesting correspondent" who gave "a graphic description of the great battle." Moreover, his account of the battle was widely considered among the best of the battle. As for his commander General Wool, he apparently was

displeased with his reportage, regarding Gregg's stories as more gossip than news, and considered him too critical of the military. By most accounts by the time of the Battle of Buena Vista, Gregg no longer considered himself officially attached to Wool's command, acting more like a freelance reporter rather than a professional correspondent. He had hoped to ride as an aide to General Zachary Taylor in some sort of official capacity but was rejected in his last-minute attempt and was forced to watch the battle from "high and commanding points" where he claimed to have been as exposed to musket and canon fire as if he were actually in the heat of battle. Following the Battle of Buena Vista he stayed in Saltillo studying the flora and working as a doctor. In 1849 he left on a business trip to the West Coast. He succumbed to sickness while exploring California's northern coastal region on February 25, 1850.

REFERENCE: Tom Reilly. War *with Mexico!: America's Reporters Cover the Battlefront*, Manley Witten, ed. 2010.

Grepp, Gerda J. Helland (1907–1940)

A Norwegian translator and journalist, Grepp covered the Spanish Civil War* for the Labour Party newspaper *Arbeiderbladet* beginning in 1936. She was the first Scandinavian female reporter to cover the conflict. She witnessed the bombing of Madrid and action on the Toledo Front. In 1937 she was in Malaga, along with the Hungarian reporter Arthur Koestler,* covering the war for England's *News Chronicle*. While the Battle of Malaga raged, she managed to escape. Koestler however was not so lucky. He was arrested and sentenced to death as a spy. Following a storm of international criticism he was released. May 1937 found Grepp covering the Basque region in northern Spain, where she reported the movements of the Republican Basque Army defensive line, known as the "Iron Belt," during the Battle of Bilbao. However, tuberculosis turned out to be her greatest nemesis, forcing

* Indicates a separate entry.

her to leave the conflict zone and return home, where she died from the disease. She was widely regarded as Norway's first female war journalist.

REFERENCE: Paul Preston. *We Saw Spain Die: Foreign Correspondents in the Spanish Civil War.* 2009.

Griffiths, Philip Jones
(1936-2008)

The self-taught photojournalist was born in Rhuddlan, Wales. He left the pharmacy business to become a freelance photojournalist in 1961. Since then he has covered the Vietnam War,* the Algerian War, the Yom Kippur War, and conflict in Cambodia and Thailand. He has served as president of Magnum Photos.

His three years covering the Vietnam conflict are chronicled in his collection of images entitled *Vietnam, Inc.,* which took four years to produce. With its emphasis on the horrors of war and its effects on civilians, it has often been described as one of the finest documents of war photography.* After its publication in the United States, the South Vietnamese government banned his return to Saigon.

In 1973 Griffiths returned to Cambodia for his third visit to the conflict, narrowly escaping death at the hands of the Khmer Rouge during an artillery attack. He was one of the first photojournalists to arrive in Israel at the outbreak of the Yom Kippur War in October 1973. With new censorship restrictions implemented since the Six Day War, Griffiths was forced to rely on his own resourcefulness to get to frontline action. He hired private drivers to help him evade Israeli roadblocks. During his three-week stay in Israel he would end up losing three cars, one of which took a direct hit by a shell. Due to prohibitive laboratory fees and military censorship he smuggled his pictures out of the country. One photograph would grace the cover of *Newsweek* magazine.

REFERENCES: *Contemporary Photographers.* 1982; Jorge Lewinski. *The Camera at War.* 1978.

Grondjis, Lodewijk Hermen
(1878-1961)

Grondjis was born in what is now Indonesia. He had the makings for a great academic career and at university studied mathematics and physics before moving on to philosophy and co-founding the *Journal of Philosophy.* He left academia in 1914 to work as war corespondent for the *Nieuwe Rotterdamsche Courant* after the First World War broke out in 1914. He covered early actions in Belgium and reported German war crimes at Leuven and the siege at Antwerp. His book *The Germans in Belgium—Notes of a Dutch Eye-Witness* chronicles his reportage during this period. He later covered the conflict in France and reported for a number of international newspapers and magazines. He was awarded the Belgian Order of the Crown for saving 50 Belgian clergymen from execution during the purported "Rape of Belgium." In 1915 Grondjis was invited by General Aleksei Brusilov to follow the Russian 8th Army as a reporter for the *Daily Telegraph.* The French weekly news magazine *L'Illustration* published many of his reports from the Eastern Front. He was especially appreciated by the Russian fighting men for the accolades he heaped on their fighting qualities in his reportage. By most accounts he enjoyed the exhilaration of wartime reporting and even fought alongside Russian forces on a number of occasions. The Russians would eventually award him the Imperial Russian Order of St. George, Order of St. Stanislaus, Order of St. Anna and Order of St. Vladimir. Grondjis would also report the onset of the Russian Revolution from Petrograd in 1917 and reported the Russian Civil War alongside the counter-revolutionary White forces. He was reportedly the only western war correspondent to follow the Volunteer Army in the Kuban Campaign in June 1918. That same year he became an accredited war correspondent for the French government. What was most perplexing was how he also won a doctorate degree in physics at the University of Charkov in 1917 despite his journalistic endeavors. Over subsequent decades he lectured against the Communist Revolution and lectured on Byzantine history and art at Utrecht University. But in the late 1930s he once more answered the siren call of war reporting, debarking for Manchuria to cover the Japanese invasion and then the Spanish Civil War.

REFERENCE: www.greatwardifferent.com/Great_War/ Reporters_East_ Front/Grondjis_00.htm.

Gross, Gad Schuster (d. 1991)

Born in Romania and educated at Harvard, Gross, representing *Newsweek* on a freelance basis, was the only journalist killed during the Gulf War.* He was killed on March 21, 1991, while traveling with several colleagues in the Kurdish region of northern Iraq.

REFERENCE: Michael Emery. *On the Front Lines*. 1995.

Grossman, Vasily Semyonovich (1905–1964)

Born in Berdichev, Russian Empire (now Ukraine), Grossman was a trained engineer and began writing short stories while studying at Moscow State University. By the mid-1930s he left engineering to concentrate on writing full-time. With the German invasion of the Soviet Union in 1941, although exempt from military service, Grossman volunteered for frontline service, where he would spend almost three years. During the war he put his writing talents to work as a war correspondent for the army newspaper, *Krasnaya Zvezda* (Red Star). He covered most of the major battles of the Soviet-German theater, including the Battle for Moscow, Stalingrad, the Battle of Kursk, and the Battle of Berlin. Many of his novels were based on his wartime experiences. First published in his newspaper, the novel *Stalingrad*, based on the siege of that city, was published in 1950. Grossman was able to collect some of the first eyewitness descriptions of the Nazi death camps as early as 1943 and was present at the

Red Army liberation of Treblinka and Majdanek. During the Nuremberg Trials, an article he had written in 1944, "The Hell of Treblinka," was used as evidence by the prosecution. Following the war Grossman often found himself in conflict with Soviet censors as he pursued a project to document the Holocaust. He wrote a number of books that would not be published until after his death in 1964 from stomach cancer.

REFERENCE: Antony Beevor and Luba Vinogradova. *A Writer at War: Vasily Grossman with the Red Army, 1941-1945*. 2006.

Gruneison, Charles Lewis (1806-1879)

Born in Bloomsbury, England, he became one of the earliest war correspondents after joining the *Morning Post* as a special and covering the Carlist army during the Spanish Civil War of 1834-1839. His dispatches were so accurate that he was arrested by the conservative Carlist supporters of Don Carlos, the pretender to the throne of Spain. Tried as a spy, he escaped with his life thanks to the intervention of the British government. Following his deportation, one Spanish officer commented that the reporter had done more damage with his pen than the Carlist generals had done with their swords, and that he would have no compunction about shooting all Carlist correspondents. In 1839, following his Spanish exploits he was made the *Morning Post* correspondent in Paris, a post he held for five years. He returned to London, where he became well known as the music critic for the *Athenaeum*. He wrote *The Opera and the Press* (1869).

REFERENCE: Robert Wilkinson-Latham. *From Our Special Correspondent*. 1979.

Guernica

One of the best-known and most controversial incidents of the Spanish Civil War* was the bombing of Guernica, a small town near the

* *Indicates a separate entry.*

Basque capital of Bilbao, in northern Spain. The Basques of Guernica supported the Republican government in its war against the Nationalists. In March 1937 Nationalist general Emilio Mola proclaimed that unless the Basques submitted to his forces he would destroy parts of their homeland. After they failed to do so Mola ordered his air force, composed of German planes and pilots, to level Guernica. Although it is uncertain how many died on April 26, 1937, estimates vary between one and two thousand.

One of the first correspondents to enter the city was George Steer* of the *Times*. His account of the bombing was featured on the front pages of the *New York Times* and the *Times* of London. What is most significant about his report is the claim that the town did not represent a military objective. When Franco's forces took control of the town several days later, the Nationalists countered with claims that the Basques destroyed the town themselves to gain sympathy for the Loyalist cause. What added to the controversy was a feature article run by the *Times* which gave credence to the Nationalist contention that the destruction of the town was due to Basque incendiaries rather than strategic bombing. Recent evidence contradicts the claim that the town was not a military objective and that the bombing was meant to demoralize the population. According to historian Hugh Thomas, Guernica could have been used as a destination for Basque and Republican forces to regroup and was thus a military objective.

This incident was but a harbinger of the age of indiscriminate bombing of civilian targets and total warfare that would characterize World War II.* Most analysts of World War II are convinced that the mass destruction and haphazard bombing of civilian targets which characterized the war had its genesis during the Spanish Civil War, in which the German Luftwaffe went through practice runs in preparation for the looming conflict.

REFERENCES: Phillip Knightley. *The First Casualty.* 1975; Phillip Knightley. *The Master Spy.* 1989.

Gulf War

In August 1990 Iraqi troops invaded Kuwait, inaugurating a new era in war journalism in which print reporters were consistently scooped by television newscasts from CNN that delivered the news instantaneously, while it took up to several weeks for print coverage to reach the public. According to media historian Johanna Neuman, the Gulf War was the "first showdown between military hardware and satellite communication, pitting global media saturation against military needs for security." The Gulf War was the beginning of an era in which television viewers did not necessarily watch warfare, but the collecting of news in a war zone. For the first time in U.S. military history Western television journalists covered war from enemy capitals and reported the damage caused by American firepower.

Perhaps no news service was impacted as strongly as CNN, which saw its viewership reach more than one million. By the time allied troops were advancing toward Baghdad, CNN was drawing a nightly audience of almost seven million, just two million shy of the major networks. The main difference between the cable network and the big three (ABC, CBS, and NBC) was that CNN's audience was worldwide. The advent of rooftop journalism* made stars of correspondents Peter Arnett,* John Holliman, Bernard Shaw, and others, as they described aerial assaults and missile attacks in "real time" to viewers around the world. The introduction of satellite journalism was unprecedented. But technology stopped at the edge of the battlefield as reporters labored to send their dispatches back to New York. Some reports took as long as two weeks to reach Dharan from the battlefield, while one photographer waited six weeks for his film to arrive. However, despite the proximity to the war zone, the American public was not bombarded by images of dead and wounded GIs, as it was during the "uncensored" Vietnam War.* Reports instead described high-tech weapons, military officers and defense experts conducting interviews, enemy soldiers surrendering to American reporters, and careful censorship.

The war consisted of two phases, a five-month buildup and then a 100-hour desert war. By the time the ground war began in February 1991, more than 1,400 journalists had arrived in Saudi Arabia to report the war. The correspondents averaged forty-seven stories during an average tour of seven weeks. Journalists were reliant on military briefings, interviews with military officials, or pooled coverage* for updated information. The war in the Persian Gulf was one of the most restricted battlefields of the modern era. Photographers were often prevented from getting anywhere near the front lines. Correspondents noted the similarities between the Gulf War and the 1982 Falklands War,* in which the media were skillfully manipulated. There were precedents in recent American military campaigns for the Gulf censorship. During the 1983 Grenada* invasion reporters were kept three hundred miles away from the action, and during the 1989 Panama incursion the press pool was kept on a U.S. air base until the fighting was over. During the Gulf War, of the initial 150 journalists chosen for the pool system, only half were allowed to accompany troops at any one time. However, by the time the brief desert campaign got under way, 159 correspondents were with American combat units, more than twice the coverage of any previous modern war.

At times there were as few as sixteen reporters covering over a half million troops. There were numerous anomalies in the press coverage. It took the vaunted *New York Times* three weeks to place a correspondent in the press pool, and only three pool positions were available for some three hundred foreign journalists. Correspondents for the radical magazine *Mother Jones* were refused coverage, while a fashion magazine was selected for a pool spot. Any infraction by the media was dealt with swiftly. After one correspondent wrote an article about Iraqi soldiers being torn apart by Apache helicopters his position was revoked, and when another reported numerous U.S. military vehicles missing, he was ejected from the press pool.

Numerous reports were censored or held up. One reporter claimed that only one third of his twenty-seven stories escaped the censor's pen. While public opinion surveys demonstrated that Americans found press coverage adequate and favored military censorship, a correspondent noted that "if World War II had been covered by pools there would never have been a national treasure named Ernie Pyle."* Coverage of the war became more difficult for reporters as the campaign pushed out into the desert. Army field phones and tactical fax machines were not adaptable to Saudi Arabia's commercial telecommunications system and most were kept off limits to the press corps. While the army had designed a pony-express-style courier system, it was understaffed and poorly trained, resulting in news copy, film, and videotape getting lost in the desert wastes.

As the ground war proceeded in February 1991, journalists left their military escorts to accompany the myriad forces advancing on Kuwait. American correspondents entered the war zone with Egyptian, Saudi, and Kuwaiti forces and arrived in Kuwait City a day before the official pool reporters. Because of press censorship and the pool system the coverage of the Gulf War was relatively superficial. Among the thousands of photographs taken by forty photographers on the battlefield there are no shots of American tanks firing during massive tank engagements and there are few pictures of dead soldiers. One correspondent designated the conflict "the Unseen War" because of the number of reports and photographs that have not been released.

REFERENCES: Michael Emery. *On the Front Lines.* 1995; John J. Fialka. *Hotel Warriors: Covering the Gulf War.* 1991; Johanna Neuman. *Lights, Camera, War: Is Media Technology Driving International Politics?* 1996.

Gwynne, Howell Arthur (1865-1950)

Born in the district of Kilvey, near Swansea, he was educated on the Continent. His chance meeting

---

Indicates a separate entry.

with the king of Rumania while on holiday, and their ensuing friendship, led to his career in journalism. He served as Balkan correspondent for the *Times* and in 1893 became the Reuters* correspondent in Rumania, beginning a ten-year relationship as a war reporter for the news agency.

He covered the Ashanti War in 1895 and the following year was with General Kitchener at Dongola. Over the next several years he reported from the Turkish side during the 1897 Greco-Turkish War* and then from Peking the following year. In 1898 Gwynne was the only civilian correspondent allowed up the Nile with Kitchener's punitive Sudan expedition after the death of Gordon, and for a short time he covered the Spanish-American War* in Cuba. With the outbreak of war in South Africa in 1899, he organized Reuters' war service there. Gwynne was in charge of almost one hundred Reuters reporters and stringers* during the Boer War.* He gave Edgar Wallace* his first position in journalism. Gwynne was present during Methuen's campaign, and the Battle of Magersfontein, and later began a long friendship with Lord Roberts, accompanying his forces into the field.

He returned to England for a short time in 1902, but soon after was with Joseph Chamberlain on a political tour of South Africa. After the murder of the Serbian king and queen in 1904 he went to Belgrade as Reuters' foreign director and later that year became editor of the *Standard*. In 1911 he began a long tenure as editor of the *Morning Post*.

REFERENCES: *DNB*, 1941-1950; Donald Read. *The Power of News*. 1992.

H

Haeberle, Ronald (b.1940)

During the Vietnam War at least 1,500 members of the various branches of the military served as war photographers, including Sergeant Ronald Haeberle of the 11th Infantry Brigade. He is best known for taking the photographs of the March 16, 1968 My Lai massacre that exposed one of the worst war crimes committed by American forces during the conflict. Following an honorable discharge he returned to the United States in 1969. The following year the *Cleveland Plain Dealer* published his photo of women and children about to be massacred by Lt. Calley's soldiers. While the pictures contributed to growing opposition to the war at home, a large percentage of Americans were not convinced they were real because no American soldiers were shown in the act of killing them. In a rare interview some 40 years after the incident Haeberle admitted after years of denials that he did have pictures of the killings in progress but decided to destroy them. Asked in 2009 if he wished he had done something differently at My Lai he responded "It's hard to say in the aftermath… You don't know. Until you're in that reality. You never know."

REFERENCES: Evelyn Theiss. "My Lai photographer Ron Haeberle admits he destroyed pictures of soldiers in the act of killing." *Cleveland Plain Dealer*, November 20, 2009; Duncan Anderson. *War A Photo History*. 2006; Susan D. Moeller. *Shooting War*. 1989.

Haidari, Aziz Ullah (1968–2001)

Born in Kabul, Afghanistan, at the age of twelve he fled to Pakistan with his family after the Soviet invasion, eventually settling in Peshawar. He began his career in journalism in 1987 working for Pashto and Persian media. In 1990 he joined Reuters* as a translator and within two years was promoted to a foreign correspondent. Haidari was in a convoy of vehicles carrying a number of journalists when it was ambushed and he was murdered along with Julio Fuentes from Spain's *El Mundo*, Australian cameraman Harry Burton, and Milan-based Maria Grazia Cutuli.* They were killed on November 19, 2001, while traveling between Jalalabad and Kabul.

REFERENCE: http://cpj.org/killed/2001/azizullah-haidari.php.

Haile, Christopher Mason (1815–1848)

Born in Rhode Island, Haile received a West Point appointment in 1836. He left the academy early and moved to Louisiana, where he joined the *Planter's Gazette* as editor. He later quit the paper for the *New Orleans Picayune* and gained a following with his satirical letters under the byline "Pardon Jones." During the Mexican-American War* he represented the paper as a war correspondent under the direction of George Wilkins Kendall.*

Indicates a separate entry.

Kendall, Haile, and another correspondent were escorted by Texas Rangers as far as Matamoras, on the Rio Grande border, where they reported the progress of the army under General Zachary Taylor. Haile accompanied General Worth's column as it advanced from the west at the Battle of Monterrey. Kendall joined Haile in the western part of the city, and their account of the battle filled nine columns of the *Picayune*. Their coverage was criticized for having only witnessed the fighting in the western part of the city, where casualties were much less, and not reporting the more bloody and spectacular struggle on the eastern side.

Following the victory Kendall left for New Orleans, while Haile remained with Taylor's troops. Haile compiled a list of the dead and wounded at Monterrey and wrote an informative account of the aftermath, listing captured arms and munitions as well as the names, ranks, places, and dates of the dead and wounded.

After Monterrey, Haile turned to less serious fare, writing light sketches in the form of reports from the quixotic "Pardon Jones" to General Taylor and President Polk. Haile was not long behind Kendall in returning to the Crescent City. However, as the war dragged on, Haile was assigned to follow the Veracruz campaign along the coast. The army made use of Haile's military training when during the siege of Veracruz he was commissioned a lieutenant, leaving Kendall the only war correspondent for the *Picayune*.

REFERENCES: Fayette Copeland. *Kendall of the Picayune*. 1943; Robert W. Johannsen. *To the Halls of the Montezumas*. 1985; Martha A. Sandweiss, Rick Stewart, and Ben W. Huseman. *Eyewitness to War*. 1989.

Halberstam, David (1934–2007)

Born in New York and educated at Harvard, he entered journalism in 1956 with the *Nashville Tennessean*. Four years later he was hired by the *New York Times*. In 1960 Halberstam covered his first conflict when he reported the Katanga uprising in the Congo. During the Vietnam War*

he quickly developed a reputation for his controversial reporting, coming under fire from the Pentagon and the White House. As a Vietnam correspondent for the *New York Times* during the 1960s, he was one of the first reporters to question the veracity of official death counts, and defeats represented as victories. He shared the Pulitzer Prize with Malcolm W. Browne* in 1964.

He left the *Times* in 1967 for *Harper's* magazine. After leaving that magazine Halberstam embarked on a highly successful career writing nonfiction, including the bestsellers *The Best and the Brightest* (1972), *The Powers That Be* (1979), *The Making of a Quagmire* (1963), *The Fifties* (1993) and *The Coldest Winter: America and the Korean War* (2007).

REFERENCES: Michael Emery. *On the Front Lines*. 1995; William Prochnau. *Once upon a Distant War*. 1995.

Hall, Sydney Prior (1842–1922)

The Cambridge-educated war artist was hired by the *Graphic* to cover his only war, the Franco-Prussian War* in 1870. The son of a prominent painter of the sporting life, Hall had achieved a reputation as an artist in his own right before taking employment as an illustrator for the newly established *Graphic*.

Following his arrival in France he came under suspicion with his sketch book, a risk assumed by all war artists. He was arrested three times by the French in August alone. In September he was arrested by the Germans. One of his colleagues described Hall as the best artist among the specials of the period; however, it is difficult to judge the quality of his work since the engravings made from his sketches for his paper were somewhat mediocre. But his book, *Sketches from an Artist's Portfolio* (1875), supports his colleague's praise. One of the preeminent war reporters of his era, Archibald Forbes,* opined that Hall's sketches of the Franco-Prussian War were so remarkable that they "can never cease to be remembered by anyone who saw them."

In October 1870 Hall arrived with the Prussian army in Paris, where he bought a horse and named it "Graphy" after his employer. He continued with the *Graphic* following the war and received recognition for his illustrations of royal tours and court functions. Later he journeyed through the American West for the *Graphic*.

REFERENCE: Pat Hodgson. *The War Illustrators.* 1977.

Halstead, Murat (1829–1908)

After graduation from college in 1851 Halstead worked for several Cincinnati newspapers before going to the *Cincinnati Commercial* in 1853, where he would be employed for the next half century. His first national assignment as a congressional reporter allowed him the opportunity to stop at Harpers Ferry en route to Washington, where he witnessed the hanging of the abolitionist John Brown.

His early criticism of the Union war effort during the American Civil War* led his competitors to give him the sobriquet "Field Marshal." He covered the Battle of Fredericksburg (1862), which he described as a "blunder and disaster" after witnessing the decimation of his home state Ohio regiments. After being told by Henry Villard* that Brigadier General Sherman had requested two hundred thousand men Halstead became convinced that Sherman was "unhinged," resulting in the headline "General Sherman Insane" in the *Cincinnati Commercial*. This misleading story was widely reprinted in other newspapers.

While he was on vacation in Paris in 1870 the Franco-Prussian War* broke out and he immediately applied for authorization to cover it. Reporting for Cincinnati, Ohio, a city and a state with a large German population, he recognized that reporting this conflict would enlarge the *Commercial's* readership. Ordinarily the *Commercial* would not be able to afford to cover the war and would rely on newsletters from English correspondents, so that Halstead's presence in Paris was quite a coup for the newspaper.

In France he was constantly harassed by military censors and endless reporting restrictions. After his application for war correspondent credentials was denied he headed to Germany, where he witnessed firsthand his only battle of the war, the Prussian victory at the Battle of Gravelotte. Also present from his vantage point were the American general Philip Sheridan, Chancellor Bismarck, and von Moltke. He wrote numerous books of history, biography, and public affairs, including his most successful book, a biography of McKinley which sold over 700,000 copies after his assassination in 1901.

REFERENCES: *DLB 23*, 155–160; Donald Walter Curl. "An American Reporter and the Franco-Prussian War," *Journalism Quarterly 49*. Fall 1972, 480–88.

Hammerl, Anton Lazarus (1969–2011)

Born in Johannesburg, South Africa, Hammerl was drafted into the South African Defense Force during the Apartheid era, serving in Angola for two years before leaving the army to study photography at Pretoria Technikon. In 1992 he caught on with the *Saturday Star* as a freelance photojournalist. He later freelanced for the Associated Press and covered the events surrounding the end of apartheid in 1994. In 1995 he was back with the *Star* and was promoted to senior photographer for several independent South African newspapers. He continued his photojournalism career in a variety of capacities with the *Saturday Star*. His last years before his death were spent as a freelance photojournalist based in London. On April 5, 2011, Hammerl and three other journalists were attacked by Libyan troops while out in a desert location moving toward the battlefront. Along with Hammerl, were James Foley,* Clare Morgana Gillis, and the Spanish photographer Manu Brabo. Soon after the gunfire erupted, Foley and Gillis reported that Hammerl yelled for help, but to no avail. Hammerl died and the other three were captured and beaten by pro-Gaddafi forces. To make

* Indicates a separate entry.

matters even worse, the Libyan government went through the charade with Hammerl's family that he was still alive for 45 days. As late as May 17, the Libyan government was promising to release the deceased photojournalist. Two days later the truth won out, and the story of his death made its way back to his family following the release of the three other journalists who had seen him perish in the desert.

REFERENCE: "Anton Hammerl," http://www.cpj.org/killed/2011/anton-hammerl-.php.

Hancock, Daniel Witt (1907–1942)

Hancock showed an interest in journalism while still in high school, reporting local sports events for his hometown Bluefield, West Virginia newspaper. Following college he worked for various newspapers in North and South Carolina before joining the Associated Press in 1929. He eagerly sought an international posting and in 1936 was assigned to England. In 1939 he arrived in Moscow to cover his most important assignment to date, witnessing the signing of the Russian-German Alliance pact at the Kremlin. He served as Moscow's AP chief for 13 months reporting on the Russian invasion of Finland, the invasion of Poland and the purported liberation of Estonia-Latvia. Hancock fled Moscow for Turkey beginning a stint there from Septemebr 1940 until July 1941. He then went to Karachi, India and moved on to cover the war in Asia. He was one of two reporters to witness the evacuation of the Dutch East Indies before the Japanese onslaught. He escaped on the *Poelau Bras*, a Dutch luxury liner debarking from South Java on March 6, 1942. However, later that day, Japanese dive bombers attacked the vessel, crippling it as its passengers fled the ship. Hancock was shot and killed as he prepared to leave the ship. According to one expert this was "the first loss of an American correspondent since the U.S. officially entered the war."

REFERENCE: Doral Chenoweth, *54 War Correspondents KIA in WWII*, Chapter 3, 2003.

Hands, Charles E. (1860–1937)

Hands entered journalism with the *Birmingham Daily Mail* while in his twenties, before moving to the *Pall Mall Gazette* and the *Star,* where as "Starman" he became well known for his descriptive writing style. In 1896 he joined the *Daily Mail* and began his career as one of the best-known war correspondents of his era.

In 1898 he covered the Spanish-American War* from Cuba and in 1900 was in South Africa reporting the Boer War* when he was wounded while attached to the Mafeking* relief force on May 12. He covered the Russo-Japanese War* in 1904, although restricted by the extraordinary Japanese press censorship.

REFERENCE: Robert Wilkinson-Latham. *From Our Special Correspondent.* 1979.

Hangen, Welles (1930–1970)

After graduation from Brown University and a stint as a foreign correspondent for the *New York Times,* news correspondent Welles Hangen, after a twelve-year career with NBC, disappeared with three television newsmen south of the Cambodian capital of Phnom Penh in May 1970. He was one of eleven correspondents to disappear along a dangerous stretch of highway controlled by the Khmer Rouge shortly before the Cambodian holocaust, which claimed over one million victims. Local villagers recounted that the missing journalists were held for three days, then killed and buried. Twenty-two years later, a U.S. Department of Defense team unearthed the remains of Hangen and several of his colleagues from their graves, along a riverbed, thirty-four miles from Phnom Penh.

REFERENCE: Charles P. Arnot. *Don't Kill the Messenger.* 1994.

Harden, Edwin W. (1868–1903)

Harden reported the Spanish-American War* from the Philippines for the *New York World.*

Harden was abroad the *McCulloch* as the Asiatic Squadron approached the Spanish fleet in Manila Harbor. Harden was one of only three correspondents to witness the Battle of Manila Bay on May 1, 1898. Commodore George Dewey's squadron sank eleven Spanish ships without the loss of any American seamen or ships. Harden's account of the battle scooped the competition.

REFERENCES: Charles H. Brown. *The Correspondents' War.* 1967; Robert W. Desmond. *The Information Process.* 1978.

Harding, George Matthews (1882–1959)

Born in Philadelphia, he studied art with Howard Pyle and others before joining the staff of *Harper's Monthly.* After the U.S. entered World War I he was commissioned one of eight official AEF artists. Harding was distinguished from his colleagues by his use of a camera in the collecting of materials for later art work. His first coverage was near Neufchatueau, France, and in June 1918 he covered the troops at Chateau-Thierry. The following month Harding accompanied the 3rd Division as it advanced across the Marne toward the battle front. In August, Harding sketched a number of drawings of captured German positions in the vicinity of Vesle, and interviewed American soldiers involved in combat operations there. The following month he covered troop movements during the St. Mihiel campaign, and witnessed battles at Varennes and Montfaucon, as the AEF began the Meuse-Argonne offensive. In October he was with troops in the Argonne forest as he continued to cover the lives of soldiers. He accompanied troop movements throughout the French campaign and at Armistiace he was with the troops at Sedan on the Mesue River. He covered the beginning of the occupation of Germany before returning to Paris. Like other artists, Harding found it was impractical to do anything but begin sketches in combat areas. His wartime artistry was almost matched by the impressions recorded in his diary, which later made the transition to canvas. His biographer

claimed Harding's drawings were "concerned with the effect of the war on the persons involved" rather than scenes of "panoramic sweeps of the battlefield." Six months after his discharge from the AEF he finished his portfolio, *The American Expeditionary Forces in Action* (1920), a set of 38 color plates that are considered among the best at capturing the American soldier's experience in the war. He sought an active role in the next war after the bombing of Pearl Harbor. Although sixty years old, he gladly accepted a commission as a U.S. Marine Corps captain and spent almost two years in the South Pacific. During this period, he produced more than 600 mostly crayon and watercolor pictures, while covering Marine landings on Bougainville, New Georgia, Munda, and Guam.

REFERENCE: Alfred Emile Cornebise. *Art from the Trenches.* 1991.

Hardman, Frederick (1814–1874)

Son of a London merchant, he rebelled against the placid life of the countinghouse by joining the lancers of the British Legion in Spain in 1834. He returned to England after being severely wounded in one of the final actions against the Carlists. Back home he became a regular contributor to *Blackwood* magazine. In 1850 he became a foreign correspondent for the *Times.* He covered the Russo-Turkish War,* in which he exposed the problems of drunkenness in the British army. Hardman witnessed the campaigns in Lombardy, Morocco, and Schleswig as well as the military actions at Tours and Bordeaux in 1870–1871 during the Franco-Prussian War.* He later became the chief correspondent for the *Times* in Paris.

REFERENCES: Robert W. Desmond. *The Information Process.* 1978; *DNB;* Joseph J. Mathews. *Reporting the Wars.* 1957.

Hardy, Albert "Bert" (1913–1955)

The self-taught photographer was born in London. He began his career using a small plate

---

* *Indicates a separate entry.*

camera that he bought for ten shillings. Later he would become one of the first photojournalists to use the early Leicas. He served as a photographer in the British army in France and Germany from 1942 to 1946. Early in the war he began his affiliation with the *Picture Post*. His pictures of the London blitz were among the best and closest to the action of any cameraman. His overseas coverage began in 1944 with the D-Day invasion and the Dieppe raid. Perhaps his best work came during the liberation of Paris and the preparation and crossing of the Rhine River into Germany. He also photographed the Greek Civil War, the Burmese war against the Karens, and the Malayan insurrection.

Hardy was once again at the front lines with the outbreak of the Korean War.* Representing the *Picture Post*, he was teamed with writer James Cameron.* Hardy and Cameron accompanied amphibious forces during the Inchon landing in 1950 and later reported the mistreatment of North Korean prisoners by South Korean troops. Although Hardy spent less than two months in Korea, his pictures are among the most memorable of the conflict. His last story of the war, on the Inchon landing, was awarded the *Encyclopedia Britannica* Award for the best picture series of the year. His war photography* is chronicled in *Bert Hardy, Photojournalist* (1975).

REFERENCE: Jorge Lewinski. *The Camera at War.* 1978.

Hare, James H. "Jimmy"
(1856–1946)

Born in London, the son of a successful camera manufacturer, Hare left college early to enter his father's trade. By the early 1880s he had become a freelance photographer before taking employment with the *Illustrated American* in 1895. He showed an early interest in naval photography. In 1898 he put it to use following the mysterious sinking of the battleship *Maine* in Havana Harbor. Hare offered his services to *Collier's Weekly*, or as one contemporary remarked, "The *Maine*

BLEW UP and JIMMY BLEW IN." He was promoted to special correspondent by the weekly on the strength of his pictures of the aftermath of the ship's explosion.

His pictures of the damaged battleship and the conditions in the internment camps in Cuba led to his elevation in status to "special photographer" for the *Weekly*. After a respite in the States, Hare returned to Cuba after war was declared. He was encouraged along with other correspondents by Sylvester Scovel* of the *New York World* to gather information that might be helpful to the military. Hare's photographs verified the position of various Spanish coastal fortifications.

On Hare's next expedition he was assigned to relay the news of American intervention in the Cuban conflict to the Cuban rebel leader General Maximo Gomez. On April 25, 1898, Hare and *Chicago Tribune* reporter Henry James Whigham and several others landed on the Cuban coast. Assisted by Cuban rebels they delivered their message personally to Gomez three days later. Following this adventure Hare covered the periphery of the conflict over the next six weeks before joining the American army near Santiago on June 29.

On July 1, Hare joined the correspondents corps, which included Stephen Crane* and Richard Harding Davis,* as they prepared to cover the American advance. He witnessed the battle at the "Bloody Bend" of the Aguadores River, when Crane came upon a friend from college mortally wounded. Hare recorded the scene for posterity, with the classmate in the center of the frame. During his first combat assignment he accompanied the charge of the Rough Riders on Kettle Hill on July 1. His coverage of the Spanish-American War* elevated him to the top ranks of the photojournalists of his day.

Following the Spanish-American War,* Hare spent the next five years covering shipwrecks, political rallies, Latin American affairs, and the travels of President McKinley. He reputably took the last photograph of McKinley, minutes before he was assassinated on September 6, 1901.

In 1904 he was in San Francisco preparing for the anticipated hostilities between Russia and Japan. *Collier's* would ultimately send fourteen correspondents to cover the war, including Frederick Palmer,* Richard Harding Davis, and Henry James Whigham. Upon arrival in Japan, the more celebrated journalists were viewed with suspicion, with Jack London* being placed under arrest for taking unauthorized pictures. After a month of waiting, a select group of reporters including Hare was allowed to proceed to Manchuria to cover the Russo-Japanese War,* but press coverage would be controlled and severely limited.

Hare accompanied Major General Kuroki's First Army along with most of the other members of the press. He witnessed the Japanese victory at the Battle of the Yalu, which Hare reported established Japan as a serious player in international affairs. Hampered by restrictions, Hare took what pictures he was allowed, such as the crude field hospitals, and was one of the first members of the press corps to cross the Yalu. After the Japanese took Hung-Sha Pass, Hare became the first newsman to enter Liaoyang, recording the entrance of Japanese troops into the fallen city. On October 17, he covered the Russian offensive at Sha-ho, where the Russians suffered 41,000 casualties.

Hare returned to the States in late 1904. The following year *Collier's* released *A Photographic Record of the Russo-Japanese War,* edited by Hare. However, due to Japanese censorship, photographers were not allowed into the trenches at the height of battles, but were required to take pictures prior to the fighting or at its conclusion. So the most of the photographic record for the Russo-Japanese War, aside from several of Hare's photos of shrapnel exploding, conformed to the restrictions set by the armed forces. The Japanese were so successful in their control of the media and their limitation on news regarding its troop movements that they set a precedent for future military censorship. In 1907 Hare was awarded a medal for his service

by the emperor of Japan. Thirty five years later, when he offered the medal to the first pilot to bomb the Imperial Palace in Tokyo he found out that it was a "phony" brass medal.

Bored with his domestic assignments, in 1912 the conflict in the Balkans drew Hare to Eastern Europe. Unfortunately, the Bulgarians modeled their system of news access after the Germans', which meant keeping correspondents away from the front. Rather than risk the divulging of military secrets, the specials were provided the news that military officials wanted them to print. He returned to America after three months of photographing supervised incidents.

The Mexican Revolution would offer a freer environment for war correspondents. In 1911 Hare had covered the battle at Ciudad Juarez from the front lines and was warned by *Collier's* that he would be no use to them "if dead or wounded." In 1914 he reported the American occupation of Veracruz and marines subduing Mexican resistance. In June and July 1914 he witnessed the Battle of Zacatecas.

In 1914, with the outbreak of war in Europe seeming imminent, Hare expected to receive his new assignment momentarily. He was astonished when *Collier's* declined to send him. Perhaps it was his age of fifty-eight or the new management, with its emphasis on fiction at the expense of news and photojournalism. After receiving this news, Hare wasted little time in offering his services to *Leslie's Weekly,* and on August 20, 1914, he was on a ship bound for England and his next war.

Reaching London a week later, Hare found such tight censorship that it was necessary to obtain a special permit for each individual photographic assignment in Great Britain. He found this out firsthand when arrested by a detective for taking pictures of cheering crowds, without the requisite permit. News restrictions were no less tight in Paris, so he left for Belgium. He was able to take pictures of the German siege of Antwerp before retreating back to England. Throughout 1915, press restrictions continued

Indicates a separate entry.

to handicap photographic war correspondents, with the threat of arrest omnipresent. While it was not a substitute for covering the front lines, on May 7, 1915, Hare rushed to the Irish coast in time to record the arrival of the survivors of the *Lusitania.*

In October 1915, after facing the same restrictions in Italy, Hare gravitated to the Balkan front and the Greek city of Salonika. In August 1916 he photographed trench warfare on the Somme. As America prepared to enter the war the following year he was called home to capture the domestic phase of the war effort. He covered the training camps, but was barred from taking pictures of soldiers leaving for Europe. On December 6, 1917, he covered the massive explosion that devastated Halifax, Nova Scotia.

Hare returned to Europe in 1918, covering the Italian army following its defeat at Caporetto. On June 23 he witnessed the Austrian advance and the Italian counteroffensive near Nervesa, locally known as the "Hog's Back." Hare followed the Italian forces in October when they beat the Austrians, effectively removing them from the war. He returned to New York at the end of the year.

He continued to work for *Leslie's* following the war and in 1920 covered the Polish war with the Russians. It would be his last conflict. At last weary of censors, and with the folding of his sponsor, *Leslie's,* he could rest on his laurels and make the lecture circuit. He died in Teaneck, New Jersey, shortly after his ninetieth birthday.

REFERENCES: Lewis L. Gould and Richard Greffe. *Photojournalist: The Career of Jimmy Hare.* 1977; Jimmy Hare and Cecil Carnes. *Jimmy Hare, News Photographer: Half a Century with a Camera.* 1940.

Harmon, Dudley Anne (?)

As a special contributor to the *Christian Science Monitor* in 1942 and 1943, Harmon was one of the few women war correspondents accredited to the Allied forces during World War II.* In 1942 she joined the information service of the Free French at Brazzaville in French Equatorial Africa. Harmon was considered somewhat of an authority on the French underground, having been introduced to its major figures in London and Africa at the outset of the war. During the Italian campaign she covered the air war for the United Press agency, and following the Normandy invasion, was among the wave of correspondents descending on France. Harmon entered Paris with the liberation forces in August 1944.

REFERENCE: Robert W. Desmond. *Tides of War.* 1984.

Harper, Fletcher (1806–1877)

Born in Newtown, Long Island, Harper entered the world of publishing with J. and J. Harper, the firm started by his two older brothers in 1817. The youngest and last of four brothers to join the family firm, Fletcher had the most impact on American Civil War* journalism. He managed his brothers' *Harper's New Monthly Magazine* in the 1850s before founding *Harper's Weekly* in 1857. This illustrated journal battled *Frank Leslie's Illustrated Newspaper* for dominance in the field of illustrated journalism during the Civil War. These two publications provided markets for the sketch artists covering both sides of the conflict. Following the war he founded *Harper's Bazaar.*

REFERENCES: *DAB;* Stewart Sifakis. *Who Was Who in the Civil War.* 1988.

Harris, Corra (1869–1935)

Harris was one of Georgia's best known women of the early twentieth century. She won national prominence for her 1910 novel *A Circuit Rider's Wife,* before gravitating to writing for national news magazines, and earning a reputation as a chronicler of the agrarian South. She would eventually publish nineteen books. She is also regarded as the first female war correspondent to cover World War I overseas between 1917 and 1918. This was her only foray into war journalism.

REFERENCES: John E. Talamadge. *Corra Harris: Lady of Purpose*, 1968; Catherine Oglesby. *Corra Harris and the Divided Mind of the New South*. 2008.

Harsch, Joseph C. (1905–1998)

Born in Toledo, Ohio, and educated at Wiliams College in Massachusetts and Cambridge University in England, he joined the *Christian Science Monitor* after college. While he also worked occasionally as a radio commentator for the BBC and CBS, he was affiliated with the *Monitor* until his retirement.

Harsch reported from most theaters of action during World War II* either by radio or through print. While reporting from Berlin prior to American entry into the war, he was prevented from covering frontline action in the Low Countries and France in May 1940 as punishment by German authorities for his reporting conditions in Denmark following the German invasion in April. Harsch described this punishment as "a badge of honor in the craft." He returned to the States in February 1941. Harsch was in Honolulu when the Japanese attacked Pearl Harbor and would later cover stories from New Zealand, Australia, and Java. His exploits are chronicled in *Pattern of Conquest* (1941) and *The Curtain Isn't Iron* (1951).

REFERENCES: Robert W. Desmond. *Tides of War*. 1984; Jack Stenbuck, ed. *Typewriter Battalion*. 1995; New York Times, June 5, 1998.

Harvest of Death

On July 5, 1863 a former Mathew Brady* assistant named Timothy O'Sullivan* set his camera up on the Gettysburg battlefield two days after the battle and took what many have called the most famous photo of the Civil War, prominent for the bloated figure of a dead Union soldier surrounded by other corpses and detritus.

REFERENCE: Duncan Anderson. *War: A Photo History*. 2006.

Hastings, Macdonald (1909–1982)

Educated at Stonyhurst, the son of noted playwright and journalist Basil Macdonald, Hastings joined the *Picture Post* in 1938. He became well known for his reporting form northwest Europe during World War II.* Following the war, he became the editor of the *Strand* and reported on big game hunting from India and Africa. In 1951 he cofounded *Country Fair* and in the 1950s became somewhat of a television personality while reporting for the BBC. He wrote over thirty books.

REFERENCE: Dennis Griffiths, ed. *The Encyclopedia of the British Press*. 1992.

Hastings, Max (b. 1945)

The son of Macdonald Hastings* was born in London and educated at University College. In the 1960s he was a researcher for the BBC before joining the *Evening Standard* in 1965. Despite intermittent stints with the BBC throughout the 1960s he continued his relationship with the *Standard* on a more permanent basis beginning in 1973. As the paper's roving correspondent for the next twelve years he reported from hot spots in more than sixty countries. He covered wars in the Middle East, Indochina, Angola, India-Pakistan, Cyprus, and Rhodesia.

He received his highest recognition while covering the Falklands War.* He accompanied British troops into Port Stanley and was designated Journalist of the Year as well as Grenada TV Reporter of the Year in 1982. In the 1980s he continued his distinguished journalism career with several other papers and was named Editor of the Year in 1988. In addition Hastings has become a formidable military historian. His books include *Ulster, 1969: The Struggle for Civil Rights in Northern Ireland* (1970), *Yoni: Hero of Entebbe* (1979), *Bomber Command* (1979), *Battle of Britain,* coauthored with Len

Indicates a separate entry.

Deighton (1980), *Das Reich* (1981), *The Battle for the Falklands* (1983), *Overlord: D-Day and the Battle of Normandy* (1984), *Victory in Europe* (1985), *The Korean War* (1987), and many others.

REFERENCES: Dennis Griffiths, ed. *The Encyclopedia of the British Press*. 1992; *Sunday Times* of London Insight Team. *War in the Falklands*. 1982.

Hastings, Michael Mahon (1980–2013)

Hastings was educated at New York University and came to prominence as a war reporter covering the Iraq War* for *Newsweek* in 2005. At this time he was living in the NATO-occupied Green Zones in Baghdad. In 2007 his fiancée, who was working for the National Democratic Institute in Baghdad, was killed along with three security guards when their convoy was ambushed. Hastings chronicled this event in his first book, *I Lost My Love in Baghdad: A Modern War Story* (2008). However, Hastings was making news rather than just reporting it in 2010 when he interviewed General Stanley McChrystal for a profile in *Rolling Stone*. The article "The Runaway General" revealed widespread contempt for civilian officials including President Obama' security team and Vice President Joe Biden by the general and his staff. The general would subsequently resign over his insubordination. Hastings was recognized for his reporting of this story with the George Polk Award* in 2010. That same year the *Huffington Post* cited Hastings and Matt Taibbi as 2010 Game Changers. Hastings documented his month-long interlude with McChrystal in Europe and Afghanistan with his 2012 book, *The Operators*. Hastings became a vocal critic of American foreign policy in 2013. He was killed in a single vehicle car crash on June 18, 2013 in the Los Angeles area, his body burned beyond recognition.

REFERENCE: http://nymag.com/news/features/michael-hastings-2013–11/.

Haviv, Ron (b.1965)

The photographer Ron Haviv is a co-founder of the VIII agency and has covered conflicts in Latin America, the Caribbean, Russia, the Balkans, the Persian Gulf, and most recently the Afghanistan and Iraq wars. His photos have been widely published in leading news magazines incuding *Time*, *Stern*, and *Paris Match*. Haviv was one of the first photographers to cover the Balkan conflict. His photos did much to demonize the Serbian side, especially after he discovered a concentration camp holding young men of military age at Trnopolje in 1992. His pictures mobilized support for the Bosnian Muslims and Croats but not before thousands were murdered. Haviv's work has been collected and published in *Blood and Honey: A Balkan War Journal* (2000) and *Afghanistan: On the Road to Kabul* (2004).

REFERENCES: www.charlierose.com//guest/view2772; www.viiphoto.com/photographer.html.

Hearst, William Randolph (1863–1951)

One of the true titans in the field of journalism, Hearst was born in San Francisco. He was expelled from Harvard prior to graduation for juvenile pranks. Hearst served a brief apprenticeship on the *New York World* before convincing his father to give him the *San Francisco Examiner*, which the elder Hearst had recently purchased. Following the death of his father in 1891 he invested family money in the acquisition of the *New York Morning Journal* in 1895. Not long after, Hearst became interested in the Cuban insurrection against the Spanish. After the mysterious explosion on board the *Maine* in Havana Harbor, Hearst, without a shred of evidence, attributed its sinking to a Spanish torpedo and urged an American declaration of war, in part because it was good for business. Prior to the outbreak of hostilities Hearst sent artist Frederic Remington* to illustrate the dispatches of correspondent Richard Harding Davis.* Remington telegraphed the home office, "Everything is quiet. There is no trouble here. There will be no war. I wish to return." Legend has it that Hearst responded, "Please remain. You furnish pictures. I will furnish war."

REFERENCE: Phillip Knightley. *The First Casualty*. 1975.

Hedges, Chris (b. 1956)

Following graduation from the Harvard Divinity School in 1979 he made the transition to freelance war correspondent. He covered wars in Central America and the Middle East before catching on with the *New York Times* shortly before the Persian Gulf War of 1991. During the rest of the decade he covered wars in the Balkans, Iraq and Afghanistan. His book *War is a Force That Gives Us Meaning* was published in 2002.

REFERENCE: Michelle Ferrari, *Reporting America at War*, 2003.

Heinzerling, Lynn Louis (1906–1983)

Heinzerling was working for the AP when he witnessed the first shots of World War II on September 1, 1939 as he watched a German cruiser bombard Danzig, Poland. Born in Birmingham, Ohio, he joined the *Cleveland Plain Dealer* in 1928 before moving to the Associated Press in 1933. He covered the opening phases of World War II including the German occupation of Denmark and the Nazi invasion of the Netherlands. He later accompanied the British Eighth Army and the U.S. Fifth Army during the campaign in Italy. From 1945 to 1946 he served as Vienna AP chief. In 1960 he covered the early stages of the Congo crisis, for which he earned a Pulitzer Prize* in International Reporting the following year.

REFERENCE: Heinz-Dietrich Fischer and Erika Fischer. *Complete Biographical Encyclopeida of Pulitzer Prize Winners, 1917–2000*. 2002.

Hemingway, Ernest (1899–1961)

Born in Oak Park, Illinois, he entered journalism with the *Kansas City Star* while still in his teens. With the outbreak of World War I* six months later, Hemingway resigned from the *Star* and joined the American Red Cross ambulance service. Assigned to the Italian campaign, he was seriously wounded and spent several months recuperating. His experiences during the war are chronicled, albeit embellished, in several short stories and his first novel, A *Farewell to Arms* (1929).

Upon his return to the States he continued in journalism as a part-time writer for the *Toronto Star* from 1919 to 1920 as he pursued his literary goals as well. Based in Paris, he served as its roving correspondent in Europe from 1921 to 1923, and on an intermittent basis until 1926. He interviewed the French wartime premier Georges Clemenceau in 1922, and from Istanbul he reported the last stages of the Greco-Turkish War of 1922–1923, including the Greek evacuation from Thrace.

With the publication of *The Sun Also Rises* (1926), Hemingway was on his way to establishing his credentials as one of the greatest writers of his era. In the 1930s he contributed articles to *Esquire* magazine on a variety of outdoors themes, war, and politics. In 1937 he returned to war correspondence when he covered the Spanish Civil War* for the North American Newspaper Alliance (NANA). This experience provided the inspiration for his books *Spanish Earth* (1938) and *For Whom the Bell Tolls* (1940). While in Spain he met the journalist Martha Gellhorn,* a war correspondent and literary talent in her own right. They married in 1940.

Hemingway's Spanish Civil War dispatches have been criticized for being meager, rambling, and self-centered, and Phillip Knightley even describes them as "abysmally bad." A literary writer, he often resorted to heavy-handed similes and contrived imagery to bring the war home to his readership. Although sympathetic to the

---

* Indicates a separate entry.

Loyalist cause, his coverage of the conflict remained politically neutral. One of his best pieces was "The Fall of Tereul."

He returned to war journalism to report the Sino-Japanese theater of World War II* for *PM*. Following this assignment he returned home and patrolled the Caribbean looking for submarines. In 1944 he was hired by *Collier's* as a feature writer in the European theater of operations. Having a preoccupation with proving his personal courage which bordered on obsession, Hemingway was not possessed with the best instincts for the journalism profession. During his World War II service his penchant for personal derring-do continually compromised his objectivity as a war reporter.

No incident exemplifies his wartime exploits better than his behavior during the Allied advance on Paris following the Normandy invasion. Having narrowly missed participation in the greatest amphibious landing in history, Hemingway was accompanying Allied forces twenty-five miles southwest of Paris when he met up with a band of French resistance fighters and used his influence to procure them weapons. In a short time, Hemingway was leading his compatriots on reconnaissance sorties, looking for hidden German troops. He was one of the first Americans to enter liberated Paris. His fellow correspondents protested to army authorities that Hemingway had seriously breached wartime press protocol. Howver, his celebrity and official connections insulated him from the chorus demanding that he surrender his accreditation.

Joining American troops in the German Huertgen Forest in November 1944, Hemingway was attired with a Thompson submachine gun draped over his shoulder, once again oblivious to press protocol. During the subsequent heavy fighting, he unslung his weapon and helped repulse a German offensive, in the process putting out of commission a German mortar. He was awarded the Bronze Star in 1947. Following the war, Hemingway continued his literary career with very few journalistic interludes. He

was awarded the Nobel Prize for literature in 1954, several years after the publication of *The Old Man and the Sea*. But, he had reported his last war, and in the late 1950s his health deteriorated, leading him to commit suicide with a shotgun in July 1961.

REFERENCES: Robert W. Desmond. *Tides of War.* 1984; Sarah R. Shaber. "Hemingway's Literary Journalism: The Spanish Civil War Dispatches," *Journalism Quarterly.* Autumn 1980; Frederick S. Voss. *Reporting the War.* 1994; William White, ed. *By-Line, Ernest Hemingway.* 1967.

Hemment, John C. (d. 1927)

As one of the leading war photographers* of the Spanish-American War,* Hemment represented the *New York Journal* and *Harper's Weekly*. He was the first newsreel* motion picture photographer to capture a battlefront. At the outset he had been hired by the federal government to take photographs of the wreckage of the *Maine* for the congressional investigation. William Randolph Hearst* had seen to it that Hemment would be the best equipped of all the photographers covering the conflict, even allowing him to use his large steam yacht, the *Silvia*, as a floating darkroom. There was apparently so much space on the yacht that besides his darkroom, he could bring duplicates of every type of equipment he needed, including cameras of several different sizes. Hemment photographed the battleground at Las Guasimas, the graves of the Rough Riders killed there, and the encampment at Sevilla. He later covered World War I* for the Hearst papers. He wrote *Cannon and Camera* (1898).

REFERENCES: Charles H. Brown. *The Correspondents' War.* 1967; Pat Hodgson. *Early War Photographs.* 1974; Joyce Milton. *The Yellow Kids.* 1989; Susan D. Moeller. *Shooting War.* 1989.

Henry, William Seton "Guy" (1816–1851)

During the Mexican-American War* he covered the Battles of Palo Alto (May 8, 1846), Resaca de la Palma (May 9, 1846), and Monterrey (September 20–24, 1846) for the *Spirit of the Times,* and the Battle of Molino del Rey (September 8, 1847) for the *New York Courier and Enquirer.* Mexican War journalism expert Tom Reilly regarded this officer and West Point graduate attached to the 3rd Infantry Division as "One of the war's most important and prolific military writers." He was able to get around military censorship, like most of his colleagues with a nom de plume, in this case G** de L**. His reports were written in the form of daily diary entries. Following the war Henry remained in the military and sporadically sent articles to his former paper from scattered frontier outposts. He died on March 5, 1851, while posted in New York City.

REFERENCE: Tom Reilly. Wa*r with Mexico!: America's Reporters Cover the Battlefront,* Manley Witten, ed. 2010.

Henty, George Alfred (1832–1902)

Best known as a writer of adventure stories for children, Henry was born at Trumpington near Cambridge. Bedridden for much of his youth with rheumatic fever, he turned to writing poetry. To fend off youthful critics of such a dandified pastime he became proficient in pugilism as well. He cut short his academic studies at Cambridge to enlist with his brother in the Crimea*-bound British army. His brother died of cholera shortly after. *The Morning Advertiser* published George Henty's letters describing the siege of Sebastopol, which led to his being hired in 1859 by the *Standard* as a correspondent. In 1866, accompanying Giuseppe Garibaldi's Italian forces in the Tyrolese campaign, he was aboard an Italian ship when he witnessed the naval battle of Lissa on July 20.

Over the next decade he would cover Lord Napier's expedition to Abyssinia (1867–1868), the opening of the Suez Canal (1869), the Franco-Prussian War,* the Paris Commune (1871), the Russian conquest of Khiva (1873), Lord Wolseley's Ashanti expedition (1873–1874), and the Carlist insurrection in Spain (1874).

His coverage of the Napier expedition was collected in the book *The March to Magdala* (1868).

While Henty was covering the Ashanti War, fellow correspondent Henry Stanley,* to break the monotony between battles, proposed a trip to the mouth of the Volta River in a boat owned by the *New York Herald.* His intention was that they would watch the British expedition, whose mission was to put down the tribes of the Volta and who were about to launch an attack on Kumasi. Their mission resulted in informative news dispatches and the near drowning of Henty.

His last assignment as a special correspondent was to follow the Turkish army during the Turko-Serbian War of 1876. Although he continued his affiliation with the *Standard* he devoted most of his remaining years to writing juvenile fiction, due to the fact that success had eluded him as a writer for adults. Regarded as the most imperialist of the imperialists for his Victorian attitudes, he published more than eighty titles over the next quarter century.

REFERENCES: *DNB;* Robert Wilkinson-Latham. *From Our Special Correspondent.* 1979.

Herbaugh, Sharon (1954–1993)

Born in Lamar, Colorado, she joined AP in 1978 and worked in several American cities before transferring to New Delhi, India in 1998 where she won distinction as the news editor of the year in 1989. The following year she was selected to lead the AP bureau in Islamabad. She covered the civil war in Afghanistan for three years, but her career was cut short when she died in a helicopter crash in the mountains there. She became "the first AP newswoman and bureau chief to die on assignment."

REFERENCE: AP Wall of Honor, www.ap.org/wallof-honor/1980_1999.html.

Herbert, St. Leger Algernon (1850–1885)

Born in Kingston, Canada, and educated at Oxford, he toiled in the Canadian Civil Service

* Indicates a separate entry.

before his appointment as secretary to Sir Garnet Wolseley in 1878. He accompanied Wolseley in his campaigns in Cyprus (1878) and South Africa (1879) and was awarded the Companion of the Most Distinguished Order of St. Michael and St. George in 1880 after taking part in the storming of Sekokoeni's Mountain.

Herbert had begun his journalism career in 1878 with the *Times*. In 1883 he joined the *Morning Post* as its special in Egypt and in the Sudan campaign, and was present at the battles of El Teb and Tamai, where he was shot through the leg. On January 19, 1885, he was killed with fellow correspondent John Alexander Cameron* of the *Standard* at the Battle of Abu Kru. Conspicuously dressed in his red jacket, Herbert was found dead among the camels following the battle. He is one of seven war correspondents killed in the Sudan campaign, commemorated by a plaque in St. Paul's Cathedral.

REFERENCES: *DNB*; Frederic Villiers,* *Pictures of Many Wars*. 1920; Robert Wilkinson-Latham. *From Our Special Correspondent*. 1979.

Herbst, Josephine Frey (1892–1969)

Born in Sioux City, Iowa, Herbst attended the University of Iowa, where she gravitated toward a literary career. During World War I* she drifted toward radical politics and moved to Berkeley, California. Over the ensuing two decades she performed social work, hobnobbed with the literati, and published her first novel in 1928.

Increasingly drawn into the orbit of radicalism, she began writing for the *New Masses* during the Depression. By the 1930s she had published several more novels. Her star began to rise when she turned to journalism in the turbulent years before World War II.* Prior to American intervention she covered the underground movement in Cuba, the rise of Hitler in Germany, and the Spanish Civil War,* where she developed a reputation for courage under fire. Her wartime experiences are chronicled in her 1941 novel *Satan's Sergeants* and in the play *The Spanish Road*, written to raise funds for Loyalist Spain in 1938.

REFERENCES: *DAB*; Peter Wyden. *The Passionate War: The Narrative History of the Spanish Civil War*. 1983.

Herr, Michael (b. 1940)

A native of Syracuse, New York, after graduation from Syracuse University he began his career in journalism in the early 1960s writing for *Holiday*. He began covering warfare in November 1967 when he covered Vietnam for *Esquire* as a freelance correspondent. His best known book is *Dispatches* (1977). He also put his Vietnam experience to work as co-author of the screenplays for the movies *Apocalypse Now* (1979) and *Full Metal Jacket* (1987).

REFERENCE: Raymond Paredes. "Michael Herr." Heath Anthology of Literature Website, Cengage.

Hersey, John (1914–1993)

Born in Tientsin, China, to missionary parents, he spent the first decade of his life there. He attended college at Yale and Cambridge. After serving as secretary for Sinclair Lewis he was employed by *Time* in 1937. In 1939 he covered events in Asia. After 1942 he covered the Pacific and European theaters of World War II* for *Life* and *Time* and published three books on the war: *Men on Bataan* (1942), *Into the Valley* (1943), based on an incident during the Battle of Guadalcanal, and *Hiroshima* (1946), which originally began as a story for the *New Yorker* on the effects of the atomic bomb on the inhabitants of the city. In 1944 he won the Pulitzer Prize for his novel about the American occupation of Sicily, A *Bell for Adano*. Following the war he had a successful career as a novelist and wrote several books of nonfiction.

REFERENCE: Frederick S. Voss. *Reporting the War*. 1994.

Hersh, Seymour (b. 1937)

Born in Chicago and educated at the University of Chicago, Hersh was a former Pentagon correspondent for the Associated Press when he heard about the My Lai incident from former members of William L. Calley's army unit. Hersh received a grant to travel as a freelance reporter to interview the participants in the tragedy. After he pieced together the story of what actually happened on March 16, 1968, when hundreds of Vietnamese civilians were murdered by American troops, it was published by the Dispatch News Service, a fledgling news syndicate. Prior to his taking the story to the Dispatch News Service, no major news organization would touch it, including *Look* and *Life*. His first My Lai article was carried in three dozen papers, including the *St. Louis Post-Dispatch*, on November 13, 1969. The following year Hersh was unanimously awarded the Pulitzer Prize.

REFERENCE: Phillip Knightley. *The First Casualty*. 1975.

Hetherington, Timothy Alistair Telemachus "Tim" (1970–2011)

The war photographers Tim Hetherington and Chris Hondros* died from shrapnel wounds while covering the conflict in Misrata, Libya on April 20, 2011. Hetherington was best known for co-directing the Academy Award-nominated film *Restrepo** with Sebastian Junger.* After graduation from Oxford, Hetherington traveled extensively for several years. It was during this trip that he decided to study photojournalism, graduating from Cardiff University in 1996. Over the following decade he chronicled war zones and political crises in West Africa, reporting from Liberia, Sierra Leone, Nigeria, and elsewhere. He changed his focus to Afghanistan in 2007 and won the World Press Photo award for a photo of a soldier during a day of fighting in the Korengal Valley of Afghanistan. In 2007 and 2008 he accompanied author Sebastian Junger on several extended forays into Afghanistan.

They collaborated on *Restrepo,* which received the Grand Jury Prize for best documentary at the 2010 Sundance Film Festival. Hetherington was honored with the 2008 Rory Peck Features award for broadcast work in the Korengal valley, that aired as *Afghanistan—The Other War* on ABC News's *Nightline*. After his death in Libya the city of Ajdabiya honored him by renaming its largest square after him. Sebastian Junger filmed the documentary *Which Way Is the Front Line From Here? The Life and Times of Tim Hetherington* to honor his friend in 2013. At a memorial service for Hetherington in New York City four American veterans of the Battle Company of the 173rd Airborne in Afghanistan who had shared the frontline dangers with Junger and Hetherington presented two American flags to the late filmmaker's family and his life partner and co-filmmaker Idil Ibrahim.

REFERENCE: C.J. Chivers, "Restrepo Director and Photographer Are Killed in Libya," New York Times, Apr. 21, 2011.

Hibben, Paxton Pattison (1880–1928)

From a well-to-do Indianapolis family, Hibben, or "Pax" as he was better known, began covering World War I in 1915 almost two years before the U.S. became involved. After the U.S. entered the war in 1916 he was commissioned as a lieutenant of field artillery and later a captain. By the time he began his stint as a war reporter Hibben had already achieved a remarkable academic record at Princeton (1903) and then Harvard Law School before becoming a diplomat at various foreign embassies. His reporting career took him throughout Europe; and in Athens he became "the only AP reporter known to have fought a duel." Hibben left Greece after a year and returned to New York and left journalism for good. His greatest achievement was leading a humanitarian effort to rescue starving children in Russia during the 1921–1923 famine.

Indicates a separate entry.

REFERENCES: "Paxton Hubben, Writer and Soldier, Succumbs. Schenectady Gazette, December 6, 1928; Stuart Hibben. *Aristocrat and Proletarian: The Extraordinary Life of Paxton Pattison Hibben.* 2006.

Hicks, Tyler (b. 1969)

Born in São Paulo, Brazil and educated at Boston University, this photojournalist began working as a contract photographer for the *New York Times* in 1999, initially covering foreign affairs and conflict in East and West Africa. Following the 9/11 terrorist attacks in America he began covering Afghanistan and was present at Kabul when the Northern Alliance took the city back from the Taliban. He has covered the Balkans conflict and the war between Eritrea and Ethiopia for the *Times* and photographed personal projects that took him to Haiti, Albania, and Kosovo.

Hicks rose to international prominence covering stories in Libya and Kenya. In March 2011 he was reported missing along with three other journalists while covering the revolution in Libya. Six days later they were released by the pro-Qaddafi forces that had captured them. In February 2012 he was working with *Times*' Beirut Bureau chief Anthony Shadid,* covering the Syrian civil war.* when Shadid died from an asthma attack. To Hicks's credit, he managed to bring Shadid's body by horseback across the border back to Turkey. In 2014, Hicks, who lives in Nairobi, was on the scene during the bloody attack at Nairobi's Westgate shopping center in September 2013. His on-the-spot photo coverage at the mall and the ensuing search for the terrorists won him the Pulitzer Prize for breaking news photography in 2014. Hicks has been the recipient of numerous awards, including sharing the 2009 Pulitzer Prize for International reporting with a team from the *Times*, for their coverage of conflict in Pakistan and Afghanistan. In 2006 he was named Newspaper Photographer of the Year by Pictures of the Year International.

REFERENCE: Tyler Hicks, "Bearing Witness in Syria: A Correspondent's Last Days," New York Times, Mar. 3, 2012.

Hiett, Helen (1913–1961)

Born in Chenoa, Illinois, after graduating from the University of Chicago in 1934 she headed for Europe on a scholarship. In 1939 she left graduate school at the London School of Economics and moved to France. The following year she became one of the first female correspondents to report for NBC. Among her radio news scoops was the fall of France in 1940. Fleeing France just ahead of the Nazi advance, she made it to Madrid, where Spanish news censorship prevented her from sending out news dispatches. She won the National Headliners Award for her scoop of the bombing of British Gibraltar. She returned to America the following year.

In 1944 Hiett returned to Europe for the Religious News Service. She was in Milan days before the arrival of Allied forces and was present when Mussolini's body was still hanging from the lamppost. After the war she transferred to the *New York Herald Tribune*. She died on August 22, 1961, from injuries sustained in a mountain climbing accident in France.

REFERENCE: David H. Hosley. As *Good As Any*. 1984.

Higgins, Marguerite (1920–1966)

Higgins was born in the crown colony of Hong Kong. She was stricken with malaria during infancy and sent to recuperate in Vietnam. Her family moved to Oakland, California in 1923, and Marguerite attended the University of California at Berkeley, where she wrote for the campus newspaper. After graduating with a degree in journalism in 1942 she joined the *New York Herald Tribune*.

Higgins entered the ranks of professional journalism at an opportune time, with many male reporters joining the armed forces in the 1940s. By 1943 she was one of the few *Herald Tribune* staffers to receive a byline. Rebuffed in her attempts to secure a position as a foreign correspondent, Higgins violated protocol by going over the heads of her superiors to the owner's wife, Helen Rogers Reid. Besides taking an active role in the management of the paper, Reid was known for her support of feminist issues, and in 1944 Higgins was on the *Queen Mary* bound for England with seven other war correspondents.

Confined to the London bureau, Higgins was determined to report from the battlefront. In 1945, during the closing days of the war, she finally got her opportunity when she was assigned to the Berlin bureau. In March 1945 she received her first taste of conflict when the Eighth Army Air Force offered to allow journalists to view the aftermath of German bombing raids. Although she served as war correspondent for only six weeks, she managed to witness the liberation of the concentration camps at Buchenwald and Dachau, as well as the capture of Munich. She was awarded the Army Campaign Ribbon for outstanding service under difficult conditions and the New York Newspaper Women's Club Award as best foreign correspondent of 1945 for her coverage of the events surrounding the liberation of Dachau. She went on to report the Nuremberg trials, the treason trial of Petain, the Berlin Blockade, and the developing Cold War.

With her reputation as a war correspondent firmly established by 1947, Higgins was elevated to Berlin bureau chief for the *Herald Tribune,* but prone to pettiness and competitive to a fault, she was ill suited for a supervisory position. In May 1950 Higgins was transferred to Tokyo, which, according to fellow correspondent Keyes Beech,* she found "about as exciting as a duck pond." She could little have known that her new position as Far East bureau chief would lead to her greatest story when North Korea crossed the thirty-eighth parallel on June 25, 1950, inaugurating the Korean War.*

Higgins covered the fall of Seoul for the *Herald Tribune,* barely eluding Communist forces. Shortly after, she was joined by a more seasoned war reporter, Homer Bigart,* with whom she would have a legendary rivalry. Management wanted Higgins to return to her post in Tokyo,

and when she refused was given the ultimatum to either return or lose her job. She stayed and reported the first actions of the war. However, she was forced to leave when the commander of American forces in Korea issued an edict banning all women. Higgins again beseeched Helen Rogers Reid to aid her in circumventing protocol. Appealing the decision directly to General Douglas MacArthur won Higgins permission to return to the battlefront.

Higgins covered many of the major campaigns of the conflict, including landing with the U.S. Marines under fire at Inchon. She gained the respect of her male counterparts as well as the foot soldiers for sharing in their hardships. Her reports continued to appear in the *Herald Tribune,* occasionally on the same page as her competitor Bigart's. In October 1950 *Life* magazine ran a feature on Higgins with an array of photographs of her in battle fatigues, further adding to her legend as a war reporter. In 1951 she published *War in Korea,* which became a best-seller. That same year, along with five other correspondents, she was awarded the Pulitzer Prize* in the international-reporting category, the first woman to be so honored. Over the next several years she received dozens of awards, including the Overseas Press Club's George Polk Award and the 1951 Woman of the Year Award from the Associated Press.

In 1953 she was in Vietnam covering the siege at Dien Bien Phu when her friend and colleague Robert Capa* was killed by a land mine nearby. Shortly after, Higgins received word that she had been granted a visa to visit the Soviet Union, the first American granted such access since the death of Stalin. Her book *Red Plush and Black Bread,* published in 1955, chronicled her 13,500-mile excursion through Russia. With the publication of *News Is a Singular Thing* that same year she became recognized as an expert on Russian affairs.

Her journalistic instincts led her again to a hot spot when she covered the Congo crisis in 1961, the first *Herald Tribune* journalist to report on that region since Henry Stanley* came in search of David Livingstone in 1877. Higgins returned to Vietnam* in 1963. In the prescient *Our Vietnam Nightmare* (1965), she described the dangers of American intervention. She left the *Herald Tribune* in late 1963 but kept her hand in journalism by writing weekly columns for *Newsday* and continuing to travel abroad. Her tenth trip to Vietnam proved her undoing when she contracted the tropical disease leishmaniasis. She was hospitalized at Walter Reed Hospital and died two months later. Higgins was buried at Arlington National Cemetery.

REFERENCES: Julia Edwards. *Women of the World.* 1989; Richard Kluger. *The Paper: The Life and Death of the New York Herald Tribune.* 1986; Antoinette May. *Witness to War: A Biography of Marguerite Higgins.* 1983.

Hill, Gladwin (1914–1992)

Best known today as a pioneering reporter on the environment, after graduating from Harvard he joined the Associated Press. In 1942 he was sent to London to cover the war, which he did for two years primarily covering the Allied air war against Germany. He was the first reporter to fly aboard an American bomber on a raid into Germany, and witnessed the Allied invasion of France in 1944 while aboard a bomber. He would also reopen the AP office in Paris. In 1945 he moved over to the *New York Times* and covered the Allied troops moving east. Hill was among the first reporters to enter Berlin as well as one of the first to cross into Poland. He was a member of the ill-fated Writing 69th* and survived the war to write books on politics and the environment in California.

REFERENCES: Richard Perez-Pena. "Gladwin Hill, a Pioneer Reporter on the Environment, Is Dead at 78." New York Times, September 21, 1992; Jim Simpson. The Writing 69th. 2005.

Hill, James (b. 1967)

Born in London, Hill took up photography in 1991 after graduation from Oxford University and the London College of Printing. He spent a decade covering Russia from Moscow for the *New York Times*. He covered the conflict in the wartorn republics of the former USSR, as well as the early battles in Afghanistan after the U.S. led invasion in 2001. In 2003 he chronicled the invasion of Iraq for the *New York Times* and *Time* magazine. His coverage of Afghanistan during a three-month stint earned him the 2001 Pulitzer Prize. His Web journal of his weeks with U.S. troops, "In the Heart of the Fight," earned him the NPPA Award for Best News Picture Story on the Web. In 2005 he won the 1st place prize in general News Stories at the World Press Photo Awards for his images from the Beslan tragedy in southern Russia.

REFERENCES: http://www.contactpressimages.com/photographers/hill/hill_bio.html; http://mjrhill.com.

Hill, Russell (b. 1919)

Following graduation from Columbia University in 1939, he turned down a scholarship to Cambridge to pursue a career in journalism. That year he traveled to Berlin, where he was hired by the *New York Herald Tribune*. He became an assistant to Ralph Barnes of the *Tribune* and then to William L. Shirer* of CBS. During the German invasion of Holland, Belgium, and Luxembourg in May 1940, Hill accompanied the German *Wehrmacht*. On the day before the signing of the French surrender in the Compiegne Forest in June 1940, both Hill and Barnes were expelled from Germany for critical pieces they had written.

Following his expulsion, Hill went to the Balkans and covered the Yugoslav and Greek campaigns, making a daring escape from the Germans in a small fishing boat with fellow correspondents Leigh White* of CBS and Robert St. John* of the AP. Their boat was strafed by enemy aircraft on several occasions, with White and St. John sustaining serious injuries.

As one of the youngest correspondents of the war, Hill next relocated to Cairo and would cover events and military affairs in Syria and Iran. During the North African campaign he covered the British Eighth Army's action against Rommel's Afrika Corps. His exploits in North Africa were chronicled in two well-received books, *Desert War* and *Conquest of Africa*. In 1944 he reported the Italian campaign and the Allied advance on Rome. Hill's closest brush with death occurred in October 1944 near the German city of Aachen on the Belgian border. While he was covering mopping-up operations around the recently captured city, his jeep triggered an antivehicular Teller mine. Hill suffered a broken arm, cuts, and bruises, and the army driver and passenger David Lardner* of the *New Yorker* magazine were killed. Hill continued to report the Allied advance into Germany and was one of the first Western correspondents permitted to tour the Soviet zone of Germany following V-E Day.

REFERENCES: Richard Collier. *Fighting Words.* 1989; Robert W. Desmond. *Tides of War.* 1984.

Hillegas, Howard Clemens (1872–1918)

Born in Pennsburg, Pennsylvania, following graduation from Franklin and Marshall College in 1894 he moved to New York City and joined the *New York Herald*. The following year he left the paper for the *New York World*. The paper sent him to South Africa in 1895 and he became the first correspondent to report the oputbreak of hostilities between the Boers and the British. He returned to the U.S. in 1898. He had befriended Boer commander General "Oom Paul" Kruger during the war and in 1899 published the book *Oom Paul's People*. In 1900 he published *The Boers in the War* and *With the Boer Forces*. Having covered the war with the Boers, Hillegas's work had difficulty getting published in England due to its obvious pro-Boer bias. He continued his newspaper career with various papers ending it where he began with the *New York Herald*.

REFERENCE: *New York Times* obituary. January 30, 1918.

Hindus, Maurice Gerschon (1891–1969)

Born in Bolshoye Bikovo, Russia, he immigrated with his family to New York City in 1905. After graduating from Colgate University and attending Harvard University's graduate school for one year he turned to freelance writing. In 1920 he published his first book, *The Russian Peasant and the Revolution*. His observations of a Russian emigre community in Canada resulted in a series of articles published by *Century* magazine. Impressed by his work, the magazine assigned him to return to Russia and observe the collective farming system. He chronicled this experience in *Humanity Uprooted* (1929) and *Red Bread* (1931).

Although his work focused on Russian peasant life, he served three years as a war correspondent during World War II,* covering the Russo-German war. Employed by the *New York Herald Tribune,* he wrote the book *Mother Russia* (1943), which captures wartime conditions in the Soviet Union. Hindus was present when the first flight of U.S. bombers from African bases reached the Soviet airfields in June 1943. During the Cold War he became a recognized authority on Soviet affairs. He played an important role in establishing sympathy for the Soviet Union during the war, but became increasingly critical of Soviet policy during the postwar years. Ever critical of the Soviet hierarchy, he always maintained an affinity with the Russian people. A prolific writer of twenty books and numerous articles, Hindus traveled widely throughout the 1940s. His books include *Russia and Germany, We Shall Live Again,* and *Russia and Japan.*

REFERENCES: *DAB 8;* Robert W. Desmond. *Tides of War.* 1984; *New York Times.* July 9, 1969.

Hollingworth, Claire (b. 1911)

Educated at the University of London, she entered journalism with *The Daily Telegraph* at the

---

* *Indicates a separate entry.*

outset of World War II,* as the only British reporter present to inform the world that the invasion of Poland had begun on September 3, 1939. She also reported the conflict from the Balkans and the Western Desert. Following the war she covered the Greek Civil War and the Palestine conflict.

Although stationed in Paris for the *Manchester Guardian* until 1963, she covered the Algerian War, Egypt, Aden, and Vietnam.* From 1967 to 1973 she was a roving correspondent for the *Daily Telegraph*, and reported the Vietnam War. After the Vietnam conflict she served as defense and China correspondent for her paper. Among her books are *Poland's Three Weeks War* (1940), *There's a German Just Behind Me* (1945), and *Front Line* (1990). In 2014 Hollingworth celebrated her 103rd birthday at home in Hong Kong.

REFERENCE: Anne Sebba. *Battling For News*. 1994.

Holme, Christopher (?)

Holme covered the Ethiopian War* for Reuters* and then the Spanish Civil War.* In 1937 he covered one of the most controversial episodes of the war when he accompanied George L. Steer* of the *Times* to the town of Guernica* in the Basque region of Spain. They were in the village of Ambacegui, several miles from their destination, when German planes attacked them from the direction of Guernica. The planes strafed the village and attempted to kill the two correspondents before continuing on. Holme and Steer responded to a rumor that Guernica had been leveled and decided to check it out, by now joined by Noel Monks* of the *Daily Express*. The destruction of Guernica, a city that was not a military objective, became a major news sensation and heralded a decade of total war.

REFERENCE: Phillip Knightley. *The First Casualty*. 1975.

Homer, Winslow (1836–1910)

Born in Boston, the best-known artist of the American Civil War* was apprenticed to a local

lithographer at the age of nineteen. During his two years he learned to draw directly on wood for engraving. He opened his own studio at the age of twenty-one and began sending engravings to the pictorial press. In October 1861 *Harper's* sent him to sketch the first Lincoln inauguration, and then the siege at Yorktown, Virginia, at the start of McClellan's Peninsular campaign. The sketches he sent back were translated into engravings for the journal's pages. More interested in art than reporting, after covering the action at Yorktown and Fair Oaks in May 1862 he returned to the studio, where he used his wartime sketches and engravings as models for more serious paintings. He subsequently made occasional visits to the battlefront as a freelance artist, up to the siege of Petersburg, Virginia, toward the end of the war.

Homer had not risen to prominence at the time of the Civil War. He was always more comfortable illustrating the more mundane activities of camp and civilian life than the carnage on the battlefield, and his wartime experiences were limited to operations against the Confederate Army of Northern Virginia. Unlike many of his colleagues, Homer did not draw a complete battle scene. His technique is exemplified by his sketch "The Sharpshooter" of 1863, in which he shows only a solitary soldier, hiding in a tree, demonstrating the new kind of impersonal warfare. Besides his work published in *Harper's* he produced a book of lithographs entitled *Campaign Sketches* in 1863.

REFERENCES: Pat Hodgson. *The War Illustrators*. 1977; Philip Van Doren Stem. *They Were There*. 1959.

Hondros, Chris (1970–2011)

Born in New York City, Hondros studied English literature and worked on the campus university newspaper at North Carolina State University and went on to earn a Master's degree at the Ohio University School of Visual Communications. In 1998 he moved to New York City to focus on international reporting. During the late 1990s he covered conflicts including those in Kosovo, Angola, Sierra Leone, Afghanistan, Kashmir, the West Bank, Iraq, and Liberia. After the 9/11 attacks he photographed the devastation at Ground Zero and in 2003 covered the Liberian Civil War. His images of conflict in Iraq earned him international recognition. In January 2005 he chronicled the shootings of an Iraqi family by U.S. troops after it failed to stop at a checkpoint in Tal Afar, fearing it was a suicide bomber. In April 2011 he suffered a fatal head injury during a mortar attack by Gaddafi forces while covering the Libyan War* in Misrata. The photojournalist Tim Hetherington* was also killed in the same attack. Hondros' photojournalism was recognized by several Pulitzer Prize nominations and other awards, including the Robert Capa Gold Medal for his work in Iraq in 2006.

REFERENCES: http://lightbox.time.com/2014/04/20/remembering-chris-hondros/; http://www.chrishondros.com/bio.htm.

Honscheid, Johannes-Matthias (1922–2001)

Born in Eitorf, Germany and educated in Frankfurt, he covered World War II as a war correspondent while serving as a *Leutnant* of the Reserves. In 1942 he served as a war correspondent for the Luftwaffe and the German/Italian newspaper *Il Popolo di Sicilia* in Catania. He later transferred to the Wehrmacht and during the Battle of Monte Cassino was credited with destroying seven enemy tanks. Captured by the British, he escaped, but was badly injured. He returned to action in 1944 and served in the capacity of *Referatleiter*, which required him to position journalists, act as a military censor, and as a liaison to the upper ranks. He received the prestigious Knight's Cross of the Iron Cross for extreme battlefield bravery. He was also the only Wehrmacht war correspondent to receive this award. He fought and reported on several battlefronts, including the North African campaign,

Operation Husky, and the Allied invasion of Italy, where he ultimately earned his Iron Cross. Following the war he remained in journalism working as an editor and publisher in Munich.

REFERENCE: "Honscheid, Johannes-Matthias," http://en.ww2awards.com/person/31014.

Hooper, Jim (?)

Formerly a television documentary writer and professional skydiver, Hooper turned to war reporting in 1984. Since then he has covered wars exclusively in Africa, covering conflicts in Chad, Sudan, Uganda, South Africa, Namibia, and Angola. He was one of the first Western journalists to be given almost unrestricted access to the bush war in Southwest Africa/Namibia, when he accompanied the Koevoet, the deadly counterinsurgency unit, against the revolutionary South West Africa People's Organization (SWAPO). A freelance defense photojournalist, he has written articles for the *Economist, International Defense Review, Jane's Defense Weekly,* and *Armed Forces.* His book *Beneath the Visiting Moon: Images of Combat in Southern Africa* is a chronicle of his career as a modern war correspondent.

REFERENCE: Jim Hooper. *Beneath the Visiting Moon.* 1990.

Hopkinson, Tom (1905–1990)

Best known as the editor of *Picture Post* in England, the Oxford-educated Hopkinson worked as a freelance journalist and in advertising and publicity before moving into editorial work. He resigned from the *Picture Post* during the Korean War* when the owner suppressed a story by Bert Hardy* and James Cameron* which reported the mistreatment of North Korean prisoners by the South Koreans.

Hopkinson traveled extensively in Africa beginning in 1958, when he edited the magazine *Drum* in South Africa. He covered the Congo conflict and the fighting in Katanga when Moise

Indicates a separate entry.

Tshombe set up his separate state. Between 1963 and 1966 he trained African journalists on behalf of the International Press Institute.

REFERENCES: Tom Hopkinson, ed. *Picture Post 1938–50*. 1970; Jorge Lewinski. *The Camera at War*. 1978.

Horne, Walter H. (1883–1921)

Home was born in Hallowell, Maine. He worked in his family tanning business as a young boy before leaving for New York City shortly after the turn of the century. After contracting tuberculosis he moved to El Paso, Texas, in 1905, hoping to improve his health. He found an outlet for his entrepreneurial skills when he entered the picture postcard* business in 1911 after the outbreak of the Mexican Revolution just across the border. He traveled widely, visiting military encampments and taking photographs. He eventually took thousands of pictures of American troops along the border, who would then buy the images to send to family back home. By 1914, his picture postcard business was booming, at one point making five thousand postcards a day. He claimed to have taken the best photographs of the Second Battle of Ciudad Juarez in November 1913. His best-selling card was reportedly of a triple execution of three Mexicans in Ciudad Juarez in 1916.

REFERENCE: Paul J. Vanderwood and Frank N. Samponara. *Border Fury*. 1988.

Hottelet, Richard Curt (1917–1914)

The son of non-English speaking German immigrants, Hottelet was born in Brooklyn and educated at Brooklyn College. In the late 1930s, since he had relatives in Germany, his father encouraged him to move there to continue graduate work at the University of Berlin. As the Nazis rose to power he left the university and found work with United Press in Berlin. In 1938 he covered the German annexation of the Sudetenland

region of Czechoslovakia, followed in close succession by the German invasion of Belgium and France in May and June 1940, as well as the evacuation of Allied troops from Dunkirk, France. Hottelet also covered the Allied bombing raids on Berlin. In March 1941 he was arrested for "suspicion of espionage" and endured a number of interrogations and four months' imprisonment in Berlin jails, but was never physically abused. He was released in July along with another reporter and exchanged for three Germans held in the United States. He recounted his months in prison in a widely published article in August 1941. He continued to work for UP after his release and joined the Office of War Information in London, putting his German language skills to good use making broadcasts in Germany and writing propaganda to be dropped over Germany.

At the end of 1943 he went to work for Edward R. Murrow* at the CBS London bureau beginning in January 1944, becoming the youngest member of the so-called "Murrow Boys," an esteemed group that included Cecil Brown,* Winston Burdett,* Charles Collingwood,* Bill Downs,* Thomas Grandin, Larry LeSeur,* William L. Shirer,* Eric Sevareid,* Howard K. Smith,* and Mary Marvin Breckinridge.* Hottelet would go on to witness the D-Day invasion of Normandy from a B-26, flying so low he could feel the percussive force of explosions and smell the aftermath of ground explosions. He made it back to London in time to become the first CBS reporter to broadcast an eyewitness report of the historic invasion. He was, besides Edward R. Murrow, the only reporter heard on radio on June 6 and in the days following the invasion. In 1944 he would report street fighting in Aachen, Germany and then the Battle of the Bulge. The following year he was forced to bail out of a B-17 bomber when it was hit by aircraft fire over France. In April he covered the linkup of American and Russian troops at the Elbe River and the liberation of the Dachau concentration camp. He was with the U.S. 2nd Armored

Division when it entered Berlin, and was the first correspondent to report from there. Following the war Hottelet covered Cold war events from the Soviet Union and West Germany. In the 1960s he once more covered conflicts, including the Congo crisis in 1960 and the Six-Day War between Israel and its Arab neighbors. From 1960 until he retired in 1985 he covered the United Nations beat for CBS, the last of the Murrow Boys.

REFERENCES: Richard Goldstein, "Richard C. Hottelet, CBS Newsman and Last of 'Murrow Boys,' Dies at 97," New York Times, Dec. 17, 2014; Braden Hall, "Richard C. Hottelet," *American World War II Correspondents*, Jeffrey B. Cook, ed. 2012, 125–130.

House, Edward Howard (1836–1901)

Born in Boston, Massachusetts, he studied music composition before joining the *Boston Courier* as its music and drama critic in 1854. He transferred to the *New York Tribune* in 1858 and covered John Brown's raid on Harpers Ferry the following year. With the outbreak of the American Civil War,* he was made special correspondent with Union forces in the Virginia campaign. He was present when Colonel Elmer E. Ellsworth, commander of a New York regiment, was shot and killed by a secessionist business proprietor in Alexandria, Virginia, while at the head of his troops. Although hostilities had not yet officially erupted, Ellsworth was the first Union death of the war. House also witnessed the First Battle of Bull Run.

Following the war he became involved in theater management before returning to the *Tribune* in 1868. He joined the *New York Times* two years later, and in 1871 he obtained a university teaching position in Tokyo. He developed an instant affinity for Japan, where he spent the next several years as journalist and teacher. In 1873 he accompanied a punitive expedition to Formosa as war correspondent for the *New York Herald*. He returned to America in 1880

and then moved to London, where he worked on Edwin Booth's British tour. He suffered a stroke in 1883 but continued to write articles and work toward popularizing Western music in Japan. House eventually returned to Japan, dying in Tokyo in 1901.

REFERENCES: J. Cutler Andrews. *The North Reports the Civil War*. 1955; *DAB*; David Shavit. *The United States in Asia*. 1990.

Hovey, Graham (1905–2010)

Following graduation from the University of Minnesota, Hovey worked for two years as a war correspondent for the International News Service (INS). Beginning in 1943 he covered the Allied landings in North Africa at Casablanca, Oran, and Algiers, covered the 1944 Italian campaign, and was with the forces entering Rome in June 1944. He also reported the invasion of France and the advancing Allied forces at the Rhine River. Hovey later worked for the Associated Press, the *New Republic*, and the *New York Times* before returning to academia as director of the Michigan Journalism Fellows Program.

REFERENCES: Robert W. Desmond. *Tides of War*. 1984; Jack Stenbuck, ed. *Typewriter Battalion*. 1995; *NY Times*, Feb. 28, 2010.

Howard, Hubert (1871–1898)

A lawyer by trade, Howard was war correspondent for the *Times* and the *New York Herald* during the conflict in the Sudan in the 1890s. He began his career covering the front lines in 1894 when he accompanied Cuban insurgents in their rebellion against the Spanish. He next covered the Matabele War in South Africa and in 1896 was present at the attack on Sekombo's Kraal, in which he acted as adjutant and took part in the fighting. He returned to South Africa in 1897 when conflict again erupted in Matabeleland and Mashonaland. The following year he was with Lord Kitchener's forces as they moved against the dervish army near Khartoum.

* Indicates a separate entry.

During the battle of Omdurman Howard rode with Winston Churchill* in the charge of the Twenty-first Lancers. Following the charge, Howard was inspecting the Khalifa's palace when it was hit by several artillery shells. He was killed instantly when a shell fragment struck the back of his head.

REFERENCE: Robert Wilkinson-Latham. *From Our Special Correspondent*. 1979.

Howard, James William "Phocion" (1833–1893)

Howard was a member of the so-called Bohemian Brigade,* which covered the American Civil War,* and was apparently the only one to cover the American Indian Wars* as well. Born in Rising Sun, Indiana, on Independence Day, he left his studies at the seminary to work as an apprentice in a newspaper shop, which led to his affinity for reporting. He worked for several papers in Kentucky and Illinois before serving in the Civil War.

Following the war he moved to Chicago and a job with the *Chicago Tribune*. He reportedly had covered at least one army expedition into Sioux country prior to General Alfred Terry's 1876 mission against the Sioux after the Custer defeat. Howard joined infantry reinforcements in Bismarck before embarking on a thousand-mile steamboat trip to Terry's camp near the Rosebud River in 1876.

Howard's reports from Indian territory, which appeared under his pen name "Phocion," were written more for entertainment value than news. In one column, he noted that Sitting Bull had learned French from the legendary Father DeSmet and was able to read the history of the Napoleonic Wars in French and therefore borrow Napoleon's tactics. Howard soon tired of Terry's uneventful campaign and returned to Chicago, where he continued his journalism career, specializing in political writing.

REFERENCE: Oliver Knight. *Following the Indian Wars.* 1960.

Howland, John Dare (1843–1914)

Born in Zanesville, Ohio, he ran away from home at the age of fourteen, joined the American Fur Company at St. Louis, and traveled up the Missouri River. By the time he was fifteen he had hunted buffalo, traded with the Sioux, and tried his luck at the Pike's Peak gold mines. With the outbreak of the American Civil War* he joined the Colorado Volunteers and fought in New Mexico. He soon took up the brush and quill, becoming a sketch artist and correspondent for *Harper's Weekly*. He saved enough to study art in Paris for two years following the war.

Returning to America in 1867 he served as secretary of the Indian Peace Commission for two years while continuing his affiliation with *Harper's* covering the American Indian Wars.* Howland was one of the earliest artists to reside in the Rockies. He designed the Civil War monument near the Colorado state capitol.

REFERENCE: Peggy and Harold Samuels. *Samuels' Encyclopedia of Artists of the American West.* 1985.

Hudson, Frederic (1819–1875)

Born in Quincy, Massachusetts, he entered journalism with the New York-based Hudson's News Rooms, a newsgathering agency founded by his older brother. Assigned to scour the waterfronts for news from abroad for the agency, he made the acquaintance of James Gordon Bennett,* who hired him for the *New York Herald* in 1837. In 1845, Bennett was approached by the editor of the *New York Journal of Commerce* with a proposition to establish together a news-gathering agency. With the outbreak of the Mexican War* the following year, this proposal seemed most timely. While Bennett was in Europe for much of the war, Hudson set up lines of communication extending to New Orleans, the major news center for the war. War news was transmitted from the battlefront to New Orleans and then the East Coast by means of a series of relays using horse express, railroad, and telegraph.

Hudson eventually was promoted to managing editor and played an important role in refining methods of collecting news and developing newsroom organization by coordinating copy and directing reporters in the field. As the outstanding managing editor of his day, he was responsible for choosing all of the war correspondents for his paper during the American Civil War.* He stayed with the *Herald* until he retired in 1866. He died in 1875 in a railroad accident. Hudson wrote *Journalism in the United States from 1690 to 1872* (1873), the first comprehensive history of American journalism.

REFERENCE: J. Cutler Andrews. *The North Reports the Civil War*. 1955.

Huet, Henri (1927–1971)

Born in Da Lat, Vietnam (formerly French Indochina), combat photojournalist Huet was educated in France and came back home to cover the first Indochina war with the French navy. In 1965 he joined Saigon's AP branch to cover the Vietnam War. In 1965 he suffered shrapnel wounds while on assignment that necessitated a lengthy recuperation and he did not return to the combat zone until 1970. The following year he was killed along with four other photographers after their helicopter was shot down over Laos.

REFERENCES: www.ap.org/wallof honor/1970_1979.html.

Hull, Peggy (1889–1967)

Born Henrietta Eleanor Goodnough in Bennington, Kansas, she began her journalism career as a typesetter with the *Junction City* (Kansas) *Sentinel*. Following her marriage to George Hull they moved to Hawaii, where she worked as a reporter for the *Honolulu Star*. Four years later she divorced Hull, after his drinking led him to climb a flagpole in the nude.

After returning to the States, she was with the *Cleveland Plain Dealer* in 1916 when the Ohio National Guard was sent to Texas to join Pershing's punitive expedition to capture Pancho Villa.

When her request to cover the guardsmen was rebuffed she quit and went to Texas on her own. In El Paso she worked for several papers, and although she never actually made it to the front, Hull did accompany the troops on a ninety-mile, two-week training march into the desert. In one incident she became separated from the troops in a sandstorm and was rescued by an Indian family.

In February 1917, her story of the return of the Pershing expedition appeared on the front page of the *El Paso Morning Times*. She almost stole the thunder from Pershing when newsreel* cameramen convinced her to mount a horse and pull alongside the general's. The image of the female reporter and Pershing leading troops out of Mexico appeared in newspapers around the world under the caption "American girl correspondent leads troops out of Mexico with General Pershing."

With America's entrance into World War I,* Hull headed for France at her own expense, with her paper agreeing to publish her articles if she was able to get to the front. She was able to connive her way to Paris in time to witness the first appearance of the Allied Expeditionary Forces (AEF) on July 4, 1917. Newspapers were required to post a $10,000 bond to ensure the good behavior of accredited correspondents. Peggy first needed sponsorship by a newspaper. After rejection by fifty newspapers she was finally endorsed by the Newspaper Enterprise Association, affiliated with the Scripps-Howard press service.

Army accreditation officers continued to deny her requests to cover combat. However, in September 1918 Hull became the first woman correspondent accredited by the U.S. War Department to cover a modern war zone in the 20th century. After obtaining accreditation, she became the only American reporter to cover the American expedition to guard supplies for the White Army in Siberia, which was still in a civil war with Bolshevik forces. She was in Russia when the armistice was signed ending the war in Europe. Hull spent nine months covering the atrocities and horror along the Siberian railroad, one of the few reporters to do so, but saw no warfare.

---

* Indicates a separate entry.

She was in Shanghai in 1932 when Japanese troops invaded, and she reported the fighting for the *New York Daily News*. Hull received accreditation to cover the Pacific conflict in November 1943 and covered most of the major campaigns, including Guam, Saipan, Guadalcanal, and the New Hebrides. Although her stories chronicled GI life much like Ernie Pyle's,* she witnessed her share of violence, including the deaths of Japanese soldiers outside her tent on Guam, and baskets of amputated feet on Saipan. She died in Carmel, California, at the age of seventy-seven.

REFERENCES: Emmet Crozier. *American Reporters on the Western Front, 1914–1918.* 1959; Julia Edwards. *Women of the World: The Great Foreign Correspondents.* 1989.

Hunt, Frazier "Spike" (1885–1967)

Born at Rock Island, Illinois, in 1885, Hunt filed dispatches from south of the border during the Mexican Revolution, before reporting World War I* and the Russian Revolution. In early 1918 he went to France as war correspondent for *American Red Cross Magazine* before transferring to the *Chicago Tribune* later that year. He reported naval operations, troop convoy movements, and fighting at the front before being sent to cover the American expeditionary force in northern Russia. His dispatches from the Russian Civil War were influential in bringing about the withdrawal of American troops from this theater of operations. As the first reporter to enter Petrograd in six months, he continued to cover the conflict, reporting pogroms, famine, and various atrocities. His reports were unique for this era in predicting victory for the Bolsheviks. He wrote several books, including *Blown in by the Draft* (1918) and *The Rising Temper of the East* (1922).

REFERENCES: Eugene Lyons. *We Cover the World.* 1937; Lloyd Wendt. *Chicago Tribune.* 1979.

Hurley, James Francis "Frank" (c. 1885–1962)

Born in Sydney, Australia, he covered his first major story in 1911 when he was the official photographer on the Australian Antarctic expedition. In 1914 he performed the same function with Sir Ernest Shackleton's ill-fated expedition, which was trapped by ice for a year. During World War I* he was made official Australian war photographer* in 1917, recording the Battles of Ypres, Menin Road, and Passhenduck. Following the war he traveled widely before making the transition to motion picture photography. During World War II* he headed the Australian Imperial Photographic Unit and there was director of British Army Features and Propaganda. Never without his camera equipment, he made dozens of films and documentaries, including *With Allenby in Palestine* (1917), *Siege at Tobruk* (1941), and one depicting the Battle of Jericho in 1922. Hurley also wrote numerous books.

REFERENCE: Turner Browne and Elaine Partnow. *Photographic Artists and Innovators.* 1983.

Huynh, Thanh My

See MY, HUYNH THANH.

Huynh, Ut Cong

See UT, HUYNH CONG .

Huyshe, Wentworth (1846–1934)

At his death on December 2, 1934, he was reputedly the oldest war correspondent in England. He served on the staff of the *New York Herald* during the Russo-Turkish War* and the *Times* during the Sudan campaign, where he witnessed the bloody Battle of Suakin on March 22, 1885. Following the war he worked for various papers, including the *Graphic* and the *Daily Graphic*.

REFERENCES: Dennis Griffiths. *Encyclopedia of the British Press.* 1992; Robert Wilkinson-Latham. *From Our Special Correspondent.* 1979.

I

Iraq War

In 2006 Vietnam War era and Pulitzer Prize winning war correspondent David Halberstam* noted that the government criticism of news reporters covering Iraq had a number of parallels to the way he and others were viewed by government officials while covering the Vietnam War. Halberstam conceded that reporters in Iraq are "the bravest correspondents that we have ever sent out to cover a war, because it's infinitely more dangerous there than it was in Vietnam," adding "in the old days, if you were in Vietnam, you could sort of rest in Saigon. There's no safe zone in Iraq." AP reporter Robert H. Reid added that he felt that by 2004 the security environment for journalists was tenuous at best. Suggesting that "the press card guaranteed no immunity," more reporters were less likely to cover news outside their lodgings, reporting from the safety of their compound, thus leaving news gathering services to depend more heavily on Iraqi reporters; nonetheless they faced as much danger as Western reporters due to the bloody sectarian and tribal conflicts that characterized the internal war. As of 2008 the Iraqi War had indeed proved to be the most dangerous one for war correspondents, taking more of their lives than the conflicts of World War II, Vietnam, the Balkans, and Korea. Different measures have been used to measure the number of deaths. For example, the International Federation of Journalists, based in Brussels, claimed 2006 was "a year of tragedy," pointing

to a total 155 deaths caused by murder, assassination and unexplained deaths. On the other hand, Reporters without Borders asserts that more than 80 journalists were killed in 21 countries that year, "the highest total since 1994." In its statistical breakdown of media deaths in Iraq between 2003 and 2009, the CPJ reported deaths by nationality as follows: Iraqi (117); European (13); Other Arab countries (3); United States (2); and other countries (5). Of these, 128 were men and 89 were classified as murder. The number broke down by job as follows: Photojournalists, photographers and camera operators (36); reporters and editor (85); producers (9); and technicians (7). The Iraq War was the first war where the Pentagon called up its press corps for a military boot-camp in preparation for covering the war. According to Julian Borger this was a result of U.S. troops in Afghanistan complaining "of having to wait for flabby, unfit journalists to keep up with them." These training sessions were scheduled to begin in 2003 on bases along the U.S. East Coast. The courses were to be a combination of classroom and field preparation, including proper procedures for getting on and off helicopters. The boot camp was not considered "obligatory" for military journalists but by most accounts those that avoided it had a lesser chance of accompanying troops into battle.

Between the first Gulf War of 1990–91 and Iraqi War that began in 2003, news reporting made the huge leap from analog to digital technology. Digital technology has transformed the

---

* Indicates a separate entry.

way journalists now cover the war zone as equipment has become much smaller and lighter. For example, while covering the battle of Fallujah, one reporter sent his stories to a computer server in the US utilizing a laptop computer and a telephone-sized contraption called a Regional Broadband Global Area Network (RBGAN) satellite modem. During this process, video is sent using File Transfer Protocal (FTP) which "few journalists with rival networks knew how to do." As a virtual one-man unit, soldiers respected his "self-reliance" and ability to shoot, write and transmit reports without a crew. The reporter also maintained an independent weblog, something NBC permitted him to do since he had freelance status.

The U.S. began withdrawing its troops in the winter of 2007–2008. The withdrawal accelerated under the Obama administration and by the end of 2011 American forces had been formally withdrawn from Iraq. However, the killing of journalists in Iraq did not end. By most accounts Iraq was the "deadliest place on earth for media professionals" each year between 2003 and 2008, as well as in 2010, 2011 and 2013. In 2014 at least 14 joirnalists were killed in Iraq, although these figures vary according to databases available from Reporters Without Borders (4), the Committee to Protect Journalists (6), and the Iraqi Journalists Syndicate (14).

REFERENCES: Associated Press. "Halberstam Finds Key Links in Iraq and Vietnam Coverage." Nov. 21, 2006; Paul L. Moorcroft and Philip M. Taylor. *Shooting the Messenger.* 2008; Julian Borger. "Flabby journalists sent to boot camp." www.guardian.co.uk/media/2002/nov/01/usnews.iraq.; http://cpj.org/reports/2008/07/journalists-killed-in-iraq.php; Dirk Adriaensens, Global Research, The Brussells Tribune, February 1, 2015.

Irvin, George Bede (1910–1944)

Born in Des Moines, Iowa he worked for several newspapers before catching on with the AP in Kansas City in 1936. He started covering World War Two in 1943, the "first American photographer assigned by the AP to cover the war in Europe in preparation for D-Day." He was killed on July 25, 1944 when an Allied bomb mistakenly hit his position north of St. Lo, France during the beginning of the Allied drive out of Normandy. He was in the process of diving for cover when he went to grab his camera and was killed by a bomb fragment. He was buried with military honors at the U.S. Cemetery near La Cambe, France.

REFERENCE: AP Wall of Honor, www.ap.org/wallof-honor/1940_1949.html.

Irwin, Virginia (1908–1980)

Born in Quincy, Illinois, and educated at Lindenwood College and Gem City Business College, Irwin entered journalism with the *St. Louis Dispatch* in 1932. With the onset of World War II* she covered the home front, and after she was rebuffed in her attempts to gain accreditation as a war correspondent she went to Europe to work for the Red Cross. She finally managed to get her credentials from the War Department shortly before the Normandy invasion in 1944.

Irwin arrived in France the following month and covered the conflict in Belgium, Holland, Luxembourg, and Germany. In April 1945 she bypassed official channels and went to Berlin, where she witnessed the final bloodletting of the war in Europe. Irwin was also present when U.S. patrols linked up with the Red Army on the Elbe River on April 25. Her unauthorized trip to Berlin with Andrew Tully of the *Boston Traveler* resulted in the first eyewitness account by any Western correspondent of the devastated capital and seemed a sure scoop for the intrepid reporters. However, for acting without official permission, their credentials were revoked and the publication of their stories was delayed. She continued with the *Post-Dispatch* at its New York bureau until 1960.

REFERENCE: Robert W. Desmond. *Tides of War. 1984.*

Irwin, William Henry (1873–1948)

Irwin was born in Oneida, New York, and educated at Stanford University. In 1900 he joined the *San Francisco Chronicle,* and after stints with the *New York Sun* and *McClure's Magazine* he took a respite from journalism to write fiction. While employed by *McClure's,* he wrote one of his best-known stories when he covered the San Francisco earthquake and fire. Although he was not given a byline, the story was quickly credited to him and he was forever linked to the city by the bay.

With the outbreak of World War I* he returned to reporting with the *New York Tribune, London Times,* and the *Daily Mail.* In 1915 he reported but did not witness the entire First Battle of Ypres in Belgium, including a German poison gas attack in which he was himself injured by gas residue following the battle. He discovered that due to censorship the British public was unaware of the heroic victory by the British soldiers three months previously at Ypres. Irwin defied the British War Office and, using confidential government sources, described a battle costing 50,000 British soldiers out of 120,000 engaged, a proportional loss unequaled in any previous war. His article "The Splendid Story of the Battle of Ypres" was written with the power of observation that a three month perspective would offer and had an incredible impact when it ran in British papers. Its publication elevated Irwin to the top ranks of the war's correspondents; however, he would be forever resented by his colleagues in the British press, who had been curtailed by censorship. In addition Irwin lost his credentials and was blacklisted by both the French and British.

After marrying for the second time in 1916 he returned to the battlefront after a two-year hiatus, this time for the *Saturday Evening Post,* and was promptly injured by a shell explosion in Italy, resulting ultimately in deafness in his right ear.

After the war he crusaded for international peace and the League of Nations. A prolific writer, he continued to produce journalistic and fiction pieces. During World War II* he wrote for the North American Newspaper Alliance and other syndicates. He died following a series of strokes in 1948.

REFERENCES: Emmet Crozier. *American Reporters on the Western Front, 1914–18.* 1959; *DLB 25.*

Isaq, Mohamed (1989–2014)

Isaq was a Somalian cameraman for Kalsan TV. He had covered the news in the south central town of Baidoa for the past couple of years, including the Somalian government takeover of the town from Al-Shabaab militants. He was killed along with 14 others inside a restaurant after a suicide bomber detonated his car as he rammed it into the business. Also killed was journalist Abdulkadir Ahmed.* Al-Shabaab has targeted journalists claiming they are spies.

REFERENCE: https://cpj.org/killed/2014/mohamed-isaq.php.

Islamic State (ISIS, ISIL)

In October 2014, the FBI issued a bulletin to news organizations warning that the Islamic State was targeting reporters and media personalities in response to the American-led air campaign. As a result of this warning and the recent beheadings of Western reporters, the United States is now involved, according to journalist Thomas L. Friedman, "in the first prolonged war in the modern Middle East that American reporters and photographers can't cover on a daily basis."

REFERENCE: Thomas L. Friedman, "Flying Blind in Iraq and Syria," New York Times, Nov. 2, 2014, 11.

Italo-Ethiopian War

See ETHIOPIAN WAR.

* Indicates a separate entry.

J

Jacob, Alaric (1909–1995)

Formerly a Reuters* correspondent in the Middle East, Jacob arrived in Tobruk to cover the North African desert campaign in August 1941. He had earlier spent six years as Washington correspondent and tended toward Marxist views. He covered the crucial Battle of El Alamein in 1942. Jacob left Reuters for the *London Daily Express* in 1942 and the following year covered the Burma front. In January 1944 he reported the war in Russia.

REFERENCE: Richard Collier. *Fighting Words.* 1989.

Jacoby, Melville (1916–1942)

Jacoby began his career in journalism with the *Stanford Daily* and then the *San Francisco Chronicle* following graduation from Stanford University. When war broke out in the Far East, Jacoby was studying at Lignan University in Canton, China. He joined the staff of *Time* and *Life* in 1940 and left China for the Philippines, where he covered the Japanese siege of the islands. His dispatches to *Time* magazine were some of the most vivid accounts of the fighting around the Philippines. On a more controversial note, Jacoby's reports formed the basis for John Hersey's* 1940s bestseller *Men of Bataan.* Jacoby had been under the impression that the magazine would use his dispatches in the magazine, but instead *Time* allowed Hersey to use the cables for his book. In compensation they offered Jacoby and his wife $450 for his research.

With the fall of Manila, Jacoby and his wife, *Time* correspondent Annalee Whitmore, and reporter Clark Lee* fled by boat to the island fortress of Corregidor and then to the Bataan Peninsula. Several weeks later they fled by boat to Australia, where Jacoby perished in a freak airplane accident on April 29, 1942, only weeks after their arrival. Jacoby was waiting with others, including Brigadier General H. H. George, to board a plane when the propeller detached from an out-of-control fighter plane and crashed into the bystanders, killing all of them. His short career as a war correspondent is commemorated by his alma mater in the form of the annual Melville Jacoby Fellowship at Stanford University for a graduate student in journalism specializing in Far Eastern affairs.

REFERENCES: Robert W. Desmond. *Tides of War.* 1984; Peter Rand. *China Hands.* 1995.

Jacquier, Gilles (1968–2012)

Born in Evian-les-Bains, France in 1968, the French photojournalist and reporter began his career for France 3 Lille in 1991. Between 1994 and 1998 he covered foreign affairs and conflicts around the world. He worked for France 2 between 1999 and 2006 and rose to prominence covering warfare in Iraq, Afghanistan, and Kosovo. Despite wearing a bulletproof vest, he was wounded near a refugee camp in the West Bank while covering the Second Intifada for France 2 in 2002. He recovered from his shoulder wound and since 2006 was working for *Envoye Special,* a documentary program that appears on France 2. During his more than two decades in the field he filmed conflicts in Afghanistan, Algeria, Iraq, the Democratic Republic of Congo, the former Yugoslavia, and the tribulations of the Arab Spring (2010–2012).

Jacquier became the first Western journalist killed covering the Syrian civil war.* He crossed into Syria in 2012 after receiving a visa to cover the conflict. Along with cameraman Christopher Kenck, the journalist made it to Homs. He supposedly had permission from the Syrian government to cover the opposition there. On January 11, 2012 he was interviewing various Syrian residents and headed toward a local hospital while a pro-Bashar al-Assad demonstration was taking place nearby. By most accounts the French reporter was killed along with seven others in a rocket attack while conducting his interviews. However, his wife Caroline Poiron, a reporter and photographer for Paris Match, claimed he was targeted by the Syrian secret police and was either killed by gunshot or knife. She was not the only doubter, with several other Swiss reporters and others claiming the Syrian government was behind the death of Jacquier. Jacquier's wife co-authored with the two Swiss journalists, Patrick Vallelian (*L'Hebdo*) and Sid Ahmed Hammouche the 2013 book, *Attentat Express,* which made a case for the Syrian government's complicity in the death of the French reporter. His reportage received numerous awards including the Albert Londres Prize (2003), the TV Journalism Ilari Alpi (2007), the Jean-Louis Calderone prize (2009), and in May 2012 he was posthumously given the International Journalism and Human Rights award by the Barcelona Human Rights Film Festival.

REFERENCES: "Syria Unrest: French Journalist Gilles Jacquier Killed," BBC News, June 11, 2012.

Jagielski, Wojciech (b. 1960)

Born and educated in Warsaw, Poland, he began his career in 1986 with the Polish Press Agency. Although his stated preference was to cover Africa, his managers were more interested in what was going on in the Caucasus, and soon he was regarded as an expert on the region. He has covered conflicts in the Transcaucasus, the Caucasus, Central Asia and Africa. His writing technique has been compared to that of his mentor and friend, Rysard Kapuscinski.* Between 1992 and 2001 he visited Afghanistan numerous times, chronicling the fratricidal wars there in his book *Pray for the Rain* (2002). He covered the war in Chechnya, producing the book *Towers of Stone: The Battle of Wills in Chechnya* (2009), and more recently examined the plight of Uganda's child soldiers and the crimes of God's Army leader Joseph Kony (2012).

REFERENCES: http://www.polishculture-nyc.org/?itemca tegory=30817&personDetailId=675; http://culture.pl/en/ work/the-night-wanderers-wojciech-jagielski.

James, Edwin "Jimmy" L. (1890–1951)

Prior to World War I* he was on the staff of the *New York Times,* covering the state capital scene in Albany. James was a principal correspondent with the American Expeditionary Force in 1918 during World War I* for the *New York Times.* He had been sent as a replacement for the recently expelled Wythe Williams.* James was present when French and American forces stopped the Germans at Chateau-Thierry on the Marne River, but when he returned to press headquarters at Neufchateau to file his story he found that headquarters had been moved back to Paris, almost two hundred miles away. Having not been apprised of the change he missed perhaps his greatest scoop, as he was forced to wait several hours before sending his cable. He later was with occupation forces in Germany and in 1919 became Paris bureau chief and director of its

European service. In 1930 he returned to New York and two years later became managing editor of the *Times*. After one of his correspondents was killed flying as an observer on a World War II* bombing mission he advised his reporters not to take unwarranted risks.

REFERENCES: Emmet Crozier. *American Reporters on the Western Front 1914–18.* 1959; Robert W. Desmond. *Windows on the World.* 1980.

James, Lionel (1871–1955)

James left his indigo plantation in India to join Reuters* at the age of twenty-four. In 1895 he accompanied the relief expedition to Chitral on India's North West Frontier. He reported the campaign for the *Bombay Times of India* and for the *Calcutta Englishman,* as well as taking part in the fighting. In 1898 Reuters assigned him to cover the warfare in the Sudan. Shortly afterward he moved over to the *Times.* During the Boer War* he was among the contingent of correspondents holed up during the siege of Ladysmith.*

The *Times* was the first news organization to make use of the wireless as a means of transmitting war reports; James pioneered the new technology during the Russo-Japanese War.* Following his exploits in South Africa, James had gone to South America and then the Balkans when war broke out in the Far East. He rushed to the front lines of the Russo-Japanese War in a chartered steamer outfitted with a mobile radio station. He had persuaded the *Times* to charter the *Haimun,* a 311-ton steamer in Hong Kong, and had a radio transmitter installed. However, the ever vigilant Japanese officials agreed to let him operate only if he allowed an intelligence officer of the Japanese navy to accompany the vessel. James planned to send his messages to a shore station in neutral China; they would in turn be relayed back to London without being tainted by Japanese press censorship. James was able to assemble important data on naval actions, most significantly the sinking of the Russian flagship

by a mine off Port Arthur, with eight hundred deaths, including that of Admiral Stepan Osipovich Makarov. James is credited with sending the first telegraphic report of a naval engagement directly from the scene of operations to the office of a news agency. He also reported the Japanese naval blockade at Port Arthur. After three months this operation was ended by pressure from the Japanese military. Later James would report the Balkans conflict of 1912 and warfare between Russia and Turkey.

REFERENCES: Robert W. Desmond. *The Information Process.* 1978; Robert W. Desmond. *Windows on the World.* 1980; Dennis and Peggy Warner. *The Tide at Sunrise: A History of the Russo-Japanese War.* 1974.

Jarban, Ferzat (d. 2011)

In November 2011, Jarban became the first Syrian journalist to perish during the Syrian civil war.* A Syrian freelance cameraman, his body was found the day after he had been arrested covering the antigovernment clashes and protests in Al-Qusayr. His work was featured on a number of Arab news outlets. He was arrested on November 19 in full view of numerous witnesses as he videotaped the protests. When his body was found the following day it had been mutilated, including having his eyes gouged out and bearing two bullet wounds.

REFERENCE: https://cpj.org/killed/2011/ferzat-jarban.php.

Jeffries, Joseph M. N. (1880–1960)

Jeffries was one of the outlaw* correspondents who bypassed official channels and went directly from England to France to cover World War I* for the *Daily Mail.* He served as Paris bureau chief and reportedly set a record by reporting the conflict from at least seventeen countries prior to 1918. Among the countries he visited were Egypt, Albania, Greece, Italy, Austria, Belgium, and France. In August 1918 he covered the landing of British and French forces in the Black Sea area of Russia. Jeffries continued his affiliation with the *Mail* until 1933.

REFERENCE: Robert W. Desmond. *Windows on the World*. 1980.

Jenks, Paul (1965–1992)

Primarily a freelance photographer, he was killed by a sniper near the city of Osijek while covering the Yugoslavian conflict. As a correspondent for the European Picture Agency, he was on his third tour covering the civil war when he became the first British victim in the conflict. Jenks was the twenty-third combat journalist to die in Yugoslavia.

REFERENCE: Dennis Griffiths, ed. *The Encyclopedia of the British Press*. 1992.

Jessica Lynch Hoax

One of the biggest news stories to come out of the early war in Iraq in 2003 was the manufactured story about the rescue of Private Jessica Lynch by US Special Forces. The only elements of the story that were actually true were that she was indeed captured and was being treated in a hospital in Nassiiriya, and was "taken from there" by US Special Forces. However, the rest of the world was given an alternative version that was meant to be a piece of well-needed feel-good propaganda. Lynch was a 19-year-old army clerk from West Virginia when she was captured on March 26, 2003 after her company caravan took a wrong turn and was ambushed on the outskirts of Nassiriya. She was transferred to a hospital for treatment. A BBC documentary entitled *War Spin* revealed the actual turn of events that led to her "rescue" eight days later. Contrary to reports that she had suffered bullet and stab wounds she had a broken arm, a broken thigh and a dislocated ankle, the result of a road accident and according to Iraqi doctors received the best medical treatment available. According to

the Penagon story line she had been mistreated and only rescued after a "courageous Iraqi lawyer" revealed her whereabouts. The US Special Forces were videotaped storming the hospital and carrying the "hostage" out on a stretcher. However, there were no Iraqi insurgetnts or soldiers present, despite the military posturing and loud explosions as the assault was quickly carried out. Shortly after, a grainy videotape of the "rescue" was shown to the corps of war correspondents who naturally delivered the story to the American public and in the process created the "first hero" of the war.

REFERENCES: Phillip Knightley. *The First Casualty*. 2004 edition; *The Guardian*. "The Truth About Jessica." May 15, 2003.

"Joan" (?)

The *Charleston Courier* was apparently the first Confederate newspaper to employ a woman war correspondent, beginning in 1861. Her real name is lost to posterity, since her dispatches appeared under the pseudonym "Joan." She initially offered her services as a Virginia correspondent so she could be near her son, who was in Johnston's army. Her first letter appeared shortly after the First Battle of Bull Run. Over the next four months she wrote several dispatches in the form of letters describing the war in Virginia from a woman's perspective. She spent two months in Richmond reporting from the home front before securing permission to see her son at the front. Reporting from Richmond in August, "Joan" noted the prevalence of disease and overall poor medical conditions among the Confederate troops.

REFERENCE: J. Cutler Andrews. *The South Reports the Civil War*. 1970.

Johnson, Edd (d. 1954)

Johnson worked as a war correspondent for the *Chicago Sun* during World War II.* He covered

---

* *Indicates a separate entry.*

the 1944 Italian campaign and later that year followed Allied forces on the advance through France to the Rhone River Valley. Johnson was the recipient of a special citation for aiding wounded soldiers while under fire during the advance of the Seventh Army. In another incident he rode into Grenoble in a tram with another correspondent and was greeted by the inhabitants as the liberators of the town. Johnson was among the twenty-five victims of a plane crash in Mexico in 1954.

REFERENCES: Robert W. Desmond. *Tides of War.* 1984; Jack Stenbuck, ed. *Typewriter Battalion.* 1995.

Johnson, Thomas M. (?)

The veteran *New York Sun* correspondent and military historian began covering World War I* in October 1917, when he was accredited to the American Expeditionary Force. He arrived at Neufchateau in time to report his first war story when he covered General Petain's visit to American headquarters. In May 1918 he covered the advance at Cantigny and the fighting at Chateau-Thierry, where American forces stopped the German drive on the Marne and saved Paris. Johnson reported but did not witness the Battle of Belleau Wood. He attended the 1919 Paris Peace Conference and following the war wrote *Without Censor* (1928).

REFERENCE: Emmet Crozier. *American Reporters on the Western Frontier 1914–18.* 1959.

Johnston, Stanley (1900–1962)

Born in Australia, he joined an artillery unit during World War I* at the age of seventeen. Following the war he returned home and attended the University of Sydney. Later, he fled France when it fell to the Nazis in 1940 and joined the London office of the *Chicago Tribune.* He reported the Battle of Britain and in 1942 was assigned to the South Pacific theater. His coverage of the Battle of the Coral Sea is considered

a classic example of war reportage. Johnston's book *Queen of the Flat-Tops* chronicles his experiences on the aircraft carrier *Lexington.* He was aboard the ship when it was sunk during the Battle of the Coral Sea. Johnston was recommended for a citation for bravery for risking his life attempting to save others.

REFERENCE: Robert W. Desmond. *Tides of War.* 1984.

Jones, Roderick (1877–1962)

Born in England, Jones moved in his youth to South Africa, where he entered the newspaper business with the *Pretoria Press* and the *Pretoria News* while still in his teens. In 1896 he scored his first scoop when Paul Kruger granted him the first interview with Dr. Jameson after the latter's capture during his unsuccessful raid on Johannesburg. Jones later joined the Reuters* bureau in Cape Town and reported for the *Cape Times.* In 1900 he accompanied British forces under Field Marshal Roberts in the Boer War* and two years later served a brief stint at Reuters headquarters in London. He returned to Cape Town in 1905 and for the next ten years supervised the news bureau offices in South and Central Africa. In 1915 he returned to London as general manager of Reuters and the following year became its principal owner. He was knighted in 1918.

REFERENCE: Donald Read, *The Power of News.* 1992.

Jouvenal, Peter (b. c. 1958)

A former officer in a British parachute regiment who made the transition to BBC cameraman, Jouvenal has covered events in Afghanistan as a cameraman for almost thirty years. He was one of the founders of the Frontline News* agency and then the Frontline Club*. He began covering Afghanistan shortly after the Soviet invasion around 1980. He made more than 70 dangerous excursions into Soviet-held Afghanistan and over the years has become one of the world's best known war zone cameramen. He is among the few to have filmed Mullah Omar of the Taliban and Osama bin Laden (1987), whom he famously described as "rather like a bank manager." He was the first cameraman to film Stinger missiles in Afghanistan and was the first western cameraman into Kabul after the fall of the Taliban. Jovenal witnessed the battle of Tora Bora as well in 2001. He has also covered conflicts in Iraq and Chechnya.

REFERENCES: Charles Sennott. "Afghanistan at the Tipping Point." Carnegi.org/publications; Denis D. Gray. "Kabul lodge honors 'Flashy' scoundrel of fiction." www.salon.com, February 22, 2010.

Juma, Adam (d. 2015)

Juma was a reporter and television presenter for a local radio station when he was killed along with four other journalists in South Sudan on January 25, 2015. By most accounts, unidentified gunmen ambushed a convoy they were traveling in from the roadside. The victims were shot then attacked with machetes before being set on fire. The journalists were following a local commissioner as he visited families of those killed in a recent attack.

REFERENCE: https://cpj.org/killed/2015/adam-juma.php.

Junger, Sebastian (b. 1962)

Junger is a journalist probably best known for his best-selling book (turned blockbuster movie in 2000), *The Perfect Storm: A True Story of Men against the Sea* (1997). He was born in Belmont, Massachusetts and educated at Wesleyan University. Following *Perfect Storm*, Junger developed an affinity for adventure nonfiction. In 2001 he was hired by ABC News and *Vanity Fair* as special correspondent to cover the war zone in Afghanistan. His book *Fire*, is a collection of articles covering dangerous occupations in

dangerous regions of the world. It includes Junger's interview with Afghan Northern Alliance leader Ahmad Shah Massoud (The Lion of the Panjshir), who fought first the Soviets and then the Taliban, before being assassinated two days before 9/11. Junger rose to further prominence with his 2008 film *Restrepo,** co-directed with Tim Hetherington.* He chronicled his coverage of Afghanistan in 2007 and 2008 in his 2010 book *War*. He went on to produce the HBO film *Which Way is the Front Line From Here? The Life and Time of Tim Hetherington* (2013), and *Korengal,** a sequel of sorts to *Restrepo*, but made in the aftermath of his friend and colleague Tim Hetherington's* death in Libya. Junger has reported from numerous war zones, including Liberia, Cyprus, and Kashmir.

REFERENCES: David Fear, "Life during Wartime: Sebastian Junger on Korengal," Rolling Stone, June 2, 2014; http://www.barnesandnoble.com/writers/writerdetails.asp?cid=883401#top.

Just, Ward (b. 1935)

Born into a newspaper family he worked as a reporter for his family newspaper in Waukegan, Illinois before landing a position with *Newsweek*, which led to postings in London and Cyprus. He next worked for the *Washington Post*, for which he began covering the Vietnam War beginning in 1965. The following year he narrowly escaped death when he was wounded by grenade fragments. He was applauded for refusing to be evacuated until all of the wounded soldiers had been airlifted. He returned home to recuperate and then came back to Vietnam. He left journalism for fiction in 1968. That same year saw the publication of his Vietnam memoir, *To What End?*

REFERENCE: Michelle Ferrari and James Tobin. *Reporting America at War: An Oral History*. 2003.

Kahn, Ely Jacques "E. J." (1917–1994)

Born in Manhattan, after graduation from Harvard in 1937 he began a fifty-seven-year association with the *New Yorker*. Serving in the army from 1941 to 1945, he wrote accounts of his life as a chief warrant officer in the South Pacific, which were published in the *New Yorker*. He also served as war correspondent for the magazine during the Korean War,* an experience which resulted in the book *The Peculiar War: Impressions of a Reporter in Korea* (1952). Kahn wrote twenty-seven books, including *The Stragglers* (1962), which chronicles the stories of Japanese soldiers who hid in the jungles for decades following World War II.*

REFERENCE: *New York Times*. May 29, 1994.

Kalischer, Peter (1915–1991)

Kalischer arrived in Korea with the first American troops in 1950 as war correspondent for the UP. Along with Tom Lambert* of the AP, he was later prohibited from covering the combat zone for giving "aid and comfort to the enemy" by using the term "lost battalion" to describe a unit in turmoil with high casualties. General Douglas MacArthur would later reinstate them. Kalischer covered the Vietnam War* sporadically for CBS. In 1975 he delivered the first bulletin announcing the fall of Saigon.

REFERENCE: Michael Emery. *On the Front Lines*. 1995.

Kaltenborn, Hans V. (1879–1965)

Born in Milwaukee, Wisconsin, and educated at Harvard, Kaltenborn was the son of a former Hessian officer. He is best known as the dean of radio commentators and is considered one of the creators of "electronic journalism." He served in the Spanish-American War* before beginning a twenty-five-year affiliation with the *Brooklyn Eagle* in 1902. In 1914 he reported German war preparations, but returned to the States prior to the outbreak of hostilities. In 1927 he resigned to devote himself to radio. He joined CBS as a full-time commentator in 1930 and rose to prominence with his broadcasts from the French-Spanish frontier in August and September 1936, the first radio broadcasts of battle in history.

Kaltenborn broadcast virtually every aspect of the diplomatic crisis emerging in Germany before, after, and during the Munich conference. However, by 1939 press censorship was imposed on foreign correspondents, and when Kaltenborn flew to Berlin intending to broadcast for CBS, he was forced to return to London on the next flight. The following year he moved to NBC and continued his work from New York.

REFERENCE: Michael Emery. *On the Front Lines*. 1995.

Kaplan, David (1947–1992)

Kaplan was in the first day of a special assignment for ABC news when he was killed by a sniper's bullet in the war-torn Bosnian capital city of Sarajevo. Kaplan had two decades of experience as a television news producer, including the Gulf War,* when he arrived in Yugoslavia to interview Prime Minister Milan Panic. It is unknown which side of the conflict was responsible for the bullet fired at Kaplan's motor vehicle, clearly marked with a large "TV" sign. He was the first American journalist killed while on assignment in the former Yugoslavia and the fortieth journalist killed since the conflict had begun the previous year.

REFERENCE: Charles P. Arnot. *Don't Kill the Messenger.* 1994.

Kapuscinski, Ryszard (1932–2007)

Born in Pinsk, Poland, he began his career in journalism in 1958, after studying Polish history at Warsaw University. While employed by the Polish Press Agency between 1958 and 1980, often as its only foreign correspondent, Kapuscinski covered twenty-seven revolutions and coups, primarily in Third World nations. In 1960 he was stationed in the Congo, when Patrice Lumumba was assassinated. Escaping to neighboring Burundi, he was sentenced to death in absentia. On several other occasions he was sentenced to death. He covered the hundred-hour "Soccer War" following the World Cup between Honduras and El Salvador in 1969.

In the 1970s he was in Cyprus when violence broke out between Turkey and Greece (1974), between Ethiopia and Somalia (1976), in Algeria (1965), in Nigeria (1966), and in Angola (1973). He recounts most of these incidents in his book *The Soccer War* (1991). His other books include *The Emperor: Downfall of an Autocrat* (1978), which chronicles the fall of Ethiopia's Haile Selassie, and *Shah of Shahs, About the Iranian Revolution.*

REFERENCES: *International Who's Who.* 1976; *Who's Who in the World.* 1978, 1979; The Guardian, Jan. 26, 2007; Adam Bernstein. "War correspondent, Author Ryszard Kapuscinski." The Washington Post, January 25, 2007.

Karnow, Stanley (1925–2013)

Born in Brooklyn, a city then awash in daily papers, Karnow early on was drawn to the craft of news reporting. He served in the Air Force during World War II and graduated from Harvard in 1947. In the 1950s he served as a Paris correspondent for *Time* magazine, covering Western Europe and North Africa. In 1958 he covered the Algerian war of independence from France. The following year found him covering conflict in Southeast Asia. His career as a correspondent was distinct from his counterparts. In the 1950s and early 1960s, while most Western reporters worked for one publication and were dropped into war zones or political hotspots to write a few articles and then typically moved on, the erudite Karnow often worked for multiple employers at the same time, writing for newsmagazines and other periodicals without the weight of deadlines to worry about. Karnow could be depended on for thoughtful and more analytical coverage of news events. He is probably best known for his Pulitzer-Prize winning career as historian of the Vietnam War.* He had first visited Vietnam in 1959 and was in country when the first American advisors were killed. Likewise, he was there at the denouement of the conflict gathering interviews with former fighters, refugees, and various others who had experienced the French and American conflicts. He chronicled his research in the magisterial *Vietnam: A History*, published to great acclaim in 1983. He paralleled this success with the 13-hour PBS documentary *Vietnam: A Television History*, one of the most successful series ever shown on the network and an eventual winner of six Emmy Awards as well as the Peabody and Polk awards. In 1990 he followed up his accomplishments on Vietnam with the Pulitzer Prize for history for *In Our Image: America's Empire in the Philippines* (1989). Karnow wrote numerous other books, most revolving around Southeast Asia.

REFERENCE: Robert D. McFadden, "Stanley Karnow, Historian, Is Dead at 87," New York Times, Jan. 28, 2013.

* *Indicates a separate entry.*

Kazickas, Jurate (b. 1943)

Born in Soviet Lithuania after World War II,* she escaped with her family to the free world and finally America. Kazickas was a freelance photojournalist who covered the Vietnam War* beginning in February 1967. Prior to the war she worked for *Look* magazine. Rebuffed in her attempts to secure accreditation as a war correspondent, she won enough money on a television game show to buy herself a one-way ticket to Saigon. She published her first article in *Mademoiselle* magazine several months later. After several requests to report the war in the field she was allowed to accompany a marine unit on a five-day patrol into the jungle looking for a North Vietnamese regiment.

She was tested under fire for the first time at Pleiku in June 1967. Kazickas continued to report from the front lines, leading marines to believe she was a jinx since each time she appeared an artillery attack would soon follow. In November 1967 she reported the battles at Dak To and the following year was in the besieged camp of Khe Sanh interviewing one of the officers when it came under a rocket attack. Kazickas suffered shrapnel wounds to her cheek, legs, forearm, and buttocks. She left Vietnam for good in May 1968 after a failed love affair and sudden fears for her own mortality.

REFERENCE: Virginia Elwood-Akers. *Women War Correspondents in the Vietnam War, 1961–1975.* 1988.

Keim, Randolph Debenneville (1841–1914)

Born in Reading, Pennsylvania, he attended Beloit College in Wisconsin for a short time. After organizing the City Zouaves of Harrisburg, Pennsylvania, in the heady days following the attack on Fort Sumter, Keim joined the *New York Herald* as a correspondent. He covered twenty-six battles of the American Civil War* prior to the surrender at Appomattox. Some sources claim that his flattering coverage of Grant's command led to the latter's promotion to commander of the Union Army. In the course of war reporting he developed lasting relationships with several officers who would play important roles in the post-Civil War American Indian Wars.*

Following the war Keim became the premier Washington correspondent. In 1868 he was assigned to cover General Phil Sheridan's successful winter campaign on the southern Plains. Keim missed perhaps his greatest story and a place in the pantheon of great journalists while out of the country on a visit to Ceylon. He just missed a letter from his editor offering him the assignment to find the explorer and missionary David Livingstone, who had been missing in Africa for three years. When Keim failed to respond to editor James Gordon Bennett's* offer, the assignment was given to correspondent Henry Stanley.*

Keim acted as a defender of Sheridan's strategy of total war against the Cheyennes and their allies during the five-month winter expedition. Keim's dispatches appearing in the *Herald* under the heading "Indian War" provide a fairly comprehensive account of military conditions on the plains of western Kansas. Most of his reports were mailed to his paper rather than telegraphed. Keim is credited with giving the name to the "Battle of the Washita" in his report of Custer's engagement along the Washita River, because neither Custer nor Sheridan referred to the action using this term. In 1870 he published what is considered one of the three best memoirs of the Indian Wars by a correspondent, *Sheridan's Troopers on the Borders: A Winter Campaign on the Plains.* Following the war in the West he returned to his position as Washington correspondent and was said to be the only reporter granted access to the White House during the Grant years. Keim wrote numerous books, including a series of tourist handbooks for various Washington area sites. He died from complications of diabetes.

REFERENCES: Randolph DeBenneville Keim. *Sheridan's Troopers on the Border,* with foreword by Paul A. Hutton. Reprint 1985; Oliver Knight. *Following the Indian Wars.* 1960.

Kellogg, Marcus Henry
(1833–1876)

Kellogg was the only reporter to accompany Lieutenant Colonel George Custer's fatal expedition to the Little Big Horn. Born in Vermont, by the 1850s he was training to be a telegraph operator in Wisconsin. He entered journalism after meeting the editor of the *La Crosse Democrat* while he was still working as a telegrapher. After an unsuccessful run for political office in 1867 and a short stint as editor for the Council Bluffs *Daily Democrat* he returned to La Crosse in 1870, where he returned to telegraphy. In the early 1870s his articles under the pen name "Frontier" appeared in the *St. Paul Pioneer.* He worked as a stringer* for various newspapers as he followed construction of the Northern pacific Railroad from Minnesota to North Dakota.

In 1873 he was employed by the *Bismarck Tribune* as a staff writer and stringer. While working for the Dakota Territory paper he met George Armstrong Custer. Custer violated an order against bringing journalists with him on his expeditions when he invited Clement A. Lounsberry,* the *Tribune's* publisher, to accompany his expedition to the Little Big Horn. Unfortunately for Kellogg, Lounsberry sent him in his place when his wife fell ill.

When Kellogg perished with Custer's command, no less than five papers claimed him as their own, including the *New York Herald* and the *Chicago Tribune.* In reality, besides the *Bismarck Tribune,* he did contribute to several St. Paul papers and probably the Western Associated Press. Kellogg wrote in his most quoted and last dispatch, "We leave the Rosebud tomorrow and by the time this reaches you we will have met and fought the red devils, and what result remains to be seen. I will go with Custer and will be at [sic] the death."

Kellogg had little to write about prior to his last battle. His dispatches portrayed Custer with sycophantic zeal-brave, dashing, and fearless. When Kellogg's horse expired he shifted to a mule. No special favors would be granted him as they continued on to the Little Big Horn. Editor Lounsberry forwarded Kellogg's last dispatches to the *New York Herald,* which published the most complete account of the Custer debacle.

REFERENCES: Oliver Knight. *Following the Indian Wars.* 1960; Lewis O. Saum. "Colonel Custer's Copperhead: The Mysterious Mark Kellogg," *Montana, the Magazine of Western History.* October 1978.

Kendall, George Wilkins
(1809–1867)

Kendall was the most celebrated war correspondent of the Mexican-American War.* Born in Mount Vernon, New Hampshire, he worked as a printer and for Horace Greeley's *New Yorker* before relocating to New Orleans, where he cofounded the *Picayune* in 1837.

He joined General Zachary Taylor's command soon after the Mexican War broke out in 1846. At the Battle of Chapultepec he was wounded in the leg. During the Battle of Monterrey he captured a Mexican flag and sent it home as a war souvenir to his newspaper. Kendall is credited with inventing General Zachary Taylor's famous order "A little more grape [shot], Captain Bragg."

There was intense competition among members of the press during the conflict. Kendall organized his own pony express service in Mexico to scoop his adversaries. This courier service, better known as "Mr. Kendall's Express," also carried official dispatches. He went on to witness the capture of the San Patricio flag at the Battle of Churubusco, the carnage at Cerro Gordo, and the peace negotiations following the fall of Mexico City. As the lone witness from the press corps at the Battle of Churubusco he reported the desertion trial of the San Patricio battalion.

* Indicates a separate entry.

After the war, Kendall covered revolutions in Europe before returning to Texas and a ranching career. Besides his newspaper reports he wrote *Narrative of the Texas Santa Fe Expedition* (1844) and collaborated with Carl Nebel on *War Between the United States and Mexico* (1851).

REFERENCES: Fayette Copeland. *Kendall of the Picayune.* 1943; Martha Sandweis, Rick Stewart, and Ben Huseman. *Eyewitness to War: Prints and Daguerreotypes of the Mexican War, 1846–1848.* 1989.

Kenichi, Kimura (1905–1973)

Born in Hiroshima, he was an army photographer when he was assigned to document the aftermath of the atomic bombing of his hometown. The Tokyo Medical Army Museum requested that he photograph the wounded of the city. His wife perished in the attack. His work has been published in the *Chugoku* newspaper.

REFERENCE: Frances Fralin, ed. *The Indelible Image.* 1985.

Kennan, George (1845–1924)

Kennan was born in Norwalk, Ohio. His father was a lawyer enamored of the technology of the electric telegraph. He passed his preoccupation with telegraphy to his son, who demonstrated an early proficiency in its use. Rebuffed in his attempts to enlist in the American Civil War,* Kennan worked as a military telegrapher in Cincinnati. His expertise brought him to the attention of the Western Union Telegraph Company, which selected the twenty-year-old Kennan as a member of its Siberian expedition team, whose purpose was to survey a possible telegraph route from the United States to Siberia by way of Alaska and the Bering Strait. The expedition concluded two years later when word arrived that the Atlantic cable had successfully been introduced. Kennan's exploits are chronicled in *Tent Life in Siberia* (1870), published to wide acclaim.

He returned to Russia in 1870 to study the culture and traditions of the Caucasus region. He became an acknowledged authority on Russia and was a highly sought-out lecturer. He wrote *Siberia and the Exile System* (1891), which detailed the abuses of the Romanov government. Its publication had great ramifications for the future Russian Revolution.

Kerman turned to war reporting during the 1898 Spanish-American War.* He covered the Cuban campaign for *Outlook* magazine and volunteered for the Red Cross. His exploits are recounted in *Campaigning in Cuba* (1899). During the Russo-Japanese War* he reported from the Japanese side. Although he never attended college, Kerman became fluent in Russian and a world-respected scholar and journalist. He also wrote *The Tragedy of Pelee* (1902), the story of the devastating Martinique eruption; *Folk-Tales of Napoleon* (1902), which is based on folk tales surrounding the march on Moscow; and a biography of E. H. Harriman.

REFERENCES: Charles H. Brown. *The Correspondents' War.* 1967; *DAB.*

Kennedy, Edward (1905–1963)

Born in Brooklyn, New York, and educated at Carnegie Tech, in 1931 he joined the Paris bureau of the *Herald Ledger* after stints with several other papers. The following year he joined the Associated Press. Kennedy covered the Spanish Civil War* and the developing conflict in the Balkans and the Middle East. In 1940 he was with General Archibald Wavell's British Expeditionary Force sent to help the Greek resistance when German parachutists captured Crete. He was the only American reporter to witness the British capture of Tobruk. He later reported the Italian campaign and the landing at Anzio. In 1945 he promised to delay reporting the capitulation of the Germans for twenty-four hours, but he broke his pledge and was fired by the AP and stripped of his press credentials. Following the war he worked for newspapers in Santa Barbara and Monterey, California.

REFERENCE: John Hohenberg. *Foreign Correspondence.* 1964.

Kerimov, Farkhad (1948–1995)

Born in Moscow, he lived most of his life in the capital city of Baku, Azherbaijan, where he graduated with a degree in Physics and Mathematics. He later made the transition to journalism as a free-lance cameraman. Since 1990 he has covered the ethnic and civil conflicts in the Caucasus region including Georgia, Tajikistan, and Moldova as well as the battle over the enclave of Nagorno Karrabaskh. He was killed while covering Chechnya for AP as a television cameraman outside the city of Grozny.

REFERENCE: AP Wall of Honor, www.ap.org/wallof-honor/1980–1999.html.

Kertesz, Andre (1894–1985)

Born in Budapest, Hungary, Kertesz graduated from the Academy of Commerce in 1912 and entered business. He showed an early proclivity for photography and in 1914 was drafted into the Hungarian army. He barely escaped death in 1915 during World War I* when shot near the heart on the Polish front, resulting in paralysis of his left hand for a year. Following experimental surgery he regained its full use. He took his first war photographs during the war, few of which have survived.

In the 1930s he became a serious freelance photographer while covering the Spanish Civil War* and in 1936 moved to the United States and began his relationship with Conde Nast publications. He went on to photograph World War II* and the Korean War.*

REFERENCE: Robert E. Hood. *12 at War.* 1967.

Kessel, Dmitri (1902–1995)

The Russian-born war photographer* was serving in the Ukraine army when one of his superiors smashed his camera over his head, outraged at Kessel's photographing of the massacre of a Polish army unit. In 1923 he moved to the United States and joined the staff of *Life.* He covered the Greek Civil War, the German retreat during World War II,* and conflicts in the Middle East and the Congo.

REFERENCE: Frances Fralin, ed. *The Indelible Image.* 1985; *The Independent,* April 6, 1995.

Khaldei, Yevgeni (1916–1997)

Khaldei covered the greatest battles of the Russian theater of World War II.* Reporting for TASS News Agency and *Pravda,* he covered the conflict in Rumania, Bulgaria, Yugoslavia, Austria, and finally Berlin. His most famous photo showed the Red Flag being held above the Reichs Chancellery on May 1, 1945. It turned out to have been a tablecloth on which were attached the hammer and sickle. Interestingly enough, it had to be retouched prior to publication because the flag-bearing soldier's right arm was initially full of wristwatches that had been probably looted earlier. He was present at the Potsdam Conference and the Nuremberg trials. Following the war he joined the magazine *Soviet Culture,* or *Sovyetskaya Kultura.*

REFERENCES: Daniela Mrazkova and Vladimir Remes, eds. *The Russian War: 1941–1945.* 1975; M. Grosset, *Un Photoreporter en Union Sovietique,* 2004; Duncan Anderson. *War A Photo History.* 2006.

Salem Khalil.

See YOUSEF EL-DOUS.

Kilgallin, James Lawrence (1888–1982)

Born in Pittston, Pennsylvania, he attended college in Chicago, where he entered journalism with the *Chicago Tribune.* After stints with several smaller papers he joined the International News Service in 1921. Following the attack on

---

* Indicates a separate entry.

Pearl Harbor he went to Honolulu and later covered the Pacific theater with the navy. Kilgallin would see action in almost every theater of operations, including Africa, Italy, France, Germany, and the Pacific. In 1944 he reported the Italian campaign and was made INS chief in Naples. He accompanied Allied forces during the capture of Rome. He was among the twenty-one media representatives selected to witness the German unconditional surrender to the Allies in May 1945.

REFERENCE: Robert W. Desmond. *Tides of War.* 1984.

Kilgore, Margaret (?)

Following graduation from Syracuse University, Kilgore spent fifteen years with the UPI*, covering the congressional and White House beat for half the time. Interested more in the politics of war than in actual warfare, she arrived in South Vietnam for UPI in 1970. She had the misfortune of arriving at the same time that America was reducing its presence in Vietnam, making it difficult to gain access to air transportation that was formerly accessible to war correspondents. As the war crossed the borders into neighboring countries reporters were faced with strict censorship in Laos and a dearth of communication facilities in Cambodia, where correspondents had to make it to Phnom Penh to transmit dispatches.

Although she considered herself more an observer and political commentator than an actual war reporter, this did not save her from confronting firsthand the horrors of war. During her tenure in the supposedly safe confines of South Vietnam she survived a midnight rocket attack and a near miss by enemy fire while aloft in a helicopter. By 1971 an alarming trend was developing as correspondents were being killed and captured on a regular basis. She returned to the States after covering the 1971 South Vietnamese elections and left foreign reporting for public relations work.

REFERENCE: Virginia Elwood-Akers. *Women War Correspondents in the Vietnam War, 1961–1975.* 1988.

Killing Fields, The

The 1984 motion picture *The Killing Fields* was based on the wartime experiences of *New York Times* reporter Sydney Schanberg.* Schanberg was the recipient of the Pulitzer Prize for his coverage of the war in Cambodia. In the film, war reporter Schanberg returns to the United States after the conflict and is faced with the reality that his journalistic aspirations might have been responsible for the death of his interpreter and friend Dith Pran. Schanberg embarks on a Conradian odyssey of repentance in an attempt to find his loyal assistant.

REFERENCE: Howard Good. *The Image of War Correspondents in Anglo-American Fiction.* 1986.

Kingsley, Mary (1862–1900)

Known primarily for her exploits as an explorer in West Africa, she covered the Boer War* for the *Morning Post* in 1900. In addition to her duties as a special correspondent, Kingsley volunteered to minister to sick Boer soldiers. She became ill with enteric fever and died on Whitmonday, 1900, at the age of thirty-eight. She was buried at sea at her request. She is best known for her works *West African Studies* (1899) and *Travels in West Africa* (1897).

REFERENCE: Robert Wilkinson-Latham. *From Our Special Correspondent.* 1979.

Kingston, William Beatty (1837–1900)

Kingston became the Berlin correspondent for the *Daily Telegraph* in the 1860s. He would spend a decade reporting from Central Europe, including Vienna, and in 1870 he covered the Prussian army during the Franco-Prussian War.* Accompanying the Prussian army, he was with the headquarters staff in Versailles when the siege of Paris began. There he managed his greatest coup, scooping his British competitors with news of the fall of Paris.

In 1877 he covered the Russian side during the Russo-Turkish War.*

REFERENCE: Robert W. Desmond. *The Information Process.* 1978.

Kinnear, Alfred (d. 1912)

One of the most widely traveled war correspondents of the Victorian era, when not attached to the Central News Agency he reported for such papers as the *Pall Mall Gazette* and *Chambers' Journal.* His career spanned conflicts in North and South America, India, China, Russia, Japan, and West Africa. As the veteran reporter for the Central News Agency he reported the Boer War* from Magersfontein to the capture of Bloemfontein, covering most of the battles of the war, including Belmont, Graspian, and the Modder River. He wrote *To Modder River* (1900) and *Across Many Seas* (1902).

REFERENCE: Robert Wilkinson-Latham. *From Our Special Correspondent.* 1979.

Kinross, Albert (1870–1929)

The London-based Kinross covered the Russo-Japanese War* for the *Morning Post.* Following the war he left journalism to become a novelist. He returned to journalism during World War I,* serving as a captain in France and the Middle East, where he set up the *Balkan News* and the *Palestine News* for the armed forces.

REFERENCE: Dennis Griffiths, ed. *The Encyclopedia of the British Press.* 1992.

Kipling, Joseph Rudyard (1865–1936)

Kipling's name is synonymous with the literature of the British Empire. He worked as a reporter for the Lahore-based *Civil and Military Gazette* in 1882, and in the following years the imperialist-minded reporter attained literary acclaim with such works as *Soldiers Three* (1890)

and *Plain Tales from the Hill* (1886). His articles continued to appear in the leading British periodicals. While he was stationed in South Africa in 1900 the Boer War* started. Offered a huge sum by the *Daily Mail* to act as its war correspondent, Kipling joined the staff of the *Bloemfontein Friend,* the official army newspaper. He continued his prodigious literary output after the war, receiving many accolades, many of which he refused. He became the first English writer to be awarded the Nobel Prize in 1907. Following his death on January 18, 1936, he was laid to rest in Westminster Abbey.

REFERENCES: *DNB;* Joseph J. Mathews. *Reporting the Wars.* 1957.

Kirk, Donald (b. 1938)

Don Kirk is an Ivy–League educated correspondent who has covered conflict zones for more than forty years. He started his journalism career as a metro reporter for the *Chicago Sun-Times* and the *New York Times* before relocating to Asia, working in Indonesia covering the so-called "Year of Living Dangerously" in 1965–1966, which included the fall of Sukarno and mass murders in Java and Bali. Before the decade was out he had covered the Vietnam War* from most theaters of action, including Cambodia, Laos, and the Tet Offensive. During the late 1970s and into the 1980s he worked for the *London Observer,* reporting the 1979 assassination of President Park Chung-hee in South Korea and the 1980 Gwanju revolt. In 1982 he covered the Israeli invasion of Lebanon from both countries. That same year he joined *USA Today,* and continued to chronicle crises and conflicts around the world through the end of the Cold War. He covered the civil war in Lebanon, civil wars in El Salvador and Nicaragua, the demise of Ceausescu in Romania, the Tiananmen Square uprising in 1988, and the Gulf War. In 1974 Kirk won the Overseas Press Club of America Award for his Asian coverage and the following year the

George Polk Award for foreign reporting, for his articles exposing corruption in Vietnam and Cambodia. Kirk's recent correspondence and reporting can be accessed at http:///www.donald-kirk.com. He has written a number of books on Asia, including *Korea Witness: 135 Years of War, Crisis and News in the Land of the Morning Calm* (co-edited with Choe Sang-hun (2006) and *Looted: The Philippines After the Bases* (1998).

REFERENCE: http://en.wikipedia.org/wiki/Donald_Kirk.

Kirkpatrick, Helen (1909–1998)

Born in Rochester, New York, Kirkpatrick was educated at Smith College and the University of Geneva. Following graduation she worked for the Geneva-based *Research Bulletin*. At a hub for international news, Kirkpatrick made contacts with various newspapers. Soon after, she quit the *Bulletin* to work as a stringer* for the *Manchester Guardian,* the *London Daily Telegraph,* and the *New York Herald Tribune*. During World War II* she served as foreign correspondent for the *Chicago Daily News* in London from 1939 to 1944. Through her well-placed connections she scooped her competitors with her prediction that Hitler was preparing to invade neutral Belgium. Well informed on international issues, she wrote *This Terrible Peace* (1938) and *Under the British Umbrella* (1939).

In London she witnessed the blitz and quickly achieved a reputation as one of the best journalists in Europe. However, when Edward R. Murrow* attempted to hire her, he was overruled. CBS opted for a younger, inexperienced, more important, male correspondent, named Charles Collingwood,* who would go on to a stellar career in this field. Kirkpatrick was disappointed, but continued to cover the war.

In 1942 Kirkpatrick and Mary Welsh* became the first women to be accredited to accompany the Allied forces. She accompanied the Free French forces, covering the Normandy invasion and the liberation of Paris. In the later stages of the war she reported Allied operations from North Africa to Italy, in France, and at the end of the war, in Germany. After the war Kirkpatrick joined the *New York Daily Post* and continued her journalism career.

REFERENCES: Julia Edwards. *Women of the World.* 1989; Frederick S. Voss. *Reporting the War.* 1994; NY Times, January 7, 1998.

Kirtland, Helen Johns (1890–1979)

Raised in Yonkers, New York and educated in Germany, Kirtland was a French-based correspondent for *Leslie's Illustrated Weekly* during World War I. By most accounts she was "the first and only woman correspondent allowed at the front" following the 1917 Italian retreat from Caporetto, which resulted in the capture of 275,000 troops. She covered battles near the Piave River in northern Italy and photographed the Austrian trenches captured by the Italians. Several of Kirtland's photos were included in *Leslie's Photographic Review of the Great War* (1919). Following the war she continued her photojournalism career in Europe and Asian, often working together with her husband, the reporter Lucian Swift Kirtland. Their collaborations appeared under her husband's name in a variety of newspapers and magazines, but her photographs were rarely attributed to her. Today the Library of Congress holds the Kirtland Collection featuring close to 200 of her photos from the war and its conclusion.

REFERENCES: Paula E. Calvin and Deborah A. Deacon. *American Women Artists in Wartime, 1776–2010.* 2011; "Women Photojournalists: Helen Johns Kirtland," http://www.loc.gov/rr/print/coll/womphotoj/kirtlandintro.html.

Kluckholn, Frank (1907–1970)

Born in St. Paul, Minnesota, and educated at the University of Minnesota and in Spain, he joined the *St. Paul Dispatch* in 1926 and then the *Boston Globe* in 1929. Later that year he moved to the *New York Times*. Kluckholn covered the Spanish Civil War* in 1936 from the insurgent side. He was the first to get the news out that Italian and German planes manned by pilots from those countries had reached Spain. When Franco found out about this news scoop, Kluckholn was stripped of his accreditation by the insurgents and narrowly escaped with his life. He was a presidential correspondent in the years leading up to World War II.* He reported the war beginning in 1942, when he landed with Allied forces in North Africa. At the conclusion of the campaign he was assigned to the Pacific theater in New Guinea, where he witnessed the marine landing at New Britain.

In 1943 he returned to North Africa to cover the Allied landings at Casablanca, Oran, and Algiers. He reported the clashes with Vichy forces and flew with paratroopers who captured an airfield near the Algerian-Tunisian border. Kluckholn arrived in Casablanca shortly before the conference met, but became embroiled in a controversy over censorship and was disciplined by being barred from the front for ten days. He was with the U.S. First Army as it ended German and Italian resistance in Tunisia. Following the Japanese surrender he interviewed Emperor Hirohito.

REFERENCE: Robert W. Desmond. *Tides of War.* 1984.

Klyan, Anatoly (c. 1946–2014)

The veteran cameraman was working for Russian Channel One when he was wounded as his bus came under fire while en route to the "self-declared Donetsk People's Republic" in eastern Ukraine. At 68 years old, Klyan was one of the oldest correspondents covering the conflict. He was reportedly on an excursion organized by pro-Russian separatists on June 29, 2014 to film the surrender of a Ukrainian army unit. Klyan was not wearing any protective armor, neither

helmet nor flak jacket and later died at a hospital from bullet wounds in his abdomen. President Vladimir Putin posthumously awarded him the Order of Courage.

REFERENCES: "Anatoly Klyan," http://cpj.org/killed/2014/anatoly-klyan.php; "Moscow Pays Last Respects to Cameraman," Voice of Russia, July 2, 2014.

Knickerbocker, Hubert Renfre (1898–1949)

Born in Texas and educated at Columbia University and in Europe, Knickerbocker began his newspaper career in 1920 on the staff of the *Newark Morning Ledger*. In 1924 he went to Germany as a foreign correspondent for the *New York Evening Sun Post* and the *Philadelphia Public Ledger*. He was awarded the Pulitzer Prize in 1931 for correspondence and in 1935 began covering the Ethiopian War* for the International News Service (INS) in Addis Ababa. Knickerbocker moved on to the Spain next, where he covered the outbreak of the Spanish Civil War.* At one point he was among several correspondents abducted by rebels and declared missing for several days.

In 1941 he joined the *Chicago Sun* as director of foreign service and the following year was covering the war in the Far East from Java and Sumatra. Knickerbocker fled to San Francisco as the Japanese seized the East Indies. He next covered the developing Pacific war from Honolulu, Batavia, and then Australia. In 1942 he covered the Allied landings in North Africa. Two years later he was accredited to Allied Force Headquarters (US-UK) during the Italian campaign and in June of that year covered the invasion of France. He witnessed the capture of the port of Cherbourg from bluffs overlooking the city. Knickerbocker wrote seven books dealing with the repercussions of the war.

REFERENCE: Robert W. Desmond. *Tides of War.* 1984.

* *Indicates a separate entry.*

Knight, Edward Frederick
(1852–1925)

The Cambridge-educated Knight was a successful barrister, soldier, and journalist. Joining the *Morning Post*, he reported conflicts from many parts of the world, beginning in the early 1870s, before answering the call of the bar. In 1891, he returned to journalism, covering the Hunza-Nagar campaign for the *Times*. Throughout the 1890s he was in constant action, covering the conflict in Matabeleland (1893–1895), the French seizure of Madagascar (1895), the Sudan campaigns of 1896–1898, the Greco-Turkish War,* and the Spanish-American War.*

He was reporting the Boer War* for the *Morning Post* when he was severely wounded in the right arm while covering Lord Methuen's forces at an engagement near Belmont. Shortly after, the arm was amputated at the shoulder on November 23, 1900. After his recovery, his final battlefield reports came from the Russo-Japanese War* in 1904 and the conflict in Turkey in 1908. His experiences as a war correspondent are chronicled in *Letters from the Sudan* (1897) and *Reminiscences: the Wanderings of a Yachtsman and War Correspondent* (1923).

REFERENCES: F. Lauriston Bullard. *Famous War Correspondents*. 1914; Robert Wilkinson-Latham. *From Our Special Correspondent*. 1979.

Knight, Gary (b. 1964)

Knight began his career as a photographer in 1987. He is one of the cofounders (along with the late Alexandra Boulat,* Ron Haviv,* Antonin Kratochvil, Christoher Morris,* James Nachtwey* and John Stanmeyer) of VII Photo Agency, established in 2001, and regarded as a "model for the 21ˢᵗ century photo agency." He started his career in Thailand and covered Southeast Asia for about five years, often covering conflicts that had broken out following the denouement of the Cold War. In 1993 he moved to Yugoslavia to cover the conflict in Bosnia and other war zones. More recently Knight has chronicled the invasion of Iraq and the civil war in Kashmir, as well as events in South Africa, Israel, Palestine, and Afghanistan. A freelancer until 1998, since then he has been a contract photographer for *Newsweek*. In June 2008 Knight inaugurated a new quarterly magazine called *dispatches*, which is devoted to "the greatest global challenges of our time."

REFERENCES: http://www.viiphoto.com/more-photographer.php?photographer=Gary Knight; http://cpn.canon-europe.com/content/ambassadors/gary_knight.do.

Knox, Thomas Wallace
(1835–1896)

Born in Pembroke, New Hampshire, Knox followed his father into the shoemaking trade before becoming a teacher and establishing his own academy in Kingston, New Hampshire. He followed a gold strike to Colorado in 1860 and became a reporter for the *Denver Daily News*. With the outbreak of the American Civil War,* he enlisted in the Union Army and served in the southwestern theater. Knox covered the 1861 Missouri campaign for the *New York Herald*. He was present at the Battle of Wilson's Creek, and in 1862 he witnessed a gunboat battle near Memphis. He was wounded and after returning to active duty served on the staff of the California National Guard.

Like many reporters during the war, Knox earned the wrath of General Sherman for his reporting and was actually court-martialed for disobeying orders. Following the edict known as General Order No. 8, all civilians were excluded from army encampments, and anyone who reported the western campaign on the Mississippi River near Vicksburg would be arrested and treated as a spy. For violating this proclamation Knox lost his accreditation and returned to civilian life in New York. A sample of his wartime dispatches is collected in *Camp fire and Cotton field* (1865).

In 1866 he was again in the employ of the *Herald* when he accompanied a Western Union expedition on its attempt to survey a telegraph route from America to Siberia. His main accomplishment during this adventure was gaining a patent for transmitting battlefield plans by telegraph. His account of this survey was published as *Overland Through Asia* (1870). An inveterate tinkerer, he invented an instrument for telegraphing by Morse code the exact location of each bullet's impact on a target. In the late 1870s he explored parts of the Far East and continued to produce a couple of books a year. He wrote numerous travel books for young boys.

REFERENCES: J. Cutler Andrews. *The North Reports the Civil War.* 1955; *DAB.*

Kodak Box Cameras

Hand-held Kodak box cameras were invented in the United States in the late 1880s. They proved especially popular among British officers seeking to document their campaigns in Africa. One officer of the Grenadier Guards was able to keep taking pictures during the 1898 Battle of Omdurman. He captured General Kitchener giving commands, his own troops waiting with fixed bayonets protected by a thorn bush zariba as the Mahdi's army attacked, and some of the most memorable war photos taken at the end of the 19th century.

REFERENCES: Duncan Anderson. *War A Photo History.* 2006.

Koestler, Arthur (1905–1983)

Born in Budapest, Hungary, and educated at the University of Vienna, Koestler spent stints as a foreign correspondent in the Middle East and Europe. In 1932 he became a member of the Communist Party and after visiting the Soviet Union covered the Spanish Civil War* for the *News Chronicle* in 1937. He was among the correspondents who reported the conflict from both sides. After reporting from the Republican side he was captured by the Fascist insurgents following the fall of Malaga, and sentenced to be executed for spying. After a hundred days on death

row he was exchanged for another prisoner. His experiences in Spain are chronicled in *Spanish Gladiators* (1937), which was published five years later in America as *Dialogue with Death,* and *The Gladiators* (1939). He had resigned from the Communist Party by the time the second book was published.

During World War II* Koestler served in the French and British armies. Although he wrote exclusively in German until his mid-thirties, he became a leading English-language writer after moving to England in 1940. He wrote several novels and works of nonfiction. He was granted permanent residence in the United States by a special act of Congress in 1951. During the 1960s he wrote for the *Observer.*

REFERENCE: Robert W. Desmond. *Tides of War.* 1984.

Kolenberg, Bernard (1927–1965)

This AP photographer was the first journalist to be killed covering the Vietnam War. He had initially reported from Vietnam for five weeks the previous year and had sent back several photos that were published in the *Albany Times-Union.* He had been working for them since the 1940s. He was killed when the jet bomber he was riding in collided with another bomber in the skies over central Vietnam on October 2, 1965.

REFERENCE: AP Wall of Honor, www.ap.org/wallofhonor/1960_1969.html.

Korean War

On June 25, 1950, Communist North Korean troops crossed the thirty-eighth parallel and invaded South Korea, inaugurating the Korean War. Almost simultaneously, journalists began to arrive from the United States and from the Tokyo bureaus. Prior to the war there were only twenty-seven correspondents accredited with the Far East Command. Over the first few months of the war about 280 correspondents from nineteen different countries came to Korea. However,

Indicates a separate entry.

it is estimated that less than a quarter of that number were at the front at the same time. Several hundred more would join their ranks by the end of the war three years later.

The only regular journalist in Korea when the invasion began was *Chicago Tribune* correspondent Walter Simmons.* Simmons had arrived in Seoul to cover the South Korean national assembly and had decided to stay over a couple of extra days. His scoop was the first by someone other than a wire service reporter. Among the first to respond was veteran correspondent Keyes Beech,* who reported the fighting at the Changjin reservoir. Other American correspondents included Hal Boyle, Don Whitehead,* Stan Swinton, Bill Shinn, Relman Morin,* and Tom Lambert* for the Associated Press; Homer Bigart* and Marguerite Higgins* for the *New York Herald Tribune;* Jim Lucas* for Scripps-Howard; Phillip Potter for the *Baltimore Sun;* Carl Mydans* for *Life* magazine; Bob Considine for Hearst newspapers; Edward R. Murrow* for CBS; Hal Levine for *Newsweek;* and Peter Kalischer,* Peter Webb, and Rutherford Poats for the UP. In 1951 Higgins, Beech, Bigart, Morin, Fred Sparks of the *Chicago Daily News,* and Whitehead received Pulitzer Prizes for their reporting of the Korean War. Three other Pulitzers would be awarded over the final two years of the conflict.

Numerous British correspondents could be found among the foreign press corps, including Christopher Buckley* of the *Daily Telegraph,* Ward Price* of the *Daily Mail,* James Cameron* of *Picture Post,* Rene Cutforth of the BBC, Ian Morrison* of the *Times,* and Jack Percival of *News Chronicle.* Cameron was assisted by veteran photographer Bert Hardy.* Among the more critical journalists concerning American war aims were Cameron and Reginald Thompson of the *Daily Telegraph* and author of the 1951 book *Cry Korea,* a vitriolic account of the war and his fellow journalists.

Correspondents faced myriad problems including censorship and poor communications.

At one command post seventy reporters had to share one military telephone to Japan. Soon after the outbreak of hostilities, General MacArthur instituted a policy of self-censorship, which he explained as the only recourse because of the dearth of qualified censors. Correspondents were never completely sure what information would be construed as giving aid and comfort to the enemy. This system was arbitrary, resulting in several unjust prosecutions for violating censorship restrictions. MacArthur was later forced to set up a more conventional system. According to a Reuters* journalist, "Ninety percent of the correspondents in Korea have indicated they would prefer open censorship" to MacArthur's capricious system.

Unlike previous wars, correspondents felt there was no place to hide, which meant that if you were in the field you were consistently under attack. According to one reporter, "It was not like other wars. In other wars you had a pretty good idea of where the enemy was and where you were. In Korea you didn't."

Journalists were assisted by the Army Signal Corps, which operated two radio-teletype machines enabling dispatches to reach Tokyo from Korea in less than two hours; this compared with twelve to twenty-four hours at the outset. The best coverage of the war was provided by the *New York Herald Tribune* team of Bigart and Higgins, who received as much publicity for their much-publicized feud as they did for their Pulitzer Prize-winning reportage.

The Korean War was considered one of the more hazardous frontline assignments, with six American correspondents losing their lives in July 1950 alone. On July 10, Ray Richards of the INS and Ernie Peeler of *Stars and Stripes** were the first two correspondents to die when their position was overrun by North Korean troops. When Albert Hinton of the *Norfolk Journal and Guide* was killed in a plane crash on July 27, he became the first black war correspondent killed during the three major wars of the first half of the twentieth century. By the time the conflict ended in 1953, of the total of 350 correspondents accredited to the United Nations headquarters in Korea a total of eighteen correspondents and photographers had perished, including ten Americans.

REFERENCES: Michael Emery. *On the Front Lines.* 1995; John Hohenberg. *Foreign Correspondence: The Great Reporters and Their Times.* 1964; Phillip Knightley. *The First Casualty.* 1975; Trevor Royle. *War Report: The War Correspondent's View of Battle from the Crimea to the Falklands.* 1987; M. L. Stein. *Under Fire.* 1968.

Korengal

A followup to his (and Tim Hetherington's*) award-winning film *Restrepo,** Sebastian Junger* filmed the soldiers of Battle Company 2/503 during and in the aftermath of their service in the Korengal Valley of Afghanistan. This film is as much as a portrait of men as it is a penetrating examination of the psychological impact of war on soldiers. It was released in 2014.

REFERENCE: David Fear, "Life during Wartime: Sebastian Junger on Korengal," Rolling Stone, June 2, 2014.

Kornelyuk, Igor (1977–2014)

Born in the Ukrainian city of Zaporozhie, this correspondent for the Russian station VGTRK died from wounds suffered in a mortar attack while covering the conflict in eastern Ukraine on June 17, 2014. He was traveling with a team of colleagues near the village of Metallist to cover the plight of local residents caught in the conflict. The team apparently arrived at a separatist checkpoint when they separated. Shelling by Ukrainian forces mortally wounded Kornelyuk and killed sound engineer Anton Voloshin. None of the team members were wearing protective gear. Kornelyuk died while in surgery at a nearby hospital.

REFERENCE: "Igor Kornelyuk," http://cpj.org/killed/2014/igor-kornelyuk.php.

Krauss, Hansjoerg "Hansi" (1963–1993)

Born in Germany, Krauss first started working for the AP as a photographer in 1989 in Berlin, where he covered the fall of the Berlin Wall. He covered conflict first in Bosnia-Herzegovina and then Somalia where he was killed with three other journalists. The four were stoned to death on July 12 by a crowd in Mogadishu, incensed by an American helicopter attack on local militia buildings.

REFERENCE: AP Wall of Honor, www.ap.org/wallof-honor/1980_1999.html.

Kudoyarov, Boris (1903–1973)

Kudoyarov was one of the pioneers of Soviet photojournalism. He became a platoon deputy commander in the Red Army during the Russian Civil War while still in his teens. Prior to the outbreak of World War II* he wrote for several news magazines. During the war he was a foreign correspondent for the Moscow-based *Pravda.* As the only photographer to survive and record the entire 900-day siege of Leningrad, he produced an incredible photographic account of a battle in which one thousand Russians died each day. Ironically, he died in a peacetime motor vehicle accident while working in Tashkent.

REFERENCES: Jorge Lewinski. *The Camera at War.* 1978; Daniela Mrazkova and Vladimir Remes, eds. *The Russian War: 1941–1945.* 1975.

L

Labouchere, Henry "Labby" Du Pre (1831–1912)

After graduating from Cambridge in the early 1850s Labouchere traveled widely throughout the United States. Upon his return to Europe he entered the British diplomatic service, and after stints in Russia, Sweden, Prussia, Italy, and Turkey, he returned to England, where he became a member of Parliament and in 1868 part owner of the *London Daily News*. Labouchere covered the Franco-Prussian War* for his newspaper after he found himself trapped in Paris when the siege broke out in 1870, and remained in the city for four months. His reports were smuggled through the Prussian siege forces by means of a not so dependable balloon service. His dispatches appeared in his paper and the *New York Tribune* under his initials "H. L." Following the war his letters were collected and published in *Diary of a Besieged Resident*. In 1877 he began publishing a weekly magazine called the *Truth*.

REFERENCES: Robert W. Desmond. *The Information Process*. 1978; DNB, 1912–1922.

Ladysmith, Siege of

From November 2, 1899, to February 28, 1900, the city of Ladysmith, Natal, was besieged by a force of five thousand Boer farmers. Close to twelve thousand British soldiers were reduced to slaughtering their horses for food during the two-month-long siege. Also inside were eight

British war correspondents, including Henry W. Nevinson* and George Lynch* of the *Daily Mail*, William T. Maud* of the *Graphic*, John Stuart of the *Morning Post*, Harry Pearse* and Ernest Smith* of the *Daily News*, William Maxwell* of the *Standard*, Melton Prior* of the *Illustrated London News*, and Lionel James* of the *Times*. In addition George W. Steevens* of the *Daily Mail* perished from enteric disease. Lynch managed to escape, while Winston Churchill* was captured near Ladysmith shortly after the siege was under way.

Correspondents resorted to every type of innovation to get their dispatches out of the besieged town. Some used a British heliograph service, a form of code system, but newspapers were restricted to only thirty words per day. Others hired Kaffir couriers to attempt to break through Boer siege lines. Steevens and Prior reportedly paid a runner more than $400 at one point.

REFERENCES: Robert W. Desmond. *The Information Process*. 1978; Kenneth Griffith. *Thank God We Kept the Flag Flying: The Siege and Relief of Ladysmith*. 1974.

Lamb, Christina (b. 1966)

Born in London and educated at University College, Oxford and a former Nieman fellow at Harvard University, Lamb began her journalism career with the *Financial Times*, where she fell under the sway of the roving foreign correspondents and the lives they lived. In 1987 she had the

Indicates a separate entry.

good fortune to score an interview with Benazir Bhutto in London. Later that year she was invited to Bhutto's wedding in Pakistan and was soon on her way to cover the war in Afghanistan. As she traveled along the fringes of the conflict she made numerous contacts among the populace that would help her in the future, including future President Hamid Karzai. However, the current regime opposed her reporting and she was deported back to England by Pakistan's notorious Inter-Services Intelligence (ISI). She was then posted to Brazil, where she covered corruption and politics before moving to South Africa during the postapartheid years. Over the next decade she covered conflicts and foreign affairs from London, Portugal, Zimbabwe, Brazil, Iraq, Pakistan, and Afghanistan. Over the years, Lamb's work has been widely disseminated in most leading newspapers and other media sources. In 1988 she received the Young Journalist of the Year in the British Press Awards for her coverage of the Soviet invasion of Afghanistan. She was recognized for her war journalism with the prestigious Prix Bayeux Calvados* in 1988 for her reporting in Afghanistan and has been named Foreign Correspondent of the Year five times in the British Press Awards. Lamb authored and collaborated on a number of books, including *Small Wars Permitting: Dispatches from Foreign Lands* (2008), and most recently co-authored the autobiography of the young human rights activist, Malala Yousafzai on *I Am Malala: The Girl Who Stood Up for Education and Was Shot by the Taliban* (2013).

REFERENCE: "About Me," http://www.christinalamb.net/pages/aboutme.html.

Lambert, Tom (1912–1995)

Lambert covered the Korean War* for the Associated Press. He found himself trapped along with reporters Marguerite Higgins,* Keyes Beech,* and Gordon Walker at the tiny airport of Suwon, as North Korean troops advanced toward it. Lambert and Beech attained a measure

of heroism when they rescued a jet fighter pilot who had crashed his plane near the airport. The correspondents made it to safety three days ahead of the invading forces. At one point Lambert was barred along with Peter Kalischer* from covering the front when he characterized an army battalion as the "lost battalion" because of its high death counts and confusion surrounding its status. He was later reinstated. His assignment was not without its risks, as demonstrated when he broke his foot. He later reported the Israeli Six Day War from Lebanon.

REFERENCE: Michael Emery. *On the Front Lines*. 1995.

Landells, Robert Thomas (1833–1877)

Trained as an engraver, the London-born war artist-correspondent* covered his first action for the *Illustrated London News* when he was sent to report the end of the Crimean War* in 1856. In 1863 he reported the war between Denmark and Prussia over Schleswig-Holstein and received decorations from both armies.

In 1866 he was attached to the staff of the Prussian crown prince during the Austro-Prussian War.* Landells put his knowledge of Prussian affairs to good use when he covered the Franco-Prussian War* in 1870–1871. Fluent in German, Landells joined the Prussian staff at Versailles and was with Prussian forces throughout the siege of Paris. He was rewarded for his services as an artist and ambulance driver with the Prussian Cross and Bavarian Cross for valor. Following the conflict he gave up war reporting and returned to his painting career.

REFERENCES: Dennis Griffiths, ed. *The Encyclopedia of the British Press*. 1992; Pat Hodgson. *The War Illustrators*. 1977.

Landon, Percival (1869–1927)

As special correspondent for the *Times,* the Oxford-educated Landon first saw action covering the Boer War* in 1900. In between practicing law and a short-lived position as assistant to the governor of New South Wales, he covered the British expedition to Tibet for the *Times*. Joining the *Daily Telegraph* in 1905, over the next twenty years he rose to become one of its most respected staff writers. Prior to World War I* he covered conflicts in Russia, Egypt, Sudan, and Mesopotamia. During World War I he was assigned to the western front (1914–1915) and the Italian campaigns. Following the war he covered the Peace Conference and continued to report from the Middle and Far East. Among his books are *Lhasa* (1905) and *The Story of the Indian Mutiny* (1907).

REFERENCES: Robert W. Desmond. *The Information Process*. 1978; Dennis Griffiths, ed. *The Encyclopedia of the British Press*. 1992.

Langham, Samuel F. (1866–1898)

One of the most popular and experienced war correspondents of the Press Club, he covered the Ashanti War in 1873. He went on to report the Sudan campaign for the *Morning Post* and *Black and White* and the Abyssinian campaign for the *Daily Mail* (1898). Shortly after Abyssinia, he returned to England in ill health and committed suicide by taking poison and lying down on a busy railway track.

REFERENCE: Dennis Griffiths, ed. *The Encyclopedia of the British Press*. 1992.

Lardner, David (1919–1945)

A son of noted writer Ring Lardner, he was killed while covering his first war assignment for the *New Yorker* magazine on October 19, 1945. He was riding in a jeep, returning from the captured city of Aachen on the Belgian border, when it struck an antivehicle Teller land mine.

REFERENCE: Robert W. Desmond. *Tides of War*. 1984.

Lardner, John Abbott (1912–1960)

A son of the writer Ring Lardner, he was born in Chicago, Illinois. He attended private schools and showed an early proclivity for journalistic writing; a family friend published a column of the ten-year-old Lardner's work. After graduation from Harvard in 1929 he studied at the Sorbonne and worked for the *New York Herald Tribune* for a few months. Upon his return to the States in 1931 he joined the *Herald Tribune* fulltime. Less than three years later he quit the paper and was hired by the North American Newspaper Alliance (NANA), an affiliation he would hold until 1948.

He reported World War II* as a war correspondent for *Newsweek,* beginning two months after Pearl Harbor. His coverage appeared throughout the war years under the caption "Lardner Goes to the Wars." He reported from the European and Pacific theaters, the North African and Italian campaigns, and the last major battles at Iwo Jima and Okinawa. During the war years he continued to publish in NANA papers, as well as in major magazines such as the *Saturday Evening Post* and the *New Yorker*. Many of these pieces are collected in *Southwest Passage: The Yanks in the Pacific* (1943).

Lardner lost two brothers during the European conflicts. His brother James was killed fighting for the Loyalists in the Spanish Civil War* and David,* a war correspondent for the *New Yorker,* was killed while covering World War II. Following the war Lardner wrote a variety of articles for the top periodicals. A man of diverse interests, he was best known for his sportswriting. By 1958 his health was in decline due to multiple sclerosis. He fulfilled his prediction that he would die young when he passed away before his forty-eighth birthday.

REFERENCES: *DAB 6;* Ring Lardner, Jr. *The Lardners: My Family Remembered*. 1976; *New York Times*. March 25, 1960.

Larrabee, Constance Stuart (1914–2000)

Born in England, she became an American citizen in 1953. Larrabee became South Africa's first woman war correspondent in World War II.* She was accredited to the South African magazine *Libertas* as a war photographer.* Larrabee covered the European theater during the last two years of the war. Her illustrated war diary, *Jeep Trek*, was published in 1946. She developed an international reputation for her coverage of World War II and for her tribal documentary photography.

REFERENCES: Frances Fralin, ed. *The Indelible Image: Photographs of War-1846 to the Present.* 1985; NY Times, August 4, 2000.

Lathrop, Barbour (1846–1927)

Born in Virginia and educated at Harvard, Lathrop was the only war correspondent of the American Indian Wars* to come from a background of wealth. In July 1876, several years after moving to San Francisco, he went out to the frontier to report the aftermath of the Custer story. He joined General George Crook's Sioux campaign as a representative of the *San Francisco Evening Bulletin*. However, the spartan conditions and poor management of Crook's command led Lathrop to transfer to Alfred Terry's for the remainder of the campaign. Most of Lathrop's reports emphasize the grumbling of the soldiers rather than any actual combat. By September Lathrop was on his way back to San Francisco as the expedition grounded to a halt.

After inheriting a fortune later in life he became a philanthropist and supporter of the plant importations of horticulturist David G. Fairchild. Lathrop took the entomologist and plant explorer on a trip around the world and continued to finance his travels after Fairchild created the Section of Seed and Plant Introduction for the Department of Agriculture. As a result, seedless raisin grapes from Italy, Chilean avocados, nectarines, new varieties of okra, onions, red peppers, cucumbers, and peanuts became staples of the American kitchen.

REFERENCE: Oliver Knight. *Following the Indian Wars.* 1960.

Laurent, Michel (1945–1975)

Born in France, Laurent was employed as a war photographer* for the Associated Press and then the Paris-based Gamma Photo Agency. He covered conflict in Africa, the Middle East, and Asia, including the Nigerian civil war and the 1973 Arab-Israeli War. In 1972 he shared the Pulitzer Prize with Horst Faas* of the Associated Press for photo coverage of soldiers bayonetting traitors during the 1971 India-Pakistan War. Their widely published photo essay was entitled "Death in Dacca." Laurent covered his final war in 1975 when he became the last journalist killed during the Vietnam War.*

REFERENCE: Turner Browne and Elaine Partnow. *Macmillan's Encyclopedia of Photographic Artists and Innovators.* 1983.

Lawless, Peter (1890–1945)

The former professional rugby player was killed in action while reporting the war in Europe for the *Daily Telegraph.* Formerly a sports reporter for the *Morning Post,* he joined the *Daily Telegraph* in 1937. Between September 1939 and May 1940 he accompanied the Royal Air Force in France. He joined the Army Intelligence Corps after the fall of France in 1940. In 1944 he returned to the *Telegraph* as a special correspondent with the American First Army after the Normandy Invasion. He was killed by shell fire in March 1945, while covering the taking of the Remagen bridge, one of the last intact bridges over the Rhine River. As one of the last journalistic casualties in the war, his death brought the number of Allied newspapermen killed in action to forty-six-sixteen British and thirty American.

REFERENCE: Dennis Griffiths, ed. *The Encyclopedia of the British Press.* 1992.

Lawley, Francis Charles (1825–1901)

Born in Yorkshire, England, and educated at Oxford, the wellborn Lawley joined the *London*

Times in 1862 after a brief political career which included a stint in Parliament and a position as private secretary to Chancellor of the Exchequer and future prime minister Gladstone. He was assigned to replace W. H. Russell* as "special correspondent" covering the Southern side of the American Civil War* after Russell was recalled for angering federal authorities with his unflattering portrayal of the Confederate rout of Union troops at the First Battle of Bull Run.

Lawley became a sympathetic admirer of the Southern war effort. As "special correspondent" he wrote approximately one hundred letters for the *Times,* which appeared under the heading of "The Southern Confederacy" or the "Confederate States." His coverage of the Battles of Fredericksburg (1862), Chancellorsville (1863), and Gettysburg (1863) are considered classics. His close relationships with Generals Lee, Stuart, and Longstreet accorded him the rare opportunity to observe these battles with the Confederate leaders from the best vantage spots. One source claimed that he was the only correspondent to witness the wounding of Jackson at Chancellorsville, the surrender at Appomattox, and the final meeting between Lee and Longstreet. Lawley had his detractors as well, who labeled him a propagandist for the Confederacy. After the Civil War he returned to England to accept a better-paying position with the *Daily Telegraph*. In 1870, he covered the Franco-Prussian War.*

REFERENCE: William Stanley Hoole. *Lawley Covers the Confederacy.* 1964.

Lawrence, William H. (1916–1972)

Lawrence was born in Lincoln, Nebraska, and entered journalism after dropping out of the University of Nebraska. After stints with several papers he joined the United Press in 1936 and five years later moved over to the *New York Times*. After reassignment to Moscow in 1943 he visited the site of the Babi Yar massacre in Kiev and the Majdanek concentration camp near Lublin,

Poland. He subsequently covered the war in the Pacific in Guam and Okinawa and was an observer on bombing raids over Japan. He landed in Japan with the occupation forces in 1945.

Lawrence was known as "Political Bill" at his paper to differentiate him from fellow reporter William H. Laurence, whose moniker was "Atomic Bill." Following World War II* he reported from Eastern Europe and South America and covered the Korean War* for the *Times*. Later he served as Washington correspondent for the *Times* and as White House correspondent for ABC beginning in 1961.

REFERENCES: Robert W. Desmond. *Tides of War.* 1984; Library of America. *Reporting World War H.* 1995.

Lawton, Kerem (1970–2001)

Born in Brussels, Belgium and raised in the UK he was fluent in his parents' native languages, Turkish and English. Lawton was killed by mortar fire while covering the border between Kosovo and Macedonia for the Associated Press. He had previously covered the war in Kosovo and the Kurdish insurgency in southeast Turkey, and in Albania.

REFERENCE: AP Wall of Honor. www.ap.org/wallof-honor/2000_2008.html.

Lea, Tom (1907–2001)

Born Thomas Calloway, the El Paso muralist was already a well-known artist when he was hired as artist-correspondent* by *Life* magazine to cover World War II.* He accompanied Allied troops to North Africa, the Pacific, and China. His battlefield sketches were turned into grim oil paintings of war once he was back in the studio. One of his most graphic paintings depicts the assault on the Pacific island of Peleliu in September 1944. When his controversial painting *The Price* appeared in *Life* magazine an avalanche of letters protested the publication of an injured marine covered in blood. His combat experiences are recounted in A *Grizzly from the Coral Sea* (1944) and *Peleliu Landing* (1945). Besides his paintings, Lea also wrote several highly praised books, including *The King Ranch* (1957) and *The Brave Bulls* (1949).

REFERENCE: Anne Dingus. "War Paint," *Texas Monthly.* August 1994.

Lederer, Edith M. (b. 1943)

Educated at Cornell and Stanford, Edie Lederer joined the Associated Press in 1966. Six years later she was assigned to Saigon and in 1973 covered the Arab-Israeli War from Egypt and Syria, reporting some of the major tank battles of the conflict. In 1975 she became the first woman to head a foreign bureau for the AP when she was assigned the Peru office. However, five months later she was expelled by the military government there for writing an unflattering piece about a military training exercise. From 1978 to 1981 she was based in Hong Kong. In June 1980 she covered the Soviet invasion of Afghanistan briefly and later reported the Falklands War.* In 1990 she completed compulsory physical training in order to qualify for field coverage during the Gulf War.* The only woman correspondent during the conflict who had covered the Vietnam War,* Lederer ended up spending over five months reporting the Gulf War. She was named AP bureau chief in Dharan during the war, marking her twenty-five years of service with the news agency.

REFERENCES: Julia Edwards. *Women of the World.* 1989; Anne Sebba. *Battling for News.* 1994.

Ledru, Filippo (?)

Ledru was one of the earliest photographer correspondents. He recorded natural disasters such as the 1883 Casamicciola earthquake and the 1887 Etna eruption and covered man-made carnage while documenting the Italian colonial experience of the late nineteenth century.

He was with Italian troops in the advance on Massawa in 1885 and in 1896 during the Battle of Adwa, where he lost all of his photographic equipment.

REFERENCE: Nicolas Monti, ed. *Africa Then.* 1987.

Lee, Clark (1907–1953)

The son of the founder of the United Press was born in Oakland, California. After attending Rutgers University he joined the Newark bureau of the Associated Press and in 1933 he took over the Mexico City bureau. From 1939 until 1941 he covered the Japanese side during the invasion of China. He was warned to leave Shanghai by Japanese officers three weeks before Pearl Harbor. He had barely reached Manila when it fell to Japanese forces. Lee was able to escape to Corregidor. His notes and dispatches from the siege of Corregidor were collected and published as *Bataan Bylines* in 1942. Lee was able to escape to Australia before Corregidor fell. Out of the five hundred correspondents in England hoping to cover the Normandy invasion, Lee was one of the twenty-eight allowed to accompany the landing. He served as a roving correspondent for the International News Service covering the occupation of Japan following the war. He died of a heart attack in California at the age of forty-six. He recounted his exploits in the Philippines in his book *They Call It Pacific.*

REFERENCE: John Hohenberg. *Foreign Correspondence.* 1964.

Le Hir, Georges (?)

Le Hir wrote perhaps the best account of the 1916 Battle of Verdun during World War I.* A French journalist, he had joined the staff of Paris bureau of the *New York Times* in 1915.

REFERENCE: Robert W. Desmond. *Windows on the World.* 1980.

---

* *Indicates a separate entry.*

Lepage, Camille (1988–2014)

Born and educated in France, Lepage later studied journalism at Southampton Solent University. During her professional career she focused on photojournalism and pursued stories in Africa, first basing herself in Juba, South Sudan in 2012. Her work was published in a number of news outlets, including the *New York Times*, *The Guardian*, *Le Monde*, *Washington Post*, *Der Spiegel*, *Vice Magazine*, Al Jazeera, and the BBC. During the last six months of her life she covered the conflict in the Central African Republic (CAR) capital Bangui. Despite warnings to the contrary Lepage was drawn to cover the chaos in the CAR, as it descended toward genocide. Shortly before her death she traveled by motorbike accompanying an anti-Balaka militia to avoid African peacekeeper checkpoints in order to report a mass killing by Seleka rebels. Her body was found on May 13, 2014 by patrolling French peacekeepers in a car being driven by anti-Balaka rebels. Lepage had been covering heavy fighting in the region and apparently got caught in the gunfire near the border with Cameroon. It was the first death of a Western journalist in the CAR conflict, with French President Francois Hollande describing it as a case of murder.

REFERENCES: http://camille-lepage.photoshelter.com/#!/about; "Camille Lepage: Photojournalist Whose Career Was Dedicated to Chronicling Conflicts often Underreported by the Mainstream Media," Independent, May 23, 2014.

Leroy, Catherine (1945–2006)

The French war photographer* first rose to prominence with her coverage of the Vietnam War* from 1966 to 1968 and subsequent capture by North Vietnamese forces. While held in North Vietnam Leroy was allowed to record daily life behind enemy lines. Arriving in Vietnam with a one-way ticket, intent on becoming a photojournalist, she was hired as a stringer* by Horst Faas,* picture editor for the Associated Press in Vietnam. According to one source, Leroy covered more combat than any other woman correspondent. She garnered attention for her parachute drop with the 173rd Airborne during a battle called "Operation Junction City." Subsequently she was awarded paratroop wings with a gold star making her combat jump. Her coverage of the marine assault on Hill 881 near Khe Sanh was reprinted throughout the world and merited a six-page spread in *Life* magazine.

In May 1967 she was hospitalized after being wounded by shrapnel while with marines near the DMZ. After a month of convalescence she was back in the field and won several awards including the Capa.* During the Tet offensive she was trapped in the Communist-controlled part of Hue as it came under fire from South Vietnamese troops. She narrowly averted capture by posing as a neutral French reporter as she made her way to the U.S. military compound.

In 1974 she covered Cyprus and spent the following two years in Lebanon reporting the civil war mainly from the Progressivist side. She has also recorded conflicts in Afghanistan, Africa, and Iran.

REFERENCES: Virginia Elwood-Akers. *Women War Correspondents in the Vietnam War. 1961–1975.* 1988; Frances Fralin, ed. *The Indelible Image.* 1985; Jorge Lewinski. *The Camera at War.* 1978.

Lesage, Sir John Merry (1837–1926)

Born in Clifton, England, and educated in Bristol, the future editor of the *Daily Telegraph* worked for several small papers before joining the *Telegraph* in 1863. He served as a special correspondent covering the Franco-Prussian War,* while accompanying the Prussian army. His first news scoop was his coverage of the Prussian army entering a defeated Paris in 1871. Shortly after, he reported the Paris Commune. In 1882 he accompanied Sir Garnet Wolseley's expedition against Arabi Pasha. He went on to a forty-year career as managing editor of the *Telegraph*.

In 1918 he was awarded a knighthood for his long career in journalism.

REFERENCES: *DNB*, 1922–1930; Dennis Griffiths, ed. *The Encyclopedia of the British Press.* 1992; Robert Wilkinson-Latham. *From Our Special Correspondent.* 1979.

Leseuer, Laurence Edward (1909–2003)

The son of a *New York Herald Tribune* correspondent, Leseuer joined the United Press in 1931 following his graduation from New York University. Six years later he went to Europe as a radio commentator for the Columbia Broadcasting System (CBS). During the early years of World War II* he reported the activities of the RAF and the British army in France. Following the French surrender in 1940 he was hired as an assistant to Edward R. Murrow* in the London office of CBS. In the fall of 1941 he was assigned to Russia, where he covered the Russian war from the siege of Moscow, which he referred to as "a correspondent's purgatory," to the relief of Stalingrad. Leseuer was the first radio correspondent to broadcast from Moscow. He recounted these events in *Twelve Months That Changed the World.* In 1944 he reported the Normandy invasion and the liberation of Paris, broadcasting from the city prior to the arrival of French troops. Following the war he continued his foreign correspondence from the Middle East and Africa.

REFERENCES: Robert W. Desmond. *Tides of War.* 1984; LA Times, Feb 7, 2003.

Leslie, Frank (1821–1880)

Founder of *Leslie's Illustrated Newspaper* and American innovator in pictorial journalism, he was born Henry Carter in Ipswich, England, on March 29, 1821. Artistically inclined, he had several drawings published in the *Illustrated London News* under his pen name "Frank Leslie" in the late 1830s. Immigrating to the United States in 1848, he went to work for several early picture magazines as a wood engraver before launching *Frank Leslie's Ladies' Gazette of Fashion* and the *New York Journal of Romance* in 1854.

In 1855 he established the first successful illustrated news weekly, *Leslie's Illustrated Newspaper,* which became the most successful of its kind in America. Its rise paralleled and was helped by the opening of the American West and the coverage of the American Civil War.* With the outbreak of the Civil War, Leslie's newspaper was in the position to dominate pictorial news coverage as the most experienced and largest staff of artists and engravers. However, by the end of the war it had lost ground to its competitor *Harper's Weekly.*

During the Civil War *Leslie's Illustrated Newspaper* assumed a strong neutral stance, offering to buy sketches from both Union and Confederate soldiers. The objectivity of Leslie's paper stands in contrast to *Harper's,* which took an increasingly Northern stance, castigating the Southerners as rebels and barbarians. Leslie's newspaper suffered some misfortune when one artist lost months of work while covering the Red River campaign and, after the Battle of Shiloh Henri Lovie,* one of Leslie's most experienced artists, quit the campaign due to exhaustion. At the Battle of Shiloh Lovie produced perhaps his best work, resulting in a sixteen-page spread of his battle sketches. On the other hand, *Harper's* was without an artist-correspondent at the battle and was forced to create sketches from newspaper reports. However, Lovie's withdrawal from his post was a severe setback for Leslie. One historian noted that Lovie, Leslie, and Leslie's engravers formed "the outstanding artist-publisher partnership of the war." With Lovie gone Leslie was without an experienced artist in the western theater of the war.

During the Civil War, *Leslie's* would have up to a dozen correspondents in the field at one time. In addition eighty artists produced more than three thousand sketches of battles and military life. Gradually, Leslie's star began to wane. He lost artists such as Thomas Nast* to his competitors, his personal and business life became increasingly complicated, and his policy of nonpartisan coverage of the war lost him many readers.

In 1875 Leslie's enterprises had expanded to twelve different publications. Although his freespending lifestyle led to bankruptcy in 1877, he continued to manage his journals until his death in 1880.

REFERENCES: *DLB 43*; Budd Leslie Gambee, Jr. *Frank Leslie and His Illustrated Newspaper, 1855–1860*. 1964.

Leslie, Jacques (b. 1947)

Leslie covered Indochina in the 1960s and 1970s. He arrived in Vietnam in 1972 as a correspondent for the *Los Angeles Times* and subsequently became a critic of the war, while clashing with his bureau chiefs. He wrote several stories that portrayed the South Vietnamese government unfavorably. Following the 1973 ceasefire agreement he went to Vietcong-held territory and returned with a report that asserted that the "rebels" were in control of vast swaths of Vietnam. When he wrote a subsequent story about corruption, the regime deemed that it had taken its last hit from Leslie, and expelled him in the summer of 1973. He next ventured to Phnomn Penh and covered the coming of the Khmer Rouge. He left Cambodia but returned in 1975 shortly before the end of the Lon Nol regime. In 1977 Leslie left the *Los Angeles Times* and has had a highly successful career as a freelance author and journalist. His work has appeared in many leading magazines including the *Atlantic, Harper's, New York Times Magazine,* and *Mother Jones.* He covers these events and more in his memoir, *The Mark: A War Correspondent's Memoir of Vietnam and Cambodia* (1995).

REFERENCES: Jacques Leslie. The Mark. 1995; www.mekong.net/cambodia/the_mark.htm.

Leventhal, Richard Gary (b. 1960)

An American reporter and senior correspondent for Fox News Channel since 1997, Leventhal has reported from a number of war zones. He has made numerous tours to Iraq, Afghanistan, and Israel over the past 15 years. He has covered conflict in Albania, Macedonia, and Libya. In 2003 he was embedded with the U.S. Marine Corps for nine weeks in Kuwait and Iraq, and was present as they advanced on Baghdad. In 2001 he had covered the devastation at the World Trade Center and later traveled to Bahrain and Afghanistan. During this time he was embedded with the Marines at Camp Rhino and Kandahar Airport as they prepared to launch the so-called "War on Terror."

REFERENCES: http://www.imdb.com/name/nm0505297/bio; http://www.netlibrary.net/articles/rick_leventhal.

Lewis, Flora (1922–2002)

Lewis was born in Los Angeles and graduated from UCLA and then Columbia with a graduate degree in journalism in 1942. She started her journalism career with the AP during World War II. She then did freelance work in Europe for a number of news outlets. Being a freelancer was probably not of her own choosing. When she married *New York Times* foreign correspondent Sydney Gruson, the newspaper's policy of not employing married couples led her to cover Cold War events in Eastern Europe for the *New York Post,* and later, the 1967 Arab-Israeli War and Vietnam for *Newsday.* After divorce in 1972 she returned to the *Times* now a single woman and worked for the paper until her death at the age of 79. She wrote four books dealing with foreign policy, the last, *Europe: Road to Unity,* in 1992.

REFERENCES: Craig R. Whitney. "Flora Lewis, Astute Observer of Wolrd Affairs for the Time and Others, Dies at 79." *New York Times,* June, 2, 2002; Richard Pearson. "Journalist, Author Flora Lewis Dies." *Washington Post,* June 3, 2002.

Lewis, George (b. 1943)

During his long career with NBC News, Lewis has become one of its most honored correspondents, winning three Emmys, the George Foster Peabody Award and the Edward R. Murrow Award. He began his career in 1970 covering the Vietnam War. After almost two years there he left but returned to cover the fall of Saigon. Based in Los Angeles, he has covered both Iraq wars, was in Iran during the 444-day hostage crisis in 1979, and in Lebanon during the 1982 Israeli invasion. He has also covered the Tiananmen Square massacre, and revoloutions and conflict in Romania, Latin America, and Asia.

REFERENCE: http://www.msnbc.com.

Lewis, Sir Wilmott Harsant (1877–1950)

Lewis was born in Cardiff, Wales, and educated at the University of Heidelberg and the Sorbonne. He first entered journalism while traveling in the Far East, reporting the Boxer Rebellion* in 1900 and then the Russo-Japanese War* for the *New York Herald* before moving to the Philippines in 1911, where he began a six-year stint with the *Manila Times*. His international expertise came to the attention of General John Pershing in 1919, when he requested that Lewis come to France to cover the Paris Peace Conference for the American information and propaganda services. From 1920 to 1948 Lewis represented the *Times* as its Washington correspondent. He was knighted in 1931 and died in Washington on January 4, 1950, two years after retirement.

REFERENCES: Robert W. Desmond. *The Information Process*. 1978; *DNB*, 1941–1950.

Libyan Insurgency

Following successful uprisings in Tunisia and Egypt in 2011 during the so-called Arab Spring, Libyan rebels began their revolution against Libyan strongman Muammar Gaddafi in February 2011. In late August Tripoli was under rebel control and in October Gaddafi had been captured and killed. In the aftermath of the insurgency the National Transitional Council was set up in Benghazi and plans were made to rebuild the country. The war proved a dangerous posting for journalists, although the number of casualties is still in dispute. At least five foreign correspondents and one Libyan journalist were killed before the death of Gaddafi on October 20, 2011.

REFERENCE: Reporters without Borders, *Upheaval in the Arab World: Media as Key Witnesses and Political Pawns*, Report, Nov. 2011, 8–9.

Liebling, Abbott Joseph "A. J." (1904–1963)

Born in New York City, Liebling graduated from Columbia University's Pulitzer School of Journalism in 1925. After jobs with several newspapers he was hired by the *New Yorker* in 1935. During World War II,* beginning in 1939, he covered the London blitz and the invasions of North Africa and Normandy, and in 1944 he witnessed the liberation of Paris. His war reports were published in several collections, *The Road Back to Paris* (1944) and *The Republic of Silence* (1947). In 1952 France awarded him its Legion of Honor medal for his war service. A prolific writer, his wartime articles were collected posthumously in *Mollie and Other War Pieces* in 1964. The overweight gourmand suffered from a variety of maladies, including gout. In 1963 a bout of pneumonia led to heart failure and renal collapse on December 28.

REFERENCES: Library of America. *Reporting World War II: Part Two*. 1995; A. J. Liebling. *Liebling Abroad*. 1981.

Liefde, Jacob B. De (1847–1878)

Educated in Holland, Liefde was a war correspondent for the *Daily News* during the Franco-Prussian

War.* Posted to the Prussian army, along with most of the English-based reporters, he worked closely with Archibald Forbes.* He was in Paris for the fall of the Paris Commune. He wrote *Great Dutch Admirals* (1873).

REFERENCE: Dennis Griffiths, ed. *The Encyclopedia of the British Press.* 1992.

The Light That Failed

Rudyard Kipling's* 1899 novel was published during the so-called golden age of war correspondents. Its protagonist is a young artist-correspondent* named Dick Heldar who is accompanying a British column in the relief of General Charles Gordon at Khartoum. As a result of a head wound suffered while he was engaged in hand-to-hand fighting with the dervishes he loses his sight several months after returning to England. Unable to accompany his friends back to the Sudan in a new campaign against the Mahdi, Heldar catches up to the expedition at the moment the dervishes attack. He asks his friends to be put in the forward defense and he is dropped almost immediately with a bullet through the head.

REFERENCES: Howard Good. *The Image of War Correspondents in Anglo-American Fiction.* 1985; Rudyard Kipling. *The Light That Failed.* 1899.

Lindbaek, Lise (1905–1961)

Born in Copenhagen, Denmark, she later moved to Norway. In 1924 she began working as a foreign correspondent in Italy for Oslo newspapers. Like her compatriot Gerda Gregg,* she has also been credited as being the first female Norwegian war journalist when she too covered the Spanish Civil War*. She covered the war for the *Dagbladet* newspaper and arrived several months after Gregg. Lindbaek's biographer claims that Gregg might have preceded Lindbaek in Spain, but Lindbaek should be accorded the distinction of first Norwegian female war correspondent on

the strength of the fact that she covered Mussolini's rise to power and the Reichstag fire in 1933, several years before Gregg covered the Spanish imbroglio. Lindbaek chronicled the exploits of the German- and Scandinavian-speaking Thalmann Battalion of the International Brigades in her book, *Bataljon Thalmann* (1938). She committed suicide, drowning herself in the sea in 1961.

REFERENCE: http://en.wikipedia.org/wiki/Lise_Lindb%C3%A6k.

Linebaugh, John H. (c. 1812–1864)

Linebaugh was a leading Southern war correspondent during the American Civil War,* whose dispatches were filed under the pen name "Shadow." Prior to the war Linebaugh was an Epsicopal clergyman. The *Memphis Appeal* special correspondent was attending church services in Chattanooga when Union forces began bombarding the city. He fled the city shortly before the Battle of Chickamauga and in September 1863 his arrest was ordered by General Braxton Bragg, about whom he had written several critical pieces. In late 1864 Linebaugh was on his way to Hood's army to represent the Associated Press Association when he drowned. He was one of only two Southern war reporters to perish in the conflict. Linebaugh was on a steamboat, five days out of Richmond, when it ran aground along the Alabama River. He attempted to swim to shore with other passengers but was lost in the swift current.

REFERENCE: J. Cutler Andrews. *The South Reports the Civil War.* 1970.

Liohn, Andre (b. 1974)

Born in Botucatu, Brazil, he moved to Norway in his twenties. He came to photojournalism rather late, beginning in 2004. In 2011 he became the first Latin American photojournalist to win the Robert Capa Gold Medal* in recognition of his coverage of the Libyan civil war.* The focus of his work often veers toward the daunting challenges faced by health care workers in war zones.

REFERENCE: https://www.facebook.com/pages/ Andr%C3%A9-Liohn/459960177375173?sk=info&tab= page_info.

Lipskerov, Georgei (1896–1977)

A seasoned photographer at the outset of World War II,* Lipskerov became the oldest Russian photojournalist to record the war. As a member of the staff of a Russian army newspaper he covered the entire war from the battlefront. Unlike other war photographers unencumbered with military affiliation, Lispkerov did not have the opportunity to roam freely; instead he spent the war with his unit. His unit defeated the Sixth Army Corps of Field Marshal Paulus near Stalingrad, affording Lispkerov the chance to take the first pictures of one of the greatest victories of the Russian theater of the war. Following the war he remained active in the field of photography.

REFERENCE: Daniela Mrazkova and Vladimir Remes, eds. *The Russian War: 1941–1945*. 1975.

Lloyd, Anthony (b. 1966)

Lloyd served with the British Army in Northern Ireland and in the first Gulf War. He left the military for war photography, first covering the war in Bosnia. He got his first start as a journalist filling in for a correspondent working for the *Daily Telegraph* who had been wounded by a mine. He then found employment with the *Times of London*. He has covered conflicts in the Balkans, Chechnya, Afghanistan, and Sierra Leone. He has published two books that chronicle these experiences. In 2001 he published *My War Gone By, I Miss It* about Bosnia and Chechnya and then *Another Bloody Love Letter* (2007) covering his exploits in the former Yugoslavia, Sierra Leone, Afghanistan, and Iraq.

REFERENCES: Anthony Lloyd. *My War Gone By, I Miss It*. 2001; *Another Bloody Love Letter*. 2007.

Lloyd, James (c. 1828–1913)

The British painter and photographer moved to Natal, South Africa, in the early 1850s. He was one of the first two press photographers in Natal. His sketches were reproduced in the *Illustrated London News*. He came to public attention with his photographs from the 1879 Zulu War.

REFERENCE: Frances Fralin, ed *The Indelible Image*. 1985.

Lloyd, Terrence Ellis "Terry" (1952–2003)

Born in Derby, England, Lloyd, the son of a policeman, started his journalism career with the Raymonds News Agency in his hometown. In 1983 he joined ITN and for the next twenty years would cover danger zones in the Middle East and the Balkans. He first covered the frontlines in the mid-1980s as he covered the internecine carnage of the Lebanese civil war. The British television journalist rose to prominence in 1988, breaking the story that Saddam Hussein used chemical weapons on the Kurds in Halabja, killing more than 5,000. In 1994 he was the first to report the discovery of mass graves in Vukovar in former Yugoslavia. Many observers credited his coverage with having major influence on subsequent Western policy in the region. He won acclaim in 1999 as the first foreign journalist to enter Kosovo in 1999. On March 22, 2003 he was covering the invasion of Iraq for ITN (Independent Television News), while working as an unembedded reporter, reporting on the advance of coalition forces. Lloyd and his team were caught in the crossfire between U.S. and Iraqi forces during the battle for Shatt Al Basra Bridge in Basra, Iraq. Following the battle, the bodies of Lloyd and his Lebanese interpreter were found shot dead, from what proved to be

---

Indicates a separate entry.

American fire. The French cameraman Frederic Nerac's body has never been found and was presumed dead. Terry Lloyd was the first ITN war reporter in almost a half century of covering international conflicts to be killed on the job. Among the many accolades directed at Lloyd after his untimely death, was that of his friend of nearly thirty years, David Nicholas, who praised him as never being afraid of "the story."

REFERENCE: David Nicholas, "Terry Lloyd, Veteran TV War Reporter Who Revealed the Attacks on Iraq's Kurds," Guardian, Mar. 24, 2003.

Lochner, Louis Paul (1897–1975)

Born in Springfield, Illinois, and educated at the University of Wisconsin, Lochner joined the Associated Press in 1921 and was AP correspondent in Berlin from the years 1924 to 1941, the last fourteen of which he was bureau chief. In 1939 he was the recipient of the Pulitzer Prize for distinguished correspondence as foreign correspondent and became the first foreign correspondent to follow the German army into Poland. He then covered action on the German western front in Holland, Belgium, and France, where he witnessed the Channel coast action as the Germans advanced on the British at Dunkirk. In 1941 he was with the German army in Yugoslavia, Greece, Finland, and Russia. When Germany declared war on the United States that December, he was interned in Bad Nauheim along with other American correspondents. The following year he was repatriated to America. Shortly after he returned to France. He recounted his life in Germany in the book *What About Germany?* In March 1945 he accompanied the Allied advance into Germany, but in June was seriously injured in a jeep accident when a Red Army vehicle plowed into it and left without stopping. It took Lochner several weeks to recuperate from a concussion and other injuries.

REFERENCE: Robert W. Desmond. *Tides of War.* 1984.

Lochridge, Pat (1916–1998)

The daughter of the editor and publisher of the *Austin Statesman* (Texas), Pat graduated from Wellesley and the Columbia School of Journalism before starting her career in journalism with a small newspaper in Missouri. Following the attack on Pearl Harbor she moved to Washington to work for the Office of War Information. The following year she went to work for the publisher of *Collier's* and *Woman's Home Companion,* for whom she would finally get selected to report the war from the Pacific in 1945. She covered the Battle of Iwo Jima from a hospital ship off the coast while assisting doctors and nurses. She reported she could (barely) see the American flag being lifted on Mount Suribachi. Unlike other women such as Dickie Chapelle* Lochridge managed to actually go ashore on the island where she helped medical personnel. Lochridge also reported from the Dachau concentration camp. After the war she continued in journalism in Arizona and did a stint in public relations with UNICEF. As the European theater came to a close Pat was in Berchtesgaden for the surrender of Hermann Goering. According to her biographer Nancy Caldwell Sorel, Goering surrendered to press members as the Seventh Army approached. They found the corpulent Nazi's car stuffed with fried chicken and wine. The food and libations were liberated by the hungry members of the Fourth Estate. It was here that Goering's art collection was discovered in secret tunnels under his villa and valued in the billions of dollars. Although Lochridge died in 1998 she was once more making news in 2007 after her son revealed that his mother had been given permission to select a piece of art from a warehouse full of art and controlled by U.S. forces in southern Germany. She chose *Cupid Complaining to Venus* by Lucas Cranach the Elder (c. 1525). At the time of this revelation there was increased interest in the provenance of looted European masterpieces. Lochridge had apparently sold the painting in the 1960s.

REFERENCES: Lilya Wagner. *Women War Correspondents of World War Two.* 1989; Nancy Caldwell Sorel. *The Women Who Wrote the War.* 1999; Nicholas Glass. "Getting the Nazi Stolen Art Bak." www.channel4.com, March 27, 2007.

Logan, Lara (b. 1971)

Born in Durban, South Africa, Logan had been in the journalism business for fourteen years before coming to international prominence with CBS News beginning in 2002. She was educated in Natal and speaks French, Afrikaans and basic Portuguese. She has covered conflicts in Afghanistan, the Middle East, and Africa for various news agencies and served as a freelance correspondent for CNN in 1998–1999, covering the embassy bombings in Nairobi and Tanzania, the conflict in Northern Ireland and the war in Kosovo. Since February 2006 Logan has been CBS News chief foreign correspondent and has been a correspondent for the program *60 Minutes.* She has covered the Iraq War since 2003 and was according to CBS, "the only journalist from an American network in Baghdad when the U.S. military invaded the city." In 2005 she was covering a battle along the Afghanistan-Pakistan border when her vehicle hit a double-tank mine. She escaped with minor injuries while two soldiers were seriously wounded. She has received an Emmy Award, an Overseas Club Award and an Edward R. Murrow Award for her 2006 report on American troops under fire in Ramadi, Iraq while embedded* with an American military unit. In 2011, Logan and her CBS crew were in Egypt covering the Egyptian Revolution, when they were detained, blindfolded and handcuffed by the Egyptian Army. They were warned to leave the country and urged to leave Egypt. It soon came out that Logan had not only been beaten, but had also been sexually assaulted. She claimed she had been covering the celebrations at Tahrir Square after Hosni Mubarak stepped down. After about an hour of filming, her camera battery ran out and one of her Egyptuan assistants told her it was time to leave, as the crowd of hundreds

of men began making lewd comments about her. For more than 20 minutes an estimated 200–300 men groped her and began pulling off her clothes and tearing at her hair. She was only saved from further injury when a group of Egyptian women became involved, protecting her from further harm. In 2013 Logan was forced to take a leave of absence from 60 Minutes after errors in a report on her Benghazi incident were revealed.

REFERENCE: www.cbsnews.com/stories/2002/12/02/broadcasts/main531421; Joe Hagan, "Benghazi and the Bombshell," *New York Magazine,* May 4, 2014.

London, John "Jack" (1876–1916)

Born in San Francisco, after a youth filled with poverty and adventure at sea he turned to writing in 1893. After winning an essay-writing contest that year he began to submit stories to various publications with little success. In 1900 his career was jump-started by the publication of the collection of short stories entitled *The Son of the Wolf.*

In 1902 he was hired by the American Press Association to travel to South Africa to report on the Boer War* and its repercussions on British colonies. But he abruptly changed his plans and went to London instead. After several weeks observing life in the crowded slums he wrote *The People of the Abyss.*

Well established as a novelist, London covered his first war in 1904 when he reported the Russo-Japanese War* from Korea for the *New York Journal.* Among the other war correspondents that sailed on the SS *Siberia* with London were Lionel James,* Frederick Palmer,* and James Hare.* The day before he debarked he put the finishing touches on *The Sea Wolf.* Like most correspondents during the war, London was faced with endless restrictions imposed by Japanese authorities. He had several encounters with the Japanese military command, leading to his arrest on two occasions. In one incident he was held for court-martial after he assaulted a Japanese officer. However, he was soon released and headed back to the United States. While he

* Indicates a separate entry.

did not witness actual combat, his reports give a vivid description of behind-the-lines activity during the Russo-Japanese War.

In May 1914 London was hired by *Collier's Weekly* magazine to cover the United States marine landing at Veracruz, Mexico. On May 30 he was stricken with dysentery and was forced to return to the United States nine days later. London died just two years later.

REFERENCE: King Hendricks and Irving Shepard, eds. *Jack London Reports.* 1970.

Long, Tania

See DANIELL, TANIA LONG.

Lorch, Donatella (b. c. 1962)

Conversant in English, French, Italian, Spanish and Chinese, she was educated at Columbia University and Columbia University, where she completed her graduate work. Lorch began her more than twenty-year career covering wars and conflicts in 1987, when she reported on what was then the little-known Afghan Mujahidin in its war against the Soviet occupation. She was hired by the *New York Times* to cover the region. Based in Peshawar, Pakistan, she took numerous trips into the war zone and was, according to her home page, "the first reporter and only woman journalist to be smuggled into Kabul to document the guerrilla underground." In Pakistan she covered the assassination of President Zia ul-Haq, the election of Benazir Bhutto, and the country's growing nuclear capability. She has gone on to cover war zones in South Asia, the Middle East, Africa, and Europe for the *New York Times*, NBC News, and *Newsweek*. She has chronicled Operation Desert Storm in Iraq and the fall of Kabul to Afghan Mujahidin in 1992. In Africa she covered the Somalian civil war and famine as well as the U.S. and UN intervention experiences. In southern Sudan she accompanied rebels and reported on the terror campaign of the Lord's Resistance Army in

northern Uganda. Of all of the brutal stories she has witnessed, none plagued her memory more than the Rwandan genocide. She was among the small group of journalists to travel into Kigali just days after the murders began. Over the next year she would document the massacres, refugee crises, and efforts to rebuild the country. Lorch joined NBC News in 1996 and began tracking Bosnian war criminals, the conflict in Kosovo, the developing refugee crisis in the Balkans, and the U.S. embassy attack in Kenya. Lorch returned to the war zone in 2002 and then again in 2003 in Afghanistan, embedded with a U.S. Army Special Forces A Team. During these tours she reported on stalled efforts at reconstruction in the Taliban stronghold of Southeastern Afghanistan.

REFERENCE: "Donatella Lorch-War Correspondent," http://www.donatellalorch.com/bio.html.

Loti, Pierre

See VIAUD, LOUIS MARIE JULIEN.

Lounsberry, Clement A. (1843–1926)

Lounsberry was the owner of the *Bismarck Tribune* and had planned to accompany General Alfred Terry's Yellowstone expedition as war correspondent, when his wife became sick. Changing his plans at that fateful moment, he assigned in his place Mark Kellogg,* a part-time telegrapher and writer, who would be the only reporter to perish with Custer at the Little Big Horn. Lounsberry and Custer were both from Michigan and had begun their friendship during the American Civil War.* When Custer arrived at Fort Abraham Lincoln in 1873 they renewed their relationship. In 1874 Custer's official dispatch rider brought Lounsberry the scoop that gold had been discovered in the Black Hills. Custer's leaks to various newspapers led to his testifying in front of a congressional committee and to his losing the command of not only the 1876 Sioux expedition, but his own regiment as well.

Lounsberry had to write General Terry for permission to send another reporter in his place. After he obtained it, the ill-fated Kellogg rode with Terry's forces, riding the horse meant for Lounsberry, and wearing his supervisor's Civil War belt. Before leaving for the Rosebud and his death Kellogg wrote to Lounsberry, "I go with Custer and will be at [sic] the death."

From notes made by Kellogg and interviews with various survivors of the Terry expedition, Lounsberry wrote a comprehensive, eighteen-thousand-word account of the Custer battle and forwarded it to the *New York Herald* at a cost of almost $3,000. It took more than two hours for the telegraph transmission to be completed. Controversy developed for Lounsberry, who attempted to capitalize on having the only accredited correspondent with the Custer expedition, when both the *New York Herald* and the *Chicago Tribune* claimed Kellogg represented their papers.

REFERENCES: Oliver Knight. *Following the Indian Wars.* 1960; The Bismarck Tribune, Oct. 6, 1926.

Lovie, Henri (1829–1875)

Born in Berlin, Germany, Lovie was the senior artist-correspondent* for *Frank Leslie's Illustrated Weekly* during the American Civil War.* Besides working as a sketch artist for the newspaper, he supported his family with a lithograph business in Cincinnati. He was first assigned to follow Lincoln from Springfield to Washington in 1861. Following the inauguration he accompanied Mc-Clellan's army. At the beginning of the campaign he covered the Battle of Philippi. His work method is aptly demonstrated by his coverage of this battle. At Philippi he moved out of harm's way to a vantage point above the carnage on a hillside, providing himself a panoramic view. Following the fighting he would walk the field sketching the detritus and debris of battle. He would then tour the encampments interviewing the exhausted soldiers. His methods were not without risks—several times he was questioned for spying and he became a target for more than one sentry.

Lovie sketched the Battle of Rich Mountain, Fremont's Missouri campaign, and the western naval war, including the capture of Forts Henry and Donelson. He had his greatest scoop with his dramatic sketches of the Battle of Shiloh in April 1862. As the only artist to record the entire two days of the epic battle, he received great acclaim for his work. According to one historian, no other artist in the war illustrated a battle as well as Lovie covered Shiloh. In 1863, tired of covering the war, he invested in cotton and retired from *Leslie's*. Lovie died soon after Appomattox.

REFERENCES: Pat Hodgson. *The War Illustrators.* 1977; W. Fletcher Thompson, Jr. *The Image of War.* 1959.

Lucas, James Griffing (1914–1970)

Lucas was born in Checotah, Oklahoma, and attended the University of Missouri before joining the *Muskogee Daily Phoenix* in 1934. He tried his hand at broadcasting and then worked for the *Tulsa Tribune* before joining the marines as a combat correspondent during World War II.* Technical Sergeant Jim Lucas began his affiliation with the Scripps-Howard newspapers toward the end of World War II and used his prior newspaper experience to his advantage as a marine combat correspondent, covering the Battles of Guadalcanal, Iwo Jima, and Tarawa, where he was listed killed in action for three days. He received the 1943 National Headliners Award for his coverage of the Battle of Tarawa, which has been described as the most vivid eyewitness account of the landings there. In 1944 he was promoted to second lieutenant when he covered the Marianas campaign.

During the Korean War* he won the Pulitzer Prize in the field of international reporting and the Ernie Pyle* Memorial Award, which he would win again during the Vietnam War* in 1964. Lucas had been on hand when the French were defeated in Indochina in 1954. As the only correspondent for an American daily newspaper assigned to troops in the field he covered the buildup in Vietnam from the Mekong Delta for five months in 1964. Lucas

Indicates a separate entry.

recounted this experience in *Dateline: Vietnam* in 1966. He shared with David Halberstam* the opinion that the press had done a poor job covering the war zone, exemplified by the fact that in the middle of 1964 there were only two dozen correspondents in all covering the developing conflict. He was the recipient of numerous other awards as well as eight battle stars, the Bronze Star, and the Presidential Unit Citation as combat correspondent with the U.S. Marines in World War II.

REFERENCE: Michael Emery. *On the Front Lines.* 1995.

Lumley, Arthur (1837–1912)

Born in Dublin, Ireland, Lumley immigrated to the United States in the 1850s. For several years he supported his art school education by selling illustrations to *Leslie's Illustrated Weekly*. With the outbreak of the American Civil War* he was assigned by the magazine to cover army encampments on the perimeter of Washington, D.C., and cover the Army of the Potomac. He covered the First Battle of Bull Run, where he sketched the bayonet charge of the New York City Fire Zouaves, one of the most heroic images of the war. Frustrated with endless sketching of camp life, Lumley left *Leslie's* for the *New York Illustrated News*. That year (1862) he covered McClellan's Yorktown campaign, the Battle of Fair Oaks near Richmond, and the Seven Days' Battles. During the seven days of incessant battles, he produced as many sketches as his four competitors combined. Lumley was so exhausted following this series of battles he needed to return to New York to recuperate and oversee the engraving of his sketches. On several occasions Lumley made sketches from the vantage point of a balloon. He also illustrated several executions and sketched scenes from the Battles of Chancellorsville and Fredericksburg. Lumley retired from the battlefront toward the end of 1863 and continued his career as an illustrator. He never returned to the battlefield.

REFERENCES: Philip Van Doren Stem. *They Were There.* 1959; W. Fletcher Thompson, Jr. *The Image of War.* 1959.

Lumsden, Francis Asbury (1808–1860)

Born in North Carolina, Lumsden cofounded the *New Orleans Picayune* with George Wilkins Kendall* in 1837. This would be the first inexpensive paper in the South, joining perhaps a dozen other papers in the Crescent City in the heady days of the penny press. In the late 1830s he made a trip to the Republic of Texas to check on circulation possibilities. In 1842, after Kendall was imprisoned following the ill-fated Santa Fe expedition, Lumsden traveled to Mexico in an attempt to have his partner and friend released. But it would be months later before Kendall was freed.

With the outbreak of the Mexican-American War* in 1846, Lumsden began organizing volunteers into the Orleans Regiment. However, when a better-equipped company from Georgia known as the Gaines Rangers elected Lumsden as its captain, he ended his recruitment drive and left for the border with the Rangers. Perhaps he should have kept to his original plan, for after reaching the Mexican border word came that the ship carrying their supplies and ammunition had gone down in a storm. So they disbanded in Matamoros shortly after their enlistment period ended.

Lumsden stayed in Mexico and was among the *Picayune* staff strategically placed throughout Mexico to record war news for their paper. He covered General Scott's Veracruz campaign in early 1847 as an aide to the staff of General Shields. In September 1860, Lumsden and his family were among the three hundred passengers who drowned when the steamer *Lady Elgin* sank in a storm on Lake Michigan following a collision with another boat.

REFERENCE: Fayette Copeland. *Kendall of the Picayune.* 1943.

Lutfallah, Aswan (1971–2006)

Known by his moniker "The Eagle," Lutfallah covered the war in his native Iraq as a cameraman for APTN from 2005 till his death. He had a well-earned reputation for fearlessness, which probably brought him to his final story. He was in a car repair shop in Mosul in northern Iraq when he left to cover a firefight between police and insurgents, who apparently turned their weapons on him when they saw him filming them. The insurgents then took all of his possessions including his camera equipment and press ID.

REFERENCES: AP Wall of Honor, www.ap.org/wallof-honor/2000_2008.html.

Lyman, Ambrose William (1848–1898)

Born in Warren, Ohio, he entered journalism with *The Cleveland Leader* and then caught on with the *New York Tribune* around 1885. He later moved out West to manage the *Helena Independent* in Montana. He held that position for eight years, before returning to New York City in 1897. He then joined the AP, for whom he covered the Spanish American War* in Cuba in 1898. He became gravely ill with yellow fever yet was able to cover the short war to its conclusion at the Battle of Santiago. He returned to New York where he succumbed to the malady later that year.

REFERENCE: AP Wall of Honor, www.ap.org/wallof-honor/1876_1899.html.

Lynch, Arthur Alfred (1861–1934)

Born in Smythesdale, Victoria, Australia, Lynch graduated from the University of Melbourne. He later attended graduate school at the University of Berlin and practiced medicine in Paris before turning to journalism in 1889. He covered the 1896 Ashanti campaign for the *Evening News* and joined the staff of the *Daily Mail* later that year. With the outbreak of the Boer War* in 1899 he went to Pretoria for the Paris-based *Le Journal*. However, upon his arrival in January 1900 he joined the conflict on the Boer side, and was appointed colonel of a group composed of seventy men from virtually every country in Europe. After six months he returned to Paris.

His participation in the Boer conflict led to a parliamentary seat representing Galway, but when he left Ireland to take his seat in England he was arrested for treason and sentenced to death. His sentence was commuted to life imprisonment, but he was released within the year. In 1908 he returned to the practice of medicine. He was elected to Parliament again in 1909, and his vigorous support of the war efforts against the Germans prior to 1918 led to his vindication for supporting the Boers.

REFERENCE: *DNB*, 1931–1940.

Lynch, George (b. 1868)

Lynch covered the Spanish-American War* from Cuba for the *Daily Chronicle*. He was accredited as war correspondent by the *Morning Herald*, the *Echo*, and the *Illustrated London News* during the Boer War* and was bottled up with twelve thousand British soldiers during the siege of Ladysmith.* He was the only correspondent to get out of Ladysmith during the siege, although he was captured by Boer forces not far from the siege lines. Lynch was imprisoned at Pretoria and released following the capitulation of the town.

When the siege of Peking and the Boxer Rebellion* broke out in 1900 he hurried to the scene, representing the *Daily Express* and the *Sphere*. He next reported the Russo-Japanese War* for the *Daily Chronicle*. Later he reported World War I* for the *London Illustrated News*. One of his greatest contributions to the conflict was his invention of a special pair of gloves for handling the ubiquitous barbed wire.

REFERENCES: Robert W. Desmond. *The Information Process*. 1978; Kenneth Griffith. *Thank God We Kept the Flag Flying: The Siege and Relief of Ladysmith*. 1974; Robert Wilkinson-Latham. *From Our Special Correspondent*. 1979.

Lynch, Jessica Hoax

See JESSICA LYNCH HOAX.

* Indicates a separate entry.

Maccosh, John (1805–1885)

Soldier and pioneer photographer John Mac-
Cosh was one of the earliest war photographers.
He was a surgeon during the Second Sikh War
of 1848–1849, when he took pictures of his fellow officers. In 1852–1853 he had perfected his
techniques enough to allow him to photograph
troops and the captured cities of Rangoon and
Prome during the Second Burma War.

REFERENCES: Pat Hodgson. *Early War Photographs.*
1974; Jorge Lewinski. *The Camera at War.* 1978.

MacDonald, Roderick (c. 1914–1944)

MacDonald worked for various Australian
newspapers and on Fleet Street in the 1930s before becoming a war correspondent for the *News
Chronicle* and the *Sydney Morning Herald* during World War II.* In 1941 he was sent by the
Sydney Morning Herald to Chungking to cover
the Japanese invasion of China. He was assigned
to the Burma theater following the bombing of
Pearl Harbor and later was posted to North Africa. During the Sicilian campaign he was the
only journalist to land with the glider-borne
troops. He was captured, but quickly freed by
British troops. In May 1944 he was killed along
with Cyril Bewley* by a land mine near Cassino.

REFERENCE: Robert W. Desmond. *Tides of War.* 1984.

Maceda, Jim (b. 1949)

During a career of more than forty years, the
Stanford-educated Maceda covered numerous war zones, including Rhodesia, Lebanon,
Chechnya, the Balkans, and Northern Ireland.
He began his journalism career as an associate
producer for CBS News in Paris between 1973
and 1976. During the rest of the 1970s he reported
and produced for French TV. He joined NBC
News' Paris bureau in 1980 and over the next
three years reported on the Middle East from
Tel Aviv. He covered the annexation of the Go-
lan Heights and the 1982 Lebanon War. He was
lauded for producing the 17-part "Lebanon Diary" series. During the second half of the 1980s
Maceda was a senior news producer in London.
He covered the first Palestinian Intifada, winning
an Emmy for his reportage in 1988. From 1988 to
1990 he was posted in Manila as an NBC News
Asia reporter and producer. During this period
he covered the Cambodian War, the Burma Revolt, and the Panama Invasion. He was recognized with an Emmy in 1989 for his coverage of
the Tiananmen Massacre in Beijing. In 1990 he
became the NBC News Moscow correspondent, covering most major events in the region
and then the Somalian civil war and the failed
American peacekeeping mission there. He was
relocated to Germany in 1994, covering Eastern
Europe, the Bosnian civil war, and peacekeeping
missions in former Yugoslavia and Haiti. Over

the past decade he was a veteran of numerous embeds in Afghanistan and Iraq, reporting on American forces, insurgents, and civilians in lands torn by warfare.

REFERENCES: nbcnews.com/id/3688817/ns/nbc_nightly_news_with_brian_williams-about_us/t/Jim-maceda

Macgahan, Januarius Aloysius (1844–1878)

The preeminent American war correspondent of his day was born in rural Ohio. At the age of twenty-four he traveled to Europe with the intention of improving his general education. He was in Brussels when France declared war on Prussia. In 1871 Macgahan offered his services to the *New York Herald*, and his amazing seven-year career as a journalist had begun. During the Franco-Prussian War* he covered the defeat of the Algerian Boubaki before heading to Paris to witness the Paris Commune. Suspected of spying, he was arrested and narrowly averted hanging thanks to the intervention of an American diplomat. Following the siege of the Paris Commune he traveled widely for the *Herald*. In his most celebrated exploit for his paper he made a one-thousand-mile horseback trek in 1873 across the unknown stretches of the Kyzil Kum desert of Central Asia to join the advance of the Russian army against the khanate of the ancient city of Kiva. On his treacherous journey he eluded Cossack and Turkoman forces who were responsible for enforcing the Russian prohibition against news correspondents.

Before returning from Asia he rode with Cossacks in their subjugation of Turkoman tribesmen. Macgahan next covered the Carlist War in Spain in 1874. While accompanying the forces of Don Carlos, the pretender to the throne, he witnessed the major battle of the war at Abarzuza-Estella. The following year he was assigned to cover an Arctic expedition searching for the fabled Northwest Passage aboard the ship *Pandora*.

The year 1876 found the intrepid Macgahan investigating reports of Turkish atrocities in Bul-

garia.* After a disagreement with James Gordon Bennett* of the *Herald* he left the paper for the *London Daily News*. His dispatches to the *Daily News* were credited with instigating the Russo-Turkish War* of 1877–1878 and were published as *The Turkish Atrocities in Bulgaria* in 1876. Today he is remembered in Bulgaria as the "champion of Bulgarian freedom," with streets and statues commemorating his investigative reporting.

He covered the war from the crossing of the Danube through the signing of the peace treaty, including the Battle of Plevna. His dispatches from the major battlefields are considered classics of the genre. Shortly before his thirty-fourth birthday he died of typhus in Constantinople. Five years later he became the first war correspondent to be conveyed to the United States after death by a warship, when the cruiser *Powhatan* brought his body back to lie in state at New York city hall before interment near his birthplace in Ohio.

REFERENCES: F. Lauriston Bullard. *Famous War Correspondents*. 1914; Dale L. Walker. *Januarius MacGahan*. 1988.

MacGowan, Gault (1894–1970)

After service in France and the Middle East during World War I,* MacGowan covered the North West Frontier of India in 1923 as a correspondent for the Associated Press. The following year he was hired as editor of the *Times of Mesopotamia*, but resigned in 1925 and returned to London and the *Times*. In 1926 he became Paris correspondent for the *Daily Press*.

After stints with the *Evening Express* and *Londoner's Diary* he was the managing editor for the *Trinidad Guardian* from 1929 to 1934. He traveled widely as foreign correspondent for the *New York Times* and reported the Spanish Civil War* for the *New York Sun* prior to World War II.*

During the world war he reported the Battle of Britain and the Battle of the Atlantic, and accompanied commandos on a mission. In June 1944,

Indicates a separate entry.

after covering the landings at Normandy beach, he was captured by Germans while accompanying the Allied advance to Paris. He later escaped and fought alongside the Maquis French resistance forces. He went on to witness the Potsdam Conference (1945) and the first United Nations meetings in London (1946). Later that year he was promoted to European manager of the *New York Sun*. His last years in journalism were spent with the magazine *European Living* as editor and publisher.

REFERENCE: Jack Stenbuck, ed. *Typewriter Battalion*. 1995.

MacHugh, Lieutenant-Colonel Robert Joseph (1863–1925)

During his first stint as a war correspondent in the 1890s, he was an officer in the London Royal Garrison Artillery. He covered the Cuban campaign during the Spanish-American War* for the *Daily Telegraph* in 1898. The following year found MacHugh covering the Boer War* for the *Telegraph*. His book *The Siege of Ladysmith** resulted from his coverage of the war.

In 1904 he covered the Russo-Japanese War* while attached to the Japanese army on the staff of General Baron Kuroki. He accompanied the Japanese First Army throughout the war, reporting the Battles of the Yalu, Mo-tien-ling Pass, and Liaoyang, in the process earning a campaign medal.

He returned to his military career in England when he joined the Territorial Army in 1908. In 1912 he reported the Balkan War while accompanying the Serbian army for the *Daily Telegraph*. The following year he reported the Mexican Revolution. During World War I* he served with the Royal Field Artillery in France.

REFERENCE: Dennis Griffiths, ed. *The Encyclopedia of the British Press*. 1992.

MacKay, Charles (1814–1889)

Born in Scotland, he reported the American Civil War* for the *Times* beginning in February 1862,

after the departure of W. H. Russell* and Bancroft Davis. MacKay exaggerated opposition to the Lincoln administration in the North and like his counterparts was denied special access to most policy makers due to the sympathetic treatment accorded the Confederacy by the British press. MacKay was already a minor poet and experienced newsman when he arrived in America. Although he witnessed little on the battlefield he reported the fall of New Orleans, political developments in the North, the New York draft riots, the Wilderness campaign, the Confederate raid on Washington, the fall of Savannah, the fall of Charleston, and Lincoln's reelection and assassination.

REFERENCE: Ian F. W. Beckett. *The War Correspondents: The American Civil War*. 1993.

Mackenzie, Frederick A. (1869–1931)

Born in Quebec, he arrived in London in the 1890s, where he joined the staff of the recently established *Daily Mail* in 1896. In 1900 he reported the Boer War* as correspondent for the *Daily Mail*. After covering the Russo-Japanese War* in 1905, he wrote *From Tokyo to Tiflis: Uncensored Letters of the War*.

Mackenzie became the *Times* Berlin correspondent, a post he would hold until war broke out in 1914. He was one of the first reporters allowed to report from Russia after the Revolution. In 1921 he resigned from the *Mail* and became special correspondent for the *Chicago Daily News* in Russia and northern Europe for the next five years. Upon his return to England at the end of the decade he wrote several nonfiction books.

REFERENCES: Robert W. Desmond. *Windows on the World*. 1980; Dennis Griffiths, ed. *The Encyclopedia of the British Press*. 1992.

MacMillan, Thomas C. (1850–1935)

Born in Scotland, he came to America with his family at the age of seven. MacMillan left the

University of Chicago without graduating to enter journalism with the *Chicago Inter-Ocean* in 1873. He was one of five correspondents covering General George C. Crook's 1876 Black Hills expedition against the Sioux. This was MacMillan's second trip to the West, having covered the Jenny-Newton expedition to the Black Hills the previous summer.

MacMillan participated in the Battle of the Rosebud along with his fellow newspaper colleagues. He suffered from a hacking cough throughout his tenure with Crook's troops, necessitating his departure from the column. Following the 1876 campaign he remained in Chicago with the *Inter-Ocean* until 1895. He left the paper to serve as clerk for the federal district court and served in the Illinois House of Representatives from 1885 to 1889. The civic-minded MacMillan would go on to serve his community in a variety of capacities, as chairman of the Senate Committee on the World's Fair and author of the first woman's suffrage act in Illinois, while remaining active in the Chicago Council of Congregational Churches through 1910.

REFERENCE: Oliver Knight. *Following the Indian Wars.* 1960.

Mafeking, Siege of

Following the outbreak of the Boer War* in October 1899, Boer forces besieged the cities of Mafeking and Kimberley in the British Cape Colony. Mafeking was finally relieved by British forces on May 17, almost one month after the relief of Kimberley. The first reports of the relief of Mafeking were provided by Reuters* correspondent William Hay Mackay on May 18, 1900, seven months after the siege began. The news was greeted with such excitement in London that the word "mafficking," a derivation from "Mafeking" meaning "to celebrate hilariously," was added to the English language. Mackay would be one of the only two Reuters correspondents to perish in the Boer War.

Also reporting from Mafeking during the siege was Colonel Robert Stephenson Smyth Baden-Powell, who commanded British troops within the city and acted as a part-time correspondent for Reuters. Charles E. Hands* of the *Daily Mail* was wounded in the relief campaign for Mafeking, and two of the paper's stringers,* Lady Sarah Wilson and the enigmatic Mr. Hellawell, were able to smuggle out dispatches on a regular basis.

REFERENCES: Robert W. Desmond. *The Information Process.* 1978; Byron Farwell. *The Great Anglo-Boer War.* 1976.

Malaparte, Curzio

See SUCKERT, KURT.

Manning, Paul (d. 1995)

Manning worked along with Edward R. Murrow* for CBS Radio and the Mutual Broadcasting System during World War II. He was one of the eight reporters that made up the Writing 69th* in 1943. Following the war he became a speechwriter for Nelson Rockefeller. Manning wrote several books including *Hirohito: The War Years* (1986) and *Martin Boormann: Nazi in Exile* (1981).

REFERENCE: Jim Hamilton. *The Writing 69th.* 2005.

Mariano, Ann Bryan

See ANN BRYAN.

Marko, Dalia (d. 2015)

Marko was covering the conflict in South Sudan in 2015 for local radio station RAJA FM, when her convoy was ambushed by unidentified gunmen on January 25, 2015. Her two-car convoy was on its way back from Sepo to Raja when the ambush occurred. According to witnesses the five journalists were shot and slashed with machetes and then set on fire. The reporters were with the county commissioner on their way to visit families of victims killed in another ambush several days earlier. The other reporters killed with Marko were Musa Mohamed and Randa George. While there was no firmly established motive for the attacks, a spokesman for the South Sudanese Army claimed the perpetrators were most likely Ugandan rebels.

REFERENCE: "Dalia Marko," https://cpj.org/killed/2015/dalia-marko.php.

Maron, Karen (b. 1975)

An Argentinian war journalist, producer, and writer, Maron has focused much of her reportage on war zones and global politics. She covered wars in Iraq, Syria, Lebanon, Colombia, Libya, and the Palestinian-Israeli conflict from the Second Intifada to the Gaza Strip offensive in 2009. Since 2001 she has covered the Arab Spring rebellions in Libya and Egypt and the conflict in Syria. Between 2004 and 2009 she reported as a freelance correspondent based in Iraq for a host of news outlets including BBC World (UK), NBC-Telemundo (US), Azteca Television (Mexico), Folha de São Paulo (Brazil), and many others. For much of 2004 and 2005 she was the only Latin American journalist in Iraq, working for up to 12 different communications media at a time. While her purview has been conflict zones, Maron has also reported widely on postconflict developments in the Middle East, Colombia, Peru, and Cyprus. She has devoted much of her time to the education of journalists operating in high-risk areas. Maron developed the Curricular Program of the International Course for correspondents in conflict zones and Peace Operations.

REFERENCE: http://en.wikipedia.org/wiki/Karen_Maron.

Martin, Boutros (d. 2015)

Martin was a cameraman for South Sudan Television and was among the five journalists killed in the January 25, 2015 ambush in South Sudan's Western Bahr al Ghazal state. Eleven members of the two-car convoy were shot, macheted, and set on fire. They had been following Raja county commissioner James Marodama Benjamin as he paid condolences to the families of the victims of another recent ambush.

REFERENCE: https://cpj.org/killed/2015/boutros-martin.php.

Mathews, L.H. (1830–1896)

Born in Ireland, he came to the United States in 1848 and moved to Florida where he began his reporting career with the *Pensacola Observer*. He reported on the Civil War* for a number of papers under the pen name, "Nemo." Despite his mild-mannered mien, Mathews was no shrinking violet when it came to challenging authorities as he pursued news stories in the opening weeks of the conflict. He apparently got on the wrong side of General Braxton Bragg by sending a report to the *Observer* detailing Bragg's plans to attack the lightly defended Union Fort Pickens. The article came out shortly before the attack and Mathews was arrested for treason and sent to Montgomery, Alabama for trial in April 1861. Charged with publishing news that could have alerted the enemy to his plans to capture Fort Pickens, Mathews became the first of many civilians to be arrested by the Confederate Army.

REFERENCE: Henry H. Schulte, "L.H. Mathews: General Bragg's Nemesis," *Knights of the Quill*, 2010, 181–199.

Matthews, Herbert Lionel (1900–1977)

Matthews was born in New York City and educated at Columbia University. Following service in the U.S. Army in World War I,* he joined the staff of the *New York Times* in 1922, beginning an affiliation that would endure for forty-five years. Matthews covered the Ethiopian War* of

1935–1936 from both sides and was awarded the Italian War Cross (Croce de Guerra) in 1936 for "valor in the East African campaign." That same year he reported the Spanish Civil War.* From 1939 to 1942 he headed the Rome bureau and was briefly imprisoned in Siena.

Following the outbreak of World War II* he reported from India in 1942 and the next year covered the last weeks of the Sicilian campaign. In 1944 he witnessed the landing at Salerno and the advance toward Naples. He was one of seven correspondents permitted to fly as observers on the first bombing raid over Rome and was among the first correspondents to enter the city following its capitulation. In August he accompanied the Allied push to Germany.

Among his reporting coups was the earliest interview with Castro, at the head of an army of less than twenty men in 1957, which made the revolutionary into an international figure. Matthews has won many awards for his reporting, including the George Polk Memorial Award and the Chevalier of the French Legion of Honor. His books include *Eyewitness in Abyssinia, Two Wars and More to Come, The Cuban Story, Cuba,* and *A World in Revolution* (1971).

REFERENCES: John Hohenberg. *Foreign Correspondence: The Great Reporters and Their Times.* 1964; Herbert L. Matthews. *A World in Revolution.* 1971.

Maud, William Theobald (1865–1903)

Described as the best war illustrator for the *Daily Graphic,* W. T. Maud was trained at the Royal Academy. Prior to his joining the *Graphic* some of his sketches appeared in *Punch.* His first assignment as artist-correspondent* was to cover the Armenian massacres in 1895. The next year he reported the rebel insurrection in Cuba, and in 1897 he accompanied the Greek army in Thessaly during the Greco-Turkish War* and witnessed the Greek retreat from Velestino.

Later in 1897 he was in the Sudan covering the advance on Abu Hamed. After a brief stay on the North West Frontier of India, Maud returned to Africa in May 1898, to participate in the advance on Omdurman. Although Kitchener attempted to bar the press from accompanying his expedition, the intercession of the prime minister resulted in sixteen members of the press corps joining the column. Maud covered the Battle of Omdurman and the reconquest of the Sudan through 1898. Unwilling to wait for mail boats or conventional modes of transportation, he hired local tribesmen to carry his sketches in waterproof packets in their turbans while they swam down the Nile to the nearest steamer. The only criticism of his work suggests that his expertise was in showing scenes of camp life or anecdotal episodes rather than in sketches encompassing larger-than-life studies such as epic battles like Omdurman.

In September 1899 Maud was sent to cover the Boer War.* He shared a house with correspondent G. W. Steevens* during the siege of Ladysmith,* although Steevens would die from enteric fever before it ended. Maud sent a steady stream of sketches back to London, but many did not make it through until the siege was lifted. Following Steevens' death, Maud joined the army as an aide to General Ian Hamilton, after he assured his paper it would not interfere with his sketching. As British troops entered Ladysmith, Maud too was stricken with enteric fever from the tainted water supply. Although he survived and returned to the battlefront, his health was shattered and he died in Aden in 1903 while on his journey back to England.

REFERENCES: Pat Hodgson. *The War Illustrators.* 1977; Robert Wilkinson-Latham. *From Our Special Correspondent.* 1979.

Mauldin, Bill (1921–2003)

Born in New Mexico, Mauldin demonstrated an early interest in the cartooning profession. After abruptly leaving the Chicago Academy of Fine Arts he returned to the Southwest but found no outlet for his pictorial satire. In 1940, with no prospects in sight, he enlisted in the army, where his talents for cartoon commentaries depicting army life led to a part-time position with the Forty-fifth Division news. By 1943 his position had become fulltime as his division was shipped off to the Mediterranean to take part in the invasion of Sicily and Italy.

During the Italian campaign Mauldin's talents came to the attention of the European edition of the army's daily *Stars and Stripes,** and in 1944 he joined its staff. Following a laudatory story on Mauldin by war correspondent Ernie Pyle,* his cartoons were picked up by the United Feature Syndicate, and by the summer of 1944 his work was carried in dozens of American newspapers.

Mauldin's most recognizable work as the cartoon chronicler of the war featured the exploits of two prototypical GIs, Willie and Joe. The two characters were imbued with a darker side, untypical for cartoons, but a side that reflected the pathos and capriciousness of the war front as they journeyed together through war-torn Europe. Mauldin spoke through these two characters, taking regular trips to the front searching for new material. In one of his most ironic commentaries he recounts being slightly nicked by shrapnel and his subsequent attempts to reject a Purple Heart foisted on him by medics, which military regulations required that he accept.

His work was not without its critics. While General Mark Clark on one occasion requested his presence in his jeep so he could get an original drawing, General George Patton wrote a letter to the editors of *Stars and Stripes** threatening to ban the paper from the entire Third Army if it did not stop what he characterized as Mauldin's attempts to undermine military discipline. But, Mauldin was too popular among the rank and file, and Allied commander General Dwight Eisenhower knew that banning his work would

harm morale. In 1945 Mauldin won the Pulitzer Prize* for Editorial Cartooning for his "Up Front with Mauldin" series in *Stars and Stripes.*

Numerous collections of his cartoons have been published, including *Star Spangled Banter* (1941), *Sicily Sketch Book* (1943), *Mud, Mules and Mountains* (1943), and *This Damned Tree Leaks* (1945). His annotated collection *Up Front* was a best-seller in 1945. In 1959 he won a second Pulitzer Prize, and in 1962 he joined the staff of the St. *Louis Dispatch.* In 1971 his autobiography *The Brass Ring* was published.

REFERENCES: Frederick S. Voss. *Reporting the War.* 1994; Todd DePastono, *A Life Up Front,* WW Norton and Co, 2007.

Mavroleon, Carlos (1958–1998)

The son of a Greek shipping tycoon and heir to a 100 million pound fortune, Mavroleon was working as a freelance television producer and cameraman on assignment for the CBS program *60 Minutes* in August 1998 when he was found dead of a heroin overdose in his hotel room in Peshawar, Pakistan. He had just arrived there several days earlier to cover the American retaliative strikes against Osama bin Laden's training camps after the attacks on the U.S. embassies in eastern Africa earlier in the month. Although the coroner's report ruled it a self-administered heroin overdose, friends of Mavroleon thought that it was maybe something more sinister involving his investigative work. He had arrived in Peshawar on August 23, and on the 25th he was detained and jailed for the night, on the Pakistan border with Afghanistan. He was interrogated and then released on August 26th. According to a producer for *60 Minutes* Carlos told him "I'm in big trouble" and then "they're onto me in a big way." There was a general impression that he had been mistaken for a spy. But none of these claims have ever been substantiated. Mavroleon seemed to have had it all. He was heir to an Etonian fortune, had been a Wall Street broker and then a charismatic war correspondent. He had even led an Afghan unit of Mujahedin against the Soviets in the late war. Others were not so surprised by his demise since by most accounts he had been a regular user of a wide range of potent drugs for most of his adult life. It is worth noting that at his death he possessed accoutrements that would have made any other freelance reporter jealous (or cringe), including a satellite phone, small video camera, Sony shortwave radio, a translation of the Koran, books on Islamic history and four syringes. For almost a decade Mavroleon covered world conflicts in the aftermath of the Soviet-Afghan War that ended in 1989, including trips to Somalia, Sudan, Burma, Angola, Rwanda, and Afghanistan, and finally Pakistan.

REFERENCES: Jason Burke. "Carlos Mavroleon." Guardian.co.uk. August 20, 2000; http://cpj.org/killed/1998/carlos-mavroleon.php.; David Loyn. *Frontline*. 2005.

Maxwell, Charles

See DELLA CASA, NICK.

Maxwell, Sir William (d. 1928)

Maxwell was assigned by the *Standard* to replace John Cameron* in the Sudan when the latter perished with the Hicks relief expedition in 1885. As war correspondent, he covered Kitchener's army on its advance on Khartoum in 1898 and witnessed the defeat of the Mahdi's forces at the Battle of Omdurman.

He covered the Boer War* after traveling in the Middle East, as well as the first peace conference at the Hague. He was with British forces besieged at Ladysmith* and following the relief of the garrison accompanied Lord Roberts' forces in each of its actions, from the capture of Bloemfontein to the Battles of Lydenburg and Komati Port. In 1905 he resigned from the *Standard* and joined the *Daily Mail* as correspondent to cover the Russo-Japanese War.* He was with General Kuroki's army from the Yalu to Port Arthur and received the Order of the Rising Sun.

Prior to World War 1* he covered the Balkan War (1912) while accompanying Bulgarian forces. During World War I he reported for the *Daily Telegraph* and was attached to the Belgian army until its defeat by German forces. Maxwell went on to witness the Battles of the Marne and Aisne, following which he entered the army as a captain assigned to the general staff. He later rose to head of section in the Secret Service and was knighted in 1919. He wrote *From Yalu to Port Arthur* (1906).

REFERENCES: Robert W. Desmond. *Windows on the World*, 1980; Dennis Griffiths, ed. *The Encyclopedia of the British Press*. 1992.

McClanahan, John R. (d. 1865)

Colonel John McClanahan, a Mexican War* veteran, coedited with Benjamin F. Dill, the *Memphis Appeal*, the most important Memphis paper during the American Civil War.* These two men were models of the indomitable Southern spirit as they continually moved the paper one step ahead of federal troops, publishing at various times from Mississippi, Georgia, and Alabama. The peripatetic editors were able to keep the *Appeal* afloat by offering half-price subscriptions to soldiers in the field. Following Appomattox McClanahan returned to Memphis, where he died in a fall from a hotel window.

REFERENCES: J. Cutler Andrews. *The South Reports the Civil War.* 1970; Stewart Sifakis. *Who Was Who in the Civil War.* 1988.

McCoan, James Carlile (1829–1904)

Born in Dunlow in Tyrone County, Ireland, McCoan attended various London schools before graduating from London University in 1848. He left the practice of law to cover the Crimean War* as war correspondent for the *Daily News*. Following the war he traveled extensively in Georgia and Circassia before arriving in Constantinople, where he returned to the practice of

* Indicates a separate entry.

law until 1864. McCoan established the *Levant Herald,* the first English-language newspaper in Turkey. After selling the paper in 1870 he returned to England. He continued to travel widely, publishing several books on Egypt, *Egypt As It Is* (1877) and *Egypt Under Ismail: A Romance of History* (1889). He was accused of disloyalty over his support for Gladstone's land bill while representing Wicklow County in Parliament in the 1880s.

REFERENCE: *DNB,* 1901–1911.

McCormick, Frederick
(1870–1951)

McCormick was born in Brookfield, Missouri, and got his start in journalism with *Harper's Weekly* and the *London Graphic* covering the Boxer Rebellion* in 1900. He next worked as a special correspondent in the Far East for the *New York Sun* and Laffan's Bureau before representing Reuters* and the Associated Press during the Russo-Japanese War.* He spent almost two years as the only foreign correspondent covering the Russian side of the war in Manchuria. He accompanied General Danieloff on a mission to evacuate prisoners and later witnessed the first official Russian visit to Japan following the war. He covered the Bolshevik uprising and reported from Russia and China into the late 1920s.

REFERENCES: Robert W. Desmond. *The Information Process.* 1978; *Who Was Who.* 1951.

McCullagh, Francis (1874–1956)

Born in Dungannon, Ireland, McCullagh began his long career in journalism with a Glasgow paper before moving to a number of others over the next half century. In 1904 he covered the Russo-Japanese War* and the *New York Herald* published his account of the opening naval battle. He worked first for a Japanese newspaper and then moved to a Russian one. He was with the beaten Russian forces as they retreated from Mukden.

He was taken prisoner and sent to Japan. He was free in time to cover the peace negotiations in Portsmouth, New Hampshire. Following this he covered conflict in the Balkans alongside the Turkish Army and was captured once more, this time by the Bulgars. After his release he traveled throughout the Near East until war broke out between Italy and Turkey in 1912. He covered the conflict with Italian troops as they descended on Tripoli. He chronicled this war in his book *Italy's War for a Desert: Being Some Experiences of a War Correspondent with the Italians in Tripoli* (1912). During most of this time he was sending dispatches to the *New York Herald* or the *Daily News.* When World War I broke out he accompanied the Czar's Army and witnessed the Germans' first attack at Warsaw. He put down his pen to fight in the British Army first with the Twelfth Worcesters and then in 1915 the Royal Irish Fusiliers, whom he was with at the Dardanelles disaster. The British secret service made use of his knowledge about Europe and Russia and he worked as an intelligence officer in Serbia and then Siberia. He was captured by the Bolsheviks and held prisoner until 1920. McCullagh went on to cover the Spanish Civil War* as well.

REFERENCES: Quebec Daily Telegraph, April 24, 1923.

McCullagh, Joseph Burbridge
(1842–1896)

Born in Dublin, Ireland, McCullagh went to sea as a boy, arriving in New York in 1853, where he became an apprentice printer for the *New York Freeman's Journal.* Soon after, he left for St. Louis and positions on the *Christian Advocate* and the *St. Louis Democrat.*

At the outset of the American Civil War* he was commissioned in the Union Army. Shortly after, he left the army to serve as war correspondent for the *Cincinnati Gazette.* In one of his early dispatches he criticized the bad conduct and drunkenness of Grant's officers during the Tennessee campaign. However, his paper refused to print the critical article. Disappointed by the rejection, he joined the *Cincinnati Commercial* in 1862. He was given free rein with this newspaper, and his articles on the Civil War appeared regularly under his pen name "Mack."

With the growing popularity of his war reports he was promoted to Washington correspondent in 1863 and became the first newspaper reporter to interview a president of the United States when he was given a meeting with Andrew Johnson. He covered the siege of Vicksburg and Sherman's march though Georgia. Apparently McCullagh was too good at his job. His success in anticipating events led to his reassignment in the fall of 1863 when he too accurately predicted Union troop movements. He was sent to Washington, D.C., as capital correspondent.

Following the Civil War McCullagh experienced a checkered career, serving as editor, major shareholder, and managing editor in a succession of newspapers. While he never regained the popularity he enjoyed during the war years he is credited with being one of the founders of the new journalism. He served as managing editor of the *St. Louis Globe-Democrat* from the early 1870s until his death on December 31, 1896.

REFERENCES: Charles C. Clayton. *Little Mack: Joseph B. McCullagh of the St. Louis Globe-Democrat.* 1969; Stewart Sifakis. *Who Was Who in the Civil War.* 1988.

McCullin, Donald (b. 1935)

Born in England, he was a freelance photojournalist, with his pictures first appearing in the *Observer* in 1958, before becoming a war correspondent for the *Sunday Times* for eighteen years. For thirty years he recorded the horrors of the combat zone and in the process was wounded in Cambodia, gassed in Northern Ireland, and severely wounded in El Salvador. He has covered wars in Vietnam,* Cyprus, the Congo, and Biafra. Among his books are *Homecoming, Hearts of Darkness, The Destruction Business, Beirut: A City in Crisis, Is Anyone Taking Notice?,* and *Open Skies.*

REFERENCE: Don McCullin. *Unreasonable Behaviour.* 1992.

McCurry, Steve (b. 1950)

McCurry is the recipient of numerous awards for his photojournalism including the Robert Capa Gold Medal* for Best Photographic Reporting from Abroad. He began his career covering war zones when he disguised himself in indigenous garb in order to make his away across the Pakistan border into rebel-held territories in Afghanistan during the build-up to the Soviet invasion in 1989. Following his exploits on this journey, his rolls of film carefully sewn into his clothing, were published. These were among the first images to chronicle the conflict. He achieved international prominence with the iconic photograph, *Afghan Girl*, published in *National Geographic* magazine. He won the Capa Award for this feat. Since 1986 he has been a member of Magnum Photos.* He has covered a number of conflicts, including the Iran-Iraq War, civil wars in Afghanistan, Lebanon and Cambodia, the Islamic insurgency in the Philippines, and the Gulf War. McCurry was awarded the Royal Photographic Society's Centenary Medal in 2014 to honor his "sustained, significant contribution to the art photography."

REFERENCE: http://stevemccurry.com/biography.

McCutcheon, John Tinney (1870–1949)

Born near South Raub, Indiana, McCutcheon attended Purdue, Notre Dame, and Northwestern Universities. The well-known cartoonist and writer covered the Spanish-American* and Boer Wars* for the *Chicago Daily Tribune* and witnessed the 1898 Battle of Manila Bay in the Philippines, which he chronicled in his book *Stories of Filipino Warfare* (1900). In 1914 he accompanied the U.S. Navy in the assault on Veracruz. However, after a telegram informed him of developments in Europe he took the first train back to Chicago.

Indicates a separate entry.

Assigned to cover World War I,* he missed the *Lusitania* by three days. Before departing he was given over five thousand dollars in gold weighing over nineteen pounds, to be used for the assistance of associates and prominent Chicagoans stranded in London and Paris. As American reporters arrived at the Belgian front despite restrictions hampering free movement of the press, it became a common practice among the Germans to detain the interlopers as spies. McCutcheon was arrested as a spy along with Will Irwin* and Harry Hansen during the German push through Belgium in 1914. In the winter of 1914–1915 many correspondents returned to the United States during a period described by one source as the "Dark Age of war correspondence." His autobiography *Drawn from Memory* was published in 1950.

REFERENCE: Emmet Crozier. *American Reporters on the Western Front 1914–1918.* 1959.

McEvers, Kelly (?)

Born in Lincoln, Illinois, she received an MA in journalism from Northwestern University. She began her journalism career with the *Chicago Tribune* in 1991. Between 1999 and 2000 she covered Cambodia for the BBC, followed by reporting stints in Indonesia, Malaysia, and Singapore in the aftermath of 9/11. She worked as a freelance journalist covering stories around the world. In 2004 she began a two-year job covering the former Soviet Union for PRI's *The World.* She has also covered the Middle East as an independent journalist for NPR beginning in 2010, covering the Arab Spring, the Iraq War, and the Syrian civil war. She made the radio documentary about her war reporting exploits, called *Diary of a Bad Year* (2013). Her work has appeared in a number of media outlets including the *New York Times Magazine, Christian Science Monitor,* the *New Republic, and the San Francisco Chronicle.*

REFERENCE: http://www.npr.org/people/131876588/ kelly-mcevers.

McGurn, William Barrett (1914–2010)

McGurn covered the Central Pacific theater of operations for *Yank** magazine for 14 months during World War II.* Prior to the war he was on the staff of the *New York Herald Tribune.* Teamed with artist Bob Greenhalgh, McGurn was wounded by mortar fire during the Second Battle of Bougainville. He returned to action in time to cover the Battle of Peleliu. Following the war he returned to the *Herald Tribune* as chief of the Rome bureau, and then the Paris and Morocco bureaus. He continued to cover the battlefront, reporting conflict in Tunisia, the Algerian and Moroccan Wars, and the Hungarian revolution. In 1957 he was awarded the Overseas Press Club of America award for covering the many mid-century insurgencies. He was expelled from Egypt by Nasser. McGurn is the author of six books including *Yank, The Army Weekly* (2004).

REFERENCE: Art Weithas. *Close to Glory.* 1991.

McIntosh, Burr William (1862–1942)

McIntosh was born in Wellsville, Ohio, and attended Princeton and Lafayette College. He entered journalism with the *Philadelphia News* in 1884. He was a war photographer* for *Frank Leslie's Illustrated Weekly* during the Spanish-American War,* where he was stricken with yellow fever and forced to leave the conflict prior to its conclusion. Among his most noted photographs is the unusual shot of the deceased Sergeant Hamilton Fish, Jr. of the Rough Riders, killed in the Riders' first action at Las Guasimas. Fish became one of the most recognized heroes of the conflict, his family well known and his photographs published throughout the land. McIntosh lost sixty-five of the eighty-four pictures he had risked his life taking when they were ruined by quarantine officers who insisted on disinfecting the container they were in. His

Cuban adventures are recounted in *The Little I Saw of Cuba* (1898).

REFERENCES: Charles H. Brown. *The Correspondents' War.* 1967; Susan D. Moeller. *Shooting War.* 1989.

McKay, Alex (b. 1837)

Born in Rhode Island, McKay came to California in 1871. He was working in Yreka, California, as a surveyor in 1872 when he acted as special correspondent for the *San Francisco Evening Bulletin* and the *Yreka Union* during the 1872–1873 Modoc Indian War. He was among the reporters granted interviews by Captain Jack in his stronghold and was nearby when the members of the peace commission were murdered by the Modocs in April 1873.

During the Three Days Fight he was among the retinue of reporters pooling their reports. Generally one of the correspondents would remain in camp with access to headquarters information and troop movements. The others would accompany various forces in the field and could telegraph stories from the front to their colleagues' newspapers. As the only nonprofessional newsman to report the conflict, McKay has been credited for a workmanlike performance. He was one of only three to see the conflict to its conclusion. His career following the Modoc War is unknown.

REFERENCE: Oliver Knight. *Following the Indian Wars.* 1960.

McLaughlin, Kathleen (1898–1990)

Born in Greenleaf, Kansas, she found her fiurst job in journalism with the Atchison Globe before catching on with the *Chicago Tribune* in the 1920s. During World War II* she was hired by the *New York Times* bureau in London. She reported on the treatment of the wounded, the evacuation of Holland by the Germans, and the subsequent de-Nazification trials. She also covered

the post-war Nuremburg Trials. McLaughlin later covered the Cold War from Germany until 1951, reporting on the Berlin blockade and the occupation of Germany. She retired in 1968 after a number of years covering the United Nations for the *New York Times.*

REFERENCES: Lilya Wagner. *Women War Correspondents of World War II.* 1989; Ishbel Ross. *Ladies of the Press.* 1974 edition.

McMillan, Richard D. (c. 1924–2008)

Prior to the outbreak of World War II,* McMillan had spent sixteen years as a United Press correspondent in Europe. He was the first war correspondent to be licensed by the British Expeditionary Forces (BEF), and accompanied British forces in most of their campaigns in the European and African theaters of the war. Following the fall of France he was stationed in London before covering the Greek army in Albania. Over the next two years he reported the conflict in Egypt, Libya, the Middle East, and Tunisia. His exploits reporting the African theater are chronicled in *Mediterranean Assignment.*

While covering the Sicilian campaign in July 1943 he was among the seven correspondents permitted to fly as observers on the first bombing raid over Rome. During the Normandy invasion he landed with British troops in France. Later, while covering the assault on Cherbourg he was wounded in the back by shrapnel but continued to stay at his post. After a short respite in England for recovery he returned to France and was on hand for the liberation of Paris. McMillan remained with Allied troops as they advanced on the Rhine and Germany.

REFERENCE: Robert W. Desmond. *Tides of War.* 1984.

Meisalas, Susan (b. 1948)

Born in Baltimore, Maryland and educated at Harvard University, during the late 1970s she

---

* *Indicates a separate entry.*

chronicled the Sandinista revolution in Nicaragua and human rights issues in Latin America. Her photographs taken in conjunction with journalists Raymond Bonner and Alma Guillermoprieto have been widely published in Nicaraguan textbooks. In 1981 she reported from a village destroyed by El Salvadoran government forces. She was recognized in 1978 with the Robert Capa Gold Medal for "outstanding courage and reporting" by the Overseas Press Club for her work in Nicaragua.

REFERENCES: Profile at Magnum Photos, http://magnumphotos.com; official website, http://susanmeiselas.com.

Memorials to War Correspondents

One of the earliest memorials to journalists killed in action commemorates seven British correspondents killed during the 1883–1885 Sudan campaigns. A tablet in St. Paul's Cathedral remembers "the Gallant Men who in the discharge of their duty as Special Correspondents fell in the Campaigns in the Soudan 1883–1884–1885." Listed on the tablet are Edmund O'Donovan,* Frank Vizetelly,* Frank Power,* John Alexander Cameron,* St. Leger Algernon Herbert,* William Henry Gordon, and Frank J. L. Roberts.*

In 1896 a War Correspondents Arch was built in Meyersville, Maryland, by former American Civil War* correspondent George Alfred Townsend,* to honor the artists, writers, and photographers who covered the Civil War. World War II* correspondents who lost their lives while serving with the U.S. military are remembered by a memorial placed in the Pentagon by Secretary of the Defense James Forrestal in 1948. Twenty-four years later the War Correspondents Corridor in the Pentagon was dedicated to the Americans killed while reporting World War II, Korea, and Southeast Asia.

War correspondents killed during the Korean War* are memorialized by a plaque dedicated in 1976 and on permanent display at the Foreign Correspondents Press Club of Japan and by a memorial unveiled the following year in Munson, Korea, by the International Cultural Society of Korea. In 1981, on the thirty-seventh anniversary of D-Day, former World War II correspondents dedicated Normandy Park in Athens, Ohio, to war correspondents killed while covering the European theater of World War II.

In 1985 a memorial was dedicated honoring journalists killed by terrorists. The Committee to Protect Journalists, the National Press Club, and No Greater Love unveiled the plaque at the National Press Club in Washington, D.C. The next year a memorial tree and stone was dedicated in Arlington National Cemetery by the Society of Professional Journalists, the Overseas Press Club of America, Inc., the National Press Club, and No Greater Love to honor all journalists killed in the line of duty. On the stone are the words "This tree grows in memory of journalists, who died while covering wars and conflicts, for the American people. One who finds a truth lights a torch."

REFERENCES: Charles C. Arnot. *Don't Kill the Messenger.* 1994; Robert Wilkinson-Latham. *From Our Special Correspondent.* 1979.

Merton, Arthur (d. 1942)

Born in England, Merton embarked for Egypt in 1903 to enter the banking and shipping business. In 1912 he was employed by the Ministry of Agriculture when he became the Cairo correspondent for the *Times.* During World War I* he was employed in Allenby's Palestine intelligence service and in 1922 was the first journalist permitted access to the recently opened tomb of Tutankhamen. His reports of the discovery were widely read. He later went to work for the *Daily Telegraph* and by World War II* was one of the most recognized journalists in the Middle East. Despite his advanced age by the time war broke out, he still covered a number of campaigns before he was killed in a car crash near Cairo on May 28, 1942. One of his surviving traveling companions was Winston Churchill's son, Randolph, who was only injured.

REFERENCES: Robert W. Desmond. *Tides of War.* 1984; Dennis Griffiths, ed. *The Encyclopedia of the British Press.* 1992.

Mexican-American War

A new era in reporting national and world affairs was inaugurated with the birth of the modern war correspondent during the Mexican-American War of 1846–1848. There were numerous correspondents involved in the coverage of the war. Besides approximately ten fulltime reporters, most representing New Orleans papers, there were many freelance writers. Some reporters had made arrangements to send dispatches to their hometown papers prior to enlisting. Editors as well as their subordinates joined the army, with sixteen from Massachusetts alone. Representatives of the press were often referred to as "printers" during this era, and virtually no company was without one.

War reporters were in such abundance in part due to the fact that so many had enlisted to fight the Mexican army. At least twenty New Orleans printers were found in a single company of volunteers. Among them were three correspondents for the *New Orleans Delta,* including James Freaner,* J.G.H. Tobin,* and John H. Peoples.* None was more celebrated than George Wilkins Kendall,* cofounder of the *New Orleans Picayune* in 1837. Often referred to as the first modern war correspondent, Kendall was so anxious to witness warfare himself he temporarily left General Zachary Taylor's command to join the Texas Rangers under Captain Ben McCulloch. Kendall covered most of the battles of Generals Taylor and Scott, including Chapultepec, Monterrey, Cerro Gordo, and Churubusco.

Kendall's partner, Francis Lumsden,* attempted to raise his own New Orleans regiment, but ended his recruiting drive abruptly when a better-equipped mounted company from Georgia on its way to the Mexican border elected Lumsden as its leader. Also representing the *Picayune* was West Point graduate Christopher Mason Haile,* who joined Scott's staff during the siege of Veracruz.

One of Kendall's chief rivals was James L. Freaner of the *Delta,* whose dispatches appeared under his sobriquet "Mustang." Although most newspapers outside the Deep South did not send correspondents, others were present. In 1846 the *New York Herald* claimed five correspondents, and one Lucian J. Eastin reported for the *Jefferson Inquirer* under the initial "E." In addition there were numerous correspondents and printers who founded newspapers collectively referred to as the Anglo-Saxon Press* in Mexico's occupied cities.

The only woman reporter to cover the front lines was Jane McManus Storms* whose dispatches appeared under the pseudonyms "Cora Montgomery" or "Montgomery" in the *New York Sun.* She became the only member of the press to report from behind Mexican lines and was one of the few to criticize American military efforts as well as her fellow reporters.

Following the invention of the daguerreotype* process in 1839, the Mexican-American War became the first war to be covered by war photographers,* although the identity of those who took the photographs of the Mexican War remains a mystery.

REFERENCES: Fayette Copeland. *Kendall of the Picayune.* 1943; Robert W. Johannsen. *From the Halls of the Montezumas: The Mexican War in the American Imagination.* 1985; Tom Reilly. "Jane McManus Storms: Letters from the Mexican War, 1846–1848," *Southwestern Historical Quarterly.* July 1981.

Meyers, Georg N. (1915–2007)

Born in Kansas City, Missouri, he covered the Aleutian Islands campaign during World War II* for *Yank* Magazine. As its Aleutian correspondent-photographer Meyers was one of the few journalists to witness the Japanese invasions of Attu and Kiska. His biggest scoop was his

Indicates a separate entry.

coverage of "the first Banzai charge on American soil." After the war he continued his career in journalism with the *Seattle Times* until his retirement in 1984.

REFERENCES: Craig Smith. "Georg N. Meyers, ex-Times sports editor dies." Seattle Times. March 7, 2007; Art Weithas. *Close to Glory*. 1991.

Middleton, Drew (1913–1989)

Born in New York City and educated at Syracuse University, Middleton worked for several small papers before joining the Associated Press. Shortly after being assigned to London as a sportswriter he moved into war reporting. He was reportedly the youngest correspondent with the British Expeditionary Forces in France during World War II.* He garnered his first scoop in June 1941, when after a briefing with Anthony Eden he learned that Germany was about to invade Russia.

In 1942 he moved over to the *New York Times*. Based in London, he witnessed the tragic raids on Dieppe and St. Nazaire. After joining the *Daily Telegraph* later that year he reported from the front lines in North Africa and on Omaha Beach during D-Day. Later in the war he covered the second front in Germany and Belgium and after the war was stationed in Moscow. Following the war he reported the conflict of the Cold War for six years, including the 1949 Berlin airlift. He continued with the *New York Times* in various capacities in Europe until his appointment as military correspondent* in 1970. He retired in 1984 and died five years later. The staunch Anglophile was awarded an honorary Order of the British Empire (1947) and Commander of the British Empire (1985). Among his books were *The Struggle for Germany* (1949), *The British* (1957), *The Sky Suspended* (1960), and *Crossroads of War* (1983).

REFERENCES: Robert W. Desmond. *Tides of War.* 1984; Dennis Griffiths, ed. *The Encyclopedia of the British Press.* 1992.

Middleton, Henry J. (c. 1876–1904)

Middleton joined the AP in London while still in his teens. He was promoted to French bureau chief where he reported the Dreyfuss Affair. He was setting up a cable department for the San Francisco office when he left to report from first Japan, then Seoul, Korea. When the Russo-Japanese War* broke out in 1904 he left to cover it from Manchuria. However, before he could get into the thick of the action he became gravely ill from dysentery and died in June in Manchuria where he was buried with full Russian military honors.

REFERENCES: AP Wall of Honor, www.ap.org/wallof-honor/1900_1939.html.

Milewicz, Waldemar (1956–2004)

Milewicz was working as a reporter for Polish State Television (TVP) when he along with his production assistant Mounir Bouamrane were killed in a drive-by shooting in Latiifya, Iraq, some twenty miles south of Baghdad. He had been working for the TVP since 1984 and was considered an experienced war correspondent having previously covered conflicts in the Balkans, Chechnya, Cambodia, and Rwanda. Milewicz had been awarded the journalism prize by Johns Hopkins University in 1995 for his coverage of Chechnya and in 2001 was named Poland's reporter of the year. The incident provoked an uproar when a Polish tabloid published graphic photos of the killings. A number of journalists and news organizations signed an open letter of condemnation directed at the *Super Express* tabloid. The other passengers in the car escaped with their lives. The two journalists had only been in Iraq for several days at the time of their deaths.

REFERENCES: Kehrt C. Reyher. "Death of a War Correspondent." Poynter Online. May 11, 2004; BBC News. "Polish Crew Attacked in Iraq."

Military Correspondents

The *London Times* began employing specialists on military affairs beginning in the late nineteenth century. The most notable and influential correspondent to hold this position was Colonel Charles a Court Repington* beginning in 1904. His articles appeared under the heading "From Our Special Correspondent," as was the newspaper practice. Unlike war correspondents, who covered the battlefront, their military counterparts were more inclined to hold court on issues shaping defense policy at the highest level or discoursing on military strategy and related subjects. In a sense the introduction of the military correspondent created a new field of British journalism, one that would be popularized by future writers such as Basil Liddell Hart.

REFERENCES: Office of the *Times*. *The History of the "Times": The Twentieth Century Test, 1884–1912*. 1947; Oliver Woods and James Bishop. *The Story of THE TIMES*. 1983.

Millard, Thomas Franklin Fairfax (1868–1942)

Born in Missouri, Millard attended the University of Missouri before embarking on a newspaper career that would earn him recognition as the dean of China hand journalists. He began his journalism career as a drama critic for the *New York Herald* in the 1890s. His lifelong interest in China and Japan was stimulated when he covered the Boxer Rebellion* in 1900 for the *New York Herald*. He came to prominence as a war correspondent in the early twentieth century, earning a disfiguring facial scar in the process. Covering the Boer War* in South Africa he developed a lifelong case of Anglophobia, and his writings on the Afrikaner struggle so enraged the British commander, Lord Kitchener, that Millard was expelled from the country before the cessation of hostilities.

In 1904 he was in Manchuria reporting the Russo-Japanese War.* He remained in the Far East following the war active in both journalism and business, and in 1911 combined the two avocations when he cofounded the *China Express* with Dr. Wu Ting-fang, former Chinese envoy to the United States. This Shanghai daily became the first U.S.-owned newspaper in China, excluding missionary publications. Millard edited the paper for six years before establishing *Millard's Review of the Far East*, a weekly Shanghai publication. In 1922 the experienced correspondent was named advisor to Li Yuan-hung, president of the Chinese Republic. He left this post in 1925 to become Shanghai correspondent for the *New York Times*, an affiliation he would maintain for the next sixteen years.

REFERENCES: Robert W. Desmond. *Windows on the World*. 1980; Peter Rand. *China Hands*. 1995.

Miller, James (1968–2003)

Born in Haverford-west, Pembrokeshire, Miller had won a number of awards in the television business before moving into documentary film making and winning an Emmy and a Peabody award. Miller was a freelance cameraman who joined the Frontline News* group in 1995. He worked in a variety of capacities making films in dangerous hot spots including in Chechnya (*Dying for the President*), Afghanistan and in the Occupied Territories. He was killed in 2003 while filming in Gaza during the intifada. In 2008 the Isreali government agreed to pay his family $3.5 million USD to close the case as long as the request to extradite the soldiers involved was withdrawn. Miller was in Gaza documenting the impact of violence on Israeli and Palestinian children. His death was captured on tape, and showed him and a colleague approaching Israeli troops, carrying a white flag as they left a refugee camp. One of the soildiers fires a shot in their direction, and after Miller responds "We are British journalists" another shot is fired,

Indicates a separate entry.

mortally wounding Miller in the neck. He was just one of four foreign observers to be killed or injured by the Israeli Defense Forces at the peak of the 2003 intifada in April and May. The film he was working on, *Death in Gaza*, was released the year after his death.

REFERENCES: Sheera Frenkel. "Israel to pay 1.75£ to family of James Miller in deal over killers," *London Times* online, April 23, 2008; David Loyn. *Frontline*. 2005.

Miller, Keith (?)

Miller began his journalism career in Los Angeles. Over a career spanning thirty years he has covered conflict zones and other events in almost 80 countries. He has covered the "war on terrorism" from Egypt, Jordan, Israel, and Iraq. He covered the Israeli-Palestinian conflict, Afghanistan, and Pakistan as a NBC New foreign correspondent often based in London. Beginning a six-year stint as chief Asian correspondent in 1988 he covered the People Power revolution in the Philippines, the student uprising in South Korea, and the assassination of India's President Indira Gandhi. During the Iranian Revolution in 1979–1980 he covered the fall of the Shah, the takeover of the American Embassy, the Soviet Invasion of Afghanistan, the Iran-Iraq War, the civil war in Lebanon, the rise of the Red Brigades terrorist group in Italy, the U.S. bombing of Libya during the Reagan era, and the Bosnian civil war. Miller has extensively covered a number of African stories, including the American military incursion into Somalia, the Rwandan genocide, and the fall of apartheid in South Africa.

REFERENCE: http://www.nbcnews.com/id/3688864/ns/nbc_nightly_news_with_brian_williams-about_us/t/keith-miller/#.VRhVo_nF_Nw.

Miller, Lee (1907–1977)

Born Elizabeth Miller in Poughkeepsie, New York, she studied theater and art in Paris before becoming a model for *Vogue* in 1927. In 1929 Miller established her own photography studio while living with the artist and photographer Man Ray and in 1932 opened a studio in New York. With the outbreak of World War II* she joined the London staff of *Vogue* in 1940. She photographed the London blitz and British war efforts. Her pictures were published in *Grim Glory: Pictures of Britain Under Fire* (1940) and *Wrens in Camera* (1942). Although she was employed primarily as a fashion photographer, Miller convinced her magazine to run more war-related pieces. She was more identified for her fashion photography during the war, in which she demonstrated women coping with wartime conditions.

In June 1944 Miller represented *Vogue* during the Normandy invasion and also witnessed the siege of St. Malo, the liberation of Paris, fighting in Luxembourg and Alsace, and the Allied advance into Germany. While covering the front Miller wore a helmet of her own devising, with a movable front that would allow her to take pictures without taking it off. After photographing the historic linking of Russian and American forces at the Elbe she chronicled the liberation of the Dachau and Buchenwald concentration camps.

REFERENCE: Frederick S. Voss. *Reporting the War.* 1994.

Miller, Robert C. (1915–2004)

The United Press war correspondent landed with the first assault by U.S. Marines on Guadalcanal on August 7, 1942, and was the only member of the press to cover both the first and last battles of the Guadalcanal campaign. While he was traveling with the U.S. invasion fleet during the Normandy invasion in 1944, Miller's ship was sunk by a torpedo during the landings, and he spent two hours in the Channel before being rescued. He was taken back to England but shortly after returned to the beaches of Normandy and accompanied Allied troops in the liberation of Paris.

REFERENCE: Robert W. Desmond. *Tides of War.* 1984.

Miller, Webb (1892–1940)

Born in Dowagiac, Michigan, Miller joined the United Press in 1916 and on his first assignment covered the punitive expedition into Mexico led by General John J. Pershing. His service to the UP took him through the Mexico City, Chicago, Washington, and New York bureaus before he landed in Europe to cover World War I* on both the American and British fronts in 1918. He witnessed the carnage at the Battles of Chateau-Thierry, the Vesle, and the Argonne. After the armistice he covered the Spanish front in Morocco during the war against the people of the Riff Mountains. Serving as director of a large staff of correspondents, he preferred to cover events personally. He was present at the explosive events leading to World War II,* including the Spanish Civil War* and the Ethiopian War,* which he reported from the Italian front lines. During the Ethiopian War he was nominated for the Pulitzer Prize for a forty-four-minute scoop on the announcement of the beginning of the war there.

In 1939 he served as correspondent with the British army in France and with the Finnish army, and the next year became the first U.S. correspondent to be killed covering World War II, albeit in rather unheroic fashion. As the general manager for the United Press in Europe, he had departed France to report the Russo-Finnish War. Forced to lay over in London while awaiting the proper paperwork to allow his entry into Norway, he was killed in a freak railway mishap. Since there were no witnesses to record his death, a reconstruction suggested that during the wartime blackout he must have fallen onto the railroad tracks expecting a station platform as he stepped out in the pitch darkness while changing trains. When it was announced in 1943 that each Liberty Ship would bear the name of a war correspondent killed in action, the first to be recognized was Webb Miller. The *Webb Miller* was christened by his wife and the following year carried U.S. forces onto Normandy beaches during the D-Day invasion.

REFERENCES: Robert W. Desmond. *Tides of War.* 1984; Webb Miller. *I Found No Peace.* 1936.

Millet, Francis Davis (1846–1912)

Millet was born in Mattapoisett, Massachusetts, and educated at Harvard. He got his baptism in warfare as a drummer during the American Civil War.* Following graduation from Harvard in 1869, he studied lithography and painting in Europe. As artist-correspondent* for the *New York Herald,* Millet covered the Russo-Turkish War* in 1877–1878. He was awarded the Cross of St. Stanislaus and the Cross of St. Anne by the Russian Czar for his service during the war. In 1893 he was master of ceremonies at the World's Columbian Exposition.

In 1899 he returned to the battlefield as artist-correspondent for the *London Times, Harper's Weekly,* and the *New York Sun* during the Spanish-American War* and the Philippine insurrection. In 1912 he was killed on the fateful voyage of the *Titanic* when it sank on its way to America.

REFERENCE: Rupert Furneaux. *News of War.* 1964.

Moats, Alice-Leone (1908–1989)

Born in Mexico, by the age of 12 she was fluent in five languages. Educated in Europe, Mexico and the United States she published her first book, an etiquette book for girls, at the age of 25. She then turned to journalism, writing magazine articles, and in 1940 she was sent to Russia by *Collier's Weekly,* where she made the transition to correspondent. She reported the heroism of Moscow's residents as the city endured bombing raids. She left Russia in October 1941 and did not return to the war front until 1944, trekking over the Pyrenees Mountains from neutral Spain to occupied France with French resistance fighters. She chronicled these events in *No Passport for Paris* and returned to freelance writing. During her career

Indicates a separate entry.

as a war correspondent Moats traveled widely, reporting from Russia, Iran, Egypt and Africa. Moats authored nine books during her career in journalism.

REFERENCES: Lilya Wagner. *Women War Correspondents of World War II*. 1989; "Alice-Moats, 81, Journalist, Is Dead." *New York Times* Obit, May 16, 1989.

Mohr, Charles (1929–1989)

Mohr was a White House correspondent at the age of twenty-seven, chief of the New Delhi bureau, and then chief of Southeast Asia coverage, all for *Time* magazine. Initially based in Hong Kong, by 1963 he was *Time* magazine's regular correspondent in Vietnam* at the outset of the conflict. He was often teamed with freelancer Mert Perry.* Mohr was in the habit of always being armed, usually with a customized Beretta handgun and a standard issue M-16 rifle. In 1965 he became the first American war correspondent to be wounded in the conflict. In 1967 he covered the Six Day War in the Middle East. Mohr was back in Vietnam covering the Battle of Hue during the Tet offensive when he found himself pinned down with marines under heavy fire. Along with two other correspondents, Mohr risked his life to pull an injured soldier to safety. In 1980, five years after the end of the war, the three correspondents were awarded the Bronze Star for bravery, the only reporters so decorated during the Vietnam conflict.

REFERENCES: Michael Emery. *On the Front Lines*. 1995; William Prochnau. *Once upon a Distant War*. 1995.

Mohyeldin, Ayman (b. 1978)

Born in Cairo, Egypt and educated at American University, he began his journalism career as a desk assistant for NBC before getting his first major assignments in the wake of the 9/11 terrorist attacks. He has covered most major news events in the Arab world since then. He covered the Iraq War,* the Israeli withdrawal from the Gaza Strip, and the 2005 bombings at the Sharm al-Sheikh resort (July) and the Jordan Hotel (November). Mohyeldin covered the Israeli attack on Gaza in 2008–2009 and has covered conflicts during the Arab Spring and more recently the Ukraine, Iraq, and Syria war zones. In July 2014 Mohyeldin witnessed and reported the deaths of four Palestinian children killed during the Gaza conflict. He had just minutes before been kicking a soccer ball with the young boys when two missiles landed among them. NBC ended up pulling him from Gaza and allowing Richard Engel* to report the story from Tel Aviv. Engel replaced him in Gaza and NBC was ultimately bombarded with criticism by independent media sources for these actions, which have still not been explained.

REFERENCE: http://blogs.aljazeera.com/profile/ayman-mohyeldin.

Monks, Noel (1907–1960)

Born in Tasmania, Monks reported the Ethiopian War* in 1936 as a freelancer before returning to London and employment with the *Daily Express*. Shortly thereafter, he departed to cover the Spanish Civil War* for two and a half years for the *Express*. He was captured by insurgents and threatened with execution before being expelled on Franco's orders. He returned to report from the side of the Republic. After joining the staff of the *Daily Mail* to report World War II* he was sent to France as one of the first correspondents to cover the war. His book *Squadrons Up* recounted his excursions with the RAF in 1939 and was the first bestselling book about the war. Monks was present on virtually every Allied front during the European theater, witnessing such pivotal events as the D-Day invasion, Dunkirk, and the attack on Berlin. After 1945 he continued his reporting for the *Daily Mail,* covering the Korean War,* the Malaysian insurgency, and other flash points throughout the world.

REFERENCES: Robert W. Desmond. *Tides of War.* 1984; Noel Monks. *Eyewitness.* 1955.

Montagu, Irving (1842–1901)

A childhood friend of the artist-correspondent* Robert Landells,* Montagu was determined to emulate him. He was hired as an artist by the *Illustrated London News* when the Franco-Prussian War* began. He found that the quickest way to get to the front from Switzerland was to accompany the ambulance corps. He covered the siege of Paris and in 1874 the Carlist War in Spain.

During the 1877–1878 Russo-Turkish War* Montagu and *Times* correspondent R. Coningsby disguised themselves as merchants to avoid the Russian prohibition on news correspondents. They survived a Turkish shell attack on their carriage and an attack on their camp by wolves on the outskirts of Plevna. Coningsby reported that they fended off the animals with one of Montagu's sketches. When the wolves returned, Montagu responded in kind, chasing them off by reading one of Coningsby's columns from the *Times.* Following the war Montagu wrote his recollections of his wartime exploits, *Wanderings of a War Artist* (1889), no doubt embellished with events both real and imaginary. He also published *Camp and Studio* (1890).

REFERENCE: Pat Hodgson. *The War Illustrators.* 1977.

Montague, Evelyn A. (1900–1948)

An Oxford graduate and medalist at the 1924 Paris Olympic Games, Montague was a third-generation journalist with the *Manchester Guardian.* He began his affiliation first as a business reporter in 1928 and then as sportswriter in 1931. With the outbreak of World War II* he turned to war reporting, covering the London blitz and the fall of France. When the war be-gan, the *Guardian* was undercapitalized, leading to the practice of using war reportage provided by other papers such as the *Times.* In one major exception Montague accompanied the British First Army in the Allied landing in North Africa. He followed the campaign until the fall of Tunis and then covered the British Eighth Army during the conquest of Sicily and the campaign in Italy.

Military commentators such as Captain B. H. Liddell Hart praised his battlefield accounts for their dependability, and the *Times* often requested reprints of his dispatches. In 1944 he returned to England when his wife fell ill. He arrived home the day after the funeral. Tuberculosis prevented him from returning to the front later that year and would kill him three years after the end of the war.

REFERENCE: David Ayerst. *The Manchester Guardian: Biography of a Newspaper.* 1971.

Moore, William Arthur (1880–1962)

Born in County Down, Ireland, and educated at Campbell College, Belfast, and Oxford, he was elected president of the University debating society and general club in 1904. In 1908 he joined the *Times* as special correspondent, covering the Young Turk rebellion. The following year he witnessed the hundred-day siege of Tabriz in Persia. He covered the Middle East for three years and then reported from India, Egypt, Russia, Spain, and Portugal before covering an insurrection in Albania in 1914. Also that year his book *The Orient Express* was published.

During World War I,* he was one of the first war correspondents to arrive in France. His coverage of the retreat from Mons in 1914 was his most famous scoop. Initially his dispatch was heavily censored, but before it was printed the head of the London bureau, F. E. Smith, replaced the excised passages, printing the original report. Later that year he was captured by a German cavalry patrol and then released.

Indicates a separate entry.

In 1915 he joined the Rifle Brigade and saw action in the Dardanelles. Two years later he traded a rifle for wings, when he transferred to the Royal Flying Corps, in which he rose to squadron leader. Following the war he resumed his affiliation with the *Times*, stationed in the Middle East. In 1924 he joined the *Calcutta Statesman* as an assistant editor and two years later was elected to the Legislative Assembly at Delhi.

His account of a round-the-world air voyage in 1941 was published as *This Our War*, and the following year he retired from journalism. Subsequently he became an advisor to Lord Mountbatten and established his own weekly journal in Delhi. He continued to publish articles in various periodicals.

REFERENCES: Dennis Griffiths, ed. *The Encyclopedia of the British Press*. 1992; Times Publishing Company. *History of the "Times,"* Vol. IV, Part 1. 1952.

Moore, William R. (1910–1950)

Born in Nowata, Oklahoma, Moore joined the AP in 1937. He served in the US Army in Korea in World War II.* After the war he went to Korea as a correspondent for the AP and was there until his death covering the Korean War* on July 31, 1950, just a month into the war. He had apparently put his notepad down to help a wounded Army lieutenant during a North Korean attack near Chinju when he was killed by a mortar round. He was initially reported missing until a corporal who had been captured in the same action reported that he had seen Moore earlier on the day he was killed.

REFERENCE: AP Wall of Honor, www.ap.org/wallofhonor/1950_1959.html.

Moorehead, Alan Mcrae (1910–1983)

Born in Melbourne, Australia, and educated at Melbourne University, Moorehead began working for the *Melbourne Herald* while still a stu-dent. After receiving his law degree he became a full-time journalist with the *Herald* for six years before joining the *Daily Express* in England and becoming its top war correspondent during World War II.* Before the outbreak of the war he covered the Spanish Civil War* as a stringer* and courier for the *Daily Express*.

He gained wide recognition for his war reporting from North Africa through the campaigns in Europe. With the outbreak of war he left Rome in 1939 to report from Athens and then Cairo. Beginning in 1940 he covered the campaign of the British Eighth Army in Africa. Moorehead next reported from Persia, where he investigated German espionage activities, and in 1942 accompanied the Allied invasion of Africa. The following year he reported the Casablanca Conference and the campaign in Italy. His books on the African campaign, *The March to Tunis* and *Eclipse*, were popular successes. In 1944 he was an early arrival on the beaches of Normandy after the D-Day invasion and at one point was arrested by a British unit on suspicion of being a spy. He was quickly identified and released. He accompanied Allied forces through the liberation of Paris and was with the British Second Army on its advance into northern Belgium and Holland.

After resigning from the *Daily Express* immediately following the war he embarked on an unsuccessful fiction-writing career and returned to England four years later to work as a press officer at the Ministry of Defence. In 1952 he began a successful nonfiction-writing career. Among his works were *The Traitors* (1952), *Gallipoli* (1956), *The Russian Revolution* (1958), *The White Nile* (1960), and *The Blue Nile* (1962). In 1966 his writing career was cut short when he suffered a debilitating stroke, which kept him from writing or speaking coherently for the remainder of his life. He died on September 29, 1983.

REFERENCES: Richard Collier. *Fighting Words*. 1989; Robert W. Desmond. *Tides of War*. 1984; Alan Moorehead. *A Late Education: Episodes in a Life*. 1976.

Moreno de Mora, Miguel Gil (1967–2000)

Born in Barcelona, Spain, he gave up corporate law for journalism. Working as a photographer and cameraman for the Associated Press Television News (APTN) he covered conflicts in Bosnia, Chechnya, Kosovo, Congo, and Sierra Leone, where he was killed along with veteran Reuters* reporter Kurt Schork* in an ambush by rebels belonging to the Revolutionary United Front. Moreno de Mora and Schork were in two different cars accompanying soldiers of the Sierra Leone Army (SLA) when they were fired on and killed along with four of the soldiers. Moreno de Mora won the 1998 Rory Peck* photographic prize and the 1999 Television Technician of the Year Award from the Royal Television Society.

REFERENCES: AP Wall of Honor, www.ap.org/wallof-honor/2000_2008.html; Associated Press Committee to Protect Journalists, May 24, 2000.

Morgan, Wallace (1873–1948)

Born in New York City, Morgan worked part-time for the *New York Sun* to support his studies at art school. He covered the 1902 Mt. Pelee volcano distaster on the island of Martinique. In 1914 he was hired by *Collier's*, but left the job in March 1918 when he was hired as an official artist for the American Expeditionary Forces in France. Morgan often accompanied the 2nd Division Marine brigade and thus saw action at Chateau-Thierry and Belleau Wood. He then followed the troops ino the St. Mihiel salient and then the Argonne Forest. It was at this time that he tried to capture the action while it was "still fresh in his mind." Following the Armistance, Morgan was with the AEF occupation forces, as they made their way into Luxembourg and Germany. In 1919 he returned to civilian life and a long career as an illustrator for the works of such authors as H.G. Wells, John Erskine,

Damon Runyon,* Richard Harding Davis,* and P.G. Wodehouse. By most accounts Morgan was viewed as "one of the best artists in black-and-white" of his era.

REFERENCE: Afred Emile Cornebise. *Art from the Trenches*. 1991.

Morin, Relman "Pat" (1907–1973)

Following graduation from Pomona College he worked for the *Shanghai Evening Post*. After returning to the United States he was called back to China when Japan invaded in 1931. By August 1941 he was the AP Tokyo bureau chief and on assignment in Indochina when he witnessed the invasion of Japanese forces. He was subsequently captured and incarcerated in Saigon before being returned to Tokyo. Following his repatriation he covered the Sicilian campaign, the landing at Salerno, Italy, and the advance on Naples. A two-time winner of the Pulitzer Prize, Pat Morin received his 1951 Pulitzer for his on-the-spot coverage during the Korean War* for the Associated Press. Six years later he received his other Pulitzer for his domestic reporting of the desegregation of Arkansas schools.

REFERENCES: John Hohenberg. *Foreign Correspondence: The Great Reporters and Their Times*. 1964; John Hohenberg. *The Pulitzer Prizes*. 1974; M. L. Stein. *Under Fire: The Story of American War Correspondents*. 1968; The Free-Lance Star, July 27, 1973.

Morris, Christopher (b. 1958)

Morris was one of the founding members of the VII Photo agency in 2001. Born in California, he has documented at least eighteen conflicts including the U.S. invasion of Panama, the invasion of Iraq, the Persian Gulf War, the drug war in Colombia, Afghanistan, Chechnya, Somalia, and Yugoslavia. Among his many awards are the Robert Capa Medal and the Oliver Rebbot Award from the Overseas Press Club. He is

* *Indicates a separate entry.*

now embedded with the 3rd Brigade of the U.S. Army's 3rd Infantry Division as a contract photographer for *Time* magazine.

REFERENCES: www.viiphoto.com/photographer.html.; www.time.com.

Morris, David J. (b. 1971)

Prior to becoming a journalist in 2004, Morris served as an officer in the U.S. Marines in the 1990s. Between 2004 and 2007 he covered the Iraq War* for *Salon*, the *Virginia Quarterly Review*, and *NPR*. He was embedded* with the American forces in Fallujah, Ramadi, and Baghdad and reported on the carnage and violence taking place. When Morris left Iraq in 2007 he was suffering from posttraumatic stress syndrome (PTSD)* and went through therapy. His subsequent experiences dealing with PTSD and the Department of Veterans Affairs led him to write a wide-ranging book on the subject entitled *The Evil Hours: A Biography of Post-Traumatic Stress Disorder*, published in 2015.

REFERENCES: David J. Morris. *The Evil Hours: A Biography of Post-Traumatic Stress Disorder*. 2015; Carter Malkasian, "War Correspondent Sheds Light on PTSD," Houston Chronicle, Feb. 15, 2015, G5.

Morris, Jr., Joe Alex (c. 1928–1979)

Following graduation from Harvard, Morris worked as a reporter for several metropolitan newspapers before joining the *New York Herald-Tribune* in 1957 as its Cairo correspondent. In 1961 he covered the Bay of Pigs invasion and in 1963 he joined *Newsweek* and was posted back to the Middle East. During a twenty-year career he covered war zones in Israel, Syria, Lebanon, Iran, and Cyprus. In 1965 he became the *Los Angeles Times* correspondent in Beirut. Morris was killed in early February 1979 by either an errant bullet or sniper as he covered a clash between Iranian air force cadets and army troops in east-

ern Tehran. He was the first reporter killed during the 15 months of street fighting. When fellow *Los Angeles Times* correspondent William Tuohy* heard the news, he hired a Learjet and proceeded to Tehran Airport. Even though the airport was closed to traffic and occupied by Iranian Revolutionary Guards, after some negotiation Tuohy received the body and was able to bring Morris back to his family.

REFERENCES: "US Reporter Killed in Iran Clash," Milwaukee Journal, Feb. 10, 1979; "Slain Reporter Lived Amid Middle East Violence," Chicago Tribune, Feb. 11, 1979.

Morrison, Chester (1899–1966)

The Philadelphia native was educated at Rutgers and served in the navy in World War I.* Following the war he worked for the Associated Press, the *Boston Transcript*, and the *Boston Herald* before joining the staff of the *Chicago Sun*. During World War II* he served as war correspondent in the North African campaign for both the *Sun* and CBS. Beginning in October 1942 he was attached to the British Eighth Army under the command of Field Marshal Montgomery. In 1944 he was among the seventeen correspondents covering naval and ground operations resulting in the capture of the island of Elba off the Tuscany shore.

REFERENCE: Robert W. Desmond. *Tides of War*. 1984.

Morrison, George Ernest (1862–1920)

Born in Geelong, Victoria, Australia, and educated at Melbourne and Edinburgh Universities, he was certified as a surgeon and doctor. In 1882 he walked 2,043 miles alone across Australia in 123 days. That same year he sailed to the New Hebrides to recruit farm laborers for Australia. His reports of this expedition created quite a stir. After mounting a poorly planned expedition to New Guinea, he was attacked by natives, suffering two spear wounds.

He arrived in Edinburgh to practice medicine in 1884, still carrying in his thigh part of a spear, which was then promptly removed by his tutor. Three years later he served for a short time as court physician in Morocco before traveling from Shanghai to Burma. His 1895 book, *An Australian in China,* is an account of this 3,000-mile adventure. Following this exploit he was hired as Peking correspondent for the *Times.* He was in Peking during the Boxer Rebellion* and siege from June to July 1900. His reports were the first eyewitness accounts of this conflict.

He next covered the Russo-Japanese War,* which according to the historian Trevor-Roper he openly promoted, leading some to call the war at its outset "Morrison's War." He accompanied victorious Japanese troops into Port Arthur and covered the signing of the armistice at the Portsmouth Peace Conference. Returning to China he continued his peripatetic existence, traveling to every province of China except for Tibet. His attachment to the country led him to resign from the *Times* in 1912 to become political advisor to the newly elected first president, Sun Yat-sen.

REFERENCES: Office of the *Times, The History of the "Times": The Twentieth Century Test, 1884–1912.* 1947; Cyril Pearl. *Morrison of Peking.* 1967.

Morrison, Ian F. M. (1913–1950)

The son of war correspondent Dr. George Ernest Morrison* was educated at Trinity College, Cambridge. From 1935 to 1937 Morrison was an English Professor at Hokkaido University, Japan, and then private secretary to the British ambassador in Tokyo. In 1941, following employment with the Far Eastern Bureau of Information, Singapore, he turned to war journalism with the *Times.* Morrison covered the British retreat in Malaya, was wounded during the New Guinea campaign in 1942, and covered the Burma campaign in 1945. During the war in the Far East he was stricken with dengue fever, tropical ulcers, amoebic dysentery, and malaria, and survived

two plane crashes. His accounts of the war were published in *This War Against Japan* (1943) and *Malayan Postscript* (1943). On August 12, 1950, shortly after the outbreak of the Korean War* he was killed when his vehicle struck a land mine.

REFERENCES: Richard Collier. *Fighting Words.* 1989; Dennis Griffiths, ed. *The Encyclopedia of the British Press,* 1992.

Morriss, Mack (1919–1976)

Born in Baltimore, Maryland, Morriss became one of the top writers for *Yank** magazine during World War II.* He served as staff writer from 1942 to 1945, covering campaigns on Guadalcanal and New Georgia in the Solomon Islands and on the Siegfried Line and in the Huertgen Forest in the European theater. In May 1945 he was one of the first correspondents to enter the defeated city of Berlin. During much of the war he was teamed with artist Howard Brodie.* However he lost his SHAEF (Supreme Headquarters Allied European Forces) credentials by defying the Allied ban on entering the fallen capital. He received the Legion of Merit for his stellar career with *Yank.* Following the war Morriss worked for *Life* and as a freelance writer. He wrote the war novel *The Proving Ground* in 1951. After a newspaper career in Elizabethton, Tennessee, he became its mayor in 1966.

REFERENCE: Art Weithas. *Close to Glory.* 1991.

Morse, Ralph (1917–2014)

Morse took some of the best known photographs of World War II.* He was a staff photographer for *Life* magazine when he took such iconic images of the Marines on Guadalcanal, the takeoff of the Doolittle Raid on Tokyo, Patton's drive across France, and the liberation of Paris,. He was the only civilian photographer to cover the surrender of the German armies to General Eisenhower, who was famously photographed flashing the "V" for victory hand gesture. In the 1950s and 60s he covered the space program and the lives of the Mercury Seven astronauts so zealously they referred to him as the "Eighth Astronaut." Morse spent 1942–1972 with *Life* and finished his career with *Time* magazine from 1972–1988.

REFERENCE: David J. Marcou. "Witnessing History With a Camera: Ralph Morse Gets 'er Done." *Photography*, July 19, 2009, http://quazen.com/arts/photography.

Morton, Joseph (1911–1945)

Raised in St. Joseph, Missouri, he began his journalism career with the AP in 1937. During the early 1940s he gained exclusive interviews with Yugoslavian Josip Broz Tito and King Michael of Romania. In late 1944 he was with several American intelligence officers who were on their way from Italy to Slovakia where their goal was to foment a rebellion against the Nazis. As Nazi forces approached, the Americans sought refuge in the mountains and several hours before Christmas 1944 they were captured. They were tortured and ultimately executed at the Malthausen concentration camp in Austria. Morton is unique as the only foreign correspondent executed by the Nazis during the war.

REFERENCE: AP Wall of Honor, www.ap.org/wallofhonor/1040_1949.html.

Morton, Paul (d. 1992)

He had covered the Italian theater of World War II for the *Toronto Daily Star* for about a year, but mostly just interviewing soldiers and Italians caught between the Allied forces and the German Army. He was in Rome when it fell to the Allies on June 4, 1944, but his correspondence lost significance once the Normandy Invasion usurped its headlines two days later. By most accounts Morton feared the war ending without having seen actual combat himself. He saw a way to rectify this when the British Special

Operations Executive (SOE) asked him to parachute behind enemy lines to cover Italian partisans in north Italy, which was then an underdocumented theater of the war. He might have been fluent in Italian, but the risks were high. The last journalist to accept such an assignment was the AP's Joe Morton,* on a mission for the American Office of Strategic Services (OSS). In this case the reporter, Joe Morton, was captured in Slovenia and executed in a German concentration camp.

The night before he was to leave on assignment he was enjoying a farewell drink in the Rome officers' mess with several British commando instructors. It wasn't long before their well-lubricated conversation began focusing on his ability to defend himself with his .45 sidearm. Egged on by his drinking pals, he fired several rounds at bottles on a shelf behind the bar and was kicked out of the mess. The jump went off on schedule several hours later. Morton and his escort officer successfully landed but were met by a competing band of partisans—communist partisans—rather than the pro-Monarchist ones they were expecting. Soon Germans were hot on their heels. After making good their escape they found their way to the Monarchist partisans they had been looking for. Over the next two months Morton survived a number of close calls before making his escape into France with several others.

By the time he made it back to Rome he received a rather cool reception at British and Canadian headquarters. He wrote nine stories for his newspaper, but first they had to get through the censors. It wasn't long before he was being accused of "inappropriate conduct" for his marksmanship in the mess hall months earlier. Canadian Army authorities then revoked his accreditation. Days later he was fired with no reason given. Only one of his articles was published by the *Star*. His other pieces apparently painted too positive an image of the Communist partisans and as they say in journalism parlance, were "spiked." British agents manufactured a story that Morton did not even parachute behind enemy lines, labeling him a fraud, an accusation that would ruin his journalism career. By the 1960s Morton had sunk into alcoholism and was working as a logger in Ontario. In 1964 he received a letter from former Italian partisans requesting him to write a memoir of his time with them. He evidently sobered up enough to do this and followed up by demanding to have his wartime exploits recognized by the British Ministry of War, which it did by confirming his mission. Next, he asked the *Star* for an apology in order to restore his reputation as a journalist. According to Morton's biographer, the *Star* never apologized and "today claims to have no records or correspondence regarding" this brave man. Don North chronicled his investigation into the case of Paul Morton in his book *Inappropriate Conduct: Mystery of a Disgraced War Reporter* (2013).

REFERENCES: Don North. *Inappropriate Conduct: Mystery of a Disgraced War Reporter*. 2013; Don North, "Inappropriate Conduct: Mystery of a 'Disgraced' Reporter," Consortium News, Sept. 28, 2010.

Mosler, Henry (1841–1920)

Born in New York City, the son of a lithographer, Mosler moved to Cincinnati on the 1850s and taught himself the art of wood engraving and painting. He joined *Harper's Weekly* as special artist in 1861, covering the western theater of the American Civil War* in Kentucky and Tennessee from 1861 to 1863, including the second day of the Battle of Shiloh. In 1863 he continued his studies in painting in Europe, settling in Paris, where he remained until 1894, when he returned to New York to open his own studio.

REFERENCE: W. Fletcher Thompson, Jr. *The Image of War*. 1959.

Mosley, Leonard Oswald (1913–1992)

Born in Manchester, England, after a short journalism career at home he moved to Hollywood to write motion picture screenplays. In 1939, as a reporter for the *Daily Sketch*, he made the acquaintance of Hitler in Bayreuth. During World War II* he reported from the Middle East, Asia, Italy, Germany, and France. In 1941 he was accredited to the British Middle East Command in Egypt but left in October 1942 prior to the Battle of El Alamein. The following year he covered the Italian front and in 1944 represented the *Daily Telegraph* when he jumped with paratroopers near Cherbourg during the D-Day landings. In the latter stages of the war he was with the British Second Army as it pushed into Holland and Belgium. Following the war he returned to the *Daily Press* as a foreign correspondent, film critic, and feature story writer.

REFERENCES: Richard Collier. *Fighting Words*. 1989; Robert W. Desmond. *Tides of War*. 1984.

Moth, Margaret (c. 1950–2010)

Margaret Moth served as a war photographer in a number of conflicts in the 1980s and 1990s. Often risking life and limb she narrowly survived being shot in the face while covering the Bosnian War from Sarajevo. Much of her work was for CNN. Noted correspondent Christiane Amanpour* reportedly was inspired to enter the trade by Moth's career. Moth died from cancer at age 59. During an interview for an upcoming CNN documentary shortly before she died, she laughingly noted that she thought she "would have gone out with a little more flair."

REFERENCE: Chris Baldwin. "Pioneer Down: Renowned former Houston photojournalist/war correspondent dies." http://culturemap.com/newsdetail/03–21–10, 3/23/2010.

* *Indicates a separate entry.*

Mowrer, Edgar Ansel (1892–1977)

The younger brother of war correspondent Paul Scott Mowrer* was born in Bloomington, Illinois, and educated at the Sorbonne and the University of Michigan. Following graduation in 1913 he returned to Paris to embark on a literary career. At the outset of World War I* he was on the staff of the *Chicago Daily News* Paris bureau. In 1915 he was assigned to Rome, where he met Benito Mussolini and observed the Italian Fascists take over the country. During the conflict he acted as war correspondent, reporting battles in Belgium at Louvain and at the Marne in France, except for a brief interlude when he was expelled and deported to England. He later toured occupied Belgium with Herbert Hoover's relief commission and was reassigned to Berlin in 1923.

Mowrer was stationed in Germany in 1933 when the Reichstag mysteriously burned on February 27, leading to Adolph Hitler's rise to dictator. Mowrer, an outspoken critic of the Nazis, suggested in a dispatch to the *Daily News* that the Nazis set the fire themselves as a ploy to solidify their grip on Nazi Germany. In 1933 Mowrer received the Pulitzer Prize for his German correspondence collected in *Germany Puts the Clock Back*. Between 1933 and the outbreak of World War II* he served as president of the Foreign Press Association, reported from Paris, covered the beginning of the Spanish Civil War,* and visited the Soviet Union. He continued his career in journalism as editor, columnist, and feature writer until retirement in 1969.

REFERENCES: Robert W. Desmond. *Windows on the World*. 1980; Robert W. Desmond. *Crisis and Conflict*. 1982; Robert W. Desmond. *Tides of War*. 1984; Michael Emery. *On the Front Lines*. 1995.

Mowrer, Paul Scott (1887–1971)

The older brother of Edgar Ansel Mowrer* was born in Bloomington, Illinois, and attended the University of Michigan. He left school early to join the *Chicago Daily News* as its Paris correspondent in 1907. He covered the conflict in the Balkans in 1911–1913 and then World War I* beginning in 1914. He was assigned to French General Headquarters until the end of the war in 1918. Although he was not present, he put together a comprehensive account of the British defeat at Mons. Because of British censorship he was able to get the story to Chicago days before it was known in England. Mowrer covered the arrival of American force in July 1917 and reported the Chateau-Thierry campaign.

Following the war he became a well-known diplomatic correspondent. He wrote several prescient books on European affairs, including *Balkanized Europe* (1921) and *Our Foreign Affairs* (1924). In 1928 he was recognized with a Pulitzer Prize for his work as a foreign correspondent. He married Hadley Richardson, the former wife of Ernest Hemingway,* in 1933 and wrote eleven books of poetry beginning in 1918. After leaving the *Chicago Daily News* in 1944 he joined the *New York Post* as its European editor until 1949.

REFERENCES: Emmet Crozier. *American Reporters on the Western Front 1914–1918*. 1959; Michael Emery. *On the Front Lines*. 1995.

Mtawe'e, Zaher (d. 2014)

During the Syrian civil war* Mtawe'e covered frontline action, selling his reports and photos to various local news outlets. Originally trained as an electrician, when war broke out he quit his job and began documenting the bloodletting with his camera. He joined an opposition media group, the Zebdine Coordination Committee, becoming one of three reporters covering the government advance to regain control of the small town of Zebdine and other towns on the outskirts of Damascus. This committee was established early in the war, and was part of a greater consortium of news outlets, the Local Coordination Committees. Members didn't just report on the war, but also organized protests and delivered humanitarian aid. He was shot in the head and killed by a sniper as he covered a battle from the fourth floor of a building some 700 meters away from the action.

REFERENCE: https://cpj.org/killed/2014/zaher-mtawee.php.

Munday, William (1910–1943)

Born in Sydney, where he started his career in journalism, he moved to London in the 1930s. In 1940 he returned to his homeland and the *Sydney Morning Herald*. With the outbreak of World War II* he covered Australian troops in the Middle East. His columns also appeared in the *News Chronicle*. In late 1941 he was transferred to Burma, where he filed his most significant reports, including "On the Road to Mandalay," and "Why We Were Beaten in Burma." He was among the last reporters to pull out of Burma.

After his escape along an almost impassable 1,200-mile road in a small car, he was next assigned to the Mediterranean theater, where he covered the British amphibious landing at Salerno. Never far from the front lines, he was killed during the advance on Naples in October 1943.

REFERENCE: Dennis Griffiths, ed. *The Encyclopedia of the British Press*. 1992.

Munro, Ross (1913–1990)

Munro was born in Ottawa, Canada, and educated at the University of Toronto. After serving in the Canadian militia in 1940 he became the third generation of his family to enter journalism, working for the Canadian press. During World War II* he covered the Spitzbergen operation in 1941 and the ill-fated raid on Dieppe the following year. His coverage of the destruction of Canadian forces in this operation appeared in the *Daily Telegraph*. He returned to Canada after this debacle and went on the lecture tour describing the failed attack.

He returned to the battlefront, covering the landing at Sicily, and accompanied the first troops on to the shores of Normandy during D-Day. Following the war he reported the Nuremberg

trials before returning to Canada, where he signed on with the Southam News Services. He went on to cover the Korean War* in 1950 and continued his career in journalism with various Canadian papers. He was awarded the Order of the British Empire in 1946 and was made officer of the Order of Canada in 1975.

REFERENCES: Richard Collier. *Fighting Words: The War Correspondents of World War H*. 1989; Dennis Griffiths, ed. *The Encyclopedia of the British Press*. 1992.

Murphy, Caryle (?)

Murphy survived one of the most harrowing feats of war reporting during the Gulf War.* On assignment for the *Washington Post*, she hid in Kuwait for almost a month after the Iraqi invasion while continuing to send out reports by telephone. She ultimately escaped and was awarded the Pulitzer Prize.*

REFERENCE: Michael Emery. *On the Front Lines*. 1995.

Murrow, Edward (Egbert) Roscoe (1908–1965)

Born Egbert R. Murrow near Greensboro, North Carolina, he became Edward while attending Washington State College from 1926 to 1930. Murrow began his career with CBS in 1935 and rapidly rose to prominence as one of the best-known radio and television personalities of his era.

In 1938 he was assigned to cover Adolph Hitler's arrival in Vienna following the annexation of Austria. Murrow is most identified with his coverage of the bombing of London in 1940. He often risked his life reporting from rooftops as bombs, antiaircraft guns and sirens blared in the background, giving listeners the ultimate sensory experience. Later Murrow accompanied American bombers on twenty-five missions over Germany.

Following the war he returned to the States as CBS vice president. In the 1950s he made the transition to television with his program *See It Now.* His most famous broadcast was in 1954 when he exposed Joseph McCarthy's bogus crusade against Communism. He left television in the 1960s disenchanted with commercial broadcasting. Forever identified with his omnipresent cigarette, he died of lung cancer on April 27, 1965.

REFERENCES: Joseph E. Persico. *Edward R. Murrow: An American Original.* 1988; R. Franklin Smith. *Edward R. Murrow: The War Years.* 1978.

Musgrove, Helen "Patches"
(1918–1988)

Born in Nebraska, Musgrove joined the Coast Guard as a registered nurse during World War II* and was the first woman to be sworn into the Women's Auxiliary of the Coast Guard. She was stationed in Alaska, where she conducted radio broadcasts for soldiers in the Pacific theater of the war as "GI Jill."

Following the sudden death of her husband she established a dressmaking business in Hong Kong. Musgrove became a war correspondent in a rather serendipitous fashion. On a stopover in Saigon in 1964 she witnessed a firefight in the distance and was intrigued with the brightly hued skies. For two years these images remained with her until 1966, when she successfully sought accreditation as a correspondent with the Joint United States Public Affairs Office (JUSPAO). She witnessed bloodshed for the first time at Chu Lai several days later.

Musgrove was based in Saigon, where she contributed to seventy different newspapers, but most often for the *Jacksonville Journal.* Each month she spent twenty days in the field, traveling whenever possible with the military, eschewing the company of journalists. She earned the nickname "Patches" for her collection of patches from various units and in 1969 legally changed her name from Helen to Patches. By late 1967 she was the only woman correspondent who spoke out in favor of American involvement in the conflict.

Patches Musgrove covered the 1968 Tet offensive from Saigon, where she was cut off from communication with her newspaper editors for two weeks. In August 1969 she was the lone correspondent to participate on a "Shadow operation," when she flew in an AC 119 gunship on a combat mission. The following year she was made an "Honorary Shadow" for her "Outstanding service to Shadow operations in the Republics of Vietnam and Cambodia." In 1971, the fifty-three-year-old Musgrove collapsed in the field. Diagnosed with heart disease, she returned to the States for successful surgery. Following the war she remained an implacable supporter of the war in Vietnam.

REFERENCE: Virginia Elwood-Akers. *Women War Correspondents in the Vietnam War, 1961–1975.* 1988; Orlando-Sentinel, June 12, 1988.

Muybridge, Eadweard
(1830–1904)

Born in Kingston-on-Thames, England, he emigrated to the United States in 1852. He was a San Francisco photographer and bookseller and friend of Leland Stanford. He began taking landscape photographs in the Yosemite region in the mid-1860s and conducted several government photographic surveys along the California coast.

After a jury acquitted him of killing his wife's lover he worked for the railroad magnate Stanford, photographing American railroads and then Indian ruins in Central America. He documented the small-scale Modoc Indian War of 1872–1873 in northern California and southern Oregon. According to his biographer, Muybridge covered the war only from May 2 to May 14, 1873 and he "appears to have been the first photographer the U.S. Army hired directly to document a war." During the short conflict Muybridge produced a number of stereoscopic photos that *Harper's Weekly* published as magazine engravings andwhich have been subsequently used in most books on the subject of the Modoc War. His coverage of the war has been compared to the coverage of the Civil War, capturing sedentary images of battlefields and camp life but no images of actual warfare. He achieved his greatest fame with his studies in time-lapse photography and animal locomotion. In 1893 he devised a photographic machine that projected pictures on the screen in a rapid, sequential order, a precursor of motion pictures.

REFERENCES: Jorge Lewinski. *The Camera at War.* 1978; Keith A. Murray. *The Modocs and Their War.* 1959; Rebecca Solnit. *River of Shadows.* 2003.

My, Huynh Thanh (1937–1965)

My joined the AP in 1963, where he worked as as freelancer for CBS covering a battle in the Mekong Delta when he was offered a job by Horst Faas.* He quickly established himself as one of the bravest and best AP photographers. His career was cut short in 1965 when he was wounded and, while waiting for helicopter evacuation, was killed by enemy rifle fire. His brother "Nick" Ut* would follow him to AP and would win a Pulitzer Prize in 1973.

REFERENCE: AP Wall of Honor, www.ap.org/wallofhonor/1960_1969.html.

Mydans, Carl (1907–2004)

Born in Boston and educated at the Boston University School of Journalism, this peripatetic photographer joined the staff of *Life* magazine in 1936. In 1939 he covered Great Britain's wartime preparations and the following year was on hand to chronicle the ill-fated attempts of the Finnish army to stop the invasion by the Russian army. Later that year he was sent to Italy to report on the public posturings of Mussolini despite almost constant harassment by the Fascist Blackshirts. After witnessing the fall of France in 1940, Mydans headed for the Far Eastern theater of the war, where he reported the Japanese invasion of China.

Mydans was in the Philippines when the Japanese in quick succession attacked Pearl Harbor and then Manila the following day. Unable to escape the onslaught of the imperial army Mydans and his wife Shelley,* a writer for *Life* magazine, along with many other American citizens became prisoners of war. They would ultimately spend twenty-one months as prisoners in the Santo Tomas camp just outside of Manila. They were released in a prisoner exchange in late 1943. Mydans returned to the battlefront in 1944, covering both the European and Pacific campaigns. Among his most celebrated photographs were the triumphant return of MacArthur to the Philippines, wading onto the beach at Luzon in 1944; the unconditional surrender of the Japanese on board the battleship *Missouri*; and the execution of a French collaborator. After the war he became a Tokyo bureau chief for *Time-Life International*. Mydan's resume as war photographer would later include the Chinese Civil War, the defeat of the French in Vietnam, and the Korean War.*

REFERENCES: Carl Mydans. *More Than Meets the Eye.* 1959; Frederick S. Voss. *Reporting the War.* 1994; NY Times, Aug. 18, 2004.

Mydans, Shelley (1915–2002)

Born Shelly Smith in Palo Alto, California, daughter of a Stanford University English professor, she was first employed as a journalist by the *Literary Digest*, which folded in the mid-1930s. In 1936, she was hired by the new *Life* magazine, where she met the photographer Carl Mydans,* whom she married in June 1938. The Mydanses were sent to Europe, as the first *Life* correspondents to cover the outbreak of war in 1939 as a photo-reporter team. While Carl was sent to Finland and other battlefronts, Shelley was faced with assignments unrelated to combat reportage such as background stories.

As Europe became embroiled in conflict the Mydanses were called back to the States. In 1940 they were sent to cover the war between Japan and China. They were in the Philippines when Pearl Harbor was attacked and were eventually interned by the Japanese after the fall of Manila. In December 1943 they were freed and returned home. Returning to the Pacific theater of the war, Shelley became the first woman assigned to CINCPac (Commander in Chief of the Pacific), headquarters of MacArthur, and was probably the first woman correspondent to enter Manila. Following the war she worked as *a Time* broadcaster and correspondent in Tokyo. Her novel *The Open City* (1945) is based on her internment experience in Manila. She wrote several other historical novels and coauthored with her husband Carl *The Violent Peace* (1968).

REFERENCES: Lilya Wagner. *Women War Correspondents of World War H*. 1989; NY Times, March 9, 2002.

Nabaa Media Foundation

In May 2014 a number of Syrian opposition news services consolidated into one unified news outlet. Among the regional news sources were the Daraa Media Union and the Consolidated Media Assembly. The foundation covers the opposition forces, issuing breaking news and daily updates about the conflict in southern Syria. It also covers human rights, social issues, and military news, releasing its reports on Facebook and YouTube.

REFERENCE: "Atallah Bajbouj, Nabaa Media Foundation," http://cpj.org/killed/2014/atallah-bajbouj.php.

Nabbous, Mohammed "Mo" (1983–2011)

Born in Benghazi, Libya, Nabbous graduated university with a degree in mathematics. He earned a reputation in international journalism as a blogger and information technologist and for establishing Libya Alhurra TV on February 17, 2011. His news channel used nine cameras enabling it to stream 24 hours a day. As its communications became more sophisticated Nabbous was able to take the cameras with him to record the destruction and casualties caused by incessant shelling by government forces. His station's reports were broadcast on the Internet and later rebroadcast by international media outlets including Al Jazeera English. Nabbous was covering a reported cease-fire by the Gaddafi

government when he was shot in the head by a sniper. He was in the back of a truck on a mobile phone recording the continuing violence when he was shot.

REFERENCE: Matt Wells, "Moahmmed Nabous, Face of Citizen Journalism in Libya, is Killed," London Guardian, Mar.19, 2011.

Nachtwey, James (b. 1948)

The American war photographer James Nachtwey has covered conflicts in Northern Ireland, the Middle East, and Central America. Affiliated with the *Albuquerque Journal* until 1980, he later joined the Black Star photo agency.

REFERENCE: Frances Fralin, ed. *The Indelible Image.* 1985.

Nagai, Kenji (1957–2007)

This Japanese photojournalist covered numerous wars and conflict zones. He worked for Tokyo's AFP News and from 1997 to 2007 reported from Afghanistan, Cambodia, the Palestinian territories, and Iraq. However, he did not become internationally prominent until his death in 2007. He was in Burma covering anti-government protests when soldiers fired into the demonstraters, killing Nagai and injuring another journalist. While the Burmese government claimed it was a random shot that killed him, video footage later obtained by a Japanese television station company showed a Burmese soldier firing the fatal shot at point blank range, while Nagai was clearly on the ground. What's more, a photo taken by Andrees Latif documented the soldiers standing over the supine Nagai as he grasped his camera in one hand. This photo of the fatal shooting earned Latif a 2008 Pulitzer Prize* for Breaking News Photography. Subsequently the Burma Media Association created an award to commemorate Nagai's death. The Kenji Nagai Award recognizes individuals who have reported the truth about the Burmese dictatorship.

REFERENCES: Bridget Johnson. "Kenji Nagai-Japanese Journalist Killed in Myanmar." http://worldnews.about.com; Committee to Protect Journalists. "Japanese Photographer Killed as Burmese Trroops Crack Down on Protestors". September 27, 2007.

Nasmyth, Charles (1825–1861)

Nasmyth was born in Edinburgh, Scotland, and was a commissioned officer with the Bombay Artillery in the East India Company. At home on sick leave at the outset of the Crimean War,* he was hired as a stringer* by the *Times*. His first assignment was to cover the Turkish forces on the Danube River. He went beyond the call of duty while stationed at Omar Pasha's camp, when he led Turkish sorties against the Russians besieging Silistri. Although he neglected to file his dispatches, his newspaper commended him for the credit his exploits brought to the *Times*. He went on to cover the Battle of Alma and the siege of Sebastopol. Following the war he continued his army service in Ireland and Australia. He died in France on June 2, 1861.

REFERENCE: Dennis Griffiths, ed. *The Encyclopedia of the British Press*. 1992.

Nasser, Maya (1979–2012)

This Syrian journalist covered the Syrian civil war* for the English-language broadcasting service, Press TV. Having previously reported from Lebanon, Jordan, Egypt, and the Bahrain, she was no stranger to the battlefield and earned acclaim for her coverage of events at Aleppo. She was killed on September 26, 2012 while covering an attack at the Syrian army headquarters in Umayyad Square. By most accounts Nasser was shot through the neck by a rebel sniper, becoming the 46th journalist killed in the conflict.

REFERENCE: http://rt.com/news/press-correspondent-killed-syria-007/.

Nast, Thomas (1840–1902)

Born in Landau, Germany, Nast was brought at the age of six to New York City, where he would become the preeminent American cartoonist and first American caricaturist. He was virtually self-taught and was providing sketches to *Leslie's Illustrated Weekly* while still in his early teens. He covered Garibaldi's campaigns in Europe as artist-correspondent* for the *New York Illustrated News*, the *Illustrated London News*, and the Parisian *Monde Illustre* in 1860. He returned to America in 1861 and the next year began his twenty-five-year affiliation with *Harper's* as sketch artist covering the American Civil War.* Like fellow artist Winslow Homer,* Nast contributed little to the contemporary pictorial coverage of the war, directing his efforts instead toward more symbolic images such as "The Press on the Field," and supporting the weekly's various patriotic campaigns. Lincoln testified to Nast's effectiveness as a political cartoonist, noting in 1864, "Thomas Nast has been our best recruiting sergeant."

In 1863 Nast witnessed several skirmishes in the aftermath of the Battle of Gettysburg and then the New York draft riots. Following the war Nast established his reputation as a political cartoonist. Among his most enduring creations as a wood engraver were the Democratic donkey, Republican elephant, and the Indian symbol of Tammany Hall. Nast is also credited for creating the image of Santa.

REFERENCES: Philip Van Doren Stem. *They Were There.* 1959; W. Fletcher Thompson, Jr. *The Image of War.* 1959.

Neely, Bill (b. 1959)

Born in Belfast, Ireland and educated at the Queen's University of Belfast, he began his journalism career with BBC Northern Ireland in 1981 during the peak of the Republican hunger strikes. He covered "the Troubles" in Northern Ireland until 1987. Two years later he left for Sky News, helping launch the English television channel in 1989. Later that year he joined ITN's ITV News and covered the fall of the Berlin Wall, the collapse of the Soviet Union, both Gulf wars, the genocide in Darfur, the siege of Beslan, and many other international stories. For his coverage of the terrorist attack at Beslan, Neely was nominated for an Emmy, one of the four Emmys he has received over his stellar career. He has covered political elections and natural disasters around the world. He also covered the killing of Osama bin Laden and Arab Spring revolutions in Libya, Egypt, and Syria, and more recently the Syrian civil war and the war in Gaza. In 2013 he was voted one of the 100 most influential journalists in the world covering violence. That same year he joined NBC News.

REFERENCES: http://tvnewsroom.org/biography-images/bill-neely-3341/; "How Covering the Troubles Helped Bill Neely Win a Bafta," Belfast Telegraph, Apr. 29, 2009.

Neil, Jr., Edward Joseph (1900–1938)

Neil was originally a sportswriter for the AP and received a Pulitzer Prize honorable mention when he was given his first assignment abroad. During the 1930s he covered the coronation of King George VI, the Italian conquest of Ethiopia, and the Arab uprising in Palestine. He was covering the Spanish Civil War* from the Teruel front on January 2, 1938 when he was mortally wounded while covering one of the war's biggest battles.

REFERENCE: AP Wall of Honor, www.ap.org/wallof-honor/1900_1939.html.

Neilly, Emerson (?)

He was one of a number of correspondents holed up in besieged Mafeking* during the Boer War.* Neilly represented the *Pall Mall Gazette* throughout the siege. He chronicled the siege in *Besieged with Baden-Powell* (1900).

REFERENCE: Robert Wilkinson-Latham. *From Our Special Correspondent.* 1979.

Neuffer, Elizabeth (1956–2003)

A journalist known for her reportage of war crimes, human rights abuses and postconflict societies, Neuffer began her career covering Capitol Hill and the Clinton Administration for the *Boston Globe.* Prior to this she covered the resignation of Gorbachev, the dissolution of the Soviet Union and the 1991 Gulf War,* covering it from Saudi Arabia and Kuwait. By most accounts war reporting held little allure for Neuffer. Despite her reluctance to cover war zones, the early 1990s found her back on hazardous duty. In 1994 she was among the few reporters present in Sarajevo in February when a bomb killed 68 civilians in a marketplace, ultimately bringing NATO into the conflict. She covered the Bosnian war and postconflict resolution there, while under threats by Bosnian Serbs for her articles on war crimes. She was also the first American correspondent to report Dutch UN forces' culpability in allowing the massacre of thousands of Bosnian Muslims after the fall of the purported UN safe haven in Srebrenica. She went on to cover civil unrest in Albania and violence in Kosovo. In 1996 she covered the return of thousands of Hutu refugees from Zaire back to Rwanda following the genocide. In 1998 she was recognized with the Courage in Journalism Award from the International Women's Media Foundation. In 2002 she spent time covering the war in Afghanistan and despite her reservations about covering conflict zones

* Indicates a separate entry.

2003 found Neuffer covering the war in Iraq. She was killed on May 9, 2003 in a car crash two weeks before she was supposed to return home.

REFERENCE: "Veteran Globe Reporter Elizabeth Neuffer Killed in Car Accident in Iraq," Boston Globe, May 9, 2003.

Neville, Robert (1905–1970)

Born on a ranch in Oklahoma, he earned a graduate degree in journalism from Columbia University in 1929. While studying for his degree, he worked as a reporter for the *New York Times* and several other New York papers. The *Herald Tribune* sent him to cover the Spanish Civil War* in 1936. His reports were also carried by the *New Republic*, a more liberal leaning weekly. He spent a year covering the conflict before returning to New York, where he took a position as foreign news editor with *Time*. During the months leading up to World War II* he traveled to Poland and witnessed the German invasion of Poland, the first day of the war on September 1, 1939. He returned to the States and worked for *Picture Magazine (PM)* until the Pearl Harbor attack in 1941, when he entered the military at the advanced age of 36. He moved up the ranks quickly to staff sergeant and was assigned to the publications division. Posted to North Africa, he co-founded the *Stars and Stripes** edition devoted to the Mediterranean and Middle East theaters of the war. His last war zone posting was in Rome after its liberation. He would eventually earn the rank of lieutenant colonel. After the war he worked for *Time* and as a freelance writer.

REFERENCE: "Robert Neville, Writer, Is Dead; a Former Time Correspondent," New York Times, Feb. 18, 1970.

Nevinson, Christopher Richard Wynne (1889–1946)

Born in Hampstead, England, Nevinson studied painting at several art schools before being advised to pursue another profession. Following service with an ambulance unit during World War I* and a subsequent bout with rheumatic fever he returned to painting. A 1916 exhibit of his war pictures opened to great acclaim. Influenced by the Cubists, his paintings portrayed the participants in war as robotic pieces in a war machine. His work, which deglamorized war, was so influential it led to the appointment of several artists as official war artists. Nevinson would be the first in 1917. During World War II* he continued to capture the senselessness of war. His subjects included the London blitz and the ill-fated raid at Dieppe in 1942, which he witnessed while accompanying the British commandos. The next year he suffered a stroke, which ended his career.

REFERENCE: DNB, 1941–1950.

Nevinson, Henry Wood (1856–1941)

Born in Leicester and educated at Oxford, he joined the *Daily Chronicle* as a correspondent in 1897 covering the Greco-Turkish War,* including the decisive Battle of Grinboro. In 1900 he reported the Boer War,* including the 118-day siege of Ladysmith.* In 1905 he was assigned to Russia to cover the abortive revolution.

After a brief stint with the *Manchester Guardian* in 1907 he moved over to the *Daily News,* but resigned to protest the paper's position against women's suffrage in 1909. Returning to the *Manchester Guardian,* he covered the Balkan War in 1912 from the Bulgarian side. After the outbreak of World War I,* Nevinson covered the war in France and then the Dardanelles, where he was wounded. He chronicled his exploits there in his *Dardanelles Campaign* (1918). He also covered the organized relief for the Macedonians (1903), and investigated slavery in Portuguese Angola, resulting in A *Modern Slavery* (1906). He wrote several other books and was a regular contributor to the *Nation.* He died on November 9, 1941.

REFERENCES: David Ayerst. *The Manchester Guardian: Biography of a Newspaper*. 1971; Robert W. Desmond. *Windows on the World*. 1978; *DNB*, 1941–1950; Rupert Furneaux. *News of War*. 1964; Angela V. John. *War, Journalism and the Shaping of the Twentieth Century: The Life and Times of Henry W. Nevinson*. 2006.

Newsreel Companies

The Spanish-American War* was the first war photographed by American motion picture producers. The Edison Company made some of the earliest films with its coverage of the funeral procession for victims of the *Maine* sinking. In recent years questions have arisen concerning the authenticity of early war footage, although much of the film stock has been proven genuine, including the embarkation of Teddy Roosevelt's Rough Riders for Santiago and U.S. troops landing at Baiquiri in Cuba. Obvious fakes include most action footage taken in Cuba and the Philippines. However, the Vitagraph Company followed Roosevelt to Cuba and photographed scenes of the Rough Rider assault on San Juan Hill.*

The Boer War* was one of the first military conflicts to be recorded on film. It was more thoroughly covered by British cameramen than any by others; the most prominent was W.K.L. Dickson of the British Mutoscope and Biograph Company, who traveled in a horse-drawn cart with a gigantic camera, summoning up images of the late Mathew Brady* during the American Civil War.* Dickson spent more than a year with the British army as motion picture correspondent. He filmed armored trains with troops, the siege of Ladysmith,* various sorties, and campsites. He was given remarkable freedom compared to photographic restrictions of subsequent wars. There is evidence to suggest that military officials confided secret plans of future military operations so that he could set up his equipment to record the action.

The Mexican Revolution, beginning in 1911, received some of the best newsreel coverage of any war prior to World War II.* All of the major newsreel companies, as well as many of the smaller ones, sent correspondents to the border. In one of the most controversial uses of newsreel motion pictures, Pancho Villa made arrangements to fight battles during the daylight hours and waited until cameras were in place before launching attacks. In the winter of 1913–1914 Villa had let it be known that he was offering motion picture rights to his war to any entrepreneurial producer with enough money to pay for exclusive coverage of his campaign. In 1914 Mutual Film Corporation secured the rights to cover the campaign. Under the contract Villa was to receive $25,000 and fifty percent of the motion picture royalties. In return he guaranteed to bar any other cameramen from recording the conflict. Apparently, Villa made good on his promise and even delayed his attack on the city of Ojinaga until Mutual had its cameras in place.

During World War I* military officials were reluctant to allow civilian cameramen to record near the battlefront, instead using military cameramen to man the cameras. Newsreel coverage of World War I, grainy, superficial, and inadequate, paled in comparison with that of World War II,* and much of it has been proven to be faked. Cameramen during the conflict found the efforts of frontline censors to be more taxing than the battlefield dangers. Wartime cameramen resorted to various techniques to secure footage, including climbing up trees and telephone poles to obtain panoramic shots of the battlefront or hiding in second-story rooms secretly photographing enemy troops passing below.

The Chinese-Japanese war of the 1930s provided some of the most graphic motion picture images of the period. Before American entry into the war, American newsreel cameramen were granted access to both sides of the conflict. The Japanese bombing of Shanghai was recorded by American cameramen Harrison Forman of the *March of Time* and Hearst representative Wong Hai-sheng, better known as "Newsreel" Wong. The most unforgettable image to emerge from

Indicates a separate entry.

the conflict was of a solitary baby crying in the rubble of a bombed-out Shanghai train station. The scene was captured by "Newsreel" Wong and the photo was reproduced throughout the world. The footage has been alleged to have been staged, but this has never been proven. More than one hundred million people are estimated to have seen either the newsreel or the print. One of the most publicized uses of newsreel footage during this period came in December 1937, when the United States gunboat *Panay* was bombed by Japanese planes on the Yangtze River. Fortunately, two cameramen were on board and took valuable footage of the incident. When the footage was returned to the States it was promoted at movie theaters like a Hollywood premiere.

American censors went to work as soon as Pearl Harbor was bombed. Military photographers took excellent shots of the bombing, but these were suppressed immediately by military censors. Most still pictures and motion pictures of the attack were not released for more than a year. During World War II civilian war photographers and cameramen were given the same rating as war correspondents once their accreditation was approved in Washington, D.C. They would then be assigned to a particular combat unit, where they were subject to the orders of the military or naval command to which they were attached, and were required to accompany it into battle unless otherwise ordered.

During World War II most of the combat that played on American theater screens was filmed by the U.S. Signal Corps and navy photographers as combat photography passed from civilian hands to the armed forces. While civilian cameramen were still present on the front lines, their footage was pooled with the service cameramen and heavily censored before it was released to the newsreel companies. Initially many movie theater chains were reluctant to show war footage in their newsreels, and some displayed signs which read "No War News Shown Here." However, according to *Look* magazine, from 1942 to 1946 four-fifths of all newsreel footage was war-related.

When the war ended in 1945, so did the newsreel as television came into existence. By the late 1940s the commercial television industry was well established and postwar television news coverage had improved significantly. By the next decade many newsreel theaters had closed across the country. Motion picture coverage would become virtually obsolete on the battlefield beginning in Vietnam,* when almost instantaneous coverage became available by satellite.

REFERENCE: Raymond Fielding. *The American Newsreel, 1911–1967.* 1972.

Nicholls, Horace H. (1867–1941)

Nicholls was a British photojournalist and war photographer.* After covering news stories and working in Chile and Johanessburg, South Africa he rose to prominence capturing images of the Boer War*. He was with the British retreat to Ladysmith. His most indelible images captured the British army slogging through heavy rain, and leaving in their wake a trail of equipment, as sick and weary soldiers sat along the road. According to one war photography historian these images summoned up similar retreats during the Napoleonic Wars almost a century earlier.

REFERENCE: Duncan Anderson. *War: A Photo History.* 2006.

Nichols, Francis Henry (1868–1904)

Nichols covered the Spanish-American War* for the *New York World* and was a member of the expedition sent to inform Cuban rebel leader General Gomez that the United States had declared war on Spain. Nichols followed the Ninth and Tenth Regiments up San Juan Hill.* Following the war he moved to China as a correspondent for the *Christian Herald* and wrote a book about his travels in secluded Shensi Province, where he died at the age of thirty-six.

REFERENCES: Charles H. Brown. *The Correspondents' War.* 1967; Joyce Milton. *The Yellow Kids.* 1989.

Nicholson, Michael (b. 1937)

Born in Romford, Essex, England and educated at the University of Leicester, Nicholson is one of the world's most recognized correspondents as well as the longest serving British television correspondent. He joined ITV in 1964 and for the next forty years reported from close to 20 different war zones, including Biafra, Israel, Vietnam Cambodia, Congo, Cyprus, Afghanistan, Rwanda, Rhodesia/Zimbabwe, Indo-Pakistan, Northern Ireland, Falklands, Bosnia, Croatia, Kosovo, the Gulf Wars, "Desert Storm" 1991, and "Shock and Awe" from Baghdad in 2003. He covered a number of events leading to the fall of Saigon during the Vietnam War,* including the Battle of Newport Bridge (*Cau Tan Can*) and was present at the embassy compound as panicked civilians and others attempted to flee the Vietcong onslaught. He covered the Soweto riots in South Africa and the Rhodesian war of independence. He was the first foreign journalist to interview Robert Mugabe following his prison release. In 1978 Nicholson, along with his cameraman and sound recordist were trapped in the African bush for more than four months, making a trek of 1,500 miles to escape capture by Cuban mercenaries working for Angola's MPLA government. Between 1976 and 1986, Nicholson was mostly working as a television newscaster, returning to the field as a war reporter to cover the Gulf War in 1991 and the Balkan War the following year. He received a number of awards for his war reporting including the Falklands and Gulf Campaign Medals. The movie *Welcome to Sarajevo* was based on his book, *Natasha's Story*.

REFERENCE: http://www.goodreads.com/author/show/114586.Michael_Nicholson.

Niedringhaus, Anja (1965–2014)

Born in Hoexter, Germany, she began her career as a freelance photojournalist at the age of sixteen working for her local newspaper. She covered the fall of the Berlin Wall, with her fine work earning her a position with the European Press Photo Agency (EPA) in 1990. Over the next eleven years she focused much of her attention on the conflict in the former Yugoslavia. In 2002 she joined the Associated Press, covering war zones in Israel, Palestine, Iraq, Afghanistan, and Pakistan. She met her untimely death on April 4, 2014 after an Afghan policeman opened fire on her car at a checkpoint on the outskirts of Khost City. She was traveling in a convoy of election workers purportedly protected by the Afghan National Army and Afghan police to cover the presidential election when the incident occurred. By most accounts she was sitting in the backseat with another AP journalist, when an Afghan police unit commander walked up to the car and opened fire on the two women while yelling *Allahu Akbar*, God is Great. The other journalist, Kathy Gannon, survived. The assailant was convicted of murder and sentenced to death. The German photojournalist was the only woman on a team of eleven AP photographers honored with the 2005 Pulitzer Prize for Breaking New Photography, while covering the Iraq War. That same year she was also recognized with the International Women's Media Foundation's Courage in Journalism Prize. She published *Fotografien* (2001) and *At War* (2011).

REFERENCE: http://www.anjaniedringhaus.com/vita.

Nivat, Anne (b. 1969)

Nivat is an award winning journalist and author who is best known for covering the Chechen conflict in 1999. She has dressed like a local woman in each conflict she has covered. She has criticized war correspondents for traveling with bodyguards and bullet-proof vests suggesting that this type of approach is not likely build trust with sources or readers. Her best known books include her first, *Chienne de Guerre: A Woman Reporter Behind the Lines of the War in*

Chechnya (2000), which was awarded the Albert Londres Prize in 2000, and *The Wake of War: Encounters with the People of Iraq and Afghanistan* (2006). She now reports for *Le Point*.

REFERENCE: Kevin Matthews. "War Correspondent tells stories of ordinary people caught in chaos of war," *UCLA Today*. Feb. 17, 2010.

Noel, Frank E. "Pappy" (1905–1966)

The American photographic war correspondent covered the campaign in Malaysia following the attack on Pearl Harbor. He then reported from the India-Burma theater. He won the Pulitzer Prize in 1943 for his photograph of a seaman in a lifeboat holding his hand out for water. This took place when Noel was adrift in a lifeboat with survivors of a ship torpedoed in the Indian Ocean. After the war he was assigned to the Mediterranean, where he covered the postwar Palestinian conflict for four years. Noel was captured during the Korean War* and spent 1950 to 1953 interned in a prisoner of war camp. While imprisoned he was able to photograph captured United Nations soldiers and after an unsuccessful escape attempt spent seven weeks in solitary confinement.

REFERENCE: Robert W. Desmond. *Tides of War*. 1984.

Noonan, Jr., Oliver (1939–1969)

This son of a *Boston Globe* reporter, Noonan was covering the Vietnam War for the AP when his helicopter was shot down southwest of Danang. According to his AP Wall of Honor biography, he was carrying a large metal camera case that day and had joked to a comrade that "If they shot at the helicopter, I'll hide behind it." He died on August 19, 1969 along with an infantry battalion commander and six other soldiers.

REFERENCE: AP Wall of Honor, www.ap.org/wallof-honor/1960_1969.html.

Norris-Newman, Charles L. "Noggs" (d. 1920)

A retired army captain, Norris-Newman crossed into Zululand with the British army on January 11, 1879. Reporting for the *Natal Times* and the *London Standard,* he was reportedly the first white man to cross the river into Zululand. He had somehow attached himself to the staff of the Natal Native Contingent under Commandant Lonsdale. Norris-Newman was equipped much like the native regiment, which was not issued uniforms; rather, for identification they wore a twisted piece of red cloth around the head, which "Noggs" tucked around his sun helmet.

As the British army camped at Isandhlwana on January 21, it turned out that Norris-Newman was the only English newspaper correspondent in Natal, since most papers back in England felt the campaign would be so short it would not be worth sending representatives. The next morning he left with a column to reinforce Major Dartnell's forward party, which had spotted Zulu warriors about twelve miles away. Norris-Newman was fortunate that he had the zeal to pursue the story, for the following day the British army suffered its worst military disaster of the late nineteenth century when over 1,300 soldiers were wiped out at Isandhlwana. His account of the debacle was relayed by telegraph to Cape Town, where it was put aboard a ship bound for London and the *Standard*.

REFERENCE: Robert Wilkinson-Latham. *From Our Special Correspondent*. 1979.

Norton, Howard (1911–1994)

Born in Haverhill, Massachusetts, Norton majored in journalism at the University of Florida in 1932 and was soon working as a foreign correspondent for the Whaley-Eaton Service, a business-news oriented service. As its Japan-China correspondent, based in Tokyo, Norton was responsible for placing its reporters at various posts around the world. In the last half of the 1930s he worked as a foreign correspondent for a host of American papers, ending up with the *Baltimore Sun* in 1940. He began reporting on World War II* in Europe in late 1942 but did not cover the actual battlefront until October 1943 when he began reporting from the Asian theater of the war. He first landed in the Fiji Islands, but due to security precautions was forced to dateline his coverage as "Somewhere in the South Pacific." As a *Baltimore Sun* reporter his first stories focused on Maryland's contributions to the war effort, focusing on the work of nurses and doctors from the state's medical schools in treating tropical maladies and war wounds. Later in the year he reported from Australia and was back in the war zone in December 1943 chronicling events in New Guinea. The following year found Norton accompanying the 2nd Marine Division to the Mariana Islands, as they landed on Saipan. His coverage captured the horrors of war, describing the "stench of death" and the many fallen bodies along the beachhead. He continued to cover the Battle of Saipan until an American victory almost a month later. In August he was injured when the submarine chaser he was aboard came under Japanese mortar fire of the coast of Guam. He returned to Washington, D.C., the next month and reported on the war from the safe confines of the United States until March 1945 when he was posted to cover the Allied campaign in Italy. Norton was with a coterie of journalists rushing toward Milan after the Allies broke through the German lines, hoping to interview the now-deposed dictator Benito Mussolini. In late April he filed the first published eyewitness account of Mussolini's death. His last reports were filed from the States, covering the sinking of the USS *Indianapolis* in July 1945 and the subsequent court-martial of its commander. During the remainder of his journalism career Norton covered the Cold War and the American political beat, and in 1947 he won a Pulitzer Prize for Public Service for an investigative series on corruption in Maryland.

REFERENCES: Peter J. Zeller II, "Howard Norton," *American World War II Correspondents*, Jeffrey B. Cook, ed. 2012, 181–188; Norris P. West, "Howard Norton, Pulitzer Winning Reporter for *Sun*," Baltimore Sun, Mar. 14, 1994, 3B.

O

Ochlik, Remi (1983–2012)

Born in Thionville, France, Ochlik developed an early interest in photography. In 2002 he started his career as a photographer for an agency in Wostok. Three years later he left to form his own business, IP3 Press, earning his first French press card in the process. He covered French politics and then the Democratic Republic of the Congo in 2008. His photos were published in most of the leading magazines including *Esquire, Time, Le Figaro, Le Monde,* and *Paris Match.* He made an early mark in photojournalism covering riots in Haiti in 2004 during the presidential elections, and would return in 2010 and 2011 to cover the Haiti cholera outbreak for his own IP3. In 2011 and 2012 his photos of the Arab Spring revolutions in Tunisia, Egypt, and Libya brought him international acclaim. His photos titled, "The Fall of Tripoli," "Egypt Tahrir Square," and "The Jasmine Revolution" earned him the Grand Prix Jean-Louis Calderon in 2011. The following year he was awarded first prize in the World Press Photo contest for his picture of a Libyan rebel fighter. Ochlik was covering the Syrian Civil War* in 2012 when he was killed along with journalist Marie Colvin* near the city of Homs after a rocket destroyed the house they had been using as a media center. Three others were injured, including William Daniels, Paul Conroy, and Edith Bouvier. Daniels was able to retrieve Ochlik's camera from the ruins. Three of his photos appeared in his posthumously published book, *Revolutions.* In 2012, to honor Ochlik the Young Reporter Award given out by the city of Perpignan, was renamed the Olchik Prize.

REFERENCES: Angelique Chrisafis, "Remi Ochlik: I Expected to See Horrible Things. Yes, I Was Afraid," Guardian, Feb. 22, 2012; Kerri McDonald, "Parting Glance: Remi Ochlik," New York Times, Feb. 22, 2012.

O'Donovan, Edmund (1844–1883)

Born in Dublin, O'Donovan studied medicine at Trinity College before beginning his career in journalism with the *Irish Times* in 1866. In 1870 he served in the French Foreign Legion during the Franco-Prussian War* before being wounded and taken prisoner.

Following the war he moved to London. As a war correspondent for various British newspapers he covered the Carlist rising in Spain (1873) for the *Times* and the *Hour* and reported from Bosnia and Herzegovina (1876) for the *Daily News.* After various travels in Asia and the Caspian region he accompanied the relief force under Hicks Pasha to the Sudan for the *Daily News.* O'Donovan was killed along with correspondent Frank Vizetelly* when Hicks' force was ambushed and massacred near Obeid sometime between November 3 and November 5, 1883. A brass tablet in the crypt at St. Paul's Cathedral commemorates the death of O'Donovan and six other journalists who perished in this expedition.

REFERENCES: Rupert Furneaux. *News of War.* 1964; *Modern English Biography*, 1214–1215. 1965.

---

* Indicates a separate entry.

O'Kelly, James J. (1845–1916)

The Irish-born O'Kelly had already lived a life of adventure before entering journalism. He left home at the age of eighteen to join the French Foreign Legion and had fought in three wars before joining the *New York Herald*. He covered the Franco-Prussian War* for the *Daily News* while serving with the French army in 1870–1871.

Upon joining the *Herald*, he was originally employed as an art critic before transfer to foreign correspondence, when he was requested to find a way through Spanish lines to interview Cuban rebel leaders in 1873. He was completing an assignment escorting a foreign dignitary on a tour of the United States when he was assigned to cover the Sioux campaign in 1876. The week following the deaths of General George A. Custer and his column, the *New York Herald Tribune* sent O'Kelly to cover General Alfred Terry's command on the Yellowstone River.

O'Kelly's main goal was to gather the true story behind the Custer story. Arriving at Custer's headquarters in Bismarck he reportedly espied the book the late general was reading prior to his fatal march. He interviewed Custer's colleagues Colonel Frederick Benteen and Major Marcus Reno. Over the next two months he continued to put together Custer's story and demanded a government investigation into what had transpired. O'Kelly was the first to report that Sitting Bull rather than Crazy Horse had commanded the Indian forces at the Battle of the Little Big Horn.

Following his coverage of the Custer defeat he returned to Ireland and a career in politics and Parliament. However, he covered one more battlefield when the *London Daily News* sent him to the Sudan in 1885, where he became lost in the desert for several months and was given up for dead before turning up along the Nile River near Khartoum.

REFERENCES: Oliver Knight. *Following the Indian Wars*. 1960; Robert Wilkinson-Latham. *From Our Special Correspondent*. 1979.

Oliphant, Laurence (1829–1888)

Born in Cape Town, South Africa, he later moved with his family to Ceylon, where he served as an assistant to his father, the chief justice. In 1852, after a trip to Russia, he published *The Russian Shores of the Black Sea in the Autumn of 1852, and a Tour Through the Country of the Don Cossacks*, which received great acclaim. He was present with his father at the siege of Sebastopol during the Crimean War.*

When the Franco-Prussian War* broke out in 1870, in the scramble to recruit war reporters the *Times* hired the novice Oliphant. He was dispatched to southern France, where he was the only English correspondent to accompany the French army. Because of his political connections he remained one of the only reporters allowed to move around unimpeded. One of his most insightful stories described the impact of the German troops on France. This article contributed to a shift in British sympathy from the Germans to France. Oliphant noted the German propensity to quarter troops directly within the civilian population rather than providing their own accommodations, eschewing tents and bivouacking. Reports of Prussian depredations and the civilian backlash led to an anti-German fervor in England. He covered fighting at Orleans, Beaugency, the destruction of Chateaudun, and the siege of Paris.

Oliphant was still in Paris for the *Times* when the Germans withdrew and the city dissolved into civil war. Amidst the Paris Commune he was reportedly unpopular with Communard leaders. He was accompanying one of their demonstrations when the National Guard fired into them point-blank. Ever the mystic, Oliphant took his narrow escape from this episode as a sign that he should leave. He left Paris for America that very evening.

REFERENCE: Anne Taylor. *Laurence Oliphant*. 1982.

---

* Indicates a separate entry.

Oliphant, Tom (?)

He was the Washington correspondent for the *Boston Globe* during the Vietnam War.* In 1972 Oliphant uncovered figures indicating the tonnage of bombs dropped in the war in Southeast Asia. Prior to his discovery no correspondent had reported the monthly figures, although he discovered that the numbers were readily available through the South-East Asia Section of the Public Information Office of the Defense Department. Oliphant published his findings in *Ramparts* magazine in 1972.

REFERENCE: Phillip Knightley. *The First Casualty.* 1975.

Omaar, Rageh (b. 1967)

Born in Mogadishu, Somalia and educated at New College, Oxford, he rose to prominence covering the Iraq War* for the BBC. In 2006 he moved to Al Jazeera English and became a well-known documentary presenter, focused on investigative reporting. In 2013 he joined ITV News and became its international affairs editor in 2014. Besides Iraq, he covered conflict in his native Somalia, and Afghanistan, for which he earned a BAFTA award. While covering the Iraq invasion for weekday BBC, the *New York Post* named him the "Scud Stud" for his telegenic presence as he became a familiar face reporting the invasion of Iraq from a hotel rooftop in Baghdad. He wrote *Revolution Day: The Real Story of the Battle of Iraq* (2006).

REFERENCES: "Rageh Omaar," http://www.itv.com/news/meet-the-team/rageh-omaar; Megan Lane, "Our Man in Baghdad," BBC News Online; John Plunkett, "Rageh Omaar Joins ITV News," Jan. 8, 2013.

O'Reilly, John "Tex" (1907–1981)

The son of journalist and soldier of fortune Major Edward S. "Tex" O'Reilly, John O'Reilly joined the reportorial staff of the *New York Herald Tribune* after attending Columbia University for one year. His first major assignment was the 1937 New London, Texas, school explosion, which killed hundreds of children. In 1942 he was accredited to cover the North African theater of operations during World War II.* He reported French actions near Lake Chad and Cairo and later from Iran, before being assigned to the Tunisian front, where he accompanied British desert forces throughout the entire campaign. He was present when the Afrika Corps of 250,000 German soldiers surrendered on May 9, 1943. After the African theater he covered the Italian and Sicily campaigns, landing with forces at Salerno. In late 1943 he was stricken with malaria and after hospitalization was sent back to the States for recuperation.

He returned to Europe in time to cover the Normandy invasion. In March 1945 he temporarily left the war when he went to the United States aboard a hospital plane and wrote several articles on how wounded soldiers were flown home for treatment. He later flew back to France and reported the last days of the war, including the Allied push into Germany.

REFERENCES: Robert W. Desmond. *Tides of War.* 1984; John Hohenberg. *Foreign Correspondence: The Great Reporters and Their Times.* 1964.

Orwell, George

See BLAIR, ERIC ARTHUR.

Osbon, Bradley Sillick (1827–1912)

Known for his daredevil feats during the American Civil War,* Osbon was the preeminent Union naval war correspondent of the war, enduring twenty-seven combat actions and seven war-related wounds. Osbon was born in Rye, New York. Continually drawn to the sea since joining the crew of a sailing ship while barely into his teens, he served on whaling ships, fought pirates in the South China Sea, and enjoyed a brief stint in the Argentine navy before returning to the States and a new career.

Osbon joined the staff of the *New York World* in 1860. On April 12, 1861, he was aboard a U.S. naval vessel in Charleston Harbor in the dual capacity of signal officer and reporter when Fort Sumter was attacked. His account of the Union surrender of the fort elevated his reputation in the journalistic ranks. That same year he joined the *New York Herald* as naval editor and was awarded a roving commission which enabled him to accompany naval expeditions. Using this to his advantage, he covered the Battle of Port Royal in 1861 and the expeditions against New Orleans and Fort McAllister, Georgia.

In early 1862, Osbon was able to slip aboard the ironclad *Merrimac,* which the South was busy rebuilding. His story caused a minor sensation. In 1863 he wrote his last Civil War dispatch when he witnessed the ironclad *Monitor's* unsuccessful assault on Fort McAllister in Georgia. He left the staff of the *Herald* in 1864 to establish his own naval news bureau, which supplied coverage to over a dozen newspapers. When one of his reports of an impending Union attack on Wilmington, North Carolina, was reprinted in a Confederate paper he was arrested and charged with violating the Articles of War. He finally was acquitted after spending six months in prison. He continued to publish his *Nautical Gazette* until he sold it in 1884. After a checkered career, which involved other newspaper endeavors as well as unsuccessful business ventures which left him destitute, Osbon died on May 6, 1912.

REFERENCE: J. Cutler Andrews. *The North Reports the Civil War.* 1955.

O'Shea, John Augustus (1839–1905)

Born in Ireland and educated at the Catholic University in Dublin, he left his medical studies to join the Irish Battalion of Pope Pius IX. In 1860 he reported the siege of Ancona for an American newspaper. Following his military service he was hired by the *New York Herald* to cover the 1866 Austro-Prussian War.* He began his twentyfive-year affiliation with the *Standard* as special correspondent in 1869 and the

following year reported the outbreak of the Franco-Prussian War.* While covering the Battle of Metz he was sentenced to death for spying by the French, and was only saved by the intercession of the French emperor after various appeals by fellow war correspondents. His exploits during the Franco-Prussian War are chronicled in *Iron-Bound City* (1886).

O'Shea covered the siege of Paris and the Carlist civil war in Spain in 1873 and 1875. The next few years were spent covering the great famine in India (1877–1878). After retiring from the *Standard* he continued to write for various newspapers and published several books, including *Leaves from the Life of a Special Correspondent* (1885), and *Roundabout Recollections* (1892).

REFERENCES: *DNB,* Supp., 1901–1911; Dennis Griffiths, ed. *The Encyclopedia of the British Press.* 1992.

Osman, William (1819–c. 1908)

During the Mexican-American War,* Osman covered the battle of Buena Vista. The experienced journalist was editor of the *Ottawa (Illinois) Free Trader* and served with the Illinois Volunteers. He ran the *Free Trader* for more than sixty years, still regularly reporting for work in 1903.

REFERENCES: Tom Reilly. *War with Mexico!: America's Reporters Cover the Battlefront,* Manley Witten, ed. 2010; *The Successful American,* Vol. 7, Part 1-Vol. 8, Part 1, 1903.

O'Sullivan, Timothy H. (c. 1840–1882)

He was born in either New York City or Ireland; little is known about his early life. He began his apprenticeship in the craft of photography while employed at Mathew Brady's* galleries in New York and Washington, D.C. With the outbreak of the American Civil War* in 1861, Brady and several assistants, O'Sullivan among them, went into the field to document the war. In the fall of 1861, O'Sullivan was assigned to record

General Thomas W. Sherman's South Carolina campaign. He returned to Washington the following May and quit Brady to work for Alexander Gardner.* Under Gardner, O'Sullivan was appointed "superintendent of the field or copy work to the Army of the Potomac." He took some of the most outstanding images of the conflict following the Battles of Gettysburg, Fredericksburg, and Petersburg, and the surrender at Appomattox. One of his greatest scoops took place on May 21, 1864, when O'Sullivan climbed to the top of a building and photographed General Grant's council of war in the courtyard of the Massapomax church shortly before the Battle of Cold Harbor.

Though he is best known for his Civil War photographs, his western landscape work is highly regarded for its remarkable clarity and an aesthetic approach heralding the modem era. As the official photographer of the U.S. Geological Survey, he accompanied the 1867–1869 Clarence King expedition along the fortieth parallel through Nevada, Utah, and California. He also was with the Thomas O. Selfridge expedition to Panama (1870), the George Wheeler expeditions to California, Nevada and Arizona (1871–1875), and the Wheeler survey along the hundredth meridian (1870, 1873–1874). In 1880 O'Sullivan was appointed chief photographer for the Department of the Treasury. The following year he was stricken with tuberculosis. His wife died several months before he expired on January 14, 1882.

REFERENCES: Pat Hodgson. *Early War Photographs.* 1974; James D. Horan. *Timothy O'Sullivan: America's Forgotten Photographer.* 1966.

Ottley, Roi (1906–1960)

Born in New York City, Ottley grew up during the so-called "Harlem Renaissance." Evidently it influenced his life, one that would bring him prominence as an award-winning author, playwright, and journalist. His biographer claimed he "was the first African-American World War II war correspondent to report for a mainstream American publication." He began his professional journalism career with the *New York Amsterdam News* in 1930. It wasn't until 1944 that he was able to receive assignments to cover the war in Europe. Thanks to a Julius Rosenwald Fellowship to conduct research on African-American soldiers fighting in Europe and an assignment as a war correspondent for *Picture Magazine* (PM) and *Liberty* magazine, Ottley was given the bona fides to cover war stories in Europe, Africa, and the Middle East. Like his white peers, he was also given a rank similar to a captain in the army. He was not the lone AfricanAmerican war reporter, for at least two dozen others covered the conflict for nationally distributed black-owned publications. What distinguished Ottley's work, was that it was for a mainstream publication, *Liberty,* which was at that time competing with the *Saturday Evening Post.* Most of his black counterparts were directed toward covering black units stationed in North Africa and Italy. Ottley on the other hand, representing the more traditional media, was able to act with less constraints, and unlike the others always identified himself as a war reporter rather than simply as a black correspondent. After his contracts expired in 1945 he left the battlefront for the homefront, having visited almost two dozen countries. He became the first African-American journalist to meet with the pope (Pope Pius XII) in 1945. In 2011 a book was published based on the journals he kept during his war journalism career. Edited by Mark A. Huddle, *Roi Ottley's World War II: The Lost Diary of an American Journalist,* chronicled the pioneering reporter's experiences throughout Europe and North Africa. Ottley died from a heart attack.

REFERENCES: Carla W. Garner, "Roi Ottley," *American World War II Correspondents,* Jeffrey B. Cook, ed. 2012, 189–193; "Roi Ottley Dies: Wrote on Negro. Reporter for Chicago Tribune Compiled a History of His Race in the United States," New York Times, Oct., 2, 1960, 84.

Ourdan, Remy (b. 1969)

This war correspondent began his career in 1992 reporting hostilities in the Balkans. He covered the siege of Sarajevo and the Bosnian War for four years. He also covered the Kosovo war, Serbia, and the fall of Slobodan Milosevic. He went on to cover the Rwandan genocide and conflicts in the Congo, the Eritrean-Ethiopian War, and the civil war in Sierra Leone. He would cover the rise of the international criminal justice movement, including the trials for crimes against humanity and war crimes trials at various venues of the International Criminal Courts, including the Yugoslavian prosecution in The Hague and the Rwanda trial in Arusha.

He covered the American wars in Afghanistan and Iraq beginning in 2001, serving as Baghdad correspondent for *Le Monde*. Between 2005 and 2008 he served as the paper's foreign editor and later as deputy editor (2013). Ourdan covered the convulsions of the Arab Spring in Egypt and Libya, the conflict in the Central African Republic, and the Islamic State.* In April 2012, he organized a reunion to mark the 20th anniversary of the fall of Sarajevo. Out of this he helped establish the *WARM Foundation*. Among his accolades was the Bayeux-Calvados Award* for war correspondents in 2000 for his coverage of conflict in Sierra Leone for *Le Monde*. He won it again in 2012 for chronicling the Mexican drug war in Ciudad Juarez.

REFERENCE: "Remy Ourdan," www.warmfoundation. org/member/remy-ourdan.

Outlaw Correspondents

Following the outbreak of World War I,* the British secretary of state for war, Lord Kitchener, issued orders that would bar war correspondents from obtaining credentials to cover the British Expeditionary Forces in France. Kitchener proclaimed that any British correspondent reporting the conflict in France or Belgium would be treated as an "outlaw," risking arrest and prosecution. This did little to stem the flow of correspondents to Europe, but it did interfere with the transmission of their reports to their home offices. The most effective alternative to official channels was to personally carry dispatches to London. Despite the risks, a fairly large contingent of outlaw correspondents kept the British public informed during the early months of the war. Additional news dispatches came from neutral correspondents from the United States who were in Belgium and France, unburdened by the outlaw label.

REFERENCE: Robert W. Desmond. *Windows on the World*. 1980.

---

* Indicates a separate entry.

Pacific War Correspondents Association (PWCA)

Established in Honolulu by twenty-two war correspondents, its goal was to maintain communications between correspondents and Admiral Nimitz' CINCPAC (Commander in Chief of the Pacific) headquarters. It was imperative to maintain a liaison that could eliminate censorship and transmission difficulties as well as attempt to improve facilities for traveling and news gathering. All accredited correspondents in the Pacific theater of World War II* were eligible for membership.

REFERENCE: Robert W. Desmond. *Tides of War*. 1984.

Packard, Eleanor (1905–1972)

Born in New York City, she attended the University of Washington and the Columbia University School of Journalism. The longtime Rome correspondent for the *New York Daily News* covered the Italian invasions of Ethiopia and Albania, the Spanish Civil War,* and the Sino-Japanese war of the 1930s. With the outbreak of World War II* she reported from the Sudetenland, Italy, and Germany. Following the war she left the UP for the *Daily News* in 1948. She served as its Rome correspondent until her death in 1972.

REFERENCE: Robert W. Desmond. *Tides of War*. 1984.

Packard, Reynolds (1903–1983)

Born in Atlantic City, New Jersey, he attended Bucknell University before moving to Buenos Aires to study Spanish. While in Argentina he joined the United Press before moving for a brief time to the *Chicago Tribune*. He returned to the UP and reported from the capitals of Europe. Following his marriage to Eleanor Packard,* they pursued a joint career as foreign correspondents. He covered the Ethiopian War* and the Spanish Civil War.* After a transient career they settled in Rome, where he headed the Italian bureau of the UP and she was the top reporter on his staff of correspondents. In April 1941 the Packards were with Italian forces during the Axis invasion of Greece and Yugoslavia. The Packards stayed in Italy until June 1942, but the last six months following the American entry into the world war were spent in a prison camp. After a brief return to the States following their release they went back to Italy to cover the Allied invasion for the UP.

In May 1943 Reynolds and Eleanor Packard flew with other correspondents in a massive bombing raid over Palermo, Sicily. In September Reynolds covered the Allied landing at Salerno and the following January was one of fourteen correspondents to report the landings at Anzio in Operation Shingle. He was joined by his wife during the subsequent Italian campaign, and they were among the first contingent of correspondents to enter Rome. Reynolds carried with him the key to the Rome UP office, which he was forced to abandon the day following Pearl Harbor. Packard wasted no time in reopening his office and resuming his position as bureau manager three years after fleeing the German onslaught. In August 1944 he headed a four-man team covering Allied invasion forces on the French Riviera advancing toward Germany. Several months later he was sent to Greece to reopen the UP office there. He coauthored with his wife *Balcony Empire*.

REFERENCE: Robert W. Desmond. *Tides of War.* 1984.

Theo, Padnos

See PETER THEO CURTIS.

Page, Charles Anderson (1838–1873)

Born in Illinois, prior to the American Civil War* his only journalism experience had been editing the *Mt. Vernon News,* a small Iowa weekly newspaper. At the outbreak of the war he was a clerk in a government office in Washington. In June 1862 his offer to cover the battlefront was accepted by the *New York Tribune,* and later that month he was reporting the Peninsular and Seven Days' campaigns. Page evaded army restrictions which forbade reporters from visiting army encampments by serving as a hospital worker during the Second Bull Run campaign of 1862.

According to one source, his descriptive account of the Peninsular campaign was unsurpassed. His columns then began appearing under his own byline "C.A.P." in 1863. In that year he covered the Gettysburg campaign with the Army of the Potomac. In 1864 he again represented the *Tribune* during the Battle of the Wilderness. Following the Civil War he resigned from the paper when he was appointed consul to Switzerland. He stayed on after his diplomatic career and

became involved in the evaporated milk business. He died in London.

REFERENCES: J. Cutler Andrews. *The North Reports the Civil War.* 1955; Louis M. Starr. *Bohemian Brigade.* 1954.

Page, Timothy John (b. 1944)

Born in Tunbridge Wells, Kent, England, Page learned the photographic craft without formal training. He credits fellow war photographers* Horst Faas,* Larry Burrows,* and others for mentoring him in the craft. He photographed his first war in 1963–1965, covering the Laotian civil war and Hanoi-supported guerrillas in Thailand. Best known for his coverage of the Vietnam War,* he originally covered the conflict as a freelancer. From 1965 to 1969 his pictures were published by Time-Life, *Look, Life, Paris-Match,* the UPI, the AP, and many others. While covering Vietnam with Sean Flynn,* son of the noted actor, he experimented with a camera that could be attached to a rifle and would simultaneously record the death of the victim when the rifle was fired.

Page was severely wounded several times, the first time at the Battle of Chu Lai, and then more seriously in 1966 while covering the Buddhist riots. After recovering from shrapnel wounds to his head, chest, and arms he was back in action the following year. In 1967 he was the victim of friendly fire when a B-57 fired on a U.S. Coast Guard ship, killing several crew members and putting Page in a hospital for several weeks. His closest brush with death occurred in 1969 when a colleague stepped on a land mine, sending shrapnel deep into Page's brain. After eighteen months of recuperation he returned to journalism. Since 1979 Page has worked as a freelancer for *Observer Magazine, Newsweek,* the BBC, and SIPA Press in Paris.

REFERENCES: Phillip Knightley. *The First Casualty.* 1975; Jorge Lewinski. *The Camera at War.* 1978; Tim Page. *Page after Page.* 1988.

Indicates a separate entry.

Paget, Henry Marriott (1856–1936)

Paget was a newspaper artist for the *Sphere*, covering the First Balkan War in 1912–1913. He was the only artist-correspondent* on the scene when Nazim Pasha was assassinated in Constantinople, making Paget's rendering of the event the only pictorial record of the incident.

REFERENCE: Dennis Griffiths, ed. *The Encyclopedia of the British Press*. 1992.

Paget, Walter Stanley (1863–1935)

Walter Paget and his brother Sydney were well-known illustrators in Victorian-era England. Walter covered his only war as sketch artist for the *Illustrated London News* with the Suakin expedition (1884–1885) to rescue general Gordon at Khartoum. Paget joined the *Sphere* when it was founded in 1900 and illustrated the classic books *Treasure Island* (1899), *Pilgrim's Progress* (1906), and *Arabian Nights* (1907).

REFERENCES: Dennis Griffiths, ed. *The Encyclopedia of the British Press*. 1992; Pat Hodgson. *The War Illustrators*. 1977.

Paine, Ralph Delahaye (1871–1925)

Paine was born in Lemont, Illinois. Since his father had fought in the Battle of Inkerman and the American Civil War,* it was perhaps only natural that the son would be drawn to the battlefield. In 1894, following graduation from Yale, he joined the *Philadelphia Press*. He served as war correspondent during the Spanish-American War.* William Randolph Hearst* chose Paine to transport a jeweled sword to the Cuban rebel leader General Maximo Gomez on behalf of the *New York Journal*. His quixotic mission ended when, after a journey of over five thousand miles, he was forced to send Gomez the sword through an intermediary.

Paine's coverage of the 1900 Boxer Rebellion* in China for the *New York Herald* is chronicled in his books *Dragon and the Cross* (1912) and *Roads of Adventure* (1922). In 1902, he led a successful campaign against the beef trust, and following a short interlude with the *New York Telegraph* left journalism to devote himself full-time to fiction and historical writing. Harkening back to his days at Yale, most of his nonfiction work focused on the history of Yankee shipping, including *The Ships and Sailors of Old Salem* (1909), *The Old Merchant Marine* (1919), and *The Fight for a Free Sea* (1920). He wrote numerous novels and boys' stories. During World War I* Paine was made a special observer of the Allied fleets. He died in Concord, New Hampshire.

REFERENCES: Charles H. Brown. *The Correspondents' War*. 1967; *DAB*.

Painter, Uriah H. (1837–1900)

A Quaker from West Chester, Pennsylvania, Uriah Painter reported the American Civil War* for the *Philadelphia Inquirer*. Because of the astuteness and the proficiency of his reportage, the twenty-four-year-old war correspondent quickly became a confidant of Secretary of State Edwin Stanton, who relied heavily on Painter's dispatches, ensuring him access to military telegraph lines.

Painter covered the First Battle of Bull Run in 1861 and was the first newspaper correspondent to report the appearance of Lee's army crossing into Maryland shortly before the Battle of Antietam in 1862. Painter missed perhaps his greatest story when he left the front briefly on what a fellow correspondent termed a "Union mission," which in reality was his marriage in Ohio. The following year he made amends when he reported the Battle of Gettysburg.

REFERENCES: J. Cutler Andrews. *The North Reports the Civil War*. 1955; Louis M. Starr. *Bohemian Brigade*. 1954; *NY Times*, October 21, 1900.

Painton, Frederick C. (d. 1945)

During World War II,* this war correspondent for *Reader's Digest*, beginning in 1942, became one of the most versed journalists on tank warfare. Much of his experience was gleaned from covering the North African campaign against Field Marshall Erwin Rommel's Afrika Corps. Painton had first witnessed the frontlines in World War I,* this time as a sergeant in France. He later worked for *Stars and Stripes** and had studied at Columbia University while working nights as a rewrite man for several New York newspapers prior to the Second World War. Following the attack on Pearl Harbor he persuaded the War Department to permit him to enlist in the Army for a week. From this experience he brought the reading public up-to-date on how soldiers were trained in preparation for war. He accompanied a submarine patrol, flew in naval coastal bombers, and took part in practice beach landings with the Marines. After covering four long campaigns from Africa to Southern France with American forces he published "This War is Down Our Alley" in the December 16, 1944 edition of the *Saturday Evening Post*. Painton covered the Anzio beach landing in Italy and the invasion of southern France. His May 1943 *Reader's Digest* article, "Secret Mission to North Africa," chronicled General Mark Clark's landing with four commandoes in North Africa months ahead of the African D-Day. While on his way to cover the story his troop ship was torpedoed and he was fished out of the sea by an escort vessel. His last reportage came from the last stages of the Pacific theater, covering the carnage on Iwo Jima. It was during this time that his health began to fail. He died of a heart attack on Guam as he raised his arm to bid goodbye to a pilot taking off in April 1, 1945. His close friend Ernie Pyle* cabled a message lamenting the death of the war reporter, commenting "…I'm glad he didn't have to go through the unnatural terror of dying on the battlefield." Pyle would be killed in action just eighteen days later.

* Indicates a separate entry.

REFERENCE: Doral Chenoweth, "-30-: A Gripping Account of 54 War Correspondents K.I.A. in WWII 1940–1945," http://www.54warcorrespondents-kia-30-ww2.com/chapter16.html.

Palmer, Frederick (1873–1958)

Born in Pleasantville, Pennsylvania, and educated at Allegheny College, Palmer joined the *New York Press* as London correspondent in 1895. His career as a war reporter lasted almost fifty years and he became the first war journalist to win the Distinguished Service Medal. No less a personage than Theodore Roosevelt declared him "our best war correspondent." In 1897 he reported the Greco-Turkish War,* beginning a long career as war correspondent. In fact for both Palmer and fellow reporter Stephen Crane,* they would be witnessing warfare for the first time. By 1897 he was affiliated with the *New York World* and *Collier's Weekly*. That year he reported a gold rush in the Klondike of northwestern Canada before moving to the Philippines to cover the Moro insurrection in the aftermath of the Spanish-American War.* In the summer of 1900 he left the Philippines to cover the Boxer Rebellion* in China. He next reported the Boer War* and then the 1904–1905 Russo-Japanese War.* He covered the Battle of Mukden in June 1905 which was at that point according to his biographer "the longest battlefront in world history."

Palmer reported the 1912 Balkans conflict for the *New York Times,* the first war he covered for that newspaper, while accompanying the Bulgarian army. Two years later he was arrested in Mexico City while covering the Veracruz and Tampico incidents for *Everybody's Magazine*. Following his release he crossed the Atlantic to report the developing conflict in Europe. Palmer was the first and only American journalist accredited with the headquarters of the British Expeditionary Forces in France when tight controls were imposed shortly after the German advance westward in 1914. Palmer attained a reputation for investigating battles after they occurred (besides during the actual engagement) allowing him to earn a better understanding of the action he was reporting.

While he was in Washington, D.C., for a brief respite in April 1917 the United States declared war on Germany. James Gordon Bennett, Jr.,* offered Palmer the position of chief correspondent in Europe for the *New York Herald* at an extraordinary salary of $40,000 per year. Prior to leaving the nation's capital he renewed his friendship with General John Pershing, whom he had met in the Philippines in 1899. Pershing updated him on the war situation in France.

While they sailed together on the *Baltic* to France, Pershing cajoled Palmer into accepting a commission to oversee the Press Section of G-2 at only $2,400 per year. At a fraction of what he would have received for the *New York Herald,* Palmer, ever the patriot, accepted the role with the full knowledge that he would be supervising the accreditation of war correspondents for the American Expeditionary Force (AEF) as well as directing censorship of the press. Now known as Colonel Palmer, he quickly shed his cloak as journalist for his new role as army officer and censor, becoming increasingly penurious at releasing information to his former colleagues. Palmer covered one of his last conflicts in the early 1930s, when he reported the rebellion against the Machado government in Cuba for the *New York Herald Tribune.* He donned a uniform for the last time while covering General Douglas MacArthur's final campaigns in the Pacific theater of World War II. He had also covered the campaigns of MacArthur's father, Major Gneral Arthur MacArthur, from the same region during the Philippine Insurrection of 1899. Palmer carried out his last reporting assignment in July 1946, when he covered the atomic tests off the Bikini atoll from aboard the U.S.S. Appalachian. He wrote 31 books, with at least a dozen related to war reportage including *Going to War in Greece* (1897), *The Ways of the Service* (1901), *With Kuroki in Manchuria* (1904), *My Year of the War* (1915), My *Second Year of the War* (1917), and *Our Greatest Battle (The Meuse-Argonne)* (1919).

REFERENCES: Emmet Crozier. *American Reporters on the Western Front 1914–18.* 1959; Robert W. Desmond. *Windows on the World.* 1980; Phillip Knightley. *The First Casualty.* 1975' Nathan A. Haverstock. *Fifty Years at the Front.* 1996.

Palmer, Royden Keith (1907–1943)

Born in New Zealand, Palmer was the first Australian war correspondent to be killed in the South Pacific during World War II.* He was killed while covering American operations at Bougainville. At his death he had been filing dispatches for the *Melbourne Herald* and *Newsweek* magazine. On November 7, 1943 he was killed when a Japanese bomber dropped a bomb that leveled the press tent at Bougainville. According to one witness he was sleeping in the tent along with several Marine combat reporters. Previous to this he covered the war beginning in 1942 as a representative of the combined Australian Press, as a correspondent for the Royal Navy. In 1944 a Liberty ship, the *Keith Palmer,* was launched to commemorate his contributions to the war effort.

REFERENCES: Australian War Memorial, https://www.awm.gov.au/people/P10676622/; Neil McDonald, "Damien Peter Parer," *Australian Dictionary of National Biography,* http://adb.anu.edu.au/biography/parer-damien-peter-11339

Palmos, Frank (b. 1940)

Born in Melbourne, Australia, he was educated at the University of Melbourne and earned a PhD from the University of West Australia in 2012. Palmos was most prominent for his coverage of foreign affairs in Southeast Asia beginning in 1961. He spent five tours as war correspondent covering the Vietnam War* between 1965 and 1968. He accompanied 33 land and air missions from bases in Da Nang and Saigon and survived a close call during the Tet Offensive in 1968, when he was the only survivor of an ambush that killed five other western war reporters. He chronicled many of his war experiences in *Ridding the Devils* (1990). It is considered the first Western book on the war to be translated from English into Vietnamese (by Phan Thanh Hao). It was broadcast in serial form between 1990 and 1991 over Vietnam National Radio.

REFERENCES: http://www.extension.uwa.edu.au/tutor/383; http://en.wikipedia.org/wiki/Frank_Palmos

Panama Invasion

In 1989 U.S. forces invaded Panama to remove dictator Manuel Noriega from office after he refused to abide by democratic elections that repudiated his regime. Following the Grenada invasion* press debacle a new system of media coverage had been approved by the Pentagon. According to the Sidle Commission directed by Major General Winant Sidle, the press had agreed to a pool system in which select journalists and photographers representing various media giants would share their coverage with other media members waiting at the Pentagon. However, the Pentagon did not fulfill its end of the agreement completely, resulting in the Washington pool arriving at the scene hours after the fighting began. It was not until the conclusion of the invasion that the Pentagon offered what one source has described as "journalism's equivalent of a cleanup mission."

REFERENCE: Johanna Neuman. *Lights, Camera, War.* 1996.

Parer, Damien Peter (1912–1944)

Born in Melbourne, Australia, Parer displayed an early interest in photography and motion pictures. By the time World War II* broke out he was an accomplished stills and motion picture photographer and was appointed as official movie photographer for the Australian military.

His early war photography was filmed on the high seas as he made his way from Australia to the Middle East. He was aboard the HMAS *Ladybird* when it shelled Bardia and later advanced with the infantry at Derna, where he experience his first close action in a war zone. Parer demonstrated a penchant for putting himself in harm's way from the very beginning as he endeavored to capture battle action. Sometimes he was filming in advance of the troops, with one observer predicting that Parer was doomed to die on the battlefield. Parer filmed war zones in Greece and Syria from a variety of vantage points—from the deck of a ship, from aircraft, and alongside the infantry on the ground. After covering the Western desert front by mid-1942 he was covering the Japanese theater of the war in New Guinea. He captured some of his best war sequences during this phase of the war, especially at Salamaua and the Kodoka frontline. As he filmed battles he was always trying to demonstrate the conditions under which his fellow Australians were fighting during the New Guinea campaign. His documentary, *Men of Timor*, chronicled the guerrilla war being fought on Timor in 1942. He returned to New Guinea where he embarked on several bombers conducting a series of operations against Japanese shipping in the Bismarck Sea. He also filmed the assault on Timbered Knoll in the Salamaua area.

He left his position with the Australian Department of Information in 1943 and began working for America's Paramount News, filming air raids over New Guinea. In 1944 he was with the U.S. Marines on Guam and then during the Peleliu operation. He was killed by a staccato burst of Japanese machine gun fire on September 17, 1944. He was focused on capturing shots of the faces of advancing soldiers, walking backwards behind a tank filming marines advancing under heavy fire when he was killed. Parer's most important work was accomplished in the New Guinea campaign, leading to his films *Assault on Salamaua* (1943) and the Academy-Award winning *Kokoda Front Line* (1942).

Indicates a separate entry.

REFERENCE: Contact: Photographs and the Modern Experience War, Australian War Memorial.

Park, Sarah (1927–1957)

Educated at American University and the University of Hawaii, in 1950 Park was hired by the *Honolulu Star-Bulletin* and in 1952 began covering the Korean War.* Park broke a number of gender barriers still holding back women from covering war zones. She gained a following for her coverage of the war and her attempts to boost morale among troops at the front. When she reported that soldiers lacked electricity on the frontlines, it jump-started a "Candles for Korea" campaign in Hawaii that resulted in 150,000 candles being sent to South Korea. Her critical reporting of the conflict led a Soviet magazine to label her and seven other American reporters, including Marguerite Higgins* and Hal Boyle as "extra-gangsters of the pen." According to the founder of the Korean American Journalists Association, Park is probably the only Korean-American whose name is on the Journalists Memorial at the Newseum in Washington, D.C. Moreover, Park was "likely the first Korean-American journalist to cover a war." Park was killed in a plane crash on March 9, 1957 off Laie while covering a tsunami.

REFERENCE: "Star-Bulletin Reporter Killed on Duty Earns Place of Honor," Honolulu Star-Bulletin, Nov. 24, 2008.

Parris, Jr., John A. (1914–1999)

Born in Sylvia, North Carolina, Parris attended North Carolina College before joining the United Press in 1934. In 1943 he was working in the London office when he was selected as one of the five UP correspondents to accompany the Allied landings in North Africa. He went on to cover the Italian campaign and report the D-Day landings from London. He coauthored *Springboard to Berlin* with Ned Russell,* Leo Disher,* and Phil Ault.

REFERENCE: Robert W. Desmond. *Tides of War*. 1984.

Parslow, E. G. (d. 1899)

Parslow was a correspondent for the *Daily Mail* during the Boer War.* While in the besieged town of Mafeking* he became assistant editor of one of the Boer siege newspapers,* the *Mafeking Mail*. In November 1899 he got into an argument with an artillery officer in a hotel bar. When Parslow told the officer, "You're no gentleman," the officer drew his pistol and killed the correspondent. To save embarrassment at home Parslow's death was listed as an accident.

REFERENCE: Robert Wilkinson-Latham. *From Our Special Correspondent*. 1979.

Paterson, Andrew Barton (1864–1941)

Born in Australia, he is probably best known as the alleged creator of the country's national song, *Waltzing Matilda*. After leaving his solicitor's practice he covered the Boer War* for the *Sydney Morning Herald* and the *Melbourne Argus*. The popularity and precision of his dispatches led the Reuters* agency to use his reports, which appeared under his nickname "Banjo," after the racehorse.

Following the campaign in South Africa he reported the Philippines insurrection for the *Sydney Morning Herald* as well as the Boxer Rebellion* in China. During World War I* he covered the western front, and ended up enlisting in the Australian Remount Service as an ambulance driver. At the conclusion of the war he had risen to major. His personal recollections were published as *Happy Despatches* (1934).

REFERENCE: C. Semmler. *The Banjo of the Bush*. 1966.

Patterson, Joseph Medill (1879–1946)

Born in Chicago and educated at Yale, the son of *Chicago Tribune* publisher R. W. Patterson got his first taste of war reporting when he covered the 1900 Boxer Rebellion* during his summer break from Yale University. After graduating the following year he joined the staff of the paper. He left journalism in 1903–1904 for a stint in the Illinois state legislature and then in 1905–1906 was commissioner of public works in Chicago. In 1908 he left the paper to pursue literary interests, producing a novel and cowriting a play. On the death of his father in 1910 Patterson became copublisher of the *Chicago Tribune* with his cousins, but this would not deter him from returning to the combat zone in the pursuit of news.

In 1914 Patterson covered the occupation of Veracruz by American marines before promptly setting out for the Belgian front with the outbreak of World War I* just weeks later. Before departing for Europe he started a Mexican edition of the *Tribune* for the troops. He had brought along his own photographer, Edwin F. Weigel, who was assigned to bring along a motion picture camera and the requisite film. Weigel shot footage of U.S. Marine and Naval operations in Mexico. Upon his arrival in Europe, Patterson convinced a French pilot to fly him over French positions in Flanders. In addition he was able to obtain aerial photographs of bombed-out Ypres. Patterson covered the German army early in the conflict, which was much more cooperative than the heavily censored British and French forces. Patterson's account of the war prior to American entry was published as *Notebook of a Neutral* and serialized in the *Tribune* in 1915.

In 1916 he rejected an offer of a commission in the Illinois National Guard, but with American intervention in 1917 he enlisted as a private in the artillery. He eventually rose to the rank of captain, serving in France in 1918, where he was gassed and wounded in five engagements. In 1918 Patterson cofounded the New York tabloid newspaper, the *Illustrated Daily News*. Within several years its name was changed to the *New York Daily News*.

REFERENCES: Robert W. Desmond. *Windows on the World*. 1980; Lloyd Wendt. *Chicago Tribune*. 1979.

Mary Marvin Breckinridge Patterson.

See MARY MARVIN BRECKINRIDGE.

Patton Slapping Incident

General George S. Patton, Jr., also known as "Old Blood and Guts," was commander of the U.S. Seventh Army. In August 1943, wearing his pearl-handled revolvers, Patton visited a military hospital evacuation tent in Sicily. When he came across a soldier whom he suspected of faking illness he slapped the soldier across the face in full view of medical staff. This incident was initially unreported. But, several days later Patton visited another hospital tent. After asking a soldier what injury he was recuperating from, Patton slapped him when he answered that it was for a nervous disorder. Calling the soldier a coward, Patton kicked him when he attempted to flee. As the general left the tent he was overheard by war correspondent Noel Monks* shouting that there was no such thing as shell shock.

It turned out that the victim had heroically served in the Tunisian and Sicilian campaigns and was only hospitalized after a doctor attempted for over a week to convince him to seek convalescence. The correspondents' pool of almost two dozen reporters decided that rather than leak the story they would send a courier to General Eisenhower in an attempt to have Patton apologize to the soldier. After receiving confirmation from other sources Eisenhower ordered Patton to apologize to both soldiers and all witnesses to the incidents, as well as to other members of the soldiers' divisions, or else lose his command. Although Patton complied, he was punished by being barred from action until after the invasion of Normandy almost a year later.

While literally thousands of servicemen were privy to what had occurred, it had still not been announced in the press. Eisenhower convinced the war correspondents not to break the story because it could provide grist for enemy propaganda and embarrass the military hierarchy. For almost three months secrecy prevailed, until Washington columnist Drew Pearson got wind of the story. Incensed that the scoop was credited to a columnist rather than a war reporter, AP correspondent Edward Kennedy* published his account of the incident, making worldwide headlines, although it was months out of date.

REFERENCES: Robert W. Desmond. *Tides of War.* 1984; Phillip Knightley. *The First Casualty.* 1975.

Pearl, Daniel (1963–2002)

Pearl began his journalism career in 1990 reporting for the *Wall Street Journal* from Atlanta. In 1993 he moved to its Washington bureau. Three years later he was covering the Middle East from London and then the Balkans from Paris. The videotaped murder of *Wall Street Journal's* Daniel Pearl in Pakistan in 2002 created outrage around the world. Following this tragedy numerous North American newsmen enrolled in a crash course on survival techniques, offered in Virginia by the British Royal Marines. Pearl was investigating the background of British Muslim Richard "the shoe bomber" Reid when he was kidnapped, tortured and had his throat cut just eight days after his capture.

REFERENCES: Duncan Anderson. *War: A Photo History.* 2006; Herbert N. Foerstel. *Killing the Messenger.* 2006.

Pearse, Harry H. S. (?)

The accomplished artist-correspondent* accompanied the 1884–1885 Gordon relief expedition for the *London Daily News* and the *Illustrated London News,* reporting and taking part in the Battle of Abu Klea. He witnessed and reported the Battle of Abu Kru during the reconquest of the Sudan in 1898. When not engaged by the *Graphic* in times of conflict, he wrote on hunting for the *Morning Post.* While besieged in Ladysmith* during the Boer War* he coproduced the free illustrated newspaper the *Ladysmith Bombshell.*

REFERENCES: Byron Farwell. *The Great Anglo-Boer War.* 1976; Pat Hodgson. *The War Illustrators.* 1977; Robert Wilkinson-Latham. *From Our Special Correspondent.* 1979.

Peck, Rory (1956–1993)

This freelance cameraman was killed while covering the 1991 coup attempt in Russia. He famously replied to a question by author David Loyn about why he covered dangerous conflicts, "You get paid to travel to the most interesting places at the most interesting time. What do you lose? Each time you lose a little bit of your heart." Peck was born in Cambridge, Massachusetts and was one of the growing group of cameramen who preferred to work alone. He was a founding partner of Frontline News* and had tried the Army but the military lacked appeal to him. In the mid-1980s he went to Peshawar to cover the Afghan War against the Soviets. Starting out as a still photographer he made the transition to the television camera. He returned to England in 1989 and went to Bucharest to film the end of the Ceausescu regime for the BBC. He covered the first Gulf War from Baghdad and the failed Soviet coup in August 1991. He subsequently covered Sarajevo and the Balkans from the Muslim side of the conflict. He was living in Moscow when he was mortally wounded while covering a shoot-out around the Ostankino television station there.

REFERENCES: Obituary. The *Independent.* October 5, 1993; David Loyn. *Frontline.* 2005.

Peixotto, Clifford (1869–1940)

Born in San Francisco, he attended various international art schools and by the 1890s was exhibiting his pictures in a Paris salon. In the late 1890s he worked for *Scribner's* and *Harper's.* In the first decade of the 1900s he chronicled the American

Southwest and various Hispanic countries in a series of articles and books which he also illustrated. In 1918 he was selected as an official artist by the AEF. He was considered among "the most active of the artists." He covered the Chateau-Thierry front and action in the vicinity of St. Mihiel. He witnessed the French Army under General Henri Petain and the Americans under General John J. Pershing as they entered St. Mihiel on September 13, 1918. Peixotto accompanied the American advance at Clermont-en-Argonne but was forced by sickness to return to Paris where he witnessed the Armistace.

REFERENCE: Alfred Emile Cornebise. *Art from the Trenches*. 1991.

Pelcoq, Jules (?)

Jules Pelcoq was a Parisian book illustrator who covered the French side for the *Illustrated London News* during the Franco-Prussian War.* While covering the 1870 siege of Paris, Pelcoq dispatched his work by balloon to London. Wood engravings were then made from his sketches once they arrived in England. His work captures the attempt by Parisian troops to break through the surrounding Prussian army and the plight of citizens on the edge of starvation forced to eat animals from the Parisian zoo.

REFERENCE: Pat Hodgson. *The War Illustrators*. 1977.

Pellegrin, Paolo (b. 1964)

Born in Rome, and educated there at the Istituto Italiano di Fotografia, his early photojournalism focused on Italian social issues before broadening his range to cover subjects in the Balkans in the 1990s and working on projects dedicated to HIV/AIDS in Europe, Mexico, and Africa, winning his first World Press Photo Award for this work in 1995. In 1997 he published his work on children in post-war Bosnia, *Bambini*, and the following year collaborated with Medecins Sans Frontieres to produce *Cambodia*. In 1998 he covered

blood feuds in Albania with reporter Scott Anderson* for the *New York Times*. Over the next two years he covered the Balkans conflict and its aftermath in Kosovo, Albania, Macedonia, and Serbia. In 2001 he reported on counter terrorism in Algeria and traveled frequently to cover events in the Middle East and Africa. In 2007 his coverage of the war in Lebanon with Scott Anderson was published in the book *Double Blind*. The book *Dies Irae* (2011) covered the Arab Spring revolutions in Egypt and Tunisia. Pellegrin won numerous awards for his photojournalism including ten World Press Photo Awards. Solo and Main Group exhibitions of his work have been featured throughout the world, including New York, Germany, Italy, Russia, Sweden, France, Italy, Spain, Switzerland, and Australia.

REFERENCE: Official website, http://www.magnumphotos.com/PaoloPelegrin.

Pelley, Scott Cameron (b. 1957)

Born in San Antonio, Texas and educated at Texas Tech University, Pelley rose to prominence as a correspondent for the CBS news magazine *60 Minutes* and as the anchor for the nightly CBS *Evening News*. He started his journalism career in 1975. His first stints in war journalism came in 1990 and 1991 while covering the Persian Gulf crisis and the invasion of Iraq. Since then he has reported often from war zones. Pelley and his reporting team accompanied U.S. Special Forces in Afghanistan in 2001 and two years later, he was part of a *60 Minutes* team that broke the news of the 2003 invasion, from an outpost in the DMZ (Demilitarized Zone) between Iraq and Kuwait. Pelley's team decided to forego being embedded and covered the invasion independently from its beginning to the fall of Baghdad. Pelley continued to cover the conflict over the years. He covered reports of genocide in Darfur and in 2007 he was even credited with helping a Sudanese rebel group organize an armed reconnaissance effort in Darfur. Pelley has followed a number of U.S. Army and Marine Corps units during combat operations. In 2011 Pelley was selected to replace Katie Couric as the anchor of the CBS *Evening News*. Pelley and his reporting team won the George Foster Peabody Award in 2007 for covering civilian deaths during a Marine battle in Haditha, Iraq. According to the citation, the investigation revealed not just the "worst single killing of civilians since Vietnam" but put into "better perspective…the terrible choices" the Iraq War presents to soldiers and civilians alike.

REFERENCES: http://www.cbsnews.com/team/scott-pelley/; http://www.webcitation.org/5gXojcn0j.

Peoples, John H. "Chaparral" (d. 1850)

A New Orleans printer, he had originally volunteered for a three-month enlistment during the Mexican-American War.* Following his discharge he continued to follow American forces as a war correspondent for the *New Orleans Delta* and then the *New Orleans Crescent*. Peoples, whose dispatches appeared under the byline "Chaparral," was among the veteran newspaper printers who published their own army newspapers for the invading troops. While running the *American Flag* from Matamoros he established the *Vera Cruz Eagle* after the American occupation of the coastal city. One of the most enterprising publishers during this conflict, he later established the *American Star No. 2* in Puebla, Mexico, shortly before General Winfield Scott's march on Mexico City. All of these camp newspapers were partially supported by printing contracts with the American army. Peoples joined Scott's forces as they left for the Mexican capital, where he would soon bring out the *American Star, Mexico*. He was later hired by the *New Orleans Picayune* to cover the California gold rush. He drowned during an expedition on the northern California coast.

REFERENCES: Fayette Copeland. *Kendall of the Picayune.* 1943; Robert W. Johannsen. *To the Halls of the Montezumas.* 1985; Tom Reilly, *War with Mexico!*, 2010.

Perez-Reverte, Arturo (b. 1951)

Best known as a popular author of historical novels, Perez-Reverte worked as a war correspondent between 1973 and 1994 for RTVE (Corporación de Radio y Televisíon Española). Born in Cartagena, Murcia, Spain he began working in journalism for the Madrid *Pueblo*. In the 1970s he was twice reported missing, in the Sahara in 1975, and in Eritrea in 1977. He covered the Falklands War in 1982 as well as conflicts in Cyprus, El Salvador, Nicaragua, Chad, Lebanon, Sudan, Mozambique, Angola, the Persian Gulf, Croatia, and Bosnia-Herzegovina. Since the 1990s he has devoted himself to his fiction writing career and in the process became among the best-selling authors in Spain.

REFERENCE: Keith F. Hatcher, Mini Bio, http://www.imdb.com/name/nm0702416/bio.

Perkins, William T. (1947–1967)

Marine corporal Perkins was serving as an American military correspondent and combat photographer in South Vietnam when he threw himself on a grenade and saved the lives of several soldiers on October 12, 1967. He was posthumously awarded the Congressional Medal of Honor.

REFERENCE: Charles P. Arnot. *Don't Kill the Messenger.* 1994.

Perlin, Bernard (1918–2014)

War artist Bernard Perlin was hired by the Office of War Information to create posters for the Domestic Section in 1942. The following year he was discharged because of a budget shortfall. In 1943 he joined *Life* as its artist-correspondent* in the Sudan and Eritrea. When he arrived in Cairo he came to the realization that there was no war-related activity in progress at his destination and made other plans without consent from *Life*. His magazine meanwhile forgot all about him and he spent several months of rest and recuperation in Cairo.

Perlin was soon restless and feeling a little guilty, so he created his own assignment without the authorization of his employers. In May 1944 he made his way by boat to the German-occupied island of Samos in the Aegean Sea. His traveling companions included a British military observer and some Greek soldiers on a mission to create a bit of havoc and plant disinformation among the Germans concerning the looming Allied invasion of Europe. The mission was only moderately successful from a military perspective, but Perlin reaped his greatest journalistic scoop with his sketches of Greek resistance fighters.

REFERENCE: Frederick S. Voss. *Reporting the War: The Journalistic Coverage of World War II.* 1994.

Perry, George Session (1910–1956)

This Texas-born novelist was orphaned at age twelve. His 1941 book *Hold Autumn in Your Hand* was reportedly the first Texas book to be awarded the National Book Award. During World War II* he was prevented from joining the military outright due to various medical problems but managed to join the fray as a war correspondent for *Harper's Weekly* and the *Saturday Evening Post.* He accompanied troops on invasions of Italy and France. After the war he was quoted as saying that his experiences had "defictionalized" him for life, and ne never wrote fiction again after 1944, preferring to write nonfiction and journalism. In 1956, suffering from depression, alcoholism and various physical ailments he walked into a river near his home and vanished. His body was found months later and his death was ruled an accidental drowning.

REFERENCE: Maxine Cousins Hairston. *George Sessions Perry.* 1973.

Perry, Henry (?)

At the outset of the American Civil War* Perry came to Richmond to cover the Confederacy for the *New Orleans Picayune.* He covered

Confederate operations at Manassas and Norfolk in Virginia before moving to Memphis in March 1862 to cover the western theater of operations. He reported the Corinth campaign and a Memphis gunboat battle. When New Orleans fell in April 1862 the *New Orleans Picayune* came under federal control, forcing Perry to transfer to the pro-Confederate *Memphis Appeal.*

REFERENCE: J. Cutler Andrews. *The South Reports the Civil War.* 1970.

Perry, Mert (1929–1970)

He was the freelance partner of Charles Mohr,* Vietnam War* correspondent for *Time* magazine. Perry had been initially sent to Vietnam by UPI, but resigned to work for *Time.* In 1962 he reported what was then the largest assault in the history of helicopter warfare as fifty H-21 helicopters loaded with two hundred American advisors and six hundred ARVN (Army of the Republic of Vietnam) troops lifted off for the war zone just north of Saigon. By 1963 he was in his second year covering the conflict and had already developed an excellent reputation for his work. According to fellow journalist David Halberstam,* Perry was the most favored correspondent among military officers. In 1963 Perry and Mohr had come under fire from both the Diem regime and American censors, leading both to resign from the magazine. Vietnam was the high point of Perry's journalistic career. After resigning from *Time* in 1963, he was never able to recapture the controversial success he enjoyed when he worked with Mohr for *Time.* He died of a massive heart attack at the age of forty-one.

REFERENCES: Michael Emery. *On the Front Lines.* 1995; William Prochnau. *Once upon a Distant War.* 1995.

Peyton, Katherine "Kate" (d. 2005)

Born in Bury St. Edmonds, England, she was drawn to journalism and broadcasting while at the University of Manchester. Her first job was with BBC Radio Suffolk. She moved to South Africa for the South African Broadcasting Corporation and worked as a freelancer for the BBC in the 1990s. The BBC correspondent was shot and killed by gunmen from a car as she was entering a Mogadishu hotel to meet with a member of Somalia's transitional parliament. According to Reporters without Borders, her killers were part of a powerful local clan keen to show its control over the capital city and to send a message against foreign meddling in Somali affairs. Further investigation by the United Nations tied her death to an Al-Qaeda affiliate. Controversy arose concerning the tradition of having journalists assigned to dangerous locations or risk losing their job. The BBC was ruled not liable for her death.

REFERENCES: Reporters without Borders, "Swedish Freelance Photographer Gunned Down on Mogadishu Street," June 23, 2006; Times newspaper obituary.

Philby, Harold Adrian Russell "Kim" (1912–1988)

Best known as a Soviet spy, the Cambridge-educated Philby journeyed to Spain to report the Spanish Civil War* for the *Times* from the Nationalist side. After graduating from college in 1933 Philby worked as a freelance journalist in Vienna and then for the *Review of Reviews* in London. He was in Spain in 1936 when war broke out. The following year he replaced George Steer,* who had left the *Times* for the *Daily Telegraph*. Philby remained in Spain for the duration of the conflict. He was awarded the Cross of the Order of Military Merit for bravery on the battlefield by General Franco. Philby later became the head of the anti-Soviet section of the British Secret Intelligence Service until it was revealed he was a longstanding member of the Soviet KGB.

During the Spanish Civil War Philby was a secret agent for the Comintern and continued to act in this capacity while representing the *Times* in Berlin in 1939. The following year he became a double agent in the British Secret Service while reporting from France as a war correspondent. Philby continued as a journalist after the war, working for the *Sunday Observer* in Beirut and covering the Middle East. It was during this period in the 1950s that Philby became a triple agent, adding the American Central Intelligence Agency to his list of employers. In 1963 he fled to the Soviet Union.

REFERENCES: Robert W. Desmond. *Tides of War*. 1984; Phillip Knightley. *The Master* Spy. 1989; Phillip Knightley, with Bruce Page and David Leitch. *The Philby Conspiracy*. 1975.

Phillips, Percival (1877–1937)

The American-born correspondent began his newspaper career in Pittsburgh before becoming a foreign correspondent in 1897 covering the Greco-Turkish War* with the Greek Army for the *Chicago Inter-Ocean*. The next year he reported the Spanish-American War* for the *New York World*. Joining the *Daily Express* in 1901, Phillips covered the Russo-Japanese War,* several natural disasters, the Italo-Turkish War, the Balkan Wars of 1912–1913, and World War I.* During World War I he became a British citizen and was knighted for his reportage of the conflict. Phillips remained with the British Expeditionary Forces headquarters throughout the war. He was with the Belgian army in 1914 and in 1918 accompanied the occupation forces into Germany.

In 1922, now known as Sir Percival Phillips, he joined the *Daily Telegraph* for the remaining fifteen years of his life. In the early 1930s he traveled through China as a roving correspondent before covering the Ethiopian War* of 1935–1936. He became ill while reporting from Tangier at the outset of the Spanish Civil War* in 1936. He returned to London, where he died the following year.

REFERENCES: Robert W. Desmond. *Windows on the World*. 1980; Robert W. Desmond. *Tides of War*. 1984; John Hohenberg. *Foreign Correspondence*. 1964.

Pickerell, James (b. 1936)

The photojournalist James Pickerell covered the Vietnam War* from 1963 to 1967. His pictures have appeared on the cover of *Newsweek* magazine and in other periodicals. His book *Vietnam in the Mud* (1967) chronicles the conflict from the level of the foot soldier. Beginning in 1967 he covered the White House and Congress and has gone on assignment to dozens of countries. Presently he reports the corporate scene.

REFERENCE: Frances Fralin, ed. *The Indelible Image*. 1985.

Picture Postcards

In 1869 the Austro-Hungarian Empire issued the first postal card. By 1873 the U.S. Post Office Department had begun issuing these cards to postmasters as a method for streamlining short communications between businesses. However, it was not until 1901 that the phrase "post cards" became legal in the United States, when postal regulations against the moniker were relaxed.

The golden age of picture postcards coincided with the 1910 Mexican Revolution and the subsequent American war preparedness efforts along the border. During this era entrepreneurial photographers captured the exploits of Pancho Villa, General "Black Jack" Pershing, the U.S. naval invasion of Veracruz, and the Mexican attack on Columbus, New Mexico. Thousands of inexperienced American troops were mobilized along the Rio Grande River. All of these events were depicted on postcards, many of them graphically violent in nature, which were bought by the participants as proof of their proximity to the action and mailed by the millions throughout the world. These picture postcards remain an underappreciated component of war photojournalism during this era.

The picture postcard boom was facilitated by the invention of a postcard printer in 1910 by the Rochester Optical Company, a subsidiary of Eastman Kodak. It was inexpensive at only $7.50, with a forty percent discount to professionals, since George Eastman realized the windfall he would reap through the sale of postcard-backed paper and processing chemicals. Among the most successful practitioners of this process were such giants as the International Film Service and the Max Stein Company. Smaller enterprises included the Mexican War Photo Postcard Company and Kavanaugh's War Postals. There were numerous one-man operations as well, including that of Walter H. Horne* of El Paso, who reported during 1916 producing five thousand cards a day.

REFERENCE: Paul J. Vanderwood and Frank N. Samponaro. *Border Fury*. 1988.

Pigott, John (?)

Pigott was the Reuters* correspondent with the Gordon relief expedition who broke the news of the death of the Victorian war hero. Pigott had a long career as a war correspondent prior to the Sudan expedition, having covered the Zulu, Afghan, Egyptian, and Burmese campaigns.

REFERENCE: Donald Read. *The Power of News*. 1992.

Pike, Albert T. (1809–1891)

Born in Boston, Massachusetts he arrived at Santa Fe in 1831. Between 1836 and 1844 he was the first reporter of the Arkansas Supreme Court. During the Mexican-American War* Pike covered the battle of Buena Vista for Little Rock's *Arkansas Advocate* while attached to the Arkansas volunteer cavalry as an officer. He helped raise what became known as the Little Rock Guards, which was then incorporated into the Arkansas cavalry regiment led by Colonel Archibald Yell. He wore many hats in his time; recognized as a poet, author, political journalist, and lawyer, the correspondent-poet returned to his law practice in Little Rock after the war. During the war he was often critical of what he regarded as incompetent leadership and made the mistake of sharing this with his readers back home. Much of his vitriol targeted Lieutenant Colonel Selden Roane. After Roane got wind of a particularly scathing piece, he challenged Pike to a duel near Fort Smith. They exchanged fire with neither one the worse for wear and both agreed that their honor had been satisfied. In later years he served in the American Civil War* as a Confederate brigadier general and was a well-known leader in the Scottish Rite of the Masonic Order. His nom de plume was "H. Von S." Prior to the publication of his three-column account of the battle, one of his poems titled "Buena Vista" appeared in the New York magazine *Spirit of the Times*.

REFERENCES: Tom Reilly. Wa*r with Mexico!: America's Reporters Cover the Battlefront*, Manley Witten, ed. 2010; Carl Moneyhon, "Albert Pike," *The Encyclopedia of Arkansas History and Culture*, online.

Pilger, John (b. 1939)

Born near Sydney, Australia, Pilger began his career in journalism as a copy boy in 1958. He has lived and worked for London newpspapers since the early 1960s. His long career as a journalist and filmmaker have been marked by controversy. As a witness to the assassination of Robert F. Kennedy in 1968, he has always claimed there was another gunman besides Sirhan Sirhan. As a war correspondent he has covered conflicts in Vietnam, Cambodia, Egypt, India, Bangladesh and Biafra. He has made more than sixty documentaries beginning in 1970 with his study of U.S. soldiers in Vietnam, *The Quiet Mutiny*. Pilger collaborated on the ITV film *Year Zero: The Silent Death of Cambodia* which eventually was used to raise more than four million pounds for Cambodian charities in the wake of the Khmer Rouge horrors under Pol Pot. One of the themes that underlies much of Pilger's reportage is a critique of American and Western

imperialism in regions such as Latin America and Southeast Asia. Nonetheless he has taken great risks in his investigative journalism in revealing some of the darkest moments of the twentieth century. His film *Death of a Nation: The Timor Conspiracy* covered the Indonesian occupation of East Timor since 1975 and contributed to the country's withdrawal from East Timor in 2000. He has won a number of awards and honorary degrees for his documentaries, many of them covering crimes against humanity. In the 1970s one of Pilger's critics, English writer Auberon Waugh, introduced the term "to pilger" which became shorthand for presenting information "in a sensationalist manner to reach a foregone conclusion." However, his supporters such as Noam Chomsky suggest the terms "pilger" and "pilgerise" were coined by "journalists furious about his incisive and courageous reporting."

REFERENCES: "John Pilger". *New Statesman.* http:www.newstatesman.com/writers/john_pilger. Retrieved 4/1/2010; Charles Nevin. "Captain Moonlight—in a word—," *The Independent*, 11.28/1993; Noam Chomsky, Chomsky Answers Guardian, 11/13/2005, zcommunications.org; The Films and Journalism of John Pilger, http://www.johnpilger.com.

Pinney, Roy (1911–2010)

Born Pinyehrae Schiffer to Polish immigrants on the Lower East Side of Manhattan, he changed his name at the age of eighteen. He is among the oldest survivors of the 500 war correspondents who covered the Normandy invasion in 1944, where he was wounded with shrapnel, while covering the invasion from Omaha Beach for *Liberty Magazine*. He would eventually give up war journalism for nature writing and photography in the 1970s and 1980s, but not before covering conflicts in Afghanistan, Guiana, Spanish Morocco, Colombia, the Philippines and South Africa. In 1973 he covered the Yom Kippur War from the Gaza Strip. Pinney wrote 24 books, mostly related to animals, spelunking and natural history.

REFERENCES: www.wikipedia.org/wiki/index. html?curid=3761256.

Politkovskaya, Anna (1958–2006)

The child of Soviet diplomats, Politkovskaya was born in New York City (other sources suggest Ukrainian), but was raised in Moscow and graduated from Moscow State University's school of journalism. Between 1981 and 1993 she worked as a reporter for *Izvestia* before moving on to a seven-year stint with the biweekly *Novaya Gazeta*. It was here that she honed her investigative skills that would bring her critical acclaim and lead to her early death. She rose to prominence with her award-winning work about Chechnya and life in Putin's Russia. As a special correspondent for Moscow's independent newspaper, *Novaya Gazeta*, she wrote extensively about human rights abuses by the Russian military during the seven years she covered the second Chechen War.

In 1999 she chronicled the Russian bombardment of an old people's home in Grozny, while helping evacuate its elderly inhabitants. Her books *A Dirty War* (2001) and *A Small Corner of Hell* (2003) are some of the best accounts of the war. During her career she was jailed, physically threatened, forced into exile, and even poisoned. In 2006 the Committee to Protect Journalists* named her "one of the world's top press freedom fighters of the past 25 years." She drew the ire of the Russian security apparatus for explaining the government's harassment of journalists attempting to cover the Chechen campaign and the bloody 2004 Beslan siege. Politkovskaya was on her way to cover the school siege when she became seriously ill aboard her flight after drinking tea that was allegedly tainted with some type of poison. In 2001 she was picked up by security agents and charged her with crossing into Chechnya without accreditation. She was jailed for three days, kept in a pit without food and water. Following her release she endured regular threats on her life and went so far as to flee to Vienna for safety. In 2001 she was recognized with the Amnesty International Global Award for Human Rights Journalism. In 2002 she clandestinely went back into Chechnya to catalogue allegations of human rights abuses. That same year she served as a mediator between the armed Chechen insurgents and Russian forces during the ill-starred Moscow theater standoff that left 129 hostages dead.

Her stinging criticism in word and print of President Putin and his security apparatus did little to endear her to the authorities, especially after the publication of *Putin's Russia* in 2004. Few were surprised when she was found dead from gunshots in the lift to her Moscow apartment on October 7, 2006, coincidentally Putin's birthday. She was shot three times in the upper body and once in the head at point blank range. Most observers believed members of the Russian Federal Security Service (FSB) played a role in her death. Although several Chechens have been sentenced to long prison sentences for the crime, no member of the FSB has been brought to account for the crime. In 2007 the human rights organization, Reach All Women in War (RAW in War), created the annual Anna Politkovskaya Award in her honor.

REFERENCE: "Anna Politkovskaya," https://cpj.org/killed/2006/anna-politkovskaya.php.

Polk, George (1913–1948)

Polk was a CBS correspondent who was assassinated in 1948 while attempting to reach insurgent leaders for an interview during the civil war in Greece. Beginning in 1949, the George Polk Award has been conferred annually to foreign correspondents in memory of the late Polk. The award is sponsored by Long Island University's Brooklyn Center and its Department of Journalism.

REFERENCES: Kati Marton. *The Polk Conspiracy*. 1990; Elias Vlanton and Zak Mettger, Who Killed Polk?, Temple University Press, 1996.

---

* Indicates a separate entry.

Pond, Elizabeth (?)

Pond studied international relations at Harvard before entering journalism. More interested in the political ramifications of the Vietnam conflict than the military aspects, Pond began covering the war for the *Christian Science Monitor* beginning in August 1967. Initially assigned to report on South Vietnamese politics, by 1968 she was writing about the rampant corruption in South Vietnamese government and the rise to power of Nguyen Van Thieu.

Following the 1970 American invasion of Cambodia, Pond decided to get a firsthand perspective of conditions in Cambodia herself. Driving with several correspondents on Highway 1 between Saigon and Phnom Penh they were taken prisoner. After five and a half weeks of being moved from village to village and rounds of interrogation they were released unharmed. Pond chronicled her experience in captivity in a five-part series for the *Monitor*. The journalists considered themselves exceedingly fortunate to have survived since twenty-nine journalists had been captured or were missing in Cambodia. She returned to the United States soon after this harrowing incident. Pond continued to cover world politics for the *Monitor*, reporting from South Korea and then Europe.

REFERENCE: Virginia Elwood-Akers. *Women War Correspondents in the Vietnam War, 1961–1975.* 1988.

Pooled Coverage

Following the almost unrestrained reporting that characterized coverage of the Vietnam War,* the Pentagon and officialdom have initiated a number of ploys to reduce the autonomy of war reporters. This went into full force during the brief military invasions of Grenada* (1983) and then Panama* (1989).* The Grenada invasion was the first Amercan military operation from which the Defense Department successfully excluded all journalists. Once these operations were concluded the press was given controlled access to the war front. "Pool coverage" was in-

troduced in which a system of supervised visits to military units were offered to small groups of correspondents. When the reporters returned from the front they were expected to share their information mostly provided by military officials, with the entire press corps. It is not surpising that this new form of censorship was opposed by the various press contingents. Others have suggested that the "pooled system" was necessary to accommodate such a large press corps during the Grenada invasion. In the aftermath of the 1991 Gulf conflict new ground rules were imposed on reporters favoring a principle of independent reporting and limiting the use of controlled pools.

REFERENCE: Charles P. Arnot. *Don't Kill the Messenger.* 1994.

Post, Robert Perkins (1910–1943)

A graduate of Harvard University, Post's family was apparently well connected and even knew President Franklin Roosevelt. During the 1930s Post was the *New York Times* White House correspondent before moving over to the London bureau in 1937. During the war years Post witnessed the Battle of Britain and in 1941 was one of the first to report the parachuting of Rudolf Hess into Scotland. Post died on the first and last voyage of the Writing 69th* perishing with eight others when his plane was blown out of the sky on a bombing run over Germany on February 26, 1943.

REFERENCES: Jim Hamilton. *The Writing 69th.* 2005; www.greenharbor.com/wr69/Biographies.html.

Posttraumatic Stress Disorder (PTSD) and War Journalists

First officially diagnosed and treated during World War I, it wasn't until the Vietnam War that PTSD entered the public consciousness as returning vets confronted complicated psychological trauma. It was around this time that the American Psychiatric Association's Diagnostic and Statistical Manual of Mental Disorders led to its official recognition. Formerly, PTSD was mostly diagnosed as a malady of combat veterans. However, in recent years more and more war correspondents and frontline reporters have been diagnosed with similar disorders. In books and articles written by soldiers and reporters, it is easy to see how in many respects, especially in combat they share similar experiences including psychological afflictions. Both have witnessed the terrible devastation of war, ranging from the remains of a suicide bomber to the deaths of young civilian noncombatants. Some have suggested that unlike traditional warfare in the past, that usually took place on the battlefield between two armies of identifiable combatants, today's battles are fought among the civilian population, in neighborhoods where there are no uniforms to distinguish the combatant from the noncombatant. In this environment, where the enemy can be anywhere, soldiers and reporters alike are under almost constant duress as they try and sort out the civilians from the insurgents. One psychiatrist has argued that the current conflicts "are the first in the history of modern warfare where combatants were sent back to the combat zone again and again." One reporter believes that the war correspondents most likely to suffer from PTSD are those that are "emotionally invested in the story." According to Dr. Anthony Feinstein,* a groundbreaking researcher in this arena, almost a third of "war journalists are at risk of developing PTSD during their careers."

REFERENCES: Adam McCauley, "Overexposed: A Photographer's War with PTSD," *The Atlantic*, Feb. 20, 2012; David J. Morris. *The Evil Hours: A Biography of Post-Traumatic Stress Disorder.* 2015; Elisa E. Bolton, "Journalists and PTSD," http://www.ptsd.va.gov/public/community/journalists-ptsd.asp.

Potter, Kent (1947–1971)

Born in Philadelphia, he began working as a photographer for United Press International in 1963. Five years later he was in Saigon reporting the Vietnam War.* In May 1969 he was promoted to UPI Newspictures manager for Vietnam. Potter is believed to be the youngest American war journalist killed in the Vietnam War, perishing in a Vietnamese helicopter crash over Laos.

REFERENCE: Charles P. Arnot. *Don't Kill the Messenger.* 1994.

Powell, E. Alexander (1879–1958)

Born in Syracuse, New York Edward Alexander Powell, the scion of a family of horse breeders, developed an early affinity for travel and adventure, which he would pursue in his vocation as travel writer and foreign correspondent. He was in Beligium when the First World War broke out and he caught on with the *New York World.* He was in Antwerp where he witnessed the first aerial bombing of a city during wartime during a Zeppelin attack on August 25, 1914. He made use of his connections to gain access to the frontlines in Belgium. Prior to America's entry into the war in 1916 Powell took advantage of his standing as a neutral to cover the early campaigns of the war and after observing the German entry into Antwerp set to writing his first book *Fighting in Flanders* (1914). He claimed to have finished the book in eleven days by dictating it to stenographers as he recuperated from injuries in a hospital. He continued to report throughout the war and published a number of books based on his war reporting including *Vive la France* (1915), *Italy at War* (1916), *Brothers in Arms* (1917) *The Army Behind the Army* (1917–18), and *Slanting Lines of Steel: Adventures of a War Correspondent.* Following the war his wanderlust took him from the Middle East and Africa through Central, Asia, India, and the Soviet Union.

REFERENCES: www.greatwardifferent.com/Great_War/E_Alexander_Powell.

Power, Frank Le Poer (1858–1884)

Born in Ireland, the son of a bank manager, Power was educated at Clongowes. He witnessed

---

warfare for the first time when he served in the Austro-Hungarian army and was besieged with Russian forces in Plevna. His first position as war correspondent was on the Bulgarian frontier during the Russo-Turkish War.* When he returned home he joined the staff of *Saunders's* in Dublin.

In 1883 he agreed to go the Sudan with Edmund O'Donovan* of the *Daily News,* with the idea of collaborating on a book on the Sudan. Power was also commissioned to make sketches for the *Pictorial World.* They accompanied the Hicks Pasha expedition into the Sudan along with British correspondent Frank Vizetelly.* Power had the good fortune to fall ill at the start of the journey and was returned to Khartoum for recuperation, thus saving his life. However, the Hicks expedition of almost ten thousand Egyptian soldiers and two British war correspondents was wiped out near El Obeid on November 5, 1883. When news reached Cairo of the disaster a month later Power provided the *Times* with the only firsthand account of events leading to the debacle.

In 1884 he would not be as fortunate. He was one of the two Britons cut off with British general Gordon in the besieged town of Khartoum. Power was entrusted by Gordon to drum up support in London for men and money to defeat the Mahdi. On April 1, a letter from special correspondent and now acting British consul Power appeared in the *Times* noting the dire straits of the garrison-the first authentic news of the critical situation in Khartoum. By the 16th telegraph lines had been cut and messages could only be smuggled out at great risk. Power's dispatches from Khartoum were instrumental in compelling the British government to launch a relief force up the Nile. After pressure from both the public and the press a relief effort was finally mounted led by General Garnet Wolseley. Unaware of the relief force, Power left Khartoum with a British officer attempting to run the Nile blockade and send out a message to Cairo, but both men were murdered on the way. Power and six other correspondents who died in the Sudan campaigns are commemorated by a tablet in St. Paul's Ca-

thedral which bears their names. Power's letters from the Sudan were collected and published in 1885 as *Letters from Khartoum.*

REFERENCES: Office of the *Times. The History of the "Times ": The Twentieth Century Test, 1884–1912.* 1947; Robert Wilkinson-Latham. *From Our Special Correspondent.* 1979; Oliver Woods and James Bishop. *The Story of the "Times."* 1983.

Press Association of the Confederate States

See CONFEDERATE PRESS ASSOCIATION.

Price, Byron (1891–1981)

Born in Topeka, Indiana, Price turned to journalism while still in college. Upon graduation from Wabash College in 1912 he went to work first for the United Press and then began his twenty-nine-year career with the Associated Press. He served in the army during World War I* and received several commendations for bravery.

Following the bombing of Pearl Harbor, Price was requested by President Roosevelt to organize and direct the government's Office of Censorship, with the goal of balancing wartime security with freedom of the press. In early 1942 he described press censorship as a "necessary evil" in wartime. Price agreed that some censorship was necessary, but as a professional journalist and advocate of press freedom he insisted that he should be responsible only to the president and that he should have a free hand in developing his agency's policies. In addition, he wanted the system of censorship to be for the most part voluntary, which meant convincing the nation's newspapers, magazines, and other media to police their own news sources. Roosevelt acceded to these requests and in 1942 the Office of Censorship was formally established with Price as its director.

Price's staff totaled over fourteen thousand employees, who were responsible for censoring all communications between the United States and Europe. The censorship office issued pamphlets setting guidelines for what war-related stories were fit to print. Emphasis was placed on the question "Is this information I would like to have if I were the enemy?" The censorship code worked well enough to keep secret the 1942 Allied invasion of Africa, the D-Day invasion, and the building of the atomic bomb. Its obvious targets included news leaks concerning troop movements and locations of important military installations.

When the war ended Price wasted no time in closing down the censorship office. Following word that the Japanese had surrendered on August 14, 1945, he received permission to close down the agency the next afternoon. After the war President Truman appointed him to investigate relations between the American occupation forces and the German populace. Price later served as vice president of the motion picture censorship board and held other offices connected with the movie industry. He was also an important figure in the moving of the United Nations headquarters to its current site.

REFERENCE: Frederick S. Voss. *Reporting the War.* 1994.

Price, George Ward (1895–1961)

Educated at Cambridge, Price was hired as a reporter for the *Daily Mail* while still a student. After covering the Balkan War he was stationed in Paris. During World War I* he covered the disastrous Dardanelles campaign and the Italian front, where he witnessed the Battle of Caporetto. After attending the Paris Peace Conference and subsequent meetings in Cannes and Genoa in 1922, he traveled widely for the paper. In 1933 he was with the French Foreign Legion during the Moroccan conflict. In the years leading up to World War II* he interviewed Hitler and Mussolini and covered the invasion of the Sudetenland. He was one of the earliest war reporters in France and covered the southeastern theater of the war in Europe. He went on to report the North African campaign and the Korean War.*

He wrote *Extra-Special Correspondent* in 1957.

REFERENCES: Robert W. Desmond. *Tides of War.* 1984; Dennis Griffiths, ed. *The Encyclopedia of the British Press.* 1992.

Price, Morgan Philips (1885–1973)

The great-grandson of a cofounder of the *Manchester Guardian*, Price covered the Russian front for the newspaper during World War I.* He was the only British correspondent with the Russian army on the eastern front when Czar Nicholas abdicated. By the time he arrived in Petrograd in 1917 he had become one of the best-informed correspondents covering events in Russia prior to the October Revolution. Price was not a newcomer to Russian affairs. His family had been importing lumber from there since the 1850s and Price had even learned the Russian language by 1910, when he joined a scientific expedition to Siberia.

In 1914 he was assigned to follow events in Russia for the *Guardian*. He subsequently reported much of the war and the Russian Revolution. Next to John Reed,* he was probably the foremost Russian correspondent of his era. Price and Reed were the only correspondents to witness the Bolshevik seizure of power, resulting in a news scoop for Price and the *Guardian*. But his greatest scoop came when he convinced Trotsky to allow him to print the secret treaties between the deposed Czar and the Allies. Price translated the document through the night. Among the most provocative plans was the Sykes-Picot agreement, which would have divided the Arab world among the Allies after World War 1. This treaty caused great embarrassment in England when it was published by the *Guardian* in November 1917.

Following the Russian withdrawal from the war effort in February 1918, Britain, Japan, France, and the United States organized an Allied expeditionary force to intervene in the Russian Revolution on the side of the Whites. Price was the only Western correspondent to report the intervention from the Russian side in a bid to counteract anti-Bolshevik reporting. In an attempt to

* Indicates a separate entry.

win the propaganda war, the Soviet Foreign Office printed fifty thousand copies of Price's pamphlet *The Truth About the Allied Intervention in Russia*, criticizing the British censor for blocking the publication of almost all of his dispatches since the Allied intervention. Price later reported from the Middle East, won a seat in Parliament, and continued to travel widely through the Balkans and the Soviet Union for the *Guardian*.

REFERENCES: David Ayerst. *The Manchester Guardian: Biography of a Newspaper*. 1971; Phillip Knightley. *The First Casualty*. 1975.

Prior, Melton (1845–1910)

Prior was born in London and attended various art schools before breaking into journalism as a print artist with the *Penny Miscellany* while still in his teens. He began his affiliation with the *Illustrated London News* in 1873 and served his first stint as war artist and correspondent covering Sir Garnet Wolseley's forces during the Ashanti War. For thirty years he covered the major wars and conflict between the Ashanti War and the 1904 Russo-Japanese War.*

In 1874 he recorded the events surrounding the Carlist uprising in Spain. Two years later he covered the Balkan conflicts, including the war between Serbia and Bulgaria, and the Russo-Turkish War,* and also accompanied Austrian forces during the Bosnian conflict. He witnessed many of the South African campaigns between 1877 and 1881, including the Kaffir, Basuto, and Zulu Wars. During the 1879 Zulu War Prior had a premonition of impending death, so he enlisted the services of another artist, who was killed on the march to Eshowe. Prior accompanied the burial detachment assigned to the field of Isandhlwana following the destruction of the British force there by Zulu forces. He covered the First Boer War through its conclusion at Majuba Hill on February 21, 1881.

In 1882 Prior accompanied English forces as they entered Cairo during the Arabi Revolt and two years later was with Baker Pasha's forces at the Battle of El Teb. In 1884–1885 Prior

followed Lord Wolseley's relief expedition up the Nile. He witnessed the Battle of Abu Klea while ensconced within the British square. After accompanying Sir Gerald Graham's forces in his 1885 Sudan campaign he was with Sir Frederick Roberts during the 1886–1887 Burma expedition. Between 1889 and 1892 he sketched revolutionary conflicts in Brazil, Argentina, and Venezuela. During the next eight years he covered frontline action in South Africa (1896), the Greco-Turkish War,* war on the North West Frontier of India, and the 1898 Cretan uprising. He was among the first correspondents to reach South Africa in 1899 during the resumption of hostilities and was with British force besieged at Ladysmith* between November 2, 1899, and February 28, 1900.

Following the Somaliland expedition in 1903 he covered his last war when war broke out between Russia and Japan in 1904. He accompanied Japanese forces under General Oku during the Liaotung Peninsula campaign. Prior reportedly spent only one year at home during his remarkable thirty-year career as war artist for the *Illustrated London News*. His life is commemorated by a tablet bearing his name in the crypt at St. Paul's Cathedral. He wrote *The Campaigns of a War Correspondent* (1912).

REFERENCES: *DNB*, 1901–1911; Robert Wilkinson-Latham. *From Our Special Correspondent*. 1979.

Price, Walter Crawfurd

See CRAWFURD-PRICE, WALTER.

Pulitzer Prize

During the nineteenth century Joseph Pulitzer exemplified the growing power of the press. His crusade against corruption and his ongoing rivalry with William Randolph Hearst* transformed newspaper business. He started the *New York World* and the *St. Louis Post-Dispatch*, two papers that "reshaped newspaper journalism." Named for Joseph Pulitzer, the first Pulitzer Prize was awarded in 1917. For a journalist, writer or photographer, winning the Pulitzer Prize has been compared to an actor or director winning an Academy Award. Some of the more notable recipients (for covering war zones either as writers or photographers) include Louis Lochner,* Laurence Allen,* Frank Noel,* Daniel DeLuce,* Joe Rosenthal,* Malcolm Browne,* Horst Faas,* Peter Arnett,* Eddie Adams,* Michel Laurent,* and Huynh Cong (Nick) Ut.* When he died in 1911, Joseph Pulitzer left funding in his will that allowed Columbia University to start a journalism school. The famed newspaperman is credited with launching a number of modern journalistic traditions and was among the first to argue for the training of journalists in college. The original Pulitzer Prizes were awards for journalism, letters, and drama, one for education, and four traveling scholarships. Today there are more than 20 different categories. The boost for one's career after winning a Pulitzer cannot be overstated, but this prestigious award has been controversial over the years; critics point out its propensity for being awarded to journalists from major newspapers such as *The New York Times* and *Washington Post,* and the fact that only articles published by U.S.-based newspapers (print or online) are eligible for consideration. The prize is given each year in April in an award ceremony by Columbia University's Graduate School of Journalism in New York City. Prospective winners must submit materials for consideration along with a $50 fee, and those award categories to be considered. Applicants can place their work in up to two categories.

REFERENCES: Doug Brinlee. "What is the Pulitzer Prize?" http://www.askdeb.com/books/pulitzer; J. Douglas Bates. *The Pulitzer Prize: The Inside Story of America's Most Prestigious Award.* 1991.

Pyle, Ernest "Ernie" Taylor (1900–1945)

The most popular reporter of World War II,* Pyle was born near Dana, Indiana. In 1923 he dropped out of Indiana University just short of graduation to begin his journalism career at the *La Porte Herald.* Shortly thereafter he became reporter for the Scripps Howard-owned *Washington Daily News.*

Pyle witnessed war for the first time in 1940, when he arrived in London to report the Battle of Britain. His columns, characterized by an understated humor, developed a following in the States. He quickly developed an affinity for the English and their culture as he reported the devastating raids by the Luftwaffe. From 1941 to 1942 he remained in the United States sorting out an increasingly troubled personal life just as his popularity was on the rise. Returning to wartime assignments he covered the training and minutiae of everyday life in the military. His meteoric rise to a household name in the States began in 1942 when he landed with American troops in North Africa. He covered the Tunisian front and was on hand for Field Marshal Erwin Rommel's rout of American troops at Kasserine Pass. In 1944 Pyle accompanied Allied forces to Normandy beach and then on to the liberation of Paris. That same year he won the Pulitzer Prize* for his war reports.

He returned to the States briefly before being persuaded by the navy to cover the Pacific war. Despite premonitions of his death he landed with marines on Okinawa. On April 17 he arrived on the tiny island of Ie Shima and the following day accompanied a patrol which came under sniper fire. Pyle was fatally wounded by three gunshots that went under his helmet, striking him in the left temple. Among his books are *Ernie Pyle in England,* a collection of his columns on the Battle of Britain, and *Here Is Your War,* an account of his experiences in the Tunisian campaign. Pyle's writings were unprecedented in the annals of war reportage in that they focused more on the individual combatants than on the leaders and their battle strategies. The 1945 movie *The Story of G.I. Joe* recounted his exploits in World War II. Pyle is buried at the National Memorial Cemetery near Honolulu.

REFERENCES: Lee G. Miller. *The Story of Ernie Pyle,* 1950; David Nichols, ed., *Ernie's War.* 1986.

Quiet American, The

Graham Greene's 1955 novel *The Quiet American* offers one of the most discerning portraits of a war reporter. Fowler, the narrator of the story, is in the tradition of British expatriates who go native in exotic locales, this time in Saigon as the United States looks to inherit France's colonial war against the Viet Minh. The "quiet American" referred to in the title is an intelligence agent named Pyle who leads a misguided campaign to establish a democratic alternative to Communism and colonialism. Fowler's dilemma is whether to expose the clandestine agitator who is supplying explosives to a terrorist group or to finger him for Communists who would undoubtedly kill him. The book was adapted to the big screen in the 1958 film of the same title.

REFERENCES: Howard Good. *Images of the War Correspondent in Anglo-American Fiction*. 1985; Graham Greene. *The Quiet American*. 1955.

Quin, Windham Thomas Wyndham (1841–1926)

Quin was born in Adare, Limerick County, Ireland, and educated in Rome and at Oxford University. He entered the military service in 1862, joining the First Life Guards as cornet. During his career in the military he exhibited a tendency toward wanderlust, taking several leaves of absence to report foreign wars, participate in steeplechase competition, and exercise his passion for sailing.

In 1867, he joined Sir Robert Napier's military expedition against Abyssinia as war correspondent for the *Daily Telegraph*. He witnessed the capitulation of Magdala. His dispatches appeared under "Mr. Adare." During the final advance on Magdala he showed Henry Stanley* of the *New York Herald* where hundreds of murdered prisoners were dumped. Quin also represented the *Telegraph* during the 1870 Franco-Prussian War.* In 1871 he won a seat in the House of Lords and traveled to the American West to hunt buffalo with frontiersmen Buffalo Bill and Texas Jack. Three years later he explored the Yellowstone region with Dr. George Henry Kingsley. Quin chronicled his exploits with Kingsley in *The Great Divide*, published in 1876. Over the next quarter century Quin, better known as the Earl of Dunraven, pursued sports and politics in equal measures. He is best remembered as a yachtsman and as a mediator in land reform legislation in Ireland.

REFERENCES: *DNB*, 1922–1930; Windham Thomas Quin, *Past Times and Pastimes*, 1922.

---

* Indicates a separate entry.

R

Raddatz, Martha (b. 1953)

Born in Idaho Falls, Idaho, Raddatz served as chief correspondent at the ABC News Boston affiliate before joining National Public radio in 1993, where she focused on foreign policy and defense issues. From 1993–1998 she covered the Pentagon and in 1999 became the ABC News State Department correspondent. For more than a decade she has covered conflict in the Middle East as well as crises in Africa, Pakistan, and India. She has traveled to war zones dozens of times, including more than 29 times to Iraq. She was on the last convoy to leave Iraq and the only television reporter permitted to cover a combat mission over Afghanistan in an F15 fighter jet. She covered the hunt for Abu Musab al-Zarqawi in Iraq and was the first correspondent to report his death in a U.S. airstrike north of Baghdad on June 8, 2006. In 2011 she reported exclusive details on the raid that killed Osama Bin Laden. Besides war zones, Raddatz has earned a stellar reputation over the past twenty years covering most aspects of American foreign policy. She wrote the 2007 *New York Times* bestseller, *The Long Road Home: A Story of War and Family*, chronicling the war in Sadr City, Iraq

REFERENCE: "Martha Raddatz," http://abcnews. go.com/Politics/print?id=127431.

Ralph, Julian (1853–1903)

Born to English parents in New York City, Ralph left school early to serve an apprenticeship with a small New Jersey newspaper, where he learned most facets of the newspaper business. After a failed attempt at launching his own paper he moved on to several others before finding employment with the newly created *New York Daily Graphic* in 1873. In 1875 his work came to the attention of Charles A. Dana of the *New York Sun,* where Ralph would be employed for the next two decades. During his career with the *Sun* he became one of the most highly respected reporters in the country, covering politics and major events including the end of the Molly Maguires, the funeral of Ulysses S. Grant (1885), the New York blizzard of 1888, and the trial of Lizzie Borden (1893).

Since the *Sun* did not give its writers a byline, not until 1890, when Ralph's articles began appearing in *Harper's Weekly* and *Harper's Monthly,* did he win a wider following and name recognition. During the 1890s several collections of his works were published, including *Our Great West* (1893) and *Dixie; or Southern Scenes and Sketches* (1895). He also wrote numerous works of fiction, short stories, and poetry.

In 1895 he left the *Sun* for Hearst's *Journal,* for which he reported his first wars. In 1897 he covered the Greco-Turkish War,* and in 1899 he went to South Africa to cover the Boer War* for the *London Daily Mail* and *Collier's* magazine. Along with his son Lester, who was an accomplished illustrator and journalist, he covered the major campaigns of Field Marshal Lord Roberts. He joined other British correspondents at

Indicates a separate entry.

Bloemfontein in editing the *Friend,* a daily newspaper for the army in the field. He saw his health decline during the war after he was wounded, thrown from a horse, and stricken with enteric fever. He returned to the States in 1902 and died after a long illness the following year.

REFERENCES: *DAB 8;* "Julian Ralph," *Outlook.* 240. January 31, 1903. Frank O'Brien. *The Story of the "Sun."* 1918.

Ranthom, John Revelstoke (1868–1923)

The Australian-born Ranthom accompanied British forces in the reconquest of the Sudan in 1898, the youngest journalist with the expedition. Following the Egyptian and Sudan campaigns he moved to the United States. He reported the Spanish-American War* for the *Chicago Herald* and then expeditions to New Guinea and Alaska. In 1910 he moved to Rhode Island as editor of the *Providence Journal.* His career as war correspondent effectively finished, Ranthom served stints with the Associated Press, the *Daily Telegraph,* and other periodicals during the last decade of his life.

REFERENCE: Robert W. Desmond. *The Information Process.* 1978.

Rather, Dan (b. 1931)

Born in Wharton, Texas, following graduation from Sam Houston State Teachers College Rather worked for the UPI and the *Houston Chronicle.* In the mid-1950s he entered the field of broadcast journalism with a CBS affiliate in Houston before rising to chief of CBS's southwestern bureau in Dallas in 1961. He was posted to London by CBS news in 1964, where he began a stint as foreign correspondent covering stories in Greece and India. In the fall of 1965 and early 1966 he requested reassignment to Saigon, spending the next several months covering the Vietnam War.* According to former Vietnam war correspondent William Prochnau, Rather's

adoption of safari jackets for his field reports made them "de rigeur for television," and in the process made the Saigon tailor who manufactured them wealthy overnight.

In 1966 Rather returned to Washington, D.C., and was designated to replace Harry Reasoner at the White House. In 1974 he was named anchorman-correspondent for *CBS Reports* and seven years later replaced Walter Cronkite* on the *CBS Evening News.*

REFERENCES: Gary Paul Gates. *Air Time: The Inside Story of CBS News.* 1978; William Prochnau. *Once upon a Distant War.* 1995.

Ray, Michele (b. 1938)

Born in Nice, France, Ray seemed an unlikely candidate for war reporter. A fashion model for the House of Chanel, Ray had a predisposition for adventure and risk taking. She had tried amateur racing and organized an all-women motor vehicle expedition from Alaska to Tierra del Fuego. Her account of the expedition was published in the French magazine *Elle.*

In 1966 Ray arrived in Vietnam without accreditation or a visa, but in no time became affiliated with the Agence France-Presse. She accompanied Green Berets on her first combat mission, which they dubbed "Operation Michele." In 1967 she became the news story when she was captured by the Viet Cong on the central coast. She was released after three weeks of Communist indoctrination. In high spirits and good health following her release, Ray was accused of staging her capture. She left the country not long after this incident.

REFERENCE: Virginia Elwood-Akers. *Women War Correspondents in the Vietnam War, 1961–1975.* 1988.

Raymond, Henry Jarvis (1820–1869)

Born near Lima, New York, Raymond is probably best remembered as the founder and editor of the *New York Times*. Reportedly able to read by the age of three, he graduated from the Genesee Wesleyan Seminary, later to be known as Syracuse University, and the University of Vermont.

In the early 1840s he entered journalism, working for Greeley's *New Yorker* and then the *New York Tribune*. He left for an editorship position with the *Morning Courier and New York Enquirer* in late 1843. After a short political career he became managing editor of the recently established *Harper's New Monthly Magazine* in 1850. In 1851, Raymond and two partners cofounded the *New York Daily Times*.

In 1857 he moved his family to Europe. Two years later Raymond, accompanied by *Times* correspondent William Johnston, traveled to Solferino in preparation for the looming battle during the Austro-Italian War.* They would be the only Americans to report the battle. Raymond wrote most of the dispatch, which was taken by courier to Paris, where Mrs. Raymond was to send it by steamer to New York. Although it was published over two weeks after the battle, well after other accounts had been published, his was the first eyewitness account printed in America.

During the American Civil War* Raymond again acted as war correspondent for his own paper. He was often at the front supervising the activities of his reporters while contributing coverage of his own. He has often been credited with inventing the display headline in 1865. Raymond was among the reporters at Bull Run who incorrectly reported a Union victory prior to the eventual outcome. He reported the Peninsular campaign and the Battle of Roanoke.

REFERENCE: J. Cutler Andrews. *The North Reports the Civil War*. 1955.

Rayner, Pendil Arthur (c. 1909–1943)

Born in Papua, New Guinea, Rayner was one of Australia's most prominent World War II* correspondents. He was killed on December 26, 1943 while on assignment in the South Pacific for the

Brisbane Telegraph. He began his journalism career with this paper in 1928 and at his death had reached the pinnacle of the profession. He was widely experienced in most phases of journalism and had taken voluntary military training prior to the conflict. He was accredited as a war correspondent with U.S. forces beginning in June 1942 and earned acclaim for his account of the Bismarck Sea battle during New Guinea operations. He also covered the American occupation of Kiriwana and the landing of paratroopers in the vicinity of Markham Valley. He accompanied Australian forces through the valley and reported their attack on the Japanese stronghold of Lae. He covered the beachhead landing at Arawe in New Britain and then returned home to Australia for a well-deserved rest. Rayner was with three Allied correspondents on a reconnaissance flight from Port Moresby to follow a U.S. Marine landing on Cape Gloucester in New Britain when their B-17 crashed.

REFERENCE: Doral Chenoweth, "-30-: A Gripping Account of 54 War Correspondents K.I.A. in WWII 1940–1945," http://www.54warcorrespondents-kia-30-ww2.com/chapter5.html.

Rea, George Bronson (1869–1936)

Born in Brooklyn, New York, and educated in private schools, he worked in Cuba as an engineer for five years prior to the Cuban War for Independence. He disagreed with the portrait drawn by the yellow press* of Spanish treatment of the Cubans. From 1895 on he blasted American press coverage of conditions in Cuba and wrote *Facts and Fakes About Cuba*, in an attempt to tell his side of the story. Rea had traveled widely through Cuba and reportedly found little evidence of Spanish atrocities.

In 1896 he was hired by the *Herald* to report rebel activity on the island. He spent the better part of nine months covering the insurrection with Generals Gomez and Maceo. However, in 1897 he became embroiled in an argument with the rebel leader General Gomez over an article

* *Indicates a separate entry.*

critical of the Cuban cause. After Gomez threatened to have him shot Rea left the island and returned to New York.

Rea returned to Cuba shortly before the Spanish-American War.* Unlike most of his colleagues, Rea was sympathetic to the Spanish side and not content to simply remain in Havana, basing his stories merely on interviews with rebel spokesmen. He was seated in a Havana cafe with Sylvester Scovel* of the *World* the night the *Maine* exploded. Rea was later assigned to study San Juan Harbor and its fortifications. He was with Cuban forces during the battle of El Caney.

Following the Spanish-American War, he settled in the Philippines, where he held several posts in the occupation government. In 1904 Rea founded the *Far Eastern Review* and during World War I* he was military attache to Spain. In 1918 he moved to Peking as advisor to the Chinese government. After a falling out over economic policy matters Rea left for a post in the Japanese puppet state of Manchukuo, a position which he admitted was "the kind of job I have always wanted. The whole world is agin [sic] me."

REFERENCES: Charles H. Brown. *The Correspondents' War.* 1967; Joyce Milton. *The Yellow Kids.* 1989; G.J.A. O'Toole. *The Spanish War.* 1984.

Reade, William Winwood (1838–1875)

Born in Oxfordshire and educated at Oxford, he first made his name as an explorer in West Africa in 1856. Reade returned to West Africa in 1871, and two years later covered the Ashanti War for the *Times*. He ended up participating in the action as well, fighting with the Forty-second Highlanders at the Battle of Amoaful and distinguishing himself at the Battle of Abakrampa, where he fought beside the Royal Navy and Marines, fending off hundreds of Ashanti warriors at a besieged church. Following his third expedition to Africa his health began to deteriorate. He died soon after returning to England. He wrote a number of books based on his experiences as an

explorer and war correspondent in West Africa, including *Savage Africa, a Tour* (1863); *The African Sketch-book,* two volumes (1873); and *The Story of the Ashantee Campaign* (1874).

REFERENCES: *DNB;* Robert Wilkinson-Latham. *From Our Special Correspondent.* 1979.

Redfern, John (1903–1990)

Born in Chesterfield, England, he began his journalism career with the *Derbyshire Times,* and worked for several other small papers before signing on with the *Daily Express* in 1934. As a war correspondent during World War II,* he covered the campaigns of the First and Eighth British armies in North Africa, Sicily, Italy, and northwestern Europe. Following the war he continued in his role as foreign correspondent for the *Express*. Based in Africa much of the time, he covered many of the independence movements there. He retired in 1968.

REFERENCES: Robert W. Desmond. *Tides of War.* 1984; Dennis Griffiths, ed. *The Encyclopedia of the British Press.* 1992.

Redkin, Mark (1908–1987)

Redkin was schooled in war journalism while working for the Russian army newspaper *Krasnaya Zvezda* prior to World War II.* During the Russian war he worked as a photojournalist for TASS and *Frontovaya Illustracia*. He covered most of the significant events of the war, including the fall of Berlin. Following the surrender of Germany he reported the war against Japan. After the war he worked for the Planeta publishing house in Moscow.

REFERENCE: Daniela Mrazkova and Vladimir Remes, eds. *The Russian War: 1941–1945.* 1975.

Redpath, James (1833–1891)

The Scottish-born Redpath moved to America at a young age. He developed an early affinity for newspaper writing, having published letters in the *New York Tribune* from the South before the outbreak of the American Civil War.* On one occasion he interviewed John Brown in Kansas. Some sources have described this as the first real newspaper "interview," or possibly the first use of the term "interview" to describe this method of news gathering. Redpath continued his affiliation with the *Tribune* throughout the war. He covered General Sherman's march through Georgia to the Atlantic coast in 1864 and the evacuation of Charleston in 1865. Following the war he established the Redpath Lyceum Bureau in Boston in 1868, supervising this organization for seven years. It is considered the first lecture bureau in the United States. He returned to the *Tribune* in 1879 and covered the controversial land question measures in Ireland for several years. He wrote several books, including *Echoes of Harpers Ferry* (1860), *The John Brown Invasion* (1860), *Life of John Brown* (1860), and *John Brown the Hero* (1862).

REFERENCES: J. Cutler Andrews. *The North Reports the Civil War.* 1955; Robert W. Desmond. *The Information Process.* 1978.

Reed, David (1927–1990)

Reed covered conflicts in Africa beginning in 1953. He reported the Mau Mau uprising in Kenya and in 1960 the independence movement in the Congo as a staff correspondent for *U.S. News and World Report.* His fluency in Swahili has led to interviews with important African statesmen, including Patrice Lumumba. He traveled widely throughout the continent in the 1960s before becoming foreign affairs editor for *Reader's Digest.* In the late 1960s he began covering the Vietnam War.*

REFERENCE: David Reed. *111 Days in Stanleyville.* 1965' Washington Post, Nov. 26, 1990.

Reed, John Silas (1887–1920)

Reed was born in Portland, Oregon, and educated at Harvard College. He entered journalism

with the *New York Globe* and then *the American* magazine. In 1913 he published a book of poetry about life in the artistic enclave of Greenwich Village and began to gravitate toward radical politics. That same year he briefly left mainstream journalism and joined the radical *Masses.* Soon after this he was hired by *Metropolitan* magazine and the *New York World* to cover the Mexican Revolution.

After making contact with the rebel forces of Pancho Villa, he accompanied them through four months of battles. His portrait of Villa softened the latter's image in the minds of the American public. His war reports and several essays written for the *Masses* were collected and published as *Insurgent Mexico* in 1914. He was promoted as "America's Kipling" by his employers, and his columns became a forum for his radical politics as he wrote sympathetically of the peon cause. He spent two tours covering World War I* beginning in 1914 for the *Metropolitan,* focusing on the daily life of the common soldier in the trenches and later writing *The War in Eastern Europe* (1916). During his second trip to cover the war he traveled from the Aegean coast through Serbia to Russia, and then back to Constantinople, Rumania, and Bulgaria. He was nearly executed by czarist soldiers in 1915 who thought he was a spy.

After he married the radical left journalist Louise Bryant in 1916, they went to Russia to cover the Bolshevik Revolution for the *Masses* and other socialist journals. Returning to the United States to successfully fight a sedition charge, he went on the lecture circuit, describing the revolution and arguing against American participation in World War I.* His involvement in radical politics led to several arrests and the publication of his most noted work and the best eyewitness account of the revolution, *Ten Days That Shook the World* (1919). He fled the United States for Russia to avoid facing federal charges for subversion, and immersed himself in the revolution. He died in Moscow of typhus, and was buried in the Kremlin on October 19, 1920, the

Indicates a separate entry.

first American so honored. Reed was the greatest radical journalist of his time. *Reds* a 1981 movie directed by and starring Warren Beatty, was based on Reed's Russian experiences.

REFERENCES: *DAB* 15, 450–451; Granville Hicks. *John Reed: The Making of a Revolutionary.* 1930; Tamara Hovey. *John Reed: Witness to Revolution.* 1975.

Reid, Samuel Chester, Jr.
(1818–1897)

The son of a prominent sea captain, Reid went to sea as a merchant sailor while still in his teens. He studied law in Mississippi, spent a term as U.S. Marshal, and served with the Texas Rangers during the Mexican War.*

Reid became one of the best-known and best-paid special correspondents covering the Confederacy during the American Civil War.* His weekly pay as a war correspondent for the *New Orleans Picayune* in 1862 began at twenty five dollars per week. By the end of the following year he was receiving four times that amount from the *Mobile Tribune*. In addition he was given a feed allowance for his horse. According to one source, over a thirty-month period he earned almost twelve thousand dollars from various newspapers. Reid counted the *Memphis Appeal*, the *Mobile Register*, the *Montgomery Advertiser*, and the *Atlanta Intelligencer* as employers during the war.

Reid accompanied Albert Sidney Johnston's army on its march to Pittsburg Landing and reported the Battle of Shiloh in April 1862. When Union forces captured New Orleans Reid joined fellow reporter Henry Perry* and joined the staff of the *Memphis Appeal*. Soon afterward Reid became the special correspondent for the *Mobile Register* when Peter Alexander* resigned. Reid was vilified by his fellow correspondents when he was accused of breaching security with a dispatch. The matter led to a crackdown on press coverage during the evacuation of Corinth.

In 1862 Reid interviewed President Jefferson Davis and covered the Richmond scene. He arrived in Chattanooga just as federal troops began their bombardment of the city. In November he covered the Battle of Perryville and the following January the Battle of Murfreesboro for the *Richmond Examiner*. When he attempted to telegraph his account of the battle to the *Mobile Register*, General Braxton Bragg refused permission, sensitive about critical press reports concerning his decisions. In retaliation Reid omitted Bragg's name from his battle account when he mailed it to the paper the next day. However, Reid provided the best account of the battle from the Southern point of view.

Reid was in Charleston, South Carolina, during the 1863 siege. In June he reported the Battle of Chancellorsville from Virginia and then traveled to Chattanooga to accompany the Army of Tennessee. He resigned from the *Mobile Register* in April over disagreements with the editors concerning military policy, and joined the competing *Mobile Daily Tribune*. Although he did not personally witness the Battle of Chickamauga, his elaborate recounting of the battle was reportedly the most complete Confederate newspaper account. He worked for two weeks on his ten-thousand-word account, and it was published in pamphlet form as *Great Battle of Chickamauga* at Mobile in November 1863.

By October Reid was also representing the *Atlanta Intelligencer* at the Battle of Lookout Mountain and during the Battles of Chattanooga. Reid followed Joseph Johnston's army at the beginning of the Atlanta campaign but missed most of the fighting. Reid faced increasing restrictions as military censorship became more intense with each Confederate loss. Having fallen ill the day before the Battle of Kennesaw Mountain, Reid was disabled back in Atlanta; however, he did manage to return shortly after its denouement to gather enough information to file a report. By late 1864, Reid was confined to bed in Charleston with rheumatism and his career as a Civil War special correspondent had come to a close.

REFERENCE: J. Cutler Andrews. *The South Reports the Civil War.* 1970.

Reid, Whitelaw (1837–1912)

Reid reported the American Civil War* for the *Cincinnati Gazette* beginning in 1861 when he was assigned to follow Ohio's troops under the command of George B. McClellan. In a series of dispatches under the pseudonym "Agate," Reid detailed the camp life of the fledgling Union Army in all its monotony and squalor.

During his tenure with the Union forces, Reid, as aide-de-camp to McClellan, was permitted full access to the generals or any other staff members he wished to accompany. He reported his first battle in July at Rich Mountain, Virginia, where Confederates under the command of General Robert Seldon Garnett were routed by federal troops. Later, at Carricks' Ford, Reid witnessed for the first time soldiers dying in battle, as Union forces caught up with Garnett's fleeing troops. Despite Garnett's death in the battle, most of the Confederate forces were allowed to slip away. In his reportage of the battle Reid blamed McClellan for failing to destroy the enemy when they were within his grasp. Reid's accounts of McClellan's ineptitude foreshadowed the general's reputation for hesitancy and caution that would cost him his command of the Army of the Potomac.

After a brief respite back in Ohio, Reid resumed his position as war correspondent, this time joining William Rosecrans's staff at Clarksburg, Virginia. In 1862 Reid honed his skills while covering the bloodshed at Carnifex Ferry. Again his reportage was laced with scathing criticism of the federal leadership. His penchant for critiquing the Union war effort, from its leadership to the inadequacy of medical care and defective ammunition, led to his banishment from Camp Nevin, where he was stationed between battles.

Shortly after returning to Cincinnati, Reid was dispatched to the western theater, where he witnessed the Battles of Fort Donelson and Fort Henry, both successful actions led by Brigadier General Ulysses S. Grant. Reid resumed his letters to the *Gazette* under his pen name Agate. His trenchant coverage of every aspect of the army's activities portrayed a much more positive appraisal of federal efforts than the year before. In April 1862 he produced what became the classic newspaper account of the Battle of Shiloh. With his reputation made by his nineteen-thousand-word account of this Union debacle, Reid had earned a national reputation as his war reporting was reprinted throughout America.

After Shiloh the *Gazette* sent him to cover the tumult of Washington, D.C. In 1863 Reid witnessed bloodshed for the last time at the Battle of Gettysburg before embarking on the next stage of his journalistic career reporting military affairs from his headquarters in the nation's capital. Besides his war reports, Whitelaw Reid wrote many books, including *Ohio in the War: Her Statesmen, Her Generals, and Soldiers,* two volumes (1868). He died in London after a successful career in journalism which included owning the *New York Tribune* from 1872 to 1912.

REFERENCES: Royal Cortissoz. *The Life of Whitelaw Reid,* 2 vols. 1921; Bingham Duncan. *Whitelaw Reid: Journalist, Politician, Diplomat.* 1975.

Reisner, Georg (1911–1940)

Born in Breslau, Germany, he graduated from the *Gymnasium* in Breslau before studying law and medicine at universities in Breslau and Freiburg. Because of his affiliation with the Socialist Party, he had to cut short his studies and flee to France when Hitler came to power. He took up photography in Paris and began freelancing in 1934. He reported the Spanish Civil War* from 1936 to 1937. *Life* published some of his work in the early phases of the developing war in Europe. In 1939 he was arrested and jailed by the French,

---

* Indicates a separate entry.

but managed to escape. He fled to Marseille, where he committed suicide rather than face internment in a French concentration camp.

REFERENCE: Turner Browne and Elaine Partnow. *Photographic Artists and Innovators.* 1983.

Remington, Frederic Sackrider (1861–1909)

Born in Canton, New York, Remington had a career as a writer, illustrator, and painter of the American West that overshadowed his short career as a war correspondent. Son of an American Civil War* cavalry officer and newspaper publisher, he fared poorly at school, necessitating a three-year stint at various military schools. In 1878 he entered the Yale School for Fine Arts in preparation for a painting career. He dropped out the following year, but not before selling his first illustration. He toiled unsuccessfully at a succession of jobs before taking his first trip West in 1881. Consequent to the trip, *Harper's Weekly* published one of his cowboy sketches that same year. Remington tried his hand at various western livelihoods, only to find that he disliked ranching, and that he could make a good income as an investor in a saloon. In 1886, he was hired by *Harper's Weekly* and assigned to the Southwest. The 1880s saw him increasingly successful as an artist as his illustrations appeared for two years in *Harper's* as well as in Theodore Roosevelt's *Ranch Life and the Hunting Trail.*

Remington was never merely an artist, for he possessed considerable literary ability as well. During the late 1880s and into the 1890s he followed the last days of the Indian-fighting cavalry in the West. He covered the developing Indian problems at the Sioux reservation at Pine Ridge, South Dakota, in 1890 for *Harper's*, which published one of his drawings of the ghost dance ceremony. When the bloodshed at Wounded Knee occurred on October 29, 1890, Remington was fifty miles away, although he filed his story of the event as if he had witnessed the actual story.

Known for his attention to detail, Remington the artist and painter spent parts of two decades covering the military in the Southwest, and like most reporters he developed a close camaraderie with the soldiers. However, this did not keep him from castigating the Indian management system under the Department of the Interior in his columns for *Harper's.*

Remington had always wanted to test his mettle as a war correspondent. Although he hoped to cover some monumental campaign in Europe, his opportunity came instead in 1896 when Hearst sent him and Richard Harding Davis* to Cuba for the *New York Journal.* Remington was assigned to illustrate the reports of Davis, but the two correspondents proved ill suited for working together as they searched fruitlessly for the Cuban resistance leader General Gomez. When their search for the colonial rebellion and the elusive Gomez proved futile, Hearst supposedly responded, "You furnish the pictures and I'll furnish the war." Remington resolved to return home to the States. When the battleship *Maine* was sunk mysteriously in Havana Harbor Hearst and Remington had their war. Once in Cuba, the rotund reporter quickly became unpopular with the rank and file as he ate more than his share of the limited rations. One account reported that Remington had "a jovial way of going up and joining messes," after which he ate messmates "out of house and home." Officers, on the other hand, were put off by his consumption of more than his share of the dwindling liquor supply. He eventually managed to witness actual combat at the Battle of San Juan Hill,* although his view of the fight was from a thousand yards in the rear, where he hid from snipers' bullets in a brush-covered hollow. As the American flag was raised on top of the hill, Remington finally left his sanctuary in the thick brush to join them. In the end Remington was disappointed in his "great war," a precursor of the jungle wars of the twentieth century. Hoping to record the frontline spectacle like Richard Harding Davis, Remington instead became the "chronicler of the battle's rear." Ill suited physically and temperamentally for on-the-spot war reportage, Remington was a dismal failure as a war correspondent, and the Spanish-American War* would be his last to cover.

REFERENCES: Douglas Allen. *Frederic Remington and the Spanish American War.* 1971; Douglas C. Jones. "Remington Reports from Badlands: The Artist as War Correspondent," *Journalism Quarterly.* Winter 1970; Peggy and Harold Samuels. *Frederic Remington: A Biography.* 1982.

Repington, Colonel Charles a Court (1858–1925)

Repington was appointed the military correspondent* of the *Times* on January 1, 1905. Educated at Eton and Sandhurst, by the age of forty-six he had established a reputation as a serious student of military literature. He served as an officer in the Omdurman campaign and in the Boer War* before resigning from the army in 1902 due to an indiscretion. His first posting as a war reporter was with the *Morning Post* before joining the *Times* in time for the Russo-Japanese War.* Under the customary heading "From Our Military Correspondent" his articles became an instant success. His classic reporting of this conflict was revised and republished as *The War in the Far East: 1904–1905* (1905).

No attempt was made to define his capacity as war correspondent for the *Times* until the conclusion of the Russo-Japanese War. He was assigned the role of critic of the British military establishment and became an ardent advocate of continental intervention and an end to British isolation in the years preceding World War I.* Repington concluded that if Britain intended to hang onto India it would be necessary to become a continental power and maintain a continental army. Most of his theorizing on military reform was meant to thwart Russian expansion. His views underwent revision in 1906 as he concentrated his editorializing on the Franco-German military situation and sending British forces to France in the event of war with Germany. His

other works included *The First World War* (1920) and *After the War* (1922).

REFERENCES: Office of the *Times. The History of the "Times": The Twentieth Century Test, 1884–1912.* 1947; Charles a Court Repington. *The War in the Far East.* 1905.

Reporters Instructed in Saving Colleagues (RISC)

The stated mission of RISC is to provide "first aid training free of cost to freelance journalists working in all media—photography, print, and broadcast—to help mitigate the many physical threats they face in the field." It was founded by Sebastian Junger* and Tim Hetherington.* The stimulus for creating this organization was the wounding and death of photographer Hetherington while covering the Libyan conflict in 2011. By most accounts his wounds were indeed life threatening, but his death might have been averted if any of the journalists with him were trained in life-saving techniques during what was a short drive to a hospital. More than 400 untrained freelance conflict journalists applied for RISC's first medical training in April 2012. Between 2012 and 2014 almost 200 journalists took the course, including 70 in 2014 alone. According to the RISC website the ages of participants have ranged from 17–19 to 50–58 years old. While more than 30 nationalities have taken the training, the majority came from the United States. Of the 7 major forms of journalism, more than half the trainees were photographers. In 2014, the total cost of training in New York City was $971, for four days of training, eight hours each day. This seems a bargain when the actual costs for training each journalist is itemized at $23,296. In 2014 courses were also given in Kosovo and Nairobi, Kenya. RISC remains "the only nonprofit devoted exclusively to training" freelance combat reporters. It remains dependent on fundraising and charitable contributions.

REFERENCE: Sebastian Junger, "RISC 2015: A Year in Review," http://risctraining.org/annual-report/2014.

Indicates a separate entry.

Restrepo

Restrepo was an outpost where Sebastian Junger* was embedded, and was named for the combat medic Pfc. Juan Restrepo who was killed in action there. Junger and British photographer Tim Hetherington* made this Oscar-nominated film about an American platoon's 15-month deployment in Afghanistan's deadly Korengal Valley. Both were on assignment for *Vanity Fair*, hence the film was made from video recorded to chronicle their experience. This film is distinguished by its nonpartisan nature and the avoidance of interviewing high- ranking generals, instead relying on the daily lives of the soldiers on the frontlines. It was nominated for the 2011 Academy Award for Best Documentary.

REFERENCE: David Carr, "Valley of Death: One Platoon's Tour of Duty," New York Times, June 16, 2010.

Reuters

This London-based international news agency was created in 1851 by Julius Reuter. Its heyday was the late nineteenth century, as Britain's imperial power was fading. Reuters correspondents based in Cairo accompanied the British relief column to rescue General Charles Gordon at Khartoum. While the fall of Khartoum was reported by official news sources, the fate of Gordon was unknown. On February 9, 1885, Reuters correspondent John Pigott* telegraphed the news scoop that Gordon had been killed.

During the African campaigns Reuters served the dual function of not only providing news from the British army but also relaying news to the army. In 1885 the Cairo office contributed to the morale of the desert-bound troops by providing daily telegraphic news summaries free of charge addressed to the "Army up the Nile." This tradition was continued until after World War II.*

Typically, whenever a war broke out, Reuters would appoint several correspondents who were given detailed instructions. William Wallace,

who covered the 1896 Niger-Sudan campaign, was to follow a protocol in which he was required to file daily reports of fifty words.

During the Greco-Turkish War* of 1897 Reuters correspondents reported from both sides of the battlefields. Among the reporters in action were Howell Arthur Gwynne,* who covered the Turkish army, and Kinnaird Rose, who was with the Greeks. Gwynne was in charge of Reuters correspondents during the Boer War.* Censorship restrictions required reporters to write all messages in English, eschewing codes, ciphers, and other languages. The agency's greatest coup during the conflict was its scoop of the relief of Mafeking.*

Reuters' next scoop occured during the 1904 war in Tibet. It was a traditional method for Reuters representatives to establish a good working relationship with high officials. So when correspondent Henry Newman arrived at Lhasa, he did just that. While normal protocol required that war correspondents wait until two hours after the official dispatches had been communicated to deliver their own telegraphic accounts, Newman was permitted to send his account of the Battle of Guru Younghusband prior to the official communique, giving Reuters a two-hour beat on the story.

With the outbreak of World War I,* Reuters correspondents were dispatched to every front in which British or German forces were in action. The first correspondents attached to British forces in Flanders were assigned to headquarters and except for infrequent visits to the battlefront were generally barred from witnessing the action. Five correspondents were eventually allowed to report from the British front in France. Most newspapers were not represented at the front and relied heavily on the dispatches from Reuters.

During World War I Reuters correspondents were required to pay their way with the British army, supplying their own food, transport, and accommodations. If they were offered a military rank or position, correspondents generally refused, afraid it could compromise their integrity. Reporters were expected to file separate reports each day for both editions of the news.

Prior to World War II, war correspondents from Reuters covered the Ethiopian War* of 1935 and the Spanish Civil War.* Eight full-time reporters plus assorted stringers* covered both sides of the African conflict, while only four reported from Spain. Dick Sheepshanks reported both conflicts and was killed with three other correspondents when a shell shattered a car in which they were sitting on the last day of 1937. The only survivor was the future Soviet spy Harold Philby,* then reporting for the *Times.*

During World War II five Reuters war correspondents were killed while reporting and another eight staff members died as members of the armed forces. Some of Reuters' best coverage of the war came from the European war at sea. Arthur Oakeshott participated in numerous convoys to Russia, and John Nixon covered the pursuit of the German battleship *Bismarck* and the sinking of the British battle cruiser *Hood.* Often scooped by the better-represented and better-capitalized UP and AP, Reuters was unsurpassed in its coverage of the eastern front between Germany and Russia. Harold King was the outstanding Reuters reporter in this theater.

In preparation for D-Day, the news agency began recruiting more journalists beginning in 1943. Among the most notable was Doon Campbell,* who had been rejected from military service because he wore a prosthetic device due to a birth defect. Campbell would be the youngest war correspondent at Normandy beach. In September 1944, Jack Smyth landed with paratroopers in the ill-fated Arnhem landings. He was eventually wounded, captured, and brutally interrogated by the Gestapo. Among Reuters' scoops during the war were Gestapo chief Heinrich Himmler's offer to surrender to the Allies and the suicide of Goebbels.

REFERENCE: Donald Read. *The Power of News.* 1992.

Reynolds, Quentin (1902–1965)

He was born in the Bronx, New York, and educated at Brown University. After studying law at Brooklyn Law School he opted for a career in journalism, joining the *New York World-Telegram* in 1928. Due to cost cutting he lost his job in 1932 but was hired by the International News Service. He left the news service to report World War II* for *Collier's,* an affiliation that would last until 1949. He rose to the top of the profession in England with his reporting of the Battle of Britain. In 1942 he accompanied Allied forces during Operation Jubilee, which was an attempt to test German defenses along the French coast and to destroy strategic installations. That same year he reported the North African desert campaign. In 1943 he reported the Sicilian campaign and later the Dieppe raid, the fall of France, and the Russian war.

In 1949 he was embroiled in a libel suit with columnist Westbrook Pegler. Following a Reynolds book review in which he implied that Heywood Broun* died as a result of his stressful relationship with Pegler, the columnist wrote a series of columns charging Reynolds with having been an absentee war correspondent, a war profiteer, and a scoundrel. In the resulting fray *Collier's* fired Reynolds. His career in shambles, having in quick order lost his television and radio jobs and any lecture opportunities, he sued Pegler, and in 1954 a jury awarded the former war correspondent $175,000 in punitive damages, a record at that time for a libel judgement.

Reynolds was a prolific writer of books and news articles. His admitted lack of research led to his involvement in a hoax that was a minor literary sensation in 1952. His book on George DuPre, who claimed to have worked as a British agent during the war, and a subsequent article based on his exploits for *Reader's Digest* damaged his credibility when it emerged that DuPre was a poseur. In response, his supportive editor at Random House, Bennett Cerf, simply promoted his book as a work of fiction instead.

* Indicates a separate entry.

He wrote numerous books, including *Convoy, London Diary, Dieppe: The Story of a Raid, The Curtain Rises,* and the best-selling *The Wounded Don't Cry* (1941). In 1965 he died after a short bout with abdominal cancer.

REFERENCES: Robert W. Desmond. *Tides of War.* 1984; *DAB 7;* Quentin Reynolds. *By Quentin Reynolds.* 1963.

Riboud, Marc (b. 1923)

Born in Lyons, France, he studied engineering in college and was self-taught in photography. During World War II* he served in the French resistance and the Free French army. Since 1953 he has been a freelance photographer and photojournalist and a member of Magnum Photos, Inc. In 1971 he was present when a Bangladeshi official publicly bayonetted four Bengali prisoners to death, probably for the benefit of Western journalists who were present. Riboud was among the few cameramen who refused to photograph the executions. He covered the Vietnam War* and in 1968 went to Hanoi, where he took the pictures for his book *Face of North Vietnam* (1970).

REFERENCE: Jorge Lewinski. *The Camera at War.* 1978.

Rich, Jr., John Hubbard (1917–2014)

Born near Cape Elizabeth, Maine and educated at Bowdoin College, where he edited the school newspaper, Rich began his journalism career with the *Kennebec Journal* in Augusta. He started his service as a war journalist with the *Portland Press Herald* before the United States entered World War II* by interviewing the survivors of the USS *Reuben James,* the first U.S. ship sunk in the war; and this was five weeks prior to Pearl Harbor. He was commissioned a major in the U.S. Marines and learned Japanese at the Navy Language School. He took part in four battle landings in the Pacific, including Kwajalein, Saipan, Tinian, and Iwo Jima, picking up a Bronze Star in the process. Following the war he began working for Hearst's International News Service (INS), going on to interview General Douglas MacArthur and accompany Emperor Hirohito and his American lawyer as an interpreter. He also covered the fall of Shanghai following the Chinese Civil War, barely escaping the Communist victors aboard a fleeing U.S. gunboat. Rich covered the International War Crimes Tribunal in Tokyo and interviewed "Tokyo Rose." Barely a week after the North Korean invasion of South Korea, Rich left Japan for Pusan with an American artillery division, covering the Korean War* for the next three years, broadcasting the signing of the armistice in 1953 for NBC. He went on to cover the French war in Indochina and the 1955 Argentine Revolution, where he made the first radio broadcast from Mendoza's revolutionary headquarters. Rich chronicled the violent uprising in the Belgian Congo during the era of Patrice Lumumba and the events of the Cold War and covered the Vietnam War* for a decade. He was a recipient of the Peabody Award for his photojournalism in 1950 during the Korean conflict.

REFERENCE: "John Hubbard Rich, Jr., Obituary," Portland Press Herald, Apr. 12, 2014.

Richardson, Albert Deane (1833–1869)

Born in Massachusetts, Richardson worked for several newspapers in Pittsburgh and Cincinnati before joining the *Boston Journal* to cover the sectional conflict in Kansas. During the American Civil War* Deane became the chief correspondent in the West for the *New York Tribune.* Adventurous and self-assured, he risked being hanged as a spy to travel through the South as a secret correspondent for the *Tribune* in 1861.

Richardson accompanied Hooker's forces at the Battle of Antietam and at the Battle of Vicksburg he attempted to run the Confederate batteries aboard a hay barge with fellow *Tribune* correspondent Junius Henri Browne* when the barge was hit by enemy gunfire, killing the captain and three crew members. Richardson and Browne survived but were captured and imprisoned in the military prison at Salisbury, North Carolina. The following year the intrepid correspondents escaped. After a daring four-hundred-mile, four-week journey through the Blue Ridge Mountains they reached Knoxville, Tennessee.

He wrote several successful books about his Civil War exploits, including *Secret Service: The Field, the Dungeon and the Escape* (1865), *Beyond the Mississippi* (1866), and *Personal History of U.S. Grant* (1868). Richardson met a tragic end shortly after his engagement to the recently divorced Abby Sage McFarland on November 25, 1869, when her ex-husband fatally shot him at his desk in the *Tribune* office. Richardson and McFarland were wed in a deathbed ceremony by Henry Ward Beecher.

REFERENCES: J. Cutler Andrews. *The North Reports the* Civil War. 1955; Stewart Sifakis. *Who Was Who in the Civil War.* 1988.

Richardson, David (1916–2005)

In 1940, shortly after receiving his journalism degree from Indiana University, Richardson joined the *New York Herald Tribune.* With the outbreak of war in 1941 he was inducted into the army. In 1942 he began covering World War II* for *Yank,** a weekly news magazine the army published for its enlisted soldiers, notable for its lack of editorial restraints.

During the war he accompanied General Douglas MacArthur's Southwest Pacific forces and participated in or witnessed almost every phase of jungle warfare. He reported the Battle of Buna on New Guinea in 1942, and unhappy with his position as a passive observer, he volunteered as waist gunner on a B-24 and participated in combat against Japanese Zero fighters over the Solomon Islands. Later he transferred to a PT boat, where he learned to handle a Browning automatic rifle. Richardson would also parachute behind Japanese lines in Burma with an Office of Strategic Service team

and spent five months attached to the elite force Merrill's Marauders. He covered the siege of the Burmese city of Bahmo. As a homage to American fighting forces none of his dispatches were written in the first person. Richardson was one of the most decorated soldier correspondents of the war, receiving seven battle stars, the Legion of Merit, the Bronze Star, Combat Infantryman's Badge, and several others. Following the war he went on to a distinguished half-century career in journalism.

REFERENCES: Bob Tutt. "Combat Reporter with True Grit," *Houston Chronicle.* August 15, 1993; Art Weithas. *Close to Glory.* 1991; Washington Post, January 30, 2005.

Rider-Rider, William (1889–1979)

As of 1978 he was reportedly the only World War I* photographer still alive. He went to work for the *Daily Mirror* in 1910. Due to poor vision he was drafted relatively late in the war. After serving a stint as a bayonet instructor he was transferred to the Canadian army and accredited as their only official photographer in the French theater of the war. Promoted to lieutenant, he was given freedom along the entire Canadian sector near Vimy Ridge. He photographed the attack on Hill 70, the Passchendaele debacle, and the final stages of the conflict.

Rider-Rider took almost four thousand pictures during the war, which were printed and developed in a field darkroom and then sent to censorship headquarters and forwarded to London for distribution by the Central Agency. Following the war he somehow managed to find most of his plates and return them to Canada, where they reside in the Public Archives.

REFERENCE: Jorge Lewinski. *The Camera at War.* 1978.

Ridley, Yvonne (b. 1959)

A native of Durham County, England. Ridley works for the Iranian-based English language news, Press TV. Ridley rose to international

Indicates a separate entry.

prominence when she was captured by the Taliban in September 2001 while covering post-9/11 Afghanistan for the *Sunday Express*. After being refused entrance into the country she crossed illegally, disguised in a burqa (following the lead of BBC reporter John Simpson*). She was released on "humanitarian grounds" the following month. Intrigued by Islam during her captivity, two years later she converted and since has become a supporter of Islamic issues. Ridley chronicled her captivity in the 2003 book *In the Hands of the Taliban: Her Extraordinary Story*. That same year she began working for Al Jazeera and helped inaugurate the English-language incarnation of its website. She was fired for insubordination soon after. More recently Ridley has worked in various capacities for the Iranian English language news channel Press TV. Meanwhile she has covered the Palestinian-Israeli conflict from Gaza.

REFERENCES: Gil Swain. "The Women in the War Zone. *The Independent*, October 2, 2001; Yvonne Ridley. *In the Hands of the Taliban*. 2003.

Rinehart, Mary Roberts (1876–1958)

The best-selling American mystery novelist was born in Allegheny, Pennsylvania. In 1914 she volunteered to assist the Allied field hospitals for the Red Cross during World War I.* Reporting from the Belgian front, she was unable to corroborate stories of German atrocities. The *Saturday Evening Post* refused to run her cabled report that the Germans used poison gas against Allied troops for fear of its impact on public opinion and the possibility of drawing America into the war.

REFERENCE: Charlotte McLeod. *Had She But Known*. 1994.

Riordan, Bartholomew (1839–1897)

Born in Virginia, after graduating from Mount St. Mary's College he began his journalism career in the nation's capital with the *Washington Union*. However, he quickly realized he wasn't cut out for a traditional journalist's life and moved to New Orleans to work in the cotton industry. However, he was once again drawn back to journalism as a reporter for various New Orleans papers. While covering the 1860 Democratic convention in Charleston, South Carolina, he decided to relocate there and soon was managing the *Charleston Mercury*.

The week following the outbreak of the Civil War, Riordan went north and began correspondence with his newspaper under the pseudonym, "Adsum." He reported South Carolina troop movements in Richmond, Virginia, and offered detailed descriptions of camp life. He was struck by the poor quality of armaments and the diligence of the amateur Confederate soldiers. He was able to make his way into Washington, D.C., from Alexandria in 1861. With all roads in and out of the city guarded, he faced the challenge of persuading Alexandria coach drivers to risk losing their teams of horses in Federal territory. His reporting often focused on the plight of civilians caught between two clashing armies. Unfortunately, most of his letters back to the *Mercury* never made it back in time due to rampant postal delays. Riordan was often supervising the activities of other war journalists from the South, including George W. Bagby, Jr.* Besides his editorial activities he still found time to write for the Press Association of the Confederate States of America* in 1863. He covered that year's siege of Charleston, sending out fifty word briefs on it twice a day. The war would ultimately leave his beloved Charleston in ruins. He covered the heavy bombardment of Fort Sumter that it left in rubble. Riordan's war reportage from South Carolina appeared in numerous Confederate newspapers. He would not flee Charleston until its evacuation in February 1865. He would return home and return to journalism; in the 1880s he decided to move to New York City and return to the cotton business, while keeping his hand in the world of newsprint. Partially paralyzed from a stroke he died in New York in 1897.

REFERENCE: Patricia G. McNeely, "Bartholomew Riordan: Spying on Washington, D.C.," *Knights of the Quill*, 2010, 127–139.

Robb, Inez (1901–1979)

Born on a cattle ranch in Middletown, California she studied journalism at the University of Missouri and after graduation began reporting for the *Tulsa Daily World* before heading to Chicago and then the *New York Daily News*, where she rose to prominence covering New York society. She went to Europe to report World War II in 1943 and was with the first two companies of the Women's Auxiliary Army Corps heading to the war theater. She covered action in North Africa. She returned to New York shortly after and left war journalism for the society pages.

REFERENCES: Lilya Wagner. *Women War Correspondents of World War II.* 1989.; M.L. Stein. *Under Fire.* 1968.

Robert Capa Gold Medal

Named for noted war correspondent Robert Capa,* this award was introduced in 1955. It has been issued annually by the Overseas Press Club of America for the "best published photographic reporting from abroad requiring exceptional courage and enterprise." Howard Sochurek won the first award.

REFERENCE: "OPC Awards: The Robert Capa Gold Medal," http://opcfamerica.org/opc_awards/archive,byaward/award_capa.php.

Roberts, Frank J. (d. 1885)

Roberts was a Reuters* war correspondent attached to General Graham's forces in the Sudan when he died at Suakin of enteric fever on May 15, 1885. His name is inscribed on a tablet in St. Paul's Cathedral which commemorates the deaths of seven special correspondents during the Sudan campaigns of 1883–1885.

REFERENCE: Robert Wilkinson-Latham. *From Our Special Correspondent.* 1979.

Robertson, James (1813–1881)

Robertson was a gifted and pioneering photographer who arrived in the Crimea shortly after the photographer Roger Fenton* left the Crimean War* and returned to England. Until about 1850, he was the chief engraver of the Imperial Mint at Constantinople. Prior to arriving in the Crimea he began his partnership with Felice Beato,* which lasted from 1852 to 1856. Some of his early pictures captured the arrival of allied troops at Constantinople en route to the Crimea in 1854. Many of his prints were used by the *Illustrated London News* as a basis for engravings.

Perhaps inspired by Fenton, Robertson arrived in the Crimea in March 1855 and stayed until the summer of the next year. Most of his photographs capture camp life and sites of battles. He was at liberty to shoot what he chose and he sent home many of his prints to the *Illustrated London News.* Robertson's work during this war was overshadowed by the more famous Fenton's. Neither took pictures showing corpses, although both were afforded many opportunities to do so. In 1857 Robertson was appointed official photographer of the British military in India. His photographs of the siege of Lucknow in 1857 while associated with Beato are considered among the greatest war photographs ever taken. With his partner Beato, Robertson covered the Indian Mutiny and photographed a variety of scenes which included battle casualties.

REFERENCES: Pat Hodgson. *Early War Photographs.* 1974; Lawrence James. *Crimea, 1854–56.* 1981.

Robertson, Nic (b. 1962)

An electrical and electronic engineer, Robertson joined CNN in 1990 and was credited with making the first live satellite broadcasts out of Iran, Ethiopia, and Iraq. He was the only CNN engineer in Baghdad during the first Gulf War and was able to set up the first satellite link that allowed for reporting from behind Iraqi lines. He has continued to contribute innovations

Indicates a separate entry.

to newsgathering on a number of fronts while gravitating more toward international reporting. He covered the break-up of Yugoslavia and between 1992–1995 was CNN's lead producer in Sarajevo, often working in tandem with Christiane Amanpour.* He covered the American mission in Somalia and the Rwandan genocide, and reported from Kabul in 1996 when the Taliban took control of Afghanistan. He was one of the few Western television reporters in this area during the events when the terror attacks on September 11, 2001 unfolded in the U.S., and was one of the last journalists to be kicked out of Afghanistan by the Taliban. Robertson has reported widely from Iraq as well, and as an embedded* correspondent covered the 2004 battle of Fallujah and the 2008 battle for Sadr City. Over more than twenty years Robertson has covered conflicts around the world including the NATO bombing campaign in Serbia and Kosovo in 1999, the Israeli-Gaza conflict, and the 2006 Israeli-Lebanon war. He has risen to further prominence covering terrorism. He has been the recipient of numerous awards including Emmys for covering Somalia (1992), Bosnia (1995), and Afghanistan (2002), and has been recognized for his innovative war reporting technology related to satellite telephoning and digital news gathering.

REFERENCE: http://edition.cnn.com/CNN/anchors_reporters/robertson.nic.html.

Robinson, G. T. (?)

Robinson was an architect in St. Peter's Square and the art critic for the *Manchester Guardian* when he arrived in Paris shortly before the siege of Metz during the Franco-Prussian War.* When informed that all English correspondents had been chased out of the city, the intrepid Robinson departed for Metz, where he would be the only English correspondent to record the siege. At one point he was arrested as a spy by the French and later made several unsuccessful attempts to cross Prussian lines. Together with a French engineer he set up a field post replete with

balloons in order to deliver messages to his parent newspaper. However, the French commander soon put a stop to it, and for the remainder of the siege the *Guardian* was cut off from its correspondent.

When victorious German troops entered the city after it capitulated following the seventy-day siege, a *Times* correspondent, noting Robinson's straw hat, mentioned that his hat had been singled out by Prussian marksmen. Shortly after the end of the siege Robinson left Metz when he was notified that his name had been handed over to the Prussians by the French commander on a list of dangerous persons. His account of the siege was carried in the *Guardian* and was republished as *The Fall of Metz* in 1871.

REFERENCE: David Ayerst. *The Manchester Guardian: Biography of a Newspaper.* 1971.

Robinson, Sir Harry Perry (1859–1930)

The Oxford-educated Robinson led a peripatetic existence in America following graduation. He tried his hand at gold mining and various journalistic endeavors before joining the *Times* in 1910, reporting from the West Indies. With the outbreak of World War I* he covered the German invasion of Belgium, barely escaping the fall of Antwerp in 1914. He went on to report from the Balkans and the western front, where he was stationed when the war ended. For his wartime service, he was rewarded by the French government with the Chevalier Legion of Honor in 1919. His recounting of his wartime activities and the Battle of the Somme were published in *The Turning Point* (1917).

REFERENCE: Robert W. Desmond. *Tides of War.* 1984.

Robinson, Henry Crabb (1775–1867)

Born in Bury St. Edmunds, Crabb Robinson was one of the earliest war correspondents. Educated to be a lawyer, he had his first dispatch published by the *Times* in 1807, when he recorded the fall of Danzig and then the French victory over the Russians at the Battle of Friedland. Upon his return to England in late 1807, he was promoted to editor. The following year he was posted to Spain, where he covered the Peninsular campaign between Britain and France. Robinson witnessed the final battles of the Spanish campaign, the death of the British commander, Sir John Moore, and the departure of the British troops from the Peninsula. Soon after his return to England in 1809, he left journalism to continue his legal career. He would count Lamb, Coleridge, and Wordsworth as friends, as well as continue an association with his old employer the *Times*. His memoirs, *Diary Reminiscences and Correspondence of Henry Crabb Robinson*, were published in 1869.

REFERENCE: Robert W. Desmond. *The Information Process*. 1978.

Rochhelli, Andrea "Andy" (1984–2014)

The Italian photojournalist covered conflicts and the human rights beat for a number of news enterprises. He was the founder of the Cesura photo agency and had been published in leading news sources including *Newsweek* and *Le Monde*. He was covering skirmishes between the Ukrainian army and pro-Russian separatists when he was killed on May 24, 2014, near Sloviansk while covering fighting in eastern Ukraine. The attack took him and his minder by surprise, and wounded French journalist William Roguelon as well. Rocchelli took cover in a ditch during a mortar attack and died from shrapnel wounds.

REFERENCE: "Andrea Rocchelli," http://cpj.org/killed/2014/andrea-rocchelli.php.

Rodger, George (1908–1995)

Rodger was born in Hale, Cheshire, England, and educated at St. Bees College, Cumbria.

Following service in the British merchant navy from 1926 to 1929, he joined *Life* as a war correspondent during World War II.* He was awarded eighteen campaign medals between 1939 and 1945. His photographs were some of the most outstanding pictures to appear in *Life* during the war. One of the most memorable photo essays was his sequence capturing the bombing raid on Coventry, England, and its aftermath. He covered the London blitz and was the only British photographer to cover the North African campaign. His coverage of the North African campaign was published as *Desert Journey* in 1944. Rodger accompanied the second diversionary expedition to Ethiopia and then covered the conflict with the Free French and the war in Libya before leaving to photograph the campaigns in Burma and on the North West Frontier of India.

He covered the rearguard actions by British and Chinese forces from the fall of Rangoon in 1942 until the conclusion of the campaign during the battles for Lashio in northern Burma. In order to escape Japanese forces he had to walk across Pungsao Pass into India. His book *Red Moon Rising* chronicles his exploits in Burma. He returned from the Burma theater to capture the Allied landings in Italy and Sicily. He covered the successful Allied campaign in Italy, including the carnage during the Battle of Monte Cassino. He landed with the first wave on Gold sector during the Normandy invasion and was with Allied forces in the drive across France and Germany. However, after witnessing the liberation of the German death camps Rodger resolved to end his career as war correspondent. Following the war he was one of the four cofounders of the Magnum Agency in 1947. He concentrated the remainder of his photographic career in Africa.

REFERENCES: *Contemporary Photographers*. 1982; Jorge Lewinski. *The Camera at War*. 1978.

Romulo, Carlos Pena (1899–1985)

A graduate of the University of the Philippines in 1918 and recipient of a master's degree from

Columbia in 1921, Romulo was a member of the Philippines Independence Commission and an officer in the Philippines Army Reserve in 1941. As editor for the *Manila Bulletin,* he undertook the assignment to alert the United States that Japan was about to unleash an aggressive campaign in the Pacific and that the United States would surely be drawn into the hostilities. In a series of articles distributed by the King Features Syndicate in the United States, Romulo predicted that the Western powers would lose most of their colonies during the conflict and that America would in the end prevail. Less than a month after Romulo's series the Japanese attacked Pearl Harbor and the Philippines. After Manila fell Romulo, as colonel on the staff of General Douglas MacArthur, helped lead the ill-fated defense of Bataan and Corregidor. Romulo was one of the last men to escape to Australia following the Japanese victory. In 1942 he won the Pulitzer Prize* in journalism, the first Asian to win the award. In June 1945 he returned to the Philippines with General MacArthur, wading ashore at Leyte. He wrote *I Saw the Fall of the Philippines* and *Mother America.*

REFERENCES: Robert W. Desmond. *Tides of War.* 1984; John Hohenberg. *The Pulitzer Prizes.* 1974; Beth Romulo, "Unforgettable Carlos P. Romulo," Readers Digest, June 1989.

Rooftop Journalism

With the introduction of satellite television, the era of rooftop journalism was inaugurated during the Gulf War.* "Rooftop journalism" refers to the new generation of war coverage in which cable news viewers can watch late-breaking events as they unfold. In the words of one authority, it is a "real-time clock on war." Disaster reporters rather than bona fide war correspondents familiar with local language and customs are now sent to cover international incidents. Trained in crisis, rather than countries and culture, their mission is to search out stories and colorful anecdotes that will draw television ratings. CNN was a prime source for this form of journalism during the Gulf War as correspondents such as Charles Jaco, Peter Arnett,* Arthur Kent, and others reported from the tops of Middle Eastern buildings as Scud missiles landed nearby, giving audiences the vicarious experience of being in a war zone.

REFERENCE: Johanna Neuman. *Lights, Camera, War.* 1996.

Rooney, Andy (1919–2011)

Known to modern audiences as the irascible commentator on CBS *60 Minutes,* Rooney grew up in Albany, New York. He worked as a war correspondent during World War II. He covered the Normandy invasion as well as the subsequent drive across France to Germany. Rooney worked for *Stars and Stripes** in London where he first came under fire covering the London Blitz. He was distinct from most other war correspondents because he was an army draftee. Originally assigned to England as a battery clerk, he used some "imaginative resume writing" to win a job in 1942 with the *Stars and Stripes.* During the war Rooney was decorated with a Bronze Star for courage under fire at Saint-Lo while covering a story. He also received the Air Medal for five excursions he took on bombing raids over Germany with the 8th Air Force. He was one of only six correspondents to fly in the first American bombing of Germany. Rooney was also among the first American journalists to visit and write about the German concentration camps. A friend of the late reporter Ernie Pyle,* in 2003 Rooney was awarded the Ernie Pyle Lifetime Achievement Award. He chronicled his war experience in his memoir, *My War* (1997).

REFERENCES: Herbert N. Foerstel. *Killing the Messenger.* 2006; Andy Rooney. *My War.* 1997.

Roos, Tielman Johannes De Villiers (1875–1935)

Roos covered the Boer side of the Boer War* for Reuters,* which fielded correspondents for both sides of the conflict. He reported the Battle of Colenso and described General Botha's headquarters and the conditions in which his staff and officer corps worked. Following the war he became auditor general in the government of the Union of South Africa.

REFERENCE: Byron Farwell. *The Great Anglo-Boer War.* 1976.

Rosen, Nir (b. 1977)

Rosen has been a regular contributor to *Atlantic Monthly*, the *Washington Post*, the *New York Times*, *Harper's* and other news sources. He is best known for his writings on the rise of violence in Iraq since the 2003 invasion. He spent two years in Iraq covering the occupation by Coalition forces and the civil war and has written extensively against the surge in Iraq, notably in his 2008 *Rolling Stone* piece, "Myth of the Surge." His book *In the Belly of the Green Bird: The Triumph of the Martyrs in Iraq* (2006) as well as much of his other works examine the other side of the U.S. war on terrorism. His 2010 book *Aftermath: Following the Bloodshed of America's Wars in the Muslim World* covers the occupation, counterresistance, sectarianism, and civil war from Iraq to Lebanon to Afghanistan. Rosen was a fellow at the Center on Law and Security at the New York University School of Law until he resigned over his comments about the sexual assault of Lara Logan* in Egypt. Over the years Rosen has reported widely from conflict zones, including Afghanistan, Pakistan, former Yugoslavia, the Democratic Republic of the Congo, Uganda, Kenya, Mexico, Palestine, Lebanon, Syria, Jordan, Yemen, Turkey, and Egypt.

REFERENCE: www.nirrosen.com/blog/.

Rosenthal, Joe (1911–2006)

The World War II* photographer took probably the most famous photograph of the war during the Battle of Iwo Jima. He received the Pulitzer Prize for his often reproduced shot of six soldiers straining to raise the American flag over Mount Suribachi on February 23, 1945. Perfectly composed, this image has been described as possessing "a dramatic sense of action, sculptural clarity, and heroic patriotism." The picture would become the inspiration for wartime posters and a three-cent stamp, and was the model for the Iwo Jima Memorial near Arlington National Cemetery.

The flag raisings that day, four days after the marines landed at Iwo Jima, marked the first time the American flag had flown over Japanese territory. Ironically, Rosenthal missed the first raising of a flag that turned out to be too small. Hearing of plans to raise a second, larger flag, he was in time to capture a much larger stars and stripes at noon. Rosenthal never received any royalties for the photo.

REFERENCE: Frederick S. Voss. *Reporting the War.* 1994; NY Times, August 22, 2006.

Round, Derek Leonard (1935–2012)

Born in New Zealand, Round was educated at Canterbury University and entered journalism in the mid-1950s as editor for his university newspaper. In 1960 he was hired as a bureau chief for Reuters* and was based in Singapore and Hong Kong. He covered the Asian beat throughout the 1970s. Round's war journalism career was spent mostly covering the Vietnam War* and he was one of the last New Zealand reporters to leave as Saigon fell. Round was murdered in his Wanganui, New Zealand home at the age of 77.

REFERENCES: "Distinguished journalist Derek Round dead," 3 NEWS, May 18, 2012; "Former Journalist Killed in Attack," New Zealand Herald.

Rowland, Jacky (b. c. 1965)

She was educated at Oxford University and joined the BBC in 1989. Rowland has covered conflicts in the Balkans and the Islamic world for more than 16 years. She moved from the BBC to *Al Jazeera* and is based in Jerusalem. In 2009 she reported from the West Bank and two year later she was in Tahrir Square covering the Egyptian revolution.

REFERENCES: Gill Swain. "The Women in the war Zone." *The Independent*, October 2, 2001.

Royal, Dennis Lee (1922–1971)

During a three-decade career as an Associated Press photographer he covered various disasters and tragedies and covered wars in the Congo in 1960 and 1961, unrest in East Africa in 1964, and the bloodshed accompanying the independence movements in Kenya, Cyprus and elsewhere. Royal also covered wars in the Middle East and India and the Hungarian revolution in 1956. He was most prominent for his photos of the starving children of Biafra during the Nigerian Civil War. By most accounts his coverage led to increased relief efforts. Most observers commented on the irony that he survived so many dangerous incidents only to perish in a helicopter crash over the English Channel while taking pictures of NATO naval exercises.

REFERENCES: AP Wall of Honor, www.ap.org/wallof-honor/1970_1979.html.

Rue, Larry (1893–1965)

Born in Fosston, Minnesota, Rue entered journalism with the *Duluth News Tribune* in 1913. During World War I* he gained experience as an air corps pilot, and later as a correspondent he piloted his own plane while on assignment. Rue joined the *Chicago Tribune* in 1919 and early on covered the Middle East, North Africa, and southern Europe. He witnessed the Fascist takeover of Rome in 1922 and Hitler's "beer hall putsch" the following year. In 1931 he began working for the *New York Daily News* and in 1939 covered the opening events of World War

II* for both the *Tribune* and the *News*. He was in Holland when the Nazis invaded and had no way to relay his story to his home office. He designed a phony document which identified him as a VIP and successfully used it to drive through almost half of Europe and back to his London office.

REFERENCES: Robert W. Desmond. *Crisis and Conflict*. 1982; M. L. Stein. *Under Fire*. 1968.

Ruhl, Arthur (1876–1935)

Born in Rockford, Illinois, prior to World War I* Ruhl was the music critic for the *New York Tribune*. He became the most active correspondent for *Collier's Weekly* during the war beginning in 1914, when he covered the fronts in Belgium and France. The following year he reported from Germany and Austria, before shifting to Russia for 1916 and 1917 to chronicle the war from both sides. He returned to France in 1918 and then reported from the Baltic states following the end of hostilities. He returned to the *New York Tribune* in the 1920s.

REFERENCE: Robert W. Desmond. *Windows on the World*. 1980.

Runyon, Damon (1884–1946)

Born in Manhattan, Kansas, the well-known chronicler of Broadway and author of the musical *Guys and Dolls* first entered journalism while still in his teens for the *Pueblo Evening Press*. During the Spanish-American War* he spent eighteen months in the Philippines. Following the war he worked for several papers in the West before landing with the Denver-based *Rocky Mountain News* in 1906.

In 1910 he moved to New York City and the sports department of Hearst's *New York American*. He would remain with the paper in various capacities until its demise in 1937. In 1912 he covered the Madero revolution in Mexico and four years later accompanied General John J. Pershing's pursuit of Pancho Villa in Mexico for bandit depredations in America. In 1918 Runyon was in France with the American Expeditionary Force in the waning days of World War I.* After the war his reputation was soaring and his articles were widely syndicated. By the 1930s he was identified not only as one of the preeminent sportswriters but also as the chronicler of Broadway life. Among his many works are *Guys and Dolls* (1931), *Blue Plate Special* (1934), and *Take It Easy* (1938). Hollywood would buy many of his stories, making Runyon a wealthy man by the 1940s. He died of throat cancer in December 1946.

REFERENCES: Tom Clark. *The World of Damon Runyon.* 1978; *DAB* Supp. 4; Patricia Ward D'Itri. *Damon Runyon.* 1982.

Russell, Andrew J. (1830–1902)

Born in Vermont, he reportedly worked in Mathew Brady's* New York studios prior to the outbreak of the American Civil War.* Russell is little known in the annals of the Civil War because many of his photographs have been credited to others. He was the only official army photographer to record the war.

Previously commissioned as a captain in a New York company, in 1863 he was reassigned to the Union military railroad chief in the capacity of official photographer. Russell was supposed to document railroad installations and personnel, but in his free time he often deviated from this task, taking pictures of various fortifications and battle sites. When not assigned to the railroad he was with the Army of the Potomac. He photographed dead horses and rebels at Chancellorsville in the aftermath of the fighting. These widely reprinted images were among his most enduring exposures. In the last months of the war Russell was fired over a salary dispute and questions over ownership of the negatives. Following the conflict he was employed by Union Pacific.

REFERENCE: Stewart Sifakis. *Who Was Who in the Civil War.* 1988.

Russell, Edmund "Ned" Allen (b. 1916)

Russell was born in Baltimore, Maryland, and began his newspaper career while still in his teens as sportswriter for the *Los Angeles Examiner.* He joined the United Press in 1936 and in 1940 covered the Battle of Britain. Beginning in 1942 Russell reported the desert war and Allied landings in North Africa, as well as the 1943 winter campaign in Tunisia while attached with the U.S. First Army. He was among the contingent of seasoned North African correspondents covering the Sicily invasion and the Italian campaign. In 1944 Russell joined the *New York Herald Tribune* in preparation for the D-Day landings, which he ended up covering from the safety of England. He coauthored the book *Springboard To Berlin* with Leo Disher,* John Parris, and Phil Ault.

REFERENCE: Robert W. Desmond. *Tides of War.* 1984.

Russell, Sir Herbert (1869–1944)

Born in Northumbria, England, he entered journalism with the *Newcastle Chronicle* in 1893. Russell joined Reuters* in time to cover World War I,* reporting the Gallipoli debacle and the western front from June 1915 to November 1918. As one of the first five Reuters members to win assignment to the British front in France, he became the best-known war correspondent for the agency during the conflict in Europe. Russell covered the first day of the Battle of the Somme on July 1, 1916, when sixty thousand British troops were killed or wounded. Following the war he was made a Chevalier of the Legion of Honor by the French government and in 1918 was knighted for his coverage of the war.

REFERENCE: Donald Read. *The Power of News.* 1992.

Russell, Sir William Howard (1820–1907)

Often referred to as the "father of modern war reporting," Russell was born in Dublin and

Indicates a separate entry.

attended Trinity College without graduating, before joining the *Times* in 1841. Originally assigned to report on political affairs, he covered his first war in 1850 when he covered the Danish conflict over Schleswig-Holstein. He received a slight flesh wound covering the Battle of Idstedt.

When the Crimean War* broke out in 1854 Russell's career as a war correspondent began. Soon after debarking at Gallipoli his critical reports of the British army began appearing in the *Times*. The British suffered more from a shortage of weapons, medicine, fuel, and clothing than from their Russian opposition. It has been claimed that his dispatches reflecting the gross negligence of the War Office led to the resignation of Lord Aberdeen's cabinet. On October 25, 1854, he used the phrase "the thin red line" for the first time, as he described the Battle of Balaklava. Later that day he produced his account of the charge of the Light Brigade. Both reports are considered classic examples of war journalism. Rudyard Kipling* admitted borrowing Russell's words "thin red line of heroes" for his poem "Tommy." Russell's story is also often credited with inspiring Tennyson's poem "The Charge of the Light Brigade." Russell continued to publicize the deprivations of the British army. Although he was criticized by the British brass, at least one officer, Sir Evelyn Wood, believed that Russell's muckraking saved what was left of the army.

The *Times* considered his coverage of the Indian Mutiny in 1857 the best work he had done. In 1859 friends convinced him that there would be great interest in a magazine devoted exclusively to issues dealing with national security, the defense, and the various armed forces. These conversations led him in 1860 to found the *Army and Navy Gazette*. For the rest of his life he remained its major shareholder and editor. In April 1861 Russell was sent to America on the eve of the American Civil War* to investigate the growing sectional crisis. With the outbreak of war, the pro-Union Russell was entrusted by the Confederate-sympathizing *Times* to cover the

war. His account of the Southern rout of Union forces at Bull Run so displeased Lincoln that he was barred from accompanying Northern forces, whereupon he returned to England.

In 1864 he witnessed Denmark's defeat by Prussia and Austria, and in 1866 the Austro-Prussian War.* He followed Prussian forces while reporting the 1870 Franco-Prussian War,* but apparently was being scooped by other papers whose reporters had gravitated quickly to the new technology of the electric telegraph.

His last war was the South African Zulu War (1879), which he reported for the *Daily Telegraph* while accompanying the forces of Sir Garnet Wolseley. His journalism career was not over, for he would report the rebellion of Arabi Pasha in Egypt (1882) and travel to South America (1889) before being knighted in 1895. Upon his death on February 10, 1907, he was buried in the crypt of London's St. Paul's Cathedral. The legend on his grave notes for posterity "The First and Greatest of War Correspondents."

REFERENCES: Alan Hankinson. *Man of Wars: William Howard Russell of the "Times."* 1982; W. H. Russell. *My Diary North and South*, 2nd ed. Edited by Fletcher Pratt. 1954; W. H. Russell. *Russell's Despatches from the Crimea, 1854–1856.* Edited by Nicholas Bentley. 1967.

Russo-Japanese War

The Russo-Japanese War began on February 8, 1904, when Japanese forces attacked the Russians at Port Arthur. The attack followed five months of fruitless negotiations as the Japanese attempted to get Russia to remove its troops from Korea. The subsequent war was fought at sea and in Manchuria, resulting in a final Japanese victory in May 1905.

Correspondents headed for Japan prior to the outbreak of hostilities. Almost two hundred members of the press covered the conflict. Many of the reporters were veterans of recent conflicts such as the 1900 Boxer Rebellion,* the Boer War,* the 1898 Spanish-American War,* and the Philippine insurrection.

Most correspondents covered the war from the Japanese side, while a contingent arrived in Russia bound for the Asian mainland by means of the Trans-Siberian Railroad. Correspondents arriving in Tokyo were confronted with restrictions that prevented most groups from covering the battlefront until after June 1904. Once permitted to get closer to the action the reporter pools were strictly controlled and never permitted to get within three miles of the front lines. Many chafed under the censorship and departed for home.

The Russo-Japanese War was the first conflict in which a wireless was used for transmitting dispatches from observers near the battlefield directly to their home offices. It was also the most expensive war to cover up to that time, in part due to the high cost of transmitting reports to London, New York, and other news centers. Several correspondents died covering the conflict. Lewis Etzel of the *Daily Telegraph* was killed in Manchuria and Henry J. Middleton of the Associated Press died from an illness.

Among the more recognizable names covering the conflict were Francis McCullagh of the *New York Herald* and *Manchester Guardian*, Melton Prior* for the *Illustrated London News*, Frederic Villiers* for the *Graphic*, Bennet Burleigh* of the *Daily Telegraph*, Edward Frederick Knight* of the *Morning Post*, Richard Harding Davis* for *Collier's Weekly*, Jack London* for the *New York Journal*, George Denny and Frederick McCormick* for the AP, Stephen Bonsal,* William Dinwiddie,* Thomas F. Millard,* and Wilmott Harsant Lewis* for the *New York Herald*, Luigi Barzini* of the *Corriere della Sera*, John T. McCutcheon* of the *Chicago Tribune*, Percival Phillips* for the *Daily Express*, William Maxwell* for the *Standard*, Ellis Ashmead-Bartlett* for the *Daily Telegraph*, and Charles E. Hands* of the *Daily Mail*.

The Russo-Japanese War established Japan as a world power. It was the first modern war in which a Western nation was beaten by an Asian power. In the end Japanese censorship prevented the hordes of correspondents from witnessing most of the decisive battles. Censorship was strict because the Japanese suspected that many of foreign journalists were spies. On the other hand the Japanese allowed their own correspondents more freedom than their Western counterparts. Any complete study of the Russo-Japanese War must consider the dispatches in the *Asahi*, *Mainichi*, and *Jiji*, whose correspondents were allowed to witness most of the pivotal battles.

REFERENCE: Robert W. Desmond. *The Information Process*. 1978.

Russo-Turkish War

Following reports of Turkish atrocities against Bulgarian Christians, Russia declared war on Turkey in April 1877. In its declaration of war Russia made no mention of the strategic value of Turkish access to the Mediterranean.

During the war close to eighty correspondents would visit the front lines. While some accompanied Turkish forces or were based in Constantinople, the majority were with the Russians. Each correspondent was equipped with a wagon outfitted with necessities, horses, and servants or couriers for assistance. Correspondents usually carried gold specie to pay for telegraph tolls. Cabling facilities were located in Bucharest, Rumania, and were moderately censored by Russian officials. Unlike previous wars, correspondents were assigned numbers by Russian officials. Initially they wore accreditation badges before these were changed to simple armbands. In addition all reporters were required to take an oath that they would not compromise Russian security and were to pass all copies of their newspapers through Russian censors. Among those accused of violating wars and expelled was Frederick Boyle* of the *Standard*. Turkish restrictions were no less strict, as Antonio Gallenga* of the *Times* found out when he was expelled.

The *Daily News* was the best-represented newspaper during the war, just as it had been

* *Indicates a separate entry.*

during the late Franco-Prussian War.* Among its most prominent correspondents were Januarius MacGahan* and Archibald Forbes.* Along with Frederic Villiers* of the *Graphic,* these three journalists witnessed some of the most crucial engagements of the war, including the Battles of Plevna and Schipka Pass. On one occasion *Daily News* war correspondents managed to bypass Russian censors through the implementation of a pony express service, using eight men and horses to deliver dispatches over the Carpathian Mountains to neutral Austria. *Daily News* correspondents on the Turkish side included Edmund O'Donovan* and Frank A. Scudamore.* At the outset of the conflict the newspaper exchanged dispatches with the *New York Herald,* which was represented by John P. Jackson and Francis D. Millet.*

Other notable reporters on the scene were Melton Prior* of the *Illustrated London News,* Frank le Poer Power* for a Dublin paper, three representatives of the *Daily Telegraph,* William Beattie Kingston* with the Russians, and Drew Gay and Campbell Clarke with the Turks. The war came to an end in January 1878 after Turkey appealed to Russia for an armistice. The peace process was formalized by the Treaty of San Stefano several months later.

REFERENCE: Robert W. Desmond. *The Information Process.* 1978.

Ryan, Cornelius John (1920–1974)

The Dublin-born Ryan joined Reuters* in 1941 and two years later left for the *Daily Telegraph.* He covered both theaters of World War II* and then the first Arab-Israeli War (1946–1947). He continued his career as a journalist for various American publications in the 1950s and 1960s, including *Time, Life,* and *Reader's Digest.* Ryan established a career as a bestselling writer of military history. Among his books were *The Longest Day* (1959), *The Last Battle* (1966), and *A Bridge Too Far* (1974), all of which became best-sellers.

REFERENCE: Dennis Griffiths, ed. *The Encyclopedia of the British Press.* 1992.

S

Sacco, Joe (b. 1960)

Born in Malta and raised in Australia and Los Angeles, Sacco took an early interest in journalism while still in high school and earned a degree in it from the University of Oregon in 1981. Looking for work he returned to Malta where he worked on local guidebooks. But he always came back to the format of expression he liked best, which was comic books. He came back to the States in 1985 and after several stabs at journalism went on the road once more in 1988. In 1991 he began applying his comic skills to the coverage of warfare during the 1991 Gulf War. He studied Middle Eastern politics and began traveling in Israel and the Palestinian territories. He then travelled to Sarajevo and Gorzde and covered the conclusion of the Bosnian War. According to a *Mother Jones* profile in 2005, Sacco "occupied a unique spot in the no-man's land between underground cartoonist and war correspondents." Sacco has won a following by combining his first hand reporting in hot spots and chronicling his insights in "gritty black and white comics." Among his most prominent works are *Safe Area Gorazde: The War in Eastern Bosnia, 1992–1996* (2002) and *Footnotes in Gaza: A Graphic Novel* (2009). His work has also been published in such print news outlets as *The Guardian* (2005) and *Harper's* magazine (2007). Sacco's work has been the recipient of an American Book Award (1996) and a Guggenheim Fellowship (2001).

REFERENCES: Dave Gibson. "The Art of War: An Interview with Joe Sacco." *Mother Jones*, July/August 2005;

Sack, John (1930–2004)

At his death in 2004 an *Esquire* obituary noted he "was the only person to have reported from every American war since Korea." Following graduation from Harvard in 1951 he joined the Army and worked as a combat correspondent for the *Pacific Stars and Stripes* in Korea. He came to prominence reporting the Vietnam War for *Esquire* in his 33,000 word piece "M Company" published in October 2006, the longest story ever published by the magazine. It was published as "*M*" in 1967. In it he followed an infantry company from its training at Fort Dix to the battlefield in Vietnam. He also won acclaim for his 1970 interviews with Lieutenant William Calley, the only person convicted for the My Lai massacre. Sack was threatened with arrest for refusing to turn over his interview tapes to prosecutors. In 1971 Viking published his book *Lieutenant Calley: His Own Story* and in 1983 Sack's autobiography *Fingerprint* was published. *Esquire* also claimed that Sack was "the only journalist in an armored vehicle during the ground phase of the first Gulf War" in 1991. In 2002 he witnessed and wrote what has been called "the definitive account" of the bloody battle dubbed Operation Aanaconda in Afghanistan's Shah-i-kot Valley. He also reported from Iraq and Yugoslavia during his career.

* Indicates a separate entry.

REFERENCES: "John Sack (1930–2004)," *Esquire*, June 2004, p. 24; *NYT* Obituary, March 31, 2004, p. C13.

Safer, Morley (b. 1931)

Best known as an anchor on the popular *60 Minutes* television newsmagazine show, the Canadian-born Safer first came to prominence while covering the Vietnam War* for CBS. In 1966 he was the recipient of the Overseas Press Club Award for best television reporting, with a controversial film story showing American troops burning the Vietnamese village of Cam Le, near Danang, as villagers pleaded to be allowed to remove their possessions. Safer was soundly criticized by U.S. officials in Vietnam for what was taken to be reporting detrimental to the war effort. Safer had several close brushes with death while reporting from battlefronts. Prior to Vietnam he reported the Congo and Cyprus conflicts, the 1967 Arab-Israeli War, the Soviet invasion of Czechoslovakia, the religious strife in Northern Ireland, the Nigerian civil war, and the American withdrawal from Cambodia.

REFERENCES: M. L. Stein. *Under Fire: the Story of American War Correspondents.* 1968; Clarence R. Wyatt. *Paper Soldiers: The American Press and the Vietnam War.* 1993.

St. George, Ozzie (1915–2007)

St. George covered the Southwest Pacific theater of World War II, witnessing battles at Port Moresby, Salamaua, and Leyte. He wrote for *Yank* magazine*. Following the war he continued a career as a news reporter out of St. Paul, Minnesota.

REFERENCE: Art Weithas. *Close to Glory.* 1991.

St. John, Robert (1902–2003)

He served in World War I* at the age of sixteen. Following the war he became a reporter for the *Hartford Courant* and then the *Chicago Daily News,* before briefly editing his own newspaper in Cicero, Illinois, the stronghold of the Capone mob. He left Cicero after being savagely beaten by gangsters for his attempts at exposing the activities of Al Capone's younger brother Ralph. St. John moved to Vermont and then joined the *Philadelphia Record*. In 1931 he moved to the Associated Press, but gave that up for rural life in New Hampshire.

With the war years approaching he rejoined the Associated Press in 1939. He arrived in Paris just as the Nazis were invading Poland and covered the conflict in the Balkans, including campaigns in Yugoslavia, Greece, and Crete. His bestselling book *From the Land of Silent People* (1942) chronicles the various resistance groups who opposed the German invaders.

At the outset of the European war St. John was headquartered in Budapest, Hungary, which gave him an edge over his competition in covering the Central Europe and the Balkans. After the fall of Rumania and Bulgaria St. John reported from Yugoslavia. As the German onslaught continued and ultimate capitulation of Yugoslavia seemed a foregone conclusion, he attempted to escape the country. Along with three other reporters, St. John debarked by boat from the Dalmatian coast for Greece, narrowly escaping the German forces. Upon reaching Greece he was faced with a situation similar to the one he just escaped from. Although wounded during a German air attack, St. John made it to safety in Egypt with the help of the British navy. He returned to America in 1941 to a job as news commentator with NBC and spent the remainder of the war broadcasting from England.

REFERENCES: Frederick S. Voss. *Reporting the War.* 1994; Washington Post, Feb. 8, 2003.

Sala, George Augustus Henry (1828–1896)

Sala was educated in Paris and studied drawing in London. After a succession of jobs as clerk, scene painter, and illustrator he began contributing articles to *Household Words* and in 1856 was assigned to cover the Crimean War.* Sala wrote regularly for the *Daily Telegraph* from 1855 to 1893. He was one of the few British correspondents to cover the American Civil War.* He also reported parts of the Italian unification campaigns in 1858–1861, the Austro-Prussian War,* the Franco-Prussian War,* and the Carlist war of 1873–1876 in Spain. Sala was not specifically a war correspondent. Although he was more content to chronicle "areas to the rear" in wartime, his dispatches were some of the most frequently reprinted from the wars he reported. In 1881 he was assigned to St. Petersburg, Russia, to report the funeral of Alexander II and did not return to England for two years.

REFERENCE: Joseph J. Mathews. *Reporting the Wars.* 1957.

Sale, Stewart (1905–1943)

A protege of Edgar Wallace,* Sale reported for the *Buckingham Mail,* the *Sunday News,* and the *Daily Telegraph* before joining Reuters.* During World War II* he flew as an observer in a bombing raid over Berlin, covered the Salerno landing, and reported other parts of the Italian campaign. In August 1943 he was posted to Allied headquarters and the Fifth Army in North Africa, where he wrote his dispatch on the landing at Salerno. The following month he was killed along with two other correspondents when a German half-track fired on their jeep in the push to Naples. Also killed were veteran war correspondents Alexander Berry Austin* and William J. Munday.*

REFERENCES: Robert W. Desmond. *Tides of War.* 1984; Donald Read. *The Power of News: The History of Reuters.* 1992.

Salisbury, Harrison Evans (1908–1993)

Salisbury was born in Minneapolis, Minnesota, and educated at the University of Minnesota. He began reporting for the *Minneapolis Journal* while still a college student. He joined the United Press in 1930 and during the New Deal was assigned to the Washington bureau, where he began freelancing under a variety of pseudonyms. He got his first foreign posting in 1943 when he was transferred to London as bureau manager in 1943. He reported World War II* from the Middle East, North Africa, and Great Britain. In 1944 he was assigned to the Soviet Union for six weeks and ended up staying for eight months. He returned to New York and completed *Russia on the Way* (1944).

After a bout with depression and a stint in a psychiatric clinic he joined the *New York Times* as a correspondent in its Moscow bureau. He stayed on for six years and developed a growing affinity for the country. Upon his return to the States he wrote a series of articles on Communist Russia and its leaders, winning the Pulitzer Prize for international reporting in 1955.

In 1966 he became the first American reporter allowed into North Vietnam when he spent a month reporting from Hanoi, and in 1967 he won his second George K. Polk Award. He retired from the *Times* in 1973. Salisbury eventually wrote over twenty books and became a recognized specialist in Russian affairs.

REFERENCE: Harrison Salisbury. A *Journey for Our Times.* 1983.

Salter, Cedric (b. 1907)

Born in Oxford, England, Salter covered the Spanish Civil War* for three years, first with the *London Daily Telegraph* in 1937, and then the *News Chronicle* and the *Daily Mail.* Attached to neither the Loyalists nor the Franco forces during the conflict, he was able to cover various battlefronts. He was in Spain from the outbreak of the war and witnessed the bombing of Barcelona and Granollers. In his book *Try-Out in Spain* he recounts helping two nuns escape to a destroyer and interviewing General Durutti after he condemned eight hundred women to be executed.

Salter developed a reputation as "the most chased about of British correspondents" during the late 1930s and early 1940s. He continued his work for the *Daily Mail* during World War II,* covering the Polish campaign until the Germans captured Warsaw, before reporting various phases of the developing Eastern European theater of the war. With the Gestapo in hot pursuit Salter recorded events in Rumania, Bulgaria, and Turkey until 1941, when he accompanied British forces into the Far East, where he witnessed the fall of Singapore. Barely escaping Japanese forces, he returned to Burma and was the last correspondent to leave Rangoon before it fell to the Japanese. He continued to cover the war in China, India, and Tibet before returning to Ankara as the Turkish correspondent for the *Daily Mail.*

REFERENCES: Cedric Salter. *Flight from Poland.* 1940; Cedric Salter. *Try-Out in Spain.* 1943.

Sandburg, Carl August (1878–1967)

Best known as a poet and biographer of Lincoln, Sandburg was born in Galesburg, Illinois. He worked in journalism for over two decades in Milwaukee and Chicago. In 1898 he served with the army in the Spanish-American War.* His first effort in journalism appeared in the *Galesburg Daily Mail,* when it published his letters sent from Puerto Rico recounting his wartime experiences. In 1918 he was stationed in Stockholm, Sweden, where he reported the final months of World War I* and the Russian Revolution for the *Chicago Daily News.*

REFERENCES: Harry Golden. *Carl Sandburg.* 1961; *New York Times.* July 23, 1967.

San Juan Hill, Battle of

The most famous battle of the Spanish-American War* was the Battle of San Juan Hill on July 1, 1898. The famous charge up the hill by the Rough Riders, led by Colonel Theodore

Roosevelt, would catapult Roosevelt into the presidency three years later. The charge was witnessed by correspondents Stephen Crane,* James Hare,* Richard Harding Davis,* and other less well known reporters. This charge has been immortalized by the press, artists, and editorial writers who embellished the event to such an extent as to obscure the fact that the soldiers were not mounted and the charge was unnecessary, leading to at least one critic of Roosevelt to describe the event as the "myth of San Juan Hill."

REFERENCE: Joyce Milton. *The Yellow Kids.* 1989.

Sankova, Galina (b. 1904)

Galina Sankova was the most outstanding woman photojournalist covering the Russian front during World War II.* She honed her craft in the 1930s before overcoming enormous obstacles to record the war. Professionally trained as a nurse at the outset of the war, and then as a driver and mechanic, Sankova took a circuitous route to her career as photojournalist. She photographed the fighting on the western front, the Briansk and Don campaigns near Stalingrad, and the northern offensive of 1944 in the beleaguered city of Leningrad. Throughout the war she was affiliated with *Frontovaya Illustracia.*

Sankova was one of only five Russian women to photograph the war. In addition to her wartime coverage she recorded the construction projects of the Five- and Seven-Year Plans as well as events in Siberia. She was twice wounded during the war and often volunteered as a nurse at the front. After the war she remained in journalism as staff writer for *Ogonyok* magazine.

REFERENCE: Daniela Mrazkova and Vladimir Remes, eds. *The Russian War: 1941–1945.* 1975.

Savin, Mikhail (1915–2006)

Prior to the outbreak of the Russian war in 1941, Savin had been a correspondent based in Byelorussia for the TASS News Agency. He covered the war as a photojournalist for the *Krasnoarmeyskaya Pravda* or *Red Army Pravda*, the army newspaper for the western front. After the war he remained active in the field as photographer for *Ogonyok* magazine.

REFERENCE: Daniela Mrazkova and Vladimir Remes, eds. *The Russian War: 1941–1945.* 1975.

Sawada, Kyoichi (1936–1970)

Born in Japan, Sawada was killed while covering the Cambodia conflict. While covering the Vietnam War* as a photojournalist for United Press International he had several close brushes with death and was captured once. In 1966 Sawada won the Pulitzer Prize.

REFERENCE: John Hohenberg. *The Pulitzer Prizes.* 1973.

Sayre, Joel Grover (1900–1979)

Sayre was born in Marion, Indiana, and served with the Canadian Expeditionary Forces in Siberia in 1917. Following stints as a crime reporter and screenwriter, he joined the *New Yorker* as a war correspondent covering the Persian Gulf Command during World War II.* His accounts of this conflict were published as *Persian Gulf Command: Some Marvels on the Road to Kazvin* in 1945.

REFERENCES: *New York Times.* September 14, 1979; David Shavit. *The United States in the Mideast.* 1988.

Schanberg, Sydney H. (b. 1934)

Born in Clinton, Massachusetts, and educated at Harvard, he joined the *Times* as a copyboy in 1959. In 1960 Schanberg filed his first story as a reporter. In rapid succession he headed news bureaus for the paper in Albany, New York; New Delhi, India; and Singapore. In April 1975 he covered the invasion of Cambodia by Communist forces and was present at Phnom Penh when the country capitulated to the invaders. Schanberg stayed behind with several other

correspondents and was able to escape to Thailand, where he filed some of the best dispatches of the conflict. He received the Pulitzer Prize for his work in 1976. He later became metropolitan editor for his paper in 1977.

REFERENCE: Haing Ngor, with Roger Warner. *Haing Ngor: A Cambodian Odyssey.* 1987.

Schell, Francis H. (c. 1834–1909)

Born in Germantown, Pennsylvania, and raised in Philadelphia, he was trained in lithography at age sixteen. During the American Civil War* he became one of the foremost artist-correspondents* for *Frank Leslie's Illustrated.* He covered the siege of Vicksburg and other action in the west. Following the war he joined a coterie of Civil War artists including the Waud* brothers, Edwin Forbes,* and Henri Lovie* as illustrators for *Beyond the Mississippi,* which was composed of historical views of America from the Mississippi River to the Pacific Coast after 1857. Schell headed the *Leslie's* art department after the war and then became partners with fellow illustrator Thomas Hogan for thirty years.

REFERENCES: Peggy and Harold Samuels. *Samuels' Encyclopedia of Artists of the American West.* 1985; W. Fletcher Thompson, Jr. *The Image of War.* 1959.

Schonberg, Johann Nepomuk (1844–1913)

The son of a noted engraver and lithographer, Johann Schonberg was born in Austria and educated at the Academy of Vienna before embarking on a career as a sketch artist with various French illustrated newspapers. In 1866 he began an affiliation with the *Illustrated London News* when he reported the Austro-Prussian War* from the Austrian side. Nine years later he was back in the field for the *Illustrated* covering the Serbo-Turkish War of 1875–1876, and then the Russo-Turkish War* of 1877–1878.

Indicates a separate entry.

After military service in Egypt he fought with Serbian forces against Bulgaria in 1885, while continuing to hone his war artist skills. Schonberg joined the *Sphere* as artist-correspondent* during the Boer War.* Masquerading as a German press representative, he was given preferential treatment by the Boers. However, his ruse fell short of success when the *Sphere* blew his cover with an ill-timed telegram identifying him as its London correspondent, and he was expelled from the Boer camp. Later, Schonberg was assigned to cover the 1900 Boxer Rebellion* for the *Illustrated London News,* but did not reach Peking until well after the fighting had ended.

REFERENCE: Pat Hodgson. *The War Illustrators.* 1977.

Schork, Kurt (1947–2000)

Born in Washington, D.C. and a Rhodes scholar in 1969, Schork was covering the conflict in Sierra Leone when he was ambushed and killed along with cameraman Miguel Gil Moreno* on May 24, 2000. Schork had previously covered conflicts in the Balkans, Iraq, Chechnya, Iraq, Kurdistan, Sri Lanka, and East Timor. He was held in such high regard in Sarajevo, Bosnia and Herzegovina that a street was dedicated to memorialize his untimely death.

REFERENCE: Emma Daly. www.ksmemorial.com/emma.htm;

Schrier, Matt (c. 1978)

Born in Syosset, New York and educated at Hofstra University, Schrier was a prisoner of Syrian rebels for seven months. As a freelance photographer, Schrier left New York for Turkey and Jordan where he covered the plight of Syrian refugees. He then traveled to Syria where he covered the civil war for 18 days, before being kidnapped by Syrian rebels from a taxicab on the last day of 2012. He was held in a rebel-controlled jail in Aleppo. His captivity included several bouts of torture, which he has graphically described in subsequent interviews. For most of his captivity he was housed with Peter Theo Curtis.* Schrier escaped by squeezing through a basement window and was rescued in Aleppo. However, his cellmate was left behind and would not be released until the following year.

REFERENCE: C.J. Chivers, "American Tells of Odyssey as Prisoner of Syrian Rebels," New York Times, Aug. 23, 2013.

Schultz, Sigrid (1893–1980)

Born in Chicago, she was a daughter of the renowned European portrait artist Herman Schultz. Fluent in five languages, the Sorbonne-educated Sigrid Schultz was hired by the *Chicago Tribune* to work as an interpreter at its Berlin bureau in 1919. Stationed in Germany, she interviewed many Nazi leaders, including Hitler, and warned of the coming conflict. The war reporter Quentin Reynolds* called her "Hitler's greatest enemy." Although allowed to stay in Germany at the outbreak of World War II,* she was prevented by German officials from covering the battlefronts. In 1941 she suffered a shrapnel injury while covering the bombing of Berlin.

Working for *McCall's* and *Liberty* magazines in 1944, she covered the Battle of the Ruhr and the American advance on Berlin, and was one of the first reporters to witness the liberation of Buchenwald. After covering the Nuremberg war trials she retired from war reporting. She wrote *Germany Will Try It Again* (1944) and was at work on a history of German anti-Semitism at her death.

REFERENCES: Julia Edwards. *Women of the World.* 1989; Lilya Wagner. *Women War Correspondents of World War II.* 1989.

Schuyler, Philippa (1932–1967)

Schuyler first saw Vietnam as a guest of Ambassador Henry Cabot Lodge in 1966. Because she was an accomplished pianist, Lodge had invited her to entertain wounded soldiers at a Saigon hospital. A former child prodigy who made her concert debut at age four and could read at two, in her early teens she accompanied the New York Philharmonic Symphony Orchestra. Prior to the trip, Schuyler had already formulated plans for a career in journalism. She had previously reported from the battlefront in 1960 while covering the civil war in the Belgian Congo. Her articles from this first campaign were collected and published as *Who Killed the Congo?* in 1962.

During the Vietnam War* she contributed articles to William Loeb's *Manchester Union-Leader* and became increasingly unpopular with American officials for her reports on American racism and how American policy was flawed because of a lack of understanding of the Vietnamese. On May 9, 1967, she was killed in a helicopter crash as she attempted to evacuate children from the besieged city of Hue.

REFERENCE: Virginia Elwood-Akers. *Women War Correspondents in the Vietnam War, 1961–1975.* 1988.

Scoop

Evelyn Waugh* wrote this satirical novel on war reporting in 1937. Waugh had covered the Ethiopian War* in 1935 for the *London Daily Mail* and was struck by the competitiveness and moral dissolution of his colleagues fighting to get news scoops. In the book, the correspondents are issued identity cards that were originally used to register prostitutes. Waugh himself was a dismal failure at this trade, sending back little news and eventually being fired. This novel foreshadows future incarnations of war correspondents as unscrupulous and shiftless creatures trading on the misfortunes of others. In *Scoop,* the protagonist William Boot is assigned to cover a war in the East African country of Ishmaelia for the *Beast,* an appropriately named newspaper. In Waugh's words, the newspaper stood for "strong mutually antagonistic governments everywhere."

REFERENCES: Howard Good. *The Image of War Correspondents in Anglo-American Fiction.* 1985; Evelyn Waugh. *Scoop.* 1937.

Scott, Jack Denton (c. 1916–1995)

Born in Elkins, West Virginia, Scott studied literature at Columbia and Oxford Universities. During World War II he worked as a war correspondent for *Yank** magazine in London, Cairo, and Florence. He was a member of the Writing 69th* and flew on at least one bombing raid over France. He was considered "the most prolific writer" of the eight reporters that comprised the unit. He wrote 41 books and 1,500 magazine articles during a career that spanned almost sixty years. His books ranged from cookbooks to mystery novels and included many children's books.

REFERENCES: Wolfgang Saxon. "Jack Denton, Cookbook Author and Novelist, 79," *New York Times,* January 6, 1995; Jim Hamilton. The Writing 69th. 2005.

Scott, Sir James George (1851–1935)

Scott was born in Dairsie, Fife, and left Oxford short of graduation because of a lack of finances. He accompanied the 1875–1876 punitive expedition to Perak, Malaya, as special correspondent for the *London Standard.* Following the campaign he moved to Burma as headmaster for an Anglican mission school, where he introduced association football. He later returned to England and attempted to land a law scholarship. Narrowly missing the selection process, he returned to his beloved Burma and in 1882 published the two-volume *The Burman: His Life and Notions.* His reputation as an authority on Burma led him again to the attention of newspaper editors in search of a war correspondent in Asia. In 1884 the *Standard* hired Scott to cover the French armies in pursuit of the conquest of Tonkin. He chronicled this experience in *France and Tongking: A Narrative of the Campaign of 1884, and the Occupation of Further India* (1885).

In 1885 he was appointed to the Indian civil service, where he performed the service of peacemaker as British forces attempted to establish rule in the Shan states and quell a civil war among Burmese tribes. In 1891 he was appointed resident for the northern Shan states at Lashio and in 1902 was given a similar position for the southern Shan states. He retired from the civil service in 1910 and returned to London shortly after. He also wrote the five-volume *Gazeteer of Upper Burma and the Shan States* (1900–1901).

REFERENCE: *DNB.*

Scott, Roddy (1971–2002)

Scott was a British television journalist. The son of an RAF officer, he was descended from a former editor and owner of the *Manchester Guardian*. He was educated at Edinburgh University and entered print journalism covering the Middle East. However, seeking a larger audience, he made the transition to film and television journalism. He covered conflicts in Sierra Leone, north Iraq, Kosovo, Turkey, and finally Chechnya. where he was killed on the border with Georgia. Scott was covering a fire-fight between Russian and Chechen rebels when a Russian bullet penetrated the eyepiece of his camera while filming. His body was not immediately identified until several days later. Over the years he had sold footage to Frontline News* and others.

REFERENCES: "Briton Killed in Chechen Rebel Skirmish." BBC News. September 26, 2002; Pelin Turgut. "Roddy Scott" obituary. www.independent.co.uk, October 4, 2002.

Scovel, Henry Sylvester (1869–1905)

Better known by his middle name Sylvester, or simply Harry, Scovel was born at Denny Station, Allegheny County, Pennsylvania. He left college early to work at a variety of occupations before landing in the newspaper profession. Since he had carved out a reputation for aggressiveness, both the *Pittsburgh Dispatch* and the *New York*

Herald felt he had the makings of a correspondent and sent him to cover the conflict in Cuba in 1895. Spanish authorities quickly wearied of his persistence and had him arrested the following year. He escaped shortly after, and was next hired by the *New York World* to report the events leading up to the Spanish-American War.* He became one of the most prominent personalities of the conflict. Scovel's columns for the *World* promoted the cause of Cuban independence and elicited American support and sympathy. He lived with Cuban insurgents for almost a year, covering the guerrilla campaign and hardships until he was captured for a second time in early 1897. However, the intervention of the American government gained Scovel a quick release.

Following his escapades in Cuba, he covered the Greco-Turkish War* in 1897, returning to the States only after the sinking of the *Maine*. Scovel served as war correspondent throughout the subsequent Spanish-American War. One of his most publicized exploits was his attempt to find rebel leader General Gomez to apprise him that America had declared war on Spain. Scovel undertook several other dangerous fact-finding missions for American authorities during the hostilities. He reported the formal capitulation of Spanish forces in Havana on New Year's Day, 1899, which ended the Spanish presence on Cuba. Consistently at odds with American authorities, Scovel attempted to punch General William Shafter in the nose at ceremonies marking the end of the conflict because the general refused to allow him to be included in the official victory photograph.

Following the war, Scovel remained in Cuba as a consulting engineer to the customs service of the U.S. military government. He left this post to pursue commercial development opportunities in Havana. When he was confined to his bed by malaria in late 1904, physicians detected an abscess on his liver. In February 1905 they operated to remove it, but the wound became infected and Scovel died when doctors operated a second time.

REFERENCES: Charles H. Brown. *The Correspondents' War*. 1967; *DAB*; Joyce Milton. *The Yellow Kids*. 1989.

Screws, William Wallace
(d. 1913)

He was a lawyer in Alabama with no formal journalism training when the Civil War* began. He almost immediately left his law practice to enlist. His reportage was featured in his hometown *Montgomery Advertiser*, which like most Southern papers relied on the correspondence of soldiers in the field. During the conflict he wrote under several monikers, including "43." He rose to prominence after he became another journalistic victim of General Braxton Bragg who had him arrested and charged with publicizing troop movements in 1862. Ten days later he was released and returned to the battlefront as a soldier. During the war he fought in numerous battles, despite the fact that his poor health would have exempted him from being drafted. In 1864 he was shot through the left shoulder, but he still recovered and returned to fight another day. Most of what is known about his war reporting was lost when the files of his newspaper were destroyed by fire during the Federal taking of Montgomery, Alabama in April 1865. In 1868 Screws bought the *Advertiser*, controlling it until his death in 1912.

REFERENCE: Amy Ransford Purvis and Bradley J. Hamm, "William Wallace Screws: 'Most Useful Citizen of His Day,'" *Knights of the Quill*, 2010, 265–275.

Scudamore, Frank (1859–1939)

Scudamore covered his first war while still in his teens, reporting the Russo-Turkish War* in 1877 with Archibald Forbes* for the *Daily News*. In 1883 he covered the British campaign in the Sudan. He accompanied Baker Pasha's forces in the relief of Sinkat and Tokar after the Mahdi's massacre of Hicks' ten-thousand-man force. He later reported the Armenian massacres in 1894–99 and three years later returned to the Su-

dan with Kitchener's forces to defeat the Mahdi. According to one of his fellow correspondents, among his baggage, carried by two camels, was "his drink camel," which carried his supply of alcohol and soda. He was said to have concocted the "Abu Hamed," a drink consisting of gin, lime juice, vermouth, Angostura, and soda, a remedy for what G. W. Steevens* described as the unquenchable "Sudan thirst."

REFERENCE: Robert Wilkinson-Latham. *From Our Special Correspondent*. 1979.

Sedgwick, Alexander Cameron "A. C." (1902–1996)

Born in Sedgewick, Massachusetts, he graduated from Harvard in 1924 before joining the *New York Times* in 1925. Three years later he left the paper to write a novel, supporting himself as a sherry salesman. He returned to the paper in 1937 as its Athens correspondent. When Greece was threatened by German invasion at the onset of the war he took a post in the Middle East, where he covered military matters. Sedgwick covered the British Eighth Army's desert campaign in North Africa during World War II* for the *New York Times*. He is best remembered for his coverage of the defeat of Rommel's Afrika Corps at the Battle of El Alamein in 1942. He was wounded by shrapnel fire during the battle but made no mention of it in his report. In 1945 Sedgwick published his second novel and was made a member of the Order of the British Empire.

REFERENCE: *New York Times*. January 21, 1996.

Seldes, George (1890–1995)

Born in Alliance, New Jersey, he was hired for his first newspaper job with the *Pittsburgh Leader* in 1909. After briefly attending Harvard he returned to journalism and in 1916 took the post of managing editor of *Pulitzer's Review* in New York City. He covered the American Expeditionary

Force as a member of the press section in 1917. As the first American to enter St. Mihiel on September 13, 1918, he was received as both war hero and liberator hours before the anticlimatic arrival of Pershing and his staff. He covered the Irish uprisings in 1919 and the war in Damascus in 1926, as well as the capture of the capital city, Soueida, from the Druses. As war correspondent for the *New York Post* from 1936 to 1937 he reported the Spanish Civil War.*

A vocal critic of press censorship since being expelled from Russia while reporting the Bolshevik purges in 1923, and from Italy for his reportage of Mussolini's rise to power in 1925, he published *You Can't Print That: The Truth Behind the News* in 1929. Seldes is probably best remembered for his attacks on the American Newspaper Publishers Association in his books *Freedom of the Press* (1935) and *Lords of the Press* (1938), which became bestsellers. In 1982 he was awarded the George Polk Award in Journalism.

REFERENCES: Eugene Lyons. *We Cover the World*. 1937; George Seldes. *Witness to a Century*. 1987.

Sevareid, Eric (1912–1992)

Born in Velma, South Dakota, he entered journalism with the *Minneapolis Journal* when he was eighteen years old. He graduated from the University of Minnesota in 1935 and continued to work for the paper until he left for Europe to study political science at the London School of Economics. While in France he reported for the *New York Herald Tribune's* Paris edition and was employed as night editor for the United Press.

Shortly before the outbreak of World War II* he joined a stellar cast of newsmen assembled by Edward R. Murrow* to report the coming war. From 1939 to 1940 he covered the French army and air force in France and Belgium. He moved to London following the capitulation of France to Germany in 1940. In 1943 Sevareid left to report the battlefront in the China-Burma-India theater of the war. When his plane went down over the Assam jungle, Sevareid was forced to bail out with nineteen others and for a brief time lived among local headhunters. He returned to Europe and covered the Italian campaign and the advance of the first American troops into southern France. Sevareid went on to cover a wide assortment of stories in Yugoslavia, France, Germany, and Britain before returning to the States after the war.

It would be over two decades before he would witness the battlefront again, when he reported from Vietnam in 1966 for CBS news. He went on to become one of the most respected television journalists and worked for CBS until forced retirement in 1977. Among his awards were two Overseas Press Club Awards and the George Polk Memorial Award.

REFERENCES: Library of America. *Reporting World War Two: Part Two, American Journalism 1944–1946*. 1995.

Seymour, David "Chim" (1911–1956)

Born David Szymin in Warsaw, Poland, to the world of photography he was known simply as "Chim." He fled with his family to the Ukraine in 1914 when the German army invaded. By the age of eight he was fluent in two of the eight languages he would eventually master. Son of an early publisher of Hebrew and Yiddish authors, Seymour was drawn early to the arts. While studying graphic arts at the Leipzig Academy he began to develop his photographic skills as a hobby. With anti-Semitism sweeping through Eastern Europe he fled to Paris, where he studied at the Sorbonne and established lifelong friendships with the photographers Henri Cartier-Bresson* and Robert Capa.* All three would cover the Spanish Civil War.* Chim chose noncombatants for his subject material to demonstrate the impact of war on the refugees and floating populations.

He went on to cover World War II* in Europe and find out that most of his family and friends had been murdered by the Nazis. His pictures of the uprooted survivors of Europe following the war appeared in *Life* in 1948. As always Chim concentrated on the survivors of wars, especially the children. In 1954, when his friend Capa was killed in Vietnam, Seymour became president of Magnum Photos. In 1956 he left an assignment in Greece to cover the Arab-Israeli War in the Suez. Four days before the end of hostilities, on November 10, 1956, he was killed with photographer Jean Roy, when nervous Egyptian soldiers sprayed their jeep with machine-gun fire as they passed Anglo-French forces only six hundred feet away.

REFERENCE: Robert E. Hood. *12 at War: Great Photographers Under Fire.* 1967.

Sgrena, Giuliana (b. 1948)

Born in Masera, Italy and educated in Milan she became a vocal pacifist and leftist in the 1980s. The Italian journalist was the child of a World War II soldier and one of the founders of the 1980s peace movement in Europe. She earned her stripes as a reporter with the Italian daily *Guerra e Pace* and *Il Manifesto*. She has been a war reporter for the communist *Il Manifesto* since 1988 and has covered conflicts including the Algerian Civil War, the Somalia conflict, and the current war in Afghanistan. She refused to be embedded* to cover the 2003 Iraq War and as a result played a central role in one of the more controversial stories to come out of the war. In February 2005 she was kidnapped outside Baghdad University. Despite her affinity for the Arab plight and her clearly anti-war reporting the kidnappers held her for a month before releasing her for a $6 million ransom on March 4, 2005. She was transported by car to the Baghdad International Airport along with a Major General Nicola Calipari from the Italian military service and another agent. However, as they approached a roadblock American forces opened fire on the car killing

Calipari and wounding Sgrena and the other agent. Both survivors claim no warning was given first. A hue and cry was raised in Italy leading to a diplomatic imbroglio between the U.S. and Italy.

REFERENCE: Edward Wong and Jason Horowitz. "Italian Hostage Returns Home after 2nd Brush with Death." *New York Times International.* March 5, 2005.

Shadid, Anthony (1969–2012)

An American of Lebanese descent, Shadid was born in Oklahoma City. He became fluent in Arabic as an adult and earned a bachelor's degree in political science and journalism from the University of Wisconsin in 1990. He later joined the Associated Press, reporting from Cairo, before moving to the *Globe* in 2001. He was with the *Washington Post* from 2003 until 2009, when he joined the *New York Times* as the Baghdad bureau chief, and became the newspaper's bureau chief in Beirut, Lebanon. No stranger to war zones, in 2002 he was shot in the shoulder by an Israeli sniper in Ramallah while covering the West Bank for the *Boston Globe*. In 2011 he was reported missing along with three other reporters while covering the uprising against Gaddafi in eastern Libya. Several days later he was released along with his colleagues. Shadid won two Pulitzer Prizes for International Reporting in 2004 and 2010 for his coverage of the Iraq war. His 2006 book *Night Draws Near* covers the impact of the war on the Iraqi civilian population. He has been the recipient of a number of other awards. He died from an asthmatic attack while covering the Syrian War. *New York Times* photographer Tyler Hicks* returned his body back to Turkey.

REFERENCE: Rick Gladstone, "At Work in Syria, Times Correspondent Dies," New York Times, Feb. 16, 2012.

Shanks, William F. G. (1837–1905)

The Kentucky-born Shanks became one of the most outstanding war correspondents covering

the western theater of the American Civil War*
while still in his twenties. Reporting for the *New
York Herald,* Shanks began his battlefield coverage in the Kentucky-Tennessee war theater in the
summer of 1862. He was with General Lovell H.
Rousseau's division as it left Nashville in September of that year. Shanks would serve the dual role
of volunteer aide to Rousseau and reporter for the
Herald during the Battle of Perryville, and the next
January he witnessed the Battle of Murfreesboro.

Shanks reported the Battle of Chickamauga
from the front lines and after leaving Chattanooga narrowly escaped death in a train accident
between Nashville and Bowling Green. He was
traveling with fellow correspondent William S.
Furay, and both leaped from the train just before
the train's engineer, a Southern sympathizer, deliberately caused a collision with another train.
After he telegraphed his account of the Battle of
Chickamauga to the *Herald,* the paper claimed it
was "the best account of that battle" and "the best
account written of any battle ever fought." However, Shanks was later castigated for portraying
this battle as a federal defeat.

Shanks subsequently covered the Battles of
Chattanooga, Wauhatchie, and Lookout Mountain, and the charge up Missionary Ridge. He published his *Personal Recollections of Distinguished
Generals* shortly after the war and in 1871 covered
the Franco-Prussian War.*

REFERENCES: J. Cutler Andrews. *The North Reports the
Civil War.* 1955; Louis M. Starr. *The Bohemian Brigade.* 1954.

Shaplen, Robert Modell
(1917–1988)

During World War II* Shaplen covered one of
the first major advances along the northern coast
of New Guinea for *Time* magazine. He filed the
first eyewitness account of the atomic bombing of
Nagasaki for *Newsweek* magazine and later reported the early days of the Vietnam War* for the
New Yorker magazine beginning in 1962. Based in
Hong Kong, he was one of the few correspondents

to cover the war from start to finish. A seasoned
chronicler of the Asian scene, he was regarded as
one of the most knowledgeable correspondents of
the Vietnam press pool.

REFERENCE: Clarence R. Wyatt. *Paper Soldiers.* 1993.

Shaykhet, Arkadi (1898–1959)

Shaykhet came to prominence with his photographic account of the Russian Revolution. He
was a leading pioneer Soviet photojournalist
in the 1920s and 1930s, and his antiwar photograph "Thank You, Sons," is considered one of
the most evocative images to come out of the
Russian war with Germany.

REFERENCE: Daniela Mrazkova and Vladimir Remes,
eds. *The Russian War: 1941–1945.* 1975.

Sheean, James Vincent
(1899–1975)

Sheean was born in Pana, Illinois, and educated
at the University of Chicago. He reported for the
Chicago Daily News and the *New York Daily
News,* before moving to Italy as foreign correspondent for the *Chicago Tribune* in the early
1920s. On his first day as a foreign correspondent
he reported Benito Mussolini's march on Rome
in 1922. In 1925 he evaded French and Spanish
forces to become one of the few reporters to see
the Riffs during the Moroccan Riff War. He interviewed both brothers Abd el-Krim and the
Raisuli after his capture by the Riffs. The movie
The Wind and the Lion is thinly based on the exploits of the Raisuli in 1904 when he kidnapped
a wealthy Greek-American citizen named Ion
Pedicaris. Sheean traveled widely through the rebel countryside, where he witnessed evidence of
the rebel rout of the Spanish army several months
earlier. His reports indicated he was convinced
of the intelligence of the Abd el-Krims as well
as the sincerity of their patriotic cause. Sheean
found that contrary to reports of mistreatment,
European prisoners were treated no better or

worse than the Arab and Berber captives. He chronicled his exploits among the people of the Riff in *An American Among the Riffi* (1926).

Following the Moroccan campaign he turned to freelancing and reported the 1929 riots in Jerusalem, the Ethiopian War,* the early days of the revolution in China, and the Spanish Civil War.* During World War II* he served in army intelligence in North Africa and Italy. On assignment to interview Mahatma Gandhi in 1948 he witnessed his assassination. Sheean published numerous works of nonfiction, including studies of Gandhi, Nehru, Verdi, and King Faisal, as well as memoirs of Dorothy Thompson, Sinclair Lewis, and Edna St. Vincent Millay. His bestselling autobiography *Personal History* (1953) is one of the most powerful reminiscences of a foreign correspondent.

REFERENCES: Raymond Strock. "The Works of Vincent Sheean: The Dust of an Honest Man," *Journalism History*. Autumn/Winter 1984; David S. Woolman. *Rebels in the* Rif. 1968.

Sheehan, Neil (b. 1936)

Sheehan was born in Holyoke, Massachusetts, and following graduation from Harvard in 1958 joined the army. He became a member of the United Press International's Tokyo bureau in 1962 and began covering the developing Vietnam conflict from Saigon. In January 1963 he reported the Ap Bac disaster, where Viet Cong guerrillas shot down at least five helicopters, killing several American crew members. The Saigon press corps drew heavy criticism for its critique of the U.S.-advised Vietnamese troops.

In 1964 Sheehan moved to the *New York Times,* and after a stint in New York he returned to the Far East, reporting from Indonesia and then reporting the Vietnam War* in 1965. While on assignment at the Pentagon in 1966, he was posted to the USS *America* in the eastern Mediterranean during the Arab-Israeli Six Day War in 1967. From 1968 on he covered the White House beat. Perhaps his greatest scoop was his obtaining the Pentagon Papers in 1971. He

is the author of *The Arnheiter Affair, After the War Was Over,* and his Pulitzer Prize-winning A *Bright Shining Lie* (1988).

REFERENCES: Michael Emery. *On the Front Lines.* 1995; William Prochnau. *Once upon a Distant War.* 1995.

Sheldon, Charles Mills (1866–1928)

Charles Sheldon was born in Indiana and gained his first experience in journalism working for his publisher father. In the 1880s he traveled throughout the South as a correspondent for the American Press Association and then opened an engraving business in Kansas. In 1890 he moved to Paris and began submitting sketches to various European publications before covering the Sudan campaign as an artist-correspondent* six years later. In 1898 he chronicled the Spanish-American War* in Cuba before moving on to South Africa and the Boer War* the following year. His sketches appeared sporadically in *Frank Leslie's Weekly* and the *Black and White* in England.

REFERENCES: Charles H. Brown. *The Correspondents' War.* 1967; Pat Hodgson. *The War Illustrators.* 1977.

Sheldon-Williams, Inglis (1870–1940)

Born in England, he moved with his family to Canada in 1886. He joined the *Sphere* as an illustrator and covered the Boer War* and the Russo-Japanese War.* During the Russo-Japanese War the *Sphere* made an arrangement with *Collier's Weekly* which allowed both journals to publish each other's pictures and battle reports. Although both periodicals gave readers the illusion that the reproduced sketches were reprints from the actual battlefront they were usually redrawn from sketches by artist-correspondents.* Following the war Sheldon-Williams accompanied the Canadian Expeditionary Forces as their official war artist during World War I.*

REFERENCE: Pat Hodgson. *The War Illustrators.* 1977.

---

* Indicates a separate entry.

Shepard, Elaine (1913–1998)

Born in Olney, Illinois, she moved to Hollywood, California, in her teens in an attempt to break into motion pictures. After starring in several serials she left films for marriage. Following a divorce she pursued a career in journalism. In 1959 she covered her first foreign assignment when she was assigned to follow Vice President Nixon's visit to Moscow. Over the following years she traveled widely as a foreign correspondent and was the only woman reporter to accompany President Eisenhower's eleven-nation tour. Later she received an exclusive interview with Indian Prime Minister Nehru and in 1961 covered the civil war in the Belgian Congo.

Shepard arrived in Saigon in 1965 and began covering Operation Rolling Thunder that March. Her account of the night-bombing missions is chronicled in her book *Doom Pussy* (1967). The title of the book is drawn from a Vietnamese translation which refers to an emblem worn by the pilots of the bombers consisting of a large yellow cat with a patch over its right eye and an airplane clenched between its teeth. During the war she eschewed Saigon for frequent forays into the field to record the real war. On a visit to a Montagnard village she removed her shirt to gain the trust of the barebreasted women who were the subjects of some of her photographs.

Vehemently anti-Communist, she became a critic of the peace movement in the States as well. During the war she was awarded two citations for her coverage of helicopter assault missions, and in 1966 she returned to the United States to complete her book and marshal support for American servicemen overseas. She continued to publish pieces on the conflict and remained to the end a staunch advocate of American intervention.

REFERENCE: Virginia Elwood-Akers. *Women War Correspondents in the Vietnam War, 1961–1975.* 1988.

Shepardson, Dr. William G. (c. c. 1830)

Shepardson was one of the most outstanding reporters for the Confederate press during the American Civil War.* He began the conflict representing the *Mobile Register* and the *Columbus Times* of Georgia, for whom he reported the First Battle of Bull Run. In September he tranferred to the *Richmond Dispatch*. During his first six months with the paper his dispatches regularly appeared over his pseudonym "Bohemian" and were reprinted in numerous Southern newspapers.

In January 1862 Shepardson wrote his last dispatch for the Richmond paper. His resignation was in part due to General Joseph E. Johnston's General Order No. 98, which prohibited all war correspondents from covering his Army of the Potomac. Johnston's action was partly in response to a security breach committed by Shepardson, who had identified the location of various brigades in a report to the *Dispatch*.

Shepardson arrived in Norfolk in time to catch a steamer for Albemarle Sound, where he reported the successful Union assault on Roanoke Island in February 1862, before being captured by federal troops. Following his parole he was back with the *Mobile Register* reporting the Richmond news scene in May 1862. In the last years of the war Shepardson attempted to relieve the monotony of city reporting by occasionally working as a naval surgeon. He sporadically sent dispatches on life in the fledgling Confederate Navy to his old Richmond paper.

REFERENCE: J. Cutler Andrews. *The South Reports the Civil War.* 1970.

Shepherd, William G. (1878–1933)

An early member of the United Press staff in New York City, Shepherd personally detected the outbreak of the Triangle Shirt Waist Company fire that killed 145 people in 1911. Three years later he was in Veracruz, Mexico, reporting the landing of the U.S. Marines. When World War I* broke out prior to the withdrawal of troops from Mexico, Shepherd headed for Europe. He left London for Belgium after being granted an incredible interview with the first lord of the Admiralty, Winston Churchill.

Shepherd was the first American reporter permitted to cover the British front in France. He reported the fall of Antwerp and was the only journalist to the witness the Battle of Ypres. Along with war correspondent Will Irwin,* Shepherd was credited with being the first correspondent to report the German use of poison gas in warfare at the Battle of Ypres in the fall of 1914. He reportedly saw more of the battle than any other American reporter and during the Second Battle of Ypres was the only correspondent on the British front. Shepherd was also the first to report zeppelin raids over London in September 1914.

Although he returned to the States for a respite in the winter of 1914–1915, he remained active on the war fronts between 1914 and 1916 before joining General Pershing's staff in 1917. Following the war he covered the 1919 Paris Peace Conference for the *New York Evening Post*. His exploits were chronicled in his book *Confessions of a War Correspondent* (1917).

REFERENCES: Emmet Crozier. *American Reporters on the Western Front, 1914–18*. 1959; Robert W. Desmond. *Windows on the World*. 1980.

Sherrod, Robert (1909–1994)

Born in Thomas County, Georgia, and educated at the University of Georgia, Sherrod entered journalism in 1929 working for the *Atlanta Constitution* and a succession of other southern newspapers. During World War II* he served as correspondent for *Time* and *Life*. He was the first of *Time's* correspondents to go overseas with American forces. In 1942 he covered the first convoys for Australia. He spent six months

reporting from New Guinea and in May 1943 was assigned to Attu. He was present during the Japanese attack and witnessed the invasion of Kiska. He would later report the marine landings on Tarawa, Saipan, and Iwo Jima. Sherrod was twice decorated by the navy for bravery. Following the war he served as Far East editor for the *Saturday Evening Post*. During the Vietnam War* he reported for *Life* magazine, flying his first combat mission since 1945, and his first in a jet. Among his works on war are *Tarawa: The Story of a Battle* (1944), *On to Westward: War in the Central Pacific* (1945), and *History of Marine Corps Aviation in World War II* (1952).

REFERENCE: Library of America. *Reporting World War Two: Part Two, American Journalism 1944–1946*. 1995.

Shimamoto, Keisaburo (1937–1971)

He was a Tokyo-based photographer for the Asia Newspaper Alliance from 1963 to 1967. He was covering the war in South Vietnam as a freelancer for *Newsweek* and other journals when he died in a helicopter crash over Laos. Also perishing on the flight were Larry Burrows,* Henri Huet, and Kent Potter.*

REFERENCE: Charles Arnot. *Don't Kill the Messenger*. 1994.

Shinn, Bill (1918–2002)

Born Shinn Wha-bong in Korea, the American-educated Shinn began working as a stringer for the Associated Press in 1948. He broke the story of Douglas MacArthur's September 15, 1950 invasion of Inchon during the Korean War.* He was denied permission to use the military telephone from Korea to Tokyo. He famously circumvented the Army-imposed news blackout by using South Korean sources to get the news out. He wrote *The Forgotten War Remembered, Korea 1950–1953: A War Correspondent's Notebook & Today's Danger in Korea* (1996).

* *Indicates a separate entry.*

REFERENCE: Steven Casey. *Selling the Korean War: Propaganda, Politics, and Public Opinion in the United States, 1950–1953.* 2008.

Shirer, William Lawrence (1904–1993)

Born in Chicago, Illinois, he was educated at Coe College in Cedar Rapids, Iowa, where he first entered the world of journalism with a local paper. In 1927, his coverage of Lindbergh's landing in France won him a job as a foreign correspondent for the *Chicago Tribune.* He covered the League of Nations and the rise of Mussolini before being assigned to report Gandhi's resistance movement in India. After being fired in 1932 he was hired by the *New York Herald* Paris office. By 1937 he was in Berlin as chief correspondent for the Universal News Service covering the Third Reich. As one of the correspondents who would sound the alarm in Hitler's Germany in the 1930s, he would later call his years there "the nightmare years."

In 1938 he covered the *Anschluss* and the Sudeten crisis for CBS. Faced with having to fly to London to use the cable, he was instructed to coordinate the transmission of shortwave news broadcasts in Europe to cover the approaching conflict, setting a pattern which would be relied on throughout the war. At the outset of the war Shirer reported from the German side and was in Berlin when Germany invaded Poland in 1939. He continued his broadcasts from there until faced with increasing censorship restrictions the following year. Shirer was injured during a British bombing, losing his sight in one eye, and in 1941 he published the best-selling *Berlin Diary: The Journal of a Foreign Correspondent, 1931 to 1941.*

He covered the Allied war effort and following the war covered the Nuremberg trials and the establishment of the United Nations. He was blacklisted for five years when he refused to denounce the Hollywood 10 and made his living on the college lecture circuit. His most enduring work was the highly acclaimed best-seller *The Rise and Fall of the Third Reich,* which won the National Book Award.

REFERENCES: William Shirer. *Midcentury Journey.* 1952; William Shirer. *Twentieth Century Journey.* 1976.

"Shooting The Messenger"

By most accounts the ancient Greeks so disliked bad news that messengers carrying the bad news from one place to another were sometimes executed, leading to this timeworn adage.

REFERENCES: Paul L. Moorcraft and Phlip M, Taylor. *Shooting the Messenger.* 2008.

Sidebotham, Herbert (1872–1940)

Sidebotham was born in Manchester, England, and educated at Oxford. Upon graduation he joined the *Manchester Guardian* as a lead writer, a position he would hold for almost a quarter century. A keen student of military history, he was the paper's military critic during the Boer War,* with his columns appearing under the pseudonym "Student of War." He filled the role again during World War I* and in 1918 left the paper to become the military critic for the *Times.* He remained with the *Times* until 1921. An avid Zionist, he wrote numerous articles and several books on the subject between 1918 and 1937.

REFERENCES: David Ayerst. *The Manchester Guardian: Biography of a Newspaper.* 1971; *DNB,* 1931–1940.

Signal

Signal was the best-selling magazine in German-occupied Europe. It was published by the *Wehrmacht* beginning in the spring of 1940 and supervised by Joseph Goebbels and his Ministry of Propaganda. By most accounts it was influenced by the success of America's *Life* Magazine. Edited by the journalist Fritz Solm. *Signal* enjoyed incredible financial support. In 1940–1941 two and one half million dollars was spent on salaries alone. Its sales peaked in 1943 when it enjoyed a readership of two and a half million in twenty different languages. *Signal* also had a large circulation in the United States until December 1941 and it was published in the Irish Free State throughout the war years. It was initially created with the intention of convincing Europeans that any resistance was futile and that the Nazi war machine was invincible. Its earliest issues reflect the heady days of German success on the battlefield. One of the first periodicals to publish color photographs by its war photographers at the front, in its heyday the magazine was unmatched in color photography and military reportage. However, by the end of 1943 *Signal* began to decline in both its quality and its readership. Due to wartime exigencies, supplies of good quality paper stock were limited, and the quality of the magazine began to deteriorate. In addition, with its headquarters in Berlin coming under attack from Allied air raids it became increasingly difficult to sell an optimistic vision of the outcome of the war to German readers. By 1944 the magazine had stopped publishing regularly, but would continue to operate intermittently until March 1945, when the editor moved its archives and staff to the west in order to avoid being captured by the Soviets.

REFERENCES: S. L. Mayer, ed. *"Signal": Years of Retreat, 1943–44.* 1979; Duncan Anderson. *War A Photo History.* 2006.

Silk, George (1916–2004)

Born in Levin, New Zealand, Silk learned the craft of photography while working in a camera store in Auckland. Silk began covering the Middle East campaign during World War II* in 1940, joining Damien Parer* as Australia's second official war photographer. His photographs from Greece, Syria, and Lebanon, as well as the siege of Tobruk are considered among the best photos of these campaigns. He was captured with Australian troops at Tobruk, Libya by the forces of German Field Marshal Erwin Rommel, but

was able to escape ten days later. He resigned his position with the Australian Department of Information, like Parer, chafing at censorship and other restrictions that prevented some of his photos from seeing the light of day. In 1943 he joined *Life* magazine, for whom he covered the war in both the Pacific and European theaters, including the Battle of the Bulge. Silk later published *War in New Guinea*. While covering American troops in Europe he was the only survivor of a glider crash in southern France and was later wounded by a grenade while crossing a river into Germany. Risking radiation exposure in 1945, he took some of the first pictures in Nagasaki after the atom bomb was dropped on it.

REFERENCES: Myrna Oliver, "George Silk, 87; Life Magazine Photographer Chronicled WWII," Los Angeles Times, Oct. 28, 2004; awm.gov.au/exhibitions/focus/george-silk.asp

Simon, Bob (1941–2015)

Simon was born in the Bronx, New York and educated at Brandeis University. He has been an American Foreign Service Officer (1964–1967) and a Fulbright scholar. He joined CBS News in 1967 as a reporter. He has covered conflicts in Vietnam, the Balkans, Lebanon, Grenada, Somalia, Haiti, civil wars in Central America, the Turkish invasion of Cyprus, the North Ireland troubles, the Falkland Islands War, the Yom Kippur War and the Gaza Intifada. Between 1971 and 1977 he reported extensively from the Vietnam War. He has been the recipient of a number of awards including 23 Emmy Awards and a Lifetime Achievement Emmy in 2003. Since 1996 he has worked on both incarnations of the show *60 Minutes* and *60 Minutes II* from 1999–2005. Simon was killed in a car crash in February 2015, after his livery cab lost control and slammed into a median. He was not wearing a seatbelt.

REFERENCE: www.cbsnews.com/stories/1999/01/04/60II/main26916.shtml; Ashley Southall, "Bob Simon, Correspondent Who Covered Wars and Riots," *New York Times*, February 13, 2015.

* *Indicates a separate entry.*

Simmons, Walter (1908–2006)

Prior to World War II* Simmons had been the city editor for the *Sioux Falls Argus-Leader*. In 1944 he joined the *Chicago Tribune* and was assigned to report the war in the Pacific theater. In January 1945 he accompanied General MacArthur's troops back to Luzon, Philippines. Following the war he was chief of the *Tribune's* North Pacific bureau when the Korean War* broke out. He was in Seoul, South Korea, covering the opening of the new government under President Syngman Rhee in June 1950 when the city came under attack and war erupted. Since he was the only American correspondent on the entire front, his dispatches turned into his greatest news scoop. He would spend three months at the front before returning to Tokyo for a brief recuperation. Simmons returned in time to cover the first American troops cutting off the Communist advance, the Inchon landing, the drive to the Yalu River, and the subsequent retreat.

REFERENCE: Lloyd Wendt. *Chicago Tribune*. 1979.

Simonov, Konstantin (1915–1979)

The well-known Russian poet and novelist was born Kiril (later changed to Konstantin) Mikhailovich Simonov in St. Petersburg. His father took part in the Russian Revolution. Simonov attended university in the 1930s and graduated with a literature degree from the Gorky Institute of Literature in 1939. That same year he covered the Khalkhin Gol campaign at the end of the Soviet-Japanese campaign in Mongolia as a war correspondent. In 1941 he was served as correspondent for the journal *Red Star*. His wartime dispatches were widely read. This Soviet writer was covering the Russian front when he came under Nazi bombardment. He reported the early days of the Soviet-German war in late 1941. He wrote in December 1941: "A tremendous, magnificent change has taken place in the psychology of our troops. Our army has learnt how to conquer the Germans." He covered the war on virtually all fronts including from Romania, Bulgaria, Yugoslavia, Poland, and Germany, where he reported the Battle of Berlin. His war correspondence has been collected in the postwar publications, *Letters from Czechoslovakia, Slav Friendshio, Yugoslavian Notebook*, and *From the Black to the Barents Sea, Notes of a War Correspondent*.

REFERENCES: *Biographical Dictionary of the Former Soviet Union*. 1992; *Encyclopedia of World Literature in the 20th Century*, 1993.

Simplot, Alexander (1837–1914)

Descended from a prominent Dubuque, Iowa, family, at the outset of the American Civil War* Simplot won a commission as special artist for the trans-Mississippi West on the strength of a sketch he submitted to *Harper's Weekly*. He was educated at Rock River Seminary and then Union College in New York. Following graduation he taught school briefly before whimsically sending his sketch of hometown troops marching off to war to *Harper's*. During the war he would submit sketches rejected by *Harper's* to the *New York Illustrated News* under the pseudonym "A. S. Leclerc."

Simplot initially covered army encampments and war preparations before his magazine convinced him to go into the field with the armies. He attached himself first to the forces under General John C. Fremont, commander of the armies in the West at the start of the war, before covering the outbreak of the western naval war during the winter of 1861–1862. He accompanied Ulysses Grant's Mississippi squadron on the land-river assault against Confederate forts along the Tennessee and Cumberland Rivers. Simplot sketched the Battle of Fort Henry, the aftermath of the victory at Fort Donelson, and the surrender of Island Number 10. However, it soon became apparent that Simplot did not possess the fortitude to be a successful war artist. One source described him as the unluckiest artist of the war. While Simplot sketched the relatively insignificant taking of Island Number 10, he missed the Battle of Shiloh, one of the most important battles of the war, and following the Battle of Fort Henry he dallied long enough to miss the more pivotal Battle of Fort Donelson.

General Henry Halleck ordered all war correspondents with the Army of the Tennessee to vacate the front lines in the summer of 1862. Simplot managed to circumvent the prohibition by returning to the field posing as a sutler. Following the Battle of Shiloh, Simplot covered the Corinth campaign with Halleck's forces. He left the field briefly to recuperate back home in Dubuque but by November 1862 was campaigning with Grant's army in Tennessee. Simplot resigned from *Harper's* in early 1863, unable to find a cure for the chronic diarrhea that had plagued him since the Shiloh campaign. Simplot hung up his sketch artist's pen and entered business in Dubuque, while *Harper's* replaced him with the vastly superior combat artist Theodore R. Davis.*

REFERENCES: Philip Van Doren Stem. *They Were There.* 1959; W. Fletcher Thompson, Jr. *The Image of War.* 1959; John Patrick Hunter, "Alexander Simplot, Forgotten Bohemian," Wisconsin Magazine of History, Vol. 41, Issue 4, 1957–1958.

Simpson, John (b. 1944)

This longtime English foreign correspondent has spent his career with BBC News. According to his autobiographical writings, he has covered stories in more than 120 countries, including thirty war zones. He started his career with the BBC in 1966 and became a reporter in 1970. His most onerous assignments include the first Gulf War in 1991 when he was expelled by the authorities and his reporting the 1999 Kosovo War from Belgrade. He was one of the earliest reporters to enter Afghanistan in 2001 and was present during the U.S. and allied invasion. In 2003 he was injured by friendly fire in northern Iraq while covering the conflict in a non-embedded capacity. The attack occurred after a U.S.

warplane misidentified the American-Kurdish convoy he was travelling in. Simpson's books include *News From No-Man's Land* (2002), *The Wars Against Saddam: Taking the Hard Road to Baghdad* (2004), and *Twenty Tales from the War Zone* (2007).

REFERENCE: www.londonspeakerbureau.co.uk/john_ simpson.aspx.

Simpson, William (1823–1899)

Born in Glasgow, Scotland, with little formal education he was apprenticed to a lithographer at the age of fourteen. In 1851 he became a lithographic artist in London and rose to prominence with his plates of the Crimean War.* Although he served as a frontline artist during the conflict he was not affiliated with any newspaper or illustrated press. Rather, he was there on behalf of the London print seller, Colnaghi, for whom he was to supply paintings for a proposed series of lithographs, *The Seat of the War in the East.* In his autobiography Simpson noted that war artists were less suspect than correspondents because they were less critical in their portrayals, hence soldiers and staff treated them better.

Simpson traveled once again for Colnaghi in 1859, when he went to India to record the aftermath of the Indian Mutiny. In 1865 he joined the *Illustrated London News.* During the 1868 Abyssinia campaign he missed the action, reaching Napier's forces soon after the fall of Magdala and the death of King Theodore. But his sketches were still valuable in giving the English public an idea what conditions were like.

Following Abyssinia, he traveled widely, covering the opening of the Suez Canal, the Middle East, and the Crimea once again. With war between Germany and France looming, he reached Paris shortly after war was declared. Joining the assemblage of correspondents near Metz, he was attacked by an angry crowd who suspected his sketching of the emperor's carriage was a front for some espionage mission. France was afflicted with spy paranoia and self-doubt after

* *Indicates a separate entry.*

two costly defeats, and any artist with a sketch-book was suspicious. Simpson thought about sketching on cigarette papers, which in the event of apprehension could be made into a cigarette, eliminating any evidence. He drew the Battle of Sedan on the back of a piece of wallpaper and witnessed the siege of Strasbourg, after which he accompanied the defeated French army back to Paris. Simpson returned to France in April 1871 to cover the Paris Commune before going back to London in June.

In 1873 he arrived in California in time to report the outbreak of the Modoc Indian War. He made a series of sketches of the Lava Beds, Captain Jack's hideout, and the assassination of General Canby. Simpson reported Schliemann's archeological discoveries at Troy and Mycenae before embarking for his last battlefront during the Afghan War (1878–1880). He quit the *Illustrated London News* in 1885.

REFERENCES: Pat Hodgson. *The War Illustrators*. 1977; William Simpson. *Autobiography of William Simpson*. 1903.

Singer, Jack (1917–1944)

A former New York sportswriter, Singer was killed aboard the aircraft carrier *Wasp* during the Battle of the Solomon Islands. Reporting for the International News Service (INS), he was the first correspondent to accompany a Navy torpedo plane mission. Following the torpedo attack that killed Singer, navy officers on board the vessel completed his last dispatch and sent it to the INS. He was awarded the Purple Heart, posthumously.

REFERENCES: Robert W. Desmond. *Tides of War*. 1984; M. L. Stein. *Under Fire*. 1968.

Sino-Japanese War

On August 1, 1894, Japanese forces attacked Seoul, Korea, seized the king, and declared war on China. The war ended by February 1895 after Chinese forces were destroyed on land and sea. This was the first war in Asia to receive Western press coverage. Most reporters covering the conflict were either stringers* or special correspondents. Barred from accompanying Chinese forces, they found Japanese press restrictions not much better, setting a standard which would be repeated in 1904–1905 during the Russo-Japanese War.*

Correspondents generally languished in Tokyo and Peking, although they were present at the Port Arthur massacre committed by the Japanese in December. The most prominent correspondents included Frederic Villiers* of the *Graphic,* James Creelman* of the *New York World,* Stephen Bonsal* for the *New York Herald,* and Julian Ralph* of the *New York Sun.*

REFERENCE: Robert W. Desmond. *The Information Process.* 1978.

Sites, Kevin (b. c. 1963)

Sites has covered conflicts in virtually every medium, ranging from print and photography to the Internet. He earned an Edward R. Murrow Award for his coverage of the war in Kosovo and has worked as a television producer for NBC's *Nightly News* and ABC's *This Week with David Brinkley.* In 2005 he was hired by Yahoo as a war correspondent. Sites rose to international prominence in 2004 for videotape he shot for NBC that showed the killing of an unarmed Iraqi prisoner by a soldier in a Fallujah mosque. Some saw Sites's new arrangement with Yahoo as a publicity gimmick since he was hired to cover every conflict zone on earth in a single year. His plan was to travel "by himself" throughout 2005 and 2006, although he would hire translators, drivers, and bodyguards when necessary. This project was chronicled in the book and DVD as *In the Hot Zone: One Man, One Year, Twenty Wars* (2007). He began his tour in Somalia in September 2005 and ended it covering the Israel-Hezbollah conflict in the summer of 2006. Sites has covered anti-drug operations in the jungles of Colombia, and the fall of the Taliban in Afghanistan; and was captured by Saddam Hussein loyalists while covering the beginning of the U.S. invasion of Iraq in 2003. He shot some of the earliest video of the conflict including its first American casualty, the wounding of a journalist during a Taliban mortar attack.

REFERENCES: http://kevinsitesreports.com/KS/KSabout/KSabout.html; Saul Hansell. "Yahoo Hires Journalist to Report on Wars." *New York Times*, September 12, 2005.

Skinner, John Edwin Hilary
(1839–1894)

Skinner was born in London and graduated from the University of London in 1861 with a law degree. He joined the *Daily News* in 1864 as a special with the Danish army during the war with Prussia. His book *Tale of Danish Heroism* was one of the more insightful accounts of the Schleswig-Holstein controversy. For his service during the war he was awarded the Order of Dannerbrog by King Christian IX.

He covered the Austro-Prussian War* in 1866 and then the Franco-Prussian War* in 1870, during which he was attached to the staff of the Prussian crown prince. He reported most battles from Worth to Sedan. Following the Battle of Sedan he attempted to outmaneuver W. H. Russell* in an attempt to get his account into print in England. To their dismay, both correspondents were outscooped by Archibald Forbes,* whose telegraph dispatch preceded theirs by two days. In 1882 he covered the invasion of Egypt.

REFERENCE: Robert Wilkinson-Latham. *From Our Special Correspondent*. 1979.

Smalley, George Washburn
(1833–1916)

Born in Franklin, Massachusetts, the Yale- and Harvard-educated Smalley was barred from American Civil War* military service because of poor vision. Hired by the *New York Tribune* because of his abolitionist leanings, he was assigned to Port Royal, South Carolina, from November 1861 to April 1862. His first report was an eyewitness account of the capture of Fort Pulaski. However, when the *Tribune's* Greeley was notified that Smalley had neglected to cover other skirmishes nearby he was sharply criticized.

Attached to Major General John C. Fremont's Union command in spring 1861 Smalley witnessed the Battles of Fort Republic and Cross Keys. After a brief respite in Washington, D.C., the next phase of his journalistic career found Smalley as a volunteer aide to Major General Joseph Hooker at the Battle of Antietam, where he wrote what has been described as one of the "best single pieces of reporting done during the Civil War." On September 17, 1862, Smalley traversed the battlefield delivering orders for the wounded Hooker, and in the process gained the perspective not only to write a complete account of the battle but to scoop the other war reporters as well. His account was reprinted in over a thousand American newspapers, and he was rewarded by the *Tribune* with an editorship in New York, where he spent the duration of the war.

In 1866 he continued his career as a war reporter when he covered the Austro-Prussian War.* The following year he opened the *Tribune's* London bureau and directed its European bureau for twenty-eight years. During the Franco-Prussian War* of 1870–1871, one of Smalley's reporters assigned to cover the Prussian army scooped the world on the French defeat at the Battle of Sedan. Smalley was one of the first journalists to make extensive use of the telegraph and cable. From 1895 to 1905 he served as American correspondent for the *London Times*. Among his published works was a two-volume autobiography, *Anglo-American Memories* (1911 and 1912).

REFERENCES: J. Cutler Andrews. *The North Reports the Civil War*. 1955; Joseph Mathews. *George W. Smalley, Forty Years a Foreign Correspondent*. 1973.

---

* Indicates a separate entry.

Smedley, Agnes (1894–1950)

Born in rural Missouri, Smedley grew up in the mining town of Trinidad, Colorado. At the age of sixteen, following the death of her mother, Agnes left the family for the Southwest. She taught school in New Mexico and studied for brief periods at the Tempe Normal School in Arizona and the University of California at Berkeley. In San Diego she made the acquaintance of the anarchist Emma Goldman and became involved in the free speech movement. Increasingly drawn to political affairs, she moved to New York City and protested America's participation in World War I.* She was arrested and charged with violating the Espionage Act in 1918, but was released after several months in prison. She left America the following year and would spend most of the remainder of her life abroad.

She lived in Berlin until 1928 with Indian nationalist leader Virendranath Chattopadyaya. Ever the political activist, Smedley helped organize Germany's first public birth control clinic and actively worked in behalf of Indian nationalism. In 1929 she published her first book, *Daughter of Earth,* a thinly veiled critique and fictionalization of her life in America.

In 1928, Smedley arrived in China as correspondent for the *Frankfurt Zeitung* and became an advocate and supporter of Communist forces in rebellion against the government of Chiang Kai-shek. In 1930 Smedley joined the *Manchester Guardian* as its foreign correspondent, although she was not allowed into Communist-held areas until 1937.

After Edgar Snow* evaded nationalist forces in July 1936 and made his way to Mao Tsetung's stronghold, scoring a great journalistic coup with the first Western interview with the Communist leader, Smedley attempted to replicate the feat. That December, Smedley scored her own reporting coup when she was the only Western journalist present in Sian when Chiang Kai-shek was kidnapped and held captive temporarily by rebellious Manchurian troops. She continued to work on behalf of Communist forces from 1937 to 1940.

After Japan invaded China in 1937 she traveled with the Eighth Route Army following the wartime conciliation of the Red Army and Chiang's forces, as they formed a united front against the Japanese. Her book *China Fights Back: An American Woman with the Eighth Route Army* (1938) chronicles her exploits with the Red Army. During the late 1930s she periodically filed reports with the *Manchester Guardian.* In 1941, critically ill from malnutrition and malaria, she was forced to return to the States for medical treatment. She remained in America until 1949. That year General Douglas MacArthur's intelligence staff singled Smedley out as a Communist spy, and after she threatened libel actions the charges were withdrawn. But, her connections to her Communist past made it increasingly difficult for her to make a living in a postwar America living in fear of the Red menace. In November 1949 she moved to England, hoping to eventually return to China. She died in an Oxford nursing home of pneumonia on May 6, 1950. Ultimately, she returned to China when her deathbed request to be buried there was granted. She is one of only two foreigners buried in Communist China's equivalent of Arlington Cemetery.

REFERENCES: *DAB;* Peter Rand. *China Hands.* 1995.

Smith, Colin (b. 1944)

Born in Birmigham, England, Smith worked as a roving reporter for the *Observer* for almost thirty years, reporting from war zones in the Middle East, Africa, and Asia. He covered the terrorist Black September aircraft hijackings in 1970 and the Arab-Israeli War of 1973. In 1971 he reported the Bengali uprsing of former East Pakistan and then the last stages of the Vietnam War. He was captured by Katanga rebels during their invasion of Zaire in 1977 and was ambushed several times during the invasion of Cyprus by Turkey.

Smith has also chronicled the first Gulf War, accompanying the US Marines into Kuwait City, the siege of Sarajevo and the Rwandan massacres. In 1974 and 1984 he was recognized as International Reporter of the Year. He has written a number of books, including the novel *The Last Crusade*, and the non-fiction works *Singapore Burning* (2005) and *England's Last War Against France* (2009)

REFERENCE: Dennis Griffiths, ed. *The Encyclopedia of the British Press*. 1992; http://www.colin-smith.info/about_colin.htm.

Smith, Dan (1865–1934)

Born in Ivugtut, Greenland, and raised in New York City, he went to Copenhagen at fourteen to study art. In 1890 he joined the staff of *Leslie's* as a sketch artist. He covered the 1890–1891 Indian troubles on the Pine Ridge Reservation and Wounded Knee. Until 1897, he traveled the West sketching Native American and outdoor scenes. He left for Hearst's newspapers in 1897 and worked as artist-correspondent* during the Spanish-American War.* For the next twenty years his illustrations appeared in the *Sunday World* magazine section and were syndicated nationally.

REFERENCE: Peggy and Harold Samuels. *Samuels' Encyclopedia of Artists of the American West*. 1985.

Smith, Elias (?)

In July 1862 Smith scooped the competition with his account of the Peninsular campaign during the American Civil War* for the *New York Times*. On February 7, Smith witnessed the Battle of Roanoke Island when he accompanied General Ambrose E. Burnside's expedition to seize the island in order to stop Confederate blockade running. In late 1863 Smith again was with Burnside during the siege of Knoxville for the *New York Tribune*. His dispatches on the fall of Atlanta in 1864 are considered among the best accounts of the campaign. Later that year he covered the Battle of Cedar Creek.

REFERENCES: J. Cutler Andrews. *The North Reports the Civil War*. 1955; Louis M. Starr. *Bohemian Brigade*. 1954.

Smith, Ernest (c. 1865–1935)

Smith was born in Hampshire, England, and worked for several smaller papers before moving to the *Daily News* in 1890s. In 1900 he joined the *Morning Leader* and the *Star* as a special correspondent covering the Boer War.* Employed as both photographer and writer, he covered the siege of Ladysmith.*

REFERENCE: Robert W. Desmond. *The Information Process*. 1978.

Smith, Frederick Edwin "F. E." (1872–1930)

Best known in later years as Lord Birkenhead, he was selected to head Great Britain's Government Press Bureau during World War I, which was set up to censor news and telegraphic reports from the British military and to release vetted information to the London and worldwide press. He went on to a distinguished career as a stateman and lawyer.

REFERENCES: *Time* magazine obituary, October 13, 1930; www.answers.com/topic/f-e-smith-1st-earl-of-birkenhead.

Smith, Howard Kingsbury (1914–2002)

Born in Ferriday, Louisiana, Smith graduated from Tulane University in 1936 and the following year won a Rhodes scholarship to Oxford. During World War II* he joined the staff of CBS and reported from Berlin until America entered the war in December 1941. Like many of his fellow journalists he quickly fell into disfavor with the Nazis and was forced to flee Germany after the attack on Pearl Harbor. He managed to escape to Switzerland on the last train from Berlin for Americans. Smith spent the remainder of the war broadcasting for CBS from Berne, Switzerland. The

Indicates a separate entry.

following years saw the publication of his book *Last Train from Berlin*. He covered the battlefront as the Ninth Army correspondent in France, Holland, and Germany, ultimately winning much critical claim and four consecutive Overseas Club Awards. He returned to the United States and a career in radio and television, winning the George Polk Award in 1960. In 1966 he reported the expanding war in Southeast Asia for ABC.

REFERENCE: Robert B. Downs and Jane B. Downs. *Journalists of the United States*. 1991.

Smith, J. Andre (1880–1959)

Born in Hong Kong, he relocated with his family ten years later to New York City. By 1911 he was considerd an established etcher and painter and had developed more importantly, "an ability to work accurately and rapidly, which would serve him well on the battlefields of Europe." Since he had the aptitude for working quickly he produced more art than any of the other official artists of the AEF during the last year of World War I. He was also the only one of the eight artists to receive formal military training and the first of them to arrive in France. He often worked together with his fellow AEF artist Peixotto*. Folowing the Armistace he followed American troops to Germany. He subsequently published *In France with the American Expeditionary Forces*, which offered one hundred selected drawings (but few reflected the battlefield). During his officer training before he became an official AEF artist, Smith had cut his leg on barbed wire in 1917. It continued to plague him throughout the war and in 1924 he had to have the leg amputated below the knee.

REFERENCE: Alfred Emile Cornebise. *Art from the Trenches*. 1991.

Smith, Vaughan (b. 1963)

Smith served as an officer in the British Army's Grenadier Guards, with tours in North Ireland, Cyprus and Germany. He worked as a microlight test plane pilot before turning fulltime to journalism as an independent cameraman and video news journalist in the 1990s, covering conflicts in Iraq, Afghanistan, Bosinia, Chehnya, and Kosovo, where he survived a sniper's bullet which lodged in his cell phone. He was a founder of the Frontline Club* and of Frontline News TV.* He has conducted journalist safety programs and worked on the acclaimed documentary *The Valley* about the war in Kosovo. According to his biography he "filmed the only uncontrolled footage of the Gulf War in 1991 after he bluffed his way into an active duty unit disguised as a British soldier."

REFERENCES: www.bloodtrailfilm.com/vaughan-smith. php; David Loyn. *Frontline*. 2005.

Smith, W. Eugene (1918–1978)

He was born in Wichita, Kansas, and educated at the University of Notre Dame on a special photography scholarship. He entered journalism with various Wichita newspapers while still in his teens and in 1937 joined the staff of *Newsweek* magazine. He was fired from his job for using a miniature camera against company policy. He freelanced for a variety of publications during a period which he described as his "creative immaturity." His career as a photojournalist took off when *Life* magazine published some of his work, leading to an on-and-off position on the staff from 1939 to 1955.

He injured himself accidentally in 1942 while making a photograph of simulated battle conditions for *Parade* magazine. Unable to serve in the armed forces due to defective hearing as a result of the explosion, he served as a war correspondent for the Ziff-Davis Publishing Company. In 1943 he became a war correspondent for *Flying* magazine and flew sixteen combat missions in the Pacific. His photographs are memorable for his employment of dramatic techniques using aerial angles and harsh contrasts. He was known in the press corps as "Wonderful Smith" to differentiate him from other Smiths by using his first initial. Originally he covered the Atlantic theater before switching to the Pacific. He was aboard the aircraft carrier *Independence* covering the second raid on Wake Island and then the *Bunker Hill* during the attack on Rabaul. He reported the Battles of Tarawa and Naru Island, and had flown over sixteen air strikes before taking respite in San Francisco in March 1944. Much to his dismay he found, as most combat photographers during World War II* would, that censors had blocked the release of almost half of his photos. He resigned from Ziff-Davis and joined the ranks of *Life*.

He covered the invasion of Saipan in June 1944 and the invasion of Guam the following month. After bouts with dengue fever he was forced to recuperate at Pearl Harbor, where he soon rejoined the *Bunker Hill* and became the only combat photographer to accompany air raids over Tokyo in February 1945. Smith was with the marines for the assault on Iwo Jima. He covered virtually every phase of the Pacific theater as the war moved toward conclusion. He covered the invasions of Guam and then Okinawa, where he was severely injured by shell fire, requiring evacuation to Guam. Due to his injuries he was not in Japan to cover the treaty signing and spent the next two years undergoing treatment for his wounds.

His postwar career saw Smith return to freelancing after *Life* refused to give him control over his photo essay on Albert Schweitzer. During the 1960s and 1970s he photographed the industrial landscape of Japan and the devastating impact of mercury poisoning at Minimata, Japan, receiving worldwide accolades. He was severely beaten by thugs for his exposure of the Minimata poisoning in 1972, leading to a temporary loss of sight.

REFERENCES: Jim Hughes. *W. Eugene Smith: The Life and Work of an American Photographer.* 1989; W. Eugene Smith. *W. Eugene Smith: His Photographs and Notes.* 1969.

Sneed, James Roddy (1818–1889)

Born in Georgia, Sneed covered the Civil War* for the *Savannah Republican* and helped found the Press Association of the Confederate States of America (Confederate Press Association).* He covered the war beginning with the siege of Fort Sumter and Charleston in April 1861. While he was one of the Confederacy's first war correspondents, according to his biographer he spent most of the war in an editorial or administrative capacity. Like most southern newspaper editors he was hamstrung by a lack of materials required for putting out his paper. His editorials sometimes focused on the inability to find paper, ink, and other supplies from the outset of the war. One of the ways he found to get around this was to make the newspaper smaller and increase subscription rates. The latter was especially necessary due to the increasing costs of paper, lack of advertising dollars and the tripling of telegraphic costs. He proved among the more vocal critics of the army's heavy-handed control of all information and the lack of press freedom. Sneed and two other journalists put together a set of resolutions chastising General Joseph E. Johnston's proclamation to oust all reporters from the army. However, this did little to stop Confederate generals from expelling reporters from the battlefront during the war. Following the war he moved to Savannah, where he became locally known for his "colorful" poetry. He served as postmaster of the U.S. Senate for several years in the 1880s and as an auditor of the U.S. Treasury under President Grover C. Cleveland.

REFERENCE: Bruce Mallard, "James Roddy Sneed: 'There Can Be No Greater Tyranny Than a Muzzled Press,'" *Knights of the Quill*, 2010, 341–361.

Snow, Edgar (1905–1972)

Born in Kansas City, Missouri, Snow attended the University of Missouri and the Columbia University School of Journalism. In 1928 he joined the Hong Kong staff of the *China Weekly Review* and then the *Chicago Tribune*. Within two years he became a correspondent for the Consolidated Press Association. He traveled widely throughout Asia on assignment, and in 1933 he published his first book, *The Far Eastern Front*, while teaching at Yenching University in Peking. Shortly after leaving the university he set out to cover the Chinese Communists. Snow claimed to be the first person to penetrate the 1936 civil war blockade and interview Mao Tse-tung, Chou En-lai, and other leaders of the Chinese Red Army in his book *The Other Side of the River: Red China Today* (1962). His coverage of the civil war for the *New York Sun* and the *London Daily Herald* proved to be his greatest reporting coup, resulting in the international best-seller *Red Star over China* (1937). He covered the Chinese Civil War until 1940, when he returned home to a post as world correspondent and associate editor for the *Saturday Evening Post*.

REFERENCE: John Hohenberg. *Foreign Correspondence: The Great Reporters and Their Times.* 1964.

Soloviev, Andrei (1955–1993)

He entered photojournalism with ITAR-TASS news agency. In 1989 he covered the Romanian reveolution and then the 1991 Persian Gulf War. In 1991 he was honored with a World Press Photo "Golden Eye" Award for his work covering ethnic bloodletting in the Caucasus Mountains, Moldova and Tajikistan. Soloviev met his death while covering fighting between Georgian and Abkhazian troops over the breakaway republic of Abkhazia. An experienced war photographer who often wore a bullet-proof vest, he was working as a Russian free-lance photographer on assignment for AP when a bullet passed through his unprotected shoulder and into his chest. Soloviev had previously suffered two gunshot wounds while covering conflict in the former Soviet Union republics; the second occasion was just a week before he was killed.

REFERENCE: AP Wall of Honor, www.ap.org/wallofhonor/1980_1999.html.

Somers, Luke Daniel (1981–2014)

Born in London, Somers grew up in the United States and was educated at Beloit College in Wisconsin. In 2008 he began traveling in the Arab world, settling in Yemen, where he worked as a freelance journalist and photographer. His work appeared in the BBC, Al Jazeera, and the *Yemen Times*. In September 2013 he was kidnapped by Al-Qaeda in the Arabian Peninsula (AQAP) in Yemen's capital, of Sana'a. At the end of December 2014 Al-Qaeda released a proof-of-life video telling the United States that it had three days to meet an ultimatum or the hostage would be killed. However, specific demands were never elucidated. News and human rights organizations, family, and friends cooperated in a campaign for his release, pleading for mercy and reminding his captors that Somers had been a force for good during his years in Yemen. Behind the scenes, the Pentagon had already launched an unsuccessful rescue mission earlier in the month. While it had been successful in rescuing six other captives, all Western hostages had been moved several days earlier. The same day that the United States released details of the mission (December 4, 2014), AQAP announced it would execute Somers if their unspecified demands were not met. Two days later, another special operations force was sent in to rescue Somers and a South African teacher, Pierre Korkie. The rescue forces, which included the Yemeni military, followed on the heels of a drone strike near the compound but were spotted by the captors. When American soldiers broke into the facility where the captives were held following a firefight they found both hostages wounded and on the verge of death. Both died shortly after being lifted off onto V-22 Ospreys, where medical teams performed airborne surgery to no avail.

REFERENCES: "Luke Somers, American Killed in Yemen, Had Wanderlust," Huffington Post, Dec. 6, 2014; "US

Hostage Luke Somers Dies after Rescue Bid," BBC News, Dec. 7, 2014; https://cpj.org/killed/2014/luke-somers.php.

Sotloff, Steven Joel (1983–2014)

Sotloff grew up in Miami and majored in journalism at the University of Central Florida. He specialized in reporting on the Arab world and had worked for a variety of major U.S. news sources, including *Time, Christian Science Monitor, Foreign Policy,* and *World Affairs.* He was kidnapped near Aleppo, Syria in 2013 and held captive by militants from the Islamic State of Iraq and the Levant (ISIL).* In one of his more prominent news reports for *Time* he chronicled the shipping of weapons and the migration of Al-Qaeda fighters from Libya to Syria to help topple the Assad regime. Sotloff was one of the reporters who visited the Benghazi compound after the U.S. ambassador and three other Americans were killed on September 11, 2012. Sotloff was kidnapped along with his fixer and several others as they crossed into Syria from Turkey. After his capture, all strings were pulled to prevent him being identified as Jewish and as an Israeli-American, especially after his ISIL captors showed him in the beheading video with James Foley.* Despite entreaties for his release by his family and human rights groups he was beheaded around September 2, 2014. His editor at *Media Line* described Sotloff as "one of the most courageous, talented and insightful journalists that I have met."

REFERENCE: "Steven Sotloff," http://cpj.org/killed/2014/steven-sotloff.php.

South African War

See BOER WAR.

Southworth, Alvan S. (1846–1901)

Born in Lockport, New York, Southworth attended the U.S. Naval Academy before joining the *New York Herald.* Prior to 1871 he covered the Fenian uprising in Canada and the Franco-Prussian War,* including the Paris Commune. In 1871 he was assigned to investigate the disappearance of Sir Samuel Baker, who was in the Sudan on a military mission to suppress the slave trade and annex the upper Nile for Egypt. His travels to Khartoum, the Red Sea, and Egypt are detailed in *Four Thousand Miles of African Travel: A Personal Record of a Journey up the Nile and Through the Soudan to Central Africa* (1875). Following his African adventure he returned to the United States and a career in the railroad business.

REFERENCE: *New York Times.* January 8, 1901.

Spanish-American War

In the 1890s reports of Spanish brutality against the Cubans began to attract American interest and stimulate sympathy for the Cuban independence movement. With the outbreak of the Cuban insurrection in 1896 and the subsequent declaration of independence from Spain, American newspapers provided their readership with lurid, sensationalist accounts of the growing Cuban conflict. When the U.S. battleship *Maine* exploded mysteriously in Havana Harbor on February 15, 1898, Congress recognized Cuba's independence and demanded that Spain give up the island. In response Spain broke off diplomatic relations with the United States, and on April 25 Congress declared war on Spain.

Most of the action took place in Cuba and Puerto Rico between June and July 1898. Although it was of short duration, the Spanish-American War was covered by more reporters than any previous event in history. Estimates of the number of war correspondents covering the conflict range as high as five hundred. However, Charles H. Brown, an authority on the conflict, believes the numbers were much lower. He found reference to approximately three hundred members of the press, including seventeen British journalists and three from Canada. Charles

Indicates a separate entry.

Sanford Diehl,* who represented the Associated Press during the war, placed the number as low as two hundred.

Many members of the press had noted the winds of war as early as April and were already in Cuba when hostilities broke out between America and Spain. Early arrivals included neutral British observers such as Edward Frederick Knight* for the *Times,* John B. Atkins* for the *Manchester Guardian,* George Lynch* of the *Daily Chronicle,* Charles E. Hands* for the *Daily Mail,* Seppings Wright* of the *Illustrated London News,* and H. A. Gwynne of Reuters.*

The Spanish-American War was one of the most expensive wars to cover, with the main expense involving communications. Cables connecting the island were cut at the outset of the war, forcing correspondents to rely on dispatch boats to get their reports to the nearest telegraph or cable office. The most popular transmission stations were located in Key West, Florida; Kingston or Port Antonio, Jamaica; St. Thomas in the Virgin Islands, and other West Indies ports. Companies chartering boats to the newspapers reaped a windfall profit, with fees of five to six thousand dollars a month not atypical. Telegraph dispatches from Key West to New York averaged five cents a word, with payment required in gold specie.

New York papers were the best represented of the American papers. William Randolph Hearst's* *New York Journal* provided sixty to seventy correspondents, including Hearst himself. Some of the more noteworthy journalists for the paper included James Creelman,* Frederic Remington,* and Stephen Crane,* late of the *New York World.* Present for the *New York Herald* were Richard Harding Davis,* Francis Millet,* and Stephen Bonsal.* Other notable correspondents included Charles Sanford Diehl, John P. Dunning,* and Reuben Briggs Davenport* of the AP, W.A.M. Goode,* George Bronson Rea,* Ralph D. Paine,* and Percival Phillips.* In addition to the hundreds of male reporters three women recorded the conflict at various times.

Katherine White reported for the *Chicago Record* while engaged as a Red Cross nurse, and Josephine Miles Woodward and Katherine Blake Watkins* provided sporadic service.

Although the war did not produce a photographer on par with Mathew Brady,* there were several war photographers on hand who managed to obtain excellent pictures. Among them were James Burton,* William Dinwiddie,* A. D. Brittingham, and others. Physical conditions presented formidable barriers to the intrepid photographers, including tropical heat, a superabundance of light, and frequent rain. Film stock and plates were often ruined by the extreme moisture. Inside their darkrooms photographers turned to innovation by using alcohol to hasten the drying of negatives in order to prevent the gelatin from congealing in the tropical heat. By the time they had adapted to the new climate the war was over. Some photographers took their skills to the Philippines, where their techniques were well suited.

Few professional photographers bothered to cover the war. Among the most prominent were James Hare* of *Collier's Weekly* and John C. Hemment,* working for William Randolph Hearst. As Hearst's personal photographer, Hemment was afforded a well-equipped floating darkroom on Hearst's boat the *Sylvia.* However, his images paled in comparison to Hare's, taken in the heat of battle with a small box camera, heralding the future use of light cameras such as the Leicas in the twentieth century. Several war correspondents brought along cameras as well. Richard Harding Davis* and Burr McIntosh* supplemented their print journalism with photographic images.

War artists supplemented the photographic record and their work was often considered superior. Among the most noted artists were Frederic Remington,* John T. McCutcheon* of the *Chicago Tribune,* Howard Chandler Christy,* and William J. Glackens, a future member of the "ashcan school" of art.

The Spanish-American War was a watershed of sorts in the history of war journalism.

No previous war had been so heavily covered, as American newspapers introduced true mass circulation. In addition the war brought advances in news photography and introduced motion picture photography as a supplement to news reporting.

REFERENCES: Charles H. Brown. *The Correspondents' War.* 1967; Frank Friedel. *The Splendid Little War.* 1958; Joyce Milton. *The Yellow Kids.* 1989.

Spanish Civil War

On July 18, 1936, army generals Francisco Franco, Emilio Mola, and Jose Sanjuro began a revolt against the Popular Front government of the Spanish Republic formed by Manuel Azafia the previous February. The revolt was secretly sponsored by Nazi Germany and Fascist Italy. Within two days the entire country was embroiled in civil war. The war ended in March 1939 with Republican forces defeated and a new government headed by General Franco. Franco's forces were identified as insurgents, Nationalists, or Falangists, while government troops were referred to as Republicans or simply "government" forces.

In July 1936 foreign intevention on behalf of Franco's forces began with Fascist Italy and Nazi Germany sending men and equipment to the insurgents. This story was first reported by *New York Times* correspondent Frank Kluckholn,* who was with Franco's troops. Once it was revealed who broke the story Kluckholn was forced to flee for his life.

The war would prove both confusing and dangerous for the legion of correspondents descending on Spain. Journalists faced every manner of barrier in covering the war. Difficulties included problems of housing, transportation, food, news gathering, censorship, health, and language. Four journalists were ultimately killed, many wounded, and several were jailed and expelled. On New Year's Eve 1937 Harvard graduate Brad Johnson, representing *Newsweek*, and Edward J. Neil, Jr., became the only

two American correspondent war deaths of the conflict. They were killed when artillery fire hit the car they were traveling in.

Since the Spanish press could not be depended on for accurate coverage of the war, and those of the Axis countries were controlled by the government, coverage was best provided by the neutrals, many of whom came to the conflict with prior experience in the recent Ethiopian War.* The scoop announcing the outbreak of the war was delivered by Lester Ziffren of the United Press, who was soon joined by Kluckholn and his *Times* colleague Lawrence A. Fernsworth. Veteran correspondents of the Ethiopian War included Vincent Sheean* for the *Chicago Tribune*, Webb Miller* and Reynolds Packard* of the UP, Herbert L. Matthews* for *New York Times*, John T. Whitaker* of the *New York Herald*, Floyd Gibbons* and Karl H. Von Wiegand for the International News Service (INS), Ladislas Farago of the *New York Times*, Ernest Richard Sheepshanks of Reuters,* George L. Steer* of the *London Times*, and Percival Phillips* of the *Daily Telegraph*.

Other experienced correspondents who arrived in Spain included Leland Stowe* of the *New York Herald Tribune*, George Seldes* of the *New York Post*, O'Dowd Gallegher* and Noel Monks* of the *Daily Express*, Henry T. Gorrell* of the UP, Arthur Koestler* of the *News Chronicle*, and Harold "Kim" Philby* of the *London Times*. Martha Gellhorn,* representing *Collier's Weekly*, was one of five women reporting the war, and her future husband Ernest Hemingway* was with Republican forces for North American Newspaper Alliance (NANA). Photographer Robert Capa* and his lover Gerda Taro,* the latter of whom would die in the conflict, were there for *Life* magazine. In addition to the dozens of other less well known journalists from Great Britain and the United States reporting the war were many representatives of the French press.

Most of the correspondents were committed ideologically to the Republicans and covered the

---

* Indicates a separate entry.

war with a passion unmatched in previous wars. Many saw Spain as a place to stop the spread of fascism. Their idealism providing a lure to prominent literary figures and the best journalists of the era. Objectivity often suffered as numerous correspondents joined the Republicans at the battlefront. At various times Hemingway, Claud Cockburn,* and Eric Blair* brandished weapons against the Nationalists. Others participated as a cover for Commintern activities, including the Soviet agent Philby and Arthur Koestler. While correspondents were quick to publicize Nationalist atrocities they generally failed to report the imperfect side of the Republicans, who were guilty of their own excesses. Among the more controversial news stories associated with the war were the bombing of Guernica* and Capa's photograph "Death of a Loyalist Soldier."

REFERENCES: Robert W. Desmond. *Crisis and Conflict: World News Reporting Between Two World Wars, 1920–1940.* 1982; Robert W. Desmond. *Tides of War.* 1984; Phillip Knightley. *The First Casualty.* 1975; Trevor Royle. *War Report: The War Correspondent's View of Battle from the Crimea to the Falklands.* 1987; Peter Wyden. *The Passionate War: The Narrative History of the Spanish Civil War.* 1983.

Spratt, Leonidas W. (1818–1903)

Born in the vicinity of Fort Mill, South Carolina, he was a first cousin of President James K. Polk. He was educated at what was then South Carolina College before taking up the legal practice and by 1850 was practicing in Charleston. As an editor and publisher of the *Charleston Southern Standard* in 1853, he used it as a vehicle for promoting the reopening of the slave trade (outlawed in 1808). When South Carolina became the first state to secede from the Union, Spratt was the only correspondent to sign the South Carolina Ordinance of Secession. When hostilities broke out he headed out to the battlefront to cover the war for the *Charleston Mercury*. In May he was covering the conflict from Charlottesville, Virginia, under his initials, "L.W.S."

His writings focused on the poor condition of the Confederate soldiers, the strategic value of Harpers Ferry, and just ordinary camp life. He covered the Federal invasion of Virginia, hoping to cover enemy forces by following in a buggy, but it never showed up and he had to leave behind all of his possessions as he headed to Manassas Junction, where he would report on the First Battle of Bull Run (Manassas) on July 21, 1861. He was among an entourage of war reporters that included Felix Gregory de Fontaine* (*Charleston Courier* and *Richmond Enquirer*), William G. Shepardson* (*Columbus (Ga.) Dispatch* and *Montgomery Advertiser*), and David G. Duncan (*Richmond Dispatch*). However, in their rush to reach the frontlines they left behind their field glasses with which they planned to watch the battle. They were saved at the last moment when an officer loaned them a "powerful opera glass."

Spratt would write several lengthy reports of the battle, including his most famous, which contained the anecdote that gave General Stonewall Jackson his famous moniker, "Stonewall." In Spratt's article he reported the death of General Barnard E. Bee, including his purported immortal last words after being mortally injured, "There is JACKSON standing like a stonewall." The legend of Stonewall Jackson traveled quickly as it was picked up and recounted in newspapers and around Confederate campfires. Just several days after his famous report, Riordan abruptly quit his job as *Mercury* war correspondent. He never quite explained why he did this, but one of his biographers claimed it had to do with the difficulty in gathering information for his reporting. He left journalism for several months to deliver a series of lectures on the war and to help raise money for sick and wounded soldiers. Before 1861 had concluded he joined Martin's Regiment of the South Carolina Militia and rose through the ranks. Unscathed in battle, he was injured in a train accident. Returning to the battlefield following his recovery in 1862 he was appointed a judge in General

James Longstreet's military court, a position he apparently held through the end of the war. He returned to Charleston after the Confederate surrender at Appomattox Court House and continued his law career.

REFERENCE: Patricia G. McNeely, "Leonidas W. Spratt: Preserving the Legend of 'Stonewall' Jackson," *Knights of the Quill*, 2010, 140–159.

SS-Standarte Kurt Eggers

This German Waffen SS unit, primarily a war correspondents unit, was formed in 1940 as the *SS-Kriegsberichter-Kompany*. It was initially made up of four platoons of war correspondents along with support staff. The platoons could operate separately from each other and were each provided with still and movie cameras that allowed them to document the actions of SS Waffen units in battle. Each unit was attached to a different Waffen-SS combat unit, reporting combat through France and the Low Countries. By 1941 the number of Waffen-SS units had increased so it was necessary to increase the number of war correspondent units to accompany all of them. In 1943 after the death of the editor of the *Das Schwarze Korps*,* Kurt Eggers,* the unit was renamed SS-Standarte Kurt Eggers in his honor. Members of this unit included photographers, movie cameramen, writers, broadcasters and recorders that served in the field of operations. The unit also had several foreign correspondents (multi-lingual) who reported the war from Germany's frontlines for their papers at home. Although it is hard to substantiate, the axis history website claims it had three English volunteers, two U.S. citizens, and several others from Sweden and New Zealand.

REFERENCES: Waffen-SS Units. www.axishistory.com/index.php?id=2008; www.search.com/references/SS-Standarte_Kurt_Eggers;

Stackpole, Peter (1913–1997)

Born in San Francisco, he worked with Alfred Eisenstaedt, one of the earliest staff photographers for *Life*. He worked for the magazine from 1936 to 1960. Until 1943 he mainly photographed Hollywood celebrities. However, as a photographer-correspondent during the invasion of Saipan in 1943–1944, he took some of the most memorable pictures of World War II.*

REFERENCES: Jorge Lewinski. *The Camera at War.* 1978; NY Times, May 14, 1997.

Stanley, Sir Henry Morton (1841–1904)

Better known as an explorer, Stanley was born in North Wales as John Rowlands. Taking the name of his adoptive father, who resided in New Orleans, he became an American citizen. He returned to Louisiana from California shortly after the outbreak of the American Civil War.* He joined the Confederacy as a private but was soon taken prisoner by Union forces at the Battle of Shiloh. Switching his allegiance to the North, he was assigned to the ironclad *Ticonderoga* at the rank of ensign.

Following the Civil War he entered journalism as a special correspondent for the *Missouri Democrat* at fifteen dollars per week plus travel expenses. He supplemented his income by supplying articles for several other papers, including the *New York Herald*. In 1867 he covered the American Indian Wars* for the St. Louis-based paper, accompanying Major General Winfield Scott Hancock's force against the southern Plains Indians. While Stanley published many dispatches during the expedition, it proved uneventful. During this stint he conducted an interview with noted Western scout and gunfighter "Wild Bill" Hickok.

Soon after the conclusion of the expedition Stanley resigned and headed for New York, where he was hired by the *New York Herald*. In 1867 he was assigned to cover the British expedition to Abyssinia. Stanley accompanied Sir Robert Napier's expedition on its march to Magdala, where he reported the storming of the fortress and the entry of British forces into King

Theodore's stronghold. During this conflict the novice reporter firmly established his reputation as a journalist. Prior to his arrival in Abyssinia he had made arrangements for his dispatches to be given priority handling, resulting in his scoop of the fall of Magdala for the *Herald*.

In 1868 Stanley was given his most famous assignment when he was ordered to "find Livingstone," David Livingstone being a missionary lost in Africa. Successfully completing this mission in 1871, Stanley returned to London the following year and was awarded the Gold Medal of the Royal Geographical Society.

The next phase of his career began in 1873, when he covered Sir Garnet Wolseley's Ashanti campaign for the *Herald*. In 1874 he was commissioned by both the *Daily Telegraph* and the *New York Herald* to find the sources of the Congo and Nile Rivers. The years 1879 to 1884 saw Stanley in the employ of King Leopold of Belgium, exploring the Congo territory. In March 1887 he was hired to rescue the German naturalist Eduard Schnitzer, better known as Emin Pasha, which he accomplished the following year. He died a year after suffering paralysis in 1903. He published numerous books on African exploration. His account of his African military exploits was released as *Coomassie and Magdala* in 1874, and in 1909 *The Autobiography of Sir Henry Morton Stanley* was posthumously published.

REFERENCES: *DNB*, 1901–1911; Robert Wilkinson-Latham. *From Our Special Correspondent*. 1979; Tim Jeal. *Stanley*. 2007.

Stars and Stripes

Stars and Stripes was published under the supervision of the Press Section of the Censorship and Press Division of the Intelligence Branch of the General Staff of the Allied Expeditionary Force (AEF). This newspaper was produced by the armed forces for the military beginning in World War I.* It was the premier troop newspaper of its era beginning with its first issue on February 8, 1918. An eight-page weekly, it appeared every Friday until June 13, 1919. At its peak it was produced by a staff of over three hundred. Created by order of General Quarters of the AEF, its initial goals were to keep units as well informed as possible and to function as an outlet for creative contributions by members of the AEF. It was also to provide information from home, along with general news and war reports, and to emphasize the role of the United States in the war. At first it was published at AEF Field Press headquarters in Neuchateau, but was soon relocated to larger quarters in Paris.

During World War II* the newspaper was revived as a daily in almost thirty editions and reclaimed its place as the best-known troop paper in Europe. Most sources indicate that President Roosevelt suggested resurrecting the paper. The World War II editions began in London in 1942 as the Thirty-fourth Infantry Division prepared to leave for the North African landings. A month following the Allied landings the Mediterranean edition was established in a Red Cross building in Algiers. Other editions soon followed with the opening of each new front. By January 1945 circulation exceeded 1,200,000 issues daily.

By most accounts the World War I edition was the superior of the two. Judged on its literary and technical merits it was truly first-rate. While it was faced with censorship restrictions imposed by a board of control, the content of each issue still reflected the concerns of a staff of writers drawn from the enlisted ranks who in the end exercised control over the newspaper and its operations. During World War II there were significantly more high-level officers who consistently interfered with the production of the newspaper.

Following World War II *Stars and Stripes* continued in two editions. With the outbreak of war in 1950, the Korean War* edition of the paper was created by a staff that eventually grew to almost seventy. One authority on armed forces newspapers noted that the World War I edition is best described as "famous" compared to the

World War II incarnation, which was "professional," but that by the time of the Vietnam War* it had become simply an "organization newspaper."

REFERENCE: Alfred Emile Cornebise. *Ranks and Columns: Armed Forces Newspapers in American Wars.* 1993.

Stavisky, Samuel E. (1914–2008)

Born just outside Boston and educated at Boston University, Stavisky had several journalism jobs before catching on with the *Washington Post* in 1937. Within the year he had begun his meteoric rise from copy reader to reporter and then assistant city editor. Following the attack on Pearl Harbor on December 7, 1941 he tried to enlist, he was rejected for poor vision, first by the army and then by the navy. He returned to the newsroom and in early 1942 he was accepted as part of a group of special combat correspondents (CCs) who would fight alongside regular marines and chronicle their experiences as a way of winning support for their activities at home.

Despite resistance to sending the myopic Stavisky to fight at the front by the Marine Corps, his persistence paid off when he was given a waiver and sworn into the Corps after some prodding by the publisher of the *Chicago Daily News* on May 25, 1942. After nine weeks of basic training at Parris Island, South Carolina, Stavisky spent most of his time interviewing marines returning from combat on Guadalcanal in the Solomon Islands. He accompanied an elite squadron known as the Third Raiders as they landed on Pavuvu in the Russell Islands. However, the Japanese had already vacated their defenses. He continued to interview sailors and marines about actions around Guadalcanal. In May 1943 he boarded a troop transport headed to Rendova, the largest of the New Georgia Islands. As he landed with the marines they were strafed by Japanese aircraft, forcing Stavisky to drop his typewriter and rifle as he sought cover. He continued to seek opportunities to cover action in the area until stricken with malaria.

According to his reports he was often in the middle of the action whenever possible and was proud to write about his own exploits killing enemy soldiers. As both a marine and a war correspondent, Stavisky reported on the invasion of New Britain and later received permission to fly on a bombing raid on Japanese airfields in Hollandia. His last taste of combat would be during the invasion of Hollandia. He left the war for good after this and was discharged from the Marine Corps in March 1945, picking up where he left off with the *Washington Post*. He continued his career in journalism writing for a range of nationally circulated magazine and in 1954 left journalism to create his own public relations firm. In 1999, Stavisky published *Marine Combat Correspondent: World War II in the Pacific.*

REFERENCES: Brandon Haase. "Samuel E. Stavisky," *American World War II Correspondents*, Jeffrey B. Cook, ed. 2012, 269–273; Patricia Sullivan, "Samuel Stavisky; Newsman, Combat Correspondent," Washington Post, Sept. 24, 2008, B5.

Stedman, Edmund Clarence (1833–1908)

Born in Hartford, Connecticut, Stedman joined the *New York World* in 1860. He covered the Virginia front during the first year of the American Civil War* before leaving, reporting next for the attorney general's office and then Wall Street. He wrote poetry during these years, earning the moniker "the Bard of Wall Street." He covered the Battles of Ball's Bluff and Williamsburg. His account of the First Battle of Bull Run was among the best of the campaign. During the war he wrote the poem "John Brown's Invasion" and the campaign song "Honest Abe of the West."

REFERENCES: Stewart Sifakis. *Who Was Who in the Civil War.* 1988; Louis M. Starr. *Bohemian Brigade.* 1954.

Steele, Archibald T. (1903–1992)

The Canadian-born Steele attended Stanford University before working for various Pacific

* Indicates a separate entry.

Coast newspapers. In 1932 he reported from Manchuria and North China for the *New York Times* and from 1933 to 1935 covered Shanghai for the Associated Press. In 1937 he witnessed the capture of Nanking by Japanese forces. Reporting for the *Chicago Daily News,* he described the evacuation of the city and the slaying of thousands as "four days of hell."

In 1941 he was among the twelve correspondents permitted to view sanitized war zones by Soviet officials. In 1942 he escaped to India just ahead of Japanese forces that had closed the Burma road. Following the Japanese capitulation in 1945 he resumed covering China for the *New York Herald Tribune.*

REFERENCES: Robert W. Desmond. *Tides of War.* 1984; *NY Times*, March 4, 1992.

Steele, Jon (b. 1950)

Born Denis Lynn Steele in Spokane, Washington, he changed his name to Jon Steele in 1974. His initial foray into journalism was as a freelance radio producer and announcer for several Colorado radio stations before joining NPR in Washington, D.C., in 1982. He covered news stories throughout the world as a cameraman and editor. In 1993 he earned acclaim for his coverage of the fall of the town of Sukhumi during the civil war in the Soviet Republic of Georgia. The Royal Television Society awarded him "Story of the Year" for his report and Le Press Club de France cited him for bravery (along with ITN reporters Julian Manyon and Oleg Yuriev). The following year he accompanied ITV reporter James Mates to cover the Rwandan genocide. Both men were caught in the crossfire as Tutsi forces laid siege to Kigali. They filmed the desperate efforts of Canadian General Romeo Dallaire to protect the residents and his UN Peacekeeping force. Steele filmed the last battle and its aftermath near Kigali Airport that was followed by the mass exit of Hutu military groups and civilians to Zaire (now the Democratic Republic of the Congo). That same year Steele, along with

ITN reporter Terry Lloyd* covered the conflict in the Balkans. In Sarajevo Steele filmed the killing of a young girl in the so-called "Sniper Alley." When he returned from the field of conflict he collapsed at Heathrow Airport. He was later diagnosed with posttraumatic stress disorder.* Like most other war correspondents he declined to seek treatment.

In 1996 Steele covered the Taliban takeover of Kabul alongside ITN reporter Mark Austin. They were able to escape the city and joined up with the Afghan warlord Ahmad Shah Massoud, as he led the advance of Northern Alliance soldiers in the attack on the Taliban in Kabul. In 1998 Steele was once more in the Balkans covering the conflict between Serbian forces and the Kosovo Liberation Army, as it morphed into the War in Kosovo. He was among the pool of cameramen selected to accompany the British Army-led NATO advance into Pristina. In 2000 he covered the Second Intifada in Jerusalem and over the next several years concentrated on chronicling the Israeli-Palestinian conflict. During the lead-up to the Second Iraq War in 2003 he spent almost five months based in Baghdad. For what he claimed were professional and personal problems, Steele left ITN on March 19, 2003, just one day before the war began. That night he left Baghdad for the Jordanian border where he witnessed the bombing of Iraqi positions by Coalition jets. Despite entreaties from ITN for him to reconsider, he left the field and went into seclusion in southern France for almost a year.

Steele followed the ongoing conflicts in Iraq and Afghanistan in 2007 and was startled at the number of American soldiers committing suicide following tours in both war zones. The next year he received permission from the U.S. Army to travel by himself to Combat Outpost Cahill in the Southern Bowl region of Iraq. Here he joined Baker Company of the 15th Infantry Regiment, 3rd Infantry Division as it surged toward an Al-Qaeda stronghold. He was able to record more than 100 hours of tape while conducting unrestricted and uncensored interviews with the soldiers of Baker Company over a three-month period. His work was edited into a four-part documentary, *Baker Boys: Inside the Surge.* It first aired in 2010 on HDNet and was honored with a number of awards. Steele's life as a news cameraman was chronicled in Jon Blair's *Reporters at War* in 2004 and in Martyn Burke's *Under Fire: Journalists in Combat* in 2012. He has written several novels and auto-biographical works including *War Junkie: One Man's Addiction to the Worst Places on Earth* (2002), which covered a year in the life of a battlefront cameraman.

REFERENCE: http://www.jonsteele-author.com.

Steer, George Lowther (1909–1944)

Steer was a British war correspondent killed during World War II.* Born in Cambridge, South Africa, and educated at Oxford, he was hired by the *Times* in 1935 to cover the Italian invasion of Abyssinia and the subsequent Ethiopian War.* Probably the best informed of the foreign correspondents, although not always a witness, Steer reported the Battles of Tembien and Aradam. He was in Addis Ababa before its capitulation to the Italians and recorded one of the most famous descriptions of Emperor Haile Selassie as he prepared to flee the city in April 1936. Assigned to report the war from the Ethiopian victim's point of view, Steer was expelled from the country by Italian authorities.

In April 1937 he reported the Spanish Civil War,* witnessing the destruction of the Basque town of Guernica.* His report in the *Times,* which was the only paper to implicate the Germans, noted that the village was of no military significance and that Nazi Luftwaffe squadrons accompanied Spanish Nationalist forces.

In 1938 he left the *Times* for the *Daily Telegraph,* covering World War II in Africa. During the war he joined the Intelligence Corps as a lieutenant-colonel and was killed in a motor

vehicle accident in Asia on Christmas Day 1944. Among his highly praised books based on his exploits are *Caesar in Abyssinia* (1936), *The Tree of Guernica* (1938), *Judgement on German Africa* (1939), *A Date in the Desert* (1940), and *Sealed and Delivered* (1942).

REFERENCES: James Dugan and Laurence Lafore. *Days of Emperor and Clown: The Italo-Ethiopian War 1935–1936.* 1973; Franklin Reid Gannon. *The British Press and Germany, 1936–1939.* 1971.

Steevens, George Warrington (1870–1900)

Born in Sydenham, England, he achieved a distinguished academic record as a classical scholar while at Oxford. In 1893 he was hired by the *Pall Mall Gazette* but left for the recently established *Daily Mail* in 1896. In 1897 he reported the Greco-Turkish War,* accompanying the Turkish army under Edhem Pasha to Thessaly. His dispatches were published under the heading "With the Conquering Turk." In 1898 he accompanied Kitchener's army to the Sudan as special correspondent. His collected dispatches to the *Daily Mail* were later published in his most successful book, *With Kitchener to Khartoum.* In 1898 he covered the installation of Lord Curzon as viceroy of India and the following year the second trial of Captain Alfred Dreyfus.

With the outbreak of the Boer War* in October 1899, Steevens left for South Africa, where he joined British forces under Sir George White. The following month, the British were trapped in the siege of Ladysmith.* Three weeks later Steevens was afflicted with enteric fever. On January 15, 1900, he died holding a glass of champagne. His last words were reportedly "This is a sideways ending to it all." His collected dispatches from South Africa were published posthumously as *From Cape Town to Ladysmith.* Lord Kitchener, the adversary of most war journalists, paid Steevens the highest compliment when he wrote, "He never gave the slightest trouble. I wish all correspondents were like him."

Indicates a separate entry.

REFERENCES: *DNB*, 1226–1227; Rupert Furneaux. *News of War*. 1964; Robert Wilkinson-Latham. *From Our Special Correspondent*. 1979.

Steichen, Edward Jean (1879–1973)

Born in Luxembourg to peasant parents, Steichen became one of the most influential photographers of the twentieth century. His family arrived in America less than two years after his birth, settling in Michigan and then Wisconsin, where he apprenticed himself to a photographer at the age of fifteen. He made the transition from commercial photography to taking more artistic shots in the late 1890s. Moving to Paris in late 1899, he was given encouragement by the great pioneer of this art, Alfred Stieglitz, who bought several of his prints. By the age of twenty-three, Steichen was already famous, having made portraits of Rodin, Matisse, and other artists. Returning to the States he photographed Theodore Roosevelt, G. B. Shaw, and other celebrities of the era.

With the outbreak of World War I* he expressed an interest in becoming a photographic reporter like Mathew Brady.* He enlisted in the Signal Corps, commissioned as a lieutenant. Placed in charge of the photographic operations, Steichen demonstrated great managerial expertise as he fulfilled General Mitchell's request for aerial photographs before the Second Battle of the Meuse-Argonne and for a mobile photo section for the Meuse-Argonne offensive. At the battlefront his photo team worked all night developing film and printing pictures of the various battles. After the senseless trench warfare and carnage of the war Steichen apparently fell into a deep depression, a common reaction of those that survived among so many who did not.

After the war he returned to commercial photography for Conde Nast, billed as the "greatest living portrait photographer." With the outbreak of World War II,* America's most famous cameraman returned to action.

Commissioned as a second lieutenant, the sixty-two-year-old Steichen organized a team of photographers to record naval activities. Serving in the Pacific theater aboard the carrier *Lexington*, he recorded the Gilbert and Marshall Islands campaign when the carrier came under air attack. He returned with the ship to the United States. He made one more visit to the battlefield, arriving at Iwo Jima the day after the battle ended. In the aftermath he made powerful images of dead Japanese soldiers partially covered by debris with hands curled and outstretched. Following the war he continued his remarkable career, organizing exhibitions such as the hugely successful *The Family of Man* exhibition at the Museum of Modem Art, and taking classic photos.

REFERENCE: Robert E. Hood. *12 at War: Great Photographers Under Fire*. 1967.

Steinbeck, Jr., John Ernest (1902–1968)

Better known as a Nobel Prize-winning author of socially influential novels, Steinbeck was born in Salinas, California. He attended Stanford University and worked in a variety of occupations before gaining fame with his novel *Of Mice and Men* in 1937. In 1943 he covered the war in Europe as correspondent for the *New York Herald Tribune*. He reported the campaigns in North Africa, Sicily, and Italy from June to October, including participation in naval commando raids with a special operations unit in the Mediterranean. Aligned with the hawks in the debate over the Vietnam War,* in 1966, at the age of sixty-four, he covered the conflict as correspondent for the New York newspaper *Newsday*.

REFERENCES: *DAB 8;* Warren French. *John Steinbeck*. 1975.

Steinbeck IV, John (1946–1991)

The second child of Nobel Prize winning author and war correspondent John Steinbeck,* he was drafted into the U.S. Army in 1965 and served in the Vietnam War. He worked as a journalist for Armed Forces Radio and TV and acted as a war correspondent for the Department of Defense. After his stint in the Army he returned to Vietnam in 1968 to cover the war and along with Sean Flynn* began the Dispatch News Service, which was the first to publish the account of the My Lai massacre by Seymour Hersh.* In 1969 Steinbeck recounted his experience covering the war in the book *In Touch*. In 1971 John was awarded an Emmy for his work with Walter Cronkite* on the CBS documentary *The World of Charlie Company*. He died in 1991 soon after going through corrective surgery for a ruptured disc.

REFERENCE:www.nancysteinbeck.com.

Stenin, Andrei (1981–2014)

A photojournalist for the Russian-owned news agency Rossiya Segodnya, Stenin disappeared while covering the civil war in eastern Ukraine on August 5, 2014. Two of his colleagues went in search of him and found a car similar to Stenin's near the town of Snizhe. It was a burned-out hulk by then, containing three charred bodies with professional camera equipment in the trunk. It wasn't until the following month that Russian authorities officially announced his death, which probably took place the day after he was reported missing. According to a subsequent Russian investigation, Stenin was killed during an attack by Ukrainian forces. Like so much else that has occurred during the Ukrainian conflict many questions remain unanswered.

REFERENCE: "Andrei Stenin," http://cpj.org/killed/2014/Andrei-stenin.php.

Stevens, Edmund (1911–1992)

Stevens was born in Denver, Colorado, and educated at Columbia University. Following graduation he moved to Moscow to study Russian. During the 1930s he contributed articles to the *Manchester Guardian* and the *Daily Herald*. At the outset of World War II* he covered the Finnish winter campaign in 1940 and the Italo-Greek campaign for the *Christian Science Monitor*. Stevens and Leland Stowe* of the *Chicago Daily News* were in Norway during the British naval blockade of the Norwegian port of Narvik, which was a crucial link for shipping Swedish ore to Germany. They were in Oslo reporting this story on April 8, 1940, when the German invasion began. Stowe scooped the competition on the story, filing the last cable from Norway.

Stevens later reported Orde Wingate's attempt to restore Haile Selassie to the throne in Ethiopia, and beginning in 1941 he accompanied General Montgomery's forces in Africa from the march to El Alamein to Tripoli. Following the war he became the Moscow correspondent for the *Monitor* for the next forty years. He published in other papers as well and in 1950 won the Pulitzer Prize for "This is Russia-Uncensored." Among his books were *Russia Is No Riddle* (1946) and *North Africa Powderkeg* (1955).

REFERENCE: Robert W. Desmond. *Tides of War*. 1984.

Stevens, George (1905–1975)

The great American film director of such films as *Shane, A Place in the Sun, Giant,* and the *Diary of Anne Frank* was responsible for much of the black and white film coverage of Allied campaigns in Europe during 1944 and 1945. Stevens left Hollywood in 1942 to serve in the American army in North Africa and Europe, and in 1943 he assembled the Special Coverage Unit of the U.S. Army Signal Corps (SPECOU) to improve the quality of motion picture coverage. The unit was attached to the Supreme Headquarters Allied Expeditionary Force;, and novelist Irwin Shaw and playwright William Saroyan wrote descriptions and captions for the footage.

According to army regulations all official footage had to be shot in black and white, reportedly because this was the standard for movie newsreels* around the world. The Technicolor process was too costly and technically cumbersome for the mobile army units of this era. Stevens apparently was never without a 16mm home movie camera, which he brandished in 1944 and 1945, sending home to the States rolls of exposed films for processing. Upon his death his son found over five hours of color footage of World War II,* virtually the only color films of the war in Western Europe.

REFERENCE: Max Hastings,* *Victory in Europe.* 1985.

Stewart, Bill (1941–1978)

A general assignment reporter for ABC news, the West Virginia-born Stewart had covered the Middle East and the fall of the Shah in Iran when he was assigned to war-torn Nicaragua. As he approached a National Guard post from his van, which was clearly labeled as "Foreign Press," he gripped a white flag. A soldier motioned Stewart to lie down and kicked him the side before summarily shooting him with a rifle at point-blank range. The film footage from this incident was broadcast throughout the world. Subsequently a third of the foreign correspondents, including most of the Americans, were airlifted out of the country.

REFERENCE: Charles Arnot. *Don't Kill the Messenger.* 1994.

Stewart, Ian (b. 1967)

Ian Stewart was the Abidjan-based Associated Press West African bureau chief, when he was critically wounded on January 10, 1999. He was riding in a car through Freetown, Sierra Leone with two other journalists when they were fired on by a rebel fighter. AP television producer Myles Tierney died in the attack and Stewart suffered a critical gunshot wound to the head, but would eventually make a full recovery. It was later determined that the assailant was actually

a boy soldier who had been pressed into service for the rebel Revolutionary United Front (RUF).

During the 1990s Stewart reported wars throughout Africa. Prior to his African experiences he covered pre-Taliban Afghanistan, post-Khmer Rouge Cambodia, Sri Lanka, Pakistan, and Kashmir. In one seven-year stint overseas Stewart travelled to 46 countries to cover eight major coups, insurgencies, and other regional conflicts. In his 2002 book, *Ambushed: A War Reporter's Life on the Line*, he chronicled his recovery both from his physical wound and crippling emotional scars, the result of having witnessed years of carnage. He would still be dealing with the aftereffects of posttraumatic stress disorder* (PTSD) some ten years later. Since his close call in Sierra Leone, Stewart completed his PhD from the University of Michigan's Doctoral Program in Anthropology and History, where he focused on contemporary forms of slavery, including the capture and exploitation of children as soldiers in West Africa. He now teaches at the University of New Mexico's International Studies Institute.

REFERENCES: "Canadian Journalist Ian Stewart, Wounded in Sierra Leone, Making Steady Recovery," Canadian Journalists for Free Expression, Feb. 4, 1999; Ian Stewart. *Ambushed: A War Reporter's Life on the Line.* 2002.

Stillson, Jerome Bonaparte (1841–1880)

Born in East Aurora, New York, Stillson covered the American Civil War* for the *New York World*. He received unflattering reviews for his reporting of Grant's overland campaign in 1864, but he redeemed himself with his coverage of Sheridan's Shenandoah Valley campaign later that fall. His reportage of the Battles of Winchester and Cedar Creek are considered among the best of the war. He also reported the surrender at Appomattox.

He gave up his position as managing editor of the *New York World* in 1876 and joined the *New York Herald*. He reported the last Sioux war and was granted an interview with Sitting

Bull following the defeat of Custer. In 1877, Stillson was accompanying President Hayes on a trip in the West, when he was assigned to cover the Ute war in Colorado. Stillson did not personally witness the fighting, employing a legman to report the action. By the time of the Ute war Stillson was suffering from neuritis, and he died in Denver shortly after.

REFERENCES: Oliver Knight. *Following the Indian Wars.* 1960; Louis M. Starr. *Bohemian Brigade.* 1954.

Stone, Dana (1939–1970)

He was last seen riding on a motorcycle with Sean Flynn* of *Time* magazine while covering the Khmer Rouge in Cambodia. Stone was working for CBS news at the time and was reportedly traveling behind enemy lines attempting to shoot film of Communist forces in action. He was reportedly executed by the Khmer Rouge.

REFERENCE: Perry Deane Young. *Two of the Missing.* 1975.

Stoneman, William H. (1904–1987)

Stoneman was born in Grand Rapids, Michigan, and educated at the University of Michigan. He began his long affiliation with the *Chicago Daily News* in 1925. Three years later he became a foreign correspondent, spending several years based in Scandanavia, Rome, and Moscow. He covered the Ethiopian War* while stationed in the Near East and in Ethiopia from 1935 to 1936, when he was assigned to the London bureau. He covered the North African landings and in 1943 earned a Purple Heart when he was ambushed and wounded in the Ousseltia sector of Tunisia.

After a short leave in the States he was back in action covering the landings at Salerno and then at Anzio during Operation Shingle. Stoneman was among the first correspondents to report from the beaches of Normandy following the D-Day invasion. Several weeks later he was

among the correspondents who witnessed the capture of the port of Cherbourg from the Germans. In 1945 he accompanied Allied forces advancing toward Berlin.

REFERENCE: Robert W. Desmond. *Tides of War.* 1984; *NY Times*, April 14, 1987.

Storms, Jane McManus (1807–1878)

Born near Troy, New York, Storms moved to Matagorda, Texas, with her father in the mid-1830s, beginning her lifelong interest in Texas. During her stay she met many of the influential figures of the day, including Sam Houston and Mirabeau B. Lamar. In 1839 she returned to New York City and a career as lobbyist and writer. She became affiliated with the *New York Sun,* the nation's first successful penny press newspaper. Her articles found their way into other papers as well, usually under her pen names "Montgomery" and "Cora Montgomery."

During the Mexican-American War,* in late 1846, Storms accompanied a secret mission to sound out peace sentiments in Mexico City. On inspecting the seaport of Veracruz, she noted that it would resist American invasion and continued to criticize the U.S. Navy. As General Winfield Scott began his assault on Veracruz, Storms was requested to undertake a perilous two-hundred-mile journey from Mexico City to Veracruz to apprise the general of conditions in the Mexican capital. Arriving at Veracruz before its capitulation, she was in time to witness the bombardment and conclusion of the siege.

Storms remained a stern critic of the American military, although her sentiments were in favor of annexing all of Mexico to the United States. She continued to be one of the few critics of the American forces as well as of her fellow journalists. Her career as a war correspondent concluded in May 1847, upon her return to Washington. She continued to publish articles and books based on themes ranging from the

* Indicates a separate entry.

annexation of Cuba to American Indian policy. She died when her ship went down off Cape Hatteras in December 1878.

REFERENCE: Tom Reilly. "Jane McManus Storms: Letters from the Mexican War," *Southwestern Historical Quarterly*. July 1981.

Story of G.I. Joe

Directed by William Wellman and released in 1945, the *Story of G.I. Joe* starring Burgess Meredith, recounts Ernie Pyle's* experiences covering frontline soldiers during World War II. Pyle had railed against press censorship throughout the war. Although he had been killed by a sniper's bullet a year earlier, he still faced posthumous censorship of a kind. Soon before the film's release the Hays Office of the Motion Picture Producers and Distributors of America held it up, objecting to some of the "coarseness of soldier talk" and would not grant it its seal of approval until "certain lines of dialogue" (such as "oh heck') had been removed. The studio hesitated but eventually changed the lines and the picture was released. Pyle's wife attended the advance screening of the film before the National Press Club. At its conclusion an Army general and Navy admiral jointly presented his wife a posthumous Medal for Merit on behalf of both military branches and the State Department before a gathering of war correspondents, members of Congress, and other luminaries. The world premiere was attended by two thousand people, including 300 wounded vets whose ten dollar tickets were paid for by grateful civilians. No less a critic than General and future president Dwight Eisenhower pronounced the film "the greatest war picture I've ever seen." And soldiers from the Fifth Army in Italy, including a number who had fought in the battles shown in the movie, said after seeing film, "This is it." By most accounts this film resonated among civilians and servicemen alike and was considered among the best visualized portrayals of soldiers in action on celluloid up to that time.

REFERENCES: David Nichols, ed. *Ernie's War*. 1986; Lawrence H. Suid. *Guts and Glory*. 1978.

Stouman, Lou (1917–1991)

Born in Springtown, Pennsylvania, Stouman graduated from Lehigh University in 1939. During World War II* he served as photographer-correspondent on the staff of *Yank.** He also contributed photos to the New York-based *PM* magazine. Following the war he continued his career as a photojournalist and since 1966 has taught film production at UCLA. He has won two Academy Awards for documentary film work.

REFERENCES: Art Weithas. *Close to Glory*. 1991; *NY Times*, October 10, 1991.

Stowe, Leland (1899–1993)

Stowe was born in Southbury, Connecticut, and educated at Wesleyan University, where he held his first newspaper job as campus reporter for the *Springfield Republican*. Following graduation he reported for the *Worcester Telegram* and then the *New York Herald* from 1922 to 1926. He was awarded the Pulitzer Prize in 1930 for his coverage of a 1929 conference that produced a plan for reducing and extending Germany's World War I* reparations and created the Bank for International Settlements.

Throughout the 1930s Stowe covered international developments, including events leading up to the Spanish Civil War.* In 1939 he was rebuffed by the *Herald Tribune* when he requested assignment as war correspondent. Barely an hour after being deemed too old for a foreign posting he was hired by the *Chicago Daily News*, which was then considered to have the best foreign service of any American newspaper. He covered the Russian invasion of Finland in December 1939 and the subsequent Russo-Finish conflict, although usually from afar.

In 1940 Stowe barely escaped the Nazi invasion of Norway, making his way to Stockholm to transmit his scoop. Later that year he reported the Italian invasion of Greece. He also covered the war in the Balkans, Russia, and Eastern Europe. Stowe was assigned to report from China in 1941, where he uncovered evidence of massive theft and graft as Chiang Kai-shek's army attempted to hide Lend-Lease arms for later use against the Chinese Communists rather than against the Japanese. Stowe filed a series of articles exposing Chiang's subterfuge with his newspaper only to have the State Department block its publication after pressure from the Chinese ambassador. Stowe was then reassigned to the Soviet Union, where he was the first Western war correspondent to accompany Russian forces in action. He published twenty-two dispatches which appeared next to his byline "With the Russian Army." In 1942 he was one of the first correspondents to cover the Burma campaign.

Following the war he worked as a commentator for ABC radio, foreign editor of the *Reporter*, news director for Radio Free Europe, and professor of journalism at the University of Michigan. He wrote eight books, including *Nazi Means War* (1933) and *No Other Road to Freedom* (1941).

REFERENCES: Robert W. Desmond. *Tides of War.* 1984; *Who's Who in America, 1984.* 1984.

Strahorn, Robert (1852–1944)

Born in Center County, Pennsylvania, and educated in the printing trade, Strahorn entered the newspaper profession as a printer and writer at the age of fourteen. He joined the staff of the *Rocky Mountain News* in 1871. Strahorn accompanied the George C. Crook expedition against the Black Hills Sioux in 1876. His articles, under the pen name "Alter Ego," appeared during the campaign in the *Rocky Mountain News* and occasionally in the *Chicago Tribune, Omaha Republican, Cheyenne Sun,* and *New York Sun.*

He was the only correspondent to follow Crook until the surrender of Crazy Horse. He

apparently injured his vocal cords during the winter campaign when he strained his voice in a battle during subfreezing temperatures. Sources indicate that the strain interfered with his speech for the remainder of his life and that he would lose his voice completely when sick. Maintaining good relations with Crook, he saved the latter's life by warning him of an ambush near the Red Cloud Agency.

Strahorn witnessed and took part in the Battle of the Rosebud and was among the four correspondents who followed the campaign into the Big Horn Mountains. In September 1876 he left the expedition to visit the Centennial Exposition in Philadelphia but returned in 1877 in time for the Powder River campaign and the surrender of Crazy Horse. Following his return from the American Indian Wars* he wrote a highly acclaimed guidebook to Wyoming, which came to the attention of railroad entrepreneur Jay Gould. Strahorn was hired by Gould to direct the Union Pacific publicity bureau and to travel the West promoting migration. He traveled the West for six years gathering intelligence for railroad tycoons. He went on to a successful career conducting irrigation and power projects and became the president and director of various railroad and utility ventures in the Pacific Northwest. He was the last of the Indian war correspondents when he died in 1944.

REFERENCE: Oliver Knight. *Following the Indian Wars.* 1960.

Street, Albert (d. 1864)

The Northern-born Street covered various phases of the American Civil War* for the Confederate *Mobile Daily Advertiser and Register* and the *Savannah Register.* Under his pen name "N'Importe" Street reported the existence of division among Confederate commanders in Mississippi and the deficiencies of the equipment provided the Quartermaster's Department in Richmond. In December 1862 he spent to weeks as a prisoner in the North. Street died from an accidental gunshot wound in May 1864.

REFERENCE: J. Cutler Andrews. *The South Reports the Civil War.* 1970.

Stringer

The term "stringer" refers to part-time, non-staff correspondents covering stories and locations for newspapers or news agencies operating elsewhere. Often working for one or more organizations, stringers are compensated on a fee-per-story basis. The term originated in small-town America, where local newspapers made arrangements with "country correspondents" to contribute letters and news stories from the outlying communities. Contributors were usually stalwart community members such as schoolteachers, housewives, retirees, or clerics. Compensation was determined by pasting each month's material together so that it formed a column-width "string," which was measured; the writer was then paid per column inch. The system of stringers is much more sophisticated today with professional journalists maintaining links with several papers at the same time and reporting from around the world. The string measure of compensation has been replaced by retainer fees and supplementary compensation. But non-staff writers are still known as "stringers."

During the Vietnam War,* local Vietnamese were often ruthlessly exploited as stringers and were required to supply photographs with great personal risk and little compensation. Their pictures were then published without attribution.

REFERENCE: Robert W. Desmond. *The Information Process.* 1978.

Stringer, Ann (1918–1990)

Born in Eastland, Texas, Stringer graduated from the University of Texas with degrees in English and journalism. While in college she met her future husband Bill Stringer, whom she married in 1941. With the outbreak of World War II,* Bill went to work for Reuters,* while Ann was employed with the Associated Press. In June 1944 Bill was killed when caught in a crossfire on D-Day. Shortly afterward Ann went to Europe to report for the UP. Reputably one of the most beautiful war correspondents, she was labeled along with Iris Carpenter* and Lee Carson as one of the three "Rhine maidens." Hindered from covering the battlefront because of a rule that prevented female reporters from going beyond the perimeter where female military personnel were restricted, she ignored orders to return to Paris for violating this code. Some attributed her risk taking to a death wish after the tragic death of her husband.

Stringer covered the American assault on the Rhine, witnessing the battle of Remagen bridge and the convergence of the Russian and American armies near the Elbe River. She also reported the liberation of the concentration camps at Buchenwald and Dachau and the Nuremberg trials.

REFERENCES: Julia Edwards. *Women of the World.* 1989. Lilya Wagner. *Women War Correspondents of the World.* 1989; NY Times, January 12, 1990.

Suckert, Kurt (1898–1957)

Better known as Curzio Malaparte and the author of the war novel *Kaputt*, Suckert covered the Russian theater of World War II* for the Italian newspaper *Corriere della Sera*. Born in Prato, Italy, Suckert was the son of a German master dyer. He had fought in World War I* and was the recipient of decorations from both Italy and France. Following the war he turned to journalism, reporting on the darker sides of the rise of fascism and Communism. In 1933 he was arrested in his home country for his anti-Fascist activities and imprisoned for three years off the coast of Sicily.

Prior to reporting from the eastern front, Suckert had covered the German occupation of

Poland and the tragedy of the Warsaw Ghetto. He is credited with providing the best war reporting from this theater of operations. Suckert followed German forces eastward beginning in 1941. He correctly predicted the effectiveness of the Russian resistance to the German *Blitzkrieg* and was the first correspondent to demonstrate an interest in the developing siege of Leningrad.

REFERENCE: Phillip Knightley. *The First Casualty*. 1975.

Sully, Francois (1928–1971)

Sully was one of the earliest journalists to cover the Vietnam War.* He was no stranger to the battlefield, having been wounded in Paris as a member of the underground resistance to the Nazis. Following his release from the French army in Saigon in 1947 he stayed on to cover the last years of the war in Indochina and the fall of Dien Bien Phu. In 1961 he began his affiliation with *Newsweek* magazine, covering American involvement in Vietnam. The following year he was expelled from Vietnam for the first time for critical pieces on the Diem regime. Following Diem's assassination in 1963, Sully returned to Vietnam. He continued to send dispatches to *Newsweek* chronicling negative aspects of the American war effort. He was finally silenced in May 1971 when he was killed in a Vietnamese helicopter crash over Laos. He left his insurance policy of eighteen million piasters to Vietnamese orphans.

REFERENCES: Michael Emery. *On the Front Lines*. 1995; William Prochnau. *Once upon a Distant War*. 1995.

Sulzberger, Cyrus Leo (1912–1993)

C. L. Sulzberger was born in New York City and educated at Harvard. He joined the United Press after a stint with the *Pittsburgh Press*. As correspondent for the *London Evening Standard* in 1938 he reported the events leading up World War II* from Austria, Czechoslovakia, and the Balkans. He began a thirty-nine-year affiliation with the *New York Times* in 1939. Sulzberger

was among the last journalists to flee Yugoslavia during the 1941 German invasion, escaping aboard a small fishing boat. He reported the 1940 Italian invasion of Greece and was in Istanbul when the Germans attacked Russia. He received the Overseas Press Club Award in 1941 for his reportage of the Russian war.

Moving to Moscow to cover the conflict, he was faced by Soviet press restrictions which allowed correspondents to make eight trips to the front lines, but only after the fighting and only after victories. In 1943 he covered the Allied invasion of North Africa and for the next two years would be stationed in Cairo. During the winter of 1943–1944 he reported from the Italian front and in early 1944 won acclaim for his coverage of Marshal Tito's Yugoslav partisans.

REFERENCES: Robert W. Desmond. *The Tides of War*. 1984; Library of America. *Reporting World War II*. 1995.

Sutherland, Thomas A. (1850–1891)

Born in California and educated at Harvard, he was the only accredited war correspondent to cover the Nez Perce Indian war of 1877. Affiliated with the *Portland Standard*, he also filed stories for the *New York Herald* and the *San Francisco Chronicle*. Sutherland characterized the conflict as one continuous chase, although he reported three inconclusive battles. Accompanying General O. O. Howard's troops, he later wrote *Howard's Campaign Against the Nez Perce Indians*. He stayed with the *Standard* for the remainder of his life, except for a brief interval in Washington, D.C., as clerk of the House Committee on Manufacturers.

REFERENCE: Oliver Knight. *Following the Indian Wars*. 1960.

Swing, Raymond Edwards (1887–1968)

Swing was born in Cortland, New York. An indifferent student, Swing attended Oberlin

Indicates a separate entry.

College briefly before being suspended for poor academic progress. He began his newspaper career in 1906 with the *Cleveland Press* as a cub reporter. During his six years on various Ohio and Indiana newspapers his reporting took on an increasingly liberal complexion as he dabbled in social work and investigated political corruption. Shortly after marriage in 1912 he joined the *Chicago Daily News* as a foreign correspondent in Berlin. As the war years approached he covered developments in the Balkans and Turkey. During World War I* he witnessed the naval battles in the Dardanelles and made inspections of the trench warfare at Gallipoli. When America joined the war effort Swing returned home and worked for the War Labor Board.

Following the war he returned to Berlin as a reporter for the *New York Herald*. In 1921 he covered the revolutionary activity in the Soviet Union, but his paper refused to print many of his columns since America refused to recognize the Communist state. He left the *Herald* for the *Philadelphia Public Ledger* and the *New York Post* in 1924. During the 1920s he reported the complex political developments in Europe as a second European conflict loomed on the horizon. He returned to Washington, D.C., in 1933 and was one of the earliest correspondents to make the transition to broadcast journalism. He filed the American end in weekly broadcasts between British and American journalists which were transmitted by shortwave. He was later teamed with fellow American Edward R. Murrow* during World War II.* As one of the most respected commentators during the war years he worked as nightly commentator for the Mutual Broadcasting Company before transferring to the National Broadcasting Company and then the American Broadcasting Company. He later became a political commentator and worked for the State Department before retiring in 1963. His broadcasts are collected in *How War Came* (1939), *Preview of History* (1943), and *In the Name of Sanity* (1946).

REFERENCES: Robert W. Desmond. *Windows on the World*. 1980; *DAB 8*.

Swinton, William (1833–1892)

Born near Edinburgh, Scotland, Swinton emigrated to Canada with his family at the age of ten. After preparation for the ministry at Knox College and a stint teaching languages at a seminary he joined the *New York Times* in 1858. He covered the Army of the Potomac from 1861 until 1864, when he was expelled from the front lines. He reported the Battle of Fredericksburg, the naval attack on Charleston, and the Battle of Chancellorsville.

Swinton was constantly at odds with Union commanders, defying their instructions not to discuss military matters or criticize generals. In several instances Generals Grant and Burnside threatened to have him shot. In one incident Swinton was caught eavesdropping on Grant and Meade, lying outside Grant's tent while the two generals discussed the Battle of the Wilderness. Finally Grant stripped Swinton of his credentials, permanently barring him from covering the Army of the Potomac. Shortly afterward he wrote *The Times Review of McClellan; His Military Career Reviewed and Exposed*. He also wrote *Campaigns of the Army of the Republic* (1866), *The Twelve Decisive Battles of the War* (1867), and *History of the New York Seventh Regiment During the War of the Rebellion* (1870). Following the war he moved to California, becoming a professor of English at the recently established University of California in Oakland. He left the university five years later to pursue a successful career writing grade school textbooks. He died in Brooklyn, New York, on October 24, 1892.

REFERENCES: *DAB*; Stewart Sifakis. *Who Was Who in the Civil War*. 1988; Louis M. Starr. *Bohemian Brigade*. 1954.

Swope, Herbert Bayard (1882–1958)

Swope entered the newspaper business while still in his teens, at the *St. Louis Post-Dispatch* and in 1909 joined the staff of the *New York World*. As

World War I* erupted in 1914 Swope delivered his greatest wartime scoop when he reported the sinking of three British warships by German submarines. He also was among the first journalists to report the entrance of German military forces into Belgium. He reported the war from the Berlin bureau from 1914 to 1917. Swope wrote a series of articles for the *World* in 1917 following American intervention. These pieces were collected and published as *Inside the German Empire in the Third Year of the War* that same year. He was awarded the Pulitzer Prize in 1918 for "a distinguished example of a reporter's work" for his coverage of wartime Germany. Swope was the first reporter to receive this distinction. In 1918 he reported the war from both France and Russia, one of the few war correspondents to actually witness combat from both sides.

In 1919 he covered the Paris Peace Conference at Versailles and from 1920 to 1929 served as executive editor of the *World*. In 1929 he left the newspaper to become director of the National Radio Press Association.

REFERENCE: Robert W. Desmond. *Windows on the World*. 1980.

Symonds, Gene (1926–1955)

Symonds covered the Korean War* for the United Press and in 1955 was beaten to death by a mob while covering a Communist demonstration in Singapore.

REFERENCE: M. L. Stein. *Under Fire: The Story of American War Correspondents*. 1968.

Syrian Civil War

By 2012 most American news agencies were pulling back their coverage from the dangerous Syrian region. As 2014 came to a close, Syria ranked as the deadliest country for the press for the third year in a row. However, the media still had to slake the thirst of the public for stories on the civil war. With larger and traditional news organizations prohibiting the use of freelancers in Syria and similar conflict zones, the vacuum to fill the void in frontline coverage was filled by freelancers such as the ill-fated James Foley.* As Jonathan Mahler put it, "The bar for entry was low. No credentials were required. All you needed was a smartphone that shot video," some notebooks, and a laptop. According to the Committee to Protect Journalists (CPJ),* there were signs that it was becoming less dangerous since the conflict began in 2011. Compared to the previous year, in 2014 less journalists were killed, imprisoned, and kidnapped. Between 2011 and the end of 2014 at least 79 journalists were killed due to their reporting. CPJ reported that next to Iraq, since 1992 when CPJ began keeping records, Syria was the second deadliest conflict zone. In 2014, 29 journalists were killed, compared to 29 the previous year. Most of the journalists killed since the war began (75 percent), had been killed in crossfire or while covering combat. However, in 2014 it became clear that there had been an increase in the targeted killing of reporters, from 10 percent in 2013 to 18 percent in 2014. The beheadings of James Foley* and Steven Sotloff* were probably the most prominent; dozens of others have been executed for just doing their jobs as well. CPJ suggests that in years past journalists could expect a degree of protection due to their noncombatant status, but this could no longer be expected, and in many cases identifying one's self as a journalist could turn a reporter into a target.

REFERENCES: Jason Stern, "In Syria, Fewer Journalist Deaths but Danger Has Never Been Greater," http://cpj.org/2014/12/in-syria-fewer-journalist-deaths-but-danger-has-never-been-gr.php; Jonathan Mahler, "James Foley," New York Times Magazine, Dec. 28, 2014, 22–23.

Szathmari, Karl Baptist Von (Carol Popp De Szathmari) (1812–1887)

Several sources consider him the "first war photographer."* Prior to the Crimean War* he was an amateur painter and photographer living in Bucharest. He first photographed military operations between Russia and Turkey at the outbreak of war in Wallachia, where his growing reputation allowed him to photograph the Russian army of occupation. When their Turkish adversaries occupied Bucharest, Szathmari was permitted to photograph the Turkish commander Omar Pasha, as well as other officers, and camp life. He covered warfare in the Danube basin with a photographic carriage much as Roger Fenton* followed troop movements during the Crimean War.

In 1854 he made his way to the Crimea to photograph the conflict. The following year he displayed two hundred of his photographs at the Universal Exhibition in Paris. Copies of his photo albums were presented to Queen Victoria, the French emperor Napoleon III, and Franz Joseph of Austria. Contemporary descriptions of his work compare it favorably to Fenton's pictures. Although only an engraving made from one of his plates survives, they were reportedly highly praised in their time. Full descriptions survive of the work shown in Paris. Among the photographs are shots of Russian staff officers watching a battle, troops deploying, and the disorganized withdrawal of Russian troops from Wallachia. These images are probably the closest to troops actually engaged in combat that would be taken before the twentieth century.

REFERENCES: Helmut and Alison Gernsheim. *Roger Fenton: Photographer of the Crimean War.* 1973; Pat Hodgson. *Early War Photographs.* 1974; Lawrence James. *Crimea, 1854–56.* 1981; Jorge Lewinski. *The Camera at War.* 1978.

Szulc, Tad (1926–2001)

Born in Warsaw, Poland, Szulc became a top investigative reporter covering foreign affairs and the Department of State for the *New York Times* in the 1950s and 1960s. He reported the Argentine revolt against Peron in 1955, revolutions in Venezuela and Cuba, and guerrilla warfare in Colombia. In 1959 he was covering the Dominican crisis when he was arrested and expelled from the country on orders from Trujillo and sentenced to two years in absentia in prison. In the spring of 1965 he landed with U.S. Marines as civil war broke out on the island. He chronicled these events in *Dominican Diary* (1965). In 1961 he reported the Cuban invasion buildup in Miami and later inspected the battlefield with Castro after the Bay of Pigs fiasco. He recounts this debacle in *The Cuban Invasion: The Chronicle of a Disaster* (1962). Szulc also is the author of *Twilight of Tyrants, The Winds of Revolution,* and *Latin America.*

REFERENCES: Tad Szulc. *Dominican Diary.* 1965; NY Times, May 22, 2001.

T

Taro, Gerda (1911–1937)

Born Gerda Pohorylles in Stuttgart, she became the lover and partner of war photographer-correspondent Robert Capa.* Capa trained the German-born Taro in the basics of photography in two weeks. They arrived in Spain together in early 1936 to record the civil war and collaborated on the book *Death in the Making,* chronicling the Spanish Civil War.* *Life* posthumously published a series of her pictures under the heading "The Spanish War Kills Its First Woman Photographer." Nicknamed "La Pequena Rubita," or "little red head," Taro was crushed by a Loyalist tank in July 1937 shortly before the publication of *Death in the Making,* and Capa dedicated the book to her.

REFERENCES: Jorge Lewinski. *The Camera at War.* 1978; Peter Wyden. *The Passionate War: The Narrative History of the Spanish Civil War.* 1983.

Taylor, Benjamin Franklin (1819–1887)

Born in Lowville, New York, and educated at the Hamilton Literary and Theological Institute, Taylor moved to Michigan in search of employment shortly after graduation. After a stint teaching he moved to Chicago, where he joined the *Chicago Daily Journal* in 1845. He left his position as literary editor to become one of the most outstanding reporters with the western army several years into the American Civil War.*

His coverage of the Chattanooga campaign, including the battles of Missionary Ridge, Lookout Mountain, and others, was widely reprinted. Taylor's accounts were later collected and published as *Mission Ridge and Lookout Mountain, with Pictures of Life in Camp and Field* in 1872.

He was among the numerous journalists targeted for censorship by General Sherman and in May 1864 was accused of revealing too much military information, resulting in his subsequent flight to evade prosecution. He fled to Virginia, where he covered the Shenandoah campaign. Following the Civil War, Taylor left the *Chicago Evening Journal* to pursue freelance writing and lecturing. He published several books of poetry and travelogues, including *The World on Wheels* (1874) and *Between the Gates* (1878).

REFERENCES: J. Cutler Andrews. *The North Reports the Civil War.* 1955; *DAB*; Louis M. Starr. *The Bohemian Brigade.* 1954.

Taylor, Cora (1868–1910)

Correspondent and novelist Stephen Crane* was accompanied by Cora Taylor while reporting the Spanish-American War.* Taylor, posing as Crane's wife, had been with him in Greece during the 1897 war with Turkey. The former hotel and nightclub owner had no experience in journalism. While she is credited with filing several dispatches with the *New York Journal* under the pseudonym "Imogene Carter" during both the Greco-Turkish War* and the Spanish-American

War, some sources claim that Crane himself was the actual author.

REFERENCE: Anne Sebba. *Battling for News: The Rise of the Woman Reporter.* 1994.

Taylor, Jr., Henry (1929–1960)

Taylor was the son of the U.S. ambassador to Switzerland and a correspondent for the Scripps-Howard newspaper chain. In September 1960 he was accompanying one hundred elite soldiers representing the Congo government of Premier Patrice Lumumba as they advanced on the eastern Congo when they were attacked by up to one thousand Baluba tribesmen. During heavy fighting Taylor was killed instantly by machine-gun fire.

REFERENCE: Charles P. Arnot. *Don't Kill the Messenger.* 1994.

Taylor, James Earl (1839–1901)

Born in New York City, he graduated from the University of Notre Dame at sixteen. By 1860 he was employed as sketch artist with *Frank Leslie's Weekly*. Taylor joined the Union Army in 1861 and in 1863 began covering the war as an artist-correspondent* for *Leslie's*. In 1864 he sketched the Thanksgiving celebrations of the Army of the Potomac. He reported Sheridan's campaign up the Shenandoah and was later sent to cover Sherman's army as it advanced through Savannah. He reported Sherman's scorched-earth campaign in the South, including the demolition of a cotton press and railroad station outside Columbia, South Carolina. He also witnessed and sketched the liberation of a Southern prison camp in Columbia. However, most of Taylor's war illustrations were not published by *Leslie's* until April 1865, shortly before the end of the hostilities.

Following the Civil War, Taylor was assigned to cover the Indian peace commission of 1867. His coverage of cattle ranching in Texas was one of the first national reports on the cattle trade. Throughout the 1860s and into the 1870s he sketched Native American and frontier life, leading to his identification as a chronicler of Indian life. He quit *Leslie's* in 1883 and embarked on a career as an independent artist. He collected and published *With Sheridan up the Shenandoah Valley in 1864: Leaves from a Special Artist's Sketch Book and Diary*.

REFERENCE: W. Fletcher Thompson, Jr. *The Image of War.* 1960.

Teichner, Martha (b. 1950)

Born in Traverse City, Michigan and educated at Wellesley College and the University of Chicago, she began her career in journalism on radio and as a general assignment reporter. In 1977 she joined CBS News, beginning her career as a foreign correspondent. Teichner covered the Lebanon War and the conflicts in the Balkans, the collapse of the Soviet Union, and the Romanian revolution. She was among the small cadre of journalists permitted by the military to accompany U.S. troops during the Persian Gulf War, where she spent almost six weeks embedded with the 1st Armored Division in the Saudi desert. She has also covered conflicts in El Salvador, Kuwait, Jordan, and Israel for CBS.

REFERENCE: "Martha Teichner," http://www.cbsnews.com/team/martha-teichner.

Tell Sparta

Alexander Cameron Sedgwick's* novel *Tell Sparta* is a roman a clef that harkens back to Evelyn Waugh's* satire of war correspondents in Ethiopia in his novel *Scoop*. The novel reinforces images of war correspondents sipping drinks safely in a friendly bar and then writing eyewitness accounts of the "action." In this case, the correspondents covered the Italian invasion of Greece, a theater of operations Sedgwick was familiar with.

REFERENCES: Howard Good. *The Image of War Correspondents in Anglo-American Fiction.* 1985; A. C. Sedgwick. *Tell Sparta.* 1945.

Thiele, Reinhold (1856–1921)

Thiele was a German photographer living in London when commissioned by the *Graphic* to cover the Boer War* in late 1899. He accompanied Lord Methuen's Kimberley force, recording the bombardment of the Magersfontein hills and the retreat to the Modder River. Thiele made use of a ten-by-twelve-inch plate camera with a newly invented Dallmeyer lens. He recorded the British victory at Paardeberg, which led to the relief of Kimberley. Thiele was also present at the subsequent surrender of General Cronje's forces following the victory.

REFERENCE: Pat Hodgson. *Early War Photographs.* 1974.

Thomas, Lowell Jackson (1892–1981)

Best known as a world traveler, pioneer radio broadcaster, and confidant of Lawrence of Arabia, Thomas was born in Woodington, Ohio. He attended the University of Northern Indiana and the University of Denver before joining the staff of the *Chicago Journal* in 1912. In 1915 he received an M.A. from Princeton University and took his first trip to Alaska, inaugurating what would become a life of adventure.

From 1917 to 1918 Thomas made films and prepared material for lectures in support of the war effort for the U.S. government's Committee on Public Information. Teamed with cameraman Harry Chase, Thomas covered the Italian front and then Egypt and the Middle East. It was during this period that Thomas entered the American consciousness when he introduced Lawrence of Arabia to the world. While covering the Middle Eastern theater he met Colonel T. E. Lawrence, a British officer fighting the Turks in Palestine, who would become better known as Lawrence of Arabia. Lawrence had been ignored by other correspondents, but Thomas befriended him and promoted his exploits as Lawrence of Arabia in his highly romanticized book *With Lawrence in Arabia,* published in 1924.

At the conclusion of World War I,* Thomas became the first reporter to enter Germany and return with an eyewitness account of the German revolution. In 1930 he began an almost fifty-year affiliation with CBS as television and radio news broadcaster. In 1935 he became recognized as the narrator of the Fox Movietime Newsreel company. Until his retirement in 1974 he continued to travel widely, filming travelogues and writing over fifty books.

REFERENCE: Norman R. Bowen, ed. *Lowell Thomas: The Stranger Everyone Knows.* 1968.

Thomas, Sir William Beach (1868–1957)

Born in Huntingdonshire and educated at Oxford, in 1892 he became a schoolmaster. In 1897 he joined the *Globe* shortly before its demise and then worked as a freelancer for over twenty-eight different papers before representing the *Daily Mail* as war correspondent during World War I.* He covered the conflict in France for four years and was knighted in 1920. He continued to travel, writing books and articles on nature and travel themes.

REFERENCE: Dennis Griffiths, ed. *The Encyclopedia of the British Press.* 1992.

Thompson, Donald (1884–c. 1930s)

Born in Topeka, Kansas, the diminutive combat photographer came to prominence as one of the pioneering war photographers of World War I.* His photographs were published in his local newspaper while he was still in his teens. In 1914 he set his sights on covering the early days of the First World War. He landed in England with a group of Canadian reporters heading to the frontlines in Belgium. With censorship at the front rampant it took him nine attempts to reach the action from Paris. By the following year his pictures, taken under heavy fire, were appearing in the *Topeka Daily Capital* and other Kansas papers. Especially valuable to a news-starved public, was his motion picture footage of the Battle of Mons, which he sold to the American Moving Picture World; his still pictures, meanwhile were selling for exorbitant fees and he was hired to cover the war for a newspaper syndicate for $800 a week plus expenses, a fortune in that era. As he made his way through Belgium, the intrepid correspondent carried a camera, field glasses, a revolver, and 300 films. The noted war correspondent, Edward Alexander Powell,* upon meeting him described Thompson as having "more chilled-steel nerve than any man I know."

Thompson operated as a freelancer, selling his photographs and motion pictures to whoever bid the highest. His work appeared in the *New York Times,* the *New York World, the Chicago Tribune, London's Daily Mail,* and the *Illustrated London News.* In 1915 he returned home to visit his family in Topeka and to deliver lectures and show his battlefront footage. By then he had witnessed more than 30 battles, taken more than 2,700 stills and shot 16,000 feet of film in the combat zone. Like many other American newspaper reporters who covered the war behind German lines prior to American involvement in the war, Thompson asserted he never saw any German atrocities, contradicting the widely disseminated anti-German propaganda stating otherwise. Thompson would cover the Russian army on the eastern front when he returned to Europe later in 1915. This time he traveled in the company of the *Chicago Tribune* publisher, Robert R. McCormick; their collaborative efforts, McCormick as reporter, and Thompson as photographer, were published in the *Chicago Tribune.* During their coverage of action in the Carpathian Mountains, Thompson took what McCormick described as

"the first 360 degree panoramic sweep of a battle front ever put on film." When Thompson returned to the States he edited his eastern front footage into the 90-minute film, *Somewhere in France.* According to Thompson's biographer, the title was "an allusion to the censors' ban on revealing place names."

In 1916, he covered the Allied front in the Balkans and then attached himself to the French army. In the process he was selected as its official cinematographer. He was wounded for the second time in the war in France, preventing him from covering the Battle of the Somme. The following year found Thompson back in Russia, traveling with *Leslie's Weekly* correspondent Florence Harper. Due to the exigencies of the European conflict they were forced to travel to Russia by sailing first to China and then crossing Russia by train. He filmed from the frontlines, as well as the street fighting and demonstrations taking place in the months leading up to the Russian Revolution that October. Little information on Thompsons' postwar career is available. He apparently continued to dabble in film as a producer in the 1920s and 1930s, mostly in relation to his own war footage and travel films. Not surprisingly he ended up in Hollywood for a time. According to his biographer he returned to Europe to cover the events leading up to World War II as well as the Italian Ethiopian campaign.

REFERENCES: David Mould, "Donald Thompson: Photographer at War," Kansas History, Autumn 1982, 154–167; Kevin Brownlow. *The War the West and The Wilderness.* 1979.

Thompson, John Hall (1908–1997)

Thompson was born in Chicago and educated at Williams College. While representing the *Chicago Tribune* in 1942, he became the first war correspondent to parachute with the armed forces into a combat situation when he jumped into the fray near Tebessa, Algeria, during the North African campaign. He later repeated this feat, dropping behind enemy lines in Sicily. He was with the first troops landing on Normandy beach in 1944 and was reportedly the first Allied correspondent to meet the Soviet Army during its historic linkup with Allied troops on the Elbe River in the latter days of the war. Thompson was the first war correspondent to be awarded the Medal of Freedom and was also the recipient of a Purple Heart.

REFERENCES: Robert W. Desmond. *Tides of War.* 1984; M. L. Stein. *Under Fire: The Story of American War Correspondents.* 1968.

Thorpe, Thomas Bangs (1815–1878)

Thorpe was a noted western humorist and painter prior to the Mexican-American War* of 1846–1848. Born in Massachusetts, Thorpe moved to Louisiana in 1836 to pursue literary and artistic fame. He scored on at least one count, developing a following for short stories of southwestern humor. He initially accompanied General Zachary Taylor's troops as war correspondent for the *New Orleans Tropic* in May and June 1846. He arrived in Matamoros following the battles along the Rio Grande. Almost immediately he began recording firsthand accounts from interviews with the participants through sketches and narrative. He quickly returned to New Orleans to turn his materials into a book for a public clamoring for war news. His book *Our Army on the Rio Grande* was published in August 1846. Not long afterward he followed with *Our Army at Monterey,* which was less successful.

REFERENCES: Milton Rickels. *Thomas Bangs Thorpe: Humorist of the Old Southwest.* 1962; Martha A. Sandweiss, Rick Stewart, and Ben W. Huseman. *Eyewitness to War: Prints and Daguerreotypes of the Mexican War, 1846–1848.* 1989.

Thrasher, John S. (1817–1879)

Born in Portland, Maine, he spent his teenage years in Cuba, his mother's native land. In 1849 he turned to journalism, buying the *Faro*

Industrial, a newspaper he used to support the developing resistance movement in Cuba against Spanish rule. He left the paper in 1851 after a failed insurrection and was soon arrested. After his release he relocated to New Orleans where he was once more publishing a journal critical of the Spanish colonial rulers. Prior to the American Civil War* he worked as a roving journalist before moving to Texas, where he married into a well-connected family. They relocated to Macon, Georgia, where he joined southern newspaper editors in 1862 in Atlanta trying to find solutions to their reporting problems, namely establishing telegraphic links after the Union shut down wire services. He would eventually play an important part in establishing the Press Association of the Confederate States of America.* As superintendent of the Press Association he introduced a number of standards for guaranteeing objective news reporting. According to his biographer these guidelines would introduce a new style of reporting that would "result in a dead uniformity in its publication." He would travel to meet with various Confederate generals hoping to mend fences and build relationships between reporters and the military establishment. He met with the most contentious opponents of press freedom, Generals Joseph Johnston and Braxton Bragg, hoping to alleviate the press association's censorship problems, but by most accounts, to little avail. As the war turned against the South after 1863, Thrasher and others were forced to rely more on soldiers' battle accounts, due to the paucity of official press sources. He moved back to Texas after the war and became one of the editor-owners of the *Galveston Civilian* newspaper.

REFERENCE: Janice Ruth Wood, "John S. Thrasher: Journalistic Revolutionary and Reformer," *Knights of the Quill,* 2010, 362–375.

Threlkeld, Richard (1937–2012)

Born and raised in the Midwest, he was educated at Ripon College, Northwestern University and Columbia University. He joined CBS News in

---

* *Indicates a separate entry.*

1966 before moving to ABC for seven years in the 1980s. He returned to CBS after that. He served as a writer, reporter, anchor and bureau chief for CBS during an almost thirty year career. He covered the first Persian Gulf War, the Vietnam War, and the invasions of Panama and Grenada. He has covered the Middle East peace talks, the 1990 Soviet Revolution and the demonstrations at Tiananmen Square. He wrote *Dispatches from the Former Evil Empire* (2001). He died in a car accident in New York.

REFERENCE: Richard Threlkeld." www.medill,northwestern.edu/alumni/hallofachievement.aspx?id=117363; Dennis Hevesi, "Richard Threlkeld, 74, Award-Winning Journalist," *New York Times*.

Tice, Austin (b. 1981)

Tice is a freelance journalist who disappeared in Syria on August 13, 2012, just three months after his arrival. One of seven children, raised in Houston, Texas, the former U.S. Marine and law school student at Georgetown University crossed the Syrian-Turkish border to cover the civil war from Damascus. He initially entered the fray as a photojournalist for McClatchy Newspapers and the *Washington Post*. In September 2012 he appeared blindfolded but apparently physically unharmed on a video that appeared on YouTube. His captors were garbed in traditional Islamic outfits. But what has been most perplexing is that no group has sought ransom or claimed to hold him. In 2014 Tice was one of at least 119 journalists kidnapped. According to Reporters without Borders, at the end of the year 40 were still being held, including 22 in Syria. By most accounts, by having had a career in the military, it gave Tice's stories a perspective lacking in mostly nonmilitary accounts. His stories covered discussions of the Syrian rebels' weapons as well as interviews with civilians and fighters. His plight is currently featured in Reporters Without Borders #FreeAustinTice campaign. In February 2015, Tice's parents joined a growing chorus of critics requesting the U.S. government to do more to help hostages held overseas by revisiting the country's hostage policies. On February 19, 2015, a banner featuring the Tice case appeared on the websites of close to 270 U.S. newspapers and media companies, urging readers to sign a petition urging the government to do more to save Tice. This was the first time so many American media organizations joined together to call for a reporter's release.

REFERENCES: Emma S. Hinchliffe, "Pleas Go Out for Return of Reporter," USA TODAY, Feb. 18, 2015, 2B; St. John Barned-Smith, "News Sites Helping Hostage Campaign," Houston Chronicle, Feb. 19, 2015, B1, B12.

Timrod, Henry (1828–1867)

The poet Henry Timrod was born in Charleston, South Carolina, and educated at Franklin College. He wrote for several literary publications before joining the Confederate Army of the West as a war correspondent for the *Charleston Mercury* shortly after the Battle of Shiloh in 1862. Writing under the pen name "Kappa," Timrod covered the Corinth campaign in Mississippi and the South Carolina campaign until the burning of Columbia, South Carolina. In later years he suffered from tuberculosis and various ailments that he in part associated with his miserable experience covering the western war.

REFERENCE: J. Cutler Andrews. *The South Reports the Civil War*. 1970.

Tobey, William C. (d. 1854)

In September 1847, during the Mexican War,* Tobey was the war correspondent for the *Philadelphia North American*. As a member of what has been called the Anglo-Saxon press,* he founded *The North American, Mexico* as an extension of his paper in Mexico City. His articles appeared over the signature of "John of York."

REFERENCES: Fayette Copeland. *Kendall of the Picayune*. 1943; Robert W. Johanssen. *To the Halls of the Montezumas*. 1985; Tom Reilly, *War with Mexico*, 2010.

Tobin, George H. (?)

Born in Wicklow, Ireland and educated at Dublin's Trinity College, Tobin later moved to the United States. Tobin, who was among the fisrt New Orleans journalists to voluneteer when the Mexiacn War broke out, was a war correspondent and printer for the *New Orleans Delta* during the Mexican-American War.* His dispatches appeared under "From Captain Tobin's Knapsack." He originally debarked from New Orleans as captain of one of the New Orleans volunteer groups for the war. He covered the Battle of Buena Vista.

REFERENCE: Fayette Copeland. *Kendall of the Picayune.* 1943; Tom Reilly, *War with Mexico!*, 2010..

Tolstoy, Leo Nicolayevich (1828–1910)

Tolstoy was born at Yasnaya Polyana in the Tula Province of Russia and educated at the University of Kazan. In 1851 he enlisted in an artillery regiment in the Caucasus. Following the outbreak of the Crimean War* he volunteered for active service and joined the beleaguered garrison at Sebastopol in late 1854. Tolstoy attempted to publish a periodical during the conflict that would express his views on the war. He had intended that his journal, the *Military Gazette,* would bolster the morale of soldiers at the front. However, it met its demise before the first issue was completed. The Czar had refused permission to publish the journal on the grounds that the *Army and Navy Gazette,* which specialized in military literature, already existed. Tolstoy recorded the siege and after its conclusion wrote *The Sebastopol Sketches* (1856), which established his reputation as a writer. The book is divided into three phases-December, May, and August,-re-creating the appalling conditions that Tolstoy witnessed in the winter of 1854. Tolstoy, like his English counterpart William Howard Russell,* has been referred to by some sources as the first modern war correspondent.

Over the next several decades he wrote his masterpieces *War and Peace* (1865–1868) and *Anna Karenina* (1874–1876) and became an extreme moralist and rationalist, rejecting the state and the church, and during the 1904 Russo-Japanese War* became an advocate of nonviolence.

REFERENCES: Leo Tolstoy. *The Sebastopol Sketches.* 1856; Henri Troyat. *Tolstoy.* 1967.

Tomalin, Nicholas (1931–1973)

Born in London, following graduation from Cambridge he worked for several papers before joining the *Sunday Times* in 1967. His coverage of the Vietnam War* reportedly brought home to Britons the manifest tragedy of the conflict. In October 1973 he was in Israel covering the Arab-Israeli War when, shortly after his first dispatch to the *Sunday Times,* he was killed by a Syrian missile.

REFERENCES: Dennis Griffiths, ed. *The Encyclopedia of the British Press.* 1992; Nicholas Tomalin. *Nicholas Tomalin Reporting.* 1975.

Tomara, Sonia (1897–1982)

Tomara was born in St. Petersburg, Russia, to wealthy White Russian parents. She was educated at the University of Moscow, and her fluency in several languages contributed to her success as a war correspondent. With the outbreak of the Russian Revolution Sonia fled with her mother and sisters, while her father stayed behind and was probably executed by revolutionary forces. In 1928, Sonia was hired by the *New York Herald Tribune.* In 1939 she covered the outbreak of World War II* in southeastern Europe, where she witnessed the fall of Poland. The following year Tomara was in Paris when the Germans invaded. She would go on to cover the Balkan conflict, the Chinese-Burma-India theater, and the Allied summit meetings in Cairo, Teheran, and Algiers. In 1944 she was the first woman journalist into liberated Paris, where she was also

Indicates a separate entry.

reunited with her family. She later covered the Seventh Army's advance through Alsace. In 1945 Tomara resigned from the *Herald Tribune* and married federal judge William Clark.

REFERENCES: Julia Edwards. *Women of the World.* 1988; Lilya Wagner. *Women War Correspondents of World War II.* 1989.

Topping, Seymour (1918–2002)

A graduate of the Missouri School of Journalism, Topping served in the Pacific theater during World War II.* After the war he became a stringer for the International News service (INS), flying from Manila to Peking to cover the Chinese Civil War. In 1948 he joined the Associated Press as a foreign correspondent in China and Southeast Asia, allowing him to cover the fall of Nanking in 1949 to the Communists. When AP opened a bureau in Saigon in 1950 he was posted there to cover the French Indochina War. By most accounts he was the first American correspondent stationed in Indochina after World War II ended. Two years later he was covering the diplomatic beat in London and then Berlin. In 1959 he joined the *New York Times* and was posted to Moscow. Over the next few years he would shuttle between continents covering the Cuban Missile Crisis and Cold War events and in 1963 he was back in Southeast Asia as the chief correspondent for the *Times.* Over the next few years he would cover the wars in Indochina before returning to the United States in 1966 and rising through the management ranks of the *Times.* In 2010 he published *On the Front Lines of the Cold War, An American Correspondent's Journal from the Chinese Civil War to the Cuban Missile Crisis and Vietnam.*

REFERENCE: "Seymour Topping," http://journalism. missouri.edu/alum/seymour-topping/.

Torgerson, Dial (1928–1983)

Torgerson was Mexico City bureau chief for the *Los Angeles Times.* On June 21, 1983, he was killed along with freelance photographer Richard Cross near the Honduran-Nicaraguan border when their car was hit by a rocket grenade fired from the Nicaraguan side.

REFERENCE: Michael Emery. *On the Front Lines.* 1995.

Townsend, George Alfred (1841–1914)

Born in Delaware, he covered the American Civil War* for the *Philadelphia Inquirer* and the *Philadelphia Press,* two years after beginning his journalism career. He later transferred to the *New York Herald,* for which he reported the Peninsular campaign and the Battle of Cedar Mountain. He reported the 1865 spring campaign for the *New York World,* and his coverage of the Battle of Five Forks elevated him into the upper echelon of the era's reporters.

Following the Civil War he covered the Austro-Prussian War* of 1866 and went on to a long career as a feature article writer and political satirist under the pen name "Gath" for the *Chicago Tribune,* the *Cincinnati Enquirer,* and other papers. He established a fund-raising campaign to erect a monument commemorating Civil War correspondents. A sixty-foot stone arch was finally erected in 1896 near his home in South Mountain, Maryland, bearing the names of 151 artists and reporters.

REFERENCES: J. Cutler Andrews. *The North Reports the Civil War.* 1955; Louis M. Starr. *The Bohemian Brigade.* 1954.

Toynbee, Arnold J. (1889–1975)

The Oxford-educated British historian Arnold Toynbee reported the Greco-Turkish war of the 1920s from Anatolia as a special correspondent for the *Manchester Guardian.* Sixty-five of his dispatches appeared in the newspaper between January 25 and October 4, 1921. It was during this experience that he began the outline of what would become his chief work, A *Study of History.*

REFERENCE: David Ayerst. *The Manchester Guardian: Biography of a Newspaper.* 1971.

Trakhman, Mikhail Anatol'evich (1918–1976)

Born in Moscow, he worked as a documentary film cameraman from 1934 to 1939 before joining the Soviet Information Bureau as a photographer-reporter from 1939 to 1941. He became a war photographer-correspondent with the Red Army and TASS in 1941. His photographs capture the lives of guerrilla fighters and civilians behind the enemy lines. He covered the Battle of Leningrad. Trakhman found nothing romantic about the horrors of war and left war photography after covering World War II.* Following the war he was chief correspondent for the Moscow-based *Literaturnaja Gaseta* (Literary Gazette). Among his publications are several collaborations with poets and other photographers including *Zarevo* (1970) and *Ozvobozhdenye* (1974).

REFERENCES: *Contemporary Photographers.* 1982; Jorge Lewinski. *The Camera at War.* 1978.

Treanor, Tom (1909–1944)

In 1940 Treanor was a roving correspondent in France reporting on the developing war in Europe. At the beginning of the Sicily campaign in July 1943, he flew as an observer with six other correspondents on a five-hundred-plane bombing raid over Rome. During the Italian campaign he contributed articles to *Collier's* magazine. The *Los Angeles Times* reporter often promoted his dispatches with the phrase "The only American foreign correspondent from west of Chicago." Following D-Day he covered the fighting in France for the Central Broadcasting Service and the *Los Angeles Times* until he was killed on August 14, 1944, when a U.S. Army tank ran over his jeep.

REFERENCE: Robert W. Desmond. *Tides of War.* 1984.

Tregaskis, Richard J. (1916–1973)

Born in Elizabeth, New Jersey, and educated at Harvard, he entered journalism while still in college, writing for the *Boston American*. Employed by the International News Service during World War II,* Tregaskis was with the first wave of marines landing on Guadalcanal on August 7, 1942. He remained there through most of August and September, witnessing the early stages of the first major successful Allied offensive against a strategic Pacific stronghold. He was present at the Battle of Bloody Ridge, where U.S. Marines repulsed Japanese attempts to recapture the island's airfield. He completed his best-selling *Guadalcanal Diary* (1943) while aboard a bomber on the way back to the States.

In November 1943 he was severely wounded when a German shell fragment pierced his skull while he was covering the advance of the Fifth Army into Italy, but he miraculously survived. He was unable to speak or move for several weeks. Six months after treatment at Walter Reed Hospital in Washington, D.C., and the insertion of a metal plate into his skull, he was back in the field. In June 1944 he was awarded a Purple Heart. Following his recuperation he followed the U.S. First Army from Normandy to Aachen. He later flew on five B-29 bomber missions in the Pacific theater and accompanied a torpedo squadron. His experiences in Italy are chronicled in *Invasion Diary* (1944). After the war he wrote for various periodicals. He also wrote several other books, including *Seven Leagues to Paradise* (1951), *X-15 Diary* (1961), *John F. Kennedy and PT 109* (1962), and *Vietnam Diary* (1963), which was awarded the George Polk Award. He died at the age of fifty-six, apparently by drowning in Honolulu.

REFERENCES: Library of America. *Reporting World War Two: Part One, American Journalism 1938–1944.* 1995; Frederick S. Voss. *Reporting the War.* 1994.

---

* *Indicates a separate entry.*

Truman, Benjamin Cummings (1835–1916)

Born in Providence, Rhode Island, Truman joined the *New York Times* in 1859 as a compositor and proofreader. With the outbreak of the American Civil War* he moved to the *Sunday Morning Chronicle* and became a war correspondent. He became one of the leading reporters of the western theater of the war, eventually covering the Battle of Murfreesboro, the Atlanta campaign, and the capture of Atlanta. Besides his journalistic activities, on various occasions he acted as an aide to Andrew Johnson, military governor of Tennessee, and was on the staffs of Generals J. S. Negley, John H. King, and Kenner Garrard.

Following the war, President Andrew Johnson assigned Truman to act as his confidential agent, investigating conditions in the Deep South. He testified before Congress during Reconstruction and later served as a special treasury agent in South Carolina and Florida and as a special agent for the Post Office Department in California. He returned to journalism in 1872 in various capacities with various California newspapers. In addition to his newspaper work, Truman wrote several books, including *The Field of Honor* (1883), a history of dueling; *Semi-Tropical California* (1874); and *Life, Adventures, and Capture of Tiburcio Vasquez, the Great California Bandit and Murderer* (1874).

REFERENCES: J. Cutler Andrews. *The North Reports the Civil War.* 1955; *DAB.*

Trumbull, Robert (1917–1992)

Trumbull covered the war in the Pacific during World War II* beginning in 1943. The former editor of the *Honolulu Advertiser* reported the Battles of Tarawa and Makin for the *New York Times.* Early in 1944 he became chairman of the Pacific War Correspondents Association.* In June and July 1944 he reported but did not witness most of the landings in the Solomon, Gilbert, Marshall, and Caroline Islands. Toward the end of the war in Asia and the Pacific, Trumbull left Guam and returned to Honolulu. He would eventually return to the Pacific aboard the British battleship *King George V. In* 1948 Trumbull was one of the first reporters on the scene when Gandhi was assassinated in Delhi, India.

REFERENCE: Robert W. Desmond. *Tides of War.* 1984; NY Times, October 13, 1992.

Tuohy, William (1926–2009)

Born and raised in Chicago, Tuohy entered the newspaper business as a copyboy with the *San Francisco Chronicle.* He moved to *Newsweek* in the 1960s and shortly after covering the 1964 presidential campaign was made Saigon bureau chief. In 1966 he joined the *Los Angeles Times* and served as its Vietnam War* correspondent, winning a Pulitzer Prize for international reporting in 1969. During his stints in Vietnam he accompanied Green Berets on riverboat patrols, and reported the Battle of Hue and the siege at Khe Sanh. During the 1970s Tuohy also covered the Jordanian civil war in 1970, the 1973 Arab-Israeli War, the Iranian Revolution, the 1978 Israeli invasion of Lebanon, and the conflict in Northern Ireland. Among his three books is *Dangerous Company*, which chronicles his days as a war reporter.

REFERENCE: William Tuohy. *Dangerous Company.* 1987.

Turgut, Serif (?)

Turgut has been credited as being the first Turkish female war journalist. She was drawn to reporting war after seeing brutal photographs from several death camps run by the Army of Republika Srpska in the early months of the Bosnian War. She went to Bosnia as a freelance journalist with the intention of staying a couple of weeks and stayed for close to five years documenting the carnage of the war for Turkish television ATV (Actual Television). She would also cover war zones in Kosovo, Iraq, Algeria, the Western Sahara, and Chechnya. She has won numerous awards for her journalistic accomplishments and served for more than three years as the United Nations Head of Public Information Office for Central Liberia, where she focused on various issues related to postconflict transition.

REFERENCE: http://en.wikipedia.org/wiki/%C5%9Eerif_Turgut.

Tweedie, Penny (1940–2011)

Born in England, she worked as a photographer-correspondent for the *Sunday Times*. Her war photographs have appeared in *National Geographic, Time, Paris Match* and many journals. Tweedie has also participated in charitable causes such as Shelter and Oxfam, and in organizations providing assistance for refugees in Vietnam and Cambodia, Montagnard orphans, and famine victims in India. While covering the 1971 conflict in Bangladesh, she took some of the most graphic images of human violence when she witnessed the bayonetting of four Bengali prisoners in a crowded Dacca football stadium. One authority is convinced that the executions would not have taken place if not for the presence of cameras. Tweedie covered the 1973 Arab-Israeli War and the Vietnam War.*

REFERENCES: Frances Fralin, ed. *The Indelible Image.* 1985; Jorge Lewinski. *The Camera at War.* 1978.

Tyomin, Viktor (1908–1982)

The veteran Soviet photojournalist has covered assignments in almost thirty different countries for various publications, but he is most identified with his work during World War II.* As special correspondent for *Pravda,* he was one of the first correspondents to photograph the raising of the Soviet Banner of Victory over the Reichstag after the fall of Berlin and was one of the small pool of photographers selected to witness the executions of Nazi war criminals after the Nuremberg trials. Tyomin covered all of the major fronts during the war, witnessing the surrender ceremonies of both the Germans and the Japanese, and participating in combat during the war in Finland. After the war he became a special correspondent for the USSR Press Center.

REFERENCE: Daniela Mrazkova and Vladimir Remes, eds. *The Russian War: 1941–1945.* 1975.

Indicates a separate entry.

Ukrainian Conflict

The Ukrainian war that began in 2014 became one of the most dangerous conflicts for war reporters. By most accounts not only were journalists becoming casualties under murky circumstances, but both sides in the war increasingly viewed them as actual participants in the conflict. In 2014, Ukraine was in the top five deadliest destinations for journalists. By July 2014 five journalists had been killed and at least 200 wounded. Abuses have been catalogued on both sides, with even pro-Russian rebels seeking support from Reporters without Borders.* In the first three months of 2015 alone, 8 journalists had been killed.

REFERENCES: Allison Quinn, "Journalists Become Walking Targets in Ukraine's Information War," The Moscow Times, July 1, 2014; "Press Logo Makes You a Target: Killing Journalists Should Be a War Crime, AP Chief Says, http://rt.com/news/245489-ap-journalists-targeting-killing, Mar. 31, 2015.

Under Fire

The 1983 movie *Under Fire,* starring Nick Nolte and Gene Hackman, is about war correspondents covering the 1979 Nicaraguan revolution and how they risk their professionalism by becoming personally involved in the conflict. Director Roger Spottiswoode described the film as "about the complexities of journalism, about journalists coping with the difficulties of being objective and yet having feelings and sensitivities about their subjects." In the film Nolte plays a photographer who fabricates a picture in order to help the rebels and perhaps reduce the bloodletting.

REFERENCE: Howard Good. *The Image of War Correspondents in Anglo-American Fiction.* 1985.

Unembedded Journalists

See UNILATERALS.

Unger, Frederic William (1875–1949)

Born in Philadelphia and educated at the University of Pennsylvania, Unger reported the Boer War* for the the *Daily Express* of London. His experiences covering the action from both sides of the conflict are chronicled in *With Bobs and Kruger: Experiences and Observations of an American War Correspondent in the Field with Both Armies* (1901). He came to prominence after gaining an interview with the Boer leader Paul Kruger and was eventually awarded the South African War Medal for his service as an official service rider for Lord Roberts. He later represented London newspapers in Japan, Korea, and Manchuria during the Russo-Japanese War.*

REFERENCE: Robert Wilkinson-Latham. *From Our Special Correspondent.* 1979.

* Indicates a separate entry.

Unilaterals

Since the 1980s the military has depended more and more on "embedded" journalists to cover the battle front in a type of de facto censorship, as the authorities exert control over news stories by offering journalists protection and transportation as long as they stay with the "party line." Those journalists that prefer to go their own way, or assert their independence, are referred to by the military as "unilaterals" or "unembedded journalists."

REFERENCE: Michael S, Sweeney. *The Military and the Press*. 2006.

United Press (UP)

See UNITED PRESS INTERNATIONAL (UPI).

United Press International (UPI)

The United Press was established on June 21, 1907 after the Associated Press* denied its service to Scripps' papers. In the mind of its founders it was "overturning the Associated Press' monopolistic grip on U.S. news dissemination." At its inception it had contracts to sell its daily news reports to 369 newspapers. It was the brainchild of Edward "E.W." Wyllis Scripps, principal owner of what became the Scripps-Howard chain who led the merger of Publisher's Press with Scripps-McRae Press Association and Scripps News Association. At the time there were several organizations using the moniker "United Press," and it would take several years of legal battles to gain ownership of the name. With a paucity of financial resources few could have foreseen its future growth and competition to the venerable AP,* which boasted 800 members and an expense budget in 1910 of almost $3 million, especially, since UP only turned a profit of $1,200 its first year in operation. In the early 1920s UP made inroads on the AP hold on the European news market and also began servicing paper in Asia. UP correspondents were known

as "Unipressers" and according to UPI its wire service reporters were the first to conduct interviews and the first to put bylines on stories. In 1935 UP became the first major U.S. news service to supply news to radio stations. In 1958 UP merged with Hearst's International News Service (INS) to form the United Press International. Throughout the years there has been a healthy competition between UP and AP. According to one former Unipresser "You could easily tell a U.P. man from an A.P. man, because a Unipresser worked alone and A.P. men traveled in packs to blanket the story." Noted UP alumni include Walter Cronkite,* William L. Shirer,* and Howard K. Smith.* For much of its history UP has operated at a loss. In 1982 during its 75th anniversary it was sold to Media News Corporation. At the time of its sale it had 2,000 full time employees and served more than 7,500 newspapers, radio and television stations, and cable systems in more than 100 countries. In 1985 UPI declared bankruptcy and filed for Chapter 11 protection. Over the next 20 years it went through a series of new owners and reorganizations and began the transition to new technologies.

REFERENCES: John Hohenberg. *Foreign Correspondence: The Great Reporters and Their Times*. Syracuse University Press, 2nd edition, 1995; UPI History, http://100years.upi.com/history.html; United Press International, Inc.-Company History, http:funduniverse.com/company-histories/United-Press-International-Inc.

Upton, George Putnam (1834–1919)

Upton was born in Roxbury, Massachusetts, and received a master's degree from Brown University in 1854. He broke into journalism with *the Chicago Evening Journal* in 1855 before beginning a fifty-seven-year affiliation with the *Chicago Tribune* in 1860. During the American Civil War* Upton covered the Mississippi naval flotilla in the western theater of operations and reported the capture of Island Number 10, New Madrid, and Fort Pillow. In 1868 he became the *Tribune's* music and drama critic and later served as editorial writer and Tribune Company director.

REFERENCE: Lloyd Wendt. *Chicago Tribune: The Rise of a Great American Newspaper*. 1979.

Ustinov, Alexander (1909–1995)

A longtime photojournalist for *Pravda*, Ustinov covered much of the Russian war with Germany. He recorded the last two years of the conflict with the First Ukrainian Front, where he chronicled the exploits of the First Czechoslovak Army Corps in late 1944 and later the liberation of Czechoslovakia by the Red Army. One of his most memorable pictures was of the linkup of Soviet and American forces on the Elbe River near Berlin in 1945.

REFERENCE: Daniela Mrazkova and Vladimir Remes, eds. *The Russian War: 1941–1945*. 1975.

Ut, Huynh Cong (b. 1951)

Best known as "Nick", the Vietnam War photojournalist was born in the Mekong Delta province of Long An when it was part of French Indochina. His older brother Huynh Thanh My,* who was also a photographer, had been killed covering action in the Mekong Delta on October 10, 1965 while on assignment for the Associated Press. Ut's mother brought the then fourteen-year old Nick to Saigon's Associated Press office and in 1966 he was hired by his brother's old boss Horst Faas.* Initially he was hired to work in the photo darkroom, where Ut remembers that he "learned by seeing the photographers' work and what every day war looked like." Nick rose to prominence on his own work in 1967 and during the 1968 Tet offensive was showcasing his courage and technical abilities while covering the heavy fighting. During this era Ut was wounded a number of times, including twice during the Cambodian theater of the war. Another time he suffered a shrapnel wound from a mortar round. By the time he was twenty-one he had been

covering the war for seven years. In 1972 he also took one of the most famous and controversial pictures of the war, the photo of nine-year old Phan Thi Kim Phuc fleeing from a napalm attack screaming in agony. Ut was awarded the 1973 Pulitzer Prize for photography. Among the many other awards he won for this picture were the World Press Photo Award, George Polk Memorial Award, and the Overseas Press Club Award. Ut left Vietnam for the Phillipines in April 1975, having covered the war for eight years. He ended up in the United States where he continues to work as a photographer. The Vietnamese girl survived her injuries. Ut made sure Kim Phuc recived the best medical treatment possible and after 17 skin transplants she recovered and went on to marry and raise a family. When the original picture was taken one of the AP editors refeused to run the picture because it showed frontal nudity. But Horst Faas argued by telex that in this case an exception to the AP rule against showing frontal nudity should be made. On the other hand President Nixon reportedly commented that he doubted the authenticity of the picture. As a postscript and an indictment of the state of modern photojournalism and news coverage, Ut did not come into prominence again until June 2007 when his photos of hotel heiress Paris Hilton crying in the back of a police car were published around the world, almost thirty-five years to the day that he took his Pulitzer Prize winning photo.

REFERENCE: Horst Faas and Marianne Fulton. "Nick Ut—Still a Photographer with the Asscoiated Press." http://digitaljournalist.org/issue0008/ngg.htm.

Utley, Clifton Garrick (1939–2014)

Born in Chicago and educated at Carleton College, Minnesota, Garrick Utley's parents were both broadcasters and reporters. Utley joined NBC in 1963, after being recommended by family friend John Chancellor. He made the transition from office clerk to war correspondent in his first year, and was soon covering conflict in Indochina and the developing Vietnam War.* In 1964 he was among the first network reporters posted in Saigon and developed a reputation for offering wider perspectives on political issues and battlefield developments in the years that Vietnam was entering the American consciousness. Utley covered the Soviet invasion of Czechoslovakia in 1968, the 1973 Yom Kippur War, and numerous Cold War stories. Fluent in Russian, German, and French, Utley reported from more than 70 countries in a versatile career, including thirty years with NBC. He was a familiar presence on television, hosting and moderating various magazine programs. He covered the 1991 Iraq War, moderated *Meet the Press* from 1989–1991, was chief NBC correspondent in the 1980s covering foreign and domestic events, and joined CNN, working for the network from 1997–2002. Utley published a memoir, *You Should Have Been Here Yesterday: A Life in Television News*

(2000), and received the Peabody Award and the Overseas Press Club's Edward R. Murrow Award. He died of prostate cancer.

REFERENCE: Robert D. McFadden, "Garrick Utley, Pioneering Vietnam Reporters, Dies at 74," New York Times, Feb. 22, 2014, A17.

Uzlyan, Alexander (b. 1908)

Uzlyan has worked as a photographer for various Russian news organizations, including *Izvestiya, Pravda,* and *Ogonyok.* During World War II* he accompanied the Black Sea Fleet, better known as the "Black Death" to the Germans, for the Soviet Information Bureau. His photographic record of Soviet naval exploits during the war have been described as giving "an impression of movement that is almost like a motion picture."

REFERENCE: Daniela Mrazkova and Vladimir Remes, eds. *The Russian War 1941–1945.* 1975.

---

* *Indicates a separate entry.*

Vandam, Albert Dresden (1843–1903)

The London-born special correspondent was educated in France before embarking on his career with various English newspapers covering the Austro-Prussian War* in 1866. In 1870 he reported the Franco-Prussian War* for the American press. He returned to London the following year to continue his career as a reporter for various newspapers.

REFERENCE: *DNB*, 1901–1911.

van de Velde, Willem "the Elder" (1610–1693)

Van de Velde made the transition from sailor to widely hailed painter of maritime subjects before the age of twenty. As the official artist of the Dutch fleet in the 1660s, his work was so revered by the Dutch states that he was given a small vessel that he could utilize to follow the Dutch fleets into battle. He was able to witness and paint a number of battles between English and Dutch vessels from "very close quarters." He sketched the Four Days Battle on June 1–4, 1666 and the St. James Day battle, July 25, 1666. His son Willem van de Velde the Younger was among several other Dutch artists that captured the Dutch fleet in battle on canvas.

REFERENCE: Walter Armstrong, "Van de Velde, Willem (1610–1693)," London, *Dictionary of National Biography, 1885–1900*, Vol. 58.

van Lynden, Aernout (b. 1954)

This Dutch-British journalist began his more than twenty years as a war correspondent in 1979 with the *Haagsche Courant*. He was one of the only Western journalists in Iraq to cover Iraq's attack on Iran. He went on to freelance for BBC Radio, the *Observer,* and the *Washington Post*. He covered the mujahedeen resistance to the Soviet invasion and in 1982 he was posted to Beirut by the *Observer*, where he reported the Lebanese civil war and subsequent regional hot zones. He chronicled the Soviet retreat from Afghanistan and the Romanian Revolution in 1989, the Gulf War* in 1990–1991, the breakup of Yugoslavia, and the Palestinian Intifada. In 1993 he was recognized for his coverage of the Bosnian conflict with several international awards and during the early 1990s was one of the few journalists present during the siege of Sarajevo.

REFERENCE: http://www.aernoutvanlynden.com/biography/.

Veremiy, Vyacheslav (1981–2014)

Veremiy covered the war in Ukraine for Kiev's newspaper *Vesti*. He was injured in January 2014 as he covered protests in Kiev, when a stun grenade exploded near him wounding his left eye and arm. The following month he was in a taxi with another reporter on his way home from work when attackers stopped his taxi, beating

* Indicates a separate entry.

the reporters with baseball bats. Veremiy was also shot in the chest and died the following day on February 19, after being treated for severe blood loss. A subsequent investigation revealed that the dead journalist was specifically targeted when he began filming the attackers from inside the cab. A local news website later published a witness's video of the killing. Further investigation suggested that he had been fatally injured by progovernment protestors known in the region as "titushki."

REFERENCE: "Vyacheslav Veremiy," http://cpj.org/killed/2014/vyacheslaw-veremiy.php.

Verlon, Claude (1958–2013)

A veteran sound engineer, Verlon was killed along with Radio France Internationale (RFI) reporter Ghislaine Dupont* in Mali on November 2, 2013. The journalists were waylaid while leaving an interview with a leader from the Tuareg separatist group, the National Movement for the Liberation of Azawad (MNLA). They were kidnapped at gunpoint as they prepared to leave. Accounts vary somewhat on how they were killed, with the Committee to Protect Journalists* describing their bodies riddled with bullets. In Mali to cover the first round of the presidential election since July, this was Verlon's second trip to Kidal. He had been with RFI since 1982 and had worked with news crews in various hotspots, including Afghanistan, Lebanon, Iraq, and Africa. Al-Qaeda in the Islamic Maghreb later claimed to have killed them.

REFERENCE: Committee to Protect Journalists, "Claude Verlon, Journalists Killed," https://cpj.org/killed/2013/claude-version.php

Vermillion, Robert (1915–1987)

Vermillion covered fighting in Italy, Sicily, and Africa during World War II* as war correspondent for the United Press. In London in August 1943 he miraculously escaped injury when a German two-ton "blockbuster" bomb, dropped during a previous air raid, exploded less than three hundred yards from where he stood. He was saved only when the irregular terrain deflected the blast. Following the war he headed the UP bureau until the outbreak of the Korean War.* He cofounded the *Okinawa Morning Sun* in Japan in 1954 before returning to the United States three years later. He worked for *Newsweek* from 1957 to 1977.

REFERENCES: Robert W. Desmond. *Tides of War.* 1984; Jack Stenbuck. *Typewriter Battalion.* 1995.

Viaud, Louis Marie Julien (1850–1923)

Best known as the novelist Pierre Loti later in life, Viaud was a lieutenant with the French navy in Indochina in the 1880s when he began war reporting for the French newspaper *Le Figaro.* He covered campaigns in 1883 near Tonkin and Hue, and in 1900 the Boxer Rebellion* in China.

REFERENCE: Robert W. Desmond. *The Information Process.* 1978.

Vietnam War

The Vietnam War was probably the most thoroughly covered war in history. Hundreds of war correspondents covered the Vietnam War between 1961 and 1975. The typical Vietnam war correspondent was between twenty-five and thirty-five years old. Representatives for the major news organizations usually brought years of foreign reporting experience but had little if any experience reporting unconventional or guerrilla warfare. Correspondents for the print media were usually limited to terms of twelve to eighteen months, with six months the norm for broadcast representatives.

Almost seventy women reported the war for such media giants as the *New York Times, Newsweek,* and the *Christian Science Monitor.* Of the forty-five correspondents and photographers killed in action, two were women. Three

---

* Indicates a separate entry.

women were wounded in action and another four taken prisoner. Numerous photographers were killed while covering the war, including Kyoichi Sawada,* Larry Burrows,* and Henri Huet. United Press International lost Charles Eggleston, Hiromichi Mine, and Kent Potter.* Other casualties included Dickey Chapelle* of the *National Observer,* Robert J. Ellison of Empire/Black Star, Bernard Kolenberg of the AP, and noted Indochina war historian Bernard Fall.* Most journalists were killed either in helicopter crashes or by mines and snipers. The most hazardous field of operations for war correspondents was Cambodia following the 1970 invasion, with eleven journalists disappearing in the first week of April 1970 alone.

By the early 1960s several correspondents had already risen to prominence, including Malcolm Browne* of the United Press, Neil Sheehan* for United Press International, David Halberstam* for the *New York Times,* and Francois Sully* for *Newsweek,* who had been in Vietnam since Dien Bien Phu in 1954. Other early correspondents of note were photojournalist Horst Faas* and Peter Arnett* of the Associated Press, Homer Bigart* for the *New York Times,* Peter Kalischer* for CBS, Charles Mohr* for *Time,* and freelance journalist Beverly Deepe.*

Coverage of the early war years was marked by deep dissension between different generations of correspondents. Old-line war correspondents who were veterans of Korea* and World War II* tended to support American intervention. Marguerite Higgins* of the *New York Tribune,* Keyes Beech* of the *Chicago Daily News,* and Jim Lucas,* representing Scripps-Howard, were frequent critics of the interpretations and reporting of Browne, Sheehan, Halberstam, and Kalischer.

Four correspondents won Pulitzer Prizes during the conflict. Horst Faas won in 1965, Kyoichi Sawada of the UPI was a recipient the following year, Toshio Sakai won for UPI in 1968, and in 1969 Eddie Adams* of the AP won for his disturbing photo of the Saigon police chief executing a Viet Cong captive during the Tet offensive. In June 1964, Jim Lucas won the Ernie Pyle Award, and in 1967 David Douglas Duncan* of *Life* won the Robert Capa Award. However, the most controversial episode of the war escaped the attention of the vaunted Saigon press corps. It took Washington freelance writer Seymour Hersh* to uncover the story of the My Lai massacre. A former AP Pentagon correspondent, Hersh won the 1970 Pulitzer Prize for international reporting for a story he had to market through the relatively unknown Dispatch News Service.

The main focus of the American press in Vietnam was combat coverage. Pacification, South Vietnamese affairs, and other stories were generally not a priority. The fact that at its peak the press corps consisted of six hundred accredited members is somewhat misleading. Their numbers were usually lower than the number accredited. According to security regulations anyone involved in news gathering who required access to military facilities had to be accredited. So the figure of six hundred would include any employee, from the bureau chief down to the secretary, who was assigned to pick up press releases from public-affairs offices. Press corps numbers were also exaggerated because most journalists were accredited for at least six months, regardless whether they were just staying days or hours. Journalists' names would remain on the roster of accredited correspondents in the country even after they left for home.

Vietnam was the first war in which journalists were routinely accredited to the armed forces but not subject to strict censorship. Unlike World War II* there was no formal censorship. Compared to subsequent wars accreditation was relatively easy to secure in Vietnam, but correspondents were required to accept certain limitations. The process involved first acquiring accreditation from the South Vietnamese government by presenting a valid passport and entrance visa, a letter from a publishing or broadcasting group, and a record of immunization. Finally, journalists obtained accreditation from the Military Assistance Command-Vietnam (MACV) by presenting a letter from an employer in the realm of news reporting stating that the employer took full responsibility for the actions of the press representative. One of the major changes associated with war reporting in Vietnam was the omnipresence of television coverage. Technical innovations such as lightweight sound equipment, satellites, and faster transportation facilitated the transmission of images back to the United States. Vietnam was the first television war, heralding the era of rooftop journalism* in the 1990s.

Former members of the Vietnam press corps have been holding reunions since 1995, beginning in 1995 and 2000 in Ho Chi Minh City (Saigon). Plans were made for the next one in 2005, once again on the roof of the Rex Hotel. In previous years a highlight was reuniting with Vietnamese journalists and others who worked with western news media during the conflict. A number of Vietnamese newsmen, cameramen and soundmen who had fled the country often returned for the reunions including the Associated Press's Nick Ut* and napalm victim Dang Van Phuoc.

REFERENCES: Virginia Elwood-Akers. *Women War Correspondents in the Vietnam War, 1961–1975*. 1988; Daniel C. Hallin. *The "Uncensored War": The Media and Vietnam*. 1986; William Prochnau. *Once upon a Distant War: Young War Correspondents and the Early Vietnam Battles*. 1995; Clarence R. Wyatt. *Paper Soldiers: The American Press and the Vietnam War*. 1993; Horst Faas, "Vietnam War Correspondents' Reunion Preparations Now Underway," Feb. 2005, http://digitaljournalist.org/issue0502/faas.html.

Villard, Henry (1835–1900)

Born in Bavaria and educated at universities in Munich and Würzburg, Ferdinand Heinrich Gustav Hilgard arrived in America in 1853, where he became Henry Villard and one of the leading journalists of his era. After working for a German-language paper he joined the *Cincinnati Commercial* in 1859. He covered mining camps in the West and the 1860 Republican convention in Chicago. Shortly after the convention he was hired by the *New York Herald*.

With the outbreak of the American Civil War,* Villard covered the First Battle of Bull Run throughout the day and evening while other correspondents rushed off the field to telegraph premature reports of a Union victory. He returned to the nation's capital the next day with the first news of the Confederate victory. He joined the *New York Tribune* in time to report the Union defeat at Fredericksburg. His paper refused at first to publish the story without confirmation from another source. Villard was nonplussed, having risked capture and imprisonment for violating the Union commander's prohibition of correspondents heading north with news of the defeat.

He made it to the Battle of Shiloh but found no telegraph facilities. After only two hours of fact-finding he departed on the first mail boat in an attempt to scoop his competitors. However, upon his arrival at Cairo, he found out that *Herald* correspondent Frank Chapman* had already scooped him. In 1863 Villard was the only reporter to accompany Admiral DuPont's fleet in its unsuccessful attack on Charleston.

Following the war he served a short stint as an American correspondent in Europe. Returning home he became a railroad promoter and financier of newspapers. Villard would ultimately gain control of the Northern Pacific Railroad and buy the *New York Evening Post*. He married the only daughter of William Lloyd Garrison. Villard died in Dobbs Ferry, New York, at the age of sixty-five.

REFERENCES: J. Cutler Andrews. *The North Reports the Civil War*. 1955; Stewart Sifakis. *Who Was Who in the Civil War*. 1988; Henry Villard. *Memoirs of Henry Villard*, 2 vols. 1904.

Villiers, Frederic (1852–1922)

One of the preeminent war artist-correspondents* of the Victorian era, he was born in

London and educated in France. Villiers was hired by the *Graphic* in 1876 to cover the Serbian War, where he was teamed with Archibald Forbes* for the first time. The following year he covered the Russo-Turkish War,* where he witnessed the siege at Plevna, which ended when the Turks were starved into submission.

In 1878 he accompanied General Frederick Roberts' command in the Afghan War. After an around-the-world assignment for the *Graphic* he covered the battlefront again in Egypt in 1882, witnessing Lord Beresford's attack in Alexandria Harbor and Sir Garnet Wolseley's victory at the Battle of Tel-el-Kebir. Villiers barely escaped drowning in the Nile shortly before covering the battles of Abu Krea and Abu Kru in January 1885. However, he suffered the death of his fellow reporter and good friend John Cameron* of the *Standard* at Abu Kru.

He covered the Serbian invasion of Bulgaria in 1886 and the following year reported conflict in Burma. With relative peace in the world for the next seven years he went on the lecture tour in the United States and Canada. In 1894 he reported the Japanese invasion of Korea from the invader's vantage point.

In 1897, while covering the Greek army in the short Greco-Turkish War,* Villiers became the first person to use a bicycle* as transportation while on a military campaign. During this conflict he also introduced the use of the cinematograph camera to the coverage of warfare for the first time. The next year he was with British forces in the Sudan, where he witnessed the pivotal battle of Omdurman, accompanied by his trusty bicycle and moving picture camera. For the rest of the nineteenth century and into the first two decades of the next, Villiers was occupied by the seemingly inexhaustible little wars of the Victorian era. He covered the Boer War* and the Russo-Japanese War,* where he was the only war artist with Japanese forces at the siege of Port Arthur. In 1911 he reported the Italian invasion of Tripoli, then the 1912 Balkan War, and World War I.* Villiers earned his place in

the pantheon of war correspondents, covering twelve major conflicts as well as many lesser ones. Rudyard Kipling* reportedly based the character of one of his war artists in *The Light That Failed** on Villiers. Among his published works are *Pictures of Many Wars* (1903), *Port Arthur* (1905), *Peaceful Personalities and Warriors Bold* (1907), and *Villiers: His Five Decades of Adventure* (1921).

REFERENCES: Pat Hodgson. *The War Illustrators*. 1977; Robert Wilkinson-Latham. *From Our Special Correspondent*. 1979.

Vincent, Steven (1955–2005)

Vincent was abduced along with his translator in the port city of Basra, Iraq while covering the Iraqi conflict. While his translator survived several gunshots, Vincent did not and he became "the first American journalist kidnapped and killed in Iraq" since the 2003 invasion and just five hours after his abduction. In his book *In the Red Zone: A Journey into the Soul of Iraq*, published the year before he died, he chided reporters for lacking courage to leave the sanctity of the protected Green Zone. Some of his fellow journalists suggest he might have been targeted for his outspoken support for the war and his criticism of the Shiites. Journalist Chris Albington suggested that Vincent's actions were "seen as a checklist of what not to do."

REFERENCE: Chris Albington, "The Death of a True Believer," nymag.com, August 7, 2005.

Vizetelly, Edward Henry (1847–1903)

Born into a family tradition of war reporting, Vizetelly was educated in France before entering journalism in time to report the Franco-Prussian War* for the *Daily News* and the *New York Times*. He next reported the 1876 Turko-Serbian War and then the Russo-Turkish War* for the *London Standard*. He traveled widely over the next decade and contributed to a variety of newspapers. In 1881 he witnessed the British bombardment of Alexandria for the *Daily News* prior to the Battle of Tel-el-Kebir. In 1889, James Gordon Bennett* hired him to go to Zanzibar to wait for Henry Stanley's* return from the African interior. He delivered his scoop of the return of Stanley in a 1,400-word dispatch to the *New York Herald* in December 1889 and was rewarded with a large bonus. Following his last adventure he retired to Paris and then London.

REFERENCES: F. Lauriston Bullard. *Famous War Correspondents.* 1914; Robert W. Desmond. *The Information Process.* 1978.

Vizetelly, Ernest Alfred (1853–1897)

Together with his father, the war correspondent Henry Richard Vizetelly,* Ernest Vizetelly covered the Franco-Prussian War* (1870–1871) and witnessed the siege of Paris at the end of the war. His dispatches appeared in the *Illustrated London News,* the *Pall Mall Gazette,* and the *Daily News.*

REFERENCES: Dennis Griffiths, ed. *The Encyclopedia of the British Press.* 1992; Henry Vizetelly. Paris in *Peril.* 1888.

Vizetelly, Frank (1830–1883)

Born in London and educated in Boulogne, the brother of war correspondent Henry Richard Vizetelly* was hired as special correspondent and artist for the *Illustrated Times,* which was established by his brother in 1855. His first assignment was to cover the Austro-Italian War.* In 1860 he was with Garibaldi's Red Shirts during the invasion of Sicily. His account of the action at Palermo took three weeks to reach London. Upon his return from Italy, Vizetelly represented the *Illustrated London News* in America when the American Civil War* broke out. He covered Union troops at Bull Run in 1861 and the following year accompanied General Burnside's forces during its victorious

Roanoke Island expedition. When Secretary of War Edwin Stanton withdrew the correspondents' permits, fellow reporter W. H. Russell* returned to Britain, while Vizetelly transferred to the western campaign under Halleck's command. Halleck attempted to dissuade civilians from observing his forces in action by forcing correspondents to supply their own transportation.

On one occasion, Vizetelly, who favored the South, visited Confederate general Jeb Stuart's headquarters, making several sketches in the process of camp life. He was inside Fort Fisher when it was captured by a Union amphibious assault in 1865.

After an unsuccessful stint running his own periodical with his brother James in the late 1860s he returned to the battlefield for the *Times* as a special correspondent with the forces of Don Carlos (1873–1875) in the Spanish Carlist War. In 1883 he reported the Mahdist uprising in the Sudan and was with the ill-fated Hicks Pasha column as it left Khartoum for El Obeid. Vizetelly and *Daily News* columnist Edmund O'Donovan* perished along with the poorly trained Egyptian relief force when the entire column was annihilated by dervish forces.

REFERENCES: F. Lauriston Bullard. *Famous War Correspondents.* 1914; Pat Hodgson. *The War Illustrators.* 1977; Robert Wilkinson-Latham. *From Our Special Correspondent.* 1979.

Vizetelly, Frank Horace (1864–1938)

A son of Henry Richard Vizetelly,* he worked as a lexicographer and writer in New York City. Unable to acquire accreditation to cover the Boer War* as a war correspondent, he was lauded for visiting Boer prisoners of war in British prison camps in Bermuda. He was the only citizen permitted to inspect and record his impressions of the captivity. He chronicled this experience for the *Illustrated London News* and several other dailies.

REFERENCE: F. Lauriston Bullard. *Famous War Correspondents.* 1914.

Indicates a separate entry.

Vizetelly, Henry Richard (1820–1894)

Born in London, he was an early innovator in illustrated press journalism. In 1855 he cofounded the *Illustrated Times*. Appointed Paris correspondent for the *Illustrated London News,* his account of the siege of Paris during the Franco-Prussian War* and the Paris Commune are remembered for his graphic coverage. His two-volume *Paris in Peril* (1888) was written with his son Ernest.* Soon after, he ended his career as foreign correspondent and returned to the publishing business.

REFERENCE: F. Lauriston Bullard. *Famous War Correspondents.* 1914.

Wade, William (1918–2006)

Born in Manhattan he began working for the Bergen County, New Jersey newspaper at the age of sixteen. Following journalism school at the University of Minnesota, in 1941 he was hired by the International News Service (INS) in London. Wade was among the eight reporters of the Writing 69th.* He never made it on a bombing run in 1943 because the bomber to which he was assigned had engine trouble. Instead Wade wrote a short story about the canceled flight entitled "This Local Boy Didn't Make Good." Following the war he did graduate work at the London School of Economics and served for a number of years as a writer, editor and on-air reporter for the Voice of America in Europe.

REFERENCES: Jim Hamilton. The Writing 69th. 2005; Diana Walsh. "William Warren Wade—WWII Correspondent," *San Francisco Chronicle*, March 29, 2006.

Wallace, Sir Donald Mackenzie (1841–1919)

Born in Boghead, Dumbartonshire, England, he was a perpetual college student at various universities until he was twenty-eight years old. While studying law in Germany he was invited to Russia to study a little-known cultural group in the Caucasus. He spent the next six years studying Russia in general. Following his return to England he published the two-volume *Russia* in 1877. It is considered the standard text on pre-Revolutionary Russia.

Wallace joined the staff of the *Times* in time to cover the 1877–1878 Russo-Turkish War.* Assigned to St. Petersburg, he also covered the Berlin Congress, where he assisted Henri de Blowitz* of the *Times* and helped provide the paper one of its greatest scoops when he smuggled to Belgium the details of the Berlin Treaty sewn into the lining of his coat. From 1878 to 1884 he reported from Constantinople and demonstrated a growing interest in problems in the Balkans. Following the Battle of Tel-el-Kebir in September 1882, he was sent on a special mission to Egypt, recounted in his 1883 book *Egypt and the Egyptian Question*. Over the next few years he traveled widely in the Middle East, before being selected to accompany the future czar Nicholas II of Russia as political officer on his Indian tour in 1890–1891. He returned to the *Times* as director of its foreign department and in 1899 was appointed to coedit the tenth edition of the *Encyclopedia Britannica*, which was then being published by the *Times*. In 1905 he covered his last major story for the paper when he attended the Portsmouth Conference in New Hampshire, which mediated an end to the Russo-Japanese War.*

REFERENCES: *DNB* Supp., 1912–1921; Dennis Griffiths. *The Encyclopedia of the British Press.* 1992.

Wallace, Edgar (1875–1932)

Born in Greenwich, England, he covered the Boer War* for Reuters* and the *Rand Daily Mail*. His dispatches were often a blend of fact and fiction. One of his stories described Boer atrocities such as the murder of British soldiers. Lord Kitchener was called in to investigate and found that Wallace's report was unsubstantiated. Wallace's most notable accomplishment during the Boer War was scooping the peace treaty signing nearly a day before it was officially announced. He was assisted in this feat by a soldier guarding the camp who on cue was to blow his nose with a white handkerchief as a prearranged signal when the treaty was actually signed. This act earned Wallace the ire of Kitchener, who vowed to end his tenure as war correspondent.

He was known for his vivid style as a war reporter, and it served him well beginning in 1905 when he found his true calling as a writer of thrillers, detective stories, and plays. Before his untimely death in Hollywood on February 7, 1932, he had published twenty-three books, eight in 1930 alone.

REFERENCES: Byron Farwell. *The Great Anglo-Boer War*. 1976; Edgar Wallace. *Unofficial Dispatches*, reprint edition. 1975.

War Correspondent (average salary)

It should not be surprising that war correspondent salaries vary according to the news outlet they are working for and reporting their experience. In 2010 the Bureau of Labor Statistics put war correspondents in a category that included other professionals in the photographic medium. It was calculated that the average salary in the professional field was almost $36,000. The top ten percent could expect more than $63,000, with those in the bottom ten percent likely to make around $17,000. According to a 2012 U.S. Bureau of Labor Statistics report, the middle half of news correspondents and reporters earned between $26,000 and $53,260.

REFERENCES: www.ehow.com/info_8604031_salary-war-photojournalist.html; www.google.com/?gws_rd=ssl.

Ward, Edward, Viscount Bangor (1905–1993)

The British foreign correspondent attended Harrow and the Royal Military Academy at Woolwich before joining Reuters* as its Far East correspondent. He then moved to the BBC, where he established his reputation as one of its finest reporters during World War II.* He covered the conflict in Finland (1939–1940), the fall of France (1940) and the campaign in the Middle East, where he was captured by Rommel's forces in November 1941. Following his release later in the war he covered the meeting of American and Russian forces at the Elbe River in 1945. He continued his career with the BBC until 1960. He wrote *I Lived like a Lord* (1970).

REFERENCE: Richard Collier. *The Warcos: The War Correspondents of World War II*. 1989.

Ware, Michael (b. 1969)

The Australian born journalist rose to prominence while reporting from Baghdad for CNN and *Time* magazine. He holds a law degree and a degree in political science. His reportage was especially valuable since he was among the few international journalists to live in Iraq almost continuously throughout the Iraq conflict. He first alighted in the region in 2001 covering the Afghanistan invasion in late 2001 and then preparations for the 2003 invasion of Iraq. While he has won acclaim for his work as an embedded journalist* with American forces he has also been criticized for reporting from various terrorist bases and offering their perspective as a a corrective to Western war reporting. His most controversial moments came in 2006 after he provided narration and edited for a CNN broadcast purported showing footage of snipers shooting and killing American troops. This led for calls to remove CNN embedded reporters during the conflict. In 2004 he endured a brief captivity by the forces of Aby Mousab al-Zarqawi while covering the growth of al Qaeda in Iraq. That same year he was selected as *Time*'s Baghdad Bureau Chief. Embedded with forces during the battle of Tal Afar, he produced a video accout of the battle that was later featured in a *Frontline* documentary and a *60 Minutes* report. Ware also reported the Israeli invasion of Lebanon in 2006 and the 2008 South Ossetia War between the Russian Federation and the Republic of Georgia. In 2010 he took a one year leave of absence from CNN to be treated for post-traumatic stress disorder*. He left CNN for good the following year but continues to write and produce films on his time in Iraq.

REFERENCES: Official CNN Bio. http://www.cnn.com/ CNN/anchors_reporters/ware.michael.html, retrieved 4/1/2010; "House Defense Chair Asks Pentagon to Remove Embedded CNN Reporters." http://www.kesq.com/Global/story.asp?S=5569487, retrieved October 21, 2006.

Warland, John H. (1807–1872)

Warland was born in Cambridge, Massachusetts and rose to prominence in the world of journalism for his pro-Whig editorials in the *Lowell Courier*, where he served as editor. During the Mexican-American War* he sent back about 40 letters from Mexico to various newspapers.

REFERENCE: Tom Reilly, *War with Mexico!: American Reporters Cover the Battlefront*, Manley Witten, ed., 2010.

War Photography

The first examples of war photography can be traced back to the Mexican-American War* (1846–1848), only seven years after the invention of the daguerreotype.* The daguerreotype process, however, was more suitable for portraiture than action because each picture needed an exposure time of five minutes. There were no negatives, so each picture was an original.

By the time of the Crimean War* in 1854 photography was still a novelty. Besides the Mexican-American War, several war photographs were taken during the Burma War of 1852, but the Crimean War was the first campaign systematically covered by photographers. Various photographers have been described as the "first war photographer," including Roger Fenton* and Mathew Brady,* but recent evidence suggests the title belongs to Karl Baptist von Szathmari,* an amateur photographer from Bucharest who photographed Russian generals and camp scenes during fighting in the Danube Valley between Turks and Russians in 1853.

Roger Fenton owes his reputation in part to his conversion to the calotype process in 1847. The calotype was invented by Henry Fox Talbot. Its advantage over the daguerreotype was that it produced a negative from which multiple positive images could be produced. In addition it was a simpler process and produced sharper, more detailed images when compared to the almost mirror-like quality of daguerreotype images. Fenton's brush with war photography came about in 1855 when he accompanied the British expedition to Crimea. Fenton is the best-known war photographer of his era only because most of his images survive. Felice Beato,* James Robertson,* and Szathmari were reportedly superior war photographers but less of their work survives, and we must rely on contemporary assessments for the quality of Szathmari's work, which has been lost except for one picture.

One interesting characteristic of war imagery is that in every war from the American Civil War* to the Vietnam War* the images released to the public in the latter stages of the conflict have been more grim and graphic than in the early stages. This is true for both battle sketches and photographs. The first American war to be extensively recorded by camera was the Civil War. The most prominent name associated with this phase of war photography is Mathew Brady. It was through his efforts that Americans observed for the first time images of slaughtered countrymen on the battlefield. Brady was supremely fortunate to have fine assistants who would later earn great acclaim on their own, including Timothy O'Sullivan* and Alexander Gardner.* Brady and his staff reportedly took more than 3,500 negatives of the war, although camera speed did not yet allow cameramen to photograph motion. The Confederacy lacked a counterpart to Brady, but most towns had a photographer. Southern photographers were much less prolific because the main suppliers of photographic chemicals were in the North. Smugglers hid the chemicals in quinine containers since medical supplies were allowed South through the blockades.

Concomitant with the rise in war photography was the decline in popularity of other forms of pictorial representation. The artist's sketchbook could not compete with the sharply detailed images of the photograph. Civil War photographers were hampered in the field by cumbersome equipment and bulky cameras better suited to the portrait studio than portable studios. Most of the operatives were trained in portrait photography prior to the war. But true war photography would have to wait for quicker camera speeds. Although Civil War photographs were lifelike they retained a static quality. The shock and frenzy of battle, the cavalry charge, and hand-to-hand fighting were integral ingredients of battlefield behavior, yet only the artist-correspondents* could bring home images of men in action.

In 1855 the pioneer photographer Nadar first experimented with aerial photography. Throughout the Civil War balloon photography was used for reconnaissance. The success and popularity of war photography during the 1860s led European armies to explore the potential of military photography. Photographers were present during the 1866–1867 Abyssinian War, the 1859 Austro-Italian War,* and the Austro-Prussian War* of 1866. The 1870–1871 Franco-Prussian War* was covered by a staff of German photographers, but their work is considered inferior. The Paris Commune of 1871 produced the majority of the images of this conflict.

The British colonial wars, referred to by Rudyard Kipling* as the "savage wars of peace," resulted in some excellent war photographs. Among the most competent photographers were John Burke,* who covered the Second Punjab War in 1878–1880 and Rene Bull,* who covered the 1897 Greco-Turkish War* and the Boer War.* Before the end of the century technical advances in photography would allow amateurs in the military ranks to include cameras with their campaign gear.

By the 1890s photojournalism was still a relatively new profession. Although pictorial newspapers had originated in the early 1840s, it was not until the advent of the halftone process in 1880 that newspapers could reproduce the photographic image on the page. The first halftone photograph was published in the *New York Daily Graphic* in March 1880. But most periodicals continued to rely on woodblock engravings because they provided more "character, tonal range, and detail."

The rise of general interest magazines such as *Cosmopolitan* and *McClure's* in the early 1890s signaled the emergence of the photojournalism profession. By relying on halftones over engravings publishers were able to cut the price of their publications by more than half. Mass circulation resulted, and the demand for photographic news essays heralded a new day in journalism. One of the most popular and effective photographers of this era was James Hare,* who rose to prominence covering the Spanish-American War* for *Collier's Weekly.* The Spanish-American War was the first American war photographed by amateurs and participants using Kodak cameras. Other notable photographers followed Hare to Cuba, including J. C. Hemment,* James Burton,* William Dinwiddie,* and Frances Benjamin Johnston. New photographic technology allowed cameramen to take pictures which conveyed actual battle conditions but it was still not possible to take action shots.

During World War I* the War Department made sure there would be a firsthand graphic history of the war through staff artists with the American Expeditionary Force and the staff photographers of the Army Signal Corps. One of the main barriers faced by war correspondents was that they were not permitted anywhere near the front. Matters were even worse for war photographers. In the early years civilian photographers were totally barred from frontline coverage under penalty of death. At the outset of the war two army officers were accredited to photograph the front with the goal of assembling a record of the conflict. They were prohibited from sharing their pictures with newspapers. While tens of thousands of photographs were taken during the conflict, to this day they still lack adequate documentation. Little information survives as to who was responsible for the pictures. It is perplexing that such a momentous event as World War I did not produce one outstanding photographer readily identifiable with the war on par with a Brady or a Fenton. One exception to the overwhelming anonymity of the World War I photographers during the first years of the war was William Rider-Rider,* who managed to retrieve most of his work after the war and take it to Canada, where it is now safely deposited in the Public Archives.

By 1917, more professional photographers were permitted to record the battlefront as the importance of photography, as a propaganda and reporting tool began to dawn on military authorities. In the latter years of the war the threat of capital punishment was removed for taking photographs at the front. Realizing that many American correspondents were supplementing their reports with photographs taken in secret and that French official photographers were making their pictures available to various American news services, General Pershing officially removed the former prohibitions against cameramen. Beginning on Christmas Day 1917 Pershing allowed "official photographers of the Allied Armies to take photographs in our army areas" and "accredited and visiting cor-

respondents ... to take photographs, subject to our censorship, to illustrate our articles." For the remainder of the war close to two dozen photographers would continue to contribute to the photographic record of the war. Between May and July 1918, over 1,600 photographs would pass through the censors on the way to American publications. Among the more prolific photographer-correspondents were Arthur Ruhl* of *Collier's Weekly,* George Seldes* for the Marshall Syndicate, Junius Wood* of the *Chicago Daily News,* Frank Taylor of the UP, and Joseph Timmons for the *Los Angeles Examiner.*

Photographers were subjected to the same censorship as their print counterparts. Among the prohibited subject matter were pictures that depicted troop movements, specific war materials, and any subject deemed injurious to AEF morale. This could include photographs of soldiers improperly dressed, dead Americans, destroyed tanks or airplanes, and wounded or mutilated servicemen.

In the course of World War I none of the American civilian photographers were killed and only one military photographer perished. The American fatality was First Lieutenant Edwin Ralph Estep of the Signal Corps, hit by shell fire days before the end of the war.

In 1926 the introduction of the Leica 35mm range finder camera to the market revolutionized the war photographer's craft. Lightweight cameras that could fit in a jacket pocket allowed photojournalists to get closer to the action and the danger and create a new market in combat photography.

By the 1930s a disturbing new trend began to develop in war photography. Since the American Civil War and the Crimean War, certain photographs have been posed and faked. This was often an alternative when technical limitations precluded using the unwieldy photographic equipment on the battlefield. However, increasingly restricted war zones led some cameramen to stage pictures for their editors. Limited

Indicates a separate entry.

by strict censorship, photographers of both the Ethiopian War* and the Spanish Civil War* of the 1930s produced numerous staged combat photographs.

World War II* was the most photographed war in history. The Imperial War Museum in London alone boasts over two million negatives from the war. With regard to the number of photographers, just taking into account the four hundred Canadian cameramen attending a reunion in 1971 testifies to the numbers involved in recording the conflict.

World War II photographers can be classified in three categories. One group consisted of those affiliated with the armed forces; another was composed of freelancers employed by various periodicals; and the final group included amateur photographers who were often either civilians or soldiers. By the end of the war in Europe most soldiers had acquired a small camera.

Government censors were intent on providing a view of the war that restricted the publication of photographs of wounded GIs, victims of Allied bombing raids or chemical warfare experiments, shell-shocked GIs, and pictures that conveyed racial strife, disunity, or confrontations between members of the Allied forces. There was a particular aversion against pictures that depicted soldiers losing control and casualties sustained in accidents. Censors also prohibited any photograph that showed American war dead being handled like inanimate objects. During the first two years of the conflict censors withheld all photographs of American casualties except for images which were deemed "comforting."

In 1943 President Roosevelt lent his voice to the chorus requesting less censorship of the photographic image. Part of the rationale behind this turn of events was of domestic origin. In part it was thought that graphic photographs could give a lift to the lagging Red Cross blood drives. In addition, *Life* magazine editors argued convincingly that pictures of wounded and dead American soldiers would help morale rather than hurt it, by bringing the war home to Americans.

The most important photographs taken during the Korean War* were taken by David Douglas Duncan,* Bert Hardy,* and Carl Mydans.* Duncan covered the conflict from the beginning for *Life* magazine and became the first photographer to accompany a jet fighter strike, taking photos of a bombing run at six hundred miles per hour. Under contract with the British *Picture Post,* Hardy made a memorable team with correspondent James Cameron.* Their stories and photographs of South Korean atrocities were the most controversial of the war. Mydans and Hardy took some of the best pictures of the landing at Inchon.

Prior to the Vietnam War,* most American wars fought in the twentieth century were photographed by government or public agencies. However, during the Vietnam War photojournalists were given unprecedented access to the battlefield, making it the freest war to cover in the modern era. Photojournalists not only were uncensored, but were also encouraged to report the conflict and were transported by the military to whatever destination they requested.

In addition to the civilian correspondents there were hundreds of military photographers sent from the Army Pictorial Center in New York City beginning in 1962. In the spring of 1962 the Pentagon created the Department of the Army Special Photo Office (DASPO) to provide worldwide coverage of military activities. However, as the American buildup began in earnest in 1965 DASPO photographers were joined by combat photographers from every branch of the armed forces. Their mandate included fully documenting activities of the U.S. military in Southeast Asia.

Photo-essays from this unpopular war led to a public backlash against the war itself, proving that photography can make a difference and sway hearts and minds. It was not unheard of during the war for television reporters to hire GIs to stage battles in the background for their broadcasts or for civilian photographers to purchase pictures from combat photographers and hire Vietnamese photographers for combat assignments. The Vietnam experience perhaps explains why the U.S. government barred photographers from covering the Grenada* and Panama invasions.*

REFERENCES: Helmut and Alison Gemsheim. *Roger Fenton: Photographer of the Crimean War.* 1973; Louis L. Gould and Richard Greffe. *Photojournalist: The Career of Jimmy Hare.* 1977; Pat Hodgson. *Early War Photographs.* 1974; Lawrence James. *Crimea, 1854–56: The War with Russia from Contemporary Photographs.* 1981; Jorge Lewinski. *The Camera at War.* 1978; Library of Congress. *An Album of American Battle Art.* 1947; Peter Maslowski. *Armed with Cameras: American Military Photographers of World War II.* 1993; Nick Mills. *The Vietnam Experience: Combat Photographer.* 1983; Susan D. Moeller. *Shooting War: Photography and the American Experience of Combat.* 1989; George H. Roeder. *The Censored War: American Visual Experience During World War Two.* 1993; Martha A. Sandweiss, Rick Stewart, and Ben W. Huseman. *Eyewitness to War: Prints and Daguerrotypes of the Mexican War, 1846–1848.* 1989; Philip Van Doren Stern. *They Were There: The Civil War in Action As Seen by Its Combat Artists.* 1959.

"War Porn"

Thanks to the wonders of modern communications, soldiers in foreign wars can post bloody images and video clips instantly on the Internet. During the Iraq War* it was revealed that American soldiers were posting gruesome photos on a website called Nowthatsfuckedup.com in exchange for pictures of other individual's girlfriends. Sites such as MySpace and YouTube have all featured gruesome images of war dead from Iraq and Afghanistan, photos often taken by American soldiers. The French social theorist Jean Baudrillard has drawn attention to the way in which the explicit images of brutality coming back from recent modern wars "borrowed from the aesthetics and production values of modern porn." the *Guardian* writer James Harkin and others have noted that the well-known photos of prisoners being humiliated at Abu Ghraib prison were shot on digital cameras with the intention of distributing them privately. The difference

between war porn and traditional pornography which is designed to titillate, is that the former is used to humiliate and horrify its audience. "Like pornography," says Harkin, "its producers heighten their sense of reality by videotaping themselves in the act." In 2014 the photographer Christoph Bangert published the book *War Porn*, which contains photos he took in Iraq and other conflict zones, most depicting graphic death and violence. Bangert's book, which confronts the arguments and ethics over violent imagery, has asserted the book is an experiment to determine, "What would happen if we suppress our need for self-censorship, for once?"

REFERENCES: Jean Baudrillard (trans. Paul A. Taylor), "War Porn," International Journal of Baudrillard Studies, Vol. 2, Jan. 2005; Christoph Bangert and Alan Chin, "Bangert and Chin Debate Value of 'War Porn," http://dartcenter.org/content/war-porn, Nov. 4, 2014; James Harkin, "War Porn," Guardian, Aug. 11, 2006.

Wasson, Joe (1841–1883)

Wasson was one of the first reporters to cover the American Indian Wars* in the West following the American Civil War.* Wasson reported General George C. Crook's expeditions in Idaho, Oregon, and northern California for the *Owyhee Avalanche* of Silver City, Idaho, a ghost town today. Wasson was nineteen years old when he came out west from Wooster, Ohio, with a company of gold seekers. He demonstrated a lifelong interest in mining. He also developed a lifelong enmity toward Indians when his wagon train was attacked by hostiles on his initial trip. In 1865 he cofounded with his brother the *Avalanche,* Silver City's first newspaper.

Beginning in the summer of 1867, Wasson would accompany Crook's Idaho campaign for four months. In addition to his own paper, his reports appeared in the *San Francisco Evening Bulletin.* He followed a set routine on each expedition of writing stories in chronological order and adding to them each day, noting whether it was Camp Number 1 or Number 2, and so on.

* *Indicates a separate entry.*

He then sent his stories, written in the form of a letter, to his paper by army courier. Most of his dispatches are simply signed "Joe." In August he received a copy of his newspaper in the mail, which much to his chagrin indicated that he no longer owned the *Avalanche,* his brother having sold it. Wasson remained a correspondent for the new owners nonetheless. He reported and participated in the Battle of Infernal Caverns, the one battle of the campaign.

Following his coverage of the Crook expedition he traveled around the West. He founded the *Winnemucca Argent* in Aurora, Nevada, and with his brother the *Arizona Citizen* in Tucson. Nine years later in 1876, he joined Crook's Black Hills expedition, while employed by the *New York Tribune, San Francisco Alta Californian,* and the *Philadelphia Press.* He witnessed and took part in the Battle of the Rosebud and later that summer was one of four correspondents accompanying Crook's forces toward the Little Big Horn Mountains.

Following his campaign with Crook, he tackled several news stories in Europe before settling down in California. According to one account, Wasson's affinity for mining paid off in the California mining business. After stints in the state legislature and as a U.S. consul to Mexico he died in San Blas, Mexico, in 1883.

REFERENCE: Oliver Knight. *Following the Indian Wars.* 1960.

Watkins, Kathleen "Kit" Blake
(1866–1915)

The Irish-born Catherine Ferguson Willis arrived in Canada in 1884. In order to mask her true origins she changed her name and conveniently subtracted eight years from her age. Five years later, following a brief marriage and divorce, she entered the journalism profession in 1889. Beginning as a columnist for the *Toronto Daily Mail,* over the next twenty-five years Kit Watkins established an international reputation as travel writer and war reporter.

Although at least two other female correspondents were already in Cuba by the time she arrived to cover the Spanish-American War,* the *Daily Mail* heralded Watkins as the first woman war correspondent accredited to cover a war in June 1898. However, by June 23 most of the war correspondents were already in Cuba while Watkins was left behind, barred by military officials and male correspondents who considered war reporting a province of the male domain. One other explanation has surfaced that could better explain why she was left behind. According to one source she may have been arrested for violating censorship rules by sending coded messages that informed her editor that American troops were poised to embark for Cuba from Florida. In one missive her editor noted how furious he was with her for getting caught.

Kit remained undaunted in her attempts to reach the battlefields, even in the aftermath of the conflict. After waiting three months she arrived in Cuba in late July 1898. Noting that the war had ended in one of her dispatches, she still felt an obligation to visit the various battle sites and record the evidence of combat. While camping outside the city of Santiago Watkins reported sleeping "in a boy's rubber suit," to protect herself from rape and murder. Her reports are filled with graphic accounts of the scenes of battle and the suffering of American forces, who lost more men to disease than in battle. Following her Cuban adventure she noted that her brief career as a war correspondent was over. As the "first woman to be accredited as a war correspondent by the US government" Watkins won a devoted international following during the Spanish American War.

REFERENCES: Charles H. Brown. *The Correspondents' War.* 1967; Barbara M. Freeman. "An Impertinent Fly": Canadian Journalist Kathleen Blake Watkins Covers the Spanish-American War," *Journalism History.* Winter 1988.

Watson, Paul (b. 1959)

Born in Weston, Ontyaruio, Watson was awarded the 1994 Pulitzer Prize for Spot New Photography for his coverage of the "Black Hawk Down" incident in Somalia for the *Toronto Star* in October 1993. He narrowly evaded death at the hands of Somalis who decided to spare him so his photographs of the dead American Ranger being dragged through the streets of Mogadishu would reach an international audience. These photos played a major role in convincing then President Bill Clintom to withdraw from the country. During a career of more than thirty years, Watson has covered conflict zones in Eritrea, Somalia, southern Sudan, Angola, Mozambique, South Africa, Romania, Serbia, Kosovo, Afghanistan, Pakistan, Kashmir, Iraq and Syria. His 2007 book, *Where War Lives*, chronicled his life as a war journalist and won the 2007 Drummer General's Award. He followed this up with *Magnum Revolution: 65 Years Fighting for Freedom*, co-authored with Jon Lee Anderson.* In 2013 his book of poetry *War Reporter* was published to wide acclaim. In recent years Watson has traded the war zone for Arctic exploration. In 2014 he was the only journalist on board a Canadian Coast Guard icebreaker during the Victoria Strait Expedition when archeologists found the historic wreck of Sir John Franklin's flagship

REFERENCE: Duncan Anderson. *War: A Photo History*. 2006; http://www.thestar.com/authors.watson_paul.html.

Waud, Alfred "Alf" Rudolph (1828–1891)

Born in London, after an apprenticeship as a decorator and studying art at the School of Design at Somerset House in London Waud left for the United States in 1850. He exhibited his work at the National Academy of Design, but made his living illustrating books and periodicals. He became the greatest of the American Civil War*

artist-correspondents* while engaged primarily by *Harper's Weekly*. As its leading artist, he furnished the paper with detailed accounts of the Virginia theater of the war from 1861 through the Appomattox campaign. Of all the sketch artists, it was said he possessed the rarest combination of talents in that he could write as well as he could draw. Waud was one of a handful of artists to spend most of the time in the field as opposed to the studio.

He originally covered the Civil War in 1861 for Barnum and Beach's *Illustrated News*, getting his first taste of action at Bull Run. Joining *Harper's Weekly* the following year he followed McClellan's Peninsular campaign as an accredited correspondent, recording the violent clashes at Fair Oaks, Gaines' Mill, and Second Bull Run, where he was captured by rebels. As a prisoner of the Confederates, Waud relished the opportunity to make sketches of the Virginia cavalry troops, which were published in *Harper's*. He went on to cover the Wilderness, Fredericksburg, Cold Harbor, and Petersburg. The most prolific Civil War sketch artist, Waud published 344 illustrations, many of which received front-page treatment. He continued his association with *Harper's* after the war, contributing illustrations to *Picturesque America* (1872) and *Battles and Leaders of the Civil War* (1887). He later published on his own *My Diary in America in the Midst of the War*. He died in 1891 after being stricken by a heart attack while sketching Georgian battlefields.

REFERENCES: Pat Hodgson. *The War Illustrators*. 1977; Library of Congress. *American Battle Art, 1755–1918*. 1947; Philip Van Doren Stern. *They Were There*. 1959; W. Fletcher Thompson, Jr. *The Image of War*. 1960; Frederic E. Ray. *"Our Special Artist."* 1994.

Waud, William (c. 1820–1878)

An immigrant to the United States in the late 1850s, he is not as well known as his correspondent brother Alfred.* In 1851 he served as an assistant to Sir Joseph Paxton while the latter

---

* Indicates a separate entry.

designed the London Crystal Palace, and he spent the first two years of the American Civil War* contributing drawings to *Frank Leslie's Illustrated Newspaper* before becoming a special roving correspondent to *Harper's* in 1864.

One of his first exclusives was the coverage of the bombardment of Fort Sumter. Waud saw little action until the spring of 1862, when he covered Admiral Farragut's naval expedition against New Orleans. He later recorded the Battle of Petersburg. After the Civil War he continued his career as artist and writer.

REFERENCES: Pat Hodgson. *The War Illustrators*. 1977; W. Fletcher Thompson, Jr. *The Image of War*. 1960.

Waugh, Evelyn Arthur St. John (1903–1966)

The well-known British novelist was born in Hampstead and educated at Oxford University. Following graduation he served as a schoolmaster for three years, all the while honing his writing talent. He quickly established his literary reputation with *Decline and Fall* (1928) and *Vile Bodies* (1930). He first developed his interest in foreign correspondence when he visited Abyssinia in 1930 to cover the coronation of Emperor Haile Selassie for the *Graphic*. He traveled extensively throughout Africa following this assignment, gaining experience which resulted in *Remote People* (1931) and *Black Mischief* (1932). In 1935, as war correspondent for the *Daily Mail*, he reported the Italian invasion of Abyssinia and the subsequent Ethiopian War.* He chronicled this event in *Waugh in Abyssinia* (1936), which has been criticized for its strongly pro-Italian slant. His satirical novel on war reporters, *Scoop** (1938) was thinly based on his experiences in Africa. He went on to a distinguished writing career, producing several travel books and such novels as *Brideshead Revisited* (1945), *The Loved One* (1948), and his trilogy *Men at Arms* (1952), *Officers and Gentlemen* (1958), and *Unconditional Surrender* (1961), based on his military service during World War

II.* He died unexpectedly on April 10, 1966, after church services on Easter Sunday.

REFERENCES: *DNB*, 1961–1970; James Dugan and Laurence Lafore. *Days of Emperor and Clown*. 1973; Christopher Sykes. *Evelyn Waugh*. 1975.

Webb, Catherine "Kate" (1943–2007)

The New Zealand-born Webb arrived in Vietnam as a freelance journalist in 1967, before joining the staff of the UPI. Prior to arrival in South Vietnam she had been working in Australia covering the Australian New Zealand Army Corps troops bound for the conflict for the *Sydney Daily Mirror*. While on this assignment she noted that there were no Australian or New Zealand correspondents covering the war, so she left Sydney for a five-week hiatus in South Vietnam. Webb was in Saigon as the 1968 Tet offensive broke out and recorded the battle raging within the formerly secure South Vietnamese city. Her record of the battle, which she described live on an audiotape, was a minor sensation when released in Europe. Webb left Saigon to record the offensive at Pleiku, the scene of heavy fighting.

In 1971 Webb was promoted to UPI bureau chief in Phnom Penh, Cambodia. On April 7 she was captured with five other correspondents as they were drawn to a new offensive. After three weeks they were released. One week earlier the remains of a Caucasian woman had been found with other bodies and had been identified as Webb. The remains were cremated according to Cambodian military custom and her death was reported in the American press at the same time she was being released. Suffering from injured feet and malaria, Webb recuperated in Hong Kong, before returning to Cambodia in September. After the war Webb left journalism for public relations work.

REFERENCE: Virginia Elwood-Akers. *Women War Correspondents in the Vietnam War, 1961–1975*. 1988.

Weber, Olivier (b. 1958)

Born in Montlucon, France, Weber studied anthropology and economics at leading French universities, receiving the PhD from the University of Nice. His journalism career took him first to Africa where he covered various conflicts before finding employment with *Le Point*, becoming a war correspondent covering some twenty wars and regional conflicts, including the Iraq War, Afghanistan, Burma, Kurdistan, Chechnya, Israel and the Palestinian territories, Iran, Eritrea, Algeria, Pakistan, and many others. Weber has gained a reputation not just for his reporting, but for his literary quality and support of indigenous peoples and lost causes. This was especially on display in his exposure of the child slave trade in Sudan and his coverage of the plight of boat people in the China Sea. His campaign against human trafficking by the Tamil Tigers in Sri Lanka led to death threats and in one incident his plane was purposely shot down between Jaffna and Colombo. He lived to embark on many other humanitarian missions, earning even more death threats from such high profile actors as the Taliban and Al-Qaeda. He has published several books, including *The Afghan Hawk: A Journey to the Land of the Taliban* (2001), *Memory Murdered* (2004), *Road of Drugs* (1996), and *The White Death* (2007). He has received numerous awards including the Prix Albert Londres (1992), the Special Prize of War Correspondents (1997) and the Prize Joseph Kessel (1998).

REFERENCE: http://en.wikipedia.org/wiki/Olivier_Weber.

Weithas, Arthur (1911–2006)

Born in the Bronx, he planned and laid out the original copy of the Army Weekly, Yank.* During World War II he covered the Central and Southwest Pacific theater of the war as an artist and photographer, putting an art school education to work. He covered the invasion of the Philippines and the capture of Manila, and saw action at Corregidor and with the landing at Mindanao. He later collaborated with noted author James Jones in the creating of the book WWII. His 1991 book Close to Glory chronicles the "untold stories" of Yank corrspondents during the late war. He was awarded the Legion of Merit medal for his military service.

REFERENCES:New York Times Obituary. May 10, 2006; Art Weithas. Close to Glory. 1991.

Wellard, James (1909–1987)

Born in London and educated at the Universities of London and Chicago, he became a war correspondent in North Africa for the *Chicago Times* in 1942. He reported the 1943 Casablanca Conference and then the Italian campaign. Wellard reported the advance on Naples and later covered action in France shortly after the Normandy invasion. Following the war he taught at the University of Illinois and was a Fulbright scholar at the University of Teheran in Iran. He is the author of more than twenty books of fiction and nonfiction. He is probably best known for covering General George S. Patton from Tunisia in 1943 through the summer of 1945. His book *General George S. Patton: Man of Mars* was published in 1946 and has been re-released in 2015 as *War Correspondent James Wellard with General George S. Patton and the Third Army*.

REFERENCE: Robert W. Desmond. *Tides of War.* 1984.

Weller, George (1907–2002)

Weller was born in Boston and educated at Harvard University. Following a student exchange fellowship to Austria he traveled extensively in Central and Mediterranean Europe. After a stint with the *Boston Journal,* he spent four years as Balkans correspondent for the *New York Times* beginning in 1932. He served in the same position for the *Chicago Daily News* starting in 1941. He was in Greece when German forces

* Indicates a separate entry.

invaded and was the last American correspondent to flee Salonika, escaping aboard a small fishing boat, only to be arrested and conveyed to Berlin by the Gestapo upon reaching Athens. After a two-month detainment he escaped to Africa and landed an exclusive interview with General Charles de Gaulle.

Weller covered the Pacific theater next, witnessing the fall of Singapore, chronicled in his book *Singapore Is Silent*. He fled Singapore for Java, Batavia, and finally Australia, where he earned qualification to jump with American paratroopers. In 1943 he was awarded the Pulitzer Prize for his reporting following the fall of Singapore. He also covered the 1942–1943 New Guinea campaign. In October 1944 he covered the Allied landing in Greece. In 1945 he parachuted with U.S. and Burmese guerrillas known as the Jingpaw Raiders behind enemy lines in Burma. He was also the recipient of the George K. Polk Memorial Award and a Neiman fellowship.

REFERENCE: Robert W. Desmond. *Tides of War*. 1984; *New York Times*, December 29, 2002.

Welsh, Mary (1908–1986)

She dropped out of journalism school at Northwestern University to write for the magazine *American Florist*. After a stint with the *Chicago Daily News* and unsuccessful attempts to win a foreign posting she was hired by the *London Daily Express*. She was reportedly the only female reporter to accompany the British forces at the outbreak of World War II.*

On July 10, 1940, Welsh resigned from the London paper in order to report for an American one. During the 1940s she was regularly employed by the London bureau of *Time, Life,* and *Fortune*. Welsh covered the London blitz for the BBC and the liberation of Paris for *Life* magazine, as well as the treatment of U.S. Army casualties after the D-Day landings. Separated from her husband Noel Monks,* she met Ernest Hemingway* during her years covering the war

in London and Paris. She filed her last article as a journalist on April 21, 1945, reporting the reaction of GIs to the death of President Roosevelt. Welsh became the fourth wife of Hemingway the following year. Her best-known work was her autobiography, *How It Was,* published after the death of her husband.

REFERENCES: Bernice Kert. *The Hemingway Women;* 1983; M. L. Stein. *Under Fire.* 1968; Lilya Wagner. *Women War Correspondents of World War Two.* 1989.

Wharton, Edith (1862–1937)

The Pulitzer Prize winning novelist covered World War I* as a correspondent, mostly for *Scribner's Magazine*. Wharton had moved to France in 1913 and the following year she became involved with helping Belgian and French refugees. She went as far as establishing the Children of Flanders Rescue Committee, which was devoted to caring for children displaced by the bombardment of their towns. The French government honored her by presenting her with title of Chevalier in the French Legion of Honor in 1916. In 1915 Wharton began visiting troops on the frontlines, touring battlefilelds, and tending to the sick and wounded. Her reports of wartime France over the course of one year were published in *Scribner's*. She traveled to Argonne, Verdun, Lorraine, the Vosges, Ypres, and Alsace, where she was granted permission by the French government to tour the Western Front and interview soldiers. She chronicled her peregrinations and observations in *Fighting France, From Dunkerque to Belfort* (1915) and *The Marne* (1918).

REFERENCE: Alan Price. *The End of the Age of Innocence: Edith Wharton and the First World War.* 1996.

Wheeler, Keith (b. 1911)

Born in Carrington, North Dakota, Wheeler was a reporter for the *Chicago Times,* accredited to the navy during World War II.* In 1942 he was the first correspondent to reach the Aleutians when American forces defended the islands from Japanese incursions. He was aboard the aircraft carrier *Hornet* in the naval expedition launching bombing raids on Japan. Covering the Gilbert Islands campaign in the South Pacific, Wheeler went ashore with the marines at Tarawa Island and in 1944 he was among the twenty-two correspondents who organized the Pacific War Correspondents Association.*

Toward the end of the Pacific war he reported what came to be known as the Second Battle of Bougainville, when Japanese forces attacked American positions in Empress Augusta Bay in the Southwest Pacific. Wheeler also was present during the landings in the Marianas and the Battle of Iwo Jima, where he was seriously wounded when a bullet cut a neck artery and smashed his jaw.

He left the *Chicago Times* for *Life* and *Time* magazines in 1951. Wheeler was the author of six books and was the recipient of the Sigma Delta Chi Award in 1942, the National Headliners' Club Award in 1945, and the Overseas Press Club Award in 1956.

REFERENCE: Robert W. Desmond. *The Tides of War.* 1984.

Whitaker, John T. (1906–1946)

Born in Chattanooga, Tennessee, and educated at the University of the South in Sewanee, Tennessee, Whitaker began his newspaper career as a reporter on the *Chattanooga News*. He later joined the staff of the *New York Herald Tribune* and was assigned to the Geneva office from 1931 to 1935, reporting the League of Nations. Beginning in 1936 he reported the latter part of the Ethiopian War* and then the Spanish Civil War.* During the Ethiopian War he accompanied Italian troops and in May 1936 he was awarded the Italian War Cross for "valor in the East African campaign."

In 1937 Whitaker moved to the *Chicago Daily News* as a roving correspondent. From 1937 to 1938 he covered the developing conflict in Europe and the following year was in Peru reporting

the Eighth Pan American Conference from Lima. He continued to cover the South American scene, investigating Italian and German propaganda campaigns south of the American border. In mid-1939 he returned to Europe, posted to Rome until his expulsion in 1941. Whitaker was the third *Daily News* correspondent to be banished from Italy in two years, whereupon the paper decided to close its Rome office.

REFERENCES: Robert W. Desmond. *Crisis and Conflict.* 1982; Robert W. Desmond. *Tides of War.* 1984.

White, Leigh (b. 1914)

Born in Vermont, White began his career as a correspondent in 1937 writing articles on the Spanish Civil War* for the *Nation*. In 1939 he returned to the States and joined the staff of the *New York Herald Tribune*. The following year he covered the Balkans. When the Germans invaded Yugoslavia White made a desperate escape attempt on a small fishing craft with correspondents Russell Hill,* Terence Atherton, and Robert St. John.* However, his exploits as a war correspondent ended rather abruptly when his femur was shattered during a Luftwaffe attack on their boat. White ended up in an Athens hospital for five months. With Athens firmly in the grip of the German army, there was some doubt concerning White's status. However, since war had not yet been declared he was still a neutral. After he had undergone four operations and had lost fifty pounds, the Germans allowed him to return to the States. He finally recovered from his wounds by 1944 and returned to Russia for the *Daily News*.

REFERENCES: Robert W. Desmond. *Tides of War.* 1984; Leigh White. *The Long Balkan Night.* 1941.

White, Theodore Harold (1915–1986)

Better known as a political journalist and best-selling author, "Teddy" White was born in Boston and educated at Harvard. Following graduation

---

Indicates a separate entry.

he won a fellowship that allowed him to continue his Asian studies in China, where he also began his career as a journalist, sending dispatches to the *Boston Globe* and the *Manchester Guardian*. In 1939 John Hersey* hired him for *Time* as an East Asian correspondent during World War II.* Soon after, White headed off to get a firsthand glimpse of the Chinese-Japanese war. His dispatches from Shensi solidified his standing with his editors as he journeyed to areas untouched by journalists in the province. White interviewed Communist and Nationalist Chinese soldiers, inspected damage inflicted by Japanese troops in southeastern Shansi, and witnessed the Communist guerrilla campaign to capture rural China. In 1942 he became the China-Burma-India theater war correspondent for *Time*. Stationed in Chungking, he flew as an observer on numerous bombing runs with the Eleventh Bombing Squadron.

After a falling-out with Henry Luce over the politics of China in 1945, White quit the magazine. He coauthored the best-seller *Thunder out of China* with Annalee Jacoby in 1946. He left a position with the *New Republic* to edit the World War II memoirs of General Joseph Stilwell, and then moved to Paris in 1948. He chronicled postwar Europe in *Fire in the Ashes* in 1953. Returning to the United States, he began the next and most familiar stage of his career chronicling the American political scene with highly successful books such as *The Making of the President* (1960), *The Making of the President-1972* (1973), and *Breach of Faith: The Fall of Richard Nixon* (1975).

REFERENCE: Peter Rand. *China Hands*. 1995.

Whitehead, Donald F. (1908–1981)

Born in Kentucky, Whitehead covered World War II* for the Associated Press. He accompanied General Montgomery's British Eighth Army prior to American involvement in the war and later took part in five amphibious assault landings in Italy, France, and North Africa. He was awarded two Pulitzer Prizes during the Korean War.*

REFERENCES: Robert W. Desmond. *Tides of War*. 1984; M. L. Stein. *Under Fire: The Story of American War Correspondents*. 1968.

Whitney, Caspar (1861–1929)

Born in Boston, Massachusetts, he is best known for having originated the "All-American Football Team" in 1889 while working as a sportswriter. He covered the Spanish-American War* in Cuba for *Harper's Weekly* beginning in 1898. He was with Chaffee's brigade during the Battle of El Caney. Whitney later served as editor of *Outing* magazine and represented the *New York Tribune* in Europe during World War I.* From 1917 to 1919 he was one of the strongest voices of opposition to wartime censorship restrictions.

REFERENCES: Charles H. Brown. *The Correspondents' War*. 1967; *DAB 1*.

Wild, Richard (1978–2003)

This Cambridge University graduate was the seventeenth journalist killed since the beginning of the Iraq conflict. He had worked as a banker and art curator before gravitating to journalism. He inititally interned with ITN. Wild was drawn to covering Iraq as his first war reporting experience and had made arrangements with Frontline News* to sell his pictures. Before he could make his mark he was shot to death in Baghdad as he waited for a taxi. He was the first journalist to die in Baghdad after U.S. forces entered the city in April 2003.

REFERENCES: Libby Brooks. "Murdered at Museum," Guardian.co.uk, July 8, 2003; David Loyn. Frontline. 2005.

Wiley, Bonnie (c. 1910–2000)

Born in Portland, Oregon, she began working for the Yakima Daily Republic in 1927. She came late to war journalism beginning in 1945. She was reportedly the only woman war correspondent for the Associated Press in the Pacific theater of the war. Wiley covered the Battle of Iwo Jima, the Japanese surrender aboard the U.S.S. Missouri in Tokyo Bay, and the war crimes trial of General Tomokuki Yamashita in Manila. At the age of 78 she took a position as an editorial advisor for the Xinhua News in Beijing. In 1989 UNESCO presented her with its award for outstanding contributions to international journalism.

REFERENCES: Mary Adamski. "Bonnie Wiley Dies at 90." Hawaii Star Bulletin. 2000; Lilya Wagner, Women War Correspondents of World War II. 1989.

Wilkeson, Samuel (1817–1889)

Born in Buffalo, New York, he was a son of one of the city's founders. He studied law at Union College before turning to journalism. He worked for several papers in Buffalo and Albany before joining the *New York Tribune*. During the American Civil War* Wilkeson wrote federal propaganda for foreign newspapers and served as Washington bureau chief and war correspondent for the *Tribune* and the *New York Times*.

Wilkeson's accounts of the 1862 Peninsular campaign were considered unsurpassed, and at the Battle of Fair Oaks he received a special mention for his bravery while serving as a volunteer aide to General Heintzelman. While reporting the Gettysburg campaign, he covered his saddest story when he learned that his nineteen-year-old son, Lieutenant Bayard Wilkeson, had been killed in the first day's fighting. He later learned that his son had been wounded in the leg and left to die in a building avoided by surgeons. He wrote his account of the battle while sitting next to the body of his dead son. Wilkeson witnessed the bombardment on Seminary Ridge, one of the most intense artillery assaults of the war, and in 1864 he reported the Petersburg mine disaster. Following the war he left the *Tribune* to work for Jay Cooke and Company selling war bonds. He then entered railroading, rising to president of the Northern Pacific Railroad.

REFERENCES: J. Cutler Andrews. *The North Reports the Civil War*. 1955; Louis M. Starr. *The Bohemian Brigade*. 1954.

Wilkie, Franc Bangs (1832–1892)

Born in West Chariton, New York, Wilkie supported himself at Union College by writing and setting type for a local newspaper. He would become one of the most outstanding correspondents covering the western theater of the American Civil War.* Wilkie was the city editor of the *Dubuque Daily Herald* at the outset of the war and in 1861 enlisted with the First Iowa. On the strength of his report of the Union defeat at Wilson's Creek, which originally appeared in his home newspaper, he was hired by the *New York Times*. Under the pen name "Galway" Wilkie covered the attacks on Forts Henry and Donelson and the Vicksburg campaign, and criticized the inefficiency of the army's medical department. In the fall of 1863 he left war reporting for a desk job with the *Chicago Tribune*. He continued his association with the paper for twenty-five years. His book *Pen and Powder* (1888) is considered one of the best memoirs by a member of the Union press corps.

REFERENCES: J. Cutler Andrews. *The North Reports the Civil War*. 1955; Stewart Sifakis. *Who Was Who in the Civil War*. 1988.

Wilkins, George Hubert (1888–1958)

Born in Mount Bryan East, South Australia, Hubert Wilkins was a virtual renaissance man, climatologist, naturalist, polar explorer, aviator, and war correspondent, serving in World War I* as an official war photographer. Prior to his appointment he had covered the First Balkan War between Turkey and Bulgaria in 1912–1913 for Britain's *Daily Chronicle*. During this period he was credited as the first person to take film footage of combat, using an aeroplane as a way to gather photographic intelligence. He had originally enlisted in the Australian Flying Corps with the intention of becoming a pilot. His medical inspection put this plan to rest when he was showed to be color-blind. Thus, he transferred to the Australian War Records Section and headed to Europe as the "designated record photographer" for the Australian military. Wilkins had a well-deserved reputation for bravery, which many claimed bordered on recklessness while trying to photograph soldiers in action. He was recognized with two Military Crosses for bravery. His pictures are among the best to chronicle the Western Front during his two years at war. He was with Charles Bean* in 1919 when they went to Gallipoli to photograph Australian battlegrounds from the 1915 campaign. In 1918 the Australia Imperial Force (AIF) published Wilkins' edited work, *Australian War Photographer: A Pictorial Record from November 1917 to the End of the War*. When the Second World War broke out he offered to repeat his previous service as a war photographer but was rejected by the British and Australian governments due to his age.

REFERENCES: Australian War memorial, https://www.awm.gov.au/publications/contact/hubert-wilkins.asp; R.A. Swan, "Wilkins, Sir George Hubert," *Australian Dictionary of Biography*, Vol. 12, 1990.

Wilkinson, Henry Spenser (1853–1937)

Wilkinson was born in Manchester, England, and educated at Owens College and Oxford University. He developed an interest in military affairs and history in the 1870s before joining the bar in 1880. Wilkinson understood the complexities of warfare quite well. Already fluent in German and French, he had founded the Oxford University Kriegspiel Club, named after the military training game *Kriegspiel,* which he had brought back from Germany while still a college student. Wilkinson was also founder of the Manchester Tactical Society and a volunteer military officer.

He turned from law to journalism in 1882 when he wrote a series of columns on the Egyptian campaign for the *Manchester Guardian.* The Egyptian campaign was the first war for which the paper provided maps of the conflict, beginning a long tradition of excellent war coverage. Wilkinson prepared the maps himself, drawing from many sources, including Admiralty charts and War Office staff maps. In 1884 he represented the *Guardian* when he covered the Berlin Conference, which determined the partition of colonial Africa. He remained affiliated with the paper as special correspondent and military commentator until 1892. During his tenure with the paper he wrote several books on military topics, including his first book, *Citizen Soldiers* (1884), and translated numerous German military books. According to one source his most significant contribution to British military affairs was his appraisal of the German general staff system in *The Brain of an Army* (1890). He followed this work with *The Brain of the Navy* in 1895.

Wilkinson joined the *Morning Post* as drama critic in 1895. He remained an influential military writer, especially during the Boer War* and World War I.* He left the *Post* in 1914 to teach military history at Oxford. He wrote *The French Army Before Napoleon* (1915) and *The Rise of Napoleon Bonaparte* (1930).

REFERENCES: David Ayerst. *The Manchester Guardian: Biography of a Newspaper.* 1971; *DNB,* 1931–1940.

Williams, Brian Douglas (b. 1959)

Born in Elmira, New York, Williams attended George Washington University and the Catholic University of America, but left before graduation. He began his news broadcasting career in 1987 in New York City and joined NBC News in 1993. He became a familiar network presence and in 1996 he was promoted to anchor and managing editor of *The News with Brian Williams,* broadcast on MSNBC and CNBC. In 2004 he replaced retiring anchor Tom Brokaw as anchor of the *NBC Nightly News.* In February 2015, Williams was making news rather than reporting it, when he was suspended for six months for misrepresenting his coverage of the 2003 Iraq invasion. Williams gave an on-air apology on February 4, for his misrepresentation of an event during the war, in which he claimed to have been in a helicopter when it was "forced down after being hit by an RPG." Williams came under verbal fire when crew members and others reported that Williams actually arrived almost an hour after the event happened to another chopper. This episode might not be the end of the story as some of his other reporting has come under scrutiny, including his reporting on Hurricane Katrina.

REFERENCES: "Brian Williams," http://www.nbcnews.com/id/3667173; Travis J. Tritten, "Brian Williams Recants Iraq Story after SoldiersP," Stars and Stripes, Feb. 4, 2015; Jonathan Mahler, Ravi Somaiya, Emily Steel, "With an Apology, Brian Williams Digs Himself Deeper in Copter Tale," New York Times, Feb. 6, 2015.

Williams, Charles (1838–1904)

Born and educated in Ireland, he was sent to the American South to recover his health. Soon after, he participated in the Nicaragua filibustering expedition, which resulted in his first taste of battle. He returned to London, where he was hired by the *London Evening Herald* and then the *Standard* in 1859, beginning a twenty-five-year affiliation with the paper, most notably as war correspondent.

In 1870 he was with the French army during the second phase of the Franco-Prussian War,* and was one of the first reporters to enter Strasbourg after its capitulation. Williams was with Turkish forces under Ahmed Mukhtar Pasha in 1877 during the Russo-Turkish War,* which he chronicled in *The Armenian Campaign* (1878). Although tarnished by its pro-Turkish slant, Williams's book presents a solid account of the war through the treaty signing at San Stefano in 1878.

Williams next reported the British military campaigns in Afghanistan at the end of 1878, and the following year published *Notes on the*

Operations in Lower Afghanistan, 1878–9, with Special Reference to Transport. In 1884 he accompanied the Nile expedition sent to relieve General Charles Gordon at Khartoum. His account of Gordon's death was published in the *Fortnightly Review* the following year.

He left the *Standard* in 1884 for the *Morning Advertiser* (soon to become the *Daily Chronicle*). He was reportedly the only British war correspondent to accompany the Bulgarian army in its war against Serbia in 1885. He covered the 1897 Greco-Turkish War* from the Greek side. Williams noted in the *Fortnightly* that the Greeks were vanquished because of the meddling of politicians. He would witness his last war in 1898 while in the company of Lord Kitchener's army during the 1898 Sudanese campaign. He covered the advance of General William Gatacre's forces up the Nile and was present at the Battle of Omdurman, where he suffered a minor bullet wound in the cheek. His account of this pivotal battle was published in the *Daily Chronicle*. Declining health barred his coverage of the Boer conflict and ended his career as a war correspondent, although he continued to contribute pieces on military affairs to the *Morning Leader*.

REFERENCES: *DNB*, 1901–1911; Robert Wilkinson-Latham. *From Our Special Correspondent*. 1979.

Williams, Eric Lloyd (1915–1988)

At his death in 1988 he was regarded as "South Africa's most distinguished war correspondent of the Second World War" an accolade that echoed the 1944 quote in the *Cape Town Argus* that referred to him as "the outstanding South African war correspondent of this war". The South African-born reporter covered the war for the South African Press Association and *Reuters.* Williams rose to prominence covering the British Eighth Army during the North African campaign. He covered the Battle of El Alemain in 1942 and the following year accompanied Allied forces into Tunis just hours after its

---

capitulation. That same year he was once more with the Eighth Army when it invaded southern Italy from Sicily. In 1943 he was awarded the South African Society of Journalists trophy for best news story of 1943 for his Italian coverage, citing "his report of the 100-mile dash he and two other war correspondents made from the night Army spearhead at Nicastro across no-man's land to American headquarters at Salerno." During his time in North Africa he was accorded the moniker "Benghazi", after the Libyan port city that changed hands several times during the conflict in 1941–1942. He continued in journalism and then public relations until his retirement in 1975.

REFERENCE: www.statemaster.com/encyclopedia/Eric_Lloyd-Williams.

Williams, George Forrester (1837–1920)

Born on the Rock of Gibraltar, Williams, the son of a British military officer, spent his youth in Africa. He joined the staff of the New York Times in 1856. Prior to the American Civil War* he had covered the 1857–1858 campaign against the Mormons and barely escaped a firing squad while accompanying William Walker's filibustering expedition to Nicaragua. He was a veteran reporter by the outbreak of the Civil War. In 1860, the Times called on Williams to undertake a tour of the South disguised as an naive English tourist. It was thought that Williams, a gifted mimic and aided by his British background, could best pull off this factfinding expedition into the heart of secessionist territory. On several occasions he fell under suspicion, but his mission was a success as the Times used his dispatches for editorials or printed his letters using fictitious names and dates.

Williams covered the Shenandoah campaign for the Times and just missed the Battle of Frederick. But this did not keep him from filing a report. Upon reaching the town Williams met a farmer who had witnessed the entire battle and

was able to give Williams a rambling but descriptive account, including the colors of the different generals. After paying the farmer for his trouble Williams telegraphed his account, replete with casualty figures, to his home office. The following day the New York Times printed one of the best accounts of the battle, leading one general to comment on its accuracy, remarking that he had not noticed the correspondent on the field of battle that day.

Williams later delivered the first account of the Battle of Winchester to Washington and was invited to give the details in person to President Lincoln. He was provided a red-letter pass which enabled him to pass through all army checkpoints without any special credentials. He was rewarded for his scoop by being made chief correspondent for the New York Times with the Army of the Potomac. He also reported the Battles of Cold Harbor, Yorktown, Chancellorsville, and Gettysburg, and other important engagements, and survived serious wounds at Malvern Hill and during the Wilderness campaign. Following the Civil War, Williams covered the Franco-Prussian War,* witnessed the execution of Emperor Maximilian at Queretaro, Mexico, and campaigned in South America.

REFERENCES: J. Cutler Andrews. The North Reports the Civil War. 1955; Louis M. Starr. Bohemian Brigade. 1954.

Williams, Wythe (1881–1956)

Williams joined the New York Evening World in 1910. Four years later he left the paper for the New York Times and was in the London bureau when World War I* began. Soon afterward he transferred to the Paris office, where he worked with Walter Duranty.* He inaugurated a clever system for sending dispatches back to London through a series of innocuous-seeming telegrams. In May 1915 he was briefly jailed in Paris for covering German military action in France. Soon after, French military authorities dropped the prohibition against war correspondents. He wrote several excellent accounts from the battle-fronts in France and Italy. In 1917 he began his affiliation with *Collier's Weekly* and became one of the first war correspondents accredited to the Allied Expeditionary Force headquarters, but he had his accreditation suspended in February 1918 for violating censorship regulations.

REFERENCES: Emmet Crozier. *American Reporters on the Western Front, 1914–18.* 1959; Robert W. Desmond. *Windows on the World.* 1980.

Wills, Stanley (1906–1944)

Educated in Northhampton, he worked for several papers before joining the *Daily Herald* as an editor in 1934. In 1943 he finally fulfilled his ambition to report from the battlefront. After covering the Allied headquarters in Algiers he was assigned to Burma, and in 1944 he was the only war correspondent to witness the relief of the Seventh Indian Division after its long siege by the Japanese. His coverage of this story received many accolades. On March 24, 1944, he was with correspondent Stuart Emeny* accompanying General Orde Wingate on a flight over Burma when the plane went down, killing all on board.

REFERENCE: Dennis Griffiths, ed. *The Encyclopedia of the British Press.* 1992.

Wilmot, Reginald William Winchester "Chester" (1911–1954)

Wilmot was born in Melbourne, Australia, and educated at the University of Melbourne. The son of a journalist, Wilmot joined the Australia Broadcasting Commission (ABC) as a radio war correspondent in August 1940. He covered Australian forces in the Middle East and Greece campaigns.

Wilmot then reported the North African campaign. He covered the first Libyan campaign from Bardia to Beda Fromm, where he was the sole correspondent to witness the defeat of an Italian armored division in the great tank battle there. Rather than bask in the glory of such a scoop, he shared the news with fellow correspondents. He also was present at the siege of Tobruk, and his dispatches from within the fortress were broadcast around the world, adding to his growing reputation and coming to the attention of the BBC. His book *Tobruk, 1941* (1945) chronicled the siege. Following the attack on Pearl Harbor that December, Wilmot was recalled to Australia. He lost his accreditation to cover Australian forces after he was accused by the Australian commander of Allied land forces of making critical statements concerning the Australian war effort.

In 1944, Wilmot had his accreditation restored by the BBC, and he left for London to cover the Normandy invasion. The BBC had assembled a team of forty-eight correspondents to report the D-Day landings. All were given special training by the army, issued uniforms, and assigned to specific units. By June 1944, the BBC had developed new broadcasting and recording equipment, more durable and compact than anything previously available, revolutionizing war reporting, eliminating the need for radio trucks and cumbersome technical gear. For the invasion Wilmot was assigned to the Sixth Airborne Division, made up of two paratroop brigades and an airborne glider force. Its hazardous mission was to protect the Orne River bridges against an expected German counterattack. His bravery and coverage of the fighting following D-Day only enhanced his standing with the BBC as Wilmot became one of its most popular voices. Perhaps his greatest skill was an ability to interpret complex events to listeners in simple terms.

Wilmot generally eschewed "color" pieces on daily military life, the mainstay of the reporting profession, concentrating instead on analysis. He continued to report from the front lines as the war in Europe came to a close. He recorded the last fighting in Germany and delivered the scoop of the German surrender on May 4, 1945. Following the war he remained in Europe covering

---

* *Indicates a separate entry.*

the Nuremberg trials for the BBC. In 1952, after six years of work, his account of the war, *The Struggle for Europe,* was published to high acclaim. He continued in radio during the 1950s and seemed ready to make the transfer to television when he was killed in a plane crash on assignment in Asia for the BBC.

REFERENCE: Trevor Royle. *War Report.* 1987.

Wing, Henry Ebenezer (1840–1925)

Born in Connecticut, following law school Wing enlisted in the Twenty-seventh Connecticut in September 1862. He covered the early stages of the American Civil War* for the *New Haven Palladium.* At the Battle of Fredericksburg he was severely wounded, losing several fingers and the full use of one of his legs, and was discharged from the army. He then reported the conflict for the *Norwich Bulletin.*

In 1864 a long-standing dispute between the War Department and the press came to a head when a proclamation was issued specifying that no civilians other than those already there would be allowed at the war front. Since every accredited *New York Tribune* correspondent was at that time stationed in the nation's capital, the proclamation would leave the paper without a war reporter. However, Wing managed to elude Union pickets and make his way sixty miles to the safe confines of a Union army encampment. He was rewarded with accreditation and a job as war correspondent by the *Tribune.*

Wing covered the first day of the Wilderness campaign and volunteered to deliver the pooled reports for his colleagues through Confederate territory. In a bizarre series of events he was escorted by the Confederate Mosby's irregulars, then chased by them, fed by New York cavalry, arrested by rebel cavalry, and finally ordered arrested as a spy by Secretary of War Stanton. When he at last reached a telegraph reserved for official military use Stanton asked him for his report. Wing replied, not until he could first send his scoop to the *Tribune.* The secretary ordered his arrest, but not before Lincoln interceded, agreeing to allow him to send in his reports. The president sent a train for Wing so he could give a more complete report in person. Arriving at the White House at 2 a.m., he was kissed by the president for the encouraging news he brought from Grant concerning the high morale of the army. Wing's greatest story was the only information received from the front that day.

Lincoln provided Wing an escort back to the front the following day, where he would remain through the completion of the war. Following the war he joined the *Litchfield Enquirer* as copublisher. Later he worked in advertising, practiced law, and then joined the ministry.

REFERENCE: J. Cutler Andrews. *The North Reports the Civil War.* 1955.

Wirgman, Charles (1832–1891)

Born in London, the war artist and editor of *Japan Punch* was hired by the *Illustrated London News* in 1857 and was assigned to cover the conflict in Asia between China and Great Britain. He witnessed the assault on Canton as well as the march on Peking. He barely escaped the British legation by crawling under his quarters to safety when the compound was overrun by Chinese forces on July 5, 1861. Following the conflict he moved to Japan, where he remained for the rest of his life. He continued his career in journalism, establishing the *Japan Punch* and becoming well known as an artist. He died on February 8, 1891.

REFERENCE: Dennis Griffiths, ed. *The Encyclopedia of the British Press.* 1992.

Wolfert, Ira (1908–1997)

Born in New York City, he attended the Columbia University School of Journalism. He joined the North American Newspaper Alliance in

1929. In 1941, he was the only newspaperman to accompany the Free French expedition which captured the French islands of St. Pierre and Miquelon off the coast of Newfoundland without incident, one of the first acts to touch North American shores directly.

In 1942 he switched to the Pacific theater, witnessing one of the greatest sea battles of the war near the Solomon Islands, with the Japanese losing nineteen ships to American forces. Wolfert was flying over the *President Coolidge,* which had been converted into a troop transport, when it hit a mine and sank. His coverage for the North American Newspaper Alliance was awarded a Pulitzer Prize in 1943. That same year he published *Battle of the Solomons* and *Torpedo 8: The Story of Swede Larsen's Bomber Squadron.*

He was with the invasion fleet during the Normandy invasion and covered the subsequent French campaign and the liberation of Paris. Wolfert continued to follow the action into Germany, but by the end of October he had returned to the States for rest and recuperation. He claimed that he had become "bored with being afraid." Following the war he turned to screenwriting and fiction. His screenplay *An American Guerrilla in the Philippines* was based on actual events in the Pacific during World War II.*

REFERENCE: Robert W. Desmond. *Tides of War.* 1984; Jack Stenbuck. *Typewriter Battalion.* 1995.

Wood, Junius (1877–1957)

Wood covered the Veracruz expedition in 1914 for the *Chicago Daily News* as well as the Pershing punitive expedition against Pancho Villa. During World War I* he was an accredited correspondent with the American Expeditionary Force until 1919 and one of the first to report the German breakthrough at Chateau-Thierry.

REFERENCE: Emmet Crozier. *American Reporters on the Western Front, 1914–18.* 1959.

Woodruff, Robert "Bob" Dawson (b. 1961)

Educated at the University of Michigan Law School and Colgate University, and fluent in Mandarin and German, Woodruff practiced law before becoming a journalist not long after getting a taste of the craft while working as a translator during the Tiananmen Square uprising in 1989. Best known for his work for ABC News, he has worked for the company since 1996. He covered the Justice Department for ABC News in the late 1990s and in 1999 began covering foreign conflicts including the Yugoslavian conflict and the war in Iraq. He became his own major story on January 29, 2006 when he was seriously wounded by a roadside bomb while covering U.S. and Iraqi security forces near Taji, Iraq. Although he suffered horrific brain injuries he returned to reporting just thirteen months later. Since then he has reported from North Korea, Syria, and Jordan. He has continued to cover the plight of thousands of soldiers who suffered similar injuries to his and in 2008 he earned a Peabody Award for his coverage. He chronicled his recovery in the book *In an Instant: A Family's Journey of Love and Healing* (co-authored with his wife Lee) in 2007.

REFERENCE: http://abcnews.go.com/print?id=127761.

Woods, Henry Charles (1881–1939)

As special correspondent for the *Times,* he covered the Italo-Turkish War and in 1912–1913 reported the Balkan Wars for the *Evening News.* At the outset of World War I* he was made military and diplomatic correspondent for the *Evening News* and the *Weekly Dispatch.*

REFERENCE: Dennis Griffiths, ed. *The Encyclopedia of the British Press.* 1992.

Indicates a separate entry.

Woodville, Richard Caton
(1856–1927)

The ex-officer of the Royal North Devon Hussars was an artist for the *Illustrated London News* during the Russo-Turkish War* and the 1882 Egyptian campaign. In 1891 he visited the United States to cover the Sioux uprising, although it was already over and he never witnessed any actual fighting. His art worked more as heroic propaganda during the late Victorian era than as realistic renderings.

REFERENCE: Pat Hodgson. *The War Illustrators.* 1977.

Woodward, David (?)

A member of the staff of the *News Chronicle* between 1936 and 1943, Woodward served as its war correspondent in the Middle East before joining the *Manchester Guardian* to cover General Montgomery's forces. On June 9, 1944, he was one of the three reporters to land in France with a glider and parachute unit. In the process he was wounded and returned briefly to England for recuperation. He returned to France in July and followed the campaign to its conclusion and the liberation of Paris.

REFERENCE: David Ayerst. *The Manchester Guardian: Biography of a Newspaper.* 1971.

World War I

The United States sent more correspondents and photographers to cover World War I than did any other country. In 1914, the first year of the conflict, there were from fifty to seventy-five staff and stringers* on the scene. By the last year of the war several hundred American press representatives were on the western front or prowling the streets of the capital cities of Europe. Prior to American intervention reporters from the States could move freely through the cities of Berlin and Vienna. However, the U.S. Army refused to accredit women to action on the western front, even though they had been active before America formally entered the conflict. As an alternative three women did cover the war on the Russian front.

By comparison, Great Britain applied the Official Secrets Act of 1911 to the British press contingent. Conditions looked particularly bleak for correspondents at the outset of the war with Lord Kitchener, a veteran of the Sudan campaigns and an inveterate enemy of war reporters, as secretary of state for war. Kitchener ordered that no credentials were to be granted to journalists applying to accompany the British Expeditionary Forces to France. The official view was that the British public could not handle bad news. He ruled that any British correspondent reporting the war in France and Belgium would be labeled an outlaw* and would be arrested and summarily prosecuted. In order to give the appearance that the British people were being kept informed of the conflict Kitchener appointed an officer known as the "Eye-Witness"* to prepare daily reports about the progress of the war which would bear his stamp of approval. After the first ten months of the war British correspondents were given accreditation but were still tightly controlled.

Prior to the American intervention, correspondents accredited to the British Expeditionary Forces (BEF) headquarters were classified as either British, French, or neutral, with limited numbers of each. They were required to wear identifying armbands and uniforms, to view the battlefront only in the company of British officers, and to present their reports to official censors. In return they were fed and billeted, with access to communication and transportation facilities. By May 1915 the outlaw classification was ended as well.

During the war freedom of the press all but vanished in France as the military insisted on strict censorship. Besides the five French representatives at BEF headquarters there was very little initiative demonstrated by the French press, indicating that they were more willing to accept the war news provided by the French government.

In the early years of the war Germany and Austria were more forthcoming and lenient with foreign members of the press than their Allied counterparts. In the later years, however, this would reverse as the Allied forces gained the upper hand in the conflict. While foreign correspondents were afforded unaccustomed luxury, their own correspondents worked under strict supervision. Austria provided complimentary assistance to accredited correspondents ranging from motor vehicles and servants to haute cuisine, wine, and tobacco. Over one hundred reporters from around the world would accept Austrian hospitality in the first year of the war.

In 1915 German military news and censorship activities were placed under the Kriegpresseamt (War Press Office), which was controlled by the general staff. It encouraged the development of trench newspapers, sponsored conferences of journalists, and prepared and distributed periodicals such as the *German War Weekly Review,* as well as propaganda publications.

With American intervention in 1917, it was only natural that there would be a heightened interest in the conflict in the United States. That July a press base was established in Paris for the American Expeditionary Force (AEF). Soon after, another base was established two hundred miles away at Neufchateau in association with the Army Intelligence Section. Prior to the summer of 1918 fifty journalists were accredited to the AEF. Twenty-one of them were print correspondents and the remaining twenty-nine were either photographers or artists. Accredited correspondents were given more perks than the "visiting" correspondents and representatives of small-town papers who continued to arrive throughout the latter stages of the war. One accredited correspondent was assigned to each division and was provided transportation and cable facilities. The rest of the press corps were not afforded cars, cable facilities, or allowed to travel outside the zone of the division they were with.

Photographers were distinguished from print correspondents by a blue armband with a white letter "P" on it, while their counterparts were identified by a green brassard with a red letter "C." Accredited correspondents held the status of officer and wore uniforms without identifying insignias or emblems. To prepare for Europe, American correspondents were advised to bring telegraph credit cards, a typewriter, copy paper, topographical maps, and a small rubber bathtub. Perhaps war correspondent and World War I censor Frederick Palmer* described the changing rules for war correspondents best when he said, "There was not the freedom of the old days, but there can never be again for the correspondent." World War I turned out to be one of the safest conflicts for American Journalists. Although a number of correspondents were wounded, none of the civilian correspondents were killed during the war. Reuters,* by comparison, lost at least 15 out of 115 correspondents, with several unaccounted for. The best-covered campaigns of the war were on the western front in France and Belgium; coverage was relatively sparse on the eastern front.

REFERENCES: Emmet Crozier. *American Reporters on the Western Front, 1914–18.* 1959; Robert W. Desmond. *The Information Process.* 1978; Joseph J. Mathews. *Reporting the Wars.* 1957.

World War II

Of the approximately 3,000 correspondents that covered the war, the United States had the largest number with 1,646 accredited around the world, including at least 100 women correspondents. Countless others were accredited by Allied and neutral countries. Thirty-seven American reporters and photojournalists would perish in the conflict, with 112 wounded. The Associated Press and the United Press each lost five journalists and the *New York Times* and *Time-Life* lost three each.

During World War II, combination or "pool" reporters were selected by American military officials in consultation with news executives for special access to battlefields and important events,

Indicates a separate entry.

providing that reporters agreed to sharing their news with nonmembers of the pool and submitted to military censorship, ground rules, and other constraints. The pool system was continually criticized for its abuse of military censorship to support political positions and public relations rather than merely to protect military secrets.

By the time war broke out in 1939, correspondents had access to many new technical innovations for news transmission. Worldwide radio broadcasts had been introduced in 1930, and Western Union had instituted a process for sending high-quality news photos by cable across the Atlantic. However, censorship initially negated some of the advances. Delays in dispatches from London rose from one to five hours shortly after war was declared.

World War II has been referred to as "the censored war" for the pervasiveness of news censorship. The news censorship process appeared in a variety of incarnations. The U.S. government took its hesitant first step toward news control when it formally established the Office of Censorship, headed by Byron Price,* in January 1942. This agency was solely a civilian enterprise, assigned to monitor war-related news coming from the United States.

Military censorship, on the other hand, was controlled by various branches of the armed forces, which supervised the release of combat news. In addition there was the Office of War Information, which served as a clearinghouse for war news and determined what news should be released to the public.

Each theater of operations offered varying degrees of press freedom. During the North African desert campaign in 1942 war correspondents were given unprecedented freedom. This was in part due to the immense tracts of desert terrain, which encouraged freedom of movement. Under these conditions correspondents accompanied particular units and developed attachments to the unit. During the war British correspondents were distinguished by the gold letter "C," worn usually as a cap badge.

On their left shoulder they were required to wear a green felt strip with "Foreign War Correspondent" emblazoned in gold letters. Military authorities regarded the war correspondents as vital elements of the war effort and often provided them current information with the unspoken agreement that they would produce favorable reports. Prior to the invasion of Tunisia, General Eisenhower went as far as to comment publicly that he considered the press part of the military organization and believed it should be treated as such. But this was true only as long as reporters produced favorable copy. Journalists for the most part were inclined to maintain their partnership with the military, since the war would be virtually impossible to follow without the assistance of the armed forces.

World War II was a much more difficult war to cover than previous wars. During World War I* and the Spanish-American War* there might have been different fronts, but usually there was only one major battle or campaign in progress. Whereas in previous wars there was a certain esprit de corps and camaraderie among the pool of correspondents, reporters during World War II were so scattered around the world that correspondents met few of their colleagues.

REFERENCES: Richard Collier. *Fighting Words.* 1989; Robert Desmond. *Tides of War.* 1984; M. L. Stein. *Under Fire.* 1968.

Wounds in the Rain

Wounds in the Rain (1900) is Stephen Crane's* collection of short stories and recollections of the Spanish-American War.* Among the stories is "The Lone Charge of William B. Perkins," which satirizes the war correspondent through the character of William B. Perkins, a whiskey-besotted reporter who arrives in Cuba "with no information of war, and no particular rapidity of mind for acquiring it." Another story has a contingent of novice war correspondents coming face-to-face with the romantic myths of the profession during the Greco-Turkish War.*

REFERENCES: Stephen Crane. *Wounds in the Rain.* 1900; Howard Good. *The Image of War Correspondents in Anglo-American Fiction.* 1985.

Wright, Henry Charles Seppings (c. 1849–1937)

Born in England, the son of a minister turned to art following a short naval career. He joined the *Illustrated London News* as an artist-correspondent* in the 1870s. He covered the discovery of Kimberley diamond fields in South Africa, the 1893 Ashanti expedition, and Kitchener's advance on Dongola in 1896. The next year Wright covered the conflict in Greece. He also sketched battles in the Spanish-American War* and the Russo-Japanese War.* He wrote several books chronicling his wartime experiences. During World War I* he witnessed the Russian and French fronts.

REFERENCES: Pat Hodgson. *The War Illustrators.* 1977; Robert Wilkinson-Latham. *From Our Special Correspondent.* 1979.

Wright, Robin (b. 1948)

Born in Ann Arbor, Michigan and educated at the University of Michigan, Wright has covered the Middle East and Africa as a roving correspondent, covering wars and revolutions for more than forty years for such august news sources as the *Washington Post,* the *Los Angeles Times,* the *New Yorker,* the *New York Time Magazine,* the *Atlantic,* and many others. In Africa she covered war zones in Congo, Angola, and Rhodesia, where she noted that she "lost a great love of my life in the Rhodesian Civil War. People don't understand the risks taken by foreign correspondents." In the Middle East she covered the Iran-Iraq War in the 1980s, the Kuwait War in the 1990s as well as most other conflicts in the region during this period, beginning with the 1973 Arab-Israeli War. Having reported from more than 140 countries and known for her erudition and historical perspective, Wright is a much sought-out columnist and lecturer. She received the National Magazine Award for her reportage from Iran for *The New Yorker* and the Overseas Press Club Award for "best reporting in any medium requiring exceptional courage and initiative" for reporting on wars in Africa. The author of many books, in 2011 her book *Rock the Casbah: Rage and Rebellion across the Islamic World* was published.

REFERENCE: Robin Weaver, "Woman around Town: Robin Wright-Fearless Historian," womanaroundtown.com, June 27, 2011.

The Writing 69th

In early 1943 the United States Eighth Air Force ran a training program for eight civilian and military journalists with the goal of preparing them to cover high-altitude bombing missions over Germany. The eight men included Homer Bigart,* Walter Cronkite,* Gladwin Hill,* Paul Manning,* Robert Perkins Post,* Andy Rooney,* Jack Denton Scott* and William Wade.* This group was initially referred to as the "Flying Typewriters" and "the Legion of the Doomed." However the reporters preferred "the Writing 69th." The week long training course was conducted in Bovingdon, England and included such lessons as adjusting to high altitude flights, identifying enemy planes, and how to parachute. Although non-combatants were prohibited from firing weapons in combat they were still trained to use weapons. Six of the eight reporters flew on separate planes on their first and last mission on February 26, 1943. However, one of the planes was shot down over Oldenberg, Germany killing eight Air Force crew members and reporter Robert Perkins Post. Post's death mostly put a stop to reporters flying on bombing missions. What is probably most amazing about the first and last run of the 69th was that two crew members survived the mid-air explosion and ended up in a German POW camp.

REFERENCES: Jim Hamilton. *The Writing 69th.* 2005; www.greenharbor.com/wr69/Biographies.html.

* Indicates a separate entry.

Ximenes, Edoardo (1852–1932)

Born in Sicily, he studied art in Naples before moving to Milan, where he cofounded the *Illustrazione Italiana,* which became the most widely circulated illustrated magazine in Italy. Ximenes often worked as a special correspondent for the magazine and in 1896 he directed the illustrated gazette *La Guerra Italo-Abissinia,* or *The War Between Italy and Abyssinia.* He witnessed the war himself, and his sketches and photographs of the war are reportedly the most memorable images of the conflict. Ximenes left the magazine in the 1920s but continued his career as a journalist.

REFERENCE: Nicolas Monit, ed. *Africa Then.* 1987.

Y

Yamamoto, Mika (1967–2012)

Born in Tsuri, Japan, in 1990 she began her career in journalism as a reporter for Asahi Newstar, a satellite television channel of TV Asahi. She rose through the ranks before leaving for the Japan Press in 1995. Working out of Tokyo, Yamamoto was recognized for her preference for using handheld cameras and doing her own editing. She covered dangerous assignments in Kosovo, Bosnia, Indonesia, and Afghanistan in 2001, Iraq in 2003, and then Uganda. In 2003 she survived a coalition airstrike on Baghdad's Palestine Hotel that killed several other international reporters. She returned to Japan as a news presenter and was recognized for her war coverage with the Vaughn-Uyeda Memorial Award Prize. In 2011 she once again found herself in the danger zone covering the Syrian civil war.* She was with several colleagues accompanying members of the Free Syrian Army when they were attacked in Aleppo. She was killed by government troops after suffering a gunshot to the neck. Other accounts have her dying during an artillery attack. An autopsy revealed she had been shot nine times.

REFERENCE: https://cpj.org/killed/2012/mika-yamamoto.php.

Yank Magazine

In the tradition of army newspapers such as the *Stars and Stripes** begun during World War I,*

Yank was created during World War II.* Unlike the *Stars and Stripes,* for which officers supervised and controlled editorial commentary, *Yank* was edited and written by noncommissioned personnel. Officers were only involved in administrative capacities. These officers were often called on to act as a buffer between the enlisted soldiers and the brass who objected to this new kind of journalism, exemplified by its motto, "By and for the enlisted man."

By the end of the war the magazine had established twenty-one separate editions in virtually every theater of operations. Its peak circulation was as high as two million paid subscribers, with a readership estimated at five times that number. The magazine opened its New York headquarters in May 1942 under the direction of the Army Information and Education Division of the War Department's Army Service Forces. The first issue of *Yank* was published on June 17, 1942, at five cents an issue and with no advertising allowed.

Originally only published in the United States, as the war progressed overseas editions were requested, with the first one being published in London on November 8, 1942. The usual protocol for setting up overseas publication was to send several representatives to the new location to set up new facilities and make arrangements with local printers. The members of the magazine staff filled the dual role of enlisted soldier and journalist, with many seeing action in both the European and Pacific theaters. The magazine

---

* *Indicates a separate entry.*

suffered the deaths of four correspondents in action. Eight reporters received Purple Hearts in the European theater and an equal number in the Pacific. *Yank* is credited with being the first enlisted man's magazine and the first publication to carry George Baker's* popular cartoon character "Sad Sack."

REFERENCES: Alfred Emile Cornebise. Ranks *and Columns: Armed Forces Newspapers in American Wars.* 1993; Art Weithas. *Close to Glory.* 1991; Barrett McGurn, *Yank, The Army Weekly: Reporting the Greatest Generation,* 2004.

Year of Living Dangerously, The

This 1983 film, starring Mel Gibson and Sigourney Weaver, revolves around a young Australian reporter on his first foreign assignment. With violent unrest surrounding the fall of the Sukarno regime in 1965 Indonesia as the backdrop, the film conveys the dangers and culture clashes faced by Western correspondents reporting conflicts in Third World countries.

REFERENCE: Howard Good. *The Image of War Correspondents in Anglo-American Fiction.* 1985.

Yellow Journalism

Yellow journalism became synonymous with sensationalist reporting in the late nineteenth century. It has been argued that the press war between Hearst's *Journal* and Joseph Pulitzer's *World* promoted war fever with sensationalistic accounts of Spanish outrages in Cuba. Many sources lay the blame for the Spanish-American War* on the shrill hysteria created by the Hearst* papers and yellow journalism.

The term has traditionally referred to the *New York World's* use of a yellow-ink cartoon strip on its front page. William Randolph Hearst liked the cartoon so much that an incarnation of the "Yellow Kid" soon appeared in the pages of the *World's* main competitor, the *New York Journal.* With both papers featuring this yellow cartoon they became identified as purveyors of yellow journalism and prime examples of the yellow press. Recent research by W. Joseph Campbell suggests that the traditional assumptions about the origins of the reference to yellow journalism more likely came from the *New York Post* and that the rivalry over the use of the "Yellow Kid" "was not the immediate inspiration for the term." Furthermore, according to Campbell, the term was not inaugurated until January 1897, almost three months after Hearst and Pulitzer both ran versions of the cartoon.

REFERENCES: Joyce Milton. *The Yellow Kids.* 1989: W. Joseph Campbell. *Yellow Journalism.* 2001.

Yevzerikhin, Emmanuel (1911–1984)

Yevzerikhin covered World War II* as a photographer-correspondent for the TASS News Agency. His photographs have an aesthetic appeal absent from most war photographs. After the war he worked as a freelance journalist and professor at the Peoples' University of Photography in Moscow.

REFERENCE: Daniela Mrazkova and Vladimir Remes, eds. *The Russian War: 1941–1945.* 1975.

Yon, Michael (b. 1964)

Yon, who left the military in 1987, is an ex-Green Beret who turned to journalism in 2004. He has covered the wars in Iraq and Afghanistan while embedded* and is the author of *Moment of Truth in Iraq* (2008), recounting his experiences as a war correspondent. Yon publishes an online magazine called MichaelYon-Online.com. According to the *New York Times* Yon has spent more time embedded with combat units than any other journalist in Iraq. He began covering the war in Afghanistan in 2008. His work and photographs have been widely published and cited in a number of News outlets, including CNN, FOX, the *Wall Street Journal,* and the *New York Times.*

REFERENCE: http://bighollywood.breitbart.com/author/myon.

Takama Yoshihide.

See NAKAYAMA GISHU.

Young, Alexander Bell Filson (1867–1938)

Born and educated in Manchester, England, Young went directly from grammar school into business. He began working for the *Manchester Guardian* on a part-time basis in 1896. He was engaged as war correspondent for the paper in 1899 to cover the Boer War,* but was notified that due to prohibitive telegraph costs he should mail in his longer dispatches and only send telegrams of short news stories. Young returned to England after reporting the relief of Mafeking.* During World War I* he accompanied the British Expeditionary Forces as a correspondent for the *Times*. He continued his career with various other periodicals and the BBC. He wrote *The Relief of Mafeking* (1900).

REFERENCE: David Ayerst. *The Manchester Guardian: Biography of a Newspaper*. 1971.

Young, John Russell (1840–1899)

Born in Tyrone County, Ireland, Young immigrated with his family to America, where he entered the newspaper business as a copyboy for the *Philadelphia Press* at the age of seventeen. In 1861 he was made war correspondent and wrote one of the earliest accounts of the Union defeat at Bull Run. He was probably the first to report the actual facts concerning the defeat and the retreat. In 1862, partly due to his reporting abilities, he was made managing editor of the *Philadelphia Press*, and two years later he covered the Red River expedition to northern Louisiana.

Following the war he joined Greeley's *Tribune*, becoming editor in June 1866. He was discharged in 1869 for allowing AP news to be published by a non-subscribing paper. Young executed several secret missions to Europe for various cabinet officials and in 1872 became foreign correspondent and editor for the *New York Herald*. In 1877, Young was in London when ex-president Grant asked him to be his guest on his around-the-world tour. He chronicled this voyage and the close friendship that developed between the two in *Around the World with General Grant* (1879). In 1882 he was made minister to China, thanks to his relationship with the former president. He would eventually return to the *Herald* and serve as Librarian of Congress.

REFERENCES: J. Cutler Andrews. *The North Reports the Civil War*. 1955; *DAB*; Stewart Sifakis. *Who Was Who in the Civil War*. 1988; Louis M. Starr. *Bohemian Brigade*. 1954.

Young, Perry Deane (b. 1941)

Born in Asheville, North Carolina, and educated at the University of North Carolina at Chapel Hill, Young covered the Vietnam War* for the UPI beginning in 1968. He arrived in the country just prior to the Tet offensive. Young reported the Battles of Hue and Khe Sanh. He chronicled the lives and deaths of fellow war correspondents Dana Stone* and Sean Flynn* in the book *Two of the Missing: A Reminiscence of Some Friends in the War* (1975).

REFERENCE: Perry Deane Young. *Two of the Missing*. 1975.

Yugoslavian Conflict

The Balkans had collapsed into virtual anarchy after the collapse of the Soviet Union in 1989 as Yugoslavia broke up into a number of independent states. Brutal civil wars ensued that pitted Serbs, Croats, and Muslims against one another. There was much to be desired from the war reporting that emerged in the mid-1990s with journalists tending to identify various factions as the good guys or bad guys. To top it off NATO and the international community were not inclined

---

* Indicates a separate entry.

to become involved in another European war. Once NATO members decided to launch an air campaign against the forces of Serbian leader Slobodan Milosevic in 1999, in reaction to the so-called "ethnic cleansing" of Albanians in Kosovo, the region became a magnet for reporters. The subsequent war attracted 2,700 representatives from the media who tagged along with NATO forces as they moved into Kosovo following the bombing campaign (compared to some five hundred at peak of Viet Nam War). Nonetheless, according to historian Alistair Horne, the campaign "turned out to be the most secret campaign in living memory."

REFERENCE: Phillip Knightley. *The First Casualty*. 2004 edition.

Yznaga, Antonio (?)

During the Mexican-American War* he was the People's Spanish-section editor for the *Mexico City American Star*, and was present in Mexico City to watch the city's handover to American forces, leaving in time to depart on the last army ship out.

REFERENCE: Tom Reilly, *War with Mexico!: America's Reporters Cover the Battlefront*, Manley Witten, ed., 2010.

Z

Zelma, Georgi Anatolyevich (1906–1984)

A pioneer in Soviet photojournalism, Zelma was born in Tashkent, Uzbekistan, Russia, studied photography in Moscow, and was apprenticed with the Russfoto agency in Moscow from 1923 to 1924. During World War II* he served as war correspondent and photographer with the Red Army and for the newspaper *Isvestiya*. Zelma covered the nine-hundred-day siege and Battle of Stalingrad, the conflict in Odessa, and the front against Germany from 1941 to 1945. His war reportage is collected in *Stalingrad: July 1942-February 1943* (1966) and *Living Legend* (1967).

REFERENCES: *Contemporary Photographers*. 1982; Jorge Lewinski. *The Camera at War*. 1978; Daniela Mrazkova and Vladimir Remes, eds. *The Russian Front: 1941–1945*. 1975.

---

* *Indicates a separate entry.*

Primary Documents & Photographs

1840 – 1899

Introduction 416

Mexican-American War
New Orleans Picayune:
    Express to California 419
    Victory of Monterey 419
    Near Matamoras 420
    Map of Monterey 420

Crimean War
    Roger Fenton's Photographic Van (photo) 421
    Valley of Death (photo) 421
    Balaklava Harbour (photo) 422
    The Interior of the Redan (photo) 422

Indian Mutiny
    Interior of the Secundra Bagh (photo) 423
    Part of Barracks held by General Wheeler (photo) 424

Chinese Wars
    Embrasure (photo) 425

American Civil War
    Savage Station (photo) 426
    Dunker Church (photo) 426
    Federal Wagon Trains (photo) 427

Franco-Prussian War
    Execution Scene Paris Commune (photo) 428

Spanish-American War
    Notes of A War Correspondent 429
    Men with the Bark On (photos) 432–434

1900 – 1949

Boer War
    The Battlefield: Spion Kop (photo) 435

Russo-Japanese War
    With Kuroki in Manchuria 436

World War I
    And They Thought We Wouldn't Fight 440

1900 – 1949 (continued)

Spanish Civil War
    Loyalist Militiaman at Moment of Death (photo) 444

World War II
    Typewriter Battalion..445
        Shot by Shot Stories of D-Day...445
        Last Fantastic Battle in the Reich..450
    They Were There..451
        Going Ashore 451
        Dieppe..455
    Ernie's War: The Best of Ernie Pyle's World War II Dispatches.........................458
        A Long Thin Line of Personal Anguish 458
        The Horrible Waste of War 459
    U.S. Marine Cradles Near-Dead Infant (photo)...461
    U.S. Flag Raised Atop Mt. Suribachi (photo)..461
    Basic Field Manual: Regulations for Correspondents 462

1950 – 1999

Korean War
    Koreans Crossing the Mostly Destroyed Bridge (photo) 481

Vietnam War
    A Dead Marine is Carried (photo)..482
    A Wounded GI Reaches Out (photo) 482
    Former POW Lt. Col. Rob Stirm (photo) 483
    My Lai Massacre (photo)..483

Lebanon
    Massacre of Palestinians by Christian Phalangists (photo) 484
    Bombing of U.S. Marine Barracks (photo) 485

Gulf War
    U.S. Sergeant Mourns Death of Fellow Soldier (photo)...................................486

2000 – 2009

Wars in Iraq and Afghanistan
    Flag-draped caskets of U.S. Air Force Staff Sergeant Phillip Myers (photos) 488
    Setting the Standard 489
    The Green Book..490
    Embedding Media During Possible Operations/Deployments in the
        U.S. Central Command...508
    Dispatches from Media Boot Camp...515
    Charter for the Safety of Journalists Working in War Zones or Dangerous Areas....................519

2010 – 2015

Adam Ray 521

Iraqi Soldier Stands Guard (photo) 523

U.S. Army Soldier at Scene of Blast (photo) 523

Soldiers cleaning Weapons before Returning Home (photo) 524

Army Soldiers celebrate After Crossing Iraqi Border (photo) 524

Guide to Safely Using Satphones 525

Global Safety Principles and Practices 566

ISIS Behead U.S. Journalist James Wright Foley (photo) 569

Press Photojournalist photographer (photo) 569

Introduction

The documents and photograph that follow are meant to complement and supplement the A-Z entries of the book. They intend to give the reader a better and more visceral appreciation of the changing nature of journalism, photography and warfare since the Mexican-American War. Through these documents and photographs, the reader will better understand the continuities in war journalism, as well as new dimensions of warfare and war reporting, especially outside influences such as the vexing censorship and restrictions that inhibit today's war journalists from capturing most aspects of frontline military action.

In 2009, the 18-year ban on media coverage of fallen soldiers being returned to the United States was lifted following a campaign by the National Press Photographers Association. U.S. Defense Secretary Gates noted "We believe that the Department of Defense ban on media coverage of the return of our fallen heroes, which in turn prevents the public from seeing images of these events, violates the very principles of free speech and free exchange of ideas, for which these very heroes have died." That important statement can be applied to all war photographic images. Viewing the photographic images in this section can help the researcher gain a better understanding of several topics.

One major characteristic of war-photo-journalism that distinguishes one era from another is the difference between earlier photographic technology and the digital era of today. This affects how fast the information reaches the public as well as what subject matter is transmitted. Looking at the photos of Fenton, Robertson, and Beato from the wars of the Victorian era, it is evident that the people and places are posed, and that these early photos were taken long after the battle.

By the American Civil War and the Franco-Prussian War, however, battlefield coverage had changed. War photos were of actual dead soldiers lying on battlefields not long after the battle. Mathew Brady and his colleagues would soon offer gallery exhibitions of these photos, reaching a larger audience than ever before. These pictures challenged the heroic portrait of warfare so accepted during the Napoleonic and Victorian eras of conflict. Anyone witnessing these uncensored images would have, no doubt, reacted much the same way audiences did when watching the movie *Saving Private Ryan*, whose stark realism and bloodletting proved such a counterpoint to John Wayne's bloodless heroics in countless Hollywood war epics.

By the end of the nineteenth-century, advances in technology allowed photos and news stories to reach a larger, more literate audience and thus have an even stronger impact on public opinion. During World War I, however, freedom of the press all but vanished. According to World War I censor Frederick Palmer, "There was not the freedom of the old days but there can never be again for the correspondent." By the Second World War, the media was expected to offer a balanced story, if it was to be published. Descriptions of American setbacks or tragedies had to be followed with uplifting passages and morale boosters.

World War II was perhaps the first American War to be referred to as the "censored war" due to pervasive news censorship. For specific examples, see the following entries: **Byron Price**; **WW II**; **Elmer Davis**; **Patton Slapping Incident**; **Stars and Stripes**; **War Photography**; and **Eye-Witness**. The following individuals were among those impacted by censorship: **Edward Kennedy**; **William Shirer**; **Frank Kluckholn**; and **Bill Mauldin**.

Fast forward to coverage of the Gulf War and beyond. The following entries help compare censorship in the two eras: **Gulf War; Embedded Journalists; Pooled Coverage; Iraq War; Unilaterals; WW II;** and **Michael Ware.**

Also compare the images from WW II with those from Vietnam and Lebanon, which tell a more complicated story. Can you pick out the soldiers? The casualties? The good guys vs. bad guys? What do these photos tell us about the nature of warfare that previous accounts do not? Compare, further, the U.S. Marine cradling the injured infant during World War II to the dead infants and civilians shown at the My Lai massacre. Has the nature of warfare changed? Or has the nature of the audience changed, now accustomed to the bloodshed and violence of the twentieth and twenty-first centuries?

How might have the photos and documents throughout this section impacted public opinion about various wars? Which would be most influential? Would they garner support for the war or against? In almost every war between the American Civil War and the Vietnam War images — and often news stories — released to the public in the latter stages of the conflict are more grim than those released in the war's early stages. What would account for this? A sign of war fatigue in the various corridors of power, resulting in fewer restrictions in bringing the war home to Americans? Do these documents and images promote or hurt morale at home? In the field?

By 2010, America's wars in Iraq and Afghanistan were the longest running wars in the nation's history. They were also the most journalistically censored, controlled and restricted of the modern era. Again, see the entries on the **Gulf War, Embedded Journalists, Pooled Coverage, Iraq War, Unilaterals,** and **Michael Ware.** If the ban on photographing the war dead was lifted earlier than 2009, would American support for these conflicts have been impacted?

As evidenced by the documents and photographs in this section, from the Mexican-American War to the current conflict in Afghanistan, one common denominator is the sheer horror of warfare experienced by those who fought or witnessed it. The earliest excerpt featuring the horrible wounds suffered by young men and the challenges they faced when returning to civilian life resonates with the modern avalanche of life-altering injuries faced by modern-day soldiers adapting to life on the home front. It was not until the Civil War photographs of Mathew Brady and Alexander Gardner were widely reproduced that the public was finally forced to reappraise its Victorian notions of war and glory. Surely there is little glory to be found in the following photos of Antietam battlefield, the Paris Commune, the Battle of Saipan, the massacres at My Lai and the Palestinian refugee camps, and the Beirut Marine Barracks. Nor do the accounts of bayonet combat during the Russo-Japanese War, being shot in the eye near the Battle of Chateau-Thierry during World War One, and the human detritus on D-Day beach elicit an urge to participate in what was once regarded as a gallant and noble endeavor.

Any consideration of the changing nature of war journalism must include the revolution in technology that has affected not only how news is covered but how quickly it is delivered to the public. The ease of transmission often saturates the public with so much immediate information that there is barely time to digest it. In some cases "war fatigue" is felt by readers and viewers who become inured to constant war coverage. As future generations of war journalists cover unavoidable new and horrific conflicts, advances in communication and technology will continue to determine how war is portrayed to an always-eager American public, hungry for news of war and glimpses of the battlefield.

Over the past five years, reporting from conflict zones has become increasingly more dangerous for all types of journalists. But, this hasn't stopped legions of amateurs and freelancers from attempting to get to the battle front in the hopes of capturing an exclusive story or photo. Communication and photographic technology have made the dissemination of news much easier for those not affiliated with major news organizations. The increasing sophistication of communications technology is illustrated by the inclusion of the new document, *Guide to Safely Using SATPHONES*. This guide elucidates the best practices for safely using communication technologies in war zones. Other new documents illustrating the measures that reporters should take to retain a modicum of safety include "Global Safety Principles and Practices" and a "Charter for the Safety of Journalists Working in War Zones or Dangerous Areas." War journalists have increasingly become targets in modern conflicts and cannot expect the traditional safety and treatment as neutrals as in recent conflicts. Moreover, the rise of the Islamic State and its beheading of **James Foley, Steven Sotloff, Kenji Goto** and others has demonstrated the sophistication of terrorist groups and other non-state actors as they broadcast images of executions and the destruction of cultural landmarks on various Internet sites.

Many of the ongoing conflicts have degenerated into local and regional conflicts, such as in **Somalia, Ukraine, Libya,** and the rise of the **Islamic State.** As a result the overwhelming majority of today's journalists that are killed, abducted, and imprisoned are local journalists. As this update to the 2nd edition demonstrates, thanks to the record keeping and reporting of such organizations as Reporters Without Borders and the Committee to Protect Journalists, researchers can now identify non-Western reporters and casualties who have become essential for the reporting of recent conflicts, such as in the case of many new entries in the 3rd edition.

Mexican-American War

Although rudimentary war correspondence existed prior to the Mexican-American War, with newspapers publishing unaccredited accounts of battles such as the Battle of New Orleans (1812), the modern war correspondent came of age during the Mexican-American War. This was accomplished due to advances in printmaking, the advent of photography and the telegraph ("the Victorian Internet") and better printing presses, which allowed news to be reported faster and farther. The following are dispatches from the New Orleans Daily Picayune. *Strategically located close to the Gulf of Mexico, it became the leading newspaper source for war news around the country. These excerpts demonstrate the continuum of war reporting between 1846 and 2010. The difficulties of reporting a large battle front (Oct. 17, November 4, 1846), the horrible wounds suffered by young men in war and the challenges they face when they return to civilian life (Nov. 14, 1846) are common themes throughout the ages. A main difference is time. What once took weeks and months by mail, steamboat, pony express and telegraph is now transmitted within moments of the action.*

New Orleans Daily Picayune
October 17, 1846

Express to California—The N.Y. *Sun* regards the conveyance of the news of the war from Washington to California as an extraordinary performance, well worthy of note. The declaration of the existence of war was made by the United States on the 13th of May, at Washington. Com. Sloat's proclamation of the conquest of California at Monterey is dated 6th July, fifty-four days after the United States declaration, and fifty-eight days after the victories on the Rio Grande. It speaks of the declaration of war by the United States, and of Gen. Taylor's taking

Matamoras. In conveying the news to the Pacific ocean, says the *Sun*, at the lowest calculation it would take six days from Washington to New Orleans, fifteen days thence to Chagres, two to Panama, and at least thirty-three days to Monterey—in all, about fifty-six days without steam.

New Orleans Daily Picayune
November 4, 1846

Victory of Monterey!

[SPECIAL CORRESPONDENCE]

Operations of the 1st and 3d Divisions in the attack on Monterey on the 20th, 21st, 22nd, and 23d September, 1846.

Editors Picayune—Having been with the 2nd Division during the operations of the Army against Monterey, I find no easy task to become familiarly acquainted with all the movements of the troops under the immediate command of Gen. Taylor. By riding over the ground with officers who participated in those sanguinary engagements, by many inquiries, and frequently referring to the reports and private journals of officers, as well as to the official maps, and by carefully noting down the information thus obtained, I feel confident that I can now give as correct an account of the operations of the divisions under Gen. Twiggs and Gen. Butler as will be published before the appearance of the regular reports. I only regret that it is impossible, in one, to furnish the public with those details which would possess so much of interest. This can only be done in the form of sketches and in that manner I propose to present to your readers the particulars of the gallant behavior of the different corps, as fast you will find room to publish them. At present I can only speak of the general operations on the east of the town. On the 19th

---

Source: *New Orleans Daily Picayune*: "Express to California," October 17, 1846; "Victory of Monterey," November 4, 1846; "Near Matamoras," November 14, 1846; "Map of Monterey," November 17, 1846.

September, the enemy opened their battery upon the mounted Texans, who acted as Gen. Taylor's escort. A reconnaissance was ordered this day....

H. (Christopher Haile)

New Orleans Daily Picayune
November 14, 1846

Near Matamoras, Nov. 1st, 1846

"....There is a young man with us, on his return home...who lost his right arm in battle at Monterey. I have frequently observed him since we started, for he walked nearly all the way from Monterey to Camargo with the short stump of his arm (not yet healed) dangling by his side. He cannot be more than 21, and has an intelligent countenance. Capt. Downing says he possesses great firmness and energy of character and behaved heroically in battle. He has likewise a fine mind, and would with, with a good education, undoubtedly become a valuable professional man. Young Williamson is a mechanic, and has, by the loss of his arm, been deprived of the means of educating, if not supporting himself. Our government will never remunerate him for the sacrifice he has made, or if it does in such cases, come too late. *Now* is the time for him, and others in his situation, to feel that his countrymen, *the people of his own State* particularly, are the friends of the brave and unfortunate who have so nobly shed their blood in the defense of the country's honor. Soon after Williamson was shot he passed by his commander with his gun in his left hand, and his right arm hanging down by the strips of skin not shot away, started for camp, two miles distant, was chased by the enemy's lancers, but succeeded in reaching camp with his gun and accoutrements, and went to the soldier to have his arm taken off! He has been walking about every days since."

H. (Christopher Haile)

New Orleans Daily Picayune
November 17, 1846

[written by editor in response to dispatch by reporter Haile]

Map of Monterey—We shall issue our extra to-day or to-morrow, containing a more full account of the part taken by Gen. Worth's division in the capture of Monterey than has yet appeared, accompanied by a true and faithful map of the city and its approaches. The latter was drawn by Lieut. Benjamin, and has been lithographed in excellent style by Messrs. Manouvrier & Snell of this city. The letters of our correspondent, Mr. Haile, have given a graphic synopsis of the part taken by Gen. Worth's Division, yet in the haste in which they were written many incidents were unavoidably omitted which possess interest. The present account would have appeared sooner but for the delay occasioned by the slow process of lithographing a sufficient number of maps.

Crimean War

Compared to the Mexican-American War, which was mostly covered by solitary correspondents, the Crimean War attracted groups of correspondents on foreign assignment, in numbers not seen before, with most representing the London press. It was also the first war systematically covered by photographers. Less than 50 years after the Napoleonic Wars, the Crimean War was the first collaboration between the former enemies France and England, a relationship that presaged their entente during World War I. War reporting and photography were still in their infancy and correspondents were expected to be self-supporting, providing their own meals, shelter and transportation as witnessed by Roger Fenton's portable darkroom which functioned as his quarters and his studio.

When photographer Roger Fenton made the transition from daguerreotype and calotype photography to the new wet-plate method (developed in 1852) he was faced with a major barrier; the glass plate for the negative had to be sensitized immediately with a coating of distilled water and silver nitrate before exposure and then developed immediately after. This necessitated transporting a complete darkroom in order to take picture and develop it in semi-darkness.

Before leaving England to cover the Crimean War, Fenton converted a wine merchant's vehicle, fitted it with yellow window panes, shutters, a cistern for water, and racks for dishes and chemical bottles into his trademark "photographic van." It was designed especially for the field and also contained a bed and washing facilities. His van was often the target of enemy artillery, perhaps mistaking it for an ammunition wagon. Since it took from three to twenty seconds per exposure his pictures were by necessity little more than posed sets. Fenton was sick for most of the three months he spent in the Crimea but his 360 photographs provide one of the best examples of early war journalism. Pictured is one of Fenton's assistants. *Photo, Roger Fenton, 1855*

This site is often referred to as the scene of the Charge of the Light Brigade, a well-known spot and frequently mentioned in letters written home by soldiers. By most accounts it was a coincidence that Alfred Lord Tennyson selected the title "Valley of Death" for his poem depicting the Charge of the Light Brigade, which more accurately was actually the Battle of Balaclava, and took place on the plain above Balaclava and not in a valley. *Photo, Roger Fenton, 1855*

Source: *Roger Fenton's Photographic Van* (1855) Roger Fenton, Victoria and Albert Museum, London; *Valley of Death* (1855) Fenton/James Robertson, Library of Congress.

The British considered Balaklava Harbor their lifeline, since it was from here that the army received all of its weapons and ammunition, supplies, food and animals required for its subsistence. *Photo, James Robertson, 1855*

The aftermath of the British assault on the Redan, a large Russian battery, which contained several guns and was protected with sand bags and big round baskets stuffed with earth called "gabions." After a three-day bombardment which saw almost 100,00 rounds of shot and shells launched on the Russian positions, the British briefly held it before being forced to withdraw after a Russian counter-attack. *Photo James Robertson, 1855*

Source: *Balaklava Harbour* (1855) James Robertson, National Army Museum, London; *The Interior of the Redan* (1855) James Robertson, National Army Museum, London.

Indian Mutiny

Variously known as the Sepoy Rebellion, the Indian Mutiny and India's First War of Independence when it broke out in 1857, the rebellion is thought to have been caused by the high caste officers in the Bengal Army, or by a rumor that ammunition was greased in either pork fat (unclean for Muslims) or beef tallow (unclean for Hindus). The British East India Company had an army of 40,000 British soldiers *and 200,000 Indian Sepoys, a combination of Muslim and Hindu soldiers. Felice Beato along with James Robertson took the most noted photographs of the Indian Mutiny. Their photographic business was known as Robertson, Beato and Company. Their pictures are distinct for showing some of the first photographs of battle casualties dead on the battlefield.*

Located outside of Lucknow, Secundra Bagh was the site of a fierce battle in November 1857. It was estimated that 2,000 Indians were killed and left to rot outside, where they were fed on by vultures and jackals. This picture was taken almost six months after the battle. Some suggest that Beato had these bones exhumed to liven up the picture. *Photo, Felice Beato, 1858*

Source: *Interior of the Secundra Bagh* (1858) Felice Beato, National Army Museum, London.

The garrison at Cawnpore, which Major-General Sir Hugh Wheeler tried to defend, pictured with British soldiers after the battle. After a three-week siege Wheeler surrendered the garrison with the promise of safe conduct by the Indian leader. Instead they were attacked and Wheeler reportedly killed near the broken building pillar on the left. *Photo, Felice Beato, 1858*

Source: *Part of the Barracks held by General Wheeler at Cawnpore after Bombardment* (1858) Felice Beato, National Army Museum, London.

Chinese Wars

*B*etween 1856 and 1860 the Chinese were engaged in a series of wars with the British over free trade issues. Much of the friction stemmed from the illegal importation of opium by British merchants.

The Taku Forts guarding Peking were surrounded by an elaborate system of obstacles that the Chinese had built. This photo was taken soon after the battle and British scaling ladders can still be seen on the left of this gun embrasure as well as bodies of dead defenders. One witness reported that Beato had asked the soldiers tasked with burning the dead to wait until the photo was taken. *Photo, Felice Beato, 1860*

Source: *Embrasure, Taku Fort (1860)* Felice Beato, National Army Museum, London.

American Civil War

The Union field hospital at Savage Station following the Battle of Fair Oaks, about a month after the May 31, 1862 battle. On June 29, 1862 Confederate troops attacked Savage Station. The following day Union troops retreated leaving behind most of these wounded and sick, who became prisoners-of-war. According to photographic historian Pat Hodgson the wounded are "waiting dejectedly to be taken prisoner." *Photo, James R. Gibson, 1862*

Considered one of the best images taken at the Battle of Antietam, this photo shows rows of dead soldiers in front of the Dunker Church. The shoes in right hand corner were probably removed as part of the traditional looting that followed battles. Oliver Wendell Holmes, while searching for his wounded son later wrote of such scenes, "Let him who wishes to know what war is look at this series of illustrations." *Photo, Alexander Gardner, 1862*

The first federal wagon train entering Petersburg, Virginia following the end of the siege. *Photo, John Reekie, 1865*

Franco-Prussian War

The Franco-Prussian War lasted for only ten months but witnessed one of the great battle in history—the Battle of Sedan. This war signaled a new era in war reporting, marking the first use of the wireless for transmitting news from the scene of battle. It was also one of the most thoroughly covered European conflicts up *to 1870, and the last war reported by the legendary William Howard Russell. Following his departure from the scene, a new era of war journalists would depend on the telegraph and cable facilities to speed news reports to the public no matter the costs.*

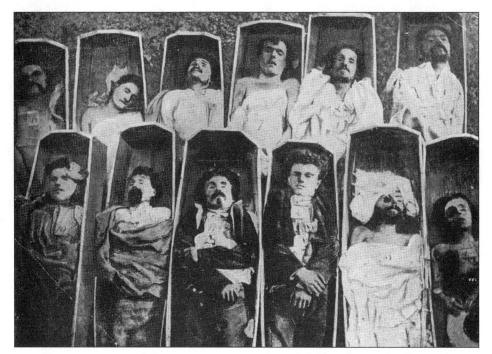

Versailles troops massacred almost 20,000 men, women and children during what became known as the "Bloody Week" between May 21-28, 1871. The dead were numbered, laid out for identification and buried in mass graves. *Photographer unknown, 1871*

Source: *Execution Scene Paris Commune* (1871), E. Appert, Radio Times Hulton Picture Library/Getty Images.

Spanish-American War

*D*espite being fairly short, the Spanish American War was covered by more reporters than any previous war in history. Estimates for journalists, photographers and artists have ranged as high as 500, although the actual number is probably much lower. Fought on the island of Cuba and later the Philippines, it was the most expensive war to cover until that time, with most costs related to communications. At the beginning of the war cables to the island had been cut forcing reporters to rely on dispatch boats to get their reports to the nearest telegraph or cable offices in Key West, Jamaica and the Virgin Islands.

Covered by Richard Harding Davis, the most eminent war journalist of his era, the fighting of Teddy Roosevelt's "Rough Riders" near San Juan Hill helped create the legend that eventually catapulted Roosevelt into the White House and the Rough Riders to iconic status. This classic account features a journalist in the heat of the action as men fall wounded and killed and the "fog of war" contributes to the confusion [and] names of wounded and dying (much of which would be censored today). Davis noted how much different his account was from the illustrations and pictures that immortalized the battle. "It was not heroic then, it seemed merely absurdly pathetic... I have seen many illustrations and pictures of the charge on the San Juan Hills, but none of them seem to show it just as I remember it."

Excerpt from: *Notes of A War Correspondent*

THE BATTLE OF SAN JUAN HILL

The enemy saw the advance and began firing with pitiless accuracy into the jammed and crowded trail and along the whole border of the woods. There was not a single yard of ground for a mile to the rear which was not inside the zone of fire. Our men were ordered not to return the fire but to lie still and wait for further orders. Some of them could see the rifle-pits of the enemy quite clearly and the men in them, but many saw nothing but the bushes under which they lay, and the high grass which seemed to burn when they pressed against it. It was during this period of waiting that the greater number of our men were killed. For one hour they lay on their rifles staring at the waving green stuff around them, while the bullets drove past incessantly, with savage insistence, cutting the grass again and again in hundreds of fresh places. Men in line sprang from the ground and sank back again with a groan, or rolled to one side clinging silently to an arm or shoulder. Behind the lines hospital stewards passed continually, drawing the wounded back to the streams, where they laid them in long rows, their feet touching the water's edge and their bodies supported by the muddy bank. Up and down the lines, and through the fords of the streams, mounted aides drove their horses at a gallop, as conspicuous a target as the steeple on a church, and one after another paid the price of his position and fell from his horse wounded or dead. Captain Mills fell as he was giving an order, shot through the forehead behind both eyes; Captain O'Neill, of the Rough Riders, as he said, "There is no Spanish bullet made that can kill me." Steel, Swift, Henry, each of them was shot out of his saddle.

Hidden in the trees above the streams, and above the trail, sharp-shooters and guerillas added a fresh terror to the wounded. There was no hiding from them. Their bullets came from every side. Their invisible smoke helped to keep their hiding-places secret, and in the incessant shriek of shrapnel and the spit of the Mausers, it was difficult to locate the reports of their rifles. They spared neither the wounded nor recognized the Red Cross; they killed the surgeons

---

Source: Richard Harding *Davis. Notes of A War Correspondent*. New York: Charles Scribner's and Sons. 1912. Chapter: "The Battle for San Juan Hill." Pp. 77-99.

and the stewards carrying the litters, and killed the wounded men on the litters. A guerilla in a tree above us shot one of the Rough Riders in the breast while I was helping him carry Captain Morton Henry to the dressing-station, the ball passing down through him, and a second shot, from the same tree, barely missed Henry as he lay on the ground where we had dropped him. He was already twice wounded and so covered with blood that no one could have mistaken his condition. The surgeons at work along the stream dressed the wounds with one eye cast aloft at the trees. It was not the Mauser bullets they feared, though they passed continuously, but too high to do their patients further harm, but the bullets of the sharp-shooters which struck fairly in among them, splashing in the water and scattering the pebbles. The sounds of the two bullets were as different as is the sharp pop of a soda-water bottle from the buzzing of an angry wasp.

For a time it seemed as though every second man was either killed or wounded; one came upon them lying behind the bush, under which they had crawled with some strange idea that it would protect them, or crouched under the bank of the stream, or lying on their stomachs and lapping up the water with the eagerness of thirsty dogs. As to their suffering, the wounded were magnificently silent, they neither complained nor groaned nor cursed.

"I've got a punctured tire," was their grim answer to inquiries. White men and colored men, veterans and recruits and volunteers, each lay waiting for the battle to begin or to end so that he might be carried away to safety, for the wounded were in as great danger after they were hit as though they were in the firing line, but none questioned nor complained.

I came across Lieutenant Roberts, of the Tenth Cavalry, lying under the roots of a tree beside the stream with three of his colored troopers stretched around him. He was shot through the intestines, and each of the three men with him was shot in the arm or leg. They had been

overlooked or forgotten, and we stumbled upon them only by the accident of losing our way. They had no knowledge as to how the battle was going or where their comrades were or where the enemy was. At any moment, for all they knew, the Spaniards might break through the bushes about them. It was a most lonely picture, the young lieutenant, half naked, and wet with his own blood, sitting upright beside the empty stream, and his three followers crouching at his feet like three faithful watch-dogs, each wearing his red badge of courage, with his black skin tanned to a haggard gray, and with his eyes fixed patiently on the white lips of his officer. When the white soldiers with me offered to carry him back to the dressing-station, the negroes resented it stiffly. "If the Lieutenant had been able to move, we would have carried him away long ago," said the sergeant, quite overlooking the fact that his arm was shattered.

"Oh, don't bother the surgeons about me," Roberts added, cheerfully. "They must be very busy. I can wait."

As yet, with all those killed and wounded, we had accomplished nothing—except to obey orders—which was to await further orders.

Colonel Roosevelt, on horseback, broke from the woods behind the line of the Ninth, and finding its men lying in his way, shouted: "If you don't wish to go forward, let my men pass." The junior officers of the Ninth, with their negroes, instantly sprang into line with the Rough Riders, and charged at the blue block-house on the right.

I speak of Roosevelt first because, with General Hawkins, who led Kent's division, notably the Sixth and Sixteenth Regulars, he was, without doubt, the most conspicuous figure in the charge. General Hawkins, with hair as white as snow, and yet far in advance of men thirty years his junior, was so noble a sight that you felt inclined to pray for his safety; on the other hand, Roosevelt, mounted high on horseback, and charging the rifle-pits at a gallop and quite alone, made you feel that you would like to cheer. He wore on his sombrero a blue polka-dot handkerchief, *à la* Havelock, which, as he advanced, floated out straight behind his head, like a guidon. Afterward, the men of his regiment who followed this flag, adopted a polka-dot handkerchief as the badge of the Rough Riders. These two officers were notably conspicuous in the charge, but no one can claim that any two men, or any one man, was more brave or more daring, or showed greater courage in that slow, stubborn advance, than did any of the others. Some one asked one of the officers if he had any difficulty in making his men follow him. "No," he answered, "I had some difficulty in keeping up with them." As one of the brigade generals said; "San Juan was won by the regimental officers and men. We had as little to do as the referee at a prize-fight who calls 'time.' We called 'time' and they did the fighting."

I have seen many illustrations and pictures of this charge on the San Juan hills, but none of them seem to show it just as I remember it. In the picture-papers the men are running uphill swiftly and gallantly, in regular formation, rank after rank, with flags flying, their eyes aflame, and their hair streaming, their bayonets fixed, in long, brilliant lines, an invincible, overpowering weight of numbers. Instead of which I think the thing which impressed one the most, when our men started from cover, was that they were so few. It seemed as if some one had made an awful and terrible mistake. One's instinct was to call to them to come back. You felt that some one had blundered and that these few men were blindly following out some madman's mad order. It was not heroic then, it seemed merely absurdly pathetic. The pity of it, the folly of such a sacrifice was what held you.

They had no glittering bayonets, they were not massed in regular array. There were a few men in advance, bunched together, and creeping up a steep, sunny hill, the tops of which roared and flashed with flame. The men held their guns pressed across their chests and

stepped heavily as they climbed. Behind these first few, spreading out like a fan, were single lines of men, slipping and scrambling in the smooth grass, moving forward with difficulty, as though they were wading waist high through water, moving slowly, carefully, with strenuous effort. It was much more wonderful than any swinging charge could have been. They walked to greet death at every step, many of them, as they advanced, sinking suddenly or pitching forward and disappearing in the high grass, but the others waded on, stubbornly, forming a thin blue line that kept creeping higher and higher up the hill. It was as inevitable as the rising tide. It was a miracle of self-sacrifice, a triumph of bull-dog courage, which one watched breathless with wonder. The fire of the Spanish riflemen, who still stuck bravely to their posts, double and trebled in fierceness, the crests of the hills crackled and burst in amazed roars, and rippled with waves of tiny flame. But the blue line crept steadily up and on, and then, near the top, the broken fragments gathered together with a sudden burst of speed, the Spaniards appeared for a moment outlined against the sky and poised for instant flight, fired a last volley, and fled before the swift-moving wave that leaped and sprang after them.

The men of the Ninth and the Rough Riders rushed to the block-house together, the men of the Sixth, of the Third, of the Tenth Calvary, of the Sixth and Sixteenth Infantry, fell on their faces along the crest of the hills beyond, and opened upon the vanishing enemy. They drove the yellow silk flags of the cavalry and the flag of their country into the soft earth of the trenches, and then sank down and looked back at the road they had climbed and swung their hats in the air. And from far overhead, from these few figures perched on the Spanish rifle-pits, with their flags planted among the empty cartridges of the enemy, and overlooking the walls of Santiago, came, faintly, the sound of a tired, broken cheer.

Photos from *Men With the Bark On*

Remington Illustrations

A double threat with pen and brush, the war artist and journalist Frederic Remington covered the Spanish-American War often alongside reporter Richard Harding Davis. Remington illustrated some of Davis's articles as well as wrote his own. He famously wrote newspaper publisher William Randolph Hearst upon his arrival there, "Everything is quiet. There is no trouble here. There will be no war. I wish to return." Hearst responded even more famously, "Please remain. You furnish the pictures. I'll furnish the war." He kept his word and Remington captured virtually every facet of the three-month war. The following four illustrations capture the combat and casualties during the Battle of Santiago. The best known actions during the battle took place near San Juan and Kettle Hills. It was here that Teddy Roosevelt became an American hero.

"AT THE BLOODY FORD OF THE SAN JUAN"

Source: Frederic Remington. *Men With the Bark On*. New York: Harper and Brothers Publishing. 1900. Chapter: "With the Fifth Corps." Pp. 171-209.

"BEFORE THE WARNING SCREAM OF THE SHRAPNEL"

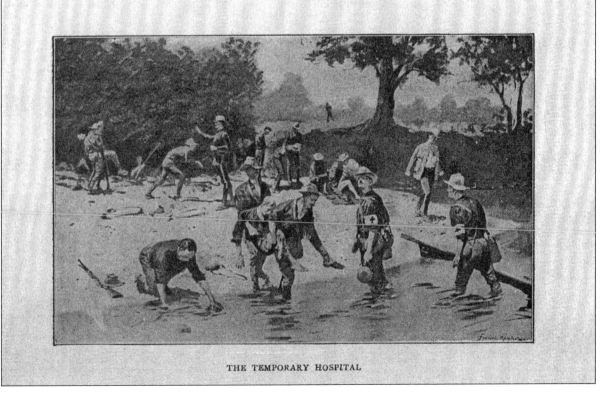

THE TEMPORARY HOSPITAL

"IN THE REAR OF THE BATTLE—WOUNDED ON THE SAN JUAN ROAD"

Boer War

The Boer War was the most widely reported British war before the twentieth century, with more than 300 correspondents covering the conflict. It was the bloodiest engagement fought by the British between the end of the Napoleonic Wars in 1815 and World War I. Fifteen *British correspondents would die in the conflict. However, what most distinguished the war coverage was the number of photographers and the first cameramen, with London's illustrated papers reportedly surviving solely on Boer War photographs.*

Photos of dead British soldiers such as this were used as propaganda by the Boers not only to encourage their own troops with pictures of mass British casualties but to bring the folly of war home to a British public unused to such realistic carnage. The British suffered 1,200 casualties while attempting to take this high point on the hills guarding the route to Ladysmith. *Photographer unknown, 1900*

Source: *The Battlefield: Spion Kop* (1900) Boer photographer, Radio Times Hulton Picture Library/Getty Images.

Russo-Japanese War

This was the first conflict in which a wireless was used for transmitting dispatches to home offices. More than 200 journalists covered the war, the majority from the Japanese side. However, battlefront coverage was strictly controlled and correspondents were never permitted to get closer than three miles from the front lines. As a result, many departed before the conflict ended. The following excerpts collected in Frederick Palmer's book With Kuroki in Manchuria *offer a microcosm of what most journalists were up against while covering the war. He describes the challenges of what he called the "Great System." Following the Japanese forces, Palmer witnesses the battle front from a distance and only gets close after it is over. It is at this point that he is best able to bring the horror of conflict home to his readers, describing the death and destruction left in the wake of battle. Ultimately Japanese censorship prevented western correspondents from witnessing most of the decisive battles, concerned that foreign journalists might be acting as spies. Palmer took advantage of some down time to interview soldiers, one of whom instructs the reporter on the utilization of the bayonet in combat.*

Excerpt from: *With Kuroki in Manchuria*

A Correspondent's Life in Manchuria

This is less about myself than about those who have intimately concerned my existence for the last four months, with results sometimes strange and sometimes humorous. While the army has waged occasional battles, the correspondent has waged a continuous one.

When the original sixteen assigned to the First Army started, we had a contract with a Mr. Yokoyama to feed us and transport our baggage. On demand he was to keep up with a column that was going at the rate of fifteen miles a day. Mr. Yokoyama was the victim of misinformation, a delusion, and the correspondents, and we were the victims of Mr. Yokoyama.

In order to feed us in a mess, naturally he had to keep us together. We were landed at Chenampo over two hundred miles from the front. Possibly the staff had that fifteen miles a day in view and thought that we would arrive in a decorous body, for that was four months ago, I repeat, when the Great System that serenely plays havoc with Russian inefficiency had as yet had no field experience with one phase of war – the correspondents – for which the Great System had not duly provided. The sixteen did not wait on fifteen miles a day. They went as many miles as they could, each his own way, whether donkeyback, horseback, or on foot. The canteen struggled on, coolie borne, after individuals who cared little whether they were fed or not till they reached their destination.

These draggled, muddy men in all kinds of habits rode into a general's headquarters which was the centre of the precise movement of fifty thousand men in one uniform, and boldly they looked if they did not ask the question: "Now bring on your battle! We're all ready."

The Great System was busy. It really had no place for spectators, particularly at rehearsals. It set the limits of the correspondents' observations on the hither side of hills that hid the portentous work of engineers on the river bank. There the strange order of beings that had run away from their transport – the only beings in all that vast hive of industry who were not moving a pontoon, digging a gun position, building a road or doing something toward the army's object – dwelt grimly in isolation in a group of Korean houses. They had traveled ten thousand miles; they had waited two months in Tokio, and bitter memory reminded them that they had been sent to the front as war correspondents.

Source: Frederick Palmer. *With Kuroki in Manchuria*. New York: Collier's Weekly and Charles Scribner's. 1904. Chapter XVIII: "A Correspondent's Life in Manchuria." Pp. 219-231.

. . .

The Great System decided that one correspondent might come from their "compound" each day and get the news for all. This was like standing outside the inclosure and having a man on the fence tell you who has the ball on whose fifteen-yard line. The Great System could not understand that it existed solely for getting a "beat" for each individual paper. Some correspondents had previously complained that they had not had the privileges accorded to others. This led the Great System to make a point of insistent impartiality. Then there were growls because it was not partial. Truly the Great System must have been sorely puzzled. When the Great System was ready to give our cue, we were taken to heights where we saw the artillery duel of one day and the battle of the next. Still some correspondents were inclined to demand their money back at the box-office. No one man had seen more than any other.

Meanwhile, the canteen in broken parts had arrived and set up its tent among the Korean houses where the correspondents were encamped. Mr. Yokoyama had not come to Korea himself. His affairs were in the hands of a manager. The manager could not speak any English. This saved him many comments, which were toned down by indirection. One can not in reason send for an interpreter to say things that are better not printed, such, for example, as "Oh, ---."

Mr. Yokoyama had taken his idea of a campaigner's diet from the tourists who frequent the hotels of Japan. He thought they subsisted entirely upon meat. He had brought only a little to eat, and that consisted mostly of canned sausage.

Aside from feeding us for the stipulated sum, the canteen was to bring mineral waters on sale. In mentioning our wants before we left Tokio, one correspondent had remarked that a little champagne was good in case of sickness. Evidently Yokoyama thought that we were all going to be ill all the time. (For there is a bar in the Imperial Hotel frequented by tourists.) He brought far more bottles of champagne than sausages – and the champagne was as sugary sweet as ever Latin drank. Our meals became town meetings, where individuals – and there are as many individuals among the correspondents as there are divisions in the army – set out their likes and dislikes.

. . .

The Battle Front

From a hill nearby Liaoyang was visible, and I could see in the gathering dusk the positions of the forces. The town was no longer a patch of silence on the plain. It lay between two hells. On one side, on the plain, were the Japanese batteries; and on the other, across the river, were the Russian. You marked their positions as you would a line of gas-jets. The air was full of the lightning of shrapnel bursts. I was witnessing the last act in the drama. Only a rearguard remained yet to cross the bridges and then destroy them.

The Second and Fourth Armies were held back by a stream which could be forded by only a few men at a time in a few places. Kuropatkin's whole force of two hundred thousand was on the same side of the Taitse as the First Army. Facing the line of the enemy's retreat, Kuroki must be a spectator of its passing. His two divisions and his extra brigade were before six or seven times their number. Fresh reserves were marching in from Mukden and the divisions that had fought Oku and Nodzu were crowding against our left. Though the onlookers could not see the Russian columns, we realized the pressure of their mass as you realize by the draught that the door of a darkened room has been opened. There was imminent danger of the Twelfth being enveloped. Kuroki sent for the Guards to cross the river in reinforcement. They came – as many of them as had the strength. Those who had not fell asleep in their tracks, with hot stones for pillows.

At this critical juncture our communication with the main army was cut. We were isolated – a fair prize, indeed, for Kuropatkin's divisions if he realized his opportunity. Probably he did realize it and probably his soldiers were as tired as ours. The staff which I had watched on many fields for the first time gave the order to retreat. But no sooner were the orders for the Twelfth to fall back received over the wires than communication with Grand Headquarters was resumed and the pressure from the Russians ceased.

. . .

After the Battle

Vaguely, the army comprehended that it had won a victory. Definitely, it realized only that it had won the right to rest. The observer, with all restrictions removed, on the morning of the 4th hurried to Hayentai through the paths in the *kowliang* that the ammunition ponies had made. Mounds of earth with ideograph posts surmounting them did not cover all the Japanese that had fallen in the fight for the "little hill." Many more were being burned on the Japanese side of the slope.

On the Russian side, the Russian dead were being dragged to trenches. Looking west from the summit, Hayentai descends to level fields, which, a little to the right, are cut by a sunken path that carries away the heavy rains of summer. This had given the Russians cover for their assault. This had called to them in their panic, when the Japanese forced them to flee. Here the faces of the dead were upturned like the faces of passengers coming up a gangway and looking aloft to the people on the next deck.

As a hog roots up the turf for nuts, so the Japanese common shells had ploughed the earth. Brass cartridge-cases, shrapnel bullets, bits of "first-aid" bandages and bits of Russian brown bread and buttons and clothing overspread the position. In a pile was such of the harvest of victory as was worth collecting. Russian and Japanese pannikins, punctured by rifle-fire and torn by shrapnel, and Russian and Japanese caps, slashed by bayonets, were thrown together.

I picked up a number of cartridges which bullets had struck. There was a bayonet that a bullet had bent into a triangle; there were rifle butts that had been shattered by shells into kindling wood. The most pathetic of all were the little blue-bound books which every Russian soldier carries. In these are entered his name, the time of his enlistment and other facts for identification. On more than one the last entry was made by a bullet and the ink it used was blood. The four drums were, in a sense, pathetic too. Their heads were in ribbons.

In this age of high organization, some officers who sit in routine facing rows of pigeon-holes will tell you that war is entirely made with brains nowadays. All such should have seen Hayentai. There they would have learned that the taking of critical points which are essential to academic plans still depends upon brute butchery or brute courage. The visitor would have slipped in blood instead of dew. Like round figures on a carpet, the clots were set off on the earth where the grass was matted and worn away by struggle. It needed mincing steps to touch every one if you walked in a straight line. In a dozen places I saw red paths where wounded men had dragged themselves away into the *kowliang*. Following one of these, I came to the coagulation which told the story of the death agony.

The marvelous thing was that, at one period of the struggle, if a wounded man could only take himself ten feet to the rear, he was safe. Where the rounding crest dipped on either side, twenty feet apart, for a time the Russian and the Japanese lines had lain in the dark firing at the flashes of each others' rifles. Slipping down the hillside, with the bullets whistling overhead like a gale through the rigging, you were as much out of the danger zone temporarily as if you had been in Mukden. The positions were clearly marked by the systematic arrangement of the blood-clots.

Was not there ugly work? Was quarter always given? I have been asked. My answer is that all was ugly work. Any one who does not palliate it, in order to be consistent, must let a burglar in his own house shoot at him without firing in response. In such a situation, soldiers are not waiting on injunctions from a court to restrain the enemy's violence. Their articulations become less like human speech than like savage cries. They are the ghosts of the individuals who line up on parade; ghosts trying to fight their way out of hell. The big man thrust at every little man, and the little man thrust at every big man; and the big man used his bayonet in powerful lunges as the bull does his horns; the little man as a panther uses his claws. The Japanese officer, disregarding the sword of Europe – that decadent product of social functions – carried their *samurai* blades, which are made for killing.

When I visited the military schools in Tokio in 1901, as I watched the cadets fencing according to Japanese fashion, I remarked: "That must be splendid training for the eye, and grand exercise."

"And extremely useful," an officer replied.

It was about this time that Herr Bloch got his name frequently printed in all the papers on account of his book, which held that modern arms of precision would not allow armies to approach each other.

. . .

Soldiers and Bayonets

I spoke with one of the veterans, a Sendai man. "You want to use your bayonet with your arms, not your body." (He spoke as a cook would say: "The whites of two eggs well beaten:, etc.) "The Russky uses his bayonet with his body. He sticks his head down and rushes at you. If he catches you, you are spitted for good. His is such a big fellow that he lifts you fairly off your feet. If you are quick on your legs, though, you can step to one side, and then you have him; the only way with little men with short arms is to get in close.

"The first time I went into a night attack I kept thinking of all that my officer told me. I felt like I did when I went in as a recruit, and the surgeon felt me all over."

"Stage fright," I suggested.

But a country boy from Sendai, though he had studied his English primer well, and tried to improve himself so as to rise in the world, did not understand that. At least, I did not think he did, by the operation of his Japanese smile.

"The first time I struck a Russian I could feel my bayonet grate on his bone," he went on. "I did not think of it at the time, but when I thought of it afterward it seemed very awful. I had seen him coming like a big black shadow, and I had just time to dodge, and I felt his bayonet go by my cheek like a razor does over your face. I pulled my bayonet out and sunk it in his neck before he had time strike me. If I had not killed him he would have killed me. It is that way always. Night before last, I----"

He told me many other things, this intelligent private. Among them was how it happened that frequently he forgot to fire when firing would have been much wiser. Many who have died from bayonet thrusts have had cartridges still in their rifle chambers. When a man comes to close quarters he seems instinctively to grapple. He reverts from science to nature, and nature's method.

World War I

More correspondents and photographers from America covered this war than from any other country. It also turned out to be one of the safest wars to cover. No civilian correspondents were killed in the war although a number were wounded. In the following excerpt, noted reporter Floyd Gibbons describes how it felt to be shot and the story behind his trademark eye patch. It also conveys the perils of covering battles on one's own initiative. Although he was told that he could "Go wherever you like" he was warned that "it's damn hot up there" where he was headed.

Excerpt from: *And They Thought We Wouldn't Fight*

. . .

Wounded – How It Feels To Be Shot

Just how does it feel to be shot on the field of battle? Just what is the exact sensation when a bullet burns its way through your flesh or crashes through your bones?

It happened on June 6th just to the northwest of Chateau-Thierry in the Bois de Belleau. On the morning of that day I left Paris by motor for a rush to the front. The Germans were on that day within forty miles of the capital of France.

"Go wherever you like," said the regimental commander, looking up from the outspread maps on the kitchen table in the low-ceilinged stone farm-house that he had adopted as headquarters. "Go as far as you like, but I want to tell you it's damn hot up there."

An hour later found us in the woods to the west of the village of Lucy le Bocage, in which German shells were continually falling. To the west and north another nameless cluster of farm dwellings was in flames. Huge clouds of smoke rolled up like a smudge against the background of blue sky.

The ground under the trees in the wood was covered with small bits of white paper. I could not account for their presence until I examined several of them and found that these were letters from American mothers and wives and sweethearts – letters – whole packages of them, which the tired, dog-weary Marines had been forced to remove from their packs and destroy in order to ease the straps that cut into aching grooves in their shoulders. Circumstances also forced the abandonment of much other material and equipment.

Occasional shells were dropping in the woods, which were also within range from a long distance, indirect machine gun fire from the enemy. Bits of lead, wobbling in their flight at the end of their long trajectory, sung through the air above our heads and clipped leaves and twigs from the branches. On the edge of the woods we came upon a hastily dug out pit in which there were two American machine guns and their crews.

The field in front of the woods sloped gently down some two hundred yards to another cluster of trees. This cluster was almost as big as the one we were in. Part of it was occupied by the Germans. Our machine gunners maintained a continual fire into that part held by the enemy.

Five minutes before five o'clock, the order for the advance reached our pit. It was brought there by a second lieutenant, a platoon commander.

"What are you doing here?" he asked, looking at the green brassard and red "C" on my left arm.

"Looking for the big story," I said.

"If I were you I'd be about forty miles south of this place," said the Lieutenant, "but if you want to see the fun, stick around. We are going forward in five minutes."

Source: Floyd Gibbons. *And They Thought We Wouldn't Fight*, New York: George Doran Co. 1918. Chapter XVI: "Wounded—How It Feels to be Shot." Pp. 305-322.

That was the last I saw of him until days later, when both us, wounded, met in the hospital. Of course, the first thing he said was, "I told you so."

We hurriedly finished the contents of the can of cold "Corned Willy" which one of the machine gunners and I were eating. The machine guns were taken down and the barrels, cradles and tripods were handed over to the members of the crew whose duties it was to carry them.

And then we went over. There are really no heroics about it. There is no bugle call, no sword waving, no dramatic enunciation of catchy commands, no theatricalism — it's just plain get up and go over. And it is done just the same as one would walk across a peaceful wheatfield out in Iowa.

But with the appearance of our first line, as it stepped from the shelter of the woods into the open exposure of the flat field, the woods opposite began to cackle and rattle with the enemy machine gun fire. Our men advanced in open order, ten and twelve feet between men. Sometimes a squad would run forward fifty feet and drop. And as its members flattened on the ground for safety, another squad would rise from the ground and make another rush.

They gained the woods. Then we could hear shouting. Then we knew that work was being done with the bayonet. The machine gun fire continued in intensity and then died down completely. The wood had been won. Our men consolidated the position by moving forward in groups ever on the watch-out for snipers in the trees. A number of these were brought down by our crack pistol shots.

At different times during the advance runners had come through the woods inquiring for Major John Berry, the battalion commander. One of these runners attached himself to Lieutenant Hartzell and myself and together the three of us located the Major coming through the woods. He granted permission for Lieutenant Hartzell and me to accompany him and we started forward, in all a party of some fifteen, including ten runners attached to the battalion commander.

Owing to the continual evidences of German snipers in the trees, every one in our party carried a revolver ready in his hand, with the exception of myself. Correspondent, you will remember, are non-combatants and must be unarmed. I carried a notebook, but it was loaded. We made our way down the slope of the wooded hillside.

Midway down the slope, the hill was bisected by a sunken road which turned forward on the left. Lying in the road were a number of French bodies and several of our men who had been brought down but five minutes before. We crossed that road hurriedly knowing that it was covered from the left by German machine guns.

At the bottom of the slope there was a V-shaped field. The apex of the V was on the left. From left to right the field was some two hundred yards in width. The point where we came out of the woods was about one hundred yards from the apex. At that point the field was about one hundred yards across. It was perfectly flat and was covered with a young crop of oats between ten and fifteen inches high.

This V-shaped oat field was bordered on all sides by dense clusters of trees. In the trees on the side opposite the side on which we stood, were German machine guns. We could hear them. We could not see them but we knew that every leaf and piece of greenery there vibrated from their fire and the tops of the young oats waved and swayed with the streams of lead that swept across.

Major Berry gave orders for us to follow him at intervals of ten or fifteen yards. Then he started across the field alone at the head of the party. I followed. Behind me came Hartzell. Then the woods about us began to rattle fiercely. It was unusually close range. That lead traveled so fast that we could not hear it as it passed. We soon had visual demonstration of the hot place we were in when we began to see the dust puffs that the bullets kicked up in the dirt around our feet.

Major Berry had advanced well beyond the centre of the field when I saw him turn toward me and hear him shout: "Get down everybody."

We all fell on our faces. And then it began to come hot and fast. Perfectly withering volleys of lead swept the tops of the oats just over us. For some reason it did not seem to be coming from the trees hardly a hundred yards in front of us. It was coming from a new direction – from the left.

I was busily engaged flattening myself on the ground. Then I heard a shout in front of me. t came from Major Berry. I lifted my head cautiously and looked forward. The Major was making an effort to get to his feet. With his right hand he was savagely grasping his left wrist.

"My hand's gone," he shouted. One of the streams of lead from the left had found him. A ball had entered his left arm at the elbow, had travelled down the side of the bone, tearing away muscles and nerves of the forearm and lodging itself in the palm of his hand. His pain was excruciating.

"Get down. Flatten out, Major," I shouted, and he dropped to the ground. I did not know the extent of his injuries at that time but I did know that he was courting death every minute he stood up.

"We've got to get out of here," said the Major. "We've got to get forward. They'll start shelling this open field in a few minutes."

I lifted my head for another cautious look.

I judged that I was lying about thirty yards from the edge of the trees in front of us. The Major was about ten yards in front of me.

"You are twenty yards from the trees," I shouted to the Major. "I am crawling over to you now. Wait until I get there and I'll help you. Then we'll get up and make a dash for it.

"All right," replied the Major, "hurry along."

I started forward, keeping as flat on the ground as it was possible to do so and at the same time move. As far as was feasible, I pushed forward by digging in with my toes and elbows extended in front of me. It was my object to

make as little movement in the oats as possible. I was not mistaken about the intensity of fire that swept in the field. It was terrific.

And then it happened. The lighted end of a cigarette touched me in the fleshy part of my upper left arm. That was all. It just felt like a sudden burn and nothing worse. The burned part did not seem to be any larger in area than that part which could be burned by the lighted end of a cigarette.

At the time there was no feeling within the arm, that is, no feeling as to aches or pain. There was nothing to indicate that the bullet, as I learned several days later, had gone through the bicep muscle of the upper arm and had come out on the other side. The only sensation perceptible at the time was the burning touch at the spot where the bullet entered.

I glanced down at the sleeve of my uniformed coat and could not even see the hole where the bullet had entered. Neither was there any sudden flow of blood. At the time there was no stiffness or discomfort in the arm and I continued to use it to work my way forward.

Then the second one hit. It nicked the top of my left shoulder. And again came the burning sensation, only this time the area affected seemed larger. Hitting as it did in the meaty cap of the shoulder, I feared that there would be no further use for the arm until it had received attention, but again I was surprised when I found upon experiment that I could still use it. The bone seemed to be affected in no way.

Again there was no sudden flow of blood, nor stiffness. It seemed hard for me to believe at the time, but I had been shot twice, penetrated through by two bullets and was experiencing not any more pain that I had experienced once when I dropped a lighted cigarette on the back of my hand. I am certain that the pain in no way approached that sensation which the dentist provides when he drills into a tooth with a live nerve in it.

So I continued to move toward the Major. Occasionally I would shout something to him, although, at this time, I am unable to remember what it was. I only wanted to let him know I was coming. I had fears, based on the one look that I had obtained of his pain-distorted face, that he had been mortally shot in the body.

And then the third one struck me. In order to keep as close to the ground as possible, I had swung my chin to the right so that I was pushing forward with my left cheek flat against the ground and, in order to accommodate this position of the head, I had moved my steel helmet over so that it covered part of my face on the right.

Then there came a crash. It sounded to me like someone had dropped a glass bottle into a porcelain bathtub. A barrel of whitewash tipped over and it seemed that everything in the world turned white. That was the sensation. I did not recognize it because I have often been led to believe and often heard it said that when one receives a blow on the head everything turns black.

Maybe I am contrarily constructed, but in my case everything became pure white. I remember this distinctly because my years of newspaper training had been in but one direction – to sense and remember. So it was that, even without knowing it, my mind was making mental notes on every impression that my senses registered.

I did not know yet where I had been hit or what the bullet had done. I knew that I was still knowing things. I did not know whether I was alive or dead but I did know that my mind was still working. I was still mentally taking notes on every second.

The first recess in that note-taking came when I asked myself the following question: "Am I dead?"

I didn't laugh or didn't even smile when I asked myself the question without putting it in words. I wanted to know. And wanting to know, I undertook to find out. I am not aware now that

there was any appreciable passage of time during this mental progress. I feel certain, however, that I never lost consciousness.

How was I to find out if I was dead? The shock had lifted my head off the ground but I had immediately replaced it as close to the soil as possible. My twice punctured left arm was lying alongside my body. I decided to try and move my fingers on my left hand. I did so and they moved. I next moved my left foot. Then I knew I was alive.

Then I brought my right hand up toward my face and placed it to the left of my nose. My fingers rested on something soft and wet. I withdrew the hand and looked at it. It was covered with blood. As I looked at it, I was not aware that my entire vision was confined to my right eye, although there was considerable pain in the entire left side of my face.

This was sufficient to send me on another mental investigation. I closed my right eye and – all was dark. My first thought following this experiment was that my left eye was closed. So I again counselled with myself and tried to open my left eye – that is, tried to give the mental command that would cause the muscles of the left eye to open the lid and close it again.

I did this but could not feel or verify in any way whether the eye lid responded or not. I only knew that it remained dark on that side. This brought me to another conclusion and not a pessimistic one at that. I simply believed, in spite of the pain, that something had struck me in the eye and had closed it.

I did not know then, as I know now, that a bullet striking the ground immediately under my left cheek bone, had ricochetted upward, going completely through the left eye and then crashing out through my forehead, leaving the eyeball and upper eyelid completely halved, the lower eyelid torn away, and a compound fracture of the skull.

Spanish Civil War

*T*he Spanish Civil War proved to be one of the more confusing and dangerous wars for correspondents descending on the conflict. Most of the correspondents were committed ideologically to the Republican side and covered the war with a passion unmatched in previous conflicts. As a result, objectivity often suffered as many correspondents joined the Republicans at the battle front.

Typically referred to as "The Falling Soldier" this is one of the most controversial war photos of all time. It depicts a Loyalist soldier being shot and falling as he attacked Republican lines. The authenticity of the photo has been challenged for more than 40 years. As of 2010 there is still no consensus as to its authenticity. Capturing a soldier at the moment of death has long been the "Holy Grail" for war photographers as the debate over this photo continues. *Photo, Robert Capa, 1936*

Source: *Loyalist Militiaman at Moment of Death* (September 5, 1936) Robert Capa, Magnum Photos.

World War II

*I*t has been estimated that more than 3,000 correspondents covered the various phases of World War II. Each theater of the war offered varying degrees of press freedom and war correspondents were regarded as vital components of the war effort as long as they produced favorable reports. Due to the exigencies of covering a world conflict journalists found it almost impossible to follow the action without the assistance of the military and therefore were prone to offer less critical accounts.

The following accounts by Richard Strout, James Wellard, George Sessions Perry, Quentin Reynolds, and Ernie Pyle, capture various operations in the European theater of the war. In "Shot-by-Shot" Strout, watches the Normany Invasion from the relative safety of a ship, commenting that he "never imagined it would be like this." He noted that "We can't really tell what's happening," but was careful to put a patriotic plug in for the Allies by adding, "but we can't lose."

James Wellard observes the "Last Fantastic Battle" in Germany in May 1945, which he compares to a "scene [that] was like something out of Dante's inferno" along the river bank. George Sessions Perry describes scenes from the 1943 invasion of Sicily, and Quentin Reynolds offers his account of what was an unsuccessful attack on Dieppe, France. He explains the complexities of sea to shore operations and the incumbent dangers of both positions. With such a complicated operation he asks himself, "had the raid been a success?" On one hand he critiques the strategy of not using parachute troops and air bombardment but makes sure to extol the virtues of the Allied soldiers, noting, "Given the opportunity, the British and Canadians fight like Russians. That is nice to know."

Ernie Pyle captures the tragic aftermath of D-Day in "A Long Thin Line of Anguish." He walks the beaches and finds human detritus along the beach — silent testimony to the young

lives lost — including a tennis racket, a lost dog, and lifebelts. He offers insight into what he calls the "Horrible Waste of War" by focusing on the "awful waste and destruction of war."

Excerpt from: *Typewritter Battalian*

Shot-by-Shot Stories of D-Day

ON BOARD THE HEAVY CRUISER U.S.S. QUINCY OFF FRANCE, June 7, 1944-This is a round-by-round story of the invasion of France and the opening of the Second Front.

It covers the secret passage of the invasion fleet under fire and the most glorious sight of the arrival by glider of 10,000 air-borne troops.

The battle continues as this is written.

The ship jolts with the explosion of shells.

But one thing is certain. Our beachhead is established.

The degree of organization disclosed is so amazing as to augur Hitler's overthrow.

The story begins on the open bridge of a United States heavy cruiser (the U.S.S. Quincy), Capt. Elliott M. Senn, United States Navy, commanding.

It is 2 p.m. Monday, June 5. I am standing under the sky. I am dictating this story as it happens.

We have just left our anchorage. We are headed almost due east in a single line of capital ships flanked by outriders. History hangs on the weather.

On our left are the cliffs of England. We are in an Anglo-American task force. The ships' names mingle like a chant. Those of the British have come down through history. The American names sing of the New World.

Our vessel, with its home port at Boston, is one of the fleet's newest and finest. There is another task force. The combined flotilla with

Source: Richard L. Strout. "*Shot-by-Shot Story of D-Day*," Christian Science Monitor, June 7, 1944, Reprinted in Jack Stenbuck, ed. *Typewriter Battalion*. New York: William Morrow and Company. 1995. Pp. 163-172.

landing craft will be vast. There are French, Dutch and Norwegian ships.

Already, another convoy is visible carrying its own barrage balloons.

The sky is overcast. The sea is lead-colored but quiet. There is hardly any wind. Even a squall no worse than last night's would hamper landing craft, result in thousands of casualties, maybe upset the whole show. Well, we have done what we can-the weather is nature's business.

This high, open bridge covers three sides. Forward and below are three decks and gunturrets. The biggest turrets carry triple sticks of long range, dangerous-looking guns.

The prow comes to a razor edge. Like most of man's weapons, this appears beautiful. It is slim as a race horse, rhythmic as a poem. It is so new that 1,000 of its crew are green. They speak every American accent. This spot is a magnificent grandstand seat for history's greatest show.

P.M. We have overtaken and are passing the landing craft fleet formerly seen on the horizon. They make slow headway; their barrage balloons tied front and stern of larger craft tug ahead as though pulling.

These craft are chock-full of assault troops and supplies. They will catch up to us as we anchor in the night.

6 P.M. We have hoisted a fresh, clean battle flag. It will fly there till the engagement is over. Blue-coated figures in steel helmets are sweeping the sky and sea around me, chanting observations like football quarterbacks.

The air is tense and the men are consciously trying to break the suspense by horseplay. This has gone on for weeks. Our ship has known its mission and has been sealed. Now that it is coming the gun crew is skipping rope.

We are leaving England. The great adventure begins. The coast-line fades as we steam slowly. Right under the haze close to the distant shore is another line of vessels, alternating big and little ones, moving our way stealthily under the shore line.

We look and wonder. Something marvelous is going on. All the world's ships seem to be going our way.

Rumors fly about. Yesterday, at the peak of uncertainty, came the radio news that a New York press association had falsely reported the invasion already under way. I have been asked dozens of times if this kills the whole thing.

7 P.M. A voice breaks the silence over the loudspeaker system. A battle message has been received for this task force.

"I will read it," says the voice. It is terse, pungent, without false heroics.

"Let's put the Navy ball over for a touchdown," it concludes. The sailors chuckle.

And now the chaplain offers the final prayer before the battle. All over the ship, out here in the breeze and down in the engine room beneath the surface of the sea, the men pause with bared heads.

The voice goes over the ship and into the evening air: "Our help is in the Lord."

"Ask and it shall be given, seek and ye shall find," the solemn voice concludes.

8:30 P.M. Zero hour tomorrow is 6:30. There will be general quarters tonight (which means battle stations) from 10:30.

That is the loudspeaker announcement. A hush falls on the crew, only two hours before night and day watches set in, with compartments sealed watertight.

Hurried last minute preparations are made. I walk through the compact crew compartments. Some men sit by themselves, others write letters home, some are on bunks in the canvas tiers. The voices are cheerful.

I turn in for a final nap.

10:30 P.M. The boatswain just piped, followed by the electrifying cry, "All hands man your battle stations!" Now the bugle blows "general quarters."

The sky is overcast. Somewhere up there the moon is one night from being full. Behind us are a few red streaks of sunset. Will this thick cloud conceal us? Is it possible German planes haven't spotted these great ship lines? All afternoon the number has been swelling. But the enemy has given no sign.

Midnight. It is June 6, D-day.

The breeze has freshened. France is off ahead. There is a spurt of distant tracer bullets and a falling meteor that is really a falling airplane.

There is a gray light and we can see one another. We keep peering out, wondering when the enemy will go into action, but nothing happens.

Here is a wonderful thing: Out here in the open Channel we are following mine-swept safety lanes clearly marked so even a landsman can read them, for there are little pinpricks of buoys. Nothing that has happened has so given me the sense of extraordinary preparation.

We steam slowly. Our ship is flanked by shadowy destroyers. Only occasionally does a muffled signal flash, and even on ships in the corridors, there are only red battle lights. Now and then there is a hint of moon in the cloud blanket.

1 A.M. For an hour, airplanes have gone over us. Occasional star shells fall off there in France. Once, the moon glowed out and cast us in full relief and a silvery patch. As I dictate this, suddenly a batch of lights twinkles like July 4 sparklers. Anti-aircraft stuff! Now it is gone.

I keep thinking of home. It's 7 P.M. there now. The family is just finishing supper. It's the same in millions of American homes, children doing home work, mothers at dishes, fathers reading papers. And here we are on the dark sea moving at half speed toward history.

2 A.M. France is just over there twelve miles off. There must be hundreds of ships around us. It is impossible to see. I couldn't have believed we would get so far undetected. The Germans must know we are here. But nothing happens. Just bombers.

A few minutes ago a great flock came back from France flying low and scudding past like bats showing the prearranged signal of friends.

Behind tiny wedges come stragglers, some with limping motors.

Again and again the lights blaze on the French coast. The moon dodges in and out.

Something extraordinary in bombing must be going on. When I was a child, I could see the distant glow of fireworks at Coney Island. This is like that. Just as I dictate, a fountain of sparklers sprays upward-dotted lines of tracer bullets shoot out. This must seem pretty bad on shore, but they don't know what's to come.

3 A.M. We have arrived. And the slower landing craft meet us here. Then we go in with them to six miles offshore. There will be simultaneous attacks by the Americans and British. Our beachhead is the one farthest north, the one nearest Cherbourg. Here on the open bridge I hear the order, "Be ready to fire." It just doesn't seem possible they don't see us. If they do, why don't they fire?

This must be the greatest concentration of bombing in the war. Everything is going off. We strain to read its meaning. The only thing we know is that we are in Act 2. Our performance is to reverse Dunkerque.

4 A.M. Well, this is the most spectacular bombing display of all. This must be the commotion kicked up by our parachute landings. As I write, the roar of planes is like an express train going over a viaduct. I dictate this to Chief Yeoman Charles Kidder. As I speak now, flares blaze out in fifteen to twenty clusters. I can read my watch. Flames still drop. They coil out long wriggling trails of white smoke. The water seems jet. I am so wrought up I can hardly hold still. The tension on the ship is reaching a peak.

We are going inshore. The bombs on land are so near and so big I feel the concussions. Our big guns are trained ahead.

Everybody is tense for the shore battery which does not come. The moon is gone and it is darker than it has been. We are getting an acrid smell of torn-up soil. The eerie flares have gone out. Well, here we go!

4:50 A.M. We are a few miles offshore. And no comment from the enemy. More fireworks stuff. I never imagined anything like it. The most horrible thing was two falling planes-ours, I suppose-that crashed down with great bubbling bursts of oily flames when they hit.

All nine big guns are pointed at the beach. It's getting lighter. There are yellow streaks in the cloud blanket.

5:30 A.M. It's come!

This is the bombardment. Our ears pound. Our big guns are just under me and every time they go off-as just then-I jump and the ship jolts.

We all have cotton in our ears, but it is noisy just the same and we feel the hot blast on our faces.

We crouched behind the rail for the first one and are bolder now. We will pound the beach for an hour, picking up where the bombers quit.

I hear the crunch of our neighbors' big guns. We all are pounding away for miles off the coast.

Here is the picture:

Dawn is breaking. There's more light every second. The sea is calm as a lake. The sky is mostly overcast.

By moving around the semi-circular bridge, I can see two-thirds of the horizon. We are in a sort of bay. We have moved in and the landing craft are coming in.

Dawn found us on Germany's doormat like the milk bottle.

The big ship to our left is firing tracers and they go in like pitched baseballs.

The whole bowl of sky echoes with our din. While we are concerned mostly with our own beach, we see tracers from other ships zipping ashore, see the flame from guns and a few seconds later, get the report.

I can see the flag waving at our mast and the long streaks of suntouched cloud are like its stripes.

6 A.M. We bang away regularly like a thunderbolt worked by clockwork. The individual drama goes on all around. Somehow I never imagined it would be like this.

I thought it would be all a motion picture close-up. Actually, the immensity of sky and land dwarfs everything and you have to strain at

the binoculars to see what is going on. I guess that is true of all battles.

If you are right in them, you can't figure what is happening. But here are details:

An airplane laying a smoke screen for the landing just crashed. It looked as though it was hit in midair.

We are smashing in salvos at specific objectives and every time the guns go off the whole ship jumps and so do I.

A sound like milk cans is the shells being ejected from the five inch batteries.

Our third salvo seems to have silenced one shore battery and we have moved to the next.

Now at 6:30 the landing craft should be hitting the beaches.

It is H-hour.

7 A.M. An American destroyer has been hit. It is heartbreaking to watch. The enemy fire splashes again and again. We shift our guns to knock off a battery.

A whaleboat leaves the destroyer.

Distress signals blink. A cloud of steam or smoke appears. A sister ship moves in right under the fire to pick up survivors. Forty-five minutes later, the same din, the same animated scene. A line of ships goes ashore. And empties are coming back. A little French village with a spire nestles at the cliffs that look so like England across the Channel.

The drama has shifted from ship to harbor.

Things probably are moving fast, but it seems amazingly slow.

8 A.M. The sun shines gloriously. This probably is the best weather ever picked for an invasion-cloudy at night, bright by day now. Our destroyers are practically walking on the beach, blazing into the cliffs as they move. We get radio word that one emplacement is in concrete and the destroyer can't rack it. Our turrets sweep around.

Bang they go! Now a second time!

It is almost impossible to stand still, so great is the will to urge that long new line of invasion barges forward. Any one of the runny little amphibious beetles makes a story in itself.

It is like picking a particular ant.

Here in my binoculars I see an ugly squarish little craft making for shore with a lace of foam in front. It reaches the beach, the white disappears, it waddles up. I can't see, but its guns are probably going.

On the sands are hulks of other boats-motionless. They have hit mines.

9 A.M. No sleep-and a plate of beans for breakfast. It seems as though it must be afternoon.

Our radio has just picked up a German radiocast denying any troops are ashore. They seem thoroughly befuddled.

They say we made an attempt at Dunkerque and Le Havre. It seems a complete surprise.

Noon. Everything depends on speed. We have a landing, but we had that at Dieppe. Can we stick and can we go in fast enough to pinch off Cherbourg?

The whole drama is that line of ships. What it looks like is an ant line.

One line moves an army with crumbs and another returns to the crust. Here they are moving like that-little black ships, but all sizes.

A big one with a whole rear end that unfolds on the beach or a little one with a truck or two. They are all pretty squat and ugly and the most beautiful sight I ever saw.

Yet it looks so quiet and peaceful. The splashes of water look like top splashes. Except when the splashes come in our direction. There is one persistent battery that keeps trying to get us. It quiets after we fire and then comes on again after we shift to something else.

One earlier target we got in the first salvo.

2 P.M. I have just had on the head phones in the communications room. Shore groups with walkie-talkies are telling the parent control what they find.

It is all in a jargon of communications nomenclature. The parent voice calls out loudly and commandingly through the static. More and more crackling static. Suddenly a quiet voice identifies itself.

"I am pinned down," says the quiet voice. "I am between machine-gun and pill-box cross fire." So that's it.

And now our radio leaves him.

A station reports that "firing from the bluff is continuing." It reports that the water obstacles are being taken care of. The incoming tide is helping.

That's what a battle sounds like under the scream of shells. We can't really tell what's happening. We are in it, but we might be losing for all we know.

4 P.M. Well, things are going well. We know because we have just heard a BBC broadcast! BBC seems delighted. It says reports are splendid. O.K. by us.

That far bluff is still spitting fire, though, and the elusive shore battery has splashed us with water. What does BBC advise?

But we are so weary now we are going to sleep on our feet anyway.

6 P.M. Six of the clumsy LCM's go by-the most angular craft ever built. Their front end, that ought to be high, is low, and vice versa. Not even its mother could love it. They are like wallowing watering troughs.

They carry a five-man crew and will lug a tank ashore. They come in abreast closer than anything so far. Those six, somehow, epitomize the whole affair. I can pick out figures-almost faces-with any glasses. To the men on shore they must look like ministering angels.

I can see the burly captain and even at this distance notice his arms akimbo. He is contemptuously looking at our towering warship and staring it out of counterance.

Then he sweeps the battle with uncomplimentary eye-the very image of a Hudson River tugboat captain. If I talked to him, I bet he would have a tough Jersey accent and would take back-talk from nobody, see-not from the Germans, nor from a warship.

We let go an eight-inch gun salvo over his right ear that must at least establish a feeling of joint respect.

All the time I have been typing, the ship has been blasting ahead. The typewriter jumps with the jolt.

Midnight. We are, I think, winning the battle. And here is the place to stop because I have just seen the most glorious sight of all. The paratroopers have come in. It was a scene of almost unbelievable romance and it probably revolutionizes warfare.

Right out of the east came suddenly a bigger and bigger roar of sound, as if all the planes in England were droning, and then here appeared line on line of big bombers, each towing a glider.

They curved over us in a mighty crescent and sped over the shore into the sunset.

Then, as the first batch passed and the second appeared, the bombers of the first were coming back again singly, this time having released their gliders filled with crack troops to reinforce the weary invasion companies that have battled all day.

Just at 11 o'clock, a new batch, even bigger than before, skimmed over in the late dusk of double summer time. They were so close you could see the rope that bound plane and glider taut as a fiddle string-all in perfect formation.

In each of the three earlier flights, there were many planes and as many gliders. Just now there are even more.

It was a fantasy out of the future.

Last week, when correspondents on the battle fleet were briefed, we were told something about airborne troops. It seemed fantastic the number was so large. But I am beginning to believe it.

What a sight that overhead reinforcement must have been to the muddy, blackened men below. It had the dash and elan of a cavalry charge.

After seeing the things I have in the past 24 hours, I know one thing-the road may be tough, but we can't lose.

Excerpt from: *Typewritter Battalian*

Last Fantastic Battle in the Reich

TANGERMUENDE ON THE ELBE, May 7, 1945-Today I saw the last battle in Germany. It was fought between thousands of disorganized, hysterical, screaming Germans and implacable, ruthless Rus- sian tanks and infantry, two hundred yards from where I sat atop an American tank.

Had this tank opened fire, it would have slaughtered hundreds of Germans at point blank range.

I saw things so fantastic that they surpassed anything I have witnessed in four years of war.

I saw Russian shells burst in the middle of a blue-gray mass of German soldiers and civilians waiting to cross Tangermuende bridge onto the American side of the Elbe. Scores of men, women and children were killed or wounded.

I saw German soldiers pushing old women out of boats in which they were trying to cross the river. I saw a German officer stripped naked, paddling a rubber boat loaded with two German soldiers, three women, their baggage and bicycles.

Two German soldiers swam the river in their vests, climbed up on the west bank and were sent straight back to the east side, still in their vests.

I arrived at Tangermuende about 10 this morning. It is here that 50,000 German soldiers have passed into our lines as prisoners within the last three days.

They built themselves a catwalk along the blown-out bridge, which lies awash in the Elbe river. Across this catwalk they have been streaming night and day for five days.

Behind them the Russians have been steadily closing in. Today, about noon, the Russian tanks were only about 1,000 yards from the river bank.

Source: James Wellard. "Last Fantastic Battle in the Reich," *The Chicago Times*. May 7, 1945, Reprinted in Jack Stenbuck, ed. *Typewriter Battalion*. New York: William Morrow and Company. 1995. Pp.345-347.

Some German rear guards were still trying to hold off the Russians. That's why the war continued in this place.

I stood and watched as the Germans came streaming over the wreckage of the bridge, SS, paratroopers, generals, high-ranking staff officers, nurses, tankmen, Luftwaffe personnel, every description of Wehrmacht soldier, ran across wild-eyed. At the end of the bridge, they saw a huge sign in German which said, "This you can thank your Fuehrer."

American guards told them to throw down their equipment and run to a field, from where long lines wove down the road. The pile of Luger pistols, field glasses, rifles, cameras and wrist watches was nearly as high as the dome of St. Paul's Cathedral.

About noon, the Russians broke out of the woods. The fury and horror of the scene became indescribable. Russian shells and mortars cracked smack into the middle of crowds of Germans.

Out of the woods and the town across the river poured thousands of German soldiers, running every way, like ants coming out of a broken ant-hill. Russian mortars fell among them.

Down on the river bank, the scene was like something out of Dante's inferno. The Germans, men and women, kept leaping into the fast-moving river and kept being washed back on shore. Dead, dying and living were scrambled.

The Americans were permitting only those who could cross by the bridge to span the river. But hundreds would not wait. They pushed off into the stream on planks, rafts, amphibious jeeps and rubber boats, or swam.

Meanwhile, behind me, long lines of prisoners were marching up the road as far as I could see-whole units in battle formation, singing Nazi songs. They had forgotten their comrades on the other side, where a hell of fantastic proportions had broken loose.

A party of Russian tommy-gunners had fought their way out of the fields and almost down to the river bank, where they were ambushed by SS men hiding among parked trucks, hundreds of them. The Germans were burning the trucks as fast as possible and ammunition within them was exploding, sending cascades of flames skywards.

By this time, the German soldiers were for the most part safely across the bridge. They had precedence over the women and children. I myself saw that they were more concerned with saving their own skins than in helping even the wounded children.

The conclusion I drew was that the SS brought down upon their own people this fury of death from the Russian guns. We could have massacred the whole Inob, but we didn't.

Excerpt from: *They Were There*

Going Ashore

JULY 13, 1943-The village of Scoglitti Pies in the center of a scimitar of white sandy beach on the southeastern coast of Sicily. It has much the appearance of the village in Elliot Paul's Life and Death of a Spanish Town. The houses, so simple and natural that they have a kind of beautiful rightness among the dunes and dry hills around them, are low and white, made of stone and mortar with shallow sloping roofs. Scoglitti is a poor town whose people have never had much more than bread and wine and fishes, religion and the simple natural merriment of healthy hard-working folk. Bread they made in little stone igloos adjacent to their modest houses. Wine they grew in near-by fields, thankful that the vine is one of the few things that sometimes bear their best fruit in poor soil. Fishes came out of the warm blue sea that comes almost to their doorsteps and which, until the advent of Il Duce and his Fascism, could still be spoken of with affectionate pride as Mare Nostrum. As for the merriment, the lively Saturday nights in cantinas and all that, it slowly vanished as the young men of Scoglitti left their boats and fields for Ethiopia,

---

Source: George Sessions Perry. "Going Ashore." *The Saturday Evening Post.* 1943. Reprinted in Curt Riess, ed. *They Were There.* New York: G.P. Putnam's Sons. 1944. Pp. 566-571.

or as still older men were called up for service in Libya and Tunisia. Their religion was centered in the cathedral whose fine square stone tower dominated the town.

It was on July eleventh, one day after the town had surrendered to the Americans, that a group of snipers with machine guns, no doubt attracted by some notion of sanctuary as well as by the thickness of the walls, gathered in the cathedral and sprayed the streets until their position was neutralized by one of our cruisers. That was on our second day at Scoglitti.

For the ship to which I was assigned, as well as for all other American ships standing off the beach in this sector, July eleventh was a day of much greater action and strain than had been the initial day of invasion. That first day things had worked better than any of us expected because of the light resistance we encountered on the beaches. The division charged with the protection of the immediate shoreline was regional troops, poorly equipped and wanting in any real will to resist.

However, there was more determined resistance encountered a few miles from Scoglitti, near the town of Gela. Here troops equipped with tanks and artillery fought our soldiers to a standstill, once they had made their initial dash inland. And by the second day, according to a wounded American soldier brought back to one of our ships, the enemy had forced one of our battalions to retreat fourteen miles and had killed some of our men. Now the fighting was proceeding little more than four miles inland as our destroyers and cruisers fired over the heads of our own men to support them and to stem the enemy advance.

From dawn of this second day, cannonading by our warships was continuous. From the signal bridge of the ship I was on, shell bursts both from our guns and from those of the enemy were clearly visible. Nevertheless, our ships continued to move closer to this area, where supplies and reinforcements were apparently badly needed. Just to the right of this fighting was a deep ravine

which wound through hills, and from it enemy bombers would periodically dart, drop their bombs over the ships and dart back into the ravine. As my ship and others in its group lay, this action was some twenty-five hundred yards distant.

Most of the planes that bombed our group during that second morning did so from high or medium altitudes. But there was such urgency to get our ship unloaded before she might be sunk that we soon dispensed with dashing into battle stations for each attack. The first phase of our job-getting men ashore in small boats-was done. The second and equally important one of landing their supplies intact largely remained to be accomplished. For the rest of the day then, except when bombers came in force, men who weren't needed for unloading were ordered to the gun pits to put up such a barrage as their numbers allowed, while the rest went on dis-charging cargo into whatever landing craft we could get alongside. By now any of the small landing craft we had brought with us on our decks were swamped on the beach. In any case, they bounced about so much while they were alongside, and held so little once they were loaded, that they weren't very effective cargo lighters.

By noon of the second day, with every available man bearing a hand, all holds were virtually cleared except No. 1, located up in the bow. It still contained about a hundred tons of ammunition. It was naturally this cargo of which we were most conscious each time bombs started down.

I made two trips ashore during the morning with boatloads of motorized guns and ammunition. Despite the endless lines of broached landing craft and the Gargantuan influx of supplies there was still order, people to unload boats and places to put supplies once they got ashore. The beaches were well marked; boatmen could be sure which beach was which. Steel netting ran down graded beaches and forked out into three prongs as it reached and entered the surf. Here were facilities for unloading three separate vehiclebearing craft simultaneously.

These beaches, like the ships, were being bombed and strafed. I was there on one such occasion, dived into a ditch and though it may seem the reaction of a lunatic I felt a certain smugness, even pleasure, at feeling around me the warm, nonexplosive earth. Every other time I had been on something that if hit at all would blow up. For there are unfortunately no foxholes on an ammunition-laden transport. Each man knows that his person isn't the extent of the target he presents, but that the skin of the ship is his own skin and that he is vulnerable to all its hurts. But from the vantage point of this wonderful Sicilian ditch the planes were another and altogether less menacing thing.

On the way back to the ship we passed a tank-landing ship. Amphibious trucks called ducks were running in and out of the ship like waterbugs with windshields. By now a landing barge was alongside our ship receiving ammunition. This was in the neighborhood of two o'clock. Hardly had I gone aboard and reached the signal bridge when a flight of from twenty to forty enemy bombers roared over and dropped more than a hundred bombs, but our ship kept on unloading.

By midafternoon the ammunition barge was loaded and its lines cast away. Some fifty tons of ammunition remained. From this time until six o'clock we dribbled such loads as we could into what small landing craft were available. Many of these boats' crews hadn't left their boats since they had been lowered over the side to hit the beach the first time. Some had jugs of mud-as sailors call coffee-and sacks of sandwiches in their boats.

Some had boxes of field rations. As for loading masters who had been loading boats all this time, their voices had long since vanished. Only hand signals were now being passed from loading masters to winchmen. Sporadic raiding by enemy planes in ones and twos, sometimes four or five, continued. And all of us suspected that once night fell they would swarm on this mass of

ships-perhaps two hundred were in this immediate area-that they would light the sky with flares and the sea with burning ships. There was no use kidding ourselves, it was in the cards-such heavy concentrations of ships along enemy coastlines is one of the inescapable embarrassments of amphibious assaults. And for that matter none of us had ever expected this job to be as tame as the North African landing. At this stage in the operation we had no air fields closer than Malta, and the enemy had at least twenty on this island. It was therefore not hard to guess what was going to happen after nightfall.

At six in the afternoon we got good news! A tank-landing ship was coming alongside to receive the rest of our ammunition. Our small-boat problems were over. Unloading would proceed much faster, now that we had something which would hold what we had to unload without having to be constantly running to the beach itself to unload. It wouldn't be dark until after nine o'clock or so. Perhaps in that length of time with every man doing his utmost we could clear the holds and have the ship ready to get under way before mass bombings began. That way we would be in a position to maneuver and fight back, have a chance to put out such fires as bombs started, minimize our damage and fully exploit whatever possibilities a transport may have in a fight with planes. But until that ammunition was gone our job, no matter what happened, was to stay put and unload it.

At this point some thirty-five tons of ammunition remained aboard. It still covered the No. 1 hold to a depth of twelve feet. In addition many barracks bags belonging to troops who had been our shipmates remained aboard. These bags were piled ten feet deep over the portside of the boat deck and there was no way to transfer them to the opposite side and forward except for men to muscle them over there.

Now that the transfer of cargo had begun up forward every man not necessary to the unloading, or to stand a gun watch, formed a double line that ran the breadth of the ship down to the main deck level and forward for a hundred feet. In this line were medical officers, colored mess cooks, myself, bluejackets from every department that could spare them.

The bags weighed from seventy to ninety pounds each, but once one of them was picked up it passed over the heads of the men in line and wasn't lowered until it reached the transfer point on the main deck. Once or twice we stopped our work to go to battle stations when planes came over, dropping bombs, but that was only the barracks-bags gang. The ammunition people went right on working. Except for these crises the work never stopped. And as the number of bags passed grew from hundreds to beyond the thousand mark, some of these people who had been working furiously without sleep for three days were reeling with exhaustion. Once, when the pace slowed somebody yelled, "Switch your tails and pass them to bags along."

Then twenty-nine-year-old Doctor John Hope, of Mobile, said, "Let's sing," and struck up "Praise the Lord and Pass the Ammunition." By 9:30 the bags were off the ship, but we found now that the rest of the ammunition wouldn't be unloaded until midnight, no matter how hard the men on both ships worked. Those of us not in the holds, at winches or engines, had, without knowing it, exactly fifteen minutes in which to rest, grab sandwiches, a cup of coffee or smoke a cigarette. By now a cool night was beginning, with a bright half-moon to light the sky and sea. There was too much noise of every kind to hear the engines of the first planes as they sailed far overhead. We found they were there when flares, in all their ghastly brilliance, began to light up our ships as brightly as the sun might have. Then we knew they were up there, their own eyes shaded from the glare of flares by the parachutes that held the flares aloft. We were marvelously illuminated sitting ducks. The first bombs came down and the ships began to saw open the night.

Down in the engine room the chief water tender was watching how each time something came over the phone the men's heads would snap around with an electric movement to hear what they hoped had happened. The boilers had steam up and there was ammunition left. The ship's first lieutenant said, "Sometimes you gotta take long chances, so you take 'em and to hell with it." Those of us on deck could see that every time a bomb found its mark great sheets of enveloping flame would race out laterally and then slowly materialize into a huge, deep red spheroidal bloom. In the forward forty-millimeter gun pit, where men were begging for the order to open fire, Gunner's Mate Lee, lanky, slow-speaking, level-headed man from Mt. Vernon, Indiana, was ordering his men to be silent. "Excited people talking leads from one thing to another." Our captain withheld the order for our own ship to open up. Tied up as we were to that ammunition barge we presented a double target to which the captain wasn't eager to direct the enemy's attention. And as the night blazed with gunfire and bursting bombs our people went on unloading the usual thousands of gallons of oil in tanks.

In the sick bay it was worse. Some of the patients had been committed that day for treatment of burns, but the majority were shrapnel cases, their nerves were shot from pain and some were trying to climb out of bed, particularly when planes came so low that the roar of their engines was loud.

After a half hour there came a lull. Perhaps it lasted ten minutes. I don't think anyone knows positively. In that period those of us not unloading wandered about, watching fires burn. In passing, people made little pleasantries and passed the time of day. Nobody doubted that planes were coming back and anybody with an ounce of brains knew we were looking death by burning in the face. Yet everybody in action and word was chipper, even though the color was gone out of many a face. So far, only one person had become a little hysterical. Another had lost his power of speech.

Then the planes did come back and lighted us up and poured it on so hot and heavy that there was no longer any conceivable advantage in withholding our fire. In a matter of minutes every twenty-millimeter gun barrel was dull cherry-red as our lads watched the fire of a nearby destroyer while they enlarged and helped increase the density of its pattern.

And when forty-millimeter guns got driving with their powerful whong, whong, whong, you could feel the projectile push against the ship as it started off, and it traveled so fast that its whoosh through the air could be heard above the surrounding clamor.

Then a great orange pool of flame materialized quickly in the sky as the ships scored the first positive hit and our people cheered like hyenas. The planes must have been impressed by our lack of success with our guns during the day, for now they were pulling in close for a real kill, coming well into range of our twenties. Another plane exploded in the air. Soon we had them burning overhead, in the sea and on the shore all at once. In perhaps five minutes we bagged seven.

At the end of five minutes they either ran out of bombs or decided we were no bargain. Again action broke off. The time was roughly 1:15. Unloading hadn't even paused, but the barge with that growing pile of ammunition on deck was still tied alongside and would be there for another hour. That was the longest hour most of us have ever spent. Then finally, before the planes came back, that wonderful order to cast off lines came over the loud-speaker and was performed by willing hands.

The relief with which we watched distance increase between the two craft was inexpressible. Now as soon as the first convoy of empty ships was ready to pull out we would be waiting to join it. With this consolation and the enormously satisfying knowledge that despite all the fire which the enemy could throw at us we had done our jobs, those of us with no watch to stand

crawled into our bunks and slept the brick-heavy sleep of the utterly exhausted and-at least for the moment-victorious.

Excerpt from: *They Were There*

Dieppe

THE sun had climbed now nearly overhead and it was blood red through the blanket of smoke which lay over Dieppe and the harbor. The greatest raid by sea in modern warfare was now at its height. Even standing there on the deck of a destroyer half a mile from shore, it was hard to believe that this was really happening, that when the men next to you suddenly swayed and gasped, they had actually been hit. It was warfare in Hollywood dress and with Hollywood sound effects. There was only one difference: The bullets were real, the shells and the bombs were real, and the agony on the faces of the wounded was real.

Major General James Roberts in charge of all military affairs on shore sat in a small room on our destroyer getting reports from his men. He directed the entire show from that one small room. He looked worried because he knew that his Canadians were in the forefront of that deadly fire. Four-fifths of the landing force had been Canadians; the rest had been British Commandos in whose ranks were some Americans and Free French. Our destroyer was rapidly filling up with wounded now. They were lying below decks, in gangways, in cabins, on the floor of the wardroom. And still they came. A barge pulled alongside to discharge a dozen Commandos. They looked fierce with their blackened faces and with their thin daggers in their belts. But they were laughing.

It was very funny, a tall Yorkshireman said. "We're the headquarters staff of No. 3 Commandos," he explained. "We're signalers and runners and liaison men. There were twenty of us, and then there were the four hundred who were supposed to do the work. We had orders to put out a gun battery on the west flank. But on the way to

Source: Quentin Reynolds. "Dieppe." Crowell-Collier Publishing Co. 1942. Reprinted in Curt Riess, ed. *They Were There*. New York: G. P. Putnam's Sons.1944. Pp. 261-265.

shore, an E-boat attacked us and two armed trawlers got after us. In the darkness we all got separated. We twenty found the rendezvous but no one else showed up. They all went, I guess, or landed somewhere else. The young major who was our CO said, `We have orders to land. What in hell are we waiting for?' So we landed.' We only had rifles because we aren't supposed to be the fighting men on the Commandos. We crept near their six-inch gun battery. They were opening up at you chaps out here. We started sniping at them, and the damn' fools turned their six-inch guns on us. We kept moving from tree to tree always under cover. The bloody fools thought they were surrounded. We kept moving and sniping at them and they never did get a chance to give it to you properly. It was a lot of fun."

A lot of fun? Twenty men had done the work that hundreds had been assigned to do. Twenty men had kept a battery of six-inch guns busy, a battery that would otherwise have taken a terrible toll among the vulnerable destroyers and barges and motor launches lying within range. A lot of fun? A brisk breeze came from the east, which was bad because it dispersed the smoke which had to some extent hidden us from the shore batteries. When it cleared we could see the Spitfires overhead darting everywhere, usually in flights of four with each flight being protected by a "Tail-end Charlie" who kept weaving this way and that, acting as the eyes of the flight.

Twice, groups of Dorniers tried to penetrate our umbrella of aircraft; twice, Dorniers went down in flames.

Then an aircraft that was neither a Spitfire nor a Dornier came wobbling toward us. It looked like an Me-iog. The ack-ack started to bark angrily, and the approaching plane was framed now by ugly black bursts of smoke. But fortunately not one bullet found its mark. Fortunately, because as it wobbled closer, we saw that it had R.A.F. markings; it was an American Mustang. It seemed out of control and then it glided down to land on the water twenty feet from us. It hit with a great splash and the pilot, as though shot from a cannon, catapulted out of his seat into the water. A motor launch picked him up

and brought him to us. He was a tall, good-looking Canadian. His motor had been put out of commission by ack-ack over Dieppe. Instead of bailing out, he had decided to glide into the water as close to our destroyer as he could.

"Only one thing worried me," he said as he stripped off his wet clothes. "Our own ack-ack."

In the control room, General Roberts kept getting reports. The main attacking forces did not penetrate far into the city itself. Suddenly, Roberts, who had gotten older during the past two hours, looked at the plans of the time schedule and said softly, "Bring them home."

His two aides gave orders through the microphones. We knew this would be welcome news to those poor devils on shore.

Roberts said, "Tell Fighter Command to give us cover for the withdrawal."

It was just eleven o'clock and now officially the raid was over. More wounded arrived. Our decks were covered with them now. One bedraggled, soaking-wet figure stumbled aboard. He was a doctor who had been with the landing forces and happily he was unwounded. Our ship's doctor uttered a cry of relief when he saw that help had come. The two went to work. The two doctors had no time to operate or to dig for shrapnel and bullets. They could only clean wounds and give the merciful needle of morphine to deaden the agony.

In the wardroom, there were twenty men lying on the floor. When bombs fell near our four-inch guns [making] the whole ship tremble, they never moved. All of them were a little stunned by the tremendous noise and blast that had lasted now for six hours. One man who seemed familiar stumbled into the room. He tried to stand straight but then he collapsed as I grabbed a bottle of brandy and put it to his lips.

"It's a hell of a story, isn't it?" he grinned and then he passed out again. I was pretty proud of my profession then. This was Wallace Rayburn of the *Montreal Standard*, one of the two correspondents who had managed to reach shore. I helped strip his wet clothes off. He had been hit by shrapnel, not seriously, but he had also been forced to swim for it and he was exhausted.

A tall blond kid looking very Midwestern came into the wardroom in his Ranger uniform. He was Sergeant Kenneth Kenyon of Minneapolis, Minnesota, and he was looking for his Ranger pal Sergeant Matchel Swank, also of Minneapolis, but Swank wasn't with us.

"It was bad on shore," young Kenyon said. "But, my God, how those Canadians can fight!"

Just then Sergeant Swank appeared. He'd been looking for Kenyon. His right arm was bandaged. It was only a small piece of shrapnel. I gave them each a drink of brandy. Neither had ever tasted it before and they didn't like it.

"Does the wound bother you?" I asked him.

"No," he laughed. "I knew nothing could happen to me. My father gave me a small Bible to carry with me. It brought him through the last war and it's going to bring me through this one. Pop's in the Army too." (Confidential note to Sergeant Major Swank, Camp Dix: That kid of yours is only nineteen but he's a good man. Congratulations!) I walked on deck for a last look. Dieppe was burning in three places. All of the men had been embarked and it was time to go home. The Destroyer Berkeley steamed by us slowly. Once a single Dornier drove through the Spits to drop its bombs. They missed us, but the Berkeley wasn't so lucky. She was hit directly, and a thin splinter of flame shot forty feet in the air.

It was a bad hit. The ship listed slowly and you knew she had received her death blow. Motor launches came hurrying, motor torpedo boats came at fifty miles an hour to help. Men tumbled from her sloping sides into the sea to be picked up. We circled the stricken ship looking for survivors.

A moment after the last man had been plucked from the water, another British ship blew up the Berkeley according to orders. She sank within twenty seconds.

Now there was a movement among the ships all around us. The raid was over. We were on our way home, but our ship remained where she was. One by one the others formed in line and headed away from Dieppe. Our engines finally started to hum and we too moved, but we moved not away from Dieppe but toward it. Roberts was going in

again on the chance that we might find a few survivors in the water near the beaches.

The next twenty minutes were not pleasant. All the shore batteries still in action turned on us. The Dorniers and the Focke-Wulfs saw what they thought to be a crippled straggler and they came at us again and again. Shells and bombs threw up huge jets of water close to us, but we steamed steadily on.

I went into the wardroom. If we were hit, the men down there wouldn't have a chance. The wardroom was below the water line. A little Yorkshire steward whose name was Joe Crowther was going from one man to another. Joe is twenty-one. He told reassuring lies.

"We're on our way home now," he said in his slow Yorkshire accents. "It won't be long. Dieppe is far behind us."

Then we were hit. The bomb landed forward and the ship trembled.

The noise reverberated from one steel wall to the other, and your head rang with the concussion. Through the noise, the laughter of Joe Crowther came. "That's our new six-inch gun they're firing," he told the wounded. "If you didn't know better you'd think it was a bomb."

The wounded who had lain tense, their faces drained of color, relaxed.

The color came back, and Joe went among them saying, "A nip of brandy; it'll warm you up. Isn't often you can drink free on His Majesty's Royal Navy."

Joe looked at me and winked. We had no six-inch guns on board, but these wounded didn't know that. If I were handing out V. C.'s leading Mess Steward Joe Crowther of Bradford, Yorkshire, would be the first to be given one.

Finally, Roberts was satisfied that no useful purpose could be served by remaining any longer. Reluctantly he gave the order to return. It was nice to hear the throaty roar of the motors sending us along at fifteen knots. They still tried to get us with their bombs, and a Focke-Wulf almost made it. I was on deck when it came from nowhere. It was only a hundred feet above us and it raked us from stem to stern with its cannon and machine guns. It dropped two bombs, one of which hit us. I reeled into the gangway, knocked sideways by the blast. Then it was gone with the discomfited Spits giving chase.

We went on toward England. We caught up with the flotilla just before entering the ten-mile German mine field. Roberts had told his men that he'd be first through the mine field. We slipped ahead of the others for the tortuous one-hour trip. We were all exhausted and a little punch-drunk from the nine hours of constant battering.

I found four U. S. Ranger soldiers sitting together with not a wound among them. They'd been with the No. 4 Commandos. They were Staff Sergeant Kenneth Stemphen of Russell, Minnesota, Corporal William Brady of Grand Forks, North Dakota; Sergeant Alex Szima of Dayton, Ohio; and Corporal Franklin M. Koons of Swea City, Iowa. They were tired but happy. They could talk of nothing but the Commandos.

"I'd like to get hold of that louse back home," husky Corporal Brady said, clenching his big hands, "who told me that the British can't fight. My God, I never saw anything like it!"

"We'd have been dead a dozen times if it hadn't been for our superior officers," Szima added. "They're the greatest fighters in the world. They make us look like sissies."

"How about that sergeant major we carried out?" Koons said. "He had a hole in his belly you could stick your fist through and yet every few minutes he'd yell 'Down!' and we'd drop flat, and sure enough, machinegun bullets would go over his head."

"I fell for that propaganda at home myself," Stemphen said. "Who the hell started it anyhow? Talk about the Russians! If they're half as good as these British they're terrific."

We steamed on, and now the mine field was behind us. The Spitfires flew sedately overhead. They had the sky pretty much to themselves. We relaxed a bit and laughed a little and drank brandy, and even the wounded joked about the blood on their uniforms. We were able to check up a bit.

Our crew had been hit badly. Many of them were casualties. All of the "walking wounded" stuck to their posts. It's true what they say about the British navy.

Then ahead we saw a very sweet sight, the shores of England. That shore looked almost as good as the shore of America would have looked. We steamed on and, looking back to the great line of little ships that steamed on so proudly, you couldn't help but choke a little. Nearly all had come back.

Had the raid been a success? Our casualties had been heavy. But quite definitely the raid proved a lot of things and taught us a lot. It had taught us that a large landing force can be transported across the Channel with a reasonable chance of arriving there. It proved that tanks can be landed.

My own view is that the two things lacking were a terrific air bombardment before the landing, and the use of parachute troops. It is true that when you do a preliminary bombing you forfeit the element of surprise.

It is also true that only by bombing or dive bombing can gun batteries effectively be silenced and troops allowed to land without having to face a suicidal fire. Parachute troops dropped a few miles inland could have taken the pill boxes which bothered our men so and could have prevented reinforcements from coming up from the rear.

But the greatest lesson of all that we learned at Dieppe was this. Given the opportunity, the British and Canadians fight like Russians. That is nice to know.

Excerpt from: ***Ernie's War: The Best of Ernie Pyle's World War II Dispatches***

A Long Thin Line of Personal Anguish

NORMANDY BEACHHEAD, June 1-, 1944-In the preceding column we told about the D-day wreckage among our machines of war that were

Source: David Nichols, ed. *Ernie's War: The Best of Ernie Pyle's World War II Dispatches*. New York: Random House. 1986. Chapter: "A Long Thin Line of Personal Anguish." June 17, 1944. Normandy Beachhead. Pp. 282-283.

expended in taking one of the Normandy beaches.

But there is another and more human litter. It extends in a thin little line, just like a high-water mark, for miles along the beach. This is the strewn personal gear, gear that will never be needed again, of those who fought and died to give us our entrance into Europe. Here in a jumbled row for mile on mile are soldiers' packs. Here are socks and shoe polish, sewing kits, diaries, Bibles and hand grenades. Here are the latest letters from home, with the address on each one neatly razored out-one of the security precautions enforced before the boys embarked.

Here are toothbrushes and razors, and snapshots of families back home staring up at you from the sand. Here are pocketbooks, metal mirrors, extra trousers, and bloody, abandoned shoes. Here are broken-handled shovels, and portable radios smashed almost beyond recognition, and mine detectors twisted and ruined.

Here are torn pistol belts and canvas water buckets, first-aid kits and jumbled heaps of lifebelts. I picked up a pocket Bible with a soldier's name in it, and put it in my jacket. I carried it half a mile or so and then put it back down on the beach. I don't know why I picked it up, or why I put it back down.

Soldiers carry strange things ashore with them. In every invasion you'll find at least one soldier hitting the beach at H-hour with a banjo slung over his shoulder. The most ironic piece of equipment marking our beach-this beach of first despair, then victory-is a tennis racket that some soldier had brought along. It lies lonesomely on the sand, clamped in its rack, not a string broken.

Two of the most dominant items in the beach refuse are cigarets and writing paper. Each soldier was issued a carton of cigarets just before he started. Today these cartons by the thousand, water-soaked and spilled out, mark the line of our first savage blow.

Writing paper and air-mail envelopes come second. The boys had intended to do a lot of writing in France. Letters that would have filled those blank, abandoned pages.

Always there are dogs in every invasion. There is a dog still on the beach today, still pitifully looking for his masters.

He stays at the water's edge, near a boat that lies twisted and half sunk at the water line. He barks appealingly to every soldier who approaches, trots eagerly along with him for a few feet, and then, sensing himself unwanted in all this haste, runs back to wait in vain for his own people at his own empty boat.

Excerpt from: *Ernie's War: The Best of Ernie Pyle's World War II Dispatches*

The Horrible Waste of War

NORMANDY BEACHHEAD, June 16, 1944-I took a walk along the historic coast of Normandy in the country of France.

It was a lovely day for strolling along the seashore. Men were sleeping on the sand, some of them sleeping forever. Men were floating in the water, but they didn't know they were in the water, for they were dead.

The water was full of squishy little jellyfish about the size of your hand. Millions of them. In the center each of them had a green design exactly like a four-leaf clover. The good-luck emblem. Sure. Hell yes.

I walked for a mile and a half along the water's edge of our many-miled invasion beach. You wanted to walk slowly, for the detail on that beach was infinite.

The wreckage was vast and startling. The awful waste and destruction of war, even aside from the loss of human life, has always been one of its outstanding features to those who are in it. Anything and everything is expendable. And we did expend on our beachhead in Normandy during those first few hours.

For a mile out from the beach there were scores of tanks and trucks and boats that you could no longer see, for they were at the bottom of the water-swamped by overloading, or hit by shells, or sunk by mines. Most of their crews were lost.

Source: David Nichols, ed. *Ernie's War: The Best of Ernie Pyle's World War II Dispatches*. New York: Random House. 1986. Chapter: "The Horrible Waste of War." June 16, 1944. Normandy Beachhead. Pp. 280-282.

You could see trucks tipped half over and swamped. You could see partly sunken barges, and the angled-up corners of jeeps, and small landing craft half submerged. And at low tide you could still see those vicious six-pronged iron snares that helped snag and wreck them.

On the beach itself, high and dry, were all kinds of wrecked vehicles. There were tanks that had only just made the beach before being knocked out. There were jeeps that had burned to a dull gray. There were big derricks on caterpillar treads that didn't quite make it. There were half-tracks carrying office equipment that had been made into a shambles by a single shell hit, their interiors still holding their useless equipage of smashed typewriters, telephones, office files.

There were LCT's turned completely upside down, and lying on their backs, and how they got that way I don't know. There were boats stacked on top of each other, their sides caved in, their suspension doors knocked off.

In this shoreline museum of carnage there were abandoned rolls of barbed wire and smashed bulldozers and big stacks of thrownaway lifebelts and piles of shells still waiting to be moved.

In the water floated empty life rafts and soldiers' packs and ration boxes, and mysterious oranges.

On the beach lay, expended, sufficient men and mechanism fora small war. They were gone forever now. And yet we could afford it.

We could afford it because we were on, we had our toehold, and behind us there were such enormous replacements for this wreckage on the beach that you could hardly conceive of their sum total. Men and equipment were flowing from England in such a gigantic stream that it made the waste on the beachhead seem like nothing at all, really nothing at all. A few hundred yards back on the beach is a high bluff. Up there we had a tent hospital, and a barbed-wire enclosure for prisoners of war. From up there you could see far up and down the beach, in a spectacular crow's-nest view, and far out to sea.

And standing out there on the water beyond all this wreckage was the greatest armada man has ever seen. You simply could not believe the gigantic collection of ships that lay out there waiting to unload.

Looking from the bluff, it lay thick and clear to the far horizon of the sea and on beyond, and it spread out to the sides and was miles wide. Its utter enormity would move the hardest man.

As I stood up there I noticed a group of freshly taken German prisoners standing nearby. They had not yet been put in the prison cage. They were just standing there, a couple of doughboys leisurely guarding them with tommy guns.

The prisoners too were looking out to sea-the same bit of sea that for months and years had been so safely empty before their gaze. Now they stood staring almost as if in a trance.

They didn't say a word to each other. They didn't need to. The expression on their faces was something forever unforgettable. In it was the final horrified acceptance of their doom.

If only all Germans could have had the rich experience of standing on the bluff and looking out across the water and seeing what their compatriots saw.

The juxtaposition of the infant and the man-of-war makes this an iconic war photo, capturing the tenderness and horror of war. It was taken during the Battle of Saipan, when the soldier found the infant wedged face down under a rock while clearing out a cave where Japanese soldiers were hiding. *Photo, W. Eugene Smith, 1943/44*

This Pulitzer-Prize winning photo is one of the most memorable images of the war, taken during the Battle of Iwo Jima atop Mt. Suribachi. The six Marines raising the flag has inspired several sculptures honoring U.S. heroism, including the Iwo Jima Memorial near Arlington National Cemetery. Three of the six men died in the battle. This marked the first time an American flag was raised over Japanese territory. *Photo, Joe Rosenthal, 1944*

Source: *U.S. Marine Cradles Near Dead Infant in Saipan* (1944) W. Eugene Smith, Time Life/Getty Images; *U.S. Flag Raised Atop Mt. Suribachi, Iwo Jima* (1945) Joe Rosental, Associated Press.

World War II has been referred to as "the censored war" for the pervasive news censorship that existed beginning in 1942 after the U.S. government established the Office of Censorship. Many of its guidelines are explained in this manual. All correspondents were required to sign an agreement to "submit for the purposes of censorship all statements, written material, and all photography intended for publication."

FM 30-26

BASIC FIELD MANUAL

REGULATIONS FOR CORRESPONDENTS ACCOMPANYING U. S. ARMY FORCES IN THE FIELD

Prepared under direction of the
Chief of Staff

Including C 1, 24 April 1942; C 2, 25 July 1942; and C 3, 23 December 1942.

Note: This is not a revision; this manual contains only the above changes to the 21 January 1942 edition placed at back following original text, and will not be issued to individuals possessing that edition.

Source: War Department. *Basic Field Manual: Regulations for Correspondents Accompanying U.S. Army Forces in the Field.* FM 3026. January 21, 1942. Pp. 1-18.

TABLE OF CONTENTS

	Paragraph
General	1
Definition	2
Status of correspondents	3
Privileges	4
Application	5
Limit on number	6
Agreement	7
Credentials	8
Uniform	9
Transportation	10
Reporting upon arrival	11
Filing of material	12
Censorship of articles for publication	13
Photographic censorship	14
Signal and mail service	15
Relief from appointment	16
Discipline	17
Visiting correspondent	18

WAR DEPARTMENT,
Washington, January 21, 1942.

FM 30–26, Regulations for Correspondents Accompanying U. S. Army Forces in the Field, is published for the information and guidance of all concerned.
[A. G. 062.11 (12–24–41).]

BY ORDER OF THE SECRETARY OF WAR:

G. C. MARSHALL,
Chief of Staff.

OFFICIAL:
E. S. ADAMS,
Major General,
The Adjutant General.

DISTRIBUTION:
X.
(For explanation of symbols see FM 21–6.)

II

BASIC FIELD MANUAL

REGULATIONS FOR CORRESPONDENTS ACCOMPANYING U. S. ARMY FORCES IN THE FIELD

■ 1. GENERAL.—The Army recognizes that correspondents perform an undoubted public function in the dissemination of news concerning the operations of the Army in time of war. Correspondents accompanying troops in the field occupy a dual and delicate position, being under the necessity of truthfully disclosing to the people the facts concerning the operations of the Army, and at the same time of refraining from disclosing those things which, though true, would be disastrous to us if known to the enemy. It is apparent that this important function can only be properly performed under reasonable rules and regulations.

■ 2. DEFINITION.—The term "correspondent" as used in this manual includes journalists, feature writers, radio commentators, motion picture photographers, and still picture photographers accredited by the War Department to a theater of operations or a base command within or without the territorial limits of the United States in time of war. Correspondents are classed as "accredited" and "visiting." This manual pertains principally to the former. See paragraph 18 for instructions concerning visiting correspondents.

■ 3. STATUS OF CORRESPONDENTS.—a. Correspondents in time of war accompanying the armies of the United States, both within and without the territorial jurisdiction of the United States, although not in the military service, are subject to military law (AW 2(d)) and are under the control of the commander of the Army force which they accompany.

b. They are not entitled to the benefits provided by laws enacted exclusively for persons in the military service and they are subject to the provisions of the Selective Training and Service Act of 1940, and regulations prescribed thereunder.

3–5 BASIC FIELD MANUAL

c. In the event of capture by enemy forces they are entitled to be treated as prisoners of war, provided they are in possession of a certificate from the military authorities of the armed forces which they are accompanying. (Geneva Conference, July 27, 1929, Title VII, Art. 81.)

d. Correspondents will not exercise command, be placed in a position of authority over military personnel, nor will they be armed. They are under the same restrictions as other military personnel as regards the settlement of accounts, compliance with standing orders, and the conducting of themselves with dignity and decorum.

e. A correspondent becomes subject to military law from the time at which he commences to accompany troops or personnel who are on active service. This will generally be upon his arrival at the field force to which he is accredited, but may commence earlier if he travels to the field force via Government transportation.

■ 4. Privileges.—*a.* Correspondents will be given the same privileges as commissioned officers in the matter of accommodations, transportation, and messing facilities. All courtesies extended them in such matters must be without expense to the Government.

b. Every reasonable facility and all possible assistance will be given correspondents to permit them to perform efficiently and intelligently their work of keeping the public informed of the activities of our forces within the limits dictated by military necessities.

c. So far as the exigencies of the service permit, correspondents will receive, without charge, the same medical treatment as that accorded officers.

d. Correspondents are free to converse with troops whenever they wish to do so, subject to the approval of the officer present with the troops in question. They are requested and expected, however, to refrain from conversing with troops at work or on guard, or from discussing subjects or soliciting answers to matters which are clearly secret.

■ 5. Application.—*a.* Application to accompany U. S. Army forces in the field will be submitted by the individual or by the agency concerned to the Director, War Department Bureau of Public Relations, Washington, D. C.

b. The application will state the name and address of the individual; qualifications and past experience in his field of work, including names of former agencies for which he worked; citizenship and place and date of birth; general health condition; the particular force it is desired he accompany; and any other pertinent information which will assist in the consideration of his application.

■ 6. LIMIT ON NUMBER.—*a.* The number of correspondents which will be accredited to a particular field force will be within the quota set by the War Department and based upon the recommendation of the force commander as determined by the size of the force, the distance from the usual media of news dissemination, and the availability of accommodations within the command or adjacent communities.

b. Representation with any one field force will be limited to one correspondent each from press associations, publications, radio, news, and picture syndicates; sole exception to this ruling will be the accrediting of a two man crew in the case of news reels. The War Department objective being the widest possible distribution of information to the American people, preferences in the consideration of applications will be given to agencies representing the largest possible news or picture dissemination.

c. In view of the importance of the work of correspondents in the field, and the necessary limitations as to the numbers of correspondents accredited to the field forces in any one theater of operations, the War Department will accredit only experienced newspaper men; all other conditions being equal, preference will be given to newspaper men with past military experience or past experience in the coverage of large maneuvers.

d. No officer, enlisted man, or civilian employee of the military forces serving in the theater of operations will be permitted to be a correspondent for any publication without the written permission of the theater or base commander. Correspondents will not use military titles in signing dispatches.

■ 7. AGREEMENT.—Before final acceptance a correspondent will be required to sign an agreement, in triplicate, as follows:

BASIC FIELD MANUAL

WAR DEPARTMENT

Bureau of Public Relations

Washington

(Date)

AGREEMENT

In connection with authority granted by the War Department to me, the undersigned, to accompany ----------------- for the purpose of securing news or story material, still or motion pictures, or to engage in radio broadcasting, I subscribe to the following conditions:

(Name of field force)

1. That, as a civilian accredited to the Army of the United States within or without the territorial limits of the United States, I am subject to the Articles of War and all regulations for the Government of the Army issued pursuant to law.

2. That, I will govern my movements and actions in accordance with the instructions of the War Department and the commanding officer of the Army unit to which I am accredited, which includes the submitting for the purposes of censorship all statements, written material, and all photography intended for publication or release either while with the Army or after my return, if the interviews, written matter, or photography are based on my observations made during the period or pertain to the places visited under this authority.

3. That, I waive all claims against the United States for losses, damages, or injuries which may be suffered as a result of this authority.

4. That, this authority is for the period ---------- to ----------, and subject to revocation at any time.

Signed: --------------------

Representing: ---------------------

(Company, syndicate, or agency)

Witnessing officer: -----------------

(Name)

(Grade and organization)

This form will be executed in triplicate for disposition as follows:

> 1 copy to War Department Bureau of Public Relations, for file.
>
> 1 copy to GHQ for transmittal to the commanding general of the field force concerned.
>
> 1 copy to correspondent.

■ 8. CREDENTIALS.—*a.* When an application for appointment as a correspondent is approved, the applicant will be furnished credentials and a Correspondent's Identification Card by the director of the War Department Bureau of Public Relations. The card is similar to W. D., A. G. O. Form No. 65–1 (Identification Card—Officers, Army of the United

States), but green in color, and identifies him as an accredited correspondent.

b. Correspondents will produce their identification cards whenever called for by any officer, warrant officer, or enlisted man in the execution of his duty. Failure to do so will subject the correspondent to arrest or detention.

c. In addition to the War Department credentials, the particular field force commander may issue a pass or credentials with regulations governing their use.

■ **9. UNIFORM.**—*a.* The proper uniform for accredited correspondents is that of an officer, but less all insignia of grade or arm or service, and without black and gold piping on field caps, officers' hat cords, or officers' insignia on the garrison cap if worn.

b. The uniform includes the wearing of the official brassard on the left arm. The brassard is a green cloth band, 4 inches wide, with the appropriate word, "Correspondent," "Photographer," "Radio Commentator," "Correspondent Chauffeur," "Photographer Chauffeur," "Radio News Chauffeur," "Correspondent Messenger," "Photographer Messenger," or "Radio News Messenger," in white block letters 1¼ inches in height. This will be furnished by the War Department Bureau of Public Relations at the time of appointment.

c. Articles of special clothing and equipment which are issued to officers and enlisted men in cold climates may be issued to correspondents. These articles must be turned in prior to departure from the theater of operations or base command.

d. Accredited correspondents will not wear civilian clothing while serving with the field force.

■ **10. TRANSPORTATION.**—*a.* Government transportation may be given accredited correspondents with the accommodations of an officer whenever such transportation—water, troop train, air, or automobile—is available and essential military personnel is not displaced or inconvenienced.

b. The baggage of correspondents will be moved with that of the headquarters to which attached. Its weight will be within the limits prescribed by the commander concerned.

■ **11. REPORTING UPON ARRIVAL.**—*a.* Upon arrival in the theater of operations or base command to which accredited, correspondents will report to the intelligence officer of the com-

11–13   BASIC FIELD MANUAL

mand, presenting their credentials. It is the intelligence officer, or his assistant in charge of public relations, who will exercise control of correspondents in the name of the field force commander, and it is to him correspondents should turn for assistance and guidance, or to register complaints if believed justified.

b. All correspondents are officially attached to the headquarters of the field force commander. They may, however, at their own request be placed on duty with a subordinate headquarters nearer to the scene of action. All changes of their base of operations will be done only upon the approval of the field force commander and contingent upon the availability of accommodations at the unit they wish to accompany.

■ 12. FILING OF MATERIAL.—a. All dispatches will be delivered, in duplicate, to the intelligence officer, or his assistant, for censorship prior to filing or mailing. In the process of censorship no changes will be made by the censor in dispatches except through deletion. Correspondents, unless the occasion is unusual, will be permitted to see their dispatches after being censored in the event they desire to make a revision, or to note the objectionable portions for future avoidance, or to recheck on wordage for cable charges.

b. Copy must be submitted for censorship on all broadcast interviews or news broadcasts.

■ 13. CENSORSHIP OF ARTICLES FOR PUBLICATION.—a. General.—In general, articles may be released for publication to the public provided—

(1) They are accurate in statement and implication.

(2) They do not supply military information to the enemy.

(3) They will not injure the morale of our forces, the people at home, or our allies.

(4) They will not embarrass the United States, its allies, or neutral countries.

b. Time element.—Intelligence officers charged with the censorship of articles for publication will take into consideration the time interval between the occurrence of events reported and the publication of the article concerning these events. If events are reported by cable, telegraph, or radio very shortly after their occurrence, the closest supervision will be necessary. If, on the other hand, the articles are forwarded by mail for printing in magazines or books, the time interval may be such as to render the information contained in the articles of little value to the enemy. Censorship regulations will be applied after consideration of this time element.

c. Specific rules governing censorship of articles for publication.—(1) The identity of organizations in the combat zone and in the communications zone will be announced only in official communiqués. When announced, they will never be associated with the name of a place.

(2) The name of an individual may be used whenever an article is materially helped by its use.

(3) Officers will not be quoted directly or indirectly nor anonymously on military matters except as specifically authorized by the theater commander.

(4) Within the combat zone no sector will be said to have any American troops in it until the enemy has established this as a fact.

(5) No town or village in the combat zone will be identified as holding American or allied forces except as an essential part of a story of an engagement and after the fact.

(6) No base port or communication center or other point of a line of communication will be mentioned by name or description as having anything to do with the activities of our forces.

(7) Ship or rail movements, real or possible, will not be discussed except as authorized by official communiqués.

(8) Plans of the Army, real or possible, will not be discussed.

(9) Numbers of troops as a total or as classes will not be discussed except as authorized by official communiqués.

(10) The effect of enemy fire or bombardment will not be discussed except as authorized in official communiqués.

(11) Articles for publication in the theater of operations or in allied countries or in neutral countries contiguous to the theater will be scrutinized carefully to make sure they do not hold possibilities of danger which the same stories printed in the United States would not hold. This applies not only to military information, which would thus be in the hands of the enemy within the day of writing, but also to an emphasis on small exploits which it may be extremely desirable to print in the United States but quite undesirable in the theater.

(12) Exaggerations of our activities accomplished or contemplated are prohibited.

13-14   BASIC FIELD MANUAL

(13) References to numbers of our own casualties will be based on the statements in official communiqués. Individual dead or wounded may be mentioned by name only when it is reasonably certain that the facts are correct and that some definite good end, such as offering examples of heroism, will be served by printing them. Mention by name will be allowed not earlier than 24 hours after the official cablegram announcement of such individual casualties has been sent to the War Department.

■ 14. PHOTOGRAPHIC CENSORSHIP.—*a. Still pictures.*—(1) All photographic negatives taken by official or accredited civilian photographers may be processed in the Signal Corps field laboratory or in such other laboratory installations as the theater commander may designate. Photographs will then be censored by a representative of G-2.

(2) No negatives or prints will be released except by authority of the theater commander. Such released prints or negatives will bear the censorship stamp and will be accompanied by suitable captions. A record of all such releases will be kept.

(3) Negatives and prints of accredited commercial correspondents not released by the censor will become the property of the United States Government, and will be forwarded through channels to the Military Intelligence Division, War Department General Staff, Washington, D. C., accompanied by full information sheet as to captions and the agency which took the photographs.

(4) Films or prints which cannot be processed locally, such as color film, will be delivered to a representative of G-2 marked, "Undeveloped film. Do not open." This will be forwarded by the fastest practicable means to the Military Intelligence Division, War Department General Staff, Washington, D. C.

(5) Regardless of the number of accredited correspondents any one agency has in the field, photographs from theaters of operation by newspaper photographers will be "rotoed." Photographs from theaters of operation of weekly magazine photographers will be rotoed.

b. Motion pictures.—(1) All exposed and undeveloped negative together with the dope sheets of accredited cameramen will be turned over to a representative of G-2 marked, "Unexposed film. Do not open."

(2) G–2 will forward this negative by the fastest practicable means to the Military Intelligence Division, War Department General Staff, Washington; D. C.

(3) In certain tropical climates where motion picture film deteriorates rapidly, it may be processed under the supervision of G–2 and the developed negative forwarded as directed in (2) above.

(4) By agreement between the War Department and the newsreel companies, all newsreel film from the theaters of operation will be rotoed by the Bureau of Public Relations, War Department, Washington, D. C.

c. Writers accredited as correspondents will not be permitted to take photographs.   Photographers accredited as correspondents will not be permitted to file stories.

d. For the privileges of "exclusive" photographs, see paragraph 18.

■ 15. SIGNAL AND MAIL SERVICE.—*a.* The signal system will be open to correspondents' dispatches, after censoring, when such use does not interfere with military needs.   Dispatches will be sent in the order of filing.   The intelligence officer under whom the correspondent serves is authorized to limit the number of words or otherwise to make an equitable adjustment of the use of the signal system among the correspondents when the system is inadequate to carry the complete text of all dispatches submitted.   If commercial cable or telegraph facilities are available, credit cards may be useful.

b. All mail, including personal letters, will be through the established censorship system.   The use of "blue envelopes" for the censoring of personal mail by the base censor is authorized, but these may not be used to mail photographs or dispatches for publication to avoid censoring by the immediate headquarters under which the correspondent serves.

■ 16. RELIEF FROM APPOINTMENT.—*a.* An accredited correspondent will not leave the theater of operations or base command without the written permission of the commander.

b. If serving with troops beyond the territorial limits of the United States, relief does not become effective until arrival in the United States, if the journey is made by Government transportation.

9

c. Upon termination of appointment as a correspondent, either on the application of the individual or his employer, by the request of the commander concerned, or by the expiration of the period of the appointment, the individual will surrender his credentials to the War Department Bureau of Public Relations and will cease wearing the official uniform of a correspondent.

■ **17. DISCIPLINE.**—*a.* A correspondent will be suspended from all privileges for the distortion of his dispatches *in the office of the publication which he represents,* and also for the use of words or expressions conveying a hidden meaning which would tend to mislead or deceive the censor and cause the approval by him of otherwise objectionable dispatches.

b. In the presence of the enemy he will conform to the actions of the troops, and will not jeopardize the safety of the command or compromise the scheme of maneuver in progress.

c. He may be subject to disciplinary action because of an intentional violation of these and other regulations, either in letter or in spirit, and in extreme cases of offense, where investigation proves the circumstances warrant, the correspondent may be placed in arrest to await deportation or trial by a court martial.

■ **18. VISITING CORRESPONDENT.**—*a.* A visiting correspondent, as differentiated from an accredited correspondent, is one who has permission from the Commander in Chief or the Secretary of War to visit the field force for the purpose of securing information or photographic material for publication *after* return from the visit.

b. Visiting correspondents will be limited to a specific itinerary as outlined in their letter of authorization, and will be accompanied ordinarily by a conducting officer. When not so accompanied, they will carry a letter from the intelligence officer of the field force. They are treated more in the nature of visitors than correspondents. They will comply with the regulations governing accredited correspondents, with the following modifications:

(1) They will not be required to wear the prescribed uniform but will wear the proper brassard.

(2) As a measure of protection to the accredited correspondents serving with the field forces, visiting correspond-

REGULATIONS FOR CORRESPONDENTS   **18**

ents will not be permitted to mail or file dispatches or
photographs intended for publication or release *during* the
period of their visit. So-called "spot" news will be reserved
for the accredited correspondents.

(3) Visiting photographers will have exclusive right to
their photographs and may not be required to "roto."

FM 30–26
C 1

BASIC FIELD MANUAL

REGULATIONS FOR CORRESPONDENTS ACCOMPANY-
ING U. S. ARMY FORCES IN THE FIELD

CHANGES No. 1	WAR DEPARTMENT, WASHINGTON, April 24, 1942.

FM 30–26, January 21, 1942, is changed as follows:

■ 9. UNIFORM.

*   *   *   *   *   *   *

b. The uniform includes the wearing of the official brassard on the left arm. The brassard is a green cloth band, 4 inches wide, with a white block letter, 2 inches in height, "C" for journalists, feature writers, and radio commentators; "P" for photographers. This brassard will be furnished by the War Department Bureau of Public Relations at the time of appointment.

*   *   *   *   *   *   *

[A. G. 062.11 (2–6–42).]   (C 1, April 24, 1942.)

BY ORDER OF THE SECRETARY OF WAR:

G. C. MARSHALL,
Chief of Staff.

OFFICIAL:

J. A. ULIO,
Major General,
The Adjutant General.

FM 30–26
C 2

BASIC FIELD MANUAL

REGULATIONS FOR CORRESPONDENTS ACCOMPANY-ING U. S. ARMY FORCES IN THE FIELD

CHANGES ⎫
No. 2 ⎭   WAR DEPARTMENT,
WASHINGTON, July 25, 1942.

FM 30–26, January 21, 1942, is changed as follows:

■ 2. DEFINITION.—The term "correspondent" as used   *   *   * pertains principally to the former. See paragraph 18 for instructions concerning visiting correspondents. Correspondents have the status of noncombatants.

    [A. G. 062.11 (7–20–42).]   (C 2, July 25, 1942.)

■ 7. AGREEMENT.—*a. Accredited correspondents.*—Before final acceptance an accredited correspondent will be required to sign an agreement, in triplicate, as follows:

   *   *   *   *   *   *   *   .

5. That at the termination of my assignment, I will surrender my credentials without delay to the Bureau of Public Relations, War Department.

   *   *   *   *   *   *   *

(Grade and organization)

b. Visiting correspondents.—Visiting correspondents will sign the following form:

WAR DEPARTMENT
Bureau of Public Relations
Washington

Date

AGREEMENT (Visiting)

In connection with recognition as a war correspondent outside the continental limits of the United States, granted by the War Department to me, the undersigned, for purpose of securing news or story material, still or motion pictures, or to engage in radio broadcasting I subscribe to the following conditions with reference to United States military and naval activities:

14

BASIC FIELD MANUAL

1. That as a civilian recognized as a war correspondent outside the continental limits of the United States, I am subject to the Articles of War and all regulations for the government of the Army issued pursuant to law, when with such forces.

2. That I will govern my movements and actions in accordance with the instructions of the War Department and the commanding officer of any Army or Navy unit which I may visit or observe, which includes the submitting, for purposes of censorship, all statements, written material intended for publication, and the undeveloped negatives of all film exposed while visiting or observing any Army or Navy unit. I further agree that I will submit for purposes of censorship all such material even though written after my return, if the interviews, written matter, or other material, including photographic prints, are based on my observations made during the period or pertain to the units visited or observed under this authority.

It is further understood and agreed that undeveloped film which cannot be processed and passed by the unit intelligence officer will be forwarded by him to the War Department.

3. That I waive all claims against the United States for losses, damages, or injuries which may be suffered as a result of this authority.

4. That this authority is subject to revocation at any time.

5. That at the termination of my assignment I will surrender my credentials without delay to the Bureau of Public Relations, War Department.

Signed: _____

Representing: _____

(Company, syndicate, or agency)

Witnessing officer: _____

(Name)

_____

(Grade and organization)

c. Disposition.—These forms will be executed in triplicate for disposition as follows:

*   *   *   *   *   *   *

[A. G. 062.11 (7–20–42).]   (C 2, July 25, 1942.)

9. Uniform.

*   *   *   *   *   *   *

REGULATIONS FOR CORRESPONDENTS

b. The uniform includes the official brassard worn on the left sleeve. This is a green cloth band, 4 inches wide, with a 2-inch white block letter "C" or "P", indicating the function of the correspondent. Journalists, feature writers, and radio commentators will wear "C" brassards. Photographers operating still or motion equipment will wear "P" brassards.

*   *   *   *   *   *   *

[A. G. 062.11 (7–20–42).]   (C 2, July 25, 1942.)

BY ORDER OF THE SECRETARY OF WAR:

G. C. MARSHALL,
Chief of Staff.

OFFICIAL:

J. A. ULIO,
Major General,
The Adjutant General.

16

FM 30–26
C 3

BASIC FIELD MANUAL

REGULATIONS FOR CORRESPONDENTS ACCOMPANYING U. S. ARMY FORCES IN THE FIELD

CHANGES }   WASHINGTON, December 23, 1942.
No. 3   }   WAR DEPARTMENT,

FM 30–26, January 21, 1942, is changed as follows:

■ 7. (AS changed by C 2.) AGREEMENT.—*a. Accredited correspondents.*

*   *   *   *   *   *   *

WAR DEPARTMENT

Bureau of Public Relations

Washington

                                            (Date)

AGREEMENT

*   *   *   *   *   *   *

2. That, I will govern * * * under this authority. I further agree that I will submit for purposes of censorship all such material even though written after my return, if the interviews, written material, or statements are based on my observations made during the period or pertain to the places visited under this authority. This includes all lectures, public talks, "off the record" speeches, and all photography intended for publication or release, either while with the armed forces or after my return, if they are based upon my observations during this period or pertain to the places visited.

b. Visiting correspondents.

*   *   *   *   *   *   *

WAR DEPARTMENT

Bureau of Public Relations

Washington

                                            (Date)

FM 30–26
C 3   BASIC FIELD MANUAL

AGREEMENT (Visiting)

*   *   *   *   *   *   *

2. That, I will govern my movements and actions in accordance with the instructions of the War Department and the commanding officer of the Army unit to which I am accredited, which includes submitting, for purposes of censorship, all statements or written material, lectures, public talks, "off the record" speeches, and all photography intended for publication or release either while with the Army or after my return, if the interviews, written matter, lectures, public talks, or "off the record" speeches are based on my observations made during the period or pertain to the places visited under this authority.

It is further *   *   *   the War Department.

*   *   *   *   *   *   *

[A. G. 062.11 (11–19–42.)]   (C 3, Dec. 23, 1942.)

BY ORDER OF THE SECRETARY OF WAR:

G. C. MARSHALL,
Chief of Staff.

OFFICIAL:
J. A. ULIO,
Major General,
The Adjutant General.

O

Korean War

The Korean War proved to be one of the more hazardous frontline assignments. Six American correspondents were killed there in the first year of the war alone. By the time the war ended, of the 350 correspondents accredited to the United Nations headquarters in Korea, a total of 18 correspondents and photographers had lost their lives. Most of the action took place in its first year, when there was little censorship or restrictions for press contingents and photographers seeking to cover the frontlines.

This Pulitzer Prize winning photo shows South Korean civilians fleeing across the destroyed Tae-dong River Bridge. Civilians and the military joined the mass of people fleeing the onslaught of North Korean and Chinese Communist forces pushing south. *Photo, Max Desfor, 1950*

Source: *Koreans Crossing the Mostly Destroyed Frozen Bridge at Taedong River* (1950) Max Desfor, Associated Press.

Vietnam War

U.S. Marines hurriedly carrying their fallen comrade to a waiting helicopter, near the Demilitarized Zone in South Vietnam. To the right of the soldiers is French photographer Catherine LeRoy. *Photo, Larry Burrows, 1966*

This iconic photo of a wounded GI reaching out to a stricken comrade at a first-aid center during Operation Prairie, shows the deep camaraderie between soldiers at war regardless of race, during a time of civil rights struggles and upheavals in the U.S. at home. *Photo, Larry Burrows, 1966*

Source: *A Dead Marine is Carried by his Buddies to a Helicopter … near DMZ* (1966) Catherine Leroy, Time Life/Getty Images; *A Wounded GI Reaches Out to a Stricken Comrade* (1966) Larry Burrows, Time Life/Getty Images.

Returning POW Lt. Col. Robert Stirm being greeted by his family at Travis Air Force Base in California, after being shot down over Hanoi in 1967. This classic coming-home photo seemingly represents the "everyday soldier" however, Stirm's received a "Dear John" letter from his wife three days earlier and they were divorced within the year. *Photo, Sal Veder, 1973*

Perhaps the greatest war crime of the Vietman conflict, the My Lai Massacre killed 300 men, women and children. This, and other photos by Sergeant Haeberle, not published until he left the military in 1970, did much to fuel the growing antiwar movement at home. *Photo, Ronald Haeberle, 1968*

Source: *Former POW LT Col. Rob Stirm Greeted by Family* (March 17, 1979) Sal Veder, Associated Press; *My Lai Massacre* (March 1968) Ronald Haeberle, Time Life/Getty Images.

Lebanon

*K*nown as the Lebanon War, the First Lebanon War and in Israel as Operation Peace
for Galilee, it began June 6, 1982 when Israel invaded southern Lebanon following the assassination attempt against Israel's Ambassador to
the United Kingdom. Targets of the operation

were the Palestinian Liberation Organization
(PLO) and Syrian forces that protected them. After Israel agreed to withdraw, international
peace keeping forces were sent in to keep the
truce. The Marines killed at the barracks were
part of this force.

Named World Press Photo of the Year, this was taken following the massacre of Palestinians men,
women and children at the Sabra and Shatila refugee camps by Christian Phalangist militiamen
supported by the Israelis in September 1982. *Photo, Robin Moyer, 1982*

Source: *Massacre of Palestinians by Christian Phalangists at Shatila Refugee Camp* (1982) Robin Moyer, Black Star/Time.

British soldiers helping rescue American soldiers following the terrorist bombing of the U.S. Marines barracks in Beirut. Of the 241 servicemen that were killed, 220 were Marines. This incident and the accompanying media coverage led to the withdrawal of American forces from Lebanon soon after. *Photo, Bill Foley, 1983*

Source: *Bombing of US Marine Barracks as Brit Soldiers Help Rescue Wounded Americans* (Oct. 23, 1983) Bill Foley, Associated Press

Gulf War

The first war in the Persian Gulf was one of the most restricted battlefields of the modern era. Photographers were often prevented from getting anywhere near the frontlines. Numerous stories were censored or held up. Among the thousands of photos taken by some *forty photographers on the battlefield there are no shots of American tanks firing during massive tank engagements and few pictures of dead soldiers. That is what makes the photo below so startling.*

This winner of the 1991 World Press Photo of the Year shows a U.S. sergeant just after realizing his best friend had died. It was taken on the last day of the Gulf War and is a poignant reminder of the realities of war. *Photo, David Turnley, 1991*

Source: *US Sergeant Mourns Death of Fellow Soldier by Friendly Fire Last Day of Gulf War, Iraq (1991)* David Turnley, Black Star/Detroit Free Press.

Wars in Iraq and Afghanistan

*M*ired in restrictive press pools and censorship, the Iraq and Afghanistan wars of the 21st century have become the most journalistically managed wars in history. They are also the most dangerous for correspondents. By 2008 more war correspondents were killed in Iraq than in the conflicts of World War II, Vietnam, the Balkans, and Korea combined (the vast majority were Iraqis). The Iraq War was the first American war where the Pentagon called its press corps for a military boot camp in preparation for covering the war. Journalists need Pentagon approval to cover both wars, introducing the journalistic expression "embedding" to the lexicon, although the principle of military control of the media can be found as far back as the 19th century Crimean War.

Embedding the Media

The Department of Defense (DOD) Pentagon established policies and procedures for embedding the news media in 2003, policies that have been revised over time. In 2009, U.S. military command banned journalists who were embedded with forces in eastern Afghanistan from videotaping or photographing soldiers killed in action. This was considered a response to the release of the photo of Lance Cpl. Bernard after he was fatally shot and at the center of the story "Death of a Marine." In a 2008, *New York Times* story reporters Michael Kamber and Tim Arango claimed that "After five years and more than 4,000 American combat deaths, searches and interviews turned up fewer than half-dozen photographs of dead American soldiers." Under the new Obama administration, the longstanding ban against photographing dead American soldiers flag-draped caskets at Dover Air Force Base in Delaware was lifted in April 2009, providing next of kin gave permission. See photos on following page.

This two-photograph sequence by *Reuters* photographer Joshua Roberts depicts eight soldiers carrying the casket of U.S. Air Force Staff Sergeant Phillip Myers of Hopewell Virginia as it is transferred to the United States from Iraq at Dover Air Force Base. Myers was fatally injured by an improvised explosive device (IED) on April 4, 2009 near Helmand Province in Afghanistan. The second photo shows the eight soldiers returning to the plane after leaving the casket on the ramp in preparation for transfer. For 18 years it had been Pentagon policy to forbid the press from covering the return of the nation's war dead. Marking an historic occasion in war journalism, President Obama overturned the prohibition in 2009 allowing the media to document the "dignified transfer" of a dead soldier for the first time since the First Gulf War in 1991. As prescribed by protocol the eight members are wearing white gloves and camouflage battle fatigues as they carry the flag-draped casket from the huge plane. Not seen in these photos are the airman's family members and a large press contingent here to witness this historic event on a "cool clear night" in April. *Photos, Joshua Roberts, 2009*

Source: *Flag-draped Casket of US Air Force Staff Sergeant Phillip Myers Returns to Dover Air Force Base* (2009), Joshua Roberts, Reuters.

*I*mmersed in two of the most dangerous wars in history for war journalists the British and American military have established a number of safeguard guidelines. Below is a set of standard safety guidelines written by major news agencies and news broadcasters, including CNN, BBC, ITN, Reuters, and APTN, for their war journalists, intended to limit their risks and protect them in hostile environments.

Excerpt from *Setting the Standard*

Safety Guidelines

Three major news broadcasters and the two major TV news agencies have joined together to establish common guidelines for their journalists working in war zones.

CNN, BBC, ITN, Reuters and APTN will publish their joint code of practice at the News World Conference in Barcelona. (Fira Palace Hotel, 16th November, Frontline Session and Journalists in Peril)

As well as agreeing a code of practice to protect journalists in the field they have also agreed to regularly share safety information and to work with other organisations, including international agencies, to safeguard journalists in war zones and other dangerous environments.

Speaking on behalf of the group, Richard Sambrook, Deputy Director of BBC News said: "This agreement represents unprecedented co-operation between competitors in the broadcast news industry to try to protect all journalists, staff and freelance, working in dangerous conditions. It's a starting point, not a final position. Our aim is to limit risk and to take responsibility for anyone working on our behalf in war zones or hostile environments. We have all signed up to these principles and agreed that safety can never be a competitive issue. We'd be delighted to talk to any other broadcast news organisations about further ways of safeguarding our teams."

The guidelines are:

- The preservation of human life and safety is paramount. Staff and freelances should be made aware that unwarranted risks in pursuit of a story are unacceptable and must be strongly discouraged. Assignments to war zones or hostile environments must be voluntary and should only involve experienced newsgatherers and those under their direct supervision.

- All staff and freelances asked to work in hostile environments must have access to appropriate safety training and retraining. Employers are encouraged to make this mandatory.

- Employers must provide efficient safety equipment to all staff and freelances assigned to hazardous locations, including personal issue kevlar vest/jackets, protective headgear and properly protected vehicles if necessary.

- All staff and freelances should be afforded personal insurance while working in hostile areas including cover against death and personal injury.

- Employers to provide and encourage the use of voluntary and confidential counselling for staff and freelances returning from hostile areas or after the coverage of distressing events. (This is likely to require some training of managers in the recognition of the symptoms of post traumatic stress disorder)

- Media companies and their representatives are neutral observers. No member of the media should carry a firearm in the course of their work.

- We will work together to establish a data-bank of safety information, including the exchange of up to date safety assessments of hostile and dangerous areas.

- We will work with other broadcasters and other organisations to safeguard journalists in the field.

CNN, BBC, ITN, Reuters and APTN

Source: *Setting the Standard: A Commitment to Frontline Journalism; An Obligation to Frontline Journalism.* The Freedom Forum European Centre, September 20, 2000. Safety Guidelines, Page 3 http://www.freedomforum.org.

In the so-called Green Book by the United Kingdom Ministry of Defence (MOD), the British formally recognized the issue of safety in war in its media operational procedures, This is the first time the MOD has offered a chapter on journalist safety in its working arrangements agreement with the media. The British joined with U.S. forces in the "Operation Enduring Freedom" invasion of Afghanistan in October 2001 in the wake of the 9/11 terrorist attacks. Since 2002 the UK has led its own military operation dubbed "Operation Herrick" as part of its own war on the Taliban and its allies. The British produced its MOD Green Book with the cooperation of the nation's main media organizations including the BBC, ITN, Sky News and the Newspaper Publishers Association. It has undergone periodic revision. With the increasing number of British casualties in Afghanistan the MOD responded by restricting access to combat zones. As a result British journalists, like their American counterparts, have found it almost impossible to reach or report from the frontlines. One British correspondent remarked in 2009 that "dealing with the Ministry of Defence is genuinely more stressful than coming under fire." British journalists had much freer access in the beginning of the war but were gradually forced to email their news reports to the military's press officers before publication. This has led reporters to tone down any criticism for fear they would not be allowed back into the war zone.

The *Green Book* chapters on the following pages includes suggestions for independent war correspondents, as well as for those who are embedded.

FOREWORD BY THE MINISTRY OF DEFENCE
DIRECTOR OF NEWS

This document has been produced in consultation with editors and press and broadcasting organisations as a general guide to the procedures that the United Kingdom Ministry of Defence (MOD) will adopt in working with the media throughout the full spectrum of military operations.

It covers the practical arrangements for enabling correspondents[1] to report on operations, including the MOD's plans for representative numbers of correspondents to accompany British Forces. It also addresses the policy and principles that will facilitate and may limit the activities of journalists during operations.

In short, the document sets out what editors can expect from the MOD and what the MOD seeks from the media. It is the result of continuing dialogue between the MOD and media organisations and representatives which began after the Falklands Conflict, was reviewed in the wake of the 1991 Gulf War and now takes account of lessons learned from subsequent operations.

The document remains a statement of intent and should be read in conjunction with specific advice that will be discussed with the media and issued by the MOD as part of the planning and preparation for each assignment.

SIMON WREN

The following media organisations have participated in this revision of the MOD Green Book:

- The Newspaper Publishers Association
- The Newspaper Society
- National Union of Journalists
- The British Broadcasting Corporation
- ITN
- Sky News
- The Scottish Daily Newspaper Society
- The International News Safety Institute
- The Independent Defence Media Association
- The London News Security Group

The MOD is also grateful to Michael Meyer (British Red Cross), who provided comments for and on behalf of the International Committee of the Red Cross and the British Red Cross.

MOD Director News welcomes comments on the MOD Green Book from all media organisations and will seek to address their comments in future revisions.

---

[1] In the context of this document, the term correspondent includes reporters, producers, photographers, cameramen, technicians and media support staff (e.g. drivers, logisticians, translators and security).

INDEX

Introduction   1
Initial Meetings with Editors and Media Organisations   2
Safety Advice   2
Security   3
Media Operations Staff   3
Operational Media Assignments   4
Media Accreditation   4
Selection of Accredited Correspondents   5
War Correspondents   6
Embed Assignments   7
Facilities in the UK   7
Briefings   7
Pooling   8
Control of Information   9
        Restrictions on Reporting   9
        Control of the Release of Information   10
        Embargoes   11
        Casualty Reporting   11
        Aircrew Interviews   13
        Prisoners of War   14
Assistance with Travel and Life Support   14

MOD WORKING ARRANGEMENTS WITH THE MEDIA FOR USE
THROUGHOUT THE FULL SPECTRUM OF MILITARY OPERATIONS

INTRODUCTION

1.   In an armed conflict and during military operations involving UK Forces, the Ministry of Defence (MOD) aims to provide the media with a range of facilities to enable reporting on operational and tactical military and defencerelated activity. In addition, the Department will seek to understand editors' and correspondents' requirements and provide an accurate, objective and timely information service.

2.   Prior to and during each assignment, editors and correspondents will be briefed as required at various levels and locations so that a regular and frank flow of information is maintained, with the aims of ensuring that the overall situation and the operational response is understood and that the British public and international audiences can be properly and fully kept abreast of developments and events.

3.   At the outset of an operation, the MOD will provide briefings ranging from those by ministers to officials and military officers as well as visits to units and other facilities as appropriate to each assignment. These will be arranged to demonstrate ongoing preparations to mobilise and deploy and, later, to give up-to-date information about progress of operations and the political situation. These facilities will always be tempered by the likely speed of deployment and the media's overall focus.

4.   In the theatre of operations, a media service will be established at the UK, Allied or coalition headquarters. Dependant on the geographical spread of the deployment and the specific command structure in place, further facilities will be provided to enable balanced access for as many correspondents as possible to represent the media as a whole with UK units and formations.

5.   The MOD and the Armed Forces will strive to give as many facilities and as much information as possible, subject to operational and security constraints. Where it is necessary to impose security checks, the MOD will seek the co-operation of editors in achieving a system which is fair and even handed and which is applied only in the interests of national or operational security, to safeguard UK, Allied or coalition operations or lives.

6.   The MOD recognises that correspondents are free to look for information in the area of operations and to communicate it back to the public. However, it is important to understand that this implies no specific obligation on the part of UK forces to protect individuals or installations over and above the rights of all civilians working in conflict zones set out in the Geneva Conventions and their Additional Protocols[2].

INITIAL MEETINGS WITH EDITORS AND MEDIA ORGANISATIONS IN TIMES OF CRISIS

7.   As a crisis evolves and/or when military action is anticipated, the MOD's Director of News, will have discussions with editors and media organisations. The dialogue will continue, as necessary, as events develop.

8.   Discussions will be in line with provisions outlined in this document and will cover practical and policy issues of mutual concern. These are likely to include:

- The number and nature of facilities for the media
- The safety of correspondents
- The MOD's security requirements
- Restrictions (if any) on numbers and allocation of places for correspondents
- Pooling arrangements
- Accreditation
- Relations with the UK's coalition partners/Allies, where applicable
- Communications and emission control
- General advice for editors and correspondents to assist their own preparations

SAFETY ADVICE

9.   The MOD recognises and understands the concerns of correspondents working in operational areas and other hostile environments regarding their own safety and protection. Correspondents who gain access to operational areas, other than under the auspices of MOD or Media Operations (Ops)

staffs, do so at their own risk. The MOD and Media Ops staffs can neither be held responsible for their safety nor guarantee to provide assistance.

---

[2] The four Geneva Conventions of 1949 and their two Additional Protocols of 1977 *only* apply to situations of armed conflicts, including military occupation. They are intended to alleviate the effects of armed conflict by protecting those not, or no longer, taking a direct part in hostilities and by regulating the means and methods of warfare. Journalists are considered civilians and thus must not be the object of attack unless and for such time as they take a direct part in hostilities (Article 79, Additional Protocol I). If captured they must be treated humanely. More detailed rules are contained in the Fourth Geneva Convention (dealing with "protected persons") and the Additional Protocols, where applicable (dealing with persons in the hands of a party to the conflict). Special rules apply to war correspondents when in enemy hands, see Art. 13(4), First Geneva Convention, Art. 13(4), Second Geneva Convention and Art. 4A(4), Third Geneva Convention. For further information on the Geneva Conventions, the Additional Protocols and the protection of journalists, you may contact the International Committee of the Red Cross (general enquiries: webmaster.gva@icrc.org; press and media: press.gva@icrc.org) or the British Red Cross (information@redcross.org.uk).

10.	It is also important to understand that UK Forces on operations will never deliberately target either individual correspondents or civil media facilities. However, media representatives also need to recognise that operations, and particularly those involving war-fighting, create extremely hazardous environments in which lethal force may be employed. In the often challenging situations that this engenders, mistakes resulting from mis-identification, weapons systems failure or mal-location, may result.

11.	Media representatives at all levels need to understand the challenges the military faces in working in often confused and fluid environments, and accept that blanket protection of media personnel will not be possible. Accordingly, correspondents who expect to work in these types of environment should be trained in risk evaluation and the fundamentals of working alongside the military. Too often, correspondents' lives are placed in danger through their own lack of understanding or knowledge. The responsibility rests with the individual and/or the individual's employer to ensure that they are appropriately prepared and trained for the assignment.

SECURITY

12.	The MOD Director News will maintain a dialogue with editors on the issue of security and security checks. If required, written guidance will be issued on security matters. This document sets out the principles governing the activities and conduct of correspondents attached to UK Forces. In addition, if required, a 24-hour advisory service will be maintained via the Duty Defence Press Officer, which editors may consult if in any doubt about security issues.

MEDIA OPERATIONS STAFF

13.	Specialist Media Ops staff[3] will be dispatched to the theatre of operations with the first troop deployments to assist with the provision of media facilities and the dissemination of information at UK, and Allied/coalition headquarters, and with units in the field. Their role is to support the military Commander in the execution of his mission. The Media Ops staff will endeavour to ensure that correspondents are provided with sufficient information, access and facilities to enable the media to develop a coherent understanding of the key issues involved and to pursue storylines as required.

---

[3] The term "Media Ops officer" covers both serving officer and MOD civilian staff engaged on Media Ops duties.

OPERATIONAL MEDIA ASSIGNMENTS

14.   **Accredited Correspondents**.   All correspondents on operational media assignments with UK Forces will require accreditation. During an armed conflict involving UK Forces (sometimes referred to as a high intensity operation) every accredited correspondent accompanying any element of the operational force will be designated as a **War Correspondent** (see under **WAR CORRESPONDENTS**).

15.   **Types of Assignment**.   The types of assignments that may be offered to accredited correspondents are as follows:

- Embed Assignments: Correspondents who are attached to specific units/sub-units.
- Centralised Assignments: Correspondents who are assigned to Press Information Centres/Media Ops teams at centralised/formation level locations.
- Individual Assignments: Correspondents who are working independently but participate in individual MOD/Media Ops staff arranged facilities.

16.   **Media Facilities**.   A range of media facilities may be offered by MOD/Media Ops staff. These may be one or a combination of the following:

- Press Conferences
- Interviews
- Briefings
- Visits
- Unit/sub-unit attachments

MEDIA ACCREDITATION

17.   All correspondents on assignments arranged under the auspices of the MOD Green Book will be required to obtain media accreditation with the military authorities to gain recognition as bona fide correspondents.

18.   On operations involving UK Forces only, accreditation can be obtained by application either to the Media Ops team within the MOD Directorate of News or to the Media Ops staff in theatre. On Coalition/Allied operations, the accreditation of media representatives may be carried out either through national or Coalition/Allied channels. Alternatively, host nations may insist on registering all media at national centres.

SELECTION OF ACCREDITED CORRESPONDENTS

19.   The MOD will accredit all correspondents before accepting them to accompany a British unit on any operation. This will be necessary to protect operational security in view of the high degree of operational access that it is planned to give.

20.   Accreditation will be at the discretion of the MOD, which will reserve the right to decide on numbers and to withhold or withdraw accreditation. However, the MOD will not employ accreditation to influence the choice of individuals. The reasons for any limitations on numbers will be the subject of discussion and explanation.

21.   The MOD will decide on the numbers of correspondents that can be accepted on any facility, having regard to all the operational and practical factors in each case. The MOD will also decide the composition of groups. If possible, representatives of the UK national and regional press, news agencies, broadcasters, and international media (in no particular order), will be included in every facility (using the table at **ANNEX D** as a guideline), with the aim of ensuring fair and balanced media representation.

22.   Having announced the numbers and composition of a facility, the MOD believes that the choice of which titles and individual correspondents should represent the media as a whole should be left to editors and media organisations   In the case of the press, the Newspaper Society, the Newspaper Publishers' Association and Scottish Daily Newspaper Society, in consultation with editors, will be invited[4] to select which newspapers will be allocated places on each facility. In the case of the broadcast media and agencies, where there are no corresponding associations, individual managements will be asked to reach mutual agreements. Editors of all titles selected will be expected to nominate individual correspondents. The MOD does not intend to be involved in this selection process unless news organisations are unable to reach agreement.

23.   Details of accreditation formalities are contained in the **Correspondent Accreditation Form** at Annex B.

24.   When selecting correspondents for facilities in the front line, editors should have regard to their physical stamina and ability to endure difficult and dangerous environments, since commanders will have the right to refuse access to a unit if, by reason of unfitness or temperament, an individual is thought likely to jeopardise operations, or the safety of personnel.

25.   If accreditation is refused, the MOD will inform the individual's editor, explaining the reasons for refusal. This also applies in cases where accreditation is withdrawn or where an individual is removed from an embed assignment. None of these occurrences will necessarily prejudice other nominations from the individual's organisation.

---

[4] Not all of these organisations will be approached on every occasion.

WAR CORRESPONDENTS

26.   Correspondents accompanying UK Forces during an armed conflict will need to be accredited to the armed forces if they are to attain the special status provided for them by Art. 4A(4) of the Third Geneva Convention. This will mean as an accredited 'War Correspondent' they will be required to carry an identity card (mentioned later in the Green Book) as a means of proof of such authorisation (see ICRC Commentary to the Third Geneva Convention (1960), p. 65.). War Correspondents will also be provided with distinguishing media insignia while working with units in the field. They will not be permitted to carry arms.

27.   Prior to deployment, War Correspondents will be placed at a number of days or hours of notice to move. The period of notice will alter as the situation develops. When placed on notice to move, War Correspondents will be expected to prepare themselves so that they are ready in all respects. In addition to the actions in **Preparations by War Correspondents Placed at Notice to Move** at Annex C the MOD will offer further advice and assistance as appropriate.

28.   Whilst the MOD recognises there is an undeniable interest on the part of the public in the progress of an armed conflict involving UK Forces, and that war correspondents should be free to communicate this, there may be exceptional circumstances when it is necessary to place limits on this freedom. It should though be understood that War Correspondents will not be 'controlled' by an MOD 'Minder'. This has often proved to be a source of friction in the past and has proved to be of little benefit to either the media or the military. However, they may still be required to submit their material for security checking and to undertake not to publish or divulge any operationally sensitive information gained as a member of a unit, without the specific permission of commanders (see under **CONTROL OF INFORMATION**). In addition they will have to agree not to cover events from the opposing side at any later stage, without the prior agreement of the MOD.

29.   Each correspondent's status as a War Correspondent will be protected by the issue by the MOD of internationally-recognised identity cards (Form 108). This accords correspondents a specific status under the terms of the Third Geneva Convention and gives them (officer status) prisoner of war protection should they be captured[5]. In other words the War Correspondent must be treated as a prisoner of war when captured, while at the same time keeping the status of civilian when accompanying British Forces on one essential condition, they must carry on them the authorisation issued by UK military authorities.

EMBED ASSIGNMENTS

30.   The purpose of embedding correspondents with units and formation headquarters' is to enable the media to gain a deeper understanding of the operation in which they are involved, particularly through largely unfettered access to personnel and commanders. They will be afforded all possible briefings and other facilities, including the opportunity to accompany British troops during war-fighting operations. Their individual requirements will be met wherever possible. In return, they will be subject to some military orders and training, both for their own safety and that of the unit.

31.   Once assigned to a particular unit or formation, it will not normally be possible for embedded correspondents to move between units. However, in some circumstances, editors may apply for their representatives to be re-assigned or replaced and, if it is practically possible, the MOD will make every effort to meet this request.

32.   Subject to conditions at the time, the MOD will aim to embed War Correspondents with UK combat units as a multi-discipline group of about five to seven accredited correspondents assigned to an individual combat unit; in ships at sea, with naval battlegroups; or at air bases.

33.   Embedded correspondents will live and work alongside the troops, sharing their food, accommodation and basic domestic chores. Within operational constraints, embedded correspondents will be given as many front line facilities as possible.

34.   The host unit will be responsible for assisting embedded correspondents with the dispatch of material, subject to the prevailing controls on emission, and for arranging security checking.

FACILITIES IN THE UK

35.   The MOD Director News will hold detailed discussions with editors and media organisations to ensure adequate practical provision for outside broadcast units, briefing and interview facilities and, wherever possible, to meet individual requirements. A programme of regular press conferences, briefings and facilities will be organised and individual briefing and interview requirements met where possible.

BRIEFINGS

36.   In the UK and in theatre the MOD will provide briefings in various forms, depending upon the scale of the operation:

- High level meetings with editors or senior editorial staff to resolve operational and facility difficulties and as an aid to understanding strategic thinking and the background to events

---

[5] Art. 4A(4)

7

- A 24-hour media enquiry service provided by the MOD Press Office

- A 24-hour high-level MOD advisory service for editors

- Open Press conferences by ministers, senior officers and/or officials

- Background briefings for defence correspondents. (These will be limited to recognised specialist defence correspondents, although the MOD may accept nominated deputies at these briefings, provided that they have relevant experience and can maintain continuity. This will be to ensure that the value and content of background briefings are not degraded).

37.   MOD and military spokesmen will offer these briefings at various levels under one of the following terms. The conditions of any briefing will be stated in advance:

- **Attributable**: The information is for use and can be quoted in full. It will be either "directly attributable" (where the spokesman can be identified by name), or "indirectly attributable" (where the person providing the information cannot be identified by name but can normally be described as "an MOD official ", "a UK military spokesman", etc).

- **Unattributable**: The information may be used but may not be attributed to a named source, either an individual or the organisation involved. Hence, for example, "military sources", or "Whitehall sources", but not "Ministry of Defence sources", or "4th Armoured Division sources".

- **Background**: the information is given to aid greater understanding. It will be stated at the time whether it may be used but, if used, may not be attributed in any way, except as though from a journalist's own knowledge.

- **Not for Use**: The information may not be published and is given only to aid greater understanding. The term "off the record", is sometimes misinterpreted, misunderstood and misused. It will not be employed.

POOLING

38.   Pooling arrangements will apply whenever demand exceeds capacity on a facility. In such cases, the MOD will endeavour to provide as many places as possible, so that the media as a whole will be represented. By making a wide range and number of facilities available and by adopting the pooling system, both in the UK and in theatre, it is intended that editors will be represented fairly and will gain a complete overall picture of events from a variety of sources.

39.   News organisations, editors and correspondents will have to agree among themselves about matters of style and presentation, resolve any differences about selection and representation and establish mutually acceptable working practices for pools and distribution of material. Editors whose representatives accept a pooled facility will be asked to make their own arrangements for making material available to the rest of the media.

40.   If pooling occurs it will mean that all written material and photographs and unabridged copies of broadcast tapes and film produced by all correspondents resulting from the facility will have to be made available to all media outlets on request.

41.   The MOD does not wish to interfere in matters of working practices or representation and selection, except in cases of unresolved differences among the media, when it may be forced to make the decisions in the greater public interest.

42.   Wherever possible, pooling arrangements will be made at news organisation/editor level but, at times, facility opportunities may arise in theatre at short notice. In these circumstances, the MOD would hope that arrangements with the media could be made locally by the Media Ops staff through a "pool co-ordinator" appointed by the media corps in theatre.

CONTROL OF INFORMATION

RESTRICTIONS ON REPORTING

43.   Correspondents must accept that, in the conditions under which they will be operating, the appropriate operational commander has the right to restrict what operational information can be reported and when. Correspondents will be advised on current restrictions (which will differ from operation to operation) by the nominated Media Ops officer, acting on behalf of the senior commander. Subjects that correspondents may not be allowed to include in copy, or radio or television reports without specific approval may include at least some of the following:

    a.   Composition of the force and the locations of ships, units and aircraft (see separate subsection on aircrew interviews).

    b.   Details of military movements.

    c.   Operational orders.

    d.   Plans or intentions.

    e.   Casualties (see separate sub section below).

    f.   Organisations.

    g.   Place names.

    h.   Tactics, details of defensive positions, camouflage methods, weapon capabilities or deployments.

i.   Names or numbers of ships, units or aircraft.

j.   Names of individual servicemen.

k.   Prisoners of War (see separate section).

CONTROL OF THE RELEASE OF INFORMATION

44.   In the interest of the security of the force and of the individual, correspondents must accept that, on certain occasions, they may be required to submit all written material, voice items intended for radio or television, films or video recordings produced for television, associated scripts or voice accompaniments, and still photographs for security checking clearance before transmission. Details of how this will be applied and actioned will be given by the nominated Media Ops officer. Applicants and their sponsors acknowledge this by signing the accreditation form at Annex B.

45.   The purpose of security checking material is to ensure only that no information is inadvertently made public which might be of benefit to an enemy, or would endanger an operation, or the lives of British or allied Servicemen or civilians.

46.   Security checking will be exercised in theatre. It will be an operational function of the UK Force Commander and will be conducted by operational officers, separate from the Media Ops function. The MOD will not impose a second tier of checking in London. Matters of taste and presentation will be for the media - although the MOD reserves the right to make its views known and make representations to editors where particular sensitivities arise.

47.   The aim will be to achieve a system which is fair, enlightened and efficient and to establish a relationship with the media based on openness and co-operation, leading to understanding and the acceptance of advice as to what is and what is not genuinely, operationally sensitive.

48.   Wherever possible, Media Ops staff and commanders, in London and in the theatre of operations, will attempt to explain the reasons why information cannot be given, or must be delayed. They will not attempt to deceive journalists or use them deliberately and unwittingly in furthering deception plans, although there will be, of course, occasions when operations are mounted to deceive the enemy when their true purpose will not be disclosed.

49.   The MOD recognises that views on what is and what is not of security value are subjective and that individual checking officers may apply different judgements. However, it will strive to achieve a system which is fair and even-handed. In the field, Media Ops staff will represent the views of correspondents to security checking officers in cases of disagreement, and they will liaise with senior officers in theatre, and with the MOD, to ensure that decisions are made for appropriate operational reasons.

50.   On the home front, editors should be aware that analysis of events and capabilities by well-informed specialists, such as academics, or retired officers and officials, could be of assistance to an enemy. They are requested, therefore, to take special care when inviting speculation from such experts.

EMBARGOES

51.   For the convenience of the media, there may be occasions when editors or correspondents are provided with operational information on the understanding that it will be embargoed. This will prevent information being published that would be of value to the enemy but will allow early briefing of the media when it would otherwise not be possible, thereby giving the media time to prepare material, or to plan for an event.

52. The MOD undertakes not to use an embargo unnecessarily, or for other than operational reasons. The reasons for its imposition will be explained, wherever possible, at the time it is declared and it will be in force for the minimum amount of time necessary.

53.   It should be understood that this could mean at times that a correspondent in theatre might be entrusted not to communicate information even to his or her editor until the expiry of the embargo. This will be made clear at the outset of the embargo by Theatre Media Ops staff.

54.   Information supplied under embargo implies considerable trust. Breaches will, therefore, be viewed seriously and may result in loss of accreditation and withdrawal of all facilities.

CASUALTY REPORTING

55.   The MOD is anxious to maintain close co-operation with editors during hostile operations on the question of casualties. It recognises that casualty information is of legitimate interest to the media and the public but it faces the difficulty that reports of casualties from individual operations could be of intelligence value to an enemy.

56.   However, while there may be occasions when the MOD will be forced to delay the release of casualty information for security reasons, in general it will aim to make announcements of losses and numbers of casualties as soon as possible after they are confirmed. (For practical purposes, this might be at set times).

57.   Casualty numbers will be provided by the relevant category e.g. as "killed (died on active service)", "injured", or "missing". It is unlikely that the MOD will be able to give details during the course of operations about the individual circumstances surrounding all casualties.

58.   It may be necessary to identify an individual group, unit, or ship which has been lost and to give details of the scale of casualties and/or survivors before next of kin have been informed - either to minimise anxiety which might be caused to families whose loved ones are not involved, or to counter enemy propaganda.

59.   However, the names of casualties will not be released or confirmed until the next of kin have been told officially and have been given a reasonable further period of time to inform their wider families.

60.   Once the next of kin have been informed, the names, ages, marital status, units, and home areas (not addresses) of those killed will be announced by the MOD in London as soon as practical.

61.   The names of personnel who are injured will not normally be released but the MOD, in some circumstances, may be prepared to confirm information obtained from other sources.

62.   Journalists may be aware of the names of individual casualties before official announcements are made. Because of the danger that it could be of value to an enemy, editors are urged not to publish such information, gained from whatever source - even if it comes directly from a next of kin - until it is released or confirmed by the MOD.

63.   The question of "missing" personnel poses a particular problem in this respect. In some circumstances it may be necessary for the MOD to withhold information about missing personnel for a considerable period - e.g. if a rescue operation is planned, or there is the likelihood they will evade capture. Editors should be aware that simply reporting that an individual is missing could be of value to the enemy, if they were unaware that he was evading capture. Similarly, personal information published about a missing serviceman could assist his interrogators if he were to be taken as a prisoner of war.

64.   For this reason, aircrew or other service personnel who might be captured by the enemy should not be identified with a particular operation without first seeking advice from MOD. Editors are urged not to publish any information, from whatever source, which might identify these personnel or give details of their personal backgrounds. Details of their families, homebase and home-town addresses and any other information, including photographs, which could assist an interrogator, or be exploited for propaganda purposes, should be similarly protected.

65.   The MOD would hope to enable the media to report the repatriation of wounded and, subject to the agreement of individuals and medical advice, would anticipate being able, on occasions, to offer facilities at reception points and hospitals for interviews with wounded personnel.

66.   The MOD is anxious, however, that the families of those killed, wounded, or missing should not be subjected to undue stress. The MOD urges extreme discretion by editors in approaching next of kin, particularly before official announcements are made.

67. Editors are also requested to ensure that their staffs do not approach the welfare organisations and casualty "helpline" services which will be set up to assist the families of servicemen during times of armed conflict. Direct enquiries could seriously hamper the work of these organisations. Casualty information and information about welfare activities will be available from the MOD Press Office. Media facilities with the welfare organisations will be arranged by the MOD Press Office and Media Ops staff in the commands.

AIRCREW INTERVIEWS

68.   Requests for interviews with operational aircrew and others who face the risk of being captured by the enemy may be considered subject to operational circumstances.

    a.   Correspondents should avoid the following:

- Any linkage between aircrew names and addresses (either home-base or home-town).

- Showing aircrew in flying suits which bear names, squadron badges or flying brevets.

- Film or photographs which reveal constituted crews. Shots of individual pilots, navigators etc are acceptable, as are shots of crews mixing together.

- Details of operations - e.g. heights and speeds employed, sortie frequency, time on task, and so on.

    b.   If the above guidelines are adhered to, there is no requirement to avoid showing aircrew faces; the following areas are perfectly
acceptable:

- Film and photographs of aircrew and groundcrew:
  o Briefing and debriefing (avoid crew linkage).
  o Walking to/from their aircraft.
  o Cockpit shots showing strapping in/unstrapping. o
  Refuelling and arming aircraft.

- Film and sound interviews focussed on the stated aim of the detachment, and general information about life on the detachment.

- Interviews may be given by the detachment commander, aircrew and groundcrew, provided that the individual from whom the interview is to be obtained agrees to the request.

13

PRISONERS OF WAR[6]

69.   The numbers of prisoners of war and the circumstances under which they are taken is a matter of legitimate public interest - but such publicity is constrained by the terms of the Geneva Conventions. Specifically, Article 13 of the Third Geneva Convention of 1949 protects prisoners of war from insults and public curiosity. In essence, this prohibits the public transmission of images of prisoners of war either as identifiable individuals or which undermine their personal dignity.

70.   The MOD and the UK Armed Forces will, therefore, attempt to provide accurate and up-to-date information and, where possible, will allow filming and photography to illustrate the scale and nature of capture. However, they will not offer any facility, or co-operate in any media activity, which contravenes the Geneva Convention. Interviews with prisoners, or close-up photography which focuses on individual prisoners will not normally be permitted. Media Ops staff will work closely with accredited correspondents to enable them to act prudently and discreetly when reporting on prisoners of war, bearing in mind the effect of publication or transmission of their work on prisoners of war or their families.

71.   The names of enemy prisoners of war and enemy dead held by UK Forces will not be made public by the MOD but will be released to the International Committee of the Red Cross (ICRC) in accordance with the terms of the Geneva Convention. The ICRC will normally divulge names only through official government channels or to the next of kin.

72.   The names of UK military prisoners of war, or those killed, whose bodies are held by the enemy, will normally be announced by the MOD once official confirmation has been received from the ICRC. Until that time, either their names will not be released, or they will be listed as "missing."

ASSISTANCE WITH TRAVEL AND LIFE SUPPORT

73.   The precise travel and life support arrangements, which will apply for each assignment, will be determined by the MOD in consultation with editors and freelance correspondents in advance of each assignment. The following paragraphs provide general amplification.

74.   **Visas**.   Correspondents will be responsible for making their own arrangements to obtain any visas that may be required.

75. **Travel to Theatre**.   The MOD will seek, wherever possible, to provide military transport to and from the theatre of operations (normally from the UK) for correspondents on embed and centralised assignments. However, editors and freelance correspondents should be prepared to make their own arrangements where viable commercial alternatives exist. In exceptional circumstances, and on a case-by-case basis, the MOD will consider providing transpor from the theatre of operations for those on independent assignments.

---

[6] The same measures apply to security internees held in Custody by UK Forces as an Occupying Power as provided for in Article 27 of the Fourth Geneva Convention.

76. **Transport within Theatre**. The MOD will provide transport for correspondents on embed and centralised assignments. Correspondents on independent assignments will be expected to make their own arrangements to get to media facilities, but they may be offered transport between a package of media facilities.

77. **Food and Accommodation**. Correspondents on embed and centralised assignments will be provided with food and accommodation by their host formation/unit. However, a charge may be raised for food and accommodation. Correspondents on independent assignments should expect to be self-sufficient and not rely on the military for support.

78. **Communications Equipment**. Correspondents will be expected to provide their own communications and transmission equipment. If absolutely necessary, assistance with communications may be given using military or MOD-controlled civil facilities. However, since the actual act of transmission could endanger an operation, or the safety of a unit under some circumstances, the use of both military and correspondents' own equipment will be at the discretion of commanders. Charges may be raised for the use of Service equipment.

79. **Medical Treatment**. Correspondents should seek medical advice from their doctor prior to travel. Correspondents on MOD-arranged assignments are entitled to receive Service medical treatment free in the operational area, but will be charged for such treatment outside the area. In an armed conflict, any sick or wounded correspondent would be entitled to medical treatment under the Geneva Conventions and Additional Protocols, see for example the definition of "wounded" and "sick" under Article 8(a) of Additional Protocol I, in conjunction with Art. 10, or Common Art. 3(2) to the four Geneva Conventions, and Art. 7 of Additional Protocol II.

80. **Casualties**. If an accredited correspondent is killed or injured whilst on an MOD-arranged assignment, the MOD will inform his or her employer as soon as the information is confirmed. It will be the employer's responsibility to inform the next of kin. The MOD will assist with arrangements for the repatriation of the dead or injured, however a charge may be raised. If judged appropriate, the MOD, without prejudice, will help with enquiries into the circumstances surrounding a death or injury.

81. **Dress and Equipment**. Correspondents will be expected to equip themselves with their own personal protective equipment (e.g. body armour, helmet). However, accredited correspondents may be issued with appropriate specialist protective clothing (as well as provided with any required training in its use) and combat clothing as worn by operational troops, but in the case of war correspondents with special media shoulder titles/armbands.

Embedding Media During Possible Operations/Deployments in the U.S. Central Command

PUBLIC AFFAIRS GUIDANCE (PAG) FOR MOVEMENT OF FORCES INTO THECENTCOM AOR FOR POSSIBLE FUTURE OPERATIONS.

1. PURPOSE. THIS MESSAGE PROVIDES GUIDANCE, POLICIES AND PROCEDURES ON EMBEDDING NEWS MEDIA DURING POSSIBLE FUTURE OPERATIONS/ DEPLOYMENTS IN THE CENTCOM AOR. IT CAN BE ADAPTED FOR USE IN OTHER UNIFIED COMMAND AORS AS NECESSARY.

2. POLICY.

2.A. THE DEPARTMENT OF DEFENSE (DOD) POLICY ON MEDIA COVERAGE OF FUTURE MILITARY OPERATIONS IS THAT MEDIA WILL HAVE LONG-TERM, MINIMALLY RESTRICTIVE ACCESS TO U.S. AIR, GROUND AND NAVAL FORCES THROUGH EMBEDDING. MEDIA COVERAGE OF ANY FUTURE OPERATION WILL, TO A LARGE EXTENT, SHAPE PUBLIC PERCEPTION OF THE NATIONAL SECURITY ENVIRONMENT NOW AND IN THE YEARS AHEAD. THIS HOLDS TRUE FOR THE U.S. PUBLIC; THE PUBLIC IN ALLIED COUNTRIES WHOSE OPINION CAN AFFECT THE DURABILITY OF OUR COALITION; AND PUBLICS IN COUNTRIES WHERE WE CONDUCT OPERATIONS, WHOSE PERCEPTIONS OF US CAN AFFECT THE COST AND DURATION OF OUR INVOLVEMENT. OUR ULTIMATE STRATEGIC SUCCESS IN BRINGING PEACE AND SECURITY TO THIS REGION WILL COME IN OUR LONG-TERM COMMITMENT TO SUPPORTING OUR DEMOCRATIC IDEALS. WE NEED TO TELL THE FACTUAL STORY - GOOD OR BAD - BEFORE OTHERS SEED THE MEDIA WITH DISINFORMATION AND DISTORTIONS, AS THEY MOST CERTAINLY WILL CONTINUE TO DO. OUR PEOPLE IN THE FIELD NEED TO TELL OUR STORY - ONLY COMMANDERS CAN ENSURE THE MEDIA GET TO THE STORY ALONGSIDE THE TROOPS. WE MUST ORGANIZE FOR AND FACILITATE ACCESS OF NATIONAL AND INTERNATIONAL MEDIA TO OUR FORCES, INCLUDING THOSE FORCES ENGAGED IN GROUND OPERATIONS, WITH THE GOAL OF DOING SO RIGHT FROM THE START. TO ACCOMPLISH THIS, WE WILL EMBED MEDIA WITH OUR UNITS. THESE EMBEDDED MEDIA WILL LIVE, WORK AND TRAVEL AS PART OF THE UNITS WITH WHICH THEY ARE EMBEDDED TO FACILITATE MAXIMUM, IN-DEPTH COVERAGE OF U.S. FORCES IN COMBAT AND RELATED OPERATIONS. COMMANDERS AND PUBLIC AFFAIRS OFFICERS MUST WORK TOGETHER TO BALANCE THE NEED FOR MEDIA ACCESS WITH THE NEED FOR OPERATIONAL SECURITY.

2.B. MEDIA WILL BE EMBEDDED WITH UNIT PERSONNEL AT AIR AND GROUND FORCES BASES AND AFLOAT TO ENSURE A FULL UNDERSTANDING OF ALL OPERATIONS. MEDIA WILL BE GIVEN ACCESS TO OPERATIONAL COMBAT MISSIONS, INCLUDING MISSION PREPARATION AND DEBRIEFING, WHENEVER POSSIBLE.

2.C. A MEDIA EMBED IS DEFINED AS A MEDIA REPRESENTATIVE REMAINING WITH A UNIT ON AN EXTENDED BASIS - PERHAPS A PERIOD OF WEEKS OR EVEN MONTHS. COMMANDERS WILL PROVIDE BILLETING, RATIONS AND MEDICAL ATTENTION, IF NEEDED, TO THE EMBEDDED MEDIA COMMENSURATE WITH THAT PROVIDED TO MEMBERS OF THE UNIT, AS WELL AS ACCESS TO MILITARY TRANSPORTATION AND ASSISTANCE WITH COMMUNICATIONS FILING/TRANSMITTING MEDIA PRODUCTS, IF REQUIRED.

2.C.1. EMBEDDED MEDIA ARE NOT AUTHORIZED USE OF THEIR OWN VEHICLES WHILE TRAVELING IN AN EMBEDDED STATUS.

2.C.2. TO THE EXTENT POSSIBLE, SPACE ON MILITARY TRANSPORTATION WILL BE MADE AVAILABLE FOR MEDIA EQUIPMENT NECESSARY TO COVER A PARTICULAR OPERATION. THE MEDIA IS RESPONSIBLE FOR LOADING AND CARRYING THEIR OWN EQUIPMENT AT ALL TIMES. USE OF PRIORITY INTER-THEATER AIRLIFT FOR EMBEDDED MEDIA TO COVER STORIES, AS WELL AS TO FILE STORIES, IS HIGHLY ENCOURAGED. SEATS ABOARD VEHICLES, AIRCRAFT AND NAVAL SHIPS WILL BE MADE AVAILABLE TO ALLOW MAXIMUM COVERAGE OF U.S. TROOPS IN THE FIELD.

2.C.3. UNITS SHOULD PLAN LIFT AND LOGISTICAL SUPPORT TO ASSIST IN MOVING MEDIA PRODUCTS TO AND FROM THE BATTLEFIELD SO AS TO TELL OUR STORY IN A TIMELY MANNER. IN THE EVENT OF COMMERCIAL COMMUNICATIONS DIFFICULTIES, MEDIA ARE AUTHORIZED TO FILE STORIES VIA EXPEDITIOUS MILITARY SIGNAL/COMMUNICATIONS CAPABILITIES.

2.C.4. NO COMMUNICATIONS EQUIPMENT FOR USE BY MEDIA IN THE CONDUCT OF THEIR DUTIES WILL BE SPECIFICALLY PROHIBITED. HOWEVER, UNIT COMMANDERS MAY IMPOSE TEMPORARY RESTRICTIONS ON ELECTRONIC TRANSMISSIONS FOR OPERATIONAL SECURITY REASONS.

MEDIA WILL SEEK APPROVAL TO USE ELECTRONIC DEVICES IN A COMBAT/HOSTILE ENVIRONMENT, UNLESS OTHERWISE DIRECTED BY THE UNIT

Source: *Public Affairs Guidance (PAG) on Embedding Media During Possible Operations/Deployments in the U.S. Central Command (CENTCOM) Area of Responsibility (AOR)*, http://fl1.findlaw.com.

COMMANDER OR HIS/HER DESIGNATED REPRESENTATIVE. THE USE OF COMMUNICATIONS EQUIPMENT WILL BE DISCUSSED IN FULL WHEN THE MEDIA ARRIVE AT THEIR ASSIGNED UNIT.

3. PROCEDURES.

3.A. THE OFFICE OF THE ASSISTANT SECRETARY OF DEFENSE FOR PUBLIC AFFAIRS (OASD(PA) IS THE CENTRAL AGENCY FOR MANAGING AND VETTING MEDIA EMBEDS TO INCLUDE ALLOCATING EMBED SLOTS TO MEDIA ORGANIZATIONS. EMBED AUTHORITY MAY BE DELEGATED TO SUBORDINATE ELEMENTS AFTER THE COMMENCEMENT OF HOSTILITIES AND AT THE DISCRETION OF OASD(PA). EMBED OPPORTUNITIES WILL BE ASSIGNED TO MEDIA ORGANIZATIONS, NOT TO INDIVIDUAL REPORTERS. THE DECISION AS TO WHICH MEDIA REPRESENTATIVE WILL FILL ASSIGNED EMBED SLOTS WILL BE MADE BY THE DESIGNATED POC FOR EACH NEWS ORGANIZATION.

3.A.1. IAW REF. A, COMMANDERS OF UNITS IN RECEIPT OF A DEPLOYMENT ORDER MAY EMBED REGIONAL/LOCAL MEDIA DURING PREPARATIONS FOR DEPLOYMENT, DEPLOYMENT AND ARRIVAL IN THEATER UPON RECEIPT OF THEATER CLEARANCE FROM CENTCOM AND APPROVAL OF THE COMPONENT COMMAND. COMMANDERS WILL INFORM THESE MEDIA, PRIOR TO THE DEPLOYING EMBED, THAT OASD(PA) IS THE APPROVAL AUTHORITY FOR ALL COMBAT EMBEDS AND THAT THEIR PARTICULAR EMBED MAY END AFTER THE UNIT'S ARRIVAL IN THEATER. THE MEDIA ORGANIZATION MAY APPLY TO OASD(PA) FOR CONTINUED EMBEDDING, BUT THERE IS NO GUARANTEE AND THE MEDIA ORGANIZATION WILL HAVE TO MAKE ARRANGEMENTS FOR AND PAY FOR THE JOURNALISTS' RETURN TRIP.

3.B. WITHOUT MAKING COMMITMENTS TO MEDIA ORGANIZATIONS, DEPLOYING UNITS WILL IDENTIFY LOCAL MEDIA FOR POTENTIAL EMBEDS AND NOMINATE THEM THROUGH PA CHANNELS TO OASD(PA) (POC: MAJ TIM BLAIR, DSN 27-1253; COMM. 703-697-1253; EMAIL

TIMOTHY.BLAIR@OSD.MIL). INFORMATION REQUIRED TO BE FORWARDED INCLUDES MEDIA ORGANIZATION, TYPE OF MEDIA AND CONTACT INFORMATION INCLUDING BUREAU CHIEF/MANAGING EDITOR/NEWS DIRECTOR'S NAME; OFFICE, HOME AND CELL PHONE NUMBERS; PAGER NUMBERS AND EMAIL ADDRESSES. SUBMISSIONS FOR EMBEDS WITH SPECIFIC UNITS SHOULD INCLUDE AN UNIT'S RECOMMENDATION AS TO WHETHER THE REQUEST SHOULD BE HONORED.

3.C. UNIT COMMANDERS SHOULD ALSO EXPRESS, THROUGH THEIR CHAIN OF COMMAND AND PA CHANNELS TO OASD(PA), THEIR DESIRE AND CAPABILITY TO SUPPORT ADDITIONAL MEDIA EMBEDS BEYOND THOSE ASSIGNED.

3.D. FREELANCE MEDIA WILL BE AUTHORIZED TO EMBED IF THEY ARESELECTED BY A NEWS ORGANIZATION AS THEIR EMBED REPRESENTATIVE.

3.E. UNITS WILL BE AUTHORIZED DIRECT COORDINATION WITH MEDIA AFTER ASSIGNMENT AND APPROVAL BY OASD(PA).

3.E.L.UNITS ARE RESPONSIBLE FOR ENSURING THAT ALL EMBEDDED MEDIA AND THEIR NEWS ORGANIZATIONS HAVE SIGNED THE "RELEASE, INDEMNIFICATION, AND HOLD HARMLESS AGREEMENT AND AGREEMENT NOT TO SUE", FOUND AT

HTTP://WWW.DEFENSELINK.MIL'NEWS/FEB2003/D20030210EMBED.PDF. UNITS MUST MAINTAIN A COPY OF THIS AGREEMENT FOR ALL MEDIA EMBEDDED WITH THEIR UNIT.

3.F. EMBEDDED MEDIA OPERATE AS PART OF THEIR ASSIGNED UNIT. AN ESCORT MAY BE ASSIGNED AT THE DISCRETION OF THE UNIT COMMANDER. THE ABSENCE OF A PA ESCORT IS NOT A REASON TO PRECLUDE MEDIA ACCESS TO OPERATIONS.

3.G. COMMANDERS WILL ENSURE THE MEDIA ARE PROVIDED WITH EVERY OPPORTUNITY TO OBSERVE ACTUAL COMBAT OPERATIONS. THE PERSONAL SAFETY OF CORRESPONDENTS IS NOT A REASON TO EXCLUDE THEM FROM COMBAT AREAS.

3.H. IF, IN THE OPINION OF THE UNIT COMMANDER, A MEDIA REPRESENTATIVE IS UNABLE TO WITHSTAND THE RIGOROUS CONDITIONS REQUIRED TO OPERATE WITH THE FORWARD DEPLOYED FORCES, THE COMMANDER OR HIS/HER REPRESENTATIVE MAY LIMIT THE REPRESENTATIVES PARTICIPATION WITH OPERATIONAL FORCES TO ENSURE UNIT SAFETY AND INFORM OASD(PA) THROUGH PA CHANNELS AS SOON AS POSSIBLE. GENDER WILL NOT BE AN EXCLUDING FACTOR UNDER ANY CIRCUMSTANCE.

3.1. IF FOR ANY REASON A MEDIA REPRESENTATIVE CANNOT PARTICIPATE IN AN OPERATION, THEY WILL BE TRANSPORTED TO THE NEXT HIGHER HEADQUARTERS FOR THE DURATION OF THE OPERATION.

3.J. COMMANDERS WILL OBTAIN THEATER CLEARANCE FROM CENTCOM/PA FOR MEDIA EMBARKING ON MILITARY CONVEYANCE FOR PURPOSES OF EMBEDDING.

3.K. UNITS HOSTING EMBEDDED MEDIA WILL ISSUE INVITATIONAL TRAVEL ORDERS, AND NUCLEAR, BIOLOGICAL AND CHEMICAL (NBC) GEAR. SEE PARA. 5. FOR DETAILS ON WHICH ITEMS ARE ISSUED AND WHICH ITEMS THE MEDIA ARE RESPONSIBLE TO PROVIDE FOR THEMSELVES.

3.L. MEDIA ARE RESPONSIBLE FOR OBTAINING THEIR OWN PASSPORTS AND VISAS.

3.M. MEDIA WILL AGREE TO ABIDE BY THE CENTCOM/OASD(PA) GROUND RULES STATED IN PARA. 4 OF THIS MESSAGE IN EXCHANGE FOR COMMAND/ UNIT-PROVIDED SUPPORT AND ACCESS TO SERVICE MEMBERS, INFORMATION AND OTHER PREVIOUSLY-STATED PRIVILEGES. ANY VIOLATION OF THE GROUND RULES COULD RESULT IN TERMINATION OF THAT MEDIA'S EMBED OPPORTUNITY.

3.N. DISPUTES/DIFFICULTIES. ISSUES, QUESTIONS, DIFFICULTIES OR DISPUTES ASSOCIATED WITH GROUND RULES OR OTHER ASPECTS OF EMBEDDING MEDIA THAT CANNOT BE RESOLVED AT THE UNIT LEVEL, OR THROUGH THE CHAIN OF COMMAND, WILL BE FORWARDED THROUGH PA CHANNELS FOR RESOLUTION. COMMANDERS WHO WISH TO TERMINATE AN EMBED FOR CAUSE MUST NOTIFY CENTCOM/PA PRIOR TO TERMINATION. IF A DISPUTE CANNOT BE RESOLVED AT A LOWER LEVEL, OASD(PA) WILL BE THE FINAL RESOLUTION AUTHORITY. IN ALL CASES, THIS SHOULD BE DONE AS EXPEDITIOUSLY AS POSSIBLE TO PRESERVE THE NEWS VALUE OF THE SITUATION.

3.0. MEDIA WILL PAY THEIR OWN BILLETING EXPENSES IF BILLETED IN A COMMERCIAL FACILITY.

3.P. MEDIA WILL DEPLOY WITH THE NECESSARY EQUIPMENT TO COLLECT AND TRANSMIT THEIR STORIES.

3.Q. THE STANDARD FOR RELEASE OF INFORMATION SHOULD BE TO ASK "WHY NOT RELEASE" VICE "WHY RELEASE." DECISIONS SHOULD BE MADE ASAP, PREFERABLY IN MINUTES, NOT HOURS.

3.R. THERE IS NO GENERAL REVIEW PROCESS FOR MEDIA PRODUCTS. SEE PARA 6.A. FOR FURTHER DETAIL CONCERNING SECURITY AT THE SOURCE.

3.S. MEDIA WILL ONLY BE GRANTED ACCESS TO DETAINEES OR EPWS WITHIN THE PROVISIONS OF THE GENEVA CONVENTIONS OF 1949. SEE PARA. 4.G.17. FOR THE GROUND RULE.

3.T. HAVING EMBEDDED MEDIA DOES NOT PRECLUDE CONTACT WITH OTHER MEDIA. EMBEDDED MEDIA,

AS A RESULT OF TIME INVESTED WITH THE UNIT AND GROUND RULES AGREEMENT, MAY HAVE A DIFFERENT LEVEL OF ACCESS.

3.U. CENTCOM/PA WILL ACCOUNT FOR EMBEDDED MEDIA DURING THE TIME THE MEDIA IS EMBEDDED IN THEATER. CENTCOM/PA WILL REPORT CHANGES IN EMBED STATUS TO OASD(PA) AS THEY OCCUR.

3.V. IF A MEDIA REPRESENTATIVE IS KILLED OR INJURED IN THE COURSE OF MILITARY OPERATIONS, THE UNIT WILL IMMEDIATELY NOTIFY OASD(PA), THROUGH PA CHANNELS. OASD(PA) WILL CONTACT THE RESPECTIVE MEDIA ORGANIZATION(S), WHICH WILL MAKE NEXT OF KIN NOTIFICATION IN ACCORDANCE WITH THE INDIVIDUAL'S WISHES.

3.W. MEDIA MAY TERMINATE THEIR EMBED OPPORTUNITY AT ANY TIME. UNIT COMMANDERS WILL PROVIDE, AS THE TACTICAL SITUATION PERMITS AND BASED ON THE AVAILABILITY OF TRANSPORTATION, MOVEMENT BACK TO THE NEAREST LOCATION WITH COMMERCIAL TRANSPORTATION.

3.W.1. DEPARTING MEDIA WILL BE DEBRIEFED ON OPERATIONAL SECURITY CONSIDERATIONS AS APPLICABLE TO ONGOING AND FUTURE OPERATIONS WHICH THEY MAY NOW HAVE INFORMATION CONCERNING.

4. GROUND RULES. FOR THE SAFETY AND SECURITY OF U.S. FORCES AND EMBEDDED MEDIA, MEDIA WILL ADHERE TO ESTABLISHED GROUND RULES. GROUND RULES WILL BE AGREED TO IN ADVANCE AND SIGNED BY MEDIA PRIOR TO EMBEDDING. VIOLATION OF THE GROUND RULES MAY RESULT IN THE IMMEDIATE TERMINATION OF THE EMBED AND REMOVAL FROM THE AOR. THESE GROUND RULES RECOGNIZE THE RIGHT OF THE MEDIA TO COVER MILITARY OPERATIONS AND ARE IN NO WAY INTENDED TO PREVENT RELEASE OF DEROGATORY, EMBARRASSING, NEGATIVE OR UNCOMPLIMENTARY INFORMATION. ANY MODIFICATION TO THE STANDARD GROUND RULES WILL BE FORWARDED THROUGH THE PA CHANNELS TO CENTCOM/PA FOR APPROVAL. STANDARD GROUND RULES ARE:

4.A. ALL INTERVIEWS WITH SERVICE MEMBERS WILL BE ON THE RECORD. SECURITY AT THE SOURCE IS THE POLICY. INTERVIEWS WITH PILOTS AND AIRCREW MEMBERS ARE AUTHORIZED UPON COMPLETION OF MISSIONS; HOWEVER, RELEASE OF INFORMATION MUST CONFORM TO THESE MEDIA GROUND RULES.

4.B. PRINT OR BROADCAST STORIES WILL BE DATELINED ACCORDING TO LOCAL GROUND RULES. LO-

CAL GROUND RULES WILL BE COORDINATED THROUGH COMMAND CHANNELS WITH CENTCOM.

4.C. MEDIA EMBEDDED WITH U.S. FORCES ARE NOT PERMITTED TO CARRY PERSONAL FIREARMS.

4.D. LIGHT DISCIPLINE RESTRICTIONS WILL BE FOLLOWED. VISIBLE LIGHT SOURCES, INCLUDING FLASH OR TELEVISION LIGHTS, FLASH CAMERAS WILL NOT BE USED WHEN OPERATING WITH FORCES AT NIGHT UNLESS SPECIFICALLY APPROVED IN ADVANCE BY THE ON-SCENE COMMANDER.

4.E. EMBARGOES MAY BE IMPOSED TO PROTECT OPERATIONAL SECURITY. EMBARGOES WILL ONLY BE USED FOR OPERATIONAL SECURITY AND WILL BE LIFTED AS SOON AS THE OPERATIONAL SECURITY ISSUE HAS PASSED.

4.F. THE FOLLOWING CATEGORIES OF INFORMATION ARE RELEASABLE.

4.F.1. APPROXIMATE FRIENDLY FORCE STRENGTH FIGURES.

4.F.2. APPROXIMATE FRIENDLY CASUALTY FIGURES BY SERVICE. EMBEDDED MEDIA MAY, WITHIN OPSEC LIMITS, CONFIRM UNIT CASUALTIES THEY HAVE WITNESSED.

4.F.3. CONFIRMED FIGURES OF ENEMY PERSONNEL DETAINED OR CAPTURED.

4.F.4. SIZE OF FRIENDLY FORCE PARTICIPATING IN AN ACTION OR OPERATION CAN BE DISCLOSED USING APPROXIMATE TERMS. SPECIFIC FORCE OR UNIT IDENTIFICATION MAY BE RELEASED WHEN IT NO LONGER WARRANTS SECURITY PROTECTION.

4.F.5. INFORMATION AND LOCATION OF MILITARY TARGETS AND OBJECTIVES PREVIOUSLY UNDER ATTACK.

4.F.6. GENERIC DESCRIPTION OF ORIGIN OF AIR OPERATIONS, SUCH AS "LAND-BASED."

4.F.7. DATE, TIME OR LOCATION OF PREVIOUS CONVENTIONAL MILITARY MISSIONS AND ACTIONS, AS WELL AS MISSION RESULTS ARE RELEASABLE ONLY IF DESCRIBED IN GENERAL TERMS.

4.F.8. TYPES OF ORDNANCE EXPENDED IN GENERAL TERMS.

4.F.9. NUMBER OF AERIAL COMBAT OR RECONNAISSANCE MISSIONS ORSORTIES FLOWN IN CENTCOM'S AREA OF OPERATION.

4.F.10. TYPE OF FORCES INVOLVED (E.G., AIR DEFENSE, INFANTRY, ARMOR, MARINES).

4.F.11. ALLIED PARTICIPATION BY TYPE OF OPERATION (SHIPS, AIRCRAFT, GROUND UNITS, ETC.) AFTER APPROVAL OF THE ALLIED UNIT COMMANDER.

4.F.12. OPERATION CODE NAMES.

4.F.13. NAMES AND HOMETOWNS OF U.S. MILITARY UNITS.

4.F.14. SERVICE MEMBERS' NAMES AND HOME TOWNS WITH THE INDIVIDUALS' CONSENT.

4.G. THE FOLLOWING CATEGORIES OF INFORMATION ARE NOT RELEASABLE SINCE THEIR PUBLICATION OR BROADCAST COULD JEOPARDIZE OPERATIONS AND ENDANGER LIVES.

4.G.1. SPECIFIC NUMBER OF TROOPS IN UNITS BELOW CORPS/MEF LEVEL.

4.G.2. SPECIFIC NUMBER OF AIRCRAFT IN UNITS AT OR BELOW THE AIR EXPEDITIONARY WING LEVEL.

4.G.3. SPECIFIC NUMBERS REGARDING OTHER EQUIPMENT OR CRITICAL SUPPLIES (E.G. ARTILLERY, TANKS, LANDING CRAFT, RADARS, TRUCKS, WATER, ETC.).

4.G.4. SPECIFIC NUMBERS OF SHIPS IN UNITS BELOW THE CARRIER BATTLE GROUP LEVEL.

4.G.5. NAMES OF MILITARY INSTALLATIONS OR SPECIFIC GEOGRAPHIC LOCATIONS OF MILITARY UNITS IN THE CENTCOM AREA OF RESPONSIBILITY, UNLESS SPECIFICALLY RELEASED BY THE DEPARTMENT OF DEFENSE OR AUTHORIZED BY THE CENTCOM COMMANDER. NEWS AND IMAGERY PRODUCTS THAT IDENTIFY OR INCLUDE IDENTIFIABLE FEATURES OF THESE LOCATIONS ARE NOT AUTHORIZED FOR RELEASE.

4.G.6. INFORMATION REGARDING FUTURE OPERATIONS.

4.G.7. INFORMATION REGARDING FORCE PROTECTION MEASURES AT MILITARY INSTALLATIONS OR ENCAMPMENTS (EXCEPT THOSE WHICH ARE VISIBLE OR READILY APPARENT).

4.G.8. PHOTOGRAPHY SHOWING LEVEL OF SECURITY AT MILITARY INSTALLATIONS OR ENCAMPMENTS.

4.G.9. RULES OF ENGAGEMENT.

4.G.10. INFORMATION ON INTELLIGENCE COLLECTION ACTIVITIES COMPROMISING TACTICS, TECHNIQUES OR PROCEDURES.

4.G.11. EXTRA PRECAUTIONS IN REPORTING WILL BE REQUIRED AT THE COMMENCEMENT OF HOSTILITIES TO MAXIMIZE OPERATIONAL SURPRISE. LIVE BROADCASTS FROM AIRFIELDS, ON THE GROUND OR AFLOAT, BY EMBEDDED MEDIA ARE PROHIBITED UNTIL THE SAFE RETURN OF THE INITIAL STRIKE PACKAGE OR UNTIL AUTHORIZED BY THE UNIT COMMANDER.

4.G.12. DURING AN OPERATION, SPECIFIC INFORMATION ON FRIENDLY FORCE TROOP MOVEMENTS, TACTICAL DEPLOYMENTS, AND DISPOSITIONS THAT WOULD JEOPARDIZE OPERATIONAL SECURITY OR LIVES. INFORMATION ON ON-GOING ENGAGEMENTS WILL NOT BE RELEASED UNLESS AUTHORIZED FOR RELEASE BY ON-SCENE COMMANDER.

4.G.13. INFORMATION ON SPECIAL OPERATIONS UNITS, UNIQUE OPERATIONS METHODOLOGY OR TACTICS, FOR EXAMPLE, AIR OPERATIONS, ANGLES OF ATTACK, AND SPEEDS; NAVAL TACTICAL OR EVASIVE MANEUVERS, ETC. GENERAL TERMS SUCH AS "LOW" OR "FAST" MAY BE USED.

4.G.14. INFORMATION ON EFFECTIVENESS OF ENEMY ELECTRONIC WARFARE.

4.G.15. INFORMATION IDENTIFYING POSTPONED OR CANCELED OPERATIONS.

4.G.16. INFORMATION ON MISSING OR DOWNED AIRCRAFT OR MISSING VESSELS WHILE SEARCH AND RESCUE AND RECOVERY OPERATIONS ARE BEING PLANNED OR UNDERWAY.

4.G.17. INFORMATION ON EFFECTIVENESS OF ENEMY CAMOUFLAGE, COVER, DECEPTION, TARGETING, DIRECT AND INDIRECT FIRE, INTELLIGENCE COLLECTION, OR SECURITY MEASURES.

4.G.18. NO PHOTOGRAPHS OR OTHER VISUAL MEDIA SHOWING AN ENEMY PRISONER OF WAR OR DETAINEE'S RECOGNIZABLE FACE, NAMETAG OR OTHER IDENTIFYING FEATURE OR ITEM MAY BE TAKEN.

4.G.19. STILL OR VIDEO IMAGERY OF CUSTODY OPERATIONS OR INTERVIEWS WITH PERSONS UNDER CUSTODY.

4.H. THE FOLLOWING PROCEDURES AND POLICIES APPLY TO COVERAGE OF WOUNDED, INJURED, AND ILL PERSONNEL:

4.H.1. MEDIA REPRESENTATIVES WILL BE REMINDED OF THE SENSITIVITY OF USING NAMES OF INDIVIDUAL CASUALTIES OR PHOTOGRAPHS THEY MAY HAVE TAKEN WHICH CLEARLY IDENTIFY CASUALTIES UNTIL AFTER NOTIFICATION OF THE NOK AND RELEASE BY OASD(PA).

4.H.2. BATTLEFIELD CASUALTIES MAY BE COVERED BY EMBEDDED MEDIA AS LONG AS THE SERVICE MEMBER'S IDENTITY IS PROTECTED FROM DISCLOSURE FOR 72 HOURS OR UPON VERIFICATION OF NOK NOTIFICATION, WHICHEVER IS FIRST.

4.H.3. MEDIA VISITS TO MEDICAL FACILITIES WILL BE IN ACCORDANCE WITH APPLICABLE REGULATIONS, STANDARD OPERATING PROCEDURES, OPERATIONS ORDERS AND INSTRUCTIONS BY ATTENDING PHYSICIANS. IF APPROVED, SERVICE OR MEDICAL FACILITY PERSONNEL MUST ESCORT MEDIA AT ALL TIMES.

4.H.4. PATIENT WELFARE, PATIENT PRIVACY, AND NEXT OF KIN/FAMILY CONSIDERATIONS ARE THE GOVERNING CONCERNS ABOUT NEWS MEDIA COVERAGE OF WOUNDED, INJURED, AND ILL PERSONNEL IN MEDICAL TREATMENT FACILITIES OR OTHER CASUALTY COLLECTION AND TREATMENT LOCATIONS.

4.H.5. MEDIA VISITSAREAUTHORIZED TO MEDICAL CARE FACILITIES, BUT MUST BE APPROVEDBYTHE MEDICAL FACILITY COMMANDER AND ATTENDING PHYSICIANANDMUST NOT INTERFERE WITH MEDICAL TREATMENT. REQUESTSTOVISIT MEDICAL CARE FACILITIES OUTSIDE THE CONTINENTAL UNITED STATES WILL BE COORDINATED BY THE UNIFIED COMMAND PA.

4.H.6. REPORTERS MAY VISIT THOSE AREAS DESIGNATED BY THE FACILITY COMMANDER, BUT WILL NOT BE ALLOWED IN OPERATING ROOMS DURING OPERATING PROCEDURES.

4.H.7. PERMISSION TO INTERVIEW OR PHOTOGRAPH A PATIENT WILL BE GRANTED ONLY WITH THE CONSENT OF THE ATTENDING PHYSICIAN OR FACILITY COMMANDER AND WITH THE PATIENT'S INFORMED CONSENT, WITNESSED BY THE ESCORT.

4.H.8. "INFORMED CONSENT" MEANS THE PATIENT UNDERSTANDS HIS OR HER PICTURE AND COMMENTS ARE BEING COLLECTED FOR NEWS MEDIA PURPOSES AND THEY MAY APPEAR NATIONWIDE IN NEWS MEDIA REPORTS.

4.H.9. THE ATTENDING PHYSICIAN OR ESCORT SHOULD ADVISE THE SERVICE MEMBER IF NOK HAVE BEEN NOTIFIED.

5. IMMUNIZATIONS AND PERSONAL PROTECTIVE GEAR.

5.A. MEDIA ORGANIZATIONS SHOULD ENSURE THAT MEDIA ARE PROPERLY IMMUNIZED BEFORE EMBEDDING WITH UNITS. THE CENTERS FOR DISEASE CONTROL (CDC)-RECOMMENDED IMMUNIZATIONS FOR DEPLOYMENT TO THE MIDDLE EAST INCLUDE HEPATITIS A; HEPATITIS B; RABIES; TETANUS-DIPHTHERIA; AND TYPHOID. THE CDC RECOMMENDS MENINGOCOCCAL IMMUNIZATIONS FOR VISITORS TO MECCA. IF TRAVELING TO CERTAIN AREAS IN THE CENTCOM AOR, THE CDC RECOMMENDS TAKING PRESCRIPTION ANTIMALARIAL DRUGS. ANTHRAX AND SMALLPOX VACCINES WILL BE PROVIDED TO THE MEDIA AT NO EXPENSE TO THE GOVERNMENT (THE MEDIA OUTLET WILL BEAR THE EXPENSE). FOR MORE HEALTH INFORMATION FOR TRAVELERS TO THE MIDDLE EAST, GO TO THE CDC WEB SITE AT TTY //WWW EL,/MIDEAST.HTM.

5.B. BECAUSE THE USE OF PERSONAL PROTECTIVE GEAR, SUCH AS HELMETS OR FLAK VESTS, IS BOTH A PERSONAL AND PROFESSIONAL CHOICE, MEDIA WILL BE RESPONSIBLE FOR PROCURING/USING SUCH EQUIPMENT. PERSONAL PROTECTIVE GEAR, AS WELL AS CLOTHING, WILL BE SUBDUED IN COLOR AND APPEARANCE.

5.C. EMBEDDED MEDIA ARE AUTHORIZED AND REQUIRED TO BE PROVIDED WITH, ON A TEMPORARY LOAN BASIS, NUCLEAR, BIOLOGICAL, CHEMICAL (NBC) PROTECTIVE EQUIPMENT BY THE UNIT WITH WHICH THEY ARE EMBEDDED. UNIT PERSONNEL WILL PROVIDE BASIC INSTRUCTION IN THE PROPER WEAR, USE, AND MAINTENANCE OF THE EQUIPMENT. UPON TERMINATION OF THE EMBED, INITIATED BY EITHER PARTY, THE NBC EQUIPMENT SHALL BE RETURNED TO THE EMBEDDING UNIT. IF SUFFICIENT NBC PROTECTIVE EQUIPMENT IS NOT AVAILABLE FOR EMBEDDED MEDIA, COMMANDERS MAY PURCHASE ADDITIONAL EQUIPMENT, WITH FUNDS NORMALLY AVAILABLE FOR THAT PURPOSE, AND LOAN IT TO EMBEDDED MEDIA IN ACCORDANCE WITH THIS PARAGRAPH.

6. SECURITY

6.A. MEDIA PRODUCTS WILL NOT BE SUBJECT TO SECURITY REVIEW OR CENSORSHIP EXCEPT AS INDICATED IN PARA. 6.A.1. SECURITY AT THE SOURCE WILL BE THE RULE. U.S. MILITARY PERSONNEL SHALL PROTECT CLASSIFIED INFORMATION FROM UNAUTHORIZED OR INADVERTENT DISCLOSURE. MEDIA PROVIDED ACCESS TO SENSITIVE INFORMATION, INFORMATION WHICH IS NOT CLASSIFIED BUT WHICH MAY BE OF OPERATIONAL VALUE TO AN ADVERSARY OR WHEN COMBINED WITH OTHER UNCLASSIFIED INFORMATION MAY REVEAL CLASSIFIED INFORMATION, WILL BE INFORMED IN ADVANCE BY THE UNIT COMMANDER OR HIS/HER DESIGNATED REPRESENTATIVE OF THE RESTRICTIONS ON THE USE OR DISCLOSURE OF SUCH INFORMATION. WHEN IN DOUBT, MEDIA WILL CONSULT WITH THE UNIT COMMANDER OR HIS/HER DESIGNATED REPRESENTATIVE.

6.A.1. THE NATURE OF THE EMBEDDING PROCESS MAY INVOLVE OBSERVATION OF SENSITIVE INFORMATION, INCLUDING TROOP MOVEMENTS, BATTLE PREPARATIONS, MATERIEL CAPABILITIES AND VULNERABILITIES AND OTHER INFORMATION AS LISTED IN PARA. 4.G. WHEN A COMMANDER OR HIS/HER DESIGNATED REPRESENTATIVE HAS REASON TO BELIEVE THAT A MEDIA MEMBER WILL HAVE ACCESS TO THIS TYPE OF SENSITIVE INFORMATION, PRIOR TO ALLOWING SUCH ACCESS, HE/SHE WILL TAKE PRUDENT PRECAUTIONS TO ENSURE THE SECURITY OF THAT INFORMATION. THE PRIMARY SAFEGUARD WILL BE TO BRIEF MEDIA IN ADVANCE ABOUT WHAT INFORMATION IS SENSITIVE AND WHAT THE PARAMETERS ARE FOR COVERING THIS TYPE OF INFORMATION. IF MEDIA ARE INADVERTENTLY EXPOSED TO SENSITIVE INFORMATION THEY SHOULD BE BRIEFED AFTER EXPOSURE ON WHAT INFORMATION THEY SHOULD AVOID COVERING. IN INSTANCES WHERE A UNIT COMMANDER OR THE DESIGNATED REPRESENTATIVE DETERMINES THAT COVERAGE OF A STORY WILL INVOLVE EXPOSURE TO SENSITIVE INFORMATION BEYOND THE SCOPE OF WHAT MAY BE PROTECTED BY PREBRIEFING OR DEBRIEFING, BUT COVERAGE OF WHICH IS IN THE BEST INTERESTS OF THE DOD, THE COMMANDER MAY OFFER ACCESS IF THE REPORTER AGREES TO A SECURITY REVIEW OF THEIR COVERAGE. AGREEMENT TO SECURITY REVIEW IN EXCHANGE FOR THIS TYPE OF ACCESS MUST BE STRICTLY VOLUNTARY AND IF THE REPORTER DOES NOT AGREE, THEN ACCESS MAY NOT BE GRANTED. IF A SECURITY REVIEW IS AGREED TO, IT WILL NOT INVOLVE ANY EDITORIAL CHANGES; IT WILL BE CONDUCTED SOLELY TO ENSURE THAT NO SENSITIVE OR CLASSIFIED INFORMATION IS INCLUDED IN THE PRODUCT. IF SUCH INFORMATION IS FOUND, THE MEDIA WILL BE ASKED TO REMOVE THAT INFORMATION FROM THE PRODUCT AND/OR EMBARGO THE PRODUCT UNTIL SUCH INFORMATION IS NO LONGER CLASSIFIED OR SENSITIVE. REVIEWS ARE TO BE DONE AS SOON AS PRACTICAL SO AS NOT TO INTERRUPT COMBAT OPERATIONS NOR DELAY REPORTING. IF THERE ARE DISPUTES RESULTING FROM THE SECURITY REVIEW PROCESS THEY MAY BE APPEALED THROUGH THE CHAIN OF COMMAND, OR THROUGH PA CHANNELS TO OASD/PA. THIS PARAGRAPH DOES NOT

AUTHORIZE COMMANDERS TO ALLOW MEDIA ACCESS TO CLASSIFIED INFORMATION.

6.A.2. MEDIA PRODUCTS WILL NOT BE CONFISCATED OR OTHERWISE IMPOUNDED. IF IT IS BELIEVED THAT CLASSIFIED INFORMATION HAS BEEN COMPROMISED AND THE MEDIA REPRESENTATIVE REFUSES TO REMOVE THAT INFORMATION NOTIFY THE CPIC AND/OR OASD/PA AS SOON AS POSSIBLE SO THE ISSUE MAY BE ADDRESSED WITH THE MEDIA ORGANIZATION'S MANAGEMENT.

7. MISCELLANEOUS/COORDINATING INSTRUCTIONS:

7.A. OASD(PA) IS THE INITIAL EMBED AUTHORITY. EMBEDDING PROCEDURES AND ASSIGNMENT AUTHORITY MAY BE TRANSFERRED TO CENTCOM PA AT A LATER DATE. THIS AUTHORITY MAY BE FURTHER DELEGATED AT CENTCOM'S DISCRETION.

7.B. THIS GUIDANCE AUTHORIZES BLANKET APPROVAL FOR NON-LOCAL AND LOCAL MEDIA TRAVEL ABOARD DOD AIRLIFT FOR ALL EMBEDDED MEDIA ON A NO-COST, SPACE AVAILABLE BASIS. NO ADDITIONAL COSTS SHALL BE INCURRED BY THE GOVERNMENT TO PROVIDE ASSISTANCE IAW DODI 5410.15, PARA 3.4.

7.C. USE OF LIPSTICK AND HELMET-MOUNTED CAMERAS ON COMBAT SORTIES IS APPROVED AND ENCOURAGED TO THE GREATEST EXTENT POSSIBLE.

8. OASD(PA) POC FOR EMBEDDING MEDIA IS MAJ TIM BLAIR, DSN 227-1253, CMCL 703-697-1253, EMAIL TIMOTHY.BLAIR@OSD.MIL.

During the past decade war journalists have made the jump from the traditional media to digital technology, transforming the way journalists cover the war zone. Many reporters are now able to operate as virtual one-man news units with the ability to shoot, write and transmit their reports without a crew. The print media has made the transition as well. Many of the most popular news journals are only available online while others offer both print and Internet versions. The following dispatches by New York Times *reporter Mark Mazzetti were published in* Slate *while he was on the staff of* US News and World Report *in November 2002. In this excerpt he describes going through the media boot camp in 2002.*

Dispatches From Media Boot Camp

Updated Friday, Nov. 22, 2002, at 11:02 AM ET

Iwo Jima

Posted Monday, Nov. 18, 2002, at 1:17 PM ET

It doesn't take long for the 6-foot swells off the North Carolina coast to have their way with 20 reporters sandwiched in a hovercraft heading out to sea. Sitting in jump seats normally occupied by Marines in full combat gear, we watch each others' faces turn unnatural shades, and the whole group fights the urge to toss up the ham-bologna-and-cheese sandwich served on the bus. Two colleagues soon succumb. Just as I hand a plastic bag to the newspaper reporter sitting next to me-who looks about ready to follow suit-the Navy's "Landing Craft Air Cushion" hops its final wave and slides into the belly of the USS Iwo Jima.

Thus begins media boot camp. For seven days, 58 journalists from 31 news organizations are training for war-or, at least as much of the war as the Pentagon will allow us to see. If the Bush

administration actually proceeds with a war against Saddam Hussein, the Defense Department is planning to "embed" journalists with military units before they head into Iraq. So for the first time ever, the military is training reporters en masse for the rigors of life in a combat zone.

After receiving requests from more than 400 reporters, the Pentagon chose an initial group of 58 (including one reporter from the United Arab Emirates and another from Russia's Tass News Service) and plans several more boot camps before any shooting starts in Iraq. The Defense Department picks up most of the tab for the program, with the exception of the meals served during the week. (The cost of the bologna sandwich several of the reporters "refunded" was $3.60.) The idea behind the boot camps is simple: The more reporters experience military life, the less chance there is they will slow down, screw up, or report inaccurately about the military unit they are embedded with. It's also a way to make the military brass comfortable with once again letting reporters bum rides on the way to war-a policy that, for the most part, was abandoned after Vietnam.

The Navy was in charge of the first two days of the program, with the Marine Corps handling the next five at Quantico, Va. As the media trainees see it, the weekend with the Navy was the calm before the storm. Despite the nausea-inducing trip out to the Iwo Jima, the Navy training was primarily a slate of briefings about shipboard safety procedures and the capabilities of Tomahawk cruise missiles (Shameless Microsoft plug for Slate-readers: The computers the Navy uses to fire Tomahawks run on Windows NT). With the Marines, however, we are expecting the first hour of Full Metal Jacket.

Aboard the Iwo Jima, a large-deck amphibious ship sailing off the Atlantic Coast, we are first briefed by the ship's commanding officer, Capt. John Nawrocki. Our job, he tells us, is to "drink from the veritable fire hose of knowledge." But we also get a taste of the literal fire hose. During a drill simulating a small-boat attack on the Iwo

Jima (similar to al-Qaida's 2000 attack against the USS Cole), several reporters don protective gear on the helicopter hangar deck and are sprayed by the ship's emergency fire team. After that, there's the pipe patching drill, where reporters team up with crewmen under a broken pipe to plug a massive surge of water before it floods the ship.

The biggest concern for most reporters slated to cover Gulf War II is that Saddam will use chemical or biological weapons, so media boot camp includes seven hours of training to protect against weapons of mass destruction. The Marines are planning to deliver the bulk of the training, including time in a gas chamber (dubbed the "confidence chamber" by Marines with a clumsy sense of euphemism.) But the Navy briefed us about the standard military-issue chem/bio suit and mask and what they protect against. The good news: They protect against nerve agents like Sarin gas. The bad news: They don't protect against "blood agents" like cyanide, which restrict the ability of blood to absorb oxygen. But there's a silver lining, according to Chief Petty Officer Dave Rawlin: "The good thing about blood agents is that if you don't die within the first couple of minutes, you're going to live." All are not comforted by this.

We leave on Monday afternoon for Quantico, where the Marines are waiting to get their hands on us.

Posted Wednesday, Nov. 20, 2002, at 1:32 PM ET

In case anybody forgot that the Marines had taken over our training, the slogan above the classroom was a reminder: "Retreat, hell. We just got here." Then there was the stocky general from Jersey City, N.J., standing in front of the lecture hall, who seemed to relish what lay ahead for the group who had just finished three days with the Navy. "Your days of clean sheets and hot meals will be over for you," said Brigadier Gen. George Flynn, commanding general of the Marines' training command. They spared us the angry drill sergeant banging on a trash can,

but we did get a loud rap on our barracks door at 5 a.m.

We have yet to be asked what "our major malfunction" is, but the Marines must have figured that asking a group of journalists that question might result in a long answer. In reality, the Quantico experience thus far is less Full Metal Jacket than Stripes: an attempt to turn 58 pen-toting pantywaists into 58 ... well, people who are less pantywaistish than when they arrived. The Marines are giving us an abbreviated version of the six-month course they give to young lieutenants. And while our trainers know it's impossible to stuff six months into five days, like good Marines, they're doing their damnedest to give it a shot.

Upon arrival at Quantico, we were issued helmets, canteens, camouflage jackets, and first-aid kits. On the packing list provided before we departed for boot camp, we were also told to bring a "1/2 roll of toilet paper in a Ziploc bag" for any contingencies that might arise during outdoor training. Some of the reporters confide that they secretly packed an entire roll, just in case. And, after a morning of briefings with one of the military's most lethal weapons, the PowerPoint slide, we finally got out into the field.

The first afternoon of training was composed of four hours of weapons orientation and land mine awareness. The Marines blew up rusted armored vehicles and wooden posts in a display of what millions of dollars of machinery could do but turned down the requests from some of the more gung-ho members of our group to test out the weapons themselves. Things turned sober when two Marines took shots at a Kevlar flak vest hanging on a post with a "squad automatic weapon"-the same flak vest all of us were decked out in. The .556 caliber bullets blew the stuffing out of the vest. Though comforting, the term "body armor" is less than accurate.

Although few of the military trainers mention the "I" word unless pressed by reporters in the group, Iraq was mentioned as among the four countries most densely populated with land mines (along with Afghanistan, Cambodia, and Angola). For the many of us who had received land mine awareness training before covering Afghanistan, Tuesday's training at Quantico confirmed what we already knew: Once you realize you are surrounded by land mines, it's probably too late. Your best bet is to poke around with a large stick to navigate the hazards. But, as Marine Capt. Nicole Dube admitted, "It's not ideal, and that's why it sucks."

As the afternoon progressed, reporters dipped into their day packs and dined on an assortment of "Meals Ready to Eat."

The four-course meals have a shelf life of more than a decade, and the menu includes pork chow mein, beef burritos, and something called "ham slice." (In Afghanistan, the MRE swap meet was a favorite pastime for reporters, who bartered freeze-dried bags of pound cake, peanut butter, and pasta alfredo like fourth-graders at recess. There, the military taught us some culinary delicacies of the forward deployed, such as "ranger pudding": one part crushed saltines, one part hot-chocolate mix, one part water. Emeril wouldn't eat it, but it goes well with goat stew.)

The first full day at Quantico concluded with two hours on first aid for shock, abdominal injuries, and "sucking chest wounds." And a helpful tip should we get to Iraq: Don't smoke while using a military latrine. The smoke could mix with the chemicals used to decompose human waste, and you might blow up. Our parting gifts after Tuesday's classes were tubes of camouflage face paint in three shades: mud brown, flat black, and leaf green. They are meant to outfit us for Wednesday's festivities of loading up in helicopters, dropping into a "hot" landing zone, tagging along as Marines assault a mock city, and sleeping out under the Virginia sky.

Posted Friday, Nov. 22, 2002, at 11:02 AM ET

"Gas! Gas! Gas!" shouts the Marine instructor and begins counting down from nine. Across the lecture hall, reporters drop doughnuts and spill cups of coffee as they fumble for their masks. As the count hits zero, a quarter of the room is still breathing Saddam's chemicals, and 15 of our group have become battlefield casualties. One scribe, clearly frustrated by the quick countdown, asks why only nine seconds. "Because at 10 seconds you die," answers the instructor. Got it.

It's weapons of mass destruction day, and the attention span of 58 sleep-deprived reporters just got longer. The group is burnt after six days of 5 A.M. wake-up calls, but looking at gruesome picture of mustard gas victims from the Iran-Iraq War has a way of waking people up. The instructors spend all morning running the gamut of deadly chemical and biological agents and teaching about the best way to respond to a battlefield attack. In a nutshell: The chem/bio (MOPP) suits give protection, but the short response time punishes the slow. Should symptoms of chemical exposure (nausea, drooling, convulsions) set in, a series of Atropine injections to the leg are required. If two don't do the job, you "throw the Hail Mary" and give the third. For the first time all week, every reporter in the room is diligently taking notes.

After class, it's time to show off what we've learned. We gear up in a MOPP suit, mask, boots, and gloves, and troop off to the "confidence chamber." The squat, cinderblock building is hardly a welcoming site, and one reporter who covered the Tim McVeigh execution remarks how similar it looks to the death chamber in Terre Haute, Ind. The purpose of the exercise is to expose us to a gas environment-in this case, tear gas-and allow us to become more confident with the ability of the chem/bio gear to protect us.

But in short, "confidence" isn't high. After an entire morning hearing the details about sarin, anthrax, and cyanide, some of us begin to reconsider our line of work-and wonder whether it might be a safer bet to start covering the Department of Transportation beat. Nevertheless, in groups of 10, we file into the hazy chamber and line up against the wall. Upon orders from the Marine instructor, we take the masks on and off, and practice "clearing" techniques to blow tear gas out of the mask. Despite various degrees of burning eyes and skin, our level of exposure is no worse than the average protester at a WTO convention.

As if getting sprayed with tear gas isn't enough for one day, after the confidence chamber we have the pleasure of spending an hour with Master Sgt. William DuBose, who leads the physical training portion of the program. His biceps are larger than most of our waists, and he seems to have a perverse love of "diamond" pushups. As he swaps off with the other Marine NCOs in leading calisthenics, some of my media brethren begin to run out of steam. But ever a hardy lot, we don't sustain any casualties. Fortunately, one hour with Master Sg. DuBose entitles us to spend the rest of

Thursday night at the bar-the only place at Quantico where a group of reporters can hold their own against their Marine instructors.

Friday is "media crucible" day. It's the day the Few, the Proud, the Reporters get a final shot at glory with a 5-mile tactical road march. The word around the campfire is that we might get ambushed with a faux chemical attack, and there may be other surprises along the way.

Whatever happens will likely end up on CNN, since other members of the media have been invited on base for the day to watch us suffer. So not only do we get to lug out packs up and down the hills of Quantico, but we get to do it in front of members of our profession who dodged media boot camp. The pansies

Charter for the Safety of Journalists Working in War Zones or Dangerous Areas

The safety of journalists working on dangerous assignments is not always guaranteed, even if international law provides adequate protection on paper, because warring parties these days are showing less and less respect for that law. News-gatherers cannot get assurances from belligerents that they will be fully protected.

Because of the risks they run to keep the public informed, media workers, journalists and their assistants (whether permanent staff or freelance) working in war zones or dangerous areas are entitled to basic protection, compensation and guarantees from their employers, though protection must never be taken to mean supervision by local military and governmental authorities. Media management also have their own responsibility to make every effort to prevent and reduce the risks involved.

The following eight principles shall apply:

Principle 1 - Commitment

The media, public authorities and journalists themselves shall systematically seek ways to assess and reduce the risks in war zones or dangerous areas by consulting each other and exchanging all useful information. Risks to be taken by staff or freelance journalists, their assistants, local employees and support personnel require adequate preparation, information, insurance and equipment.

Principle 2 - Free will

Covering wars involves an acceptance by media workers of the risks attached and also a personal commitment which means they go on a strictly voluntary basis. Because of the risks, they should have the right to refuse such assignments without explanation and without there being any finding of unprofessionnal conduct. In the field, the assignment can be terminated at the request of the reporter or the editors after each side has consulted the other and taken into account their mutual responsibilities. Editors should beware of exerting any kind of pressure on special correspondents to take additional risks.

Principle 3 - Experience

War reporting requires special skills and experience, so editors should choose staff or freelances who are mature and used to crisis situations. Journalists covering a war for the first time should not be sent there alone, but be accompanied by a more experienced reporter. Teamwork in the field should be encouraged. Editors should systematically debrief staff when they return so as to learn from their experiences.

Principle 4 - Preparation

Regular training in how to cope in war zones or dangerous areas will help reduce the risk to journalists. Editors should inform staff and freelances of any special training offered by nationally or internationally qualified bodies and give them access to it. All journalists called upon to work in a hostile environment should have first-aid training. Every accredited journalism school should familiarise its students with these issues.

Principle 5 - Equipment

Editors should provide special correspondents working in dangerous areas with reliable safety equipment (bullet-proof jackets, helmets and, if possible, armoured vehicles), communication equipment (locator beacons) and survival and first-aid kits.

Principle 6 - Insurance

Journalists and their assistants working in war zones or dangerous areas should have insurance to cover illness, repatriation, disability and loss of life. Media management should take all necessary steps to provide this before sending or employing personnal on dangerous assignments. They should strictly comply with all applicable professional conventions and agreements.

Principle 7 - Psychological counselling

Media management should ensure that journalists and their assistants who so desire have access to psychological counselling after returning from dangerous areas or reporting on shocking events.

Principle 8 - Legal protection

Journalists on dangerous assignments are considered civilians under Article 79 of Additional Protocol I of the Geneva Conventions, provided they do not do anything or behave in any way that might compromise this status, such as directly helping a war, bearing arms or spying. Any deliberate attack on a journalist that causes death or serious physical injury is a major breach of this Protocol and deemed a war crime.

Reporters Without Borders — Reporters sans fronti res
March 2002

A *former soldier, war correspondent Michael Yon is heir to a tradition of the soldier-as-war journalist that dates back at least to the Victorian era. An ex-Green Beret, Yon is also representative of the 21st century war reporter who has won an admiring following in the digital era with his online magazine called MichaelYon-Online.com. His work has been widely published and cited. Here, he conveys the capricious tragedy of war as he recounts the death of 23-year-old soldier Adam Ray.*

Excerpt from: ***MichaelYan.OnlineMagazine***

Adam Ray

On Feb. 9th, in a field near a road, an Afghan soldier squatted to relieve himself. He picked the wrong spot. A bomb exploded, blowing off a leg, and he died. Captain John Weatherly, Commander of Charlie Company of the 4-23 Infantry at FOB Price in Helmand Province, mentioned that in passing as he described the series of events that led to the death of Specialist - now Sergeant - Adam Ray, a vigorous 23 year old, born in Tampa, Florida. The bomb the Afghan stumbled upon was near the IED that struck Adam.

Without the thousands of culverts underneath, the roads of Afghanistan would be flooded and washed away during the snow melts and rains. In safe countries, drivers pay as little attention to culverts as we would to telephone poles. As a practical matter they are invisible to us.

In the war zone that is Afghanistan, life and limb depend on noticing normally mundane things like culverts. They are a favorite hiding spot for the Taliban to plant bombs intended to kill Americans driving the roads. Hundreds, even thousands of pounds of explosives can be stuffed inside, launching our vehicles into the sky, flipping them over and over, sometimes killing all. And so, in some areas, soldiers on missions must stop dozens of times to check culverts for explosives. Since we do this every day in front of thousands of Afghans, they know our patterns. In addition to planting bombs in culverts, they plant mines and other bombs near culverts, to get men who stop to check.

The U.S. military has been taking inventory of the culverts, identifying their exact locations, and documenting them with photos and maps. The military has embarked on a program to place barriers on culverts over which our troops cross on any regular basis. The enemy tries to remove or circumvent the barriers, and so night and day we have SKTs (Small Kill Teams) who move from place to place watching culverts. The SKTs frequently call fire that kills men who come to place bombs. When more enemy comes to collect the bodies, we kill them, too. But the SKTs can't be everywhere all the time, and so this wily adversary lands hard blows every day.

The main route west from Kandahar is Highway 1, the jugular for ground transport in Afghanistan, which also connects to major cities like Kabul. Donor nations have invested hundreds of millions of dollars to construct and attempt to safeguard this crucial passageway. Yet the enemy is always there, leaving convoys smoldering and bullet-riddled bodies slumped over steering wheels or crumpled on the road.

Between Kandahar and just east of FOB Tombstone most of the culverts have been blocked with obstacles such as concertina razor wire, yet ten remained open.

And so on Tuesday, 9 February 2010, Charlie Company from the 4th Battalion 23rd Infantry of the 5/2 Stryker Brigade Combat Team from Fort Lewis, headed out to conduct "culvert denial." The Soldiers know the risks of approaching the culverts, yet they do it anyway.

Staff Sergeant Christine Jones from the 4th Combat Camera Squadron was along on the mission. Company Commander Captain John Weatherly was away at a meeting when 3rd Platoon arrived west of Maiwand, just off the

Source: *Iraqi Soldier Stands Guard* (2010) Hadi Mizban, Associated Press; *U.S. Army Soldier at Scene of Blast* (2010), Associated Press.

south side of Highway 1, near the village of Yakhchal, a Taliban stronghold.

The unreleased combat photos show that the morning was clear and bright. Soldiers can be seen unwinding concertina wire at the mouth of one side of the culvert. Specialist Adam Ray walks across the road to the other side of the culvert, down in the drainage area, and a photo catches dust in the air. A flock of birds can be seen taking flight. The meta-data on the image indicates it was 9:30 AM. A white 4-door car sped away, over the culvert, and Sergeant Jones quickly snapped to get the plate. Subsequent investigations indicated the car was not involved. The soldiers' discipline speaks for itself; nobody shot at it.

Adam Ray was among the three soldiers who had been wounded by the small explosion.

Captain Weatherly got the radio call and headed over, as did Army medevac helicopters. Adam's feet and legs were fine; the explosive was buried higher up, near the road at the side of the culvert. He had been hit in the neck. The other two soldiers had arm wounds that were not severe. Despite the danger of more bombs, the photos show soldiers and medics diving straight in to help. Adam was patched and put onto a litter, and soon an Army helicopter with a red cross landed in the dust. The wounded were loaded and flown to Camp Bastion where Adam Ray, the third of five children, beloved son of a minister and a devoted mother, a soccer player and a flirt, who tutored dyslexic kids and was known to ask less popular girls to dance at school events, died. He was 23 years old.

This two-photo sequence of scenes in Iraq, shows the aftermath of increased violence in that country as American combat troops continue to withdraw toward their goal of 50,000 remaining by the end of the summer, 2010. Top: An Iraqi soldier stands guard outside the office of the Al-Arabiya television station in Baghdad after a suicide bomber driving a minivan struck. *Photo, Hadi Mizban, July, 2010.* Bottom: An American soldier at the scene of a fatal suicide car bomb in Ramadi, west of Baghdad, killing civilians standing in line at the post office. *Photo, AP, August, 2010*

U.S. Army soldiers clear their weapons as they wait to board a military aircraft in Baghdad, as they begin their journey home, part of American troop drawdown. *Photo, Maya Alleruzzo, August 13, 2010*

Two U.S. soldiers of the last combat brigade to leave Iraq during the drawdown of U.S. forces, celebrate as they cross over the border from Iraq into Kuwait. *Photo, Maya Alleruzzo, August 16, 2010*

SMALL WORLD NEWS'

GUIDE TO SAFELY USING SATPHONES

VERSION 1.0 / MARCH 2012

THE GOALS OF THIS GUIDE

This guide provides a comprehensive look at potential uses for sat-phones in repressive regimes. It contains the best practices on keep-ing safe while communicating effectively with the least chance for detection & observation.

TABLE OF CONTENTS

OVERVIEW

01 WHAT IS A SATPHONE?

02 OPERATING A SATPHONE
2.1 Activation
2.2 Connection
2.3 Using a Satphone, a Walkthrough

03 KNOWN RISKS FROM SATPHONES
3.1 Phone confiscation
    3.1.1 Call Log
    3.1.2 Sent folder
    3.1.3 Phonebook
3.2 Signals Interception
    3.2.1 Radio Signals Transmissions
    3.2.2 GPS Location Transmissions
3.3 Encryption Decoding

04 PRECAUTIONS FOR LIMITING RISK
4.1 Delete all records
4.2 Disguise your phone
4.3 Deceive by Speaking in Code
4.4 Destroy your simcard and phone

TABLE OF CONTENTS

**05 USING YOUR SATPHONE
     MORE SAFELY**
     5.1 Voice Calls
     5.2 SMS
     5.3 EMAIL

**06 CHOOSING WHAT BRAND
     YOU SHOULD USE**
     6.1 Thuraya
     6.1.1 Background
     6.2.2 Thuraya's Problems
     6.3 Inmarsat / iSatphone

**07 HOW TO IMPROVE THE SAFETY
     OF AN ISATPHONEPRO**
     7.1 Lock Your Phone
     7.2 Clear your Call Log
     7.3 Delete your Sent folder
     7.4 Delete your Phonebook
     7.5 Use a Bluetooth headset to minimize suspicion
     7.7 Disable your phone

OVERVIEW

Satellite phones, also known as satphones, are becoming popular communication tools. In areas with low access to traditional communication tools or where communications have been cut off, activists may need satphones to reach the outside world. Using a satphone presents particular risks.

For example, when you depend on this complex technology it is impossible to know exactly how your communication can be monitored. Also, satphones are often banned by repressive governments, and those governments may search for people using them. This guide will assist you to maintain a low profile and improve your chances to evade detection and monitoring from the authorities.

1.0 WHAT IS A SATPHONE?

A **satellite telephone**, **satellite phone**, or **satphone** is a type of mobile phone that connects to orbiting satellites instead of terrestrial cell sites. They provide similar functionality to terrestrial mobile telephones; voice, short messaging service and low-bandwidth internet access are supported through most systems.

Satphones are complicated radio transmitters. Radios and cell phones use antennas on earth to send out a signal, either a radio broadcast or a phone calls. Satphones send the signal to a satellite in orbit around the earth. The satellite then broadcasts the signal back to earth, to a "Ground Earth Station," or GES. From the GES the signal is sent to the proper communications service provider and to its destination, the receiver of the call. The GES acts as a gateway between your satphone, traditional cellular mobile phone networks, landline networks, and other satphones.

Transmitting information **to** the satellite in orbit is the "uplink." Receiving information **from** the satellite is the "downlink." This information can be data or voice. A phone's signal can be intercepted anytime it has an active connection with the satellite: during the uplink or the downlink.

 If you communicate with someone outside the satphone's service provider network your communications are subject to any observation happening on the other user. Communicating with other satphones from the same service provider is much safer. Even this method is not entirely secure, but following these basic steps will limit your risks.

This guide provides the techniques necessary to increase your safety, but is not a guarantee of secure communications.

2.0 OPERATING A SATPHONE

Satphones may look like very large mobile phones, but differ in some key elements. The **Activation** process is relatively similar, while the **Connection** process poses notable differences.

2.1 ACTIVATION

Satphones require activated simcards and must have a plan associated with the simcard. The plan may be prepaid or postpaid. If prepaid the phone must have minutes associated with the simcard. Minutes can be paid for and added online or directly from the phone by submitting scratch card codes via **SMS**.

See **Section 7.2** for details on adding credit to an iSatphonePro satphone.

2.0 OPERATING A SATPHONE

2.2 CONNECTION

Satphones do not connect automatically to their network. Satphones speak directly to one or more satellites in orbit far overhead.

To obtain a signal you must stand still and aim the phone's antenna towards the sky and wait for the phone to locate a signal. Your phone will first obtain a GPS Location fix, then it will connect to the network. This process may take over a minute.

 The time needed to connect with the network is the first major security risk.

While you are waiting for the phone to connect you may be observed by the authorities. In **Section 4.2** we will discuss steps you may take to disguise your phone. This can reduce your risk.

NOTE: In order to obtain a signal, the phone must be "deployed" meaning the antenna must be in the on position. Unlike a cellular mobile phone, a satphone will NOT receive calls simply by being turned on. Satphones should not be able to communicate unless the user intentionally connects to the network. This makes it difficult to have unscheduled calls with other satphone users. Therefore, satellite phones should not be depended on for urgent or emergency communications.

2.0 OPERATING A SATPHONE

2.3 USING A SATPHONE, A WALKTHROUGH

This is a complete overview for the steps involved in making a phone call or sending a message from a satphone.

01. Turn on the phone
02. Find a clear view of the sky
03. Engage the antenna to look for a signal
04. The phone obtains a GPS fix.
05. The phone connects to the satellite network
06. Make the call or send an SMS/email
07. The phone uplinks to the satellite
08. The satellite downlinks with a Ground Earth Station (GES)
09. The GES transmits the information to the intended recipient
10. The GES records the phones's GPS locations while transmitting
11. Complete the call or SMS/email
12. The phone logs its GPS Location, the number called, and length of the call
13. Close your antenna
14. Turn off and store the phone

3.0 KNOWN RISKS FROM SAT PHONES

3.1 PHONE CONFISCATION

In many cases, you and your colleagues will be your own worst enemies. There are many technical risks with satellite communication, but the most likely risk is user-generated. These risks are often overlooked because they are primarily caused by normal operation. In repressive states, phone features such as the call log, phone book, and sent folder can endanger your life and the lives of others.

These features help you keep your contacts handy, but they also provide an easily accessed record for the authorities to track your calls, even if they do not have access to your transmissions.

When a file on a computer is deleted, it is not completely destroyed and may be reconstructed without further measures. It is also possible your satphone's logs can be reconstructed from the satphone or data from the service provider.. Deleting information is not a complete fail-safe, but will make it harder for authorities to access information on a confiscated phone.

3.0 KNOWN RISKS FROM SAT PHONES

3.1.1 CALL LOG

By default, your phone will keep a log of everyone you have called. Be sure to delete this every time you make a phone call. Any number you have left in the log will be at risk if your phone is confiscated. It may be suspicious to have an empty call log, but will have less impact on your colleagues.

3.1.2 SENT FOLDER

Similar to the **Call Log**, your phone will maintain a list of **SMS** and **Email** message sent from the phone. Be sure to **Delete** these after every delivery.

3.1.3 PHONEBOOK

Your phonebook is also provides a checklist for the authorities. Any person listed in the phonebook will be at risk if your phone is confiscated. It may be suspicious to have an empty phonebook, but will have less impact on your colleagues.

3.0 KNOWN RISKS FROM SAT PHONES

3.2 SIGNALS INTERCEPTION

All phones are radio transmitters. Satphones send a Radio Signal to a satellite in orbit around the earth. The satellite then broadcasts the signal back to earth, to a "Ground Earth Station," or GES. From the GES the signal goes through another communications system to its destination, the receiver of the call. A phone's signal can be intercepted anytime it has an active connection with the satellite: during the uplink or the downlink, when the satellite is sending the receiver's voice back down to you.

Depending on the equipment available to the authorities, there are different potential risks for signal interception, outlined in this section.

3.0 KNOWN RISKS FROM SAT PHONES

3.2.1 RADIO SIGNALS TRANSMISSIONS

Satellite communications use Radio Signals to transmit information. These transmissions can be triangulated with affordable, even homemade tools. Triangulation uses two or more signal receivers to determine the location of a radio signal transmitter. The location is determined by the receiver based on the axes of the angles of receivers. Highly developed countries with advanced technical security are likely to have this capacity, less developed states and even non-state actors may be able to develop the capacity. For these reasons, keep all transmissions as short as possible.

In some cases the authorities may have the proper equipment to "listen in" on your transmissions, however this requires highly advanced and sophisticated technology. Review section **4.3 Decieve by Speaking in Codes** for tips on how to communicate more safely if you suspect your calls are being monitored.

3.0 KNOWN RISKS FROM SAT PHONES

3.2.2 GPS LOCATION TRANSMISSIONS

Satellite communications require a **GPS Location** for optimal functionality. GPS means Global Positioning System. Your GPS location gives exact coordinates for authorities to find your location. This provides the potential for an individual using any satellite device to be located with exact coordinates. Your location may be logged at the service provider's Ground Earth Station (GES). The GES data may be accessible to many different groups including local or nearby governments, shareholders, local service partners and anyone who is able to hack the GES security systems.

If the authorities possess the correct technology, or have the specific encryption and transmission codes of your satphone brand they may use your phone's GPS coordinates to locate and detain you.

3.0 KNOWN RISKS FROM SAT PHONES

3.3 ENCRYPTION DECODING

Satellite transmissions are encrypted, but many governments are capable of defeating the encryption used by these phones. Standard encryption may deter detection and monitoring but cannot guarantee security.

 Thuraya's encryption has been broken, and more advanced governments may be able to break the encryption of other satphones. To learn more see Section 6.2.2

3.0 KNOWN RISKS FROM SAT PHONES

3.3 ENCRYPTION DECODING (CONTINUED)

Satellite communications are vulnerable to prying ears and eyes, who may review voice, message, and data transmissions. Even if the necessary equipment and capability to break the encryption may not be available to the authorities in your area they may be able to break it over time. If the authorities can intercept your Transmissions, and they are capable of recording the signals, it is likely they will eventually break the signal's encryption and review the content of your calls or messages.

> In February 2012, two German researchers demonstrated the capability to decode the GMR-1 and GMR-2 encryption standards. These standards are not used by all satphones, but Thuraya and the Inmarsat iSatphonePro both use this standard. The method is fairly technical, however the potential is documented and it is likely that governments will soon begin obtaining the necessary technology.

Given the potential for authorities to obtain such equipment, you should **NEVER** share personal, life threatening, or other critical information via satellite. If you must, please remember to **Speak in Codes** to deter the authorities from understanding.

4.0 PRECAUTIONS FOR LIMITING RISK

Satphones are closed technology, and not easy to modify. Because of this it is impossible to have completely secure communications with a satphone. However, these basic precautions can be used with any satphone to increase your safety and decrease the risk of observation or detention by authorities.

4.1 DELETE ALL RECORDS

Do not save communications information on the satphone. Although security services may obtain calling records through other means, do not make it easy for them. Even without names a list of phone numbers, cellular or satellite, for authorities to track and locate could be catastrophic. Each phone manufacturer has a different system, so become familiar with the steps to delete records on your phone as soon as possible.

 See **Section 7.0** for specific steps to make the Inmarsat iSatphonePro safer.

When communicating with individuals who may be threatened or under surveillance, be sure to maintain their information in a safe and secure location.

4.0 PRECAUTIONS FOR LIMITING RISK

4.2 DISGUISE YOUR PHONE

When using the phone for calls, do not leave it out in the open. Always pair with a headset, so it will appear you are using the local cellular network not making a satellite call. Using a Bluetooth headset will make it easier to disguise the phone, however there are additional security risks, listed in section 7.5.

Keep the phone hidden at all times and disguise it if you have time. Place the phone in a location with a good angle toward the satellite's position, but disguise its physical location as much as possible. Put the phone inside an open bag, or behind some bushes. This may be difficult as the phone needs a clear view of the sky. If possible experiment in a safe location to see how you can evade observation without interfering with the phone's connection.

4.0 PRECAUTIONS FOR LIMITING RISK

4.3 DECEIVE BY SPEAKING IN CODE

In cases where you are communicating with collaborators, fellow activists, etc. hide your true intentions. Use codes, discuss common subjects that you are likely to share, yet have double meanings. Do not discuss your intentions directly.

EXAMPLE:

Use memorable phrases and terms with double meanings, or use familiar subject matter such as specific religious verses. For example, use a term to indicate authorities such as "uncle."

When checking with a contact to first determine whether the contact is safe from authorities, one might ask, "Has your uncle come to town?" Yes may indicate it is not a good time to talk, no indicates it is safe.

This enables further codes, your contact could say "My uncle was here, but he left, I'm going to be busy for the next few days," indicating it's inadvisable for you to try and reach your contact in the near future.

Additionally "My Uncle was here, he reminded me that the family reunion is happening soon," could indicate the authorities may be planning to interrogate you or your other colleagues soon.

4.0 PRECAUTIONS FOR LIMITING RISK

4.3 DECEIVE BY SPEAKING IN CODE (CONTINUED)

You may also want to consider codes that are don't have such a direct relationship, where the combination of subjects discussed provides information. Also providing false or misleading information, such as a location, can confuse anyone who may be listening in.

For example "Did I tell you about my cousin's wedding that is coming up? She is marrying a very good man from Aleppo." In this case the term "wedding" and "very good man" could be operative phrases, where wedding indicates the authorities may be looking for you soon, and "very good man" indicates the specific security service involved. Using another phrase such as "wealthy merchant" will indicate a different office.

Covering your intentions may save your life or others.

4.0 PRECAUTIONS FOR LIMITING RISK

4.4 DESTROY YOUR SIMCARD AND PHONE

If your phone is confiscated, the simcard will provide information that can be used against you and your colleagues. Keep the simcard out of the phone so it can be quickly destroyed. If possible destroying your phone may further limit your risk, however its more important to follow the previous 3 precautions and attempt to avoid detection by the authorities.

5.0 USING YOUR SATPHONE MORE SAFELY

The previous section outlined basic precautions you can take with any satphone. This section explains specific techniques for using your satphone more safely in each of the primary uses, making voice calls and sending SMS or email messages.

5.0 USING YOUR SATPHONE MORE SAFELY

5.1 VOICE CALLS

Voice calls are a very risky method for communicating via satellite. When making a call, be sure to keep the call as short as possible, due to the potential for interception of your phone's **Radio Signals**, or **GPS Location**.

Authorities may use your phone's **Radio Signals** to detect your position within less than three minutes. As their techniques become more sophisticated they may be able to locate a satphone even more quickly. In some cases authorities may be able to listen in to your phone call, by intercepting its **Radio Signals** transmissions. Authorities may tap the phone at the other end, if they have access to service provider.

The longer you remain on the line, the greater opportunity you provide the authorities to find your exact position via your phone's **GPS Location**.

5.0 USING YOUR SATPHONE MORE SAFELY

5.1 VOICE CALLS (CONTINUED)

When making an interview, be sure the interviewer is clear on your situation and do not remain on the line longer than you feel safe. It is best to keep your call under three minutes. Prepare your comments beforehand, and be clear that you will not discuss items outside your planned communication.

When making a Voice call to communicate with a colleague or coordinate with other activists, remember to **Speak in Codes**. This is important in order to **Deceive** anyone who may be listening in, or may break your phone's **Encryption**.

Speaking in Codes and using common phrases that have a double meaning may keep you or others safe, though you may not know your conversations are being monitored. Utilize common phrases, rather than special words you would not otherwise discuss.

Delete your phone's call log. There is nothing worse than creating an indexed archive of information that is waiting for the authorities. If you fail to do this, you will put others at risk and may increase the potential threat to yourself if your phone is confiscated.

5.0 USING YOUR SATPHONE MORE SAFELY

5.2 SMS

SMS is a highly convenient method of sending a message. When sending an SMS from a satphone that message is delivered via email, where your phone number is attached to a carrier specific server address, such as 5555555@text.phonecarrier.com.

Despite manufacturer claims, SMS does not provide secure encryption. Do not transmit sensitive information via SMS unless you are willing to have it read by the authorities. If the SMS is intercepted, it is likely to be recorded and the **Encryption** broken at a later date, if not immediately.

SMS may take less time than a voice call, so the risk of intercepting the SMS Radio Signal or exploiting the phone's **GPS Location** may be less than with voice. However it is more likely the content of your message will be retrievable by the authorities, if your **Transmission** is intercepted.

Deceive unwanted observers through the use of code phrases and terms with double meaning. **Delete** SMS from your phone's sent folder. There is nothing worse than creating an indexed archive of information that is waiting for the authorities to review in the event you are detained.

5.0 USING YOUR SATPHONE MORE SAFELY

5.3 EMAIL

Email can be sent via any satellite phone, but is delivered via the same protocols as SMS, and restricted to approximately 160 characters.

You may decide to use the email feature rather than SMS because you expect email to be more secure. This is incorrect. Email sent from your satphone does not provide the same protection as Email sent via computer or mobile data plans.

Computer and mobile internet both provide the opportunity to use additional security tools. Email can be sent by computer or mobile over an **HTTPS** connection that is far more difficult to intercept. On some mobile phones and all computers **Tor** can be used to anonymize your computers traffic and hide your identity and location. If at all possible use a secure internet connection to communicate, not a satphone.

5.0 USING YOUR SATPHONE MORE SAFELY

5.3 E-MAIL (CONTINUED)

Because, like SMS, an Email transmission may take less time than a voice call, risk of intercepting the message via the Radio Signal or exploiting the phone's GPS Location may be less than with voice. However it is more likely the content of your message will be retrievable by the authorities, if your Transmission is intercepted.

Deceive unwanted observers through the use of code phrases and terms with double meaning. Delete Email from your phone's sent folder. There is nothing worse than creating an indexed archive of information that is waiting for the authorities to review in the event you are detained.

6.0 CHOOSING WHAT BRAND TO USE

All satphones are not equal. Each brand has its limitations, though as will be explained, we recommend not using Thuraya phones if you can avoid them. That warning aside, the previous sections will still provide the best practices to follow to limit your risk.

There are a variety of satellite communications service providers, including Thuraya, Inmarsat, Iridium, and GlobalStar. Others such as MSV, ICO, Teledesic are currently non-operational or do not provide consumer services.

Based on our research, although no satphone is truly safe and secure from determined authorities, we have found that Thuraya, in particular, is unsafe, and should be avoided at all cost. We are recommending Inmarsat's iSatphonePro for ease of use, availability, and its recent rise as an entry-level device used by many journalists and activists across the Middle East.

6.0 CHOOSING WHAT BRAND TO USE

All satphones are not equal. Each brand has its limitations, though as will be explained, we recommend not using Thuraya phones if you can avoid them. That warning aside, the previous sections will still provide the best practices to follow to limit your risk.

There are a variety of satellite communications service providers, including Thuraya, Inmarsat, Iridium, and GlobalStar. Others such as MSV, ICO, Teledesic are currently non-operational or do not provide consumer services.

Based on our research, although no satphone is truly safe and secure from determined authorities, we have found that Thuraya, in particular, is unsafe, and should be avoided at all cost. We are recommending Inmarsat's iSatphonePro for ease of use, availability, and its recent rise as an entry-level device used by many journalists and activists across the Middle East.

6.0 CHOOSING WHAT BRAND TO USE

6.1 WHY NOT THURAYA?

6.1.1 BACKGROUND

Thuraya became one of the more popular satellite communications companies, due to its affordable products and broad functionality, particularly in the Middle East. Throughout 2011 the popularity of Thuraya began to decrease, due to the ease with which governments are able to block or intercept Thuraya. Blocking was first seen over 6 months in 2006 as the Libyan government engaged in massive jamming of the service from within its territory. Likely due to Thuraya's popularity in the Middle East the United States targeted this provider in particular for interception and encryption decoding.

6.2.2 THURAYA'S PROBLEMS

In 2011 Syrian activists alleged the Syrian government compromised Thuraya's network security. It is believed that Rami Makhlouf controls the Syrian subsidiary of Thuraya. Activists believe he obtained access to Thuraya's decryption codes and other records and provided these to the Syrian regime. Detained activists have later reported hearing recordings of conversations they made over satphones. We have been unable to determine if the recording happened by interception of an uplink. It seems likely the activists was communicating with someone on a local service provider that was tapped by the authorities.

In 2011 Syrian activists alleged the Syrian government compromised Thuraya's network security. It is believed that Rami Makhlouf

6.0 CHOOSING WHAT BRAND TO USE

6.2.2 THURAYA'S PROBLEMS (CONTINUED)

controls the Syrian subsidiary of Thuraya. Activists believe he obtained access to Thuraya's decryption codes and other records and provided these to the Syrian regime. Detained activists have later reported hearing recordings of conversations they made over satphones. We have been unable to determine if the recording happened by interception of an uplink. It seems likely the activists were communicating with someone on a local service provider that was tapped by the authorities.

According to Strategy Page, in 2003, "Thuraya recently announced that while the phones did transmit the GPS location periodically (to insure a good signal), the information was sent in encrypted form and only someone with access to the codes, or with powerful decryption capabilities, could get the location information (of the phone broadcasting the information)."

It is also documented that the US, and possibly Indian authorities were able to listen in on conversations between individuals using Thuraya phones, ahead of the terrorist attacks across Mumbai in 2008, "Officials say one of the phones recovered was a Thuraya satellite phone. "Once we have the number we will be able to know everyone who was called and where the calls were made from," one former intelligence office says."

Based on this information, we recommend activists avoid using Thuraya phones in any circumstance.

6.0 CHOOSING WHAT BRAND TO USE

6.2 WHY USE INMARSAT'S ISATPHONEPRO?

Why do we believe the iSatphonePro is safer than Thuraya, and relatively as safe as other brands? While Thuraya is definitely compromised, other services may be compromised as well. The contents of this guide will assist you to maintain the greatest amount of safety possible, despite the serious risks posed by satellite communications technology.

At the time of publication, January 2012, there were no known exploits of Inmarsat phones by the Syrian authorities. As a company based in the United Kingdom, there are legal constraints preventing Inmarsat from providing records to the Syrian Government. At the time of publication there were no accounts of Inmarsat phone users detained due to the operation of an Inmarsat phone.

 All satellite phones pose significant potential risks to the user, based on the very real potential for interception of the transmissions and location information.

7.0 HOW TO IMPROVE THE SAFETY OF AN ISATPHONEPRO

In many cases, you and your colleagues will be your own worst enemies. Although there are many technical risks with satellite communication, the most likely risk is user-generated. These risks are often overlooked because they are primarily caused by normal user operation.

In the case of repressive states, phone features such as the call log, phone book, and sent folder can endanger your life and the lives of others. These features keep your contacts handy, but also provide a record for the authorities to track your calls, even if they do not have access to your transmissions.

These directions will make the iSatphonePro safer and help you avoid the risks mentioned in this guide.

7.0 HOW TO IMPROVE THE SAFETY OF AN ISATPHONEPRO

7.1 LOCK YOUR PHONE

To prevent unwanted eyes from examining your phone, turn on the admin code, and pin request functions. This may be found by accessing:

Menu > Settings > Security

When choosing number codes **DO NOT** choose codes with all the same number, or easy combinations such as 1111 or 1122. By default the admin code is 123456, this code must be 6 digits. If you mis-dial your code you can reenter an unlimited number of times.

The SIM pin by default is 8888, this code must be between 4 and 8 digits. The SIM pin 2 by default is 9999, this code must be between 4 and 8 digits. If the SIM codes are entered incorrectly three times your SIM will only be unlocked by obtaining the PUK code.

7.0 HOW TO IMPROVE THE SAFETY OF AN ISATPHONEPRO

7.2 ADD PHONE CREDIT REMOTELY

To add credit to your iSatphonePro you need to first purchase credit. This can be done at a number of websites, such as: http://satphonecity.com

To check your phone's balance, make a call to this code: ***106#**

To add balance to your phone from a voucher, enter the following code: *101*VoucherNumber#

For example: *101*123456789#

7.0 HOW TO IMPROVE THE SAFETY OF AN ISATPHONEPRO

7.3 CLEAR YOUR CALL LOG

By default, your phone will keep a log of everyone you have called. Be sure to delete this every time you make a phone call. Any number you have left in the log will be at risk if the phone is confiscated. It may be suspicious to have an empty call log, but will have less impact on your colleagues.

Delete the Call Log by accessing:

Menu > Call Log > Options > Clear all

7.0 HOW TO IMPROVE THE SAFETY OF AN ISATPHONEPRO

7.4 DELETE YOUR SENT FOLDER

Similar to the Call Log, your phone will maintain a list of SMS and Email message sent from the phone. Be sure to Delete these after every delivery.

Delete SMS and Email messages by accessing:

Menu > Messaging > Sent > Options > Delete all messages

7.0 HOW TO IMPROVE THE SAFETY OF AN ISATPHONEPRO

7.5 DELETE YOUR PHONEBOOK

Your **Phonebook** also provides the authorities a checklist if it list your colleagues' phone numbers. Any number left in the phonebook will be at risk if the phone is confiscated. It may be suspicious to have an empty phonebook, but it will have less impact on your colleagues.

Delete your Phonebook by accessing:

Menu > Contacts > Phonebook > Delete all

You can delete any contacts stored on the simcard by accessing:

Menu > Contacts > Sim Contacts

7.0 HOW TO IMPROVE THE SAFETY OF AN ISATPHONEPRO

7.6 USE A BLUETOOTH HEADSET TO MINIMIZE SUSPICION

Do not leave the phone out in the open. Keep it hidden at all times and consider disguising the phone.

When using the phone for calls, if at all possible, pair with a headset. It will appear you are using the local cellular network, not making a satellite call. Place the phone in a location with a good angle toward the satellite, but disguise the phone's physical location. Using a bluetooth headset will make it easier to disguise the phone, but may result in other risks listed below.

Activate the phones' bluetooth capacity by accessing:

Menu > Settings > Bluetooth > Paired Devices > Options > Search for devices

7.0 HOW TO IMPROVE THE SAFETY OF AN ISATPHONEPRO

7.6 USE A BLUETOOTH HEADSET TO MINIMIZE SUSPICION (CONTINUED)

NOTE: When "discoverable" your Bluetooth signal will be visible to devices detecting Bluetooth transmissions within 10 meters. Always keep your Bluetooth non-discoverable. NEVER connect your satphone to an unknown Bluetooth device. Always use a headset with a "push-to-sync" button. The Bluetooth signal switches randomly among 79 radio frequencies, 1600 times per second, making it very difficult to intercept the transmission.

There is equipment on the market that will enable anyone to monitor, record, and decrypt Bluetooth audio transmissions in real time. The likelihood of authorities to have access to this equipment is unknown, though not impossible. If you are not currently being monitored, it will be difficult for the authorities to observe you, based on your Bluetooth transmissions alone. If the authorities do locate you, it is feasible they can obtain a receiver capable of picking up Bluetooth transmissions from more than a kilometer away.

7.0 HOW TO IMPROVE THE SAFETY OF AN ISATPHONEPRO

7.7 DISABLE YOUR PHONE AND KEEP YOUR SIMCARD SECURE

The satphone will not connect with the network, and should not transmit GPS or other signals when the antenna is not deployed. Remove the simcard and keep it with you, this will make it easy to destroy in the event of confiscation. Always close the antenna to **disable** the phone when not in use.

In the case of the iSatphonePro a large coin works well.

Global Safety Principles and Practices

On February 12, 2015, a coalition of major news companies and journalism organizations gathered to endorse worldwide freelance protection standards.

Over the last two years, killings, imprisonments and abductions of journalists have reached historic highs. These attacks represent a fundamental threat not just to individual news professionals, but to the practice of independent journalism.

Locally-based journalists face by far the largest threat and endure the vast majority of murders, imprisonments and abductions. We call on governments, combatants and groups worldwide to respect the neutrality of journalists and immediately end the cycle of impunity surrounding attacks on journalists. At the same time, the kidnapping and murder of reporters James Foley and Steven Sotloff brought to light the growing risks faced by international freelance journalists.

The undersigned groups endorse the following safety principles and practices for international news organizations and the freelancers who work with them. We see this as a first step in a long-term campaign to convince news organizations and journalists to adopt these standards globally. In a time of journalistic peril, news organizations and journalists must work together to protect themselves, their profession and their vital role in global society.

FOR JOURNALISTS ON DANGEROUS ASSIGNMENTS:

1. Before setting out on any assignment in a conflict zone or any dangerous environment, journalists should have basic skills to care for themselves or injured colleagues.

2. We encourage all journalists to complete a recognized news industry first aid course, to carry a suitable first-aid kit and continue their training to stay up-to-date on standards of care and safety both physical and psychological. Before undertaking an assignment in such zones, journalists should seek adequate medical insurance covering them in a conflict zone or area of infectious disease.

3. Journalists in active war zones should be aware of the need and importance of having protective ballistic clothing, including armored jackets and helmets. Journalists operating in a conflict zone or dangerous environment should endeavor to complete an industry-recognized hostile environment course.

4. Journalists should work with colleagues on the ground and with news organizations to complete a careful risk assessment before traveling to any hostile or dangerous environment and measure the journalistic value of an assignment against the risks.

5. On assignment, journalists should plan and prepare in detail how they will operate including identifying routes, transport, contacts and a communications strategy with daily check-in routines with a colleague in the region or their editor. Whenever practical, journalists should take appropriate precautions to secure mobile and Internet communications from intrusion and tracking.

6. Journalists should work closely with their news organizations, the organization that has commissioned them, or their colleagues in the industry if acting independently, to understand the risks of any specific assignment. In doing so, they should seek and take into account the safety information and travel advice of professional colleagues, local contacts, embassies and security personnel. And, likewise, they should share safety information with colleagues to help prevent them harm.

7. Journalists should leave next of kin details with news organizations, ensuring that these named contacts have clear instructions and action plans in the case of injury, kidnap or death in the field.

FOR NEWS ORGANIZATIONS MAKING ASSIGNMENTS IN DANGEROUS PLACES:

1. Editors and news organizations recognize that local journalists and freelancers, including photographers and videographers, play an increasingly vital role in international coverage, particularly on dangerous stories.

2. Editors and news organizations should show the same concern for the welfare of local journalists and freelancers that they do for staffers.

3. News organizations and editors should endeavor to treat journalists and freelancers they use on a regular basis in a similar manner to the way they treat staffers when it comes to issues of safety training, first aid and other safety equipment, and responsibility in the event of injury or kidnap.

4. Editors and news organizations should be aware of, and factor in, the additional costs of training, insurance and safety equipment in war zones. They should clearly delineate before an assignment what a freelancer will be paid and what expenses will be covered.

5. Editors and news organizations should recognize the importance of prompt payment for freelancers. When setting assignments, news organizations should endeavor to provide agreed upon expenses in advance, or as soon as possible on completion of work, and pay for work done in as timely a manner as possible.

6. Editors and news organizations should ensure that all freelance journalists are given fair recognition in bylines and credits for the work they do both at the time the work is published or broadcast and if it is later submitted for awards, unless the news organization and the freelancer agree that crediting the journalist can compromise the safety of the freelancer and/or the freelancer's family.

7. News organizations should not make an assignment with a freelancer in a conflict zone or dangerous environment unless the news organization is prepared to take the same responsibility for the freelancer's wellbeing in the event of kidnap or injury as it would a staffer. News organizations have a moral responsibility to support journalists to whom they give assignments in dangerous areas, as long as the freelancer complies with the rules and instructions of the news organization.

In conclusion, we, the undersigned, encourage all staff and freelance journalists and the news organizations they work with to actively join in a shared commitment to safety and a new spirit of collegiality and concern.

SIGNATORY ORGANIZATIONS

Agence France Press

Al-Monitor

American Society of Journalists and Authors

Association of European Journalists (Bulgaria)

The Associated Press

Belarusian Association of Journalists

Blink

Bloomberg

British Broadcasting Corporation

Canadian Journalism Forum on Violence and Trauma

Center for Journalism and Public Ethics (Mexico)

Committee to Protect Journalists

Danish Union of Journalists

Dart Center for Journalism and Trauma
Ena News Agency
European Federation of Journalists
Foreign Correspondents' Club (Hong Kong)
Foro de Periodismo Argentino
Frontline Club
Frontline Freelance Register
The Frontliner (Albania)
Global Journalist Security
GlobalPost
The GroundTruth Project
Guardian News and Media Group
International Center for Journalists
International News Safety Institute
International Press Institute
International Women's Media Foundation
James W. Foley Legacy Foundation
Journalistic Freedoms Observatory (Iraq)
Journalists in Danger (Kazakhstan)
Mashable
McClatchy DC
Miami Herald
National Press Club
National Press Photographers Association
National Union of Journalists-Philippines
Newsweek

NOS News (Netherlands)
Online News Association
Overseas Press Club of America
Overseas Press Club Foundation
PBS Frontline
Press Emblem Campaign (Switzerland)
Public Radio International's The World
Pulitzer Center on Crisis Reporting
Reporters Instructed in Saving Colleagues
Reporters Without Borders
Reuters
Rory Peck Trust
Security First (UK)
Society of Professional Journalists
Storyhunter
Trauma Training for Journalists
Union of Journalists in Israel
USA Today
Video News (Japan)
Words After War
Zuma Press

News organizations, journalist associations or advocacy groups interested in joining these guidelines should contact David Rohde, david.rohde@thomsonreuters.com.

U.S. Journalist James Wright Foley and member of ISIS speak to the camera before Foley is beheaded on video – August 2014 (Rex Features via AP images)

Press Photojournalist photographer (iStock © chameleonseye)

War Journalism Timeline

1660s

Willem van de Velde, the Elder, paints a number of battle scenes between Dutch and English vessels from "very close quarters."

1807

Henry Crabb Robinson covers the Napoleonic Wars for the *Times*, making him one of the earliest war correspondents.

1835

James Gordon Bennett founds *New York Herald*.

Morse code is invented by Samuel Morse.

First successful carrier pigeon flight links London to Paris.

1837

Shorthand is invented.

1839

The daguerreotype is developed by Jacques Mande Daguerre.

1840

The *Boston Daily Mail* uses carrier pigeons to deliver news in what became known as the "pigeon express."

1841

New York Tribune is founded by Horace Greeley.

1842

London Illustrated News is founded.

1844

Telegraph is invented.

Photographer Mathew Brady opens his first studio, Brady's Daguerrian Miniature Gallery.

Photographer Mathew Brady shifts from daguerreotypes to the wet-plate process.

1845

Earliest prototype of a facsimile (fax) machine developed by Scottish inventor Alexander Bain.

1846

George Kendall covers the Mexican-American War for the *New Orleans Picayune*, establishing himself as the first American war correspondent.

Jane McManus Storm witnesses and reports the siege of Vera Cruz.

1846-48

First examples of war photography, from Mexican-American War, the first war to be systematically covered by photographers.

1849

Associated Press is established.

1850

London inventor F. C. Blakewell obtains patent for a "copying telegraph."

1851

The London-based international news agency *Reuters* is created by Julius Reuters.

1852

Several war photographs are taken during the Burma War.

1854

William Howard Russell begins his career as war correspondent covering the Crimean War for the *Times* and uses the phrase "the thin red line" for the first time while describing the Battle of Balaclava. The works of Rudyard Kipling and Alfred Tennyson are said to have been inspired by Russell's war prose.

During the Crimean War Russian writer Leo Tolstoy publishes his accounts in *The Sebastopol Sketches* in 1856 after being rejected by military journal. The book established him as a writer and early war correspondent.

Amateur painter and photographer Karl Baptist Von Szathmari covers the Crimean War and is recognized as the "first war photographer."

1855

Pioneer photographer Nadar experiments with aerial photography.

Frank Leslie's Illustrated Newspaper is founded.

1857

Harper's Weekly is founded by Fletcher Harper.

1858

Photos by Felice Beato and James Robertson after the Battle of Lucknow are reportedly the first of dead bodies.

1860

The United States has 2,500 newspapers and almost 50,000 miles of telegraph lines.

1861

In March British war correspondent William Howard Russell arrives in the U.S. preparing to cover the looming American Civil War.

1862

In January with General Order No. 98, the Army of the Potomac bans all correspondents from covering Union troops under threat of arrest.

New York Tribune correspondent Charles D. Brigham reports battle of the ironclads *Monitor* and *Merrimac* at Hampton Roads.

In April Whitelaw Reid produces the classic newspaper account of the Battle of Shiloh.

George Washburn Smalley produces account of Battle of Antietam, considered among the best pieces of reporting during the American Civil War.

1863

In March Confederate Press Association is created to provide war news to Confederate dailies east of the Mississippi, since most cannot afford their own war correspondents.

On July 4 *New York Tribune* correspondent Aaron Homer Byington's account of the Battle of Gettysburg becomes first complete account to hit newsstands.

Journalist Samuel Wilkeson pens his account of the Battle of Gettysburg next to the body of his son, killed in the first day of fighting.

Photographer Timothy O'Sullivan takes what some call the most famous photo from of the Civil War, *The Harvest of Death*, on the Gettysburg battlefield.

1865

New York Times founder Henry Jarvis Raymond is credited with inventing the display headline for his newspaper.

First commercial telefax service (using the "Pantelegraph") introduced between Paris and Lyon, France.

1866

Freelance photographer Ridgeway Glover is killed while on his way to photograph Sioux leader Red Cloud's warriors near Fort Phil Kearny in Wyoming, making Glover perhaps the first news photographer to be killed while attempting to photograph in America.

1867

Joe Wasson becomes one of the first reporters to cover the American Indian wars in the West for the *Oyhee Avalanche* of Silver City, Idaho.

Henry Stanley establishes his reputation as a journalist and war reporter while covering the British march on Abyssinia and the subsequent Battle of Magdala.

1870

Outbreak of Franco-Prussian War heralds a new age in European war reporting by the first use of the wireless for transmitting news from the scene of battle.

Archibald Forbes scoops William Howard Russell and John Edwin Hilary Smalley by two days in getting his account of the Battle of Sedan during the Austro-Prussian War to England.

1873

During the Modoc War Eadweard Muybridge becomes the first photographer to be hired by the U.S. Army specifically to document a war.

1876

In June five correspondents cover the Battle of the Rosebud in Montana, one of the biggest battles of the American Indian Wars.

Mark Kellogg is the only reporter to perish with General George A. Custer's 7th Cavalry at the Battle of the Little Big Horn.

Correspondent Januarius Macgahan publishes rumors of Turkish atrocities in Bulgaria that are later substantiated and lead to war between Russia and Turkey in 1877.

1877

Thomas A. Sutherland is the only accredited war correspondent to cover the Nez Perce War.

1880s

Hand-held Kodak cameras are invented and prove popular with British officers on campaigns in Africa.

1880

War correspondent Archibald Forbes makes his "Ride of Death," (300 miles in fifty hours) bringing news of a British victory during the Zulu War to England before official sources.

New York Daily Graphic publishes first halftone photograph.

1881

Introduction of "scanning phototelegraph" telefax machine capable of scanning a two-dimensional original.

1893

Photographer Eadweard Muybridge devises a machine that projects pictures on a screen in a rapid sequential order, a precursor to motion pictures.

1895

New York World reporter Howard C. Hillegas becomes first correspondent to report outbreak of war between British and Boers.

Reporting for the *Daily Graphic*, future statesman Winston Churchill reports his first military action in Cuba during the insurrection against the Spanish.

1896

Newspaper magnate William Randolph Hearst tells Richard Harding Davis and Frederic Remington "You furnish the pictures and I'll furnish the war" after they fail in their search for the Cuban resistance leader.

1897

In January the term "yellow journalism" is introduced.

Journalist George Eugene Bryson writes several sensational news stories about Cuban atrocities that inflame American public opinion prior to Spanish-American War.

Serving as a special correspondent to the *Times*, Alexander Edward Murray is awarded the Victorian Cross for his actions at the Battle of Landaki in India, by most accounts the only journalist to have received this award.

While covering the Greek army during the Greco-Turkish War, Frederic Villiers becomes the first person to use a bicycle for transportation during a military campaign.

Cinematograph camera is first used to cover warfare.

1898

The U.S. Battleship *Maine* explodes in Havana Harbor on February 15 killing 268 Americans, leading to headlines that fuel pro-war sentiment.

On April 25 the United States declares war on Spain.

During the Spanish-American War Kathleen Blake becomes first woman to be accredited as a war correspondent by the U.S. government.

During Spanish American War photographer John Hemment becomes the first newsreel motion picture photographer to capture a battlefront.

The British Army prohibits Winston Churchill's dual service as correspondent-officer during the Nile campaign.

1899

Reporting the Boer War for the *Daily Telegraph*, Winston Churchill is captured and taken prisoner; his subsequent escape becomes a major story.

1900

Covering Peking for the *Chicago Record*, Robert Coltman smuggles out news scoop of Boxer siege with help from local beggar.

1904-1905

Covering the Russo-Japanese War for the *Times*, Lionel James pioneers use of radio wireless technology as means of transmitting war reports.

1905

Italian journalist Luigi Barzini is only correspondent to cover the Battle of Mukden during Russo-Japanese War.

1907

William Howard Russell is buried in the crypt of London's St. Paul's Cathedral, remembered by the inscription "The First and Greatest of War Correspondents."

1912-1913

George Hubert Wilkins becomes first person to film combat footage from an aeroplane during the First Balkan War.

1914

E. Alexander Powell reports the first aerial bombardment of a city in wartime from Antwerp, Belgium.

Frederick Palmer becomes the first and only American journalist accredited with the headquarters of the British Expeditionary Forces in France.

William G. Shepherd is only journalist to witness the Battle of Ypres and with reporter Will Irwin, brakes the story about the German use of poison gas.

William G. Shepherd is first to report zeppelin raids over London in September.

Remote fax for photo and news reporting championed by Edouard Belin.

1916-1917

Under contract to Pancho Villa, pioneer cameraman Otis A. Aultman covers Mexican Revolution, including the raid on Columbus, New Mexico.

1917

Morgan Philips Price and John Reed are only two correspondents to witness Bolshevik takeover of power in Russia.

Covering women soldiers at the Russian front during the World War I for the *New York Evening* Mail, Rheta Childe Dorr notes in a dispatch that half were casualties.

Corra Harris is credited as being the first female war correspondent to cover World War I overseas.

Helen Johns Kirtland becomes "first and only woman correspondent allowed at the front" during WW I.

1918

First issue of *Stars and Stripes*, the premier troop newspaper of its time which stopped publishing the following year.

Herbert Bayard Swope becomes one of the few reporters to cover the World War I from France, Germany and Russia and wins Pulitzer Prize for his coverage of wartime Germany.

1924

Lowell Thomas publishes the highly romanticized book, *With Lawrence of Arabia*, exploits of British office Colonel T.E. Lawrence, fighting in the Middle East theater of World War I.

1926

Introduction of the Leica 35mm range finder camera revolutionizes war photography.

1935

Wilfred C. Barber becomes only correspondent to die during the Ethiopian War and receives the Pulitzer Prize posthumously for his "distinguished service."

Author Evelyn Waugh covers the Ethiopian War for the *Daily Mail*.

1936

Jay Allen becomes first correspondent to interview general and future president Francisco Franco during Spanish Civil War.

Robert Capa takes photo "Death of a Loyalist Soldier" during Spanish Civil War.

1936-1940

Edgar Snow covers the Chinese civil war and is the first Westerner to interview Mao Tse-Tung.

1937

George Lowther Steer witnesses and reports the Nazi Luftwaffe attack on Guernica in Spain's Basque region.

1939

Lynn Heinzerling witnesses and reports the opening shots of World War II — a German cruiser bombarding Danzig, Germany.

1940

Edward R. Murrow rises to international prominence for his rooftop coverage of the London Blitz.

The German Waffen SS creates a war correspondent unit known as SS Standarte Kurt Eggers in honor of a deceased SS war correspondent.

In November Ralph W. Barnes is shot down in a British bomber over Yugoslavia, becoming the first American correspondent killed in World War II, a year before America entered the conflict.

1941

Melville Jacoby becomes first American correspondent to die in a combat theater after Americas's official entry into WW II.

Yank cartoonist George Baker creates cartoon character "Sad Sack."

In December Cecil Brown survives sinking of the British battleship *Repulse* and is honored by CBS for his subsequent broadcast.

1942

Byron Price is selected to organize and direct the government's Office of Censorship by President Roosevelt.

Stars and Stripes is resurrected after its brief run in 1918.

Laurence Edmund Allen receives Pulitzer Prize for his coverage of the British Navy in the Mediterranean.

Helen Kirkpatrick and Mary Welsh become the first women to be accredited to accompany Allied forces.

Chicago Tribune reporter John Hall Thompson becomes first war correspondent to parachute with armed forces into a combat zone during North African campaign.

Carlos Romulo becomes first Asian to win Pulitzer Prize in journalism for his coverage of the Philippines theater of World War II.

1943

George Weller is awarded Pulitzer Prize for coverage of New Guinea campaign.

Georg N. Myers covers the Battle of Attu in the Aleutian Islands, the only land battle fought on American soil during World War II.

War reporters Stewart Sale, Alexander Berry Austin, and William J. Munday are killed when a German half-track fired on their jeep during the push to Naples during World War II.

Novelist John Steinbeck covers campaigns in North Africa, Sicily, and Italy for *New York Herald Tribune*.

In August General George S. Patton, Jr. visits a military hospital in Sicily, where he slaps a soldier he suspected was feigning a nervous disorder.

In January Margaret Bourke-White becomes first woman to fly on an American combat mission.

On February 26th, *New York Times* reporter Robert Perkins Post and eight Air Force crewmen perish on the maiden voyage of the Writing 69th in a bombing raid over Germany, effectively ending the experiment of sending reporters on bombers to document bombing raids.

George Weller receives Pulitzer Prize for his reporting of the fall of Singapore.

Ira Wolfert is awarded Pulitzer Prize for his coverage of the Battle of the Solomons.

1944

British correspondents Stanley Wills and Stuart Emeny perish in plane crash that kills General Orde Wingate while flying over Burma.

Ernie Pyle is awarded a Pulitzer Prize for his war reporting.

Future photojournalist Larry Burrows mistakenly destroys most of Robert Capa's D-Day photos while working as laboratory technician in London's *Life* office; Burrows will twice win the Overseas Press Club's Robert Capa Award.

Daniel De Luce wins Pulitzer Prize for his coverage of Yugoslavian partisan forces the previous year.

German correspondent Johannes-Matthias Honschied becomes only Wehrmacht war correspondent to receive Iron Cross for battlefield bravery.

Roi Ottley becomes the first African-American war correspondent to report for a mainstream American publication.

1945

AP correspondent Joseph Morton is executed at the Mauthausen concentration camp, the only foreign correspondent executed by the Nazis.

On May 1 Russian war photographer Yevgeni Khaldei takes iconic picture of Red Flag being held above the Reich's Chancellery in Berlin.

On April 17 Ernie Pyle is killed while covering the Battle of Okinawa.

On February 23 Joe Rosenthal photographs the raising of the American flag over Mount Suribachi during the Battle of Iwo Jima, probably the most reproduced photo of the war, earning him a Pulitzer Prize. The photo inspires wartime posters and the three-cent stamp, and serves as the model for the Iwo Jima Memorial.

Wilfred Burchett is first Western reporter to reach Hiroshima after dropping of atomic bomb in August.

1947

Robert Capa co-founds Magnum Photos with David Seymour, George Rodger and Henri Cartier-Bresson.

1948

CBS correspondent George Polk is murdered while covering civil war in Greece, inspiring the prestigious George Polk Award honoring foreign correspondents.

1949

On July 12 a KLM passenger plane crashes the outskirts of Bombay, India killing 24 foreign correspondents who were covering the Indonesian battlefront.

1951

Marguerite Higgins shares Pulitzer Prize for reporting Korean War with Homer Bigart, becoming the first woman to win for foreign reporting.

Keyes Beech receives Pulitzer Prize for coverage of Korean War.

1952

Laurence Edmund Allen is awarded the Croix de Guerre from the French High Command for his front-line reporting during the French war in Indochina.

1954

Robert Capa, is killed by landmine while on assignment for *Life* magazine, the first of 135 combat photographers to die covering war in Vietnam.

1955

First radio-fax transmission sent across a continent.

Robert Capa Gold Medal introduced by the Overseas Press Club of America.

1956

On November 10 photographers David "Chim" Seymour and Jean Roy are killed after Egyptian soldiers spray their jeep with gunfire during the Arab-Israeli Suez War.

1960

6,000 computers operational in the United States.

1962

Pentagon creates the Department of the Army Special Photo Office (DASPO) to provide worldwide coverage of military activities.

1964

Bernard Kolenberg becomes the first journalist to be killed covering the Vietnam War.

Malcolm W. Bowne receives Pulitzer Prize for his harrowing photograph of the self-immolation of a monk in Saigon.

James Griffing Lucas wins his second Pulitzer as the only correspondent for an American daily newspaper assigned to troops in the field during the early days of the Vietnam War.

IBM introduces "word processing" with its Magnetic Tape/Selectric Typewriter.

1965

On November 4 during the Vietnam War Dickey Chapelle becomes the first American woman photojournalist killed in action.

Pressure from Morley Safer's controversial "zippo lighter" story results in the U.S. military issuing new rules of engagement designed to protect South Vietnamese civilians from unnecessary harm.

Italian Romano Cagnoni becomes first independent photographer admitted into North Vietnam after fall of Dien Bien Phu in 1954.

Photojournalist Horst Faas becomes first cameraman to win the Pulitzer Prize and the Robert Capa Award in the same year.

1966

Peter Arnett receives Pulitzer Prize for his coverage of Vietnam War.

Harrison Salisbury becomes first American reporter allowed into North Vietnam, spending a month reporting from Hanoi.

Nobel Prize-winning novelist John Steinbeck covers the Vietnam War for New York's *Newsday*.

1967

On October 12 Marine Corporal William T. Perkins is killed when he throws himself on a grenade, while serving as an American military correspondent and photographer in South Vietnam, and awarded a posthumous Congressional Medal of Honor.

1967-70

Italian Romano Cagnoni is the only photographer to cover the entire war in Biafra.

1968

In February Walter Cronkite opines on a CBS documentary about the Tet Offensive that the Vietnam War is headed for a "stalemate" prompting President Lyndon B. Johnson to comment, "Well, if I've lost Cronkite I've lost Middle America."

On March 16 more than 300 civilians are massacred at My Lai which is captured by military war photographer Sergeant Ronald Haeberle but withheld from the public until the following year.

John Steinbeck IV and Sean Flynn form the Dispatch News Service.

1969

Eddie Adams receives the Pulitzer Prize for his 1968 Vietnam War photograph of the execution of a Viet Cong prisoner by South Vietnamese Colonel Nguyen Ngog Loan, a photo that played a role in turning American public opinion against the war.

1970

Reporters Dana Stone and Sean Flynn (son of actor and matinee idol Errol Flynn) disappear in Cambodia and are reportedly executed by the Khmer Rouge.

1971

Francois Sully, one of the earliest journalists to cover the Vietnam War, is killed in a Vietnamese helicopter crash over Laos, leaving his insurance policy of 18 million piasters to Vietnamese orphans.

Journalists Keisaburo Shimamoto, Larry Burrows, Henri Huet, and Kent Potter are killed in helicopter crash over Laos and their bodies are recovered in 2008.

First e-mail sent between side-by-side computers; some suggest this happened as early as 1965, as way for shared computer users to communicate with mainframe.

1972

In June Nick Ut's photograph of a young girl running down the street screaming during a napalm bombing, is published on front page of *New York Times*, and Ut wins the 1973 Pulitzer Prize for his efforts.

1973

"Internet" is used as shorthand for "inter networking of networks."

Mid-1970s

Introduction of modern fax machine.

1975

Michel Laurent becomes last journalist killed during the Vietnam War.

On October 16 five Australian journalists are killed by Indonesian soldiers at Balibo while covering the conflict in East Timor.

Digital camera invented by Eastman Kodak Company.

200,000 computers operational in the United States.

1976

Sydney Schanberg, immortalized in the film *The Killing Fields*, is awarded the Pulitzer Prize for his coverage of the invasion of Cambodia in 1975 by Khmer Rouge.

1978

ABC reporter Bill Stewart's execution by a Nicaraguan soldier is broadcast around the world.

First public trials of cellular telephone system in Chicago with 2,000 users.

1979

Los Angeles Time correspondent William Tuohy flies to Tehran to retrieve body of his fellow war reporter, Joe Alex Morris, Jr., who had died covering Iranian street fighting.

1980

Charles Mohr is among the only three correspondents to be awarded the Bronze Star for bravery during the Vietnam War, five years after the war ended.

1981

The Committee to Protect Journalists is founded.

1982

First cellular telephone service in the U.S.

1983

In October the Granada invasion is the first American military campaign from which the Defense Department successfully excludes all journalists as a matter of policy, prompting the appointment of a commission to recommend changes for press coverage of conflicts.

"Laptop computer" concept introduced by Radio Shack.

1984

The Sidle Commission proposed the creation of the Department of Defense National Media Pool which would determine access to war zones at early stages of conflict.

1985

First registered Internet domain.

1988

Internet opens to commercial users.

1989

In December the U.S. invades Panama and arrests General Manuel Noriega for drug trafficking, but the action of Secretary of Defense Richard Cheney, prevents the press pool from being notified, or visiting scene of conflict until operation is over.

Frontline Television News, Ltd., the cooperative for freelance cameramen, is founded.

Early 1990s

Cost for satellite transmission gear is $100,000, making it affordable only to major news operations.

First recognized bloggers – individuals who keep online diaries as a way of sharing their lives with strangers; by late 1990s blogging would be increasingly used by war journalists.

1990s

Reporters file stories from anywhere in the world, almost as they happen, with just a laptop computer and modems or a satellite.

1990

In August Iraqi troops invade Kuwait inaugurating a new era in war journalism in which the print media is consistently scooped by television newscast, primarily CNN.

1991

1,400 journalists arrive in Saudi Arabia before outbreak of the Gulf War.

On March 21 Gad Schuster Gross becomes the only journalist killed covering the Gulf War.

Caryl Murphy receives Pulitzer Prize for International Reporting after eluding Iraqi forces to report from Kuwait.

Nick Della Casa, his wife Rosanna and Charles Maxwell, freelancers for Frontline News Agency, are murdered by their Turkish guide, while attempting to cross from Turkey into Kurdistan to cover Kurdish resistance to Saddam Hussein at end of first Gulf War.

Edith Lederer becomes the only woman correspondent during the Gulf War who has also covered the Vietnam War.

Vaughan Smith films the only "uncontrolled footage of Gulf War" while disguised as a British soldier.

World Wide Web is put on the Internet.

During Gulf War CNN adopts a "four-wire" telephone, thus avoiding Iraq's central phone system, which was destroyed by early air attacks.

1992

David Kaplan becomes the first American journalist killed while covering the conflict in Yugoslavia.

IBM produces "Simon", the first smart-phone (combination mobile phone and Internet), released to public the following year.

The Committee to Protect Journalists begins keeping records of journalists killed covering wars.

1993

On July 12, four Western journalists are stoned to death in Mogadishu, Somalia, after American Black-hawk strikes on militia buildings.

1994

War reporter Terry Lloyd reports discovery of mass graves in Vukovar. Many suggest that this revelation influenced Western government to become more involved in region.

1996

Qatar-based Al-Jazeera begins operation, offering a satellite news service providing news from the Arab perspective.

2000

Photojournalists Kurt Schork and Miguel Gil Moreno de Mora are ambushed and killed by rebels while covering the conflict in Sierra Leone.

There are 20 million Web sites on the Internet.

2001

The VII Photo Agency is established, regarded by many as a "model for 21st century photo agencies."

Wikipedia, a user-driven, online encyclopedia, is founded.

Satellite radio broadcast is introduced by XM Radio.

Digital Globe's QuickBird satellite offers, among other features, the ability to take a continuous stream of pictures with a field vision of almost 6-miles wide.

Portable digital audio player iPod is launched by Apple Computer.

2002

John Sack witnesses and writes the definitive account of the bloody battle dubbed "Operation Anaconda" in Afghanistan.

Eight days after being captured, *Wall Street Journal* reporter Daniel Pearl is brutally executed on film, while in Pakistan investigating Richard "the shoe bomber" Reid.

Terry Lloyd becomes first ITN war reporter to die in almost half a century.

2003

Freelance cameraman James Miller is killed by Israeli troops while covering the conflict in Gaza, and five years later the Israel government agrees to pay Miller's family $3.5 million.

The Pentagon reports the capture and "rescue," eight days later, of Private Jessica Lynch, a story that captivates news audiences until it is revealed as a fraud.

On April 4 journalist Michael Kelly becomes the first American to die in the Iraq War.

NBC reporter David Bloom dies from deep vein thrombosis and a pulmonary embolism while covering the Iraq War from his so-called "Bloom Mobile."

During Iraq War, the news media transitions from traditional telephony to satellite broadcasting.

Due to satellite technology, transmission rates drop to $20,000, one fifth of this cost for the Gulf War; this allows local news stations to compete with national services.

During the Iraq War, a fifth satellite was added to handle the huge amount of news emanating from Iraq.

War journalists broadcast news using only 15 pounds of equipment, compared to the trucks that were required to carry broadcast equipment during the 1991 Gulf War.

Online social network MySpace is launched.

Free Internet calling service Skype is founded.

2004

A firestorm of controversy erupts after Kevin Sites films the killing of an unarmed Iraqi prisoner in a Fallujah mosque.

There are 8 million U.S. blogs.

There are 50 million Web sites on the Internet.

Image and video hosting web site Flickr launched, allowing photo and video sharing.

There are 800 million people using the Internet.

Online social network FaceBook is introduced, originally limited to Harvard University students.

2005

Steven Vincent becomes first American journalist to be kidnapped and killed after invasion of Iraq.

Yahoo hires Kevin Sites to cover every conflict zone in the world within a single year.

There are 40 billion web pages.

The killing of Kate Peyton in Mogadishu provokes controversy over the tradition of signing journalists to dangerous location or losing their jobs

Jean Baudrillard publishes "War Porn."

2006

There are more than 100 million MySpace users.

Online social network service Twitter is introduced by the company Obvious.

Dr. Anthony Feinstein publishes *Journalists Under Fire: The Psychological Hazards of Covering War.*

2007

iPhone – an Internet-enabled combination mobile phone, wireless Internet device, and iPod – is introduced by Apple Computer.

2008

Sebastian Junger and Tim Hetherington's film *Restrepo* is released.

2009

Photographer Ronald Haeberle, who documented the 1968 My Lai massacre, admits to having destroyed the only photos of the actual killings in progress, after denying their existence for decades.

2010

Remains of Sean Flynn are found in Cambodia.

There are more than 400 million FaceBook users.

Video-sharing web site YouTube registers more than 2 billion views per day.

The first Pulitzer Prizes are awarded for Internet journalism.

Interview with General Stanley McChrystal by war reporter Michael Mahon Hastings published in *Rolling Stone*. Its revelations would lead the general to resign.

2011

Libyan civil war breaks out.

Ferzat Jarban becomes first Syrian journalist to die while covering Syrian civil war.

Andre Liohn becomes first Latin American photojournalist to win the Robert Capa Gold Medal.

2012

Photojournalist Tyler Hicks crosses border from Syria to Turkey returning the body of Pulitzer Prize winning journalist Anthony Shadid who had recently died covering Syrian civil war.

The French photojournalist Gilles Jacquier becomes first Western journalist killed covering Syrian civil war.

Syrian journalist Maya Nasser becomes 46th journalist to be killed during Syrian civil war.

Martyn Burke's *Under Fire: Journalists in Combat* is released.

2013

The documentary, *Which Way Is the Front Line from Here? The Life and Times of Tim Hetherington* is released.

More than 400 untrained freelance conflict reporters applied to take first course offered by Reporters Instructed in Saving Colleagues (RISC).

2014

American journalist James Foley appears on YouTube video made by ISIS entitled "A Message to America" and was then executed. Unlike subsequent beheadings of Western journalists by ISIS, the entire execution was not played on the video.

ISIS forces British war photographer and hostage John Cantlie to narrate propaganda video.

Camille Lepage becomes first Western journalist to die covering the conflict in the Central African Republic.

War photographer Ashley Gilbertson publishes *Bedrooms of the Fallen.*

The FBI issues a bulletin to news agencies warning that the Islamic State was targeting reporters and media personalities.

Syrian opposition news services create the Nabaa Media Foundation.

Video of the beheading of journalist Steve Sotloff by ISIS is released.

By end of year Syria is ranked as the deadliest country for the press for the third year in a row.

Ukrainian conflict begins

2015

ISIS releases video of the decapitation of the Japanese journalist Kenji Goto.

Reporters without Borders launch campaign to free journalist Austin Tice as media organizations joined together to work for his release and to call on U.S. government to revisit its hostage policies.

Brain Williams is suspended by NBC News for six-months for misrepresenting his wartime reporting.

Appendix A

Mexican-American War Correspondents and the Battles They Covered

Battle of Palo Alto, May 8, 1846: William S. Henry*, Thomas Bangs Thorpe*

Battle of Resaca de la Palma, May 9, 1846: William S. Henry*, Thomas Bangs Thorpe*

Battle of Monterrey, September 20-24, 1846: Samuel Chester Reid Jr., George Wilkins Kendall*, Christopher M. Haile*, William S. Henry*

Battle of Buena Vista, Feb. 22-23, 1847: George Tobin*, Josiah Gregg*, William Osman*, Rufus R.K. Arthur, Albert T. Pike*

Battle of Veracruz, March 9-28, 1847, George Wilkins Kendall*, Christopher M. Haile*, Francis A. Lumsden*, James Freaner*, John Peoples*, William C. Tobey*, Jane McManus Storms*, "Truth"

Battle of Cerro Gordo, May 17-18, 1847: George Wilkins Kendall*, John Peoples*, William C. Tobey*, George M.C. Davis

Battle of Contreras and Churubusco, August 19-20, 1847: George Wilkins Kendall*, James Freaner*, William S. Henry*

Battle of Molino del Rey, September 8, 1847: George Wilkins Kendall*, James Freaner*, William S. Henry*

Battle of Chapultepec/Mexico City, September 12-12, 1847: James Freaner*, John Peoples*, William C. Tobey*, John Warland*, James R. Barnard

Sources: Tom Reilly, *War with Mexico!: America's Reporters Cover the Battlefront*, Lawrence: University of Kansas Press, 2010, p. 43.

* *Indicates a separate entry.*

Appendix B

Crimean War Correspondents

Barkley, John, the *Times*

Beato, Felice A., photographer

Carmichael, J. W., *Illustrated London News*

Chenery, Thomas,* the *Times*

Crowe, Joseph Archer,* *Illustrated London News*

Eber, Ferdinand, the *Times*

Fenton, Roger,* photographer

Godkin, Edwin Lawrence,* *Daily News*

Hardman, Frederick,* the *Times*

Henty, George Alfred,* *Morning Post*

Kanouy, Alfred, *Le Moniteur*

Nasmyth, Charles,* the *Times*

Paton, Andrew Archibald, the *Times*

Robertson, James,* photographer

Russell, Sir William Howard,* the *Times*

Sandwith, Humphrey, the *Times*

Simpson, William,* *Illustrated London News*

Stowe, Henry, the *Times*

Szathmari, Karl Baptist von (Carol Popp de Szathmari),* photographer

Twopenny, Captain, the *Times*

Wood, Nicholas A., *Morning Herald*

Source: Robert W. Desmond. *The Information Process.* 1978

Appendix C

American Indian War Correspondents

"Albert," *St. Louis Globe-Democrat*

Allen, Charles W., *New York Herald*

Atwell, H. Wallace,* *San Francisco Chronicle; Sacramento Recorder; Chicago Inter-Ocean*

Bailey, Gilbert, *Chicago Inter-Ocean; Rocky Mountain News*

Bogart, Robert D.,* *San Francisco Chronicle*

Boyland, R. J., Jr., *St. Paul Pioneer Press*

Brown, George Center, *Cincinnati Commercial*

Budd, H. J., *Cincinnati Daily Gazette*

Bulkeley, ?, *New York Herald*

Burkholder, Alfred H., *New York Herald*

Burns, "Judge," *Chicago Times*

Butler, Guy, *Duluth Tribune*

Clark, Edward B., *Chicago Tribune*

Clover, Sam T., *Chicago Herald*

Copenharve, Charles H., *Omaha Bee*

Corbin, Captain H. C., *Washington Post; Columbus Dispatch*

Crawford, John Wallace, *New York Herald*

Cressey, Charles H., *Omaha Bee*

Curtis, William E., *Chicago Inter-Ocean*

Davenport, Reuben Briggs,* *New York Herald*

Davis, Theodore Russell,* *Harper's Weekly*

Dean, Teresa Howard,* *Chicago Herald*

Diehl, Charles Sanford,* *Chicago Times*

Fayel, William, *St. Louis Republican*

Finerty, John F.,* *Chicago Times*

Fox, Edward,* *New York Herald*

Glover, Ridgeway,* *Frank Leslie's Illustrated Newspaper*

Hall, S. F., *Chicago Tribune*

Harries, George H., *Washington Star; New York Herald*

Hawkins, Irving, *Chicago Tribune*

Howard, James William "Phocion,"* *Chicago Tribune*

Howland, John Dare,* *Harper's Weekly*

Keim, Randolph DeBenneville,* *New York Herald*

Kelley, William F., *Nebraska State Journal*

Kellogg, Marcus Henry,* *Bismarck Tribune; New York Herald*

Knox, Thomas Wallace,* *New York Herald*

Lathrop, Barbour,* *San Francisco Bulletin*

MacMillan, Thomas C.,* *Chicago Inter-Ocean*

McDonough, John A., *New York World*

McFarland, W. J., *Omaha World-Herald*

McKay, Alex,* *San Francisco Evening Bulletin; Yreka Union*

McKay, William, *San Francisco Bulletin*

Medary, Edgar F., *New York Herald*

Moorehead, Warren K., *Illustrated American*

O'Brian, Edward A., *Associated Press*

O'Kelly, James J.,* *New York Herald*

Remington, Frederic Sackrider,* *Harper's Weekly*

Reynolds, Milton W., *New York World; Kansas State Journal; Chicago Times*

Robert, Dent H., *St. Louis Post-Dispatch*

Seymour, Charles G., *Chicago Herald*

Stanley, Sir Henry Morton,* *New York Tribune; St. Louis Weekly Democrat*

Smith, Carl, *Omaha World-Herald*

Stillson, Jerome Bonaparte,* *New York Herald*

Strahorn, Robert,* *Chicago Tribune; Rocky Mountain News; Omaha Republican*

Taylor, James Earl,* *Frank Leslie's Weekly*

Tibbles, Suzette "Bright Eyes," *Omaha World-Herald; Chicago Express*

Tibbles, Thomas H., *Omaha World-Herald; Chicago Herald*

Wasson, Joe,* *Philadelphia Press; New York Tribune; Alta California*

Sources: Oliver Knight. *Following the Indian Wars.* 1960; George Kolbenschlag. *A Whirlwind Passes: Newspaper Correspondents and the Sioux Indian Disturbances of 1890-1891.* 1990; Elmo Scott Watson. "A Check-List of Indian War Correspondents, 1866-1891," *Journalism Quarterly.* December 1940; Elmo Scott Watson. "The Indian Wars and the Press," *Journalism Quarterly.* December 1940.

* Indicates a separate entry.

Appendix D

American Civil War Correspondents

NORTHERN CORRESPONDENTS

Adams, George W., *New York World*

Aldrich, Thomas Bailey,* *New York Tribune*

Ames, Mary Clemmer, *New York Evening Post*

Anderson, Finley,* *New York Herald*

Anderson, William, *Philadelphia Inquirer*

Armstrong, J., *New York Times*

Ashbrook, Sam C., *Philadelphia Inquirer*

Ashley, James Nye, *New York Herald*

Atcheson, Thomas, *New York Tribune*

Austen, J. A., *Chicago Tribune*

Avery, R. B., *Chicago Times*

Babcock, Charles T., *New York Associated Press*

Babcock, William A., *Philadelphia Inquirer*

Badeau, Adam, *New York Times*

Baker, William, *New York Tribune*

Barnard, Theodore, *New York Associated Press*

Barnes, Lucien J., New *York Tribune; St. Louis Missouri Democrat*

Barrett, Edwin Shepard, *Boston Traveller*

Barlett, David V. G., *New York Evening Post; Springfield (Massachusetts) Republican*

Beaman, George W., *St. Louis Missouri Democrat*

Beanie, W. L., *Cincinnati Times*

Bellew, Frank H., *New York Tribune*

Bentley, Henry,* *Philadelphia Inquirer*

Berford, ? , *New York Times*

Betty, Edward, *Cincinnati Gazette*

Bickham, William Denison,* *Cincinnati Commercial*

Bingham, ?, *New York Herald*

Bodman, Albert,* *Chicago Tribune; New York Herald*

Bowern, George C., Jr., *Philadelphia Inquirer*

Boweryem, George, New *York Tribune; Philadelphia Press*

Brace, Charles L., *New York Times*

Bradford, Joseph, *New York Tribune*

Brady, John A., *New York Herald*

Brigham, Charles D.,* *New York Tribune*

Brittingham, J. W., *St. Louis Missouri Republican*

Brooks, Noah, *Sacramento (California) Union*

Brown, George W., *New York Herald*

Browne, Junius Henri,* *Cincinnati Gazette; New York Tribune*

Buckingham, Lynde Walter, *New York Herald*

Buell, George P., *Cincinnati Times*

Bulkley, Solomon T., *New York Herald*

Burnett, Alfred, *Cincinnati Commercial, Times*

Burritt, Ira N., *Cincinnati Gazette*

Buxton, Frank Lacy, *New York Tribune*

Byington, Aaron Homer,* *New York Tribune*

Cadwallader, Sylvanus,* *Chicago Times; New York Herald*

Carpenter, S. M., *New York Herald*

Carroll, William, *New York Times*

Carson, Irving, *Chicago Tribune*

Carson, John Miller, *New York Times*

Cash, Thomas M., *New York Herald*

Cazaran, Augustus, *Boston Traveller*

Chadwick, James B., *New York Tribune*

Chamberlin, W. H., *Cincinnati Gazette*

Chapman, Frank C.,* *New York Herald*

Chester, Thomas Morris,* *Philadelphia Press*

Chounce, ?, *Cincinnati Commercial*

Church, Francis Pharcellus, *New York Times*

Church, William Conant "Pierrepont,"* *New York Evening Post Times*

Clark, G. C., *Chicago Tribune*

Clark, Thomas H., *Philadelphia Inquirer*

Clarke, George W., *New York Herald*

Coffin, Charles Carleton,* *Boston Journal*

Colburn, C. C., *New York Times*

Colburn, Richard T., *New York World*

Colston, ?, *New York Tribune*

Conyngham, David Power, *New York Herald*

Cook, Joel, *Philadelphia Press*

Cook, Thomas M., *New York Herald*

Cooney, Myron A., *New York Herald*

Coscorran, ?, *Chicago Post*

Crapsey, Edward, *Cincinnati Commercial, Gazette; Philadelphia Inquirer*

Creighton, F., *New York World*

Crippen, William G., *Cincinnati Times*

Croffut, William Augustus, *New York Tribune*

Crounse, Lilas Hilston, *New York Times*

Crounse, Lorenzo L.,* *New York Times, World*

Cummins, Thomas J., *New York Herald*

Cunnington, William H., *Philadelphia Inquirer*

Cureau, *?*, *New York Associated Press*

Curry, Lewellan, *Chicago Tribune*

Davenport, John I., *New York Tribune*

Davidson, A., *New York Herald*

Davidson, Nathaniel, *New York Herald*

Davis, R. Stewart, *Philadelphia Inquirer*

Davis, William E., *Cincinnati Gazette*

Dawson, J. J., *New York Herald*

Deming, Sid, *New York Associated Press*

Denyse, Edwin F., *New York Herald*

Doyle, John Edward Parker, *New York Herald*

Driscoll, F., *New York Tribune*

Dugan, James, *Cincinnati Commercial*

Dunglison, Robly, Jr., *Philadelphia Inquirer*

Dunn, John P., *New York Herald*

Eaton, D.B.M., *New York Herald*

Elliott, James, *Cincinnati Gazette*

Elliott, Thomas H., *Philadelphia Inquirer*

Evans, John, *New York Tribune*

Everett, *?*, *New York Herald*

Farrell, Charles H., *New York Herald*

Fawcette, *?*, *New York Times*

Fayel, William A., St. *Louis Missouri Democrat*

Fiske, Samuel Wheelock, *Springfield (Massachusetts) Republican*

Fiske, Stephen Ryder,* *New York Herald*

Fitzpatrick, James C., *New York Herald*

Flint, Henry Martyn, *New York World*

Forrest, Joseph K. C., *Chicago Tribune*

Foss, G. W., *Philadelphia Inquirer*

Foster, F. E., *Chicago Tribune*

Francis, R. D., *New York Herald, Tribune, World*

Fuller, Artur B., *Boston Journal*

Fulton, Albert, *Baltimore American*

Fulton, Charles Carroll, *Baltimore American*

Fulton, Edington, *Baltimore American*

Furay, William S., *Cincinnati Gazette*

Gatchell, William, *New York Herald*

George, William, *New York Times*

Gilbert, Curtis F., *Cincinnati Gazette; New York Tribune*

Gilden, G. P. van, *New York Times; Philadelphia Press*

Gilden, Ira van, *New York Times*

Gilmore, James Roberts, *New York Tribune*

Glen, Samuel R., *New York Herald*

Glenn, Joseph, *Cincinnati Gazette*

Glenn, W., *New York Herald*

Glover, Thaddeus B., *New York Herald*

Gobright, Lawrence Augustus, *New York Associated Press*

Grafffan, Charles H., *New York Herald*

Green, John H., *Cincinnati Enquirer*

Grey, T. C., *New York Tribune*

Groves, *?*, *St Louis Missouri Republican*

Gunn, Thomas Butler, *New York Tribune*

Hall, E. H., *New York Tribune*

Halpin, Charles Graham, *New York Herald*

Halstead, Murat,* *Cincinnati Commercial*

Hamilton, John R., *New York Times*

Hammond, James Bartlett, *New York Tribune, World*

Hannarm, Charles, *New York Herald*

Hanscorm, Simon P., *New York Herald*

Hardenbrook, John A., *New York Herald*

Hart, Charles H., *New York Times*

Hart, George H., *New York Herald*

Harwood, J. H., *New York Times*

Hasson, John, *New York Associated Press*

Hayes, John E., *Boston Traveller; New York Tribune*

Henderson, Thomas J., *New York Tribune*

Hendricks, Leonard A., *New York Herald*

Henry, Arthur, *New York Tribune*

Henry, Frank, *New York Times, Herald*

Hickox, Volney, *Chicago Tribune; Cincinnati Commercial*

Hill, Adams S., *New York Tribune*

Hills, Alfred Clark, *New York Herald*

Hills, William H., *Boston Journal*

Hinton, Richard Josiah, *Chicago Tribune*

Homans, Phineas, *New York Herald*

Hosmer, George Washington, *New York Herald*

House, Edward Howard,* *New York Tribune*

Houston, Alexander, *New York Herald*

Howard, Joseph, Jr., *New York Times*

Howe, O. P., *New York Herald*

Hudson, Henry Norman, *New York Evening Post*

Ives, Malcolm, *New York Herald*

Jacobs, John T., *New York Herald*

Johnson, *?*, *Philadelphia Inquirer*

Johnston, George W., *New York Herald*

Judd, David Wright, *New York Times*

Kaw, Ralph, *Chicago Tribune*

* *Indicates a separate entry.*

Keim, Randolph DeBenneville,* *New York Herald*

Kelly, Henry C., St. *Louis Missouri Democrat*

Kennedy, ?, *Philadelphia Inquirer*

Kent, William H., *New York Tribune*

Kinney, D. J., *New York Tribune*

Knox, Thomas Wallace,* *New York Herald*

Landon, Melville D., *New York Tribune*

Latham, James, *New York Herald*

Law, W.B.S., *New York Herald*

Lippincott, Sara, *New York Tribune*

Long, Francis C., *New York Herald, Tribune*

MacDuff, J., *Philadelphia Inquirer*

MacGahan, Januarius Aloysius,* *St. Louis Missouri Democrat*

Mason, Samuel W., *New York Herald*

Matteson, Andre, *Chicago Post*

Maverick, Augustus, *New York Evening Post*

Maybard, E. L., *New York Herald*

McAran, C. S., *Philadelphia Inquirer*

McBride, R. H., *Philadelphia Press*

McCormick, Richard Cunningham, *New York Evening Post; Commercial Advertiser*

McCracken, W. B., *New York Herald*

McCullagh, Joseph Burbridge,* *Cincinnati Commercial, Enquirer, Gazette*

McDevitt, J. F., *Philadelphia Press*

McElrath, Thompson P., *New York Times*

McGregor, William D., *New York Associated Press, Herald, Times, Tribune*

McKee, Henry, St. *Louis Missouri Democrat*

McKenna, John L., *New York Tribune*

McQuillan, Milton P., *Cincinnati Gazette*

Meader, William H., *Philadelphia Press*

Medberry, W. H., *Cincinnati Gazette*

Merriam, William H., *New York Herald*

Millar, Constantine D., *Cincinnati Commercial*

Miller, John C., *Chicago Journal*

Miller, Joseph W., *Cincinnati Commercial*

Miller, Wilson, *New York Tribune*

Misener, M. C., *Chicago Times*

Mitchell, Abram S., *New York Times*

Moore, William D., *Columbus Ohio State Journal*

Murdock, D., *Philadelphia Inquirer*

Murrell, Hower, *New York Herald*

Myers, ?, *New York Associated Press*

Newbould, Thomas M., *New York Tribune*

Newcomb, J. Warren, *New York Herald*

Newell, Robert Henry, *New York Herald*

Nichols, George Ward, *New York Evening Post*

Norcross, John, *Philadelphia Press*

Noyes, James Oscar, *New York Associated Press*

Nunevile, ?, *Philadelphia Inquirer*

O'Donnell, Kane, *Philadelphia Press*

Olcott, Henry S., *New York Tribune*

Osbon, Bradley Sillick,* *New York Herald, World*

Osborne, Galen H., *New York Herald*

Page, ?, St. *Louis Missouri Democrat*

Page, Charles Anderson,* *New York Tribune*

Paige, Nathaniel, *New York Tribune*

Painter, Uriah H.,* *Philadelphia Inquirer*

Paul, Edward Alexander, *New York Times*

Pedrick, A. K., *Philadelphia Inquirer*

Peters, E. T., *Philadelphia Inquirer*

Plympton, Florus B., *Cincinnati Commercial*

Pollock, ?, *New York Tribune*

Poore, Benjamin Perley, *Boston Journal*

Post, Truman A., *New York Tribune; St. Louis Missouri Democrat*

Puleston, J. H., *Philadelphia North American*

Quigg, John Travis, *New York World*

Rathbone, John F., *New York World*

Ray, Charles H., *Chicago Tribune*

Raymond, ?, *New York Herald*

Raymond, Henry Jarvis,* *New York Times*

Rea, Samuel J., *New York Associated Press; Philadelphia Inquirer*

Reden, Laura C., *St. Louis Missouri Republican*

Redfield, W. R., *Chicago Journal*

Redpath, James,* *Boston Journal; New York Tribune*

Reid, Whitelaw,* *Cincinnati Gazette*

Reilly, Frank W., *Chicago Tribune; Cincinnati Times*

Rhoads, J. S., *Philadelphia Inquirer*

Richardson, Albert Deane,* *New York Tribune*

Ricks, ?, *Cincinnati Commercial*

Ripley, Phillip, *New York World, Evening Post*

Robinson, Joseph, *Philadelphia Inquirer*

Rogers, George M., *New York Times*

Runkle, ?, *New York Herald*

Rust, George W., *Chicago Times*

Salter, George H. C., *New York Times*

Sawyer, Oscar G., *New York Herald*

Schenk, ?, *New York Herald*

School, Charles E., *Philadelphia Press*

Schrick, Julius, *St. Louis Missouri Republican*

Seward, ?, *Philadelphia Inquirer*

Seybold, Thaddeus S., *New York Tribune*

Shanahan, Charles S., *New York Herald*

Shanks, William F. G.,* *New York Herald*

Shelly, R. L., *New York Associated Press*

Shepherd, Nathaniel Graham, *New York Tribune*

Shoaff, James, *Chicago Times*

Shore, W. W., *New York Tribune, World*

Shriek, Ernest, *St. Louis Missouri Republican*

Silsby, ?, *Cincinnati Gazette*

Simonton, James, *New York Times*

Slack, ?, *New York Herald*

Slocum, J. D., *New York Herald*

Smalley, George Washburn,* *New York Tribune*

Smith, Elias,* *New York Times, Tribune*

Smith, Henry M., *Chicago Tribune*

Snell, James, *New York Herald*

Sparks, William J., *New York Herald*

Spenser, E. M., *Cincinnati Times*

Spofford, Ainsworth, *Cincinnati Commercial*

Stafford, ?, *St. Louis Missouri Democrat*

Stark, William J., *New York Herald*

Stedman, Edmund Clarence,* *New York World*

Stillson, Jerome Bonaparte,* *New York World*

Stiner, William H., *New York Herald*

Surface, D., *Cincinnati Gazette; Philadelphia Inquirer*

Swain, James Barrett, *New York Times*

Swinton, William,* *New York Times*

Swisshelm, Jane Grey, *New York Tribune*

Sypher, Josiah Rhinehart, *New York Tribune*

Taggartt, John H., *Philadelphia Inquirer*

Talcott, Alfred B., *New York Herald*

Tallman, Pelegg, *Chicago Times; New York Herald*

Taylor, Bayard, *New York Tribune*

Taylor, Benjamin Franklin,* *Chicago Journal*

Thompson, Henry, *New York Herald*

Thompson, Mortimer, *New York Tribune*

Townsend, George Alfred,* *New York Herald, World*

Tracey, ?, *St Louis Missouri Republican*

Trembly, J. R., *New York Herald*

Truman, Benjamin Cummings,* *New York Times; Philadelphia Inquirer, Press*

Tyler, George W., *New York Associated Press*

Upton, George Putman,* *Chicago Tribune*

Vaughn, W. W., *New York World*

Villard, Henry,* *New York Herald, Tribune*

Vosburg, J. H., *New York Herald*

Wallz, Lawrence W., *New York Herald; Philadelphia Press*

Wallington, William M., *Philadelphia Inquirer*

Ward, Ulysses B., *New York Herald*

Wardell, James, *New York Herald*

Warden, W. W., *Cincinnati Enquirer*

Ware, Joseph A., *Philadelphia Press; Washington Chronicle*

Warner, James C., *Philadelphia Press*

Warren, Fitz-Henry, *New York Tribune*

Wayland, H. L., *New York World*

Webb, Charles Henry, *New York Times*

Webb, William E., *St. Louis Missouri Republican*

Weed, ?, *New York Herald*

Weik, John, *Philadelphia Press*

Wells, William H., *New York Herald, Tribune*

Westfall, E. D., *New York Associated Press, Herald*

Wheeler, Charles L., *St. Louis Missouri Republican*

Whipple, T. Herber, *New York Herald*

White, Horace, *Chicago Tribune*

Whitely, L. A., *New York Herald*

Whittenmore, W. H., *New York Times*

Wikoff, Henry, *New York Herald*

Wilkes, George, *New York Tribune*

Wilkeson, Samuel,* *New York Times, Tribune*

Wilkie, Franc Bangs,* *New York Times*

Williams, George Forrester,* *New York Times*

Williams, Walter F., *New York Evening Post*

Williamson, D. B., *Philadelphia Inquirer*

Wilson, John R., *Chicago Journal*

Wilson, Theodore C., *New York Herald*

Winchell, James M., *New York Times*

Wing, Henry Ebenezer,* *New York Tribune*

Wisner, Henry Jacob, *New York Times*

Woodal, A. T., *Cincinnati Gazette*

Woods, George Z., *Boston Daily Advertiser*

Woodwell, Charles H., *Boston Post*

Young, Harry H., *New York Times, World*

Young, John Russell,* *Philadelphia Press*

Young, William, *Boston Herald; New York Herald*

Source: J. Cutler Andrews. *The North Reports the Civil War.* 1955.

* *Indicates a separate entry.*

SOUTHERN CORRESPONDENTS

Abrams, Alexander St. Clair,* *Atlanta Daily, Intelligencer*

Adams, Warren, *Mobile Daily Advertiser and Register*

Albertson, Jonathan White, Confederate Press Association

Alexander, Peter Wellington,* *Savannah Republican; Mobile Daily Advertiser and Register; Richmond Daily Dispatch*

Bagby, George W.,* *Charleston Mercury, Mobile Daily Advertiser and Register; New Orleans Daily Crescent; Columbus Daily Sun*

Barr, W. W., *Memphis Daily Appeal*

Barr, William D., *Memphis Daily Appeal*

Bass, J. N., *Atlanta Daily Southern Confederacy*

Bell, James Pinkney, *Richmond Daily Dispatch*

Britton, E. H., *Charlotte Bulletin*

Bruns, Dr. John Dickson, *Charleston Mercury*

Bunting, Robert Franklin, *Houston Telegraph; San Antonio Herald*

Carter, Captain Theodoric, *Chattanooga Daily Rebel; Montgomery Daily Mail*

Cooke, John Esten,* *Richmond Whig; Richmond Southern Illustrated News*

Courtenay, William A.,* *Charleston Mercury*

Cox, T. J., *Columbus Daily Sun*

Da Ponte, Durant,* *New Orleans Daily Delta*

Davis, Captain Richard T., *Savannah Republican*

Dawson, Andrew H., *Mobile Daily Advertiser and Register*

De Fontaine, Felix Gregory,* *Charleston Daily Courier; Daily Richmond Enquirer; Columbia Daily South Carolinian; Richmond Whig; Savannah Republican; Memphis Daily Appeal; Mobile Daily Advertiser and Register*

De Gournay, Captain Francis F., *New Orleans Daily Picayune*

DeMorse, Charles,* *Clarksville Standard*

Dill, Benjamin F., *Memphis Daily Appeal*

Douglas, James P., *Tyler Reporter*

Duncan, David Grieve, *Charleston Mercury; New Orleans Daily Delta; Savannah Morning News; Richmond Daily Dispatch*

Dupre, Colonel Louis J., *Knoxville Daily Register*

Dutcher, Salem, *Augusta Daily Constitutionalist*

Ette, Robert, *Memphis Daily Appeal*

Farris, Captain, *Atlanta Daily Register*

Flournoy, J. G., *Memphis Daily Appeal*

Foard, N. E., *Charleston Daily Courier*

Forbes, ?, Confederate Press Association

Forsyth, John,* *Mobile Daily Advertiser and Register; Atlanta Daily Southern Confederacy; Augusta Daily Contitutionalist; Charleston Daily Courier*

Fowler, W. B., *Mobile Daily Tribune*

Galbreath, W. B., *Memphis Daily Appeal*

Gibbes, Robert W.,* Press Association of the Confederate States of America*

Gibbons, Israel,* *New Orleans Daily Crescent; Mobile Daily Advertiser and Register*

Gilbert, Rensalear Reed "R.R.,: *Houston Tri-Weekly Telegraph*

Graeme, John, Jr., *Southern Associated Press;* Confederate Press Association

Gray, Alexander, *Southern Associated Press*

Hatcher, John E., Confederate Press Association; *Mobile Daily Advertiser and Register*

Hotsze, Henry, *Mobile Daily Advertiser and Register*

Hutchen, Virginius, *Columbus Daily Sun*

Jenkins, Donelson Caffery, *New Orleans Daily Delta*

Jeter, Oliver, *Mobile Daily Advertiser and Register*

"Joan",* *Charleston Courier*

Kennedy, Captain John, *Southern Associated Press*

Kirk, Charles D., *Louisville Daily Courier; Chattanooga Daily Rebel; Memphis Daily Appeal; Augusta Daily Constitutionalist*

Lane, J. J., *New Orleans Daily Delta*

Linebaugh, John H.,* *Memphis Daily Appeal*

Loommis, ?, *Southern Associated Press*

Marx, Bonhomme, *New Orleans Daily Picayune*

Mathews, L. H., *Pensacola Observer*

Matthews, Captain ?, *Memphis Daily Appeal*

Meyer, Gustave, *Richmond Daily Dispatch; New Orleans Daily Delta*

Parks, Virgil A. S., *Savannah Republican*

Perry, Major Henry H., *New Orleans Daily Picayune; Memphis Daily*

Pleasants, Hugh, *Richmond Daily Dispatch*

Posey, Ben Lane, *Mobile Daily Advertiser and Register*

Pryor, J. P., *Memphis Daily Appeal*

Purvis, Captain George E., *Atlanta Daily Southern Confederacy*

Reid, Samuel Chester, Jr.,* *Chattanooga Daily Rebel; Memphis Daily Appeal; New Orleans Daily Picayune; Montgomery Daily Advertiser; Mobile Daily Advertiser and Register; Mobile Daily Tribune; Atlanta Daily Intelligencer*

Reyburn, W. P., *New Orleans Daily Crescent*

Riordan, Bartholomew R.,* *Charleston Mercury;* Confederate Press Association

Roberts, Albert, *Nashville Republican Banner*

Rowe, George Henry Clay, *Daily Richmond Examiner*

Ryan, Lipscomb, *New Orleans Daily Crescent*

Sanderson, ?, Confederate Press Association

Screws, William Wallace,* *Montgomery Daily Advertiser*

Semple, William M., *Mobile Daily Advertiser and Register*

Sener, James Beverley, *Richmond Daily Dispatch; Daily Richmond Enquirer*

Shepardson, Dr. William G.,* *Mobile Daily Advertiser and Register; Columbus Times; Montgomery Daily Advertiser; Richmond Daily Dispatch*

Sledge, James, *Athens Southern Banner*

Smith, J. Henly, Confederate Press Association

Smoot, ?, Confederate Press Association

Smyth, Frank, *Petersburg Daily Express*

Sneed, James Roddy,* *Savannah Republican*

Sossman, ?, *Mobile Daily Tribune*

Sparnick, Henry, *Charleston Daily Courier*

Spratt, Leonidas W.,* *Charleston Mercury*

Stedman, George Clinton, *Daily Richmond Enquirer*

Stoddard, George W., *New Orleans Daily Crescent*

Street, Albert J., *Mobile Daily Advertiser and Register; Savannah Republican*

Thompson, J. H., *Jackson Daily Mississippian*

Thompson, John R., *Memphis Daily Appeal*

Thompson, William Tappan, *Savannah Morning News*

Thrasher, John S.,* *Confederate Press Association*

Timrod, Henry,* *Charleston Mercury*

Timsley, H. C., *Richmond Daily Dispatch*

"Virginia", *The Mobile Advertiser and Register*

Wagner, A. J., Confederate Press Association

Walker, Alexander, *New Orleans Daily Delta*

Ward, John S., *Atlanta Daily Register*

Watterson, Henry, *Atlanta Daily Southern Confederacy; Augusta Daily Constitution; Mobile Daily Advertiser and Register*

West, John M., *New Orleans True Delta*

Woodson, Will O., Confederate Press Association

Wright, Lieutenant T. D., *Atlanta Daily Southern Confederacy*

Wright, ?, *New Orleans Bee*

Yarington, Richard J., *Richmond Associated Press; Richmond Daily Whig; Columbus Daily Sun*

Youngblood, Captain J. W., *Memphis Daily Appeal*

Source: J. Cutler Andrews. *The South Reports the Civil War.* 1970; Patricia McNeely, Debra Reddin van Tuyll, and Henry H. Schulte, eds. *Knights of the Quill,* 2010.

BRITISH CORRESPONDENTS

Day, Samuel Phillips,* *Morning Herald*

Dicey, Edward James Stephen,* *Daily Telegraph*

Gallenga, Antonio,* the *Times*

Godkin, Edwin Lawrence, *Daily News*

Lawley, Francis Charles, the *Times*

MacKay, Charles,* the *Times*

Sala, George Augustus Henry,* *Daily Telegraph*

Vizetelly, Frank,* *Daily News*

Sources: J. Cutler Andrews. *The North Reports the Civil War.* 1955; J. Cutler Andrews. *The South Reports the Civil War.* 1970; Robert W. Desmond. *The Information Process.* 1978

Appendix E

Franco-Prussian War Correspondents

Austin, Charles, *the Times*

Cardon, Emile, *Le Gaulois*

Chabrillat, Henri, *Le Figaro*

Claretie, Jules, *Opinion Nationale*

Conway, Moncure D., *Daily Telegraph*

De Blowitz, Henri Stepan Opper,* the *Times*

Forbes, Archibald,* *Daily News*

Freytag, Gustav, *Die Grenzboten*

Hance, Joseph, *New York Tribune*

Hardman, Frederick,* the *Times*

Henty, George Alfred,* *London Standard*

Holtof, Ludwig, *Frankfurter Zeitung*

Jennerod, G., *Le Temps*

Kingston, William Beattie,* *Daily Telegraph*

Labouchere, Henry "Labby" Du Pre,* *Daily News*

Lawley, Francis Charles,* *Daily Telegraph*

Lesage, Sir John Merry,* *Daily Telegraph*

MacGahan, Januarius Aloysius,* *New York Herald*

Muller, Gustav, *New York Tribune*

Oliphant, Laurence,* the *Times*

Russell, Sir William Howard,* the *Times*

Sala, George Augustus Henry,* *Daily Telegraph*

Shea, John Augustus, *London Standard*

Skinner, John Edwin Hilary,* *Daily News*

Texier, Edmund, *Le Siecle*

Vizetelly, Edward Henry,* *Daily News*

Vizetelly, Ernest Alfred,* *Daily News*

Vizetelly, Henry Richard,* *Illustrated London News*

Voget, Hermann, *Frankfurter Zeitung*

Wachenhusen, Hans, *Kolnische Zeitung*

Wellmer, Arnold, *Neue Freie Presse*

Whitehurst, Felix, *Daily Telegraph*

Whyte, Holt, *New York Tribune*

Williams, George Douglas, *Reuters*

Source: Robert Desmond. *The Information Process.* 1978

Appendix F

Russo-Turkish War Correspondents

Clarke, Campbell, *Daily Telegraph*

Cockerill, John A., *Cincinnati Enquirer*

Forbes, Archibald,* *Daily News*

Gallenga, Antonio,* the *Times*

Gay, Drew, *Daily Telegraph*

Jackson, John P., *New York Herald*

Kingston, William Beattie,* *Daily Telegraph*

MacGahan, Januarius Aloysius,* *Daily News*

Millet, Francis Davis,* *Daily News*

O'Donovan, Edmund,* *Daily News*

Power, Frank Le Poer,* stringer

Prior, Melton,* *Illustrated London News*

Scudamore, Frank,* *Daily News*

Stickney, Joseph L., *Chicago Tribune*

Stillman, William J., the *Times*

Villiers, Frederic,* *Graphic*

Source: Robert W. Desmond. *The Information Process.* 1978.

* *Indicates a separate entry.*

Appendix G

Correspondents Covering the Sudan and Egyptian Campaigns, 1882-1899

Bass, John Foster,* *Chicago Record*

Bell, Charles Frederick Moberly, the *Times*

Bennett, Ernest W., *Westminster Gazette*

Burleigh, Bennet,* *Daily Telegraph*

Cameron, John Alexander,* *London Standard*

Chapman, J. C., *Daily News*

Churchill, Sir Winston Leonard Spencer,* *Morning Post*

Ferguson, Fergus, Reuters*

Gay, Drew, *Daily Telegraph*

Gwynne, Howell Arthur,* Reuters

Herbert, St. Leger Algernon,* *Morning Post*

Howard, Hubert,* *New York Herald*

James, Lionel,* Reuters

O'Donovan, Edmund,* *Daily News*

O' Kelly, James J., *Daily News*

Pearse, Harry H. S.,* *Daily News*

Power, Frank Le Poer,* the *Times*

Prior, Melton,* *Illustrated London News*

Rathom, John Revelstoke,* *Melbourbe Argus*

Robinson, Philip, *Daily Chronicle*

Steevens, George Warrington,* *Daily Mail*

Vayssie, Georges, Agence Havas

Vizetelly, Frank Horace,* *Daily News*

Wilkinson, Henry Spenser,* *Manchester Guardian*

Sources: Robert W. Desmond. *The Information Process.* 1978; Robert Wilkinson-Latham. *From Our Special Correspondent.* 1979.

Appendix H

Greco-Turkish War Correspondents

Atkins, John Black,* *Manchester Guardian*

Bourchier, James David,* the *Times*

Burleigh, Bennet,* *Daily Telegraph*

Chadourne, Gaston, Agence Havas

Crane, Stephen,* *New York Journal*

Creelman, James,* *New York Journal*

Davis, Richard Harding,* *New York Journal*

Dillon, Emile Joseph,* *Daily Telegraph*

Ferguson, Fergus, Reuters*

Gwynne, Howell Arthur,* Reuters

Knight, Edward Frederick,* the *Times*

Maud, W. T.,* *Graphic*

Miller, William, *Morning Post*

Nevinson, Henry Woodd,* *Daily Chronicle*

Palmer, Frederick,* *New York World*

Phillips, Percival,* *Chicago Inter-Ocean*

Prior, Melton,* *Illustrated London News*

Ralph, Julian,* *New York Journal*

Rose, W. Kinnaird, Reuters

Scovel, Henry Sylvester,* *New York World*

Scudamore, Frank, *Daily News*

Steevens, George Warrington,* *Daily Mail*

Taylor, Cora,* *New York Journal*

Villiers, Frederic,* *London Standard*

Werndel, W. H. G., Reuters

Williams, Charles,* *Daily Chronicle*

Source: Robert Desmond. *The Information Process.* 1978.

* *Indicates a separate entry.*

Appendix I

Spanish-American War Correspondents

Addington, Oscar, *New York Journal*

Akers, C. E., *London Times*

Alvarez, Ramon, *New York Herald*

Alvord, Thomas G., *New York World*

Archibald, James Francis Jewell,* *San Francisco Post*

Atkins, John Black,* *Manchester Guardian*

Barrett, John, *New York Journal*

Barry, David S., freelancer based in Washington, D.C. Bass, John Foster,* *Harper's Weekly*

Beach, Harry L., Associated Press

Bengough, William, artist, *New York Journal*

Benjamin, Anna Northend,* *Leslie's Illustrated*

Bennett, James O'Donnell, *Chicago Journal*

Betancourt, Alcides, *New York Herald*

Biddle, Nicholas, ?

Bigelow, Poultney,* *New York Herald; London Times*

Billman, Howbert,* *Chicago Record*

Bonsal, Stephen, *New York Herald; McClure's Magazine*

Bowen, William Shaw, *New York World*

Brandenberg, Earl B., *New York World*

Brown, Harry, *New York World*

Browne, Herbert J., New *York Journal*

Bryson, George Eugene,* *New York Journal*

Burgin, Fred, *New York Herald*

Burton, James,* photographer, *Harper's Weekly*

Caldwell, John R., *New York Herald*

Campbell, Floyd, artist, *New York Herald*

Cary, Henry, *New York World*

Casey, Daniel, *Chicago Record*

Chamberlain, Joseph Edgar, *New York Evening Post*

Chamberlin, Henry Barrett, *Chicago Record*

Chambers, Julius, *New York Journal*

Chapman, Carlton T., artist, *Harper's Weekly*

Charles, Cecil, *New York World*

Christy, Howard Chandler,* artist, *Leslie's Illustrated*

Coffin, George, *New York Journal*

Collins, Frank, *Boston Journal*

Cramer, Robert B., *Atlanta Constitution*

Crane, Stephen,* *New York World*

Creelman, James,* *New York World*

Crosby, Charles E., *Chicago Record*

Davenport, Reuben Briggs,* ?

Davenport, Walter, cartoonist, *New York Journal*

Davies, Acton, *New York Sun*

Davis, Oscar K., *New York Sun*

Davis, Richard Harding,* *New York Journal*

Dawley, Thomas R., Jr., *Harper's Weekly*

Decker, Karl, *New York Journal*

Delorme, Thomas, *New York Journal*

Denton, Hal, *New York Journal*

Diehl, Charles Sanford,* Associated Press

Dieuaide, T.M., *New York Sun*

Dinwiddie, William,* *New York Herald*

Dunning, John P.,* Associated Press

Emerson, Edwin, *Leslie's Illustrated*

Farman, T. F., *London Standard*

Fay, John, *Chicago Tribune; New York World*

Ferguson, David, *Chicago Tribune*

Flint, Grover, *New York Journal*

Follansbee, John G., *New York Journal*

Fox, John, Jr.*, *Harper's Weekly*

Francis, Charles R., *Minneapolis Times*

Fuentes, Manuel, *New York World*

Fulton, Harry S., *New York Journal*

Garcia, Eduardo, *New York Sun*

Gay, W. W., New *York World*

Glackens, William, artist, *McClure's Magazine*

Goode, Sir William Athelstane Meredith,* Associated Press

Goudie, Alfred C., Associated Press

Govin, Charles,* *Key West Equator-Democrat*

Graham, George Edward,* Associated Press

Halstead, Freeman, *New York Herald*

Halstead, Murat,* *New York Journal*

Hancock, H. Irving, *Golden Hours of New York*

Hands, Charles E.,* *London Daily Mail*

Harden, Edwin W.,* *New York World*

Hare, James H.,* photographer, *Collier's*

Harris, Julian, *Atlanta Constitution*

Harris, Kennett, *Chicago Record*

Hawthorne, Julian, *New York Journal*

Hemment, John C.,* photographer, *Harper's Weekly*

Herrings, J., New *York Staats-Zeitung*

Hilgert, F. J., Associated Press

Hillegas, Howard Clemens, ?

Howard, Walter, *New York Journal*

Hunt, D. V., photographer, *Harper's Weekly*

Johnson, General Bradley T., *New York World* Johnstone, E.R., Associated Press

Jones, Hayden, artist, *New York World*

Keen, Edward L., Keen-Scripps-McRae Press

Kendrick, Marion, *New York Journal*

Kenealy, Alexander C., *New York World*

Kerman, George,* *Outlook* Magazine

Knight, Edward Frederick,* *London Times*

Koelbe, Adolph, *New York World*

Laine, Honore, *New York Journal*

Langland, James, *Chicago News*

Lawrence, Frederick W., *New York Journal*

Leary, William, freelancer, New York

Leighton, Sir Bryan, ?

Lewis, Alfred H., *New York Journal*

Lewis, William E., *New York Journal*

Low, A. Maurice, *London Daily Chronicle*

Luks, George B., artist, *New York World*

Lyman, A. W., Associated Press

Lynch, George,* *London Chronicle*

Mannix, William, *Army and Navy Journal*

Marcotte, Henry, *Army and Navy Journal*

Marriott, J. Crittenden, Associated Press

Marshall, Edward, *New York Journal*

Martin, Harold, Associated Press

Masterson, Kate, *New York Journal*

Maxwell, John M., *Chicago Tribune*

McCutcheon, John T.,* artist, *Chicago Record*

McDowell, Malcolm, *Chicago Record*

McIntosh, Burr William,* photographer, *Leslie's Illustrated*

McMillan, Samuel, freelancer, Lowell, Massachusetts

McNichol, H. E., *New York Journal*

McPherson, Douglas, ?

McQueen, Peter, freelancer, Boston

McReady, Ernest W., ?

Melton, Ona, *Jacksonville Times-Union*

Michelson, Charles, *New York Journal*

Millard, Thomas Franklin Fairfax,* *New York Herald*

Millet, Francis Davis,* *Harper's Weekly; London Times*

Mumford, John K., *New York Journal*

Musgrave, George Clarke, *London Chronicle*

Nichols, Francis Henry,* *New York World*

Norris, Frank, *McClure's Magazine*

Nuttall, Frank, *London Daily Telegraph*

O'Donohue, Dennis, *Detroit News*

Ohl, Joseph, *Atlanta Constitution*

O'Shaughnessy, James, Jr., *Chicago Chronicle*

Paine, Ralph Delahaye,* *New York World; Philadelphia Press*

Peltz, Hamilton, *New York Herald*

Pendleton, C. B., *Key West Equator-Democrat*

Pepper, Charles M., *Washington Star*

Peters, G. W., artist, *Harper's Weekly*

Phillips, Percival,* *New York World*

Price, G. Ewing, *New Orleans Times-Democrat*

Quail, J.N., *New York Journal*

Quigley, W.S., *New York Mail and Express*

Ranthom, John Revelstoke,* *San Francisco Chronicle*

Rea, George Bronson,* *New York Herald*

Redding, Leo L., *New York Herald*

Remington, Frederic Sackrider,* artist, *New York Journal*

Roberts, Elmer E., Associated Press

Robinson, Philip, *London Pall Mall Gazette*

Romaine, Major, *National Tribune*

Root, Walstein, *New York Sun*

Russell, Walter, artist, *New York Herald*

Schell, Frank C., artist, *Leslie's Illustrated*

Schemedtzen, William, ?

Scovel, Henry Sylvester,* *New York World*

Seibold, Louis, *New York World*

Sheldon, Charles M.,* artist, *London Black and White*

Smith, Morton, *Atlanta Journal*

Somerford, Fred O., *New York Herald*

Steep, Thomas W., Scripps-McRae League

Stickney, Joseph L., *New York Herald*

Thompson, Howard N., Associated Press

Thrall, Charles H., *New York World*

Valesch, Eva McDonald, *New York Journal*

Walker, T. Dart, artist, *Harper's Weekly*

Watkins, Kathleen "Kit" Blake,* *Toronto Mail and Express*

Watson, Oscar, ?

Whigham, H. J., *Chicago Tribune*

* Indicates a separate entry.

White, Douglas, ?

White, Mrs. Katherine, Red Cross; *Chicago Record*

White, Trumbull, *Chicago Record*

Whitney, Caspar,* *Harper's Weekly*

Willets, Gilson, *Leslie's Illustrated*

Wilson, W. O., artist, *New York Herald*

Wright, Henry Charles Seppings,* *London Illustrated News*

Zogbaum, Rufus, artist, *Harper's Weekly*

Sources: Charles H. Brown. *The Correspondents' War.* 1967; Robert W. Desmond. *The Information Process.* 1978; Joyce Milton. The Yellow Kids: Foreign Correspondents in the Heyday of Yellow Journalism. 1989.

Appendix J

Boer War Correspondents

Amery, Leopold Charles Maurice Stennett,* the *Times*

Atkins, John Black,* *Manchester Guardian*

Baillie, F. D., *Morning Post*

Barnes, *Daily Mail*

Battersby, Prevost, *Morning Post*

Beresford, Robert, Central News

Bleloch, *Standard*

Booth, R. C., *Pearson's War News*

Bray, Charles, Central News

Bullen, Percy *Daily Telegraph*

Burleigh, Bennet,* *Daily Telegraph*

Buxton, *Cape Argus*

Cameron, J., *Daily Chronicle*

Campbell, Alister, Laffan's Agency

Carrere, Jean, *Matin*

Churchill, Winston,* *Morning Post*

Collett, Albert, *Daily Mail*

Davies, *Sphere*

Delaware, Lord, *Globe*

Dickinson, Edith Charlotte Musgrave, *Adelaide Advertiser*

Dinwiddie, William,* *Harper's*

Donohoe, Martin Henry,* *Daily Chronicle*

Dunn, Joseph S., Central News

Ewan, *Toronto Globe*

Ferrand, Alfred, *Morning Post*

Finlason, C. E., *Black and White*

Fripp, Charles Edwin,* *Graphic*

Giles, D., *Black and White*

Goldman, Charles Sydney, *Outlook*

Goldmann, S., *Daily Telegraph*

Gotto, Basil,* *Daily Express*

Graham, A., Central News

Graham, George Edward,* Central News

Gwynne, Howell Arthur,* Reuters*

Hales, A. G., *Daily News; Sydney Morning Herald*

Hamilton, Frederick, *Toronto Globe*

Hamilton, J. Angus, the *Times*, *Black and White*

Hands, Charles E.,* *Daily Mail*

Hartland, Hardtford, *Navy and Army Illustrated*

Hellawell, Mr., *Daily Mail*

Hodgetts, E. A. Brayley, *Daily Express*

Hoskier, Colonel, *Sphere*

Hutton, Reuters

Hyman, *Cinematograph*

James, Lionel,* the *Times*

Jenkins, *Daily Mail*

King, G., *Melbourne Age*

Kingsley, Mary,* *Morning Post*

Kinnear, Alfred,* Central News

Knight, Edward Frederick,* *Morning Post*

Lambie, Mr., *Melbourne Age*

Landon, P., the *Times*

Lynch, George,* *Morning Herald; Echo*

Lyons, H., *Daily Mail*

Macdonald, Donald, *Melbourne Argus*

MacDonell, the *Times*

MacHugh, Lieutenant-Colonel Robert Joseph,* *Daily Telegraph*

Mackem, *Scribner*

Mann, Harrington, *Black and White*

Manners, Lord Cecil, *Morning Post*

Martindale, W., Central News

Maud, W. T.,* *Daily Graphic*

Maxwell, Sir William,* *Standard*

Mempes, Mortimer, *Black and White*

Milne, James, Reuters*

Mitchell, Robert, *Standard*

Musgrave, George Clark, *Black and White*

Neilly, Emerson,* *Pall Mall Gazette*

Nevinson, Henry Woodd,* *Daily Chronicle*

Nissen, R.C.E., *Daily Mail*

Nissen, *Cape Times*

Owen-Scott, *Illustrated London News*

Parslow, E. G.,* *Daily Chronicle*

Paterson, Andrew Barton, *Sydney Morning Herald; Melbourne Argus; Reuters*

Paxton, R.M.B., *Sphere*

Pearse, Harry H. S.,* *Daily News*

Pollock, Major A.W.A., the *Times*

Pontin. D., *Melbourne Age*

Prater, Ernest, *Sphere*

Prior, Melton,* *Illustrated London News*

* *Indicates a separate entry.*

Ralph, Julian,* *Daily Mail*

Ralph, Lester, *Daily Mail*

Reiss, *Manchester Guardian*

Rennett, *Laffan's*

Rhodes, Colonel F., the *Times*

Rosenthal, *Cinematograph*

Rosslyn, Lord, *Daily Mail, Sphere*

Scott, *Manchester Courier*

Scull, E. D., *Chicago Record*

Seull, G. H., *New York Commercial Advertiser*

Shelley, *King*

Smith, *Canadian*

Smith, Ernest,* *Morning Leader*

Spooner, H. H., Reuters

Steevens, George Warrington,* *Daily Mail*

Stent, Vere, Reuters

Stewart, F. A., *Illustrated London News*

Story, Douglas, *Daily Mail*

Stuart, John, *Morning Post*

Swallow, W. S., Central News

Sykes, A. A., *Black and White*

Thackery, Lance, *Sphere*

Toy, Pert, *Perth Morning Herald*

Unger, Frederic William,* *Philadelphia Press*

Villiers, Frederic,* *Graphic*

Walker, F. W., *Daily Mail*

Wallace, Edgar,* Reuters, *Daily Mail*

Wester, Captain, *Midland News*

White, *Montreal Star*

Wigham, H. J., *Daily Mail*

Wilkinson, Frank, *Sydney Daily Telegraph, Melbourne Age*

Wilson, Lady Sarah, *Daily Mail*

Wollen, W. B., *Sphere*

Wright, Henry Charles Seppings,* *Daily News*

Young, Alexander Bell Filson,* *Manchester Guardian*

Sources: Robert W. Desmond. *The Information Process.* 1978; Frederic William Unger. *With Bobs and Kruger: Experiences and Observations of an American War Correspondent in the Field with Both Armies.* 1901; Robert Wilkinson-Latham. *From Our Special Correspondent.* 1979

Appendix K

Russo-Japanese War Correspondents, 1904-1905

Ashmead-Bartlett, Ellis*, the *Times*, *Daily Telegraph*

Baring, Maurice*, *The Morning Post*

Barry, Richard, *Eastern Illustrated War News*

Barzini, Sr., Luigi*, Corriere della Sera

Bass, John Foster*, *Chicago Daily News*

Bonsal, Stephen, *New York Herald*

Brill, W.H., AP, Reuters

Brindle, *Daily Mail*

Brinkley, Francis, the *Times*

Burleigh, Bennet*, *Daily Telegraph*

Clarkin, Franklin, *New York Post*

Cockran, J.M., *Leslie's Weekly*

Collins, Robert Moore*, Reuters

Davis, Oscar King*, *New York Herald*

Davis, Richard Harding*, *Collier's*

De la Salle, Georges, Agence Havas

Denny, George, AP

Dinwiddie, William*, *NY Herald*

Donald, William Henry, *NY Herald*

Donohoe, Martin*, *Daily Chronicle*

Dunn, James H., *NY Globe*

Emerson, Edwin

Etzel, Lewis, *Daily Telegraph*

Fox, John, Scribner's

Fraser, David Stewart, the *Times*

Hands, Charles E.*, *Daily Mail*

Hare, James H.*, *Collier's weekly*

James, Lionel*, the *Times*

Kennan, George*, The Outlook

Knight, Edward Frederick*, *Morning Post*

Kriegelstein, Baron Bilder von, Berliner Lokal-Anzeiger

Lewis, Wilmott Harsant*, *New York Herald*

Little, Richard H., *Chicago Daily News*

London, Jack*, *Colliers, NY Herald, Harper's, NY Journal*

MacHugh, Robert Joseph*, *Daily Telegraph*

Maxwell, William*, *The Standard*

McCormick, Frederick*, AP

McCutcheon, John T.*, *Chicago Tribune*

McCullagh, Francis*, *NY Herald*

McKensie, Frederick Arthur, *Daily Mail*

Middleton, Henry, AP

Millard, Thomas Franklin Fairfax*, *NY Herald*

Morgan, W.G., *NY Tribune*

Naudeau, Ludovic, *Le Journal*

Palmer, Frederick*, *NY Globe*

Phillips, Percival*, *Daily Express*

Ponting, Herbert G., *Harper's Weekly*

Prior, Melton*, *Illustrated London News*

Repington, Charles a Court*, the *Times*

Ricalton, James, Travel Magazine

Scull, G.H., Commericial Advertiser

Smith, Richmond, AP

Straight, Willard, Reuters

Victor-Thomas, Charles, Le Gaulois

Villiers, Frederic*, *Illustrated London News, Graphic*

Wallace, Grant, *San Francisco Bulletin*

Washburn, Stanley, *Chicago Daily News*

Sources: Great Britain War Office. *The Russo-Japanese War: Reports from British Officers Attached to the Japanese and Russian Forces in the Field.* 1908; Robert W. Desmond. *The Information Process.* 1978

* Indicates a separate entry.

Appendix L

World War I Correspondents

CORRESPONDENTS ACCREDITED TO THE U.S. ARMY ON THE WESTERN FRONT

Name	Accreditation	Organization
Heywood Broun*	July 1, 1917	*New York Tribune*
Raymond G. Carroll	July 9, 1917	*Philadelphia Public Ledger*
Junius Wood*	July 9, 1917	*Chicago Daily News*
Wythe Williams*	July 10, 1917	*New York Times* and *Collier's*
Herbert Corey	July 24, 1917	Associated Newspapers
Reginald W. Kaufman	September 17, 1917	*Philadelphia North American*
Floyd Gibbons*	October 9, 1917	*Chicago Tribune*
Thomas M. Johnson*	October 9, 1917	*New York Sun*
Lincoln Eyre	October 14, 1917	*New York World*
C. C. Lyon	October 15, 1917	Newspaper Enterprise Association
Norman Draper	October 28, 1917	Associated Press
Naboth Hedin	March 1918	*Brooklyn Eagle*
Edwin "Jimmy" L. James*	March 11, 1918	*New York Times*
Wilbur S. Forrest	March 22, 1918	*New York Tribune*
John T. Parkerson	March 30, 1918	Associated Press
Dennis S. Ford	March 31, 1918	International News Service (INS)
Fred S. Ferguson	April 8, 1918	United Press
Newton C. Parke	April 8, 1918	INS
James Hopper	April 11, 1918	*Collier's Weekly*
Don Martin	May 1918	*New York Herald*
George Seldes*	May 12, 1918	Marshall Syndicate
Frank G. Taylor	May 12, 1918	United Press
Charles S. Kloeber	July 27, 1918	Associated Press
Bernard O'Donnell	August 23, 1918	*Cincinnati Inquirer*
Guy C. Hickok	September 1918	*Brooklyn Eagle*
Charles J. Doyle	October 1918	*Pittsburgh Gazette Times*
Damon Runyon*	October 1918	Universal Service
George Applegarth	October 14, 1918	*Pittsburgh Post*
Burr Price	October 19, 1918	*New York Herald*
Maximilian Foster	November 1918	Committee on Public Information
Edwin A. Roberts	November 11, 1918	*Cleveland Plain Dealer, Chicago Tribune*
John Tinney McCutcheon*	November 19, 1918	*Chicago Tribune*
Webb Miller*	November 19, 1918	United Press
Cyril Brown	December 1918	*New York World*
Parke Brown	December 1918	*Chicago Tribune*
Ward Greene	December 1918	*Atlanta Journal*

CORRESPONDENTS SERVING AS ACCREDITED CORRESPONDENTS

H. Warner Allen, *London Morning Post*

Ellis Ashmead-Bartlett*, *London Times*

Herbert R. Bailey, *London Daily Mail*

H. Prevost Battersby, Reuters

Elizabeth, Mary Beatty,* *Good Housekeeping*

Granville Roland Fortescue*, *London Daily Telegraph*

Henry Hamilton Fyfe*, *London Daily Mail*

Philip Gibbs*, *The London War Illustrated*; *London Daily Chronicle*

Louis Grondjis*, *Nieuwe Rotterdamsche Courant* (Rotterdam); *L'Illustration* (Paris); *London Daily Telegraph*

H. Noble Hall, *London Times*

Corra Harris*.

James P. Howe, Associated Press

F. Tennyson Jesse, *Collier's*

Clair Kenamore, St. *Louis Post-Dispatch*

Robert Scott Liddell, *The Sphere*

Cameron MacKenzie, *London Chronicle*

Burge McFall, Associated Press

Lowell Mellett, United Press

Keith Murdoch, *Melbourne Herald* and *Sydney Sun*

Edward Alexander Powell, *New York World*; Scribner's; *London Daily Mail*

Philip M. Powers, Associated Press

Charles a Court Repington*, the *Times*

Mary Roberts Rinehart*, *Saturday Evening Post*

Fred A. Smith, *Chicago Tribune*

Willam Beach Thomas*, *Daily Mail*

Frederick Villiers*, *Illustrated London News*

Henry G. Wales, INS

VISITING CORRESPONDENTS OF LONGEST SERVICE

Walter S. Ball, *Providence Journal*

Adam Breede, *Hastings Daily Tribune*

Cecile Dorian, *Newark Evening News*

Elizabeth Frazier, *Saturday Evening Post*

Charles H. Grasty, *New York Times*

David W. Hazen, *Portland Oregonian*

Otto P. Higgins, *Kansas City Star*

Frazier "Spike" Hunt,* *Chicago Tribune*

W. S. McNutt, *Collier's Weekly*

George Pattullo, *Saturday Evening Post*

Arthur Ruhl,* *Collier's Weekly*

Frank P. Sibley, *Boston Globe*

Joseph Timmons, *Los Angeles Examiner*

Raymond S. Tompkins, *Baltimore Sun*

Caspar Whitney,* *New York Tribune*

Harry A. Williams, *Los Angeles Times*

Source: Emmet Crozier. *American Reporters on the Western Front, 1914-18.* 1959.

* *Indicates a separate entry.*

Appendix M

Spanish Civil War Correspondents, 1936-1939

Alving, Barbro, Dagens Nyheter

Allen, Jay*, *Chicago Tribune* and *News Chronicle*

Baron, Sam, Socialist Call

Bartlett, Vernon, *News Chronicle*

Berniard, Georges, *Le Petit Gironde*

Berthet, Daniel

Bolloten, Burnett, AP

Borkenua, Franz, *Londin Daily Express*

Botto, Georges, Havas Agency

Brut, Rene

Buckley, Henry, *Daily Telegraph* and *Observer*

Buckly, M.J., *Cork Examiner*

Cardozo, *Harold, Daily Mail*

Carney, William P., *New York Times*

Cockburn, Claud*, *Daily Worker*, *The Week*

Corman, Mathieu, C Soir

Correia, Felix, Diario de Lisboa

Cowles, Viginia*, Hearst Publications

Cox, Geoffrey*, *News Chronicle*, *Daily Express*

Dany, Marcel

Davis, Frances, *Chicago Daily News*

Delapree, Louis, Paris-Soir

Delmer, Sefton, *London Daily Express*

D'Hospital Jean, Havas Agency

Duff, Sheila Grant, *Chicago Daily News*

Farago, Ladislas, *New York Times*

Fernsworth, Lawrence, *New York Times*

Fischer, Louis, *The Nation, New Statesman* and *Nation*

Fleming, Lionel, *Irish Times*

Foltz, Charles, UP

Forrest, William, *Daily Express*

Gaffney, Gertrude, *Irish Independent*

Gallegher, O.D.*, *London Daily Express*

Gerahty, Cecil, *Daily Mail*

Gellhorn, Martha*, *Collier's Weekly*

Gibbons, Floyd*, International News Service

Gorrell, Hank*, UP

Grepp, Gerda,* Arbeiderbladet

Hanighen, Frank, *Daily Express*

Himingway, Ernest*, North American Newspaper Alliance

Hericourt, Pierre, Acyion francaise

Hillman, William, Hearst Press

Holburn, James, the *Times*

Holme, Christopher*, Reuters

Hughes, Langston, Baltimore Afro-American

Jellinek, Frank, Manchgester Guardian

Johnson, Bradish, *Newsweek, The Spur*

Jouvenal, Bertrand de, Paris-Soir

Kerrigan, Peter, *Daily Worker*

Kluckhohn, Frank L.*, *New York Times*

Knickerbocker, H.R.*, Hearst Press

Knoblaugh, H. Edward, AP

Koestler, Arthur*, *News Chronicle*

Koltsov, Mikhail, Pravda

Langdon-Davies, John, *News Chronicle*

Lechter, Roman, Naje Presse

Lindbaek, Lise,* Dagbladet

Lockwood, Rupert, *Melbourne Herald*

MacGowan, Gault*, *New York Sun*

Malet-Dauban, Henri, Havas Agency

Massock, Richard, AP

Massot, Max, *Le Journal*

Matthews, Herbert*, *New York Times*

McCullagh, Francis*, *Irish Independent*

Miller, Webb*, UP

Minifie, James M, *New York Herald-Tribune*

Monks, Noel*, *London Daily Express*

Montanelli, Indro, Il Messaggero

Moorehead, Alan*, *London Daily express*

Mortari, Curio, La Stampa

Neil, Edward J., AP

Neves, Mario, Diario de Lisboa

Neville, Robert, *New York Herald-Tribune*

North, Joseph, *Daily Worker*, New Masses

Nunes, Leopoldo, O Seculo

Packard, Eleanor*, UP

Packard, Reynolds*, *New York Herald-Tribune*

Pflaum, Irving

Philby, Kim*, the *Times*

Phillips, Percival*, *Daily Telegraph*

Rice, F.A., *Morning Post*

Robson, Karl, *Daily Express*

Rolfe, Edwin, *Daily Worker, New Masses*

Romilly, Edmond, *News Chronicle*

Rothman, Kajsa, Karlstad-tidningen

Salter, Cedric*, *Daily Telegraph, News Chronicle, Daily Mail*

Schiff, Victor, *Daily Herald*

Scott-Watson, K.

Seldes, George*, *New York Post*

Sheepshanks, Ernest, Reuters

Small, Alex, *Chicago Tribune*

Smith, Sidney, *Daily Express*

Steer, George*, *Daily Telegraph*

Stirling, William F., the *Times*

Stowe, Leland*, *Herald Tribune*

Swire, Joseph,

Strunk, Roland, Volischer Beobachter

Tangye, Nigel, *Evening News*

Taylor, Edmond, *Chicago Tribune*

Vajta, Ferenc

Watson, Scott, *Daily Herald*

Weaver, Dennis, *News Chronicle*

Whitaker, John T.*, *New York Herald Tribune*

Wiegand, Karl H. Von, International News Service

Wilkinson, Elizabeth, *Daily Worker*

Wintringham, Tom, *Daily Worker, Picture Post*

Yindrich, Jan H., UP

Ziffren, Lester, UP

References: Robert W. Desmond. *Crisis and Conflict.* 1982; Robert W. Desmond. *Tides of War.* 1984; Philip Knightley. *The First Casualty.* 1975. Peter Wyden. *The Passionate War.* 1983; Paul Preston. *We Saw Spain Die.* 2009.

* *Indicates a separate entry.*

Appendix N

World War II Accredited U.S. War Correspondents

Ackerman, Michael J., Acme News-Pictures

Ackerman, Robert, AP

Ackermann, Carl, Columbia School of Journalism

Adams, Benjamin P., Funk & Wagnalls

Adams, John B., CBS

Adams, Noel B., Group 2, Australian Papers

Adams, Phelps H., *New York Sun Times*

Agronsky, Martin, INS

Albayalde, Abe, *Filipino News*

Albright, Sydney, NBC

Alcine, Billy L., *Yank*

Aldridge, F. G., Group 2, Australian Papers

Alexander, Eben R., *Time*

Alexander, Jack, *Saturday Evening Post*

Alexander, William H., Oklahoma Publishing Company

Alexanderson, George, Ministry of Information (G.B.)

Allen, Lawrence Edmund,* AP

Allen, William C., AP

Allen, W. R., AP

Alley, Norman, *News of the Day*

Amato, Victor, War Dept., Bureau of Public Relations

Anderson, Alan F., Australian Dept. of Information

Anderson, Earl H., *Yank*

Anderson, F. David, *New York Times*

Anderson, Jack, *Desert News*

Andrew, John J., UP

Andrew, Philip, Philip Andrew Publishing Company

Andrews, Bert, *New York Herald Tribune*

Andrews, Steffan, *Cleveland Plain Dealer*

Andrica, Theodore, *Cleveland Press*

Angel, D. M., Australian Dept. of Information

Angelopoulous, A., INS

Angley, Joseph, *Chicago Sun*

Annabel, Russell F., UP

Antrobus, Edmund, *Yank*

Archinard, Paul J., NBC

Armstrong, John P., *Yank*

Armstrong, R. B., St. *Louis Globe-Democrat*

Armstrong, Richard, INS

Arnot, Charles P.,* UP

Arter, Theodore, *Altoona (Pa.) Tribune*

Atkins, Oliver F., American Red Cross

Atkinson, Brooks, *New York Times*

Atkinson, C. P., Civil & Military Gazette, Ltd.

Atkinson, Oriana T., *New York Times*

Ault, Philip, UP

Avery, Marjorie, *Detroit Free-Press*

Azrael, Louis, *Baltimore News-Post*

Babcock, Franklin L., *Time*

Babcock, Lawrence, *Fortune*

Bader, Jesse M., *Christian Evangelist*

Baer, Howard, Abbott Laboratories

Bagley, Henry W., AP

Bailey, Wesley L., *Time*

Baillie, Hugh,* UP

Bain, Leslie B., WIOD

Baird, Joseph H., Overseas News Agency

Baker, Richard, Religious News Service

Baker, Warren, *Chicago Tribune*

Baldwin, Hanson W.,* *New York Times*

Ball, Edward, AP

Band, John, Australian Dept. of Information

Banker, Franklin F., AP

Barber, Charles P., *Parade*

Barber, F., AP

Barcella, Ernest L., UP

Barden, Judy, *New York Sun*

Barker, Fowler W., *Air Transport*

Barkham, John, *Time*

Barnes, Howard, *New York Herald Tribune*

Barnes, John P., *Yank*

Barnes, Joseph, *New York Herald Tribune*

Barnett, Jack S., Fox Movietone News

Barnett, Lincoln, *Time*

Barnett, Martin, Paramount News

Barr, Richard M., CIAA

Barrett, Frank B., *Lowell Sun*

Barrett, George A., *Yank*

Barretto, Lawrence B., *Liberty*

Barrows, Nat A., *Chicago Daily News*

Barry, Joseph A., *Newsweek*

Bartholomew, Frank Harmon,* UP

Bartholomew, John B., ABC

Barton, Frederick B., *Plane Talk*

Baukhage, H. R., ABC

Baum, Arthur W., *Saturday Evening Post*

Bauman, Frank M., *Look*

Baxter, George E., UP

Baylor, David M., WGAR

Beall, Cecil C., *Collier's*

Bealmear, Henry A., AP

Beam, Oscar P., AP

Beattie, Edward W., Jr.,* UP

Beatty, Morgan, NBC

Beaufort, John D., *Christian Science Monitor*

Beeby, Nellie B., *American Journal of Nursing*

Befeler, Murray, AP

Belair, Felix, *Time*

Belden, Jack,* *Harper's*

Bell, Don, MBS

Bell, John A., *Miami Herald*

Bell, Borman, AP

Benedetti, Abraham, Reuters

Bennett, Lowell,* INS

Benny, Robert L., Abbott Laboratories

Berger, Meyer, *New York Times*

Bergholz, Richard C., AP

Bernard, Charles, UP

Bernstein, Victor H., *PM*

Bernstein, Walter,* *Yank*

Berrigan, Darrell, UP

Bess, Demaree, *Saturday Evening Post*

Bess, Dorothy, *Saturday Evening Post*

Best, Cort, AC/Photo Division

Bettencourt, Sylvia de, *Correio de Manha*

Biben, Joseph H., Biben Publishing Company

Biddle, George,* *Life*

Bienstock, Victor, Overseas News Agency

Bigart, Homer,* *New York Herald Tribune*

Billotte, William C., Jr., *Omaha World-Herald*

Binder, Carroll, *Chicago Daily News*

Bjornson, Bjorn, NBC

Black, John C., Gillett Publishing Company

Blackburn, Casper K., *Seapower*

Blair, Robert H., Fox Movietone News

Blakeslee, Howard W., Fox Movietone News

Blay, John S., *Yank*

Boatner, Charles K., *Fort Worth Star-Telegram*

Bockhurst, John A., *News of the Day*

Boggs, William, Abbott Laboratories

Boguslav, David, *Chicago Sun*

Bohrod, Aaron,* *Time*

Bolden, Frank E., *Pittsburgh Courier*

Bolling, Landrum, *Beloit Daily News*

Bongard, Nicholas, *March of Time*

Boni, William F., AP

Bonney, Teresa, Duell, Sloance & Pear

Booth, W., *Philadelphia Record*

Bordaam, William, INS

Bordas, Walter, International News Photos

Boren, Wallace R., *This Week*

Borgstedt, Douglas H., *Yank*

Boss, William,* Canadian Press

Bostwick, Albert L., Veterans of Foreign Wars

Bottomley, C., Australian Dept. of Information

Bourchet, Rene, *Ospecre Algerese*

Bourges, Fernand A., *Life*

Bourke-White, Margaret,* *Time*

Bovill, Oscar, *Pathe-Gazette*

Bow, Frank, Brush Moor Newspapers

Bowen, Lewis, American Red Cross

Bowerman, Waldo G., *Engineering-News Record*

Boyce, Ralph L., *Yank*

Boyle, Harold, AP

Boyle, John W., *Time*

Bracker, Milton, *New York Times*

Bracker, Virginia L., *New York Times*

Bradley, Holbrook, *Baltimore Sun*

Brady, Lloyd C., AP

Brag, Rubin, *Diario Carioca*

Braidwood, Nelson, *London Telegraph*

Bramley, George E., *American Aviation*

Brandao, Paul, *Correio de Manha*

Brandt, Bertram G., Acme Newspictures

Brandt, Frank M., *Yank*

Brandt, Raymond P., *St. Louis Post-Dispatch*

Branham, Leo, AP

Breckinbridge, Mary,* CBS

Breese, Howard F., AP

Bregon, John, INS

Breimhurst, Donald W., *Yank*

Brennan, John C., *Sydney Bulletin*

* Indicates a separate entry.

Brennan, Peter, NBC

Brewer, Sam, *New York Times*

Bria, George C., AP

Bridgman, Julie, *Liberty*

Briggs, Walter L., UP

Brigham, Daniel P., *New York Times*

Brines, Russell, AP

Broch, Nathan, Aneta News Agency (Dutch)

Brock, Ray, *New York Times*

Broderick, Hugh, International News Photos

Brodie, Howard,* *Yank*

Brook, Alexander, *Life*

Brooks, Deton J., *Chicago Defender*

Brooks, Olive, INS

Brooks, William F., NBC

Brown, Arthur E., *Chicago Herald American*

Brown, David, Reuters

Brown, Dickson, *London News Chronicle*

Brown, Harold P., Reuters

Brown, Harry, *Yanks*

Brown, James E., INS

Brown, Norman E., Australian Dept. of Information

Brown, Robert E., UP

Browne, Barbara, *Christian Science Monitor*

Browne, Mallory, *New York Times*

Brumby, Robert M., MES

Bruto, Frank, AP

Bryan, W. Wright, *Atlanta Journal*

Bryant, Robert, International News Photos

Bryant, Vaughn M., AP

Buckley, Christopher,* Reuters

Buddy, Edward C., *Path News*

Bullard, Arthur E., American Red Cross

Bullitt, William C., *Time*

Buntin, William, INS

Burchett, Wilfred,* *London Daily Express*

Burdette, Winston, CBS

Burke, James C., *Liberty*

Burke, James W., *Esquire-Coroney*

Burnham, L. B., UP

Bums, Douglas R., Australian Dept. of Information

Bums, Eugene, AP

Bums, George,* *Yank*

Bums, John T., AP

Burroughs, Edgar Rice, UP

Burroughs, Henry J., AP

Burrows, Ted, *Yank*

Burton, L. V., McGraw-Hill

Busch, Noel F., *Time*

Buschemi, John,* *Yank*

Bush, Asahel, AP

Butler, Eldon K., AP

Buttrose, C.O.G., *Sydney Morning Herald*

Byfield, Ernest L., *Chicago Herald American*

Cafaliere, Nicholas, *March of Time*

Calabria, Frank J., *March of Time*

Calhoun, C. H., *New York Times*

Calhoun, Millard F., *Time*

Callender, Harold, *New York Times*

Calmer, Edgar M., CBS

Calvosa, Ulrich, *Collier's*

Camp, Helen, AP

Campbell, Archibald Doon,* Reuters

Campbell, Edward L., AP

Cancellare, Frank, Acme Newspictures

Capa, Robert,* *Life*

Caparelle, Peter L., *Ring*

Carley, John 0., *Memphis Commercial-Appeal*

Carlisle, John M., *Detroit News*

Carnes, Disney C., *Saturday Evening Post*

Carpenter, Iris,* *London Daily Herald*

Can, Milton L., UP

Carroll, Loren, *Newsweek*

Carroll, Peter J., AP

Carroll, Sidney, *Esquire-Coronet*

Carson, Lee, INS

Carter, Amon G., *Fort Worth Star Telegram*

Carter, Archer N., McGraw-Hill

Carter, Arthur M., *Afro-American Newspaper*

Carty, William, Australian Dept. of Information

Case, Lewis S., Paramount News

Casey, Robert Joseph,* *Chicago Daily News*

Cashman, John, INS

Cassidy, Henry C.,* NBC

Cassidy, James F., WLW

Cassidy, Morley, *Philadelphia Bulletin*

Caswell, Donald F., UP

Catledge, William T., *New York Times*

Cellario, Alberto, *La Prensa*

Chafin, Glenn M., Bell Syndicate

Chakales, Lawrence S., AP

Chamberlain, Charles W., AP

Chandra, P. T., *India-Burma*

Chang, C. B., Central News Agency

Chao, Sam, Reuters

Chapelle, Georgette "Dickey,"* *Look*

Chappelle, Minafox, *American Home*

Chaplin, William W., NBC

Chapman, Frank M., Acme Newspictures

Chapman, John F., McGraw-Hill

Chase, Milton, WLW

Chase, William T., AP

Cheng, Hawthorne, Chinese Ministry of Information

Chernoff, Howard L., West Virginia Network

Chester, John F., AP

Chickering, William H., *Time*

Childs, Marquis, St. *Louis Post-Dispatch*

Chinigo, Michael, INS

Chipping, Chu, *TaKanpPao*

Chorlian, Edward, CBS

Clapper, Raymond Lewis,* Scripps-Howard

Clark, Edgar, UP

Clark, Edward T., *Cleveland Press*

Clark, Gregory,* *Toronto Star*

Clark, Herbert, *New York Herald Tribune*

Clark, Katherine L., WCAU

Clark, Michael, the *Nation*

Clark, Richard, UP

Clark, William E., *Life*

Clarke, Philip C., AP

Clausen, John A., War Dept., Special Services

Clausen, Walter B., AP

Clayton, Bernard, *Life*

Clayton, Frederick, American Red Cross

Cleary, Ed J., McGraw-Hill

Clements, Olen W., AP

Clover, Robert, AP

Clurman, Robert 0., AP

Cobbledick, Gordon, *Cleveland Plain Dealer*

Cochrane, Jacqueline, *Liberty*

Cochrane, Robert B., *Baltimore Sun*

Codel, Martin, American Red Cross

Coe, Donald G., ABC

Coffy, Patrick V., *Yank*

Coggins, Jack B., *Yank*

Cohen, Haskell P., *Pittsburgh Courier*

Cohn, Arthur E., INS

Cohn, David L., Houghton-Mifflin

Colburn, John H., AP

Colby, Carroll B., *Popular Science*

Coll, Ray, *Honolulu Advertiser*

Collingwood, Charles Cummings,* CBS

Collins, Walter, UP

Combas, Guerra E., *El Mundo*

Combs, George H., WHN

Conefry, Walter, Scripps-Howard

Conger, Clinton B., UP

Coniston, Ralph A., Aneta News Agency (Dutch)

Conniff, Frank,* INS

Considine, Robert B., INS

Coogan, James A., UP

Cook, Donald P., *New York Herald Tribune*

Cook, George J., *Yank*

Cook, Howard N., *Life*

Cook, Max B., Scripps-Howard

Cook, Zenas D., *Newsweek*

Cooke, David C., McBride Publishing Company

Cooke, Donald E., *Yank*

Cookman, Mary C., *Ladies Home Journal*

Cool, Robert N., AP

Cooper, Edward H., *Christian Science Monitor*

Corbellini, George, *Yank*

Cornell, Douglas, AP

Corsinia, Aralbo R., *Petroleum Magazine*

Cort, Horance W., AP

Corte, Charles, Acme Newspictures

Corum, Bill, King Features

Corwin, Norman L., CBS

Costa, Joseph C., *New York Daily News*

Courtenay, William, *London Daily Sketch*

Courtney, W. B., *Collier's*

Cowan, Howard S., AP

Cowan, Ruth,* AP

Cowles, Virginia,* NANA

Coxe, George, Alfred Knopf

Coyne, Catherine, *Boston Herald*

Craig, Elizabeth M., Gannett Publishing Company

Craig, Thomas T., *Life*

Cranston, Paul F., *Philadelphia Bulletin*

Cravens, Kathryn, MBS

* Indicates a separate entry.

Crawford, Kenneth Gale,* *Newsweek*

Crider, John H., *New York Times*

Crocker, A. J., St. *Paul Dispatch*

Crockett, E. Harry, AP

Cromie, Robert A.,* *Chicago Tribune*

Cronkite, Walter Leland, Jr.,* UP

Crost, Lyn,* *Honolulu Star-Bulletin*

Crotchett, Earl, Universal Newsreel

Crowther, Francis B., *New York Times*

Crozier, Thomas E., *New York Herald Tribune*

Crumpler, Hugh, UP

Cuddy, John M., UP

Cuhel, Frank J., MBS

Cumming, C., *Christian Science Monitor*

Cummings, Ray, *Honolulu Star-Bulletin*

Cunha, Albelardo, *Imprensa Propoganda*

Cunningham, Bill, *Boston Herald-Traveller*

Cunningham, Chris, UP

Cunningham, Ed,* *Yank*

Cunningham, Joseph, *Yank*

Cunningham, Owen, MBS

Curran, Thomas R., UP

Cumvan, Eugene A., *New York Times*

Cushing, Richard G., AP

Custer, Joseph, AP

DaFonseca, Silvio S., *Imprensa Propoganda*

Dallaire, Victor J., UP

Daly, John C., CBS

Danenberg, Elsie, NANA

Daniel, Elbert C., AP

Daniel, F. Raymond, *New York Times*

Daniel, Hawthorne, Asia *Magazine*

Daniel, James M., New *York Post*

Daniel, Tatiana, *New York Times*

Daniell, F.H.W., MacQuarie Broadcasting Company

Darnton, Byron, *New York Times*

Darrah, David H., *Chicago Tribune*

Dash, Hugh, Group 2, Australian Papers

Dashiell, Samuel, NANA

Davenport, John A., *Time*

Davenport, Russell W., *American Mercury*

Davenport, Walter A., *Collier's*

David, David R., Acme Newspicture

David, Steven A., UP

Davidson, William J., *Yank*

Davis, Gladys, *Life*

Davis, Jerome, INS

Davis, Kenneth S., Doubleday Doran

Davis, Lloyd, *Life*

Davis, Maxine, Macmillan

Davis, Myron H., *Life*

Davis, Spencer, AP

Dawes, Allen W., Group 3, Australian Papers

Day, Price, *Baltimore Sun*

Day, Richard M., American Red Cross

DeAbranches, Carlos, *Jornel de Brazil*

Dearing, Joseph A., *Collier's*

Debnam, Waldemar E., WPTF

Decormis, Anne McCormick, *Fortune*

Dees, Joseph, UP

DeGusmao, Rubin, *Coeiho Sobrinho*

Delalande, Francois, Pathe News

Delaphale, Stanto, *San Francisco Chronicle*

De Luce, Daniel,* AP

Dennehy, Edward, AP

Dennis, Gene, KMBC

Denny, Harold Norman,* *New York Times*

Denton, Nixsoin, *Cincinnati Times Star*

DeRochement, Richard G., *March of Time*

Derry, Steven, *Yank*

DeSantillana, George D., *Atlantic Monthly*

Desfor, Maxd, AP

DeSoria, Charles J., AP

Despouey, Rene, NBC

Deter, Arthur S., CBS

DeVoto, Bernard A., War Dept., Bureau of Public Relations

Dexter, Frank H., Group 1, Australian Papers

Dharma, Ernest, UP

Dick, Harold G., *Australian Depatment of Information*

Dickinson, William B., UP

Dickson, Cecil B., Gannett Newspapers

Diehl, Chandler, AP

Diggins, Mary M., INS

Disbrow, Leslie D., American Red Cross

Disher, Leo S.,* UP

Disney, Dorothy, *Saturday Evening Post*

Dixon, George H., *New York Daily News*

Dixon, Kenneth L., AP

Dixon, William R., *Pittsburgh Courier*

Dmitri, Ivan, *Saturday Evening Post*

Doan, Donald P., AP

Dodd, Howel E., AP

Dolan, Leo V., INS

Donaghey, Donald, *Philadelphia Bulletin*

Donahue, Robert F., Pathe News

Donghi, Frank, Acme Newspictures

Dopking, Al, AP

Dored, John, Paramount News

Dorsey, George, Pathe News

Dorvillier, William, UP

Dos Passos, John Roderigo,* *Life*

Douglas, Wes, *Chicago Sun*

Douglass, Richard W., *Yank*

Dowling, John G., *Chicago Sun*

Downes, Donald C., Overseas News Agency

Downs, William R.,* CBS

Doyle, Robert J., *Milwaukee Journal*

Drake, Catherine, *Reader's Digest*

Drake, Francis, *Reader's Digest*

Dreier, Alexander, NBC

Driscoll, David E., MBS

Driscoll, Joseph, *New York Herald Tribune*

Driver, Roy A., Australian Dept. of Information

Drummond, J. Roscoe, *Christian Science Monitor*

Duga, Dennis L., *Melbourne Age*

Dunbar, Rudolph, Associated Negro Press

Duncan, Raymond E., *Yank*

Dunn, Francis W., Bell Aircraft

Dunn, William J.,* CBS

Durdin, F. Tillman, *New York Times*

Durdin, Margaret L., *Time*

Duret, Fernando L., *El Universal*

Durrance, Thomas D., *Time*

Durston, John H., *New York Herald Tribune*

Dynan, Joseph E., AP

Eager, Clifton C., *Australian Press*

Ebener, Charlotte, INS

Ecker, Allan B., *Yank*

Edmonds, James E., WLW

Edmundson, Charles F., *Time*

Edson, Peter, NEA

Edwards, Clyde D., CBS

Edwards, Herman F., *Portland Oregonian*

Edwards, Leonard, Australian Broadcasting Commission

Edwards, Reginald J., Australian Department of Information

Edwards, Webley, CBS

Eitington, Lee, *Time*

Ek, Carl, Passaic *Herald-News*

Ekins, Herbert R., WSYR

Elisofon, Eliot, *Life*

Elliott, John, Australian Broadcasting Commission

Ellison, Earl J., *Look*

Emeny, Stuart,* *London News Chronicle*

Enell, George, American Red Cross

Engelke, Charles B., UP

Epstein, Clifford, *Detroit News*

Erickson, Wendell S., AP

Eunson, Robert C., AP

Evans, Druscilla, *New York Post*

Evans, Edward A., Scripps-Howard

Evans, Joe, *New York Herald Tribune*

Eyerman, J. R., *Life*

Fabinani, Henry, Paramount News

Fagans, Allen T., *Newsweek*

Falvey, William, *New York Mirror*

Faris, E. Barry, INS

Farnsworth, Clyde A., AP

Faron, Ward H., AP

Farr, Walter G., *London Daily Mail*

Fast, Howard, *Esquire-Coroney*

Faust, Frederick,* *Harper's*

Faust, Hal, *Chicago Tribune*

Feder, Sydney A., AP

Feldman, Arthur S., Blue Network

Fendell, Jack D., CBS

Feng, Paul, Central News Agency

Fenger, Austin B., Associated Broadcasters

Fenwick, Robert W., *Denver Post*

Ferber, Edna, NANA

Ferris, Dillon J., *Yank*

Ferris, Jack, *Newsweek*

Fielder, Blaine P., Group 3, Australian Papers

Filan, Frank, AP

Finan, Elizabeth S., *Harper's Bazaar*

Finch, A. Percy, Reuters

Finch, Barbara M., Reuters

Finch, Edward, *Time*

Finnegan, Herbert A., *Boston American*

Fischer, Ernest G., AP

Fisher, Alan, *PM*

Indicates a separate entry.

Fisher, William, *Time*

Fisk, James B., *National Geographic*

Fitchett, Ian G., *London Daily Express*

Fitzhenry, L. J., *Brisbane Courier Mail*

Fitzpatrick, S. H., Australian Department of Information

Fitzsimmons, Thomas J., AP

Flaherty, Pat, NBC

Flaherty, Vincent X., *Washington Times-Herald*

Flanner, Janet, *New Yorker*

Fleeson, Doris,* *Woman's Home Companion*

Fleischer, Jack,* *Time*

Fleming, Dewey L., *Baltimore Sun*

Fleming, James, CBS

Fleming, Thomas E., *Yank*

Florea, John T., *Life*

Fodor, Marcel W., *Chicago Sun*

Folkard, F. B., Group 3, Australian Papers

Folliard, Edward T., *Washington Post*

Folsom, Charles E., *Boston Post*

Folster, George T., *Chicago Sun*

Fonda, Dow H., AP

Foote, Mark, Booth Newspapers

Forbes, Ernest D., WFBM

Ford, Corey, *Collier's*

Forrest, Wilbur, New *York Herald Tribune*

Forsberg, Franklin S., *Yank*

Fort, Randolph L., AP

Forte, Aldo, UP

Foss, Kendall, *New York Post*

Foster, Cedric, Yankee Network

Foster, John, *Aviation Magazine*

Foster, Wilson K., NBC

Fowle, Farnsworth, CBS

Fowler, Homer Wick, *Dallas Morning News*

Frank, Gerold, Palcor News Agency

Frank, H. H., Overseas News Agency

Frank, June M., *This Month*

Frank, Stanley B., New *York Post*

Frankel, Lazarus, *Billboard*

Frankish, John F., UP

Frano, John J., *Yank*

Fraser, John G., Blue Network

Frawley, Harry J., AP

Frazer, William L., *Yank*

Frazier, Benjamin W., *Yank; Look*

Fredenthal, David,* *Life*

Frederick, Pauline, Western Newspaper Union

Freeman, Beatrice, *Magazine Digest*

Freeman, Edward, *Baltimore News Post*

Freidin, Seymour, New *York Herald Tribune*

Frey, Robert L., UP

Friedman, Seymour T., *Yank*

Frisby, Herbert M., Afro-American Newspapers

Frissell, Toni, *Free Lance*

Froendt, Antonio, Religious News Service

Frutchey, Fred, NBC

Frye, William F., AP

Fulton, William J., *Chicago Tribune*

Furnas, Joseph Chamberlain,* Saturday Evening Post

Gaeth, Arthur, MBS

Gaige, Richard T., *Yank*

Gale, Jack F., UP

Gallagher, James Wesley "Wes,"* AP

Gallico, Paul, *Cosmopolitan*

Gammack, Gordon, *Des Moines Register-Tribune*

Gannett, Lewis, *New York Herald Tribune*

Garland, Robin, *Saturday Evening Post*

Garrison, Omar, Reuters

Gask, Roland, *Newsweek*

Gaskill, Betty, *Liberty*

Gaskill, Gordon, *American*

Gaston, Carl D., War Dept., Bureau of Public Relations

Geiger, Richard, AP

Geis, Bernard J., *Esquire-Coronet*

Gelder, Stuart, *London Daily Express*

Gellhorn, Martha,* *Collier's*

George, Carl, WGAR

George, Collins, *Pittsburgh Courier*

Gercke, George, *March of Time*

Gercke, William F., Paramount News

Gervasi, Frank H., *Collier's*

Ghali, Paul, *Chicago Daily News*

Ghio, Robert A., *Yank*

Gilman, LaSelle, *Honolulu Advertiser*

Gilman, William, *Baltimore Sun*

Gilmore, Eddy L., AP

Gingrich, Arnold, *Esquire-Coronet*

Gingrich, Helen, *Esquire-Coronet*

Glosker, Anita, NANA

Glynn, Paul T., CBS

Goble, James B., *Yank*

Goldberg, Abraham I., AP

Goldstein, Sam, International News Photos

Goodwin, Joseph C., AP

Gopalan, J., Associated Press of India

Gorrel, Henry T.,* UP

Gorry, Charles P., AP

Goss, Frank B., CBS

Gottfried, Carl M., *Time*

Gottlieb, Sol S., International News Photos

Gould, Beatrice B., *Ladies Home Journal*

Gould, Randall, *Shanghai Evening Post*

Gowran, Clayton, *Chicago Tribune*

Graebner, Walter A., *Time*

Graffis, Herbert, *Chicago Daily News*

Graham, Frederick, *New York Times*

Graham-Barrow, C. R., Reuters

Grandin, Thomas B., Blue Network

Grant, Donald S., *Look*

Grant, Gordon N., *Tampa Tribune*

Grant, Herbert B., *Chicago Times*

Gratke, Charles E., *Christian Science Monitor*

Grauer, Benjamin F., NBC

Graves, Lemuel E., *Christian Science Monitor; Norfolk Journal and Guide*

Gray, Peyton, Afro-American Newspapers

Gray, William P., *Time*

Green, Allen, Scripps-Howard

Green, Clinton H., *New York Times*

Green, Janet, *Trans-Radio Press*

Greene, Hamilton, *American Legion Magazine*

Greene, Roger D., AP

Greenhalgh, Robert F., *Yank*

Greenwald, Edwin B., AP

Greenwald, Sanford, *News of the Day*

Greer, Allen J., *Buffalo Evening News*

Gridley, Charles O., *Chicago Sun*

Griffin, Bulkley, *Hartford Times*

Griffin, Henry, AP

Griffin, John, AP

Grigg, Joseph, UP

Grim, George H., *Minneapolis Star Journal*

Grossi, Daniel, AP

Groth, John A., *Parade*

Grover, Allen, *Time*

Grover, James A., *Time*

Grover, John, AP

Grover, Preston, AP

Grueson, Sidney, *New York Times*

Grumich, Charles A., AP

Grupp, George, *Boating*

Guard, Harold, UP

Gudebrod, Morton P., AP

Gunderson, Arthur R., UP

Gunn, Stanley E., *Fort Worth Star Telegram*

Gunnison, Royal A., *Collier's*

Gunther, John, NANA

Guptill, Charles H., AP

Guth, Oscar A., UP

Gwinn, John W., AP

Haacker, Charles, Acme Newspictures

Haaker, Edwin, NBC

Haas, Saul, *Portland Oregonian*

Hackler, Victor, AP

Haden, Allen, *Chicago Daily News*

Haeger, Robert A., UP

Hager, Alice R., *Skyways*

Hahn, Willard C., *St. Louis Post-Dispatch*

Hailey, Foster B., *New York Times*

Hairland, Patrick, *London News Chronicle*

Hales, Samuel D., UP

Haley, Pope A., AP

Hall, Charles H., *Springfield Republican*

Hall, Clarence, *Link & Chaplain Magazine*

Hall, Flem R., *Fort Worth Star-Telegram*

Halton, Matthew, *Toronto Star*

Hamburger, Edith I., *Cleveland Press*

Hamburger, Philip P., *New Yorker*

Hamm, Clarence L., AP

Hammond, Gilbert T., *Boston Herald-Traveller*

Hampson, Frederick E., AP

Handleman, Howard M., INS

Handler, Myer, UP

Hanley, Richard S., *Yank*

Hansen, Robert H., *Look*

Hanson, Ernest, *Saturday Evening Post*

Hardesty, Harriet C., UP

Hardy, Eugene J., Chilton Company

Hargest, William J., *American Machinist*

Hargrove, Charles R., *Wall Street Journal*

Harkness, Richard L., NBC

Harkrader, Charleton, *Newsweek*

Harmatz, Herbert J., Reuters

Harmon, Dudley Anne,* UP

Harper, Robert S., *Ohio State Journal*

Harrington, Oliver W., *Pittsburgh Courier*

Harris, Harry L., AP

Harris, Reginald S., *Australian Consolidated Press*

Harris, Richard, UP

Harrison, A. Paul, UP

Harrison, Joseph G., *Christian Science Monitor*

Harrison, Paul L., NEA

Harrity, Richard, *Yank*

Harsch, Joseph C.,* *Christian Science Monitor*

Hartrich, Eugene, *Chicago Sun*

Hartt, Julian, INS

Hartzog, Hazel, UP

Hatch, Willard A., Acme Newspictures

Haugland, Vernon A., AP

Hauser, Ernest O., *Saturday Evening Post*

Haverstick, John M., *Yank*

Hawkes, George H., Group 4, Australian Papers

Hawkins, Eric E., *New York Herald Tribune*

Hawkins, Henry E., Reuters

Hawkins, Lewis, AP

Hawkslet, G.G.M., Group 4, Australian Papers

Haworth, William F., *Yank*

Hay, John, *Yank*

Haynes, Weston, American Red Cross

Healy, Thomas, *New York Post*

Hearst, Dorris L., *New York Journal American*

Hearst, Joseph, *Chicago Tribune*

Hearst, William Randolph,* INS

Heath, S. Burton, NEA

Heinz, Wilfred C., *New York Sun*

Heinzerling, Lynn L., AP

Heisler, Philip S., *Baltimore Sun*

Hellinger, Mark J., Hearst Newspapers

Hemery, Clement, INS

Hemingway, Ernest,* *Collier's*

Henderson, Ralph E., *Reader's Digest*

Henle, Raymond Z., *Pittsburgh Post Gazette*

Henry T., AP

Henry, James E., Reuters

Henry, John R., INS

Henry, Thomas R., *Washington Star*

Henry, William M., *Los Angeles Times*

Henshaw, Fred W., *United States News*

Hensley, Malcolm S., UP

Herald, George W., INS

Heran, Arthur F., INS

Hercher, Wilmot W., AP

Herfort, Norman V., *Pix Pictorial*

Herlihy, Martin, Reuters

Hermann, Leopold, AP

Hersey, John,* *Time*

Hershey, Burnet, *Liberty*

Hewlett, Frank, UP

Hicks, George, Blue Network

Hiett, Helen,* Religious News Service

Higginbotham, W. R., UP

Higgins, Marguerite,* *New York Herald Tribune*

High, Stanley, *Reader's Digest*

Hightower, John M., AP

Hill, Carol, *Collier's; Redbook*

Hill, Ernie, *Miami Herald*

Hill, Gladwin A., *New York Times*

Hill, Max, NBC

Hill, Russell,* *New York Herald Tribune*

Hills, Lee O., *Miami Herald*

Himmelsbach, Gerard R., INS

Hinde, John, Australian Broadcasting Commission

Hindson, Curtis, Reuters

Hine, Alfred B., *Yank*

Hippie, William, *Newsweek*

Hirsch, Joseph, Abbott Laboratories

Hlavack, John M., UP

Hoffman, Bernard, *Time*

Holburn, James, *London Times*

Holland, Gordon P., Group 5, Australian Papers

Hollenbeck, Don, NBC

Holies, Everett R., CBS

Hollingworth, Claire,* *Time*

Holt, Carlyle H., *Boston Globe*

Hooley, John A., NBC, CBS, MBS, ABC

Horan, James D., G. P. Putnam's Sons

Homaday, Mary, *Christian Science Monitor*

Horne, George F., *New York Times*

Homer, Durbin L., *Yank*

Hoskins, Francis T., MBS

Hostick, King V., *Chicago Sun*

Hottelet, Richard,* CBS

Houle, Harry J., American Red Cross

Hovey, Graham,* AP

Howard, Ralph, NBC

Howard, Rosemary, *Newsweek*

Howe, Quincy, CBS

Howland, William S., Simon & Schuster

Hoyt, Palmer, UP

Hubbard, Lucien, Simon & Schuster

Hughes, John B., the *Oregonian*

Huie, William B., *American Mercury*

Hull, Harwood, NBC

Hull, Peggy,* *Cleveland Plain Dealer*

Hulls, Alan, Group 2, Australian Papers

Hume, Rita, INS

Humphreys, William J., *New York Herald Tribune*

Hunt, Frazier "Spike," * *Reader's Digest*

Hunt, John R., War Dept., Special Services

Hunter, Kent, INS

Hurd, Peter, *Time*

Hurd, Volney, *Christian Science Monitor*

Hurwitz, Hyman, *Boston Globe*

Huss, Pierre, INS

Hutch, Donald E., AP

Hutcheson, James M., AP

Hutton, Geoffrey, *Melbourne Argus*

Ichac, Pierre, *Vainere*

Ingraham, Herbert, *Time*

Irvin, George B., AP

Irwin, Theodore, *Look*

Isaacs, Harold, *Newsweek*

Isley, Charles C., Stauffer Publishing Company

Israels, Josef II, *This Week*

Jackson, William A., International News Photos

Jacobs, Ann L., *Young America*

Jacoby, Annalee, *Time*

Jacoby, Melville,* *Time*

Jackett, S. T., Reuters

Jameson, Henry B., AP

Jandoli, Jerome B., INS

Janssen, Guthrie E., NBC

Jarrell, John W., INS

Jencks, Hugh I., UP

Jenkins, Bums A., *New York Journal American*

John, Elizabeth B., *Cleveland News*

Johnson, Albin E., INS

Johnson, Carol L., NEA

Johnson, Edd,* *Chicago Sun*

Johnson, Hugo C., Paramount News

Johnson, John R., *National Geographic*

Johnson, Mac R., *New York Herald Tribune*

Johnson, Malcolm, *New York Sun*

Johnson, Vincent, *Pittsburgh Post Gazette*

Johnson, William M., Afro-American Newspapers

Johnson, William W., *Time*

Johnston, George H., Group 1, Australian Papers

Johnston, Paul A., *Yank*

Johnston, Richard J., *New York Times*

Jones, Alexander, *Washington Post*

Jones, Edgar L., *Atlantic Monthly*

Jones, Edward F., *Time*

Jones, Edward V., AP

Jones, George, *New York Times*

Jones, George E., UP

Jones, Joe, *U.S. Engineers*

Jones, John E., *Pittsburgh Post Gazette*

Jones, Joseph M., *Time*

Jones, Victor O., *Boston Globe*

Jones, William W., International News Photos

Jordan, John Q., *Norfolk Journal & Guide*

Jordan, Lewis E., *Yank*

Jordan, Max, NBC

Jurgens, Victor J., *March of Time*

Kadish, Reuben, *Life*

Kadison, William, American Red Cross

Kaltenborn, Hans V.,* NBC

Kammerman, Eugene L., Pics, Inc.

Kantor, MacKinlay, *Enquire*

Karant, Max, *Flying*

Kasischke, Richard, AP

Kaufman, Isador, *Brooklyn Eagle*

Kay, Leon L., UP

Keene, K. C., Group 3, Australian Papers

Kehoe, Thomas, *VFW Magazine*

Keighley, Larry, *Saturday Evening Post*

Kelley, Frank R., *New York Herald Tribune*

Kelley, Hubert W., *American Magazine*

Kelly, George M., AP

Kelly, Phillip R., *Time*

Kelty, William R., *NBC*

Kempner, Mary Jane, *Conde-Nast*

Kendrick, Alexander, *Philadelphia Inquirer*

Kennedy, Edward,* AP

Kennedy, Robert E., *Chicago Times*

Kennet, Warren H., *Newark Evening News*

Kenny, Reginald, Acme Newspictures

Kent, Carleton V., *Chicago Times*

Kent, George, *Reader's Digest*

Kern, Harry F., *Newsweek*

Kessell, Dmitri,* *Life*

Keys, Henry, *London Daily Express*

Kiek, Robert H., Netherlands Press Agency

Kilgallin, James Lawrence,* INS

Kimball, Neil W., *Foreign Service*

Kinch, Samuel, *Fort Worth Star Telegram*

King, Ernest H., AP

King, Herbert G., UP

King, James F., AP

King, William B., AP

Kintzley, Russell, *New Orleans-Times Picayune*

Kirkland, Wallace W., *Life*

Kirkpatrick, Helen,* *Chicago Daily News*

Klein, Julius, *Yank*

Klerr, Edward, INS

Kluckhohn, Frank,* *New York Times*

Knauth, Percival, *Time*

Knickerbocker, Agnes G., *Nashville Tennesseean*

Knickerbocker, Herbert Renfre,* *Chicago Sun*

Knight, Clayton, AP

Knopf, Hans, *Collier's*

Kolodin, Irving, *AAF*

Konzelman, Frederic, *Yank*

Kopf, Dorothy Thompson, Bell Syndicate

Kopf, Maximillian, *Ladies Home Journal*

Korman, Seymour M., *Chicago Tribune*

Kornfeld, Alfred H., *Time*

Kreutzberg, Edgar C., Penton Publishing Co.

Krieg, Frederick P., AP

Krueger, Jess, *Chicago Herald-American*

Krygier, Henry R., Polish News Agency

Kuh, Frederick, *Chicago Sun*

Kuhn, Irene, NBC

Kulick, Harold W., *Popular Science*

Labaudt, Lucien A., *Life*

Labez, Ricardo, *Honolulu Star-Bulletin*

LaFarge, Christopher G., *Harper's*

Laird, Stephen, *Time*

Lait, George, INS

Laitin, Joseph, *Time*

Lake, Austen R., *Boston American*

Lamport, Sara M., *New York Post*

Lancaster, Herbert, *March of Time*

Landaum, Ida B., Overseas News Agency

Landry, Robert, *Life*

Landsberg, Morris, AP

Lane, Charles G., AP

Lang, Daniel, *New Yorker*

Lang, Will, *Time*

Laning, Edward, *Life*

Lanius, Charles, Trans-Radio Press

Lardner, John, NANA

Lauterbach, Richard E., *Time*

Lavelle, Elise, National Catholic News Service

Lawrence, William H.,* *New York Times*

Lawton, Fleetwood, NBC

Lea, Tom,* *Time*

Leach, Paul R., *Chicago Daily News*

Leader, Anton, CBS

Lear, John W., *Saturday Evening Post*

Learned, Albe L., American Red Cross

Leavell, David, *Fort Worth Press*

Leavelle, Richard C., *Chicago Tribune*

Lecardeur, Maurice, Acme Newspictures

Lecoutre, Martha, *Tri-Color*

Lee, Clark,* INS

Lee, J. Edgerton, INS

Lee, Paul K., AP

Legg, Frank G., Australian Broadcasting Commission

Leggett, Dudley, Australian Broadcasting Commission

Lehrman, Harold A., *Argosy*

Leimert, Walter H., CBS

Lennard, Wallace W., Australian Broadcasting Commission

Leonard, John, Reuters

Leonard, Reginald B., Group 3, Australian Papers

Lerner, Max, *PH*

Lesever, Lawrence Edward, CBS News

Levin, Meyer, Overseas News Agency

Lewis, Boyd, NEA

Lewis, Ervin G., WLS

Lewis, Flora, AP

Lewis, Fulton, Jr., MBS

Lewis, Harley C., Acme Newspictures

Lewis, Morris, War Dept., Special Services

Lewis, Robert E., American Red Cross

Leyson, Burr W., *Skyways*

Lieb, Jack, *News of the Day*

Lieberman, Henry, *New York Times*

Liebling, Abbott Joseph "A. J.,-* *New Yorker*

Limpus, Lowell, *New York Daily News*

Lindley, Ernest K., *Newsweek*

Lindsley, James S., AP

Lippmann, Walter, *New York Herald Tribune*

Littell, Robert, *Reader's Digest*

Litz, Leo M., *Indianapolis News*

Lloyd, Rhona, *Philadelphia Evening News*

Lochner, Louis Paul,* AP

Lochridge, Mary P., *Women's Home Companion*

Lockett, Edward B., *Time*

Loeb, Charles H., Negro Newspaper Publishing Association

Loehwing, David A., UP

Logan, Walter F., UP

Long, James M., AP

Longmire, Carey, *New York Post*

Lopez, Andrew, Acme Newspictures

Lopez, Carlos F., *Life*

Loring, Paul S., *Providence Journal*

Loughlin, John, Group 1, Australian Papers

Loundagin, Nicholas F., *Newsweek*

Loveland, Reelif, *Cleveland Plain Dealer*

Lower, Elmer, *Life*

Lowry, Cynthia, AP

Lubell, Samuel, *Saturday Evening Post*

Lucas, Lenore V., Overseas News Agency

Lucas, W. E., *London Daily Express*

Luce, Henry R., *Time*

Luter, George W., *Hawaii Magazine*

Luter, John T., *Time*

MaCauley, Thurston B., INS

MacBain, Alastair, *Collier's*

MacCartney, Robert R., Group 1, Australian Papers

MacCormac, Isabel, *New York Times*

MacCormac, John P., *New York Times*

MacDonald, Grant G., AP

MacDonald, James, *New York Times*

MacKenzie, DeWitt, AP

MacKenzie, Donald, *New York Daily News*

MacKenzie, Fred M., *Buffalo Evening News*

MacLean, James A., UP

MacVeane, John, NBC

Maddox, William, J., *Worked Petroleum*

Madru, Gaston, *News of the Day*

Mahon, Jack, MBS

Maisel, Albert Q., *Cosmopolitan*

Maitland, Patrick, *London News Chronicle*

Mangan, J. J. Sherry, *Time*

Mann, Arthur, MBS

Mann, Erika, *Liberty*

Manning, Bruce, War Dept., Special Services

Manning, Paul, MBS

Marden, Luis, *National Geographic*

Margulies, Leo, *Standard*

Marien, William, *Sydney Morning Herald*

Markey, Lawrence M., *Liberty*

Marsh, Reginald, *Life*

Marshall, George, *Collier's*

Marshall, James, *Collier's*

Marshall, Joseph, *Saturday Evening Post*

Martellierre, Paul, *March of Time*

Martin, Cecelia (Jackie), *Ladies Home Journal*

Martin, David S., *U.S. Engineers*

Martin, Fletcher, *Life*

Martin, Fletcher P., Negro Newspaper Publishing Association

Martin, Frank L., AP

Martin, Robert P., UP

Martin, Robert W., *Time*

Martinez, Albert W., Reuters

Mason, Frank E., NANA

Massell, Robert, Blue Network

Massock, Richard G., AP

Mathews, Ronald, *London Daily Herald*

Mathews, William R., *Arizona Daily Star*

Matthews, Herbert Lionel,* *New York Times*

Matthews, Thomas S., *Time*

May, Ernest R., *Trans-Radio Press*

May, Foster, WOW

McAvoy, Thomas D., *Life*

McBride, William M., *Herald News*

* *Indicates a separate entry.*

McBrine, Robert J., *Yank*

McCabe, Charles R., *Time*

McCabe, Gibson, *Newsweek*

McCaleb, Kenneth, INS

McCall, Frances, NBC

McCallum, Walter R., *Washington Evening Star*

McCardell, Lee A., *Baltimore Sun*

McCardle, Carl W., *Philadelphia Bulletin*

McCarthy, Francis, UP

McCarthy, Ira B., *Kansas City Star*

McCarthy, Joseph W., *Yank*

McClure, William K., Pathe News

McConaughy, John, *Ohio State Journal*

McConnell, Raymond, *Nebraska State Journal*

McConnell, Roscoe, KOMO

McCormick, Anne O'Hare, *New York Times*

McCormick, Robert K., NBC

McDaniel, Yates, AP

McDermott, John B., UP

McDermott, William F., *Cleveland Plain Dealer*

McDonald, John F., *London Daily Mail*

McDowell, Jack S., INS

McEvoy, Joseph P., *Reader's Digest*

McFadden, Louis, *Yank*

McGee, Mary V. P., *Toronto Globe & Mail*

McGeorge, John R., *Toledo Blade*

McGill, Ralph, *Atlanta Constitution*

McGlincy, James, UP

McGovern, Raymond T., *Yank*

McGowan, Gault,* *New York Sun*

McGraffin, William, *Chicago Daily News*

McGraw, Alvin, *Yank*

McGurn, William Barrett,* *Yank*

McIlhenny, Eleanor, *Pan-American*

McKnight, Colbert A., AP

McKnight, John P., AP

McLaughlin, Kathleen, *New York Times*

McMahon, Henry O., *Washington Times-Herald*

McManus, James L., *Yank*

McManus, Robert, *Farm Journal*

McMillen, Richard P., UP

McMurtry, Charles H., AP

McNeil, Marshall, *Scripps-Howard*

McNulty, Henry P., UP

McQuaid, Bernard J., *Chicago Daily News*

McWilliams, George, INS

Mechau, Frank A., *Life*

Mecklin, John M., *Chicago Sun*

Meier, G. Lawrence, MBS

Mejat, Francois, Pathe News

Mejat, Raymond, Pathe News

Melendez, Dorothy, *Star Herald*

Meltzer, Theodore, INS

Meyer, Ben F., AP

Meyer, Jane, *Chicago Herald American*

Meyer, Robert L., UP

Meyers, Debs, *Yank*

Meyers, George N., *Yank*

Michaelis, Ralph, *Air News*

Michie, Alan, *Reader's Digest*

Middleton, Drew,* *New York Times*

Miles, Frank F., *American Legion*

Miller, Graham, *New York Daily News*

Miller, Lee,* Scripps-Howard

Miller, Merle D., *Yank*

Miller, Robert C.,* UP

Miller, William J., *Cleveland Press*

Miller, William M., *Look*

Mills, Raymond, International News Photos

Miner, Charles S., *New York Post*

Mintzer, Leonidias, *California State Guard*

Misabe, C. R., UP

Mishael, Herbert, *Melbourne Age*

Mitchell, Bruce H., *Life*

Moats, Alice L. B., *Collier's*

Moe, M. Lorimer, *Time*

Moler, Murray, UP

Montrose, Sherman, Acme Newspictures

Moody, Blair, *Detroit Free Press*

Moorad, George L., CBS

Moore, Charles M., *London Daily Telegraph*

Moore, Pugh, AP

Moore, Robert E. L., *Trans-Radio Press*

Moore, William T., *Chicago Tribune*

Moosa, Spencer, AP

Moran, Maurice, AP

Morde, Theodore A., *Reader's Digest*

Morehouse, Ward, *New York Sun*

Morgan, Edward P., *Chicago Daily News*

Morgan, Ralph F., AAF

Morgan, Wilfred R., War Dept., Bureau of Public Relations

Morin, Relman "Pat,"* AP

Moroso, John A., AP

Morphopoulos, Panos, *Newsweek*

Morris, Frank D., *Collier's*

Morris, Joe Alex, *Collier's*

Morris, John G., *Life*

Morris, John R., UP

Morrison, Chester,* NBC

Morriss, Mack* *Yank*

Morrow, Thomas, *Chicago Tribune*

Morse, Ralph, *Life*

Morton, Joseph, AP

Morton, Ralph S., AP

Most, Mel, AP

Mowrer, Edgar Ansel,* *Chicago Daily News*

Mowrer, Paul Scott,* *New York Post*

Mowrer, Richard, *Chicago Daily News*

Muchmore, Gareth B., AP

Mueller, Merrill, NBC

Mueller, William A., *Chicago Times*

Muir, John, Whaley-Eaton Service

Muir, Malcolm, UP

Muller, Edwin, *Reader's Digest*

Muller, Mary T., *Reader's Digest*

Munn, Bruce, UP

Murdock, Barbara, *Philadelphia Bulletin*

Murphy, Charles J., *Fortune*

Murphy, William, *Philadelphia Inquirer*

Murray, James E., UP

Murray, William, *Pathe News*

Murray, William R., *Yank*

Murrow, Edward (Egbert) Roscoe,* CBS

Musel, Robert, UP

Muth, Russell A., Fox Movietone News

Muto, Frank, War Dept., Bureau of Public Relations

Mydans, Carl,* *Life*

Mydans, Shelley,* *Life*

Naintre, Yves, Paramount News

Navarro, Robert, *March of Time*

Neill, Franklin F., INS

Nesensohn, Carl D., Acme Newspictures

Neville, Robert,* Stars and Stripes

Nevin, Jack E., *San Francisco Call Bulletin*

Newhall, Scott, *San Francisco Chronicle*

Newman, Albert, *Newsweek*

Newman, Larry, INS

Newton, William, Scripps-Howard

Nichols, David M., *Chicago Daily News*

Nixon, Robert G., INS

Noderer, Elvedore R., *Chicago Tribune*

Noel, Frank E. "Pappy,"* AP

Noli, Louis, AP

Norall, Frank V., *CIAA*

Nordness, Nedville, AP

Norgaard, Noland, AP

Norris, Frank C., *Time*

Norton, Howard M.,* *Baltimore Sun*

Norton, Taylor E., *Time*

Norwood, William R., *Christian Science Monitor*

Noyes, Newbold, *Washington Evening Star*

Nurenberger, Meyer J., *Jewish Morning Journal*

Nutter, Charles P., AP

O'Beirne, D. P., Reuters

O'Brien, Frank, AP

O'Brien, Mary H., Fawcett Publications

O'Connell, John, *Bangor Daily News*

O'Connell, John P., *New York Daily News*

O'Conner, James A., Group 1, Australian Papers

O'Connor, Eugene, American Red Cross

O'Donnell, James, *Newsweek*

Oechsner, Frederick, UP

Oeth, Alfred J., Paramount News

Offner, Philippa G., *Life*

O'Flaherty, Hal, *Chicago Daily News*

Oggel, Dean M., *Yank*

O'Keefe, Richard J., *Philadelphia Inquirer*

O'Kelly, Raymond, Reuters

O'Laughlin, John C., *Army & Navy Journal*

Olde, George, Springfield Newspapers

Oliphant, Homer N., *Yank*

Oliver, David R., Pathe News

Oliver, Frank, Reuters

Olsen, Alphonsus G., *Melbourne Age-Sydney Sun*

Olsen, R., *Sydney Sun*

Olson, Sidney, *Time*

Omelian, L. J., WLEU

O'Neill, James P., *Yank*

Opper, Frederick B., Blue Network

O'Quinn, Judson C., AP

* *Indicates a separate entry.*

O'Regan, Richard A., AP

O'Reilly, John "Tex,"* *New York Herald Tribune*

O'Reilly, Martin L., Pathe News

Orro, David H., *Chicago Defender*

Osbiston, Francis, Group 4, Australian Papers

Osborne, John F., *Time*

O'Sullivan, J. Reilly, AP

Oswald, George, Universal Newsreel

Ottley, Roi V.,* *PM*

Ottoway, N., Group 3, Australian Papers

Oursler, William C., Fawcett Publications

Pacine, H. J., Group 2, Australian Papers

Packard, Eleanor,* UP

Packard, Nathaniel, UP

Packard, Reynolds,* UP

Paine, Ralph D., *Fortune*

Painton, Frederick C.*, *Reader's Digest*

Palmer, Frederick, NANA

Palmer, George J., AP

Palmer, Gretta Clark, *Liberty*

Palmer, Kyle, *Los Angeles Times*

Palmer, Mary B., *Newsweek*

Palyi, Melchoir, Booth Newspapers

Parier, Damien,* Paramount News

Paris, Peter M., *Yank*

Parker, Fred, International News Photos

Parker, Jack D., WJIM

Parker, Pegge, *American Weekly*

Parker, Robert, WLW

Parr, William G., NBC

Parris, John A., AP

Parrott, L., *New York Times*

Parsons, Geoffrey, *New York Herald Tribune*

Pasley, Fred, *New York Daily News*

Patterson, Harry E., *Daily Oklahoman*

Paul, Herbert, Cowles Papers

Paul, Raymond A., Australian Broadcasting Commission

Paul, Richard H., *Yank*

Pawlak, Mason H., *Yank*

Peague, Harry H., American Red Cross

Pearson, Leon M., INS

Pepperburg, Ray L., *American Illustrator*

Percival, Jack, Group 5, Australian Papers

Perkins, Alice K., Fairchild Publications

Perlin, Bernard,* *Life*

Perlman, David A., *New York Herald Tribune*

Perry, George S., *Saturday Evening Post*

Perryman, Charles R., News *of the Day*

Person, Kriston, *Free Norwegian Press*

Peterman, Ivan H., *Philadelphia Inquirer*

Peters, Harold A., Blue Network

Peters, Walter F., *Yank*

Peterson, Elmer, NBC

Peterson, Frederick, Group 3, Australian Papers

Peterson, George L., *Minneapolis Star-Journal*

Peterson, Ralph E., NBC

Pflaum, Irving, *Chicago Times*

Phelps, Winston, *Providence Journal*

Phillips, Cecil A. C., *New York Times*

Phillips, John, *Time*

Phillips, Martha E., Afro-American Newspapers

Phillips, William L., AP

Phipps, William E., AP

Pickens, William, *Trans-Radio Press*

Pignault, Charles, *TAM*

Pimper, John A., *Yank*

Pinkley, Virgil M., UP

Pinney, Roy, *Liberty*

Pitkin, Dwight L., AP

Pitman, Frank W., AP

Plachy, Frank, *New York Journal of Commerce*

Plambeck, Herbert, WOW

Platt, Warren C., *National Petroleum News*

Pleissner, Ogden M., *Life*

Polier, Dan A., *Yank*

Poling, Daniel, *Philadelphia Record*

Polk, Catherine, *Los Angeles* News

Polk, George,* *Los Angeles News*

Poor, Henry V., *U.S. Engineers*

Poor, Peggy, *New York Post*

Poorbaugh, Earl R., INS

Pope, James S., *Louisville Courier-Journal*

Porter, K. R., Ziff-Davis Publishing Company

Porter, Leroy P., NBC

Potter, Henry O., Group 3, Australian Papers

Potter, John P., *Baltimore Sun*

Poulos, Constantine, Overseas News Agency

Powell, Hickman, *Popular Science*

Powers, John H., *Town & Country*

Pratt, Fletcher, *Harper's*

Pratt, Melbourne, Group 5, Australian Papers

Preston, Hartwell L., *Life*

Prevost, Clifford A., *Detroit Free Press*

Prewett, Virginia, *Chicago Sun*

Pribichevich, Stoyan, *Time*

Price, Wesley, *Saturday Evening Post*

Priestly, Thomas A., Universal Newsreel

Primm, Arthur, MBS

Prince, E., International News Photos

Pringle, Helena, *Women's Home Companion*

Pringle, Nelson G., CBS

Prist, Frank, Acme Newspictures

Pryer, Donald J., CBS

Purcell, John F., *Life*

Purdue, Marcus, AP

Purtell, Joseph P., *Time*

Putnam, Eva B., *Trans-Radio Press*

Pyle, Ernest "Ernie,"* Scripps-Howard

Pyle, Howard, NBC

Pyle, John, KTAR

Queen, Harold, UP

Quigg, Horace D., UP

Quigley, Karl, INS

Quinn, Stanley, MBS

Rae, William B., *New York Times*

Rae, William E., *Liberty*

Ragsdale, Warner R., *United States News*

Ragsdale, Wilmott, *Time*

Raleigh, John M., CBS

Ramage, Frederick J., Keystone-International

Ramsay, Paul, *Philadelphia Inquirer*

Ranft, Joseph, UP

Raper, Stoddard, *Columbus Dispatch*

Rappoport, Joan (Ann Hunter), WAIT

Raridan, Leo, INS

Ravenholt, Albert, UP

Rawlings, Charles A., *Saturday Evening Post*

Ray, Charles C., War Dept., Bureau of Public Relations

Raymond, Allen, *New York Herald Tribune*

Rayner, Pendil,* Group 3, Australian Papers

Rea, Gene, Il Progresso

Reading, Geoffrey, *Sydney Mirror*

Rebiere, Marcel H., *Time*

Redger, George, *Time*

Redmond, Dick A., WHP

Reed, Philip G., INS

Reed, William K., *Yank*

Reichmann, John A., UP

Reinhart, Hans, International NewsPhotos

Reiter, John H., *Philadelphia Record*

Reston, Sarah J., *New York Times*

Reuben, Robert E., Reuters

Reusswig, Martha S., *Collier's*

Reusswig, William, King Features

Reynolds, Emil G., Acme Newspictures

Reynolds, Quentin,* *Collier's*

Rhodenbaugh, Harold, *Look*

Rice, Jack, AP

Rich, Stanley, UP

Richards, Guy, *New York Daily News*

Richards, Robert W., UP

Richardson, David,* *Yank*

Richardson, Harold W., *Engineering News Record*

Richardson, Stanley P., NBC

Richardson, William H., *Yank*

Rickman, Theodore Z., *News of the Day*

Ridder, Walter, St. *Paul Dispatch*

Riemer, Harry, *Daily Trade Record*

Riess, Curt, *Trans-Radio Press*

Riggs, Robert L., *Louisville Courier Journal*

Roark, Eldon E., Scripps-Howard

Robb, Inez, INS

Robbins, Charles H., *American Weekly*

Roberts, Cletus, Blue Network

Roberts, David, *Cincinnati Inquirer*

Roberts, Edward V., UP

Roberts, Harrison B., Associated Press Photos

Roberts, Kenneth, Group 4, Australian Papers

Robertson, Ben, *New York Herald Tribune*

Robertson, Frank, INS

Robertson, Ruth A., Press Syndicate

Robinson, Iona, *Saturday Review of Literature*

Robinson, Pat, INS

Robinson, William E., *New York Herald Tribune*

Robson, William, CBS

Rocho, Ethel P., *Collier's*

Rollins, Byron H., AP

Rolo, Charles J., *Atlantic Monthly*

Roos, Leonard H., Pathe News

Root, Gordon, Southam Newspapers (Canada)

Indicates a separate entry.

Roper, James E., UP

Rosen, Fred, *Yank*

Rosenthal, Joe,* AP

Ross, Nancy W., freelance

Rouzeau, Edgar T., *Pittsburgh Courier*

Rowe, William L., *Pittsburgh Courier*

Rucker, Joseph T., Paramount News

Rue, Larry,* *Chicago Tribune*

Ruge, John A., *Yank*

Rundle, Walter G., UP

Russell, E. A., UP

Russell, Edmund "Ned" Allen,* *New York Herald Tribune*

Russell, Frank (Ted Malone), Blue Network

Russell, H. T., UP

Ryan, Cornelius John,* *London Daily Telegraph*

Ryan, Robert G., *Yank*

Sabin, Jesse, *News of the Day*

Saerchinger, Caesar, *American Historical*

Salisbury, Harrison Evans,* UP

Sample, Paul, *Time*

Sanders, Branan I., AP

Sann, Paul, *New York Post*

Santin, Miguel A., *El Mundo*

Sargint, H. J., NANA

Sasso, Arthur H., International News Photos

Satonomy, Edward, UP

Sayre, Joel Grover,* *New Yorker*

Schalben, Orville, *Milwaukee Journal*

Schedler, Dean, AP

Scheer, Sam, International News Photos

Scherman, David, *Life*

Scherschel, Frank, *Life*

Schmidt, Dana A., UP

Schneider, Lieutenant Philip, *Leatherneck*

Schuck, Hugh, *New York Daily News*

Schulman, Sammy, International News Photos

Schwartz, Robert, *Yank*

Scott, Burgess H., *Yank*

Scott, David W., Pathe News

Scott, John, *Time*

Seacrest, Joseph W., *Nebraska State Journal*

Seawood, Charles P., Acme Newspictures

Sebring, Lewis, *New York Herald Tribune*

Sedgwick, Alexander Cameron "A. C.,"* *New York Times*

Selle, Earl A., *Honolulu Advertiser*

Senick, Langdon, Fox Movietone News

Sevareid, Eric,* CBS

Severyns, Marjorie, *Time*

Shadel, W. F., *Rifleman & Infantry Journal*

Shafer, Thomas, Acme Newspictures

Shapiro, Henry, UP

Shapiro, Lionel S., NANA

Shaplen, Robert M.,* *Newsweek*

Sharp, Roland H., *Christian Science Monitor*

Shaw, Albert E., *Westminster Press*

Shaw, Charles, CBS

Shaw, Jack, MBS

Shaw, John W., American Red Cross

Shaw, William, *March of Time*

Shaw, William D., *Yank*

Shayon, Robert, CBS

Sheahan, Joseph G., *Chicago Tribune*

Shean, Vincent, *Newsweek*

Sheean, James Vincent,* *Redbook*

Sheets, Millard O., *Life*

Shehan, Thomas F., *Yank*

Shelley, John D., WHO

Shenkel, William, *Newsweek*

Shepley, James R., *Time*

Shere, Samuel, *Life*

Sheridan, Martin, *Boston Globe*

Sherman, Dean F., *Alaska Life*

Sherman, Eugene, *Los Angeles Times*

Sherrod, Robert,* *Time*

Shippen, William H., *Washington Evening Star*

Shirer, William Lawrence,* CBS

Shoemaker, Leslie, UP

Shoenbrun, David, Overseas News Agency

Shoop, Duke, *Kansas City Star*

Short, Gordon H., Australian Dept. of Information

Showers, Paul, *Yank*

Shrout, William C., *Life*

Shultz, Sigrid, *Chicago Tribune*

Siegman, Harold, Acme Newspictures

Siler, Bert, NBC

Silk, A., Australian Dept. of Information

Silk, Arthur G., *Time*

Silk, George, *Life*

Simmonds, Charles J., Group 3, Australian Papers

Simmons, Walter,* *Chicago Tribune*

Simms, William P., Scripps-Howard

Simpson, Kirke L., AP

Sinclair, Frederic M., *Buffalo Evening News*

Singer, Jack,* INS

Singleton, Alexander, AUP

Sions, Harry A., *Yank*

Skadding, George R., *Life*

Skariatina, Irina, *New York Times*

Slocum, William, CBS

Slosberg, Marvin, NBC

Small, Alex, *Chicago Tribune*

Small, W. C., *Saturday Evening Post*

Smalley, Alton D., *St. Paul Dispatch-Pioneer*

Smith, A. Merriman, UP

Smith, Ardis, Pathe News

Smith, Beverly, *Collier's*

Smith, Eugene, *Life*

Smith, Frank P., *Chicago Times*

Smith, Harold P., *Chicago Tribune*

Smith, Howard Kingsbury,* CBS

Smith, Irving I., *Universal Newsreel*

Smith, Jack, AP

Smith, John C., *New York Herald Tribune*

Smith, Joseph K., INS

Smith, Lawrence, Abbott Laboratories

Smith, William E., Ziff-Davis

Smyth, James F., *Truth & Daily Mirror*

Snow, Edgar,* *Saturday Evening Post*

Soderholm, Wallace, *Buffalo Evening News*

Solon, Samuel L., *New Leader*

Sommers, Martin, *Saturday Evening Post*

Sondem, Frederick E., *Reader's Digest*

Soong, Norman, Central News Agency

Sosin, Milton R., *Miami Daily News*

Souder, Edmund L., Blue Network

Southerland, Henry J., American Red Cross

Southwell-Keely, Terence, Group 5, Australian Papers

Spencer, Murlin, AP

Spilman, Charles, *Providence Journal*

Stanfield, Lawrence, *Los Angeles Times*

Stanford, Graham, *London Daily Mail*

Stanford, Theodore, *Pittsburgh Courier*

Starr, Donald, *Chicago Tribune*

Stavisky, Samuel,* Chicago Daily News

Stead, Ronald, *Christian Science Monitor*

Stebbins, Robert G., *Contractor & Engineer*

Steel, Johannes, WHN

Steele, Archibald T.,* *Chicago Daily News*

Steele, Earl B., UP

Stein, Gunther, *Christian Science Monitor*

Steinbeck, John Ernest, Jr.,* *New York Herald Tribune*

Steinkopf, Alvin, AP

Stephenson, Malcolm L., AP

Stern, Michael, Fawcett Publications

Stevens, Edmund,* *Christian Science Monitor*

Stevenson, Kenneth, *Yank*

Stewart, Benjamin A., *National Geographic*

Stewart, Ollie, Afro-American Newspapers

Stewart, William, *Canadian Press*

Stirling, Monica, *Atlantic Monthly*

Stoecker, Leo J., Acme Newspictures

Stokes, Richard L., *St. Louis Post-Dispatch*

Stone, I. F., *PM*

Stone, John L., WRVA

Stonehouse, Kenneth, Reuters

Stonehouse, Merlin, *Trans-Radio Press*

Stoneman, William H.,* *Chicago Daily News*

Stoody, Ralph W., Religious News Service

Stout, Rex, freelance

Stout, Wesley, *Saturday Evening Post*

Stowe, Leland,* Blue Network

Strand, William, *Chicago Tribune*

Stratton, Lloyd, AP

Strickler, Homer, *New York Sun*

Stringer, Elizabeth, UP

Stringer, William, *Christian Science Monitor*

Strock, George A., *Life*

Stromme, George L., Occidental Publishing Company

Strout, Richard L., *Christian Science Monitor*

Strozier, Fred L., AP

Struthers, I. O. Paramount News

Stumm, Loraine, *London Daily Mirror*

Sturdevant, Robert N., AP

Sturdy, Frank, *Chicago Tribune*

Studer, Boyd B., *American Legion*

Sullivan, John V., *Yank*

Sullivan, Neil, Pathe News

Sulzberger, Cyrus Leo,* *New York Times*

Summers, Harold J., Group 5, Australian Papers

Sunde, Tenold R., *New York Daily News*

* *Indicates a separate entry.*

Sutton, Donn, NEA

Suydam, Henry, *Newark News*

Sweeney, Don G., UP

Symontowne, Russ, *New York Daily News*

Tait, Jack M., *New York Herald Tribune*

Talbott, Sprague, *Look*

Taves, Brydon, UP

Taylor, Alexander, *New York Post*

Taylor, Henry, Scripps-Howard

Taylor, Robert, *Newark Evening News*

Teatsorth, Ralph C., UP

Telegian, Manual, Abbott Laboratories

Telford, Frank, Young & Rubicam

Tepling, Lloyd, UP

Terrell, John *U., Newsweek*

Terrell, Maurice E., *Look*

Terry, John B., *Chicago Daily News*

Tewkesbury, Richard, NBC

Thale, Jack A., *Miami Herald*

Thayer, Mary V., INS

Thomas, Bryon, *Life*

Thomas, Ed, UP

Thomas, Igor, *Saturday Evening Post*

Thomas, Lowell Jackson,* NBC

Thompson, Charles H., UP

Thompson, Craig F., *Time*

Thompson, Fred, *Reader's Digest*

Thompson, George F., Fox Movietone News

Thompson, J. Flynn, *Time*

Thompson, John Hall,* *Chicago Tribune*

Thorndike, Joseph J., *Life*

Thorp, Gerald R., *Chicago Daily News*

Thusgaard, Carl, Acme Newspictures

Tighe, Dixie, INS

Tobin, Richard, *New York Herald Tribune*

Toles, Edward B., *Chicago Defender*

Tomara, Sonia,* *New York Herald Tribune*

Tomlinson, Edward, Blue Network

Tondra, John A., Fox Movietone News

Travis, Roderick, Group 3, Australian Papers

Treanor, Tom,* *Los Angeles Times*

Treat, Roger L., *Washington Daily News*

Tregaskis, Richard J.,* INS

Tremaine, Frank, UP

Troutman, Stanley, Acme Newspictures

Trumbull, Robert,* *New York Times*

Tubbs, Vincent, Afro-American Newspapers

Tucker, George, AP

Tully, Andrew, *Boston Traveller*

Tupling, William L., UP

Turcott, Jack, *New York Daily News*

Turk, Raymond J., *Cleveland News*

Turnbull, James, *Life*

Turner, Ewart (Dr.), Religious News Service

Twitty, Tom, *New York Herald Tribune*

Tyree, William, UP

Uhl, Alexander H., *PM*

Ullman, Frederick, Pathe News

Vadeboncoeur, E. R., NBC

Van Atta, Lee, INS

Valnes, Evans G., UP

Vanderbilt, Sanderson, *Yank*

Vandercook, John W., NBC

Vanderlip, Candace, INS

Vandivert, Margrethe, *Time*

Vandivert, William, *Time*

Van Sluys, C. J., Aneta

Vas Dias, Arnold, Aneta

Vaughn, Miles W., UP

Ventres, Fisko, *Hartford Courant*

Vermillion, Robert,* UP

Vern, Ike, *Quick*

Veysey, Arthur, *Chicago Tribune*

Vidner, Richard, *New York Herald Tribune*

Villanova, Anthony, *Miami Herald*

Vivian, Robert E., Reuters

Von Bovene, G. A., Aneta

Von Schmidt, Harold, *Saturday Evening Post*

Waagenaar, Samuel, INS

Wade, William W., INS

Wadsworth, Horace A., *Newsweek*

Wagg, Alfred, *Chicago Tribune*

Wagner, Theodore, *St. Louis Post-Dispatch*

Wahl, Jim M., NBC

Waite, Elmont, AP

Waldrop, Frank C., *Washington Times-Herald*

Wales, Henry G., *Chicago Tribune*

Walker, Charles L., *Harper's*

Walker, Gordon, *Christian Science Monitor*

Walker, Harrison H., *National Geographic*

Walker, John H., *Time*

Walker, Milton E., *New York Herald Tribune*

Walker, Samuel, *New York Post*

Wall, Carl B., *Reader's Digest*

Wallace, Ed R., NBC

Wallenstein, Marcel H., *Kansas City Star*

Walsh, Burke, *Saturday Evening Post*

Walsh, John B., *National Catholic* WC

Walters, John B., *London Daily Mirror*

Walton, William E., *Time*

Wang, George K., UP

Ward, Henry, *Pittsburgh Press*

Warden, William, AP

Waring, Gerald H., British United Press

Warner, Dennis, *Melbourne Herald*

Warner, Eugene P., American Red Cross

Warren, Mervyn, Group 3, Australian Papers

Waters, Enoc P., *Chicago Defender*

Watson, James B., BBC

Watson, Mark, *Baltimore Sun*

Watson, Paul R., *Our Navy*

Waugh, Irving C., WSM

Wear, Joseph R., *Fort Worth Star Telegram*

Weber, Thomas, *Look*

Wecksler, Abraham N., Conover Mast

Weil, Joseph, American Red Cross

Weisblatt, Franz, UP

Weisman, Al, *Yank*

Wellard, James,* *Chicago Times*

Weller, George,* *Chicago Daily News*

Werner, Merle M., UP

Werner, Oscar L., AP

Wertenbaker, Charles, *Time*

Weston, Joe, *Time*

Weston, Mervyn C., *Argus*

Wheeler, Elliot R., AP

Wheeler, George, NBC

Wheeler, Herbert K., *Chicago Times*

Whipple, Sidney, Scripps-Howard

Whitcomb, Philip, *Baltimore Sun*

White, Elmont, AP

White, Frank, *Indianapolis Star*

White, Herbert K., AP

White, Leigh,* *Chicago Daily News*

White, O.E.D., Group 2, Australian Papers

White, Theodore Harold,* *Time*

White, Walter, *New York Post*

White, William, *New York Herald Tribune*

White, William L., *Reader's Digest*

White, William S., *Time*

Whitehead, Donald F.,* AP

Whitehouse, Arthur G., Fawcett Publications

Whiteleather, Melvin K., *Philadelphia Evening Bulletin*

Whitman, Howard J., *New York Daily News*

Whitney, Betsey C., *Washington Times-Herald*

Whitney, Peter D., *San Francisco Chronicle*

Wiant, Thoburn H., AP

Widis, Edward C., AP

Wilcher, Lester, Cowles Newspapers

Wilcox, Richard L., *Time*

Wiley, Bonnie, AP

Wilhelm, Donald, *Reader's Digest*

Wilhelm, John R., Reuters

Wilkes, Jack, *Time*

Wilkins, Ford, *New York Times*

Williams, Donald, *Stars & Stripes*

Williams, Emlyn J., *Christian Science Monitor*

Williams, Garth M., *PM*

Williams, Glenn A., AP

Williams, Gurney, *Collier's*

Williams, Henry L., Group 5, Australian Papers

Williams, Joseph F., INS

Williams, Larry W., War Dept., Bureau of Public Relations

Williams, Leonard W., *Newark Evening News*

Williams, Maynard O., *National Geographic*

Williams, Oswald M., Australian Broadcasting Commission

Williams, Thomas V., AP

Willicombe, Joseph, INS

Willis, Douglas, BBC

Wilson, Edmund, *New Yorker*

Wilson, Gill Robb, *New York Herald Tribune*

Wilson, Lon H., *Yank*

Wilson, Lyle, UP

Wilson, Richard L., *Minneapolis Star-Journal*

Wilson, Robert C., AP

Wilson, William C., UP

Winkler, Betty, Press Alliance

Winkler, Paul, INS

Winn, Mary Day, *This Week*

* Indicates a separate entry.

Winner, Howard, Pathe News

Winter, William, Overseas News Agency

Wittels, David G., *Philadelphia Record*

Wohl, Harry, St. *Louis Star-Times*

Wolfe, Henry C., *This Week*

Wolfe, Thomas, NEA

Wolfert, Ira,* NANA

Wolff, Werner, *Yank*

Wong, N.H.S., *News of the Day*

Wood, Percy S., *Chicago Tribune*

Woodbury, Clarence M., *American*

Woodward, Stanley, *New York Herald Tribune*

Woolf, S. J., NEA

Worth, Edward S., AP

Wright, James, Paramount News

Wright, McQuown, UP

Yancey, Luther F., Afro-American Newspapers

Yap, Dioadado M., *Bataan*

Yarbrough, W. T., AP

Yates, Thom, *Yank*

Young, B. J., Group 4, Australian Papers

Young, Murray G., WHK

Young, Stanley, *Cosmopolitan*

Young, Thomas W., Guide Publishing Company

Youngman, Lawrence, *Omaha World Herald*

Zaimes, Charles J., American Red Cross

Zaimes, Margaret K., American Red Cross

Zayas, George, *Collier's*

Zegri, Amando, NBC

Zinder, Harry, *Time*

Source: Barney Oldfield. *Never a Shot in Anger.* 1989 reprint.

Appendix O

BBC War Correspondents with the Allied Expeditionary Force, June 6, 1944–May 5, 1945

Barr, Robert

Bernard, David

Byam, Guy

Dimbleby, Richard*

Downing, Rupert

Duff, Robin

Dunnett, Robert

Fletcher, Alfred

Gillard, Frank

Johnston, Denis

Lefevre, Pierre

MacPherson, Stewart

Marshall, Howard

Maxted, Stanley

Melville, Alan

North, Richard

Ray, Cyril

Reid, Robert

Shepherd, E. Colston

Standing, Michael

Stevenson, Kent

Vaughn-Thomas, Wynford

Ward, Edward, Viscount Bangor*

Willis, Douglas

Wills, Colin

Wilmot, Reginald William Winchester "Chester"*

Wilson, Ian

Sources: Desmond Hawkins, ed. *War Report, D-Day to VE-Day: Dispatches by the BBC's War Correspondents with the Allied Expeditionary Force, 6 June 1944-5 May 1945. 1985.*

* *Indicates a separate entry.*

Appendix P

Korean War Correspondents

Aquino, Benigno,* *Manila Times*

Baillie, Hugh,* United Press

Barnard, Bill, Associated Press

Beech, Keyes,* *Chicago Daily News*

Bell, John, Time, Life

Bennyhoff, Robert, United Press

Bigart, Homer,* *New York Herald Tribune*

Blair, William D., Baltimore Sun

Boss, William,* Canadian Press

Bourke-White, Margaret,* *Life*

Boyle, Hal, *New York Herald Tribune*

Brines, Russ, Associated Press

Brodie, Howard,* Associated Press; CBS News

Browne, Malcolm W.,* *Stars and Stripes*

Buckley, Christopher,* *Daily Telegraph*

Burchett, Wilfred,* *London Daily Express*

Cameron, James,* *Picture Post*

Cannon III, James Monroe,* Baltimore Sun

Carson, Tom, International News

Cioffi, Lou, CBS

Conniff, Frank,* International News Service

Considine, Bob, Hearst Newspapers

Crane, Burton, New York Times

Cutforth, Rene, BBC

Davidson, Michael, Observer

Davies, John O., Newark Evening News

Dearie, Philip, International News

De Premonville, Jean-Marie, Agence France-Presse

Desfor, Max, Associated Press

Dibble, Arnold, United Press

Dille, John, Life magazine

Downs, Bill, CBS

Duncan, David Douglas,* *Life*

Emery, Frank, International News Service

Faber, Harold, New York Times

Fielder, Wilson, Time, Life

Gayn, Mark, Chicago Sun Times

Gibney, Frank, Time

Handleman, Howard, International News Service

Hardy, Albert `Bert,"* *Picture Post*

Herman, George, CBS

Higgins, Marguerite,* *New York Herald Tribune*

Hinton, Albert, *Norfolk Journal and Guide*

Hoberecht, Earnest, United Press

Inouye, Ken, Telenews

James, Jack, United Press

Jefferson, John, CBS

Jones, Charles, NBC

Jones, Eugene, NBC

Kahn, Ely Jacques "E. J.,"* *New Yorker*

Kalischer, Peter,* United Press

Karnow, Stanley,* Time magazine

Kirk, Donald,* New York Times

Lambert, Tom,* Associated Press

Landry, Bob, Life

Leseur, Larry,* CBS

Levine, Hal, *Newsweek*

Lorwin, I.R., Pix Incorporated

Lucas, James Griffing,* Scripps-Howard

Magee, Haywood, Picture Post

Martin, Harold, Saturday Evening Post

Mauldin, Bill,* *Collier's*

McDonnell, David, New York Herald Tribune

Miller, Robert C., United Press

Miller, William, United Press

Moler, Murray, United Press

Moore, William R., Associated Press

Morin, Relman "Pat,"* Associated Press

Morrison, Ian F. M.,* *Times*

Murrow, Edward (Egbert) Roscoe,* CBS

Mydans, Carl,* *Life*

Noel, Frank E., Associated Press

Park, Sarah,* Honolulu Star-Bulletin

Parrott, Lindsay, New York Times

Pearcy, Derek Arthur Gordon, Reuters-AAP

Peeler, Ernie, *Stars and Stripes*

Philomenko, Maximilen, Agence France-Presse

Pierpoint, Robert, CBS

Poats, Rutherford, United Press

Potter, Philip, *Baltimore Sun*

Price, George Ward,* *Daily Mail*

Raymond, Allen, New York Herald Tribune

Rich, John,* NBC

Richards, Ray, INS

Rosecrans, Jr, Charles D, International News

Scott, Ed, CBS

Shinn, Bill,* Associated Press

Simmons, Stephen,

Simmons, Walter,* *Chicago Tribune*

Sparks, Fred, Chicago Daily News

Stone, Thomas Jefferson, AP

Sullivan, Walter Seager, New York Times

Summerlin, Sam, AP

Supple, James O., Chicago Sun Times

Sweers, George, AP

Swinton, Stan, Associated Press

Symonds, Gene,* United Press

Thompson, Reginald, *Daily Telegraph*

Waln, Nora, Saturday Evening Post

Ward, John T., Baltimore Sun

Webb, Peter, United Press

Wershba, Joseph, CBS

Whitehead, Donald F.,* Associated Press

Wilson, Charles B., Columbus (Ohio) State Journal

Sources: Michael Emery. *On the Front Lines.* 1995; John Hohenberg. *Foreign Correspondence.* 1965; Trevor *Royle. War Report.* 1987; M. L. Stein. *Under Fire.* 1968; Korean War Educator, http://www.koreanwar-educator.org/topics/p_war_corre-spondents.htm.

* Indicates a separate entry.

Appendix Q

Vietnam War Correspondents

Adams, Edward "Eddie" T.,* Associated Press

Apple, R.W. "Johnny," *Time*

Arnett, Peter,* Associated Press

Arnot, Charles P.,* Associated Press

Becker, Elizabeth, *Washington Post, Newsweek,* NBC

Bigart, Homer,* *New York Times*

Brelis, Dean,* NBC

Brodie, Howard,* Associated Press

Browne, Malcolm W.,* Associated Press; ABC; *New York Times*

Bryan, Anne,* *Overseas Weekly*

Burrows, Larry,* *Life*

Cagnoni, Romano,* freelancer

Caputo, Philip,* *Chicago Tribune*

Chapelle, Georgette "Dickey,"* freelancer

Chauvel, Patrick,*

Cheatham, UPI

Clurman, Richard, *Time*

Collingwood, Charles Cummings,* CBS News

Cronkite, Walter Leland, Jr.,* CBS News

Deepe, Beverly,* freelancer

Downing, John,* *London Daily Express*

Dring, Simon,* *London Daily Telegraph*

Dudman, Richard, *St. Louis Post-Dispatch*

Duncan, David Douglas,* *Life;* ABC; *Collier's*

Eggleston, Charles, ?

Ellison, Robert J., *Empire/Black Star*

Emerson, Gloria,* *New York Times*

Faas, Horst,* Associated Press; *Life*

Fall, Bernard,* freelancer

Fallaci, Oriana,* freelancer

Fitzgerald, Frances,* freelancer

Flynn, Sean,* freelancer; *Time*

Foa, Sylvana,* UPI

Fox, Martin Stuart, UPI

Franjola, Matt, AP

Gellhorn, Martha,* *Manchester Guardian*

Gerretsen, Chas,* UPITN

Geyer, Georgie Anne,* *Chicago Daily News*

Goralski, Robert,* NBC

Greenway, David,* Time magazine

Griffiths, Philip Jones,* freelancer

Halberstam, David,* *New York Times*

Halstead, Dirck, *Time*

Hangen, Welles,* *New York Times*

Herndon, Ray, UP

Hersh, Seymour,* freelancer

Hillenbrand, Barry, *Time*

Hoberecht, Ernest, UPI

Hollingworth, Claire,* *Daily Telegraph*

Huet, Henri, ?

Huynh, Ut Cong,* Associated Press

Kalischer, Peter,* CBS

Kamm, Henry, *New York Times*

Kazickas, Jurate,* freelancer

Kennerly, David Hume, UPI

Kilgore, Margaret,* United Press International

Kirk, Don, Washington Star

Kolenberg, Bernard*, Associated Press

Langguth, Jack, *New York Times*

Laurent, Michel,* Associated Press

Laurie, Jim, NBC

Lederer, Edith M.,* Associated Press

Leroy, Catherine,* freelancer

Leslie, Jacques*, *Los Angeles Times*

Lucas, James Griffing,* Scripps-Howard

McCullin, Donald,* *Sunday Times*

McDonald, Glenn, ABC radio

Mine, Hiromichi, ?

Mohr, Charles,* *Time*

Morrow, Mike, Dispatch News Service

Mulligan, Hugh, Associated Press

Musgrove, Helen "Patches,"* *Jacksonville Journal*

Nicholson, Michael,* ITV

Nivolon, Francois, *Le Figaro*

North, Don, ABC, NBC

Northrup, Steve, UPI, *Time*

Oliphant, Tom,* *Boston Globe*

Page, Timothy John,* freelancer

Palmos, Frank,* freelancer

Perry, Mert,* freelancer

Pond, Elizabeth,* *Christian Science Monitor*

Potter, Kent,* United Press International

Pringle, Jim, Reuters

Prochnau, William, *Washington Post*

Raffaelli, Jean, Agence France Presse

Rather, Dan,* CBS

Ray, Michele,* Agence France-Presse

Raymond, Jack, *New York Times*

Riboud, Marc,* Magnum Photos

Robinson, Carl, AP

Robinson, Jack, NBC

Rockoff, Al, AP

Round, Derek,* Reuters

Russell, Jack, NBC

Safer, Morley,* CBS

Salisbury, Harrison Evans,* *New York Times* Sargent, Tony, CBS

Sawada, Kyoichi,* United Press

Schanberg, Sydney H.,* *New York Times*

Schuyler, Philippa,* *Manchester Union-Leader*

Sevareid, Eric,* CBS

Shaplen, Robert Modell,* *New Yorker*

Sharrock, Peter, Reuters

Sheehan, Neil,* *New York Times*

Shepard, Elaine,* freelancer

Sherrod, Robert,* *Life*

Shimamoto, Keisaburo,* *Newsweek*

Smith, Terence, *New York Times*

Southerland, Dan, UPI, *Christian Science Monitor*

Steinbeck, John Ernest, Jr.,* *Newsday*

Stone, Dana,* CBS

Sully, Francois,* *Newsweek*

Syversten, George, CBS

Terry, David, feelancer

Tomalin, Nicholas,* *Sunday Times*

Tuckner, Howard, NBC

Tuohy, William,* *Los Angeles Times*

Turner, Nick, Reuters

Ulevich, Neal, AP

Utley, Garrick,* NBC

Volkert, Kurt, CBS News

Wagner, Ken, UPI

Webb, Catherine,* UPI

Webster, Dan, CBS

Williams, T. Jeff, AP, CBS

Wolkerstorfer, Terry, AP

Young, Perry Deane,* UPI

Sources: Virginia Elwood-Akers. Women War Correspondents in the Vietnam War, 1961-1975. 1988; William Prochnau. *Once upon a Distant War.* 1995; Clarence R. Wyatt. *Paper Soldiers.* 1993.

* Indicates a separate entry.

Appendix R

Pulitzer Prizes Awarded for War Reporting, 1917-2010

WORLD WAR I

1917   Herbert Bayard Swope,* *New York World*

ETHIOPIAN WAR

1936   Wilfred C. Barber,* *Chicago Tribune*

WORLD WAR II

1939   Louis P. Lochner, Associated Press

1940   Otto D. Tolischus, *New York Times*

1941   Group award to American war correspondents

1942   Lawrence Edmund Allen,* Associated Press

1942   Carlos Pena Romulo,* *Philippines Herald*

1943   Hanson W. Baldwin,* *New York Times*

1943   George Weller, *Chicago Daily News*

1943   Ira Wolfert,* North American Newspaper Alliance

1944   Daniel De Luce,* Associated Press

1944   Ernest "Ernie" Taylor Pyle,* Scripps-Howard

1945   Mark Watson, *Baltimore Sun*

1945   Joe Rosenthal,* Associated Press

1945   Hal Boyle, Associated Press

1945   Bill Mauldin,* *Stars and Stripes**

1946   Homer Bigart,* *New York Herald Tribune*

1946   William Leonard Laurence, *New York Times*

KOREAN WAR

1951   Keyes Beech,* *Chicago Daily News*

1951   Homer Bigart,* *New York Herald Tribune*

1951   Marguerite Higgins,* *New York Herald Tribune*

1951   Relman "Pat" Morin,* Associated Press

1951   Fred Sparks, *Chicago Daily News*

1951   Donald F. Whitehead,* Associated Press

1952   John Hightower, Associated Press

1953   Donald F. Whitehead,* Associated Press

1954   James Griffing Lucas,* Scripps-Howard

VIETNAM WAR

1964   Davis Halberstam,* *New York Times*

1964   Malcolm W. Browne,* Associated Press

1965   Horst Faas,* Associated Press

1966   Peter Arnett,* Associated Press

1966   Kyoichi Sawada,* UPI

1968   Toshio Sakai, UPI

1969   Edward Adams,* Associated Press

1969   William Tuohy,* *Los Angeles Times*

1970   Seymour Hersh*, Dispatch News Service

1973   Ut Cong Huynh,* Associated Press

MIDDLE EAST WARS

1968   Alfred Friendly, *Washington Post*

INDO-PAKISTAN WAR OF 1971

1972   Peter R. Kann, *Wall Street Journal*

1972   Horst Faas,* Associated Press

1972   Michel Laurent,* Associated Press

CAMBODIA

1976   Sydney Schanberg*, *New York Times*

ISRAELI INVASION OF LEBANON

1983   Thomas L. Friedman, *New York Times*

1983   Loren Jenkins, *Washington Post*

KUWAIT AND PERSIAN GULF WAR

1991   Caryle Murphy*, *Washington Post*

1992   Patrick J. Sloyan, *Newsday*

YUGOSLAVIAN CONFLICTS

1993   John F. Burns, *New York Times*

1993   Roy Gutman, *Newsday*

1996   David Rohde, *Christian Science Monitor*

RWANDA

1995   Mark Fritz, AP

AFGHANISTAN

2002   Barry Bearak, *New York Times*

IRAQ

2004   Anthony Shadid, *New York Times*

2005   Judith Miller, *New York Times*

2010   Anthony Shadid, *New York Times*

Appendix S

War Artists

Atkinson, George *, *Illustrated London News*

Aylward, William J,*, American Expeditionary Forces (Hereafter cited as AEF) , *Scribner's, Harpers Monthly*

Baker, George*, *Yank**

Benson, Eugene*, *Frank Leslie's Illustrated Newspaper* (hereafter cited as *Leslie's*)

Biddle, George*, *Life*

Bohrod, Aaron*, *Life*

Brodie, Howard*, *Yank, Life, Collier's, AP*

Bull, Rene*, *Black and White*

Burton, James*, *New York Herald, Harper's Weekly* (hereafter cited as *Harper's*), *Leslie's*

Christy, Howard Chandler*, *Leslie's, Harper's*

Crowe, Joseph*, *Daily News, The Times*

Davis, Theodore R.*, *Harper's*

Duncan, Walter J., AEF

Dunn, Harvey T.*, AEF

Fisher, Philip D.*, *Harper's*

Forbes, Edwin*, *Leslie's*

Fredenthal, David*, *Life*

Fripp, Charlie*, *Graphic, Daily Graphic*

Giles, Geoffrey Douglas*, *Graphic*

Glackens, William J., ?

Goodall, Edward A.*, *Illustrated London News*

Hall, Sydney Prior*, *Graphic*

Harding, George M.*, AEF, *Harper's Monthly*

Homer, Winslow*, *Harper's*

Landells, Robert T.*, *Illustrated London News*

Lea, Tom*, *Life*

Leslie, Frank*, *Illustrated London News, Leslie's*

Lovie, Henri*, *Leslie's*

Lumley, Arthur*, *Leslie's, New York Illustrated News*

Maud, W.T.*, *Daily Graphic*

Mauldin, Bill*, *Stars and Stripes*

Millet, Francis Davis*, *New York Herald, London Times, Harper's, New York Sun*

Montagu, Irving*, *Illustrated London News*

Morgan, Wallace, AEF

Mosler, Henry*, *Harper's Weekly*

Nast, Thomas, *Harper's, New York Illustrated News, Illustrated London News, Le Monde Illustre*

Nevinson, Christopher Richard Wynne*, ?

Paget, Henry M.*, *Sphere*

Paget, Walter Stanley*, *Illustrated London News, Sphere*

Pearse, Harry*, *London Daily News, Illustrated London News, Graphic*

Peixotto, Ernest C.*, AEF, *Scribner's*

Peloq, Jules*, *Illustrated London News*

Perlin, Bernard*, *Life*

Power, Frank Le Poer*, *Pictorial World*

Prior, Melton*, *Illustrated London News*

Remington. Frederic*, *Harper's, New York Journal*

Sacco, Joe*, *The Guardian, Harper's*

Schell, Francis*, *Leslie's*

Schonberg, Johann Nepomuk*, *Illustrated London News*

Sheldon, Charles*, Leslie's, *Black and White*

Sheldon-Williams, Inglis*, *Sphere, Collier's Weekly*

Simplot, Alex*, *Harper's, New York Illustrated News*

Simpson, William*, *Illustrated London News*

Smith, J. Andre*, AEF

Smith, Dan*, *Leslie's*

Taylor, James Earl*, *Leslie's*

Townsend, Harry E.*, AEF

Villiers, Frederic*, *Graphic*

Vizetelly, Frank*, *Illustrated London News*

Waud, Alfred*, *Harper's*

Waud, William*, *Harper's*

Wirgman, Charles*, *Illustrated London News*

Woodville, Richard Caton*, *Illustrated London News*

Wright, Henry Charles Seppings*, *Illustrated London News*

Ximenes, Edoardo*, *La Guerra Italo-Abissinia*

Yriarte, Charles Emile, *Le Monde Illustre*

References: Pat Hodgson. The War Illustrators. 1977; Robert Wilkinson-Latham. From Our Special Correspondent. 1979; F. Laurinston Bullard. Famous War Correspondents. 1914; Philip Van Doren Stern. They Were There: The Civil War Action as Seen by Its Combat Artists. 1959; The Library of Congress. An Album of American Battle Art. 1947; Alfred Emile Cornebise. Art from the Trenches. 1991.

* Indicates a separate entry.

Appendix T

War Photographers/Cameramen

Adams, Edward*, AP

Alpert, Max*, TASS

Anannin, Mikhail*, *Pravda*

Aultman, Otis*, International News Service, Pathe

Baldwin, Herbert*, Central News Agency

Baltermans, Dmitri*, *Izvestia, Na Razgrom Varaga*

Barnard, George N.*, Military Division of the Mississippi

Barzini, Sr., Luigi*, *Corriere della Sera, London Daily Telegraph*

Beato, Felice*, British War Office

Berry, Ian*, *Daily Mail*

Boulat, Alexandra*, Sipa Press, VII Photo Agency

Bourke-White, Margaret*, *Life*

Brady, Mathew*, *Harper's Weekly, Leslie's*

Browne, Malcolm*, AP

Bull, Rene*, *Black and White*

Burke, John*, *Graphic*

Burrows, Larry*, *Life*

Burton, James*, *Harper's Weekly*

Buscemi, John*, *Yank*

Cagnoni, Romano*, *Observer, Paris-Match, Life, Stern, L-Espresso, Newsweek*

Capa, Cornell*, *Life*

Capa, Robert*, *Life, Time*

Cartier-Bresson, Henri*, professional

Chapelle, Georgette "Dickey"*, *Life*

Cook, George S.*, daguerreotypist

Davis, Neil*, Australian Broadcasting Commission

Delahaye, Luc*, *Newsweek*

Della Casa, Nick*, Frontline News

Depardon, Raymond*, Magnum

Diament, Rafail*, Russian Navy

Dinwiddie, William*, *Harper's, New York Herald*

Downing, John*, *Daily Express*

Duncan, David Douglas*, South Pacific Air Transport Command, *Life*

Fenton, Roger*, Thomas Agnew (Manchester publisher), *Illustrated London News*

Fly, Camillus S*, Fly Studio, Tombstone, Arizona

Flynn, Sean*, CBS

Garanin, Anatoli*, *Frontovaya Illustracia*

Gardner, Alexander*, Army of the Potomac

Glover, Ridgeway*, Philadelphia Photographer, *Leslie's*

Gore, William "Billy"*, *Daily Sketch, News Chronicle*

Grebnev, Viktor*, *Krasnaya Zvezda* (Red Star), *Frontovik* (Frontline Fighter)

Griffiths, Philip Jones*, freelance

Haeberle, Ron*, *Cleveland Plain Dealer*

Hardy, Albert "Bert"*, *Picture Post*

Hare, James "Jimmy" H.*, *Illustrated American, Collier's Weekly*

Haviv, Ron*, *Time, Stern, Paris-Match*

Hemment, John C.*, *New York Journal, Harper's Weekly*

Horne, Walter H.*, postcard photography

Huet, Henri*, AP

Hurley, James F.*, Australian Imperial Photographic Unit

Jenks, Paul*, European Picture Agency

Jouvenal, Peter*, Frontline Television News

Kazickas, Jurate*, *Look, Mademoiselle*

Kenichi, Kimura*, *Chugoku*

Kerimov, Farkhad,*, AP

Kertesz, Andre*, Conde Nast

Kessel, Dimitri*, *Life*

Khaldei, Yevgeni*, TASS, *Pravda*

Knight, Gary*, *Newsweek*, VII Photo agency

Kolenberg, Bernard*, AP

Kratochvil, Antonin, VII Photo Agency

Krauss, Hansjoerg "Hansi"*, AP

Kroft, Steve*, *Stars and Stripes*

Kudoyarov, Boris*, *Pravda*

Larrabee, Constance Stuart*, *Libertas*

Laurent, Michel*, AP, Gamma Photo Agency

Ledru, Filipp*, ?

Leroy, Catherine*, *Life*, AP

Lewis, George*, NBC

Lipserov, Georgei*, Russian army newspaper

Lloyd, Anthony*, *Daily Telegraph, Times*

Lloyd, James*, *Illustrated London News*

Lutfallah, Aswan*, APTN

MacCosh, John*, surgeon in 2nd Sikh War

Mavroleon, Carlos*, CBS

McCullin, Don*, *Sunday Times*

McIntosh, Burr William*, *Leslie's*

Meyers, Georg*, *Yank*

Miller, James*, freelancer

Miller, Lee*, *Vogue*

Moreno de Mora, Miguel Gil*, Associated Press Television News (APTN)

Morris, Christopher*, VII Photo Agency

Morse, Ralph*, *Life*, *Time*

Moth, Margeret*, CNN

Muybridge, Eadweard*, *Harper's*

My, Huynh Than*, AP

Mydans, Carl*, *Life*

Nachtwey, James*, *Albuquerque Journal*, Black Star photo agency

Nagai, Kenji*, Tokyo AFP News

Nicholls, Horace H*, ?

O'Sullivan, Timothy*, Army of the Potomac

Page, Tim*, Time-Life, *Look*, *Life*, *Paris-Match*, UPI, AP

Peck, Rory*, Frontline Television News

Pickerell, James*, *Newsweek*

Potter, Kent*, UPI

Redkin, Mark*, TASS, *Frontovaya Illustracia*

Reisner, Georg*, *Life*

Riboud, Marc*, Magnum agency

Rider-Rider, William*, *Daily Mirror*

Robertson, James*, *Illustrated London News*

Robertson, Nic*, CNN

Rodger, George*, *Life*

Rosenthal, Joe*, ?

Royal, Dennis Lee*, AP

Sankova, Galina*, *Frontovaya Illustracia*

Savin, Mikhail*, TASS, *Krasnoarmeyskaya Pravda* (Red Army Pravda)

Sawada, Kyochi*, UPI

Schork, Kurt*, Reuters

Scott, Roddy*, Frontline News

Seymour, David "Chim"*, *Life*

Shaykhet, Arkadi*, ?

Shimamoto, Keisburo*, *Newsweek*, Asia Newspaper Alliance

Sites, Kevin*, NBC, ABC, Yahoo

Smith, Eugene W.*, *Newsweek*, *Life*

Smith, Vaughan*, Frontline Television News

Soloviev, Andre*, TASS, AP

Stackpole, Peter*, *Life*

Stanmeyer, John, VII Photo Agency

Steichen, Edward Jean*, ?

Stevens George*, Special Coverage Unit of the U.S. Army Signal Corps

Stouman, Lou*, *Yank*

Szathmari, Karl Baptist von*, pioneer war photographer

Taro, Gerda*, *Life*

Thiele, Reinhold*, *Graphic*

Trakhman, Mikhail Anatol'evich*, TASS, Red Army

Tweedie, Penny*, *Sunday Times*, *National Geographic*, *Time*, *Paris-Match*

Tyomin, Viktor*, *Pravda*

Ustinov, Alexander*, *Pravda*

Ut, Huynh Cong "Nick", AP

Uzlyan, Alexander*, *Pravda*, *Izvestiya*, *Ogonyok*

Ware, Michael*, CNN

Watson, Paul*, *Toronto Star*

Wild, Richard*, ITN, Frontline News

Yevzerikhin, Emmanuel*, TASS

Yon, Michael*, CNN, FOX, *Wall Street Journal*, *New York Times*

Zelma, Georgi Anatolyevich*, Red Army, Isvestiya

References: Daniela Mrazkova and Vladimir, eds. *The Russian War 1941-1945.* 1975; Helmut and Alison Gersheim. *Roger Fenton: Photographer of the Crimean War.* 1973; Pat Hodgson. *Early War Photographs.* 1974; Jorge Lewinski. *The Camera at War.* 1978; Duncan Anderson. *War: A Photo-History.* 2006; David Loyn. *Frontline.* 2005.

* Indicates a separate entry.

Appendix U

Films that Portray War Correspondents

The War Correspondent (1913)

Strangers May Kiss (1931)

The Yellow Ticket (1931)

War Correspondent (1932) (aka Soldiers of Fortune)

Clear All Wires! (1933)

Four Frightened People (1934)

I'll Tell the World (1934)

Paris Interlude (1934)

Sing Sing Nights (1934)

Viva Villa! (1934)

Love on the Run (1936)

Next Time We Love (1936)

Espionage (1937)

I Cover the War (1937)

The Last Train from Madrid (1937)

The Soldier and the Lady (1937)

That Certain Age (1938)

Gateway (1938)

International Settlement (1938)

Too Hot To Handle (1938)

North of Shanghai (1939)

Barricade (1939)

Everything Happens at Night (1939)

The Light That Failed (1939)

Stanley and Livingstone (1939)

Arise, My Love (1940)

Comrade X (1940)

A Dispatch from Reuter's (1940)

Foreign Correspondent (1940)

Confirm or Deny (1941)

Penny Serenade (1941)

Affectionately Yours (1941)

Man At Large (1941)

Berlin Correspondent (1942)

Cairo (1942)

Once Upon a Honeymoon (1942)

Journey for Margaret (1942)

Somewhere I'll Find You (1942)

A Yank in Libya (1942)

This Was Paris (1942)

Three Hearts for Julia (1943)

Behind the Rising Sun (1943)

Jack London (1943)

Guadalcanal Diary (1943)

My Son, the Hero (1943)

They Got Me Covered (1943)

Action in Arabia (1944)

The Fighting Seabees (1944)

Passage to Marseille (1944)

Betrayal from the East (1945)

Blood on the Sun (1945)

Guest Wife (1945)

Isle of the Dead (1945)

Objective, Burma! (1945)

Ernie Pyle's Story of G.I. Joe (1945)

Week-End at the Waldorf (1945)

Sing Your Way Home (1945)

Salome, Where She Danced (1945)

Perilous Holiday (1946)

The Searching Wind (1946)

June Bride (1948)

Command Decision (1948)

Malaya (1949)

The Big Lift (1950)

The Tanks Are Coming (1951)

Here Comes the Groom (1951)

Assignment – Paris (1952)

Never Let Me Go (1953)

Little Boy Lost (1953)

Roman Holiday (1953)

Sabre Jet (1953)

The Last Time I Saw Paris (1954)

Love Is a Many-Splendored Thing (1955)

The Gamma People (1956)

Godzilla, King of the Monsters! (1956)

The Sun Also Rises (1957)

Another Time, Another Place (1958)

Dunkirk (1958)

The Quiet American (1958)

The Angry Hills (1959)

Island of Lost Women (1959)

The Angel Wore Red (1960)

Mysterious Island (1961)

Lawrence of Arabia (1962)

The Bedford Incident (1965)

The One Eyed Soldiers (1966)

The Venetian Affair (1967)

Hogan's Heroes: "No Names Please" (1968)

Anzio (1968)

The Green Berets (1968)

The Shoes of the Fisherman (1968)

Young Winston (1972)

Fireball Forward (1972)

The Girl From Petrovka (1974)

The Passenger (1975)

Professione: reporter (1975)

The Man Who Would Be King (1975)

M*A*S*H: "The Interview" (1976)

M*A*S*H: "Our Finest Hour" (1978)

Apocalypse Now (1979)

M*A*S*H: Co-Respondent (1980)

Reds (1981)

Das Boot (1981)

The Dogs of War (1981)

Circle of Deceit (1981)

Die Falschung (1981)

M*A*S*H: Tell It To the Marines (1981)

M*A*S*H: Blood and Guts (1982)

The Year of Living Dangerously (1982)

Angkor: Cambodia Express (1982)

The Blue and the Gray (1982)

Wrong Is Right (1982)

V (1983)

Love Is Forever (1983)

Last Plane Out (1983)

Under Fire (1983)

The Killing Fields (1984)

Eleni (1985)

Salvador (1986)

Violets Are Blue (1986)

Murrow (1986)

Full Metal Jacket (1987)

Deadline (1987)

Saigon Commandos (1987)

Scoop (1987)

Witness in a War Zone (1987)

Highway to Heaven: "The Correspondent" (1988)

Shooter (1988)

Violent Zone (1989)

China Beach: "How To Stay Alive in Vietnam" (1989)

Old Gringo (1989)

Margaret Bourke-White (1989)

Navy Seals (1990)

Cover-Up (1991)

Nambugun (1990)

Year of the Gun (1991)

The Time for Cherries (1991)

Held Hostage: The Sis and Jerry Levin Story (1991)

Coach: "Dateline Bangkok" (1992)

Double Edge (1992)

Turtle Beach (1992)

Danielle Steel's Message from Nam (1993)

Speechless (1994)

The Troubles We've Seen (1994)

Before the Rain (1994)

Pretty Village, Pretty Flame (1996)

Welcome to Sarajevo (1997)

Forbidden Territory: Stanley's Search for Livingstone (1997)

Legacy (1998)

A Bright Shining Lie (1998)

Three Kings (1999)

Beautiful People (1999)

The Trench (1999)

Harrison's Flowers (2000)

No Man's Land (2001)

War Photographer (2001)

The Quiet American (2002)

We Were Soldiers (2002)

Live from Baghdad (2002)

Escape from Afghanistan (2002)

Fire Over Afghanistan (2003)

War Stories (2003)

Law & Order: "Embedded" (2003)

And Starring Pancho Villa as Himself (2003)

Coronado (2004)

In My Father's Den (2004)

Critical Assignment (2004)

Over There (2005)

Manticore (2005)

Embedded Live (2005)

Jarhead (2005)

The Good German (2006)

* Indicates a separate entry.

Blood Diamond (2006)

Six Degrees (2006)

Kabul Express (2006)

The Situation (2006)

Retaliation (2006)

A Mighty Heart (2007)

Redacted (2007)

Interview (2007)

The Daily Show (2007)

The Hunting Party (2007)

Generation Kill (2008)

The Men Who Stare at Goats (2009)

Triage (2009)

Balibo (2009)

The Bang Bang Club (2010)

Afghan Luke (2011)

Forces Speciales (2011)

5 Days of War (2011)

Appendix V

Iraq War Correspondents (2003-2015)

Abdel-Hamid, Hoda, Al Jazeera

Anderson, Jon Lee,* New York Times

Aspell, Tom,* NBC

Ayers, Chris,* Times of London

Bangert, Christoph,* New York Times

Boettcher, Mike,* CNN

Bowen, Jeremy,* BBC

Burns, John Fisher,* New York Times

Damon, Arwa,* CNN

Engel, Richard,* NBC

Filkins, Dexter,* New York Times

Fisk, Robert,* The Independent

Garcia-Navarro, Lourdes,* NPR

Garrells, Anne,* NPR

Gilberston, Ashley,* New York Times

Gillespie, Bill, CBC News

Goldenberg, Suzanne,* The Guardian

Hastings, Michael M.,* Newsweek

Hill, Jmaes*, New York Times

Hondros, Chris,* freelancer

Jamail, Dahr, Al Jazeera

Jacquier, Gilles,* France 2

Lloyd, Terry,* ITN

Mari, Jean-Paul, Le Nouvelle Observateur

Maron, Karen,* freelancer

McEvers, Kelly,* NPR

Milewicz, Waldemar,* TVP

Miller, Keith,* NBC news

Morris, David, J.,* Salon

Nagai, Kenji,* AFP News

Nivat, Anne,* Le Point

Omaar, Rageh,* BBC

Osnos, Evan, Chicago tribune

Ourdan, Remy,* Le Monde

Pelley, Scott,* CBS News

Raddatz, Martha,* ABC News

Sites, Kevin*, NBC

Squitieri, Tim, USA Today

Steele, Jon,* ITN

Turgut, Serif,* ATV

Tyson, Ann Scott, Washington Post; Christian Science Monitor

Ward, Clarissa, CBS News

Weber, Olivier,* Le Point

Weiskopf, Michael, Washington Post; Time magazine

Williams, Brian,* NBC

Yamamoto, Mika,* Asahi Newstar

Indicates a separate entry.

Appendix W

Afghanistan War Correspondents (2001-2015)

Adario, Lynsey,* , New York Times, AP

Ahmad, Sardar*, Agence France-Press

Anderson, Jon Lee,* New York Times

Aspell, Tom,* NBC

Bangert, Christoph,* New York Times

Boettcher, Mike,* CNN

Burton, Harry, Reuters

Coll, Steve, New Yorker

Cutuli, Maria,* *Corriere della Sera*

Deghati, Reza, National Geographic

Filkins, Dexter,* New York Times

Fisk, Robert,* The Independent

Foley, James,* Stars and Stripes

Gall, Carlotta, New York Times

Gannon, Kathy, AP

Garcia-Navarro, Lourdes,* AP Televsion

Gillespie, Bill, CBC News

Gilles, Clare Morgana, Freelance

Haidari, Aziz Ullah,* Reuters

Hammerl, Anton,* freelance photographer

Hetherington, Tim,* freelancer

Hill, James,* New York Times

Junger, Sebastian,* ABC News, Vanity Fair

Leventhal, Richard Gary,* Fox News

Lorch, Donatella,* NBC

Neidringhaus, Ana,* AP

Nivat, Anne,* Le Point

Raddatz, Martha,* ABC News

Ourdan, Remy,* Le Monde

Refsdal, Pal, freelancer

Rohde, David S., Reuters

Rowland, Jacky,* BBC, Al Jazeera

Squitieri, Tim, USA Today

Weber, Olivier,* Le Point

Appendix X

Journalists Killed in Somalia, 1992-2014/motive confirmed

Mohamed Isaq,* Kalsan TV, December 5, 2014

Abdulkadir Ahmed,* Somali Channel TV, December 5, 2014.

Yusuf Ahmed Abukar, Radio Ergo, Mustaqbal Radio, June 21, 2014

Mohamed Mohamud, Universal TV, October 26, 2013

Liban Abdullahi Farah, Kalsan TV, July 7, 2013

Mohamed Ibrahim Raage, Radio Mogadishu, Somali National Television, April 21, 2013

Abdihared Osman Aden, Shabelle Media Network, January 18, 2013

Mohamed Mohamud Turyare, Shabelle Media Network, October 28, 2012

Ahmed Farah Ilyas, Universal TV, October 23, 2012

Hassan Yusuf Absuge, Radio Maanta, September 21, 2012

Liban Ali Nur, Somali National TV, September 20, 2012

Abdisatar Daher Sabriye, Radio Mogadishu, September 20, 2012

Abdirahman Yasin Ali, Radio Hamar, September 20, 2012

Ahmed Addow Anshur, Shabelle Media Network, May 24, 2012

Farhan Jeemis Abdulle, Radio Daljir, Simba Radio, May 2, 2012

Mahad Salad Adan, Shabelle Media Network, April 5, 2012

Ali Ahmed Abdi, Freelancer, March 4, 2012

Abukar Hassan Mohamoud, Somaliweyn Radio, February 28, 2012

Hassan Osman Abdi, Shabelle Media Network, January 28, 2012

Abdisalan Sheikh Hassan, Freelance, December 18, 2011

Noramfaizul Mohd, Bernama TV, Sept 2, 2011

Barkhat Awale Adan,* Hurma Radio, Aug 24, 2010

Sheikh Nur Mohamed Abkey,* Radio Mogadishu, May 4, 2010

Abdulkhafar Abdulkadir, Freelance, Dec 3, 2009

Mohamed Amin, Radio Shabelle, Dec 3, 2009

Hassan Zubeyr, Al_Arabiya, Dec 3, 2009

Mohamud Mohamed Yusuf, Radio IQK, July 4, 2009

Mukhtar Mohamed Hirabe, Radio Shabelle, June 8, 2009

Nur Muse Hussein, Radio IQK, May 26, 2009

Abdirisak Mohamed Warsame, Radio Shabelle, May 22, 2009

Said Tahlil Ahmed, HornAfrik, Feb 2, 2009

Hassan Mayow Hassan, Radio Shabelle, Jan 1, 2009

Nasteh Dahir Farah, Freelancer, June 7, 2008

Bashir Noor Gedi, Radio Shabelle, Oct 19, 2007

Abdulkadir Mahad Moallim Kaskey, Radio Banadir, Aug 24, 2007

Mahad Ahmed Elmi, Capital Voice, Aug 11, 2007

Ali Sharmarke, HornAfrik, Aug 11, 2007

Ahmed Hassan Mahad, May 16, 2007

Abshir Ali Gabre, May 16, 2007

Mohammed Abdullahi Khalif, Voice of Peace, May 5, 2007

Martin Adler*, Freelancer, June 23, 2006

Duniya Muhyadin Nur., Capital Voice, June 5, 2005

Kate Peyton*, BBC, Feb 9, 2005

Abdullahi Madkeer, DMC Radio, Jan 24, 2003

Ahmed Kafi Awale, Radio of the Somali People, Jan 26, 2000

Marcello Palmisano, RAI, Feb 9, 1995

Pierre Anceaux, Freelancer, Aug 31, 1994

Miran Krovatin, RAI-3 Television, March 20, 1994

Ilaria Alpi,* RAI 3, March 20, 1994.

Anthony Macharia, Reuters, June 12, 1993

Hansi Krauss*, Associated Press, July 12, 1993

Dan Eldon*, Reuters, July 12, 1993

Hosea Maina, Reuters, July 12, 1993

Jean-Claude Jumel, TF-1, June 18, 1993

References: Adapted from http://cpj.org/killed/africa/somalia/

---

* Indicates a separate entry.

Appendix Y

Syrian Civil War Correspondents

Al-Deeri, Mahran,* SANA

Al-Sayed,* citizen journalist

Bajbouj, Atallah,* Nabaa Media Foundation

Cantlie, John,*

Cooper, Anderson Hays,* CNN

Curtis, Peter Theo,*

El-Dous, Yousef,* Orient News

Foley, James,* GlobalPost

Didier, Francois,* French Daily Liberation

Goto, Kenji,* Independent Press

Hicks, Tyler,* New York Times

Jacquier, Gilles,*

Jarban, Ferzat,* freelancer

Kenck, Christopher,

McEvers, Kelly,* NPR

Mtawe'e, Zaher,* Zebedine Coordination Committee

Nasser, Maya,* Press TV

Neely, Bill,* ITN

Schrier, Matt,* freelancer

Shadid, Anthony,* New York Times

Sotloff, Stephen,* Media Line

Tice, Austin,* Washington Post

Appendix Z

Libyan Civil War Correspondents

Al-Jabar, Ali Hassan,* Al Jazeera

Al-Qasim, Mohammed,* Radio Rozana

Amanpour, Christiane,*

Bowen, Jeremy,*

Colvin, Mary,* Sunday Times

Foley, James,* *GlobalPost*

Garcia-Navarro,* NPR

Hammerl, Anton,* Saturday Star

Hetherington, Timothy,* freelancer

Hicks, Tyler,* New York Times

Hondros, Chris,* freelancer

Liohn, Andre,*

Nabbous, Mohammed,* Libya Alhurra TV

Ochlik, Remi,* Sunday Times

Shadid, Anthony,* New York Times

* *Indicates a separate entry.*

Appendix AA

Robert Capa Gold Medal Winners*

1955   Howard Sochurek, Magnum for Life

1956   John Sadovy, Life

1958   Paul Bruck, CBS News

1959   Mario Biasetti, CBS News

1960   Yung Su Kwon, NBC News

1962   Peter Dehmel & Klaus Dehmel, NBC News

1963   Larry Burrows*, Life

1964   Horst Faas*, Associated Press

1965   Larry Burrows*, Life

1966   Henri Huett*, Associated Press

1967   David Douglas Duncan*, Life & ABC News

1968   John Olson, Life

1969   Josef Koudelka, Look

1970   Kyoichi Sawada*, UPI

1971   Larry Burrows, Life

1972   Clive W. Limpkin, Penguin Books

1973   David Burnett, Raymond Depardon & Chas Gerretson, Gamma Presse Images

1974   W. Eugene Smith*, Camera 35

1975   Dirck Halstead, Time

1976   Catherine Leroy*, Gamma for Time

1977   Eddie Adams*, AP

1978   Susan Meiselas*, Time

1979   Kaveh Golestan, Time

1980   Steve McCurry, Time

1981   Rudi Frey, Time

1982   Harry Mattison, Time

1983   James Nachtwey*, Time

1984   James Nachtwey*, Time

1985   Peter Magubane, Time

1986   James Nachtwey*, Black Star for *Time*

1987   Janet Knott, The Boston Globe

1988   Chris Steele-Perkins, Magnum for *Time*

1989   David Turnley, Black Star for *The Detroit Free Press*

1989   Bruce Haley, Black Star for *U.S. News & World Report*

1991   Christopher Morris, Black Star for Time

1992   Luc Delahaye*, Sipa Press

1993   Paul Watson, The Tornto Star

1994   James Nachtwey*, Magnum for Time

1995   Anthony Suau, Time

1996   Corinne Dufka, Reuters

1997   Horst Faas*/Tim Page*, Random House

1998   James Nachtwey*, Magnum for Time

1999   John Stanmeyer, SABA for Time

2000   Chris Anderson, Aurora for The New York Times Magazine

2001   Luc Delahaye*, Magnum for Newsweek

2002   Carolyn Cole*, The Los Angeles Times

2003   Carolyn Cole*, The Los Angeles Times

2004   Ashley Gilbertson, Aurora for The New York Times

2005   Chris Hondros*, Getty Images

2006   Paolo Pellegrin*, Magnum

2007   John Moore, Getty Images

2008   Shaul Schwarz, Getty Images

2009   Khalil Hamra, AP

2010   Agnes Dherbys, Freelance for *The New York Times*

2011   Andre Liohn*, Prospekt Photographers, European Pressphoto Agency for Newsweek

2012   Fabio Bucciarelli*, Freelance for AFP

2013   Tyler Hicks*, *The New York Times*

Sources: OPC Awards: The Robert Capa Gold Medal, http://www.opcofamerica.org/opc_awards/archive/byaward/award_capa.php.

Appendix BB

Bayeaux Calvados Awards for War Correspondents: 1994-2014

1994:

Magazine: Philipp von Recklinghausen STERN

Photo: André Soloviev* ASSOCIATED PRESS

Daily press: Denis Arcand LA PRESSE

Radio: Alan Little BBC

Television: Elisabeth Burdot RTBF

Special prize of the jury: Paul Marchand RADIO Canada

1995

Written press: Henri Guirchoun LE NOUVEL OBSERVATEUR

Photo: Laurent Van der Stockt GAMMA

Television: Ben Brown BBC

Special prize of the jury: Patricia Coste FRANCE 2

The Ouest-France – Jean Marin Prize (written press): Xavier Gautier LE FIGARO

1996

Written pres: Patrick de Saint Exupéry LE FIGARO

Photo: James Nachtwey* MAGNUM pour TIME MAGAZINE

Television: George Allagiah BBC

Radio: Nicolas Poincaré FRANCE INTER

The Ouest-France – Jean Marin Prize (written press): Olivier Weber LE POINT

1997

Written press: Alain Bommenel et le bureau d'Alger AFP

Photo: Santiago Lyon ASSOCIATED PRESS

Television: Bob Coen, Amy Mertz CNN

Radio: François Clémenceau EUROPE 1

The Ouest-France – Jean Marin Prize (written press): Jean-Paul Mari LE NOUVEL OBSERVATEUR

The Public Prize: Luc Delahaye* MAGNUM

1998

Written press: Jean-Paul Mari LE NOUVEL OBSERVATEUR

Photo: Achmad Ibrahim ASSOCIATED PRESS

Television: Morad Aïd-Habbouche et Christian Decarné FRANCE 3

Radio: Nicolas Charbonneau EUROPE 1

The Ouest-France – Jean Marin Prize (written press): Jean Hatzfled LIBERATION

The Public Prize: Hocine AFP

1999

Written press: Gabriel Grüner STERN

Photo: James Natchwey* MAGNUM pour TIME MAGAZINE

* Indicates a separate entry.

Television: Fergal Keane BBC

Radio: Isabelle Dor FRANCE INFO

The Ouest-France – Jean Marin Prize (written press): Javier Espinosa EL MUNDO

The Public Prize: Brennan Linsley SIPA PRESS

2000

Written press: Rémy Ourdan* LE MONDE

Photo: Eric Bouvet FREE-LANCE

Television: Matt Frei et Darren Conway BBC

Radio: Madeleine Mukamabano – et Médi Elhag FRANCE CULTURE

The Ouest-France – Jean Marin Prize (written press): Patrick Saint-Paul LE FIGARO

The Lower Normandy Secondary School Students': Rageh Omaar BBC

The Public Prize: Eric Bouvet FREE-LANCE

2001

Written press: Françoise Spiekermeier PARIS MATCH

Photo: Enric Marti ASSOCIATED PRESS

Television: Ben Brown BBC

Radio: Gilles Perez RFI

The Ouest-France – Jean Marin Prize (written press) : Maureen Cofflard LE NOUVEL OBSERVATEUR

The Lower Normandy Secondary School Students': Marie-Claude Vogric FRANCE 3

The Public Prize: Jeffrey B. Russel CORBIS SYGMA

2002

Written press: Pierre Barbancey L'HUMANITÉ

Photo: Luc Delahaye MAGNUM PHOTOS

Television: FRANCE 2 – Gilles Jacquier, Bertrand Coq, Tatiana Derouet, Alexandre Berne

Radio: Arnaud Zajtman BBC

The Ouest-France – Jean Marin Prize (written press): Jean Kehayan LIBÉRATION

The Lower Normandy Secondary School Students': John Simpson BBC

The Public Prize: Yannis Behrakis REUTERS

2003

Written press: Sammy Ketz AFP

Photo: Georges Gobet AFP

Television: Grégoire Deniau et Hervé Paploray CAPA PRESSE

Radio: Renaud Bernard FRANCE INFO

The Ouest-France – Jean Marin Prize (written press): Caroline Laurent-Simon ELLE

The Lower Normandy Secondary School Students': RTBF – Philippe Lamair, Luc Cauwenberghs, Stefan Janssens, Nathalie Lucien

The Public Prize: Georges Gobet AFP

2004

Written press: James Meek et Suzanne Goldenberg THE GUARDIAN

Photo: Karim Sahib AFP

Television: Paul Wood, Adam Moose Campbell, Yousseff Shomali, Sarah Halfpenny, Nigel Sawtell, Qais Hayawi, Laith Kawther – BBC

Radio: Andrew Harding – BBC

The Ouest-France – Jean Marin Prize (written press) : Christophe Ayad LIBERATION

The Secondary School Students': BBC – Fergal Keane, Glenn Middleton, Jackie Martens, Isaac Mugabi

The Public Prize : Jaafar Ashtiyeh AFP

Jury's Prize : ELLE – Caroline Laurent-Simon

2005

Written press: Vincent Hugeux L'EXPRESS

Photo: Jim MacMillan ASSOCIATED PRESS

Television: ITN-ITV NEWS – Julian Manyon, Sacha Lomakim, Artem Drabkin, Patrick O'Ryan-Roeder

Radio: Ishbel Matheson et Dan McMillan BBC NEWS

The Ouest-France – Jean Marin Prize (written press) : Javier Espinosa EL MUNDO

The Lower Normandy Secondary School Students' : FRANCE 3 – Caroline Sinz, Christian De Carné, Salah Agrabi, Michelle Guilloiseau-Joubair

The Public Prize : Roger Lemoyne MACLEANS MAGAZINE/REDUX PICTURES/ALEXIA FUNDATION

2006

Written press: Jon STEPHENSON – METRO

Photo: Jaafar ASHTIYEH – AFP

Television: Neil CONNERY – ITN-ITV NEWS

Radio: Alex LAST – BBC NEWS

The Ouest-France – Jean Marin Prize (written press): Javier ESPINOSA EL MUNDO

The Lower Normandy Secondary School Students': Jeff KOINANGE CNN

The Public Prize: Tomas VAN HOUTRYVE FREELANCE

2007

Written press: Adrien JAULMES LA REVUE DES DEUX MONDES / LE FIGARO

Photo: Mahmud HAMS AFP

Television: Alastair LEITHEAD BBC NEWS

Radio: Angus CRAWFORD BBC NEWS

The Ouest-France – Jean Marin Prize (written press): Benjamin BARTHE LE MONDE

The Lower Normandy Secondary School Students': Orla GUERIN BBC NEWS

The Public Prize: Mahmud HAMS AFP

Young reporter: Anne GUION – LA VIE

2008

Written press: Elizabeth RUBIN – THE NEW YORK TIMES MAGAZINE

Photo: Balazs GARDI – VII Network

Television: Dominique DERDA – FRANCE 2

Radio: Mike THOMSON – BBC NEWS

Young reporter: Julius MWELU – IRIN

Lower Normandy Secondary School Students': Dominique DERDA – FRANCE 2

Ouest-France – Jean Marin Prize : Anne GUION – LA VIE

Public Prize: Yasuyoshi CHIBA – AFP

Indicates a separate entry.

2009

Written press: Christina LAMB – THE SUNDAY TIMES

Photo: Walter ASTRADA – AFP

Television: Paul COMITI – TF1

Radio: Tim FRANKS – BBC NEWS

Grand Format Television: Jeremy BOWEN – BBC NEWS

Young reporter: Mohamed DAHIR – AFP

Lower Normandy Secondary School Students' Prize : Paul COMITI – TF1

Ouest-France – Jean Marin Prize : Célia Mercier – XXI

Public Prize: Jérôme DELAY – ASSOCIATED PRESS

2010

Written press: Christophe Boltanski – Le Nouvel Observateur

Photo: Véronique de Viguerie – Paris Match / Getty Images

Television: Danfung Dennis – PBS

Radio: Florence Lozach – Europe 1

Grand Format Television: Gilles Jacquier – France 2

Young reporter: Miles Amoore – The Sunday Times

Lower Normandy Secondary School Students' Prize: Danfung Dennis – PBS

Ouest-France – Jean Marin Prize: Mélanis Bois – Elle

Public Prize: Véronique de Viguerie – Paris Match / Getty Images

2011

Written press: Jon Stephenson – Metro magazine

Photo: Yuri Kozyrev – NOOR

Television: Alex Crawford – SKY NEWS

Radio: Etienne Monin – France Info

Grand Format Television: Vaughan Smith – Frontline Club

Web journalism: Zoé Lamazou, Sarah Leduc – France 24

Young reporter: Sara Hussein – AFP

Lower Normandy Secondary School Students' Prize: Alex Crawford – SKY NEWS

Ouest-France – Jean Marin Prize: Mariana Grépinet – Paris Match

Public Prize: Yuri Kozyrev – NOOR

2012

Written press: Javier ESPINOSA – EL MUNDO

Photo: Aris MESSINIS – AFP

Television: Nic ROBERTSON – CNN

Radio: Jeremy BOWEN – BBC NEWS

Grand Format Television: Mathieu MABIN – FRANCE 24

Young reporter: Ed OU – Reportage by Getty Images

Web journalism: David Wood – Huffington Post

Lower Normandy Secondary School Students' Prize: Mathieu MABIN – FRANCE 24

Ouest-France – Jean Marin Prize: Rémy OURDAN – LE MONDE

Public Prize: Manu BRABO – ASSOCIATED PRESS

2013

Written press: Jean-Philippe REMY* – LE MONDE

Photo: Fabio BUCCIARELLI – AFP

Television: Sophie NIVELLE-CARDINALE – TF1

Radio: Marine OLIVESI – CBC

Grand Format Television: Ben ANDERSON – BBC

Young reporter: Florentin CASSONNET – XXI

Web journalism: Laurent VAN DER STOCKT et Jean-Philippe REMY – LE MONDE

Lower Normandy Secondary School Students' Prize: Sophie NIVELLE-CARDINALE – TF1

Ouest-France – Jean Marin Prize: Wolfgang BAUER – Die Zeit

Public Prize: Javier MANZANO – AFP

Selected Bibliography

A

Adie, Kate. *The Kindness of Strangers: The Autobiography.* London: Headline, 2002.

Alldritt, Keith. *Churchill, the Writer: His Life as a Man of Letters.* London: Hutchinson, 1992.

Andrews, J. Cutler. *The North Reports the Civil War.* Pittsburgh: University of Pittsburgh Press, 1955.

The South Reports the Civil War. Princeton: Princeton University Press, 1970.

Arnot, Charles P. *Don't Kill the Messenger: The Tragic Story of Welles Hangen and Other Journalistic Combat Victims.* New York: Vantage Press, 1994.

Attacks on the Press. A Worldwide Survey by the Committee to Protect Journalists. New York: Committee to Protect Journalists, 2009.

Ayers, Chris. *War Reporting for Cowards: Between Iraq and a Hard Place.* London: Murray, 2005.

Ayerst, David. *The Manchester Guardian: Biography of a Newspaper.* Ithaca, New York: Cornell University Press, 1971.

B

Baillie, Hugh. *Two Battlefronts.* New York: United Press Association, 1943.

Bangert, Christoph. *War Porn.* Berlin: Kehrer Verlag, 2014.

Beckett, Ian F. W. *The War Correspondents: The American Civil War.* Dover, N.H.: Alan Sutton Publishing, 1993.

Beevor, Anthony and Luba Vinogradova. *A Writer at War: Vasily Grossman with the Red Army, 1941-1945.* London: Pimlico Books, 2014

Bell, Martin. *Through Gates of Fire: A Journey into World Disorder.* London: Phoenix, 2004.

Bentley, Nicolas, ed. *Russell's Despatches from the Crimea, 1854-1856.* New York: Hill and Wang, 1967.

Breaking News: How the Associated Press Has Covered War, Peace, and Everything Else. New York: Princeton Architectural Press, 2007.

Brown, Charles H. *The Correspondents' War: Journalists in the Spanish-American War.* New York: Charles Scribner's Sons, 1967.

Browne, Malcolm. W. *Muddy Boots and Red Socks: A War Reporter's Life.* New York: Random House, 1993.

Brownlow, Kevin. *The War, the West and the Wilderness.* New York: Knopf, 1979.

Bullard, F. Lauriston. *Famous War Correspondents.* Boston: Little, Brown and Co., 1914.

C

Campbell, W. Joseph. *Yellow Journalism: Puncturing the Myths, Defining the Legacies.* Westport, CT: Praeger, 2001.

Carlebach, Michael L. *The Origins of Photojournalism in America.* Washington, D.C.: Smithsonian Institution, 1992.

Castellan, James W. and Ron van Dopperan. Eds. *American Cinematographers in the Great War, 1914-1918.* New Barnet, UK: John Libbey Publishing, 2015.

Churchill, Winston. *The Boer War: London to Ladysmith via Pretoria* and *Ian Hamilton's March.* First American ed. New York: W. W. Norton and Co., 1990.

Collier, Richard. *Fighting Words: The War Correspondents of World War Two.* New York: St. Martin's Press, 1989.

Cook, Jeffrey B. ed. *American World War II Correspondents,* Dictionary of Literary Biography 364, Gale Publishing, 2012

Cooper, Anderson. *Dispatches from the Edge.* New York: Harper, 2006.

Copeland, Fayette. *Kendall of the Picayune.* Norman: University of Oklahoma Press, 1943.

Crozier, Emmet. *American Reporters on the Western Front, 1914-18.* New York: Oxford University Press, 1959. *Yankee Reporters, 1861-65.* New York: Oxford University Press, 1956.

D

Deedes, W.F. *At War with Waugh: The Real Story of Scoop.* London: Pan, 2004.

Desmond, Robert W. *Crisis and Conflict: World News Reporting Between Two Wars, 1920-1940.* Iowa City: University of Iowa Press, 1982. *The Information Process: World News Reporting to the Twentieth Century.* Iowa City: University of Iowa Press, 1978. *Tides of War: World News Reporting, 1931-1945.* Iowa City: University of Iowa Press,. 1984. *Windows on the World: World News Reporting, 1900-1920.* Iowa City: University of Iowa Press, 1980.

Downs, Robert B., and Jane B. Downs. *Journalists of the United States.* Jefferson, N.C.: McFarland and Co., 1991.

Downton, Eric. *Wars Without End.* Toronto: Stoddart Publishing Co., 1987.

E

Edwards, Julia. *Women of the World: The Great Foreign Correspondents.* New York: Ballantine Books, 1989.

Elwood-Akers, Virginia. *Women War Correspondents in the Vietnam War, 1961-1975.* Metuchen, N.J.: Scarecrow Press, 1988.

Emery, Michael. *On the Front Lines: Following America's Foreign Correspondents Across the Twentieth Century.* Washington, D.C.: American University Press, 1995.

F

Farrar, Martin J. *News From the Front: War Correspondents on the Western Front 1914-1918.*Phoenix Mill: Sutton, 1998.

Farwell, Byron. *The Great Anglo-Boer War.* New York: Harper and Row, 1976.

Feinstein, Anthony. *Journalists under Fire: The Psychological Hazards of Covering War.* Baltimore: The Johns Hopkins Press, 2006 edition.

Ferrari, Michelle and James Tobin. *Reporting America at War: An Oral History.* New York: Hyperion, 2003.

Fewster, Kevin, ed. *Gallipoli Correspondent: The Frontline Diary of C. E. W. Bean.* Sydney: George Allen and Unwin, 1983.

Fialka, John J. *Hotel Warriors: Covering the Gulf War.* Baltimore: Johns Hopkins University Press, 1991.

Foerstel, Herbert N. *Killing the Messenger: Journalists at Risk in Modern Warfare.* Westport, CT: Praeger, 2006.

Fumeaux, Rupert. *News of War: Stories and Adventures of the Great War Correspondents.* London: Max Parrish, 1964.

G

Garrels, Anne. *Naked in Baghdad: The Iraq War as Seen by NPR's Correspondent.* New York: Picador, 2003

Gernsheim, Helmut, and Alison. *Roger Fenton: Photographer of the Crimean War.* New York: Arno Press, 1973.

Gilbertson, Ashley. *Bedrooms of the Fallen.* Chicago: University of Chicago Press, 2014

Glossop, Reginald. *Sunshine and Battle-Smoke: Reminiscnecs of a War Correspondent.* London: Brown, 1907.

Greenway, H.D.S. *Foreign Correspondent: A Memoir.* New York: Simon and Schuster, 2014

Gorrell, Henry T. *Soldier of the Press: Covering the Front in Europe and North Africa 1936-1943.* Columbia: University of Missouri Press, 2009.

Gould, Louis L., and Greffe, Richard. *Photojournalist: The Career of Jimmy Hare.* Austin: University of Texas Press, 977.

Grey, Elizabeth. *The Noise of Drums and Trumpets: W. H. Russell Reports from the rimea.* New York: Henry Z. Walck, 1971.

Griffiths, Dennis, ed. *The Encyclopedia of the British Press.* New York: St. Martin's Press, 1992.

H

Hallin, Daniel C. *The "Uncensored War": The Media and Vietnam.* New York: Oxford University Press, 1986.

Hamilton, Jim. *The Writing 69th: Civilian War Correspondents Accompany a U.S. Bombing Raid on Germany During World War II*, Green Harbor Press, 2005.

Hankinson, Alan. *Man of Wars: William Howard Russell of the "Times."* London: Heinemann Educational Books, 1982.

Harris, Brayton. *Blue & Gray in Black & White.* Washington, D.C.: Brassey's, 1999.

Hastings, Michael M. *I Lost My Love in Baghdad: A Modern War Story.* New York: Scribner's, 2008.

Haverstock, Nathan A. *Fifty Years to the Front: The Life of War Correspondent Frederick Palmer.* Washington, D.C.: Brassey's Inc, 1996.

Hendricks, King, and Irving Shepard, eds. *Jack London Reports.* Garden City, N.Y.: Doubleday and Co., 1970.

Hodgson, Pat. *Early War Photographs.* Boston: New York Graphic Society, 1974. *The War Illustrators.* New York: Macmillan Publishing Co., 1977.

Hohenberg, John. *Foreign Correspondence: The Great Foreign Correspondents and Their Times.* New York: Columbia University Press, 1964.

Hood, Robert E. *12 at War: Great Photographers Under Fire.* New York: G. P. Putnam's Sons, 1967.

Hooper, Jim. *Beneath the Visiting Moon: Images of Combat in Southern Africa.* Lexington, Mass.: Lexington Books, 1990.

Huddle, Mark. Ed. *Roi Ottley's World War II: The Lost Diary of an American Journalist.* Lawrence: University Press of Kansas, 2013.

Hudson, Miles and John Stainer. *War and the Media: A Random Searchlight.* Phoenix Mill: Sutton Publishing, 1998.

Hughes, Jim. *W. Eugene Smith, Shadow and Substance: The Life and Work of an American Photographer.* New York: McGraw-Hill Publishing Co., 1989.

J

James, Lawrence. *Crimea, 1854-56: The War with Russia from Contemporary Photographs.* New York: Van Nostrand Reinhold Co., 1981.

Johannsen, Robert W. *To the Halls of the Montezuma: The Mexican War in the American Imagination.* New York: Oxford University Press, 1985.

John, Angela V. *War, Journalism and the Shaping of the Twentieth Century: The Life and Times of Henry W. Nevinson.* London: I.B. Taurus, 2006.

K

Kapuscinki, Ryszard. *The Soccer War.* New York: Knopf, 1991.

Keim, de, B. Randolph. *Sheridan's Troopers on the Borders: A Winter Campaign on the Plains.* Lincoln: University of Nebraska Press, 1985.

Knight, Oliver. *Following the Indian Wars: The Story of the Newspaper Correspondents Among the Indian Campaigners.* Norman: University of Oklahoma Press, 1960.

Knightley, Phillip. The First Casualty: From the Crimea to Vietnam: The War Correspondent as Hero, Propagandist, and Myth Maker. New York: Harcourt Brace Jovanovich, 1975.

Korte, Barbara. *Represented Reporters: Images of War Correspondents in Memoirs and Fiction.* New Brunswick: Transaction Publishers, 2009.

L

Lambert, Andrew, and Stephen Badsey. *The War Correspondents: The Crimean War.* Dover, N. H.: Alan Sutton Publishing, 1994.

Lewinski, Jorge. *The Camera at War: A History of War Photography from 1848.* New York: Simon and Schuster, 1978.

Loyn, David. *Frontline: The True Story of the British Mavericks Who Changed the Face of War Reporting.* London: Michael Joseph, 2005.

Lubow, Arthur. *The Reporter Who Would Be King: A Biography of Richard Harding Davis.* New York: Charles Scribner's Sons, 1992.

M

Maslowski, Peter. *Armed with Cameras: The American Military Photographers of World War II.* New York: Free Press, 1993.

Matheson, Donald and Stuart Allan. *Digital War Reporting: Digital Media and Society Series.* Cambridge: Polity Press, 2009.

Mathews, Joseph J. *Reporting the Wars.* Minneapolis: University of Minnesota Press, 1957.

May, Antoinette. *Witness to War: A Biography of Marguerite Higgins.* New York: Beaufort Books, 1983.

McCullin, Don. *Unreasonable Behaviour: An Autobiography.* New York: Knopf, 1992.

McGurn, Barrett. Yank, *The Army Weekly: Reporting the Greatest Generation.* Golden, Colorado: Fulcrum Publishing, 2004.

McLaughlin, Greg. *The War Correspondent.* London: Pluto Press, 2002.

McNamara, John. *EXTRA! U.S. War Correspondents in Action.* Boston: Houghton Mifflin Co., 1945.

McNeely, Patricia C, Debra Reddin van Tuyll, and henry H. Schulte. *Knights of the Quill: Confederate Correspondents and their Civil War Reporting.* West Lafayette, Indiana: Purdue University Press, 2010.

Mercer, Derrik, Geoff Mungham, and Kevin Williams. *The Fog of War: The Media on the Battlefield.* London: William Heinemann Limited, 1987.

Miles, Hugh. Al Jazeera: *The Inside Story of the Arab News Channel that is Challenging the West.* New York: Grove Press, 2006.

Mills, Nick. *The Vietnam Experience: Combat Photographer.* Boston: Boston Publishing Co., 1983.

Milton, Joyce. *The Yellow Kids: Foreign Correspondents in the Heyday of Yellow Journalism.* New York: Harper and Row, 1989.

Moeller, Susan D. *Shooting War: Photography and the American Experience of Combat.* New York: Basic Books, 1989.

Monti, Nicolas, ed. *Africa Then: Photographs. 1840-1918.* New York: Knopf, 1987.

Moorcraft, Paul L. and Philip M. Taylor. *Shooting the Messenger: The Political Impact of War Reporting.* Washington, D.C.: Potomac Books, Inc., 2008.

Moore, Harold G. and Joe Galloway, *We were Soldiers Once ... and Young,* New York: Random House, 1992.

Morris, David J. *The Evil Hours: A Biography of Post-Traumatic Stress Disorder.* New York: Houghton Mifflin, 2015

Mrazkova, Daniela, and Vladimir Remes, eds. *The Russian War: 1941-1945.* New York: E. P. Dutton, 1975.

Mydans, Carl, and Shelley Mydans. *The Violent Peace.* New York: Atheneum Press, 1968.

N

Neuman, Johanna. *Lights, Camera, War: Is Media Technology Driving International Politics?* New York: St. Martin's Press, 1996.

Nichols, David, ed. *Ernie's War: The Best of Ernie Pyle's World War Two Dispatches.* New York: Random House.

North, Don. *Inappropriate Conduct: A Mystery of a Disgraced War Reporter.* iUniverse, 2013

O

O'Connor, Richard. *The Spirit Soldiers: A Historical Narrative of the Boxer Rebellion.* New York: G. P. Putnam's Sons, 1973.

Oldfield, Colonel Barney. *Never a Shot in Anger.* 2d ed. Santa Barbara, Calif.: Capra Press, 1989.

Ostroff, Roberta. *Fire in the Wind: The Life of Dickey Chapelle.* New York: Ballantine Books, 1992.

O'Toole, G. J. A. *The Spanish War: An American Epic, 1898.* New York: W. W. Norton and Co., 1984.

P

Palmos, Frank. *Ridding the Devils.* Arrow Books, 1991.

Pelton, Robert Young. *The World's Most Dangerous Places,* 5th edition, New York: Harper Collins, 2003.

Persico, Joseph E. *Edward R. Murrow: An American Original.* New York: McGraw-Hill Publishing Co. 1988.

Politkovskaya, Anna. *Dirty War*. UK: Harvill Press, 2004.

Preston, Paul. *We Saw Spain Die: Foreign Correspondents in the Spanish Civil War*. New York: Skyhouse Publishing. 2009.

Price, Alan. *The End of the Age of Innocence: Edith Wharton and the First World War*. New York: St. Martin's Press, 1996.

Prior, Melton. *Campaigns of a War Correspondent*. London: Arnold, 1912.

Prochnau, William. *Once upon a Distant War*. New York: Random House, 1995.

R

Rand, Peter. *China Hands: The Adventures and Ordeals of the American Journalists Who Joined Forces with the Great Chinese Revolution*. New York: Simon and Schuster, 1995.

Ray, Frederic E. *"Our Special Artist": Alfred R. Waud's Civil War*. 2d ed. Mechanicsburg, Pa.: Stackpole Books, 1994.

Read, Donald. *The Power of News: The History of Reuters*. New York: Oxford University Press, 1992.

Reed, John. *Insurgent Mexico*. New York: Simon and Schuster, 1969.

Reilly, Tom. *War with Mexico!: American Reporters Cover the Battlefront*, edited by Manley Witten. Lawrence: University of Kansas Press, 2010.

Reporting Vietnam, Part One: American Journalism 1959-1969. New York: Library of America, 1998.

Reporting Vietnam, Part Two: American Journalism 1969-1975. New York: Library of America, 1998.

Reporting World War II, Part One: American Journalism 1938-1944. New York: Library of America, 1995.

Reporting World War II, Part Two: American Journalism 1944-1946. New York: Library of America, 1995.

Riess, Curt, ed. *They Were There: The Story of World War II and How It Came About by America's foremost correspondents*. New York: Putnam, 1944.

Roeder, George H. *The Censored War: American Visual Experience During World War Two*. New Haven, CT.: Yale University Press, 1993.

Ross, Ishbel. *Ladies of the Press*. New York: Harper, 1974.

Royle, Trevor. *War Report: The War Correspondent's View of Battle from the Crimea to the Falklands*. London: Mainstream Publishing, 1987.

Russell, William Howard. *My Diary North and South*. 2d ed. New York: Harper and Brothers,1954.

S

Samuels, Peggy, and Harold Samuels. *Frederic Remington: A Biography*. Garden City, N.Y.: Doubleday and Co., 1982.

Sandweiss, Martha A., Rick Stewart, and Ben W. Huseman. *Eyewitness to War: Prints and Daguerreotypes of the Mexican War, 1846-1848*. Fort Worth, Tex.: Amon Carter Museum, 1989.

Sebba, Anne. *Battling for News: The Rise of the Woman Reporter*. London: Hodder and Stoughton, 1994.

Shadid, Anthony. *Night Draws Near: Iraq's People in the Shadow of America's War*. UK: Picador Books, 2006.

Shinn, Bill. *The Forgotten War Remembered, Korea 1950-1953: A War Correspondent's Notebook & Today's Danger in Korea*. Elizabeth, NJ: Hollym International Corporation, 1996.

Sibbald, Raymond. *The War Correspondents: The Boer War*. Dover, N. H.: Alan Sutton Publishing, 1993.

Sifakis, Stewart. *Who Was Who in the Civil War*. New York: Facts on File, 1988.

Simpson, John. *News from No Man's Land: Reporting the World*. London: Macmillan, 2002.

Simpson, John. *The Wars against Saddam Hussein: Taking the Hard Road to Baghdad*. London: MacMillan, 2003.

Skiba, Katherine M. *Sister in the Band of Brothers: Embedded with the 101st Airborne in Iraq*. Lawrence: University Press of Kansas, 2005.

Smart, James G. *A Radical View: The "Agate" Dispatches of Whitelaw Reid, 1861-1865*. Memphis, Tenn.: Memphis State University Press, 1976.

Snow, Jon. *Shooting History: A Personal Journey*. London: Harper Collins, 2004.

Solnit, Rebecca. *River of Shadows: Eadweard Muybridge and the Technological Wild West*. New York: Viking, 2003.

Sorel, Nancy Caldwell. *The Women Who Wrote the War*. New York: Arcade Publishing, 1999.

Starr, Louis M. *Bohemian Brigade: Civil War Newsmen in Action*. New York: Knopf, 1954.

Stavisky, Samuel. *Marine Combat Correspondent: World War II in the Pacific*. New York: Ivy Books, 1999.

Steele, Jon. *War Junkie: One Man's Addiction to the Worst Places on Earth*. Kindle, 2002.

Stein, M. L. *Under Fire: The Story of American War Correspondents*. New York: Julian Messner, 1968.

Stern, Philip Van Doren. *They Were There: The Civil War As Seen by Its Combat Artists*. New York: Crown Publishers, 1959.

Stewart, Ian. *Ambushed: A War Reporter's Life on the Line*. Chapel Hill: NC: Algonquin Books, 2002

Suid. Lawrence H. Guts and Glory: Great American War Movies. Reading, MA: Addison-Wesley Publishing, 1978.

Sunday Times of London Insight Team. *War in the Falklands: The Full Story*. New York: Harper and Row, 1982.

Sweeney, Michael S. *The Military and the Press: An Uneasy Truce*. Evanston, Illinois: Northwestern University Press, 2006.

T

Thompson, W. Fletcher, Jr. *The Image of War: The Pictorial Reporting of the American Civil War*. New York: A. S. Barnes Co., 1959.

Tolstoy, Leo. *Sebastopol*. Ann Arbor: University of Michigan Press, 1961.

Tuohy, William. *Dangerous Company: Inside the World's Hottest Trouble Spots with a Pulitzer Prize-Winning War Correspondent*. New York: William Morrow and Co., 1987.

V

Vanderwood, Paul J., and Frank N. Samponara. *Border Fury: A Picture Postcard Record of Mexico's Revolution and U.S. War Preparedness, 1900-1917*. Albuquerque: University of New Mexico Press, 1988.

Villiers, Frederic. *Port Arthur: Three Months with the Besiegers: A Diurnal of Occurrents*. London: Longman's, 1905.

Villiers, Frederic. *Villiers: His Two Decades of Adventures*. 2 vols. London: Hutchinson, 1921.

Voss, Frederick S. *Reporting the War: The Journalistic Coverage of World War II*. Washington, D.C.: Smithsonian Institution, 1994.

W

Wade, Betsy, ed. *Forward Positions: The War Correspondence of Homer Bigart*. Fayetteville: University of Arkansas Press, 1992.

Wagner, Lilya. *Women War Correspondents of World War Two*. Westport, CT.: Greenwood Press, 1989.

Walker, Dale L. *Januarius MacGahan: The Life and Campaigns of an American War Correspondent*. Athens: Ohio University Press, 1988.

Waugh, Evelyn. Scoop. London: Chapman and Hall. (1938; 1964 edition.)

Waugh, Evelyn. *Waugh in Abyssinia*. London: Metheun, (1936; 1984 edition).

Weisberger, Bernard A. *Reporters for the Union*. Boston: Little, Brown, and Co., 1953. Weithas, Art. *Close to Glory*. Austin, Tex.: Eakin Press, 1991.

Whelan, Richard. *Robert Capa: A Biography*. New York: Random House, 1985.

White, William, ed. *By Line: Ernest Hemingway*. New York: Charles Scribner's Sons, 1967.

Wilkinson-Latham, Robert. *From Our Special Correspondent: Victorian War Correspondents and Their Campaigns*. London: Hodder and Stoughton, 1979.

Woods, Oliver, and James Bishop. *The Story of THE TIMES*. London: Michael Joseph Limited, 1983.

Wyatt, Clarence R. *Paper Soldiers: The American Press and the Vietnam War*. New York: W. W. Norton and Co., 1993.

Wyden, Peter. *The Passionate War: The Narrative History of the Spanish Civil War*. New York: Simon and Schuster, 1983

Index

A

ABC, 19, 48, 76, 89, 167, 187, 289, 332, 350, 399, 401

Abend, Hallett Edward, 1

Abkey, Sheikh Nur Mohamed, 1

Abrams, Alexander St. Clair, 1–2

Abu Klea, Battle of, 53, 274

Abu Kru, Battle of, 53, 59, 166, 274, 378

Abyssinian War. See Ethiopian War accreditation system

Active Service, 2

Adams, Edward "Eddie" T., 2

Adan, Barkhad Awale, 2

Addario, Lynsey, 3

Adie, Kate, 3

Adler, Martin, 3–4

Afghanistan, 21st century war, 4, 5, 8, 13, 85, 112, 119, 124, 165, 167, 168, 170, 187, 265, 331, 333, 408

Africa, 42, 54, 73, 106, 213

"Agate." See Reid, Whitelaw

Ahmad, Sardar, 4

Ahmed, Abdulkadir, 4

Al-Deeri, Mahran, 4

Aldrich, Thomas Bailey, 4–5

Aleutians campaign, 27, 233

Alexander, Peter Wellington, 52, 94

Al-Jabar, Ali Hassan, 5

Al Jazeera, 4, 5–6, 251, 262, 308

Allen, Jay, 6

Allen, Laurence Edmund, 6–7

Allis, Sebastian Albert Dutton, 7

Alpert, Max, 7

Alpi, Illaria, 7

Alqasim, Mohammed, 8

Al-Sayed, Basil, 8

Amanpour, Christiane, 8

American Civil War, 8–10, 46, 48, 75, 94, 127, 139, 221, 300, 315, 333; and Bohemian Brigade, 39; hostility to press, 9–10

American Indian Wars, 11–12, 88, 140, 176, 190, 205, 343, 352, 353

American Star, 14, 276

Amery, Leopold Charles Maurice Stennett, 12

Amin, Idi, 103

Anannin, Mikhail, 12

Anderson, Finley, 12–13

Anderson, John R. L., 13

Anderson, Jon lee, 13

Anderson, Scott, 13

Anglo-Saxon Press, 13–14, 233, 364

Angly, Edward, 14

Ap Bac, battle, 325

Aquino, Jr., Benigno Simeon "Ninoy" , 14

Arab-Israeli Six Day War, 104, 205, 207, 314, 325

Archibald, James Francis Jewell, 14–15

Armit, R. H., 15

Army and Navy Gazette, 310, 365

Army and Navy Journal, 68

Army of the Potomac, and censorship, 10, 356

Army Signal Corps, 200, 349, 385

Arnett, Peter, 15–16, 150, 306

Arnot, Charles P., 16

artist-correspondents, 16–18, 286, 317–18, 377–78, 384, 389; techniques of Edwin Forbes, 126

Ashanti War, 152, 165, 204, 286, 292

Ashmead-Bartlett, Ellis, 18, 127, 311

Asmi, Rami. See El Dous, Yousef

Aspell, Thomas Francis "Tom", 18–19

Associated Press (AP), 19

Associated Press Television News (APTN), 135, 241

Atkins, John Black, 19–20

Atkinson, George, 20

Atlanta Campaign, 2

Atwell, H. Wallace, 20

Aultman, Otis A., 21

Ault, Philip H., 20–21

Austin, Alexander Berry, 21

Australian war journalists, 25, 28–29, 48, 89, 243, 280, 382

Austro-Hungarian Empire, and first postal card, 279

Austro-Italian War, 21

Austro-Piedmont War. See Austro-Italian War

Austro-Prussian War, 21–22

Axe, David, 22

Axelsson, George, 22

Ayers, Chris, 22

Aylward, William James, 22

B

Bagby, George W., 23

"Baghdad Pete," 15

Baillie, Hugh, 23

Bajbouj, Atallah, 24

Baker, George, 24, 408

Balaklava, Battle of. See Charge of the Light Brigade

Baldwin, Hanson W., 24

Baldwin, Herbert, 24

Balibo, 24–25

Balkan Affairs, 41, 54

Balkan War of 1912-1913, 24, 26, 40, 79, 139, 143, 227, 268, 278, 378

balloon service, 202, in siege of Metz, 304; in siege of Paris, 203

Baltermans, Dmitri, 25

Bang Bang Club, 25

Bangert, Christoph, 25
Bangladeshi war, 105
"Banjo." *See* Paterson, Andrew Barton
Barber, Noel, 25
Barber, Wilfred C., 26
Baring, Maurice, 26
Barnard, George N., 26
Barnes, Ralph W., 26–27
Bartholomew, Frank Harmon, 27
Barzini, Luigi, 27
Bass, John Foster, 28
"Battle fog" policy, 28
Bayeux-Calvados War Correspondents Awards, 28
BBC Effect. *See* CNN Effect
Bean, Charles Edwin Woodrow, 28–29
Beato, Felice A., 29, 303
Beattie, Jr., Edward W., 29–30
Beatty, Elizabeth Mary "Bessie", 30
Beech, Keyes, 30; and Georgie Anne Geyer, 137; and
      Marguerite Higgins, 168–70
Belden, Jack, 30–31
Bell, Martin, 31
Bengali prisoners, execution of, 300, 369
Benjamin, Anna Northend, 31–32
Bennett, James Gordon, 32, 176, 190, 221, 270, 379
Bennett, Jr., James Gordon, 32
Bennett, Lowell, 32–33
Benson, Eugene, 33
Bentley, Henry, 33
Berlin Congress of 1878, 93, 381
Berlin, fall of, 145, 369
Bernstein, Walter, 33
Berry, Ian, 33–34
Bewley, Cyril, 34
Biafran War, 58
Bickham, William Denison, 34
Bicycles, 34, 378
Biddle, George, 34–35
Bigart, Homer, 35; and Marguerite Higgins, 169
Bigelow, Poultney, 35
"Bill Dadd the Scribe." *See* Atwell, H. Wallace
Billman, Howbert, 35–36
Biograph Company, 38, 255
Birch, Michael, 36
Bismarck, battleship, 299
Black and White, 38, 51–52
"Black Hawk Down" incident, Somalia, 389
Black war correspondent, 200
Blair, Eric Arthur, 36
Blitz. *See* London Blitz
Bloemfontein Friend. See Friend, The
Blogger, 251
Bloom, David, 36
Blundey, David, 37
Bodman, Albert, 37
Boer War, 12, 37–38, 52, 130, 140, 184, 203, 219, 225, 409
Boer War siege newspapers, 38, 274

Boettcher, Mike, 38
Bogart, Robert D., 38–39
Bohemian Brigade, 39, 176
Bohrod, Aaron, 41
Bonsal, Stephen, 41–42
Boot camp for reporters, 179
Borthwick, Jessica Elvira, 40
Bosnian War. *See* Yugoslavian conflict
Boss, Gerard William, 40–41
Boulat, Alexandra, 41
Bourchier, James David, 41–42
Bourke-White, Margaret, 42
Bowen, Jeremy, 42
Bowlby, Thomas William, 43
Boxer Rebellion, 43
Boyle, Frederick, 43
Brabazon, James Martin, 44
Brackenbury, Charles Booth, 44
Brady, Mathew B., 44–45, 309, 383
Bragg, General Braxton, 10, 126, 139, 212, 224, 294, 321
Brand, Max. *See* Faust, Frederick
Breckinridge, Mary Marvin, 45–46
Brigham, Charles D., 46–47
Brines, Russell, 47
British Broadcasting Company (BBC), 3, 100, 185, 200,
      308, 331, 382, 399
British Mutoscope, 255
Brodie, Howard, 47, 243
Broun, Heywood, 47, 299
Brown, Cecil, 48
Brown, John: hanging of, 155; interview with, 293
Brown, Stephen R., 48
Browne, Junius Henri, 48–49, 300
Browne, Malcolm W., 49
Bryan, Ann, 49–50
Bryant, Louise, and John Reed, 293
Bryson, George Eugene, 50
Buckley, Christopher, 50
Bugbee, Charles "Charley", 50–51
"Bugbee Express". *See* Bugbee, Charles "Charley"
Bulgarian atrocities, 51; and Januarius MacGahan, 221
Bull, Rene, 51–52
Bull Run, First Battle of, 206, 218, 268, 291, 310, 326, 345,
      379, 389, 409
Bunker, William Mitchell, 52
Burchett, Wilfred, 52–53
Burke, John, 53
Burleigh, Bennet, 53–54
Burma, 247
Burma campaign (WWII), 50, 96, 251, 305, 319
Burma, War of 1852, 383
Burns, George, 54
Burns, John Fisher, 54
Burroughs, Edgar Rice, 55
Burrows, Larry, 55
Burton, James, 55
Buschemi, John, 55

Bush, Asahel "Ace", 55–56
Byington, Aaron Homer, 56
Bylines, and UPI, 371

C

Cadwallader, Sylvanus, 57
Cagnoni, Romano, 57–58
Caldwell, Erskine, 58
Caledonian, ship, 12
Callahan, Charles, 58
calotype process, 383
Cambodia, 122–23, 194, 239, 282, 317, 351, 376
Cameron, James, 58–59; and Bert Hardy, 158, 173
Cameron, John Alexander, 59, 232
Campbell, Archibald Doon, 59–60, 299
Campbell, Gerald Fitzgerald, 60
Cannon, James Monroe III, 60
Cantlie, John, 60–61
"C.A.P." *See* Page, Charles Anderson
Capa, Cornell, 61
Capa, Robert, 61–62, 92, 93
Captain Jack, interview with, 127
Caputo, Philip, 62
"Carleton." *See* Coffin, Charles Carleton
Carpensian, Mile, 62
Carpenter, Iris, 62–63
carrier pigeons, 63, 129
Carson, Lee, 354
Cartier-Bresson, Henri, 63–64
cartoonists, 24, 229, 252
Casey, Robert Joseph, 64
Cassidy, Henry C., 64
Caucasus conflict, 1990s, 142, 193
Cave, Peter, 64
CBS, 73, 81, 105, 150, 161, 170, 188, 196, 200, 209, 215,
    223, 248, 281, 290, 322, 328, 329, 335, 349, 351, 364,
    376
censorship, and American Civil War, 296; and Boer War,
    300; and frontal nudity, 372; and Grenada invasion, 151;
    and Gulf War, 151; and Korean War, 200; Office of Cen-
    sorship, 284; and Russo-Japanese War, 159, 215, 311;
    and World War I, 18, 65, 115, 181, 385; and World War
    II, 122, 256, 386, 390, 407; and Yom Kippur War, 150
Chancellorsville, Battle of, 83
Chandler, Edmund, 64–65
"Chaparral." *See* Peoples, John H. "Chapelle"
Chapelle, Georgette "Dickey", 65–66
Chapman, Frank C., 66
Charge of the Light Brigade, 80, 84, 112, 310
Chateau-Thierry, Battle of, 186, 237, 246, 401
Chauvel, Patrick, 66
Chechen conflict, 66, 142, 257, 320
Chenery, Thomas, 66
Chester, Thomas Morris, 67
Chetwyd-Talbot, John, 67
Chickamauga campaign, 294, 324

Chile Civil War, 108
"Chim." *See* Seymour, David
China, 52
China Hands, 67
Chinese Civil War, 332, 338
Chinese-Japanese War, and newsreels, 255
Chinese Revolution, 53
Christy, Howard Chandler, 67–68
Church, William Conant "Pierrepont," 68
Churchill, Sir Winston Leonard Spencer, 12, 68–69, 120
Churubusco, Battle of, and capture of San Patricio
    battalion, 191
cinematograph camera, 378
Civil War. *See* American Civil War
Clapper, Raymond Lewis, 69
Clark, Gregory, 69
Clark, Willis Gaylord, 69–70
Clarke, Sir Basil, 70
Clarke, Thomas, 70
Clifford, Alexander Graeme, 70
CNN, 15, 150, 306, 382–83
CNN Effect, 70
Cobb, Irvin Shrewsbury, 71
Cockburn, Claud, 71
Coffin, Charles Carleton, 71–72
Colburn, Robert T., 72
Cold War correspondents, 52, 171, 234
Cole, Carolyn, 72–73
Coleman, Kit. *See* Watkins, Kathleen "Kit" Blake
Collingwood, Charles Cummings, 73, 196
Collins, Robert Moore, 73
Coltman, Robert, 73
Colvin, Marie Catherine, 73–74
Committee to Protect Journalists (CPJ), 74, 179
concentration camps, liberation of, 169, 237, 306, 354
Confederate Press Association, 74–75, 337
Congo conflict (1961), 34, 116, 154, 169–70, 173–74, 293,
    319, 360
Conniff, Frank, 75
Cook, George S., 75
Cooke, George Wingrove, 75
Cooke, John Esten, 75–76
Cooper, Anderson Hays, 76
Cooper, James Lees, 76
Cooper, Robert Wright "Bob," 76
"Cora Montgomery." *See* Storms, Jane McManus
Corregidor, siege of, 207
Courtenay, William ashmead, 76–77
Cowan, Ruth, 77–78
Cowles, Virginia, 78
Cox, Sir Geoffrey Sandford, 78
Coyne, Catherine, 78
Crane, Stephen, 2, 78–79, 158, 359, 404
Crapsey, Edward, 10
Crawford, Kenneth Gale, 79
Crawfurd-Price, Walter, 79
Crazy Horse, 261, 353

Creelman, James, 79–80
Crimean War, 16, 66, 80–81, 385
Crockett, Edward Harry, 81
Croft, Steve, 81
Croix de Guerre, 7
Cromie, Robert, 81–82
Cronkite, Jr., Walter Leland, 82
Crook, General George C., 88, 120, 205, 223, 353, 388
Crosby, Charles E., 82
Cross, Henry, 82
Crost, Lyn, 82–83
Crounse, Lorenzo L., 83
Crowe, Sir Joseph Archer, 83–84
Crozier, Emmet, 84
Cuban affairs, 35, 50
"Cuban Girl Martyr," 50
Cuban Insurrection, 144, 175, 292, 320, 339
Cunningham, Alfred, 84
Cunningham, Ed, 84
Curtis, Peter Theo, 85
Custer, General George Armstrong, Little Big Horn
    debacle, 91, 99, 191, 205, 216, 261
Cutuli, Maria Grazia, 85

D

daguerreotype, 86, 233
Damon, Arwa, 86
Daniel, John Moncure, 87
Daniell, Tania Long, 87
Da Ponte, Durant, 87
Dardanelles campaign, 18, 254, 285, 356
Darnton, Byron, 88
Das Schwarze Korps (The Black Corps), 88
Davenport, Reuben Briggs, 88–89
Davies, Charles Maurice, 89
Davis, Elmer, 89
Davis, Neil, 89
Davis, Oscar King, 89
Davis, Richard Harding, 89–91; The Derelict, 98; and
    Frederic Remington, 296
Davis, Theodore Russell, 91
Dawson, Albert Knox, 91
Day, Samuel Phillips, 91–92
D-Day Invasion, 55, 61, 76, 100, 144, 241, 351, 399
Dean, Teresa Howard, 92
"Death in Dacca" photograph, 205
"Death of a Loyalist Soldier," 92–93
De Blowitz, Henri Stefan Opper, 93
Deedes, William Frances, 93–94
Deepe, Beverly, 94
De Fontaine, Felix Gregory, 94–95
Delahaye, Luc, 95
Della Casa, Nick, 95
Della Casas, Rosanna. See Della Casa, Nick
Della Gattina, Ferdinando Petruccelli, 95–96
De Luce, Daniel, 96

De Monfried, Henri, 96
DeMorse, Charles, 96–97
Denny, Harold Norman, 97
Depardon, Raymond, 97
"Derelict, The," 98
De St. Jorre, John, 98, 126
Deuell, Peggy Hull. See Hull, Peggy
Diament, Rafail, 98
Dicey, Edward James Stephen, 98
Dickenson, Edith Charlotte Musgrave, 98–99
Dickson, W.K.L., 255
Diehl, Charles Sanford, 99
Diem, Ngo Dinh, 49, 95
Dien Bien Phu, Battle of, and Bernard Fall, 117, 169, 355
Dieppe raid, 247, 254
Di Giovanni, Janine, 99
Dillon, Emile Joseph, 100
Dimbleby, Richard, 100
Dinwiddie, William, 100–01
Disher, Leo S., 101
Dispatch News Service, and My Lai, 349
Dixie, Lady Florence Caroline, 101
Dobson, George, 101–02
Dominican crisis, 358
"Don Carlos." See Crosby, Charles E.
Dong Xoai, Battle of, 116
Donohoe, Martin, 102
Dorr, Rheta Childe, 102
Dos Passos, John Roderigo, 102–03
Dowling, James Graham, 103
Downing, John, 103
Downs, Jr., William Randall "Bill", 103–04
Downton, Eric, 104
Doyle, Sir Arthur Conan, 104–05
Dozier, Kimberly, 105
Dring, Simon, 105
Dubois, Jules, 106
Dufka, Corinne, 106
Duncan, David Douglas, 106–07
Dunn, Harvey Thomas, 107
Dunn, William J., 107–08
Dunning, John P., 108
Du Pont, Ghislaine, 108
Duranty, Walter, 108–09
Durborough, Wilbur H., 109
Durivage, John "Jack" E., 109

E

Eastman Kodak Company, and picture postcards, 279
Edison Company, and Spanish-American War, 255
Edwards, Henry Sutherland, 110
Egan, Martin, 110
Eggers, Kurt, 110
Ehrenburg, Ilya, 111
Eisenhower, General Dwight, and Patton slapping
    incident, 273

El Alamein, Battle of, 182, 321, 349
El Caney, Battle of, 14, 35, 55, and James Creelman, 80, 292
El Dous, Yousef, 111
Eliot, Richard Smith, 111–12
El Salvadoran War, 81, 229
Embedded Journalists, 112
Emeny, Stuart, 112
Emerson, Gloria, 112–13
Engel, Richard, 113
Esper, George, 113
Ethiopian War, 113–14, 319
Evangelina , 50
"Eye-Witness," 115, 402

F

Faas, Horst, 116
Falklands War, 116–17; and Max Hastings, 161
Fall, Bernard, 117
Fallaci, Oriana, 117–18
Faust, Frederick, 118
Feinstein, Anthony, 118
Fenton, Roger, 118–19, 142, 383
Filkins, Dexter, 119
Fincastle, Viscount Alexander Edward Murray, 119–20
Finerty, John F., 120
Fiorillo, Luigi, 120
First Casualty, The, 120
Fisher, Philip D., 120–21
Fisk, Robert, 121
Fiske, Stephen Ryder, 121
Fitzgerald, Frances, 121
"Five O'Clock Follies," 121–22
Fleeson, Doris, 122
Fleischer, Jack, 122
Fletcher, Martin, 122
Fly, Camillus Sidney, 122–23
Flynn, Sean, 123, 246; and Timothy Page, 267, 384
Foa, Sylvana, 123–24
"Fog of War, The." See "Battle Fog" Policy
Foley, James Wright "Jim", 60, 124–25, 339
Forbes, Archibald, 125, 154, 212, 378
Forbes, Edwin, 125–26, 317
Forsyth, Fredrick, 126
Forsyth, John, 126–27
Fortescue, Granville Roland, 127
Fort Sumter, Battle of, 94
Fox, Edward, 127–28
Fox, Jr., John, 128
Franco, General Francisco, 22
Francois, Didier, 129
Franco-Prussian War, 17, 125, 128–29; And censorship, 155; new era in war reporting, 128
Fraser, David, 129
Freaner, James L., 129–30
Fredenthal, David, 130

Fredericksburg, Battle of, 76, 155
French Foreign Legion, 33, 261, 285
French Underground, and Dudley Anne Harmon, 160
Friedmann, Andre. See Capa, Robert
Friend, The, 130, 290, 293
Fripp, Charles Edwin, 130
"From Captain Tobin's Knapsack." See Tobin, J.G.H.
Frontline Club, 131
Frontline Television News Ltd., 95, 130–31, 186, 236, 274, 336, 394
Fuller, Sarah Margaret, 131
Furlong, Charles Wellington, 131–32
Furnas, Joseph Chamberlain "J.C.", 132
Fyfe, Henry Hamilton, 132

G

Gallagher, James Wesley "Wes," 133
Gallagher, O'Dowd "O. D.," 133–34; and Death of a Loyalist Soldier, 92
Gallenga, Antonio, 9, 134
Gallipoli campaign, 29, 310
Galloway, Joseph L., 134–35
"Galway." See Wilkie, Franc Bangs
Gandhi, Mahatma, assassination of, 325
Garanin, Anatoly, 135
Garcia-Navarro, Lourdes, 135
Gardner, Alexander, 135; and Mathew Brady, 44
Garibaldi's Red Shirts, 379
Garrels, Anne, 136
"Gath." See Townsend, George Alfred
Gellhorn, Martha, 136–37
General Order No. 98, American Civil War censorship, 326
Gerretsen, Chas, 137
Gettysburg, Battle of, 56, 295, 398
Geyer, Georgie Anne, 137
Ghost Dance troubles, 92, 296
Gibbes, Jr., Robert W., 137–38
Gibbons, Floyd, 138–39
Gibbons, Israel, 139
Gibbs, Sir Philip Armand Hamilton, 139
Gibney, Frank Bray, 139–40
Gilbertson, Ashley, 140
Giles, Geoffrey Douglas, 140
Gishu. Nakayama, 140
Glover, Ridgeway, 140–41
Godkin, Edwin Lawrence, 141
Goldenberg, Suzanne, 141–42
Goltz, Thomas, 142
Gomez, General Maximo, and Spanish-American War, 268, 291, 296
Goodall, Edward Angelo, 142
Goode, Sir William Athelstane Meredith, 142
Goose Green, and Falklands War, 117
Goralski, Robert Stanley, 142
Gorbatov, Boris, 143

Gordon Relief Expedition, 279, 284, 298, 397
Gore, Al, 143
Gore, William W. "Billy," 143
Gorrell, Henry T., 143–44
Goto, Kenji, 144
Gotto, Basil, 144
Govin, Charles, 144–45
Gowran, Clay, 145
Graham, George Edward, 145
Grant, General Ulysses S., 57, 66, 190, 264, 289, 356, 356, 409
Gravelotte, Battle of, 155
Grebnev, Viktor, 145
Greco-Turkish War, 2, 145–46, 404
Greek Civil War, 104
Greenway, H.D.S. "David", 146–47
Gregg, Josiah, 147
Grenada invasion, 146
Grepp, Gerda J. helland, 147–48
Griffiths, Philip Jones, 148
Grondjis, Lodewijk Hermen, 148–49
Gross, Gad Schuster, 149
Grossman, Vasily Semyonovich, 149
Gruneison, Charles Lewis, 149
Guadalcanal, Battle of, 103, 237, 367
Guernica, 149–50, 172, 347
Gulf War, 3, 15–16, 150–51, 207, 247
Gunfight at O.K. Corral, 122
Gwynne, Howell Arthur, 151–52

H

Haeberle, Ronald, 153
Haidari, Aziz Ullah, 153
Haile, Christopher Mason, 153–54
Halberstam, David, 154
Hall, Sydney Prior, 154–55
Halstead, Murat, 155
Hammerl, Anton Lazarus, 155–56
Hancock, Daniel Witt, 156
Hands, Charles E., 156
Hangen, Welles, 156
Harden, Edwin W., 156–57
Harding, George Matthews, 157
Hardman, Frederick, 157
Hardy, Albert "Bert," 58, 157–58, 173
Hare, James H. "Jimmy," 158–60
Harmon, Dudley Anne, 160
Harper, Fletcher, 160
Harper's Ferry, raid on, 175
Harris, Corra, 160
Harsch, Joseph C., 161
Harvest of Death, 161
Hastings, Macdonald, 161
Hastings, Max, 116, 161–62
Hastings, Michael Mahon, 162

Hatfield-McCoy feud, 79
Haviv, Ron, 162
Hearst, William Randolph, 162–63, 268; and yellow journalism, 408
Hedges, Chris, 163
Heinzerling, Lynn Louis, 163
heliograph service, at Ladysmith, 202
Hemingway, Ernest, 163–64, 341; and Martha Gellhom, 136
Hemment, John C., 164
Henry, William Seton "Guy", 164–65
Henty, George Alfred, 165
Herbaugh, Sharon, 165
Herbert, St. Leger Algernon, 165–66
Herbst, Josephine Frey, 166
Herr, Michael, 166
Hersey, John, 166; and "Death of a Loyalist Soldier," 92; and Melville Jacoby, 182, 394
Hersh, Seymour, 167
Hetherington, Timothy Alistair Telemachus "Tim", 167, 297, 298
Hibben, Paxton Pattison, 167
Hick's Pasha expedition, 260, 284, 321, 379
Hicks, Tyler, 168
Hiett, Helen, 168
Higgins, Marguerite, 168–70, 203
Hill, Gladwin, 170
Hill, James, 170
Hill, Russell, 170–71
Hillegas, Howard Clemens, 171
Hindus, Maurice Gerschon, 171; Hiroshima, 35, 53, 166
Holliman, John, 150
Hollingworth, Claire, 171–72
Holme, Christopher, 172
Homer, Winslow, 172
Hondros, Chris, 172–73
Honscheid, Johannes-Matthias, 173
Hood, battleship, 299
Hooper, Jim, 173
Hopkinson, Tom, 173–74
Horne, Walter H., 174, 279
Hottelet, Richard Curt, 174–75
House, Edward Howard, 175
Hovey, Graham, 175
Howard, Hubert, 175–76
Howard, James William "Phocion," 176
Howland, John Dare, 176
Hudson, Frederic, 176–77
Huet, Henri, 177
Hull, Peggy, 177–78
Hunt, Frazier "Spike," 178
Hurley, James Francis "Frank," 178
Huynh, Thanh My. See My, Huynh Thanh
Huynh, Ut Cong. See Ut, Huynh Cong
Huyshe, Wentworth, 178

I

"Imogene Carter." *See* Taylor, Cora
Inchon Landing, 169
Indian Mutiny, 303, 310
Indian Wars. *See* American Indian Wars
International News Service, 21, 122, 138, 175, 197, 207,
    332, 371, 381
Iraq War, 36, 54, 113, 119, 136, 179–80, 211, 215, 234, 238,
    242, 257, 262, 276, , 304, 323, 378, 382, 401, 408
Irvin, George Bede, 180
Irwin, Virginia, 180
Irwin, William Henry, 181
Isaq, Mohamed, 181
Islamic State (ISIS, ISIL), 181; and hostages, 60, 124, 144
Italian Wars of Independence, 95–96
Italo-Ethiopian War. *See* Ethiopian War
Iwo Jima, Battle of, 307, 348, 394–95
Izvestia, 25, 111, 281

J

Jaco, Charles, 306
Jacob, Alaric, 182
Jacoby, Melville, 182
Jacquier, Gilles, 182–83
Jagielski, Wojciech, 183
James, Edwin "Jimmy" L., 183–84
James, Jones, author, 391
James, Lionel, 184
Jarban, Ferzat, 184
Jeffries, Joseph M. N., 184–85
Jenks, Paul, 185
Jessica Lynch Hoax, 185
"Joan," 185
"Joe." *See* Wasson, Joe
"John of York." *See* Tobey, William C.
Johnson, Edd, 185–86
Johnson, Thomas M., 186
Johnston, Stanley, 186
Joint United States Public Affairs Office (JUSPAO), 121,
    248
Jones, Roderick, 186
Jouvenal, Peter, 186–87
Juma, Adam, 187
Junger, Sebastian, 187, 297, 298
Just, Ward, 187

K

Kahn, Ely Jacques "E. J.," 188
Kalischer, Peter, 188, 203
Kaltenborn, Hans V., 188
Kaplan, David, 188–89
"Kappa." *See* Timrod, Henry
Kapuscinski, Ryszard, 189
Karnow, Stanley, 189
Katyn massacre, 12

Kazickas, Jurate, 190
Keim, Randolph Debenneville, 190
Kellogg, Marcus Henry, 99, 191, 216, 217
"Mr. Kendall's Express," 191
Kendall, George Wilkins, 129, 153, 154, 191–92; and
    Francis Lumsden, 218
Kenichi, Kimura, 192
Kennan, George, 192
Kennedy, Edward, 192
Kent, Arthur, 306
Kerimov, Farkhad, 193
Kertesz, Andre, 193
Kessel, Dmitri, 193
Khaldei, Yevgeni, 193
Khe Sanh, siege of, 190, 368, 409
Kilgallin, James Lawrence, 193–94
Kilgore, Margaret, 194
Killing Fields, The, 194
Kingsley, Mary, 194
Kingston, William Beatty, 194–95
Kinnear, Alfred, 195
Kinross, Albert, 195
Kipling, Joseph Rudyard, 195, 212, 310, 378
Kirk, Donald, 195–96
Kirkpatrick, Helen, 196
Kirtland, Helen Johns, 196
Kitchener, Lord, 115, 152, 265, 347, 382, 397, 402, 405
Kluckholn, Frank, 196–97, 341
Klyan, Anatoly, 197
Knickerbocker, Hubert Renfre, 197
Knight, Edward Frederick, 198
Knight, Gary, 198
Knightley, Phillip: *First Casualty*, 120; on Hemingway's
    Spanish Civil War dispatches, 163
Knox, Thomas Wallace, 198–99
Kodak Box cameras, 199
Koestler, Arthur, 199
Kolenberg, Bernard, 199
Korean War, 23, 29, 30, 58, 106, 199–201
Korengal, 187
Kornelyuk, Igor, 201
Kosovo War. *See* Yugoslavian conflict
Krauss, Hansjoerg "Hansi", 201
Kriegpresseamt. *See* War Press Office
Kudoyarov, Boris, 201

L

Labouchere, Henry "Labby" Du Pre, 202
Ladysmith, siege of, 202, 219, 225, 254, 255, 274, 335, 347
Lamb, Christina, 202–03
Lambert, Tom, 203
Landells, Robert Thomas, 203
Landon, Percival, 203–04
Langham, Samuel F., 204
Laotian Civil war, 267
Lardner, David, 171, 204

Lardner, John Abbott, 204
Lardner, Ring, 204
Larrabee, Constance Stuart, 204–05
Lathrop, Barbour, 205
Latif, Andrees, 252
Laurent, Michel, 205
Lawless, Peter, 205
Lawley, Francis Charles, 205–06
Lawrence, William H., 206
Lawton, Kerem, 206
Lea, Tom, 206–07
Lebanon invasion. *See* "Battle fog" policy
Lebanon War, 35
Lederer, Edith M., 207
Ledru, Filippo, 207
Lee, Clark, 207
Le Hir, Georges, 207
Leningrad, siege of, 355, 367
Lepage, Camille, 208
Leroy, Catherine, 208
Lesage, Sir John Merry, 208–09
Leseuer, Laurence Edward, 209
Leslie, Frank, 209–10
Leslie, Jacques, 210
Leslie's Illustrated Newspaper. *See* Leslie, Frank
Leventhal, Richard Gary, 210
Lewis, Flora, 210
Lewis, George, 211
Lewis, Sir Wilmott Harsant, 211
Lexington, aircraft carrier, 186
Liberian conflict, 43, 72–73
Libyan Insurgency, 3, 5, 42, 74, 86, 124, 155, 167, 168, 173, 211
Liebling, Abbott Joseph "A. J.," 211
Liefde, Jacob B. de, 211–12
Life, 34, 39, 41, 46, 54, 57, 58, 61, 62, 106, 116, 130, 167, 169, 182, 193, 200, 206, 208, 244, 249, 250, 267, 276, 295, 305, 312, 323, 327, 329, 336, 341, 359, 376, 386, 392
Light That Failed, The, 212, 378
Lincoln conspirators, execution of, 135
Lindbaek, Lise, 212
Linebaugh, John H., 2, 212
Liohn, Andre, 212–13
Lipskerov, Georgei, 213
lithography, 16
Livingstone, David, 32, 170, 190, 344
Lloyd, Anthony, 213
Lloyd, James, 213
Lloyd, Terrence Ellis "Terry", 213–14
Lochner, Louis Paul, 214
Lochridge, Pat, 214
Logan, Lara, 215, 307
London Blitz, 254, 305
London, John "Jack," 159, 215–16
London Times: and Boer War, 37; and Russo-Japanese War, 184

Lone Charge of William B. Perkins, The, 404
Long, Huey, assassination of, 133
Long, Tania. *See* Daniell, Tania Long
Lorch, Donatella, 216
Loti, Pierre. *See* Viaud, Louis Marie
Lounsberry, Clement A., 191, 216–17
Lovie, Henri, 17, 217, 317
Lucas, James Griffing, 217–18
Lucknow, siege of, 29, 303
Lumley, Arthur, 218
Lumsden, Francis Asbury, 218
Lusitania, 160, 230
Lutfallah, Aswan, 218–19
Lyman, Ambrose William, 219
Lynch, Arthur Alfred, 219
Lynch, George, 219
Lynch, Jessica Hoax. *See* Jessica Lynch Hoax.

M

MacArthur, General Douglas, 107, 130, 132, 300, 306
MacCosh, John, 220
MacDonald, Roderick, 220
Maceda, Jim, 220–21
MacGahan, Januarius Aloysius, 51, 221
MacGowan, Gault, 221–22
MacHugh, Lieutenant-Colonel Robert Joseph, 222
"Mack." *See* McCullagh, Joseph Burbridge
MacKay, Charles, 222
MacKenzie, Frederick A., 222
MacMillan, Thomas C., 222–23
Mafeking, siege of, 223, 253, 272
"mafficking," 223
Magdala, capture of, 288, 343–44
Magnum Picture Agency, 34, 62, 95, 305, 323
Maine: and Randolph Hearst, 162, 164, 255, 292, 339; sinking of battleship, 48, 158, 320
Majuba Hill, Battle of, 59
Malaparte, Curzio. *See* Suckert, Kurt
Manila Bay, Battle of, 157, 229
Manning, Paul, 223
March of Time, newsreel, 255
Mariano, Ann Bryan. *See* Bryan, Ann
Marko, Dalia, 223–24
Maron, Karen, 224
Martin, Boutros, 224
Matabele War, 130, 175
Mathews, L. H., 224
Matthews, Herbert Lionel, 224–29
Maud, William Theobald, 225
Mauldin, Bill, 225–26
Mau Mau uprising, 104, 293
Mavroleon, Carlos, 226–27
Maxwell, Charles. *See* Della Casa, Nick.
Maxwell, Sir William, 227
McClanahan, John R., 227
McCoan, James Carlile, 227–28

McCormick, Frederick, 228
McCullagh, Francis, 228
McCullagh, Joseph Burbridge, 12, 228–29
McCullin, Donald, 229
McCurry, Steve, 229
McCutcheon, John Tinney, 229–30
McEvers, Kelly, 230
McGurn, William Barrett, 230
McIntosh, Burr William, 230–31
McKay, Alex, 231
McLaughlin, Kathleen, 231
McMillan, Richard D., 231
media manipulation: and Grenada, 146; and Gulf War, 150–51; Russo-Japanese War, 156, 159
Meisalas, Susan, 231–32
memorials to war correspondents, 232, 368
Merton, Arthur, 232–33
Metz, siege of, 125, 304
Mexican-American War, 7, 13, 32, 50–51, 58, 109, 111, 126, 129, 153, 164–65, 233, 263, 383, 410; and birth of modern war correspondent, 79–80, 128, 151–52, 175, 221, 222, 304, 315, 361, 374; and daguerreotypes, 86
Mexican Revolution, 21, 174; and American mobilization, 138, 158; and picture postcards, 174, 279
Mexico City Olympics, and killing of students, 118
Meyers, Georg N., 233–34
Middleton, Drew, 234
Middleton Henry J., 234
Milewicz, Waldemar, 234, 235
Military Assistance Command-Vietnam (MACV), 121, 377
military correspondents, 235
Millard's Review of the Far East, 235
Millard, Thomas Franklin Fairfax, 235
Miller, James, 236
Miller, Keith, 236
Miller, Lee, 236–37
Miller, Robert C., 237
Miller, Webb, 237
Millet, Francis Davis, 237–38
Moats, Alice-Leone, 238
Modoc War, 11, 20, 38, 52, 127, 231, 249, 332
Mohr, Charles, 238, 277, 376
Mohyeldin, Ayman, 238
Monitor and the Merrimac, Battle of, 46, 91
Monks, Noel, 239
Mons, retreat from, 132, 240
Montagu, Irving, 239
Montague, Evelyn A., 239
Monterrey, Battle of, 129, 154, 191
Moore, William Arthur, 240
Moore, William R., 240
Moorehead, Alan McRae, 240–41
Moreno de Mora, Miguel Gil, 241
Morgan, Wallace, 241
Morin, Relman "Pat," 241–42
Morris, Christopher, 242
Morris, David J., 242

Morris, Jr., Joe Alex, 242
Morrison, Chester, 242–43
Morrison, George Ernest, 243
Morrison, Ian F. M., 243
Morriss, Mack, 47, 243–44
Morse, Ralph, 244
Morton, Joseph, 244
Morton, Paul, 244–45
Mosler, Henry, 245
Mosley, Leonard Oswald, 245
Moth, Margaret, 246
Mother Jones, 151, 210, 313
Mowrer, Edgar Ansel, 246
Mowrer, Paul Scott, 246
Mtawe'e, zaher, 247
Mukden, Battle of, 27
Munday, William, 247
Munro, Ross, 247
Murphy, Caryle, 247
"Murrow Boys", 46, 104, 174–75
Murrow, Edward (Egbert) Roscoe, 196, 247–48, 332
Musgrove, Helen "Patches," 248
"Mustang." See Freaner, James L.
Mutual Film Corporation, 255
Muybridge, Eadweard, 248–49
My, Huynh Thanh, 249
Mydans, Carl, 249
Mydans, Shelley, 249–50
My Lai, massacre at, 153, 167

N

Nabaa Media Foundation, 251
Nabbous, Mohammed "Mo," 251
Nachtwey, James, 251
Nagai, Kenji, 251–52
Nanking, capture of, 346
Nasmyth, Charles, 252
Nasser, Maya, 252
Nast, Thomas, 210, 252
NBC, 113, 142, 168, 211, 332, 372–73
Neely, Bill, 253
Neil, Jr., Edward Joseph, 253
Neilly, Emerson, 253
Neuffer, Elizabeth, 253–54
Neuman, Johanna, 150
Neville, Robert, 254
Nevinson, Christopher Richard Wynne, 254
Nevinson, Henry Wood, 254
Newman, Henry, 298
newsreel cameramen, 177, 255
newsreel companies, 255–56, 361
Nez Perce campaign, 355
Nicaraguan conflict, 97; death of Dial Torgerson, 366; death of Bill Stewart, 350
Nicholls, Horace H., 256
Nichols, Francis Henry, 256

Nicholson, Michael, 257
"N'Importe." *See* Street, Albert
Nivat, Anne, 257–58
Nixon, John, 299
Noel, Frank E. "Pappy," 258
Noonan, Jr., Oliver, 258
Norris-Newman, Charles L. "Noggs," 258
Norton, Howard, 258–59

O

Ochlik, Remi, 260
O'Donovan, Edmund, 260, 284, 312
O'Kelly, James J., 261
Okinawa, Battle of, 65, 204, 287, 337
Oliphant, Laurence, 93, 261
Oliphant, Tom, 262
Omaar, rageh, 262
Omdurman, Battle of, 52, 54, 68, 82, 176, 199, 225, 227, 378, 397
O'Reilly, John "Tex," 262
Orwell, George. *See* Blair, Eric Arthur
Osbon, Bradley Sillick, 262–63
O'Shea, John Augustus, 263
Osman, William, 263
O'Sullivan, Timothy H., 263–64
Ottley, Roi, 264
Ourdan, Remy, 265
outlaw correspondents, 184, 265, 402

P

Pacific War Correspondents Association (PWCA), 266, 368, 393
Packard, Eleanor, 266
Packard, Reynolds, 266–67
Padnos, Theo. *See* Curtis, Peter Theo
Page, Charles Anderson, 267
Page, Timothy John, 267
Paget, Henry Marriott, 268
Paget, Walter Stanley, 268
Paine, Ralph Delahaye, 268
Painter, Uriah H., 268
Painton, Frederick C., 269
Palestinian conflict, 42, 258, 346
Palmer, Frederick, 269–70
Palmer, Royden Keith, 270
Palmos, Frank, 270–71
Panama invasion, 15, 271
Panay, bombing of gunboat, 256
"Pardon Jones." *See* Haile, Christopher Mason
Parer, Damien Peter, 271
Paris Commune, 96, 125, 165, 208, 261, 332
Paris, siege of in Franco-Prussian War, 128, 165, 194, 202, 203, 206, 208, 221, 304, 310, 312
Park, Sarah, 272
Parris, Jr., John A., 272

Parslow, E. G., 272
Pasha, Nazim, assassination of, 268
Paterson, Andrew Barton, 272
Patterson, Joseph Medill, 272–73
Patterson, Mary Marvin Breckinridge. *See* Breckinridge, Mary Marvin
Patton, General George, 226
Patton slapping incident, 273
Pearl, Daniel, 274
Pearse, Harry H. S., 274
Peck, Rory, 274
Pegler, Westbrook, 299
Peixotto, Clifford, 274–75
Pelcoq, Jules, 275
Peleliu campaign, 206, 230
Pellegin, Paolo, 275
Pelley, Scott Cameron, 275–76
Peninsular campaign, American Civil War, 335, 395
Peoples, John H. "Chaparral," 276
Perez-Reverte, Arturo, 276
Perkins, William T., 276
Perlin, Bernard, 276–77
Perry, George Sessions, 277
Perry, Henry, 277
Perry, Mert, 238, 277
Pershing expedition to Mexico, 138, 177, 279
"Personne." *See* De Fontaine, Felix Gregory
Peyton, Katherine "Kate", 277–78
Philby, Harold Adrian Russell "Kim," 278, 341
Philippines insurrection, 101, 127, 270, 310
Phillips, Percival, 278
Pickerell, James, 279
pictorial journalism, 16, 209
picture postcards, 174, 279
Pigott, John, 279
Pike, Albert T., 279–80
Pilger, John, 280
Pinney, Roy, 280
Plevna, siege of, 101, 221, 378
"Political Bill." *See* Lawrence, William H.
Politkovskaya, Anna, 281
Polk, George, 281
Pond, Elizabeth, 282
Pooled coverage, 282
Pool system reporting, 20; and Gulf War, 150–51; and Modoc War, 231; and Panama Invasion, 271; and World War II, 403–04
Port Arthur, massacre, 79
Post, Robert Perkins, 282, 405
Post-Traumatic Stress Disorder (PTSD), 38, 242, 282–83
Potter, Kent, 283
Powell, E. Alexander, 283
Power, Frank Le Poer, 283–84
Pran, Dith, and *Killing Fields, The,* 194
Pravda, 7, 12, 143, 193, 201, 317, 369, 372, 373
Press Association of the Confederate States.
    See Confederate Press Association

Price, Byron, 284–85
Price, George Ward, 285
Price, Morgan Philips, 285–86
Price, Walter Crawfurd. *See* Crawfurd-Price, Walter.
"printers," 233, 276
Prior, Melton, 286
Pyle, Ernest "Ernie" Taylor, 287

Q

Quiet American, The, 288
Quin, Windham Thomas Wyndham, 288

R

Raddatz, Martha, 289
radio broadcasting, 138, 188, 248, 300, 404
Ralph, Julian, 289–90
Ranthom, John Revelstoke, 290
Rasputin, killing of, 132
Rather, Dan, 290
Ray, Michele, 290
Raymond, Henry Jarvis, 290–91
Rayner, Pendil Arthur, 291
Rea, George Bronson, 291–92
Reade, William Winwood, 292
Redfern, John, 292
Redkin, Mark, 292
Redpath, James, 292–93
Reed, David, 293
Reed, John Silas, 285, 293–94
Reichstag fire, 246
Reid, Samuel Chester, Jr., 294–95
Reid, Whitelaw, 295
Reisner, Georg, 295–96
Remington, Frederic Sackrider, 162–63, 296–97
Repington, Colonel Charles a Court, 235, 297
Reporters Instructed in Saving Colleagues (RISC), 297
Reporters without Borders, 179; and Austin Tice, 364
Repulse, sinking of, 48, 67, 134
Restrepo, 298
Reuters, 9, 152, 228, 298–99, 303, 306, 309, 312, 315, 403;
    and Boer War, 37; and Falklands War, 116
Reynolds, Quentin, 299–300, 318
"Rhine Maidens, The," 354
Rhodesian conflict, 98
Riboud, Marc, 300
Rich, Jr., John Hubbard, 300
Richardson, Albert Deane, 300–01
Richardson, David, 301
"Ride of Death," 125
Rider-Rider, William, 301
Ridley, Yvonne, 301–02
Riff War, 127, 138, 237, 324
Rinehart, Mary Roberts, 302
Riordan, Bartholomew, 302
Robb, Inez, 303

Roberts, Frank J., 303
Robertson, James, 303
Robertson, Nic, 303–04
Robinson, G. T., 304
Robinson, Henry Crabb, 304–05
Robinson, Sir Harry Perry, 304
Rochester Optical Company, and picture postcards, 279
Rochhelli, Andrea "Andy", 305
Rodger, George, 305
Romulo, Carlos Pena, 305–06
rooftop journalism, 150, 306
Rooney, Andy, 306
Roos, Tielman Johannes De Villiers, 306–07
Roosevelt's Rough Riders, 31, 128, 164, 230, 255, 316
Roosevelt, Theodore, 127, 269, 316, 348
Rosebud, Battle of the, 11, 88, 120, 223, 353, 388
Rosecrans, Major General William S., 34
Rosen, Nir, 307
Rosenthal, Joe, 54, 307
Rough Riders. *See* Roosevelt's Rough Riders
Round, Derek Leonard, 307
Rowland, Jacky, 307–08
Royal, Dennis Lee, 308
Rue, Larry, 308
Ruhl, Arthur, 308
Runyon, Damon, 308–09
Russell, Andrew J., 309
Russell, Edmund "Ned" Allen, 309
Russell, Sir Herbert, 309
Russell, Sir William Howard, 9, 125, 128, 309–10, 365
Russian Revolution, 30, 101, 109, 178, 285, 316
Russo-Japanese War, 156, 159, 243, 310–11
Russo-Turkish War, 311–12
Ryan, Cornelius John, 312

S

Sacco, Joe, 313
Sack, John, 313
"Sad Sack," 24, 408
Safer, Morley, 314
Saigon, fall of, 188, 211, 257
St. George, Ozzie, 314
St. John, Robert, 170, 314
St. Paul's Cathedral, memorial to war correspondents,
    232, 310
Sala, George Augustus Henry, 314–15
Sale, Stewart, 315
Salerno landing, 315
Salisbury, Harrison Evans, 315
Salter, Cedric, 315–16
Sandburg, Carl August, 316
San Juan Hill, Battle of, 55, 90, 296, 316
Sankova, Galina, 316
Santiago, surrender of, 36, 145
Savin, Mikhail, 316–17
Sawada, Kyoichi, 317

Sayre, Joel Grover, 317
Schanberg, Sydney H., 194, 317
Schell, Francis H., 317
Schipka Pass, Battle of, 125, 312
Schleswig-Holstein War, 98, 203, 310
Schonberg, Johann Nepomuk, 317–18
Schork, Kurt, 318
Schrier, Matt, 318
Schultz, Sigrid, 318
Schuyler, Philippa, 318–19
Scoop, 319, 390
Scott, General Winfield, 130
Scott, Jack Denton, 319
Scott, Roddy, 320
Scott, Sir James Georg, 319–20
Scovel, Henry Sylvester, 158, 292, 320
Screws, William Wallace, 321
Scudamore, Frank, 321
Second Afghan War, 53
Second Boer War. *See* Boer War
Second China War, 29
Sedgwick, Alexander Cameron "A. C.," 321
Selassie, Haile, 112, 133, 189, 347, 349, 390
Seldes, George, 321–22
Sevareid, Eric, 322
Seymour, David "Chim," 322–23
Sgrena, Giuliana, 323
Shadid, Anthony, 323
"Shadow." *See* Linebaugh, John H.
Shanks, William F. G., 323–24
Shaplen, Robert Modell, 324
Sharpeville, 33
Shaw, Bernard, 150
Shaykhet, Arkadi, 324
Sheean, James Vincent, 324–25
Sheehan, Neil, 325
Sheepshanks, Dick, 299
Sheldon, Charles M., 325
Sheldon-Williams, Inglis, 325
Shepard, Elaine, 326
Shepardson, Dr. William G., 326
Shepherd, William G., 326–27
Sheridan, General Philip, 155, 190
Sherman, General William Tecumseh, 10, 155, 198, 293, 359
Sherman's "March to the Sea," 26, 229, 293
Sherrod, Robert, 327
Shiloh, Battle of, 33, 66, 217, 295
Shimamoto, Keisaburo, 327
Shinn, Bill, 327–
Shirer, William Lawrence, 170, 328
Shooting the Messenger, 328
Sicily campaign, 239, 262
Sidebotham, Herbert, 328
Signal, 328–29
Silk, George, 329
Simmons, Walter, 200, 330

Simon, Bob, 329
Simonov, Konstantin, 330
Simplot, Alexander, 330–31
Simpson, John, 331
Simpson, William, 331–32
Singer, Jack, 332
Sinn Fein rebellion, 138
Sino-Japanese War, 332
Sites, Kevin, 332–33
Sitting Bull, 79, 99, 176, 261
Skinner, John Edwin Hilary, 333
Smalley, George Washburn, 333
Smedley, Agnes, 334
Smith, Colin, 334–35
Smith, Dan, 335
Smith, Elias, 335
Smith, Ernest, 335
Smith, Frederick Edwin "F.E.", 335
Smith, Howard Kingsbury, 335–36
Smith, J. Andre, 336
Smith, Vaughan, 336
Smith, W. Eugene, 336–37
Smyth, Jack, 299
Sneed, James Roddy, 337
Snow, Edgar, 337–38
"Soccer War," 189
Solferino, Battle of, 84, 291
Solomon Islands campaign, 145
Soloviev, Andrei, 338
Somalian conflict, 1, 2, 3, 4, 7, 181
Somers, Luke Daniel, 338
Somme, Battle of the, 309
Sotloff, Steven Joel, 124, 339
South African War. *See* Boer War
Southworth, Alvan S., 339
Soviet photojournalism, 7, 201, 411
Spanish-American War, 127, 339–41
Spanish Civil War, 149–50, 212, 341–42; and Hemingway, 163
Spanish Civil War (1834-1839), 149
"special artist," 83
"specials," 10, 16
Spratt, Leonidas W., 342–43
Sri Lanka civil war, 74
SS-Standarte Kurt Eggers, 343
Stackpole, Peter, 343
Stalingrad, Battle of, 25, 104, 111, 411
Stanley, Sir Henry Morton, 32, 165, 190, 288, 343–44, 379
"Starman." *See* Hands, Charles E.
Stars and Stripes, 344–45; and Mauldin, 226
Stavisky, Samuel E., 345
Stedman, Edmund Clarence, 345
Steele, Archibald T., 345–46
Steele, Jon, 346–47
Steer, George Lowther, 150, 172, 347
Steevens, George Warrington, 321, 347
Steichen, Edward Jean, 348

Steinbeck, Jr., John Ernest, 348
Steinbeck IV, John, 348–49
Stenin, Andrei, 349
Stern Gang terrorists, 145
Stevens, Edmund, 349
Stevens, George, 349–50
Stewart, Bill, 350
Stewart, Ian, 350
Stillson, Jerome Bonaparte, 350–51
Stone, Dana, 351, 409
Stoneman, William H., 351
Storms, Jane McManus, 351–52
Story of G.I. Joe, The, and Ernie Pyle, 287, 352
Stouman, Lou, 352
Stowe, Leland, 352–53
Strahorn, Robert, 353
Street, Albert, 353–54
stringer, 354, 402
Stringer, Ann, 354
Suckert, Kurt, 354–55
Sully, Francois, 355
Sulzberger, Cyrus Leo, 355
Sutherland, Thomas A., 355
Swing, Raymond Edwards, 355–56
Swinton, William, 356
Swope, Herbert Bayard, 356–57
Symonds, Gene, 357
Syrian civil war, 4, 8, 24, 64, 111, 183, 230, 247, 252, 253, 260, 357
Szathmari, Karl Baptist Von (Carol Popp De Szathmari), 357–58; as first war photographer, 383
Szulc, Tad, 358

T

Taliban, 4, 85
Tarawa, Battle of, 217, 337, 368
Taro, Gerda, 61, 341, 359
TASS, 7, 135, 193, 292, 367, 408
Taylor, Benjamin Franklin, 359
Taylor, Charles, 44, 72
Taylor, Cora, 359–60
Taylor, Jr., Henry, 360
Taylor, James Earl, 360
Teichner, Martha, 360
telegraph, 125, 176, 184, 333, 340
Tell Sparta, 360
Tet offensive, 2, 94, 208, 238, 248, 372, 390
Texas Rangers, in Mexican War, 129, 294
Thiele, Reinhold, 361
"Thin Red Line," 80, 310
Thomas, Hugh, 150
Thomas, Lowell Jackson, 361
Thomas, Sir William Beach, 361
Thompson, Donald, 361–62
Thompson, John Hall, 362–63
Thorpe, Thomas Bangs, 363

Thrasher, John S., 363
Three Days' Fight (Modoc War), 128, 231
Threlkeld, Richard, 363–64
Tice, Austin, 364
Times. See London Times
Timrod, Henry, 364
Tito, Marshal, 33
Tobey, William C., 364
Tobin, J.G.H., 233
Tobruk, capture of, 6, 192, 329, 399
Tojo, suicide of, 54
Tolstoy, Leo Nicolayevich, 365
Tomalin, Nicholas, 365
Tomara, Sonia, 365–66
Torgerson, Dial, 366
Townsend, George Alfred, 232, 366
Toynbee, Arnold J., 366
Trakhman, Mikhail Anatol'evich, 367
Treanor, Tom, 367
Tregaskis, Richard J., 367
Triangle Shirt Waist Company, and tragic fire, 326
Truman, Benjamin Cummings, 368
Trumbull, Robert, 368
Tunisian campaign, 33, 273, 287
Tuohy, William, 368
Turgut, Serif, 368–69
Turkish Revolution of 1909, 102, 239
Turko-Serbian War (1876), 165
Tweedie, Penny, 369
Tyomin, Viktor, 369

U

Ukrainian Conflict, 197, 201, 370
Ulundi, Battle of, 125
Under Fire, 370
Unembedded Journalists. See Unilaterals.
Unger, Frederic William, 370
Unilaterals, 371
Unipressers, 371
United Press International (UPI), 371
United States Army Signal Corps. See Army Signal Corps
"Unseen War," and Gulf War, 151
Upton, George Putnam, 371–72
U.S.S. Missouri, 27
Ustinov, Alexander, 372
Ut, Huynh Cong, 372
Ute War, 351
Utley, Clifton Garrick, 372–73
Uzlyan, Alexander, 373

V

Vandam, Albert Dresden, 374
Van de Velde, Willem "The elder", 374
Van Lynden Aernout, 374
Vera Cruz (1914), American occupation of, 159, 218, 273, 327, 351

Verdun, Battle of, 103, 109, 207
Veremiy, Vyacheslav, 374–75
Verlon, Claude, 375
Vermillion, Robert, 375
Viaud, Louis Marie Julien, 43, 375
Vicksburg, Battle of, 1, 12, 37, 48, 57, 72, 300, 317
Victoria Cross, 120
Vietnam War, 2, 19, 30, 35, 46, 47, 49, 105, 124, 137, 142,
    146, 189, 375–77; compared to Falklands War, 117; first
    journalist wounded, 236; last journalist killed, 205; and
    stringers, 354, 402; youngest journalist killed, 283
Villa, Pancho, 138, 177, 255, 279, 293, 309
Villard, Henry, 377
Villiers, Frederic, 377–78
Vincent, Steven, 378
Vitagraph Company, and Spanish-American War, 255
Vizetelly, Edward Henry, 378–79
Vizetelly, Ernest Alfred, 379
Vizetelly, Frank, 379
Vizetelly, Frank Horace, 379
Vizetelly, Henry Richard, 380
Von Clausewitz, Carl, 28

W

Wade, William, 381
Wake Island, raid on, 337
Wallace, Edgar, 152, 382
Wallace, Sir Donald MacKenzie, 381
War Correspondent (average salary), 382
War Correspondents Arch, 232
War Correspondents Association, 368
War Correspondents Corridor, 232
Ward, Edward, Viscount Bangor, 382
Ware, Michael, 382–83
Warland, John H., 383
war photography, 45, 75, 86, 148, 158, 199, 213, 249, 256,
    271, 305, 307, 309, 338, 348, 358, 361, 367, 383–87;
    Brady and Civil War, 45; and Fenton, 118–19
War Porn, 25
"War Porn", 387
War Press Office, 403
Warsaw Ghetto, 355
Washita, Battle of the, 11, 190
Wasson, Joe, 387–88
Watkins, Kathleen "Kit" Blake, 388
Watson, Paul, 389
Waud, Alfred "Alf" Rudolph, 389
Waud, William, 389–90
Waugh, Evelyn Arthur St. John, 326, 390
Webb, Catherine "Kate", 390
Weber, Olivier, 391
Weithas, Arthur, 391
Wellard, James, 391
Weller, George, 391–92
Welsh, Mary, 196, 392
wet collodion process, 119

Wharton, Edith, 392
Wheeler, Keith, 392–93
Whitaker, John T., 393
White, Leigh, 170, 393
White, Theodore Harold, 393–94
Whitehead, Donald F., 394
Whitney, Caspar, 394
Wild, Richard, 394
Wiley, Bonnie, 394–95
Wilkeson, Samuel, 395
Wilkie, Franc Bangs, 395
Wilkins, George Hubert, 395–96
Wilkinson, Henry Spenser, 396
Williams, Brian Douglas, 396–97
Williams, Charles, 397
Williams, Eric Lloyd, 397–98
Williams, George Forrester, 398
Williams, Wythe, 398–99
Wills, Stanley, 399
Wilmot, Reginald William Winchester "Chester," 399–400
Wind and the Lion, The, 324
Wing, Henry Ebenezer, 400
Wingate, Orde, 112, 349
wireless, and Russo-Japanese War, 311
Wirgman, Charles, 400
"With the Conquering Turk." See Steevens, George War-
    rington
Wolfert, Ira, 400–01
women's rights, 98, 101
women war correspondents, , 4, 24, 31, 41, 46, 62, 63, 74,
    98, 99, 101, 112–13, 196, 214–15, 236, 248, 257, 272,
    340–41, 375, 402; and Spanish-American War, 388; and
    Vietnam War, 375; and World War II, 403
Wong, Hai Sheng "Newsreel," 255
Wood, Junius, 401
Woodruff, Robert "Bob" Dawson, 401
Woods, Henry Charles, 401
Woodville, Richard Caton, 402
Woodward, David, 402
World War I, 29, 90, 109, 132, 402–03; and outlaw cor-
    respondents, 265
World War II, 30, 42, 47, 52, 69, 81, 103, 106–07, 135, 139,
    151, 161, 178, 179, 390, 392, 403–04
Wounded Knee, 11, 296, 335
Wounds in the Rain, 404
Wright, Henry Charles Seppings, 405
Wright, Robin, 405
Writing 69th, The, 405

X

Ximenes, Edoardo, 406

Y

Yalu River campaign, 129
Yamamoto, Mika, 407

Yank magazine, 47, 54, 55, 84, 243, 301, 352, 407–08
Year of Living Dangerously, The, 408
Yellow journalism, 32, 291, 408
"Yellow Kid," 408
Yemen, 8, 85
Yevzerikhin, Emmanuel, 408
Yon, Michael, 408
Yoshihide, Takama. *See* Gishu, Nakayama
Young, Alexander Bell Filson, 409
Young, John Russell, 409
Young, Perry Deane, 409

Ypres, Battle of, 181, 277, 337
Yugoslavian conflict, 3, 48, 67, 96, 130, 185, 189, 198, 214, 244, 266, 304, 314, 322, 355, 401, 409–10
Yznaga, Antonio, 410

Z

Zebdine Coordination Committee, 247
Zelma, Georgi Anatolyevich, 411
Ziffren, Lester, 341
Zulu War (1879), 101, 130, 213

About the Author

Mitchel P. Roth is Professor of Criminal Justice and Criminology at Sam Houston State University. He received a Ph.D. in history from the University of California, Santa Barbara. His research interests include history, crime and punishment, prisons, terrorism and organized crime. He has published numerous articles and book chapters on topics ranging from Mexican-American war reporting to organized crime and terrorism financing in Turkey. The author of numerous books, his most recent books include *An Eye for An Eye: A Global History of Crime and Punishment* (2015), *Houston Blue: The Story of the Houston Police Department* (2012) and *Global Organized Crime* (2010).